International Directory of
COMPANY
HISTORIES

International Directory of

COMPANY

HISTORIES

VOLUME 108

Editor

Jay P. Pederson

ST. JAMES PRESS
A part of Gale, Cengage Learning

GALE
CENGAGE Learning™

Detroit • New York • San Francisco • New Haven, Conn • Waterville, Maine • London

GALE
CENGAGE Learning™

International Directory of Company Histories, Volume 108

Jay P. Pederson, Editor

Project Editor: Miranda H. Ferrara

Editorial: Virgil Burton, Donna Craft, Matthew Derda, Louise Gagné, Peggy Geeseman, Julie Gough, Sonya Hill, Keith Jones, Matthew Miskelly, Lynn Pearce, Laura Peterson, Holly Selden, Justine Ventimiglia

Production Technology Specialist: Mike Weaver

Imaging and Multimedia: John Watkins

Composition and Electronic Prepress: Gary Leach, Evi Seoud

Manufacturing: Rhonda Dover

Product Manager: Jenai Drouillard

Cover Photograph: Title Guarantee & Trust Building, Los Angeles. Courtesy Library of Congress, Prints & Photographs Division, Historic American Buildings Survey.

For product information and technology assistance, contact us at **Gale Customer Support, 1-800-877-4253.**
For permission to use material from this text or product, submit all requests online at **www.cengage.com/permissions.**
Further permissions questions can be emailed to **permissionrequest@cengage.com**

Gale
27500 Drake Rd.
Farmington Hills, MI, 48331-3535

LIBRARY OF CONGRESS CATALOG NUMBER 89-190943
ISBN-13: 978-1-4144-4104-7
ISBN-10: 1-4144-4104-5

This title is also available as an e-book
ISBN-13: 978-1-55862-771-0   ISBN-10: 1-55862-771-5
Contact your Gale, a part of Cengage Learning sales representative for ordering information.

BRITISH LIBRARY CATALOGUING IN PUBLICATION DATA
International directory of company histories, Vol. 108
Jay P. Pederson
33.87409

Printed in the United States of America
1 2 3 4 5 6 7 13 12 11 10 09

Contents

Preface

The St. James Press series *The International Directory of Company Histories* (*IDCH*) is intended for reference use by students, business people, librarians, historians, economists, investors, job candidates, and others who seek to learn more about the historical development of the world's most important companies. To date, *IDCH* has profiled more than 10,570 companies in 108 volumes.

INCLUSION CRITERIA

Most companies chosen for inclusion in *IDCH* have achieved a minimum of US$25 million in annual sales and are leading influences in their industries or geographical locations. Companies may be publicly held, private, or nonprofit. State-owned companies that are important in their industries and that may operate much like public or private companies also are included. Wholly owned subsidiaries and divisions are profiled if they meet the requirements for inclusion. Entries on companies that have had major changes since they were last profiled may be selected for updating.

The *IDCH* series highlights 25% private and nonprofit companies, and features updated entries on approximately 35 companies per volume.

ENTRY FORMAT

Each entry begins with the company's legal name; the address of its headquarters; its telephone, toll-free, and fax numbers; and its web site. A statement of public, private, state, or parent ownership follows. A company with a legal name in both English and the language of its headquarters country is listed by the English name, with the native-language name in parentheses.

The company's founding or earliest incorporation date, the number of employees, and the most recent available sales figures follow. Sales figures are given in local currencies with equivalents in U.S. dollars. For some private companies, sales figures are estimates and indicated by the abbreviation *est.* The entry lists the exchanges on which the company's stock is traded and its ticker symbol, as well as the company's NAICS codes.

Entries generally contain a *Company Perspectives* box which provides a short summary of the company's mission, goals, and ideals; a *Key Dates* box highlighting milestones in the company's history; lists of *Principal Subsidiaries, Principal Divisions, Principal Operating Units, Principal Competitors*; and articles for *Further Reading*.

American spelling is used throughout *IDCH*, and the word "billion" is used in its U.S. sense of one thousand million.

SOURCES

Entries have been compiled from publicly accessible sources both in print and on the Internet such as general and academic periodicals, books, and annual reports, as well as material supplied by the companies themselves.

CUMULATIVE INDEXES

IDCH contains three indexes: the **Cumulative Index to Companies**, which provides an alphabetical index to companies profiled in the *IDCH* series, the **Index to Industries**, which allows researchers to locate companies by their principal industry, and the **Geographic Index**, which lists companies alphabetically by the country of their headquarters. The indexes are cumulative and specific instructions for using them are found immediately preceding each index.

SPECIAL TO THIS VOLUME

This volume of *IDCH* contains an entry on the largest utility company in the world, State Grid Corporation of China; and an entry on Israel's largest conglomerate, Israel Corporation Ltd.

SUGGESTIONS WELCOME

Comments and suggestions from users of *IDCH* on any aspect of the product as well as suggestions for companies to be included or updated are cordially invited. Please write:

> The Editor
> *International Directory of Company Histories*
> St. James Press
> Gale, Cengage Learning
> 27500 Drake Rd.
> Farmington Hills, Michigan 48331-3535

St. James Press does not endorse any of the companies or products mentioned in this series. Companies appearing in the *International Directory of Company Histories* were selected without reference to their wishes and have in no way endorsed their entries.

Notes on Contributors

M. L. Cohen
Novelist, business writer, and researcher living in Paris.

Jeffrey L. Covell
Seattle-based writer.

Ed Dinger
Writer and editor based in Bronx, New York.

Paul R. Greenland
Illinois-based writer and researcher; author of two books and former senior editor of a national business magazine; contributor to *The Encyclopedia of Chicago History, The Encyclopedia of Religion,* and the *Encyclopedia of American Industries.*

Robert Halasz
Former editor in chief of *World Progress* and *Funk & Wagnalls New Encyclo-*

pedia Yearbook; author, *The U.S. Marines* (Millbrook Press, 1993).

Frederick C. Ingram
Writer based in South Carolina.

Kathleen Peippo
Minnesota-based writer.

Nelson Rhodes
Editor, writer, and consultant in the Chicago area.

Carrie Rothburd
Writer and editor specializing in corporate profiles, academic texts, and academic journal articles.

Roger Rouland
Writer and scholar specializing in company histories, literary criticism, literary essays, and

poetry; freelance photographer specializing in nature photography.

David E. Salamie
Part-owner of InfoWorks Development Group, a reference publication development and editorial services company.

Mary Tradii
Michigan-based writer.

Frank Uhle
Ann Arbor-based writer; movie projectionist, disc jockey, and staff member of *Psychotronic Video* magazine.

A. Woodward
Wisconsin-based writer.

List of Abbreviations

€ European euro
¥ Japanese yen
£ United Kingdom pound
$ United States dollar

A

AB Aktiebolag (Finland, Sweden)
AB Oy Aktiebolag Osakeyhtiot (Finland)
A.E. Anonimos Eteria (Greece)
AED Emirati dirham
AG Aktiengesellschaft (Austria, Germany, Switzerland, Liechtenstein)
aG auf Gegenseitigkeit (Austria, Germany)
A.m.b.a. Andelsselskab med begraenset ansvar (Denmark)
A.O. Anonim Ortaklari/Ortakligi (Turkey)
ApS Amparteselskab (Denmark)
ARS Argentine peso
A.S. Anonim Sirketi (Turkey)
A/S Aksjeselskap (Norway)
A/S Aktieselskab (Denmark, Sweden)
Ay Avoinyhtio (Finland)
ATS Austrian shilling
AUD Australian dollar
Ay Avoinyhtio (Finland)

B

B.A. Buttengewone Aansprakeiijkheid (Netherlands)
BEF Belgian franc

BHD Bahraini dinar
Bhd. Berhad (Malaysia, Brunei)
BND Brunei dollar
BRL Brazilian real
B.V. Besloten Vennootschap (Belgium, Netherlands)

C

C. de R.L. Compania de Responsabilidad Limitada (Spain)
C. por A. Compania por Acciones (Dominican Republic)
C.A. Compania Anonima (Ecuador, Venezuela)
C.V. Commanditaire Vennootschap (Netherlands, Belgium)
CAD Canadian dollar
CEO Chief Executive Officer
CFO Chief Financial Officer
CHF Swiss franc
Cia. Compagnia (Italy)
Cia. Companhia (Brazil, Portugal)
Cia. Compania (Latin America [except Brazil], Spain)
Cie. Compagnie (Belgium, France, Luxembourg, Netherlands)
CIO Chief Information Officer
CLP Chilean peso
CNY Chinese yuan
Co. Company
COO Chief Operating Officer
Coop. Cooperative
COP Colombian peso

Corp. Corporation
CPT Cuideachta Phoibi Theoranta (Republic of Ireland)
CRL Companhia a Responsabilidao Limitida (Portugal, Spain)
CZK Czech koruna

D

D&B Dunn & Bradstreet
DEM German deutsche mark (W. Germany to 1990; unified Germany to 2002)
Div. Division (United States)
DKK Danish krone
DZD Algerian dinar

E

E.P.E. Etema Pemorismenis Evthynis (Greece)
EC Exempt Company (Arab countries)
Edms. Bpk. Eiendoms Beperk (South Africa)
EEK Estonian Kroon
eG eingetragene Genossenschaft (Germany)
EGMBH Eingetragene Genossenschaft mit beschraenkter Haftung (Austria, Germany)
EGP Egyptian pound
Ek For Ekonomisk Forening (Sweden)
EP Empresa Portuguesa (Portugal)

ESOP Employee Stock Options and Ownership
ESP Spanish peseta
Et(s). Etablissement(s) (Belgium, France, Luxembourg)
eV eingetragener Verein (Germany)
EUR European euro

F

FIM Finnish markka
FRF French franc

G

G.I.E. Groupement d'Interet Economique (France)
gGmbH gemeinnutzige Gesellschaft mit beschraenkter Haftung (Austria, Germany, Switzerland)
GmbH Gesellschaft mit beschraenkter Haftung (Austria, Germany, Switzerland)
GRD Greek drachma
GWA Gewerbte Amt (Austria, Germany)

H

HB Handelsbolag (Sweden)
HF Hlutafelag (Iceland)
HKD Hong Kong dollar
HUF Hungarian forint

I

IDR Indonesian rupiah
IEP Irish pound
ILS Israeli shekel (new)
Inc. Incorporated (United States, Canada)
INR Indian rupee
IPO Initial Public Offering
I/S Interesentselskap (Norway)
I/S Interessentselskab (Denmark)
ISK Icelandic krona
ITL Italian lira

J

JMD Jamaican dollar
JOD Jordanian dinar

K

KB Kommanditbolag (Sweden)
KES Kenyan schilling
Kft Korlatolt Felelossegu Tarsasag (Hungary)
KG Kommanditgesellschaft (Austria, Germany, Switzerland)
KGaA Kommanditgesellschaft auf Aktien (Austria, Germany, Switzerland)
KK Kabushiki Kaisha (Japan)
KPW North Korean won
KRW South Korean won
K/S Kommanditselskab (Denmark)
K/S Kommandittselskap (Norway)
KWD Kuwaiti dinar
Ky Kommandiitiyhtio (Finland)

L

L.L.C. Limited Liability Company (Arab countries, Egypt, Greece, United States)
L.L.P. Limited Liability Partnership (United States)
L.P. Limited Partnership (Canada, South Africa, United Kingdom, United States)
LBO Leveraged Buyout
Lda. Limitada (Spain)
Ltd. Limited
Ltda. Limitada (Brazil, Portugal)
Ltee. Limitee (Canada, France)
LUF Luxembourg franc

M

mbH mit beschraenkter Haftung (Austria, Germany)
Mij. Maatschappij (Netherlands)
MUR Mauritian rupee
MXN Mexican peso
MYR Malaysian ringgit

N

N.A. National Association (United States)
N.V. Naamloze Vennootschap (Belgium, Netherlands)
NGN Nigerian naira
NLG Netherlands guilder
NOK Norwegian krone
NZD New Zealand dollar

O

OAO Otkrytoe Aktsionernoe Obshchestve (Russia)
OHG Offene Handelsgesellschaft (Austria, Germany, Switzerland)
OMR Omani rial
OOO Obschestvo s Ogranichennoi Otvetstvennostiu (Russia)
OOUR Osnova Organizacija Udruzenog Rada (Yugoslavia)
Oy Osakeyhti ???? (Finland)

P

P.C. Private Corp. (United States)
P.L.L.C. Professional Limited Liability Corporation (United States)
P.T. Perusahaan/Perseroan Terbatas (Indonesia)
PEN Peruvian Nuevo Sol
PHP Philippine peso
PKR Pakistani rupee
P/L Part Lag (Norway)
PLC Public Limited Co. (United Kingdom, Ireland)
PLN Polish zloty
PTE Portuguese escudo
Pte. Private (Singapore)
Pty. Proprietary (Australia, South Africa, United Kingdom)
Pvt. Private (India, Zimbabwe)
PVBA Personen Vennootschap met Beperkte Aansprakelijkheid (Belgium)
PYG Paraguay guarani

Q

QAR Qatar riyal

R

REIT Real Estate Investment Trust
RMB Chinese renminbi
Rt Reszvenytarsasag (Hungary)
RUB Russian ruble

S

S.A. Sociedad Anónima (Latin America [except Brazil], Spain, Mexico)
S.A. Sociedades Anônimas (Brazil, Portugal)
S.A. Société Anonyme (Arab countries, Belgium, France, Jordan, Luxembourg, Switzerland)
S.A. de C.V. Sociedad Anonima de Capital Variable (Mexico)
S.A.B. de C.V. Sociedad Anónima Bursátil de Capital Variable (Mexico)
S.A.C. Sociedad Anonima Comercial (Latin America [except Brazil])
S.A.C.I. Sociedad Anonima Comercial e Industrial (Latin America [except Brazil])

S.A.C.I.y.F. Sociedad Anonima Comercial e Industrial y Financiera (Latin America [except Brazil])

S.A.R.L. Sociedade Anonima de Responsabilidade Limitada (Brazil, Portugal)

S.A.R.L. Société à Responsabilité Limitée (France, Belgium, Luxembourg)

S.A.S. Societe Anonyme Syrienne (Arab countries)

S.A.S. Societá in Accomandita Semplice (Italy)

S.C. Societe en Commandite (Belgium, France, Luxembourg)

S.C.A. Societe Cooperativa Agricole (France, Italy, Luxembourg)

S.C.I. Sociedad Cooperativa Ilimitada (Spain)

S.C.L. Sociedad Cooperativa Limitada (Spain)

S.C.R.L. Societe Cooperative a Responsabilite Limitee (Belgium)

S.E. Societas Europaea (European Union Member states)

S.L. Sociedad Limitada (Latin America [except Brazil], Portugal, Spain)

S.N.C. Société en Nom Collectif (France)

S.p.A. Società per Azioni (Italy)

S.R.L. Sociedad de Responsabilidad Limitada (Spain, Mexico, Latin America [except Brazil])

S.R.L. Società a Responsabilità Limitata (Italy)

S.R.O. Spolecnost s Rucenim Omezenym (Czechoslovakia

S.S.K. Sherkate Sahami Khass (Iran)

S.V. Samemwerkende Vennootschap (Belgium)

S.Z.R.L. Societe Zairoise a Responsabilite Limitee (Zaire)

SAA Societe Anonyme Arabienne (Arab countries)

SAK Societe Anonyme Kuweitienne (Arab countries)

SAL Societe Anonyme Libanaise (Arab countries)

SAO Societe Anonyme Omanienne (Arab countries)

SAQ Societe Anonyme Qatarienne (Arab countries)

SAR Saudi riyal

Sdn. Bhd. Sendirian Berhad (Malaysia)

SEK Swedish krona

SGD Singapore dollar

S/L Salgslag (Norway)

Soc. Sociedad (Latin America [except Brazil], Spain)

Soc. Sociedade (Brazil, Portugal)

Soc. Societa (Italy)

Sp. z.o.o. Spólka z ograniczona odpowiedzialnoscia (Poland)

Ste. Societe (France, Belgium, Luxembourg, Switzerland)

Ste. Cve. Societe Cooperative (Belgium)

T

THB Thai baht

TND Tunisian dinar

TRL Turkish lira

TWD Taiwan dollar (new)

U

U.A. Uitgesloten Aansporakeiijkheid (Netherlands)

u.p.a. utan personligt ansvar (Sweden)

V

V.O.f. Vennootschap onder firma (Netherlands)

VAG Verein der Arbeitgeber (Austria, Germany)

VEB Venezuelan bolivar

VERTR Vertriebs (Austria, Germany)

VND Vietnamese dong

VVAG Versicherungsverein auf Gegenseitigkeit (Austria, Germany)

W–Z

WA Wettelika Aansprakalikhaed (Netherlands)

WLL With Limited Liability (Bahrain, Kuwait, Qatar, Saudi Arabia)

YK Yugen Kaisha (Japan)

ZAO Zakrytoe Aktsionernoe Obshchestve (Russia)

ZAR South African rand

ZMK Zambian kwacha

ZWD Zimbabwean dollar

ABP Corporation

—■—

1 Au Bon Pain Way
Boston, Massachusetts 02210
U.S.A.
Telephone: (617) 423-2100
Fax: (617) 423-7879
Web site: http://www.aubonpain.com

Private Company
Incorporated: 1999
Employees: 2,300
Sales: $330 million (2008 est.)
NAICS: 722210 Limited-Service Restaurants; 311811
     Retail Bakeries; 311812 Commercial Bakeries

■ ■ ■

ABP Corporation is the operator of the Au Bon Pain bakery-café chain. The chain consists of approximately 165 company-owned units concentrated in the metropolitan markets of Boston, Chicago, New York, Pittsburgh, Philadelphia, and Washington, D.C. Through franchise agreements, there are more than 60 units operating in 20 states. Au Bon Pain, through franchise agreements, also operates internationally, collecting royalty payments from stores in South Korea, Taiwan, Thailand, and the Middle East. Au Bon Pain units serve bread, pastries, sandwiches, soups, salads, and entrees. The chain's stores are located in city office buildings, suburban shopping malls, hospitals, airports, train stations, and universities.

CREATION OF A COMPANY TO BUY A CONCEPT

Twenty years before ABP was founded, the restaurant concept it acquired was created. ABP Corporation was formed in 1999 to complete the acquisition of the once-flourishing Au Bon Pain bakery-café chain, a business that was struggling to reproduce the success that had made it the darling of the fast-causal niche of the restaurant industry. ABP paid $78 million for Au Bon Pain, gaining control of a 263-unit chain with virtually accidental origins.

THE EARLY YEARS OF AU BON PAIN

Au Bon Pain, as a restaurant concept, was never intended to succeed. One of the first upscale fast-food chains in the country initially was treated like a prop in a theater production. Pavallier BVP SA, a French manufacturer of commercial ovens, opened the first Au Bon Pain in 1976, establishing the store in Boston's historic Faneuil Hall Marketplace. The store was staffed by French bakers who dutifully attended to creating authentic baked goods, such as croissants, pastries, and loaves of bread, but the ultimate aim of the original Au Bon Pain had little to do with selling baked goods for a profit. Pavallier had opened the store to promote its ovens.

The rationale for the business made its definitive turn when Louis I. Kane entered the picture. A Boston native and a 1949 graduate of Harvard College, Kane owned Kane Financial Corp., a venture-capital company involved in commercial banking, real estate, and health

care, and a frozen yogurt franchise that operated in Faneuil Hall Marketplace. He rightly sensed the growing
demand for French breads and pastries and acquired Au
Bon Pain in 1978 for $1.5 million, intending to use the
location to sell baked goods instead of ovens. Kane
struggled to turn a profit with the business until he
formed a partnership with Ronald M. Shaich, a Harvard
graduate 20 years his junior, in 1981. They formed Au
Bon Pain Co. Inc. in 1981, when there were three stores
in operation, and made important changes that led to
financial success. Production was made more efficient
and a central baking facility was established. Seats,
sandwiches, and coffee were added in 1984, converting
the Au Bon Pain concept from a bakery to a bakery
café. Kane and Shaich focused expansion in urban locations and opened 80 units by 1991, the year they took
the $70-million-in-sales Au Bon Pain Co. Inc. public.

After the stock offering, expansion accelerated. The
number of Au Bon Pain units jumped to 250 within a
few short years and, through franchise agreements, the
company expanded internationally, opening stores in
Chile, Indonesia, and Thailand, but soon the expansion
campaign screeched to halt, when finding viable locations in urban markets became increasingly difficult. In
1993, desperate to find a way to expand, Kane and
Shaich acquired the six-year-old, 20-unit Saint Louis
Bread Co., a bakery café chain focused on suburban
markets. During the ensuing three years, Saint Louis
Bread tripled in size, but expansion of the Au Bon Pain
concept stalled, forcing Kane and Shaich to make a
pivotal decision. "By 1997, we realized we had two good
businesses, but they were in different places in their life
cycles," Shaich said in the June 26, 2000 issue of
Nation's Restaurant News. "Saint Louis Bread was young,
and Au Bon Pain was mature. Saint Louis Bread was the
better public company, and Au Bon Pain needed to be
private."

OPPORTUNITY KNOCKS AND ABP ANSWERS

The partners decided to shed their company's namesake
restaurant concept and focus on the expansion of Saint
Louis Bread. In August 1998, they agreed to sell Au
Bon Pain to a private investment company, New York-
based Bruckmann, Rosser, Sherrill & Co. Inc. for $78
million. The investment firm, which owned the
California Pizza Kitchen and Acapulco restaurant chains,
completed the deal in 1999, forming ABP Corporation
to take control of the Au Bon Pain concept. Kane followed his creation, becoming chairman of ABP
Corporation, while Shaich remained with Au Bon Pain
Co. Inc. and the 97-unit Saint Louis Bread chain.
Shaich soon changed the name of Au Bon Pain Co. Inc.
to Panera Bread Company, the new name for Saint
Louis Bread, and focused on franchising units in
suburban markets. Kane, in charge of ABP, began looking for ways to invigorate growth in Au Bon Pain's
urban markets. "Au Bon Pain Co. Inc. was trying to
manage two different brands, which were competing for
management's attention and for capital," a Bruckmann,
Rosser executive said in the August 24, 1998 issue of
Nation's Restaurant News. "Au Bon Pain, being the more
mature of the two concepts, lost out."

THE SEARCH FOR AN EFFECTIVE STRATEGY

In the months leading up to the agreement with the
investment firm, Kane and Shaich had begun developing
a new design for Au Bon Pain dubbed "ABP 2000." The
changes were developed to spark sales growth, but a lack
of capital limited the scope of the renovation program
to only 10 restaurants. On his own, with the financial
backing of Bruckmann, Rosser, Kane focused on
implementing the new format chainwide. Several new
soups, salads, and sandwiches were introduced and a
new store design emphasizing self-service and the
concept's French heritage became the blueprint for the
chain. In January 2000, Frank Guidara, the former chief
executive officer of Wolfgang Puck Food Co., was hired
as ABP's chief executive officer and president to help
Kane, who was ailing. After a long illness, Kane died in
June 2000 at the age of 69, leaving Guidara on his own
to restore the vitality of the Au Bon Pain concept.

Within months of Kane's passing, ABP faced a
major change at the corporate level. In November 2000,
Bruckmann, Rosser agreed to buy the upscale dinner-
house operator Il Fornaio (America) Corp., which
touched off rumors that it was selling ABP Corporation.
The following month, the rumors proved to be true
when Compass Group North America, a subsidiary of
London, England-based Granada Compass PLC,

KEY DATES

1976: First Au Bon Pain is opened by Pavallier BVP SA.

1978: Entrepreneur Louis I. Kane acquires the Au Bon Pain location.

1984: Au Bon Pain's format is converted from a bakery to a bakery café.

1999: Bruckmann, Rosser, Sherrill & Co., an investment firm, acquires the Au Bon Pain chain and forms ABP Corporation to manage the acquisition.

2000: Bruckmann, Rosser sells ABP to Granada Compass PLC.

2004: ABP begins courting suburban clientele with a new prototype store.

2005: ABP's management acquires a 75 percent interest in their company from Granada Compass PLC.

2006: ABP signs international franchise agreements that will nearly double the size of the Au Bon Pain chain.

2008: LNK Partners acquires a majority stake in ABP.

larger than Au Bon Pain. By 2002, Panera Bread ranked as the largest bakery-café chain in the country, boasting roughly 500 stores and annual revenues of $755 million. Shaich was pursuing a target of 1,500 Panera Bread stores nationwide, while Guidara, in contrast, presided over a chain that was getting smaller with each passing year.

A DRAMATIC SHIFT IN STRATEGY IN 2004

ABP recorded encouraging success with the changes made to its stores. The company registered same-store sales increases for four consecutive years at the beginning of the decade, lifting revenues to an estimated $245 million in 2004, a 14 percent increase over the previous year's total. The changes were not enough, however, to enable the chain to expand. Panera Bread ended 2004 with 700 units in operation and $1.16 billion in revenue. The gap separating Au Bon Pain from its former sister chain was widening into a chasm, and Guidara needed to find a way to ignite his chain's growth. In 2004, he tested the waters with a profound shift in Au Bon Pain's strategy, aping the approach used by Panera Bread. A prototype for a suburban Au Bon Pain was established in Woburn, Massachusetts, signaling the beginning of a new era for the nearly 30-year-old concept.

As was often the case in ABP Corporation's history, a change in strategy occurred at approximately the same time a change in ownership occurred. Guidara left ABP in early 2005 to become the chief executive officer of Uno Chicago Grill. He was replaced by Sue Morelli, a 17-year Au Bon Pain veteran, and under Morelli's guidance ABP's management purchased 75 percent of the company from Granada Compass, a $90 million deal sponsored by PNC Mezzanine Capital. Morelli, in the August 22, 2005 issue of *Nation's Restaurant News*, described the buyout as a "mutual decision," between ABP and Granada Compass. "It was seen as a better way for Au Bon Pain to go forward," she said.

Experimenting with strategy, a decade-long theme at Au Bon Pain, continued after the management buyout. In 2006, the company adjusted its two-year-old suburban strategy after research revealed the prototype in Woburn had failed to produce the desired results. "It was not in line with what suburban folks wanted," Morelli explained in the August 21, 2006 issue of *Nation's Restaurant News*. "There was not enough differentiation from the traditional urban design," she added. As part of the redesign, store hours were expanded, a store layout was created with a visible kitchen, and the self-service format was altered to provide suburban patrons with limited table service.

acquired ABP for an estimated $108 million. ABP became part of one of the world's largest foodservice organizations, a $13 billion-in-sales conglomerate that supplied food to corporate cafeterias, airports, train stations, hospitals, and universities.

As ownership of ABP changed hands, the search for an effective retail format pressed forward. Guidara remained chief executive officer under Granada Compass ownership, spearheading an overhaul of Au Bon Pain's concept, a seemingly never-ending task at the company's Boston headquarters. He decided to eliminate table service entirely and convert the 270 units in operation into a self-service format. Krispy Kreme doughnuts, a popular item, were added to the company's menu, and the stores' interiors adopted the look of a French Bistro, incorporating bright yellow and pale blue colors. Sales increased nearly 25 percent at the redesigned units, but the chain failed to expand, finding little room to maneuver in urban markets.

Meanwhile, Shaich, over at Panera Bread, was experiencing a far different set of circumstances. When Panera Bread shed Au Bon Pain in 1999, the chain comprised 97 units. By 2001, there were 287 units, mostly franchised, in operation, making Panera Bread

AU BON PAIN PURSUES GROWTH OVERSEAS

While Morelli pinned her hopes on the success of the suburban strategy, she also looked overseas to stimulate ABP's expansion. At the end of 2006, she announced Au Bon Pain would nearly double the number of its locations by adding 200 more bakery cafés through franchise agreements with companies in Kuwait and Thailand. ABP Corporation signed an agreement with a Kuwait-based company, The Sultan Center, to open 100 new units during the ensuing decade in the Middle East and northern Africa. A similarly sized agreement was signed with ABP Thailand, a franchise organization that had been operating Au Bon Pain bakery cafés and kiosks in Thailand since the late 1990s.

LNK PARTNERS TAKES CONTROL IN 2008

Despite its troubles, ABP always piqued the interest of onlookers. Beginning with Kane, the Au Bon Pain concept attracted suitors, compelling Bruckmann, Rosser, Granada Compass, and its own management to invest substantial amounts of capital to gain control of the chain. In 2008, the chain's 30th anniversary, another name was added to the list. In January, LNK Partners, a White Plains, New York-based private-equity firm, purchased a majority stake in ABP, investing more than $100 million in the acquisition.

As ABP prepared for the future, the company continued to struggle with the same problem that had plagued the chain for roughly 15 years. The company ranked as the third-largest bakery café chain in the country, trailing Panera Bread and Einstein Noah Restaurant Group, Inc., but it had not discovered a formula for genuine success. The stewards of the Au Bon Pain chain had tinkered with various formats for more than a decade, achieving little success in creating a concept that could be expanded substantially. For the years ahead, ABP's management looked to penetrate suburban markets, where Panera Bread enjoyed a commanding lead. They also looked overseas, seeking to expand the concept through franchise agreements in Asia as well as in other international markets.

Jeffrey L. Covell

PRINCIPAL COMPETITORS

Atlanta Bread Company International, Inc.; CBC Restaurant Corp.; Einstein Noah Restaurant Group, Inc.; Panera Bread Company.

FURTHER READING

Allen, Robin Lee, "Au Bon Pain Preps French-Style Upgrades Under Guidara Regime," *Nation's Restaurant News,* May 29, 2000, p. 4.

————, "Au Bon Pain's Kane Dead at 69; Founded Bakery Chain," *Nation's Restaurant News,* June 26, 2000, p. 6.

Aronovich, Hanna, "Driving Forces," *Food and Drink,* January–February 2008, p. 60.

"Au Bon Pain Expanding Overseas," *Europe Intelligence Wire,* November 15, 2006.

Battaglia, Andy, "Help Kneaded: St. Louis Bread/Panera to Go Its Own Way, Plans to Rise Without ABP," *Nation's Restaurant News,* February 22, 1999, p. 12.

"Compass Points to Au Bon Pain Overhaul," *Restaurants & Institutions,* March 1, 2001, p. 16.

Frumpkin, Paul, "Au Bon Pain Management Buys 75 Percent Stake in Company," *Nation's Restaurant News,* August 22, 2005, p. 1.

————, "Au Bon Pain Retools Bistro Prototype in Panera Pursuit," *Nation's Restaurant News,* August 21, 2006, p. 4.

Goodison, Donna L., "Au Bon Pain Acquisition May Be Near," *Boston Business Journal,* December 1, 2000, p. 1.

Hamstra, Mark, "Au Bon Pain Bids Au Revoir to Flagship Bakery Chain," *Nation's Restaurant News,* August 24, 1998, p. 1.

"LNK Takes a Slice of Au Bon Pain," *Investment Dealers' Digest,* January 21, 2008.

Lohmeyer, Lori, "Bakery-Café Chain Au Bon Pain Goes to Market with New Image," *Nation's Restaurant News,* August 19, 2002, p. 8.

Papiernik, Richard, "Au Bon Pain Ends 1997 with Profitable Run into New Year," *Nation's Restaurant News,* March 16, 1998, p. 14.

Reidy, Chris, "Boston-Based Au Bon Pain Eatery Sold to London-Based Food Conglomerate," *Boston Globe,* December 22, 2000.

Spector, Amy, "BRS to Acquire Il Fornaio, Eyes Sale of Au Bon Pain," *Nation's Restaurant News,* November 27, 2000, p. 1.

Accenture Ltd.

Canon's Court, 22 Victoria Street
Hamilton, HM 12
Bermuda
Telephone: (441) 296-8262
Toll Free: (877) 889-9009
Web site: http://www.accenture.com

Public Company
Incorporated: 2001
Employees: 186,000
Sales: $25.31 billion (2008)
Stock Exchanges: New York
Ticker Symbol: CAN
NAICS: 541990 All Other Professional, Scientific, and Technical Services; 541618 Other Management Consulting Services

■ ■ ■

Accenture Ltd. is the world's largest consulting firm, offering consulting, systems integration, outsourcing, and technology services to corporations involved in more than 15 industries. Once a facet of Arthur Andersen's operations, Accenture broke free from the accounting firm in 2000. Accenture operates offices in more than 200 cities in 52 countries, serving *Fortune* 1,000 clients and government agencies.

ORIGINS

The consequences were manifold and profound when General Electric Co. turned to Arthur Andersen & Co. in 1953 and asked the auditing firm to do something it had never done before. It was a seminal moment. An industry was born, the world's first business computer was installed, the world's largest consulting company was created, and a schism was created within the largest accounting firm in the world, Arthur Andersen, eventually fracturing the company in half. The Accenture name did not appear until a half-century later, but the story of its development began when General Electric asked a group of accountants to be something other than accountants.

General Electric wanted to automate payroll processing and manufacturing within its appliance division based in Louisville, Kentucky. In 1953, the company asked Arthur Andersen to conduct a feasibility study to determine the best course of action. Arthur Andersen, moving into uncharted waters, researched the possibilities and recommended General Electric install UNIVAC, an acronym for Universal Automatic Computer. The world's first commercial computer, the 29,000-pound UNIVAC had debuted two years earlier, counting the U.S. Census Bureau and the U.S. Air Force as its first customers. General Electric, which heeded Arthur Andersen's advice, became UNIVAC's first commercial customer when the company acquired the machine in 1954 and hired Arthur Andersen to install the world's first commercial computer application to automate payroll processing and manufacturing at its Appliance Park facility.

To spearhead the new and unfamiliar venture, Arthur Andersen turned to one of its employees, Joe Glickauf, and established an Administrative Services division. Glickauf, regarded as the father of computer

COMPANY PERSPECTIVES

■

Our "high performance business" strategy builds on our expertise in consulting, technology and outsourcing to help clients perform at the highest levels so they can create sustainable value for their customers and shareholders. Using our industry knowledge, service-offering expertise and technology capabilities, we identify new business and technology trends and develop solutions to help clients around the world.

consulting, headed the division for its first dozen years of existence. The creation of the Administrative Services division in 1954 gave the corporate world its first data processing business, soon to become a massive industry, and represented the beginnings of Arthur Andersen's consulting business, a business that later became known as Andersen Consulting before being rebranded as Accenture.

The first project completed by Arthur Andersen's Administrative Services division established the template for the parade of consulting jobs to follow in its wake. Glickauf and his successors established Arthur Andersen as the preeminent authority on installing mainframe computer systems and customizing the systems for business customers. The consulting business branched into systems integration services, strategic services, software development, and an array of other technological services.

FAST GROWTH BREEDS DISCONTENT

The work performed by the consulting arm of Arthur Andersen, first couched as administrative services, became better known in later years as "information systems" and "information technology," one of the main pillars supporting virtually every *Fortune* 1,000 company. Arthur Andersen's consulting business thrived as a result, becoming an important financial contributor to a company owned by its partners, primarily accountants. Tension between the two sides of the company, the consultants and auditors, was palpable by the end of the 1970s, when the consultants' fees accounted for more than 20 percent of Arthur Andersen's revenue. At the end of the decade, Harvey Kapnick, the managing partner of Arthur Andersen, suggested dividing the company into two separate firms, one focused on accounting and the other on consulting, but his proposal was rejected by Arthur Andersen's auditors.

From there, a rift between the accountants and the consultants transmogrified into a chasm, setting the stage for a divorce that occurred in two phases, the first taking place a decade after Kapnick made his suggestion and the second following a decade later.

By the end of the 1970s, the consulting arm of Arthur Andersen contributed more than 20 percent of the firm's revenues. By the end of the 1980s, helping other companies install and use computer systems accounted for more than 40 percent of Arthur Andersen's revenues. The increasing importance of the Administrative Services division to Arthur Andersen's financial health aggravated emotions. Consultants grew increasingly angry, resenting the differences in the pay scale separating the consulting and accounting sides of Arthur Andersen and annoyed at the managerial control bestowed on the auditors over consulting projects. A wave of consulting partners resigned from the company, which triggered lawsuits filed by Arthur Andersen against the departing consultants. The animosity within the company ebbed for a time when the head of Arthur Andersen, Duane Kullberg, did what his predecessor had proposed. In 1979, Kapnick suggested splitting Arthur Andersen in half. In 1989, Kullberg succeeded in dividing the company, but the arrangement did not endure.

CREATION OF SEPARATE COMPANIES: 1989

In 1989, Arthur Andersen's leader looked to calm his company's internecine feud in neutral Switzerland. Kullberg turned to a Swiss cooperative formed by the company in the 1970s and renamed it Andersen Worldwide Société Coopérative, a Geneva-based umbrella organization charged with governing Arthur Andersen & Co., the auditing and tax operations, and Andersen Consulting, the former Administrative Services division. Separate, but tied together through contractual provisions administered by Andersen Worldwide, the two companies began pursuing their own agendas, soon to square off in what would be the ultimate battle for independence.

George T. Shaheen took command of Andersen Consulting upon its formation and began presiding over robust growth. Andersen Consulting was a $1.88 billion business in 1989, the year it began offering facilities management services and began taking control of a client's entire information-processing department. Shaheen also guided Andersen Consulting into the personal computer (PC) market during the first years of the company's independence, responding to changing market conditions that saw corporations move away from mainframe systems. Andersen Consulting signed reseller contracts with Sun Microsystems Inc., Hewlett-

KEY DATES

1954: Arthur Andersen & Co. diversifies into consulting, marking the birth of Accenture.

1979: Arthur Andersen's managing partner, Harvey Kapnick, suggests dividing the company into two separate firms; his proposal is rejected.

1989: Arthur Andersen's Administrative Services division becomes a separate company, Andersen Consulting.

1997: Andersen Consulting seeks complete independence and turns to the International Court of Arbitration to resolve its case.

2000: Andersen Consulting is allowed to sever its ties with Arthur Andersen.

2001: Company changes its name to Accenture Ltd. and completes an initial public offering of stock.

2004: Accenture is awarded a $10 billion contract by the U.S. government to develop a "virtual border."

2008: Revenues exceed $25 billion.

Packard Co., and Compaq Computer Corp., tailoring its services to align with the increasing use of client/server architecture. Andersen Consulting offered its clients software development services, system integration, and local and wide-area networking capabilities, and its business grew rapidly.

During the 1990s, Andersen Consulting flourished, recording 20 percent annual growth. The company's financial success sowed the seeds of discontent, however, aggravating the animosity between consultants and auditors that had been festering for decades. One of the provisions established when the consulting and accounting operations were separated called for the more profitable of the two firms to pay the other company a percentage of its net income. Andersen Consulting, growing faster and more profitable than Arthur Andersen, perennially shared as much as 15 percent of its profits with Arthur Andersen. To make the situation more egregious from Andersen Consulting's perspective, Arthur Andersen formed its own consulting business in 1994, which began to compete against Andersen Consulting. By the end of 1997, when Andersen Consulting's revenues reached $6 billion, eclipsing the $5.2 billion generated by Arthur Andersen, Shaheen had had enough.

ANDERSEN CONSULTING GOES TO COURT IN 1997

Shaheen wanted complete independence from Arthur Andersen and Andersen Worldwide. He sought the help of an international arbitrator, filing a claim for breach of contract with the International Court of Arbitration in Paris in December 1997 and ceased making payments to Arthur Andersen, putting the company's annual payments in escrow pending the ruling. Andersen Consulting faced a termination fee potentially as high as $14 billion to complete the breakup, but when Colombian lawyer Guillermo Gamba Posada issued his ruling in August 2000, Andersen Consulting was granted its wish for a fraction of the price. Andersen Consulting was ordered to pay $1.2 billion to Arthur Andersen to gain its freedom, but $800 million of the sum consisted of the payments the company held in escrow.

The ruling generally was perceived by observers as a victory for Andersen Consulting, an assessment echoed by Joe Forehand, who replaced Shaheen as the company's chief executive officer in 1999. "This is a total win for Andersen Consulting," Forehand said in the August 7, 2000 edition of the *Chicago Tribune*. "We won. It's over." The greatest loss from the ruling, one that Andersen Consulting valued at $7 billion, was its identity. Posada ordered the company to drop the Andersen name from its corporate title by the beginning of 2001, but within months even that loss turned out to be a victory.

ADOPTION OF ACCENTURE NAME: 2001

Andersen Consulting, after decades of rancor, was free to pursue its own strategy and reap the full financial rewards of its efforts. The 65,000-employee company generated $8.9 billion in revenue in 1999, a year during which it began moving away from installing computer systems and shifted its focus to transforming beyond the parameters defining a consulting company. The company attempted to become a more nimble operator, no longer able to sustain itself on lengthy systems integration projects. It began pursuing a number of different avenues, taking on shorter-term consulting jobs and delving in venture capital, business incubation, and outsourcing services. A new type of company was being created, one whose shape and scope had to be reflected in its new name, the most pressing concern after the ruling of the International Court Arbitration. The company considered more than 5,000 possible names, investigated 3,000 for trademark violations, and researched hundreds of candidates for offensive connotations in dozens of languages. Andersen Consulting hired a firm to help it create its new identity, but it ultimately embraced a suggestion from one of its employees, Kim Petersen, who worked in a branch office in Oslo, Norway. In October 2000, both "Andersen" and "Consulting" were dropped from the company's corporate title when it unveiled Accenture Ltd. as its new name.

On January 1, 2001, Andersen Consulting officially changed its name to Accenture. In February, the company, which claimed to have no headquarters, registered as a Bermuda corporation based in Hamilton, establishing its official residence in a British-controlled territory that imposed no income tax, no capital gains tax, and scant business regulation. In July, the company completed an initial public offering (IPO) of stock, raising $1.7 billion in an offering that sold 13 percent of Accenture, and proceeded to record the most successful four-month period in its history. Between September and December 2001, Accenture booked $5.6 billion in new contracts, ending the year with a 17 percent increase in revenue to $11.4 billion, a rate of growth that was more than double the industry average. Accenture thrived after its separation from Arthur Andersen, but the same could not be said of the auditors the company left behind.

THE COLLAPSE OF ARTHUR ANDERSEN

While Accenture was enjoying the most productive period in its history, Arthur Andersen endured the most devastating period in its history. One of the accounting firm's largest clients, Enron Corp., filed for bankruptcy in December 2001, two months after the U.S. Securities and Exchange Commission revealed it was investigating the company. Fraud and corruption on a massive, systematic scale emerged from the investigation, casting attention to the practices of Arthur Andersen. The company conceded in January 2002 that its employees had shredded a substantial number of Enron-related documents, which led to the firm's conviction of obstruction of justice charges later that year. Barred from offering auditing services to publicly traded companies in the United States, the company collapsed, the $7 billion value of the Andersen name, no longer an asset, transmogrified into a stigma.

Accenture, free and clear of the debacle in name and association, did not look back at the carnage left behind. In 2002, the year Arthur Andersen was convicted of its fatal crime, Forehand announced he intended to double Accenture's annual revenue in the not-too-distant future. He planned to increase the firm's government contracts, move it deeper into outsourcing, and he placed an emphasis on performance-based and fixed-price contracts, as opposed to the hourly fee model

that had been the company's lifeblood. In 2004, he passed the reins of command to William D. Green, a 26-year veteran of the firm who was promoted from his position as chief operating officer, and Green took the helm of a company continuing to enjoy enviable success. In 2004, Accenture won a $10 billion contract from the U.S. government to design and to install a system that used fingerprints, facial scans, and other technology to identify every foreigner passing into or out of the United States. The massive contract reflected the new face of Accenture, symbolizing its new capabilities and pointing to a promising future for a company whose legacy had been built on antiquated mainframe computers.

The first five years of Green's tenure made good on the predictions expressed by Forehand. Between 2004 and 2008, Accenture's financial stature swelled; a $15 billion company became a $25 billion company. Accenture divided its work into five categories: Communications & High Technology; Financial Services; Products (including automotive, consumer goods, retail, and health and life sciences); Public Service; and Resources. Directing its work along these five business lines, the company celebrated its 55th anniversary in 2009, holding sway as the vibrant vestige of the once-powerful Arthur Andersen.

Jeffrey L. Covell

PRINCIPAL SUBSIDIARIES

Accenture SRL (Argentina); Accenture Australia Holdings Pty Ltd.; Accenture GmbH (Austria); Accenture S.A./N.V. (Belgium); Partners Security Ltd.; Accenture do Brasil Ltda. (Brazil); Accenture Canada Holdings Inc.; Accenture Ltda. (Colombia); Accenture Denmark Holdings A/S; Accenture Oy (Finland); Accenture Holdings France SAS; Accenture GmbH (Germany); Accenture S.A. (Greece); Accenture Co. Ltd. (Hong Kong); Accenture Services Private Ltd. (India); Accenture Technology Solutions (Ireland); Accenture SpA (Italy); Accenture Japan Ltd.; Accenture International Sarl (Luxembourg); Accenture S.C. (Mexico); Accenture Holdings B.V. (Netherlands); Accenture A.S. (Norway); Accenture Pte. Ltd. (Singapore); Accenture Africa Pty Ltd. (South Africa); Accenture S. L. (Spain); Accenture AB (Sweden); Accenture AG (Switzerland); Accenture (UK) Ltd.; Accenture LLP (USA); Accenture Inc. (USA); Accenture Financial Corporation (USA); Avanade Inc. (USA); Random Walk Computing Inc. (USA); Accenture Insurance Services LLC (USA).

Accenture Ltd.

PRINCIPAL OPERATING UNITS

Communications & High Tech; Financial Services; Products; Public Service; Resources.

PRINCIPAL COMPETITORS

BearingPoint, Inc.; Electronic Data Systems, LLC; International Business Machines Corporation.

FURTHER READING

Banks, Howard, "House Divided," *Forbes,* November 3, 1997, p. 344.

Doler, Kathleen, "Andersen Consulting Takes Aim at Burgeoning PC Arena," *PC Week,* January 15, 1990, p. 119.

Gordon, Joanne, "A Rose by Any Name," *Forbes,* March 4, 2002, p. 86.

Kaiser, Rob, "Accenture, Formerly Andersen Consulting, Prepares to Go Forward with IPO," *Chicago Tribune,* March 22, 2001.

———, "Andersen Consulting Becomes Accenture After Much Pondering," *Chicago Tribune,* October 26, 2000.

———, "Andersen Consulting to Name 1,300 Partners in Effort to Retain Employees," *Chicago Tribune,* August 31, 2000.

Manor, Robert, "Accenture Grows into Life on Bermuda, Land of Few Taxes or Rules," *Chicago Tribune,* July 20, 2001.

———, "Accenture Ltd. Sets Price on $1.8 Billion IPO," *Chicago Tribune,* June 11, 2001.

Pearlstein, Steven, "How Accenture Seized Tomorrow," *America's Intelligence Wire,* June 4, 2004.

Sachdev, Ameet, "Accounting, Consulting Leaders Have History of Antagonism," *Chicago Tribune,* August 8, 2000.

———, "Andersen Consulting, Arthur Andersen Split Signals Industry-Wide Rifts," *Chicago Tribune,* August 13, 2000.

Schmeltzer, John, "Andersen Consulting to Give Up Name in Divorce," *Chicago Tribune,* August 7, 2000.

Semich, J. William, "Andersen Consulting," *Datamation,* June 15, 1992, p. 52.

Taylor, Paul, "Accenture Chief to Step Down," *Financial Times,* March 31, 2004, p. 20.

Wahlgren, Eric, "Accenture Goes with a Veteran," *America's Intelligence Wire,* April 9, 2004.

Access to Money, Inc.

———— ■ ————

1101 Kings Highway North, Suite G100
Cherry Hill, New Jersey 08034
U.S.A.
Telephone: (856) 414-9100
Toll Free: (800) 877-8762
Fax: (856) 414-9186
Web site: http://www.accesstomoney.com

Public Company
Incorporated: 1981 as TRM Copy Centers Corporation
Employees: 61
Sales: $88.61 million (2008)
Stock Exchanges: Over the Counter (OTC)
Ticker Symbol: AEMI
NAICS: 541990 All Other Professional, Scientific, and
    Technical Services

■ ■ ■

Access to Money, Inc., sells, leases, and rents automated teller machines (ATMs), managing roughly 12,000 ATMs throughout the United States. Access to Money provides equipment and services to convenience stores, shopping malls, supermarkets, restaurants, and other retailers. The company's support services include repairing ATMs, supplying parts and supplies, and providing custom branding and graphics programs that include logo placement, color themes, and other design elements.

SIMPLE BEGINNINGS IN 1981

In 1981, then 19-year-old Matthew J. Shawcross and two other friends combined their initials over a good idea and launched TRM Copy Centers Corporation. Using surplus used copy machines from their existing copier sales business, Shawcross and associates started their fledgling 5-cents-a-copy photocopying business out of an office in Portland, Oregon.

The company was organized around a simple contract. Under a joint agreement between TRM and the owner of each of its host retail locations, the company received a fee of $95 for each used, reconditioned copy machine it installed. In exchange, TRM agreed to repair and stock its machines, retaining only a percentage of the standard 5 cents per copy that it charged consumers. The first installations, which occurred in the greater Portland area, were relatively easy to keep stocked with paper and toner, and repairs were handled through arrangements with local service technicians. However, what was simple on a small scale became unwieldy as the company began to grow.

By 1984, with 100 copy machines installed in small retail locations throughout Oregon, the tiny company was floundering. Edwin S. Chan, a Chinese immigrant who had just ended a 27-year career as manager of over 80 branches of Copeland Lumber Yards, Inc., took the reins of management at the struggling TRM. "I had been managing a $100 million business," Chan would tell Dori Jones Yang of *Business Week*, "and now I had to make money a nickel at a time." Forgoing a salary for the first six months in lieu of an increasing share of company equity, Chan successfully introduced several efficiency and cost-saving measures, including an automated billing system and an in-house copier repair service. Within four years Chan had turned TRM around; the once-flailing company was experiencing an annual growth rate of 30 percent. By the end of 1988 net income was posted as $615,000 on sales of $5.9 million. At 5 cents per copy, this translated into over 118 million copies made at the company's 3,550 copy centers, totaling 236,000 reams of paper.

PREPARING FOR EXPANSION: 1990

By the beginning of 1990, with the previous year's sales cresting at $10 million, Chan had set TRM on a course down the road to major expansion. The company's steadily increasing sales volume allowed it to purchase paper, toner, and other supplies in bulk, thus benefiting from price discounts and further increasing the profitability of each sale. Also, by relying on a streamlined "fleet" of just two standard copier models, TRM was able to cut the cost of machine repairs by stockpiling spare parts. This homogeneity also allowed the company's repairmen to carry the most commonly used replacement parts with them when responding to service calls for individual machines. The company's increasingly centralized management and more standardized operations also minimized overhead costs. By the close of fiscal 1990, with the number of copy centers standing at 8,307, TRM's earnings had almost doubled from the previous year's level, rising to $1 million.

In the fall of 1991 TRM opened its first copy center in English-speaking Canada; it would soon enter Quebec as well. Chan was also busy laying the groundwork for expanding TRM's markets across the Atlantic, where the company's bright yellow logo would become a familiar site in London beginning in mid-1992. The company continued to increase the number of individual copy centers in its core domestic markets as well. Even with the increasing sales that these expansion efforts would generate, TRM's biggest stride

forward was yet to come. In November 1991 the company finally made the decision to go public, offering 1.8 million shares on the NASDAQ. This stock offering raised $13.8 million worth of funding and debt reduction for the growing company, which TRM augmented during the remainder of fiscal 1991 with profits from its 11,382 copy centers in 26 metropolitan areas worldwide. By the end of fiscal 1992 TRM would post net income of $2.7 million on sales of $30.5 million. In the eight years since Chan had taken command, the copy company had grown an amazing 500 percent.

TRM GOES COLOR: 1992

In 1992 with 14,000 copiers installed in 34 cities throughout North America alone, the company began to introduce color copiers in certain of its locations. By September of that year 80 color photocopy machines were available to consumers in test-market cities in Oregon, Arizona, and Washington; customers were charged 39 cents apiece for full-color copies. The company also signed buying agreements with photocopy manufacturer Ricoh that enabled it to receive favorable discounts on supplies and repair parts; it would do the same with Mita in 1993. While the company realized that its entry into the European market would require a period of adaptation to a different environment and time to acquire the requisite goodwill needed to grow sales, by August 1993 TRM had established 860 copy "centres" in London alone. In addition, plans were underway to expand northward into the industrial city of Manchester. Although management acknowledged the increased expense incurred by foreign expansion, it viewed its first overseas venture as a learning experience. Future expansion operations, both overseas and domestically, would be increasingly streamlined, with a satellite system of new copy centers receiving initial technical and managerial support from profitable, more established operations.

Meanwhile, on its own shores, the company had expanded its full-color copy centers to 298, and customer enthusiasm for this new service would continue to expand that number. During 1993 the company also formed BisCard Corporation, a subsidiary dedicated to developing new, business-oriented products. The BisCard self-service, design-and-print business card venture was test-marketed in 50 kiosks located throughout Portland during 1993. By year-end, with expansion of both locations and product, the company employed a total staff of 365 men and women to oversee its copy centers and kiosks and manage its corporate affairs. Together, these employees helped to earn TRM sales of $38.8 million, which resulted in 1993 net income of $3.3 million.

COMPETITION AT HOME, EXPANSION ABROAD, CUT INTO 1994 PROFITS

The year 1994 would witness the first copy centers to appear on the European continent, as the yellow TRM logo became visible in various retail locations throughout northern Paris. Total copy centers numbered 25,563 scattered over 50 metropolitan areas, the vast majority still in the United States. While company growth continued, it slowed relative to previous years, a result both of increased competition by new local vendors within TRM's core market and the disproportionate expenses associated with TRM's continuing expansion overseas. While 1994 sales in Europe increased more than 500 percent over the previous fiscal year, continental copy centers did not begin to outstep their associated costs and turn a profit until the end of the second quarter in December. By the following June, the end of fiscal 1994, the company posted sales of $47.9 million.

Despite an increasingly competitive retail environment, between 1991 and the final quarter of 1994 TRM had managed to successfully expand its network of copy centers from 26 to 41 urban areas in the United States

alone. The introduction, as well, of three Canadian cities and six European metropolitan areas would result in a company presence that generated combined sales of $43.7 million in North America compared with just over $4.2 million in Europe, where the United Kingdom remained home to the majority of the company's copy center outlets.

PAPER PRICES MASK RISING SALES BASE

Notwithstanding a dramatic worldwide increase in paper prices, 1995 would be a banner year for TRM. On the strength of its 570 employees, the company posted sales of $60.5 million, complemented by a jump in net income from $3.3 million to $3.7 million from the previous year. The company maintained 43 service areas in the United States, three in Canada, seven in the United Kingdom, and one in France, encompassing 28,995 individual copy centers. Of these, the TRM copy centers scattered throughout the United States accounted for 80 percent of the company's total annual revenue.

In 1995 Chan would retire as president and CEO of TRM. He was replaced by Michael D. Simon, a former vice-president of Sequent Computer Systems. This changing of the guard signaled a reorganization within the ranks of the company's middle management and a renewed commitment to upgrading skills and reevaluating key operational areas. In addition to improving profitability and continuing its policy of aggressive expansion, TRM also looked to broaden its business by finding new ways to cater to its small host retailers.

The increasing automation of company systems that had been underway since Chan's first year as CEO began to reap even more dividends. From the data generated by its centralized computer system, company analysts were able to calculate the price elasticity of various market areas throughout the world, resulting in price changes at 25 percent of TRM's copy center locations. Poorly performing machines were relocated to areas that indicated potentially higher volumes. Also, the servicing strategy for each of the company's photocopy machines changed from an "on-call" policy to scheduled servicing by field technicians, thereby enhancing timely maintenance, customer satisfaction, and the most cost-effective use of each technician through reduced drive-time to each service site.

TRM IN THE MID-NINETIES

By the close of fiscal 1996, TRM maintained over 32,000 copy centers worldwide and a field service network of 400 employees. With year-end net income of $4.1 million on sales of $67.5 million, the company was still burdened by the inflated costs of paper on the world market. However, significant growth of its European locations and TRM's continued pricing adjustments to its domestic copy centers allowed for an 11.5 percent rise in net income over the previous year.

The year also marked the beginning of company-wide efforts to integrate its field service and field sales operations; TRM's new "service selling" program would provide an incentive for each service technician to promote the TRM program to retailers within his or her service areas. In addition, the company began to investigate its market potential within both larger retail chains and through stand-alone service centers. Expanding its operations throughout Europe remained another priority: by company estimates, despite the higher costs of such consumables as paper, toner, and photocopier parts, the European market had the potential to be even more expansive than the U.S. market.

TRM ADDS ATMS IN 1998

The search for new avenues of growth steered TRM in a new direction in the late 1990s, sending the company on an adventurous, transformational ride. The impetus for the profound changes was management's dissatisfaction with the photocopier business, a business that was profitable but suffered from little growth potential. By 1998, TRM had recorded three consecutive years of flat sales, prompting the company to try a new line of business. In June, the company announced it had received a capital infusion of $20 million from a Philadelphia-based investment group, part of which it intended to use to diversify into the ATM business. TRM planned to court the same retail clientele as it did for its photocopier business, and just as it did with its photocopier business, the company would service the machines and receive a percentage of the fees paid by consumers. ATMs, like photocopiers, were seen as tools to increase foot traffic at retail locations, but ATMs, in contrast to photocopiers, represented a business with seductive growth potential.

It took nearly a year before TRM began operating as a non-bank ATM operator. The company debated whether to build the business internally or launch its foray through an acquisition. Meanwhile, senior officials talked with ATM manufacturers and the ATM transaction networks, Plus and Cirrus. Executives decided to build the business from the ground up, establishing the first TRM-managed ATM in the spring of 1999 and ending the year with 443 machines in operation. After a slow start, TRM picked up the pace of expansion during the next two years, using its network of photocopy centers as a roadmap for creating an ATM network. By the end of 2001, the company operated 33,355 self-service photocopiers at retail locations in North America and Europe and maintained 1,857 ATMs in the United States and the United Kingdom.

EFUNDS ACQUISITION TRIGGERS PROBLEMS

TRM shied away from acquisitions as a way to build its ATM network during its first five years in the business, relying on internal expansion to become the 10th-largest independent operator in the United States by 2004. The year marked a significant change in strategy, one that would haunt the company in succeeding years. TRM began acquiring ATMs in 2004, making its first push into Canada with the purchase of Mighty Cash Financial and completing a mammoth deal at the end of the year. The company acquired 17,000 ATMs from Scottsdale, Arizona-based eFunds Corp., a $150 million deal that made TRM the second-largest independent operator in the United States and the operator of the largest international network of ATMs. After the acquisition was completed, TRM operated 21,000 ATMs throughout North America and the United Kingdom.

In the wake of the eFunds acquisition, TRM struggled. The company experienced difficulties in integrating the acquired assets into its operations, difficulties that were exacerbated by a rash of ATM robberies in the United Kingdom in 2005. Financial losses and debt obligations mounted, causing the company's stock value to plunge and prompting TRM's independent auditor, in a filing with the U.S. Securities and Exchange Commission, to raise questions about whether the company could "continue as a going concern," as reported in the April 18, 2006 issue of *American Banker*.

In response to its problems, TRM began to shed assets. In June 2006, the company sold its photocopier business in the United Kingdom. After reporting a staggering $101.2 million loss during the third fiscal quarter of 2006, the divestiture program intensified. At the end of 2006, TRM sold its U.S.-based photocopier business and reached an agreement to sell its Canadian ATM operations. In January 2007, the company sold its European ATM operations.

ACQUIRING ACCESS TO MONEY:
2008

After the fire sale, TRM paused before attempting to rebuild itself. The company took its first positive step forward in April 2008, when it secured $11 million in financing. The money was used to meet some of its financial obligations and to acquire Whippany, New Jersey-based LJR Consulting Corp., a company that operated under the name Access to Money. The $15 million deal expanded TRM's U.S.-based ATM network to 12,200 machines and gave it a new identity. TRM re-branded itself as Access to Money in 2008, the year it moved its headquarters from Oregon to New Jersey, and began focusing entirely on ATM operations in the United States. In 2009, the company officially changed its name to Access to Money, Inc. "This is the final step in the long transition process associated with our acquisition of Access to Money," the company's chief executive officer said in the July 11, 2009 issue of *Investment Weekly News*. "While the TRM name had been as-sociated with leadership in the ATM industry in its early days, we believe that the name Access to Money not only describes our primary service, but is also readily identifiable with our business of distributing and servic-ing ATM machines."

Pamela L. Shelton
Updated, Jeffrey L. Covell

PRINCIPAL SUBSIDIARIES

TRM (Canada) Corporation; FPC France Ltd.; TRM ATM Corporation; TRM ATM Acquisition Corpora-tion; S-3 Corporation; Access Cash International LLC; TRM Services Limited (UK).

PRINCIPAL COMPETITORS

Cardtronics, Inc.; Electronic Cash Systems, Inc.; Global Axcess Corp.

FURTHER READING

"ATM Expansions Increase Revenues for Portland, Ore.-Based Tech Firm," *ORian,* March 7, 2001.

Breitkopf, David, "Purchase Brings TRM Corp. into Canada's ATM Market," *American Banker,* June 24, 2004, p. 7.

———, "TRM Losing Execs as Auditor Questions Viability," *American Banker,* April 18, 2006, p. 17.

———, "TRM Pins Loss on Integration Problems, Canceled U.K. Deal," *American Banker,* April 3, 2006, p. 5.

Goldfield, Robert, "Can TRM Get Beyond Copiers?" *Business Journal-Portland,* January 1, 1999, p. 10.

Jalili, H. Michael, "TRM Selling Its Canada ATMs to EZEE," *American Banker,* December 18, 2006, p. 5.

Tripp, Julie, "TRM Shares Drop in Wake of Executive's Resignation," *ORian,* March 15, 2006.

"TRM Agrees to Buy eFunds ATM Network for $150 Mil-lion," *America's Intelligence Wire,* September 20, 2004.

"TRM Corporation Announces Name Change to Access to Money, Inc.," *Investment Weekly News,* July 11, 2009, p. 391.

"TRM Sells European ATM Business," *Wireless News,* January 29, 2007.

"TRM to Acquire Travelex UK ATM Network," *Wireless News,* September 3, 2005.

Wade, Will, "Ailing ATM Operator Asserts Its Viability," *American Banker,* April 25, 2008, p. 6.

Yang, Dori Jones, "TRM Makes Millions—A Nickel at a Time," *Business Week,* June 1, 1992.

Air China Limited

Beijing Capital International Airport
Beijing, 100621
China
Telephone: (+86 10) 6146 2777
Toll Free: (800) 882-8122
Fax: (+86 10) 6146 2805
Web site: http://www.airchina.com.cn

Government-Controlled Public Company
Incorporated: 1988 as Air China
Employees: 20,494
Sales: CNY 52.91 billion (2008)
Stock Exchanges: Shanghai Hong Kong London
Ticker Symbols: 601111 00753 AIRC
NAICS: 481111 Scheduled Passenger Air Transportation; 481112 Scheduled Freight Air Transportation; 488190 Other Support Activities for Air Transportation

∎∎∎

Air China Limited is China's principal international airline, and is the designated flag carrier of the world's most populous country. Air China dominates passenger service at its home base in the capital of Beijing, as well as at China's largest city, Shanghai. Thanks to a cross-shareholding arrangement with Cathay Pacific, it is also well represented in Hong Kong.

The airline has occupied a special place in the hearts of aircraft manufacturers and foreign airlines eager for access to the untapped potential of the Asian market. In 2007 it became a member of the Star Alliance, a global group led by United Airlines. Air China's logo, made up of the letters "VIP" styled into the form of a phoenix, reflects the carrier's aspirations regarding customer service.

The most consistently profitable of China's Big Three airlines, Air China operates a fleet of some 230 aircraft on a network of about 80 domestic and 40 international destinations. It provides ground handling at Beijing Capital International Airport and has a major maintenance joint venture (Ameco) with Lufthansa. Air China has been a public company since 2004 but the Chinese government maintains a controlling interest.

ORIGINS

Air China was one of several airlines created out of the Civil Aviation Administration of China (CAAC) in the mid-1980s. This body, and its predecessors the China Civil Aviation Administration (CCAC) and the Chinese Civil Aviation Bureau (CAB), had directed China's civil air service since 1949. At first dependent on Soviet aviation technology, by the 1980s the Chinese were fielding fleets of modern Western jets as they began to compete with Western airlines on international routes.

Difficulty adapting to new marketplace competition and a series of accidents between 1979 and 1983 created pressure for the organization to change. The CAAC was reorganized in late 1984, producing the following four regional divisions: Eastern, Southern, Southwestern, and Northwestern. Air China, based in Beijing, was given chief responsibility for intercontinental flights, and took over the CAAC's long haul aircraft (Boeing 747s, 767s, and 707s, as well as medium-haul 737s) and routes

COMPANY PERSPECTIVES

The desire and orientation of Air China is an air company with an international reputation, the connotation of which is to realize four strategic targets of achieving leading competitiveness in the world, continuously developing and steadily increasing profits and providing excellent and unique travel experiences for passengers.

when it was granted its autonomy on July 1, 1988. Because of the commercial importance of Guangzhou (formerly Canton), China Southern was also cleared for international flights, along with Shanghai-based China Eastern.

The CAAC remained in existence as a kind of governmental overseer. It still controlled aircraft purchasing and worked very closely with its newly independent branches. The government also made its voice known to domestic passengers: an official letter of recommendation was a prerequisite for booking a flight until 1993.

At its launch in 1988, Air China operated 32 international routes to 31 destinations, and also connected 30 cities within China. It was China's largest carrier, and the only one allowed to carry China's national flag. In 1989, Air China posted a net profit of $106 million on revenues of $383 million. (The carrier had 6,000 employees at the time.) In that same year, Air China entered a joint venture with Lufthansa German Airlines, which provided 40 percent of the capital, or $220 million, to create the Beijing Aircraft Maintenance Center (Ameco Beijing). It specialized in the upkeep of the Boeing aircraft that constituted Air China's fleet. The venture was expanded with another $218 million (CNY 1.2 billion) in 1992. Ameco Beijing employed nearly 4,000 people, a little fewer than 50 of them from Lufthansa. *Air Transport World* reported the company preferred to source its needs through joint ventures due to the country's lack of hard currency. Its Beijing Air Catering was 40 percent owned by a large Hong Kong caterer.

EXPANSION

Air China's president, Xu Bai Ling, had years of experience piloting China's most distinguished visitors. An early priority for the airline was repairing a reputation damaged by delays, cancellations, or poor in-flight service. In the early 1990s, CAAC launched an incentive program to foster improvements. Air China hired consultants from Singapore Airlines, which was known for its stellar cabin crews. It also hired a few Russian planes and crews to fly certain routes.

Operating revenues for Air China were $1.05 billion in 1994, producing a net income of $36 million. In 1997, the airline reported sales of $1.38 billion (CNY 11.5 billion). The fleet had grown to 65 aircraft and the carrier was flying 144 routes overall. By October 1997, Air China was planning a public stock offering. China Eastern Airlines and China Southern Airlines had listed on the Hong Kong and New York exchanges earlier in the year. Air China delayed its plans due to poor financial performance and a downturn in business caused by the Asian financial crisis.

Rumors of a state-prompted merger between Air China and China Southern Airlines abounded in 1999. By this time, China Southern, based in the commercial center of Guangzhou, had become the country's largest carrier. At the time, China had 30 airlines, and Beijing wanted to group them into several, more globally competitive units. Altogether, mainland airlines lost more than ¥6 billion in 1998. *Flight International* observed that a merger with China Southern could give Air China access to the Hong Kong and New York stock markets.

About 16 million passengers flew Air China in 1998. The October 1999 opening of a new terminal at Beijing Capital International Airport, where Air China operated the vast majority of flights, promised not only to relieve travelers of cramped conditions but also to allow Air China to devote more resources to its lucrative ground handling business for international carriers. One-fifth of Air China's 15,000 employees worked in ground handling.

Although the Chinese aviation industry as a whole was expected to earn CNY 1 billion ($120 million) in profits in 1999, Air China and other individual airlines were struggling to break even and mitigate their collective losses of 1998, which totaled $300 million. Air China was not publicly traded and was not quite as open with its sales figures as were China Eastern and China Southern.

NEW FRONTIERS IN THE NEW MILLENNIUM

To demonstrate the airline's faith in its Y2K preparations, Air China chief Wang Li'an and several other top officers personally piloted several flights at the turn of the millennium. As reported in the *China Daily*, this decision generated a considerable amount of positive

KEY DATES

1984: Civil Aviation Administration of China (CAAC) is reorganized, creating four divisions, one based in Beijing.
1988: Air China becomes autonomous from CAAC.
1989: Lufthansa joins Air China in maintenance joint venture.
1991: CAAC launches incentive program to improve in-flight service and on-time performance.
1994: Operating revenues exceed $1 billion.
1997: CAAC delays Air China initial public offering (IPO) due to Asian financial crisis.
1998: Excess capacity leads China's airlines to billions in losses.
2002: In restructuring of China's airline industry, Air China takes over China Southwest Airlines and Xinjiang Airlines.
2004: Newly formed Air China Limited holds IPO on Hong Kong and London exchanges.
2007: Air China joins Star Alliance.

publicity in China. Wang had worked for the CAAC for more than 40 years before being appointed Air China's director-general in 1999.

Early in 2000, Air China teamed with China National Aviation Co. Group (CNAC), the CAAC's Hong Kong-listed commercial arm, to establish a Hong Kong branch (95 percent owned by Air China). Direct flights to London from Hong Kong soon began. Air China faced competition at its home base from Air France, which increased its four flights a week to Beijing, begun in 1997, to daily service. British Airways also wanted to increase its frequencies (it was operating 18 flights a week to China).

In mid-2000, the CAAC repeated earlier calls for a consolidation of the 10 airlines it controlled into 3. (Air China, China Southern, and China Eastern were to each acquire the smaller airlines.) Apart from the 10 CAAC airlines, there were another 24 smaller carriers that had been formed by provincial or private interests.) Price wars had proved so destructive that the government banned discounting. However, no deadlines or plans for financial support for ailing carriers were made. To aggravate the airlines' financial troubles, the CAAC blocked a proposed merger in September 2000 between Air China and China Southern on anti-competitive grounds.

In January 2001, the CAAC's 10 airlines announced they had agreed on a merger plan. Air China was to acquire China Southwest Airlines and China International Airlines, the country's fourth strongest domestic airline. This was to create a group with assets of CNY 56 billion (HKD 52.5 billion), including 118 aircraft.

Air China had completely dropped plans to merge with China Southern and was soon reported to be planning its own $500 million floatation on the New York and Hong Kong stock markets. The funding was to help Air China, which had been eclipsed in previous years by China Eastern and China Southern, to grow sufficiently to justify its status as a national flag carrier.

Later in the year, the influential Star Alliance, founded by United Airlines and Lufthansa, was reported to be considering inviting Air China to join in the alliance. This would raise Air China's profile considerably, as well as connect it to the world's largest network of air routes, reported the *South China Morning Post*. However, China's airlines were negatively impacted by the September 11, 2001, terrorist attacks on the United States. According to China Eastern Chairman Ye Yigan, the incident was expected to cost the top three airlines CNY 3.35 billion ($405 million) due to a drop in passenger demand and higher operating costs.

RESTRUCTURING

Li Jianxiang, a general from the air force, took over as company president in 2000. As *Air Transport World* described it, he set out to refocus the "defeated army," which was posting losses while its other Big Three counterparts were, for the moment, in the black. Over the next three years he cut the number of Air China subsidiaries (which included "a carpet factory, a printing plant, and even a fish farm") from more than 100 to 27. Air China made a net profit of CNY 40 million in 2001.

The long awaited restructuring of the Chinese airline industry was executed in 2002, with the Big Three each taking over two or three of the smaller carriers. In October 2002 Air China and CNAC were combined with China Southwest Airlines under the new China Aviation Group Company. China Southwest was one of the more profitable of the second-tier airlines being folded into the Big Three.

In 2004 newly formed Air China Limited held its initial public offering (IPO) on the Hong Kong and London exchanges. The vastly oversubscribed IPO raised $1 billion (CNY 10 billion). Shares were listed in Shanghai as well two years later, albeit to less enthusiastic reception. The government maintained a controlling interest.

Air China's parent followed the lead of various regional airliners when it launched a corporate jet subsidiary in 2003. In October of that year it also formed a Beijing-based cargo joint venture named International Cargo Transport Ltd. of China.

Air China managed a profit of CNY 160 million even in 2003, a year beset by the severe acute respiratory syndrome (SARS) crisis. The next year Air China's income reached CNY 2.39 billion, a record, as passenger numbers improved in Asia and Europe. Revenues rose nearly a third to CNY 30.83 billion in 2004. By 2007 revenues were up to CNY 47.72 billion ($6.99 billion); net income was CNY 4.12 billion ($603,000).

STRATEGIC PARTNERSHIPS

Hong Kong's Cathay Pacific Airways Limited had acquired a 10 percent holding in Air China just before the 2004 IPO and soon raised its stake to 17.5 percent in a cross-shareholding arrangement that strengthened ties between the two carriers. Together the pair dominated traffic between Beijing, Hong Kong, and Shanghai. Both had been minority shareholders in Dragonair, a regional airline that connected Hong Kong with the mainland. Air China sold its holding in exchange for the 17.5 percent stake in Cathay Pacific, which bought out the other Dragonair partners as well.

The need for international partners was intensified as China began to open its skies more to foreign airlines. Intense price competition prompted Air China to upgrade the interiors on some of its wide-body long-haul aircraft. Although the most international of the mainland airlines, it still suffered from a lack of brand recognition in the West.

After years of overtures to various parties, Air China finally formally joined the industry-leading Star Alliance in December 2007. It had been a United code-share partner for four years and had marketing arrangements with 20 other airlines.

The strategic situation at home was far from settled. When rival China Eastern Airlines (CEA) was entertaining a bid from Singapore Airlines (SIA), Air China suggested it would pay more for the shares, and the SIA-CEA link was ultimately rejected in January 2008.

In 2007 Air China expressed some interest in acquiring Shanghai Airlines; this plum, however, ultimately went to CEA in 2009. Shanghai remained in Air China's sights, and it was reported to be mulling its own strategic investment in China Eastern, also based there. However, by the fall of 2008 Air China's new Chief Executive Kong Dong (brother of Citic Group Chairman Kong Dan) was saying that he was more concerned with managing the group through difficult times than acquiring other companies.

Traditionally the most profitable of China's Big Three, Air China struggled in the global economic slowdown. Although sponsorship of the 2008 Beijing Olympics likely raised its international profile, this failed to translate into the desired sales increase and its duties related to the Games proved an expensive distraction.

In the same year the airline also had to contend with a devastating snowstorm, and an earthquake at Sichuan, a major hub. These disruptions contributed to a loss of RMB 1.91 billion for 2008 on revenues of RMB 52.91 billion ($7.23 billion). The airline then had about 20,500 employees, half as many as rival CEA.

Frederick C. Ingram

PRINCIPAL SUBSIDIARIES

Air China Cargo (69%); CNAC (Hong Kong; 69%); Air Macau Company Limited (Macau); Air China Group Import and Export Trading Co.; Zhejiang Air Services Co., Ltd.; Air China Shantou Industrial Development Company (51%); Air China Development Corporation (Hong Kong) Limited (95%); Shanghai Air China Aviation Service Co., Ltd.; Beijing Golden Phoenix Human Resource Co., Ltd.; Total Transform Group Limited (British Virgin Islands); Angel Paradise Limited (British Virgin Islands); Aircraft Maintenance and Engineering Corporation, Beijing (60%); Macau Asia Express Ltd. (68%); SkyWork Capital Asia Ltd. (Hong Kong; 33%); ACT Cargo (USA), Inc. (51%).

PRINCIPAL OPERATING UNITS

Southwest; Zhejiang Province; Chongqing; Inner Mongolia; Tianjin; Shang Hai; Guizhou Province; Xi Xang; South China Base; Tibet.

PRINCIPAL COMPETITORS

China Eastern Airlines Corporation Limited; China Southern Airlines Company Limited; Hainan Airlines Co., Ltd.

FURTHER READING

"Air China Launches New Service, Works on Image," *USA Today*, October 9, 1991, p. 8B.

"Air China to Stand Alone," *Airfinance Journal*, March 1995, p. 8.

Bangsberg, P. T., "Lufthansa, China Plan More Funds for Aircraft Maintenance Venture," *Journal of Commerce*, June 24, 1992, p. 2B.

Bradbury, Nicholas, "Troubled but Hopeful," *Asset Finance & Leasing Digest*, June 1994, p. 23.

"CAAC Blocks China Southern Merger with Air China," *AFX-Asia*, September 28, 2000.

Cantle, Katie, "Air China's War for Profits," *Air Transport World*, October 2007, pp. 36+.

Chan, Christine, "Link-Up Possible between Mainland Flagship and Southern Airline; Rumours Fly of Giant Merger," *South China Morning Post*, Bus. Sec., July 9, 1999, p. 4.

Chang, Leslie, "China Intends to Merge 10 Airlines into Three," *Wall Street Journal*, July 24, 2000, p. A21.

"China: Person of the Week; Making the Trans-Millennium Flight, Wang Creates a Marketable Image," *China Daily*, December 12, 1999, p. 8.

Davies, R. E. G., "Airlines of the New China," *Airlines of Asia since 1920*, London: Putnam Aeronautical Books; McLean, VA: Paladwr Press, 1997, pp. 403–24.

Flynn, Ann Amelia, "China's Airlines Take Wing," *China Business Review*, May/June 1993, p. 14.

Guo, Al, "Air China Chief Gets Top CAAC Job; Move May Sway China Eastern Minority Shareholders' Decision on SIA, Temasek Tie-Up," *South China Morning Post*, December 29, 2007, Bus. Sec., p. 1.

Harding, James, "Air China Plans Overseas Float," *Financial Times* (London), October 15, 1997.

Holland, Tom, "China Break-In," *Far Eastern Economic Review*, October 25, 2001, p. 41.

"It's a Jungle Up There: China Tries to Tame Its Unruly Aviation Sector," *ChinaOnline*, October 25, 2000.

Lo, Joseph, "Star Alliance Beckons Air China," *South China Morning Post*, May 24, 2001, Bus. Sec, p. 2.

Lo, Joseph, and Russell Barling, "Airline Merger Creates Flying Fortress; Cross-Shareholding Agreement between Cathay Pacific and Air China Expected to Raise Concerns over Competition," *South China Morning Post*, March 16, 2005, Bus. Sec., p. 1.

Lott, Steven, "Cathay, Dragonair, Air China Finalize Complex Agreement," *Aviation Daily*, June 12, 2006, p. 2.

McGregor, Richard, "Call for Mergers Leaves Chinese Carriers Up in the Air," *Financial Times* (London), August 1, 2000.

Ng, Eric, "Air China Set to Announce Lead Bank for Listing," *South China Morning Post*, July 16, 2001, Bus. Sec., p. 4.

Perrett, Bradley, "Chinese Takeover; Strategic Investment in China Eastern Would Make Air China Dominant," *Aviation Week & Space Technology*, January 14, 2008, p. 38.

———, "Clear Target; Air China Wants Shanghai Airlines to Develop a Balanced Business across the Country," *Aviation Week & Space Technology*, November 26, 2007, p. 42.

"Rise of the Phoenix," *Ground Handling International*, July 1999, p. 55.

So, Charlotte, "Air China Chief Takes Safe Route in Stormy Weather; Kong Dong Says Now Is Not Time for Mergers or Acquisitions," *South China Morning Post*, October 13, 2008, Bus. Sec., p. 14.

"Ten Chinese Airlines Prepare for Takeoff of Mergers, Alliances," *China Online*, January 11, 2001.

Vandyk, Anthony, "Air China: New Name, New Heights," *Air Transport World*, February 1991, p. 54.

Air France–KLM

45 rue de Paris
Roissy-CDG, F-95747 Cedex
France
Telephone: (33 01 41) 56 78 00
Fax: (33 01 41) 56 70 29
Web site: http://www.airfranceklm-finance.com

Public Company
Incorporated: 2004 as Air France–KLM
Employees: 107,000
Sales: EUR 23.97 billion (2009)
Stock Exchanges: Over the Counter (OTC) Euronext
   Paris Amsterdam
Ticker Symbols: AFLYY FR0000031122
NAICS: 481111 Scheduled Passenger Air Transporta-
   tion; 481112 Scheduled Freight Air Transportation;
   481211 Nonscheduled Chartered Passenger Air
   Transportation; 492110 Air Courier Services;
   488190 Other Support Activities for Air
   Transportation

■ ■ ■

Air France–KLM is one of Europe's leading air-transport companies. It flies approximately 75 million passengers a year to 244 destinations in 105 countries around the world and has a fleet of more than 600 aircraft. Cooperative pacts with Delta Air Lines, Inc., and others extend its reach even further. Passenger travel accounts for the bulk of revenues, but the group also has extensive operations in cargo and aircraft maintenance and participates in other ancillary activities.

The 2004 merger of Air France and KLM Royal Dutch Airlines is believed to be the first takeover of one of Europe's flag carriers. The group acquired a stake in Alitalia–Compagnia Aerea Italiana S.p.A. five years later, adding a strong southern European hub to its bases at Amsterdam-Schiphol and Charles de Gaulle (CDG) airport north of Paris.

KLM'S REGAL BEGINNINGS

KLM was organized by a young aviator lieutenant named Albert Plesman. In 1919 Plesman, with the financial support of an Amsterdam shipping company, sponsored the "Elta" aviation exhibition in Amsterdam to satisfy the public's fascination with the airplane. Over half a million people attended the air show. When it closed, several Dutch commercial interests decided to establish a Dutch air transport company, and Plesman was nominated to head the company.

The Royal Dutch government lent its support to Plesman's project by offering to allow him use of the title *Koninklijke,* meaning "Royal," in the company's name. On October 7, 1919, Koninklijke Luchtvaart Maatschappij, or "KLM," was founded in The Hague. It was one of the world's first commercial airline companies.

In its early years KLM transported passengers, freight, and mail to a growing number of European destinations linking Dutch cities with London, Paris, Oslo, and Athens. At that time the Netherlands had a worldwide empire with colonies in Asia and the Caribbean. Soon KLM was charting routes to link these colonies with Holland. Services to Curaçao and Trinidad

COMPANY PERSPECTIVES

Air France–KLM serves 244 destinations in 105 countries worldwide. It has the most extensive route network between Europe and the rest of the world, which is efficiently coordinated and balanced around the Roissy–Charles de Gaulle and Amsterdam-Schiphol hubs. With its new partner Alitalia, Air France–KLM is developing the leading network coordinated around a unique combination of hubs in northern and southern Europe. The partner of choice for the major air transport players, Air France–KLM is one of the founding members of the international airline alliance, SkyTeam, which enables it to extend and consolidate its reach in all of the largest markets in the airline sector across 169 countries. Some 107,000 employees contribute to the dynamism of the business, of which the main activities are passenger, cargo and maintenance. The Group is also developing ancillary activities, such as catering and leisure transport. Building on its solid fundamentals and robust balance sheet, the Group is pursuing a strategy of profitable growth together with a sustainable development policy based on respect of its commitments to environmental advances and social progress.

were opened, and in 1927 KLM established a route from Amsterdam to Batavia (later Djakarta) on the island of Java in Dutch Indonesia. The 8,700-mile trip took 11 days.

At the start of World War II German armies invaded the Low Countries and closed KLM operations. Plesman was understandably upset by the occupation and frustrated with his inability to convince the Germans to relax their grip on the Netherlands. One summer night Plesman's determination to take action led him to awaken one of his house guests, a Swedish KLM pilot named Count von Rosen. Plesman reportedly asked the count, "What can I do to stop this?" and Von Rosen replied, "You could talk to my Uncle Hermann." Suddenly Plesman realized he was speaking to the nephew of the German Reichmarschall Hermann Göring. A few days later Plesman was in Berlin discussing the possibility of a peace treaty between England and Germany with Göring.

Plesman formulated a document that was later forwarded to Winston Churchill's office in London. The peace terms would leave the British Empire intact but give Germany control of the European continent and the United States control of the Americas. The matter was "studied with much interest" and receipt of the document was acknowledged by Lord Halifax. Göring, however, became displeased with Plesman's initiative and later had him jailed. Plesman was released in April 1942 and told to remain at his house in Twenthe in the woods of eastern Holland until the end of the war. During this time he kept himself occupied by formulating strategies for the postwar operation of KLM.

POSTWAR EXPANSION

When the war ended in the spring of 1945 Plesman was largely forgiven by the public for his attempts to make peace with the Germans earlier in the war. Soon afterward he traveled to the United States to negotiate the purchase of surplus war planes for KLM. The company wasted no time rebuilding its network, but since the Dutch East Indies were in a state of revolt, Plesman's first priority was to reestablish KLM's route to Batavia. By the end of the year KLM was again flying to Indonesia. By 1948 services were opened to Africa, North and South America, and the Caribbean. Also during the immediate postwar period, the Dutch government expressed interest many times in gaining a controlling stake in KLM. Plesman, however, was a fiercely independent man and kept the company under private control while conceding only a portion of KLM's ownership to the government.

Indonesia (formerly the Dutch East Indies) gained its independence from the Netherlands in 1949. The following year the Indonesian government established its own national airline called Garuda. KLM assisted Garuda from the time of its inception and continued to aid the company with technical and financial assistance until 1982. KLM later helped to establish several other airlines in developing nations, including Philippine Airlines, Nigeria Airways, Viasa (Venezuela), Egyptair, and Aerolineas Argentinas.

In 1950 KLM entered into an agreement with Swissair and Belgium's Sabena airlines that led to the establishment of a spare-parts pool. The BeNeSwiss agreement laid the ground for a future maintenance pool called the KSSU group, which included KLM, Scandinavian Airlines, Swissair, and the privately operated French airline UTA. KLM also continued to modernize and expand during the 1950s. It was the first European airline to fly new versions of the Lockheed Constellation and Electra. In addition, several destinations in western North America were added to KLM's route structure. In 1954 the company created KLM Aerocarto N.V., an aerial survey and photography service.

KEY DATES

1919: KLM is established in the Netherlands as one of the world's first commercial airlines.

1933: Société Air France is formed from Aéropostale and other existing companies.

1948: Air France is nationalized.

1962: Air France joins British Airways in joint venture to operate the Concorde, the first supersonic airliner.

1989: KLM begins long-term strategic partnership with Northwest Airlines.

1998: Air France forms the SkyTeam global alliance with Delta Airlines.

2003: Air France ends scheduled Concorde flights.

2004: Air France and KLM merge to form the world's largest airline by revenues.

2009: Air France–KLM invests in Alitalia, gaining a southern European hub.

Plesman died on December 31, 1954, at the age of 64. Praised and decorated as a hero of the Netherlands, Plesman also received decorations from Denmark, Belgium, Sweden, Czechoslovakia, Greece, Tunisia, Lebanon, and Syria. The company he left behind was entering a difficult period in commercial aviation history. A sudden and unexplained decline in ridership caused financial reverses at KLM and most of the world's other airlines. The company also faced the burden of financing a costly conversion to jet airplanes. Moreover, by this time the government had increased its ownership of the company to two-thirds by purchasing new KLM stock issues. The board of directors, however, remained under the control of the private shareholders.

WEATHERING THE JET AGE

In 1961 KLM reported its first year of losses. The company's president, I. A. Aler, resigned and was replaced by Ernst Hans van der Beugel. Yet the change in leadership was not enough to reverse the company's financial difficulties. Aler returned to active participation and enlisted McKinsey & Company, an airline consulting firm, to make recommendations for restoring the company to profitability. Their study concluded that KLM should reduce its staff and number of airplanes. Aler, however, had already reduced the staff by one-seventh and refused to release any more personnel. In January 1963 Aler left KLM and later, suffering from exhaustion, checked into a hospital.

KLM's board of directors then elected Horatius Albarda to the company's presidency. Albarda initiated a reorganization of the company which involved further cutbacks in staff and air services. Unfortunately, Albarda's tenure ended when he was killed in a private plane crash during 1965. Albarda was succeeded by KLM's Deputy President Gerrit Van der Wal, who would adopt Plesman's attitude toward government involvement in KLM. Before his appointment to KLM Van der Wal reached an agreement with the government in that, despite its major financial holding in the company, KLM would be run as a private enterprise without interference from the government. By 1966 the Dutch government's interest in KLM had been reduced to 49.5 percent.

In 1965 the airline created a subsidiary called KLM Helicopters to transport oil workers to and from oil drilling rigs in the North Sea. The division was eventually expanded in its range of operations to include specialized and chartered airlift services. KLM created another subsidiary in 1966 to operate domestic passenger air services in the Netherlands. KLM Dutch Airlines connected a number of smaller Dutch cities with the nation's international airports in Rotterdam and Amsterdam. KLM later included flights to other European cities, and in 1976 the division's name was changed to KLM CityHopper.

In an attempt to better utilize its facilities at Amsterdam's Schiphol Airport, KLM initiated a promotion called Distrinet, in conjunction with some Dutch shipping and transport companies. Distrinet was intended to coordinate these various Dutch companies in order to establish Amsterdam as the primary continental port of entry and distribution for European cargo.

KLM was a regular customer of the McDonnell Douglas Corporation during this time. When the airline introduced jet service in 1960, it decided to employ the Douglas DC-8 rather than the Boeing Company's 707, and in 1969 the company purchased DC-9s rather than Boeing's similarly configured three-engine 727. In 1971, however, KLM purchased the first of several Boeing 747 jumbo jets. McDonnell Douglas campaigned very hard to prevent KLM from purchasing more Boeing products, but KLM opted to remain neutral, preferring to recognize the unique qualities of each company's product and avoid becoming the exclusive customer of any one company.

McDonnell Douglas's response to Boeing's production of the 747 was to manufacture the DC-10, which became available shortly after the 747. The DC-10 was smaller than the 747 and somewhat more efficient at lower passenger load factors (when a number of seats remained empty). In 1972 KLM purchased the first of several DC-10s to provide the airline with a more flexible fleet. Boeing and McDonnell Douglas, however, soon had more than just each other for competition. Several airlines, most of them European and including KLM, placed orders for a new airplane being developed by Airbus, the European aerospace consortium. KLM ordered 10 Airbus A-310 passenger jetliners scheduled for delivery beginning in 1983.

Difficult economic conditions caused by the 1973–74 oil crisis forced KLM to seek government assistance in arranging debt refinancing. In return for the government's money, KLM issued additional shares of stock to the government. By the late 1970s the government held a 78 percent majority of KLM stock. Company management, however, remained under the control of private shareholders.

Sergio Orlandini (his father was Italian and his mother Dutch) became KLM's president in 1973. Upon taking office he was confronted with a problem common to all international carriers at that time: overcapacity. KLM was flying planes with too many empty seats. The solution at other airline companies was to offer discounted fares in the belief that some income from a given seat was better than none at all. Orlandini chose another approach. His idea was to reconfigure KLM's 747s (with their huge capacity for passengers) so that they could carry a combination of passengers and freight. A partition separated the passenger cabin from the cargo hold in the rear of the airplane. Later 747s delivered to KLM (called "combis") were specifically designed for combinations of passengers and freight. KLM competed with Federal Express and DHL by specializing in high-end operations, such as shipping live horses and global sourcing.

In the mid-1980s, one-sixth of KLM's earnings came from non-airline operations, which included management consulting, technical services, staff training, hotels, duty-free shops, catering, and ground handling. Under the terms of the KSSU agreement, KLM performed maintenance on 747s and overhaul of CF6 engines. The company's diversity enabled it to survive difficult periods in the airline passenger market.

The Dutch government's share of KLM was reduced to 54.8 percent in 1986, a figure that was expected to be reduced even further as the decade progressed. Also during this time, KLM began cooperating with British Airways and several U.S. airlines in lobbying to relax airline regulations in Europe.

LIBERALIZATION

Airlines worldwide were hurt by the Persian Gulf crisis and sluggish economy that opened the 1990s. In order to survive the decade's Pyrrhic competition, KLM aimed for at least a 10 percent share of the markets served by itself and its affiliates. KLM invested heavily in its fleet, bringing its debt and lease obligations to the $2 billion level. In the short term, the carrier configured its combis to carry more freight. KLM, however, still lost money as the dollar and yen fell in value and was unable to turn a profit for 1990–91.

KLM started a three-year restructuring plan in 1990. The plan eliminated about 1,000 staff positions and focused the company on its core operations, with hopes of cutting expenses 15 percent a year. However, productivity increases were the most important component of the regimen. Pieter Bouw, a longtime KLM veteran, became its chairman in 1991. The reforms begun under Bouw were estimated to improve productivity by 60 percent within a few years. *Business Week* noted that passenger traffic rose by half without a further loss of jobs.

As the European market liberalized, KLM developed its Amsterdam hub, feeding it with traffic from 50 affiliated airlines. The most newsworthy of its partnerships was that with Northwest Airlines (NWA). KLM owned a 20 percent equity holding in NWA and although the two reaped significant benefits from their cooperation, the relationship proved notoriously difficult at times, culminating in an aborted takeover attempt on the part of KLM. Still, the relationship gave KLM the global reach it found necessary for survival in the deregulated international environment. An "open skies" agreement between the United States and the Netherlands allowed KLM and NWA to operate virtually as a single airline. The pair cut transatlantic fares and offered U.S. passengers discounts and easy connections to KLM's European and North African destinations. Even so, profits were not instantaneous for NWA, which would suffer numerous labor crises, and KLM was compelled to write off its original $400 million investment made in 1989.

KLM had its own labor concerns as well. Pilots made some concessions in 1993 in the face of further losses, when management contemplated moving back office operations from The Hague to a lower-cost area such as India.

KLM finally saw another profit in 1993–94, of $42 million on revenues of more than $5 billion. Cargo operations contributed $800 million. In 1993–94, KLM was 38.2 percent owned by the Dutch government but received no subsidies, unlike other European counterparts such as Air France, which received nearly $4 billion that year.

Meanwhile, KLM's partner NWA had posted an even larger profit, $296 million, surpassing even

American Airlines. Combined, KLM/NWA would have been the world's third largest airline in 1994, prompting notice from other U.S. carriers resentful of the pair's antitrust exemption. The partnership brought in an extra $300 million per year to the two carriers. KLM increased its stake in NWA to 25 percent, the legal limit.

In December 1995, KLM successfully bid for a 26 percent share of newly privatized Kenya Airways. The two shared codes, as Kenya Airways implemented KLM's customer service procedures and benefited from new economies in purchasing and other areas.

An operating loss of $86.8 million in 1996–97 followed high fuel prices and weak Dutch currency. The next year, however, brought reported income of $389 million. KLM's internal regimen appeared to be working under CEO Leo van Wijk. KLM's 1998 contract with its seven unions would allow for three bonuses and a permanent pay raise.

In 1997 KLM agreed to sell its shares back to NWA for $1.1 billion, an investment that was originally worth $400 million. The takeover issue put aside, the two signed a 10-year extension to their mutually beneficial arrangement.

INTO THE NEW MILLENNIUM

KLM entered into another close partnership with Alitalia–Compagnia Aerea Italiana S.p.A. in December 1998. The deal was expected to particularly benefit the pair's cargo operations. KLM also teamed with Eurowings, Braathens, Malaysia Airlines, Nippon Cargo Airlines, and others during the late 1990s. Air Engiadina and Air Alps Aviation operated flights under the brand "KLM Alps." KLM Cargo formed an alliance with EAC Logistics, based in Beijing.

Nearly 15 million passengers flew KLM in 1998, more than double the number carried 10 years earlier, and the company ordered $1.2 billion of Boeing aircraft to meet the new demand. Faced with finite capacity at its Schiphol hub, KLM aimed to develop Europe's first multi-hub system.

THE BIRTH OF AIR FRANCE

Air France emerged in the early 1930s, when the possibilities for large-scale commercial air transport were swiftly expanding. Recognizing the benefits likely to arise from coordination and an end to competition, four private French air transport companies—Air Union, SGTA, CIDNA, and Air Orient—merged in August 1933 and took over another enterprise, Aéropostale, to create Société Air France.

The new company soon became France's most prominent airline and expanded steadily during the 1930s, as the demand for air transport grew. The company created extensive networks for carrying passengers, cargo, and mail in various parts of the world until, by the start of World War II in 1939, Air France was recognized as one of the world's leading air carriers.

The outbreak of the war and the German occupation of much of France ended this period of expansion for Société Air France and crippled the company's chances of maintaining its services. Most of the airline's activities were suspended until the war ended in 1945.

POSTWAR NATIONALIZATION

The end of World War II sparked a wave of support within the French government for nationalization of key industries as the best method of harnessing the country's resources to rebuild what had been destroyed during the war and strengthen the French economy. Considered one of the country's main connections with the rest of the world, Air France was a prime target, and in 1948 Société Air France became Compagnie Nationale Air France, with the French government holding the bulk of the company's stock.

Nationalization allowed Air France access to much greater financial resources than had previously been the case, both through the government's injection of capital and the benefits of government backing in securing loans. Thus, aided by a period of global economic growth, rising demand for air transport, and dramatic improvements in aircraft technology, the company was able to sustain a long period of expansion.

During the 1950s and 1960s Air France developed an extensive network of tourist paths, increasing both the number of routes it served and the frequency of flights. The company improved its operations by using the fastest and newest propeller aircraft, including the Super Constellation, a plane capable of flying up to 500 kilometers (km) per hour. These changes enabled Air France to expand its network from a total of 250,000 km in 1953 to 325,000 km in 1960.

The development of commercial jet aircraft, which afforded larger capacity and shorter journey times, during the 1960s enabled Air France to undertake another important improvement in its operations. The company began using Caravelle and Boeing 707 jets and in 1962 became involved in a joint venture with British Airways to develop a supersonic jet aircraft, the Concorde, at an estimated cost to each partner of between £75 million and £85 million.

By 1970 Air France's network had grown to 500,000 km, and its acquisition of new jet aircraft, including the Boeing 727 and 747 and the Airbus 300, ensured its position as one of the world's leading international carriers. In the mid-1970s the company began using the newly developed Concorde for commercial flights. The Concorde project, however, proved far more expensive than originally expected: by 1982 it had cost the French and British governments a total of nearly £1.8 billion, more than 10 times the original estimates.

DEREGULATION ERA

Throughout the 1980s the world airline industry, which had remained relatively stable for decades, showed signs of change. Deregulation of the U.S. industry in the early part of the decade radically altered conditions in one of the key airline markets, while the prospect of a single European market emerging in the 1990s compelled European airlines to examine their operations, build alliances with other carriers, and diversify their business bases.

Like other airlines, Air France was affected by the changing conditions. In 1987, amid widespread rumors that he would be responsible for preparing the company for privatization, Jacques Friedmann, former head of the Compagnie Générale Maritime et Financiera, was appointed chair of Société Air France by the conservative French government of Jacques Chirac. A plan to sell 15 percent of Air France's stock on the Paris stock exchange, though, was postponed indefinitely in October.

The government deregulated the domestic French airline market by allowing charter companies to compete against Société Air France and a private carrier, Air Inter, for domestic routes. Air France responded to this change by fighting for control of Air Inter against Union des Transports Aériens (UTA), Air France's main private rival. Both companies increased their stakes in Air Inter, but the dispute ended in a stalemate with Air France and UTA each holding 35 percent of the company.

Meanwhile, Air France was building alliances with other European airlines to branch out into other industries. Among such collaborations was its investment of 25 percent of the capital to develop a joint computer reservations system called Amadeus with the German airline Lufthansa, the Spanish carrier Iberia, and Scandinavian Airlines. The consortium estimated the cost of developing the system at $300 million.

In September 1988 the newly elected Socialist government chose Bernard Attali, a prominent Socialist, to take over for Friedmann as chair of Air France. Widely regarded as a political move, the replacement

was officially linked with the crash three months before of a new Air France A320 Airbus at the Mulhouse air show, in which three people were killed.

The change in leadership removed the immediate possibility of privatization for Air France, but the company continued to seek acquisitions and new alliances. In July 1989 Air France paid FRF 240 million for a 35 percent stake in TAT, a regional passenger carrier and parcels and express delivery company based in Tours. TAT was the fourth-largest air carrier in France. In September 1989 Air France signed a cooperation agreement with Lufthansa in response to the changing conditions and to moves by British Airways, then the largest Western European airline, to build new alliances in Europe and America. The accordance entailed cooperation in all aspects of management and operations, including joint negotiations with aircraft manufacturers, harmonized aircraft acquisition programs, joint development of new long-distance routes, and the establishment of permanent management structures between the two companies.

A DIFFICULT DECADE

Air France made another crucial strategic move in January 1990, when it bought 70 percent of UTA from Chargeurs S.A., giving it authority over UTA's extensive network in tropical Africa and the South Pacific as well as control of Air Inter, which dominated the French domestic airline industry. The takeover made Air France the largest airline in Western Europe. The European Commission's (EC) competition commissioner, Sir Leon Brittan, tried to block the takeover on the grounds that it would restrict competition. After 10 months of negotiations, though, he approved the deal on the condition that the French government allow independent carriers to compete on several routes and that Air France sell its 35 percent holding in TAT.

In late 1990, however, the expansion that Air France and other airlines were planning was put to a halt. The Iraqi invasion of Kuwait pushed oil prices sharply higher and ultimately caused a huge dent in passenger demand. Citing soaring fuel costs and higher insurance premiums, Air France launched an economy drive and spending freeze in September, stopping all ground investments that had been planned for 1990, canceling all nonessential building and computer investments, and suspending recruitment.

Air France continued to look for international alliances, and in September 1990 signed a commercial agreement with US Air, a leading domestic airline in the United States, to cooperate on transatlantic routes. A worsening economic and financial climate, however, was limiting the possibilities for expansion. In November, a few days after the EC approved the UTA takeover, UTA and Air Inter announced that they were no longer making a profit. After years of growing profits, Air France recorded a loss of FRF 668 million for 1990. The group estimated that the crisis in the Persian Gulf had cost it FRF 1.7 billion in 1990 alone.

In early 1991 the EC responded to the worsening position of the airlines by suspending its restrictive competition rules, allowing them limited state support and more flexibility in pricing and assessing costs. Bernard Attali illustrated the extent of the problem in the April 12, 1992 issue of the *Guardian:* "We are in a period of very great crisis. It is the greatest crisis ever in air transport."

In May 1991 the French government announced that it would inject FRF 2 billion in fresh capital into Air France and in August gave the company approval to raise up to FRF 5 billion more from other sources. In November, after the EC had approved the government grant, the airline announced that the state-owned Banque Nationale de Paris would pay FRF 1.25 billion for an 8.8 percent stake in the company.

The worsening of the Persian Gulf crisis in early 1991 and the ensuing war was detrimental to airlines. Air France incurred a loss of FRF 1.16 billion in the first six months of 1991. The company responded to the predicament by appointing Andersen Consulting to undertake a nine-month study of how the company could cut costs in the face of increased competition from American and Asian airlines.

As a result of the study, Air France announced in September 1991 that it would merge its routes with those of UTA, cutting 3,000 jobs, or nearly 8 percent of its workforce, by the end of 1993, saving £150 million a year, and phasing out the UTA brand name. Air France also announced that it would sell its headquarters in central Paris for FRF 1.6 billion and move its offices to CDG airport by 1995. The company reported another loss of FRF 685 million for 1991. Despite a slight increase in business, a restructuring, and a slight upturn in traffic, it did not expect to make a profit until 1993 at the earliest.

In January 1992 Air France became the first Western airline to acquire shares in an existing Eastern European carrier. The company led a consortium, along with the European Bank for Reconstruction and Development and Caisse des Depots et Consignations, that paid a total of $60 million for a 40 percent stake in the Czechoslovakian airline Ceskeslovenske Aerolinie. The two carriers began combining their activities, using Paris and Prague as shared bases.

Also in early 1992, the pressures of the tight market were displayed in a series of disputes between Air France and U.S. carriers over transatlantic routes. Each side slashed prices to undercut the other, and a dispute over the amount of extra capacity the American airlines could add to their European routes during summer months resulted in France renouncing a bilateral air traffic agreement it had signed with the United States in 1946.

Air France signed a partnership agreement with the state-owned Belgian airline Sabena in April 1992. Air France agreed to acquire as much as BEF 6 billion of a BEF 15 billion issue of Sabena shares by 1994, giving it a 37 percent stake in the carrier. The companies consented to integrate their activities at Brussels, CDG, and Orly airports.

Also during this time Air France announced an in-principle accordance with Lufthansa to merge its Meridien hotel chain with Lufthansa's Kempinski chain, creating an 80-hotel group with annual sales of nearly £565 million. By June 1992, however, the only firm result was a marketing agreement between the two, and no timetable for a merger had been set.

Édouard Balladur became prime minister of France in March 1993. He proposed privatizing 21 large companies, including Air France. In the face of a paralyzing but popular strike in the fall of 1993, the government canceled plans to cut wages and eliminate 4,000 jobs. It feared similar strikes in other troubled industries. France floundered in a recession characterized by severe unemployment, afflicting nearly 12 percent of the workforce. Meanwhile Air France hemorrhaged money, losing $650 million in the first six months of 1993.

In April, Chairman Christian Blanc finally announced that the previously rejected restructuring had been approved by Air France unions. Nevertheless, it was contingent upon the EC's approval of another government bailout in the amount of FRF 20 billion ($3.4 billion). The *Economist* noted this spurred resentment among unsubsidized European carriers such as British Airways, which owned a 50 percent share of French domestic carrier TAT.

French resources were severely taxed when Flight 8969 was hijacked in Algeria by Muslim terrorists. Although three passengers were executed before the plane was allowed to leave the country, a French commando unit rescued the remainder after it refueled in Marseille.

In 1995 Air France announced plans to enter the commercial data communications business, in direct competition with France Telecom. The company's extensive computerized reservations system provided the rationale behind the venture. It already had 50 air transportation clients, and expected revenues of $40 million per year from the venture.

After losing $3.5 billion in seven years, Air France posted a profit in 1996, when earnings were FRF 394 million. Blanc cut 5,000 jobs through attrition and trimmed costs by one-fifth. Blanc also resisted Chirac's urging to buy only Airbus aircraft. Thanks to these practical, but politically unpopular efforts, Air France posted even larger profits in 1997.

Chairman and CEO Blanc, frustrated at government intervention of the airline's majority privatization scheme, resigned in September 1997. He had guided the airline to profitability, but the concessions he gained from workers rested on the promise of eventual compensation in company stock. If only a minority stake were sold, too few shares (less than 10 percent) would land on the market to make the employees' share of 30 percent very valuable. Jean-Cyril Spinetta became the company's next chairman.

French tourism was booming in 1997, again making it the most popular tourist destination in the world. During this time Air France merged with domestic carrier Air Inter. An ouster of conservatives in June 1997, however, threatened Air France's plans to go public. In February 1998 a partial privatization plan was announced that would reduce the government's share from 95 percent to 53 percent. In March this plan was postponed until autumn.

Air France pilots went on strike in June 1998. They objected to plans to cut their salaries in exchange for equity. The *Economist* reported the strike cost FRF 100 million ($17 million) per day.

In the summer of 1998, the planned privatization was rescheduled for early 1999. This plan called for the sale of only 20 percent of the company, expected to raise between FRF 15 billion and FRF 20 billion.

By November 1998, the main pilots' union had agreed to a three-year contract that would reduce costs by $90 million per year. With an initial public offering planned for 1999, most of the union's pilots opted to reduce their wages in exchange for company stock.

The government lowered its shareholding to 54.4 percent in the first phase of privatization in 1999. With the privatization in hand and the pilots' union (and 16 others) on board, the company instituted a cost-cutting program and soon exhibited a stunning, growth-oriented turnaround.

INTERNATIONAL ALLIANCES

The international aviation industry was becoming increasingly dominated by global alliances, which al-

lowed members to offer their passengers simple connections spanning the globe. A new bilateral agreement between France and the United States prompted Air France to sign code-share arrangements with Delta and Continental, and in 1999 Air France and Delta formed their own global alliance, SkyTeam, which was soon populated by other world airlines including AeroMexico, Korean Air, CSA (Czech Airlines), and Alitalia. The United States and South America became Air France's fastest-growing service areas. Air France was a particularly valuable partner as its base at Paris's CDG was the only major airport in Europe with room to expand. CDG built two new terminals in the next few years, allowing Air France to add thousands of weekly departures.

While Air France seemed more concerned with increasing transcontinental traffic, KLM rapidly built up the network of its U.K.-based Buzz airline to compete with low-cost carriers on regional routes, particularly those connecting to French destinations. Nevertheless, KLM lost a record EUR 416 million ($480 million) in 2003, a particularly dismal year for the aviation industry. Air France recorded income of $139 million for its fiscal year ending March 31, 2003, although it lost an equivalent amount ($142 million) in the first quarter of 2003.

Air France was then operating a fleet of almost 250 planes on a network of nearly 300 destinations. It had 43 million passengers a year. Air France ended the high-profile but unprofitable Concorde's scheduled operations in May 2003.

A MAJOR MERGER

Air France acquired KLM in 2004 in a deal worth 800 million. It was said to be the continent's first takeover of a national flag carrier. The two airlines continued to operate separately as a holding company, Air France–KLM, was created, in which the French government held a minority 18 percent stake.

The combination formed what was then the largest airline group in the world by revenues, and the linkup paid dividends from the start. Pretax profits rose a third to EUR 455 million ($575 million) on a pro forma basis in the combined company's first year as total revenues rose from EUR 17.8 billion to EUR 19.1 billion. Having two strong hubs, CDG and Schiphol, seemed to cushion the combined carrier from formidable industry-wide shocks such as rising fuel prices and the global economic downturn sparked by the financial crisis in the United States.

NAVIGATING CRISIS

The economic crisis ultimately prompted Air France–KLM to cut some capacity and make some layoffs. There was also further consolidation activity in the industry. Air France–KLM's U.S. alliance partner Delta Airlines merged with NWA in 2008, extending the possibilities for cooperation. After receiving antitrust immunity from the U.S. Department of Transportation, in April 2009 the four carriers began a massive transatlantic joint venture involving 200 flights a day at six hubs.

In 2009 Air France–KLM acquired 25 percent of Italy's troubled, state-owned Alitalia, long courted by KLM and others, for EUR 323 million, giving it a base in southern Europe. Air France–KLM also proposed buying another flag carrier, Czech Airlines, but demurred.

After more than a decade at the helm, in January 2009 Spinetta handed CEO duties to his longtime lieutenant Pierre-Henri Gourgeon, while retaining the position of chairman. Air France–KLM posted a net loss of EUR 814 million on revenues of EUR 24 billion in the fiscal year ended March 31, 2009. Increasingly open skies and extended range aircraft had increased competition from the United Arab Emirates and others. By this time the group was carrying nearly 75 million passengers annually on a fleet of 641 aircraft.

Air France–KLM had transformed from a troubled state-run carrier to one of the world's largest and most respected airline groups. Along the way a number of tragedies demonstrated that it was not immune to the types of dangers all airlines faced. Notable incidents included the loss of a Concorde on takeoff in Paris in July 2000, the collapse of a terminal at CDG in May 2004, and the crash of Air France flight 447 en route from Rio de Janeiro to Paris in June 2009.

Richard Brass
Updated, Frederick C. Ingram

PRINCIPAL SUBSIDIARIES

Air France S.A.; Koninklijke Luchtvaart Maatschappij, N.V. (KLM Royal Dutch Airlines).

PRINCIPAL COMPETITORS

Deutsche Lufthansa AG; British Airways plc; easyJet plc; Emirates Group; Iberia, Líneas Aéreas de España, S.A.

FURTHER READING

"Airline of the Year," *Air Transport World*, February 1998, pp. 39–40.

Allen, Roy, *Pictorial History of KLM, Royal Dutch Airlines*, London: Ian Allen, 1978.

Cottoli, Ken, "KLM, Alitalia Join Forces," *Traffic World*, December 7, 1998, pp. 37–38.

"Deja Vu," *Economist*, October 30, 1993.

Done, Kevin, "Air France–KLM Reaps Benefits of Merger," *Financial Times*, May 20, 2005, p. 26.

Ducros, Christine, "Jean-Cyril Spinetta—'Écouter n'est jamais un effort pour moi,'" *Le Figaro*, March 10, 2003, p. 32.

Egan, Jack, "Equality, Fraternity, and Inefficiency," *U.S. News and World Report*, June 23, 1997.

Emmings, Alan, "New Aircraft and Low-Cost Strategy for KLM," *Aircraft Economics*, July/August 2002, pp. 12–13.

"European 100: Air France," *Information Week*, December 11, 1995.

Feldman, Joan M., "Potential Realized," *Air Transport World*, December 1996, pp. 44–47.

Flint, Perry, "Vive l'America!" *Air Transport World*, November 1999, p. 61.

"Flying Low with Air France," *Economist*, October 30, 1993.

"Flying Tackle," *Economist*, June 6, 1998.

Glab, Jim, "Air France: 70 Years of Innovation, Elegance and Style," *Air Transport World*, August 2003, pp. 80–85.

Holly, Tricia A., "The French Connection," *Travel Agent*, September 27, 1999, pp. 64, 66.

Jones, G., *Air France*, Hinckley, U.K.: Midland, 2008.

Kingsley-Jones, Max, "French Connections Signal Major Growth for Buzz," *Flight International*, December 18, 2001, p. 9.

Matlock, Carol, "Air France's Surprising Air Show; CEO Jean-Cyril Spinetta Talks About How the French Flag Carrier Has Managed to Avoid the Woes That Are Plaguing So Much of the Industry," *Business Week Online*, May 20, 2003.

McKenna, James T., "Northwest/KLM Package Challenges Competition," *Aviation Week and Space Technology*, February 15, 1993, p. 31.

Michaels, Daniel, "Air France Delta Alliance Gets Off the Ground; Antitrust Issues Could Cause Turbulence for Partnership," *Wall Street Journal Europe*, Global Marketplace Sec., June 23, 1999, p. 4.

Morais, Richard C, "They Ship Horses, Don't They?" *Forbes*, November 7, 1994, pp. 45–46.

Nobbs, Pierre-Alain, *Air France et sa flotte de 1933 à nos jours*, Paris: Officine, 2008.

Ott, James, "KLM Boosting Productivity and Debt to Survive Airline Wars of 1990s," *Aviation Week and Space Technology*, May 27, 1991, pp. 81–82.

———, "Top Airline Competitors Share Growth Strategy," *Aviation Week and Space Technology*, August 10, 1998, pp. 53–58.

Rossingol, Denis, *Air France: Mutation économique et evolution statutaire*, Paris: Harmattan, 2009.

Samuels, David, "You Also See the Ugly Side," *International Commercial Litigation*, May 1998, pp. 10–13.

Sancton, Thomas, "Anatomy of a Hijack," *Time*, January 9, 1995.

Shiffrin, Carole A., and Pierre Sparaco, "European Carriers Regroup as Alcazar Hopes Fizzle," *Aviation Week and Space Technology*, November 29, 1993, pp. 29–30.

Thibault, Philippe-Michel, *Le roman d'Air France,* Paris: Galli-mard, 2003.

Toy, Stewart, et al., "Flying High," *Business Week*, February 27, 1995, pp. 90–91.

Tully, Shawn, "Northwest and KLM: The Alliance from Hell," *Fortune*, June 24, 1996, pp. 64–72.

"Whitewash," *Economist*, April 16, 1994.

AirBoss of America Corporation

16441 Yonge Street
Newmarket, Ontario L3X 2G8
Canada
Telephone: (905) 751-1188
Fax: (905) 751-1101
Web site: http://www.airbossofamerica.com

Public Company
Incorporated: 1989 as IATCO Industries Inc.
Employees: 750
Sales: CAD 259.41 million ($212.1 million) (2008)
Stock Exchanges: Toronto
Ticker Symbol: BOS
NAICS: 316211 Rubber and Plastics Footwear Manufacturing; 325212 Synthetic Rubber Manufacturing; 326299 All Other Rubber Product Manufacturing

■ ■ ■

Named after a line of unique segmented tires that was its original business, AirBoss of America Corporation is one of the largest rubber-mixing companies in North America as well as a leading manufacturer of chemical, biological, radiological, and nuclear (CBRN) and extreme cold weather (ECW) protective gear. Its defense division makes gas masks and rubber boots primarily for military customers in North America and Europe, but also for first response agencies, such as municipal fire departments. Rubber mixing accounts for three-quarters of sales. AirBoss focuses on makers of industrial tires and conveyor belts and it boasts a capacity of 250 million pounds of rubber a year.

ORIGINS

In the 1980s Alan Burns, a mining engineer in Perth, Australia, developed a unique segmented tire that was virtually impervious to flats. Comprising 20 separate, hollow, chevron-shaped rubber pieces bolted onto a rim, the modular design allowed damaged sections to be changed quickly in the field.

They were originally conceived for Jeeps and other off-road vehicles, but the unpressurized tires could be operated only below 30 miles per hour or they would overheat, making them unsuitable for the 4x4 market in the United States. However, they appeared ideally suited for skid-steer loaders, which were especially prone to punctures due to their debris-strewn operating environments and their high-friction method of steering. They were also more than twice as expensive as conventional tires, but promised substantial savings in time lost due to changing flats.

Burns formed Altrack Limited, soon renamed Air-Boss Limited, to commercialize his new design. According to the *Financial Times,* by 1991 he had invested at least AUD 6 million (£3 million) in the project.

A group of several investors including AirBoss Limited, formed IATCO Industries Inc. in 1989 to bring AirBoss to North America. (IATCO was actually an amalgamation of Greenstrike Gold Corp. and 846241 Ontario Limited; the acronym stood for "Industrial and Agricultural Tire Company.") One of the founders, R. L. Hagerman, would serve as its president and CEO. By 1991 Thomas Equipment was offering AirBoss tires as original equipment. It was followed a few years later by Case and then, in 1994, by Ford, New Holland Inc., and Gehl Company.

According to an October 1999 issue of *Rubber & Plastics News,* IATCO's revenues were nearly $4 million by 1994 but the company was not yet profitable. In that year, IATCO was renamed AirBoss of America Corporation. Most skid-steer loaders used one of two sizes of tire, but over the course of the decade AirBoss introduced a dozen more sizes as it grew the market into other types of construction and mining vehicles.

OTHER INTERNATIONAL FRANCHISES

The Australian company, AirBoss Limited, had also licensed its non-pneumatic tire technology to Britain's Courtwell Group plc, a corporate shell that had once owned Bear Brand hosiery as well as casinos. Courtwell was being reorganized as Select Industries PLC. In March 1991 it formed AirBoss Ground Engagement plc in Abingdon, England, to produce and market the tires for the European market.

Select had revenues of £465,000 in 1992. Losses mounted quickly, reaching £1 million in 1993 and £2 million the next year, when sales were up to £1 million. In 1996 Select outsourced the manufacturing of rubber tire segments to IATCO, keeping its own Didcot plant for assembly and marketing.

AirBoss Limited held a 50.4 percent stake in Select until 1995, when it sold most of it. AirBoss had a few other important international franchises: Japan's Fukuyama Rubber Co. and Madras Elastomers Ltd. of India.

CONTROLLED PURCHASE

In August 1995 AirBoss bought Controlled Rubber Products Inc. for $3 million. A maker of rubber injection-molded products, it had also added railway supplies and auto components to its product line. Its leased 50,000-square-foot plant in South Haven, Michigan, became AirBoss of America's first manufacturing facility of its own. The purchase also brought AirBoss a line of solid tires. The company soon moved its segmented-tire production lines there as well. Controlled Rubber was breaking even on annual sales of more than $7.5 million.

AirBoss of America's loss grew 25 percent to CAD 2.5 million in 1995 as revenues rose a third to CAD 9.6 million. The purchase of Controlled Rubber helped it turn the corner by reducing its tire production costs and providing a basis for new business lines.

INTO COMPOUNDING IN 1996

In December 1996 AirBoss acquired a superior rubber-mixing facility via the purchase of one of its suppliers, Kitchener, Ontario's International Technical Rubber Manufacturing Inc. (ITRM), in a cash and stock deal worth initially CAD 12.3 million ($9 million) with the potential for another CAD 17 million if sales targets were met. ITRM was growing quickly, experiencing a 50 percent sales leap to CAD 21 million in the 1996 fiscal year.

ITRM was an offshoot of a business formed to sell off the equipment of a former Uniroyal Goodrich tire factory after its operations were relocated to a nearby plant in 1992. At four stories and 800,000 square feet, the facility was huge, and situated on a 42-acre property. AirBoss invested in new mixers and within a few years more than doubled capacity there to 200 million pounds annually, making it one of the largest rubber-mixing facilities in North America.

Entering the late 1990s, AirBoss of America had 300 employees. It had already diversified far beyond the segmented tires that gave it its name, offering more than 250 products in all. Revenues were in excess of $50 million.

During the year, the company formed a design and marketing subsidiary in Kansas City, Missouri, called AirBoss Railway Products Inc. It sourced production to the South Haven, Michigan, and Kitchener, Ontario,

KEY DATES

1989: IATCO Industries Inc. is formed in Toronto to bring Australian-designed AirBoss segmented tires to North America.

1994: IATCO is renamed AirBoss of America Corporation.

1995: AirBoss buys Controlled Rubber Products Inc.

1996: AirBoss acquires rubber-mixing facility via acquisition of Kitchener, Ontario's International Technical Rubber Manufacturing Inc.

1998: Revenues exceed $50 million; AirBoss Railway Products Inc. is formed.

1999: AirBoss enters military market with purchase of Quebec's Acton International Inc.

2005: AirBoss sells the last of its tire units; temporary plant opens in Scotland Neck, North Carolina.

2008: AirBoss Railway Products is divested.

plants. Railroads were booming thanks in part to the North American Free Trade Agreement, noted *Rubber & Plastics News*. In 2000 the unit formed a joint venture with Ralph McKay Industries Inc. of Regina, Saskatchewan, to add metal clips to its railway-tie product line.

The U.S. company tried to keep extra capacity available to meet rush orders, Hagerman told *Rubber & Plastics News*. It also assiduously avoided competing with its customers, a policy that closed potential avenues for expansion in its tires business. Conveyor-belt manufacturers were also important users of AirBoss's rubber compounds.

INTERNATIONAL DEVELOPMENTS

Meanwhile, in Australia, AirBoss Limited had developed a one-piece CushionBoss tire in the mid-1990s, which was manufactured by Japanese licensee Fukuyama Rubber Co. A few years later it introduced ForkBoss tires for forklifts, which was also made of one piece with hollow openings across the length of the tire. AirBoss of America declined to license the designs, which would have competed with its existing rubber-mixing customers, Hagerman told *Rubber & Plastics News*.

AirBoss Limited changed its name to Sphere Investments in 2001 and set out to invest in a Mauritania

iron-ore mine. Sphere had originally become active in commodity exchanges through its Entyre Rubber Systems recycling unit. Sphere sold its last shares in AirBoss of America by the end of 2003.

INTO DEFENSE IN 1999

In 1999 AirBoss entered the military market with the $22 million purchase of Acton International Inc., which produced rubber boots at a 250,000-square-foot plant in Acton Vale, Quebec. At the time of the purchase, Acton had been supplying the Canadian armed forces for 20 years and the U.S. military for five years. Other customers included Sweden, Germany, Norway, and the United Kingdom. Annual revenues were $40 million, of which the military division then accounted for about 20 percent. Acton also had commercial footwear and industrial products divisions.

Acton had been making rubber boots since it was formed in 1928. It bought out the equipment of another venerable Kitchener, Ontario, manufacturer in the 2000 bankruptcy of William H. Kaufman Inc. However, the company's famed Sorel brand went to Columbia Sportswear Co.

More than mere galoshes, Acton's protective footwear was designed to shield against nuclear, biological, and chemical (NBC) threats. It also made boots for ECW use. Acton introduced an NBC glove by 2002. In addition to the military market, Acton was selling these to civil defense agencies as concern over CBRN threats was growing even before the September 11, 2001, terrorist attacks against the United States.

AirBoss of America's compounding business was exposed to a drop in demand from tire manufacturers in 2001 and 2002. Due to its well-timed diversification, the company nevertheless managed to maintain net income of about $2 million as annual revenues rose one-fifth to $110 million (CAD 150 million). There seemed to be plenty of room to grow the military business, which then accounted for less than 10 percent of sales. After contracting some of its more fashion-oriented footwear production to Asia, the company divested the consumer footwear business in 2004.

When Acton was acquired, officials had posited using the AirBoss facility in Michigan as a base to produce its military footwear for the U.S. market. In early 2001, however, AirBoss moved almost all of its U.S. production to its plants in Ontario and Quebec. The company had 750 employees in all, and its Canadian workforce was growing to meet rising demand in footwear and industrial products.

In 2002 AirBoss relocated its five-person headquarters to a larger facility outside Toronto. Although affected by a labor dispute at its Quebec facility, AirBoss continued to thrive in 2003 despite increased costs for materials and energy and falling demand for truck tires. Its investments in automated equipment paid off in lower costs, and the company benefited as a difficult economy thinned the ranks of its rubber-mixing competitors.

A NEW MIX

Revenues approached $150 million in 2004 and the company had more than 600 employees. In January 2005 AirBoss opened a temporary rubber-compounding plant in Waynesville, North Carolina. The company was never satisfied with quality at this plant and lost more than $1 million there. In August 2005 the company relocated the business to a new plant in Scotland Neck, North Carolina.

By this time, Air Boss of America's segmented-tire business only made up 1.5 percent of its total sales, according to *Rubber & Plastics News.* Hagerman told the journal the company could not expand into related tire and tread areas without competing with its rubber-mixing clients, so it was sold off. One of the company's sales executives, Robert Gilkenson, bought the solid-loader tire business in 2005 and relaunched it with the seven employees left at the remaining South Haven, Michigan, site as SolidBoss Worldwide Inc. In December 2008 AirBoss Railway Products, which then had just five employees and sales of $15 million a year, was sold to Amsted Rail Company Inc. in a deal worth CAD 6 million plus potential performance bonuses.

AirBoss's sales were flat at CAD 209 million in 2007 and net income slipped from CAD 6.5 million to CAD 4.1 million. It posted a net loss of CAD 1.1 million on revenues of CAD 259.4 million ($212.1 million) in 2008 as raw material costs rose and the Canadian dollar strengthened.

In 2007 the company formed a joint venture, SunBoss Chemical Ltd., to source chemicals used in rubber compounding. Rubber compounding accounted for 75 percent of total sales for AirBoss. Capacity had grown to 250 million pounds, and the company offered customers 2,000 different formulations.

Two years later, in August 2009 AirBoss announced plans to open a new plant in Burlington, Vermont, to produce CBRN protective gear for primarily the U.S. defense market. The company appeared focused on its key areas of business as it looked to the future.

Frederick C. Ingram

PRINCIPAL SUBSIDIARIES

AirBoss Produits d'Ingénierie Inc. / AirBoss Engineered Products Inc.; AirBoss Rubber Compounding (NC), Inc. (USA); SunBoss Chemical Ltd. (50%).

PRINCIPAL DIVISIONS

AirBoss-Defense; AirBoss Rubber Compounding.

PRINCIPAL OPERATING UNITS

Kitchener, Ontario; Scotland Neck, North Carolina; Acton-Vale, Quebec; Burlington, Vermont.

PRINCIPAL COMPETITORS

Biltrite Rubber (1984) Inc.; Excel Polymers L.L.C.; Avon Rubber plc; North Safety Products Ltd.; LaCrosse Rubber Mills, Inc.

FURTHER READING

"AirBoss of America Corp.," *Modern Tire Dealer,* September 1994, p. 62.

Baxter, Andrew, "Technology: Fresh Ground for the Wheel—A Tyre and Rim System That Resists Punctures," *Financial Times,* July 30, 1991, p. 9.

Deruyter, Ron, "Quietly Going About Business; Don't Be Fooled: AirBoss Factory on Glasgow Is Busier Than It Looks," *Kitchener-Waterloo Record,* February 15, 2005, p. D1.

McNulty, Mike, "Acton Finding Gold in Protective Goods," *Rubber & Plastics News,* November 15, 1999, p. 18.

———, "AirBoss Diversifies into Compounds, Parts: Reduced Dependence on the Tyre Sector as Rubber Firm Spreads into Military Goods and Custom Mixing," *European Rubber Journal,* June 1, 2002, p. 8.

———, "AirBoss Ltd. Develops One-Piece Industrial Tire," *Rubber & Plastics News,* September 20, 1999, p. 57.

———, "AirBoss Positions for End of U.S. Production," *Rubber & Plastics News,* March 19, 2001, p. 1.

———, "AirBoss Sells Last Tire Operation to Employee," *Rubber & Plastic News,* May 30, 2005, p. 1.

———, "AirBoss Takes Flight with New Growth Plan," *Rubber & Plastics News,* July 5, 1999, p. 8.

———, "AirBoss to Enter Military Market," *Rubber & Plastics News,* April 5, 1999, p. 1.

———, "AirBoss to Expand Capacity," *Rubber & Plastics News,* August 17, 1998, p. 1.

———, "AirBoss to Hike Mixing Output," *Rubber & Plastics News,* May 29, 2000, p. 4.

———, "AirBoss to Move Headquarters, Michigan Operation," *Rubber & Plastics News,* September 9, 2002, p. 42.

———, "AirBoss to Open U.S. Plant," *Rubber & Plastics News,* August 24, 2009, p. 1.

———, "AirBoss Wins Military Pacts for Gloves," *Rubber & Plastics News,* September 9, 2002, p. 1.

————, "Different Road: AirBoss Veers from Course Iatco Intended at Founding," *Rubber & Plastics News,* October 4, 1999, p. 1.

————, "Locked On: AirBoss Dominates in Segmented Tires," *Rubber & Plastics News,* September 20, 1999, p. 57.

————, "Weathering the Storm: AirBoss Continues Growth Despite Economic Turmoil," *Rubber & Plastics News,* October 6, 2003, p. 1.

Meyer, Bruce, "Making Mixing Work; Manufacturers Find There Is More Than One Way to Succeed in Custom Mixing," *Rubber & Plastics News,* March 21, 2005, p. 1.

Scholz, Nathan, "Sphere Focuses on Other Side of Globe," *Courier Mail* (Queensland), December 18, 2003, p. 40.

Shapiro, Joshua, "From the Rugged Outback, a Quick-Fix Modular Tire," *New York Times,* Bus. Sec., February 28, 1993.

Strathdee, Mike, "K-W Firm Sells Unit to AirBoss: Deal for Rubber Mixing Compound Business Worth $12 Million," *Kitchener-Waterloo Record,* January 3, 1997, p. C5.

Wilson, Enloe, "AirBoss Establishes Rail Product Subsidiary," *Rubber & Plastics News,* June 15, 1998, p. 6.

Won, Shirley, "Rubber Maker Looking for Bounce in U.S. Sales; Analysts Become Bullish on AirBoss as Conditions in the Industry Improve," *Globe & Mail* (Canada), January 15, 2005, p. B3.

Ajinomoto Co., Inc.

———■———

1-15-1 Kyobashi
Chuo-ku
Tokyo, 104-8315
Japan
Telephone: (+81 3) 5250-8111
Fax: (+81 3) 5250-8293
Web site: http://www.ajinomoto.com

Public Company
Incorporated: 1917 as S. Suzuki & Co. Ltd.
Employees: 26,869
Sales: ¥1.19 trillion ($12.15 billion) (2009)
Stock Exchanges: Tokyo Osaka
Ticker Symbol: 2802
NAICS: 325199 All Other Basic Organic Chemical Manufacturing; 311225 Fats and Oils Refining and Blending; 311411 Frozen Fruit, Juice, and Vegetable Processing; 311412 Frozen Specialty Food Manufacturing; 311421 Fruit and Vegetable Canning; 311423 Dried and Dehydrated Food Manufacturing; 311920 Coffee and Tea Manufacturing; 311941 Mayonnaise, Dressing, and Other Prepared Sauce Manufacturing; 311991 Perishable Prepared Food Manufacturing; 312111 Soft Drink Manufacturing; 325412 Pharmaceutical Preparation Manufacturing; 325414 Biological Product (Except Diagnostic) Manufacturing

■ ■ ■

Ajinomoto Co., Inc., the world's first and still-largest producer of monosodium glutamate (MSG), is one of Japan's largest food-processing companies. In addition to seasonings, Ajinomoto produces edible oils, frozen and processed foods, beverages and dairy products, sweeteners, amino acids, pharmaceuticals, and other specialty chemicals. Although the company sells its products in about 100 countries and territories around the world, it derives nearly 70 percent of its revenue in its domestic sphere.

ORIGINS AND POSTWAR ACTIVITIES

MSG, the company's mainstay throughout its history, was discovered in kelp by Kikunae Ikeda at the University of Tokyo in 1908. With help from Ikeda, Saburosuke and Chuji Suzuki (two brothers who had been extracting iodine from seaweed since 1890) formed Suzuki Seiyakusho Co. to produce the substance commercially. They began marketing it in 1909 as "AJI-NO-MOTO," which translates literally as "essence of taste." The company was incorporated as S. Suzuki & Co. Ltd. in 1917.

The company focused on international sales and established a strong base in chemical development at its inception. A New York office was opened in 1917, and between the wars production and sales offices were opened throughout Asia, giving the company a global position decades before other Japanese companies. During this time the company began to produce MSG from soybean protein, which eventually led to the production of cooking oils. World War II halted MSG production, but between 1947 and 1953 AJI-NO-MOTO became available in the United States and Europe, and the

COMPANY PERSPECTIVES

2009 is the 100th year of Ajinomoto, and an appropriate time to reflect on what it is that has made our company both successful and unique. There are perhaps three specific points to note: 1. We have pursued a scientific approach to food, sustaining development of fundamental concepts over the long term. 2. We have successfully commercialized the umami flavor and accumulated extensive associated technology and experience. 3. We have developed the most advanced amino acid technology in the world.

In looking ahead to the next 100 years, we believe that by further developing these unique characteristics we can contribute to markets and society around the world, and in doing so increase the value and significance of the Ajinomoto Group. Amid increasing concerns worldwide about health, the environment, and the safety, security and sustainability of food supply, we want to help resolve food-related issues that Ajinomoto is in a unique position to make significant contributions to, based on our strengths in amino acids.

company also began to sell cooking oil. In the meantime, the company adopted the name Ajinomoto Co., Inc., in 1946 and went public three years later. Ajinomoto opened offices in São Paulo, Paris, Bangkok, Singapore, and Hong Kong in 1954.

Emphasis on chemical research culminated in the creation of the Central Research Laboratories in 1956. Research during the 1950s brought about not only different biological and synthetic methods of MSG production but also an entry into the pharmaceutical industry. The development of crystalline essential amino acids, used for intravenous solutions, introduced Ajinomoto to pharmaceuticals. Amino acids were found to have a wide variety of applications, and before the end of the decade they were being used in the company's seasonings and animal-feed additives.

FOOD PROCESSING IN THE SIXTIES

The company took larger strides toward internationalization in the 1960s. Most overseas growth was limited to expanded production of seasonings in Asia and South America. Through joint ventures and licensing agreements with U.S. and European companies, however, Ajinomoto increased its presence on those continents and at the same time expanded its product line domestically. The first large-scale licensing agreement came in 1962 when it began marketing Kellogg's breakfast cereals in Japan. A similar agreement with CPC International Inc. to manufacture and market Knorr soups was reached in 1965. These ventures established the company as a food processor and not just a seasonings producer. After 1965, the company applied its research to the development of new seasonings, soups, margarine, mayonnaise, frozen foods, and flavored edible oils. In 1973 Ajinomoto formed another joint venture, with General Foods, to produce coffees, instant coffees, and soft drinks.

The oil crisis led most companies to consolidate in 1973 and 1974, and internal development of food products increased during the 1970s. By 1978 seasonings accounted for only 22 percent of sales, and processed food had boomed to 31 percent from 3 percent in 1965. In 1970 the company created Ajinomoto Frozen Foods and also began to collaborate with the NutraSweet Company of the United States. A 1979 joint venture with the French firm BSN-Gervais Danone (later Groupe Danone) introduced dairy products for the first time to the company's product line.

EXPANDING PHARMACEUTICAL OPERATIONS IN THE EIGHTIES

Ajinomoto's new focus on products derived from its amino acids research proved well-timed as the company entered the 1980s. Growth in the Japanese food industry slowed significantly. Although MSG sales overseas increased, the domestic market was mature. Food-related products, which made up 80 percent of the company's sales, could no longer be relied on for large-scale or long-term growth. Management initiated a plan to expand its fine chemicals divisions further while diversifying the food products made by its overseas subsidiaries. Pharmaceutical product sales were ¥20 billion in 1980; U.S. medical institutions and pharmaceutical manufacturers purchased half of the company's output. Although the reliance on exports would prove damaging to many Japanese companies as the yen appreciated in the late 1980s, Ajinomoto's extensive research investments in the 1970s gave it prominence in the field and made the division less vulnerable to international cycles.

The diversification into the pharmaceutical business was not easy. The complexity of the pharmaceutical market called for completely different marketing techniques as well as lengthy approval processes from

KEY DATES

1909: Through their company Suzuki Seiyakusho Co., Saburosuke and Chuji Suzuki begin marketing monosodium glutamate (MSG), earlier discovered by Kikunae Ikeda, as AJI-NO-MOTO.

1917: Company is incorporated as S. Suzuki & Co. Ltd.

1946: Company adopts the name Ajinomoto Co., Inc.

1949: Ajinomoto goes public.

Early 1960s: Expansion into food processing begins.

1989: Ajinomoto ventures further into fine chemicals via acquisition of Belgium-based S.A. OmniChem N.V.

2006: Ajinomoto acquires the Amoy Food Group from Groupe Danone.

2007: Company takes full control of Japanese soft drink maker Calpis Co., Ltd.

various governments. In order to defray these high research-and-development costs, Ajinomoto typically used other companies to market its drugs or used licensed companies to produce them.

In 1987 the joint Ajinomoto-CPC International venture was altered, with Ajinomoto taking full control of the Japanese joint venture firm, Knorr Foods Co., Ltd., At the same time, Ajinomoto purchased from CPC a 50 percent equity stake in CPC's seven Asian subsidiaries located in six countries. In 1990 Ajinomoto joined with Calpis Food Industry Co., Ltd., in an agreement whereby beverages and dairy products manufactured and marketed by Calpis would be distributed by Ajinomoto.

Ajinomoto's new venture department was established in 1987 with a focus on new markets and cooperative producers in the life-sciences area. The department symbolized the company's commitment to the industry, and earnings showed why. In 1988 sales rose only 0.5 percent, but earnings grew 15.4 percent, largely because of the much higher margins the company earned on life-science products. In 1989 Ajinomoto ventured further into the area of fine chemicals through the $92.4 million acquisition of S.A. OmniChem N.V. of Belgium, a maker of intermediate chemical products for the pharmaceutical and food industries.

Although the international market for research and development in pharmaceuticals made Ajinomoto less vulnerable to currency valuation cycles, a strong yen hurt the company nonetheless. In response to a reduced export market, the company turned to domestic food sales in the late 1980s, becoming more active in restaurants and foodservice and entering the fresh vegetable and fish market for the first time. The food-processing division was the only one in 1988 to show an increase in sales, to 40.6 percent of the company total, reflecting the influence of the difficult export market. Ajinomoto hoped to increase its overseas food production by taking advantage of the strong yen to acquire companies and diversify the product lines of its foreign subsidiaries.

The company continued to spend a higher percentage (3.3 percent) of sales on research than most food processors did, reflecting its interest in the fine chemical and pharmaceutical industries. In addition to this money, the Japanese government funded research on problems such as AIDS, and in the late 1980s university research became available to commercial developers. Funding from the MIT Cancer Research Institute, for example, helped support research and provide a wider variety of potential developments.

EXPANSION MOVES AND OVERCOMING DIFFICULTIES IN THE NINETIES

In the 1990s Ajinomoto expanded rapidly in the increasingly open market of China, establishing seasoning, food, and pharmaceutical operations there. The company also continued to pursue joint venture opportunities. In 1992 Ajinomoto joined with Calpis and the French food conglomerate Groupe Danone to form Calpis Ajinomoto Danone Co., Ltd., a Japanese-based marketer of chilled desserts, most of which were made from dairy products. In the pharmaceuticals sector, Ajinomoto expanded its research in the areas of immune diseases and diabetes. In 1994 the company licensed to Sandoz AG of Switzerland a diabetes treatment. Moreover, in 1996 the U.S. Food and Drug Administration recommended as a first-line therapy for AIDS a drug called dideoxyinosine that Ajinomoto had developed.

The 1990s also saw the company struggle through a number of difficulties. The prolonged Japanese economic downturn led to only moderate increases in net sales during the early and mid-1990s and stagnated profits. Results improved during the later years of the decade, with net sales increasing from ¥750.84 billion in 1996 to ¥788.4 billion in 1997 to ¥835.97 billion in 1998, while net income rose from ¥10.49 billion in

1996 to ¥15.33 billion in 1997 to ¥17.98 billion in 1998. Other troubles included a U.S. investigation into allegations of international price fixing in the food and feed additive business. The investigation led to a criminal felony case brought in August 1996 against Ajinomoto and two other Asian companies charging them with conspiring to illegally fix the worldwide price of lysine, a livestock feed additive, in concert with Archer Daniels Midland Company of the United States. In November 1996 Ajinomoto pleaded guilty to one conspiracy count and agreed to pay a $10 million fine. In early 1997 two Ajinomoto executives were indicted on charges of paying ¥6 million ($47,500) to *sokaiya* gangsters. The *sokaiya* were Japanese mob extortionists who blackmailed companies by threatening to disrupt annual shareholder meetings. This scandal led to the resignation of the president of Ajinomoto, Shunsuke Inamori, who took personal responsibility for the alleged payoffs.

The new president, Kunio Egashira, announced in early 1999 that Ajinomoto would adopt a holding company system by the year 2002 and integrate 130 domestic and overseas group companies into about 90 firms. The company also launched an effort to reduce the parent company workforce from 5,200 to 4,800 by 2005 and to cut its 150-person administrative staff in half by 2002. Through these moves to consolidate and streamline operations, Ajinomoto aimed to improve its early 21st century profitability.

DEAL MAKING AT THE FOREFRONT

Egashira was also an extremely active deal maker, completing dozens of mergers and acquisitions and entering into a number of new joint venture arrangements by the end of the 2005 fiscal year. With these deals, Ajinomoto sought to make itself more of a global player in its strongest markets. In addition, in those areas in which the company's position was somewhat weaker, Egashira pursued mergers and alliances, while even weaker businesses were jettisoned. In edible oils, for instance, Ajinomoto and Honen Corporation merged their food-oil units into a joint venture in 2002, and then two years later this venture merged with Yoshihara Oil Mill Ltd. to form J-Oil Mills, Inc., which ranked as the largest edible-oils entity in Japan. Ajinomoto retained a stake in J-Oil of approximately 25 percent.

Among other deals completed during this period, Ajinomoto strengthened its position in frozen foods with the 2003 purchase of Frec Corporation from Nippon Sanso Corporation. That same year, the company also purchased a 33.4 percent stake in spice maker Ga-

ban Co., Ltd. Ajinomoto later gained majority control of Gaban. In addition, in a two-step, $381 million transaction completed during the fiscal year ending in March 2004, Ajinomoto sold its shares in the CPC joint ventures in Southeast Asia to Anglo-Dutch consumer products giant Unilever, which had become Ajinomoto's partner in the ventures in 2000 after taking over Bestfoods. Extracting itself from this partnership enabled Ajinomoto to begin expanding its own processed food businesses in Southeast Asia, a high-growth region in the company's core fields that accounted for more than 20 percent of operating profits. Other growth initiatives announced in 2004 included the establishment of the firm's first subsidiary in India to begin marketing name-brand flavor-enhancing seasonings and a ¥21.6 billion ($195 million) expansion of the company's amino acids businesses in Brazil, China, and the United States.

Egashira's profitability drive paid off as net income rose steadily during the 2002 through 2005 fiscal years. Profits in 2005 reached ¥44.82 billion ($418.9 million) on sales of ¥1.07 trillion ($10.03 billion). Egashira stepped aside from his position as president and CEO in June 2005, becoming chairman, while his right-hand man, Norio Yamaguchi, was promoted from senior vice president to the chief executive position.

Over the next few years, Ajinomoto's financial fortunes reversed course in large measure because of the firm's susceptibility to fluctuations in the feed-use amino acid market. Stiff competition from Chinese manufacturers was a key challenge in this sector, and the company also had to contend with sharp rises in the costs of the raw materials used to produce MSG and other amino acids. To lessen the impact of the vicissitudes of the amino acid market, Ajinomoto in early 2006 acquired the Amoy Food Group from Groupe Danone for approximately ¥27.3 billion ($239 million). The addition of Amoy, producer of Chinese soy sauce and frozen-food products in Hong Kong, North America, and Europe, significantly enhanced Ajinomoto's position as an all-around food maker, not just a maker of ingredients, outside of Japan.

At this same time, Ajinomoto was seeking to expand its position in the health-food products sector. Toward this goal, the company in October 2007 acquired full control of Japanese soft drinks maker Calpis Co., Ltd., in a stock-swap deal valued at around ¥73.2 billion ($731.5 million). Calpis was best known as the producer of a fermented-milk beverage that was sold as a health drink in Japan and was also popular in Taiwan and other markets in Asia.

During the fiscal year ending in March 2009, Ajinomoto booked a net loss of ¥10.23 billion ($110.6

million) as a result of the global economic downturn, high raw material and fuel prices, intense competition, and unfavorable trends in foreign exchange rates. In June 2009 Masatoshi Ito succeeded Yamaguchi as president and CEO as the latter moved into the chairman's seat. Ito immediately launched an effort to roughly double the company's overseas food sales to ¥300 billion by fiscal 2015 in part by venturing into new markets in Africa, the Middle East, Central America, and Southeast Asia. Acquisitions were expected to be a key component of this growth initiative. Ajinomoto was also seeking deals in other areas as well, including pharmaceuticals. In July 2009 the company announced it had acquired the Japanese rights to the osteoporosis drug risedronate from Procter & Gamble Company for $210 million.

Updated, David E. Salamie

PRINCIPAL SUBSIDIARIES

Ajinomoto Frozen Foods Co., Inc.; Ajinomoto Logistics Corporation (89.4%); Ajinomoto Medica Co., Ltd.; Ajinomoto Pharma Co., Ltd.; Ajinomoto Treasury Management, Inc.; Calpis Co., Ltd.; GABAN Co., Ltd. (55. 4%); Knorr Foods Co., Ltd. ASIA: Ajinomoto (China) Co., Ltd.; Chuanhua Ajinomoto Co., Ltd. (China; 70%); Henan Ajinomoto Amino Acid Co., Ltd. (China); Lianyungang Ajinomoto Frozen Foods Co., Ltd. (China); Lianyungang Ajinomoto Ruyi Foods Co., Ltd. (China; 90%); Shanghai Ajinomoto Amino Acid Co., Ltd. (China; 60%); Shanghai Ajinomoto Seasoning Co., Ltd. (China); Shanghai House Ajinomoto Foods Co., Ltd. (China; 70%); Xiamen Ajinomoto Life Ideal Foods Co., Ltd. (China; 51%); PT Ajinex International (Indonesia); PT Ajinomoto Calpis Beverage Indonesia; PT Ajinomoto Indonesia (50%); Ajinomoto (Malaysia) Berhad (50.1%); Ajinomoto Philippines Corporation (95%); Ace Pack Co. (Thailand) Ltd.; Ajinomoto Betagro Frozen Foods (Thailand) Co., Ltd. (50%); Ajinomoto Betagro Specialty Foods (Thailand) Co., Ltd. (51%); Ajinomoto Calpis Beverage (Thailand) Co., Ltd.; Ajinomoto Co. (Thailand) Ltd. (78.7%); Ajinomoto Frozen Foods (Thailand) Co., Ltd.; Fuji Ace Co., Ltd. (Thailand; 51%); Ajinomoto Vietnam Co., Ltd. AMERICAS: Ajinomoto Biolatina Indústria e Comércio Ltda. (Brazil); Ajinomoto Interamericana Indústria e Comércio Ltda. (Brazil); Ajinomoto del Perú S.A. (99. 6%); Ajinomoto Frozen Foods U.S.A., Inc.; Ajinomoto U.S.A., Inc.; Calpis U.S.A., Inc. EUROPE: S.A. Ajino-moto OmniChem N.V. (Belgium); Ajinomoto Euro-Aspartame S.A.S. (France); Ajinomoto Eurolysine S.A.S. (France); Ajinomoto Poland Sp. z o.o.; ZAO "Ajinomoto-Genetika Research Institute" (Russia).

PRINCIPAL COMPETITORS

Archer Daniels Midland Company; McCormick & Company, Incorporated; The Nisshin OilliO Group, Ltd.; Bunge Limited; Kyowa Hakko Kirin Co., Ltd.; Global Bio-chem Technology Group Company Limited.

FURTHER READING

Abe, Nami, "Ajinomoto: Outgoing Chief Develops Firm into Global Enterprise," *Nikkei Report,* March 16, 2005.

———, "Ajinomoto's Amoy Takeover Targets Global Presence," *Nikkei Report,* January 13, 2006.

———, "Dependence on Amino Acids Hurts Results at Ajinomoto," *Nikkei Report,* August 29, 2005.

Abrahams, Paul, "Japanese Drug Group Licenses Treatment," *Financial Times,* January 20, 1994, p. 28.

Bremner, Brian, "Quenching a Thirst for New Markets: Tokyo's Ajinomoto Aims Its Energy Drinks at Health-Crazed Americans," *Business Week* (international ed.), October 25, 2004, p. 24.

Burton, Thomas M., "Archer-Daniels Faces a Potential Blow as Three Firms Admit Price-Fixing Plot," *Wall Street Journal,* August 28, 1996, p. A3.

Dawkins, William, "Ajinomoto Profits Static for Year," *Financial Times,* May 26, 1995, p. 25.

———, "Tradition on a Knife-Edge," *Financial Times,* March 13, 1997, p. 21.

Gordon, Michael, "Ajinomoto Ploughs Funds into Amino Acids Business," *European Chemical News,* August 23–September 5, 2004, p. 27.

"Honen, Ajinomoto Agree to Merge Food-Oil Units," *Asian Wall Street Journal,* August 17, 2001, p. M3.

Kilman, Scott, "Ajinomoto Pleads Guilty to Conspiring with ADM, Others to Fix Lysine Price," *Wall Street Journal,* November 15, 1996, p. A4.

Lander, Peter, "Mob Scene," *Far Eastern Economic Review,* March 20, 1997, p. 58.

Nakamoto, Michiyo, "Ajinomoto Head Quits over Scandal," *Financial Times,* April 12, 1997, p. 21.

Nakano, Keisuke, "Ajinomoto Steps Up Global Push," *Nikkei Weekly,* August 3, 2009.

Sugimoto, Akiko, "Ajinomoto Has Obstacles to Overcome," *Nikkei Report,* July 22, 2002.

Tanzer, Andrew, "We Have Our Eyes Open," *Forbes,* September 4, 1989, pp. 57+.

alfresa

Alfresa Holdings Corporation

1-1-13 Ohtemachi
Chiyoda-ku
Tokyo, 100-0004
Japan
Telephone: (+81 813) 5219 5100
Fax: (+81 813) 5219 5103
Web site: http://www.alfresa.com

Public Company
Incorporated: 2003
Employees: 10,517
Sales: ¥193.4 billion ($17.71 billion) (2008)
Stock Exchanges: Tokyo
Ticker Symbol: 2784
NAICS: 424210 Drugs and Druggists' Sundries
    Merchant Wholesalers

■ ■ ■

Alfresa Holdings Corporation is Japan's second-largest drug wholesaler. The company operates as a holding company for a network of 14 subsidiaries involved in the wholesaling, marketing, and import and export of pharmaceuticals, medical equipment and supplies, and diagnostic reagents. The group's Wholesaling Division is conducted primarily through subsidiary Alfresa Corporation, and its network of 11 subsidiaries directly controlled by Alfresa. The company also operates a range of affiliated subsidiaries in partnership with other Japanese pharmaceutical wholesalers. While wholesaling is the company's primary operation, Alfresa is also present in the pharmaceutical manufacturing sector.

Through Alfresa Pharma the company produces and markets a range of more than 90 prescription and over-the-counter medications, as well as diagnostic reagents and medical and other healthcare equipment. Alfresa was formed in 2003 through the merger of Fukujin and Azwell, amid the ongoing consolidation of the Japanese pharmaceutical wholesale sector. In October 2008, the company announced its intention to team up with market leader Mediceo Paltac to form a new company. That merger was put on hold amid the worsening economic climate at the beginning of 2009. Alfresa is listed on the Tokyo Stock Exchange and is led by Chairman Kunio Fukujin and President Arata Watanabe. The company generates annual sales of ¥193 billion ($17.7 billion).

JAPANESE PHARMACEUTICAL WHOLESALE CONSOLIDATION IN THE NINETIES

As in many markets, most of Japan's pharmaceutical and medical supplies distribution was carried out by a myriad of wholesale companies. Into the early 1990s, the country counted nearly 500 pharmaceutical wholesalers. Many of these companies also operated as pharmaceutical manufacturers, as well as producers of medical devices, equipment, and supplies.

The 1990s, however, marked a new era of consolidation for the market. Over the course of the decade and into the new century, the Japanese market saw a wave of mergers and takeover agreements. As a result, the number of players in the pharmaceutical wholesale market was trimmed dramatically, with less

COMPANY PERSPECTIVES

Group Philosophy: "Alfresa creates a fresh life for all." We meet shareholders' expectations. We are always customer centric. We value the happiness of our people. We strive for symbiosis with society, the environment and other stakeholders as a good corporate citizen.

Group Mission: Our mission is to maximize our corporate value by creating innovative value and earning the trust of society through contributions to people's health mainly in the field of medical care.

than 200 companies still sharing the market. Most of these companies, however, remained quite small. Instead, a handful of wholesale giants grew to capture a majority of the country's wholesale market. By the end of the opening decade of the 2000s, just five companies controlled more than 80 percent of the pharmaceutical wholesale market. This figure compared to the United States, where three companies accounted for 90 percent of all pharmaceutical sales. In Europe, the three largest wholesalers captured 65 percent of the market.

Alfresa emerged as one of the top Japanese wholesalers in the early 2000s, with a market share of more than 20 percent. The company's origins traced back to the early years of the 20th century. One of the oldest branches of the company stemmed from the creation of a drug company in 1913. This branch, which became Showa Pharmaceutical, moved into pharmaceutical sales with the opening of the Yokoi Pharmacy in Uchiyama-cho, Nagoya, in 1918. The founding Yokoi family remained at the head of the company into the next century.

Showa added several more pharmacy operations over the next decades. In 1964, the company separated its operations into its two primary components, those of retail and wholesale distribution and pharmaceutical manufacturing, creating a new company for the purpose, Showa Shinyaku Co. Ltd. Later known as Showa Pharmaceutical, the company went public in 1995, with a listing on the Nagoya Stock Exchange.

Soon after, however, Showa entered talks to merge with another prominent pharmaceutical group. Like Showa, Nippon Shoji Kaisha operated in both the pharmaceutical distribution and manufacturing sectors. The company traced its own origins back to the Philippines, with the founding in 1920 of Nakashima Shigeru

Shoten in order to import and distribute Japanese pharmaceutical and medical supplies to the Filipino market.

The outbreak of World War II, however, forced the company to move back to Japan, where it reincorporated in Osaka in 1939. After the war, the company changed its name, becoming Nippon Shoji Kaisha. The company continued to build its pharmaceutical distribution business. Over the following decades, however, Nippon Shoji Kaisha also launched its own pharmaceutical manufacturing operations. This effort was boosted in 1972 when the company opened its own research laboratory. That facility was later expanded in 1982, becoming known as the company's development and research headquarters.

AZWELL IN 1998

Nippon Shoji Kaisha went public in 1991, listing its shares on the Osaka Stock Exchange's Second Section. The company ran into a rough period during the early years of that decade, however. In 1993, the company codeveloped a new medication, Sorivudine, for the treatment of shingles. The product launch quickly proved disastrous, as the new drug proved fatally incompatible with a common anticancer medication. As a result, more than 14 people died in the month following the product launch.

The new drug was quickly banned by the Japanese government. Soon after, the company was rocked by a new scandal involving insider trading. The scandal spread to involve more than 175 employees, and led to the resignation of the company's president. Nippon Shoji Kaisha appeared to have put these troubles behind it, and by 1996 the company's share listing was admitted to the Osaka Exchange's First Section.

Nonetheless, the company was forced to join the ongoing consolidation of the pharmaceutical wholesale sector, and by 1999 had completed its merger with Showa Pharmaceutical, forming Azwell Inc. The new company then listed its shares on the Nagoya Stock Exchange's First Section in 1999, before moving its listing to the Tokyo Stock Exchange's main board the following year.

FORMING ALFRESA IN 2003

Azwell by then had emerged as Japan's third-largest wholesaler. Into the early 2000s, the company claimed more than 11 percent of the key regional markets in metropolitan Tokyo, Nagoya, Osaka, and Kobe. However, the company was already losing ground to its fast-growing rivals, notably to Kuraya Sanseido. That company itself had been created only in 2000, as a

KEY DATES

1918: Showa Pharmaceutical is founded as the Yokoi Pharmacy in Uchiyama-cho.

1920: Nippon Shoji Kaisha originates as an importer and distributor of Japanese pharmaceutical products in the Philippines.

1949: Fukujin is founded as a pharmacy.

1998: Showa and Nippon Shoji Kaisha merge to form Azwell Inc.

2003: Azwell and Fukujin merge to form Alfresa Holdings.

2004: Company restructures its wholesale operations into Alfresa Corporation and its pharmaceutical manufacturing business into Alfresa Pharma.

2005: Alfresa acquires a stake in a mainland China wholesale business.

2008: Alfresa and Mediceo Paltac announce plans to merge and form a new company with a 50 percent share of the Japanese wholesale market.

2009: Alfresa and Mediceo Paltac call off their merger agreement.

result of a merger, and became a major driver of the consolidation movement, buying two more major regional wholesalers in 2003.

In order to maintain its position among the country's top three wholesale groups, Azwell turned to its number four rival, Fukujin, that year. This company had been founded as a pharmacy group in 1949 by the Fukujin family, under the name Fukujin Stores Ltd. By 1960, Fukujin had become a prominent pharmaceutical wholesaler, becoming known as Fukujin Inc. in 1964. The company also developed a network of subsidiaries, in Saitama, Kanagawa, Senju, and elsewhere.

Fukujin became the centerpiece of an early consolidation movement, merging its various operations with Umeya Corporation in 1980. In 1983, the company completed another merger, becoming Kurosaki Fukujin. Over the next decades, Fukujin continued to grow strongly, completing several more acquisitions and partnerships. Into the early 2000s, the company claimed more than 8 percent of the national wholesale pharmaceutical market.

Fukujin and Azwell's merger agreement was completed in September 2003 with the creation of a

new company, Alfresa Holdings Corporation. The two companies' wholesale operations, which remained Alfresa's primary business, were restructured into a new subsidiary, Alfresa Corporation. The company's pharmaceutical manufacturing business, primarily contributed by Azwell, was then reformed into a second major subsidiary, Alfresa Pharma Corporation, in 2004.

CHALLENGING THE MARKET LEADER

Alfresa, led by Chairman and CEO Kunio Fukujin and President Futoshi Yokoi, immediately asserted its intention to claim the top position in the country's wholesale pharmaceutical market by the end of the decade. Toward this end, the company became the driving force behind a fresh consolidation wave.

The company launched a series of acquisitions, starting with the purchases of Odashima Ltd. in Iwate Prefecture, most of DAIWA Wholesalers Co. (Daiwa) in Ehime Prefecture, and Taishodo Co. in Saitama Prefecture, in 2004. The following year, the group added three more acquisitions, Kowa Yakuhin in Tokushima Prefecture, Okauchi Kankodo in Kagawa Prefecture, and Seiwa Sangyo Co. in Hiroshima Prefecture, along with the remaining shares of Daiwa. The company then reorganized its expanded operations. Okauchi, Kowa Yakuhin, and Daiwa, for example, were merged together to form a single subsidiary, Shikoku Alfresa Corporation, with its headquarters in Kokubunji-cho, Takamatsu, Kagawa Prefecture.

Alfresa completed several more acquisitions through the second half of the decade. The company acquired Meisho Co., based in Ishikawa Prefecture, in 2006, then added CS Yakuhin Co. and Ryuyaku Co. in 2007. By 2009, the company had extended its operations to a national level, with a network of 11 wholesale subsidiaries. In order to coordinate its operations, the company also put into place a centralized information technology unit, Alfresa System Corporation, based in Tokyo, created in 2007.

Alfresa's acquisition drive had succeeded in lifting the group to the number two position in Japan by 2008. At the same time, the company had also begun taking steps to prepare for future changes in the Japanese market. With the country's declining birthrate and rapidly aging population, Alfresa sought new growth avenues. The company responded to the country's changing demographics by targeting medications and other medical products designed for the senior citizen market.

At the same time, Alfresa sought an entry into the mainland Chinese market. In contrast to Japan, the

Chinese pharmaceutical wholesale market remained highly fragmented, with the largest groups controlling just 35 percent of the total market. Alfresa took its first step into China in 2005, forming a partnership with Itochu Corporation to acquire a stake in a mainland wholesaler.

In the meantime, Alfresa continued to seek the deal that would allow it to move into the top wholesaler's spot in Japan. The company appeared to have found its target when, in October 2008, it announced its intention to merge with the country's number one wholesaler, Mediceo Paltac. The merger, which was to take place on an equal basis, was expected to be completed by 2009.

However, the proposed new company was expected to control more than 50 percent of the Japanese market. As a result, the merger was subjected to a compulsory review by the Japanese Fair Trade Commission (FTC). In the beginning of 2009, the FTC announced that its review had run into delays. Amid the difficult economic climate of the time, Alfresa and Mediceo Paltac were forced to call off the merger. Despite this setback, Alfresa's business remained strong, as the company claimed a total market share of nearly 23 percent. With annual revenues of ¥193.4 billion ($17.71 billion), Alfresa was not only one of Japan's leading pharmaceutical wholesalers, it also ranked among the top wholesalers in the world.

M. L. Cohen

PRINCIPAL SUBSIDIARIES

Alfresa Corporation; Alfresa Nikken Sangyo Corporation; Alfresa Pharma Corporation; Alfresa System Corporation; Ando Co., Ltd.; CS YAKUHIN CO., LTD.; Kowa Pharmaceuticals Co., Ltd.; Meisho Co., Ltd.; Odashima Limited; QINGDAO NESCO MEDICAL CO., LTD. (China); RYUYAKU CO., LTD.; SEIWA SANGYO CO., LTD.; Shikoku Alfresa Corporation.

PRINCIPAL DIVISIONS

Wholesaling; Manufacturing.

PRINCIPAL COMPETITORS

Mitsubishi Chemical Holdings Corp.; Mediceo Paltac Holdings Company Ltd.; Marubeni Corp.; Suzuken Company Ltd.; Kanematsu Corp.; Daiichi Sankyo Company Ltd.; Toho Holdings Company Ltd.; Nagase and Company Ltd.; Meiji Holdings Company Ltd.

FURTHER READING

"Alfresa Aims to Be No. 1 Wholesaler with ¥2 Trillion Sales by 2008," *Asia Africa Intelligence Wire*, September 22, 2003.

"Alfresa HD: Profits Decline Despite Growth in Sales," *Asia Africa Intelligence Wire*, August 29, 2005.

"Alfresa Holdings Begins Developing Molecular Market Determination Reagent," *Asia Africa Intelligence Wire*, November 5, 2004.

"Alfresa Pharma, AnGes MG Sign Joint Development Contract for Atopic Dermatitis Drug," *Asia Africa Intelligence Wire*, July 11, 2005.

"Alfresa Pharma to Become Distributor of Anafranil Antidepressant," *Asia Africa Intelligence Wire*, October 15, 2005.

"Fukujin, Odashima Enter Wide-Ranging Business Tie-Up," *Chemical Business NewsBAse-Pharma Japan*, January 19, 2004.

"Fukujin to Team Up with Four Firms in OTC Drug Business," *Asia Africa Intelligence Wire*, April 12, 2004.

"Fukujin Wants to Become No. 1 Drug Wholesaler by Merging with Azwell," *Asia Africa Intelligence Wire*, January 2, 2003.

Hug, Dale, "Alfresa, Meisho to Form Comprehensive Business Alliance," *Asia Africa Intelligence Wire*, October 5, 2004.

"Itochu, Alfresa to Invest in Chinese Drug Wholesaler," *Asia Africa Intelligence Wire*, July 29, 2005.

"Japan's Mediceo Paltac and Alfresa to Merge," *Reuters*, October 8, 2008.

"Japan's Top Two Pharmaceutical Wholesalers to Merge in April," *Kyodo News*, October 11, 2008.

Nishitani, Yumiko, "Japan's Mediceo, Alfresa Scrap Merger Plan," *Reuters*, January 9, 2009.

Tsukioka, Aki, "Alfresa HD, Seiwa Sangyo to Join Hands in Pharmaceutical Wholesale Business," *Asia Africa Intelligence Wire*, September 6, 2004.

———, "Alfresa Pharma Introduces New Stop-Smoking Aid," *Japan Corporate News Network*, August 23, 2005.

Uranaka, Taiga, "Top Drug Wholesaler to Buy Two of Its Rivals," *Japan Times*, December 13, 2003.

ALSTOM

ALSTOM

3, Avenue André Malraux
Levallois-Perret, 92309
France
Telephone: (+33 141) 492000
Fax: (+33 141) 492485
Web site: http://www.alstom.com

Public Company
Incorporated: 1928 as Als-Thom
Employees: 81,500
Sales: EUR 18.7 billion ($27.04 billion) (2008)
Stock Exchanges: Euronext Paris
Ticker Symbol: ALS
NAICS: 336510 Railroad Rolling Stock Manufacturing

■ ■ ■

ALSTOM (Alstom) is a world-leading manufacturing company focused on two primary divisions: Alstom Transport and Alstom Power. The French company is the world's leading producer of hydroelectric power plants, the leading producer of conventional islands (the housing for the instrumentation and control systems) for nuclear-power plants, and the global leader in the production of environmental control systems. Alstom also holds the number one position in the very-high-speed and high-speed train sectors, and the world train speed record of 574.8 kilometers (km) per hour. The company is also the world's second largest producer of metros, tramways, suburban and regional trains, and related infrastructure and equipment.

The group's Power Systems operating unit also manufactures turnkey gas- and coal-fired power plants, and has entered the wind-powered market as well. Power Systems represents 49 percent of the group's annual sales, which neared EUR 19 billion ($27 billion) in 2008. The company's Transport unit adds another 30 percent to sales, while the Power Service unit adds another 20 percent. At the beginning of 2009, the company's total order book topped EUR 45 billion. The company operates on a global level, with a presence in more than 70 countries and more than 81,500 employees. Alstom is listed on the Euronext Paris stock exchange and is led by Chairman and CEO Patrick Kron.

ORIGINS IN THE LATE 19TH CENTURY

Created in 1928, Alstom's roots lie in the early period of both the electrical power generation and railroad industries in France in the late 19th century. The group's electric power side originated in 1893 with the founding of Compagnie Française pour l'exploitation des procédés Thomson-Houston (CFTH). This company represented a collaboration between the French Compagnie des Compteurs, founded in 1872 to repair and produce gas meters, and the U.S.-based Thomson-Houston, a pioneer in electric-powered machinery, equipment, and infrastructure, including tramways. That company had been founded in 1879 and later merged with Edison General Electric to form General Electric Company (GEC).

CFTH was initially created to serve as the French sales and marketing wing for Thomson-Houston's

Our values and ethics: Three essential values have been defined by the Group's Executive Committee: trust, team spirit and sense of action.

Trust. Alstom, with its two activities, three Sectors, numerous management structures, units, production sites and countries is, by definition, a complex company. Mutual trust between colleagues and their management is essential for the proper conduct of the business and effective management of projects.

Team. Alstom's business is based on delivering projects which require collective discipline and efforts to execute them successfully as well as networking to ensure that the Group takes full advantage of all available competencies. This team spirit, supported by the desire to develop each employee, extends to collaboration with partners and customers.

Action. Alstom commits to deliver products and services to its customers which meet their expectations in terms of price, quality and delivery schedules. To meet these commitments to customers, a sense of action is a priority for all employees throughout the Group.

machinery and tramway systems and other equipment. The French company, however, soon displayed its own technological prowess and by 1895 had received its first three patents for its designs. Over the next two decades, the group developed a portfolio of more than 30 of its own patents. Following the creation of General Electric (GE) in 1903, however, CFTH was acquired by a French investment consortium. The company kept the Thomson-Houston name, as well as the rights to incorporate GE's technology, patents, and licenses into its own production. Thomson-Houston and GE maintained their partnership into the 1950s.

Soon after becoming an independent company, Thomson-Houston launched its own expansion drive that saw the company develop into one of the largest corporations in France. One of the company's first acquisitions came in 1905, with the purchase of Postel-Vinay, which produced electrical motors and dynamos (generators) and had also been an early pioneer in the French telecommunications market. Another important purchase for the company came in 1918, when it took over L'Éclairage électrique. Into the 1920s, Thomson-

Houston also began branching out into the consumer electronics, television and radio, and other electricity-dependent markets.

MERGER IN 1928

These diversified operations would later give rise to a number of other prominent names in the French corporate landscape, including Thales, Thomson-Brandt, Alcatel, and Alstom. In 1928 Thomson-Houston saw a new opportunity to boost its operations in the development and construction of trains and train ways and pursued a merger of these operations with the locomotive and rail manufacturing operations of Société Alsacienne de Constructions Mécaniques (SACM).

SACM had been founded in 1839 by André Koechlin, who opened a self-named locomotive workshop in Mulhouse, in France's Alsace region. Koechlin had previously manufactured machinery for the textile industry; the Mulhouse workshop enabled it to become a pioneer of the French railroad industry. Koechlin later merged with Ateliers de Graffenstaden pour créer l'Elsaessische Maschinenbau-Gesellschaft Grafenstaden.

With the German annexation of the Alsace-Lorraine region in 1871, all of the French Koechlin company's operations were now located in Germany. In response, the company transferred part of its production line to SACM, a new workshop in Belfort. In this way, the company's production base had grown to three factories, in Belfort, Grafenstaden, and Mulhouse. The latter two factories produced steam locomotives, focusing on the French market following France's recovery of the Alsace-Lorraine region after World War I. The new SACM factory in Belfort became the site of the company's extension into the production of electric locomotives.

SACM's experience in electric locomotives caught the attention of Thomson-Houston, and in 1928 the two companies agreed to merge these operations into a new company, called Als-Thom. The hyphen was soon removed from the name, and Alsthom emerged as one of the leading electric-powered locomotive producers in France as well as the rest of Europe.

Alsthom completed a number of acquisitions in the years leading up to World War II. In 1932 the company bought Constructions Électriques de France. This company, based in Tarbes, was a major producer of electric locomotives and other electrical and hydraulic equipment, and provided the foundation of the company's Transport unit. In 1937 Alsthom completed a new acquisition, of Vetra, a company founded in 1925 to produce electric trolley buses.

```
┌─────────────────────────────────────────────┐
│                                               │
│              KEY DATES                        │
│                  ▪                            │
├───────────────────────────────────────────────┤
```

1893: Compagnie Française pour l'exploitation des procédés Thomson-Houston (CFTH) is founded.

1903: Thomson-Houston becomes an independent company.

1928: Thomson-Houston and Société Alsacienne de Constructions Mécaniques (SACM) merge operations to create Als-Thom (later Alsthom).

1969: Compagnie Générale d'Électricité (CGE) takes majority control of Alsthom.

1976: Alsthom enters shipbuilding through acquisition of Chantiers de l'Atlantique.

1989: CGE merges Alsthom into a joint venture with U.K. firm General Electric Company called GEC Alsthom.

1998: Alsthom becomes an independent company listed on the Paris stock exchange, and becomes Alstom.

2000: Alstom acquires full control of ABB Alstom Power.

2004: French government rescues Alstom from bankruptcy, and the company begins streamlining its operations.

2006: Alstom returns to profits and sells off 75 percent of its Marine division.

2009: Alstom announces its interest in acquiring Areva's transport and distribution division.

CGE SUBSIDIARY IN 1969

Alsthom, like parent company Thomson-Houston, suffered under the years of Germany's occupation of France during World War II, as the company's production was pressed into supporting the German war effort. This position in turn made the company's factories a prime target for Allied bombing raids. Both companies' fortunes, however, revived quickly following the war as they each became major motors for the French reconstruction effort.

The postwar period also saw the evolution of Thomson (the company simplified its name in the 1950s) into two major areas of operations, consumer electronics and military and defense. Alsthom grew as well, developing expertise in the construction of power plants. The company also began participating in the French effort to develop its domestic nuclear-power industry starting in the 1960s. Additionally, the company entered into a series of cooperation agreements with chief rival Compagnie Générale d'Électricité (CGE), setting up three joint ventures in 1965: Alsthom-Savoisienne, Delle-Alsthom, and Unelec.

The 1950s and 1960s were also marked by intense involvement of the French government in the country's industrial and other business sectors. Although the government had nationalized outright a number of industries, such as the power generation and related industries, it exerted increasing influence on the nation's industrial sector in other ways. This influence led to a wholesale restructuring of the country's electrical and heavy equipment producers in the late 1960s. As part of this process, the government pushed through the transfer of majority control of Alsthom to CGE in 1969.

HIGH-SPEED SUCCESS IN THE SEVENTIES

CGE was by then one of France's largest and most diversified conglomerates, with leading positions in a variety of industries, including construction, energy generation, and heavy equipment. As a result, Alsthom itself grew strongly under CGE. Backed by its powerful parent, the company entered an entirely new field of operations in 1976, with the acquisition of Chantiers de l'Atlantique, based in Saint-Nazaire, near Nantes. The purchase allowed Alsthom to become one of the world's leading shipbuilders, and established the company's Marine division.

One year later, Alsthom completed the major project of the installation of a 1,300 megawatt (MW) generator, which proved capable of producing 1,500 MW of power. Located at the power station in Paluel, the new plant set a world record for power generation. Alsthom was about to set another world record, as it debuted the French high-speed train project, the Trains à Grand Vitesse (TGV) in 1978.

By 1981 the first TGV had established its first train speed record, reaching 380 km per hour by 1981. Alsthom would continue to develop its high-speed train technology, setting a new record of 515.3 km per hour in 1990, with commercial speeds of 320 km per hour. By 2007 the company had raised the barrier again, setting a new world record of more than 574 km per hour. The group's commercial designs also made speed gains, with the unveiling of a prototype in 2008 capable of commercial speeds of 360 km per hour.

During the 1980s, Alsthom's other operations grew as well, particularly following the acquisition of Compagnie Électro-Mécanique (CEM) in 1983, which formed the basis of a new subsidiary, CEM Alsthom. In 1986 the company set out to achieve a new world record, as it launched the construction of a 212 MW gas turbine for French electricity utility Électricité de France.

INTERNATIONAL GROUP IN 1989

Nevertheless, Alsthom's focus on the French market threatened the company's further growth. The end of the 1970s had seen a dramatic reduction in France's economic expansion. The run-up to the European Union and the first stage of the lowering of trade barriers among member states in 1992 threatened the company with the beginning of a new era of competition. In order to meet these challenges, Alsthom sought to expand outside of France for the first time.

This led CGE to form a joint-venture partnership with British counterpart GEC in 1989. CGE contributed Alsthom to the new venture, while GEC added its GEC Power Systems subsidiary. The new company took on the name GEC Alsthom.

The company was now able to compete on a Europe-wide, and soon global, scale. In 1994 the company added operations in Germany, the third of Europe's big three economies, by acquiring LHB Salzgitter. The company also acquired a stake in MAN Energie, before taking full control of that company in 1995.

Throughout its history, Alsthom had operated as a subsidiary of another, larger company. The 1990s, however, saw a number of important market trends. The global investment community had begun to lose faith in the highly diversified industrial conglomerate model. At the same time, the electronics and defense industries were developing increasingly complex technologies. Meanwhile, the telecommunications industry had begun to experience a period of unprecedented expansion.

By 1998 CGE and GEC agreed to spin off Alsthom as an independent company in order to refocus their own operations around their telecommunications and defense electronics operations, respectively. Alsthom's operations were then transferred to another company, called Jotelec, which was already listed on the Euronext Paris stock exchange. The company then changed its name to Alstom, simplifying its spelling for the international market.

GOVERNMENT RESCUE IN THE 21ST CENTURY

Alstom appeared to start off with a bang, making a number of acquisitions at the end of the 1990s. These included Sasib Railways, in Italy, and its U.S. subsidiary General Railway Signal Company; and Télécité Inc., based in Canada, in 1999. Also that year, the company formed a joint venture with Sweden's ABB to create ABB Alstom Power. The partnership quickly broke down, however, and by the end of 2000 Alstom had taken full control of the joint venture. The move, however, came at an inopportune moment for Alstom.

For one thing, the takeover of ABB's power plant operations had proved a disaster, in part because of problems involving the high-power gas-turbine model inherited from ABB. The collapse of the global market following the September 11, 2001, terrorist attacks on the United States hit Alstom hard, all the more so because the company had already been weakened by a requirement to pay more than EUR 460 million in dividends to its former shareholders.

As a result, by 2003 Alstom teetered on the brink of bankruptcy. Nevertheless, its importance to the French economy was underscored when Nicolas Sarkozy, the French finance minister (and future president), pushed through a bailout of the company in 2004. Under terms required for approval of the bailout by the European Commission, Alstom was forced to agree to shed significant parts of its operations, including its transport and distribution division to nuclear-power specialist Areva, and its power conversion operations to Barclays Private Equity. The company completed one last major shipbuilding project, of the *Queen Mary 2* in 2004, then sold 75 percent of its Marine division to Norway's Aker Yards in 2006.

This streamlining enabled Alstom to return to profitability within two years. Into the second half of the decade, the group's operations resumed their growth, in part because of soaring demand for both high-speed trains and power plants from China, India, and other rapidly developing markets. In 2007 the company also entered the Russian market, acquiring a 49 percent stake in a joint venture with the state-owned company Atomenergomash. That same year, the group, which had achieved world-leading status in the gas, coal, and nuclear-power generation markets, extended its operations into the renewable energy category for the first time. For this, the company acquired Spain's Ecotècnia, a wind-power specialist, for EUR 350 million ($471 million).

As the first decade of the 21st century neared its close, Alstom, with the encouragement of the French government, had expressed its interest in merging with Areva, in part in order to gain control of its former transport and distribution division. By mid-2009, however, the likelihood of a full-scale merger between the two companies appeared slim. Nonetheless, Alstom remained interested in reacquiring at least the transport and distribution division. In the meantime, the company continued to achieve strong growth in the international markets through its dual core operations of transport and power systems. By 2009 the company's revenues had neared EUR 19 billion, while its total order book stood at a healthy EUR 45 billion. A world-leading manufacturer, Alstom stood as one of France's corporate flagships in the new century.

M. L. Cohen

PRINCIPAL SUBSIDIARIES

Alstom (China) Investment Co. Ltd.; Alstom (Switzerland) Ltd.; Alstom Africa Holding (Pty) Ltd. (South Africa); Alstom Asia Pacific Sdn Bhd (Malaysia); Alstom Australia Holdings Ltd.; Alstom Brasil Energia e Transporte Ltda (Brazil); Alstom Canada Inc.; Alstom Croatia Ltd.; Alstom Deutschland AG (Germany); Alstom España IB (Spain); Alstom Ferroviaria SpA (Italy); Alstom Hydro Energia Brasil Ltda (Brazil); Alstom Hydro France; Alstom Inc. (USA); Alstom Konstal Spolka Akeyjna (Poland); Alstom LHB GmbH (Germany); Alstom Limited (Russia); Alstom Ltd. (Australia); Alstom Ltd. (UK); Alstom Mexico SA de CV; Alstom Norway AS; Alstom NV (Netherlands); Alstom Portugal, SA; Alstom Power Inc. (USA); Alstom Project India Limited; Alstom Signaling Inc. (USA); Alstom SpA (Italy); Alstom Technical Services (Shanghai) Co. Ltd. (China); Alstom Technology Ltd. (Switzerland); Alstom Transport Holding US; Alstom Transport SA; PT Alstom Power Energy Systems Indonesia.

PRINCIPAL DIVISIONS

Alstom Power; Alstom Transport.

PRINCIPAL OPERATING UNITS

Power Systems; Power Service; Transport.

PRINCIPAL COMPETITORS

Siemens AG; Abengoa S.A.; MAN SE; Bombardier Inc.; Kawasaki Heavy Industries Ltd.; Titran Joint Stock Co.; Hyundai Mobis Company Ltd.; J.M. Voith AG; Rautaruukki Oyj; China South Locomotive and Rolling Stock Corporation Ltd.

FURTHER READING

"Alstom Sells Shipyard," *International Herald Tribune*, January 5, 2006, p. 13.

"Alstom's Last Stand," *Economist* (U.S.), December 6, 2003, p. 59.

Arnold, Martin, "Alstom Lives Off Its Past Glories," *Financial Times*, November 18, 2004, p. 30.

Belton, Catharine, and Peggy Hollinger, "Alstom Joins Russia Venture," *Financial Times*, April 3, 2007, p. 28.

Fishbein, Jennifer, "Alstom Surges on Upbeat Report," *Business Week Online*, January 18, 2008.

Hollinger, Peggy, "Alstom Buys Spain's Ecotecnia," *Financial Times*, February 6, 2008, p. 16.

———, "Alstom Sets Sights on Areva Unit," *Financial Times*, May 6, 2009, p. 15.

Johnson, Nicholas, "Alstom Posts a Profit After Bankruptcy Scare," *International Herald Tribune*, May 18, 2006, p. 23.

Marsh, Peter, "Not Every Marriage Is Made in Heaven," *Financial Times*, April 1, 2000, p. 18.

———, "A Turbine Triumph Propelled by a Disaster," *Financial Times*, November 19, 2002, p. 14.

Marsh, Peter, and Raphael Minder, "Alstom Chief Seeks Painless Separation from Parents," *Financial Times*, January 29, 2001, p. 32.

Minder, Raphael, "Alstom to Seek More Sell-offs," *Financial Times*, May 16, 2001, p. 28.

"Racing Its Rivals, Alstom Introduces a 360-Kilometers-an-Hour Train," *International Herald Tribune*, February 6, 2008, p. 16.

"Train Wars, Alstom v Bombardier," *Economist* (U.S.), February 10, 2007, p. 70.

Viscusi, Gregory, "Alstom Gains Contract for Plant in Bulgaria," *International Herald Tribune*, September 26, 2006, p. 22.

Wright, Robert, "Alstom Puts Brakes on Transfer of Technology," *Financial Times*, May 18, 2007, p. 29.

———, "For Alstom China Train Success Comes at a Price," *Financial Times*, October 26, 2006, p. 4.

American Public Education, Inc.

———————————————— ■ ————————————————

111 West Congress Street
Charles Town, West Virginia 25414
U.S.A.
Telephone: (304) 724-3700
Toll Free: (877) 468-6268
Fax: (304) 724-3780
Web site: http://www.americanpubliceducation.com

Public Company
Founded: 1991 as American Military University
Incorporated: 2002
Employees: 1,140
Sales: $107.1 million (2008)
Stock Exchanges: NASDAQ
Ticker Symbol: APEI
NAICS: 611310 Colleges, Universities, and Professional
   Schools; 611710 Educational Support Services;
   541512 Computer Systems Design Services

■ ■ ■

American Public Education, Inc. (APEI), is an exclusively online for-profit provider of postsecondary education directed primarily to military and public service communities. The company delivers its services through two universities, American Military University and American Public University, which together constitute APEI's one wholly owned subsidiary, American Public University System (APUS). The two universities share faculty and curriculum consisting of more than 70 degree programs and 50 certificate programs in fields related to business administration,

criminal justice, education, homeland security, intelligence, liberal arts, military studies, national security, public health, and technology. One of the few U.S. academic institutions both regionally and nationally accredited, APUS serves about 45,000 part-time students in all 50 states and in more than 130 other countries. In 2008, more than 80 percent of APUS students were either in the military or were veterans.

BEGINNING AS A PAPER-BASED, DISTANCE-DELIVERY UNIVERSITY

American Public Education, Inc., traces its lineage to one of the first 100 percent distance-delivery universities, American Military University (AMU). Founded in 1991 by retired Marine Corps officer James P. Etter, AMU was intended to address the unique educational needs of military personnel. Etter, who had taught at the Quantico Marine Corps base, launched the company to serve an adult mobile population and provide courses not typically offered by other institutions through a curriculum geared to military officers seeking degrees relevant to their professions.

AMU initially began as a paper-based university operating by mail, phone, fax, and e-mail. The institution's first courses were offered in January 1993 and, following its 1995 accreditation by the Distance Education and Training Council, in January 1996 AMU started providing undergraduate programs primarily designed for military personnel, initially marketing its courses through word of mouth. During the next three years, the university progressively expanded its military-related curriculum to include courses in civil war stud-

COMPANY PERSPECTIVES

American Public University System has evolved into one of the world's leading distance learning institutions, providing relevant, student-focused, and affordable degree programs that prepare students for service and leadership in a diverse and global society. American Public University System educates the nation's military and public service communities by providing respected, relevant, affordable, and student-focused online programs that prepare them for service and leadership in a diverse, global society.

ies, defense management, intelligence, and unconventional warfare and later added such course areas as criminal justice, emergency management, homeland security, and national security. Responding to a demand for career preparation after the military, AMU gradually increased its offerings to include liberal arts courses and extended its marketing efforts to address public-service professionals employed in police, fire, emergency-management, and national security fields.

FOUNDING OF AMERICAN PUBLIC EDUCATION, INC., AND APUS

After educating thousands of students and graduating hundreds, in 2002, AMU was reorganized and became part of the newly formed American Public University System (APUS), a wholly owned subsidiary of American Public Education, Inc. (APEI), which was established that year. At the same time, APEI founded American Public University (APU), which also became part of APUS. APU was established to extend the model of its sister university AMU to a larger arena of adult students, including individuals with no military affiliation, particularly those in the public service sector such as teachers as well homeland security, intelligence, and public safety professionals.

In 2006, APUS took significant steps to becoming increasingly profitable. APUS was granted regional accreditation from the Higher Learning Commission of the North Central Association of Colleges and Schools and given approval to begin offering seven new degree programs in education and information technology. That same year, APEI universities became eligible to provide students with federal financial aid, often a major source of for-profit company income. For 2006, APEI earned $1.8 million on revenues of $40.05 million as

course registrations increased 46 percent over the previous year, when revenues were $28.18 million and the company lost $11.9 million.

With accreditation and the ability to offer its students federal financial aid, APUS attracted greater attention in 2007 from those seeking postsecondary education, and it took strides to expand its marketability among diverse populations. With a growing student enrollment, APUS expanded its curriculum to include four new undergraduate programs in information technology and three new master's programs in education. To develop new markets for its educational offerings, the company signed several articulation agreements with community colleges to make it easier for students to transfer credits to APUS schools. APEI also increased its efforts to forge solid relationships with the various military branches. One branch, the Navy, granted APUS provisional acceptance into its College Partnership Distance Learning Program, which allowed sailors to take courses relevant to their field from anywhere in the world.

INITIAL PUBLIC OFFERING AND INCREASED PROFITABILITY

In November 2007, American Public Education, Inc., went public, offering more than 5.3 million shares of stock at an initial price of $20 per share. The initial public offering (IPO) was deemed a major success by the company and one of the three best domestic IPOs in 2007 based on stock price value at year's end. The IPO generated proceeds of $100.3 million, which were used to pay a $93.8 million special distribution to shareholders and $6.5 million in offering-related expenses. By year's end, APUS's annual enrollment numbers had increased 68 percent to more than 30,000 students while net course registrations increased 73 percent. The result was $69.1 million in revenues, a 73 percent increase that helped generate net earnings for APEI of $8.75 million.

The company continued to broaden its degree offerings in 2008. APUS expanded its master's of education teaching degree to include concentrations in elementary education and secondary social studies, and it began offering two new master's degrees in education: one in administration and a second in teaching with a concentration in instructional leadership. That same year, APUS received Higher Learning Commission approval to enhance its associate degree programs. As a result, the one APUS associate's degree (in general studies, with multiple concentration options) was transformed into several different associate's degrees.

For 2008, numerous economic indicators pointed to exceptional growth for APEI. Course registrations

KEY DATES

1991: American Military University (AMU) is established by retired Marine Corps officer James P. Etter.

1993: AMU's first classes are offered.

1995: AMU receives accreditation from the Distance Education and Training Council.

1996: University begins offering undergraduate degree programs.

2002: American Public Education, Inc. (APEI), and subsidiary American Public University System (APUS) are established; AMU is folded into APUS.

2006: APUS receives accreditation; APEI is certified to distribute federal student tuition aid.

2007: APEI goes public.

increased 55 percent, and enrollment rose 50 percent to more than 45,200 students. Earnings climbed to $16.19 million in 2008 on revenues of $107.1 million. Secondary public offerings also suggested the company was performing well. In a February 2008 public offering, stock shares were priced at $35.50, up from the $20 figure of the IPO just three months prior. In a subsequent offering later in 2008, shares were priced at $37.50. Clearly, APEI was in a strong financial position as it closed the books on 2008, having no corporate debt and more than adequate cash on hand.

APEI'S FUTURE

In 2009, APEI's results seemed just as stellar as the year before. Early in the year, when a lengthy recession appeared plausible, analysts heralded the company as recession proof. The same logic reasoned that the company was growing in spite, or because of, the poor economy which drove the underemployed and unemployed to seek additional education. After the company reported a set of extremely strong quarterly earnings in 2009, APEI became a choice pick for some analysts, including CNBC's Jim Cramer, and certain Wall Street veterans even suggested the company's earnings would double in 2009.

By October 2009, many economists had declared that the recession was ending. However, economists also suggested that a recovery of jobs would lag behind the Wall Street recovery, perhaps by years, guaranteeing a substantial group of unemployed considering returning to school. While some so-called stock-pickers were mov-

ing out of the for-profit online education market in late 2009, some analysts suggested that even with an economic recovery that included an improved job market, there could remain a long-term interest among the populace in pursuing a postsecondary education. Such a trend would also bode well for APEI.

Other trends appeared favorable to the company, too. Given APEI's performance for the first half of 2009 and online educational market projections, analysts were expecting the company's revenues and earnings-per-share growth rates for 2009 and 2010 to be in the neighborhood of more than 40 percent for both 2009 and 2010. The long-term market forecasts for the 2010s suggested U.S. postsecondary enrollment only to grow at a rate of 1.3 percent a year. However, online enrollment was projected to increase 12 percent annually, a distinct advantage for APEI.

APEI had several other advantages in terms of capturing a sizable share of that 12 percent growth. For one, the company held a distinct advantage with military personnel. By the late 1990s, there were more than 2.1 million prospective armed forces students and 1,200 schools serving them; however, only about 30 postsecondary schools offered online degree programs tailored to the military student. Moreover, as of 2009, APEI had not raised its per-credit hour tuition of $250 since 2001. That $250 figure was completely covered by the Department of Defense's Uniform Tuition Assistance Program (through a maximum benefit of $4,500 per fiscal year), making APUS education completely affordable for armed forces students. APEI also had a long tradition of understanding demanding work schedules and offering flexible course scheduling.

As APEI neared the 2010s, the company planned to build upon the strengths it had developed serving a military demographic and expand further into civilian markets. Of particular interest were public service sectors that complemented the company's strengths and core market, involving areas such as homeland and national security, intelligence, public health, and other public service areas. The company also expected to expand its liberal arts degree programs, making itself more attractive to a broader base of returning students.

Roger Rouland

PRINCIPAL SUBSIDIARIES

American Public University System, Inc.

PRINCIPAL COMPETITORS

Apollo Group, Inc.; Capella Education Company; Career Education Corp.; Corinthian Colleges, Inc.;

DeVry Inc.; ITT Educational Services, Inc.; Strayer Education, Inc.; University of Maryland University College (UMUC); Park University; Touro International University; Central Texas College; Embry-Riddle Aeronautical University.

FURTHER READING

"American Public Education Inc. at UBS Technology and Service Conference," *Fair Disclosure Wire,* June 8, 2009.

Aristotle, Rick, "The Military Secret That Can Make You Rich," *Motley Fool,* March 12, 2009.

Ashworth, Will, "American Public Education: A Rare IPO Win," *Investopedia,* http://stocks.investopedia.com/stock-analysis/2008/american-public-education-a-rare-ipo-win-apei-lope-lrn1204.aspx.

Brennan, Tom, "Back to School—on the Internet," *CNBC.com,* January 9, 2009.

Lipton, Josh, "Unemployment Favoring For-Profit Schools," *Minyanville,* September 9, 2009.

Mason, Cliff, "The Market's Only High-Growth Stocks?" *CNBC.com,* January 12, 2009.

"Morgan Stanley Education Stock Analyst Sees 12% to 15% Growth over Next 12 Months," *Wall Street Transcript Online,* September 9, 2009.

Obel, Mike, "Sector Snap: Proprietary Schools up on GAO Report," *Yahoo Finance,* September 21, 2009.

Wilton, Bill, "American Public Education, Inc.," *Zacks Investment Research,* June 17, 2009.

ArcelorMittal

19 Avenue de la Liberté
Luxembourg, L-2930
Luxembourg
Telephone: (+352) 4792 5000
Fax: (+352) 4792 2675
Web site: http://www.arcelormittal.com

Public Company
Incorporated: 2006
Employees: 315,900
Sales: $124.93 billion (2008)
Stock Exchanges: Paris New York Brussels Luxembourg
    Barcelona
Ticker Symbol: MT
NAICS: 331111 Iron and Steel Mills; 212210 Iron Ore
    Mining; 331221 Cold-Rolled Steel Shape
    Manufacturing; 331222 Steel Wire Drawing

■ ■ ■

ArcelorMittal is the world's leading producer of steel. The Luxembourg-based company, which represents the culmination of a long series of mergers within the steel industry, produces approximately 10 percent of the world's steel supply. In 2008, the company's total production topped 103 million tons, generating total revenues of $124.9 billion. ArcelorMittal operates across the full range of metal products, producing flat and long steel products, as well as stainless steel. The company is also one of the most vertically integrated in the steel market, with operations in iron ore and other metals mining, and the production of direct-reduced iron

(DRI). ArcelorMittal operates more than 60 steel mills in 20 countries. Europe accounts for 49 percent of the group's steel production, while the group's North and South American operations contribute 36 percent of its production. The remainder comes from the group's operations in such countries as South Africa, Kazakhstan, China, and Ukraine. ArcelorMittal was created in 2006 through the merger of the French-Luxembourg-Spanish group Arcelor and London-based Mittal Steel. Lakshmi Mittal, considered one of the most dynamic leaders in the modern steel industry, spearheaded the merger and is the company's CEO, chairman, and largest shareholder.

FORGING A STEEL INDUSTRY LEADER IN 2006

ArcelorMittal was created in 2006 through the merger of Mittal Steel, then the world's number one steel producer, with Arcelor, the industry's number two, in a highly controversial deal brokered by Lakshmi Mittal. The merger represented the culmination of a long series of mergers and takeovers in a process of consolidating the highly fragmented steel industry. The creation of a smaller number of major steel groups with truly global operations marked a milestone in the transformation of the traditionally cyclical steel market. Much of the credit for this transformation fell to India-born Mittal, who built his own steel empire over the course of 40 years.

Mittal, the son of a small Indian steel mill owner, had guided both publicly listed Ispat International and privately held LNM Group to the top of the global steel market. Starting in 1975 with just a single small mill in

COMPANY PERSPECTIVES

Transforming tomorrow: Our Philosophy, Our Values. We know that our position in the steel industry brings unique responsibilities. We are committed to setting globally recognised standards with the needs of future generations in mind. Our goal is to provide the leadership that will transform tomorrow's steel industry. We have a clear vision of the future, underpinned by a consistent set of values.

Sustainability: We are guiding the evolution of steel to secure the best future for the industry and for generations to come. Our commitment to the world around us extends beyond the bottom line, to include the people in whom we invest, the communities we support and the world in which we operate. This long-term approach is central to our business philosophy. Quality: We look beyond today to envision the steel of tomorrow. Because quality outcomes depend on quality people, we seek to attract and nurture the best people to deliver superior solutions to our customers. Leadership: We are visionary thinkers, creating opportunities every day. This entrepreneurial spirit brought us to the forefront of the steel industry. Now, we are moving beyond what the world expects of steel.

Indonesia, Mittal built a steel empire that entered the world's top 10 by the 1990s. From the start, Mittal focused his growing steel production on the newly developing minimill model. These were smaller production facilities that used electric-arc smelting technologies, replacing the larger and far more expensive traditional blast furnaces. Minimills had a major drawback, however, in that they relied on the use of steel scrap as their raw materials, which became increasingly expensive with the newly rising demand.

Mittal was credited with pioneering the use of DRI in the early 1980s. Through a production process that eliminated the use of expensive steel scrap in favor of directly transforming iron ore into steel, Mittal was able to slash his raw materials costs by as much as 50 percent.

By the late 1980s, Mittal's growing treasury led him to take his first steps toward building a vertically integrated business. In the late 1980s and early 1990s, Mittal acquired a number of the world's leading DRI

suppliers, including in Trinidad and Tobago and Mexico. In this way, Mittal's steel operations became one of the world's lowest-cost producers and was able to deliver finished steel products at prices less than its competitors' raw materials costs.

BUILDING A STEEL EMPIRE IN THE NINETIES

Cash-rich, Mittal launched the implementation of what many consider a visionary strategy: carrying out a long series of acquisitions across the world. When Mittal started, the steel industry remained controlled by a large number of national steel champions that tended to focus almost exclusively on their domestic market. Many of the world's steel companies were government-owned, dominated by national interests, and often inefficiently run. Despite heavy subsidies, most of these companies struggled to maintain profits, particularly during the many periods of cyclical steel industry downturns.

Into the 1990s, Mittal recognized the potential for building his own international network by bidding for the world's failing state-run steel companies. Many of Mittal's early acquisitions focused on developing markets. His first acquisition was Trinidad and Tobago's national steel company, in a two-phase deal launched in 1989 and completed in 1994. In 1992, Mittal acquired Mexican steelmaker Sicarsta, also a major DRI producer. The struggling steel companies in the former Soviet Bloc formed another attractive acquisition pool for Mittal through the middle of the 1990s. Among these the company acquired Karmet from the Kazakhstan government in 1996.

By then, Mittal had also begun targeting an expansion into key Western markets. In 1994, for example, he acquired Sidbec-Dosco in Canada. Mittal, who became a British citizen and established his permanent residence in London, acquired his first European holdings in 1996, taking over the state-owned steel mill in Hamburg, Germany, as well as Ireland's sole steel mill, Irish Steel.

By 1998, Mittal had entered the United States, buying Inland Steel, which operated one of the world's largest steel plants in East Chicago, Indiana. That purchase marked a new phase in Mittal's acquisition strategy. The steel baron's previous purchases had come quite cheaply. In the case of Sicarsta, for example, Mittal paid just $220 million to acquire a steel facility built at a cost of $2 billion. The Irish Steel acquisition price had been merely symbolic, as Mittal agreed to take over the company's debt. For Inland Steel, however, Mittal reached deep into his pockets, paying $1.43 billion.

KEY DATES

1911: Arbed is founded in Luxembourg.
1948: Usinor is founded in France.
1950: Ensidesa (later Aceralia) is founded in Spain.
1975: Lakshmi Mittal founds LNM Group and Ispat International with a steel mill in Indonesia.
1997: Arbed and Aceralia form a strategic alliance.
2002: Arcelor is created through the merger of Arbed, Usinor, and Aceralia.
2004: Ispat International acquires its parent company, LNM Holdings, and becomes Mittal Steel.
2006: Mittal Steel acquires Arcelor for $32 billion, creating the world's largest steel company, ArcelorMittal.
2009: ArcelorMittal enters India for the first time, acquiring 35 percent of Uttam Galva.

CREATING MITTAL STEEL IN 2004

The Inland Steel acquisition, which was quickly followed by the purchase of three steel mills from France's Usinor, firmly placed Mittal's steel holdings, representing a production capacity of more than 19 million tons, into the global top 10.

Fueling Mittal's later purchase was his decision to spin off Ispat International as a publicly listed company in 1997. The initial public offering (IPO) sold 20 percent of Ispat on the New York and Amsterdam stock exchanges, with Mittal retaining 80 percent of the company through LNM Group. The Ispat IPO became the largest ever in the steel industry at the time, raising $780 million. Only part of Mittal's steel holdings were placed into Ispat, however. LNM Group retained significant parts of Mittal's steel businesses, as well as a range of diversified interests, including shipping.

A new slump in the global steel market provided Mittal, by then joined by son Aditya Mittal, with fresh opportunities for expansion. With the younger Mittal, a graduate of the Wharton School's M.B.A. program, leading the group's mergers and acquisition team, both LNM and Ispat completed a number of important deals in the early 2000s. Among these were the purchase of a controlling stake in Algeria's Alfasid; the Czech Republic's Nowa Huta; Poland's Polskie Huty Stali; and Balkan Steel in Macedonia.

Aditya Mittal's next target, however, was also the family's largest. In 2004, Mittal agreed to pay $4.5 billion to acquire International Steel group, formed from the ashes of former steel giant Bethlehem Steel. The deal not only gave the Mittals control of the largest steel operations in the United States, it also raised the company to the number two spot in the world. The acquisition also provided the Mittals with the opportunity to streamline their steel holdings.

In 2004, Ispat launched the $13 billion takeover of its own parent company, LNM, and renamed itself Mittal Steel. The reorganization came in part to satisfy criticism from Ispat's minority shareholders, notably that the Mittals' acquisition strategy favored LNM over Ispat, despite their assurance, during the Ispat IPO, that future acquisitions would be carried out through the public company.

THE BIRTH OF ARCELOR

Mittal Steel became the world's number two steel company, trailing only another recently created steel giant, Arcelor, based in Luxembourg. Arcelor had been formed in 2002 through the merger of Luxembourg-based Arbed, France's Usinor, and Spain's Aceralia Corporacion Siderurgica, creating a European champion.

Arcelor's roots lay at the very heart of the European steel industry and represented decades of steel industry mergers and acquisitions in each country. Arbed itself had been formed in 1911 although parts of the company stemmed from as early as 1838. The merger of three companies, Hauts Fourneaux et Forges de Dudelange; Mines du Luxembourg et des Forges de Sarrebruck; and Forges d'Eich—Le Gallais, Metz et Cie created the dominant Luxembourg steel group Acieries Reunies de Burbach-Eich-Dudelange, or ARBED.

The company, which adopted the acronym as its official name in 1978, completed a number of acquisitions through the 20th century, including operations in neighboring Germany and Belgium. In 1962, Arbed acquired HADIR, a consortium of steel interests based in France, Belgium, and Luxembourg. Toward the end of the century, Arbed began looking beyond the Luxembourg region. In 1994, the company acquired a controlling stake in Germany's Stahlwerke Bremen. In 1997, Arbed entered Spain as well, forming a strategic alliance with Aceralia Corporacion Siderurgica there.

Aceralia's own origins reached back to the creation of Altos Homos de Vizcaya, founded through the merger of three Bilbao-region steel companies in 1902. Another key component of the future Aceralia was Empresa Nacional Siderurgica Sociedad Anonima, or ENSIDESA, which was created by the Franco government in 1950 as part of an effort to stimulate the Spanish economy. Ensidesa later took over another Spanish steel producer, Uninsa, in 1973.

FORMING ACERALIA AND USINOR IN THE NINETIES

In the early 1990s, the Spanish government began taking steps toward the privatization of its steel interests. As part of this process, the Ensidesa and Altos Homos businesses were amalgamated into a new entity, Corporacion de la Siderurgia Integral, or CSI. This company was then restructured and by 1994 the Spanish government had hived off CSI's profitable operations into a new company, CSI Corporacion Siderurgica. Following the signing of the strategic alliance with Arbed in 1997, CSI became Aceralia.

Backed by Arbed, Aceralia launched its own acquisition drive into the end of the decade. The company first acquired Aristrain, the largest producer of steel sections in Spain. In 1999, Aceralia added UC Group, which led the Spanish market in the production of wire rod and rebars. In this way, Aceralia had boosted its capacity to 10 million tons.

The third and largest part of Arcelor was Usinor, formerly France's flagship state-owned steel company until its privatization in 1995. Usinor had been formed through a long series of mergers and acquisitions in the French steel industry. The company's oldest operations dated from as far back as 1704, with the founding of the de Wendel Ironworks that year. Usinor's modern period began following World War II, when de Wendel joined with eight other French steel companies to found Société Lorraine de Laminage Continu (Sollac) in 1948. In that year as well, two major French steel companies, Denain-Anzin and Nord Est, completed the merger creating Usinor.

Sollac evolved into Sacilor in the early 1970s, and, like Usinor, found itself confronted by a major crisis in the global steel industry in the middle of that decade. The French steel industry was particularly hard hit during the decade, suffering from inefficient operations, overproduction, and often antiquated manufacturing processes. This crisis, however, set the stage for a major drive to restructure the French steel industry, as well as a massive investment in new technologies and production capacity. Much of this effort occurred under government control, when the French government nationalized Sacilor and took over 90 percent of Usinor in 1981. The two companies were then merged in 1986, becoming Usinor Sacilor, before becoming Usinor during its privatization in 1995.

ARCELOR MERGER IN 2002

Like its counterparts, Usinor started to add interests beyond its core French market from the 1990s. The company entered the United States, creating a wire rod joint venture with Georgetown Steel in 1990. In that year, Usinor moved into Germany, buying Hoechst AG's steel production operations. Other international operations added during the decade included a steel-tube joint venture with Italy's Ilva Spa and Germany's Mannesmann; Arus Corp., a joint venture with Arbed; and Germany stainless steel group Ugine SA.

The consolidation of, and increasing globalization of the international steel industry, inspired in large part by the rapid growth of Lakshmi Mittal's steel empire, got underway in earnest at the end of the 1990s. Usinor joined in on this drive in a bid to establish itself among the top players. In 1998, the company added several new purchases including J&L Speciality Steel in the United States, Cockerill-Sambre in Belgium, and Acos Especiais Itabira and Siderurgica Tubarao, both in Brazil.

The steel industry crisis amid the overall global economic downturn, encouraged the continuing consolidation of the international steel market. The steel industry found itself caught between rising raw material prices on one end, and a slump in demand on the other. Companies found themselves unable to respond quickly to the new market. As a result, the world saw a glut of steel, and prices dropped significantly.

Steel companies increasingly began seeking partners in order to form ever larger groups. This led Usinor, Arbed, and Aceralia to agree in 2001 to merge their operations. Completed in 2002, the new group became Arcelor, and took the position as the largest steel producer in the world. The company, which posted losses of nearly $630 million in its first year, quickly launched a restructuring, trimming off unprofitable businesses and reorganizing its remaining operations. By 2004, as the global market picked up again, Arcelor had become profitable, generating sales of $41.1 billion and profits of $3.1 billion.

GLOBAL STEEL LEADER IN 2006

The steel crisis also had an impact on Mittal Steel, as the company struggled both with the global production surplus at the beginning of the decade and with the precipitous drop in the price of steel industry shares. At the height of the crisis, shares in the then-Ispat plunged to just $1.50, compared to an IPO price of $27 per share. Parts of Mittal Steel, including its operations in Mexico, neared bankruptcy.

Part of the steel industry's problem, the Mittals' reasoned, was that steel companies were neither large enough nor global enough in their scope. Both the industry's key raw materials suppliers and its primary customers, especially the automotive industry, had completed a major consolidation drive. Their power over the steel industry had increased dramatically at the start of the new century. Still, the fragmented nature of the steel industry meant that steel companies were too small to be able to respond appropriately, by idling production facilities, for example, to market cycles.

In 2006, however, Aditya Mittal proposed the family's most audacious move yet, a takeover of Arcelor. Mittal Steel at first attempted a friendly approach to Arcelor, and in January 2006 offered to buy the company for $23 billion. Arcelor rejected the offer, however, despite the acknowledgment from many observers that the proposed merger would be an important step in the transformation of the historically unstable steel industry.

The battle for Arcelor proved hard fought, as the European company resisted the takeover effort. Mittal, driven by Aditya Mittal, stood firm and, after making a number of important concessions, won the day with a final offer of nearly $32 billion. In June 2006, the newly combined company took the name ArcelorMittal. As part of the takeover agreement, the Mittals had agreed to appoint Roland Junck, from Arcelor, as the group's CEO. Lakshmi Mittal, however, remained the company's largest shareholder and chairman. By November 2006, Junck left the company, replaced by Lakshmi Mittal.

CONTROLLING RAW MATERIALS SUPPLIES FROM 2007

The merger of Arcelor and Mittal created a global steel industry giant, with a highly complementary geographic presence with little overlap. The long history of investment in research and development at Arcelor and its founding companies also provided the merged company with a new base of technological expertise that could be shared across the whole of ArcelorMittal's network. In this way, the company began upgrading many of its existing operations with the technological advancements pioneered at Arcelor. This effort, as well as company-wide cost reductions, enabled ArcelorMittal to meet its promised cost reduction targets by 2008.

Meanwhile, ArcelorMittal lost no time in pursuing further international growth. Vertical integration, and particularly control over its own raw materials supplies, became an important part of the company's strategy. Toward this end, the company began acquiring mining interests around the world. These included the purchase of three mines from Russia's Severstal in 2007, and the acquisition of London Mining South America, which

held significant mining interests in Brazil, in 2008. Also in 2008, ArcelorMittal spent nearly $433 million to purchase a controlling stake in South Africa's Kalagadi Manganese, ensuring the group's supply of that important steel component. The company also received a concession to develop a hematite and magnetite mining concession in the Faleme region of Senegal in 2007.

The company also moved to boost its international steel distribution profile. This led to a number of new acquisitions, including NSD Ltd. in the United Kingdom and M.T. Majdalani Y Cia in Argentina, both in 2007. The following year, the company bought Eisen Wagener, a major steel distributor in Austria. The company also strengthened its position in the Middle East, acquiring a 60 percent stake in Dubai Steel Trading Company in January 2009.

PUT TO THE TEST IN 2009

ArcelorMittal continued to seek further expansion opportunities for its core steel production operations. The company acquired Sicarsta, a long steel producer based in Mexico, in April 2007. In September of that year, the company acquired full ownership of Arcelor Brasil, then formed a 50/50 joint venture with Turkey's Borusan to build a $500 million mill with a capacity of 4.8 million tons.

Other steel acquisitions included Galvex OU, a producer of hot dip galvanized steel in Estonia; Slovakia's OFZ, a producer of ferro-alloys; and Uruguayan steel-tube producer Cinter. ArcelorMittal also entered the fast-growing Chinese market in 2007, paying $644 million for a 28 percent stake in China Oriental Group Company Ltd. The company also acquired a 90 percent stake in wire producer Roncheng Chenshan Steelcord, based in Shandong. In 2008, ArcelorMittal raised its Chinese presence, forming a joint venture with Hunan Valin Iron & Steel Group to produce electrical steel for the Chinese automotive market.

ArcelorMittal's total production topped 100 million tons by the end of 2008, generating total sales of $124.9 billion, and net profits of nearly $9.4 billion. By then, however, ArcelorMittal found the reasoning behind its formation put to the test as the steel industry reeled through a major new global economic crisis.

In December 2008, ArcelorMittal responded to the slump in steel demand by laying off more than 9,000 sales and administrative staff, for a total cost savings of $1 billion. Importantly, the company's global footprint enabled it to provide the long sought-after response to the drop in steel demand. Through the end of 2008, the company moved to enact a dramatic reduction in its production totals. By the beginning of 2009, the company had slashed production by some 50 percent, idling a significant portion of its more than 65 steel mills throughout the world.

The reduction in output helped maintain pricing stability throughout the steel industry, and allowed ArcelorMittal to keep its competitive edge through the height of the economic crisis. As the recession appeared to ease toward the end of the year, the company found itself in a strong position to take advantage of the steel market's coming return to growth. By September 2009, ArcelorMittal had resumed its own expansion, announcing its intention to acquire a 35 percent stake in Indian steel company Uttam Galva. The purchase, part of ArcelorMittal's overall strategy of focusing on the rapidly developing Indian and Chinese markets, also marked Lakshmi Mittal's entry into the Indian steel market, more than 45 years after the Indian native had set out to build the world's leading steel company in the 21st century.

M. L. Cohen

PRINCIPAL SUBSIDIARIES

ArcelorMittal Brasil S.A.; ArcelorMittal Bremen GmbH (Germany); ArcelorMittal Commercial Sections Rayleigh Ltd. (UK); ArcelorMittal Espana S.A. (Spain); ArcelorMittal Frydek-Mistek A.S. (Denmark); ArcelorMittal Galati S.A.; ArcelorMittal Gent (Belgium); ArcelorMittal Hamburg GmbH (Germany); ArcelorMittal Lazaro Cardenas S.A. de C.V. (Mexico); ArcelorMittal Plate L.L.C. (USA); ArcelorMittal Poland S.A.; ArcelorMittal Singapore Private Ltd.; ArcelorMittal South Africa Ltd.; ArcelorMittal SSC UK Birmingham Ltd.; ArcelorMittal Staalhandel Rotterdam B.V. (Netherlands); ArcelorMittal Stainless Europe S.A. (France); ArcelorMittal Steelton L.L.C. (USA); Vinton ArcelorMittal Inc. (USA).

PRINCIPAL DIVISIONS

AACIS; Flat Carbon Americas; Flat Carbon Europe; Long Carbon Americas and Europe; Stainless Steel; Steel Solutions and Services.

PRINCIPAL COMPETITORS

GTR Inc.; Cargill Inc.; BHP Billiton Ltd.; Nippon Steel Corp.; JFE Holdings Inc.; Tata Sons Ltd.; The Indian Iron and Steel Company Ltd.; Hitachi Metals Ltd.; MAN SE; United States Steel Corporation.

FURTHER READING

"ArcelorMittal Takes First Step into India," *Associated Press*, September 4, 2009.

"ArcelorMittal to Tender an Offer to Buy Uttam Galva," *Health & Beauty Close-up*, September 9, 2009.

"Deals That Changed the Market in 2006," *Euromoney*, February 2007.

Kwok, Vivian Wai-yan, "ArcelorMittal Buys Hunk of Chinese Steel," *Forbes*, November 7, 2007.

Laurent, Lionel, "ArcelorMittal Slashing Administrative Staff," *Forbes*, November 27, 2008.

"Luxembourg-Based Steelmaker ArcelorMittal Has Completed Its Acquisition of Noble European Holdings BM," *Advanced Materials & Processes*, September 2009, p. 18.

Miller, Robert M., "Global Steel Is Coming Together," *Business Week Online*, September 14, 2006.

"Mittal & Son," *Business Week*, April 16, 2007, p. 45.

"Mittalic Magic," *Economist* (U.S.), February 16, 2008, p. 76.

Myers, Laura, "Mittal Tightens His Grip on ArcelorMittal," *Forbes*, May 14, 2008.

Ram, Vidya, "ArcelorMittal Digs Self-Sufficiency," *Forbes*, August 20, 2008.

———, "ArcelorMittal Feels the Pinch," *Forbes*, September 3, 2008.

Reed, Stanley, "Arcelor Mittal's Very Stable Shakeup," *Business Week Online*, November 7, 2006.

———, "Behind Mittal's Wrenching Cuts," *Business Week*, May 25, 2009, p. 25.

Shapland, Mark, "Stainless on 'Bumpy Road'; ArcelorMittal Eyes Merger," *American Metal Market*, September 2, 2009, p. 8.

Asahi

Asahi Breweries, Ltd.

■

1-23-1 Azumabashi
Sumida-ku
Tokyo, 130-8602
Japan
Telephone: (+81-3) 5608-5126
Fax: (+81-3) 5608-7121
Web site: http://www.asahibeer.co.jp/english

Public Company
Founded: 1889 as Osaka Beer Brewing Company
Incorporated: 1949 as Asahi Beer, Ltd.
Employees: 16,357
Sales: ¥1.46 trillion ($16.07 billion) (2008)
Stock Exchanges: Tokyo Osaka
Ticker Symbol: 2502
NAICS: 312120 Breweries; 424810 Beer and Ale Merchant Wholesalers; 312130 Wineries; 312140 Distilleries; 424820 Wine and Distilled Alcoholic Beverage Merchant Wholesalers; 312111 Soft Drink Manufacturing; 312112 Bottled Water Manufacturing; 311422 Specialty Canning; 311999 All Other Miscellaneous Food Manufacturing; 325411 Medicinal and Botanical Manufacturing; 551112 Offices of Other Holding Companies

■ ■ ■

Asahi Breweries, Ltd., is locked in a fierce battle with archrival Kirin Brewery Company, Limited, for first place in the Japanese beer market. Kirin had reigned supreme for decades until 2001, when Asahi attained the top spot and began a several-years-long run in that position. Aiding Asahi's surge to the top was the 1987 introduction of Asahi Super Dry, which in a decade became the top-selling beer in Japan, a position it held into the early 21st century. The company's beer and beer-like beverage operations, which also encompass *happoshu* (low-malt beer) and "new genre" beverage (no-malt beer) offerings, must contend with a steadily declining market in Japan, so Asahi has pushed strongly into overseas markets. In particular, the company has moved aggressively to capture a major share of the rapidly growing market in China, the largest beer market in the world. After investing in three local brewers and establishing a joint venture there, Asahi made its boldest move yet: the purchase of a 20 percent stake in Tsingtao Brewery Company Limited, the second-largest brewer in China.

In addition to its domestic and overseas brewery operations, which account for approximately 60 percent of the company's net sales, Asahi manufactures and markets other alcoholic beverages (including distilled spirits and wines), soft drinks (headed by the WONDA canned coffee and Mitsuya Cider brands), and food products (including brewer's yeast extracts and related products, breath mint tablets, and baby food); sells pharmaceuticals; and runs restaurants. Soft drinks are another area in which Asahi has sought growth overseas, most notably in China, South Korea, and Australia.

EARLY HISTORY

The history of Asahi Breweries is linked with that of virtually every other brewery in Japan. Beer had been introduced to Japan in the mid-1800s. The American in large part responsible for renewing trade relations with Japan, Commodore Matthew Perry, brought several cases of beer to Japan as a gift for the Tokugawa Shogunate. The beverage was so well liked that the Japanese government soon decided to establish a brewing industry. After an extensive search for a suitable area, wild hops were found growing on the island of Hokkaido, the northernmost island in the Japanese archipelago. As a result, in 1876 the commissioner-general for the development of Hokkaido founded Japan's first brewery in the town of Sapporo. (Coincidentally, the global beer capitals of Munich, Milwaukee, and Sapporo are all located along the 45 degrees north latitude.)

In the late 1880s the government sold its Hokkaido brewery to private interests, and thus the Osaka Beer Brewing Company, Japan Beer Brewery Company, Sapporo Brewery, and Nippon Brewing Company all came into being. In 1888 Hiizu Ikuta was sent to Germany by Osaka Beer Brewing Company to study brewing at the famous School of Weihenstephan in Bavaria. He returned the following year and was appointed manager and technical chief of the Suita Brewery, one of the individual breweries controlled by Osaka. Three years later, in 1892, his creation, Asahi Beer, was released for sale. Osaka was reorganized in 1893 as Osaka Breweries, Ltd.

In 1906 the Osaka Breweries, Sapporo Brewery, and Nippon Brewing Company were amalgamated into Dai Nippon Brewery Co., Ltd. Asahi became a separate division of the new company and began a long history of producing nonalcoholic beverages as well as beer. Asahi pioneered the soft drink industry in Japan with both Mitsuya Cider and Wilkinson Tansan, a mineral water. Mitsuya Cider was released for sale in 1907, 17 years after Asahi Beer had first been introduced to the market.

In the years leading up to World War II, particular beer brands tended to dominate local markets. The Asahi brand gained popularity in the Kansai area. The Asahi division expanded in 1921 through the completion of the Hakata brewery and in 1927 with the opening of the Nishinomiya brewery.

FORMING ASAHI BEER, LTD., IN 1949

In 1949, as a result of the enactment of the Excessive Economic Power Decentralization Law, Dai Nippon Brewery, which had cornered nearly 70 percent of the beer market in Japan, was divided into two parts, Asahi Beer, Ltd., and Nippon Breweries, Ltd. (the latter emerged as Sapporo Breweries Limited). In 1951 Asahi introduced Wilkinson Tansan mineral water to the Japanese market. That year also saw the introduction of Japan's first fruit-flavored soft drink, Bireley's Orange. In 1958 the company launched a canned version of Asahi Beer, Japan's first canned beer. Asahi's first plant exclusively devoted to the production of soft drinks was opened in Kashiwa in 1966. Six years later another Asahi soft drink plant began production in Fukushima. By the mid-1970s soft drink sales accounted for 35 percent of the company's total sales.

Asahi also enjoyed other kinds of success. Its Central Research Laboratory, charged primarily with quality control, also developed new products, including Ebios, a dry brewer's yeast introduced in 1930 and renowned in Japan for its medicinal properties. In 1965 laboratory staff invented the world's first outdoor fermentation and lagering tank (the "Asahi Tank"). The West German beer plant construction firm of Ziemann soon negotiated with the company for a license to build the tank.

The early 1970s saw Asahi take its first serious moves outside Japan and in the area of importing. In 1971, in a joint venture with Nikka Whiskey Distilling Company, Asahi established Japan International Liquor to import foreign liquors, primarily Scotch whiskeys (Dewars and King George IV). Also in 1971, Asahi was the first Japanese brewery to have its beer produced overseas under license when it concluded a technical assistance agreement with United Breweries of New Guinea, and a brewery was subsequently constructed at Port Moresby. Two years later Asahi began to import French and German wine. In January 1986 a technology transfer agreement was reached with San Miguel Corporation of the Philippines for the local production of Asahi beer. Another technical transfer agreement had previously been reached in 1979 with this same company for the use of Asahi's automatic beer gauge system for beer fermentation at other plants under San Miguel control. This system had been jointly developed by Asahi and the Toshiba Corporation.

Asahi entered the restaurant business in the early 1980s. Subsidiary companies (Asahi Kyoei and New Asahi) managed more than 100 restaurants in western and eastern Japan, respectively. The company also

KEY DATES

1889: Japanese government sells its Hokkaido brewery to private interests, simultaneously establishing Osaka Beer Brewing Company and several other brewing companies.

1892: Osaka begins production of Asahi Beer.

1893: Osaka is reorganized as Osaka Breweries, Ltd.

1906: Osaka, Sapporo Brewery, and Nippon Brewing Company are amalgamated into Dai Nippon Brewery Co., Ltd., which includes a separate division called Asahi.

1949: Dai Nippon is divided into two parts: Asahi Beer, Ltd., and Nippon Breweries, Ltd.

1958: Canned version of Asahi Beer, Japan's first canned beer, is introduced.

1987: Asahi Super Dry is introduced and becomes a blockbuster hit.

1989: Asahi Beer, Ltd., is renamed Asahi Breweries, Ltd.

1994: A push into the burgeoning Chinese market begins with the purchase of controlling interests in several breweries.

1995: Wide-ranging alliance with U.S.-based Miller Brewing Company commences.

2001: Asahi enters the *happoshu* (low-malt beer) segment; company gains the top spot in the Japanese beer market, edging past longtime rival Kirin.

2009: Company acquires a 20 percent stake in Tsingtao Brewery Company Limited and also purchases Schweppes Australia Pty Ltd.

entered into a joint venture with the U.S. company Pizza Hut to establish Pizza Hut restaurants in Japan.

TURNAROUND IN MARKET SHARE: MID-EIGHTIES

In October 1981 Asahi Chemical Industry (despite their similar names, the companies were not previously related) acquired 22 million shares of Asahi Beer, Ltd. An agreement was concluded between the two companies concerning relations involving personnel, technology, and sales. Asahi Chemical eventually held about 10 percent of Asahi stock, making it one of the brewer's 10 largest shareholders.

Another of Asahi's important shareholders at this time was Sumitomo Group, which held a 12 percent

stake. Over the preceding decades, Asahi's share of the Japanese beer market had declined significantly, from a peak of 36 percent in 1949 to 10 percent in 1981. Among Japanese brewers, Asahi was a distant third, trailing both Kirin and Sapporo Breweries. Executives at Sumitomo Bank had been placed into the president's office starting in the early 1970s, but they were unable to stop the decline. Then in January 1982 another Sumitomo Bank executive, Tsutomu Murai, was sent to Asahi to take over. Murai specialized in turning around troubled companies and had previously helped to rescue Mazda Motor Corporation.

Murai began with a reorganization aimed at improving communication between company departments. He then concluded a series of licensing agreements with foreign companies. In November 1982 the company entered into an agreement with Löwenbräu Company of West Germany to produce Lowenbrau Beer under license in Japan. Production of the German beer began the following April. Asahi also gained needed technical know-how by signing contracts with U.S., British, and German brewers to obtain technology. In 1984 Asahi's soft drink division concluded an agreement with Schweppes, which led to Asahi manufacturing several Schweppes brands in Japan, including Tonic Water, Golden French (an apple and ginger drink), Passion Orange, and Grapefruit Dry. Asahi entered into other partnerships, notably to import foreign beers and wines into Japan. Asahi in 1985 formed a partnership with the Australian wine company Lindemann's, after which Asahi sold Australian wine under the "My Cellar" brand.

Perhaps most important, Murai pushed the company to become more attuned to its customers. One by-product of this was a renewed attention to quality. Asahi abandoned its policy of buying most of its wheat and hops in Japan and began to buy the best raw materials available, regardless of cost or origin. The company also made moves to ensure the freshness of its beer, such as having salespeople visit stores where they would discard any Asahi beer older than three months.

In 1985 Murai ordered a series of market surveys. Of most significance was that 98 percent of the beer drinkers surveyed advised Asahi to change the taste of its beer. Consumers said that they wanted a beer that was rich but left no aftertaste, a combination that the company's technicians said was not chemically possible. Murai insisted that nothing was impossible, and Asahi subsequently developed and introduced in 1986 Asahi Draft, a full-bodied beer with a crisp taste. Then in March 1987 Asahi introduced Japan's first dry beer, Asahi Super Dry, which became a blockbuster hit. Super Dry, a cold-filtered draft beer, contained slightly more alcohol than other Japanese beers (5 percent compared with 4.5 percent) but less sugar and was thus lighter. It was also less bitter. The brand became particularly popular among younger drinkers and helped Asahi's market share increase to 17 percent just one year after its introduction.

Super Dry was so successful that Murai had to abandon a planned diversification that aimed to derive half of the company's revenue from nonbeer operations. Instead, beer increased in importance, making up 80 percent of sales in 1988.

LATE-CENTURY MARKETING INNOVATIONS AND GLOBALIZATION

By the end of the 1980s Asahi's market share had surpassed the 20 percent mark and the company (which was renamed Asahi Breweries, Ltd., in January 1989) leapfrogged Sapporo into second place among Japanese brewers. In addition to the new brands, Asahi's success in the late 1980s and early 1990s was also attributable to changes in marketing. In Japan, most beer was traditionally sold in small liquor stores by the bottle. Asahi targeted nontraditional customers by producing more of its beer in cans and packaging it in six-packs, and by sending the canned beer into supermarkets and convenience stores. The company also became much more aggressive in its pitches to retailers who sold beer. Asahi continued to emphasize the freshness of its product and by 1995 was able to deliver beer to stores just 10 days after brewing. By 1997 Super Dry had dethroned Kirin's Lager brand from the top spot among Japanese beer brands, and Asahi's overall market share hit 34.4 percent, up from 10 percent in 1985. During the same period, Kirin's market share had plummeted from 60 percent to 43 percent.

From the late 1980s into the mid-1990s, Asahi continued to be active in importing but at the same time stepped up its export activities. A technological agreement was reached with U.K.-based Bass Brewers Ltd. in 1988, whereby Asahi began to import the Bass Pale Ale brand. In 1996 the two companies entered into a new agreement that called for Bass to produce and market Asahi Super Dry in the United Kingdom and elsewhere in Europe.

In 1990 Asahi gained further access to manufacturing and marketing channels outside Japan by purchasing a significant stake, which stood at 20 percent in 1992, in Foster's Brewing Group Ltd., based in Australia and then the fourth-largest beer company in the world. In the succeeding years Asahi expanded its own system of overseas operations so that the purpose of the tie-in with

Foster's grew less important. Asahi consequently reduced its stake, then in mid-1997 sold its remaining 14 percent stake back to Foster's.

A 1994 license agreement with Molson Breweries brought Super Dry into the Canadian market. Asahi then targeted the two largest beer markets in the world, the United States and China. In 1995 a wide-ranging alliance with Miller Brewing Company commenced, which initially featured the introduction of the Miller Special brand in Japan (a brand brewed specifically for the Japanese market) and the Super Dry brand in the United States. In September 1996 Asahi and Miller introduced Asahi First Lady, a beer targeted toward women, in Japan and the United States. In April 1998 Asahi Beer U.S.A., Inc., was established as a U.S. marketing and sales company that would work with the Miller distribution network to increase sales of Super Dry in the world's leading beer market.

On the Chinese front, in 1994 and 1995 Asahi acquired shares in and began managing five Chinese brewing companies in Beijing, Yantai, Hangzhou, Quanzhou, and Jiaxing. Initially four of the companies sold a beer called Asahi Bichu, then in March 1998 Yantai Beer Asahi Co., Ltd., launched the production and sale of Asahi Super Dry. Meanwhile, in December 1997, Asahi entered into a joint venture with the largest beer maker in China, Tsingtao Brewery Company Limited, to construct a state-of-the-art beer plant in Shenzhen. Production of Asahi Super Dry began at this plant in May 1999.

In addition to growing market share in Japan and an increasing presence in Europe, North America, and China, further proof of the brewer's resurgence came in 1996 when Asahi posted record net sales and net income. Asahi repeated the feat in 1997. In mid-1997 the company finished construction of a new research and development center in Ibaraki Prefecture and was confidently building its ninth brewery, the Shikoku brewery, which was subsequently completed in June 1998. In March 1999 Asahi reached an agreement with Bass Brewers whereby Bass would undertake local production of Asahi Super Dry through an affiliate in the Czech Republic called Prague Breweries, A.S.

BECOMING THE NUMBER ONE JAPANESE BREWER IN THE EARLY 21ST CENTURY

In the late 1990s and into the early 21st century, the overall beer market in Japan was stagnant (in part because of the shrinking number of young people), but there was a significant shift occurring in the types of beers that Japanese people were consuming. Rapidly growing in popularity were low-malt beers known as *happoshu.* In the mid-1990s, some Japanese brewers decided to take advantage of the fact that beer in Japan is taxed according to its malt content. The tax on low-malt beers was significantly lower, resulting in a retail price about two-thirds that of a regular beer. Budget-conscious consumers snapped up the lower-priced beer in increasing numbers, so that by 2000 the *happoshu* segment accounted for 22 percent of the overall beer market. (To maintain a beer-like taste, producers of *happoshu* used various types of malt substitutes.)

For some time, Asahi had been able to ignore the *happoshu* phenomenon because Asahi Super Dry was defying the trend and continuing to gain market share. As the low-malt interlopers continued to gain market share, however, Asahi felt compelled to develop its own *happoshu* brand. Asahi Honnama launched in February 2001 and captured 22.3 percent of the *happoshu* market for 2001, despite Asahi being the last of the major Japanese brewers to enter the segment. This terrific debut helped Asahi Breweries finally surpass Kirin and claim the top spot in the Japanese beer market for 2001 with a market share of 38.7 percent.

The year 2001 also saw Asahi return to the black after posting a net loss in 2000 that was attributable to large write-offs of unrealized losses from securities holdings and pension-related liabilities. Overall sales for 2001 increased 2.4 percent over the previous year, with the ¥1.43 billion ($10.86 billion) figure being a record for the company. In addition to its successful introduction of Honnama, Asahi also was concentrating on strengthening its nonbeer alcoholic beverage operations in order to develop a more complete lineup of alcoholic products.

To that end, Asahi announced in February 2002 that it would acquire the alcoholic beverage businesses of Kyowa Hakko Kogyo Co. for ¥20 billion ($150.8 million). The deal included production and sales facilities for ready-mixed alcohol drinks, wine, and *shochu,* a distilled liquor comparable to vodka. In April 2002 Asahi reached an agreement with Maxxium Worldwide, a Dutch liquor sales firm, whereby Asahi gained the rights to market in Japan such brands as Rémy Martin brandy, Highland Park whiskey, Absolut vodka, Cointreau liqueur, and Maison Louis Latour wine. Also in April 2002 Asahi agreed to purchase the *shochu* and low-alcohol beverage operations of Asahi Kasei Corporation. Later in August 2002, as part of a strategic alliance, Asahi bought a 10 percent stake in Okinawa-based Orion Beer Co., the fifth-largest brewer in Japan with a market share of almost 1 percent.

SEEKING GROWTH OVERSEAS

With the continuing contraction of the Japanese beer market, Asahi sought new avenues for growth overseas, not only in the beer sector but also in soft drinks. In 2003, for instance, the company announced plans to make Thailand its production base for an expanded push into Southeast Asia and Australasia, targeting the beer markets of Australia, New Zealand, Singapore, Malaysia, the Philippines, Vietnam, Cambodia, and Indonesia. The following year, one of the company's joint ventures in China opened a new brewery in Beijing and reintroduced Beijing Beer into the Chinese market. In soft drinks, Asahi in 2004 joined with Japanese trading firm ITOCHU Corporation to acquire a 50 percent stake in the beverage business of Tingyi Holding Corporation, China's leading instant-noodle producer. The Tingyi beverage arm ranked number four overall in China, with the leading position in tea-based beverages and the number two position in juices. In South Korea, Asahi increased its investment in Haitai Beverage Co., Ltd., and turned it into a consolidated subsidiary. Among South Korean soft drink manufacturers, Haitai ranked third with a market share of around 13 percent.

Back home, sales of *happoshu* were hurt by the launch of so-called third beer, also known as new genre beverages, which contained no malt at all and thus were taxed at an even lower rate than *happoshu.* As was the case with *happoshu,* Asahi was a late entrant into this category, finally introducing its first new genre beverages, Asahi Shinnama and Asahi Shinnama 3, in 2005 to protect its lead in the Japanese beer market. Pursuing other avenues of growth at home, Asahi in 2005 also acquired LB, Ltd., a move that expanded its soft drink operations into the chilled beverage sector, specifically oolong, green, and other teas and yogurt-based drinks. In addition, the company's food operations were enlarged via the 2005 purchase of health-food maker Sunwell Co., Ltd., and the 2006 acquisition of Wakodo Co., Ltd., Japan's leading producer of baby food. In 2007 Asahi entered into an alliance with Kagome Co., Ltd., a producer of vegetable and chilled beverages. To spur further growth in soft drinks, Asahi turned Asahi Soft Drinks Co., Ltd., into a fully consolidated subsidiary, and the latter's stock was delisted from the Tokyo Stock Exchange in April 2008.

Through 2008, Asahi managed to hang onto the number one spot among Japanese brewers although by that year its lead over Kirin had been reduced to less than 1 market share percentage point. Asahi that year also achieved its eighth straight year of record net income, with profits hitting ¥45 billion ($494.5 million) on net sales of ¥1.46 trillion ($16.07 billion). A new series of bold overseas ventures also kicked off that year when Asahi introduced its beer and whiskey brands into India, becoming the first Japanese brewer to enter that market.

In 2009 the company ventured deeper into the world's largest beer market by acquiring a 20 percent stake in Tsingtao Brewery Company Limited, the second-largest brewer in China, from Anheuser-Busch InBev, for $666.5 million. Asahi in April 2009 further bolstered its overseas soft drinks operations by acquiring Schweppes Australia Pty Ltd. from Cadbury plc for AUD 1.19 billion ($774 million). The Schweppes unit was the second-largest producer of nonalcoholic drinks in Australia with ownership of such brands as Cottee's, Solo, and Spring Valley and production of Pepsi, Sunkist, and Gatorade under franchise agreements. Further Asahi acquisitions and alliances were quite likely at a time when the company was facing a potential new threat, a merger between Kirin and Suntory Holdings Limited under negotiation in the fall of 2009. If completed, the deal promised to create the clear number one brewer in Japan.

Updated, David E. Salamie

PRINCIPAL SUBSIDIARIES

The Nikka Whiskey Distilling Co., Ltd.; Sainte Neige Wine Co., Ltd.; Satsumatsukasa Shuzo Co., Ltd.; Asahi Soft Drinks Co., Ltd. (97.4%); LB, Ltd. (67.9%); Asahi Food & Healthcare Co., Ltd.; Wakodo Co., Ltd.; Amano Jitsugyo Co., Ltd. (80%); Asahi Beer Malt, Ltd.; Asahi Beer U.S.A., Inc. (99.2%); Buckinghamshire Golf Company Limited (UK); Hangzhou Xihu Beer Asahi Co., Ltd. (China; 55%); Yantai Beer Tsingtao Asahi Co., Ltd. (China; 51%); Beijing Beer Asahi Co., Ltd. (China; 31%); Shenzhen Tsingtao Beer Asahi Co., Ltd. (China; 29%); Asahi Beer (Shanghai) Product Services Co., Ltd. (China); Qingdao Tsingtao Beer & Asahi Beverage Co., Ltd. (China; 60%); Tingyi-Asahi-Itochu Beverages Holding Co. Ltd. (China; 50%); Haitai Beverage Co., Ltd. (South Korea; 58%); Asahi & Mercuries Co., Ltd. (Taiwan; 50%); Schweppes Australia Pty Ltd.

PRINCIPAL COMPETITORS

Kirin Brewery Company, Limited; Suntory Holdings Limited; Sapporo Breweries Limited.

FURTHER READING

Abe, Nami, "New Brews Abound as Asahi, Kirin Battle for Leadership," *Nikkei Report*, December 6, 2006.

"Asahi Breweries to Offer 'Third Beer,'" *Nikkei Weekly*, January 7, 2005.

"Asahi Flattens Kirin's King of Beers," *Nikkei Weekly*, July 8, 1996, p. 9.

Ellison, Sarah, "Asahi Beer Ads Brew Bewilderment, Taste of Tokyo for Britain's Bass PLC," *Wall Street Journal*, May 15, 2000, p. A9.

Jameson, Sam, "Team Spirit: The Case of Asahi Breweries Illustrates How Bank Rescues of Struggling Firms Help the Japanese Economy. But There Is No Guarantee of Success," *Los Angeles Times*, December 8, 1988, pp. 1, 11.

"Japan's Beer Wars," *Economist*, February 28, 1998, p. 68.

Joyce, Andee, "It's Dry, Dry Again, as Asahi Takes a Super Stab in the US," *Beverage World*, June 30, 1998, p. 8.

Kachi, Hiroyuki, "Asahi Breweries' China Plan Would Leave Rivals in Dust," *Asian Wall Street Journal*, December 15, 1997, p. 14.

———, "Asahi Continues to Catch Up to Kirin in Beer Battle," *Asian Wall Street Journal*, February 20, 1998, p. 7.

Kahn, Gabriel, "Asahi, Itochu Will Buy Chinese Drink Business," *Asian Wall Street Journal*, January 5, 2004, p. A3.

Maeno, Masaya, "Asahi Looks to Bolster China Ops via Tsingtao Brewery Stake," *Nikkei Report*, May 1, 2009.

———, "Kirin, Asahi Take Rivalry into No-Alcohol Arena," *Nikkei Weekly*, August 17, 2009.

Miller, Karen Lowry, "Can Asahi Brew Up Another Blockbuster?" *Business Week*, March 4, 1991, p. 41.

Moffett, Sebastian, "High and Dry: Asahi's Deft Moves Win Over Japan's Beer Drinkers," *Far Eastern Economic Review*, October 3, 1996, pp. 98–99.

Nakamoto, Michiyo, and Jenny Wiggins, "Asahi to Acquire Tsingtao Stake in Push Abroad," *Financial Times*, January 24, 2009, p. 10.

Pollack, Andrew, "The Company That Makes Japan's Best-Selling Beer Seeks Inroads into the U.S. Market," *New York Times*, April 20, 1998, p. D8.

"A Right Old Brewhaha in Japan," *Economist* (U.S. edition), February 24, 2001, p. 7.

Smith, Charles, "Satisfying a Dry Thirst: A Japanese Brewery Enjoys Success with a New Type of Beer," *Far Eastern Economic Review*, September 1, 1988, p. 50.

Tanaka, Hirofumi, and Fumika Murakami, "Asahi Breweries Finds First Place a Challenge," *Nikkei Report*, October 10, 2003.

Tomioka, Katsuhiko, "The Secret Behind Asahi's Growth: Interview with Yuzo Seto, President of Asahi Breweries," *Japan 21st*, November 1996, pp. 12–13.

Urry, Maggie, "Cadbury Agrees to Sell Australian Drinks Arm," *Financial Times*, December 27, 2008, p. 9.

Yamamoto, Yuri, "In Beer Battle, Kirin Goes Flat While Asahi Barrels Ahead," *Nikkei Weekly*, March 3, 1997, pp. 1, 19.

———, "Japan's Brewers Tapping Chinese Market," *Nikkei Weekly*, October 7, 1996, pp. 1, 21.

Yamashita, Akira, "Asahi Looks Super, but Firm Needs to Broaden Horizons," *Nikkei Weekly*, July 23, 2007.

Avon Rubber p.l.c.

Hampton Park West
Semington Road
Melksham, SN12 6NB
United Kingdom
Telephone: (44 01225) 896800
Fax: (44 01225) 896898
Web site: http://www.avon-rubber.com

Public Company
Incorporated: 1890 as Avon India Rubber Company Limited
Employees: 879
Sales: £44.1 million ($74.9 million) (2008)
Stock Exchanges: London
Ticker Symbol: AVON
NAICS: 339991 Gasket, Packing, and Sealing Device Manufacturing; 326113 Unsupported Plastics Film and Sheet (Except Packaging) Manufacturing; 326121 Unsupported Plastics Profile Shape Manufacturing; 326122 Plastics Pipe and Pipe Fitting Manufacturing; 326130 Laminated Plastics Plate, Sheet, and Shape Manufacturing; 326150 Urethane and Other Foam Product (Except Polystyrene) Manufacturing; 326220 Rubber and Plastics Hoses and Belting Manufacturing; 326291 Rubber Product Manufacturing for Mechanical Use; 326299 All Other Rubber Product Manufacturing

■ ■ ■

Avon Rubber p.l.c. is a supplier of specialized rubber and polymer products for military and commercial markets. Once an industry leader in tires for automobiles, bicycles, and motorcycles, Avon divested its car-tire business in 1997 and the rest of its auto-related operations in 2006. It has also pared away its sporting goods and inflatable boat businesses to become primarily a defense company. Avon focuses on respiratory protection products, such as gas masks, and liners and tubing for the dairy industry. Since 2007 Avon has been led by Sir Richard Needham.

WILTSHIRE ORIGINS

Avon Rubber p.l.c. began its history in the dairy lands of England's West Country. In 1885 E. G. Browne and J. C. Margetson bought Avon Mill on the River Avon at Limpley Stoke. First a textile mill, then a flour mill, it had been producing rubber goods for 10 years when it was acquired.

Starting with just seven employees, the enterprise soon outgrew its original site and moved to another former textile mill in nearby Melksham in 1890. This would be the company's home for more than a century.

The business was incorporated in 1890 as Avon India Rubber Company Limited (the "India" was dropped in 1963, and it became a public limited company in 1981). With two dozen workers at the new site, the company had first-year sales of £15,265 and a profit of nearly £500.

Browne sold most of his holding in the company in 1894. In spite of high demand for its products, the business was in financial trouble as it struggled to expand capacity. Concerned about the region's

COMPANY PERSPECTIVES

Avon Rubber p.l.c. is a world leader in the design, test and manufacture of advanced CBRN respiratory protection solutions to the world's military, law enforcement, first-responder, emergency services, fire and industrial markets. Avon has a unique capability in CBRN protection based on a range of advanced CBRN technologies in respirator design, filtration and compressed air breathing apparatus. This enables Avon to develop specialised solutions that take full account of user requirements.

unemployment, in 1896 local member of Parliament G. P. Fuller provided capital to prevent Avon's collapse. He started a long reign as chairman a few years later, with his son Major Robert Fleetwood Fuller succeeding him after his death in 1927.

Much of the firm's early production consisted of components for the railroads. The company also made tires for cycles and horse-drawn carriages, and solid-band tires for commercial vehicles. After installing electricity and beginning to make pneumatic car tires in 1897, Avon grew rapidly along with the rise of the automobile in the early years of the 20th century.

Revenues exceeded £100,000 in 1906, when the company had more than 300 employees. In 1908 the firm adopted a three-stone (trilith) trademark symbolizing the strength and durability of Stonehenge.

Avon became a public company in March 1933 and had its initial public offering on the London Stock Exchange. The next year, a strike closed the Melksham plant for six weeks.

AIDING THE WAR EFFORT

Avon's efforts were critical in wartime. The company supplied vast quantities of tires, munitions, and general rubber goods to the military. The Melksham plant had more than 1,000 employees in 1914 even as 300 men left to join the service. In 1915 Avon added the bankrupt Sidar Rubber Works at Greenland Mills in Bradford. Research in World War I resulted in petrol resistant tubing, a technology the company shared with competitors. During World War II the company supplied tires, tank wheels, gas masks, and other rubber products as employment swelled to nearly 2,500. The company also had to deal with shortages of raw materials.

Avon made 20 million gas masks and production of these continued in force during the civil-defense-conscious postwar years. A dedicated gas-mask plant opened in Bridgend, South Wales, in 1951. After a few years the plant switched to making rubber boots.

SPORTING GOODS AND BOATS

Avon began making golf balls around 1910 and articles for sports such as soccer and swimming were introduced between the wars. It began making stitchless tennis balls in quantity in 1921. These were sold by the House of Wisden.

Naturally, Avon was also involved in motor sports, particularly motorcycle racing. It supplied a number of champion racers as early as 1914. It launched a motorcycle racing program in 1949, but canceled it in 1963 due to the costs involved. The company began manufacturing a line of inflatable boats in 1959. It added products for commercial and military use in the 1980s and expanded into Europe with acquisition of the assets of French company Sillinger (for £1.5 million) in 1988. Avon Inflatables Limited was sold off to the newly formed Avon Marine Limited in 1994.

POSTWAR DEVELOPMENT

Avon entered a number of foreign ventures in the early postwar years. In 1952 A/B Gummifabrik began producing Avon tires in Sweden while Avon started making large auto tires under license from U.S. manufacturer Sieberling Tires. The next year Avon opened a plant in Kenya, originally used for retreads and later to supply cycle tires and footwear soles for the region.

The 1956 acquisition of George Spencer Moulton and Company marked a milestone in consolidation of the British rubber-products industry. A longtime rival, George Spencer Moulton had been founded in Bradford on Avon in 1848 by Stephen Moulton. It owned Kingston Mills in Bradford as well as other facilities including a French joint venture. Well known in the railway industry, it had like Avon produced a wide range of products from tires to tennis balls.

In the same year, Avon also bought J. W. & T. Connolly, a High Wycombe manufacturer of agricultural wheels and axles, building a new factory for it in 1961. Avon acquired Henley's Tyre and Rubber Company of Gravesend, Kent, in 1957. By the early 1960s, Avon employed 5,000 people and was exporting to 125 markets. It had revenues of £12.9 million in 1961.

In 1963 Avon took a major move into tire distribution when it bought Normeir Tire Company. Originally

KEY DATES

1848: Stephen Moulton starts rubber-products operation at Kingston Mills, Bradford on Avon.

1885: E. G. Browne and J. C. Margetson acquire Avon Mill, which is already producing rubber goods.

1933: Avon Rubber has its initial public offering on the London Stock Exchange.

1956: Avon buys George Spencer Moulton and Company.

1963: Avon acquires distributor Normeir Tire Company.

1966: Fire causes £1 million of damage to Melksham plant.

1974: Company opens first European plant, a hose factory in Belgium.

1989: Cadillac Rubber and Plastics Group of Michigan is company's largest acquisition to date; controlling interest in Motorway Tyres sold to subsidiary of Japan's Sumitomo.

1991: Kingston Mills is closed after 143 years of continuous rubber-products production.

1993: Company starts manufacturing in Czech Republic through an auto-hoses joint venture.

1997: Tire business is sold to Ohio's Cooper Tire and Rubber Company for £60 million.

1998: Wisconsin rubber dairy liner manufacturer Hi-Life Rubber L.L.C. is acquired.

2001: Five noncore units are closed or sold; company shifts more production to Czech Republic and Portugal.

2005: Avon buys U.S. breathing-equipment manufacturer International Safety Instruments Inc.

2006: Avon spins off automotive business in $115 million management buyout.

set up in a cowshed in 1921 by Albert Fox, this became the basis for the Motorway Tyres and Accessories Company, which had 140 branches by 1973. It was bolstered with the acquisitions of Tyrebatt and Kerrys in 1966 and Howcroft in 1970.

In 1964 Avon acquired David Moseley & Sons Ltd., a Manchester manufacturer of industrial products. This included a medical products business, Capon Heaton and Co. Ltd.

Wiltshire's Great Fire of August 1966 caused £1 million of damage to the Melksham plant. The company listed its wares in a 1967 display advertising in the *Times* (London): "tyres ... inflatable boats ... milker rubbers ... roller coverings ... golf grips ... railway springs ... auto components ... aerosol gaskets ... industrial hoses ... conveyor belts ... axle undergear equipment ... dialysing units ... and other specialised products for industry." Avon had also begun making skirting for hovercraft the previous year. It had subsidiaries in Switzerland, Sweden, Norway, and Denmark. Avon replaced its Stonehenge logo with a modern design in 1968. Annual revenues were about £30 million at the time.

The company began building a new £6 million tire factory in Washington, Durham, in 1968. However, it ultimately decided to concentrate its tire production at Melksham and sold the new plant to Dunlop. In 1971 the company announced the closure of its Moseley plant in Manchester due to a falloff in demand for its conveyor belts used by the mining industry.

INCREASINGLY INTERNATIONAL

The company was increasingly involved in international ventures. In 1973 it formed a Melksham-based joint venture with Ames Rubber Corporation of the United States to make rubber rollers for copy machines. The next year, it began selling a wide variety of rubber components through a new subsidiary in Chicago, Illinois. In 1974 the company also opened its first European plant, a hose factory in Tessenderlo, Belgium. Avon entered a Mississippi hovercraft-skirt venture with Bell Aerospace Textron in 1981.

Revenues exceeded £50 million before the first Arab oil embargo, which greatly affected the economy in general. Avon responded in 1975 by investing in its nascent medical equipment business with a new plant in Redditch and opening an Oregon-based joint venture with U.S. dialysis-machine manufacturer Drake Willock.

Avon returned to profitability in fiscal 1977 with a record income of £5.4 million. It soon invested in new factories at Trowbridge (automotive hoses) and Chippenham (hovercraft skirts). Avon ended the 1970s with annual revenues of £150 million.

However, a general industrial decline in the United Kingdom soon led to decreased orders and diminishing margins. There were layoffs throughout the group during the recession of the early 1980s. The company responded to difficult market conditions by investing in making its operations more efficient. By the end of the decade, Avon was posting record profits in its tire-manufacturing and industrial polymers operations. Total revenues exceeded £200 million ($225 million) in 1987.

LARGEST ACQUISITION IN 1989

The 1989 purchase of Cadillac Rubber and Plastics Group of Michigan was the company's largest acquisition to date, costing £37 million ($57 million). At 17 times Cadillac's after-tax earnings, it was considered a premium price, noted the *Times* (London). Avon was planning to use the unit to produce not just auto components but also its rubber and polymer products for the dairy and industrial markets.

Around the same time, Avon sold a 70 percent stake in its troubled Motorway Tyres business (for £16.5 million) and a 20 percent stake in Avon Tyres (£5.7 million) to the SP Tyres UK Limited subsidiary of Japan's Sumitomo Rubber Industries, Ltd. This relationship ended in 1993 with SP Tyres buying the remainder of Motorway Tyres and Avon buying back SP's stake in Avon Tyres.

In 1991 Kingston Mills closed after 143 years of making rubber products. The inflatables unit was spun off in 1994, leaving Avon with three main business areas: automotive components, technical products, and tires. The company moved its corporate headquarters to Manvers House in Bradford on Avon in 1995.

The company continued to invest in growth markets. In the mid-1990s Avon built a 100,000-square-foot factory in Chippenham to make suspension blocks for heavy trucks in collaboration with U.S. market leader Clevite Elastomers Inc. In 1998 Wisconsin rubber dairy liner manufacturer Hi-Life Rubber L.L.C. was acquired for £22 million, gaining a U.S. counterpart for its successful U.K. business.

Avon also shifted manufacturing of commodity items to areas of lower labor costs. In 1993 the company started making hoses in the Czech Republic, through a joint venture at first. It opened a hose factory, Avon Polímeros, in Portugal in 1996. The same year, the company entered a joint venture with Gold Seal to supply hoses for the emerging auto market in India.

TIRES SOLD IN 1997

In 1997 the tire-manufacturing business was sold to Ohio's Cooper Tire and Rubber Company for £60 million. Avon Tyres was profitable on annual sales of £111 million, but its global market share had shrunk to just 0.1 percent. It had come to specialize in premium, high performance tires.

Avon continued to make auto-components acquisitions into the late 1990s. It bought Cow Polymer from Unipoly Industrial BV in March 1998, paying £10.3 million. However, it was divested within several years. More enduring was the June 1999 acquisition of Spain's Industrial Flexo SA and Proflex SA for $23 million.

REFOCUSING IN 2001

Five noncore units were closed or sold in 2001. Among the casualties was the hose plant at Trowbridge, which had suffered as the strength of the British pound prompted auto manufacturers to source parts elsewhere. Avon shifted more manufacturing of commodity hoses to the Czech Republic and Portugal, while keeping production of more advanced, polymer-based hoses closer to its technical base in England. In 2004 the company set up a small headquarters for its auto operations in Hannover, to be closer to German carmakers.

After losing £1.5 million on revenues of £250.5 million in 2002, Avon posted pretax profits of £7.7 million ($13.5 million) on sales of £248.5 million in 2003. Much of the gain was attributed to the technical products business.

Avon became prime contractor for the U.S. military's Joint Services General Purpose Mask (JS-GPM), a project potentially worth in the hundreds of millions of dollars. Homeland security and first-responder markets became increasingly important after the September 11, 2001, terrorist attacks against the United States.

In 2005 Avon bought breathing-equipment manufacturer International Safety Instruments Inc. (ISI) of Lawrenceville, Georgia, in a deal worth about $20 million. The acquisition expanded on Avon's success in the U.S. gas-mask market by adding self-contained breathing apparatus capabilities.

AUTO BUSINESS SPUN OFF IN 2006

In 2006 Avon spun off its automotive business as Avon Automotive Inc. in a $115 million management buyout. It employed 3,500 people at a dozen plants in 10 countries and had annual revenues of about $350 million. The deal was backed by a New York equity group, Red Diamond Capital Partners L.P., which had ties to Mitsubishi Automotive.

After the spinoff, Avon Rubber had about 850 employees in England. In January 2007 Sir Richard Needham became chairman of Avon Rubber, succeeding Trevor Bonner who was retiring after five years of intensive restructuring activity. Once a Tory member of

Parliament, Needham had since 1995 served on the board of Dyson, the vacuum-cleaner manufacturer known for its pioneering products. He was also a vice chairman at NEC Europe.

Revenues were £44.1 million ($74.9 million) in 2008. The company had relocated its European dairy-liner business to the Czech Republic and closed its rubber-compounding operation in Wiltshire. This left Avon with a single plant in England. It had five in the United States. While the dairy industry lagged, demand for gas masks and protective hoods (for the U.S. military in particular) was booming. In August 2009 the FTSE index reclassified Avon as a defense company. The company would enter the 2010s reliant on this sector for its future growth.

Frederick C. Ingram

PRINCIPAL SUBSIDIARIES

Avon Polymer Products Ltd.; Avon Rubber Overseas Ltd.; Avon Rubber Pension Trust Ltd.; Avon Automotive Deutschland GmbH (Germany); Avon Caoutchouc S.A. (France); Avon Hi-Life Inc.; Avon Injected Rubber & Plastics Inc. (USA); Avon Milk-Rite Inc. (USA); Avon Polymeres France S.A.; Avon Protection Systems Inc. (USA); Avon Rubber & Plastics Inc. (USA); Avon Rubber Polimeros LDA (Portugal); Avon Vibration Management Systems Ltd.; Avon Zatec L.L.C. (USA); Avon-Ames Ltd.; Bell Avon Inc (USA); Cadillac Rubber & Plastics Inc (USA); Cadillac Rubber and Plastics de Mexico SA de CV; Cadimex SA de CV (Mexico); CT Rubber & Plastics Inc. (USA); Industrial Flexo SA (Spain); Nova Insurance Ltd.; Proflex S.A. (Spain).

PRINCIPAL DIVISIONS

Protection—U.S.; Protection—Rest of World; Avon Impact Management; Dairy; ISI; AEF.

PRINCIPAL COMPETITORS

Dräger Safety AG & Co. KGaA; Mine Safety Appliances Company; Scott Health and Safety Worldwide; Interspiro, Inc.; Sperian Protection Group; Skellerup Industries Ltd.; Trelleborg AB.

FURTHER READING

Andrews, Jeremy, "Avon Rubber to Pay $57m for US Car-Parts Maker," *Times* (London), Bus. Sec., June 14, 1989.

"Avon Hose Business Develops Well," *European Rubber Journal,* December 1, 2004, p. 18.

"The Connotation of the Trilith," *Times* (London), June 22, 1914, p. 6.

McNulty, Mike, "Avon Automotive to Go Solo," *Rubber & Plastics News,* May 29, 2006, p. 1.

———, "Avon Bowing Out of Custom Rubber Mixing," *Rubber & Plastics News,* February 11, 2008, p. 9.

———, "Doors Opening for Avon," *Rubber & Plastics News,* February 25, 2008, p. 23.

"A Profile of Avon Rubber," *Economist Intelligence Unit: Rubber Trends,* March 1993, pp. 50+.

Raleigh, Patrick, "Prudent Avon Seeks to Build on Profit Gains: Sale of Five Non-Core Units Leaves Avon in Better Shape as Profits Rise," *European Rubber Journal,* June 2002, p. 4.

———, "US Disposals Signal Avon Changes," *European Rubber Journal,* July 2001, p. 7.

Rooney, Brendan, *The Implementation of CIM in Rubber Manufacturing: A Flexible Response; Case Study of Avon Rubber,* Edinburgh: Research Centre for Social Sciences, University of Edinburgh, 1991.

Shaw, David, "Avon Restructures UK Operation," *European Rubber Journal,* November 1991, p. 9.

"£6m Avon Tyre Plant," *Times* (London), July 26, 1968, p. 21.

White, Liz, "Avon Acquires US Breathing Equipment Manufacturer; UK Firm Expands Its New Protection Division with Latest Buy," *European Rubber Journal,* July 1, 2005, p. 4.

———, "Avon Back in the Black," *European Rubber Journal,* January 2004, p. 12.

———, "Avon Set for Growth After Tough Times, Restructuring: Business Is More Valuable Than Two Years Ago, Says Avon Boss," *European Rubber Journal,* January 2003, p. 15.

White, Sally, "Avon Rubber Factory to Close: 515 Affected," *Times* (London), December 31, 1971, p. 11.

BAE SYSTEMS

BAE Systems plc

■

6 Carlton Gardens
London, SW1Y 5AD
United Kingdom
Telephone: (+44 0 125) 237 3232
Fax: (+44 0 125) 238 3000
Web site: http://www.baesystems.com

Public Company
Incorporated: 1978 as British Aerospace
Employees: 106,400
Sales: £18.5 billion ($34.4 billion) (2008)
Stock Exchanges: London
Ticker Symbol: BAESY
NAICS: 336411 Aircraft Manufacturing; 325920 Explosives Manufacturing; 332992 Small Arms Ammunition Manufacturing; 332993 Ammunition (Except Small Arms) Manufacturing; 332994 Small Arms Manufacturing; 332995 Other Ordnance and Accessories Manufacturing; 334511 Search, Detection, Navigation, Guidance, Aeronautical, and Nautical System and Instrument Manufacturing; 336413 Other Aircraft Part and Auxiliary Equipment Manufacturing

■ ■ ■

BAE Systems plc (BAE) is the largest defense contractor in Europe, and the second largest in the world. Its North American operations are a top-ten Pentagon contractor in their own right, and the company has several other global "homes" where it maintains a significant presence, often working in conjunction with local defense contractors. Its main markets are Australia, Saudi Arabia, South Africa, Sweden, the United Kingdom, the United States, and India, and it supplies customers in more than 100 countries in all.

Formerly known as British Aerospace plc, the firm was renamed in 2000 as it began a transformation into a global defense company. Already active in a range of military activities ranging from small arms to electronics to shipbuilding, BAE divested its commercial aviation and space operations while making large acquisitions to boost its U.S. business in particular. It remains involved in a number of advanced combat-aircraft programs either as a partner or supplier.

CONSOLIDATION OF PREDECESSORS

In the years after World War II the British aircraft industry was overpopulated with manufacturers who had an increasingly difficult time competing not only with each other but with larger U.S. manufacturers such as Boeing, Douglas (later McDonnell Douglas), and Lockheed. British companies were victimized by small orders from a government that was divesting itself of most of its empire and thus had greatly reduced military needs. Noting that the British aircraft industry was three times larger than France's, "with no obvious justification for being so," the *Economist* asked the critical question, "Does Britain need an aircraft industry?" Throughout the 1950s the health of British aviation was a major political issue and was the subject of many Parliamentary debates. Finally, in 1960, after intense lobbying from the Minister of Aviation, Member of

Parliament Duncan Sandys passed a bill that called for a "rationalization" of the British aircraft industry through the merger of several existing companies that were facing closure.

The purpose of the rationalization was to combine the talent and resources of about 20 companies and limit overall production, while avoiding the politically sensitive issue of creating unemployment or allowing the British aeronautics industry to fall victim to external economic pressures. It was hoped that the program would raise the intensity of technological development to a level equal to that of the United States. It was also noted that British aeronautic companies were diversifying themselves out of aircraft production, a trend that could have left Britain without an aircraft industry of any kind.

Early in 1960 Vickers-Armstrong, Ltd., which was originally founded in 1928, merged with English Electric (founded in 1918) and Bristol Aeroplane (founded in 1910) to form the British Aircraft Corporation (BAC). The three companies continued to operate as divisions of BAC, with Vickers and English Electric each accounting for 40 percent of the consortium's capital and the remaining 20 percent coming from Bristol. In May 1960 BAC acquired a controlling interest in another British company, Hunting Aircraft.

HAWKER-SIDDELEY

At the time of the British Aircraft Corporation merger, a second group of British aircraft companies were amalgamated to form the Hawker-Siddeley Aviation Company. Like BAC, Hawker-Siddeley's constituent companies, Armstrong Whitworth (founded in 1921), A.V. Roe & Company (1910), Folland Aircraft (1935), Gloster Aircraft (1915), and Hawker Aircraft (1920), were operated as subsidiaries. Each brought an area of expertise to the new company. Armstrong produced large cargo airplanes, Avro built smaller passenger liners, and Folland, Gloster, and Hawker were known for their Gnat, Javelin, and Hunter jet fighters. Hawker-Siddeley also acquired a controlling interest in de Havilland Holdings, Ltd., and The Blackburn Group, as well as a

50 percent share of Bristol-Siddeley, Ltd., the airplane engine manufacturer.

The amalgamation that created British Aircraft Corporation and Hawker-Siddeley also made Westland Aircraft Britain's primary helicopter and hovercraft manufacturer. Rolls-Royce (which received most of its publicity from its manufacture of automobiles but most of its profits from aircraft engine production) and Bristol-Siddeley, Ltd., became Britain's leading engine manufacturers. Handley Page, Short Brothers, Scottish Aviation, and British Executive and General Aviation were the only British companies that were not a part of the government's rationalization program.

During the 1960s BAC continued to manufacture English Electric's Lightning and Hunting's Jet Provost fighters in addition to Vickers's four-engine VC10 jetliner. The company also built a new twin-engine jetliner called the BAC-111. In 1962 BAC entered a co-production agreement with Aérospatiale of France to build the Concorde supersonic passenger transport.

Hawker-Siddeley was divided into two divisions: Aircraft, for aircraft production, and Dynamics, for missiles and rockets. The aircraft division took over production of the HS-125 executive twin-jet from de Havilland and the HS-748 turboprop airliner from Avro. In 1964 it introduced the Trident, a three-engine jetliner intended to compete against the BAC-111, Douglas DC-9, and Boeing 727. In the military field, Hawker-Siddeley assumed production of Blackburn's Buccaneer fighter and developed the HS-1182 Hawk trainer as well as a military patrol version of the de Havilland Comet called the Nimrod. The unique product of Hawker-Siddeley during the 1960s was the Harrier fighter jet.

The Harrier featured thrust nozzles that the pilot could aim either straight backward or toward the ground. When the nozzles were pointed backward the Harrier could take off on a runway like a conventional jet. When the nozzles were pointed down it could take off vertically like a helicopter. The Harrier was built in two configurations, one for the Royal Air Force and one for Royal Navy aircraft carriers.

Hawker-Siddeley Dynamics produced the Seaslug, Firestreak, and Red Top missiles. BAC also operated a missile division that manufactured the Vigilant, Blue Water, Thunderbird, and Bloodhound missiles. The Bloodhound was a particularly effective weapon, but created a scandal when details of BAC's high profits from the project were made public.

INTERNATIONAL COMPETITION

The success of the rationalization program was, however, limited, and by 1965 Britain's aerospace industry was

KEY DATES

1960: Government-directed consolidation creates British Aircraft Corporation (BAC) and Hawker-Siddeley Aviation Company from existing U.K. manufacturers.

1977: Hawker-Siddeley merges with BAC and Scottish Aviation, Ltd., to form British Aerospace (BAe).

1979: BAe joins the Airbus consortium and becomes a public company.

1987: Diversification drive launched, adding Royal Ordnance, Rover automobiles, and property-developer Arlington Securities, among others.

1991: BAe restructures and begins to divest noncore assets.

1997: BAe is part of multinational group developing the Eurofighter aircraft.

1999: BAe buys GEC-Marconi for £6 billion, gaining significant U.S. operations.

2000: BAe is renamed BAE Systems; acquires Control Systems and Aerospace Electronics Systems units of Lockheed Martin.

2004: BAE outbids General Dynamics Corporation for control of Alvis, Britain's last armored-vehicle manufacturer.

2005: BAE buys U.S. defense contractor United Defense Industries (UDI) for $4 billion.

2006: BAE sells its 20 percent stake in Airbus to EADS, the majority owner.

2007: BAE acquires Armor Holdings, Inc., for $4.5 billion.

again unable to compete with foreign competitors. Lord Plowden headed a special Parliamentary committee that recommended a second major restructuring of the aircraft industry. The Plowden Report proposed that Rolls-Royce and Bristol-Siddeley merge to form a single company that manufactured aircraft engines. This merger, which included the sale of Hawker-Siddeley's 50 percent interest in Bristol-Siddeley to Rolls-Royce, was carried out in 1966. The second proposal, a merger of BAC and Hawker-Siddeley, was abandoned.

In February 1969 the governments of France and West Germany concluded an agreement that established a consortium called Airbus Industrie to manufacture a new passenger jetliner designated the A-300. The British government was invited to join Airbus as a full partner,

but declined when it decided the project was doomed to failure. In its opinion, there was simply too little room in the commercial airliner market (dominated by Boeing, McDonnell Douglas, and Lockheed) to support another competitor. Hawker-Siddeley, however, agreed to produce wings for the A-300 as an Airbus subcontractor. Because of intense competition, BAC and Hawker-Siddeley made no plans to develop successors to the BAC-11 and Trident. Even British Overseas Airways (BOAC), Britain's state-owned international air carrier, was ordering the more advanced U.S.-made jetliners. In addition, the U.S. aircraft companies had extremely profitable military divisions that enabled them to devote large sums of money to the development of new commercial aircraft. BAC and Hawker-Siddeley had excellent military divisions, but the requirements of the domestic military establishment were small. At the same time, the international arms market was dominated by U.S. and Soviet manufacturers. U.S. arms import restrictions prevented Hawker-Siddeley from selling its Harrier to the United States, despite interest in the jet from the Pentagon.

MORE FINANCIAL DIFFICULTIES, 1977 CREATION OF BAE

British Aircraft Corporation, Messerschmitt-Bolkow-Blohm (MBB) of Germany, and Aeritalia of Italy created the Panavia partnership to develop the Tornado Interdictor Strike fighter. Separately, BAC and Breguet of France created another consortium called SEPECAT (Société Européenne de Production de L'avion E.C.A.T.) to develop the Jaguar jet fighter. Both of these programs were a financial drain on BAC, despite substantial contributions from the British government. Finally, it became apparent that BAC was unlikely to realize a profit from its costly coproduction of the Concorde with Aerospatiale. Only 16 were built (seven each for British Airways and Air France, with two remaining unsold), the first of which did not enter service until 1976. Once again the two largest British aerospace companies were in financial trouble and facing bankruptcy.

Engineers at Hawker-Siddeley designed a new short-haul 80-passenger jetliner called the HS-146. Convinced of the aircraft's commercial potential and the need for Hawker-Siddeley to remain in the commercial aircraft market, the British government pledged to share the development costs for the HS-146. To generate capital, the company's chairman, Sir Arnold Hall, authorized the sale of de Havilland of Canada to the Canadian government for $38 million. Similarly, BAC sold assembly rights for the BAC-111 to the government of Romania.

While the HS-146 was being developed, poor economic conditions and intense competition from the United States eroded the already tenuous position of the British aerospace industry. In 1975 the Plowden merger proposal for BAC and Hawker-Siddeley had been resurrected in the form of an Aircraft and Shipping Industries Bill. The following year BAC and Hawker-Siddeley were nationalized, less in an attempt to protect their finances than to force a merger upon them. In 1977, after once being rejected in the House of Lords and defeated in the Commons, the Industries Bill was successfully ushered through Parliament.

The Aircraft and Shipping Industries Bill merged the Aircraft and Dynamics divisions of Hawker-Siddeley with the British Aircraft Corporation and Scottish Aviation, Ltd. The new company, called British Aerospace (BAe), continued to be operated by the British government as a state-owned corporation. British Aerospace was divided into two divisions: Aircraft, based at the Hawker-Siddeley facility in Kingston, and Dynamics, headquartered at the BAC Guided Weapons plant in Stevenage.

Scottish Aviation, the third and smallest member of the BAe group, was established in 1935 to create employment opportunities in aviation in Scotland. Scottish Aviation built the international airport in Prestwick, which later became the forward traffic control base for flights between London and North America. Later, Scottish Aviation manufactured a series of propeller-driven general purpose aircraft.

JOINING AIRBUS CONSORTIUM IN 1979

In 1978 British Aerospace considered partnership with foreign companies to produce a new large passenger airliner. Even in its new form British Aerospace lacked the resources to develop a commercial jetliner any larger than the HS-146 (renamed BAe-146). Airbus, for which BAe was still building A-300 wings, was a candidate, as was Boeing, which was beginning work on its next generation of commercial aircraft. To join Boeing would have been politically inexpedient since Boeing was the primary source of the British aerospace industry's decline. In addition, British officials expressed concern over Boeing's size and aggressive corporate personality. Joining Airbus, on the other hand, would require a substantial entry fee for development costs already incurred by the Airbus partners.

Eventually Boeing lost interest in a partnership with BAe. On January 1, 1979, British Aerospace purchased a 20 percent share of Airbus, pledging $500 million through 1983 for incurred costs and development of a new aircraft designated the A-310.

In 1979 Sir Keith Joseph, industry secretary for the Conservative government of Prime Minister Margaret Thatcher, announced the government's intention to privatize (or sell to the public) most of Britain's state-owned corporations, including British Aerospace. At first this announcement alarmed officials, including BAe Chairman Lord Beswick, who had worked hard to reform the nation's aerospace industry. They feared that private investors would divide the company and indiscriminately sell the more profitable divisions, possibly to foreigners.

The privatization program moved slowly because of political opposition and the government's desire to offer shares only when market conditions were most favorable. In the meantime, BAe appointed a new chairman to succeed Lord Beswick. The man they chose was the chairman of Esso Petroleum, Austin Pearce. Pearce was faced with the dual task of guiding British Aerospace through the privatization while ensuring that the company's orders were being filled. The increased military budget of the Conservative government contributed to the company's backlog of orders.

BECOMING A PUBLIC COMPANY

The unconventional method in which British Aerospace was privatized established the form of future privatizations. On December 31, 1979, British Aerospace became a private limited company with authorized capital of £7 divided into seven shares, each with a par value of £1. All seven shares were held by nominees of the Secretary of State for Industry. On January 2, 1981, pursuant to the British Aerospace Act of 1980, the seven shares were split into 14, each with a value of 50p, and an additional 79,999,986 shares were created, raising the company's share capital to £40 million. On the same day, BAe adopted new Articles of Association and was registered as a public limited company. By February 4, 1981, British Aerospace's share capital was increased to 200 million shares, 50 million of which were made available to the public.

In its first year as a substantially public company, British Aerospace registered a pretax profit of £71 million. This was £6 million more than had been predicted, despite £50 million in development costs for the BAe-146 and A-310. The Panavia Tornado was past its development stages and in full production. The West German Panavia partner MBB prevented the consortium from realizing a substantial profit from the Tornado project, however, by not allowing exports of the fighter to countries outside of NATO, such as Saudi Arabia.

Management at British Aerospace was reorganized on January 1, 1983. Admiral Sir Raymond Lygo was appointed to the newly created position of managing director. Under the new system all group executives were to report to Sir Raymond. This enabled the board chairman, Pearce, to handle matters such as company finances more easily. One such external matter was British Aerospace's involvement in the Airbus A-320 project.

The A-320 was designed to carry 150 passengers and featured advanced "fly-by-wire" electronic control and navigation systems. BAe persuaded the other partners to allow it a 26 percent share of the A-320. The British government supported the company's involvement in the new Airbus project by making a £250 million line of credit available on favorable repayment terms. Under the terms of the agreement British Aerospace produced wings for the A-320.

REJECTED TAKEOVER BIDS

As a public company, BAe enjoyed greater independence in its policymaking. However, like other public companies, it also risked becoming a takeover target. On May 15, 1984, the chairman of Thorn EMI, Peter Laister, announced his company's intention to merge with BAe. Thorn EMI was a profitable electronics and leisure conglomerate, whose assets included everything from production rights for video recorders to performance rights to Placido Domingo and the rock group Duran Duran. British Aerospace, described as a company that earned money making missiles and lost it building airliners, was also profitable but involved in an entirely different line of business. The London financial community reacted to Laister's announcement with amazement. In Parliament the Labour Party asked: "Is it sensible to allow a firm which has been successful in the fields of color television, videos and the marketing of pop groups to have the responsibility of looking after the development of Britain's largest company in civil and military aviation, in missile technology and space satellites?"

The announcement also invited criticism from the managing director of Britain's General Electric Company (GEC), Lord Weinstock: On two previous occasions when GEC expressed an interest in purchasing all or part of British Aerospace, it was privately rebuffed by the government, which was concerned that GEC would become too dominant a force in the British defense industry. GEC, which was a principal owner of BAC before 1977, was fully prepared to exceed any bid submitted by Thorn EMI.

In June 1984 British Aerospace rejected Thorn EMI's takeover proposal, and the following month did the same with GEC, citing a lack of any specific proposals. The government was satisfied with the takeover rejections because it ensured that British Aerospace would remain under British ownership and that it would continue to be a part of the Airbus group.

In 1985, confident about the company's position, the British government sold its 48 percent of British Aerospace, retaining, however, a special £1 share to ensure that BAe would stay under U.K. control. The £550 million offer was tightly restricted to institutional investors. The company also was reorganized into eight functional divisions during the year, a move that was intended to economize use of engineering teams by having them specialize in the development of products in specific fields. BAe was also the prime contractor on a lucrative contract known as Al Yamamah, which was signed with Saudi Arabia in 1985. Under Al Yamamah, the largest defense export contract in British history, BAe supplied Tornado fighter-bombers and other military aircraft to Saudi Arabia. By the early 1990s, the company's contracts with Saudi Arabia accounted for about half of its defense business.

In 1986 the Lockheed Corporation reached an agreement with BAe to develop new versions of the BAe-146 for military and cargo applications. Coproduction agreements with U.S. companies were nothing new to British Aerospace, whose Harrier fighter jet had been built in the United States in conjunction with McDonnell Douglas since the mid-1970s.

SPATE OF ACQUISITIONS

In April 1987 British Aerospace acquired Royal Ordnance plc, a state-owned maker of small arms ammunition, for £190 million. Shortly thereafter, Pearce stepped down as chairman. Instead of Lygo replacing him, however, an outsider was brought in: Roland Smith, a professor of marketing who had been chairman of a number of other U.K. firms. Under Smith's leadership, which followed the predominant trend of the period, BAe diversified in the late 1980s and early 1990s through a spate of acquisitions, some of which resulted from additional British government privatizations. In 1987 the company acquired Steinheil Optronik GmbH, a German manufacturer of optical equipment, for £17 million, and Ballast Nedam Group, a Dutch construction concern, for £47 million. BAe also bought stakes that year in Reflectone Inc., a U.S.-based maker of flight simulators and other training devices, and System Designers plc, which specialized in computer software and systems and was renamed SD-Scicon plc (the latter stake was sold in July 1991).

In 1988 Smith made his biggest, and furthest afield, purchase when BAe acquired The Rover Group plc, an automobile maker, from the British government for £150 million ($255 million), a sum considered to be a steal. The following year British Aerospace continued to diversify by spending £278 million for Arlington Securities Plc, a major developer of business parks in the United Kingdom. BAe already had a large property portfolio, including substantial holdings gained with Royal Ordnance and with Rover, and the rationale for purchasing Arlington was that through streamlining and plant closings BAe would have additional property to develop and could generate profits by doing so.

Smith's last significant acquisitions were a 76 percent stake in Liverpool Airport in May 1990 and all of Heckler & Koch GmbH, a German small arms, machine tool, and general engineering company, in March 1991. By the time of the latter purchase, BAe was near collapse. A recession had severely impacted the automobile and real estate sectors, turning the acquisitions of Rover and Arlington sour. The economic downturn also wreaked havoc with the company's already troubled regional and corporate aircraft operations. Smith approached first Trafalgar House (a construction engineering and property group) and then GEC about a merger. When the BAe board found out about the talks with GEC, they ordered that the discussions be terminated. In September 1991 the company's dire straits forced Smith to attempt to raise £432 million ($755 million) through a stock offering. When current shareholders revolted, the board ousted Smith, replacing him temporarily with Graham Day, who had been chairman of Rover. During Day's brief six-month tenure, he succeeded in turning away another attempt by GEC to acquire BAe. He also restructured the company's defense operations, placing them under a single umbrella subsidiary called British Aerospace Defence Limited.

RESTRUCTURING BEGINS: 1992

In April 1992 John Cahill, former chief executive of BTR PLC, was brought in as the new chairman. By this time, thanks in large part to Smith, British Aerospace had evolved into a quite unwieldy conglomerate, with seven core activities: defense, Rover, Airbus, commercial property development, corporate aircraft, regional aircraft, and satellite communications. Under Cahill, BAe began a major restructuring aimed at concentrating the company's efforts on the first four of these seven areas. In late 1992 the company took a £1 billion write-off to close a plant belonging to its troubled regional aircraft unit and to lay off 3,000 workers. For the year, BAe posted an after-tax loss of £970 million. The company attempted to spin off the regional aircraft unit into a joint venture with Taiwan Aerospace Corporation

but the deal fell through. BAe proceeded, however, to sell its corporate jet unit to Raytheon Co. in June 1993. Earlier that year, in January, the company had secured a second-stage Al Yamamah contract with Saudi Arabia totaling $7.5 billion.

Meanwhile, behind the scenes, Cahill had approached GEC again about a merger of the two companies' defense units. When word leaked out in mid-1993 about the discussions, the BAe board once again quickly moved to scuttle the talks. Nevertheless, British Aerospace remained in financial trouble and it was expected that merger talks would soon revive. Within a matter of months, though, BAe's financial picture improved dramatically following a spate of divestments, which exceeded the initial bounds of Cahill's restructuring. In December 1993 Ballast Nedam was sold to a consortium of Hochtief AG, Internationale Nederlanden Group, and the Ballast Nedam Pension Fund. In March 1994 Rover, which was gobbling up cash and whose acquisition was proving to be a huge blunder, was sold to BMW AG, with BAe netting £529 million in the process. In July of that same year the company's satellite communications unit was sold to Matra Marconi Space for £56 million. Around this same time, another boardroom coup resulted in the ouster of Cahill, who was replaced by Bob Bauman, former CEO of U.S. pharmaceutical giant SmithKline Beecham.

EUROPEAN AEROSPACE/DEFENSE CONSOLIDATION

While BAe had been busy cleaning up its balance sheet and trying to stay independent, dramatic changes in the world scene brought new threats. Following the breakup of the Soviet Union and the concomitant end of the Cold War, the defense industry in the United States quickly consolidated into three giant firms, Boeing, Lockheed Martin, and Raytheon. In Europe, however, consolidation did not come nearly so quickly, and European companies were increasingly at a competitive disadvantage in comparison with U.S. firms. In response, a healthier BAe began to seek strategic acquisitions and, perhaps more importantly, to create numerous links with other European defense and aerospace firms in what were likely the first moves toward a Europe-wide consolidation.

In June 1995 BAe lost out to GEC in a bid for VSEL, a U.K. maker of submarines. That same month, however, British Aerospace formed a joint venture, Saab-BAe Gripen AB, with Saab AB's Saab Military Aircraft to manufacture and sell the Gripen combat aircraft. In January 1996 the company shifted its troubled regional aircraft operations into a three-way consortium, Aero International (Regional) SAS, with Aerospatiale of

France and Alania of Italy. This venture was dissolved in mid-1998, however, following disagreements among the partners. BAe in April 1996 expanded into the Australian defense market with the acquisition of AWA Defence Industries (AWADI, later renamed British Aerospace Defence Industries) for AUD 50 million. Following more than three years of negotiations, BAe and Lagardère's defense arm, Matra, merged their guided missile businesses into a £1 billion joint venture called Matra-BAe Dynamics. In October 1997 the company announced that it would bolster its defense electronics sector through the £320 million ($536.5 million) purchase from Siemens AG of Siemens Plessey businesses in the United Kingdom and Australia. One of BAe's longer-standing joint ventures, the one that had spent years developing the next-generation Eurofighter military jet, received a huge boost in December 1997 when Britain, Germany, Italy, and Spain signed a $40 billion deal to build the jet, ordering more than 600 of them. Also in 1997 BAe announced that it would cease manufacturing its Jetstream turboprop regional aircraft, further distancing the company from this troubled sector.

In April 1998 BAe announced that it would buy a 35 percent stake in Saab AB, furthering the consolidation of European defense. With this link, the two companies planned to cooperate more closely and on more projects. Around this same time, the company was contemplating the purchase of a stake in Construcciones Aeronautics S.A. (CASA), a defense and aerospace firm owned by the Spanish state and a partner of BAe's in Airbus (CASA held a 4.2 percent stake). British Aerospace was eager to join with other European companies to form a pan-European defense and aerospace firm, and the four Airbus partners (BAe, CASA, Aerospatiale of France, and DASA of Germany) had issued a report, following a request from their respective governments, in March 1998 saying that they wanted to merge although no timetable for doing so was set. A major sticking point to such a merger was that Aerospatiale was owned by the French government. Both BAe and DASA insisted that the French firm had to be privatized for a merger to work, but the French government was opposed to doing so. BAe, meantime, had ruffled some feathers of its own in November 1997 when it signed a multimillion-dollar deal with Boeing, Airbus's archrival, to make wing parts for the next generation of 737 jets.

British Aerospace continued to divest itself of non-core assets in 1998, most notably selling 16.1 percent of its 21.1 percent stake in Orange PLC, an operator of mobile telephones, for £763.8 million ($1.28 billion), netting £368 million ($616.7 million) in the process. The possibility that Arlington Securities would be divested became very real around this time. In the event of such an occurrence, BAe would have come full circle, returning to its defense and aerospace roots. Starting in May 1998, a new management team would see the steadily improving company—which in 1997 had posted profits before taxes and exceptional items of £596 million, a 31 percent gain over 1996—into whatever the future might have in store. Replacing Bauman in the chairman's seat that month was Richard Evans, who had been chief executive of the company since 1990, while John Weston, who had been in charge of BAe's defense operations, took over the chief executive slot. The two executives faced perhaps the biggest challenge in British Aerospace's chronically challenging history, merging or transforming the company into "European Aerospace."

TRANSATLANTIC TRANSFORMATION

BAe looked more toward the United States for growth, however, and soon became what it called a transatlantic company. An obvious reason for pursuing contracts across the pond was size: The U.S. defense market was 10 times as large as that of the United Kingdom and twice as large as that of the European Union. While the Pentagon was traditionally leery of awarding much business to foreign companies, BAe benefited from the special relationship between the United States and Britain, its closest military ally.

There were still significant developments in Europe. In 1999 BAe bought the Marconi defense-electronics business of Britain's GEC for £7.7 billion ($11 billion). The deal reportedly angered officials at DaimlerChrysler Aerospace AG, with whom BAe had been in merger discussions. The Marconi buy brought with it a significant presence in the United States.

Reflecting its global focus, British Aerospace took the name BAE Systems plc in May 2000. BAE Systems North America Inc., the main U.S. subsidiary, was then chiefly concerned with being a supplier to prime contractors. It had more than 18,000 employees in North America and sales of $3 billion.

In April 2000 BAE announced it was buying a flight-control-systems unit from Lockheed Martin Corp. for $510 million. An even larger, and politically more sensitive, purchase followed. In December 2000 BAE acquired the Aerospace and Electronic Systems (AES) unit of Lockheed Martin for $1.67 billion. AES had annual revenues of more than $1 billion and employed 5,000 people. The main component of AES, New Hampshire-based Sanders, was involved in highly classified electronic-warfare work for the U.S. military.

FOCUSING ON DEFENSE: 2001–03

Subsequent acquisitions and divestments honed BAE's focus on defense, across a wide range of activities relating to air, land, and sea. In 2001 the company ended its regional-jet manufacturing program while retaining a support-services business. BAE had revenues of £13.1 billion ($20 million) for the year. The United States accounted for 28 percent of sales, slightly more than Britain.

The company noted that its complex international joint ventures were less profitable than its wholly owned subsidiaries. In 2003 BAE transferred its 25 percent holding in the Astrium space business to majority-owner EADS, the pan-European defense and aerospace firm. Astrium had been formed just three years earlier by combining Matra Marconi Space and part of Daimler-Chrysler Aerospace. Although it had revenues of EUR 2 billion a year, Astrium was losing money.

The comprehensive transformation seemed to be going well; however, BAE's Chief Executive John Weston had resigned suddenly in March 2002, with Chief Operating Officer Michael Turner succeeding him. The acquisition drive continued, adding five U.S. companies in 2003 alone.

LANDING LARGE ACQUISITIONS

In 2004 BAE acquired Britain's only armored-vehicle manufacturer, Alvis, for £355 million, beating out General Dynamics. It also added DigitalNet for $595 million, lifting BAE's U.S. government IT revenues to $1 billion annually. BAE's North American unit had revenues of about $5 billion and 27,000 employees. BAE's total revenues were £15.4 billion in 2005.

BAE acquired United Defense Industries Inc. (UDI) for $4 billion in June 2005. The publicly traded defense conglomerate traced its lineage to the agricultural machines built by Food Machinery Corporation (later FMC Corporation) in the 1940s. FMC and Harsco Corporation merged their defense operations in 1994 under the United Defense name; Carlyle Group acquired it for $880 million in 1997 and took it public four years later. UDI had sales of $2.3 billion in 2004; products included U.S.-made Bradley armored vehicles and Sweden's Bofors armaments.

In 2006 BAE sold its 20 percent stake in Airbus to EADS. It also sold the Prestwick facility where it had been manufacturing Airbus wing assemblies. During the year, a British bribery probe related to the Al Yamamah contract was reportedly squelched after the Saudis threatened to withhold cooperation in antiterrorist activities.

In 2007 BAE acquired another prominent U.S. defense contractor, Armor Holdings, Inc., in a deal valued at $4.5 billion. BAE sold its Landsdale electronic surveillance business to Cobham plc for $240 million in December of that year. The acquisition drive was still underway, as BAE soon announced a deal to acquire MTC Technologies, a U.S. supplier of military support services, for $450 million.

Updated, David E. Salamie;
Frederick C. Ingram

NEW PRODUCT LINES

Orders for the Hawk trainer were dwindling, leading to layoffs in England, as other product lines were coming out of their long development cycles and entering production. The first of a new class of destroyer, the Type 45, was delivered to the Royal Navy in early 2006. After years of layoffs, there was more positive economic news in shipbuilding, as BAE's joint venture with British shipbuilding rival VT Group in May 2008 landed a long-awaited £4 billion agreement to produce a pair of aircraft carriers for the Ministry of Defence.

The Eurofighter group landed orders for hundreds of aircraft from the countries where it was being built, and Saudi Arabia ordered a few dozen. In other aerospace activities, BAE was also building 66 Hawk trainers for India, which was becoming its newest "home" market. In addition, BAE was a subcontractor for major U.S. aircraft programs, such as Lockheed Martin's F-35 Lightning II under development.

Chief Executive Mike Turner resigned in August 2008 and took the chairmanship at Cobham plc. He was succeeded by Chief Operating Officer Ian King.

PRINCIPAL SUBSIDIARIES

BAE Systems Inc. (USA).

PRINCIPAL DIVISIONS

Australia; Saudi Arabia; South Africa; Sweden; UK and Rest of World; US.

PRINCIPAL OPERATING UNITS

BAE Systems Australia; BAE Systems Products Group; CS&S International; Detica; Electronics, Intelligence & Support; BAE Systems Insyte; Land & Armaments; Military Air Solutions; Regional Aircraft; Shared Services; Submarine Solutions.

PRINCIPAL COMPETITORS

Lockheed Martin Corporation; General Dynamics Corporation; European Aeronautic Defence and Space

Company EADS N.V.; The Boeing Company; Northrop Grumman Corporation.

FURTHER READING

"BAE Systems and VT Unite as MoD Agrees £4bn Deal for New Carriers," *Independent* (London), May 21, 2008, p. 36.

Barrie, Douglas, and Robert Wall, "Strategic Revision; BAE Systems Quells Any U.S. Prime Ambitions While Bolstering Supply-Side Business," *Aviation Week & Space Technology,* September 20, 2004, p. 35.

Betts, Paul, "BAe Benefits as It Brings Its Head Out of the Clouds," *Financial Times,* June 14, 1993, p. 17.

Betts, Paul, and Tony Jackson, "Defence May Be the Best Attack," *Financial Times,* February 5, 1994, p. 6.

———, "A Flight Back to Basics," *Financial Times,* August 3, 1992, p. 10.

Buchan, David, and Bernard Gray, "BAe, Matra in £1bn Missiles Merger Move," *Financial Times,* May 14, 1996, pp. 1, 20.

Buckley, Christine, and David Robertson, "BAE Systems Cuts 600 Jobs as Orders for Red Arrows Aircraft Dry Up," *Times* (London), April 4, 2008, p. 52.

Cohen, Norma, "Cash Is the Stumbling Block in Property Separation," *Financial Times,* April 7, 1998, p. 27.

Cook, Nick, "BAe Sees United Europe as Only Way Forward," *Interavia Business & Technology,* April 1996, pp. 18+.

Davidson, Andrew, "Sir Richard Evans," *Management Today,* January 1997, pp. 38–41.

"The Defence Industry Jettisons Its Excess Baggage," *Economist,* August 8, 1992, pp. 57+.

Dwyer, Paula, "Triage for Battered British Aerospace," *Business Week,* October 5, 1992, pp. 109–10.

Elliott, Simon, "The Drive to Survive," *Flight International,* December 25, 1991, p. 17.

"Europe's Defence Companies Join the Modern World," *Economist,* December 10, 1988, pp. 67–68.

Evans, Richard, and Colin Price, *Vertical Take-Off: The Inside Story of British Aerospace's Comeback from Crisis to World Class,* London: Nicholas Brealey, 1999.

Feldman, Elliot J., *Concorde and Dissent: Explaining High Technology Project Failures in Britain and France,* Cambridge: Cambridge University Press, 1985.

"Fly Off with Me," *Economist,* October 5, 1991, pp. 70, 72–73.

"Getting Together," *Economist,* August 10, 1996, pp. 46, 48.

Goldsmith, Charles, "Airbus Prepares for Unique Restructuring," *Wall Street Journal,* August 30, 1996, p. A6.

———, "British Aerospace in Enviable Turnaround," *Wall Street Journal,* March 1, 1996, p. A10.

———, "British Aerospace Opts to Team with Lockheed on U.S. Jet Bid," *Wall Street Journal,* June 19, 1997, p. B4.

———, "Re-Engineering: After Trailing Boeing for Years, Airbus Aims for 50% of the Market," *Wall Street Journal,* March 16, 1998, pp. Al, A10.

———, "Report on Defense Restructuring in Europe Is Short on Details," *Wall Street Journal,* March 30, 1998, p. A14.

Gray, Bernard, "BAe Lands Behind Barricades in the UK," *Financial Times,* June 22, 1995, p. 23.

———, "BAe Pulls Out of £835m Bid Battle for VSEL," *Financial Times,* June 22, 1995, p. 1.

———, "An Elusive Moving Target," *Financial Times,* May 14, 1996, p. 19.

———, "How BAe Pulled Back from the Brink," *Financial Times,* December 18, 1995, p. 7.

———, "Time to Seek a Grand Alliance," *Financial Times,* December 19, 1995, p. 7.

Hayward, Keith, *International Collaboration in Civil Aerospace,* New York: St. Martin's Press, 1986.

Levine, Jonathan B., and Paula Dwyer, "Europe's Weapons Makers Start Linking Arms," *Business Week,* May 24, 1993, p. 130A.

Lidstone, Digby, "Extending the Deal; The 20-Year-Old Al-Yamamah Defence Deal Is at the Mature Stage, but Its Prime Contractor, BAE Systems, Is Confident There Are Many Years Left in the Relationship with Riyadh," *MEED Middle East Economic Digest,* January 28, 2005, pp. 29+.

Lorenz, Andrew, "Up in the Air at British Aerospace," *Management Today,* February 1995, pp. 32–36.

"Making Rover Fly," *Economist,* December 9, 1989, pp. 61–62.

"Men of Property," *Economist,* October 22, 1988, p. 62.

Michaels, Daniel, and August Cole, "BAE's Global 'Homes' Weather Defense Cuts," *Wall Street Journal,* August 13, 2009, p. A16.

Michaels, Daniel, Rod Stone, and Rebecca Christie, "BAE Faces Challenges with United Defense Deal," *Wall Street Journal,* March 8, 2005, p. B2.

Monopolies and Mergers Commission, *British Aerospace Public Limited Company and VSEL plc: A Report on the Proposed Merger,* London: HMSO, 1995.

Morrison, Murdo, and Helen Massy-Beresford, "BAE Back on Target," *Flight International,* February 27, 2007.

Morrocco, John D., "BAE Systems Focuses on U.S. Connection," *Aviation Week & Space Technology,* July 24, 2000, p. 110.

Nelms, Douglas W., "Sea Change for Ship of State: Like a Giant Oil Tanker, British Aerospace Is Slowly, Ponderously Altering Course," *Air Transport World,* December 1993, pp. 64–69.

Nicoll, Alexander, "BAe, Dasa Win Siemens Arm," *Financial Times,* October 31, 1997, p. 25.

———, "BAE Must Work Hard to Throw Off Albatross Tag: In Spite of Problems, the Defence Group's Prospects Look Good but It Must Deliver," *Financial Times,* January 13, 2001, p. 18.

———, "Re-Arming for the Battlespace as a Competitive All Rounder," *Financial Times,* April 15, 1998, p. 26.

———, "Siemens' Sale Creates Fresh Fighters," *Financial Times,* October 31, 1997, p. 27.

O'Toole, Kevin, "BAe's Brave New World," *Flight International,* March 22, 1995, pp. 28+.

Prada, Paulo, Alessandro Galloni, and Charles Goldsmith, "In a Surprise, BAE's Chief Resigns Post; Weston's Departure Comes as Contractor Faces Key Challenges," *Wall Street Journal,* International Sec., March 27, 2002, p. A13.

"Rescued by Rover," *Economist,* February 22, 1992, pp. 62+.

Robertson, David, "Typhoon Contract Race Fuels BAE's Desire to Develop a Strong Presence in India," *Times* (London), August 2, 2008, p. 53.

Skapinker, Michael, "Aerospace Groups Back Merger," *Financial Times,* March 28, 1998, p. 2.

——, "BAe Reshuffles for Wider Role," *Financial Times,* April 3, 1998, p. 25.

Taverna, Michael A., and Pierre Sparaco, "BAE Systems Exits Space Business," *Aviation Week & Space Technology,* February 17, 2003, p. 38.

Wayne, Leslie, "British Arms Merchant with Passport to the Pentagon," *New York Times,* August 16, 2006, p. C1.

Wood, Derek, "BAe Foresees Major Changes in Europe," *Interavia Aerospace World,* May 1993, pp. 30–31.

Balducci's

10411 Motor City Drive, Suite 500
Bethesda, Maryland 20817
U.S.A.
Telephone: (240) 403-2440
Fax: (240) 403-2520
Web site: http://www.balduccis.com

Private Company
Founded: 1916
NAICS: 445299 All Other Specialty Food Stores

■ ■ ■

Balducci's is an upscale specialty food market that operates six grocery stores in Connecticut, Maryland, New York, and Virginia. The company also has several small outposts in New York's JFK airport. Products offered include fresh pasta, imported cheeses, and prepared meals with a special focus on gourmet items. Balducci's also runs a catering service and sells gourmet and corporate gift baskets through its online catalog and in its stores.

SMALL FAMILY GROCERY ESTABLISHES REPUTATION FOR QUALITY: 1916–72

In 1916, Louis Balducci opened a small produce stand in Brooklyn, New York, and named it Balducci's. Born in Corato, Italy, the young entrepreneur had moved to New York in 1914 with only a third-grade education. According to family lore, he was ambitious from the start, keeping his stand open 24 hours a day and sleep-

ing about four hours a night. Eventually he married and had three children with his wife, Maria. While his eldest, Charles, went to college and became a doctor, his younger children, Grace and Andrew, grew up working in the family store and became an integral part of the business.

Thirty years after starting Balducci's, in 1946, Louis moved the family business to Greenwich Village. There, he made a name for himself by stocking exotic fruits and vegetables, which local residents, rising chefs, and food writers valued for their outstanding quality and uniqueness.

In the 1950s and 1960s, Grace and Andrew Balducci both married. While Grace and her husband, Joseph Doria, a night-shift worker at the family's store, stayed on at Balducci's, eventually sharing management responsibilities with Louis Balducci, Andrew left the family business. Of the first and second generations' focus on excellence, grandson Louis Balducci said in a 2002 *Washington Post* article: "They always looked to the best. They always looked for the hardest to find. My uncle and my grandfather were very quality conscious."

However, the Balduccis were not as keen on business growth. In 1968, Andrew Balducci returned to work at Balducci's. In a June 2000 article in the *New York Times*, he remarked: "When I went back, I found what I left. There was no progress at all." Dismayed by the lack of business development, he stepped into a leadership role and began to push for change. Although known for his abrasive personality, which caused a great deal of internal tension, "Andy was the creative and driving force," Louis Balducci, Charles Balducci's son, said in a June 2000 article in the *New York Times*. Even Andrew's critics gave him credit for the store's success, although as Louis Balducci went on to explain, "[B]ut he also had an incredible team behind him."

BECOMING A MECCA FOR GOURMET ITEMS: 1972–84

Four years later, in 1972, the Balduccis moved across the street and established their store with its signature green awnings and swirly "B" logo on the Avenue of the Americas. With more space, they were able to significantly expand their inventory to include then-rare gourmet foods including real Italian parmigiano-romano cheese, radicchio, extra virgin olive oil, truffles, crème fraîche, and prosciutto. Since many of these items were new to New Yorkers in the 1970s, Balducci's became famous as a gourmet mecca.

Unfortunately, success created power struggles within the Balducci family. Andrew Balducci's temperamental style and violent temper caused tension and, some claimed, difficult working conditions. Additionally, with the signing of the store's Greenwich Village lease, the family unevenly divided up ownership of the business. Four partners were listed as owners, with Andrew Balducci and his wife, Nina, holding 51 percent of the shares and Grace and Joseph Doria holding 49 percent. For unknown reasons, Louis Balducci did not sign the new papers. These developments would later sow the seeds of dissension that broke apart the family.

FAMILY ISSUES AND DEVELOPMENT OF CATALOG SALES: 1985–98

Over the next decade, rancor grew within the family. Then, in 1985, after years of threatening to do so, founder Louis Balducci sued for his share of the business. That same year, a feud between Grace and Andrew over the direction of the business caused Grace to claim that she also had been cheated out of a controlling interest, and she sued Andrew as well.

Several additional lawsuits followed, and the food world buzzed with gossip about the hostility among siblings. When Grace and Joseph Doria left Balducci's in 1985 to open a rival market, Grace's Marketplace, on the Upper East Side, many claimed this was the beginning of the end of the 54-year-old family business. Three years later, in 1988, Louis Balducci died; his wife, Maria, died one year later.

For the next decade, Andrew and Nina Balducci ran the business together, with Nina focusing on a successful mail-order catalog, which they had started in 1982. Catalog operations ran out of two separate buildings in Long Island City, Queens. By 1993, the catalog operation, which employed 150 people and functioned as a full catering service, selling prepared dishes and full meals, brought in significant revenue, about $4 million, which accounted for 20 percent of Balducci's total sales. Circulation of the catalog was at more than one million.

The company also began producing several of Balducci's private-label products, such as Italian pasta, which it eventually distributed via chain markets, including Sutton Place, beginning in 1997. From 1998 to 1999, the company's mail-order and online sales grew dramatically. Internet orders rose 250 percent to $2 million a year, and catalog sales climbed 25 percent, to $10 million. The Greenwich Village store's revenues were at $20 million.

SUTTON TAKEOVER LEADS TO GROWTH AND DISSATISFACTION: 1999–2003

By 1999, Balducci's had become New York's top epicurean shopping destination. That year, Zagat's listed it as the number one food specialty shop in New York, ahead of Sahadi's, Dean & DeLuca, and Zabar's.

Also in 1999, Sutton Place Group, a company with a taste for acquiring gourmet stores, approached with an offer to purchase Balducci's for $26.5 million. Balducci's had several assets Sutton Place craved, including a booming Internet and mail-order business and a huge kitchen that could support more growth. "They have an

KEY DATES

1916: Louis Balducci opens a produce stand, Balducci's, in Brooklyn, New York.

1946: Balducci's moves to Greenwich Village in Manhattan.

1972: Company moves across the street to its flagship location on Avenue of the Americas.

1982: Company's first mail-order catalog is published.

1985: Grace Balducci sells her company shares to open Grace's Marketplace.

1999: Sutton Place Group acquires Balducci's for $26.5 million.

2000: Balducci's opens a second store in Manhattan's West Side and a third in Bethesda, Maryland; Web site is launched.

2003: Flagship store in Greenwich Village closes; Bear Stearns Merchant Banking acquires Balducci's as part of its acquisition of Sutton Place Group.

2004: All Sutton Place Group stores are renamed Balducci's, creating 11 locations.

2006: New flagship Balducci's is opened in the Chelsea neighborhood of Manhattan.

2009: Both Manhattan locations are closed, along with two other Balducci's locations; Irving Place Capital sells the remaining six Balducci's stores to an investor group, Angelo, Gordon & Co.

infrastructure that's amazing," Tom Johnston, president of Sutton Place, said in a 1999 *Washington Post* article.

According to her exit contract, Grace had an option to purchase the business if sold, but she balked at the $26.5 million price tag and turned it down. Soon after, the Sutton Place deal went through. "You can take a mom and pop organization only so far," Andrew Balducci said in a 1999 article in the *New York Times* of his decision to sell.

Based in Maryland, Sutton Place ran 12 markets, including the Hay Day Country Farm Market, a chain that had become well-known for its high prices. However, its products were not of the same quality as Balducci's. The takeover prompted a backlash among Balducci's regular customers, who complained that the product quality took an immediate nosedive while prices skyrocketed.

A year after the sale, in 2000, Sutton Place Group opened a second Balducci's on Manhattan's West Side across the street from Lincoln Center. The space was slightly larger than the Greenwich Village store with 7,300 square feet of retail space. To evoke old world tradition and to signify its long history, a portrait of Louis and Maria Balducci hung over the front door.

Other initiatives that year included an aggressive expansion of Balducci's Internet operation. Sutton Place borrowed $23 million to transform its $2 million Internet business that then featured 600 products into one that listed thousands of products.

Another project included a $2.5 million renovation of an existing 30,000-square-foot Sutton Place store in Bethesda, Maryland, to include a Balducci's component, which featured Balducci's private-label products, along with meats, cheeses, and olives, and made-to-order paninis, gelato, and coffee.

However, a year and a half after takeover, regulars were still complaining. The Greenwich Village store had lost its luster and had begun to look shabby, with chipped and scratched takeout counter cases and long neglected window displays. To stave off criticism, in 2002, Sutton Place Group fixed up the Greenwich Village store, adding better lighting and new showcases, and expanding the deli and catering menus.

By 2003, sales were still stagnating, and the Web site project, Balduccis.com, had flopped. As a result, Sutton Place was saddled with crippling debt. To cut some of its losses, it quietly sold the Greenwich Village building, and the original Balducci's store closed its doors in January 2003. Meanwhile, the new store in Lincoln Square struggled to attract a following large enough to sustain its overhead.

Rumors were that Sutton Place would close Balducci's. However, Sutton Place would not give up. Throughout 2003, executives continued to search for a larger storefront in New York to compete with the gourmet market rivals. Sutton Place also planned to expand distribution of its Balducci's private-label imported items, including Italian dried pasta, prosciutto di Parma, and extra virgin olive oil, to select supermarkets in the Midwest, San Francisco, and Los Angeles.

Still, none of these initiatives alleviated Sutton Place's growing struggle with debt. Finally, at the end of 2003, Bear Stearns Merchant Banking purchased Sutton Place Group from AEA Investors and Catterton Partners (which owned Sutton Place Group). The sale included Balducci's, Sutton Place, and Hay Day Country Farm Market, with a total of 11 stores operated under the Sutton Place Group name. The selling price was $50 million.

REBRANDING THE CHAIN UNDER
BEAR STEARNS: 2003–07

Bear Stearns was optimistic that it had the winning formula to transform Sutton Place Group's holdings into a winning chain of high-end gourmet markets. The team was led by Mark Ordan, an avid foodie, who had launched Fresh Fields in New York in the 1980s, and eventually sold the chain to Whole Foods in 1991 for $150 million.

Immediate plans were to expand with 12 new Balducci's stores across the New York metropolitan area. "I could see us having six to eight stores in Manhattan," Ordan said in a 2003 *New York Daily News* article. Balducci's was to become the flagship brand for the company's high-end gourmet grocery chain. Plans were to eventually open 50 stores in upscale neighborhoods along the East Coast within five years and then make a public offering.

In 2004, Sutton Place Group announced that it would unite all 11 store operations under one name: Balducci's, with the tagline "Food Lover's Market." In a June 2004 *Gourmet News* article, Carrie Forti, spokesperson for Sutton Place Group, said: "The Balducci's name is one of the most respected names in food retailing. We are going to position the new stores as Balducci's, but not as the same small Italian grocery store."

After rebranding the chain, Ordan invested $1 million in cleaning the stores, reducing prices, and adding more everyday items, such as milk and eggs. By the end of 2004, the company announced that it would open a new Balducci's in the Chelsea neighborhood of Manhattan in the historic New York Savings Bank building. As the building underwent extensive renovations, plans were announced in the summer of 2005 that the chain would further open three new stores in the greater Washington, D.C., area and another in Annapolis, Maryland.

Finally in January 2006, the Chelsea store, which would serve as Balducci's new flagship location, was ready to open. It had 50-foot vaulted ceilings, a dome, stained glass, and about 8,000 square feet of retail space. However, 2006 also marked an important turning point: Mark Ordan left the project, and all plans for expansion halted. In his absence, the new owners struggled to find an identity for the Balducci's brand in an increasingly competitive industry that saw the rapid rise of chains, such as Whole Foods and Trader Joe's, and the expansion of gourmet items at supermarkets such as Safeway.

NEW OWNERSHIP AND NEW
HOPE IN HARD TIMES: 2008–09

By 2008, the four planned stores in Annapolis and Washington, D.C., had fallen by the wayside. Only one store had opened in D.C. Then in the spring, Bear Stearns collapsed and was taken over by JPMorgan Chase. Bear Stearns Merchant Banking spun itself into a new entity under the name Irving Place Capital.

The following April, Balducci's had to grapple with the hard economic times and increasing competition in the high-end food retailers market. Severe cutbacks were announced with the closing of the single Washington, D.C., store, along with three other locations in Ridgefield, Connecticut. Both Manhattan locations were also closed.

Then in June, an investor group, Angelo, Gordon & Co., led by Jim Demme, acquired all retail operations for Balducci's LLC, along with Balducci's licensing, catering, and gift basket operations. Only six stores remained: in Alexandria and McLean, Virginia; Bethesda, Maryland; Scarsdale, New York; and Westport and Greenwich, Connecticut. Once again, Balducci's future was in the hands of a hopeful owner with its potential dependent on a combination of leadership and vision.

Carrie Rothburd

PRINCIPAL COMPETITORS

Dean & DeLuca Inc.; Zabar's & Co. Inc.; Sahadi Fine Foods; Citarella; Whole Foods Market Inc.; Grace's Marketplace; D'Agostino Supermarkets Inc.; Trader Joe's Company.

FURTHER READING

Bagli, Charles V., "Talk of Selling the Fabled Balducci's Reopens Family Wounds," *New York Times*, May 1, 1999, p. 1.

Buckley, Cara, "Balducci's Makes a Quiet Exit from Manhattan," *New York Times*, April 27, 2009, p. A18.

Burros, Marian, "Balducci's: A House Divided Stands in Name Only," *New York Times*, June 28, 2000, p. F1.

Corrigan, J. Caruso, "Bailing Out on Balducci's: Grace Balducci Explains for the First Time Why She Didn't Buy the Family Store," *New York Post*, June 28, 1999, p. 26.

Dunaief, Daniel, "Investor Group Buys Balducci's," *New York Daily News* December 5, 2003.

Haughney, Christine, "Market's New Recipe; Some Longtime Customers Don't Like Changes at N.Y. Landmark," *Washington Post*, April 10, 2002, p. E01.

Rothstein, Mervyn, "Balducci's Finds a West Side Home for Its Goodies," *New York Times,* January 5, 2000, p. B7.

Tharp, Paul, "Balducci's Back!; Bear Stearns Buys Gourmet Grocer, Plans Growth," *New York Post*, December 5, 2003, p. 37.

Wolfe, Anna, "Banking on Balducci's," *Gourmet News*, June 2004, p. 1.

Wolff, Lisa, "Balducci's Greenwich Village Store Closed," *Gourmet News*, March 2003, p. 1.

BASF SE

—————■—————

Carl-Bosch-Strasse 38
Ludwigshafen, 67056
Germany
Telephone: (49 621) 60-4-32-63
Fax: (49 621) 60-425-25
Web site: http://www.basf.com

Public Company
Incorporated: 1952 as Badische Anilin- und Soda-Fabrik AG
Employees: 96,924
Sales: EUR 62.3 billion (2008)
Stock Exchanges: Frankfurt London Swiss Over the Counter (OTC)
Ticker Symbols: BAS (Frankfurt); BFA (London); AN (Swiss); BASFY (OTC)
NAICS: 325411 Medicinal and Botanical Manufacturing; 325320 Pesticide and Other Agricultural Chemical Manufacturing; 325211 Plastics Material and Resin Manufacturing; 325131 Inorganic Dye and Pigment Manufacturing; 325510 Paint and Coating Manufacturing; 325188 All Other Inorganic Chemical Manufacturing; 325192 Cyclic Crude and Intermediate Manufacturing; 325998 All Other Miscellaneous Chemical Product Manufacturing; 211111 Crude Petroleum and Natural Gas Extraction

■ ■ ■

BASF SE is the largest chemical company in the world, operating more than 150 manufacturing facilities around the globe. The company divides its business into six segments: Chemicals; Plastics; Performance Products; Functional Solutions; Agricultural Solutions; and Oil & Gas. The Chemicals segment comprises inorganics, petrochemicals, and intermediates. The Plastics segment includes performance polymers and polyurethanes. The Performance Products segment consists of four divisions: dispersions & pigments; care chemicals; paper chemicals; and performance chemicals. The Functional Solutions segment covers the company's involvement in catalysts, construction chemicals, and coatings. Through its Agricultural Solutions segment, BASF develops and manufactures crop protection products. The company's oil and gas exploration and production activities, constituting its sixth business segment, are conducted through a subsidiary, Wintershall AG.

ORIGINS

Since the company's founding in 1865, Badische Anilin- und SodaFabrik AG has been a major influence in the world chemical industry. As one of the three largest German chemical companies, BASF exerted an influence from 1924 to 1947 that extended far beyond dyes and nylons. When the company joined with Bayer and Hoechst to form the world's largest chemical cartel, BASF was instrumental in helping to secretly rearm Germany.

For its role during these years, the chemical cartel, known as the I.G. Farbenindustrie AG (I.G. Farben) consisting of the merger of companies such as BASF AG, Bayer AG, and Hoechst AG, was broken up by the Allies, and BASF again existed as an independent company. Despite the fact that almost half of its plant

COMPANY PERSPECTIVES

We focus our business activities on the challenges of the future. In times of economic difficulty, we continue to concentrate on innovative business areas and profit from our wide portfolio range, operating excellence, solid financing and a high-performance team. We invest early in growth markets and are present in all important markets. Our active portfolio management, acquisitions and divestitures make us economically independent and more competitive. All BASF employees contribute to affirming our number one position in the chemical industry through their creativity, individual responsibility and performance. In order to guarantee this in the future, our personnel policy centers on long-term developments, with a program on demographic change, and a stronger focus on internationality and diversity.

in Ludwigshafen, Germany, was reduced to rubble during World War II, BASF was able to reestablish its presence in the chemical industry. It is now the world's largest chemical maker, just ahead of du Pont and Bayer. In addition to its flagship production facilities in Ludwigshafen (the world's largest chemical site), BASF operates major facilities in Caojing, China; Geismar, Louisiana; Yeosu, Korea; Altamira, Mexico; Singapore; Antwerp, Belgium; Schwarzheide, Germany; and Tudela, Spain. BASF holds a significant share of the international market in chemicals, natural gas, plastics, pharmaceuticals, crop protection agents, and its original product, dyes.

EARLY HISTORY IN THE LATE 19TH CENTURY

BASF was founded in 1865 by Friedrich Engelhorn, a jeweler, along the banks of the Rhine River at Mannheim. Using the discoveries of the English scientist William Perkins, BASF became one of the first companies to manufacture dyes from coal tar. Its specialty was the bright bluish-purple known as indigo. The attraction of BASF's process lay in the fact that it took coal tar, a messy by-product of gas distillation, and transformed it into something that replaced a more expensive and unreliable organic substance.

BASF's synthetic dyes were less expensive, brighter, and easier to use than organic dyes. Profits from these dyes were used to finance BASF's diversification into

inorganic chemicals later in the century as well as new production facilities across the river in Ludwigshafen.

By the early 20th century, journalists were calling BASF "The World's Greatest Chemical Works." In 1910 the company employed over 8,000 people and by 1926 this number had grown to 42,000. Its production facilities in Ludwigshafen alone covered 2,787 acres. American journalists were impressed by BASF's charity and reported, "The company has given a great deal of attention to welfare work; especially to housing, hygiene and the care of the sick."

BASF's sanatoriums and dispensaries, along with its main production facilities, were financed in part by business arrangements that would be illegal today in either Germany or the United States. Beginning around 1900 leaders of the German chemical industry began to dream of what was, in effect, the merger of most German chemical companies. Should this cartel be formed, said Carl Duisberg, the man who eventually set up the I.G. Farben, "the now existing domination of the German chemical industry, especially the dye industry, over the rest of the world would then, in my opinion, be assured."

FORMATION OF CARTELS IN EARLY 20TH CENTURY

By 1904 two major cartels had been formed. The first of these cartels included Bayer and BASF; the second cartel was anchored by Hoechst. Not only did these firms avoid competition and fix prices, but they also set up a quota system and even shared their profits. For instance, a marketing agreement was reached for the sale of indigo, which was one of the most profitable dyes.

Both cartels played an important role during World War I. Not only was dye necessary for garments, the basic chemical formulas for dyes could be altered slightly to make mustard gas and munitions. Companies such as BASF provided gas and explosives for German troops and, previous to the United States' entry into the war, they initiated economic activities that stunted the growth of the chemical companies important to the U.S. war effort. For instance, BASF had sold aniline at below market prices to U.S. firms in order to discourage aniline production by U.S. companies. As part of the dye cartel it had also engaged in a practice called "full-line forcing." If a dealer wanted to purchase item A for example, available only from BASF, the dealer was forced to purchase the whole product line, effectively eliminating U.S. producers.

After the war the German government recognized the importance of the chemical industry, especially the dye industry. Not only did the chemical industry bring

---

KEY DATES

■

1865: Badische Anilin- und Soda-Fabrik AG (BASF) is founded by Friedrich Engelhorn in Ludwigshafen, Germany, for the production of coal tar dyestuffs.

1897: Indigo dye is first synthesized by BASF.

1908: Development of the Haber-Bosch process revolutionizes the production of nitrogen fertilizers.

1913: BASF's first ammonia synthesis plant starts operation at Oppau.

1925: I.G. Farbenindustrie AG (I.G. Farben) is founded in Frankfurt with the merger of BASF and other chemical and pharmaceutical companies, including Bayer AG (Bayer) & Farbwerke Hoechst Aktiengesellschaft vormals Meister Lucius & Bruning (Hoechst).

1939: I.G. Farben joins the war effort in Germany.

1945: Allied Control Council orders the dissolution of I.G. Farben. BASF's Ludwigshafen plant continues to operate independently.

1951: Under the name Badische Anilin- und Soda-Fabrik AG, BASF develops Styropor, a white rigid foam used as an insulating and packaging material.

1952: Company is incorporated under the name of Badische Anilin- und Soda-Fabrik AG.

1958: BASF establishes a joint venture with The Dow Chemical Company.

1965: BASF begins acquiring other companies to produce surface coatings, drugs, crop protection agents, and fertilizers.

1969: BASF acquires Wyandotte Chemicals Corporation and Wintershall AG.

1972: Company changes its name to BASF Aktiengesellschaft.

1975: BASF acquires Boots Pharmaceuticals and a majority interest in Knoll AG; company assumes full ownership of Knoll AG in 1982.

1990: BASF takes over a united Germany's Synthesewerk Schwarzheide.

1991: BASF Ecology Laboratory begins work.

1993: BASF and Gazprom establish WINGAS to market and distribute gas in Central and Eastern Europe.

1995: BASF opens its first plant in Nanjing, China.

1998: With PetroFina, BASF constructs the world's largest steam-cracker plant at Port Arthur, Texas; company founds BASF Plant Science, a worldwide research platform, with sites in Germany, Sweden, Canada, and the United States.

2000: BASF is listed on the New York Stock Exchange and the company's worldwide pharmaceutical business is sold to Abbott Laboratories, Inc.

2001: Company begins transacting business via Elemica, a neutral electronic marketplace, and sets up a global extranet platform, WorldAccount.

2006: BASF acquires Engelhard Corp. in a hostile takeover, paying $5 billion for the New Jersey-based company.

2007: Company converts to a Societas Europaea, becoming BASF SE.

2009: BASF acquires Ciba Holding AG, a Swiss specialty chemicals company.

---

in needed foreign currency, it was critical to defense. Since the buildup of the chemical industry was so important to Germany, the cartels were granted government loans as well as a 10-year tax deferment. The cartels also received a special allotment of coal, which was scarce at the time.

CREATION OF I.G. FARBEN: 1925

In 1925 the top executives in the chemical industry decided that the duplication of product lines and the maintenance of separate sales forces was wasteful. As a result, hundreds of German chemical companies (including Bayer and Hoechst) formally merged with BASF. This new corporation, headquartered at Ludwigshafen, was renamed the Interessengemeinschaft Farbenindustrie, or I.G. Farben. BASF ceased to exist as a legal entity; it operated for the next 26 years as "Betriebsgemeinschaft Oberrhein," or the upper Rhine operating unit of I.G. Farben.

The I.G. Farben set quotas and pooled profits. This large trust was more than an economic entity, however; it was a political one. I.G. Farben's executives feared that leftists might triumph in Germany's unstable political climate and that I.G. Farben itself would be nationalized. This led to the I.G. Farben's support for Adolf Hitler. As early as 1931 its directors made secret contributions to the Nazi Party.

NOTORIOUS WORLD WAR II YEARS

The I.G. Farben profited handsomely from its support of Hitler and his foreign policy, and it grew tremendously during World War II. By 1942 the cartel was making a yearly profit that was 800 million marks more than its entire combined capitalization in 1925, the year of its founding. Not only was the I.G. Farben given possession of chemical companies in foreign lands (the I.G. Farben had control of Czechoslovakian dye works a week after the Nazi invasion), but the captured lands also provided its factories in Germany with slave labor. In order to take advantage of slave labor, I.G. Farben plants were built next to Maidanek and Auschwitz.

At its peak, the I.G. Farben had controlling interest in 379 German firms and 400 foreign companies. It has been noted that one of the historic restraints on Germany was its lack of colonies to supply necessary products, such as rubber. During this time, the I.G. Farben, synthesizing many of the country's chemical needs with a native product, provided Germany with the self-sufficiency it lacked during World War I.

Near the end of the war, the BASF production facilities at Ludwigshafen were bombed extensively. While factories built during the war were often camouflaged, the old BASF factories were more visible to U.S. bombers, which often flew over Ludwigshafen on the way back from other bombing raids and dropped any leftover bombs on the ammonia and nitrogen works. During the war BASF factories sustained the heaviest damage in the I.G. Farben with 45 percent of BASF buildings destroyed.

POSTWAR REBUILDING OF BASF

With the surrender of Germany, I.G. Farben's problems had only just begun. Immediately after the war many members of the Vorstand, or board of directors of the I.G. Farben, were arrested and indicted for war crimes. There was a large amount of written evidence incriminating the Vorstand, most of it written by the directors themselves. I.G. Farben executives were in the habit of keeping copious records, not only of meetings and phone calls, but also of their private thoughts on the I.G. Farben's dealings with the government. Despite the quantity of written evidence and testimony from

concentration camp survivors, the judges at Nuremberg dealt with the Vorstand leniently. Journalists covering the 1947 proceedings attributed the light sentences, none of which was longer than four years, to the fact that all the sentences in the trials were becoming less severe toward the end, and to the judges' unwillingness to lower the standards for active participation in war crimes to include businessmen.

The Potsdam Agreement referred to the necessity of dismantling the I.G. Farben in the interests of "peace and democracy." From the very beginning, though, the Allies disagreed over the fate of the I.G. Farben. The British and French favored a breakup of the company into large separate companies, while many U.S. officials advocated that the company be divided into smaller and therefore less influential firms. Negotiations over the cartel's fate lasted for several years. The French and British plan eventually prevailed.

After operating under Allied supervision from 1947 to 1952, the I.G. Farben was divided in 1952 into three large firms—Bayer, Hoechst, and BASF—and nine smaller firms. After this reorganization BASF was once again a small corporation located on its original Ludwigshafen site. Its share of the 30,000 I.G. Farben patents had been taken away; some of its trade secrets had been sold for as little as $1. It was isolated from its previous suppliers in Eastern Europe and, in fact, most of its basic supplies, such as coal, were insufficient. The 55 percent of its buildings that had not been destroyed were filled with outdated equipment. Leading BASF from its refounding until 1965 was Board Chairman Carl Wurster, who started at the company as a chemist.

West Germany, lacking money to import chemicals from abroad, was in dire need for chemicals produced at home. By 1957, BASF's sales of nitrogen and ammonia products were approaching their wartime levels. BASF initially lagged behind both Bayer and Hoechst in profits, in part because its product line included such items as fertilizers, plastics, and synthetics which were easily challenged on the market by competitors. Between 1957 and 1962 sales grew 59 percent, less than either Bayer or Hoechst. As prices for plastics and fertilizers stabilized in 1963, however, sales for the company increased 19 percent in one year.

BASF's growth during the postwar period was impressive. In the 10 years after the dissolution of the I.G. Farben, the company increased its capital from DEM 81 million to DEM 200 million. Employing only 800 workers in the late 1940s, it employed 45,000 by 1963. Although BASF had lost all of its patents in 1952, within 10 years it had recovered a large number of them.

IMPRESSIVE GROWTH IN THE SIXTIES AND SEVENTIES

BASF began its second decade of independence from the I.G. Farben with a switch to oil as a base for most of its old, coal-based formulas. With the purchase of Rheinisch Olefinwerke, BASF added petroleum to the long list of raw materials it was able to provide. The company soon became the world's largest producer of plastic, and provided an astonishing 10 percent of the international requirement for synthetic fibers.

Despite these gains, BASF was still faced with problems. It was the possessor of the old I.G. Farben soda and nitrogen works, but these products were often in oversupply. BASF competed with other European producers who were not burdened with this product and who were situated in more petroleum-rich countries. Nevertheless, the company reached DEM 1 billion in sales during 1965. Bernard Timm, the newly appointed board chairman with a background as a physicist, attributed the company's performance in 1965 to a judicious mix of plastics, farm chemicals, and raw materials for coatings, dyes, and fibers.

In 1969, another significant year for the company, BASF purchased Wintershall, which had half of the German potash market and produced a quarter of the country's natural gas. This acquisition was the largest in German history, and with it BASF jumped over Bayer to become the nation's second-largest chemical company. A large new plastics plant at Antwerp made PVC, polyethylene, and caprolactam (a nylon intermediary) at an accelerated rate.

Following the impressive growth of BASF during the 1960s, the 1970s started slowly. After much encouragement by the state of South Carolina in the United States to build a $200 million dye and plastics plant in an impoverished area near Hilton Head, the company's plans were thwarted by an unlikely coalition of outside agitators, local residents, and Southern gentry who feared damage to the beautiful Carolina coastline. In 1971 large investments in fibers and plastics were lost due to overcapacity. Synthetic fibers, whose prices were low in relation to the petroleum used in their manufacture, continued to plague BASF throughout the decade.

Despite the problems with fibers, however, the company continued to grow. The growth plan favored by Timm, who served as board chairman until 1974, and Matthias Seefelder, chairman from 1974 to 1983 and a chemist by trade, featured vertical integration, expansion abroad, and emphasis on consumer products. Of the three successors to the I.G. Farben, BASF was the one left with the least attractive product line.

In order to remedy this situation, BASF marketed its line of magnetic cassette tapes (a product it claims to have invented) and then ventured into videotapes. As for vertical integration, the company had ample access to raw materials and chose to modify existing raw materials rather than diversify into unfamiliar fields.

U.S. EXPANSION IN THE EIGHTIES

Since there was little room to grow in Germany, the expansion into foreign markets was a cornerstone of BASF's strategy for growth. The 1980s were a decade of significant growth for BASF in the United States. In order to avoid U.S. tariffs BASF formed numerous partnerships with U.S. companies and acquired others. Wyandotte Chemicals Corporation of Wyandotte, Michigan, had been a major acquisition in 1969. The 1980s began with the purchase of Fritzsche Dodge and Olcott, Inc., the third-largest U.S. producer of flavors and fragrances, not to mention Cook Industrial Coatings and Allegheny Ludlums. This last acquisition put BASF among the top 15 pigment manufacturers in the United States. The 1985 purchase of American Enka doubled BASF's fiber capacity. Although BASF's 1980s foreign ventures were by no means limited to the United States, its emphasis on U.S. expansion was understandable. At the time, the United States consumed one-third of the world's chemical production. The company's holdings in the United States also cushioned BASF against fluctuations in the value of the deutsche mark and the dollar.

In 1986 the increasing importance of its U.S. operations was highlighted when BASF consolidated all North American operations under a new subsidiary called BASF Corporation. Within the entire BASF Group, the new company ranked second in size only to the flagship BASF AG, and generated 20 percent of overall group sales. Nearly all (90 percent) of BASF Corporation's sales were generated from products it produced in North America.

The very year of its consolidation, BASF Corporation was in the news when the Oil, Chemical and Atomic Workers Union decided to strike at a plant located in Geismar, Louisiana. Union allegations of unsafe working conditions prompted the U.S. Congress to investigate conditions at the plant. The union announced a campaign of negative publicity directed against the company. The strike surprised the management at BASF, which with the exception of World War II, generally treated workers well. Asked about the labor difficulties, a highly ranked BASF executive said, "We haven't had a strike since 1924, except a work stoppage in 1947 to protest our president being tried for war crimes." The strike, which evolved into a lockout, dragged on and on until it was finally settled with a union victory in 1989.

TRANSFORMATION OF BASF IN THE NINETIES

After Hans Albers had served as board chairman from 1983 to 1990, he was succeeded by Jürgen F. Strube. The year 1990 was a fitting one for a change in leadership. It was the 125th anniversary of the company's founding, and represented the beginning of one of the most remarkable periods in BASF history, a period of furious activity that included restructurings, acquisitions, divestments, joint ventures, and immense capital expenditures, all on a scale unprecedented in BASF history. Strube took over BASF after it had posted one of its strongest years ever in 1989, with sales of DEM 46.16 billion and net income after taxes of DEM 20.2 billion. Sales would then fall for each of the next four years, while net income fell for the next three. The levels of 1989 would not be surpassed until 1995.

The reasons for BASF's struggles were many: a cyclical downturn in the chemical industry in the early 1990s, to which the company was still highly vulnerable; a serious recession in Germany, brought on in part by the cost of German reunification; health-care reform efforts in Europe, which led to the increasing use of generic drugs to contain costs, with BASF's proprietary drug sales suffering as a result; and the Common Agricultural Policy reform effort, which reduced the amount of farmed land and the amount of chemicals used in farming it, thus hurting the sale of BASF agricultural products. The German reunification also affected BASF in a more direct way when it took over—for nothing—Synthesewerk Schwarzheide, one of the largest chemical businesses in the former East Germany. BASF converted it into BASF Schwarzheide GmbH, but then had to spend DEM 1.4 billion to modernize and expand its facilities.

Strube quickly responded to the crisis by initiating a serious cost-cutting program and by identifying businesses BASF should divest. Cost-cutting efforts included the closure of a number of plants and a gradual workforce reduction that saw BASF's employee numbers fall from a high of 136,990 in 1989 to 106,266 in 1994, a reduction of more than 22 percent. Divested operations were identified as businesses in which BASF was not competitive. These included the Auguste Victoria coal mine, which BASF had used to supply itself with coal since 1907, sold in 1990 to Ruhrkohle AG; the flavors and fragrances business of Fritzsche Dodge and Olcott, which was no longer viewed as a good fit; and the advanced materials division, which was not profitable enough to retain.

EMPHASIS ON NONCYCLICAL BUSINESSES

Strube also wanted to make BASF less susceptible to the cyclical downturns of the chemical industry by bolstering the company's noncyclical businesses. The company's consumer products area was beefed up with the 1991 acquisition of AGFA-Gevaert's magnetic tape operations, which were reorganized with BASF's existing magnetic tape business to form BASF Magnetics GmbH, producer of tapes, videocassettes, and diskettes. A more important and daring venture began in 1990 when Wintershall, BASF's oil and gas subsidiary, entered into an agreement with Gazprom (the world's largest natural gas producer, based in Russia) to build and operate pipelines for distributing Gazprom natural gas to the German market, directly challenging Ruhrgas, Germany's near-monopoly natural gas supplier. After committing itself to invest more than DEM 4.5 billion over the next decade in what was described as the largest project in company history, BASF could boast of attaining 10 percent market share in its first year of operation (1995), and aimed to reach 15 percent by 2000.

The natural gas venture was perceived by BASF as a long-term investment, as were the company's large expenditures in China. Although other countries were also targeted by BASF for significant investment in the 1990s, including Japan, Russia, India, Malaysia, and Korea, it was China that saw astounding expenditure levels. BASF's first plant in China opened in 1992 in Nanjing, a production facility for unsaturated polyester resins. By 1995 the company had committed DEM 600 million to various Chinese ventures, including plants for making pigments, textile dyes, polystyrene, and vitamins, all through various joint ventures. In 1996 another joint venture was formed to build a $4 billion petrochemical facility, also in Nanjing, in what was the single largest investment in China yet by a chemical company.

Meanwhile, acquisitions bolstered BASF's plastics operations. In 1992 the polystyrene-resins operation of Mobil was acquired for $300 million. Then, two years later, BASF paid $90 million for Imperial Chemical's polypropylene operations in Europe. Also in 1994, a new steam-cracker plant located in Antwerp became operational after an outlay of DEM 1.5 billion, the largest single capital expenditure in BASF history. Further moves in plastics came in 1996 when two joint ventures were formed, one with Hoechst in polypropylene and one with Shell in polyethylene. Because of German antitrust laws, these had to be set up as separate businesses, with joint venture partners allowed to have only limited control over their operations.

MAJOR PHARMACEUTICALS PUSH

Early in 1994, BASF reached the important decision to retain its struggling pharmaceuticals business as a core business and to pour money into its growth. The next three years saw a flurry of activity in this area. In 1994 a new biotechnology and genetic engineering research center was opened by BASF Bioresearch Corporation in Worcester, Massachusetts, to develop drugs for fighting cancer and immune system diseases. BASF gained a foothold in generic drugs that same year by acquiring the German generic drugmaker Sagitta Arzneimittel, and by entering into a 50-50 joint venture with IVAX to market generic drugs. The following year BASF's Pharmaceuticals sector received a huge boost with the acquisition of Boots Pharmaceuticals, based in England, for $1.3 billion. Boots was merged into BASF's existing drug operations, forming the new Knoll Pharmaceuticals.

Following the Boots acquisition, BASF created a new Health and Nutrition sector to highlight the importance of both Pharmaceuticals and agricultural products to the company's future. Included in this sector were pharmaceuticals, fine chemicals (notably vitamins), crop protection agents, and fertilizers. In 1996 crop protection expanded when BASF paid $780 million for the North American corn herbicides business of Sandoz, which was ordered divested as part of the merger of Sandoz and Ciba to form Novartis. Another joint venture was also initiated that year in an agreement with Lynx Therapeutics, based in California, to form BASF-Lynx Bioscience AG, for research in biotechnology and genetic engineering for the development of new pesticides and drugs. BASF planned to invest more than DEM 100 million ($66 million) in this venture, in which it held a 51 percent stake. Also in 1996, the U.S. Food and Drug Administration (FDA) approved the antiobesity drug sibutramine, developed by Boots, from which the company expected annual worldwide sales of DEM 800 million ($525 million).

As part of the restructuring that created the Health and Nutrition sector, BASF in 1995 also created an Information Systems sector. This was short-lived, as magnetic tape products were identified as a noncore business and sold early in 1997 to KOHAP of Korea. Another noncore business was potash and in 1996 BASF's holding in Kali und Salz was sold to Potash Corporation of Saskatchewan. Also in 1996, BASF purchased Zeneca's textile dye operations for $208 million, making BASF third worldwide in textile dyes, trailing only DyStar (the merger of Bayer and Hoechst's

textile dye businesses) and Ciba's spinoff specialty Chemical division.

By 1997 BASF was operating five main sectors: Plastics and Fibers, Colorants and Finishing Products, Health and Nutrition, Chemicals, and Oil and Gas. The company had plans to spend more than DEM 20 billion ($13 billion) on acquisitions in the coming years, concentrating on businesses that would counter the cyclical chemical area, notably its Health and Nutrition sector, and on strengthening itself outside Europe. These goals were met by the following acquisitions: Punch Printing Inks, Ltd. (Ireland), and Schou Trykfarver A/S (Denmark); the U.S. surfactant businesses of Olin Corporation and PPG; and a portion of Dow Benelus N.V. (Terneuzen). In a joint venture, BASF acquired a 50 percent share of Hanwha Chemical Corporation in Korea. Another long-term goal was to set up a more streamlined structure in Europe (where the conglomerate had more than 100 separate companies), one similar to the integrated BASF Corporation in the United States. To this end, the following companies were consolidated: BASF Singapore (Pte.) Ltd.; BASF South Africa (Pty.) Ltd., Polioles S.A. de C.V., Wintershall Exploration (United Kingdom) Ltd. and Wintershall (United Kingdom) Ltd.

INVESTING IN CHINA AND ELSEWHERE

Developing markets in Southeast Asia and the Far East had been a goal of BASF since the 1980s. Through joint ventures with local partners, BASF opened the first production plants in China, at Shanghai and Nanjing, the location of an integrated petrochemical site, BASF's largest investment in China.

At the heart of BASF's integrated-production strategy in North America was the construction of the world's largest steam-cracker plant, begun in 1998 with PetroFina, in Port Arthur, Texas. The Port Arthur plant was one of the largest single investments made by BASF outside Europe; other steam-cracker plants were located in Ludwigshafen (since 1965) and Antwerp, Belgium. The steam-cracking process involved the "cracking" of naphtha by adding steam at a temperature of 800 degrees Celsius to form ethylene and propylene, used to make plastics, surface coatings, solvents, raw materials, crop protection agents, and vitamins.

Through joint ventures in 1998, BASF broadened its plant biotechnology operations with research sites in Germany, Sweden, the United States, and Canada. BASF Plant Science, a worldwide research platform, was founded with Svalof Weibull, Sweden's seed producer. Shell partnered with BASF in 1999 to establish one of the world's largest polyolefin manufacturing plants. Through a joint venture with European companies Montell, Elenac, and Targor, BASF began manufacturing polyethylene and polypropylene. This paved the way for the creation of Bassell N.V. in 2000.

From the mid-1970s BASF expanded into pharmaceuticals through the acquisition of Knoll AG and U.K.-based Boots Pharmaceuticals. Although strengthening its presence in the North American market, its worldwide pharmaceutical business was sold to Abbott Laboratories, Inc., in late 2000, following settlement of legal action alleging "a conspiracy among vitamin manufacturers to fix prices, allocate markets and engage in other practices in violation of the Sherman Act and the antitrust, consumer protection and/or common laws of the various states" against BASF and other codefendants.

RECORD SALES IN 2000 AND EXPANDED E-COMMERCE CAPABILITIES

In the first and second quarters of 2000, BASF achieved record sales. Chairman of the Board of Executive Directors Strube attributed this milestone to a strategy of continuous change, the strength of an integrated approach to manufacturing (*Verbund*), global presence, and a spirit of innovation. To further enhance its global position, BASF took strategic positions in several ventures, including new Internet marketplaces for chemicals and thermoplastics. In February, BASF acquired a stake in ChemConnect, the leading U.S. online chemicals and plastics marketplace.

In June 2000, BASF shares were listed on the New York Stock Exchange under the trading symbol BF. Another milestone was reached in the United States in July when BASF made its largest acquisition, American Home Products, a crop protection program. This acquisition made BASF the world's third-largest supplier of agricultural products. The first *Verbund* site in Asia was opened as BASF Petronas Chemicals. The joint venture with the Malaysian state enterprise in Kauntan produced acrylic monomers. Other operations included the merger of its textile dye activities in DyStar as a result of a joint venture with Bayer and Hoechst. The end of 2000 recognized BASF as "number one among world chemical companies and among German businesses" in *Fortune*'s "Global Most Admired Companies."

REORGANIZATION OF BUSINESS UNITS: 2001

BASF reorganized its core business units into five segments to optimize value-adding chains by bundling product groups. These business segments were Chemicals, Plastics and Fibers; Performance Products; Agricultural Products and Nutrition; and Oil and Gas. These segments were further divided into 12 operating divisions.

BASF's Chemical segment, comprising the Inorganics, Petrochemicals, and Intermediates divisions, produced a range of products from basic petrochemicals and inorganic chemicals to specialty intermediates and related products. Based on sales in 2001, this division was one of the largest chemical producers in the world, meeting the needs of many industries, including chemical, construction, automotive, electrical, electronics, detergents, colorants, coatings, and health and nutrition industries.

The Plastics and Fibers segment produced not only plastics but also fiber products. Styrenic plastics, engineering and high-performance plastics, thermoplastics, foams, nylon fibers, nylon intermediates, and polyurethanes were products made for construction, packaging, automotive, household appliances, electrical and electronics, consumer products, textile, and carpet industries. To retain its large European market, BASF's Plastics and Fibers segment spent approximately EUR 146 million on research and development activities in 2001.

High-value chemicals such as surfactants, pigments, automotive and industrial coatings, dispersions, and adhesive raw materials were produced by the Performance Products segment. BASF also produced acrylic acid and its derivatives, as well as polymers, such as superabsorbents, which were used to manufacture sanitary care products. These products were sold throughout the world in the automotive, paper, packaging, textile, sanitary care, construction, coatings, printing, and leather industries.

The Agricultural Products and Fine Chemicals divisions, functioning under the Agriculture Products and Nutrition segment, produced a variety of agricultural products, including herbicides, fungicides, and insecticides. The Agricultural Products division was based in Mount Olive, New Jersey. Fine Chemicals produced in this segment included vitamins, carotenoids, and pharmaceutical active ingredients; polymers for pharmaceuticals, cosmetics, and human nutrition; and aroma chemicals, amino acids, and feed enzymes. This segment was previously named Health and Nutrition, prior to the 2001 selling of Abbott Laboratories, Inc. (United States).

Activities of the Oil and Gas segment, operated through BASF's subsidiary Wintershall AG and its corresponding subsidiaries and affiliates, included the exploration and production of crude oil and natural gas.

Throughout Central and Eastern Europe, natural gas marketing, distribution, and trading were handled in partnership with Gazprom of Russia. Oil and Gas operations were conducted in North Africa, the Middle East, Germany, and Argentina.

PARTNERSHIPS, NEW PRODUCTS, AND STRONG GROWTH

In 2001 BASF began transacting business in Europe and the United States via Elemica, a company-neutral electronic marketplace, allowing electronic transactions supplying neopentyl glycol between BASF, The Dow Chemical Company, and DSM in the Netherlands. These transactions provided the necessary infrastructure to link BASF's Enterprise Resource Planning (ERP) system with customers. Another important e-commerce advance was WorldAccount, an integrated, global extranet platform for customer product information resources. In early 2002, BASF joined with Dell Computer Corporation, in the United States, to introduce a worldwide corporate personal computer standard in an effort to streamline company communications and business processes.

BASF continued to make important advances in pharmaceuticals in 2002 with the introduction of Kollicoat IR, a water-soluble tablet coating designed to improve tablet strength and protect active ingredients. With other brands launched previously, BASF remained one of the leading producers of pharmaceutical excipients and active ingredients.

During the first decade of the 21st century, BASF left little doubt about its intention to remain the world's largest chemical company. The years witnessed phenomenal growth, as revenues leaped from EUR 32.21 billion in 2002 to EUR 62.3 billion by 2008. Internal growth played a role in the company's development, but acquisitions completed during the period represented the driving force behind BASF's expansion.

ACQUISITIONS: 2006–09

BASF spent nearly $14 billion during a three-year period, beginning its acquisition campaign with a hostile takeover launched at the beginning of 2006. The company wanted to acquire Iselin, New Jersey-based Engelhard Corporation, a specialty chemicals producer whose principal strengths were in car emission catalysts and paints and pigments. BASF approached Engelhard's board of directors in late 2005 and offered to buy the company in a friendly takeover, but its advances were rebuffed by Engelhard, whose senior leaders described the offer as "inadequate" and "opportunistic" in the

January 4, 2006, issue of the *America's Intelligence Wire*. BASF, led by CEO Jürgen Hambrecht, responded quickly, launching a hostile takeover in January 2006. The company, in one of the largest hostile takeovers by a German company for an overseas rival, offered $37 per share for Engelhard, submitting a $4.9 billion, all-cash bid.

Engelhard's board of directors unanimously rejected BASF's offer before the end of the month, but BASF remained steadfast in its pursuit of the company. Hambrecht extended the expiration date of his offer three times during the spring of 2006, using the time to pursue another acquisition candidate while he waited for Engelhard to accept his proposal. In March 2006, he announced BASF was acquiring the construction chemicals business belonging to Degussa AG. BASF paid $2.6 billion for the business, which operated in two segments, an admixtures systems segment that made products for the concrete industry and a construction systems segment that served contractors involved in facades, flooring, and waterproofing.

News of the Degussa acquisition occurred at the same time negotiations for the Engelhard takeover reached a turning point. In March, BASF extended the deadline for its offer for the third time, giving Engelhard's board of directors and shareholders until April to accept its proposal, and it raised its offer to $38 per share. Engelhard's board of directors rejected the proposal, but the company signed a confidentiality agreement with BASF that allowed the German company to examine its intimate financial details. BASF subsequently improved its bid a second time, offering Engelhard $39 per share in May. At the end of the month, Engelhard's board of directors agreed to the $5 billion bid, paving the way for BASF's acquisition of Engelhard the following month.

NEW LEGAL STRUCTURE: 2007

BASF's next major purchase was completed without the reluctance of its acquisition candidate. However, before the company pressed forward with the deal it made a significant change to its corporate designation. In February 2007, the company approved a plan for BASF to become a Societas Europaea (SE), or European Company, a corporate designation introduced to reduce the complexities of conducting cross-border business in Europe. As a result of the change to its legal structure, BASF AG became officially known as BASF SE.

Reports of BASF's next move on the acquisition front occurred in September 2008, when the company announced it was purchasing Swiss specialty chemicals producer Ciba Holding AG. "With the acquisition of

Ciba," Hambrecht said in the September 15, 2008, issue of the *America's Intelligence Wire*, "we are strengthening our portfolio and expanding our leading position in specialty chemicals with products and services for a variety of customer industries, in particular the plastics and coatings industries as well as water treatment." BASF offered $5.3 billion for Ciba and, after divesting several units to satisfy antitrust concerns, completed the transaction in April 2009. The acquisition made BASF the second-largest supplier of coating effect materials in the world, just one of the numerous market strengths enjoyed by the world's largest chemical company.

Updated, David E. Salamie; Carol D. Beavers;
Jeffrey L. Covell

PRINCIPAL SUBSIDIARIES

BASF Catalysts LLC (USA); BASF Corporation (USA); BASF Canada; BASF IT Services GmbH; BASF PLC (UK); BASF Coatings AG; Wintershall AG.

PRINCIPAL DIVISIONS

Inorganics; Petrochemicals; Intermediates; Performance Polymers; Polyurethanes; Dispersions & Pigments; Care Chemicals; Paper Chemicals; Performance Chemicals; Catalysts; Construction Chemicals; Coatings; Crop Protections; Exploration & Production; Natural Gas Trading.

PRINCIPAL COMPETITORS

Bayer AG; The Dow Chemical Company; E.I. du Pont de Nemours and Company.

FURTHER READING

Alperowicz, Natasha, "BASF to Idle Production in Europe," *Chemical Week,* November 21, 2001, pp. 15–16.

Alperowicz, Natasha, Lyn Tattum, and Emma Chynoweth, "Managing the Business Cycle at BASF: Gas Deal Provides Hope for Improving Results," *Chemical Week,* December 16, 1992, pp. 22–26.

Alperowicz, Natasha, Michael Roberts, and Debbie Jackson, "Domestic Pressures Turn the Screw on German Chemical Firms," *Chemical Week,* March 31, 1993, pp. 34–35.

Anderson, Curt, "Board at Engelhard Again Tells Investors to Reject BASF Bid," *America's Intelligence Wire,* March 7, 2006.

Baker, John, "BASF Invests in Chinese Future," *ECN-European Chemical News,* October 7, 1996, p. 25.

"BASF AG," *Mergent Industrial Manual,* New York: Moody's Investor Service, 2001, pp. 912–916.

"BASF: Change, Focus, Speed," supplement to *ECN-European Chemical News,* November 1995.

"BASF Claims Top Spot Among Investors in Korea," *Chemical Marketing Reporter,* September 23, 1996, p. 5.

BASF Milestones in Its History, Ludwigshafen, Germany: BASF Aktiengesellschaft, 1995.

"BASF Targets Acquisitions That Cut Cycles: The Company Also Wants to Structure European Business Like That of U.S.," *Chemical Marketing Reporter,* November 18, 1996, pp. 7, 41.

Borenstein, Seth, "BASF Sells Off Units to Win EU OK for Ciba Deal," *America's Intelligence Wire,* March 12, 2009.

Chandler, Alfred D., Jr., "The Enduring Logic of Industrial Success," *Harvard Business Review,* March/April 1990, p. 130.

"Engelhard's Board Unanimously Rejects BASF Bid," *America's Intelligence Wire,* January 23, 2006.

Gibson, Paul, "How the Germans Dominate the World Chemical Industry," *Forbes,* October 13, 1980, p. 155.

Gold, Jeffrey, "Engelhard Backs $5 Billion BASF Takeover," *America's Intelligence Wire,* May 30, 2006.

Hayes, Peter, *Industry and Ideology: I.G. Farben in the Nazi Era,* London: Cambridge University Press, 1987.

Khan, Zarar, "BASF Makes US$4.9B Offer for Engelhard," *America's Intelligence Wire,* January 4, 2006.

Layman, Patricia L., "For BASF, Big Is Still Better," *Chemical and Engineering News,* September 16, 1996, pp. 13–15, 18.

Mattar, Shafika, "Germany's BASF to Become European Company, or SE, Pending Shareholders' Approval," *America's Intelligence Wire,* February 27, 2007.

Milmo, Sean, "BASF, Lynx Form Biotech Collaboration," *Chemical Marketing Reporter,* October 28, 1996, p. 7.

"The Money Pit: Investing in Eastern Europe," *Economist,* June 22, 1991, pp. 74–75.

Moore, Matt, "BASF to Buy Switzerland's Ciba," *America's Intelligence Wire,* September 15, 2008.

Moulson, Geir, "Germany's BASF to Buy Degussa Construction Chemicals Business," *America's Intelligence Wire,* March 1, 2006.

Reier, Sharon, "Hundred Years War: How BASF Allied Itself with the Russians to Battle Germany's Gas Monopoly," *Financial World,* September 14, 1993, pp. 28–30.

Richman, Louis S., "Hans Albers: BASF," *Fortune,* August 3, 1987, p. 50.

Schroter, Harm G., "The German Question, the Unification of Europe, and the European Market Strategies of Germany's Chemical and Electrical Industries, 1990–1992," *Business History Review,* Autumn 1993, p. 369.

Sheridan, Mike, "BASF Atofina Cracker Is Finally Up and Running," *Chemical Marketing Reporter,* February 18, 2002, p. 4.

White, Aoife, "BASF Still Pursuing Engelhard, Despite Snubbed Bid," *America's Intelligence Wire,* January 24, 2006.

Winfield, Nicole, "Engelhard Terms BASF Bid Inadequate," *America's Intelligence Wire,* February 6, 2006.

Bayerische Motoren Werke AG

———■———

Petuelring 130
Munich, D-80788
Germany
Telephone: (+49 893) 822-3362
Fax: (+49 893) 821-0881
Web site: http://www.bmw.com

Public Company
Incorporated: 1917
Employees: 101,733
Sales: EUR 53.19 billion (2008)
Stock Exchanges: Frankfurt
Ticker Symbol: BMW
NAICS: 336111 Automobile Manufacturing; 423110 Automobile and Other Vehicle Merchant Wholesalers; 423120 Motor Vehicle Supplies and New Parts Merchant Wholesalers; 441110 New Car Dealers; 336991 Motorcycle, Bicycle, and Parts Manufacturing; 441221 Motorcycle Dealers

■ ■ ■

Bayerische Motoren Werke AG is a global manufacturer of automobiles marketed under the BMW, Rolls-Royce, and MINI brands. The company also manufactures and markets BMW motorcycles and accessories. BMW operates manufacturing facilities in Europe, North America, South Africa, China, and India, producing approximately 1.4 million automobiles annually. The company is known primarily as a maker of luxury automobiles, but it has begun to make more inexpensive models to increase its stature.

AN AIRCRAFT-ENGINE BUILDER FIRST

Although not officially established until 1917, BMW can trace its heritage back to 1913 when Karl Rapp started to build aircraft engines for Austria in anticipation of World War I. Rapp-Motorenwerke's top customer was Franz Josef Popp, general inspector of Emperor Franz Josef's army. Popp hired Max Friz, an aircraft engine designer from Austro-Daimler; together in Munich they established Bayerische Motoren Werke based on the engineering ideas of Rapp. Popp, an engineer, took charge of administration while Friz served as senior designer. A third associate, Camillo Castiglioni from Vienna, looked after the accounts. The trio began their enterprise at the old Rapp factory, then moved to the Moosacher Strasse factory, also in Munich, in 1918. There, Friz designed and built the company's first aircraft engine.

At the end of the war, Bayerische Motoren turned to the production of train brakes, and when in 1922 the Moosacher Strasse factory was sold to Knorr-Bremse, BMW employees moved to another Munich location, the former Ottowerke plant on the Lerchenauer Strasse. (Ottowerke had been founded by Gustav Otto, son of Nikolaus August Otto, inventor of the four-stroke internal combustion engine.)

Despite the 1923 Treaty of Versailles' ban on aircraft production in Germany, Bayerische Motoren continued to operate and thrive. Its 12-cylinder engines were used on international flights by ace pilots such as Gunther Plüschow, Wolfgang von Gronau, and Walter Mittelholzer, and more than a thousand BMW VI

COMPANY PERSPECTIVES
■

Identifying potential and encouraging growth. Knowing what we represent. Recognising where our strengths lie and making the best use of every opportunity. Following a clear strategy. Goals we have attained are in essence the point of departure for new challenges. This is the philosophy that inspires every individual at the BMW Group. It influences the company's structure and it plays a vital role in the decision-making process. Our corporate ethos finds its expression in the uncompromising pursuit of the superlative. The result? Outstanding brands with an unmistakable profile. Automobiles and motorcycles which fascinate people all over the world and which win legions of new admirers every day. And a degree of success which sees the BMW Group go from strength to strength.

engines were sold to the Soviet Union. Production continued to rise steadily through the 1930s.

The company's interests in motorcycle manufacture developed rapidly in the early 1920s. The first model, the R32, consisted of a flat twin engine and drive shaft housed in a double-tube frame, with valves in an inverted arrangement to keep the oil clean. Ernst Henne, riding an R32, broke the world motorcycle speed record at 279.5 kph (173.35 mph) in 1929; his record held until 1937.

FIRST AUTOMOBILE: 1929

In 1928, Bayerische Motoren acquired the ailing Fahrzeugwerke Eisenach, and a year later the Dixi, BMW's first luxury car, was produced at the Eisenach site. The Dixi won the 1929 International Alpine Rally, covering the mountain route in five days. Despite its success, the Dixi created major financial problems for BMW, and a merger with Daimler-Benz was discussed in detail. Meanwhile, a partnership contract was agreed upon; Dr. Wilhelm Kissel, Daimler-Benz's chairperson, and Popp, at Bayerische Motoren, joined each other's supervisory boards. A smaller six-cylinder model of the Dixi proved to be a most effective competitor in the Daimler-Benz market, however, and Popp dropped the merger plans.

Another Dixi, the DA2, based on the six-cylinder model, was introduced in Berlin in July 1929. It featured improved handling, better brakes, and a more attractive interior. Despite the stock market crash in

October 1929 and the subsequent depression (17,000 German firms were forced into bankruptcy, including one of Bayerische Motoren's shareholders, the Danat-Bank), the company avoided financial disaster. A total of 5,390 DA2s, the "mini car at a mini price," were sold in 1929; this was increased the following year to 6,792 cars.

When Adolf Hitler assumed power in 1933, Bayerische Motoren, along with other German automotive companies, was required to manufacture airplane engines for the new air force, the Luftwaffe. In the same year, BMW acquired licenses to produce the 525 horsepower Hornet engine and to develop small radial engines for sports planes. The company also launched its 300 automobile series with the 303, the first car to feature the now-familiar "kidney" shape. Lighter than comparable models, the 303 was 50 percent more powerful. Its success encouraged BMW to introduce two popular compact sports models, the 315 and the 319. Early in 1936, the 326 model was launched in both sedan and convertible versions. The all-steel bodied 327 was also introduced that year, and in September Popp unveiled the standard-production 328, which proved to be the fastest sports car of its time; it won the Italian Mille Miglia race in 1938.

The company's rising production of aircraft engines and armored motorcycles resulted in an expansion of facilities at the Milbertshofen plant on the Lerchenauer Strasse, which previously had been devoted to motorcycle manufacturing. A 1939 edict of the German Ministry of Aviation required Brandenburgische Motorenwerke to merge with Bayerische Motoren, and a new factory, Allach, was constructed with government money. The Allach buildings, tucked away in the woods near Munich, were constructed at a distance from one another to minimize damage in the event of an air raid.

WORLD WAR II

BMW played an important role in the German war effort and at the height of Nazi domination the company operated plants as far afield as Vienna and Paris. In two crucial areas of military technology, BMW was in the vanguard: With the guidance of Dr. Hermann Oestrich of the German aviation test center, the company developed the 003, the first jet engine to enter standard production; and under conditions of intense secrecy, it opened a rocket testing and production plant at Zuhlsdorf.

Intent on maintaining a plentiful supply of military aircraft, the Nazi government instructed Bayerische Motoren in 1941 to halt all motor car production. Popp, who had been at the company helm for 25 years,

KEY DATES

∎

1913: Inventor Karl Rapp opens an aircraft design shop.

1917: Rapp's original business leads to the formation of Bayerische Motoren Werke AG under the direction of Franz Josef Popp and Max Friz.

1918: First BMW aircraft engine is built.

1929: First BMW car is built.

1959: Herbert Quandt becomes BMW's dominant shareholder.

1962: Introduction of the 1500 model creates a lasting market niche for BMW.

1994: British-based Rover Group Ltd. is acquired for $1.2 billion.

2000: After years of losses due to an unsuccessful assimilation of the Rover brand, Rover Group Ltd. is divested.

2002: BMW releases the MINI, rekindling the public's affection for the original Morris Mini-Minor built in 1959.

2003: BMW takes control of Rolls-Royce Motor Cars Limited.

2005: Construction of a $1.6 billion production plant in Leipzig, Germany, is completed.

2006: After increasing annual production volume substantially, Helmut Panke retires as chief executive officer.

2008: Panke's successor, Norbert Reithofer, trims BMW's payroll in response to flagging economic indicators.

refused. He was forced to resign and narrowly avoided internment in a concentration camp. It was left to his successor, Fritz Hille, to institute Bayerische Motoren's automatic system of monitoring production, a mechanical forerunner of the computer.

After the defeat of the Nazis, Allied Command ordered the dismantling of many BMW facilities; at the same time, reconstruction of the now divided Germany got underway. In the immediate postwar years, few West Germans were in a position to buy cars, but by 1948, the year of German currency reform, there was a substantial need for motorcycles. BMW produced a new model out of spare parts provided by dealers. Known as the R24, this motorcycle was put into production and in 1949 almost 10,000 machines came off the assembly line. Production in 1950 increased to 17,000, 18 percent of which was exported.

POST–WORLD WAR II: THE EMERGENCE OF A LUXURY CAR MAKER

Bayerische Motoren's return to car manufacturing in 1951 proved to be a disappointment. The 501 model, a six-cylinder conservatively styled car with few technical innovations, was not well received; neither was its successor, the 502, which featured a V8 engine. The company pinned its hopes on the 503 and 507 models, highlights of the 1955 Frankfurt Motor Show. Both cars were designed by Albrecht Graf Goertz and were powered by Alex von Falkenhausen engines. They proved to be too expensive, however, for the majority of West German motorists. To add to BMW's woes, its motorcycle sales dropped drastically, and the Allach factory had to be sold.

The company's fortunes revived a little in the late 1950s during the era of the "bubble car." Its Isetta mini-car, a mere 2.29 meters (7.51 feet) in length and fitted with motorcycle engines, reached a speed of 53 mph. Customer interest in the machine was short-lived, but it enabled BMW to recoup some of its losses.

To capitalize on the increasing market for cars, albeit inexpensive ones, Bayerische Motoren introduced the rear-engined 700 LS model in August 1959. Available as a coupe or convertible, and powered by motorcycle engines, the 700 LS was initially unprofitable. By 1965, however, when annual sales reached 18,000 units, the car had become the company's first long-term success of the postwar years.

THE 1500: THE FIRST SPORTS SEDAN

BMW's fortunes further improved with the launching of its 1500 model. This first "sports sedan" secured the company's prominence in the automotive market for the foreseeable future. The balance sheet showed a profit of DEM 3.82 million in 1963 and a 6 percent dividend was paid. By the end of the decade, the company's long-suffering shareholders were much happier. Nine more models had been introduced, sales for 1969 set a new record of 144,788 cars, and business was up to DEM 1.4 billion.

The 1970s, a period of dramatic growth in Western Europe, proved to be a time of significant reorganization and development at BMW. All motorcycle production was moved to West Berlin, a new plant was opened, the popular 520 sports sedan was launched (1972), the Dingolfing plant in Lower Bavaria was further expanded (providing jobs for 15,000 farmworkers), and following the establishment of the European Economic Community, BMW subsidiaries were set up in member countries. Halfway through the decade, a U.S. importing, marketing, distribution, and support subsidiary was formed in Montvale, New Jersey, and later in the 1970s the company built a car plant at Steyr in Austria.

Early in the 1970s, it appeared that Bayerische Motoren's interests in motor racing, operated by BMW Motorsport GmbH, might be curtailed; however, the company was able to expand its racing activities. For some years, BMW had been the leading producer of racing car engines in the classification known as Formula 2; the company decided to compete in the Formula 1 market as well. Success was swift. In 1975, Nelson Piquet won the Formula 1 World Championship in a BMW-powered Brabham. This was the first turbocharged engine to win in the 34-year history of Formula 1 racing.

BMW IN THE EIGHTIES

The Steyr plant in Austria commenced operation in the early 1980s as a producer of turbocharged diesel engines. By the mid-1980s, the factory was a major gas engine manufacturer and at full capacity could turn out 150,000 engines a year. Another factory, at Spandau in West Berlin, opened in the spring of 1984 to make BMW's new four-cylinder, water-cooled K series of motorcycles. This machine won the January 1985 Paris-Dakar Rally, the world's toughest and longest off-road race. The company's motorcycles won this rally four times in its first six years.

BMW's car sales during the 1970s and 1980s increased along with the demand for higher-priced models, and healthy domestic sales were enhanced by the successes of foreign subsidiaries. In 1984, for example, BMW of North America sold 71,000 cars. On the other hand, motorcycle sales suffered. High unemployment, high interest rates, and loan restrictions decreased the purchasing power of a crucial motorcycle market, young Europeans; and competition from Japan became fierce.

As the company entered the 1990s, competition from Japanese car manufacturers represented perhaps the greatest threat to BMW's future growth, although high German labor costs continued to be a perennial problem. Adopting design characteristics from European luxury models, the Japanese produced cars of similar quality, yet sold the cars at substantially lower prices than those offered by European manufacturers, including BMW. Exacerbating BMW's woes, economic conditions in Europe soured during the early 1990s, portending dismal financial results for the coming years. Despite these ominous developments, however, BMW entered the decade in sound shape. BMW exhibited a vitality few other European car manufacturers could muster, thanks to robust sales during the 1980s and comparatively small debt. In this regard, BMW was the exception rather than the norm in a troubled European automobile industry. The 1990s, however, promised to be quite different from the 1980s, when luxury items and luxury cars sold extremely well, and as the company charted its future it braced itself for less profitable times.

THE ROVER SAGA

As the recession increased in intensity, BMW's financial performance suffered, but not to the extent that other European manufacturers exhibited. The most glaring decline in the company's growth took place at its U.S. operations, where the Japanese struck their first blow in the luxury car market, and the deutsche mark's strength against the dollar slowed sales and squeezed profit margins. By 1992, BMW of North America was recording a 50 percent decline in sales from the subsidiary's peak years in the mid-1980s. BMW management regarded the American situation as boding ill for its European operations. To strengthen its position in the United States, the company announced plans that year to construct an approximately $300 million assembly plant near Spartanburg, South Carolina, which, through the plant's state-of-the-art equipment, was designed to produce 72,000 cars a year. Half of this annual production volume the company planned to export overseas, which lessened BMW's dependence on its domestic production facilities and the associated high labor costs of German workers.

In 1993, Eberhard von Kuenheim ended his 23-year reign at BMW and was replaced by Bernd Pischetsrieder, who had spent his entire career at BMW. Under Pischetsrieder's stewardship, BMW concluded a momentous acquisition that promised to dramatically change the company's future and bolster its position worldwide. In January 1994, less than a year after gaining control of BMW, Pischetsrieder announced the acquisition by BMW of Rover Group Ltd., the esteemed British manufacturer of sport-utility vehicles (SUVs) and Rover Cars. The purchase, a $1.2 billion deal, immediately doubled BMW's share of the European market to 6.4 percent and gave the company a prestigious presence in the SUV market, which was growing exponentially during the early 1990s. The purchase of Rover Group stunned the industry, particularly Honda Motor Company, which held the remaining 20 percent interest in the British car manufacturer and did not learn of BMW's purchase until three days before Pischetsrieder's announcement.

BMW's prospects after the acquisition of the Rover Group were exceedingly brighter. With the addition of Rover Group, BMW gained not only an entry into the fast-growing SUV market, but also the high-volume business of Rover Cars. Pischetsrieder's bold move, made less than a year after he took the helm, was designed to usher BMW into the mainstream with a product line geared toward the mass market. One line of thinking held that BMW was too large to compete as a niche player catering exclusively to the premium segment of the car market and too small to compete as one of the major global concerns. The acquisition of Rover Group, when viewed from this perspective, represented a solution to the company's dilemma, giving it a product line that stretched from entry level models all the way through to the high-priced, luxury end of the market. Pischetsrieder's formidable task was to make the strategy work. If he succeeded, the BMW of the late 1990s and beyond would figure as a full-bodied car manufacturer, competing model against model with global heavyweights such as Ford and General Motors.

As Pischetsrieder set out to incorporate Rover Group into BMW's fold, a change of command occurred in the backdrop. The publicity-shy Quandt family, which owned nearly 50 percent of BMW, had controlled the company since Herbert Quandt became its dominant shareholder in 1959. Johanna Quandt sat on BMW's supervisory board when the Rover Group acquisition was made, but in 1997 she relinquished her post to the fourth generation of Quandt leadership, sister and brother Susanne and Stefan Quandt. When the Quandt siblings assumed control, they, like the industry analysts who were charting Pischetsrieder's progress, wanted to know why Rover Group was continuing to lose money three years after its acquisition.

The marriage between BMW and Rover Group was failing miserably, leading one BMW shareholder to describe the acquisition as the worst investment deal in German corporate history, according to the May 17, 2000 issue of the *Financial Times*. The financial losses incurred by Rover Group were numbing. As BMW poured billions of dollars into the company, all it received in exchange were successive years of financial losses, punctuated by a staggering $1 billion loss in 1998. Critics charged that BMW never properly assimilated Rover Group into its fold and that the company gave U.K. managers too much control. Consequently, the branding of BMW cars and Rover Cars never came together to form a cohesive strategy. Instead of using Rover Cars to gain entry into the mainstream market, BMW marketed the British cars as a premium brand, despite the fact that the cars were distinctly midmarket models. What BMW was left with was two premium brands that competed against one another and no solution to the dilemma that had precipitated the purchase of Rover Group in the first place.

Disaster loomed as BMW entered the last year of the 1990s, a year that would end with another $1 billion loss recorded by Rover Cars. In February 1999, a board meeting was held to determine the fate of Rover Group. By the end of the meeting Pischetsrieder had resigned, as had his deputy and heir apparent, Wolfgang Reitzle, leaving a leadership vacuum that was filled by little-known Joachim Milberg, an academic who had joined BMW a mere six years earlier. With Milberg in charge, BMW continued to suffer both from the losses incurred by Rover Cars and from the distraction the British subsidiary caused, which adversely affected the progress of BMW's luxury car business. Sales of Rover Cars fell approximately 25 percent in 1999, a year in which the launch of Rover 75, a $30,000 luxury sedan, was delayed by six months. In response, increasing numbers of BMW's research and development staff were dispatched to develop new models and improve production quality at Rover, but the rescue efforts occurred at a time when the company was under great pressure to develop new BMW models. BMW's luxury sedan business began to suffer from the distraction, as Mercedes eclipsed BMW in the lucrative U.S. market in 1999. In Europe, the company's market share fell to 3.1 percent, dropping from the 3.4 percent the company held in 1996.

BMW AND ROVER PART WAYS

As BMW entered the 21st century, the struggle to resuscitate Rover Cars continued. Milberg promised to improve quality standards and to turn Rover Cars into a profitable enterprise by 2002. To show his commitment to the ailing British subsidiary, which the German business press had dubbed "The English Patient," Milberg announced plans to invest roughly $5.3 billion in Rover Cars between 2000 and 2005, an investment that represented one-third of BMW's total projected spending during the period. By March 2000, however, the company had conceded defeat and announced it would abandon its efforts at Rover Cars. During BMW's six years of ownership it spent an estimated $4.4 billion on Rover Cars. The decision to dispose of Rover Group led to a $2.85 billion restructuring charge and left Milberg with the daunting task of formulating a future for BMW in the post-Rover era.

Rover Cars was sold to Phoenix Consortium, a loose alliance of English businessmen who paid a nominal fee of $15 for the beleaguered carmaker. Ford Motor Co. acquired Rover Group's Land Rover SUV operations. BMW retained ownership of Rover Group's Mini brand. Milberg planned to release an entirely revamped line of Mini cars in 2001. Milberg also planned to develop an entry-level BMW in the midprice segment to take on Volkswagen's $14,000 Golf, which dominated the midprice segment in Europe. The company's plans also called for the development of the luxury brand Rolls-Royce, which was set to come under BMW's control in 2003. As the company pushed forward, amid speculation that it would be acquired by a larger competitor, few certainties about its future existed, making the first years of the 21st century a critical period in BMW's history.

THE MINI DEBUTS IN 2002

BMW, eager to put the Rover debacle behind it, fared well in the first decade of the 21st century, registering its most stunning success with a vestige of the previous decade's blunder. The MINI, introduced globally in 2002, was enthusiastically embraced by the driving public, its reception exceeding BMW's expectations. Priced at under $20,000 and, at 12 feet in length, one-third larger than the original model built by British Motor Corp. in 1959, the retro-style vehicle attracted a cultlike following, leading BMW to introduce a diesel model, a convertible model, and a premium model in succeeding years. After the anguish wrought by Rover, the MINI brought joy to the company's Munich headquarters, righting a struggling company and giving it much needed momentum for the decade ahead.

The year the MINI was introduced also marked a change in leadership at BMW, as Helmut Panke, a 20-year BMW veteran with a doctorate in nuclear science, took the helm as chief executive officer. Panke led BMW toward the greatest production expansion in its history, seeking to elevate the company, ranked as the 14th-largest automobile manufacturer, to the upper tier of automobile manufacturers in terms of units shipped. Luxury models such as the company's 5 Series and 7 Series, would continue to play a prominent role in BMW's operations, but Panke sought to develop a full-range of selections, unveiling the 1 Series, an entry-level model with a base price of $25,300, roadsters, SUVs, and minivans. Panke oversaw the completion of a new $1.6 billion manufacturing facility in Leipzig, Germany, in 2005, and he presided over robust financial growth. Revenues increased from EUR 29.9 billion in 2001 to EUR 48.9 billion in 2006, Panke's last year in charge of the company.

GLOBAL ECONOMIC CRISIS

Panke reached BMW's mandatory retirement age of 60 in 2006, prompting a change in leadership that saw the company's chief of production, Norbert Reithofer, take the reins of command. Reithofer promised to continue pursuing Panke's vision, inheriting six consecutive years of sales and profit growth since the Rover disaster. When Panke became chief executive, he promised to increase annual production from 1.1 million automobiles to 1.4 million by 2008, a goal that was surpassed one year early under Reithofer's watch, when BMW produced 1.5 million automobiles in 2007.

Reithofer soon faced one of the most pernicious economic environments in a century, however, forcing him to ease back on expansion and adjust to a deteriorating marketplace. In early 2008, BMW reduced its workforce by 13,000 employees and nearly doubled the liquid assets on its balance sheet. "We took measures to absorb the effects of the economic crisis much sooner than other car makers," Reithofer said in the March 19, 2009 issue of *Business Week Online*. BMW ended the decade much as it had ended the previous decade: facing a crucible that would determine its success in the years to come.

Updated, Jeffrey L. Covell

PRINCIPAL SUBSIDIARIES

BMW INTEC Beteiligungs GmbH; BMW Bank GmbH; BMW Finanz Verwaltungs GmbH; BMW Ingenieur-Zentrum GmbH + Co.; BMW Maschinenfabrik Spandau GmbH; BMW Leasing GmbH; BMW Hams Hall Motoren GmbH; BMW Fahrzeugtechnik GmbH; BMW M GmbH Gesellschaft für individuelle Automobile; BMW Österreich Holding GmbH (Austria); BMW Motoren GmbH (Austria); BMW China Automotive Trading Ltd.; BMW Russland Trading OOO (Russia); BMW Austria Gesellschaft m. b. H.; BMW Holding B. V. (Netherlands); BMW Italia S. p. A. (Italy); BMW (Schweiz) AG (Switzerland); BMW Australia Finance Ltd.; BMW (South Africa) (Pty) Ltd.; BMW Finance N. V. (Netherlands); BMW Japan Corp.; BMW Belgium Luxembourg S. A. / N.; BMW France S. A.; BMW Canada Inc.; BMW Australia Ltd.; BMW Portugal Lda.; BMW Hellas Trade of Cars SA (Greece); BMW Korea Co., Ltd. (South Korea); BMW Automotive (Ireland) Ltd.; BMW Sverige AB (Sweden); BMW New Zealand Ltd.; BMW Nederland B. V. (Netherlands); BMW (UK) Holdings Ltd.; BMW (UK) Ltd.; BMW (UK) Manufacturing Ltd.; BMW Financial Services (GB) Ltd. (UK); BMW (UK) Capital plc; BMW Malta Ltd.; BMW España Finance S. L. (Spain); BMW (US) Holding Corp.; BMW Manufacturing, LLC (USA); BMW Financial Services NA, LLC (USA);

BMW of North America, LLC (USA); BMW US Capital, LLC.

PRINCIPAL COMPETITORS

Audi AG; Daimler AG; Ford Motor Company; General Motors Company; Toyota Motor Corporation; Volkswagen AG.

FURTHER READING

"BMW Board Set to Decide Chief's Future," *Financial Times*, February 5, 1999, p. 24.

"BMW Could Use a Little Skid Control," *Business Week*, January 24, 2000, p. 134.

"BMW: Unloading Rover May Not Win the Race," *Business Week*, April 3, 2000, p. 59.

Burt, Tim, "Europe," *Financial Times*, September 1, 2000, p. 24.

Edmondson, Gail, "BMW Keeps the Home Fires Burning," *Business Week,* May 30, 2005, p. 31.

———, "BMW's Accelerated U.S. Push," *Business Week Online,* July 25, 2006.

———, "The Mini Just Keeps Getting Mightier," *Business Week,* April 5, 2004, p. 26.

———, "Profits Take a Backseat at BMW," *Business Week Online,* May 4, 2007.

Ewing, Jack, "BMW: In Crisis Mode, Motoring Shrewdly," *Business Week Online,* March 19, 2009.

Flynn, Julia, "How BMW Zipped In—and Called Rover Right Over," *Business Week,* February 14, 1994, p. 44.

Kay, John, "A Takeover That Missed Its Marque," *Financial Times,* February 18, 1999, p. 18.

Kurylko, Diana T., "Profit Fell, BMW Discloses," *Automotive News,* January 31, 1994, p. 2.

———, "10 Years of BMW Growth Stalling Now," *Automotive News,* March 29, 1993, p. 4.

Loeffelholz, Suzanne, "Kuenheim's Complaint; The BMW CEO Spurns the Japanese and Berates Washington, Wall Street and Detroit," *FW,* January 9, 1990, p. 26.

Marquardt, Stephan, "BMW's Bold Gamble: Buying Rover Makes BMW Twice as Big as Mercedes," *Automotive Industries,* April 1994, p. 44.

McElroy, John, "Why Can't Germany Compete?" *Automotive Industries,* August 1992, p. 22.

Taylor, Alex, "Seven and the Dwarf," *Fortune,* April 15, 2002, p. 386.

———, "The Ultimate Fairly Inexpensive Driving Machine," *Fortune,* November 1, 2004, p. 130.

"Then There Were Seven," *Economist,* February 5, 1994, p. 19.

Tierney, Christine, "The Little Car That Could," *Business Week,* October 7, 2002, p. 32.

Big Fish Games, Inc.

---

333 Elliott Avenue West, Suite 200
Seattle, Washington 98119-4101
U.S.A.
Telephone: (206) 213-5753
Fax: (206) 269-3800
Web site: http://www.bigfishgames.com

Private Company
Incorporated: 2002
Employees: 350
Sales: $85 million (2008 est.)
NAICS: 511210 Software Publishers

■ ■ ■

Big Fish Games, Inc., is one of the worldwide leaders in the design, publication, and distribution of casual games through the Internet. With more than 2,000 game titles available, including several titles developed in-house, Big Fish Games distributes as many as 1.5 million games on peak days, through online play or as downloaded content. The company offers a new game daily, with one-hour of free sample play for every game anytime, and then charges a flat fee to download the full version of the game or for unlimited online play. Casual games are characterized as stress-free and simple to play. Colorful, detailed graphics are employed to engage customers for hours of addictive play. Casual game genres include puzzle, hidden object, time management, adventure, strategy, word, arcade and action, card and board, mahjong, and brain teasers. Although the emphasis is on

family fun, the games attract a primary audience of mature gamers, especially women over 30 years of age.

The company's game titles are available at its home Web site, and through game distribution sites, including Yahoo Games, MSN Games, and Electronic Arts' Pogo. Through affiliate agreements, the company hosts games for numerous casual games developers, including competitors. Big Fish Games distributes games in several languages and hosts portals in German, French, Spanish, and Japanese. The company's game development studios are located in Vancouver, British Columbia, Canada, and Cork, Ireland, as well as at its Seattle headquarters.

FOUNDER DEFINES ONLINE CASUAL GAME MARKET

Paul Thelen brought experience, fortitude, and a lifelong love of games to the venture of starting Big Fish Games. He started his first game company at 11 years of age. With a bachelor of science degree in electrical engineering from the University of Washington and an M.B.A. from Stanford University, Thelen obtained software development and management experience at various companies in Washington, D.C. In 1996, RealNetworks in Seattle offered him a position as a product developer. While at RealNetworks, Thelen cofounded RealArcade, an online game site. Then a minor, relatively unknown segment of the Internet, except to "core" game users, males in their teens and twenties, the casual game industry exploded with the launch of RealArcade. Thelen had his own ideas about the possibilities for casual gaming online, and he began writing a business plan for his own company.

Thelen left RealNetworks in 2002 to start Big Fish Games. Working 10 to 12 hours per day, Thelen struggled through a debilitating, unknown illness. One doctor gave him a terminal diagnosis, with three months to live. Suffering from nausea, fatigue, and an irregular heartbeat, Thelen continued working because it diverted his attention from his health problems. Finally, an accurate diagnosis led to removal of his gallbladder, and Thelen recovered.

After a few minor successes, Big Fish Games introduced its first hit game, *Mahjong Towers,* based on the classic Chinese tile game, in August 2002. According to game monitor ComScore Media Metrix, *Mahjong Towers* ranked number one for usage among online games in 2002. The company quickly expanded by offering proprietary games as well as by distributing games for other game developers. By the end of 2003, Big Fish Games had introduced another 14 games and revenues reached $1.2 million. Over the next year, Big Fish Games became one of the top online outlets for game developers, with distribution as high as 300,000 downloadable games per day.

"A NEW GAME EVERY DAY" INITIATIVE: 2005

In order to maintain its early lead in a rapidly growing segment of Internet commerce, Thelen proclaimed that Big Fish Games would introduce "A New Game Every Day" in 2005. The company vowed to offer a new game every day, for 365 days, either proprietary titles or titles developed by outside game developers. The company set a high standard for quality and customer fit. Only one in five games submitted for consideration by other game development studios were accepted. However, for games that showed potential, Big Fish Games collaborated with other game studios to optimize the design for the Big Fish Games site. Released at midnight, each new game drew thousands of gamers to the company's Web site every night. Private investment of $8.7 million supported the ambitious agenda.

To add to the company's internal game development, Big Fish Games acquired another leading casual games company serving the mature gamers market, Ion Thunder. IonThunder.com was renowned in the casual game market for sustained play, with gamers spending more than 40 hours per month playing on the site. The April 2005 acquisition added several social games to Big Fish Games' repertoire, including more than 40 free multiplayer bingo, card, puzzle, and casino games. Game winners received tokens that could be applied to an online lottery for cash and prizes.

Through a partnership with Nickelodeon, Big Fish Games entered the family games market. Nick Arcade, launched in July 2005, offered games in generic form, such as *Magic Ball* and *Feeding Frenzy,* as well as games featuring popular cartoon characters. The latter included *SpongeBob SquarePants Obstacle Odyssey* and *Dora's Rapido River Rafting Adventure.* The Nick Arcade Pass offered children subscriptions to download games for $7.99 per month, and games were available on a "try-before-you-buy" basis. With more than 60 games available at launch, Nick Arcade distributed more than 1.6 million game downloads during the first month of operation.

Big Fish Games' dramatic success continued in 2005 with the release of several top-selling proprietary games, such as *Magic Vines.* With more than 70,000 downloads per day, online sales of the game exceeded $6,000 per day and contributed to a 400 percent increase in game sales. Moreover, Thelen succeeded in reaching his target markets, as people over age 40 accounted for 65 percent of sales, and women accounted for 70 percent of sales.

Big Fish Games launched the third game in the *Mahjong* series in August 2005, *Mahjong Towers Eternity.* The title became the company's first major social gaming product, which allowed in-game chat, tile-set trading, messaging, and tile layout creation and sharing. During its first three months, more than two million players downloaded the game, and it was played more than 12 million times.

Another major success for Big Fish Games involved the November release of *Mystery Case Files: Huntsville.* The crime-based game featured richly detailed artwork and mood music, and players earned badges for solving each case. The game provided thousands of clues/items to find within 20 unique environments. *Mystery Case Files* broke the casual game industry record for first-day downloads, with 1,000 downloads, compared to the previous high of 450.

With a team of producers, testers, and Web developers, as well as more than 300 game designers from around the world, Big Fish Games met its goal of launching 365 new games in 2005. The program attracted 25 million unique users to the Big Fish Games Web site every month; and they purchased over 100 million games. Moreover, the company established a reputation for releasing new hit games before other game Web sites. Big Fish Games extended its commitment to offering a new game every day indefinitely.

CULTIVATING WORLDWIDE AUDIENCE

The interest in casual gaming was a worldwide phenomenon, and Big Fish Games sought to capitalize on its lead position through international expansion. The company established Big Fish Games Deutschland in 2005 to launch a German-language Internet portal. Big Fish Games Japan, established in 2006, adapted games for Japanese culture and language. Also, several games were offered in a variety of languages, such as *Mahjong Towers Eternity,* made available in 13 languages. Reflecting its worldwide base of customers, Big Fish Games adopted the marketing slogan, "Where the World Goes to Play."

Big Fish Games entered the French casual gaming market through the January 2006 acquisition of Fun-Pause EURL. Located in Montpelier, France, FunPause offered gamers a cinematic visual style and relaxing music. The company's downloadable games included the popular *Atlantis* and *Fairies* titles, both of which reached the number one slot on several game distribution sites. Renamed Big Fish Games Europe, the game design studio retained full creative freedom and, in April, introduced another top-selling title, *Mystic Inn.*

The acquisition of FunPause provided Big Fish Games entry into the Apple computer game market, through FunPause's Macintosh game site. In April, Big Fish Games released more than 20 of its existing games for Mac users. Available for download at $19.95 each, games included mahjong, puzzle, card, action, and

arcade genres, as well as the top-selling title, *Mystery Case Files: Huntsville.*

DIVERSIFYING MARKETING OUTLETS AND OPTIONS

To expand its customer base, Big Fish Games implemented a variety of marketing initiatives in 2006. The company experimented with retail distribution, introducing 10 titles offered through Activision. A new social networking site, My Game Space, provided customers with an opportunity to set up a page with their favorite games. Membership included two free games from a limited selection, and the company offered a rewards program, in which the member received cash or a discount toward new purchases for every purchase made by a friend through the member's game space page.

Big Fish Games built on the success of *Mystery Case Files: Huntsville,* which reached $1 million in sales within three months. It remained the number one digitally distributed game online in March 2006. The first sequel, *Mystery Case Files: Prime Suspects,* was released in April. That game broke the download record, with as many as 3.3 games downloaded per minute, and helped propel the company into the top 10 list of online casual gaming sites.

Travel and adventure became a source of inspiration for proprietary game titles. These included *Travelogue 360: Paris.* The *Travelogue* series featured three-dimensional images of popular tourist sites, such as the Eiffel Tower and the Champs-Élysées, where gamers searched for souvenirs. *Hidden Expedition: Titanic,* launched in 2006, featured a scuba diver searching the underwater wreckage of the *Titanic* ocean liner.

Travel and adventure games led Big Fish Games to a distribution outlet that appealed to the mature casual gamer. The release of *Hidden Expedition: Mount Everest* in 2007 coincided with the company's affiliation with *National Geographic Magazine.* The magazine offered the games on its Web site and through direct sales, providing Big Fish Games with an untapped market of potential customers. The company hoped the visual quality of its *Hidden Expedition* and *Travelogue 360* game titles would appeal to readers of *National Geographic,* a publication renowned for photographic excellence.

EXPANDING ON SUCCESS

Given its success in the new industry of online casual gaming, Big Fish Games obtained plenty of capital toward further growth. The company invested profits into marketing. By the end of 2006, sales at Big Fish Games reached $24 million, and then tripled over the next two years. Rapid growth prompted the company to hire new executive management. Jeremy Lewis, a former managing director at Goldman Sachs, became president and chief operating officer. His ascension to the chief executive position in 2007 gave Thelen time to focus on growth strategy as chairman of the company. Big Fish Games raised $83.3 million in common stock financing in mid-2008, just before a worldwide financial crisis hit and the stock market crumbled. The common stock financing drew support from Balderton Capital, General Catalyst Partners, and Salmon River Capital.

Big Fish Games applied its investment funds to a variety of international expansion initiatives. In 2008 the company launched Big Fish Games Spain and improved its portal offerings at Big Fish Games Japan. The company established a game design studio in Vancouver, British Columbia, Canada, in October 2008. That division expanded in 2009, when the company bought Vancouver-based Grubby Games, one of the company's longtime outside game developers. Popular titles included *My Tribe, Incredibots,* and *FizzBall.* Big Fish Games opened a new European headquarters in Cork City, Ireland, in 2009. Over the next three years, Big Fish Games planned to hire 100 employees to adapt existing game titles to the sensibilities of local markets.

Big Fish Games entered the market for virtual world games with the introduction of its *Faunasphere* site in 2009. *Faunasphere* originated with Thinglefin, a game developer acquired by Big Fish Games in 2007. *Faunasphere* allowed people to adopt, name, and care for dogs, horses, and other pet animals. Unlike other virtual worlds, *Faunasphere* used a Web browser to maneuver through the game. A massively multiplayer online (MMO) style of casual game, *Faunasphere* allowed casual gamers to interact with each other, even as they created their own virtual worlds. In this burgeoning aspect of the casual games market, Big Fish Games held a competitive advantage, as high levels of traffic to its Web site gave the company a large, ready market.

Big Fish Games sought to cultivate the active female audience for online causal games. In 2009 the company formed an exclusive licensing partnership with Harlequin Enterprises Ltd., publisher of women's romantic fiction. Harlequin Presents, the company's most popular series of romance novels, would provide the inspiration for new game titles. In turn, Harlequin planned to publish books based on the *Mystery Case Files* game series. A distribution agreement with *People* magazine, a publication popular with women, provided daily features of a Big Fish Games title on the online outlet People.com.

Mary Tradii

PRINCIPAL SUBSIDIARIES

Big Fish Games Deutschland; Big Fish Games Japan; Big Fish Games Spain; Big Fish Games Studios Europe.

PRINCIPAL COMPETITORS

Big Splash Games, LLC; Electronic Arts, Inc.; GameHouse, Inc.; iWin, Inc.; PlayFirst; Inc.; PlayFish Ltd.; PopCap Games, Inc.; RealNetworks, Inc.; Ubisoft Entertainment, SA.

FURTHER READING

Engleman, Eric, "Big Fish Names Big-Time President," *Puget Sound Business Journal,* July 28, 2006.

"Harlequin and Big Fish Games Announce Licensing Agreement," *Women's Health Weekly,* February 5, 2009.

Holtzman, Clay, "Game Company Aims to Be Big Fish in Market," *Puget Sound Business Journal,* October 19, 2007.

"National Geographic Distributes Video Games," *Information Week,* July 18, 2007.

Reese, Heather, "Thelen Worked Through Illness to Launch Big Fish," *Puget Sound Business Journal,* September 9, 2005.

blue sun.

Blue Sun Energy, Inc.

14143 Denver West Parkway, Suite 100
Denver, Colorado 80401-3266
U.S.A.
Telephone: (303) 865-7700
Fax: (303) 865-7705
Web site: http://www.gobluesun.com

Private Company
Incorporated: 2001 as Sunfuels, Inc.
Employees: 20
Sales: $15 million (2008 est.)
NAICS: 325998 All Other Miscellaneous Chemical Product Manufacturing

∎ ∎ ∎

Blue Sun Energy, Inc., is the leading producer of renewable, vegetable-based diesel fuel, providing premium-quality biodiesel for blending with fossil fuel diesel. Blue Sun Fusion brand biodiesel contains the company's proprietary additive, DTX, which enhances the positive characteristics of biodiesel. As an integrated renewable fuel company, Blue Sun is involved in the entire process of production and marketing, beginning with the development of oilseed feedstock.

Blue Sun Producers, a farmers' cooperative, supplies Blue Sun with the oilseed used in the production of biodiesel. Blue Sun Fusion B20, the company's main product, is distributed to more than 25 retail, municipal, and corporate fueling stations in Colorado, New Mexico, Nebraska, Utah, Idaho, and Washington.

Blue Sun Fusion B35, B50, and B70 blends are available for industrial applications.

CASUAL CONVERSATION SPURS GROUP TO ACTION

Blue Sun Energy began rather spontaneously in 2001, when friends in the Fort Collins, Colorado, area gathered for a weekend of summer fun. Company cofounder John Long happened to bring a book about biodiesel as a renewable alternative to fossil-based fuels. The book generated discussion, and over the course of the weekend, talk shifted to the idea of building a biodiesel processor. Electrical engineer Sean Lafferty, less than three years out of college but already an experienced consultant in significant alternative energy systems, brought professional experience to the project. Long's experience in the nonprofit sector garnered a $1,000 community education grant from New Belgium Brewing Company, a Fort Collins-based microbrewery. The group began holding weekly forums at Avogadro's Number, a popular hangout for progressively minded locals. By the end of the summer, as many as 40 people began attending the demonstrations of recycling restaurant oil into biodiesel. The formation of Sunfuels, Inc., followed in November, and a business plan generated seed money from family and friends.

From the start Sunfuels was concerned about the poor quality of biodiesel available in this relatively unknown area of alternative fuels. Furthermore, the group considered the specifications for performance, as determined by ASTM, a professional materials testing association, to be inadequate. Sunfuels intended to exceed those specifications by developing a fuel additive that would improve the quality of biodiesel. The company began to research and develop fuel additives while it contracted to begin oilseed extraction and biodiesel refining for commercial use.

Initially, Sunfuels served the public sector, such as fleet vehicles used by the City and County of Denver and the City of Boulder. Littleton Public Schools used the biodiesel in school buses. By the end of 2002, the economic potential and growing popularity of biodiesel as an alternative fuel began to outgrow Sunfuels' capacity to manage and market it. When Jeff Probst joined the company in January 2003, he brought much needed experience in product and brand development and marketing from positions with Duracell, EcoLab, and Gould Electronics. As president and chief executive officer, Probst became a cofounder of the newly formed Blue Sun Biodiesel.

The development of Blue Sun Biodiesel coincided with greater public awareness of the benefits of mixing biodiesel with fossil-based diesel fuel. Social concerns, such as national energy independence, air pollution, and global climate change caused by greenhouse gases, prompted interest in renewable, clean energy options. Also, biodiesel delivered better performance, as enhanced lubricity reduced wear on the engine components, creating cleaner, cooler, and quieter operation. Higher cetane (diesel octane) gave the fuel quicker ignition for greater horsepower. In addition to being more compatible with conventional diesel fuel than ethanol with gasoline, biodiesel offered a lower ratio of energy use in production. For every unit of energy burned to produce biodiesel, 3.2 units of energy were created. The combined factors made biodiesel an attractive alternative to fossil-based fuels.

DEVELOPING CANOLA FEEDSTOCK AND SUPPLIER BASE

Commercial viability of biodiesel, in comparison to fossil fuels, required Blue Sun to reduce the cost of production. With oilseed feedstock accounting for 80 percent of manufacturing costs, Blue Sun sought to maximize oil extraction. Probst, along with scientists and researchers at Blue Sun, drove many miles across the high plains of eastern Colorado to talk to farmers in search of a base of raw material. They found Colorado farmers were cautious about new investments of their time and energy. Moreover, Blue Sun discovered that purchasing soybeans on the commodities market entailed wide fluctuations in pricing and required federal price supports. Farmers expressed interest in cultivating crops that would not require participation in the volatile commodities market.

Agricultural research determined that mustard plants, such as canola and camelina, would provide several economic advantages to Blue Sun as well as to farmers. First, they were ideal for the dry, high desert plains in eastern Colorado. Soybean seed was the primary source of raw oil needed to produce biodiesel. Canola, the preferred crop for fuel in Europe, provided about 45 percent of its weight in oil, in contrast to soybeans, which provided 20 percent oil. Hence, a higher ratio of oil extraction would reduce the cost of cultivation and require less land. Also, mustard plants could be grown during the winter fallow season, along with winter wheat. Farmers could therefore provide material for biodiesel production year-round. Because the strains of mustard chosen could be grown on marginal land, unsuitable for cultivating other crops, generating fuel feedstock would not interfere with the production of food for human consumption.

Blue Sun was unusual in its use of canola oil for biodiesel production in the United States, and that attracted a U.S. Department of Energy Small Business Innovative Research program grant to research mustard plants. The $2.2 million funding enabled the company to breed varieties of canola and camelina appropriate to agricultural regions of Colorado, Wyoming, and Nebraska. Working with researchers at Colorado State University in Fort Collins, Blue Sun opened a breeding facility in nearby Torrington, Wyoming, after receiving the grant in 2003.

Having found a crop with the potential to provide farm security, Blue Sun explored the idea of forming a cooperative to foster a mutually beneficial relationship between the company and farmers. Probst sought to develop an innovative form of cooperative, whereby farmer participation included equity interest in

KEY DATES

2001: Friendly get-together results in founding of Sunfuels, predecessor to Blue Sun.
2003: New CEO Jeff Probst facilitates development of oilseed feedstock and biodiesel distribution.
2006: Blue Sun introduces its proprietary B20 Fusion biodiesel.
2007: Company releases its first hybrid seed.

manufacturing and distribution of the biologically-based fuel, as well as a predetermined price for oilseed crop. Although the farmers might receive less money for the crop than on the commodities market, the "value-added" cooperative structure mitigated the overall risks of farming. The idea appealed to independent family farmers, because the additional income from biodiesel contributed to the profitability of small farms.

Rather than pursue conventional incorporation, Blue Sun Producers was formed in 2003 as a limited liability corporation, a legal structure that allowed the profits to go to the farmers prior to taxation. Probst believed that farmers needed to be paid first in order to attract their investment and ensure their survival. Blue Sun presented the cooperative idea to farmers throughout eastern Colorado. Despite encountering some reticence, the company successfully interested enough farmer-investors. In February 2004, the U.S. Department of Agriculture and Rural Development awarded Blue Sun Producers a $450,000 Value-Added Producer Grant to assist in the transition from soybeans to canola cultivation.

BLUE SUN DEVELOPS MANUFACTURING AND DISTRIBUTION NETWORK

To ensure the continuation of its cooperative structure, Blue Sun took an integrated approach to biodiesel production, seeking control over all aspects, from oilseed cultivation to processing, blending, and distribution. Blue Sun intended to build a processing and refining facility in Johnstown, Colorado, but snafus stalled the project. Instead, the company outsourced oil refining to contractors in the Midwest. Nevertheless, by late 2003 Blue Sun began retail distribution of its B20 biodiesel. Bartkus Oil Company fuel station, in Boulder, Colorado, began to offer Blue Sun fuel in September. Bartkus obtained business from individuals driving

diesel engine cars, such as Mercedes and Volkswagen models, as well as from the University of Colorado, and the City and County of Boulder. The Denver Regional Transportation District experimented with Blue Sun biodiesel, fueling 10 small, community buses in the Boulder area.

Retail stations throughout Colorado installed biodiesel fuel pumps, dispensing Blue Sun B20 biodiesel. In November the Shoco Oil fuel center, at the busy U.S. 85 and U.S. 6 crossroads in Commerce City, north of Denver, began offering the alternative fuel. The largest retail fuel station in the United States, Shoco provided biodiesel to Commerce City Public School District, as well as to individuals. The Heartland Town and Country Store, on U.S. Highway 34 in Fort Morgan, northwest of Denver, offered alternative fuels exclusively, including Blue Sun B20. The following summer 15 retail fueling stations installed biodiesel pumps. These included locations in Colorado Springs, Denver, Fort Collins, Fort Lupton, Pueblo, Carbondale, Durango, Sterling, and Greeley. Expansion in the public sector included the city of Colorado Springs, which implemented use of Blue Sun fuel in more than 2,400 city vehicles. Denver Public Schools converted its entire fleet to Blue Sun biodiesel in 2005. Colorado legislation in 2006 requiring state-owned vehicles to use alternative fuels supported continued expansion in the public sector.

Blue Sun continued to pursue opportunities to process fuel in Colorado. In October 2004 the company received a $500,000 Renewable Energy Systems grant from the U.S. Department of Agriculture to build a biodiesel processing plant and a blending plant. Development of the processing or refining plant, located in Alamosa on the agricultural high plains of southern Colorado, was stalled by local opposition. However, the company opened a blending and distribution terminal, where diesel and biodiesel were blended in an 80/20 ratio. Outfitted to fill tanker trucks or rail cars, the facility supplied Blue Sun B20 fuel for distribution throughout the western United States.

During 2005, Blue Sun expanded distribution to New Mexico, Utah, Wyoming, Nebraska, and Idaho. Blue Sun planned to develop distribution to all 14 western states, as biodiesel proved particularly useful for engines operating at high altitudes. Biodiesel did not require the use of sulfur for lubricity, thus its use reduced pollution as well as engine wear due to harmful deposits. Biodiesel improved horsepower, and fuel efficiency increased as much as 10 percent, even for trips traveling over mountain passes.

INNOVATIONS COME TO FRUITION IN FUEL AND FEEDSTOCK

From its inception, Blue Sun labored to develop an additive that would further improve the quality of its alternative fuel. Blue Sun's controls for fuel consistency and the quality of its product attracted participation by scientists at Cummins Engine Company. After four years of research and testing, Blue Sun introduced its Fusion blend in November 2006. Blue Sun B20 Fusion addressed problems associated with the use of biodiesel, such as clogged fuel filters. By fusing Blue Sun B100, pure biodiesel, with its proprietary additive, branded DTX, Blue Sun's B20 blend attained higher horsepower and fuel efficiency, as well as a reduction of tailpipe emissions. Moreover, DTX additive improved use of biodiesel for cold weather conditions as low as minus 20 degrees Fahrenheit. Vegetable-based diesel tended to gel in cold weather, but DTX reduced viscosity in all weather. Tested over more than 400 million road miles, Blue Sun Fusion exceeded ASTM specifications.

Higher-quality fuel provided Blue Sun with new revenue streams in specialty blends with higher biodiesel ratios, including B35, B50, and B70 fuels. Specialty fuels became popular in the mining industry, where lower emissions for underground equipment improved mine air quality. Also, Blue Sun Fusion improved the effectiveness of diesel engines used at high altitudes and in cold weather, such as snowplows used at ski resorts in Idaho, Washington, and Colorado.

Another breakthrough innovation at Blue Sun involved the introduction of hybrid spring camelina seed in the spring of 2007. The release marked the transition from experimentation to commercial production of Blue Sun's hybrid varieties. Spring camelina, a non-food crop, could be grown on land where most other plants wither, especially in drought conditions. Also, the hybrid strain of mustard provided farmers with a rotation crop for irrigated or non-irrigated fallow land.

PLANS ANTICIPATE NATIONAL EXPANSION

With sources of raw material in place and market expansion continuing, Blue Sun pursued development of a new fuel processing project that would meet potential demand for biodiesel. The company formed a joint venture with ARES Corporation, an engineering firm with which the company began collaboration on fuel processing technology. The venture combined the Burlingame, California, company's fuel processing and project management talent with Blue Sun's high-quality fuel and oilseed technology. ARES Blue Sun planned to build biodiesel production facilities across North America. The first facility, located in Clovis, New Mexico, near ARES' Albuquerque office, was expected to carry annual production capacity of 15 million gallons of pure biodiesel.

To fund the project, Blue Sun turned to private sources for investment. After a proposed merger with M-Wave disintegrated, the company raised $20 million in private investment during 2007 and obtained a $3 million unsecured loan through a private source in early 2008. The company hoped to attain a credit instrument to further fund refinery development.

In anticipation of continued growth, Blue Sun created a chief operations officer position, filled by Michael Miller, who brought 15 years experience in the gas and oil industry to the company's next stage of growth. Lafferty, company founder and former operations manager, took the position of vice president of technology and strategic projects.

Blue Sun continued to expand into new uses and new markets. Aquila Energy, a power company in Pueblo, Colorado, began using Blue Sun in its power generators in 2007, and experienced an 86 percent reduction in mechanical problems. Corporate Express, a major business products company, and Republic National Distributing Company, the nation's second largest premium beer and wine distributor, began using Blue Sun Fusion in May 2008. Retail fuel stations in Santa Fe, New Mexico, and Wenatchee, Washington, began offering Blue Sun B20 Fusion.

In 2008 Blue Sun ranked number 242 on the *Inc.* 500 list of the fastest-growing private companies in the nation. For companies in the energy industry, Blue Sun ranked number 10. Revenues at Blue Sun grew 1,078 percent during the four years from 2004 to 2007, increasing from $1.2 million to $14.1 million.

Although Blue Sun intended to expand nationwide, the company's growth was restricted to the West. New retail locations opened in Cheyenne, Wyoming, and in Steamboat Springs and Golden, Colorado. Coleman Oil expected expansion to continue along the border of Washington and Idaho, in Coeur d'Alene, Spokane, and Sandpoint. A seed-crushing plant in Oklahoma was in the proposal stage. In anticipation of potential involvement in other alternative energy developments, the company changed its name to Blue Sun Energy in early 2009.

Mary Tradii

PRINCIPAL SUBSIDIARIES

ARES Blue Sun, Inc. (50%); Blue Sun Biodiesel, LLC; Blue Sun Producers, Inc.

PRINCIPAL COMPETITORS

Archer Daniels Midland Company; Cargill, Inc.; Horizon Biofuels Corporation; Pacific Biodiesel, Inc.; Renewable Energy Group.

FURTHER READING

"Biodiesel Fuel Exceeds ASTM Specifications," *Product News Network,* November 29, 2006.

"Blue Sun Biodiesel Continues to Open Retail Fueling Locations," *Space Daily,* May 14, 2008.

"Blue Sun Biodiesel Fastest Growing Biodiesel Provider," *Space Daily,* August 23, 2008.

Bushbaum, Lee, "Energy Innovators: Colorado Companies Squeeze Fuel from Crops and Coal," *Colorado Biz,* January 2006, p. 42.

Chakrabarty, Gargi, "Blue Sun Shines in Biodiesel Fuel Study," *Rocky Mountain News,* August 25, 2005, p. 2B.

"Colorado's First All Biofuels Retail Station Opens in Fort Morgan," *Brush News Tribune,* January 28, 2004.

Hartman, Todd, "Biodiesel Gets a Leg Up—Legislation Requires State-Owned Vehicles to Use Alternative Fuel," *Rocky Mountain News,* May 4, 2006, p. 25A.

Howell, Parker, "More Biodiesel Coming to Area—Lewiston Distributor to Set Up Stations with Card-Lock Fuel Pumps," *Spokesman Review,* December 13, 2007.

Lundeen, Tim, "Companies Add to Biodiesel Capacity," *Feedstuffs,* March 10, 2003, p. 31.

Raabe, Steve, "Fuel Firm Spreading the Word: Mustard," *Denver Post,* January 2, 2004, p. C1.

Schwab, Robert, "Crops Fuel Pumps That Could Save Colorado Farms," *ColoradoBiz,* December 2003, p. 9.

Thompson, Stephen, "Biodiesel with Altitude: Colorado's Blue Sun Co-op Grows Rapeseed for Biodiesel Production," *Rural Cooperatives,* November–December 2004, p. 4.

"United States: Growing Camelina Could Bring $80 Million to Colorado's Economy," *TendersInfo,* July 24, 2008.

The Boston Beer
Company, Inc.

One Design Center Place, Suite 850
Boston, Massachusetts 02210
U.S.A.
Telephone: (617) 368-5000
Toll Free: (800) 372-1131
Fax: (617) 368-5500
Web site: http://www.bostonbeer.com

Public Company
Incorporated: 1984
Employees: 775
Sales: $449.55 million (2008)
Stock Exchanges: New York
Ticker Symbol: SAM
NAICS: 312120 Breweries

■ ■ ■

The Boston Beer Company, Inc., is the largest craft brewer and the fourth-largest brewer overall in the United States, producing 2.3 million barrels of beer annually. The company sells more than 20 beers under the Samuel Adams or Sam Adams brand names, including its flagship offering, Samuel Adams Boston Lager, an all-malt Pilsner-style beer based on a 100-year-old formulation. Boston Beer also markets seven flavored malt beverage products under the Twisted Tea brand name and one hard cider product under the HardCore brand name. The company's products are made at three company-owned breweries in Ohio, Pennsylvania, and Massachusetts, and through agreements with breweries in North Carolina, New York, Pennsylvania, and Wisconsin.

1984: FOUNDED ON LIFE
SAVINGS AND HARD WORK

Boston Beer Company was founded by C. James Koch (pronounced Cook), a Cincinnati native who moved to Boston to study at Harvard's law and business schools. In the early 1980s, Koch (descended from five generations of brewmasters) noticed an increase in the sales of imported beers. In April 1984, with $100,000 of his own savings, $140,000 from supportive family and friends, and the sales savvy of Rhonda L. Kallman (his former secretary and, eventually, company marketing vice president), 33-year-old Koch quit his well-paying job as management consultant to Boston Consulting Group. Armed with a recipe formulated by his great-great-grandfather, St. Louis-based brewer Louis Koch, the young James Koch derived a beer that was more full-bodied than typical U.S. brews. Koch's recipe adhered to rigorous German beer purity laws that demanded top-quality ingredients and long brewing and fermentation periods. After cooking up the first few batches on his kitchen stove, Koch contracted with 30-year-veteran Pittsburgh Brewing Co. to manufacture his brown-bottled, premium lager in their modern plant. Door-to-door marketing of the new beer began in downtown Boston in 1985, netting Koch a customer base of 25 restaurants and bars. Shipments of Samuel Adams Boston Lager were underway by April. Ironically, Koch was unable to find a distributor willing to carry his product, so he was forced to buy a truck and do it himself.

Because of the brew's high retail cost ($20 per case, against Heineken's $17), these first sales were the hardest. Koch and Kallman used a personal approach by encouraging bartenders to sample their product and explaining why Samuel Adams was a higher-quality brew from a better company. Their dogged persistence eventually won over the New England market. By 1987 the company was poised to enter the finicky Manhattan market where, Koch contended in the *Wall Street Journal,* "New Yorkers are well behind other cities in accepting quality American beers." He added, "But we've done so well elsewhere, we're ready to invest the time and money in educating New York." By 1988, Koch and Kallman had such a strong sales base that they were able to acquire $3 million from an investment banking firm for the purchase of an old brewery within Boston's Jamaica Plain section. Although efforts to establish a full-scale brewing operation there were quickly nixed because of the prohibitive costs associated with outfitting a brewery, the location would serve as a research and development facility, as well as a tourist attraction.

1990–92: BOSTON BEER GOES NATIONAL

Boston Beer soon saw its distribution networks grow to include Washington, D.C., and Chicago. In 1990, as part of its controlled, targeted expansion strategy, the company further expanded its market by reaching an agreement with Portland, Oregon-based Blitz-Weinhart Brewing to brew and distribute its product in the western United States. It also opened the Samuel Adams Brew House in Philadelphia. Distribution increased in 1992, when California's Pacific Wine Co. agreed to distribute Boston Beer products on the West Coast. With distribution encompassing the 48 contiguous states, Koch watched 1992 sales increase 63 percent to $48.2 million, resulting in net income of $1.6 million.

Since upscale U.S. beer drinkers' tastes ran strongly to imports, marketing a new high-end brew required some creativity. As early as 1986, Koch earmarked a large portion of the company budget for marketing. He composed some quirky radio advertisements promoting the quality of his product. He also did some flag-waving, touting Samuel Adams as a Made-in-the-U.S.A. alternative to pricey foreign brews. More importantly, Koch recognized the value in focusing his efforts on a specific market segment, rather than the general beer-drinking public. In addition to such catchy slogans as "Declare Your Independence from Foreign Beer," his ads were also an impassioned attempt to educate listeners about beer in general and about what made Samuel Adams unique.

However, Samuel Adams's rise to the top had stronger foundations than the flurry of interest generated by a clever ad campaign. Boston Beer made a quality product. The company used only four age-old ingredients—hops, malt, yeast, and water—a time-honored four-vessel, all-malt process, and a secondary fermentation process called krausening to create a smoother brew. Use of relatively rare European-grown Hallertau Mittelfrueh, Spalt Spalt, Saaz, and Tettnang hops provided a distinctive aroma and spicy edge. Boston Beer watched its flagship brand win numerous awards at Denver's annual Great American Beer Festival and more medals at the 1994 World Beer Championship than any other brew. Tellingly, Koch's 1993 advertising campaign, which claimed his product as the best beer in the United States "four years running," unleashed arguments and threats of litigation by rival microbrewers in an increasingly competitive beer industry. Similarly, ads claiming that Samuel Adams was the sole U.S. beer imported into Germany ruffled feathers of more than one competitor who maintained a European market for their product. Ultimately, the hue and cry over Koch's advertising strengthened the name recognition of his company's product as consumers went to the bar to find out what all the fuss was about.

Due to both clever ad strategies and quality products, Boston Beer watched its production increase from 294,000 barrels in 1992 to 714,000 by 1994. From 1992 to 1993 the company expanded its employee base from 87 to 110; and the following year 170 people worked to produce and promote Boston Beer products. These increases in production and staff

KEY DATES

1983: C. James Koch starts The Boston Beer Company with Rhonda L. Kallman.
1985: Koch and Kallman sell the first cases of Samuel Adams Boston Lager.
1986: The White House receives its first Samuel Adams delivery.
1988: Boston Beer starts brewing in its Jamaica Plain brewery in Boston.
1990: Company begins brewing at the Blitz-Weinhard Brewing Company, in Portland, Oregon.
1993: Koch's aggressive advertising campaign causes competitors to threaten litigation.
1995: Boston Beer goes public.
1996: American Airlines selects Samuel Adams Boston Lager as its in-flight beer for first- and business-class passengers on transcontinental flights.
1997: Company buys an historic Cincinnati brewery.
1998: Boston Beer signs a distribution agreement for Japan.
2000: Company launches BoDean's Twisted Tea, a malt- and tea-based beverage.
2001: President Martin Roper is named CEO, succeeding Koch, who remains chairman.
2002: Company launches Samuel Adams Light, a new lower-calorie and lower-alcohol beverage.
2007: Boston Beer agrees to acquire a brewery in Breinigsville, Pennsylvania, for $55 million.
2008: Voluntary recall of certain Samuel Adams products contributes to a substantial decline in net income.

were the result of increased sales; the company's sales staff personally contacted customers whose collective beer tab earned the brewer a net income of more than $9 million. Well trained in brewing techniques (all company employees were required to spend a day brewing beer in Boston) company salespeople continually educated retailers about the quality of the company's products.

As sales and profits increased, so did the money the company allotted to advertising. Boston Beer sponsored bar beer nights that featured Samuel Adams giveaways including T-shirts and caps, distributed coasters, table

cards, restaurant umbrellas, and menu boards. To increase public exposure, the company also donated its products to charity events. Samuel Adams was served at each of the social balls and dinners that accompanied President Bill Clinton's ascension to the presidency in 1993. By 1995, along with other microbreweries including Mistik Beverages, Boston Beer began to consider the benefits of a television advertising campaign to promote its product; television testing was still underway through 1996.

1995: GOING PUBLIC

Prompted by its forward momentum, Boston Beer made the decision to go public in 1995, offering 3.1 million shares in November. Of those, it held back 990,000 shares, directing these toward its loyal customers. These customers included not only the bar owners, shop owners, and wholesalers who distributed company products; every six-pack of Samuel Adams sold at retail came with a mail-in coupon for discounted shares in Boston Beer's growing operation. More than 130,000 customers were quick to invest in a piece of their favorite brew. By the close of the year, the company reported net income of $5.9 million on revenues of $151.3 million. Production was a record 961,000 barrels divided among an increasing array of products that included Samuel Adams Brand Ale, Boston Lager, Cream Stout, Honey Porter, and Triple Bock, as well as such tempting seasonal variations as Cranberry Iambic and Winter Lager. In addition, the company produced and marketed beers under the Boston Lightship brand. The Oregon Original brands, brewed by the company-owned Oregon Ale and Beer Company, had also been introduced to most major markets by 1995.

Not surprisingly, Boston Beer's success spawned a host of imitators. In fact, throughout the early 1990s, approximately 55 new breweries were established each year. Of these, the company perceived a real threat in the similarly named Boston Beer Works. Although Boston Beer would sue the coattail brewery, it lost the suit in 1994.

Much of the success of Boston Beer was its ability to foster and stay on top of a niche market for the second-most popular beverage in the world (the first being tea). Unlike other microbrewers—skilled craftspeople who prided themselves on small-batch production and local distribution, often eschewing the "business" side of the business by leaving advertising to word of mouth—Boston Beer was ambitious. A tiger in the industry, it went for the jugular, directly challenging high-priced imports including Heineken, St. Pauli Girl, and Beck's. Strategically avoiding head-to-head combat with such domestic giants as Miller Brewery, Anheuser-

Busch, and Budweiser, whose highly financed promotional "lifestyle" campaigns featured frogs, dogs, and buxom, bikini-clad beach babes, Boston Beer aimed for a share of the import market. Instead of gearing its product toward 20-something middle-class males, Samuel Adams targeted connoisseurs, beer aficionados with an eye for quality and a taste for an exceptional product. Advertising the weaknesses of imported beers, namely, that foreign brews headed for the United States had fewer premium ingredients, a "lighter" taste, and were less fresh because of long shipping times (like other perishable foodstuffs, beer "goes sour" and loses its flavor and quality after as little as four months), the company prided itself on the quality of ingredients and brewing skill it brought to its products. By directly tackling the premium imports, Boston Beer created a new marketing niche, domestically brewed premium beer, and assumed a leadership position within the growing specialty beer market.

In addition to encouraging other beer-brewing entrepreneurs, the major U.S. breweries did not respond to the advances made by Boston-based upstart Koch by lying down. Watching a segment of a relentlessly sluggish beer market mushroom almost overnight would tantalize any businessperson. Beer giants Anheuser-Busch, Coors, and the Philip Morris–owned Miller Brewery used their leverage to try to restrict the supply of raw materials and national distribution network of the entire microbrewery industry, a $400 million market divided among almost 500 brewers by 1994. Their efforts forced many craft brewers to confine their distribution within regional markets, with a select few becoming the targets of takeovers as the giants maneuvered for a piece of the growing microbrew pie.

LEADER OF MICROBREWING INDUSTRY

The "if you can't beat 'em, join 'em" strategy proved to be increasingly popular. Adopting an array of small-scale guises, such as Miller's nonexistent Plank Road Brewery (Miller's original name in 1855), the major breweries attempted to cash in on the micro movement by introducing a battery of so-called craft beers into the high-end marketplace. Aesthetically appealing labels proclaiming brands such as Red Dog, Killian, Blue Moon, Elk Mountain, Eisbock, Leinenkugel, Red Wolf House, and Augsburger filled retail beer shelves and popped up in point-of-sale tavern displays. Even importers responded to the competition by distributing "micros" of their own, such as Heineken's Tarwebok and Labatt's Moretti La Rossa.

In its position as microbrewery industry leader, Boston Beer encouraged cultivation of the brewmeister's

art. In 1995 it organized the first annual World Homebrew Championships, a summer gathering of 60 judges entrusted with the task of choosing the best among brews from around the world. Three category winners were announced in 1996 and their brews successfully marketed by the company under the names Long-Shot American Pale Ale, LongShot Hazelnut Brown Ale, and LongShot Black Lager. Meanwhile, Koch continued to indulge in the brewer's art, deriving new brews for the discerning palate. During 1995 he introduced three new products, Scotch Ale, Cherry Wheat Ale, and Old Fezziwig Ale, increasing the company's product line to 14. Triple Bock, first introduced in 1994, was a dark, sherry-like barley beer aged in oak casks. An acquired taste, it was a sipping beer boasting a 17 percent alcohol level. Boston Beer's spicy Cherry Wheat Ale, introduced as a seasonal brew, became an annual product due to customer demand. The second World Homebrew Contest generated a second series of LongShot beers, which were available in limited quantities in select markets, but in 1997, the contest itself was put on hiatus.

Despite its ranking as one of the top 10 brewers in the United States, Boston Brewery prided itself on being a small fish in an ocean containing a few large sharks; in the mid-1990s, the combined sales of the entire U.S. microbrewery industry accounted for less revenue than the total sales of Michelob Light in any one year. In a market dominated by a handful of giants, tenth-ranked Boston Brewery was, in the words of Koch, "like being the 12th largest car company." Anheuser-Busch's production had reached the millionth barrel by the first week of the year, Koch explained to Greg W. Prince in the December 1994 issue of *Beverage World*. "When I tell people we're one five-hundredth of the beer business … [they] are surprised at how small we really are."

1996–97: THE MARKET SLIDES, FROM PEAK TO SOGGY

Although Boston Beer's third quarter of 1996 once again showed record results, the 294,000 barrels sold were fewer than the company had expected for its product line, sending mini-shockwaves throughout the microbrewery industry. Other small-scale brewers, many of which were fledgling operations, wondered if the wave they had been riding had crested. Even as the overall beer market continued to stagnate because of the increasing influence of health-conscious consumers, the market for upscale craft beers remained on an ascent, albeit one not quite as steep because these same consumers expressed a clear preference for quality malt liquor products when they chose to indulge. On the strength of third-quarter net sales of $46.1 million, the company went ahead with the planned purchase of Cincinnati's historic Hudepohl-Schoenling Brewing Co., its midwest contract brewery. Also in 1997, HardCore Cider Company, an affiliate of Boston Beer, launched HardCore Crisp Hard Cider and HardCore Apple Cranberry Cider in 11 cities nationwide.

Throughout 1996, beer sales began to level off across the board, with both micros and large brewers posting more moderate increases in sales. Feeling an especially acute pinch due to lackluster Budweiser earnings, Anheuser-Busch fronted a group complaint to the Bureau of Alcohol, Tobacco and Firearms (BATF) leveled against Boston Beer, Pete's Brewing Co. (makers of Pete's Wicked Ale), and fellow top-gun brewer Miller. Accusing the two micros of false advertising in their reported claims to brew "in small batches" instead of through large-scale contracted breweries, Busch and associates also demanded that Miller's parentage of both Icehouse and Red Dog be legitimized on the label rather than cloaked by its fictitious alter ego, the Plank Road Brewery.

In retaliation, in March 1996 Boston Beer petitioned the BATF to request "full disclosure" on all beer labels. This would end the widespread use of encoded freshness dates and require point-of-product origin to be clearly identified. Boston Beer had been among only a handful of brewers to print encoded freshness dates on its products, a practice it initiated in 1989. The brewer also accepted product returns after expiration dates had been reached. Boston Beer's move to raise industry accountability to its own standards quickly received the nod from *Consumer Reports,* which praised both the company's packaging and product by voting Samuel Adams the best in the United States in its 1996 craft-brewed ale taste test.

Furthermore, in April 1997, an advertising-industry watchdog resolved a dispute between Anheuser-Busch and Boston Beer. The Budweiser brewer protested the Samuel Adams claim that the company's beer came from New England, when it was also produced by contract brewers in the Midwest. The National Advertising Division, an arm of the Council of Better Business Bureaus, decided that Busch's ads, questioning the brand's New England heritage and high price, were not accurate.

Around this time Boston Beer also began efforts to bring its brew home to Boston by purchasing an abandoned brewery that it slated for renovation and planned for operation by January 1997. Meanwhile, the regional distribution of company-contracted brewing sites—which included Pittsburgh Brewing Co., upstate New York's F.X. Matt Brewing Co. and Genesee Brew-

ing Co., Cincinnati's Hudepohl-Schoenling Brewing Co., and the Stroh-owned Blitz-Weinhart—continued to ensure the freshness of its products to its large customer base outside the greater Boston area. However, Boston Beer pulled out of its contract with Pittsburgh Brewing after 1988, and in July 2001, Boston Beer and Hudepohl-Schoenling Brewing Company announced that they were not renewing their contract brewing agreement. Nevertheless in February 1999, Pabst Brewing Company assured Boston Beer that it would continue Boston's brewing contract with Stroh upon completion of the proposed sale of Stroh brands and brewing assets to Pabst.

Boston Beer also entered into a working relationship with Seagram Beverage Company. Under the terms of the agreement, in exchange for ownership of both trademark and trade name and future royalties on sales, the company agreed to aid the liquor giant in 1997 with the development and marketing of its new Devil Mountain craft beer line. Commanding a sales force of 115 people by 1996, Boston Beer began to introduce its product line internationally in Germany, Ireland, Japan, and Hong Kong. In May 1996 the company signed an agreement with England's Whitbread PLC to aid the United Kingdom's fourth-largest brewery in the development of a craft brew that catered to British tastes. The company also literally took to the skies, as Samuel Adams became American Airlines' in-flight beer on transcontinental flights beginning in mid-1996. Although pleased to have acquired an international profile, the company's efforts remained concentrated upon its domestic market. Its goals continued to be educating the consumer and developing a taste for a top-quality beer while maintaining profitability.

1998–2002: FIGHTING FLAT SALES

In 1997, the tide began to turn for the industry. Boston Beer was still experiencing growth but not the 30 to 40 percent increases the company had seen over the past five years. Smaller brewers were consolidating. In February 1998, Koch predicted on CNN that the next few years would be difficult for the smaller craft brewers. Although the healthiest of microbreweries, even Boston Beer was seeing sales and earnings fall. Looking at the saturated high-end beer market, industry analysts predicted that Boston Beer would survive because it was the only microbrewer with a national franchise. Also in 1998, as the company celebrated its 10-year anniversary since Boston Beer Company started brewing in its Jamaica Plain brewery, it introduced Samuel Adams Boston IPA, a traditional British India Pale Ale.

On January 28, 1999, addressing the bust that had hit the industry for the past two years, with Boston

Beer's stock at less than half its $20 initial public offering (IPO) price, Steven Syre wrote in the *Boston Globe,* "Boston Beer has taken no disastrous wrong turns or missed any great opportunities on the way to this predicament. It is stuck in a consumer category that lost some of its cachet and may be fighting an uphill demographic battle." The market for specialty beers in the 1990s had expanded to include not only yuppie businesspeople but also 20-something drinkers as well. These younger drinkers had gained their more sophisticated taste for malt liquors on the strength of the craft beer renaissance, a phenomenon directly attributable to Koch and Boston Beer. Industry analysts attributed Boston Beer's flat performance to competition from high-end imports such as Heineken and Corona. "Imports stole their thunder," trade newsletter editor Benj Steinman told the *Boston Globe* in the aforementioned article. "The core user base was never that large. So once they weren't expanding the experimental customer base it was tough to grow. A lot of their growth had come from trial customers." That year, Boston Beer expanded its sports marketing tie-ins, such as a March basketball promotion with ESPN.

The company posted an 8 percent volume increase in the first quarter of 2000. A contributing factor was the early 2000 launch of BoDean's Twisted Tea, a malt- and tea-based beverage. Also that year, Boston Beer and craft brewer Sleeman Breweries of Canada joined forces; Sleeman would represent the flagship Samuel Adams brand in Canada, and Boston Beer would conduct market research in the States to uncover possible markets for Sleeman brand products. In 2000, the company also undertook an effort to ensure freshness by buying back all out-of-code Samuel Adams for the month of March, an expenditure of about $2 million. (The distributor usually absorbed this cost.) Everything was recycled, the glass, the packaging, and even the beer, which was fermented into ethanol, an environmentally friendly additive for gasoline.

In January 2001, Martin Roper was named CEO, replacing Koch, who retained the title of chairman. In the second quarter of that year, the company saw an increase in gross profit margin, which it attributed to factors such as increased pricing and changes to the product mix. In July of that year, the company kicked off test-marketing for a Samuel Adams Light product in Providence, Rhode Island, and Portland, Maine, with the tagline, "Taste the revolution." On July 24, 2001, beer newsletter editor Steinman told the *Boston Globe*'s Chris Reidy, "There's a bit of a disconnect, but it's sort of a necessity for full-bodied Samuel Adams to pursue the light beer category; it's sensible given the lower-calorie/lower-alcohol sector's potential for growth." By January 2002, after test-market success, Samuel Adams

Light arrived in New England bars and restaurants, and would land in stores that March. The new brew set a record in the Reduced Calorie Lager Category in December 2001 at Chicago's World Beer Championships. "We've worked for years to develop a recipe that offers the flavor and drinkability that beer lovers want," Koch said, describing the beer's two-row malt and German Noble hops. "The world's best ingredients give Sam Light a flavor and complexity never before found in light beer."

FINANCIAL GROWTH RESUMES IN 2002

The introduction of Sam Adams Light helped invigorate sales, ushering in an era of revitalized growth at Boston Beer. By mid-2003, one year after the debut of Sam Adams Light, two million cases of the brand had been sold, giving the company a 14 percent share of what it termed the "better light beer" market. "When Sam Adams Lager came out, all domestic beers were pretty similar," Koch said in the May 2003 issue of *Beverage World.* "It opened up a whole new space for beer. Sam Adams Light is a new paradigm for light beer. My hope was that Sam Adams Light would revolutionize light beer in the same way that Sam Adams Lager revolutionized domestic beer."

Boston Beer shipped 1.29 million barrels in 2002, enabling it to post record sales for the year. Sales climbed to $215 million, ending a six-year period of stagnant revenue growth and marking the start of an equally long period of robust growth. Koch struggled to find the right marketing approach to attract a new, younger generation of Samuel Adams aficionados. "I know that Sam Adams still stands for quality, passion, authenticity, and innovation, but I don't know how to communicate that to a 23-year-old," he said in the September 1, 2003 issue of *Business Week.* Nevertheless, Boston Beer enjoyed success. Between 2003 and 2006, craft beer sales in the United States increased 31.5 percent, generating $4.7 billion in sales, and Boston Beer, as the dominant player among the nation's 1,400 small breweries, benefited from the rising popularity of the product category. The company unveiled several new varieties during the period, introducing Samuel Adams Hefeweizen in 2003, Samuel Adams Black Lager in 2005, and Samuel Adams Brown Ale in 2006, as well as new blends of its flavored malt beverage line. Revenues, stuck in the $200 million range for years, began to rise vigorously. Between 2002 and 2006, Boston Beer added $100 million to its annual volume, generating $315 million in sales in 2006 and recording $18.2 million in net income.

A NEW BREWERY, A RECALL, AND ECONOMIC MALAISE

As Boston Beer entered 2007, the mood was buoyant at company headquarters. The year would produce record financial totals, $380 million in sales and $22.5 million in net income, and it would see Koch announce plans for the addition of a brewery, something he had not done since purchasing the Cincinnati-based brewery in 1997. Koch and Roper flirted with the idea of constructing a new, $200 million brewery in Freetown, Massachusetts, but those plans were shelved when Boston Beer signed an agreement in April 2007 to acquire an existing brewery in Breinigsville, Pennsylvania. The company paid $55 million for the facility, which was expected to increase brewing capacity by 1.6 million barrels annually, and began renovating the plant, spending more than $5 million to get it ready for a June 2008 opening. As the celebratory occasion neared, however, Koch and Roper made an announcement that negated the momentum built up during the previous five years.

In April 2008, Boston Beer announced a voluntary recall of some of its beer. A routine quality control inspection at its Cincinnati brewery revealed that a run of 12-ounce bottles potentially contained small grains of glass. The recall, announced one month after Boston Beer released its rousing financial results for 2007, negatively affected the company's profit total in 2008. Despite a 17 percent increase in sales in 2008, Boston Beer's net income plummeted from $22.5 million to $8.1 million.

The recall was a temporary setback for the company, but a threat with potentially far greater staying power appeared at roughly the same time Koch and Roper watched their profits slide. A global economic crisis at the end of the decade created uncertain time for all businesses, Boston Beer included. Koch, in a May 15, 2008 interview with *Beverage World*, looked at Boston Beer's past to offer a sense of the future his company faced. "In the early 1990s there were a lot of brands flooding the market; some of them were good, others had audacious names and some were a little gimmicky. A lot of those lesser beers fell by the wayside when the category slowed in the late 1990s. The recent growth the craft category has been experiencing in the past four or five years feels different to me. It feels sturdier, and it feels as if it's driven by the drinker's real preference and appreciation for great beer. Of course, I don't have a crystal ball. I think the demand will continue to rise, but with our economy so uncertain, and prices for ingredients and transportation fuels skyrocketing, there are no certainties."

Pamela L. Shelton
Updated, Michelle Feder; Jeffrey L. Covell

PRINCIPAL SUBSIDIARIES

BBC Brands, LLC; BBC Keg Company, LLC; Boston Beer Corporation; Boston Beer Corporation Canada Inc.; Boston Brewing Company, Inc.; Freetown Acquisition Company, LLC; SABC Realty, Ltd.; Samuel Adams Brewery Company, Ltd.; Providence Street Associates, LLC; Samuel Adams Pennsylvania Brewery Company.

PRINCIPAL COMPETITORS

Anheuser-Busch InBev; Heineken USA Inc.; Miller-Coors LLC; Pyramid Breweries Inc.; Craft Brewers Alliance, Inc.

FURTHER READING

Asimov, Eric, "Beer from Boston Brewery Makes Its Way to New York," *Wall Street Journal*, June 24, 1987.

"Boston Beer Appoints CEO to Replace Koch," *Boston Globe*, February 2, 2001, p. C4.

"Boston Beer Co. Buys Pennsylvania Brewery," *Beverage Industry*, August 2007, p. 12.

"Boston Beer Sees the Light," *Beverage Aisle*, September 2001, p. 8.

"Busch to Bottle Up Ads Targeting Rival," *Newsday*, April 1, 1997, p. A43.

Cioletti, Jeff, "Still Crafty After All These Years," *Beverage World*, November 15, 2006, p. 30.

Hill, Sam, and Glenn Rifkin, *Radical Marketing: From Harvard to Harley, Lessons from Ten That Broke the Rules and Made It Big*, New York: HarperBusiness, 2000, 304 p.

Holson, Laura M., "Private Sector; The Shows Must Go On," *New York Times*, August 12, 2001, Money and Business, p. 2.

Karolefski, John, "Boston Brewin'," *BrandMarketing* (Supplement to *Supermarket News*), April 7, 1997, p. l.

Kelley, Brad, "Boston Beer Co.," *Investor's Business Daily*, June 11, 2007, p. A5.

Khermouch, Gerry, "Keeping the Froth on Sam Adams," *Business Week*, September 1, 2003, p. 54.

Krass, Peter, ed., *Industry Leaders Speak Their Minds: The Conference Board Challenge to Business*, John Wiley & Sons, 2000.

Landi, Heather, "A Revolutionary Brewer," *Beverage World*, May 15, 2008, p. 34.

Mamis, Robert A., "Market Maker," *Inc.*, December 1995.

McCarthy, Michael, "Oops!" *USA Today,* August 28, 2001, p. 3B.

McCune, Jenny C., "Finding Your Niche," *Small Business Reports,* January 1994.

Melcher, Richard A., "Those New Brews Have the Blues," *Business Week,* March 9, 1998, p. 40.

Morris, Valerie, "Brewer of Samuel Adams Beer," *CNN,* Transcript #97081502FN-L17, August 15, 1997.

Prince, Greg W., "Little Giants," *Beverage World,* December 1994.

———, "Solid Ground." *Beverage Aisle,* June 15, 2001, p. 52.

Reidy, Chris, "Anheuser-Busch Agrees to Modify Ads Targeting Sam Adams," *Boston Globe,* April 1, 1997, p. C2.

———, "Boston Beer Chooses New Advertising Agency," *Boston Globe,* August 4, 1998, p. C9.

———, "Boston Beer Company Tests Product in Maine," *Boston Globe,* July 24, 2001.

Richardson, Tyrone, "Boston Beer Set to Brew," *Morning Call,* June 7, 2008.

Rosenberg, Ronald, "IPO, Entrepreneur Hopes to Brew Interest on 'Net," *Boston Globe,* March 18, 1998, p. D4.

Syre, Steven, "Fighting Flat Sales," *Boston Globe,* January 28, 1999, p. Dl.

Theodore, Sarah, "The Next Generation: Having Secured the Top Spot Among Craft Beers, Boston Beer Co. Finds a New Segment to Take On," *Beverage Industry,* May 2003, p. 32.

Thierry, Lauren, "CEO of Boston Beer," *CNN,* Transcript #98022618FN-L03, February 26, 1998.

Turcsik, Richard, "Boston Beer, ESPN Team Up," *BrandMarketing,* March 1999, p. 8.

"US: Boston Beer Company Cheers Strong End to 2007," *just-drinks.com,* March 12, 2008.

"US: Boston Beer Company Launches Product Recall," *just-drinks.com,* April 8, 2008.

"US: Boston Beer Company Sees Product Recall Hammer FY Profits," *just-drinks.com,* March 13, 2009.

Braskem

Braskem S.A.

———————— ∎ ————————

Avenida das Nações Unidas 8501
São Paulo, São Paulo 05425-070
Brazil
Telephone: (55 11) 3576-9000
Fax: (55 11) 3576-9532
Web site: http://www.braskem.com.br

Public Company
Incorporated: 2002
Employees: 3,410
Sales: BRL 23.02 billion ($12.51 billion) (2008)
Stock Exchanges: São Paulo Madrid New York
Ticker Symbols: BRKM; XBRM; BAK
NAICS: 325110 Petrochemical Manufacturing; 325181
    Alkalies and Chlorine Manufacturing; 325211
    Plastics Material and Resin Manufacturing

∎∎∎

Braskem S.A. is Latin America's leading petrochemical producer and the third-largest Brazilian-owned private-sector industrial company. In Braskem's manufacturing processes, basic feedstocks (principally naphtha) yield basic petrochemicals, such as ethylene and propylene, which are converted into thermoplastic resins such as polyethylene, polypropylene, and polyvinyl chloride (PVC). These resins are used by a variety of companies called converters to produce an array of finished products, including disposable containers and other plastic products, synthetic fibers, and synthetic rubber. Braskem also produces related chemicals such as hydrogen and chlorine.

Although controlled by Odebrecht S.A., Latin America's largest engineering and contracting company, Braskem has significant minority participation from Petróleo Brasileiro S.A. (Petrobrás), the state-owned entity that provides it with much of the naphtha and natural gas it needs to convert these feedstocks to basic petrochemicals at Braskem's crackers in the industrial complexes at Camaçari, Bahia, and Triunfo, Rio Grande do Sul. These are then used to produce thermoplastic resins. Braskem produces slightly more than half of Brazil's output of polyethylene, polypropylene, and PVC. The bulk of the remainder is manufactured by Quattor Participações S.A., which also has significant minority participation from Petrobrás and also largely depends on that company for its feedstocks.

COPENE, A PETROCHEMICALS COMPLEX SERVING BRAZIL'S NORTHEAST: 1972–88

The heart of what became Braskem was the state-owned Petroquímica do Nordeste Copene Ltda., established in 1972 to plan, execute, and coordinate the activities at Camaçari in Brazil's underdeveloped northeast. This company, incorporated in 1974 under the name Copene Petroquímica do Nordeste S.A., was responsible for the Camaçari infrastructure. Copene was a subsidiary of Petrobrás Química S.A. (Petroquísa), a subsidiary of Petrobrás. Although Petroquísa controlled Copene and three other central companies, some 32 privately owned ones were committed to building plants in the complex.

The construction of the Camaçari complex, completed in 1978, formed part of a policy to diversify the geographical distribution of Brazil's industrial assets and promote economic growth across different regions. The Petrobrás refinery nearby, the largest in Brazil, refined crude oil into subproducts such as gasoline, diesel oil, and naphtha. Naphtha, plus natural gas, then provided the raw material for a Copene-built petrochemical complex whose core unit was an ethylene plant. Copene also constructed a utility center furnishing the complex with water, electricity, and industrial gases. Ten years later, the Camaçari complex was accounting for 55 percent of Brazil's petrochemical production.

ODEBRECHT'S VITAL ROLE IN COPENE: 1990–2000

Odebrecht entered the petrochemical business as part of a consortium, along with Petroquísa and a Japanese company, that founded Companhia Petroquímica de Camaçari (CPC). This company established a plant that began operations in 1979 in the state of Alagoas to produce PVC and became the leading producer of the resin in Brazil. Odebrecht became one of the most important of the 14 private investor groups that established Nordeste Química S.A. (Norquísa), a holding company that, by 1990, was a major shareholder of Copene. As a continuation of the Brazilian government's privatization program, Petroquísa sold some of its shares in Copene in 1995. Norquísa acquired enough of the shares to become the majority stockholder.

THE FOUNDING OF BRASKEM S.A. IN 2002

Odebrecht joined with a group of companies overseen by the Mariani family to acquire control of Norquísa in 2001. This acquisition included stakes in three polyethylene producers. The following year the Odebrecht and Mariani interests merged six different subsidiaries into Copene, which changed its name to Braskem S.A. Odebrecht was the controlling shareholder, and the head office was in the old quarters of its chemical division. Braskem began its life as Latin America's largest private petrochemicals producer.

The merged companies were consumers for the raw materials produced at Copene's petrochemical complex.

Braskem also acquired 30 percent of Companhia Petroquímica do Sul (Copesul), the second-largest Brazilian petrochemical complex, located in Triunfo, Rio Grande do Sul. Braskem had an interest in 13 factories in four states. Its research and development center was administering 6 pilot plants and 11 laboratories, and its technology and innovation center, in Triunfo, was considered to be the equal of any in Latin America.

FOCUS ON DEBT REDUCTION: 2002–05

Braskem inherited more than BRL 5.6 billion ($1.9 billion) in debts incurred by the merged companies and identified 115 projects to reduce costs and profit from synergies between these units. For the next year and a half it struggled to integrate these companies, including the Copene and Copesul crackers; Odebrecht's polyethylene and polypropylene plants at Camaçari and Triunfo, respectively; the polyethylene producer Polialden Petroquímica S.A., and polyethylene terephthalate producer Proppet S.A.; the vinyls manufacturer Trikem S.A.; and the caprolactam producer Nitrocarbono S.A. Braskem, in 2003, held 41 percent of Brazil's market for polypropylene and 29 percent of the market for polyethylene. It also held about half the PVC market in South America.

After an initial public offering (IPO) of stock on the Bolsa de Valores de São Paulo and the equivalent offering in New York, Odebrecht held 44 percent of Braskem; Norquisa, 12 percent; and Petroquisa, 11 percent. Braskem reported a net loss in 2002 but was profitable in every succeeding year until 2008. In 2004 the company completed the largest global public stock offering issued by a Brazilian company that year, totaling BRL 1.2 billion ($422 million).

Debt reduction was Braskem's chief objective at the time. At first the company had to issue a series of issues of short term debt, but over time it was able to exchange this debt for issues with longer-term maturation and lower interest rates. By the end of 2005 Braskem's debt had been reduced to $1.2 billion. This allowed it to resume making capital investments, including, in partnership with Petrobrás, construction of a polypropylene plant in Paulínia, São Paulo, and to add capacity at several factories. In 2006 Braskem increased its share of the polyethylene producer Politeno Empreendimentos Ltda. from 35 to 97 percent by means of a $111 million purchase. This company was merged into Braskem the following year.

Taking control of Copesul, Brazil's Southern Petrochemicals Complex, Petrobrás, Braskem, and

KEY DATES

1972: Copene, a government-owned petrochemicals complex, is formed.

1988: Copene accounts for 55 percent of Brazil's petrochemical production.

1995: Norquísa, a private consortium, becomes majority shareholder in Copene.

2001: Odebrecht S.A. and another group assume control of Norquísa.

2002: Copene and six other companies are merged into Braskem S.A.; Braskem also assumes a 30 percent stake in Copesul, another petrochemicals complex.

2004: Braskem completes a global stock offering in New York and Madrid.

2007: Braskem doubles its stake in Copesul.

2008: Latin America's leading petrochemicals producer, Braskem has 18 factories.

another company purchased the petrochemical assets of the Ipiranga Group for about $2.5 billion in 2007, with Braskem ultimately receiving 60 percent and Petrobrás the remaining 40 percent. These assets included Ipiranga Química and its subsidiary Ipiranga Petroquímica, and Ipiranga's 30 percent share of Copesul. The transaction, completed in 2008, doubled Braskem's own 30 percent stake in Copesul's cracker and other facilities at Triunfo and made it the third-largest petrochemical company in the Americas. More than 70 percent of Braskem's sales were coming from businesses unrelated to the original Odebrecht entities from which it partly sprang.

Copesul, Ipiranga Petroquímica, Petroquímica Paulínia, and Petroquímica Triunfo (a polyethylene plant) were merged into Braskem in 2008–09, after Petrobrás traded its stakes in these enterprises for a sizable one in Braskem itself. Polypropylene production at the new Paulínia plant, using propylene supplied by Petrobrás, began in 2008. New projects being planned by Braskem included a plant at Camaçari to produce 300,000 metric tons of propylene a year. Start-up was scheduled for 2010.

In 2007 Braskem was conducting research on producing polyethylene from ethanol, made from sugarcane, rather than from a petroleum-based raw material such as naphtha. The company later said that a plant with capacity to produce 200,000 metric tons a year of so-called green plastics, the first in the world, would be operational in 2010 in Triunfo.

Under study was a possible role in Venezuela, where state-owned Petroquímica de Venezuela S.A. (Pequiven) had formed joint ventures with Braskem with the intent to produce polypropylene and polyethylene. Exxon Mobil had withdrawn from an earlier proposal to build a cracker in eastern Venezuela because of rising royalties demanded by the government, but observers said Braskem had a better chance of coming to terms because Venezuela had better relations with Brazil than with the United States.

PLANNING FOR THE FUTURE

Braskem's consolidated gross revenues dropped by about 3 percent in 2008, and it lost BRL 2.49 billion ($1.36 billion), which the company attributed to the effects of the global financial crisis. Braskem had recorded profits in 2006 and 2007. The company had 18 production units in four states, producing basic petrochemicals such as ethane, propane, and benzene, in addition to gasoline and cooking gas. The major petrochemical products in the thermoplastic segment were polyethylene and polypropylene.

Braskem was both importing and exporting chemical and petrochemical products and fuels. Export sales came to 12.4 percent of total sales in 2008. It was providing much of the raw materials for the Camaçari and Triunfo crackers, such as steam, water, and electrical energy. It also held stakes in a number of other companies.

In August 2009 Braskem confirmed a report that it was negotiating a "strategic alliance" with Quattor Participações, its main Brazilian competitor in the petrochemicals market. A merger would make Braskem second only to Dow Chemical Company in petrochemicals production in the Americas.

Odebrecht S.A. held 62 percent of Braskem's voting capital and 39 percent of its total equity at the end of 2008. Petrobrás (by means of Petroquísa) held 31 percent of the voting capital and 24 percent of the total equity. Public shareholders held 7 percent and 32 percent, respectively, while the Brazilian development company BNDES held 5 percent of the equity.

Robert Halasz

PRINCIPAL SUBSIDIARIES

Braskam America Inc. (USA); Braskem Distribuidora Ltda.; Braskem Europe B.V. (Netherlands); Braskem Incorporated (Cayman Islands); Braskem Participações S.A.; IQ Soluções & Química; Petroquímica Paulínia S.A. (60%); Politeno Empreendimentos Ltda.

Braskem S.A.

PRINCIPAL OPERATING UNITS

Basic Petrochemicals; International Business Development; Polymers.

PRINCIPAL COMPETITORS

BASF Aktiengesellschaft; Dow Chemical Company; E.I. du Pont de Nemours and Company; Quattor Participações S.A.; Solvay & Cie. S.A.

FURTHER READING

"Aos 10 anos, a mainoridade de Camaçari," *Exame,* June 29, 1988, pp. 102–09.

"Bahia Gets Big Slice of CPI Pie in Brazil," *Chemical Week,* July 14, 1976, pp. 43, 45, 47.

Caetano, José Roberto, "Bebê vitaminado," *Exame,* September 4, 2002, pp. 72–74.

"Com a verticalização, a CPC se consolida," *Exame,* January 26, 1983, p. 41.

"An Entire Day Dedicated to Braskem at the NYSE," *Global Finance,* September 2005, p. 13.

Kapp, Michael, "Petrochem Powerhouse," *Latin Trade,* December 2003, pp. 22–23.

Rodrigues, Lino, "Braskem negocia 'parceria estratégica' na area petroquímica con rival Quattor," *O Globo,* August 25, 2009.

Seewald, Nancy, "Braskem Claims World's First 'Green' PE," *Chemical Week,* June 27, 2007, p. 9.

Sissell, Kara, "Braskem Acquires Politeno," *Chemical Week,* April 12, 2006, p. 10.

———, "Braskem, Petrobras, and Ultra Buy Ipiranga Group," *Chemical Week,* March 28, 2007, p. 7.

———, "New Lineup Takes the Field," *Chemical Week,* November 14, 2007, pp. 19–21.

———, "Regional Growth Benefits Braskem," *Chemical Week,* January 21, 2004, pp. 56–57.

———, "Sweet Prospects Hit Sour Note," *Chemical Week,* November 3, 2008, pp. 24–27.

Smith, Tony, "New Brazilian Player in Petrochemicals," *New York Times,* January 14, 2003, pp. W1, W7.

Tullo, Alexander H., "Braskem Emerges," *Chemical & Engineering News,* October 29, 2001, p. 17.

———, "Braskem's Rough Start," *Chemical & Engineering News,* May 5, 2003, pp. 25–26.

Bridgepoint Education,
Inc.

13500 Evening Creek Drive North, Suite 600
San Diego, California 92128
U.S.A.
Telephone: (858) 668-2586
Toll Free: (866) 475-0317
Fax: (858) 408-2903
Web site: http://www.bridgepointeducation.com

Public Company
Founded: 1999
Employees: 3,000
Sales: $218.3 million (2008)
Stock Exchanges: New York
Ticker Symbol: BPI
NAICS: 611310 Colleges, Universities, and Professional
    Schools

■ ■ ■

Bridgepoint Education, Inc., is an independent, for-profit provider of postsecondary educational services delivered through two wholly owned subsidiaries, Ashford University in Clinton, Iowa, and University of the Rockies in Colorado Springs, Colorado. Through these two regionally accredited universities, Bridgepoint offers associate's, bachelor's, graduate certificate, master's, and doctoral programs in business, education, health sciences, psychology, and social science disciplines. Along with providing traditional campus and online educational offerings, the two universities also are engaged in recruitment and admission activities. Federal financial aid sources provide the major source of the company's revenues. As of December 2008, Bridgepoint had more than 45,000 students (98 percent of whom attended class exclusively online) enrolled at its two universities.

EARLY HISTORY

Bridgepoint Education, Inc., was established as a Delaware corporation in 1999 by Wayne Clugston and Scott Turner to offer affordable, work-related courses to adult students who sought four-year degrees. At the time Bridgepoint was launched, Clugston was owner and founder of Advance Learning Network (ADL), a 12-year-old company that developed, licensed, and implemented regionally accredited bachelor degree completion programs. In January 2001, Clugston merged ADL into Bridgepoint Education.

In December 2003, Andrew S. Clark joined Bridgepoint as chief executive officer and a director. Clark's personal background and professional vision for the company soon began to shape Bridgepoint. Clark's father was a banker and his mother was a teacher. As Clark later told *Education Inc.*, he "was born at the nexus of education and business." He had earned his M.B.A. from the online University of Phoenix before working there and for two other online education companies in various management and executive roles. By 2002, Clark had developed his own business plan to offer affordable, quality adult education that would marry online instruction with a brick-and-mortar campus which made the college experience attractive to students. Prior to joining Bridgepoint, Clark had also consulted with private-equity firms considering investments in the postsecondary market. In the process he developed a relationship with the equity firm Warburg Pincus.

BRIDGEPOINT'S FIRST BRICK-AND-MORTAR UNIVERSITY

Beginning in 2004, Clark assembled a management team that initially included cofounders Clugston, as senior vice president of academic affairs, and Turner as vice president of marketing and business development. Also joining Clark's team in 2004 were Rodney T. Sheng, as vice president of operations; Charlene Dackerman, as director of human resources; Christopher L. Spohn, as vice president of admissions; and Ross Woodard, as director of e-commerce. In compiling his initial circle of executives, Clark tapped former management of University of Phoenix's parent company, Apollo Group, for which both Spohn and Sheng, as well as Clark, had worked.

After joining Bridgepoint, Clark spent eight months in 2004 touring small liberal arts colleges, including The Franciscan University of the Prairies in Clinton, Iowa, which appeared to him as an ideal acquisition for his business plan and for Bridgepoint. By late 2004, Bridgepoint had secured financing from Warburg Pincus and struck a deal with Franciscan University trustees. In 2004, Bridgepoint was registered as a California company, and Ashford University, LLC, was registered as a limited liability company in Iowa. Then in March 2005, Bridgepoint Education, Inc., was incorporated in Florida. Incorporation signatories for the latter included Clark; company cofounder Scott Turner; Daniel Devine, who would become Bridgepoint chief financial officer; Ryan Craig, a company director; Bill Wenrich, future

chancellor emeritus of Bridgepoint; and Mimi Strouse, Warburg Pincus technology partner. In March 2005, shortly after the Florida incorporation, Bridgepoint purchased Franciscan University, which upon acquisition became Ashford University.

At the time of the acquisition, Ashford University had about 300 students, and its first online program with just 20 students was only in its infancy. Nevertheless, enrollment numbers would soon rise. Bridgepoint kept the university's faculty and undergraduate and graduate programs but also developed online degree programs in business administration, education, organizational management, and later psychology. To target the lower-to-middle-class adult student, Ashford priced tuition fees to be highly competitive and among the lowest in the country compared to other private institutions. It also eased requirements regarding the transferability of credits. In addition, Bridgepoint began pumping funds into online advertising and hiring enrollment advisers. In 2005, the company also hired, as chancellor/president of Ashford University, Jane McAuliffe, a former president of Argosy University, Sarasota (Florida) Campus, an institution combining on-campus and online educational offerings, and a former dean in the College of Education at University of Phoenix.

For 2005, Bridgepoint, with just 10 employees, logged sales of $8 million. In 2006, with Ashford University as a wholly owned subsidiary for the entire year, Bridgepoint recorded $28.6 million in revenues.

COMPANY'S SECOND UNIVERSITY

In September 2007, Bridgepoint acquired its second brick-and-mortar campus: Colorado School of Professional School Psychology in Colorado Springs, Colorado, offering master's and doctoral programs, primarily in psychology. Concurrent with the acquisition of the private, independent graduate school, Bridgepoint renamed the institution University of the Rockies. At the time of the acquisition, the university had 75 students and offered no online programs or classes.

In 2007, Bridgepoint was named the 17th-fastest-growing private company (based on 2006 annual revenues) in the country by *Inc.* magazine. Contributing to Bridgepoint's growth, according to *Inc.*, was the fact that Ashford University offered "the savings of distance learning (tuition is 20 percent to 50 percent lower than at other schools with comparable admission standards) with all the features of a traditional campus, from dorms to sports teams." The company also was named the fastest-growing private education company in the country with 2006 revenues of $28.6 million and a

KEY DATES

1999: Bridgepoint Education, Inc., is established and incorporated in Delaware.

2001: Bridgepoint cofounder Wayne Clugston merges a company he owns, Advance Learning Network, into Bridgepoint.

2003: Andrew S. Clark joins Bridgepoint as chief executive officer.

2005: Bridgepoint acquires The Franciscan University of the Prairies and renames it Ashford University.

2007: Bridgepoint acquires Colorado School of Professional Psychology and renames it University of the Rockies.

2008: Bridgepoint is the 14th-fastest-growing private company in the United States, and the number one fastest-growing private company in the education market.

2009: Bridgepoint goes public.

growth rate of more than 4,000 percent over the previous three-year period.

By February 2008, University of the Rockies had doubled its enrollment to 150 students and launched three new options in the master of arts in psychology and two new options in the doctor of psychology degrees. In October 2008, University of the Rockies began offering an online master's program, with two specializations, and it launched the company's first online doctoral program. During the same time frame, Ashford University's enrollment was also growing, and by the end of 2008, the Iowa-based institution had 600 on-campus students and 12,600 students enrolled exclusively in online classes.

FROM PRIVATE TO PUBLIC COMPANY

In 2008, Bridgepoint for the second successive year was named the fastest-growing private education company in the United States by *Inc.*, based on its 2007 revenues of $85.5 million, and the 14th-fastest-growing private company in the country. Over the previous three years it had posted revenue growth of more than 6,700 percent. During that time, Bridgepoint's number of employees had grown from less than a dozen to 2,800. The year 2007 also marked the first in three years that the company earned a profit, netting $3.3 million.

With discernible signs of growth potential, Bridgepoint made plans in late 2008 for an initial public offering (IPO). For 2008, the company posted revenues of $218.3 million. In terms of its educational product, by March 2009, the company was offering more than 980 courses and 45 degree programs, 34 minors, and 101 specializations. Enrollment had climbed to more than 42,000 students.

In April 2009, during a tumultuous economic year with only two preceding IPOs, Bridgepoint went public, offering 15.5 million shares of stock at an initial price of $10.50 each. The share price was much less than the $14 to $16 initially sought by Warburg Pincus. On the first day's trading, though, the stock rose to $11.10 and during the subsequent summer reached a high of $21.90 a share.

TARGETING THE MILITARY AND UNEMPLOYED

Following its IPO, Bridgepoint increasingly began targeting veterans and the newly unemployed in 2009. Ashford University and University of the Rockies began participating in the GI Bill's Yellow Ribbon Education Enhancement Program, allowing the universities to match the federal government's contribution to veterans' educational costs, covered by the GI Bill benefit, dollar for dollar. Ashford University was also selected to participate in the SOCCOAST-4 degree network: a system of colleges and universities, which accepted each other's credits, offering bachelor degree programs to Coast Guard students, their adult family members, and Coast Guard civilians. In addition, Ashford was selected by the U.S. Army to participate in its Letter-of-Instruction program, resulting in the integration of the university into the GoArmyEd Web site that listed courses and services available to Army soldiers. To address the weakened job market, Ashford University launched its Auto Industry Grant Program, offering persons employed or laid off by Chrysler, Ford, and General Motors a 30 percent tuition reduction.

In 2009, Ashford University also began actively expanding its course offerings and launched several new degree programs, including those in business information systems, business economics, English-language learner studies, environmental studies, health-care studies, homeland security and emergency management, human resources management, political science and government, and public policy, as well as a new minor and specialization in operations management. The university also began offering three new master of arts degrees: in education, public administration, and health-care administration.

NEW PARTNERSHIPS AND NEW GRADUATE PROGRAMS

Bridgepoint developed partnerships and articulation agreements (officially approved agreements matching course work between schools) designed to bring more students to Ashford University in 2009. Drawing upon Bridgepoint's corporate base of operations in San Diego, Ashford inked an articulation agreement with San Diego Miramar College, allowing Miramar students to transfer up to 99 credits into one of Ashford's degree programs. Ashford entered into a similar articulation agreement with another California community college, Allan Hancock College of Santa Barbara County. Bridgepoint also forged a partnership and articulation agreement between Ashford University and the Colorado Community College System (CCCS), through which CCCS students also could transfer up to 99 units into one of Ashford's bachelor's degree programs.

In the fall of 2009, University of the Rockies launched its 15-credit, graduate certificate programs in business psychology, criminology and justice studies, general psychology, and organizational leadership. These certificate programs provided students with an opportunity to enhance their employment qualifications and resumes and move 15 credithours closer to a graduate degree.

STOCK VALUE FLUCTUATIONS AND AN AUDIT OF ASHFORD UNIVERSITY

Bridgepoint's stock took some significant hits during the second half of 2009. In August, the company announced a secondary public offering of up to 11 million shares being sold by management members and the company's largest stockholder, Warburg Pincus, with a 65 percent stake in Bridgepoint. While such a secondary offering from executives, directors, and large stockholders on the heels of an IPO was common (because such investors were barred from selling shares during a "lock-up period" immediately following an IPO), shares of the company's stock fell more than 6 percent on the news.

Worse for the company, in September 2009, Bridgepoint's stock value fell more than 15 percent, after Bridgepoint acknowledged that the U.S. Department of Education's (DoE) inspector general was in the midst of an audit of Ashford University. According to the company, the audit involved alleged misuse of student federal aid, possibly related to enrollment officer compensation, disbursement of student aid monies, and student leaves of absence documentation, according to a company release. Bridgepoint confirmed in a quarterly report filed in 2009 that it could face fines and "corrective action" from the DoE. Given the financial news emanating from the company over a two-month span, in mid-September Bridgepoint withdrew its bid for a secondary offering, citing the decline in stock value as its principal motive.

BRIDGEPOINT'S FUTURE

Bridgepoint's increases in enrollment and revenues corresponded with the decline in available jobs and the overall U.S. economic downturn of the period. Bridgepoint believed that its ability to maintain consistent growth was in part dependent upon increased demand for postsecondary education related to a poor job market. The company also thought that its financial success hinged on at least three other factors: continued federal aid financing of student tuition, decreased turnover in its enrollment advisers, and lowered advertising costs consistent with a weakened economy.

To capitalize on its position in the field, the company planned to continue acquiring colleges and was considering expansion overseas. Potential international markets included England, China, and India. Bridgepoint's ability to navigate future U.S. economic trends and related changes stemming from the federal government, and its ability to compete for business in an increasingly competitive market for lower-to-middle-class students, would be crucial to its long-term success.

Roger Rouland

PRINCIPAL SUBSIDIARIES

Ashford University, LLC; Bridgepoint Education Real Estate Holdings, LLC; University of the Rockies, LLC; Waypoint Outcomes, LLC.

PRINCIPAL COMPETITORS

Apollo Group, Inc.; Corinthian Colleges, Inc.; DeVry Inc.; American Public Education, Inc.; Capella Education Company; Grand Canyon Education, Inc.; Lincoln Educational Services Corporation; Strayer Education, Inc.

FURTHER READING

Blackford, Jill, "Close-Up: Andrew Clark: The Business of Higher Education," *San Diego Daily Transcript*, April 11, 2008.

"Bridgepoint Shares Take Beating on Wall Street," *San Diego Union-Tribune Online*, September 5, 2009.

Cowan, Lynn. "Market Rally Encourages IPO Chatter," *Wall Street Journal: Eastern Edition*, April 13, 2009, p. C2.

"Entrepreneur Profile—Andrew Clark," *San Diego Business Journal*, May 21, 2007.

"How I Did It: Andrew Clark, Bridgepoint Education," *Education Inc.*, September 2008, p. 114.

"June Stock Selection: Bridgepoint Education," *California Stock Report*, June 2009, pp. 8–9.

McKenzie, Meredyth, "Education: People Person; How to Hire the Right Employees for Your Company," *Smart Business San Diego*, March 2008.

Rossa, Jennifer, "The Perils of a Private Equity-Backed Education," *Wall Street Journal Online,* September 19, 2009.

Showley, Roger, "Bridgepoint Shares Take Beating on Wall Street: Possible Mishandling of Student Aid at Issue," *San Diego Union-Tribune*, September 5, 2009.

Smith, Jeniece, "Local Colleges See Enrollment Hikes," *Clinton (IA) Herald Online,* August 26, 2009.

Bubba Gump Shrimp Co. Restaurants, Inc.

209 Avenida Fabricante, Suite 200
San Clemente, California 92672-7544
U.S.A.
Telephone: (949) 366-6260
Fax: (949) 366-6261
Web site: http://www.bubbagump.com

Private Company
Incorporated: 1996
Employees: 500
Sales: $170 million (2007 est.)
NAICS: 722110 Full-Service Restaurants

■ ■ ■

Bubba Gump Shrimp Co. Restaurants, Inc., is a San Clemente, California-based chain of themed restaurants inspired by the 1994 Academy Award–winning film *Forrest Gump*. Although the menu is dominated by shrimp dishes and other seafood, it also includes Southern fried chicken, steak, Dixie Style Baby Back Ribs, and hamburgers and other sandwiches. The restaurants also offer theme specialty drinks, appetizers, and desserts. In keeping with the Alabama setting of much of *Forrest Gump*, the restaurants maintain what the company calls a "down-home" decor, accented by memorabilia from the film, including costumes, storyboards, still photographs from the film, and copies of script pages. The restaurants also generate about 10 percent of their income from *Forrest Gump* inspired merchandise.

Bubba Gump owns and operates about 20 restaurants in the United States, mostly situated at waterfront locations frequented by tourists. Another 10 franchised units are found in Indonesia, Hong Kong, Japan, Malaysia, Mexico, and the Philippines. Deals are also in place to open Bubba Gump restaurants throughout the Middle East. In addition, the company operates the Rusty Pelican, a more upscale seafood restaurant in Newport Beach, California; Capi's Italian Kitchen, a quick-casual Italian concept that complements the Bubba Gump restaurant at Chicago's Navy Pier; and Mai Tai Bars in Honolulu, Hawaii; Long Beach, California; and Daytona Beach, Florida.

FILM ACHIEVES WORLDWIDE POPULARITY IN 1994

Based on a Winston Groom novel, *Forrest Gump* was released in 1994 by Paramount Pictures, starring Tom Hanks as the title character, an Alabama-born idiot savant. In the film, Forrest befriends a man named Bubba Blue, who is obsessed with the shrimping business and invites Forrest to become his partner after the war. Bubba is killed in the Vietnam War and after his discharge Forrest, to honor his friend, forms the Bubba Gump Shrimp Company, which provides the foundation for his fortune. The epic tale caught the imagination of audiences, resulting in $677 million in worldwide ticket sales, the highest-grossing Paramount Pictures film to that date.

The film also received the respect of critics, garnering the Academy Award for Best Picture of 1994, as well as five other Oscars. Moreover, *Forrest Gump* enjoyed unexpected licensed merchandise sales, highly unusual for a film not targeted at children. Aside from the typical baseball caps, T-shirts, jackets, and soundtrack album, the producers secured *Forrest Gump* tie-ins for a cookbook, a book of "Gumpisms," Forrest Gump chocolates, supermarket shrimp products sold under the Bubba Gump Seafood Company name, and even table tennis sets.

Handling merchandising for the film was Viacom Consumer Products, Paramount's licensing division, which sensed there was an opportunity to develop a seafood restaurant concept around the Bubba Gump Shrimp Company idea. In the mid-1990s there was a good deal of consumer interest in themed restaurants, such as the Rainforest Café, the 1950s-inspired Johnny Rockets chain, the Harley-Davidson brand, and pop culture icon Hard Rock Café. Although Planet Hollywood paid tribute to movie stars, no restaurant had yet been developed that relied on a single film for its theme. Because Paramount was not in the restaurant business, it began searching for a partner with which to develop a Forrest Gump-theme restaurant and found it in Rusty Pelican Restaurants Inc.

PARTNERING WITH RUSTY PELICAN: 1995

Rusty Pelican was founded in 1972 in Orange County, California, as an upper-midscale seafood dinner-house concept. A decade later the company was flying high and in 1983 went public to fuel further growth. It soon ran into trouble, however, and in 1987 was acquired by Green Leaf Ventures. The chain grew to 33 units but the company had taken on excessive debt; as the economy deteriorated, Rusty Pelican was forced to close stores. Finally in 1993 it filed for Chapter 11 bankruptcy protection while simultaneously shuttering 6 of its remaining 24 restaurants. When the company emerged from bankruptcy a year later under the ownership of the Hillman Co. investment firm and some of the company's top executives, the chain was reduced to 13 seafood restaurants, with management looking to develop a mid-market concept.

When Paramount contacted Rusty Pelican's chairman, Gordon Miles, in the fall of 1995 about a joint

venture to develop a Forrest Gump-themed seafood restaurant, the timing could not have been better for Rusty Pelican. Scott Barnett, Rusty Pelican's chief executive officer, was charged with developing the concept. In the end the parties decided to focus on the family market and place at least as much emphasis on the menu as the theme, an approach they believed would be the key to long-term success. About two dozen potential markets were also identified, generally waterfront locations highly trafficked by tourists. The decor was chosen to emulate the kind of restaurant that Forrest and Bubba might have opened and incorporated a replica of Forrest Gump's shrimping boat as well as a hint of his mother's boardinghouse.

Although a minority partner in the joint venture, Paramount retained complete control over theming and menu items but it also made its props and costume department available for memorabilia to decorate the restaurants. Attention was paid to detail to such a degree that the beverage operations consultant watched the film repeatedly before creating a drink menu that featured laminated photos on binder rings attached to an actual ping-pong paddle. It would prove so popular with customers that eventually the menus had to be secured to each table with a cable to prevent them from becoming souvenirs.

OPENING OF FIRST FORREST GUMP RESTAURANT: 1996

In quick order the Bubba Gump concept was developed and the first restaurant, capable of seating 220, opened in April 1996 at historic Cannery Row in Monterey, California. Rusty Pelican anticipated first-year sales of about $3.2 million but it soon became apparent that the restaurant was more popular than was first predicted, with sales more than double the expectations. The success of the first unit then set the stage for further restaurant openings, which were handled like movie premieres, including the appearance of a Forrest Gump lookalike. In 1997 two more Bubba Gump units were added in Lahaina, Hawaii, and San Francisco's Pier 39 complex of shops and restaurants. A year later, three additional units followed, located in Chicago, New Orleans, and Breckenridge, Colorado. In 1999 Bubba Gump restaurants opened in Miami, Honolulu, and Hona, Hawaii. In addition, the company opened the Mai Tai Bar in Oahu, Hawaii. In 2000 a single Bubba Gump restaurant was opened in Charleston, South Carolina.

By 1998 Rusty Pelican decided that its future lay with the Bubba Gump concept, as demonstrated by the testing of a fast-casual version of the concept called Bubba Gump Shrimp Shack. (Primarily located at

KEY DATES

1994: Film *Forrest Gump* premieres.
1996: First Bubba Gump Shrimp restaurant opens.
1998: Chicago unit opens; chain totals six restaurants, and includes units in San Francisco, Chicago, and New Orleans.
2001: First international Bubba Gump opens in Osaka, Japan.
2003: Times Square restaurant opens; chain has total of 14 restaurants by year-end.
2007: Franchise deal is signed with Mubarak Al-Hassawi Restaurant Development Group to open a series of restaurants in the Persian Gulf region.

theme parks, the Shacks operated for the next several years.) The company began to phase out the Rusty Pelican concept, divesting some of the units in order to fund further expansion of Bubba Gump. Five of the Rusty Pelican restaurants were sold in 1999 to Houston-based Landry's Seafood Restaurants. In time, only the Rusty Pelican at Newport Beach, California, would remain.

Barnett and his management team also decided that in order to grow Bubba Gump at the rate they desired, they would have to address its high turnover rate of general managers and managers. Although the numbers were not out of the ordinary for the restaurant industry, the management team believed an improvement in manager retention could be a key element in a smooth and successful expansion effort, allowing the company to develop talent that could be transferred to new stores to provide much needed experience and continuity. Recruiting statistics were studied, leading to the reengineering of the company's training methods and career development program. A major finding was that internal promotions and employees hired through in-house referrals led to higher retention rates.

Because of the changes the company made, Bubba Gump did not lose a single general manager in 2001, resulting in nearly $500,000 in savings in recruiting and training costs. The value of using skilled managers to open new units was not as quantifiable but no less important. Moreover, the restaurants performed better the longer a seasoned manager was in place. The company retained all of its general managers in 2002 and 2003 as well.

INTERNATIONAL INTEREST IN FRANCHISING: 1999

Another benefit of the tie-in with *Forrest Gump* was the film's worldwide appeal, leading to international interest in Bubba Gump restaurants. Although the company was not looking to franchise Bubba Gump in the United States, preferring to maintain tight control over the execution of the concept, it viewed franchising and joint-venture partnerships as an excellent way to grow the business globally. The first franchise agreement was signed in 1999 for a unit to eventually be opened in Cancun, Mexico. The first international restaurant opening occurred in 2001 when a Bubba Gump restaurant was introduced in Osaka, Japan.

In 2002 Bubba Gump expanded on several fronts. A Bubba Gump unit opened in Daytona Beach, as did a second Mai Tai Bar. Another international franchised Bubba Gump restaurant was also added in Manila, Philippines. With 12 units in operation, Bubba Gump generated sales of $68 million in 2002. A year later Bubba Gump made its way to Broadway, opening a restaurant in the Times Square area of New York City. The concept was also taken to America's heartland in 2003, when an eatery opened in the Mall of America in Bloomington, Minnesota.

In 2004 a company-owned Bubba Gump restaurant was added in Long Beach and a franchised unit opened in Bali, Indonesia. In addition, the company unveiled its Capi's Italian Kitchen at Chicago's Navy Pier. The 3,500-square-foot fast-casual Italian restaurant was located near a Bubba Gump. Not only did the new restaurant serve as a hedge against competing restaurants taking away business from Bubba Gump, essentially keeping the sales within the family, but it also served as a test for a possible new concept for the parent company. For the year, the Bubba Gump chain and satellite operations generated about $100 million in sales.

10TH ANNIVERSARY: 2006

The long awaited Cancun restaurant opened in 2005. In that same year, a company-owned unit was added in Santa Monica, California. The following year the chain celebrated its 10th anniversary with a pair of domestic and a pair of international openings. New restaurants were added in Universal CityWalk in Orlando, Florida, as well as Hollywood, California, while franchised units opened in Victoria Peak in Hong Kong and Tokyo, Japan. As a result, sales increased to $125 million in 2005 and $140 million in 2006.

In 2007 several more Bubba Gump units opened. In the United States they were located in Fort Lauderdale, Florida; Gatlinburg, Tennessee; Denver,

Colorado; and Anaheim, California. Locations for international franchised units included Puerto Vallarta, Mexico, and Quezon City, Philippines. In addition, Bubba Gump signed a franchise agreement with Mubarak Al-Hassawi Restaurant Development Group to open at least 12 units by 2020 in fast-growing Dubai as well as major Persian Gulf cities in Egypt, Jordan, Kuwait, Lebanon, Oman, Qatar, and Saudi Arabia. In the meantime, Bubba Gump continued to enjoy success in Asia. A pair of units opened in Malaysia in 2009 and plans were underway to add three more restaurants in the country as well.

More than 15 years had passed since *Forrest Gump* first delighted moviegoers around the world, yet its appeal continued, due in part to the presence of the Bubba Gump restaurants that kept the Forrest Gump brand in the public eye. Although the association with the movie helped the restaurant chain and continued sales of Forrest Gump merchandise padded the balance sheet, the key to the chain's longevity and potential remained the quality of the menu. As long as Bubba Gump delivered on that front, it could expect to enjoy continued worldwide success.

Ed Dinger

PRINCIPAL SUBSIDIARIES

Bubba Gump Shrimp Co. International LLC.

PRINCIPAL COMPETITORS

Legal Sea Foods Inc.; McCormick & Schmick's Seafood Restaurants, Inc.; Phillips Foods, Inc.

FURTHER READING

Berta, Dina, "Bubba Gump: Maintaining Managers Pays Off in Profits," *Nation's Restaurant News*, June 21, 2004, p. 18.

Crecca, Donna Hood, "Staying Power: Bubba Gump Shrimp Co. Builds Its Management Bench to Ensure the Success of New Units," *Chain Leader,* November 2003, p. 85.

Elliott, Stuart, "'Gump' Sells to Viacom's Surprise," *New York Times*, October 7, 1994, p. D1.

Johnson, Greg, "Biggest Name in Shrimp," *Los Angeles Times*, March 8, 1996, p. 1.

LaVecchia, Gina, "Gump's Still Shrimpin'," *Restaurant Hospitality*, April 2000, p. 74.

Liddle, Alan, "Successful Is as Successful Does: Bubba Gump to Expand," *Nation's Restaurant News*, December 2, 1996, p. 3.

Luna, Nancy, "Bubba Gump Heading to Middle East," *Orange County (CA) Register*, March 30, 2007.

Martin, Richard, "Pelican, Paramount to Debut Bubba Gump," *Nation's Restaurant News*, March 18, 1996, p. 3.

"Reverse Product Placement: Case Study: Bubba Gump Shrimp Co.," *Brand Strategy*, May 9, 2007, p. 26.

Robertiello, Jack, "Bubba Gump Paddles Along," *Cheers*, June 1999, p. 16.

Spector, Amy, "Bubba Gump Launches Italian Sidekick Capi's," *Nation's Restaurant News*, June 7, 2004, p. 4.

Vasari, Marie, "Bubba Gump's Keeping Running," *Monterey County (CA) Herald*, January 24, 2007.

Walkup, Carolyn, "Bubba Gump Shrimp Co. Right on Track as Fourth Unit Opens," *Nation's Restaurant News*, July 20, 1998, p. 42.

CARBO Ceramics, Inc.

———— ■ ————

6565 MacArthur Suite 1050
Irving, Texas 75039
U.S.A.
Telephone: (972) 401-0090
Fax: (972) 401-0705
Web site: http://www.carboceramics.com

Public Company
Incorporated: 1987
Employees: 648
Sales: $387.8 million (2008)
Stock Exchanges: New York
Ticker Symbol: CRR
NAICS: 327999 All Other Miscellaneous Nonmetallic
   Mineral Product Manufacturing; 511210 Software
   Publishers; 541990 All Other Profession, Scientific,
   and Technical Services

■ ■ ■

CARBO Ceramics, Inc., (Carbo Ceramics) is the leading worldwide supplier of ceramic proppants to the oil and natural gas development industry. Proppants are tiny kiln-fired ceramic pellets that prop open rock fissures in order to facilitate oil and natural gas extraction from the rock formations. Carbo Ceramics offers a range of proppant products which meet a variety of underground conditions. Complementary oilfield engineering services include hydraulic fracture design and consulting. Applications for the company's ceramic pellets include industrial mineral grinding and foundry metalcasting.

Manufacturing facilities in Louisiana, Georgia, and Alabama are located near bauxite and kaolin mineral deposits owned by the company. Carbo Ceramics operates manufacturing facilities in China and Russia. Worldwide manufacturing capacity is more than 1.28 billion pounds of proppants annually. Distribution centers are located in six U.S. cities, and independent distributors sell the company's products in Europe, Southeast Asia, the Middle East, Australia, and South America.

EARLY DEVELOPMENT OF CERAMIC PROPPANTS

Carbo Ceramics originated as a division of U.S. Carborundum. A subsidiary of Standard Oil Company, Carborundum manufactured specialized abrasive tools, such as sandpaper and abrasive discs, used by the automotive, steel, aerospace, and machine tool industries when smooth surface texture was required. The formation of Standard Oil Proppants Company, Ltd. (SOPCO), in 1978, marked Carborundum's entry in the nascent ceramic proppant market. Until this time, the oil and gas industry used sand as a proppant. Deep well exploration required greater strength than sand alone could deliver. Resin-coated sand, the next step, provided additional durability.

Carborundum's experience with creating sand and synthetic abrasives similar to sand, led to the development of ceramic proppants. During the 1970s, as hydraulic fracturing became more common for depths below 14,000 feet, regular sand no longer sufficed. Resin-coated sand provided additional strength, but better alternatives were sought. Carborundum's ceramic

COMPANY PERSPECTIVES

Through the years, CARBO has followed a straightforward formula for success: product quality, superior customer service, innovative thinking and ongoing commitment to improvement.

By diligently applying these practices, CARBO has helped many other companies achieve success as our proppant, software and consulting services have enhanced the productivity and financial performance of new and existing oil and gas wells around the globe.

Today, CARBO is one of the world's leading manufacturers of environmentally friendly ceramic media. In addition to the oil and gas industry, markets for ceramic media now include foundry metal casting and industrial mineral grinding.

pellets provided strength to endure underground pressure while allowing oil or natural gas to be extracted from the reservoir.

SOPCO's strategy focused on developing premium, high-quality proppants capable of tolerating the pressure of deep oil and gas wells. In 1979 SOPCO opened a research and development laboratory and manufacturing facility in New Iberia, Louisiana. Engineers found that kiln-firing clay sand with aluminum oxide created "sintered bauxite," composed of 83 percent alumina for strength and conductivity. Superior to the quality of mined or resin-coated sand, the pellets were produced by grinding calcined bauxite into a fine powder. Combined with water and binders and processed in a high-shear mixer, the powder turned into tiny green pellets. These were baked, or sintered, in a rotary kiln at 2,500 to 3,000 degrees Fahrenheit. SOPCO initiated production of the ceramic proppant, later rebranded CarboHSP, at 20 million pounds per year.

Successful application of the proppants led SOPCO to expand. A second production line, capable of manufacturing 40 million pounds of ceramic proppants per year, began operations in 1981. That line handled production of CarboProp, introduced the following year. A lighter, less-resilient proppant made with 72 percent alumina, CarboProp was designed for oil and natural gas extraction at moderate depths.

In 1983 the company opened a second manufacturing plant in Eufaula, Alabama, near bauxite clay deposits. The 90 million pound annual capacity of the plant accommodated a new product, CarboLite, made with kaolin, which contained less aluminum. While normal oil and gas extraction did not require extra strength, the spherical shape and consistent size of CarboLite offered greater permeability for oil and gas flow than sand-based proppants. Also, the company offered the product in different sizes to accommodate different levels of desired permeability. CarboLite became available in 1984.

BECOMING AN INDEPENDENT, PUBLICLY TRADED COMPANY

The first step toward SOPCO's independence from Carborundum began through a joint venture with Dresser Industries, formed in 1984 to further development of ceramic proppants. The company took the name Carbo Ceramics in 1987, with Jesse Orsini as chief executive officer.

Profitability provided the foundation for new ventures, as Carbo Ceramics sought to diversify its business activities. The company acquired Polybau, SA, manufacturer of modular, precast drainage channels for the construction industry. The Swiss company provided Carbo Ceramics with an adjunct to abrasives, a mature industry from which the company could expect slow but steady growth, but little investment potential. After seeking a variety of industries from which to derive revenues, Carbo Ceramics eventually concentrated its activities on ceramic proppants exclusively.

The company sought growth by diversifying its product line to compete with sand and sand-based proppants. In 1992, the company introduced Ceramacore, a synthetic mullite produced with 49 percent alumina. Later renamed CarboEconoprop, the product provided the oil and gas industry with a ceramic proppant that could compete on price and other factors. Carbo Ceramics offered technical service, easy availability, and on-time delivery. In order to provide customers with the cost savings of just-in-time inventory, with delivery on an as-needed basis, Carbo Ceramics developed a distribution system that would meet customers' time and stocking constraints. The company opened stocking facilities in Rock Springs, Wyoming; Oklahoma City, Oklahoma; San Antonio, Texas; Fairbanks, Alaska; and Edmonton, Alberta, Canada. Bulk storage silos at these locations allowed the company to easily load truck trailers for product transport via truck or rail. Carbo Ceramics also operated a distribution center in Rotterdam, Netherlands.

The products and services enabled the company to secure a significant share of the ceramic proppants

KEY DATES

1979: Introduction of sintered bauxite (CarboHSP) coincides with opening of production facility in New Iberia, Louisiana.

1981: Eufaula, Alabama, production facility opens; CarboLite is introduced.

1987: Carbo Ceramics becomes an independent company.

1992: CarboEconoprop is introduced; production facilities expand.

1996: Initial public offering of stock raises funds for new production facility in Georgia.

2000: Carbo Ceramics is listed on the New York Stock Exchange.

2002: Acquisition of Pinnacle Technologies adds fracture analysis and design services.

2007: HydroProp is introduced; manufacturing facilities open in Russia and the United States.

market, which constituted 14 percent of the total proppants market. In 1993, the Eufaula unit added 70 million pounds of capacity for production of CarboLite and CarboEconoprop, for a total plant capacity of 160 million pounds.

A 20 percent increase in deep drilling of natural gas increased demand for the company's high strength products. At the New Iberia site, production of Carbo-HSP and CarboProp increased by 40 million pounds for a total of 100 million pounds in annual capacity. Carbo Ceramics added new EconoProp products in different sized pellets, which contributed to revenue increases and profitability. In 1995 Carbo Ceramics reported $58 million in revenue and $21.71 million in net income. Carbo Ceramics became the leading supplier of ceramic proppants, with 60 percent of the market worldwide. Customers included oil, gas, and petroleum exploration and services companies Shell Oil, Enron, Halliburton, and BJ Services. Expansion into international markets led the company to open distribution centers in China. International sales accounted for 37 percent of the company's $21.1 million in revenues.

Rapid growth set the foundation for an initial public offering (IPO) of stock. In April 1996 Carbo Ceramics became a publicly traded company, with an IPO on the NASDAQ. The company applied funds from the offering to expand production. The Eufaula site added 70 million pounds of production capacity for

CarboLite and EconoProp, for total production capacity of 230 million pounds. Companywide, actual production reached 330 million pounds of ceramic proppants annually. The company began construction of a 150 million pound capacity manufacturing facility in McIntyre, Georgia.

EXISTING PRODUCTS FIND APPLICATIONS IN FOUNDRY BUSINESS

Carbo Ceramics unexpectedly found an additional, complementary stream of revenue after a study of its synthetic mullite for use in the production of lost foam metalcasting led it into the foundry business. Conducted by the U.S. Department of Energy, the 1993–94 study compared Carbo Ceramics' synthetic mullites to 15 other silica and olivine sand media. Holdovers from Carborundum's abrasives business, Ceramacore 311 and 411 provided the best combination of desirable characteristics, particularly as an environmental alternative to silica sand.

As Carbo Ceramics developed its foundry supply business, the quality of the Ceramacore product attracted Ashland Chemical Company of Dublin, Ohio. In July 1997 Carbo Ceramics and Ashland signed an exclusive agreement to develop a ceramic supply business worldwide. Ashland began testing Ceramacore 311, in conjunction with zircon specialty sand, for use in sand core molds, seeking the right combination to provide a desirable casting surface finish. Products developed by Carbo Ceramics emerged under the CARBOACCUCAST brand.

RISE IN OILFIELD SERVICES SUPPLY

As business operations expanded and sales increased, Carbo Ceramics sought to gain parity in its industry as a pubic company. In May 2000, Carbo filed for a listing on the New York Stock Exchange, where most major companies in the oil and gas industry are listed. A secondary offering of stock, 1.89 million shares at $27 per share, accompanied the transfer from the NASDAQ.

The market for Carbo Ceramics' proppants increased along two paths, in the application of deep-well hydraulic fracturing for resource extraction and the use of its ceramic proppants for use in shallow wells. As hydraulic fracturing became a more prevalent method in oil and gas production, the market for ceramic proppants increased, accounting for 14 percent of the overall proppant market. To remain competitive in the premium proppant market, Carbo Ceramics introduced CARBOHSP2000, an improved version of its high-strength proppant. Revenues rose accordingly. In 2000 Carbo Ceramics' revenues reached $93.3 million.

A change in leadership occurred in April 2001, when Mark Pearson, a former oilfield manager for Arco Oil, became chief executive officer. At Arco, Pearson used Carbo Ceramics products at Alaska North Slope operations during the late 1990s. Despite the higher cost, he used the ceramic proppants for wells 6,000 to 10,000 feet in depth. Pearson showed that ceramics were cost effective for hydraulic fracturing at shallow depths. As CEO of Carbo Ceramics, Pearson planned to use his experience in Alaska to broaden the distribution of the company's products.

Carbo Ceramics initiated field studies to compare the efficacy of its product with sand, resin-coated sand, and other ceramic proppants. In cooperation with several gas development operators, the study was intended to look at conductivity, the ability of proppants to assist the flow of natural gas, in a variety of reservoir conditions.

The acquisition of Pinnacle Technologies, Inc., in the spring of 2002, facilitated the field studies as it expanded the company's operations to oilfield services. Pinnacle provided reservoir mapping and fracture diagnostic services. The acquisition included FracProPT, state-of-the-art hydraulic fracturing simulation software, and Applied Geomechanics, a leading tiltmeter technology company, for geological monitoring applications. The subsidiary contributed fracture design, engineering, and consulting services, facilitating Carbo Ceramics' ability to analyze site-specific characteristics and advise customers on the appropriate proppant product for each situation. The 2005 appointment of Gary Kotstad, a 20-year veteran of the oilfield service industry, as chief executive of Carbo Ceramics, supported the new area of business.

NATIONAL AND INTERNATIONAL DEVELOPMENTS

Although the oil and gas industry experienced fluctuations of activity in the early 2000s, Carbo Ceramics prepared for an eventual increase in proppant demand. In 2002 the company acquired raw material deposits in Georgia that would supply the company with kaolin for 15 years. Multiyear contracts secured domestic and international sources of bauxite and kaolin as well. The company initiated a $17 million upgrade of the McIntyre facility and began construction of a $63 million manufacturing plant in nearby Toomsboro, Georgia. In 2005, as proppant demand rose, production capacity increased 35 percent.

International developments supported a stable growth pattern, and the company began construction on a CarboProp and CarboLite manufacturing plant in China in 2002. A second line opened in 2004. That year, Carbo Ceramics opened a sales office in Moscow and developed distribution operations. Construction on a CarboProp manufacturing plant in Kopeysk, Russia, began in 2005. Completed in November 2007, the facility carried a 100-million pound ceramic proppant capacity.

Carbo Ceramics also developed its first major product in several years. In 2007 the company introduced HydroProp, designed to enhance the performance of ceramic proppants in slick water fractures. The low-priced product was made from kaolin at the Eufaula plant.

Due to higher costs of imported raw materials in early 2008, especially bauxite, Carbo Ceramics halted manufacturing at the New Iberia plant. Also, outdated equipment at the site made production at other facilities, with state-of-the-art efficiencies, more cost effective. Research and development, administration, and distribution facilities remained open. By the end of the year, however, high demand for specialized ceramic proppants for gas developments in the Haynesville Shale formation, in northeastern Louisiana and east Texas, prompted the company to reopen the plant. The specialized proppants could be made with few modifications to the production equipment, making it cost-effective to restore operations.

As demand for its proppants continued to rise, Carbo Ceramics added a second production line at the Toomsboro facility, bringing production capacity to 250 million pounds per year. A third line, begun in January 2008, was expected to become operational in 2010. The facility held space for potential production of one billion pounds annually.

While international sales stimulated growth in 2006 and 2007, growth in the domestic market provided the main stimulus in 2008. International sales accounted for 36 percent of total revenues in 2006 and 2007, $283.8 million and $300.0 million, respectively. In 2008, domestic sales accounted for 29 percent of the company's $387.8 million in overall revenues. The sale of the fracture and reservoir diagnostics operations of Pinnacle Technologies for $142.3 million in October 2008 contributed a $44.13 million gain from discontinued operations, leading to net income of $110.32 million.

Mary Tradii

PRINCIPAL SUBSIDIARIES

Applied Geomechanics, Inc.; StrataGen Engineering.

PRINCIPAL COMPETITORS

Curimbaba GmbH; Saint-Gobain Proppants, SA; Borovichi Refractory Plant; FORES Refractory Plant; Yixing Orient Petroleum Proppant Company, Ltd.; GuiZhou LinHai New Material Company, Ltd.; Unimin Corporation; Badger Mining Corp.; Fairmount Minerals Ltd.; Hexion Specialty Chemicals, Inc.; Ogelbay-Norton Company.

FURTHER READING

"Carbo Ceramics, Inc.," *Oil and Gas Investor,* September 1997, p. S12.

"Designing Fractures for Realistic Downhole Demands: With a Staff of Field-Proven Petroleum Engineers, a Manufacturer Works with Customers to Select the Ideal Proppant for Each Stimulation Treatment," *Oil and Gas Investor,* March 2005, p. SS28.

Elliott, Alan R., "Carbo Ceramics, Inc./Irving, Texas Where Tiny, Caviarlike Pellets Fuel Sales Growth," *Investor's Business Daily,* February 20, 2001, p. A12.

Ferguson, Carol, "Profitable Carbo Pays Way to Stock Exchange Listing," *London Times,* May 11, 1988.

Spada, Alfred, "Manufactured Alternatives to Traditional Molding Media," *Modern Casting,* April 1998, p. 45.

Carr's Milling Industries PLC

Old Croft, Stanwix
Carlisle, CA3 9BA
United Kingdom
Telephone: (44 01228) 554600
Fax: (44 01228) 554601
Web site: http://www.carrs-milling.com

Public Company
Incorporated: 1908 as Carr's Flour Mills Ltd.
Employees: 737
Sales: $677.8 million (2008)
Stock Exchanges: London
Ticker Symbol: CRM
NAICS: 311211 Flour Milling; 311119 Other Animal Food Manufacturing; 325314 Fertilizer (Mixing Only) Manufacturing; 336211 Motor Vehicle Body Manufacturing; 541330 Engineering Services

■ ■ ■

Listed on the London Stock Exchange, Carr's Milling Industries PLC is a Carlisle, U.K.-based company that divides its operations among three primary sectors: Food, Agriculture, and Engineering. The heart of the company's food business is Carr's Flour Mills, a cereal processing company serving bakers, manufacturers, and retailers. Agricultural units include Carrs Billington, a farm equipment, feed, fuel and lubricants, and services company; Carrs Fertilizer, a diverse manufacturer and blender of fertilizers for agriculture, forestry, and horticulture markets; Caltech, offering feed supplements for forage-based diets for cattle, deer, goats, horses, and sheep; and New Generation Feeds, another maker of feed supplements. Carr's engineering sector comprises three subsidiaries. Bendall's Engineering designs and manufactures process plant and equipment used by the oil and gas, nuclear power, petrochemical, pharmaceutical, process, and water industries. Focusing on the nuclear power industry, Carrs MSM produces remote handling equipment. Hinds Bendalls offers body shop and repair services for cars and commercial vehicles, including conversions, painting, and signwriting. In addition, Carr's owns B&A Travel, a specialist travel agency.

FOUNDER, JONATHAN DODGSON CARR

Carr's Milling was founded by Jonathan Dodgson Carr, born the son of a Quaker wholesale grocer in December 1806 in Highgate, Kendal, an English weaving town. After completing his schooling, Carr in 1820 became a baker's apprentice, and upon the completion of his service sought to set himself up as a baker. There was no shortage of bakers in Highgate, however, prompting the young man in 1831, after serving three years as a journeyman baker, to move to the growing community of Carlisle, soon to become connected to the railroad. According to an oft-repeated story, he walked the entire 43 miles from Highgate to Carlisle. Some accounts claim, however, that he walked only a short distance before receiving a lift from a tea merchant, a family friend who more than likely agreed ahead of time to take Carr with him. Thus, the wagon ride was probably arranged rather than the result of a chance encounter, but Carr's long walk is still remembered, if for no other

---

COMPANY PERSPECTIVES
∎

Carr's Milling Industries activities are focused on agriculture, food and engineering.

---

reason than to serve as an emblem of his life's journey from poor youth to wealthy businessman.

Funded by unknown sources, Carr set up a bakery on Castle Street in Carlisle. His ambitions extended far beyond that, however. Well ahead of his time, Carr sought to achieve some vertical integration in his business, hoping to add a milling operation to produce his own flour and a distribution operation, all under the same roof. Six years after arriving in Carlisle, Carr realized his dream, setting up shop in the impoverished Caldewgate section of Carlisle. What seemed like a risky location proved to be a key to Carr's eventual success, because shortly before his new factory opened a new railway was established nearby. The railway provided a link to a canal, which in turn provided access to distant markets. Rather than the bread he baked at his Castle Street shop, Carr planned to produce and ship fancy biscuits (known in the United States as crackers or cookies) from his new factory. Not only did biscuits last longer than bread and were easy to package, they were growing in popularity as train travel increased. Unlike stage coaches that stopped at inns for meals, train passengers could not yet rely on restaurants at train stations or dining cars, making biscuits an ideal snack for the road. Moreover, middle-class women began serving fancy biscuits at tea to project a sense of refinement.

OBTAINING A ROYAL WARRANT: 1841

Carr was a pioneer in other ways as well. He learned of a biscuit-making machine invented in the United States and had it installed at his factory to dramatically increase production. He also obtained a Royal Warrant in 1841. Four years earlier Queen Victoria had ascended the throne and began issuing warrants that bestowed a mark of distinction on a supplier. For an obscure Quaker like Carr with no political connections and a factory located in the hinterlands of England to gain a Royal Warrant was an impressive feat. While it did not guarantee success, the warrant played an important part in the successful branding of Carr's fancy biscuits and improving demand for the product. Annual output of 350 tons in 1844 more than doubled by 1851, and by the start of the 1860s doubled once again. Helping to drive demand was Carr's regular introduction of new

biscuit varieties, none of which was especially novel. They included such shapes as scrolls, boats, dogs heads, and the faces of royal personages, as well as names that appealed to consumers through association, such as Albert, Balmoral, Prince of Wales, and Osborne. Carr also offered sweet biscuits in a variety of shapes sold as a collection under the evocative Rich Desserts label.

BUSINESS CONDITIONS CHANGE: 1870–80

Two of Carr's sons, Henry and James, joined the company, the former supervising biscuit production, the latter buying grain. Both young men fell out with the Quaker faith, however, leading to their expulsion from the Society of Friends. In 1869 Jonathan Carr and his wife also left the church, and just as his personal world became unsettled so too did the climate for the biscuit business. Huntley & Palmer had emerged as England's largest biscuit maker, but Carr had been unconcerned because there appeared to be plenty of opportunity both home and abroad for everyone in the trade. Other countries, however, caught up to England in industrialization and developed their own domestic sources of biscuits that were protected by high tariffs, forcing British biscuit makers to cut prices and lower profits. At home, competition only stiffened and regional concerns now sought to compete across the country, and they proved to be increasingly adept at advertising their products. To make matters worse, a series of poor wheat harvests in England in the 1870s forced the expensive importation of wheat. In the United States, in the meantime, the invention of the mechanical reaper by Cyrus McCormick that led to the creation of International Harvester, coupled with the spread of the railroads, ushered in wheat production in the great plains of the United States. High-quality, inexpensive wheat became available in England, where farmers no longer found it profitable to grow grain. As a result, Carr realized that if he wanted to continue to produce his own flour, he would have to open mills that were located close to the ports rather than the English countryside. The aging Carr would also have to invest in a fleet of steamships.

In 1884 Jonathan Carr died from a stroke at the age of 77. He left his four sons the factory capable of producing 128 varieties of biscuits, four flour mills, a bread bakery and shop, three other shops, five ships, and depots in Liverpool and London. Henry Carr succeeded his father as the head of the company, but in time he faced a financial crisis. With the company overdrawn at its bank, he lacked the reputation of his father to secure the necessary bank funding. The bank advised the family to incorporate. As a result, a decade after the death of Jonathan Carr, in 1894, the family business was

KEY DATES

1831: Jonathan Dodgson Carr starts bakery business.
1841: Carr receives Royal Warrant to produce biscuits.
1884: Jonathan Carr dies.
1894: Company incorporates as Carr & Co. Ltd.
1908: Carr's Flour Mills Ltd. is formed.
1950: Carr's Flour Mills is renamed Carr's Milling Industries Limited.
1964: Carr & Co. is sold.
1972: Carr's Milling goes public on the London Stock Exchange.
1997: Ian Carr retires as last Carr family member involved in the company.
2001: Hoof-and-mouth disease hurts milling business.
2005: Milling operations double with Meneba UK acquisition.

restructured as a limited liability corporation and rechristened Carr & Co. Ltd. The Clydesdale Bank promptly extended credit to the company and investors eagerly purchased the shares made available to the public.

By the time of the incorporation, a third generation of the Carr family was involved in the business, in particular the son of Thomas Carr, Theodore, who was 28 at the time. He had grown up fascinated by the biscuit works and became completely devoted to the company his grandfather founded. With an engineering background, Thomas Carr made significant improvements to the factory operations, including the development of the Baker-Carr machine that could ice biscuits in a fraction of the time required by human hands, leading to the development of a new biscuit with a coffee-flavored icing called the Café Noir, which became extremely popular after its introduction in 1891. Theodore Carr also sought to make a thinner version of the popular Captain's Thin, resulting in the creation of the Table Water biscuit, which was twice the size of a Captain's thin while one-third the thickness. It became Carr's signature biscuit.

FORMATION OF CARR'S FLOUR MILLS: 1908

In 1904 Henry Carr died of a heart attack and the 37-year-old Theodore Carr succeeded his uncle as Carr's

chairman. To his surprise he found, after sorting through the poorly kept books, he had been left a company in debt. The heart of the problem was the flour mills. Rather than shut them down, as his uncle had the bread baking operation, Theodore Carr elected to borrow the money necessary to actually expand the milling operation. This led to the opening of a new mill in Silloth, England. Then, in 1908, he took the bold step of spinning off the flour-milling business from the biscuit operation, creating a new company called Carr's Flour Mills Ltd., the direct predecessor to Carr's Milling Industries PLC. Thomas Carr became the chairman and managing director of the new company, roles he also retained with Carr & Co. Although they supported one another, the companies were operated separately.

Always looking forward, Theodore Carr was committed to growing the family businesses. He acquired the shares of S. & H. Rakusen, maker of unleavened biscuits, to establish in 1910 a new company called Bonn & Co. to produce kosher biscuits. Shortly before World War I, Carr, who at one time had built his own car, motorized the company's delivery fleet. During the war, Theodore Carr also ran a munitions factory that he started up from scratch, all the while managing to keep the biscuit factory operational by replacing men called to war with women workers, who needed to be trained. The war years were also marked by tragedy when his 20-year-old son Stanley was killed in battle.

Following World War I an increasing number of non-family members became involved in the running of the Carr businesses, as Theodore and his brother Bertram became involved in politics. Nevertheless, the companies thrived in the 1920s. The biscuit business was especially buoyed by the popularity of the Club Cheese and Table Water biscuits, and a robust export business, for which Bertram Carr was most responsible. Before the war he had traveled extensively to establish depots and create a network of agents. The India operation was one of the chief reasons for Carr's recovery and prosperity following the war.

Bertram Carr retired in 1925 and died suddenly from heart failure two years later. In January 1931 Theodore Carr suffered a heart attack on a business trip and died two weeks later. The family business was a century old, and while later generations of the Carr family took the top management positions at Carr & Co. and Carr's Flour Mills, the family's grip was loosening. England was already suffering from the Great Depression of the 1930s when Theodore Carr died, and although the two Carr concerns survived as family companies they were greatly weakened. After the end of World War II, Carr & Co. faced increasingly stiff competition from other biscuit makers. As the years passed, there appeared no choice but to sell the business or merge with a rival. An offer to sell Carr & Co. was refused during the 1950s, but in 1964 the Carr family accepted a cash offer from Cavenham Foods. In 1972 Cavenham sold the business to United Biscuits, which continued to produce biscuits under the Carr's label.

CARR'S FLOUR BECOMES CARR'S MILLING: 1950

Carr's Flour Mills, meanwhile, was renamed Carr's Milling Industries Limited in 1950. It was headed by Theodore Carr's son, Ivan, until 1964 when his cousin, Ian Carr, succeeded him. Ian Carr had been with the biscuit side of the business since 1950, when he became a wages clerk. He then became an export salesman in the Middle East and India, and served as sales director until 1962 when he left to join Carr's Milling, which was still very much family controlled. Over the next 30 years, however, the Carr family's stake in the business eroded steadily, and Ian Carr would become the last family member actively involved in the running of the company.

Under Ian Carr's leadership, Carr's Milling was taken public in 1972 and gained a London Stock Exchange listing. In 1982 the company re-registered as a PLC. It was Ian Carr who successfully diversified Carr's Milling into animal feeds, fertilizers, and farm machinery. He became non-executive chairman in 1989 and then in September 1997 retired, becoming the last Carr family member to work in the company. He died in 2004 at the age of 75. Ian Carr was succeeded as chairman by David Newton, the company's former chief executive.

A year prior to Carr's retirement, the company acquired Bendalls, and in 1997 Oklahoma-based Animal Feed Supplement was acquired. Other developments in the late 1990s included the opening of a second Animal Feed Supplement plant in South Dakota, and the closure of the Silloth animal feed mill. In addition, the Carrs Billington Agriculture joint venture was formed to sell animal feed as well as other farm products and equipment.

NEW CENTURY BRINGS VARIED ACQUISITIONS

More acquisitions followed in the new century, including the purchase of a pair of animal feed mills and four retail outlets from Af PLC in 2000. Unfortunately, the next year the country faced an outbreak of hoof-and-mouth disease that crippled the cattle industry and Carr's feed operation, making diversity more important

than ever. In 2002 the engineering assets of Master Slave Manipulators were acquired. Although Carr's engineering business suffered from a downturn in the economy, cost-cutting measures helped the unit to at least break even. The feed business, in the meantime, began to recover, and in 2005 the milling operations of Meneba UK were added to more than double Carr's flour milling business. Later in the year the unit grew further through the acquisition of W&J Pye and its animal feed producing assets. Also in 2005 Carrs Billington added Wallace oils, followed in 2007 by the acquisition of Johnstone Fuels and Lubricants. The ground care equipment distributor J.M. Raine was acquired in 2008, followed a year later by the purchase of Hans Walischmiller, a German remote handling technology company serving the nuclear power industry. Carr's Milling also expanded internationally during the early 2000s. A joint venture was established in 2006 in South Africa, Afgritech, to produced animal feed supplements. In that same year Crystalyx Products GmbH was formed as a joint venture with Agravis in Germany to manufacture the Crystalyx feed supplement for forage-based diets. Revenues for Carr's Milling totaled $677.8 million in 2008. While the milling business remained the core of its success, the company had become diversified enough to position itself for reasonable growth for years to come.

Ed Dinger

PRINCIPAL DIVISIONS

Agriculture; Engineering; Food.

PRINCIPAL COMPETITORS

Archer Daniels Midland Company; Associated British Foods plc; NWF Group plc.

FURTHER READING

Blackwell, David, "Carr's Buoyed by Rising Wheat Prices," *FT.com*, August 8, 2008.

Crosland, Jonas, "Carr's Milling Rises to the Occasion," *Investor's Chronicle*, November 11, 2008.

Forster, Margaret, *Rich Desserts and Captain's Thin*, London: Random House, 1997, 284 p.

"Ian Carr Last Family Head of the Water Biscuit Dynasty, Whose Products He Sold in the Middle East, India and Blackpool," *Daily Telegraph*, June 19, 2004, p. 25.

Richards, Matthew, "Acquisitions Help Carr's Milling Rise," *Financial Times*, November 22, 2005, p. 27.

Shelley, Toby, "Carr's Milling Warns Tough Agricultural Grind," *Financial Times*, November 14, 2006, p. 25.

Tighe, Chris, "Last Carr Moves On," *Financial Times,* January 8, 1997, p. 31.

Urry, Maggie, "Carr's Reaps Benefit of Farm Revival," *Financial*

Times, April 8, 2008, p. 20.

Wallop, Harry, "Carr Ploughs a Valuable Furrow," *Daily Telegraph,* January 29, 2005, p. 2.

Cathay Life Insurance Company Ltd.

296 Jen Ai Road, Section 4
Taipei,
Taiwan
Telephone: (+886 2) 2755-1399
Toll Free: (+886) (800) 036599
Fax: (+886 2) 2708-2166
Web site: https://www.cathaylife.com.tw

Subsidiary of Cathay Financial Holdings Co. Ltd.
Incorporated: 1962
Employees: 31,051
Total Assets: TWD 2.54 trillion (2008)
NAICS: 524113 Direct Life Insurance Carriers; 524114
    Direct Health and Medical Insurance Carriers

■ ■ ■

Cathay Life Insurance Company Ltd. is Taiwan's leading life insurance provider. The Taipei-based company is also Taiwan's second-largest corporation, and, as the flagship operation of parent company Cathay Financial Holdings Co. Ltd., part of the single-largest company in Taiwan. Cathay Life provides a range of life insurance, as well as health and medical insurance, throughout Taiwan, with a network of more than 700 offices and a staff of more than 30,000 people. Although Cathay Life's market share has declined from a high of more than 50 percent of the total Taiwanese life insurance market, the company remains the country's heavyweight, controlling more than 30 percent of the market. The group has also launched an international

expansion drive at the start of the 21st century, adding operations in Vietnam as well as in mainland China.

Other parts of the Cathay Financial Holdings group include Cathay Century Insurance, Cathay United Bank, Cathay Securities Corporation, Cathay Capital Management, and Cathay Venture. The parent company, itself part of the Lin Yuan Group, posted total assets of TWD 3.75 trillion in 2008. Cathay Life remains its most profitable contributor, generating TWD 935.79 billion in revenues in 2008. Both Cathay Life and Cathay Financial were founded by the legendary Tsai Wan-lin, once Taiwan's richest person and one of the world's wealthiest billionaires, who died in 2004. Elder son and Chairman Tsai Hong-tu turned over the day-to-day operations of the group to his younger brother T. Y. Tsai in 2009.

FROM RICE TO RICHES IN POSTWAR TAIWAN

Cathay Life Insurance Company stemmed from the fortunes of the Tsai (sometimes spelled as Cai) family, which emerged from poverty to become not only the wealthiest in Taiwan, but one of the wealthiest families in the world. The Tsai family were originally poor rice farmers based in Chunan, in the Miaoli district of what was then known as Formosa while the island was still under Japanese colonial rule.

Tsai Wan-chun and his younger brother Tsai Wan-lin at first worked on their father's farm, and then began selling vegetables to their neighbors. In 1932, when Tsai Wan-lin was just eight years old, the brothers traveled to Taipei, where the younger Tsai could go to school. Older brother Wan-chun, then 16 years old, went to work selling cosmetics for a Japanese company. Before long, however, the brothers had set up their first business, selling vegetables and fruits from a market stall.

The brothers' business acumen rose quickly and soon they had invested their savings in the opening of a grocery shop. By 1938 the brothers had acquired a department store. Not long after, the brothers began making their own soy sauce, which led to the opening of a soy sauce factory as well. Throughout this time, Tsai Wan-lin attended night school, finally passing his middle school exam. Japan's defeat in World War II provided still more business opportunities for the Tsai brothers.

By the end of the 1940s, the brothers were on their way toward establishing one of the island's preeminent *quanxi qiye*. This was the term used by native Taiwanese to designate the family-controlled conglomerates that were a distinct feature of many 20th-century Asian markets. Also known as *hong* in Hong Kong and *chaebol* in Korea, these conglomerates often distinguished themselves by developing highly diversified, and yet vertically integrated operations.

The Tsai brothers' fortunes took off with the arrival of more than two million Chinese fleeing to Taiwan during the Communist takeover of mainland China in 1949. The surge in demand for housing led the brothers to move into the construction sector. By 1957 the brothers had started real estate development investment interests, which provided a major springboard for the group's entry into Taiwan's rapidly growing financial sector. Over the next decades, the Tsai family came to control vast areas of land across Taiwan, and its properties portfolio included more than 230 of Taiwan's major commercial properties.

FOUNDING TAIWAN'S FIRST LIFE INSURANCE COMPANY IN 1962

The Tsai family moved more directly into the financial sector in 1960 when the brothers acquired stakes in Taiwan's Tenth Credit Cooperative bank, based in

Taipei. In that year, also, the family took its first steps into the insurance market, launching Cathay Insurance. Two years later, the group became the first Taiwanese company to begin offering life insurance, establishing Cathay Life Insurance Company.

By the late 1970s, the Tsai family already numbered among the most prominent financial players in what was then one of the world's most rapidly growing economies. During this period, Taiwan had begun to transition from an early focus on the manufactured-goods sector to a massive investment in the high-technology sector. Into the late 1970s and through the 1980s, Taiwan emerged as one of the world's major high-tech sectors.

The corresponding rise in wealth in turn enabled the Tsai family to build its own vast financial empire. The family's real estate holdings also allowed it to benefit from the Taiwanese property boom during the 1970s. By the end of the decade, the family conglomerate had claimed the position as Taiwan's leading *quanxi qiye*, with operations in banking, insurance, asset investment, property development, construction, plastics, and retail operations.

Tsai Wan-chun and Tsai Wan-lin had been joined in the business by a third brother, Tsai Wan-tsai, as well as by Wan-chun's four sons. Tsai Wan-chun remained as the family's patriarch. Following a stroke, however, in 1977 Wan-chun decided to break up the family's financial empire. Brother Tsai Wan-lin gained the major part of the company, including Cathay Life Insurance, Cathay Construction, and, temporarily, Tenth Credit Cooperative, which by then had become fully controlled by the family. When the Taiwanese authorities objected to Wan-lin's control of the bank, its ownership was transferred to Tsai Zhenzhou, the eldest son of Tsai Wan-chun, who was also a member of the ruling Nationalist Party government.

TAIWAN'S WEALTHIEST IN THE EIGHTIES

Tsai Wan-lin regrouped his part of the family business empire into a new holding company, Lin Yuan Group. Cathay Life Insurance served as the group's flagship, as it developed an impressive network of more than 700 agencies across Taiwan. The company's payroll grew to more than 40,000, making it the largest employer in Taiwan. By the end of the 1980s, Cathay Life had established itself as the dominant player in the Taiwanese life insurance market. It enjoyed a market share of 52 percent by 1991.

In 1985 the Tsai family had completed a new reshuffling of its shared business interests. This came

KEY DATES

1962: Tsai Wan-lin and older brother Tsai Wan-chun establish Taiwan's first life insurance provider, Cathay Life Insurance Company.

1977: Following the breakup of the Tsai family's holdings, Tsai Wan-lin takes over Cathay Life, and creates the Lin Yuan Group.

1989: Tsai Wan-lin rises to the ninth position on the *Forbes* Billionaires list.

1993: Lin Yuan acquires a 45 percent stake in the Taiwan First investment trust.

2001: Cathay Life acquires Capital Securities, which leads Lin Yuan to create a new holding company for its financial assets, Cathay Financial.

2005: Cathay Life becomes the first Taiwanese insurer to enter the mainland China market through a joint venture with Eastern Air Holding.

2008: Cathay Life adds operations in Shanghai and opens its first branches in Vietnam.

about following a scandal involving Tsai Zhenzhou, who was convicted of embezzling hundreds of million of dollars from Tenth Credit Cooperative. Zhenzhou had attempted to rescue the failing Cathay Plastics business, which had been hit hard by soaring oil prices in the 1970s and 1980s. Because Tenth Credit Cooperative was allowed to lend only to individuals, Zhenzhou ordered 700 of Cathay Plastics' employees to take out loans to be used in shoring up the company. By 1983 these loans totaled $190 million. Other schemes operated by Zhenzhou, including the use of postdated checks, resulted in losses of another $225 million.

The resulting scandal, which took on a political tone due to Tsai Zhenzhou's government position, led to the further breakup of the Tsai family holdings. Tenth Credit Cooperative was taken over by the Taiwanese government, while Tsai Wan-lin and younger brother Tsai Wan-tsai, who had formed his own conglomerate, Fubon, gained control over other parts of the group. In this way, Lin Yuan added operations in the engineering and hospital management fields, while also developing its own extensive real estate holdings. The scandal, however, led to a feud between the two remaining Tsai brothers, in large part due to Tsai Wan-tsai's anger over Tsai Wan-lin's refusal to support their nephew through the scandal.

Nonetheless, this refusal helped reinforce Tsai Wan-lin's own lack of involvement in Tsai Zhenzhou's misdeeds. Instead, Tsai Wan-lin continued to focus on building his business empire. By 1989 he claimed the title of Taiwan's wealthiest person, which was underscored by his ninth-place position on *Forbes* magazine's top-ten richest persons list of that year.

EXPANDING FINANCIAL GROUP IN THE NINETIES

Tsai Wan-lin began preparing for his succession in 1990, turning over the day-to-day operations of the group to his own sons. Eldest son Tsai Hong-tu took over as the conglomerate's head. Nevertheless, Tsai Wan-lin remained highly active in the group's operations. In fact, Wan-lin had earned a reputation for micromanaging every detail of the group's sprawling operations. Although his highly paternalistic management style played a major role in the group's early growth, it also was said to have hampered the company's expansion through the 1990s. Despite the company's continued success, Tsai Wan-lin's position among the world's wealthiest dropped steadily through the decade. By the time of his death in 2004, his rank had slipped to 94th on the list of the world's wealthiest individuals.

Tsai Wan-lin, however, had continued preparing for his succession through the 1990s. In 1998 he had established a clear division of his sprawling business empire among members of his family. Control of the Lin Yuan Group passed relatively peaceably to the next generation, a rare event among Taiwanese family conglomerates.

Lin Yuan expanded its financial sector interests in the early 1990s. The group's application for a banking license was turned down by the Taiwanese government in 1991. Tsai Wan-lin, however, found a backdoor into the banking sector in 1993 when he purchased a 45 percent stake in investment trust Taiwan First. By the end of the decade, Lin Yuan had successfully leveraged that stake into a significant entry into the commercial banking market, with the establishment of Cathay United Bank.

NEW FINANCIAL MARKETS IN THE 21ST CENTURY

This move into the commercial banking market came in part in response to the increasingly competitive life insurance market in Taiwan. In 1994 the Taiwanese government announced that it would allow foreign companies to begin competing in the country's insurance sector for the first time. Cathay Life Insurance's market share began to decline steadily throughout the decade, dwindling to just 30 percent.

Another major financial sector extension came in 2001, when Cathay Life acquired Capital Securities. This purchase gave the company control of one of Taiwan's top-five securities brokerages. Following this acquisition, Lin Yuan moved to consolidate its financial operations into a new publicly listed holding company, Cathay Financial Holdings. Cathay Life then became the new company's flagship operation.

With its domestic market share slipping, Cathay Life also began looking toward expanding overseas in the late 1990s. In 1998, for example, the company announced plans to set up a subsidiary in the Bahamas, as a base for its further international expansion. The company then began focusing on two primary foreign markets: Vietnam and mainland China.

INTERNATIONAL TARGETS IN THE 21ST CENTURY

The transition to a new Taiwanese government starting in 2000 paved the way for the group's entry into the mainland Chinese market. Whereas the previous government had steadfastly resisted any form of trade with the mainland, the new government recognized the need to develop economic relations with its powerful neighbor. By 2005 Cathay Life Insurance had become the first Taiwanese company to establish insurance operations on the mainland. This came through a joint venture formed in partnership with Eastern Air Holding.

Although the joint venture struggled to get off the ground, and did not project profitability until 2013, Cathay continued to bid for licenses to operate elsewhere in China. This led the group to establish its second business in China, Cathay Insurance, based in Shanghai, in 2008. In that year, the company announced its plans to seek a new partner in order to establish itself as a national player in the Chinese market.

In the meantime, Cathay Life had also been making progress toward its expansion into the Vietnamese market. The company established its first office in Hanoi in 2004. By 2007 the company had acquired a license to operate in the country's life insurance market. This enabled the group to open its first full-scale branches there, in Hanoi and Ho Chi Minh City in 2008.

Back in Taiwan, however, the Tsai family fortune was buffeted by the worsening global economic crisis. Cathay Financial had invested heavily in the subprime loan markets in the United States, as well as in funds involved in Bernard Madoff's $50 billion pyramid

scheme. In the meantime, the group's flagship Cathay Life continued to struggle to revive its flagging market share.

By the end of 2008, Cathay Life had posted its first loss, of $49 million, since its founding in 1962. The Tsai family's own fortune had plunged by some 75 percent. These difficulties led Tsai Hong-tu to call in younger brother T. Y. Tsai to take over as the day-to-day head of the company in early 2009. Cathay Life Insurance Company, and Cathay Financial, looked toward its new leadership to ensure their position as Taiwan's financial frontrunners in the new century.

M. L. Cohen

PRINCIPAL SUBSIDIARIES

Cathay Insurance (Bermuda) Co., Ltd.; Cathay Insurance Co., Ltd. (China); Cathay Life Insurance (Vietnam) Co., Ltd.; Cathay Life Insurance Co. (China); Cathay Securities Investment Consulting Co., Ltd.; Symphox Information Co., Ltd.

PRINCIPAL COMPETITORS

China Life Insurance Company Limited; Nan Shan Life Insurance Company Ltd.; E.Sun Financial Holding Co. Ltd.; Sinon Corp.; American Life Insurance Co.; First-Aviva Life Insurance Company Ltd.; Taiwan Life Insurance Company Ltd.; Union Insurance Company Ltd.

FURTHER READING

Bangsberg, P. T., "Taiwan's Cathay Life Seeks Bermuda Subsidiary Office," *Journal of Commerce and Commercial,* October 28, 1998, p. 11A.

"Cathay Insurance Starts Operation in Shanghai," *Alestron,* September 20, 2008.

"Cathay Life Aggressive on Forming Subsidiary in M'land China," *Taiwan Economic News,* January 31, 2002.

"Cathay Life Building Elite Force for Financial Services," *Taiwan Economic News,* June 10, 2002.

"Cathay Life Expands Footholds in Mainland China," *Asia Africa Intelligence Wire,* September 15, 2005.

"Cathay Life Insurance Launches Two Products on New Life Table," *Alestron,* January 5, 2006.

"Cathay Life Insurance Opens in Vietnam," *AsiaPulse News,* July 10, 2008.

"Cathay Life Insurance Set Up Branch in Guangdong," *Alestron,* November 14, 2008.

"Cathay Life Now Taiwan's Largest Co. with US$13 BLN FY 02 Revenue," *AsiaPulse News,* May 1, 2003, p. 8888.

"Cathay Life Property Insurance JV Starts Operation," *SinoCast China Business Daily*, September 3, 2008.

"Cathay Life to Form Property Insurer in Mainland," *SinoCast LLC China Financial Watch*, November 12, 2007.

Dickie, Mure, "Cathay Life to Take Over Local Brokerage," *Financial Times*, October 18, 2001, p. 30.

Flannery, Russell, "Oh, Brother," *Forbes Asia Magazine*, July 13, 2009.

Hsu, Crystal, "Cathay Financial Positions Itself to Expand FYP Share," *Taipei Times*, August 26, 2009, p. 12.

Lai, Iris, "Taiwan's Cathay Life Invests in Blackstone Capital," *A.M. Best Newswire*, August 28, 2008.

Leonard, Andrew, "From Soybeans to Subprime," *Salon.com*, July 10, 2008.

Lin, Jackie, and Kevin Chen, "Tsai Led Family to Dominate Nation's Finance Business," *Taipei Times*, September 29, 2004, p. 10.

"Taiwan Life Plans JV in Mainland," *SinoCast, LLC China Financial Watch*, November 30, 2005.

"Taiwan's Cathay, Hontai Fall Victim to Fraud of Nasdaq Ex-Chairman Madoff," *BBC Monitoring International Reports*, December 16, 2008.

"Taiwan's Cathay Life Insurance to Set Up Office in Guangdong," *AsiaPulse News*, September 26, 2002.

"Three Taiwan Insurers Given Access to Mainland Market," *Alestron*, November 16, 2007.

"Tsai Wan-lin," *Telegraph*, October 14, 2004.

Chicago Transit Authority

—■—

567 West Lake Street
Chicago, Illinois 60661
U.S.A.
Telephone: (312) 664-7200
Toll Free: (888) 968-7282
Web site: http://www.transitchicago.com

Government Agency
Founded: 1945
Employees: 12,000
Operating Revenues: $450 million (2009 est.)
NAICS: 485113 Bus and Other Motor Vehicle Transit
Systems

■ ■ ■

Chicago Transit Authority, known simply as the "CTA" around Chicago and its sprawling suburbs, is the nation's second-largest public transportation system. With 1,190 Metra rail cars, 224.2 miles of track, and 1,971 Pace buses covering 2,517 route miles, the CTA provides service throughout the city of Chicago and 40 surrounding suburbs, averaging close to 1.75 million riders each weekday. Governed by the Chicago Transit Board and part of the Regional Transit Authority, the CTA has often been a source of controversy during its nearly 70 years in operation, concerning questionable management, service cuts, and legendary financial difficulties. Nevertheless, the CTA remains one of the country's busiest transit systems and keeps Chicagoans moving at a rapid pace.

GETTING AROUND CHICAGO: LATE 19TH TO MID-20TH CENTURY

In the early 20th century, Chicago was a bustling city gaining national exposure for its growth. Not content as the "Second City" after New York, Chicago's early movers and shakers saw the potential of the city's waterways and midwestern location. Transportation within the city began with horse-drawn carriages followed by cable cars, electric streetcars, then steam-powered trains in the 1890s.

To combat congestion and traffic, city planners and businessmen decided to follow New York City's example and built elevated rail platforms above the streets. Chicago's first elevated rail line (known as the "L" or "el") began service in 1892 traveling between Congress Parkway and 39th Street, followed by additional routes in 1893 (Lake Street), 1895 (West Side), and 1899 (Northwestern). Perhaps the greatest rail innovation of the time was Charles T. Yerkes Jr.'s Union Elevated Railroad, uniting the segments to form a loop around the city in 1897, ushering in downtown's famous nickname, "the Loop."

In 1924 the owners and operators of Chicago's elevated rail segments merged into the Chicago Rapid Transit Company (CRT). The following year, in 1925, the glittery Great Hall of the Chicago's Union Station rail hub opened. Designed by famed architect Daniel Burnham, the new train station set the stage for the city's mass transit revolution.

By the 1940s the L train system had expanded throughout the city and bus service had begun in

COMPANY PERSPECTIVES

The Chicago Transit Authority (CTA) operates the nation's second largest public transportation system—a regional transit system that serves the City of Chicago and 40 neighboring communities. CTA provides 1.7 million rides on an average weekday, accounting for over 80% of all transit trips taken in the six-county Chicago metropolitan region.

earnest as well. Chicago finally went underground with its L trains running beneath Clybourn, Division, and State streets, opening the State Street station in 1943. Two years later, in 1945, the Illinois General Assembly created the Chicago Transit Authority (CTA) as an independent governmental agency to oversee the city's mass transit systems. The CTA bought rail and bus lines with $100 million in bonds and officially began service on October 1, 1947. Exactly five years later, after acquiring the last private bus service, the CTA became Chicago's only transit operator.

BOOMS AND BUSTS: FIFTIES THROUGH SEVENTIES

The early 1950s saw the first of several rail lines built within the medians of Chicago's major arteries, beginning with the Congress (now Eisenhower) Expressway. Unfortunately, as the postwar boom subsided, CTA ridership declined. The agency closed dozens of stations, cut service on many routes, and raised fares, a move it would make many times in the future. Higher fares, however, led to even less ridership, more route cuts, and the CTA operating in the red.

The 1960s were a decade of further ups and downs. Couples and families moved away from Chicago's increasingly crowded wards, favoring the quiet of newly built homes on tree-lined streets. This was good news for the CTA as additional train stations in the western and northern suburbs were needed; conversely, though, many among the prospering middle class bought cars and drove into the city, skipping trains and buses altogether. As it had previously, the CTA responded rather badly according to observers, cutting service and raising fares, once again exacerbating rather than solving its problems.

To help shore up the struggling CTA, a new agency called the Regional Transportation Agency (RTA) was formed in 1974. The RTA oversaw the transit systems of both the city and its far-reaching suburbs. Designed to ease the CTA's perennial budget woes, the RTA soon found itself in the same situation. Luckily for both agencies, several factors led commuting drivers to ditch their cars and return to mass transit including the oil embargos and gas shortages; high parking fees and clogged highways; and growing environmental awareness, especially of air pollution and vehicle emissions.

Major developments in the 1980s included uniting suburban bus service under a single name, "Pace," in 1983 and renaming the commuter rail lines as "Metra" in 1984. The new names and logos were meant to create instantly recognizable brands and signify the unity of Chicago and its six counties' transportation system under the RTA. The CTA, meanwhile, had completed a new rail line from the city to O'Hare International Airport. The new route proved to be a popular and inexpensive alternative to taxis and convoluted bus routes.

CROOKED MILES IN THE NINETIES

In the early 1990s as the economy slumped, the cash-strapped CTA raised fares to offset losses. The increase again resulted in a backlash of reduced ridership and vocal criticism. By 1992 city ridership on the L had strengthened although the particularly hard-hit bus system remained down more than 25 percent. Suburban rail service was also down, having fallen over 15 percent from 1990 to 1992.

The CTA renamed its many rail lines with colors (Red, Blue, Brown, Green, Orange, Purple, and Yellow) in early 1993 to differentiate routes and service. The Southwest or Orange Line, running from downtown into southern Cook County, had undergone an ambitious extension to take riders from the Loop to Midway Airport, just as the Blue Line provided transportation from the city to O'Hare Airport. The Orange Line kicked off service to Midway in October 1993 and came in under a budgeted $300 million price tag. Next came the $350 million renovation of the Green Line–Lake Street railway, including an automated signal and train control system installed by Harmon Industries. The Green Line reopened in July 1996.

As the end of 1996 neared, the CTA announced it would renegotiate leases on some of its 100-plus properties throughout the city and suburbs to raise funds. This followed 1995's innovation of leasing rapid transit cars to investors, then leasing them back to raise cash. With the CTA operating with an estimated $20 million loss for 1996 and almost triple that amount projected for 1997, the deals went a long way toward shoring up the agency's budget.

KEY DATES

1859: Chicago transportation begins with horses and buggies.

1882: City's first cable car begins operation.

1890: Electric streetcars begin ferrying Chicagoans around the city.

1892: City's first section of "L," or "el," elevated trains initiate service.

1897: Charles Yerkes Jr.'s "loop" unites the L lines in the city.

1917: Chicago's first motorized bus service begins.

1924: Chicago Rapid Transit Company consolidates L owners and operators.

1943: State Street subway station opens to the public.

1947: CTA begins operations in Chicago.

1952: CTA becomes the city's sole mass transit operator.

1984: Rail service to and from O'Hare Airport begins.

1993: CTA begins using color designations; rail service to and from Midway Airport begins.

1997: Fare cards are introduced to CTA riders.

2006: Pink Line rail service is initiated.

2008: CTA ridership (both bus and train) tops 526 million for the year.

2009: CTA purchases "green" hybrid buses for use in the city and suburbs.

The biggest news for 1997, however, was not the CTA's budget but the rollout of new electronic fare cards by San Diego-based Cubic Corporation, modeled after a similar system in New York. The new collection system, which went on line in August, went surprisingly well. Although there were a few glitches such as machines becoming full too quickly or not being able to give change, the city, the agency, and riders deemed the new system a success.

The cards were also significant as a handy source for advertising. One-day and weekly cards featured ads for a variety of products from breath mints and food items to Old Navy clothing. The city's embattled bus system also initiated a new revenue stream by debuting "wrapped" buses, vehicles completely covered in a single advertiser's banner or message. Visually striking, the moving billboards earned the CTA kudos from amused riders and provided millions in needed revenue.

In 1998 the CTA reached a creative financing agreement to lease its Green Line to private investors, then lease it back, netting $20 million in the transaction. The funds were earmarked for repairs to aging buses and trains, and mirrored previous leasing deals, only leasing the entire Green Line instead of individual rail cars.

NEW MILESTONES

By the dawn of the new century, the CTA was once again fraught with problems old and new. The new, both a positive and a negative, was a vast increase in ridership to over 1.4 million customers per day; the old was funding. The CTA badly needed funds to update its fleet and strengthen an aging and overused infrastructure of rail lines and stations. The worst off seemed to be the L with overcrowding, crumbling tracks, and moldy stations.

Suburban Metra trains were also overcrowded during the morning and afternoon rush hours, but pretty open on weekends. Luckily for the CTA, legislators fought for and won extensive funding from Congress to renovate and rebuild part of the L and Metra systems, including the older Blue and Brown Lines.

In 2003 CTA riders had their fare cards upgraded into "smartcards." Like credit cards, the new cards could be refilled or reloaded with funds as necessary and provided faster service with touch pads for entry. The following year, 2004, saw part of the Blue Line restoration completed, with two stations reopening and construction continuing on six others. Next came renovations on the Brown Line and building of the Pink Line traveling well into the western suburbs, which began service in 2006.

By 2007 the CTA was back in the headlines as money woes reached crisis proportions. With a huge deficit, the economy in turmoil, and renovations causing headaches for staffers and riders alike, the embattled agency faced questions about its leadership. This, of course, was nothing new and the CTA's leadership and governing bodies struggled to find answers and solutions. Regardless, construction and renovations continued, with proposals for new service routes and connecting stations as combined ridership for CTA buses, L trains, and commuter lines grew to 526 million passengers for 2008.

In early 2009 the CTA got a new president in Richard Rodriguez, who had formerly served as Chicago's aviation commissioner, led the city's buildings department, and worked at the Chicago Housing Authority. He hoped to bring the CTA into the green, literally and figuratively, to both balance the budget and to bring greater environmental awareness to the transit agency. A step in the right direction was the city's first hybrid buses, bought with federal stimulus funds, to save millions in fuel costs, maintenance, and repairs.

Despite its critics, the CTA had remained the backbone of Chicago's transportation system, providing the city with bus and train service for close to seven decades. Often steeped in controversy, like so many other city agencies, the CTA continued to serve millions in the tristate (Illinois, Indiana, and Wisconsin) area on a daily basis and would likely do so for decades to come.

Nelson Rhodes

FURTHER READING

Cappo, Joe, "Minty-Fresh CTA Card Heralds a New Medium," *Crain's Chicago Business*, August 9, 1999, p. 8.

Hinz, Greg, "Advisers Get $9-Million Fare on CTA Lease Deal," *Crain's Chicago Business*, April 27, 1998, p. 3.

———, "CTA's Money Pit," *Crain's Chicago Business*, August 1, 2005, p. 2.

———, "CTA's Next Stop: Surviving Success," *Crain's Chicago Business*, August 27, 2001, p. 1.

———, "In Search for Cash, CTA Makes Tracts," *Crain's Chicago Business*, September 23, 1996, p. 3.

Hollenhorst, John, "Surfing the CTA," *Mass Transit*, June 2009, p. 50.

Klein, Sarah A., "Carole Brown: Chairman, Chicago Transit Authority," *Crain's Chicago Business*, May 7, 2007, p. 32.

"On Time, Under Budget," *Railway Age*, June 1992, p. 48.

Phillips-Fein, Kim, "There's Light at the End of the Tunnel for CTA," *Crain's Chicago Business*, January 5, 1998, pp. 4+.

Slania, John T., "Loop Dreams," *Crain's Chicago Business*, June 2, 2003, p. A47.

China Eastern Airlines Corporation Limited

2550 Hongqiao Road
Hongqiao Airport
Shanghai, 200335
China
Telephone: (+86 21) 6268 6268
Fax: (+86 21) 6268 6116
Web site: http://www.flychinaeastern.com

Government-Controlled Public Company
Incorporated: 1988 as China Eastern Airlines
Employees: 35,000
Sales: CNY 41.07 billion ($6 billion) (2008)
Stock Exchanges: Shanghai Hong Kong New York
Ticker Symbols: 600115 00670 CEA
NAICS: 481111 Scheduled Passenger Air Transportation; 481112 Scheduled Freight Air Transportation; 481212 Nonscheduled Chartered Freight Air Transportation; 481211 Nonscheduled Chartered Passenger Air Transportation

■ ■ ■

China Eastern Airlines Corporation Limited (CEA) is one of China's top three airlines. One of the country's first state-owned enterprises to offer shares on the New York Stock Exchange, China Eastern remains majority owned by the government through CEA Holding. CEA has invested heavily to modernize its fleet and train its personnel to Western standards. The carrier operates approximately 240 Boeing and Airbus jets on more than 400 routes, from domestic flights to intercontinental voyages as far as Europe, Australia, and the United

States. CEA is based in the bustling commercial center of Shanghai and its dominance there increased in 2009 when it took over local rival Shanghai Airlines. CEA has regional hubs in the northwest (Xi'an) and the southwest (Kunming) of the country.

ORIGINS

The China Civil Aviation Administration (CCAC) was formed on November 2, 1949, about a month after the creation of the People's Republic of China. CCAC was started with the scattered band of personnel and aircraft left as airlines sponsored by Chinese and U.S. interests fled to Taiwan to escape the Communists.

CCAC was assigned responsibility for air travel in the south of China, while the Sino-Soviet Joint Stock Company (*Ren Ming Hong Kong Kun Sze* in Chinese or *Sovietsko-Kitaysko Aktsioneren Obschestvo Grazhdanskoi Aviatsii* in Russian), commonly known as SKOAGA, was responsible for northern routes. These were merged in 1954 to form the Zhongua Ming Hong Jui (also transliterated as Minhaiduy) or Chinese Civil Aviation Bureau, which had six main regional divisions based in Beijing, Shanghai, Guangzhou, Shenyang, Si'an, and Wuhan. The Civil Aviation Bureau became the Civil Aviation Administration of China (CAAC) in April 1962.

At first, the CAAC was dependent on Soviet support. It operated, for the most part, Soviet-designed aircraft during the Cold War, except for a few leftover U.S. designs and a few modern turboprops and jets bought from Great Britain in 1961. It bought more Western aircraft in the 1970s, including some British

KEY DATES

1984: Civil Aviation Administration of China is divided into four regional airlines and one international one.

1988: China Eastern Airlines (CEA) becomes officially autonomous.

1997: Shares begin trading on New York and Hong Kong stock exchanges.

1998: Code-share agreement with American Airlines is the first of its kind between China and the United States.

2001: CEA acquires control of Great Wall Airlines in consolidation of China's airline industry.

2008: Bid to sell a strategic stake to Singapore Airlines founders when Air China suggests a rival bid.

2009: CEA acquires much coveted local rival Shanghai Airlines.

Trident jets in 1971 and 10 Boeing 707s in 1972. (A few supersonic Concordes also were ordered that year but never delivered.) CAAC also bought a few smaller Australian aircraft.

By the time it was disassembled in 1984, CAAC at least had pretensions of providing Western levels of service, that is, concerning the types of aircraft used on international routes. The carrier even had bought a few Boeing 747 wide-body jets, which were placed in service to Paris, San Francisco, and New York. After 25 years without a reported accident, a string of fatal crashes in the late 1970s gave impetus to modernizing the airline's operations.

In late 1984, CAAC was divided into one international carrier (Air China) and four regional airlines: Southern, Southwestern, Northwestern, and Eastern, based in Shanghai. Three others also were soon created in an atmosphere of explosive growth in air traffic. The result was unprecedented freedom of choice among passengers and unprecedented fiscal responsibility among the carriers.

AUTONOMOUS IN 1988

Two of the regionals, China Southern and China Eastern, were allowed to fly abroad because of the commercial importance of their home bases, Guangzhou and Shanghai. Both soon developed into major airlines in their own right. They did not become officially autonomous until July 1, 1988, although they remained under the ownership of CAAC, which had authority over aircraft purchases and the establishment of new routes. At the time, new freedoms were sweeping the country, and small independent airlines continued to spring up until the Tiananmen Square Massacre in June 1989, which emptied Chinese airliners of foreign tourists and threatened trade with U.S. aircraft manufacturers.

The Tiananmen crisis notwithstanding, CEA's planes usually flew full, averaging load factors of 80 percent. Its diverse fleet included Airbus Industrie A300 wide-body aircraft, McDonnell Douglas MD-82s, and British Aerospace BAe 146 regional jets, which were soon sold off. CEA ordered five MD-11 tri-jet wide-body transports to handle the new long-haul international routes critical to bringing in hard currency. In 1991, China Eastern carried up to 8,000 passengers a day on a total of 70 routes, including flights to several Japanese destinations and Seattle and Los Angeles in the United States. CEA employed 3,600 people at the time. Pilots and engineering personnel would remain particularly scarce for the rest of the decade.

One of the MD-11s operated as a freighter between Shanghai and Chicago. A Seattle stop was soon added and frequency increased to two flights a week. Flights to the United States ran 80 percent full and carried apparel for the most part, according to the *Journal of Commerce*. Return flights only ran at 30 percent capacity and carried items such as high-tech machinery for forwarders including Airborne Express. The beginning of passenger service on the Chicago route was delayed by late aircraft deliveries.

Annual revenues rose about 20 percent in 1992. CEA bought ten Fokker 100 regional turboprops and ordered five Airbus A340s worth $555 million. In June, CEA launched its first European route with service from Brussels, originating in Shanghai with stops in Beijing and Bahrain. A route to Madrid followed the next spring. The world's most profitable airline, British Airways (BA), was rumored to be considering an investment in CEA. BA was building a network of global alliance partners at the time.

The China Eastern Air Group, a collection of 30 companies with operations in tourism, foodstuffs, real estate, finance, and marketing, was organized in 1993. It created the largest air transportation company in China and competed directly with the CAAC and the airlines (Air China, China Southern) still under CAAC's control. Another round of expansion followed the reorganization, with new McDonnell Douglas aircraft on the way and new destinations planned in Malaysia and Vietnam.

China Eastern, along with four other Chinese airlines, contracted Northwest Airlines to train its pilots in 1994. Safety concerns continued as several CEA aircraft were involved in incidents in the mid-1990s. Hijackings, disastrous crashes, and in-flight mishaps among various Chinese carriers including CEA contributed to dwindling interest in the airline's planned flotation on the New York Stock Exchange. CEA aimed to raise hard currency in the offering to finance its purchases of new Airbus and McDonnell Douglas airliners. The new capacity was needed to keep up with China's air traffic, which grew at a rate of 25 percent per year in the mid-1990s. These planes, however, would experience low rates of utilization (about seven hours per day) and lowering load factors (about 70 percent), representing somewhat of an excess of capacity.

CEA invested CNY 100 million in a new maintenance hangar and entered into a Shanghai-based wheel and brake overhaul joint venture with AlliedSignal in 1994. It also announced plans to build a second hub outside its home province (in Qingdao, the province of Shandong), the first Chinese carrier to do so. It began flying to Seoul, in the Republic of Korea, late in the year. CEA posted a profit of $76 million on revenues of $790 million in 1995. It operated 41 aircraft at the time.

1997 PUBLIC OFFERING

Revenues for 1996 rose 10 percent to $797 million (CNY 7.3 billion) although after-tax profits fell about 7 percent to $71.2 million (CNY 591 million). CEA earned more than half of its passenger revenues on international routes, although its most profitable ones, those to Hong Kong, were reclassified as domestic routes when the territory was returned to China. Cargo revenues were lagging, however. CEA operated only one dedicated freighter (Boeing, which took over McDonnell Douglas, was scheduled to convert two of CEA's MD-11 passenger airliners into freighters in 1999).

CEA hoped to raise $250 million in exchange for 35 percent of its share capital (the maximum foreign ownership allowed by Chinese law) in simultaneous offerings on the New York and Hong Kong stock exchanges in February 1997. The listing received a lackluster response, but raised $246 million nonetheless. CEA also borrowed $130 million from the China Industry and Commerce Bank to help finance its new aircraft purchases, worth about $1 billion. A round of government-administered consolidation among China's other carriers was expected.

In September 1998, CEA became the first carrier from the People's Republic of China to enter a code-share agreement with a U.S. airline. CEA's cooperation with American Airlines had been in the works since April 1997. A code share with a Japanese carrier, All Nippon Airways, soon followed, another first. A bilateral air services agreement between the United Kingdom and China in November 1998 raised expectations regarding the entry of British airlines into the Shanghai market. Both Virgin Atlantic Airways and British Airways expressed interest.

Countering the positive developments, CEA experienced serious losses resulting from the Asian economic crisis. It posted a loss of CNY 481 million ($58 million) for 1998 although passenger and cargo traffic were up. Revenues were CNY 7.79 billion. Lowered domestic airport fees and the sale of 13 MD-82s offered some hope for financial recovery. CEA traded in the jets as part of its deal to lease ten Airbus A320s from General Electric Capital Aviation Services, which had helped the carrier dispose of its Fokker 100s earlier.

CEA installed quick access recorders in its cockpits in an attempt to nip bad flying habits in the bud. After a safety audit, CEA signed a new code-share agreement with Qantas, which was expected, ultimately, to increase passenger traffic 30 percent between China and Australia. Qantas was a member of the One-World global alliance that also included British Airways and American Airlines. CEA continued to seek such partnerships.

CEA was showing a profit again by the first half of 1999. Selling planes helped, as did favorable currency markets. CEA also trimmed domestic service heavily. It anticipated completion of the new $1.6 billion Pudong International Airport near Shanghai, the largest city in the world's fastest-growing aviation market.

CONSOLIDATION

After two decades of frenetic growth China had more than 30 airlines in all. Owing to both commercial considerations and growing safety concerns, the Chinese government directed the Big Three (CEA, China Southern, and Air China) to each take over two or three smaller carriers. At the same time, the CAAC relinquished direct ownership of the ten airlines it controlled in order to focus on its regulatory role.

CEA led the takeovers when it acquired a controlling interest in the relatively small Great Wall Airlines and China Northwest Airlines Company, a larger regional airline which was itself quite laden with debt. In 2002 Northwest and Yunnan Airlines Company were folded in with the old CEA to form China Eastern Airlines Corporation Limited. CEA also acquired control of Wuhan Airlines in 2002.

In 2003 CEA was exposed to the severe acute respiratory syndrome (SARS) crisis, which halved passenger numbers on international flights. This prompted it to cut capacity on international routes and defer deliveries of more than one-dozen aircraft on order.

Although it broke even in 2004, from 2001 to 2005 CEA accumulated losses of CNY 400 million ($50 million), and it lost another CNY 3.3 billion ($429 million) in 2006. Worse losses were to come. To many, CEA appeared vulnerable to takeover, perhaps by the smaller but more profitable Air China.

SEEKING A PARTNER

Although very weak financially, CEA had a great deal to offer in terms of strategic position, including access to the vast Chinese market as well as rights to fly beyond China, noted *Aviation Week & Space Technology*. A strategic investment from a foreign airline would help CEA, bringing not just capital but management expertise.

After an extended courtship, a bid from Singapore Airlines for a 24 percent holding in CEA was rejected by CEA's minority shareholders in January 2008 after Air China and its partner Cathay Pacific informally developed a competing proposal.

Although CEA eked out a CNY 586 million ($85 million) profit on operating revenue of CNY 43.53 billion in 2007, for 2008 the carrier posted a huge net loss of CNY 13.9 billion ($2.03 billion); unfavorable jet-fuel hedging contracts were partly responsible. Annual passenger count peaked at 39 million in 2007.

The government injected billions of dollars in capital into CEA and other airlines. The Chinese government made other moves that seemed to ensure the continued survival of CEA, which had appeared vulnerable to a takeover from the more profitable Air China.

In 2009 CEA landed a valued prize when it acquired Shanghai Airlines, coveted for its extensive presence in the bustling port that was also CEA's hometown. Although Shanghai Airlines dominated the local market, it was also losing money (CNY 1.25 billion in 2008).

Analysts told *Aviation Week & Space Technologies* that although the combined entity was expected to cut duplicate routes, political considerations made it unlikely that many jobs would be cut. With the absorption of the smaller carrier, CEA held a 50 percent market share in China's largest, fastest-growing, and most business-oriented city. It had also bulked up to tie

Air China for second place in the country in terms of passenger numbers.

Frederick C. Ingram

PRINCIPAL SUBSIDIARIES

China Cargo Airlines Co., Ltd. (70%); China Eastern Airlines Jiangsu Co., Ltd. (63%); China Eastern Airlines Development (HK) Co., Ltd. (Hong Kong; 80%); Shanghai Eastern Flight Training Co., Ltd. (95%); Eastern Airlines Hotel Co., Ltd. (86%); China Eastern Airlines (Shantou) Economics Development Co., Ltd. (55%); China Eastern Airlines Wuhan Co., Ltd. (96%); Shanghai Eastern Maintenance Co., Ltd. (60%); Shanghai Eastern Airlines Logistics Co., Ltd. (70%); Eastern Business Airline Service Co., Ltd.; China Eastern Airline Gifting Co., Ltd.

PRINCIPAL COMPETITORS

Air China Limited; China Southern Airlines Co., Ltd.; Cathay Pacific Airways Limited; Hainan Airlines Co., Ltd.

FURTHER READING

Armbruster, William, "Delays at McDonnell Hamper China Eastern," *Journal of Commerce*, May 18, 1992, p. 2B.

Bangsberg, P. T., "China Eastern Targets Cargo," *Journal of Commerce*, May 1, 1997, p. 7B.

Betts, Paul, "BA Seeks to Enter China Air Ventures," *Financial Times*, June 8, 1994, World Trade News Sec., p. 9.

Chau, Beverly, "Beijing to Bend Tax Rules for Airlines," *South China Morning Post*, June 19, 1994, Money Sec., p. 1.

———, "Crashes Dent Airlines' Foreign Fund-Raising Effort," *South China Morning Post*, June 12, 1994, Money Sec., p. 3.

Davies, R. E. G., *Airlines of Asia since 1920*, London: Putnam, 1997.

Dobson, Chris, "US Official Thought He Was Going to Die as Both Engines Ran Short of Fuel," *South China Morning Post*, May 29, 1994, p. 3.

"Dog Fight; Aviation in China (Fighting over Shanghai)," *Economist*, September 29, 2007, p. 68.

Grindrod, Barry, "Speculation Mounts over BA Link-Up with Chinese Partner," *South China Morning Post*, February 6, 1993, p. 4.

Harding, James, and John Ridding, "China Eastern Goes Traveling," *Financial Times*, January 23, 1997, Companies and Finance: Asia-Pacific, p. 25.

Hindo, Brian, "Sudden Loss of Altitude at China Eastern; Shares Fall after a Bidding War between Cathay Pacific and

Singapore Airlines, Aiming at Securing Eastern's Shanghai Market, Fails to Materialize," *Business Week Online,* September 26, 2007.

Hodgson, Liz, "Turbulence Drama Claims Second Victim," *South China Morning Post*, April 11, 1993, p. 5.

Ionides, Nicholas, "China Eastern Reports $58m 1998 Loss," *Air Transport Intelligence*, April 28, 1999.

———, "GECAS Deal to Help China Eastern Reduce Debt," *Air Transport Intelligence*, April 13, 1999.

———, "New Shanghai Airport Set to Ramp Up Operations," *Air Transport Intelligence*, October 6, 1999.

———, "Virgin, China Eastern to Hold Formal Code-Share Talks," *Air Transport Intelligence*, November 20, 1998.

———, "Virgin's Branson Meets China Eastern Boss over Tie-Up," *Air Transport Intelligence*, November 19, 1998.

Jones, Dominic, "Dragon to Get Bit in the Year of the Tiger," *Airfinance Journal*, February 1998, pp. 28–30.

———, "The Next Step for China's Big Two," *Airfinance Journal*, February 1998, pp. 24–27.

Jones, Lois, "Shanghai Shangrila," *Airline Business,* December 1997, pp. 32+.

Kang, William, "Airline Hinges Growth on Pilot Quality," *South China Morning Post*, September 10, 1994, Bus. Sec., p. 1.

Kelly, Emma, "China Eastern in Wuhan Deal," *Flight International,* August 27, 2002, p. 23.

———, "Safety Audit Seals China Eastern/Qantas Deal," *Flight International*, May 12, 1999, p. 11.

Lewis, Paul, "China Eastern to Go Public," *Flight International*, September 4, 1996.

"Listing Abroad May Backfire," *South China Morning Post*, April 17, 1994, p. 4.

Mackey, Michael, "Great Leap Forward; China Eastern Leads the Way Toward Private Ownership," *Air Transport World*, March 1997, pp. 25ff.

Ng, Eric, "Long Restructuring Haul Ahead for Merged Airlines," *South China Morning Post*, June 7, 2002.

Perrett, Bradley, "Consolidation Push; China Eastern Seeks Foreign Partner as Domestic Takeover Looms," *Aviation Week & Space Technology*, May 21, 2007, p. 49.

———, "Eastern Promise: China Eastern Angles for Help by Loosening Its Share Criterion; SIA Could Benefit," *Aviation Week & Space Technology*, January 8, 2007, p. 43.

———, "Shanghai Tie-up," *Aviation Week & Space Technology*, June 15, 2009, p. 70.

Proctor, Paul, "Upcoming Service to U.S. Fuels China Eastern Upgrade," *Aviation Week & Space Technology*, June 10, 1991, pp. 34–37.

Westhael, Michael, "Flying Starts: New Chinese Carriers Replace State Monopoly," *Far Eastern Economic Review*, February 18, 1993, pp. 54–55.

中国移动通信
CHINA MOBILE

China Mobile Ltd.

60th Fl., The Center
99 Queen's Road Central
Hong Kong,
Hong Kong
Telephone: (+852) 31218888
Fax: (+852) 25119092
Web site: http://www.chinamobileltd.com

Public Company
Incorporated: 1997 as China Telecom (Hong Kong) Ltd.
Employees: 127,959
Sales: RMB 124.37 billion ($60.37 billion) (2008)
Stock Exchanges: New York Hong Kong
Ticker Symbols: CHL; 941
NAICS: 517212 Cellular and Other Wireless Telecom-
munications

■■■

China Mobile Ltd. is the leading provider of mobile telephone services in China, commanding more than 70 percent of that country's total market. With nearly 500 million subscribers in September 2009, China Mobile is also the world's largest mobile telephone operator. China Mobile operates through a network of 32 subsidiaries, each representing one of China's provinces or autonomous regions, as well as the Hong Kong market. In this way, the company provides coverage on a national level. China Mobile also has GSM-based global roaming agreements reaching nearly 240 countries and regions throughout the world. In addition to its mobile

telephone operations, China Mobile has also been developing value-added services, such as the M.Music download service in partnership with EMI, Sony, Universal Music, and Warner Music; ringtone sales; Internet access; M-Zone, which provides services developed for the youth market; and the upscale Go-Tone service. China Mobile has also been chosen by the Chinese government to develop and deploy the country's homegrown 3G highspeed mobile telephony technology, TD-SCDMA.

Faced with growing competition at home, China Mobile has announced plans to develop its operations onto an international scale in the future. In 2007, the company reached an agreement to acquire an 89 percent stake in Paktel, the fifth-largest player in the Pakistani market. China Mobile has also opened an international headquarters in London to serve the European, Middle Eastern, and African markets. China Mobile is led by CEO and Chairman Wang Jianzhou. The company is listed on the Hong Kong Stock Exchange. In 2008, China Mobile's revenues reached RMB 124.37 billion ($60.37 billion).

CHINA'S MOBILE TELEPHONE PIONEER

China Mobile stemmed from one of the earliest cellular telephone operations in China, when the provincial government of Guangdong launched a commercial mobile telephone network based on the total access communication system (TACS) protocol in 1987. Guangdong's position on the coast of the South China Sea, as well as its proximity to Hong Kong, had made it the earliest beneficiary of the new economic reform policies instituted by the communist government in the late 1970s. By the mid-1980s, Guangdong was China's wealthiest province, and boasted an increasing number of wealthy entrepreneurs, private enterprises, and a rising middle class.

Access to the TACS network initially remained restricted to high-level officials, including the directors of the province's state-owned corporations and high-ranking government officials, but also to a number of leaders of privately held businesses in the region. Guangdong Mobile, which was formally incorporated in 1988, grew only slowly. At the end of 1991, the company's subscriber base stood at just 30,000.

The Chinese economy began its first surge forward through the middle of the 1990s. Guangdong Mobile's own operations accelerated, and by 1997 the company boasted more than 1.2 million subscribers to its TACS network. By then, that analog-based technology had become outdated. In 1995, Guangdong Mobile introduced its first digital mobile telephony services based on the newly emerging GSM (global system for mobile communications) technology. This technology, which had also been adopted as the mobile telephony standard in Europe and elsewhere, provided far greater potential for expanding the region's mobile telephony network. Within two years, Guangdong's GSM-based network had surpassed its TACS network, topping 2.5 million subscribers. The company had also established an infrastructure covering all of the province's cities and outlying counties, and had also begun its penetration of the more rural and mountainous areas.

Guangdong Mobile was not the only player in the Chinese mobile market. Other provinces had also begun to develop their own mobile telephone networks. In Zhejiang, for example, the government rolled out a TACS-based network in 1992, before launching GSM service in 1995. By 1997 the two networks had reached a subscriber base of 650,000 and 1.25 million, respectively.

INDUSTRY RESTRUCTURING IN 1998

The Chinese government in Beijing, however, recognized the importance of developing a single mobile telephony operator on a national scale. The new body was to be separated from the government and operated as a commercial enterprise. This led the government to launch a restructuring of the telecommunications sector in 1997, placing the mobile telephone sector under the auspices of a new body, MII.

MII took over all of the country's provincial mobile telephony operators. At the same time, a new company was created, called China Telecom Hong Kong BVI Limited. The new company then formed its own subsidiary, China Telecom (Hong Kong), which finally became China Mobile Ltd. in 2000. In the meantime, China Mobile took over the operations of the country's two largest mobile telephone operators, Guangdong and Zhejiang, then listed its stock on the Hong Kong Stock Exchange. China Telecom Hong Kong BVI remained China Mobile's controlling shareholder.

The movement toward national operations proceeded only slowly for China Mobile. The company added a third province, Jiangsu, in 1998, paying HKD 22.48 billion ($2.9 billion). That province, China's third-largest in terms of cellular telephone uptake, added nearly 900,000 subscribers to China Mobile's customer base. The Jiangsu acquisition was quickly joined by three more, in Fujian, Henan, and Hainan, in 1999. In that year, China Mobile formed a partnership with European mobile telephone giant Vodafone, which became a strategic investor in the Chinese group through a $2.5 billion share purchase.

EXPANDING NETWORK

The company continued to absorb new operations in the new century. In 2000, the company added the provincial mobile operators in Beijing, Guangzi, Hebei, Liaoning, Shandong, Shanghai, and Tianjin. These were followed in 2002 by a new consolidation phase, adding operators in Anhui, Chongqing, Hubei, Hunan, Jiangxi, Shaanxi, Shanxi, and Sichuan. The fifth and final phase of the assets transfer from China Telecom to China Mobile was carried out by 2004. At that time, China Mobile absorbed the mobile networks in Gansu, Guizhou, Heilongjiang, Jilin, Neimenggu, Ningxia, Qinghai, Xinjiang, Xizang, and Yunnan. The company also took over two other subsidiary entities, China Mobile Communication Company Limited and Beijing P&T Consulting and Design Institute Company Limited.

China Mobile controlled mobile telephone operations in all 31 of China's provinces and autonomous

KEY DATES

1987: Guangdong Province in China launches its first TACS-based cellular telephone service.
1992: Mobile telephone service is launched in Zhejiang Province.
1995: Guangdong Mobile and Zhejiang Mobile both launch GSM-based networks.
1997: China Telecom (Hong Kong) Ltd., which later becomes China Mobile, is created and takes over Guangdong Mobile and Zhejiang Mobile.
1998: China Mobile acquires Jiangsu Mobile in the second of five asset transfers.
2004: Final asset transfer is completed, establishing China Mobile as a national operator in all 31 Chinese provinces.
2006: China Mobile acquires China Resources Peoples Telephone Company in Hong Kong.
2007: Company acquires 89 percent of Paktel in Pakistan.
2008: China Mobile opens a London headquarters for its European, Middle Eastern, and African interests.
2009: China Mobile's subscriber base tops 500 million.

regions, as well as the special administrative zone of Hong Kong. While absorbing the existing networks accounted for part of the boost in the group's subscriber base, its growth came especially by the booming demand for mobile service in China. The combination of a rapidly growing middle class, the introduction of new tariff schedules adapted to the country's enormous working class, and the relative lack of penetration of fixed line telephones in the country, provided the foundation for growth that was to transform China into the world's single-largest and fastest-growing mobile telephone market.

By 1999, China Mobile boasted 20 million subscribers. Just two years later, the company claimed the world's number two position, behind Vodafone, with 50 million subscribers. By the end of 2003, the company's subscriber base topped 140 million as the company reached the world's number one spot. From just RMB 15 billion in 1997, China Mobile's revenues climbed to RMB 128 billion ($15 billion) by the end of 2002.

Helping to fuel this expansion, and the company's own growing revenues, was the rollout of a number of new services, such as the introduction of short-messaging services (SMS) and other value-added services. By 2002, the company's subscribers were sending more than 40 billion text messages per year. The following year, the company also began introducing a range of other services, including multimedia messaging service (MMS) and other data transmission products. The new services and products helped the company's revenues jump again, to RMB 192 billion ($23 billion) in 2004.

INTERNATIONAL ASPIRATIONS

By 2006, China Mobile's total subscriber base had grown to 300 million, nearly as many as the entire population of the world's next largest mobile telephone market, the United States. The company enjoyed dominant status at home, claiming more than 70 percent of the total mobile telephone market (against competitor Unicom), and 39 percent of the total telecommunications market, including fixed line operators such as China Telecom.

China Mobile's future growth prospects dimmed somewhat as the Chinese government moved to add new competition in the mobile telecommunications market in the second half of the decade. In 2006, the government announced its intention to distribute three licenses for the operation of new high-speed 3G (third generation) mobile telephone networks. The third license went to China Telecom. That company's position as the country's dominant fixed-line telephony player meant that China Mobile faced a new major rival for the domestic market.

At the same time, China Mobile's dominant position also meant that it was singled out to deploy its 3G network using the TD-SCDMA standard, developed in China. The company was therefore forced to struggle with the difficulties of putting into place a new and untested technology, while its competitors were able to deploy their own networks using tried-and-tested 3G technologies used in North America and Europe.

By the end of the decade, China Mobile's competitors began gaining ground on the company, claiming an increasing share of new subscribers. As a result, China Mobile began seeking new markets. In the domestic market, the company began targeting further penetration into the relatively untapped rural market, which represented a potential population of more than 700 million people, where mobile telephone penetration hovered at just 10 percent.

The company also indicated its interest in expanding into overseas markets. Among the company's first moves was an entry into Hong Kong, with the acquisition of China Resources Peoples Telephone Company, a smaller player in that market with about one million subscribers. In 2007, the company made its first entry into the international market proper, buying an 89 percent stake in Paktel, the number five player in the Pakistan mobile telephone market. Then, in 2008, the group established a headquarters in London to oversee future development in the European, Middle East, and African markets.

China nonetheless remained the group's primary market. Through the end of the century, the group began to stabilize its 3G network, while developing new product ranges, such as music downloads, mobile Internet, and television services. The group launched negotiations with Apple Corporation to roll out its hugely successful iPhone. Those talks broke down, however; instead, China Mobile began rolling out its own, similar device, the Ophone, in 2009. By then, China Mobile's total subscriber base had reached 500 million. With more than 700 million more people to sign up in China, and the company's international ambitions, China Mobile anticipated years of growth ahead as the world's largest mobile telephone operator.

M. L. Cohen

PRINCIPAL SUBSIDIARIES

China Mobile Group Anhui Company Ltd.; China Mobile Group Beijing Company Ltd.; China Mobile Group Chongqing Company Ltd.; China Mobile Group Fujian Company Ltd.; China Mobile Group Gansu Company Ltd.; China Mobile Group Guangdong Company; China Mobile Group Guangxi Company Ltd.; China Mobile Group Guizhou Company Ltd.; China Mobile Group Hainan Company Ltd.; China Mobile Group Hebei Company Ltd.; China Mobile Group Heilongjiang Company Ltd.; China Mobile Group Henan Company Ltd.; China Mobile Group Hubei Company Ltd.; China Mobile Group Hunan Company Ltd.; China Mobile Group Jiangsu Company Ltd.; China Mobile Group Jiangxi Company Ltd.; China Mobile Group Jilin Company Ltd.; China Mobile Group Liaoning Company Ltd.; China Mobile Group Neimenggu Company Ltd.; China Mobile Group Ningxia Company Ltd.; China Mobile Group Qinghai Company Ltd.; China Mobile Group Shaanxi Company Ltd.; China Mobile Group Shandong Company Ltd.; China Mobile Group Shanghai Company Ltd.; China Mobile Group Shanxi Company Ltd.; China Mobile Group Sichuan Company Ltd.; China Mobile Group Tianjin Company Ltd.; China Mobile Group Xinjiang Company Ltd.; China Mobile Group Xizang Company Ltd.; China Mobile Group Yunnan Company Ltd.; China Mobile Group Zhejiang Company Ltd.; China Mobile Hong Kong Company Ltd.

PRINCIPAL COMPETITORS

Nippon Telegraph and Telephone Corp.; Hutchison Whampoa Ltd.; SK Group; China Mobile Communications Corp.; NTT DoCoMo Inc.; Sumitomo Corp.; China Telecom Corporation Ltd.; KT Corp.; China United Telecommunications Corp.

FURTHER READING

Balfour, Frederik, "China Mobile Is Growing Rural," *Business Week Online*, December 21, 2006.

Betts, Paul, and Kathrin Hille, "China Mobile Trudges Slowly Along Lonely 3G Path," *Financial Times*, May 27, 2009, p. 14.

"China Mobile (Hong Kong) Commits to Its Investors," *Asiamoney*, May 2003, p. 8.

Einhorn, Bruce, "China Mobile Is Counting on Android," *Business Week Online*, August 21, 2009.

Hille, Kathrin, and Justine Lau, "China Mobile Loses Ground to Smaller Groups," *Financial Times*, August 21, 2009, p. 16.

Hong, Iris, "China Mobile Wants at Least 50% of Revenues from App Store," *Telecom Asia*, June 2009, p. 14.

Kwong, Robin, "China Mobile Hits Snag in Taiwan," *Financial Times*, May 13, 2009, p. 15.

———, "China Mobile Plans 100 3G Launches," *Financial Times*, August 24, 2009, p. 13.

Lau, Justine, "China Mobile Buys 10 More Networks," *Financial Times*, December 17, 2003, p. 24.

———, "China Mobile Looks to Expand Overseas," *Financial Times*, March 12, 2005, p. 9.

Leahy, Joe, "Competition Fears Put China Mobile's Dream Run at Threat," *Financial Times*, March 6, 2001, p. 35.

Parker, Andrew, "China Mobile Fights to Retain Position in New Landscape," *Financial Times*, March 6, 2009, p. 16.

Roberts, Dexter, "China Mobile Makes Its First Overseas Buy," *Business World Online*, January 23, 2007.

———, "China Mobile's Hot Signal," *Business Week Online*, January 26, 2007.

Stafford, Philip, "China Mobile in Global Expansion," *Financial Times*, February 21, 2008, p. 15.

"Will China Pick Up the Ophone?" *Business Week*, September 7, 2009, p. 20.

China National Petroleum Corporation

9 Dongzhimen North Street, Dongcheng District
Beijing, 100007
China
Telephone: (+86 10) 6209 4114
Fax: (+86 10) 6209 4205
Web site: http://www.cnpc.com.cn

Government-Owned Company
Incorporated: 1988
Employees: 1.73 million
Sales: $145.89 billion (2008)
Stock Exchanges: (PetroChina) Hong Kong Shanghai
  New York
Ticker Symbols: 857; 601857; PTR
NAICS: 424710 Petroleum Bulk Stations and Terminals;
  213111 Drilling Oil and Gas Wells; 213112 Support Activities for Oil and Gas Field Exploration;
  424720 Petroleum and Petroleum Products Merchant Wholesalers (Except Bulk Stations and Terminals)

■ ■ ■

China National Petroleum Corporation (CNPC) is China's largest oil and gas company and one of the top three in the world. CNPC controls oil and gas field concessions with reserves of more than 3 billion tons of oil and 2.67 trillion cubic meters of gas. The company's operations produce nearly 2.4 million barrels of crude and nearly 5.1 billion cubic feet of gas each day. This gives the company a 57 percent share of China's total crude oil production and 79.5 percent of its natural gas production. The company also operates more than 42,000 kilometers of pipeline, both in China and across its borders into Kazakhstan, Turkmenistan, and elsewhere. China became a net importer of oil and gas in the early 1990s; as a result, CNPC has spearheaded the development of international operations designed to ensure the supply for China's fast-growing demand. As a result, CNPC operates in more than 29 countries, primarily in Asia, including along the Russian border, as well as in Africa and the Middle East. Much of CNPC's domestic assets are grouped under its publicly held subsidiary PetroChina, which is listed on the Hong Kong, Shanghai, and New York stock exchanges. As of 2009, CNPC owned more than 86 percent of PetroChina's shares. CNPC was led by President Jiang Jiemin. The company employed nearly two million people and generated revenues of $145.89 billion in 2008.

ORIGINS

The origins of China National Petroleum Corporation go back to the earliest days of Communist China. China's first oil joint venture was launched on March 27, 1950, by an agreement with the Soviet government to establish the Sino-Russian Petroleum Co. Ltd. in order to develop Xinjiang's Dushanzi Oil Mines. On April 23, 1950, the Chinese government created the General Bureau of Petroleum Administration within the Ministry of Fuel Industry to oversee production and construction in the country's petroleum industry. The Ministry of Petroleum Industry (MOPI) was created five years later.

An exploration well struck oil in the Karamay Oilfield in Xinjiang's Junggar Basin on October 29, 1955.

Several other productive oilfields were discovered in the next 15 years, located in Qinghai, Heilongjiang Province, and Shandong Province.

A reorganization of the government's petroleum, coal, and chemistry sectors created the Ministry of Fuel and Chemistry Industries on June 22, 1970. In August of the same year, construction began on China's first long-distance pipeline, running from Daqing to Fushun.

The Ministry of Fuel and Chemistry Industries was replaced with the Ministry of Petroleum and Chemistry Industries in January 1975. That June saw the construction of the Qinhuangdao to Beijing Oil Pipeline. Soon China would be a major world producer.

In March 1978, the MOPI was restored, replacing the three-year-old Ministry of Petroleum and Chemical Industries. By the end of the year, the country would be producing 100 million tons of oil a year.

Before 1983, according to Haijiang Henry Wang, China's petroleum industry was in disarray. Its ownership was highly fragmented, divided among various corporations and government bodies. To consolidate the industry, two new companies were created in 1982 and 1983: China National Offshore Oil Corporation (CNOOC) and China National Petrochemical Corporation (Sinopec). Sinopec had authority over most refining facilities, except for certain smaller ones based at oilfields. For its part, MOPI had been given new importance under the new national energy plan and announced the ambitious goal of achieving three million barrels per day by 1990 (the figure was actually attained five years later).

One key constraint was a lack of capital and technology. To overcome this, in the mid-1980s the Chinese government cleared the way for cooperative projects with foreign companies in the south of the country, areas that China's existing equipment had been unable to exploit effectively. The first such contract was signed on May 28, 1985, between China National Oil Development Corporation and the Australian CSR Company. On September 17, 1988, China National Petroleum Corporation was established to replace the MOPI.

LOOKING ABROAD IN THE NINETIES

A restructuring in early 1993 added two new joint-venture trading companies to the traditional international trading monopoly controlled by the China National Chemicals Import and Export Corporation (Sinochem). China National United Oil Corporation (called ChinaOil or SinOil) paired Sinochem and CNPC to export crude oil. China International United Petroleum and Chemicals Corporation (Unipec) was a joint venture between Sinochem and Sinopec, China's national refining company, to market refined products.

Wang Tao, the chairman of CNPC at the time, planned to use the extra profits from the new export joint venture to fund new domestic refineries as well as more exploration and development abroad through the China National Development Company, which had been established in 1981 but was underfunded.

In the early 1990s, CNPC was producing 140 million tons of crude a year from its domestic wells. The massive Daqing oilfields were showing the first signs of depletion. Meanwhile, economic reforms put in place since the late 1970s had created a booming demand for oil and gas in the country. By 1993, the country's own oil and gas production was no longer sufficient to meet its demands, and China became a net importer of oil.

With the Chinese economy the fastest growing in the world, the company set off on a global search for oil. CNPC became the first Chinese company to acquire overseas oilfield development rights in 1993. On March 5, the company obtained operational rights in Thailand. On July 15, the company obtained rights to part of the North Twing Oilfield in Alberta, Canada. Rights at the nearby Tarara Oilfield were obtained in October. CNPC soon ventured into Latin America in partnership with Petroleos del Peru. Sites in Papua New Guinea were also being explored.

The liberalization of trade in China was accompanied by an economic boom. This reduced the amount of petroleum products available for export. In 1990, the price of crude oil was regulated between CNY 174 and CNY 500 per ton, the equivalent of $5 and

KEY DATES

1988: China National Petroleum Corporation (CNPC) is established, replacing the Ministry of Petroleum Industry.
1993: CNPC begins exporting oil and developing overseas oilfields.
2000: Company's main operating subsidiary, PetroChina, lists on the Hong Kong and New York stock exchanges.
2002: CNPC begins to shift its exploration and production focus to Central Asia and Africa, and acquires the rights to the Gumdag Oilfield in Turkmenistan, and the Tenere and Bilma blocks in Nigeria.
2005: CNPC pays $4.18 billion to acquire PetroKazakhstan.
2009: CNPC acquires the Libyan oil assets of Verenex Energy of Canada, and plans to acquire 48 percent of Kazakhstan's Mangistau-MunaiGas.

$14 per barrel, given an official exchange rate of CNY 4.78 per dollar. In 1995, the exchange rate had gone to CNY 8.31 per dollar, and the price of crude was between CNY 700 and CNY 1,200 per ton, or about $11.50 and $19.70 per barrel.

RESTRUCTURING IN 1998

A recalculation of crude oil prices by the Chinese government in 1994 allowed CNPC to show a profit for the first time in several years. However, the company remained concerned about its future due to increasing exploration and development costs. According to the China Petroleum Information Institute, CNPC was operating a total of 9,479 wells in 1995, about 10 percent of them exploratory wells. Daqing, China's largest oilfield, accounted for 2,851 of the total.

The company obtained rights to portions of the Muglad Basin in September 1995 and March 1997. After a round of competitive bidding, two oilfields in Venezuela were added to the list in July 1997. This deal was worth $358 million.

In October 1997, CNPC acquired a 60 percent holding in Aktyubinsk Oil Company, gaining access to oilfields in western Kazakhstan. CNPC paid $325 million for its shares and agreed to invest another $4 billion over 20 years, mostly to build a proposed pipeline to

China. It outbid a consortium led by U.S. oil group Amoco. During 1997, CNPC also secured a $1.3 billion contract to develop Iraq's Al Ahdab oilfield upon the lifting of United Nations sanctions.

CNPC accounted for 89 percent of China's crude oil production in 1996. The China National Offshore Oil Corporation (CNOOC) accounted for another 10 percent, while the Ministry of Geology and Mineral Resources (MGMR), local governments, and joint ventures between CNOOC and foreign companies shared the remaining 1 percent.

The China National Star Petroleum Corporation (CNSPC) was created in 1997 to develop both onshore and offshore oil and, particularly, natural gas resources on a commercial basis, through partnerships with foreign companies. It gave the existing state-owned oil companies a new competitor and was formed due to a lack of progress in staving off an impending oil shortage.

CNPC was created as an upstream conglomerate but had plans to expand its downstream (refining) sector by 2000 by forming integrated refining-petrochemical centers in Karamay, Dushanzi, Daqing, Zhongyuan, and Bohai Bay. In a 1998 restructuring of the national oil industry, CNPC acquired 19 companies from China Petrochemical Corporation (Sinopec), including several refineries, while Sinopec acquired 12 of CNPC's companies, including several oilfields.

After the swap, CNPC and Sinopec became known as "Northern" and "Southern" companies, respectively, due to the location of their assets, which in CNPC's case totaled $57.2 billion. CNPC accounted for two-thirds of both China's petroleum and its natural gas output.

CREATING PETROCHINA IN 1999

In January 1999, CNPC merged 10 pipeline enterprises into its China Oil and Gas Pipeline Bureau subsidiary, which was also given authority over four engineering construction companies, two research and design centers, a personnel training center, and a hospital. This gave the bureau assets of CNY 23 billion ($2.77 billion), including 13 oil or gas pipelines.

CNPC completed its first long-distance crude pipeline built overseas at the end of May 1999. It linked the Muglad oilfield to Port Sudan over a distance of 1.05 kilometers. By this time, China was importing 20 percent of the oil it used. This figure was projected to increase to 40 percent by 2010. The country's oilfields in the north and northeast were maturing, noted Britain's *Financial Times,* and its more recently discovered fields in the west had proved disappointing, both in terms of yields and in the cost of shipping the oil to the east coast economic centers.

By June 1999, CNPC had begun to restructure subsidiaries and trim jobs in preparations for a partial flotation. *China Daily* noted the company was plagued with an unnecessarily large number of employees, duplicated construction, high costs, and heavy debts, all relics of the centralized planning regime. The company's offshore oil exploration counterpart, CNOOC, was also planning an initial public offering (IPO) but canceled it in October. That did not dissuade CNPC management from pursuing their own flotation.

In November 1999, CNPC announced the establishment of a new limited liability company, China National Petroleum Co., Ltd. (China Petroleum or PetroChina), engaged in a variety of upstream and downstream activities. A few subsidiaries, already listed on the Hong Kong or mainstream China stock markets, were transferred to PetroChina, with the exception of China (Hong Kong) Oil Co., Ltd., which retained its position in the stock market. PetroChina was thus endowed with CNPC's most valuable assets. It would have 480,000 employees, while CNPC would retain the bulk of the other one million, most of whom were likely to be laid off.

PETROCHINA IPO IN 2000

CNPC's net profits for 1999 were about CNY 17 billion ($2 billion), more than two and a half times greater than the previous year's. Sales income was about CNY 330 billion ($39.8 billion). The company pumped 107 million tons of crude oil and 16 billion cubic meters of natural gas during the year. A government crackdown on refined oil smuggling and CNPC's own restructuring efforts were credited with the positive results.

Before its planned flotation on the Hong Kong and New York stock markets, PetroChina based the compensation of its top managers on performance, making it one of the first Chinese companies to adopt such a Western-styled incentive system. In spite of this, the PetroChina IPO, held in 2000, was disappointing.

CNPC had planned to raise $7 billion in what would have been China's largest IPO to date. However, the company only took in HKD 22.5 billion ($2.9 billion) from the offering, even after the Chinese government pressured its mainland enterprises listed in Hong Kong to buy shares in the issue. One big subscriber was the British oil giant BP Amoco PLC, which agreed to invest up to $1 billion for a 20 percent holding.

Several U.S. pension funds boycotted the issue due to alleged human rights abuses and terrorist connections

in Sudan, where CNPC was participating in a joint venture (PetroChina itself had no overseas assets), as well as environmental damage in Tibet. PetroChina shares fell markedly after listing on the New York and Hong Kong exchanges in early April 2000.

FUELING CHINA'S GROWTH IN THE 21ST CENTURY

In the new century, CNPC held a crucial role in the Chinese government's economic and political plans. The government continued to focus on rapidly building the country's economy, setting targets of at least 7 percent per year, in part in order to maintain social order, and its own control. Oil and gas provided the fuel for the country's growth, as demand soared. At the beginning of the decade, China was the world's second-largest consumer of oil and gas, trailing only the United States.

CNPC's responsibility, therefore, was to secure the energy supplies required to achieve China's growth targets. One of CNPC's primary objectives was to reduce the country's reliance on the Middle Eastern oil producers, seen as being too heavily influenced by the West, in favor of the emerging oil and gas markets in Asia, Central Asia, and Africa.

In 2002, for example, the company reached agreement with Turkmenistan to exploit the Gumdag Oilfield. The company also became a partner in the construction of the Central Asia Gas Pipeline, ultimately linking China to Turkmenistan, Kazakhstan, and other countries in the region. The company also acquired the Indonesian oilfield operations of Devon Energy that year. In Nigeria, CNPC acquired two petroleum exploration and development licenses, for the Tenere and Bilma blocks, in 2003, as well as the contract to build an integrated oilfield and refinery complex in Algeria.

CNPC made major strides into Kazakhstan as well. The Chinese and Kazakhstan governments had formed a partnership to build a 1,000-kilometer oil pipeline linking the two countries. The Kazakh government had begun to adopt oil and gas policies favoring Asian companies over Western groups. This shift enabled CNPC to buy out Chevron Texaco's operations in North Buzachi. In 2005, CNPC won a bid worth $4.18 billion to acquire PetroKazakhstan, based in Canada, which had become the country's second-largest foreign oil producer.

BUILDING GLOBAL ASSETS

Back at home, CNPC achieved some success in boosting the level of its oil and gas reserves, as well as its production. In 2002, the company located a 30 billion cubic meter natural gas reservoir in the Songliao Basin, part of its Daqing Oilfield operations. Other discoveries included a major gas reserve in Sichuan in 2003, and the Bohai Bay Basin-based Jidong Nanpu Oilfield, with a reserve of more than one billion tons of oil, in 2007. In 2008, the company began development of the Dina-2 Gas Field in the Tarim Basin, which was expected to supply five billion cubic meters of natural gas by mid-2009. By the end of 2008, the company had made another major natural gas discovery, of more than 100 billion cubic meters, at the Kelameili Gas Field in the Junggar Basin.

Accompanying these discoveries, CNPC made continued improvements in its production capacity. By 2009, the company's total production capacity topped 2.4 million barrels of crude and nearly 5.1 billion cubic feet of gas each day. In this way, CNPC became responsible for 57 percent of the country's total crude oil production, and nearly 80 percent of its natural gas production.

By then, however, domestic demand for oil and gas had far outpaced the country's ability to supply them. Into the end of the decade, CNPC continued to scramble for the world's dwindling oil and gas supplies, helping to push the price of oil to record levels in 2007. In that year, the company reached an agreement to explore and develop the Amu-Darya gas fields in Turkmenistan, which were expected to supply as much as 30 billion cubic meters per year over a 30-year period.

In 2008, CNPC acquired the contract to explore and develop the Agadem Block, as well as build a refinery and pipeline in Nigeria. The first phase of that project was expected to be operational by 2011. The company also formed a joint venture with Uzbekneftegaz to develop the Mingbulak Oilfield in Uzbekistan's Fergana Basin.

While the slump in demand, brought on by the global recession, helped ease pressure on the world's oil reserves, CNPC remained committed to securing China's oil and gas supply. The company continued to seek new deals, adding a number of contracts to build and operate refineries and related installations in Syria, Sudan, Algeria, and elsewhere.

In March 2009, the company announced that it had reached an agreement to acquire the Libyan oil assets held by Canada's Verenex Energy, primarily focused on the Ghadames Basin. The company quickly followed this agreement with the announcement that it planned to acquire 48 percent of Kazakhstan's Mangistau-MunaiGas. The world's third-largest oil and gas company, China National Petroleum Corporation hoped

to continue to quench the fast-growing Chinese economy's thirst for fuel in the new millennium.

Frederick C. Ingram
Updated, M. L. Cohen

PRINCIPAL SUBSIDIARIES

China National Petroleum Co., Ltd. (86%); China National Logging Corporation; China Oil & Gas Eastern Survey and Design Research Institute; China Petroleum Engineering and Construction (Group) Corporation; China Petroleum First Construction Company; China Petroleum Hong Kong (Holding) Limited; China Petroleum Seventh Construction Company; China Petroleum Sixth Construction Company; China Petroleum Technology Development Corporation; CNPC Service & Engineering Co., Ltd.; Dagang Oilfield (Group) Co., Ltd.; Great Wall Drilling Company; Jilin Petroleum (Group) Co., Ltd.; Ningxia Dayuan Refining and Chemicals Co., Ltd.; Qingyang Refining and Chemicals Co., Ltd.

PRINCIPAL COMPETITORS

Royal Dutch Shell PLC; Saudi Arabian Oil Co.; Petroleo Brasileiro S.A.; Elf Aquitaine S.A.; ENI S.p.A.; Statoil ASA; Kuwait Petroleum Corporation; RWE AG; SONATRACH S.p.A.

FURTHER READING

Carroll, Susan, "China Revamps Chem Operations," *Chemical Market Reporter*, August 3, 1998, p. 18.

"Chronicle for CNPC," *China Chemical Reporter*, January 26, 2008, p. 23.

"CNPC Commences Construction of Central Asia Gas Pipeline," *China Chemical Reporter*, July 16, 2008, p. 11.

"CNPC Intends to Spin Off Coalbed Methane Business in CUCMC," *China Chemical Reporter*, July 26, 2008, p. 7.

"CNPC Merges Pipeline Enterprises," *China Daily*, January 25, 1999.

"CNPC Regrouping," *China Chemical Reporter*, November 26, 1999, p. 3.

"CNPC Restructures Gas Business," *China Chemical Reporter*, May 16, 2009, p. 7.

"CNPC to Acquire Kazakhstan's Oil Assets," *China Chemical Reporter*, April 6, 2009, p. 8.

"CNPC to Acquire Libyan Oil Assets," *China Chemical Reporter*, March 26, 2009, p. 5.

"CNPC to Strengthen Exploration for Oil, Gas," *China Business Information Network (CBNet)*, January 25, 1999.

"CNPC Unloads High-Risk Businesses," *China Chemical Reporter*, February 6, 2009, p. 9.

"CNPC Ventures Need More Funds," *China Daily*, August 2, 1999, p. 5.

Corzine, Robert, "From Minor to Major: Formerly Monolithic State Oil Companies Are at Last Challenging the Western Majors on Their Home Turf," *Financial Times*, August 19, 1997, p. 13.

"Drilling for the Party," *Economist*, May 24, 2003, p. 66US.

Gesteland, Lester J., "PetroChina Falls in New York, Hong Kong," *China Online*, April 10, 2000.

Harding, James, "Chinese Oil Giant Finalises Plan to Raise Up to $10 Billion," *Financial Times*, June 29, 1999, p. 1.

Kynge, James, "China Anxious to Ensure That Oil Supplies Are More Secure," *Financial Times*, May 6, 1999, p. 6.

Landler, Mark, "China's No. 2 Oil Company Prepares to Go Public," *New York Times*, October 12, 2000, p. W1.

Ling Zhuang, "Joys and Worries in Operations of CNPC and Sinopec," *China Chemical Reporter*, October 6, 1998.

McMahon, William J., "PetroChina's Roadshow Kicks Off as Detractors Drill Its Prospects," *China Online*, March 28, 2000.

"National Petroleum Corp. Signs Up for Oil Exploration in Three Continents," *South China Morning Post*, November 22, 1993, p. 2.

"Oil Giant Rakes in Big Bucks," *China Daily*, December 29, 1999, p. 1.

"Sinopec, CNPC Reduce Gas Prices, Begin Market Competition in Shanghai," *China Online*, August 15, 2001.

"Slick Maneuvers: China's Petroleum Shake-Up Dashes Competition Hopes," *Far Eastern Economic Review*, July 2, 1998, p. 61.

"Slick Move by Petroleum Firm Creates Oil Giant," *China Daily*, November 9, 1999, p. 5.

"Strong Development Momentum in CNPC," *China Chemical Reporter*, September 6, 2003, p. 10.

Walker, Tony, "China Creates Third State Oil Company; New Operation to 'Commercialise' Oil Bureaux and Research Institutes in Attempt to Revive Sector," *Financial Times*, January 27, 1997, p. 4.

Wang, Haijiang Henry, *China's Oil Industry & Market*, New York: Elsevier, 1999.

Watson, N. J., "China Beats India to PetroKazakhstan," *Petroleum Economist*, October 2005, p. 23.

Yuan, Sy, Yi-kun Chen, and Ann M. Weeks, "An Update on China's Oil Sector Overhaul," *China Business Review*, March/April 2000.

China Southern Airlines Company Limited

278 Ji Chang Road
Guangzhou, Guangdong 510405
China
Telephone: (+86 20) 95539
Web site: http://www.csair.com

Government-Controlled Public Company
Incorporated: 1988 as China Southern Airlines
Employees: 46,209
Sales: CNY 55.29 billion ($8.07 billion) (2008)
Stock Exchanges: New York Hong Kong Shanghai
Ticker Symbols: ZNH 1055 600029.SS
NAICS: 481111 Scheduled Passenger Air Transportation; 481112 Scheduled Freight Air Transportation; 488190 Other Support Activities for Air Transportation

∎ ∎ ∎

China Southern Airlines Company Limited (CSA) has long been China's largest carrier in terms of numbers of passengers carried (58 million in 2008) and fleet size (about 350 aircraft). CSA is propelled by the robust economy of Guangzhou, its home base. It maintains its own terminals and three airports and has branches throughout China and dozens of ticket offices around the world. China Southern flies to more than 80 international destinations, including Los Angeles and Amsterdam. The carrier has also developed a cargo network. CSA participates in sizeable ventures related to airframe and engine maintenance, pilot training, and flight catering. The Chinese government owns a control-ling interest through the China Southern Air Holding Company.

ORIGINS AND INDEPENDENCE

China Southern Airlines was formed out of the China Civil Aviation Administration (CCAC), which itself had been created from the U.S.-led China National Aviation Corporation and other assets left behind by those fleeing the Communists in 1949. Five years later, CCAC merged with the Sino-Soviet Joint Stock Company, which had responsibility for air service in northern China. This created the Chinese Civil Aviation Bureau (CAB), with divisions based in Beijing, Shanghai, Shenyang, Xi'an, Wuhan, and Guangzhou, later the base for China Southern. In April 1962, the CAB became the Civil Aviation Administration of China (CAAC). Over the next 20 years, the CAAC gradually evolved from dependence on Soviet aviation technology to a customer-driven preference for British and U.S. jets, culminating in orders for Boeing 747s and Concordes, although the latter were never delivered.

A reorganization of the CAAC in late 1984 produced the following four regional divisions: Eastern, Southern, Southwestern, and Northwestern. The liberalization of the domestic market soon produced other carriers such as Xiamen Airlines, which operated on China Southern's turf. Because of the commercial importance of Guangzhou (formerly Canton), China Southern was cleared for international flights, along with Shanghai-based China Eastern. Yu Yanen, an active pilot himself, was appointed president of the airline.

COMPANY PERSPECTIVES

China Southern Airlines Co. Ltd.—the newest member of SkyTeam—is a main air transportation business of China Southern Air Holding Company. With flight operations based at Guangzhou's brand-new, award-winning Baiyun International Airport, China Southern Airlines' company logo can be seen around the globe with a brilliant red kapok delicately adorning a blue vertical tail fin.

China Southern was granted its autonomy on July 1, 1988. However, the CAAC still controlled aircraft purchasing and worked very closely with its newly independent branches. The government also made its voice known to domestic passengers: an official letter of recommendation was a prerequisite for booking a flight until 1993.

In spite of the oversight from Beijing, the airline pursued partnerships with Western aviation companies to increase its expertise and revenue potential. In 1990, China Southern set up a maintenance joint venture with Hutchison Whampoa (25 percent) and Lockheed (25 percent) called Guangzhou Aircraft Maintenance Engineering Co. (GAMECO). The center specialized in Boeing 757 and 747 aircraft and boasted labor costs one-fourth of those in the West. A flight simulator station was also under development.

China Southern carried nearly six million people in 1991, up more than sixfold from a decade earlier. Cargo traffic boomed as well. The carrier flew to 90 cities at home and 17 international destinations and operated a fleet of 38 Boeing jets. Employment was about 6,000. Tragically, one of China Southern's 737s flew into a mountain in 1992, killing 141 people. The occurrence puzzled some industry observers who had seen the vast improvements made by China's commercial airlines in the previous decade.

CSA posted a profit of $102 million on revenues of $537 million in 1992. With Air China, China Eastern, and a few dozen companies in other industries, the carrier was given special financial independence. One drawback to this was the increased cost of buying fuel on the open market and paying airport fees. China Southern also had to compete vigorously to attract qualified pilots. However, the carrier was able to shed various general aviation activities such as forestry service inherited from the 1950s.

Demand for commercial aircraft softened in the wake of the Persian Gulf War, giving Yu an opportunity to acquire the Boeing 777s needed to establish China Southern as a long-haul international carrier. Boeing lowered its price and stepped up its delivery schedule; CSA was the first Asian airline to operate this state-of-the-art jet.

OPEN TO FOREIGN INVESTMENT: 1994

The Chinese government opened its airlines to the possibility of foreign investment in 1994. United Airlines and China Southern were early to the negotiating table. CSA also began to plan for a listing on the New York Stock Exchange. It needed the capital to distance itself from other smaller, largely unprofitable Chinese airlines, among the world's most dangerous to fly. CSA entered into training and maintenance agreements with U.S. carriers. It contracted with American Airlines' sister company Sabre Decision Technologies to develop its operations control center.

Sales doubled in 1994, although profits fell due to increased costs associated with the company's growth. It added four international and 26 domestic routes in 1995. Passenger traffic exploded in the early 1990s; gross revenues reached $1.1 billion in 1996; the Xiamen Airlines unit contributed another $400 million. Net income was $1.4 billion (CNY 887 million). CSA and associated airlines were flying 15 million passengers a year. CSA's domestic subsidiaries covered 68 destinations within China.

Yu had resisted pressure to order Airbuses (and, earlier in the decade, MD-80s being manufactured in Shanghai), at least until April 1996, when the CAAC ordered 20 Airbus A320s for the company. CSA added a fifth Boeing 777 in 1997 as it expanded international services in a bid to usurp Air China's leading position. CSA had an advantage in the liberal, business-oriented climate of its southern home, compared to Air China's bureaucratic home base of Beijing. The carrier operated 63 jets, plus 15 through Xiamen Airlines and dozens more through other subsidiaries, to Air China's 50.

Even though the airline had invested heavily in bringing capacity to the international market, domestic flights accounted for almost 80 percent of its passenger revenues. The domestic carriers were an important source of feeder traffic; to keep passengers coming in from abroad, CSA signed a code-sharing arrangement with Delta Air Lines. International flights brought in vitally needed hard currency. Cargo operations provided less than 10 percent of the carrier's revenues.

In July 1997, China Southern finally made its initial public offering (IPO) on the Hong Kong and

KEY DATES

1984: Civil Aviation Administration of China divides into separate airlines.
1988: China Southern Airlines (CSA) is officially granted autonomy.
1992: Beijing grants CSA further financial independence.
1997: CSA goes public, listing on the Hong Kong and New York stock exchanges.
1998: Asian financial crisis leads to CSA's first annual loss.
2000: Dedicated cargo operation is launched.
2002: In a national industry consolidation CSA acquires China Northern and Xinjiang Airlines.
2003: CSA weathers the SARS crisis, lists shares in Shanghai.
2004: New airport in Guangzhou opens.
2007: CSA joins SkyTeam global alliance.
2008: CSA operates the first direct flight between mainland China and Taiwan in 60 years.

New York exchanges, raising approximately $700 million. A strong local economy and hub in the gateway city of Guangzhou were two key selling points. The CAAC still owned about two-thirds of CSA after the IPO. CSA reported revenues of $1.5 billion in 1997. The next year, the first loss in CSA's history, compounded by unfavorable exchange rates, amounted to CNY 544 million ($65 million) on revenues of CNY 10.6 billion. As a group, Chinese airlines lost $775 million in 1998.

Even after the IPO, CSA and Xiamen Airlines together had nearly $2 billion in debt. Within a few months, the Asian financial crisis soured investors on CSA's short-term prospects. A sharp decline in traffic manifested itself quickly. In the first half of 1998, CSA lost even more than was expected, CNY 72 million. Managers scrambled to contain costs but with cheap land, low-cost labor, and expensive new planes to maintain, their options were limited. About 600 workers were laid off and a few airplanes were returned. The prospect of growth via teaming with Delta Air Lines in the U.S. market offered some hope; CSA advertised special incentives to U.S. travel agents. The Chinese government reduced infrastructure taxes to help the struggling airlines, saving China Southern approximately CNY 500 million a year.

The domestic Chinese market showed some signs of improvement by early 1999, as the CAAC intervened to control pricing and capacity. CSA's cargo traffic improved by 12 percent in the first quarter. The CAAC also planned to merge all of China's 34 airlines into a handful of groups. A merger of China Southern with Air China was expected to lead the process. China Southern management was likely to take over the proposed entity; Air China's head had been replaced by the leader of China Eastern Airlines due to poor financial performance. In fact, Air China was not yet strong enough to launch its own public offering, despite several years of trying. Air China would bring better U.S. destinations to the merger, a key to competing with major U.S. airlines. As of mid-1999, CSA operated 99 aircraft and Air China 60, together accounting for more than a third of China's total commercial airliners and half the country's air traffic.

Although susceptible to exchange rate fluctuations, China Southern had long demonstrated an uncanny ability to navigate between bureaucratic demands of the socialist regime at home and the requirements of competition in the open market. China Southern President Yan Zhi Qing stated a goal of becoming the world's number one airline, not an altogether out of sight target, given the airline's phenomenal rate of growth and the impending merger.

CONSOLIDATION

China Southern had total operating revenue of CNY 15.2 billion in 2000 and posted net income of CNY 502 million, most of it from the sale of aircraft. Profit slipped by a third in 2001 as revenues rose 11 percent to CNY 16.9 billion. The carrier managed to maintain its profitability through a global aviation downturn with net income of CNY 513.3 million on revenues of CNY 18.8 billion in 2002.

China Southern and China Eastern remained independent of each other in the coming wave of consolidation. Instead, the Chinese government directed the "Big Three Airlines" (including Air China) to each take over a few smaller airlines. CSA's parent China Southern Air Holding Company acquired tiny Zhengzhou Airlines in 2000 and China Northern and Xinjiang Airlines in 2002.

CSA also bought a 49 percent interest in China Postal Airlines; it had launched its own cargo operation in 2000. At the same time, CSA was building an international freight hub in Shenzhen as China prepared to enter the World Trade Organization.

In 2003, directly affected by the severe acute respiratory syndrome (SARS) crisis in the first part of the year, CSA saw revenues slip to CNY 17.5 billion ($2.1 billion) and had a CNY 358.3 million ($43.3 million) loss. A stock offering on the Shanghai exchange provided funds to buy new planes and help finance a new airport at Guangzhou. The loss was narrowed to CNY 48 million in 2004.

CSA kicked off 2005 by ordering five massive Airbus 380s. An even larger order was placed with Boeing several months later, when CSA ordered 10 B787 Dreamliners from Boeing. The next year, it placed an ambitious bet on its growing cargo operations by ordering a half-dozen Boeing 777 freighters.

CSA posted a hefty CNY 1.9 billion loss on revenues of CNY 38.3 billion in 2005, attributed to rising fuel costs and challenges integrating China Northern and Xinjiang Airlines. The company returned to profitability in 2006, managing a surplus of CNY 106 million on revenues of CNY 46.1 billion. Restated results for 2007 indicated a CNY 2 billion net profit on revenues of CNY 54.4 billion.

A CHANGING WORLD

Most (80 percent) of CSA's revenues were still being produced domestically, but like the other large Chinese airlines it sought international partnerships. In 2007 CSA joined the SkyTeam global alliance.

CSA partnered with Taiwan's China Airlines after an easing of flight restrictions. On July 4, 2008, CSA operated the first direct flight between mainland China and Taiwan in 60 years, piloted by company Chairman Liu Shaoyong. Liu headed to rival China Eastern Airlines in January 2009 to attempt a turnaround there.

The airline was carrying 58 million people a year, most of them on domestic flights. CSA suffered as demand fell in the global economic slowdown. It posted a loss of CNY 4.8 billion ($700 million) on revenues of CNY 55.3 billion ($8.1 billion) in 2008. This was a record deficit for the company, but it fared much better than its Big Three rivals, in large part due to its ending of fuel-hedging contracts in September before fuel prices dropped. CSA announced in October 2008 it was building up its presence in northeast China by investing in a hub in Liaoning, home of its China Northern Airlines unit.

CSA received a capital infusion of CNY 3 billion in 2009 as part of a government bailout of the industry, but this only nudged its debt-to-equity ratio to just below 90 percent. Another handout, of CNY 1.5 billion, soon followed.

CSA began 2009 with 348 aircraft and plans to expand the fleet to 375 planes. Passenger numbers were improving. However, the airline had deferred delivery of its largest aircraft on order, the superjumbo A380 and B787, due to the slow travel market. It also postponed a planned air-cargo linkup with Air France. CSA's new chairman, Si Xian Min, told the *South China Morning Post* that he was chiefly concerned with maintaining the stability of the airline as it traversed a difficult period.

Frederick C. Ingram

PRINCIPAL SUBSIDIARIES

Shantou Airlines Company Limited (60%); Chongqing Airlines Company Limited (60%); Zhuhai Airlines Company Limited (60%); Xiamen Airlines Company Limited (60%); Guizhou Airlines Company Limited (60%); Nan Lung International Freight Limited (Hong Kong; 51%); Guangzhou Air Cargo Company Limited (70%); Guangzhou Baiyun International Logistic Company Limited (61%); China Southern Airlines Group Air Catering Company Limited; Guangzhou Nanland Air Catering Company Limited (55%); China Southern West Australian Flying College Pty Limited (91%); Xinjiang Civil Aviation Property Management Limited (51.8%).

PRINCIPAL COMPETITORS

China Eastern Airlines Co., Ltd.; Cathay Pacific Airways Ltd.; Air China Limited; Hainan Airlines Co., Ltd.

FURTHER READING

Carey, Susan, "Air Crash in China Proves Puzzling, Differing Greatly from Past Disasters," *Wall Street Journal*, November 30, 1992.

———, "China's Airlines Are Growing at Rapid Rate—Beijing Appears to Be Giving Approval and Is Limiting Amount of Interference," *Wall Street Journal*, April 13, 1992.

Chiu, Annette, "China Southern on Course for Shanghai A-Share Listing," *South China Morning Post*, March 18, 2003, p. 3.

Chung, Lawrence, "Airliners cross Straight into History; First Direct Flights between Mainland and Taiwan since 1949 Open a New Chapter," *South China Morning Post*, July 5, 2008, p. 1.

Davies, R. E. G., *Airlines of Asia since 1920*, London: Putnam, 1997.

Ernsberger, Dave, "Risk and Reward," *Aviation Week & Space Technology*, March 10, 2008, p. 40.

Feldman, Joan M., "'Independence' ... with Strings," *Air Transport World*, October 1993, p. 52.

Forestier, Katherine, "Gameco: International Ambitions," *Asian Business*, January 1992, p. 11.

Ionides, Nick, "China Southern Bids for Xinjiang," *Airline Business,* January 2001, p. 27.

Jones, Dominic, "Dragon to Get Bit in the Year of the Tiger," *Airfinance Journal,* February 1998, pp. 28–30.

———, "The Next Step for China's Big Two," *Airfinance Journal,* February 1998, pp. 24–27.

Kahn, Joseph, and Miriam Jordan, "China's Big State Airlines Are Flying in New Direction—They Seek Operating Accords, and Possibly Funds, from Foreign Lines," *Wall Street Journal,* November 1, 1994, p. B4.

Kj, Max, "China Southern to Buy and Operate 747 Freighter Fleet," *Flight International,* August 22, 2000, p. 10.

Leary, William M., Jr., *The Dragon's Wings: The China National Aviation Corporation and the Development of Commercial Aviation in China,* Athens: University of Georgia, 1976.

Mackey, Michael, "Mainland Powerhouse," *Air Transport World,* September 1997, pp. 26–32.

———, "The Right Place," *Air Transport World,* July 1996, p. 67.

Mecham, Michael, "China Southern Looks to U.S. Market for Relief," *Aviation Week & Space Technology,* March 29, 1999, p. 45.

———, "New Airport Puts Focus on Guangzhou," *Aviation Week & Space Technology,* December 9, 2002, p. 50.

O'Connor, Anthony, "Meet the Boss," *Airfinance Journal,* July/August 1996, pp. 22–23.

———, "The Tearaway," *Airfinance Journal,* July/August 1996, pp. 16–19.

Proctor, Paul, "China Southern Closes on Air China for Premier Spot," *Aviation Week & Space Technology,* March 31, 1997, p. 44.

Qian Yanfeng, "China Southern Invests in Northeastern Hub," *China Daily,* October 30, 2008.

Rocks, David, and Bruce Einhorn, "A Steep Ascent at China Southern," *BusinessWeek,* March 29, 2004, p. 22.

So, Charlotte, "Dependable Pragmatist Steers China Southern; Si Xianmin's Cautious Approach Fits Difficult Times for Airlines," *South China Morning Post,* May 18, 2009, Bus. Sec., p. 10.

Thomas, Geoffrey, "China Airline Merger Talks May Spark a Trend," *Aviation Week & Space Technology,* July 19, 1999, p. 36.

Wang Ying, "China Southern to Ride Out of Turbulence," *China Daily,* June 3, 2009.

Yu, Kai Peter, "China Southern Adds Cargo Hub," *South China Morning Post,* August 16, 2000.

The Coleman Company, Inc.

3600 North Hydraulic
Wichita, Kansas 67219-3812
U.S.A.
Telephone: (316) 832-2700
Toll Free: (800) 835-3278
Fax: (316) 832-3060
Web site: http://www.coleman.com

Wholly Owned Subsidiary of Jarden Corporation
Incorporated: 1900 as Hydro-Carbon Light Company
Employees: 3,000
Sales: $1 billion (2008 est.)
NAICS: 314912 Canvas and Related Product Mills;
314999 All Other Miscellaneous Textile Product
Mills; 326199 All Other Plastics Product
Manufacturing; 335129 Other Lighting Equipment
Manufacturing; 335221 Household Cooking Appli-
ance Manufacturing; 339920 Sporting and Athletic
Goods Manufacturing; 451110 Sporting Goods
Stores; 454111 Electronic Shopping

■ ■ ■

The Coleman Company, Inc., is one of the most
famous and successful manufacturers of camping equipment and outdoor recreational products. The well-
known Coleman lamp was invented by 1909 and the
lantern in 1914, and since that time more than 50 million of the lanterns have been sold throughout the
world. Coleman is the market leader in lanterns and
stoves for outdoor recreational use, and it has created a
loyal consumer following for a broad range of coolers,

tents, sleeping bags, airbeds, backpacks, outdoor
furniture, and other recreational accessories marketed
under the Coleman and Exponent brands. Coleman
products are sold in more than 100 countries worldwide
and can be found at outdoor retailers, sporting goods
stores, mass merchandise and discount stores, hardware
home centers, drugstores, and online retailers. In addition, the company operates about a dozen Coleman factory outlet stores in the United States and sells its
products on its own Web site.

Coleman, founded in 1900, has been a wholly
owned subsidiary of Jarden Corporation since 2005, at
which point it became the core of Jarden's Outdoor
Solutions unit. Later, in 2007, Jarden acquired sports
equipment giant K2 Inc. K2's Stearns division was
subsequently split off and merged into Coleman, which
thus added the following to its product lines: flotation
devices, towables, rainwear, waders, hunting and fishing
gear, and safety and survival equipment under the
Stearns, Sevylor, Sospenders, Hodgman, Mad Dog Gear,
Nevin, and Helium brands. The Outdoor Solutions unit
generates nearly half of Jarden's overall revenues.

BRIGHT BEGINNINGS

The founder of the company, William Coffin Coleman,
was born to a young couple who migrated west to
Kansas from New England in 1871. Coleman became a
schoolteacher in Kansas and later entered the University
of Kansas Law School. Shortly before receiving his
degree, however, Coleman ran out of money, and he
became a traveling typewriter salesman. Working the
southern part of the United States, he found himself in

COMPANY PERSPECTIVES

"Don't let life put you back on your heels. Lean into it."—Sheldon Coleman Sr.

That mantra still guides the Coleman Company. We continue to lean into the future. Ours is a company with an uncanny ability to adapt to change. A company with an intimate understanding of the consumer. A commitment to research and development that breathes vitality into every aspect of the business. A company that sets industry standards.

We are defined by our heritage. And excited about our future.

Brockton, Alabama, a poor coal-mining community with dirt streets and wood sidewalks.

According to company lore, as Coleman was taking an evening walk down one of the town's streets, he noticed the intense white glow of a lamp in a drugstore window. The lamp, which was powered by gasoline, was so bright that even with his bad eyesight Coleman was able to read under it easily. Because most people at that time used flickering gaslights, smoky oil lamps, or dim carbon-filament light bulbs, Coleman immediately saw the lamp as an important step forward.

Coleman arranged to sell this new type of lamp for the Irby-Gilliland Company of Memphis, and traveled to Kingfisher, Oklahoma, to begin his new venture. Unfortunately, he had sold only two lamps at the end of the first week. The lack of sales dismayed him, but he soon discovered that another salesman had previously sold dozens of lamps to the town's shopkeepers. Because the lamps could not be cleaned, they clogged with carbon deposits that snuffed the light out after a short time. The salesman had left a bit too quickly, and the shopkeepers felt swindled.

Unable to sell his lamps, Coleman hit upon the idea of leasing them for $1 per week and servicing them himself. If the lamps failed, the customer did not have to pay. Revenues skyrocketed. In order to remain competitive almost all the town's shopkeepers purchased his lighting service. The business flourished as Coleman reinvested profits and branched out into neighboring communities. Not long afterward, in 1900, he founded Hydro-Carbon Light Company.

With the demand for his lamps and lighting service increasing, Coleman received $2,000 from his two brothers-in-law for an 8 percent interest in the company.

In 1902 requests for his lighting service were so numerous that he decided to move the business to Wichita, Kansas, and establish a permanent headquarters. Coleman, having purchased the rights to the Efficient Lamp, improved on this product's design and began selling it as the Coleman Arc Lamp in 1903. Ever on the lookout for original ways to market his lamps, Coleman in 1905 arranged for the Arc Lamps to provide the lighting for a night football game.

WARTIME CONTRIBUTIONS

By 1909 Coleman had invented a portable table lamp with a gasoline tank designed as a small fount with a flat base. Bug screens were later added to protect the mantles during outdoor use. In 1914 the company developed the Coleman gasoline lantern for use in inclement weather. When World War I broke out, the Allies requested U.S. wheat and corn to replenish their food supplies. Realizing the need for a reliable, bright, and portable light for farmers carrying out the tasks necessary to aid the Europeans, the U.S. government declared the Coleman lamp essential for the wartime support effort and provided Coleman with both money and materials to produce the lanterns. During World War I, the company made over one million lamps for the nation's farmers.

The company grew steadily in the 1920s. Although electricity came to the smaller towns across the United States, most rural areas had to wait. Coleman thus found its largest markets in rural areas, with ever increasing sales of gasoline stoves, used both as camp stoves and cook stoves and first produced in 1923, and lamps and lanterns. The company also established international operations in 1925 with a manufacturing plant and headquarters in Toronto. Locating an office in Canada was a smart move on the part of Coleman, because the British Commonwealth gave preferential tariffs and duties to products made in member nations. By the end of the 1920s the reputation of the Coleman lantern was firmly established, and various accounts of its use were reported: Admiral Byrd used the lantern on his trip to the South Pole; on Pitcairn Island the descendants of British mutineers from the *Bounty* and their Tahitian families illuminated primitive homes with Coleman lanterns; and Coleman lantern-lit runways in the Andes made emergency landings possible.

The company was not entirely successful in developing new products and markets. During the late 1920s, Coleman made a line of waffle irons, coffee percolators, toasters, and electric irons. Coleman could not, however, compete with Westinghouse Electric Corporation and General Electric Company and withdrew these product lines quickly. William Coffin

KEY DATES

1900: William Coffin Coleman founds Hydro-Carbon Light Company.
1903: Founder begins manufacturing the Coleman Arc Lamp.
1923: First Coleman camp stove is introduced.
1951: Sheldon Coleman, son of the founder, is named company president.
1954: First Coleman cooler hits the market.
1989: Coleman family involvement ends with New York financier Ronald Perelman's hostile takeover of the firm.
1998: Perelman sells Coleman to Sunbeam Corporation.
2002: Sunbeam emerges from bankruptcy as American Household, Inc.
2005: Coleman becomes a wholly owned subsidiary of Jarden Corporation following the latter's acquisition of American Household.
2007: Jarden acquires K2 Inc. and later merges K2's Stearns division into Coleman.

Coleman (known as W. C. to the rest of the company) designed a coffeemaker for restaurants and hotels. Although it brewed excellent coffee, the machine was complicated to handle and difficult to clean. It was commercially unsuccessful and the company halted its production.

Coleman was hit very hard when the stock market crashed in 1929. During the next two years, the Great Depression severely affected almost every industry in the nation. The demand for Coleman products declined rapidly, mainly because of the searing poverty and inability of many people in rural areas to purchase anything other than food. Inevitably, the company experienced financial losses, but a good working relationship with a number of banks helped Coleman to overcome the worst years of the Depression. In 1932 the company's sales totaled a mere $3 million, but a small profit was made.

After Franklin Delano Roosevelt was elected president in 1932, he launched a massive program for rural electrification, and Coleman was faced with a decline in its market for gasoline stoves and lights. Nevertheless, Coleman found two potentially profitable markets, oil space heaters and gas floor furnaces, and by the end of the decade the company was the leading manufacturer of both products. At the same time, Cole-

man's portable stove and lantern business was making headway in the camping equipment market, and the international operation was beginning to reap significant profits. In 1941 the company reported annual sales of $9 million.

When World War II began, Coleman was called on to manufacture products for the various branches of the U.S. armed services, including 20-millimeter shells for the Army, projectiles for the Navy, and parts for the B-29 and B-17 bombers for the Air Force. In June 1942 the company was notified, by the Army Quartermaster Corps, that field troops urgently needed a compact stove that could operate at 125 degrees above and 60 degrees below zero, was no larger than a quart bottle of milk, and could burn any kind of fuel. Moreover, the Army wanted 5,000 of the stoves delivered in two months.

Coleman worked nonstop to design and manufacture a stove to the Army's specifications. The end product was better than the Army had requested: the stove could work at 60 degrees below and 150 degrees above Fahrenheit; it could burn all kinds of fuel; it weighed a mere three-and-one-half pounds; and it was smaller than a quart bottle of milk. The first order for 5,000 units was flown to U.S. forces involved in the November 1942 invasion of North Africa. Ernie Pyle, the famous World War II journalist who wrote about the common man's experience in the war, devoted 15 articles to the Coleman pocket stove and considered it one of the two most important pieces of noncombat equipment in the war effort, the other being the Jeep.

When the war ended, Coleman's business boomed. Because the company had been manufacturing products for the armed services during the war, there was an enormous backlog of demand for its regular products, which had been off the market. Sales rose to $34 million by 1950, while profits also substantially increased. At the start of the decade, there were four main divisions of Coleman products: oil space heaters accounted for 30 percent of sales; gas floor furnaces, 30 percent; camp stove and gasoline lanterns, 20 percent; and military contracts to supply Boeing Co. with airplane parts for the B-47 bomber, 20 percent.

CAMPING AND RECREATIONAL PRODUCT FOCUS IN POSTWAR PERIOD

In the early 1950s, Coleman was the leader in sales in each of its civilian product lines. At the end of the decade, however, sales for oil heaters and gas floor furnaces alone dropped 85 percent, and by 1960 the company suffered an overall loss of 70 percent in sales volume. The U.S. military had also phased out Coleman's contracts for airplane parts. In response, Coleman developed its camp stove and lantern products into an extensive line of camping equipment. Having introduced its first cooler in 1954, the company's portable ice chests and insulated jugs quickly became leaders in the field of outdoor recreation products. Coleman also expanded its line of oil, gas, and electric furnaces to manufacturers of mobile homes and began designing air conditioning equipment and furnaces for onsite homes.

During the 1960s, Coleman continued to expand its product lines in the field of camping, adding sleeping bags, tents, and catalytic heaters. Coleman soon became the leading manufacturer of camping equipment. Growing along with the mobile home industry, Coleman supplied 40 percent of the specialized furnaces and 50 percent of the air conditioning equipment for mobile homes. Sales grew from $38 million in 1960 to $134 million by 1970, and during the same period net profits increased dramatically from $278,000 to $7 million.

The two leaders of the company were Sheldon Coleman, who replaced his father as president in 1951 and as chairman of the board six years later when the founder died, and Lawrence M. Jones, a longtime employee of Coleman who possessed a doctorate from Harvard University. Sheldon had hired Jones as president of the company in 1964, and the two men collaborated on product development and market strategy. Their joint effort resulted in the manufacture of adjustable backpack frames, a compact cooler, a small backpack stove, canoes made from a petroleum-based substance that created a quieter ride than aluminum, Crosman air guns, and camping trailers. In 1977 Coleman's success continued unabated, with sales reaching $256 million. The company's outdoor recreation business seemed to be recession-proof, and profits from its mobile home products kept increasing.

END OF FOUNDING FAMILY INVOLVEMENT WITH 1989 HOSTILE TAKEOVER

For more than three-quarters of a century, Coleman had worked hard to establish and maintain a reputation for high-quality products sold at reasonable prices. This reputation paid off handsomely during the 1980s as both profits and sales increased steadily. According to *Fortune*, however, the Coleman family, who owned 25 percent of the company's stock, began withdrawing profits rather than reinvesting for product development and market expansion. Sheldon Coleman Jr. replaced his father as chairman of the board in 1988, and only one year later he decided to privatize the company in order

to reap an even larger profit. The pension plan of the company was overloaded by approximately $30 million.

The new chairman floated an offer of $64 per share for the company's stock. The bid proved too low, and ill-timed as well. Instead, New York financier Ronald Perelman entered the scene and purchased Coleman for $545 million, or $74 per share, in a 1989 leveraged buyout through his company MacAndrews & Forbes Holdings Inc. Together, Perelman and Jones sold the heating and air-conditioning business, shut down an obsolete factory, and implemented a strategy that improved efficiency and ultimately reduced inventory costs by $10 million.

Through a comprehensive restructuring of its operations, the company increased productivity significantly in 1991, and Coleman's sales that year reached $346.1 million. In 1992 sales increased to $491.9 million, proof that the company's concentration on manufacturing products in growing recreational markets was paying off. Perelman took Coleman public again during 1992 but retained an 82.5 percent stake in the company. In late 1992 Coleman reacquired the Coleman Powermate line of gasoline-powered electrical generators and high-pressure power washers. The following year the company aimed to bolster its overseas sales through acquisitions. Coleman had encountered difficulty over the years in Europe selling its propane-based camping appliances because Europeans generally preferred products running on butane gas. The purchase of British and Italian camping equipment makers in late 1993 led to the launch of dozens of Coleman-brand butane products in Europe.

At the beginning of 1994 Jones retired and was replaced as chairman and CEO by Michael N. Hammes, who had been vice chairman of The Black & Decker Corporation and president of its worldwide power tools and home products group. Acquisitions continued under the new executive. Added in 1994 were Sanborn Manufacturing Company, whose portable and stationary air compressors were folded into the Powermate division, and Eastpak, Inc., a maker of book bags, daypacks, and related products. The following year Coleman purchased Sierra Corporation of Fort Smith, Inc., maker of portable outdoor and recreational folding furniture under the Sierra Trails brand. In early 1996 the company expanded its Eastpak division by licensing the Timberland brand for a new line of packs. Coleman also acquired France-based Application des Gaz, a leading European camping equipment maker under the Camping Gaz brand. Meanwhile, the 50 millionth Coleman lantern rolled off the assembly line in 1995, the same year that Hammes moved the firm's headquarters to Golden, Colorado.

The company's aggressive pursuit of acquisitions did not come without a cost. By 1996 Coleman had shown tremendous growth since being acquired by Perelman, as revenues reached $1.22 billion, three-and-a-half times the level of 1991. However, the company also posted a net loss of $41.8 million. The loss was largely attributed to higher than expected costs related to integrating overseas sales forces following the purchase of Camping Gaz. Another key factor was mounting debt stemming from the string of acquisitions, the debt level having reached $583.6 million by the end of 1996.

On the heels of the announcement of the 1996 loss, Coleman replaced Hammes, installing Jerry W. Levin as acting CEO in February 1997. Levin had previously run the company from 1989 to April 1991 when he became CEO of Revlon Inc., another Perelman-controlled company. Under Levin's leadership, Coleman moved quickly to turn its fortunes around through a number of cost-cutting initiatives. The company closed its administrative headquarters in Golden and a regional headquarters in Geneva, Switzerland, and shifted its world headquarters back to Wichita. The 7,000-person workforce was cut by 10 percent. Four factories, three domestic and one international, were closed. Certain noncore product areas were divested, including power washers and portable spas. Finally, one-third of the company's stock-keeping units were eliminated, greatly streamlining its product offerings.

SUNBEAM/AMERICAN HOUSEHOLD ERA

In March 1998, with the company verging on a turnaround, Perelman sold his 82 percent stake in Coleman to Sunbeam Corporation for $1.6 billion plus the assumption of about $440 million in debt. At the same time Sunbeam announced two other purchases: Signature Brands USA Inc., maker of such household products as Mr. Coffee coffeemakers and Health-o-meter scales; and First Alert Inc., a maker of residential safety products, including smoke alarms and fire extinguishers. Charges of accounting irregularities and misleading earnings reports led to the ouster of Sunbeam's CEO, "Chainsaw Al" Dunlap, in June 1998. Soon thereafter, Perelman, who had gained a 14 percent stake in Sunbeam as part of the sale of his Coleman stake, installed a new team at Sunbeam, including naming Levin as CEO; Levin in turn installed Bill Phillips, a 20-year company veteran, as chief executive of Coleman. Dunlap had evidently laid plans to sell off Coleman's backpack and compressor businesses, plans that were quickly abandoned once Levin took over at Sunbeam.

In the wake of Dunlap's ouster, Coleman was left as a subsidiary of a company in extremely shaky financial condition, including being burdened by $2.2 billion in debt. Nonetheless, a year after posting losses in 1998, Coleman rebounded with strong profits based on an increase in camping and on higher shipments of lanterns, stoves, generators, and other products stemming from fears of Y2K-related equipment malfunctions. The company also benefited from strong sales of its new line of Coleman Xtreme coolers, which thanks to thick insulation and tight-fitting lids were able to hold ice for up to five days at temperatures as high as 90 degrees Fahrenheit. Early in 2000, Sunbeam acquired the last remaining publicly traded shares of Coleman stock, making the Wichita company a wholly owned subsidiary.

In 2000 and 2001, a century after the firm's founding, Coleman displayed a newfound devotion to new product development. Consumer research revealed that Coleman products were being used for much more than just camping, so the company began designing items specifically for such activities as picnicking, tailgating, and backyard lounging. In addition, Coleman launched a line of higher-end camping and hiking gear under the Exponent brand and also unveiled a selection of camping and outdoor products aimed at children. In 2000 the company entered into a licensing agreement with the National Association of Stock Car Auto Racing, Inc., (NASCAR) that led to the debut of Coleman products sporting the NASCAR logo. This partnership made much sense given the hundreds of thousands of campers who attended NASCAR races every year. To support the NASCAR-related line, Coleman began setting up trailers at racing events that featured new product displays and offered free repairs of Coleman gear. By mid-2001 the company was reporting that the NASCAR and other initiatives had helped push sales up 50 percent.

The financially troubled Sunbeam finally filed for Chapter 11 bankruptcy protection in February 2001, ending a period of uncertainty for Coleman as rumors had circulated of its impending sale. Sunbeam emerged from bankruptcy in December 2002 financially restructured and sporting a new corporate name, American Household, Inc. During this period of reorganization, Coleman closed down its outdoor grill manufacturing plant in Neosho, Missouri, and shifted the production to a facility in Wichita. A further restructuring of the manufacturing operations was completed in 2004. In this instance, a portion of Coleman's production was shifted to lower-cost locations overseas, and as part of this shift the firm's sleeping bag plant in Lake City, South Carolina, was shut down.

2005 JARDEN TAKEOVER OF AMERICAN HOUSEHOLD

In March 2004 Coleman's top two executives, Phillips and Randy Underwood, the CFO, abruptly left the company. Gwen Wisler, a former Coleman executive, was named the new president and CEO. Six months later, Jarden Corporation, a maker of consumer products such as Diamond matches and Bicycle playing cards that was based in Rye, New York, reached an agreement to acquire American Household. Jarden completed the deal in January 2005 at the price of $745.6 million in cash and the assumption of $140 million in debt. Coleman was thus once again a wholly owned subsidiary of a publicly traded company and was positioned as the core of Jarden's newly formed Outdoor Solutions unit. On completion of the takeover, Gary A. Kiedaisch was named president of Coleman Company. Kiedaisch had previous executive experience with consumer products companies specializing in sports and outdoor recreation, including NIKE, Inc.'s Bauer Nike Hockey Inc.

Later in 2005, Coleman announced a renewed effort to go after the high-end outdoor gear market by creating two separate sales forces: one for large chain retailers and one for specialty stores, including outdoor stores, sporting goods stores, department stores, and Internet retailers. It also returned to a practice from earlier in its history of designing and producing high-end goods specifically for specialty stores.

Jarden in August 2007 acquired K2 Inc., a sports equipment giant based in Carlsbad, California, in a deal valued at about $1.2 billion. Just a month later, Kiedaisch resigned from Coleman. The firm's CFO, Sam Solomon, was named interim president and CEO. He was named to that post on a permanent basis in May 2008. Solomon was thus charged with overseeing an important diversification of Coleman's product portfolio that stemmed from its parent's K2 purchase. Coleman at this time was contending with the challenging trend of fewer people camping and hiking, so Jarden elected to split the Stearns division out of K2 and merge it into Coleman and thus broaden the Wichita company's product lines. In this way, Coleman gained responsibility for flotation devices, towables, rainwear, waders, hunting and fishing gear, and safety and survival equipment marketed under the Stearns, Sevylor, Sospenders, Hodgman, Mad Dog Gear, Nevin, and Helium brands. The product lines of Coleman and Stearns were clearly complementary, with similarities in customers, marketing, and manufacturing. Perhaps most importantly, Coleman's broader array of products provided it with greater leverage with retailers. Further growth initiatives under Jarden's stewardship were likely, as evidenced by

Coleman's mid-2009 purchase of Esky, an iconic Australian brand of portable coolers.

Thomas Derdak
Updated, David E. Salamie

PRINCIPAL SUBSIDIARIES

Application des Gaz, S.A.S. (France); Australian Coleman, Inc.; Bafiges, S.A.S. (France); Beacon Exports, Inc.; Camping Gaz CS Spol S.R.O. (Czech Republic); Camping Gaz (Deutschland) GmbH (Germany); Camping Gaz International Portugal Lda.; Camping Gaz Italia S.r.l. (Italy); Camping Gaz Suisse A.G. (Switzerland); CC Outlet, Inc.; Coleman Asia Limited (Hong Kong); Coleman Benelux B.V. (Netherlands); Coleman Brands Pty. Limited (Australia); Coleman (Deutschland) GmbH (Germany); Coleman EMEA, S.A.S. (France); Coleman Guangzhou Outdoor Leisure Company, Ltd. (China); Coleman Hong Kong Limited; Coleman International Holdings, LLC; Coleman Japan Company, Ltd.; Coleman UK Limited; Coleman Worldwide Corporation; Coleman Vostok LLC (Russia); Nippon Coleman, Inc.; Productos Coleman, S.A. (Spain).

PRINCIPAL COMPETITORS

Igloo Corporation; Newell Rubbermaid Inc.; Aero Products International, Inc.; Intex Recreation Corp.; VF Corporation; Kellwood Company; Worthington Industries, Inc.; Eveready Holdings, Inc.; The Procter & Gamble Company; Spectrum Brands, Inc.

FURTHER READING

Atwater, Andi, "Coleman Chief Executive Resigns," *Wichita (KS) Eagle*, September 15, 2007, p. 6B.

Berman, Dennis K., and Henny Sender, "Jarden Is Set to Acquire American Household," *Wall Street Journal*, September 20, 2004, p. A6.

Brannigan, Martha, "For Perelman, Sunbeam Stake Turns a Bit Pale," *Wall Street Journal*, June 4, 1998, p. C1.

Brooks, Rick, and Greg Jaffe, "Sunbeam's Not So Odd Couple," *Wall Street Journal*, March 3, 1998, p. B4.

Coleman Company, *Portrait of the Coleman Company: The First Hundred Years*, Wichita, KS: Coleman Company, 1999.

Coleman, Sheldon, and Lawrence Jones, *The Coleman Story: The Ability to Cope with Change*, New York: Newcomen Society in North America, 1976, 28 p.

Dinell, David, "Coleman Planning to Move Grill-Making Unit to Wichita," *Wichita (KS) Business Journal*, June 8, 2001, p. 1.

Doherty, Jacqueline, "Bulletproof Billionaire?" *Barron's*, May 19, 1997, pp. 18, 20.

Dorfman, Dan, "Coleman: No Happy Campers," *Financial World*, April 15, 1997, p. 28.

———, "Coleman Seen Following Marvel as Perelman's Next Disaster," *Financial World*, March 18, 1997, p. 14.

Dumaine, Brian, "Earning More by Moving Faster," *Fortune*, October 7, 1991, pp. 89–94.

Fitzgerald, Kate, "Events Light Coleman's Fire: New Marketing Strategy Sparks Higher Sales," *Advertising Age*, June 18, 2001, p. 61.

Gallagher, Leigh, "Coleman Brass Flexes Muscle and Stakes Out New Terrain," *Sporting Goods Business*, April 1996, p. 28.

———, "Coleman Shutters CO Office in Cost-Cutting Strategy," *Sporting Goods Business*, May 12, 1997, p. 18.

———, "The SGB Interview: Jerry W. Levin," *Sporting Goods Business*, August 7, 1997, pp. 32–33.

Geer, John F., Jr., "Coleman: Hiking Nowhere?" *Financial World*, April 22, 1996, p. 17.

Knox, Don, "Coleman Deal Tripped 'Chainsaw,'" *Denver Post*, November 14, 1999, p. K1.

Labate, John, "Growing to Match Its Brand Name," *Fortune*, June 13, 1994, p. 114.

Laing, Jonathan R., "Into the Maw: Sunbeam's 'Chainsaw Al' Goes on a Buying Binge," *Barron's*, March 9, 1998, p. 13.

———, "Now It's Ron's Turn: Sunbeam Shareholders, Beware," *Barron's*, October 12, 1998, pp. 31–32, 34–35.

Lipin, Steven, "Sunbeam Plans $1.8 Billion in Acquisitions: Deals to Include Coleman, First Alert, and Maker of Mr.

Coffee Machines," *Wall Street Journal*, March 2, 1998, p. A3.

McEvoy, Christopher, "Acquiring Minds," *Sporting Goods Business*, August 1995, pp. 44+.

Pounds, Stephen, "Sun Capital Lands Coleman Generator Firm," *Palm Beach (FL) Post*, October 13, 2004, p. 1D.

Sommers, Novelda, "Coleman Now More Than Just Camping," *Wichita (KS) Eagle*, April 22, 2001, p. 1B.

Story, Mark, "Coleman Freed to Accelerate Global Brand Initiatives," *Wichita (KS) Business Journal*, August 24, 2001, pp. 1, 28.

Voorhis, Dan, "Back to Camping Roots," *Wichita (KS) Eagle*, January 22, 2006, p. 1C.

———, "Coleman CEO Looks Ahead," *Wichita (KS) Eagle*, June 1, 2008, p. 1C.

———, "Coleman's New Bosses Take Look Around Plants," *Wichita (KS) Eagle*, January 26, 2005, p. 1A.

———, "Coleman's New Parent Vows Stability," *Wichita (KS) Eagle*, September 21, 2004, p. 1A.

———, "Coleman to Push High-End Gear Again," *Wichita (KS) Eagle*, November 17, 2005, p. 6B.

———, "Mystery Envelops Coleman Shakeup," *Wichita (KS) Eagle*, March 4, 2004, p. 1A.

Weimer, De'Ann, Gail DeGeorge, and Leah Nathans Spiro, "Chainsaw Al Goes to Camp," *Business Week*, March 16, 1998, p. 36.

Weisz, Pam, "Camp Giant Coleman Goes Electric," *Brandweek*, November 27, 1995, p. 6.

"Will Sunbeam Make the Cut Following Coleman Co. Buy?" *Sporting Goods Business*, March 25, 1998, p. 18.

Comisión Federal de Electricidad

Reforma 164
Mexico City, D.F. 06500
Mexico
Telephone: (52 55) 5229-4400
Toll Free: (01 800) 223-3071 (in Mexico City)
Fax: (52 55) 5553-6424
Web site: http://www.cfe.gob.mx

Government-Owned Company
Founded: 1937
Employees: 78,170
Sales: MXN 269.68 billion ($19.92 billion) (2008)
NAICS: 221111 Hydroelectric Power Generation; 221112 Fossil Fuel Electric Power Generation; 221113 Nuclear Electric Power Generation; 221119 Other Electric Power Generation; 221121 Electric Power Transmission and Control; 221122 Electric Power Distribution

■ ■ ■

Comisión Federal de Electricidad (CFE), or Federal Electricity Commission, is Mexico's second-largest operational public body. It is the chief generator of electricity in Mexico and, along with a smaller public organism, has a virtual monopoly on the transmission, distribution, and sale of electricity. The commission also prepares the groundwork for new generating plants and expansion of the national grid as demand for electricity grows.

MOSTLY IN FOREIGN HANDS BEFORE 1937

The first electrical generating plant in Mexico was installed for a textile factory in 1879. Electricity was almost immediately adopted for the mining industry and, to a degree, for residential and public lighting. The public distribution of electricity was principally in the hands of three foreign-owned companies that exercised monopoly power: the Toronto-based Mexican Light and Power Company in central Mexico; the American and Foreign Power Company in the north, and the Compañia Eléctrica de Chapala, in the west. All machinery used was imported until 1943.

Federal regulation of the electrical industry began in 1926. A 1933 constitutional amendment established that the generation and distribution of electricity were activities of public utility and extended federal authority to all phases of the industry. Mexico's Congress authorized the executive branch to organize and direct a nonprofit system with the end or purpose of obtaining, at minimal cost, the greatest possible return for the benefit of the public.

ORGANIZING THE CFE: 1937–38

In 1937, when the CFE was established, only 7 million of Mexico's 18.3 million people had access to electricity. The private companies, beset by the Great Depression, were not making the investments needed to extend service. They concentrated on supplying the largest users: industrial and commercial companies that, as the most coveted customers, received preferential rates.

COMPANY PERSPECTIVES

Mission: To secure, within a framework of competence and up-to-date technology, the service of electrical energy, under conditions of quantity, quality, and price, with a proper diversification of energy sources. To optimize the utilization of physical infrastructure, business and human resources. To attain excellence in relations with our customers. To protect the environment, further social development, and respect the values of the people who live where the electrical works are located.

There was no rural electrification except in areas of major irrigation.

The CFE was governed by a five member administrative council appointed by the president of Mexico and presided over by the home secretary. The operating staff was headed by a director general who was made a member of the cabinet. The commission's mandate was to organize and direct a national system of generation, transmission, and distribution of electric energy. At the end of 1938 a law was passed that imposed a 10 percent consumption tax on electrical energy. The federal government contributed almost half of the commission's revenue from its own resources. The sale of bonds abroad accounted for another 30 percent.

INCREMENTAL PROGRESS: 1944–59

The CFE accounted for only 5 percent of Mexico's installed capacity for electricity generation before 1944, when its first big project, the Ixpantongo hydroelectric generating plant in the mountainous southern part of the state of México, began service. (A companion plant, Santa Bárbara, was later built there.) The power generated was transmitted to the Mexico City metropolitan area and distributed to hundreds of factories as well as to residences, offices, and commercial establishments.

By the early 1950s the CFE had completed a major thermal plant in Monterrey, a key industrial center. Another one, in the state of Chihuahua, was serving an important mining zone in northern Mexico and also aiding farmers by providing power for irrigation pumps in a drought prone area. Acapulco, once plunged into darkness as soon as the sun descended, was now brightly lit by a group of diesel generators, and a hydroelectric plant was under construction. This project stimulated

tourism, the nation's chief single source of hard currency.

Rural electrification advanced more slowly, even though more than 60 percent of the population lived in the countryside. Even 15 years after the founding of the CFE only about 40 small power plants had been installed in the rural communities of just 16 of Mexico's 27 states.

Distribution of electricity remained largely in private hands. In its early years, the CFE, by an informal agreement, sold three-quarters of its production to private companies for further distribution to customers. Electricity rates were kept low in the 1950s to aid private industry, and the CFE extended loans to small companies.

ACQUIRING THE PRIVATE COMPANIES: 1960–65

By 1960 the CFE was producing more than half of Mexico's electrical power and distributing about half. Only 44 percent of the population, however, had electrical service. The private companies were widely held responsible for insufficient investment and labor problems. Consequently, the government purchased both the Mexican Light and Power Company and the American and Foreign Power Company and its subsidiaries in 1960, giving the CFE control of 91 percent of the nation's installed capacity. (The Chapala company had been acquired by the CFE in 1940.) Five years later, the commission acquired 19 other private companies, which were subsequently integrated into this body.

By 1968 almost all electrical power produced in Mexico was generated by the CFE or the Compañia de Luz y Fuerza del Centro (CLFC), a parallel state-owned body that had been created in 1963 to serve the Mexico City metropolitan area and surrounding zones. It was, essentially, the former Mexican Light and Power Company in public hands. (The exceptions were private generators and Petróleos Mexicanos S.A., Pemex, Mexico's state monopoly for the production of petroleum and natural gas.)

Although nominally an independent unit, the CLFC shared the same governing board and general management and was considered by the CFE to be its central division. These two officially became the exclusive bodies for providing electric energy to the public in 1975. The CLFC generally left new generation to the CFE and dedicated itself mainly to the sale and distribution of electricity.

The rate system in use for electricity was completely overhauled in 1962. More than 150 different rate

KEY DATES

1937: Government forms the Comisión Federal de Electricidad (CFE).

1944: CFE completes its first major project, a hydroelectric generating plant.

1960: Commission gains control of Mexico's two largest power companies.

1968: Almost all electrical power is produced by the CFE and another public body.

1982: Mexico's installed electrical capacity has increased ninefold since 1960.

1987: CFE-owned nuclear power plant enters service in Laguna Verde, Veracruz.

1992: Government allows private firms to generate limited amounts of electricity.

1999: Presidential proposal to dissolve the CFE fails to gain traction in Congress.

2009: Nearly 97 percent of the Mexican population is receiving public power.

structures were in existence at the time, based on generation and distribution costs in individual plants. In general, the least developed areas of Mexico were charged the highest rates. The new system divided the nation into three areas, with an average rate fixed for all types of services. Industrial rates rose by about 40 percent in most cases as favoritism for large consumers was abandoned. Overall, rates were raised by about 17 percent, but south and southeastern Mexico, the least developed areas, benefited from considerable reductions.

RAPID GROWTH FOLLOWED BY SLOWDOWN: 1960

The next two decades saw an enormous increase in power production. Between 1960 and 1982 Mexico's installed electrical capacity increased ninefold, and the CFE's revenues increased by sevenfold. The percentage of housing with electricity grew from 28 in 1961 to nearly 74 in 1980. The last great hydroelectric project, El Infierillo, was completed in 1965. It was supplemented, and later followed, by many smaller, thermal fossil fueled plants. Installed capacity rose from 3,250 megawatts in 1961 to 7,874 in 1971 and 17,360 in 1980.

A CFE-built geothermal plant in Cerro Prieto, north of Mexicali, began operation in 1973. The com-

mission also initiated nuclear-powered commercial generation in 1987, when a plant went into service in Laguna Verde, Veracruz. A second unit at the site began operation later.

The CFE's debt was not great until the 1970s, when this sum began to grow faster than other parts of the public budget, reaching MXN 8.23 billion in 1981, compared to MXN 990 million in 1970. Meanwhile, the real average price (discounting inflation) per kilowatt hour had been allowed to drop sharply and by 1978 was little more than half of the 1962 level. Accordingly, the cost of servicing debt rose from 20 percent of the CFE's current expenditures in 1970 to 40 percent in 1980. Because of these restraints, installed capacity grew at a slower rate in the 1980s. In 1986 the federal government decided to absorb the debt itself.

SEEKING A ROLE FOR PRIVATE POWER: 1992–2007

By the early 1990s there was strong sentiment throughout Latin America in favor of privatizing state-owned companies. In 1992 the Mexican government allowed private companies to generate limited amounts of electricity for their own use or sell it to the CFE or CLFC for distribution. This program attracted very little private investment at first in what were called independent power projects, but by 2009 private generators accounted for 23 percent of installed capacity in Mexico.

In 1999 President Ernesto Zedillo sent to Congress a proposal that in essence would have eventually dissolved the CFE. It called for the commission to be replaced by several generating and distribution companies and one transmission company operating under two independent state-owned entities; open access to the national transmission grid; and the establishment of a wholesale market for electricity in which generators would sell their power. Generation and marketing would be opened to both domestic and foreign private investment. The state-owned generation and distribution companies were to be progressively privatized. This proposal, which would have required a constitutional amendment, died in Congress.

By this time some 95 percent of all Mexicans had access to electricity. However, 83,000 rural communities were still without power, and electricity losses due to transmission and distribution problems were said to be excessive by world standards. Moreover, some 35 percent of all electricity transmitted was reported to be unbilled to any user, and making the investments necessary to meet demand by a growing population and economy was competing with other demands on the government, such as spending on health and education. By 2007 no less than 233 companies were reported in the last two years to have decided to reduce their costs by building their own power plants.

THE CFE IN 2009

In 2009 President Felipe Calderón suggested another possible revenue stream for the CFE by means of a telecommunications network using two reserve sets of dark fiber optic wire to transmit voice, video, data, and Internet services at a rate of 10 megabytes per second. A pilot project for this purpose had been underway since 2003 by another means of transmission but was suspended in 2009 because of high costs. The CFE's director, however, opposed proposals to auction the wire to private parties on the grounds that it could put at risk the security and trustworthiness of the national electrical system.

The subsidies needed to support the CFE and CLFC in the first three years of the Calderón presidency (2006–09), were 32 percent higher than in the first three years of the previous administration of Vicente Fox Quesada. Because of low rates, in 2009 CFE customers were paying only 66 percent of the cost of generation.

In 2009 the CFE and CLFC had 156 central generators with an installed capacity of 38,514 megawatts. The electricity generated was reaching the public by means of about 732,000 kilometers (about 455,000 miles) of transmission wires. Nearly 97 percent of the population in 184,613 rural and 3,325 urban communities was receiving this electricity. In terms of effective capacity, the two public bodies' thermal generators accounted for 45 percent of the nation's electricity generation and hydroelectric installations for 22 percent. The CFE's nuclear generators at Laguna Verde ac-counted for 3 percent and geothermal power for 2 percent. Although the residential sector accounted for 88 percent of all customers, home sales represented only 26 percent of the total. By contrast, commercial customers accounted for less than 1 percent of the total but 56 percent of sales revenue.

In October the Mexican government announced that it was shutting down the CLFC, formally shifting the company's operations to the CFE. The move, heavily criticized by union workers, was the result of a national effort to improve services while reducing inefficiency and high utility costs.

Robert Halasz

FURTHER READING

Baker, George, and Eric R. Blume, "Zedillo's Revolution?" *Electric Perspectives,* July/August 1999, pp. 26+.

Cruz Serrano, Noé, "Creció 31.8% el subsidio a electricidad," *El Universal,* September 2, 2009.

De La Garza Toledo, Enrique, et al., *História de la Indústria Eléctrica en México,* Mexico City: Universidad Autónoma Metropolitana, 2 vols., 1994.

"Electricidad," in *Enciclopedia de México,* Mexico City: Sabeca International Investment Corporation, Vol. 5, pp. 2457–2465.

González Rubí, Rafael, "La indústria eléctrica y los 50 años de la CFE," *Comércio Exterior,* August 1987, pp. 625–31.

Kahler, Anita von, "Kilowatts for Prosperity," *Américas,* January 1953, pp. 3–5, 30–31.

Lacey, Marc, "Mexico Says It Is Closing a Provider of Electricity," *New York Times,* October 11, 2009.

Vernon, Raymond, ed., *Public Policy and Private Enterprise in Mexico,* Cambridge, MA: Harvard University Press, 1964, pp. 37–110.

Wionezek, Miguel S., et al., *Energy Policy in Mexico,* Boulder, CO: Westview Press, 1988, pp. 65–96.

Compass Diversified
Holdings

———■———

61 Wilton Road, 2nd Floor
Westport, Connecticut 06880-3121
U.S.A.
Telephone: (203) 221-1703
Fax: (203) 221-8253
Web site: http://www.compassdiversifiedholdings.com

Public Company
Incorporated: 2005
Employees: 237
Sales: $1.54 billion (2008)
Stock Exchanges: NASDAQ
Ticker Symbol: CODI
NAICS: 551112 Offices of Other Holding Companies

■ ■ ■

Listed on the NASDAQ, Compass Diversified Holdings, a statutory trust, along with sister management company Compass Group Diversified Holdings, LLC, acquires and manages small and middle-market companies. Compass makes regular distributions to investors, thus allowing them to participate in the ownership and growth of businesses while retaining liquidity in much the same way investors participate in real estate through Real Estate Investment Trusts. Acting as a leveraged-buyout firm, Compass focuses on undervalued U.S. companies, regardless of industry, that maintain a significant market share in their sector. Rather than saddle portfolio companies with excessive debt, Compass borrows money at the holding company level. Unlike some investment firms, Compass does not

set a timetable on cashing out investments, content to hold onto companies as long as they produce attractive returns for Compass shareholders. Portfolio companies include Colorado-based Advanced Circuits, maker of quick-turn, prototype printed circuit boards (PCBs); American Furniture Manufacturing, Inc., a Mississippi manufacturer of sofas, love seats, recliners, and other inexpensive upholstered furniture; Anodyne Medical Device, Inc., a Florida maker of medical support surfaces used to prevent and treat pressure ulcers on immobile patients; Fox Factory, Inc., a California producer of suspension products for motorcycles, off-road vehicles, and other modes of transportation; Halo Branded Solutions, Inc., an Illinois company specializing in customized promotional products to support branding campaigns; and CBS Personnel Holdings, Inc., a staffing services company based in Ohio that operates under the Staffmark name. Compass maintains its headquarters in Westport, Connecticut. Founder I. Joseph Massoud serves as chief executive officer.

FOUNDER: 1993 HARVARD BUSINESS SCHOOL GRADUATE

A native Californian, Joe Massoud received an undergraduate degree from Claremont McKenna College in 1989 and then went to work as a management consultant for McKinsey & Company, serving in the Los Angeles and Mexico City offices. He then continued his education, earning an M.B.A. from Harvard Business School. Upon graduation in 1993 he went to work for a Los Angeles private-equity firm, Colony Capital, that in addition to real estate invested in distressed

COMPANY PERSPECTIVES

We believe that private company owners and corporate parents looking to sell their businesses may consider us an attractive acquirer because of our ability to: Provide ongoing strategic and financial support for their businesses; Maintain a long-term outlook as to the ownership of those businesses where such an outlook is required for maximization of our shareholders' return on investment; and Consummate transactions efficiently without being dependent on third-party financing on a transaction-by-transaction basis. We believe that management teams may consider us an attractive partner due to our ability and desire to: Work with management to pursue organic and external growth opportunities; and Structure significant and creative equity incentive programs for our management teams.

companies. Massoud's next stop was Petroleum Heat and Power, where he served as vice president of finance and corporate development. While there he was recruited in 1997 by the principals of the Kattegat Trust to take charge of investments for TK Foundation, a philanthropic endeavor established by Danish shipping magnate Jens Torben Karlshoej.

In 1998 Massoud established the predecessor to Compass Diversified Holdings, Compass Group International. Investing on behalf of Kattegat Trust, whose sole beneficiaries were philanthropic entities, the Compass Group focused on acquisitions between $25 million and $150 million. No particular industry was favored. One of Compass Group's early investments was in CBS Personnel Services. The Kentucky company then used the backing of Compass Group to acquire Columbia Staffing & Health Care Services in 2000, gaining a presence in the Mid-Atlantic region as well as Florida as part of an effort to become more of a national player. In 2004 CBS Personnel acquired Venturi Staffing in a deal that allowed the company to expand to 13 states.

In 2001 Compass Group acquired California Pellet Mill (CPM), which served the feed milling market, selling pelleting and particle size reduction equipment for use in animal feed milling and oil seed processing. As was the case with CBS, Compass Group used CPM as a platform for further acquisitions. A year later CPM acquired St. Charles, Missouri-based Beta Raven, a company that sold process automation and control systems. It not only served the feed milling market but also the bakery, tortilla, and premix industries. To support CPM's further growth, Compass Group arranged financing for the company from American Capital Strategies Ltd.

PURCHASE OF SDC TECHNOLOGIES: 2004

Another Compass Group deal came in late 2004 when the firm helped the management team of SDC Technologies Inc. to buy the California-based manufacturer of eyewear coatings, renaming it Silvue Technologies Group, Inc. In that same year, Compass Group paid about $65 million for Rochester, New York-based Crosman Corporation, maker of air-powered guns and ammunition, including paintball guns as well as replicas of famous guns. In 2005 Compass Group and investment partners acquired Advanced Circuits, Inc., a maker of PCBs. Rather than compete in the low-margin commodity portion of the market dominated by Asian companies, Advanced Circuits specialized in prototypes and other low-volume, high-margin, quick-turnaround PCBs.

In order to develop an appropriate fund-raising strategy, Massoud and his team had considered a number of options before settling on creating a publicly traded investment trust. "It wasn't an 'a-ha' moment," Massoud told *Buyoutnews.com*. "It was more of an evolution." Hence, in November 2005 Compass Diversified Holdings, a trust that was 38 percent owned by Kattegat Trust, was incorporated in Delaware. Simultaneously, Compass Group Diversified Holdings, LLC, was formed as the operating company, and along with the trust was intended to acquire and manage small and middle-market businesses. Unlike other trusts, investors were not asked to contribute to a fund that could be used to acquire any manner of assets. Rather, investors were buying stakes in a portfolio of companies already under management: CBS Personnel, Crosman, Compass AC Holdings (Advanced Circuits), and Silvue.

INITIAL PUBLIC STOCK OFFERING: 2006

Many investors were confused by the Compass approach. "Half the investment bankers we talked to looked at us and said it was interesting but that they couldn't do that," Massoud told *Buyoutnews.com*. "When they said we were ahead of our time, maybe they thought we were nuts." Nevertheless, Massoud and his team carried on with a road show to promote the issue, and after several days they received enough positive

```
┌─────────────────────────────────────────────┐
│                                               │
│              KEY DATES                        │
│         ───────────■───────────               │
│                                               │
│  1998:  I. Joseph Massoud founds predecessor  │
│         company.                              │
│  2005:  Compass Diversified Holdings          │
│         incorporates.                         │
│  2006:  Compass goes public.                  │
│  2007:  Compass acquires Aeroglide            │
│         Corporation and HALO Branded          │
│         Solutions Inc.                        │
│  2008:  Company acquires Fox Factory, Inc.    │
│  2009:  Company completes secondary stock     │
│         offering.                             │
│                                               │
└─────────────────────────────────────────────┘
```

responses to conclude that their model would indeed find a place in the market. The initial public offering of stock was completed in May 2006, netting nearly $270 million. The four portfolio companies were then acquired by the trust, shares of which began trading on the NASDAQ. Just two months later Compass paid shareholders its first distribution.

Compass then added to its holdings in August 2006 when it joined forces with Hollywood Capital Inc. to form Anodyne Medical Device Inc. as a roll-up vehicle in the medical support surfaces sector. Anodyne immediately acquired two of the sector's leading companies: AMF Support Surfaces Inc., maker of such items as mattress overlays and seat cushions; and Sen-Tech Medical Systems Inc., which designed and manufactured electronically controlled air-based specialty surfaces. Later in the year Anodyne made a further acquisition, adding Anatomic Concepts Inc., designer and manufacturer of mattresses, mattress overlays, and operating room table pads. Before 2006 came to a close CBS Personnel also completed another deal, acquiring Maryland-based PMC Staffing Solutions Inc. The deal was especially important because PMC significantly bolstered CBS's footprint in Baltimore as well as Chicago.

In 2007 Compass made further changes to its portfolio. Early in the year Crosman was sold, providing Compass with a net gain of $36 million, the money used to pay off debt in the company's revolving credit facility. A month later, in February 2007, Compass brought two new companies into the fold at a combined cost of $119 million: Aeroglide Corporation and HALO Branded Solutions Inc. Founded in North Carolina in 1940, Aeroglide manufactured industrial dryers used to make such products as Kellogg's cereal, Frito-Lay chips, Kingsford charcoal, and Purina pet foods. HALO's roots reached back to Tapico, Illinois, when in 1952 the Lee Wayne Corporation was founded to make promotional items. In the early 1990s it was acquired by an advertis-

ing and marketing services company, HA-LO Industries, Inc. The domestic promotion product assets of HA-LO were then acquired in 2004 to form HALO Branded Solutions.

ACQUISITION OF AMERICAN FURNITURE MANUFACTURING: 2007

To support further growth, Compass in 2007 completed a secondary public stock offering of 9.2 million shares as well as a private placement of 1.87 million shares. Together they raised $168.7 million for the trust. The funds were soon put to use when in August 2007 Compass acquired Ecru, Mississippi-based American Furniture Manufacturing, Inc. The company was established in 1998 to produce inexpensive promotional upholstered furniture, including sofas and recliners, which it sold to retailers and major furniture distributors. When 2007 came to a close, completing Compass's first full year, combined sales of its portfolio companies totaled nearly $918 million. Net income amounted to $40.4 million.

The year 2008 began with another addition to the Compass portfolio. A controlling interest in Fox Factory Holding Corp. was purchased for about $80 million in early January. The Watsonville, California-based high-end suspension company was founded in 1974 by Bob Fox, a motorcycle racer who thought he could do a better job at producing suspensions and shock absorbers than established companies. He originally set up shop in a friend's garage and over the years expanded beyond motorcycles to develop suspension products for snowmobiles, mountain bikes, all-terrain vehicles, and off-road cars and trucks. The company had enjoyed especially strong growth in previous years, and Bob Fox decided the time had come to partner with a larger company with the financial wherewithal to support further growth. After considering several other potential partners, Fox sided with Compass, which kept him on as chief executive officer. Bob Fox also retained a 24 percent interest in the company.

EXPANDING STAFFING SERVICES WITH STAFFMARK: 2006

Later in January 2008 CBS expanded its operations through the acquisition of Staffmark Investment, LLC, for about $134 million. With offices in 29 states Staffmark was a major provider of commercial staffing services, mostly focusing on light industrial staffing, and to a lesser degree administrative and transportation staffing, permanent placement services, and managed solutions. Because the Staffmark brand was better known than CBS Personnel, all of the 300 offices spread across 30 states began doing business under the Staffmark name in 2009.

Later in 2008 Compass adjusted its portfolio, selling a pair of subsidiaries. On June 24 Aeroglide was sold for $95 million, of which Compass received $85.6 million for its majority position. As a result, Compass enjoyed a $34 million gain on the asset. One day later, Silvue was divested as well, also for $95 million. Compass's net share of the proceeds was about $71.3 million, resulting in a net gain on the sale of $39.4 million. The remaining portfolio companies combined to generate $1.53 billion in 2008.

Compass continued to expand its slate of subsidiaries in 2009. HALO in March of that year bought Advertising Novelties Company, a Tulsa, Oklahoma-based promotional products distributor, adding the company's 17-member sales team to HALO's Sterling, Illinois headquarters. In June 2009, Advanced Circuits grew through acquisition as well, adding Haverhill, Massachusetts-based Circuit Board Express, Inc., a company, established in 1993, that was well established in the quick-to-market PCB sector. Also in June 2009 Compass completed another secondary stock offering, netting another $42.1 million. Aside from improving the company's cash position, the success of the offering demonstrated the continued support for Compass in the capital markets. Compass had also established a reputation for being a poor man's Berkshire Hathaway, a fund like that of legendary investor Warren Buffett that displayed patience and was willing to hold onto companies that were performing well, rather than buy

and sell assets within a predetermined window. While hardly in the same league as Berkshire Hathaway, Compass was nevertheless well positioned to carve out a profitable niche in the years to come.

Ed Dinger

PRINCIPAL SUBSIDIARIES

Advanced Circuits, Inc.; American Furniture Manufacturing, Inc.; Anodyne Medical Device, Inc.; Fox Factory, Inc.; Halo Branded Solutions, Inc.; CBS Personnel Holdings, Inc.

PRINCIPAL COMPETITORS

Apax Partners Holdings Ltd.; Blum Capital Partners, L.P.; The CapStreet Group, LLC.

FURTHER READING

Formosa, Nicole, "Connecticut Holdings Group Acquires Fox Racing Shox," *Bicycle Retailer and Industry News,* February 1, 2008, p. 6.

Malik, Naureen S., "A Poor Man's Berkshire Hathaway," *Weekday Trader,* January 27, 2009.

"Medical Roll-Up Formed," *Los Angeles Business Journal,* March 13, 2006, p. 10.

"Private Equity Fund Takes Public Route," *Corporate Financing Week,* May 15, 2006, p. 1.

"Putting on a Public Face: I. Joseph Massoud," *Buyoutnews.com,* August 11, 2006.

Thimangu, Patrick, "Staffing Firm Extends Reach," *Business Courier Serving Cincinnati–Northern Kentucky,* October 20, 2000, p. 3.

CVS Caremark
Corporation

One CVS Drive
Woonsocket, Rhode Island 02895
U.S.A.
Telephone: (401) 765-1500
Fax: (401) 766-2917
Web site: http://www.cvscaremark.com

Public Company
Incorporated: 1922 as Melville Shoe Corporation
Employees: 215,000
Sales: $87.47 billion (2008)
Stock Exchanges: New York
Ticker Symbol: CVS
NAICS: 446110 Pharmacies and Drug Stores; 454110 Electronic Shopping and Mail-Order Houses

∎ ∎ ∎

CVS Caremark Corporation is the largest pharmacy and pharmacy benefit management (PBM) company in the United States. With more than 6,950 drugstores in 44 states and the District of Columbia, CVS Caremark fills more than one billion prescriptions annually. Prescriptions can be requested over the Internet, through six mail-order pharmacies, or through the stores themselves. CVS Caremark is also the top specialty pharmacy in the country, with 19 specialty mail-order pharmacies and 58 specialty retail pharmacies. These offer special services for patients with long-term health conditions, such as HIV/AIDS and multiple sclerosis, which require complex and expensive drug regimens.

CVS Caremark operates a PBM business that provides services to managed care and other organizations. Services to individuals are intended to support positive health outcomes and include Proactive Pharmacy Care, a refill reminder and counseling service designed to improve adherence to prescription medicine programs. Bridge Supply allows customers to obtain a small supply of pills at a local CVS pharmacy while waiting for a mail-order prescription to arrive. Maintenance Choice offers qualified participants the option to pick up 90-day prescription refills at mail-order prices. MinuteClinics, available in more than 500 CVS stores, offer customers a convenient alternative to a regular doctor's appointment when seeking help for minor ailments. MinuteClinics accept insurance coverage, and uninsured patients receive care as an affordable alternative to the physician's office. Although CVS trails archrival Walgreen Co. in terms of overall revenues, CVS's private-label products, including cosmetics, foodstuffs, and over-the-counter health products, give the company a competitive edge in front-of-the-store sales.

CVS OPERATES UNDER UMBRELLA OF THE MELVILLE CORPORATION

The history of CVS is intertwined with that of Melville Corporation, whose own history dates back to the late 19th century but ends in 1996 when it changed its name to CVS Corporation. For much of its life, Melville was known chiefly for its chain of discount footwear stores, Thom McAn. During the late 20th century, however, Melville acquired more than a dozen

Our Vision: We strive to improve the quality of human life. Our Mission: We provide expert care and innovative solutions in pharmacy and health care that are effective for our customers. Our Values: Accountability, Respect, Integrity, Openness, Teamwork.

other retailing operations. Among these was the Consumer Value Stores (CVS) retail drug chain, which Melville acquired in 1969, six years after that chain was founded. Melville continued as a retailing conglomerate into the mid-1990s, when the company then decided to concentrate on its best performing chain, CVS. The company divested the last of its non-drugstore chains in 1997.

CONCENTRATING ON SHOES: LATE 19TH CENTURY TO EARLY SIXTIES

Melville Corporation traces its roots back to 1892, when Frank Melville, a shoe jobber, took over the three stores owned by his employer, who had left town under a cloud of debt. Melville parlayed the three New York shops into a small but thriving chain. In 1909 he brought his son, John Ward Melville, into the family business. The younger Melville, who dropped the "John" and was known by "Ward," was named vice president in 1916 and became the driving force behind much of the company's growth. He ran the corporation for nearly half a century and served as chairman of the board until the day he died in 1977 at the age of 90.

While serving in the army during World War I, Ward Melville struck up a profitable friendship with J. Franklin McElwain, a New Hampshire shoe manufacturer. Together they devised a method to mass-produce shoes and distribute them at low prices through a chain of stores, which they decided to name after a Scottish golfer, Thomas McCann, shortened to Thom McAn. They opened the first Thom McAn store in New York in 1922, offering a few simple styles of men's shoes at the fixed price of $3.99. That same year, Melville Shoe Corporation was incorporated.

Despite the lack of variety, the discounting scheme was an immediate success, and new stores were opened all over the Northeast. By 1927 when the Thom McAn chain had grown to more than 300 stores, demand outstripped the capacity of McElwain's Nashua, New Hampshire plant, which produced 20,000 pairs a day. Consequently, McElwain acquired a new plant in Worcester, Massachusetts.

Melville Shoe, like other businesses, suffered during the Great Depression. In 1932, for example, sales dropped more than 21 percent from 1931 levels, from $26.2 million to $20.5 million. Despite rumors of bankruptcy that circulated in 1933, Melville Shoe weathered the storm with careful management, prudent expansion, and financial innovation. Melville made a public stock offering in 1936, taking its place on the New York Stock Exchange. Throughout the 1930s, Melville continued to open more outlets. By 1939 Melville operated 650 Thom McAn stores and also marketed its products through its smaller John Ward and Frank Tod shoe store chains.

In 1939 Ward Melville moved to centralize and unify the entire production and marketing operation under one corporate head. He proposed that Melville merge with McElwain's manufacturing company, J.F. McElwain Company, which then produced about 11 million shoes annually for Melville. The stockholders of both companies approved the merger in December 1939. The following year, J. Franklin McElwain and Ward Melville participated in a ceremony to commemorate the production of their 100 millionth pair of shoes.

In 1940 as the economy started climbing out of the Depression, Melville posted sales topping $40 million for the first time. Sales continued to climb through the war years. The growth continued unabated until 1952, when total sales actually fell for the first time since the Depression. The decline from $92 million to $90 million signified the first inkling of a weakness in Melville's time-tested strategy of producing a few styles of relatively inexpensive shoes. In an expanding and competitive economy, diversity and specialization became increasingly necessary. Accordingly, Melville began to add more women's and children's shoes in an effort to diversify.

In 1952 Melville acquired Miles Shoes, a chain of 151 stores. With this acquisition, better results were realized immediately: sales for 1953 increased about 20 percent, topping $108 million. By 1955 Melville had grown to include 12 factories and 850 stores. The following year, Ward Melville, then 69, was named chairman of the board, although he retained his post of chief executive officer. Robert C. Erb assumed the post of president, which Melville had vacated. As part of a sustained effort to increase market penetration, Melville created a new division in 1960. The new unit, Meldisco, was dedicated to leasing and supplying family shoe

KEY DATES

1892: Frank Melville, a shoe jobber, takes over three stores owned by his employer.

1909: Melville's son, Ward Melville, joins the company and will eventually become the driving force behind much of the company's growth.

1922: Company opens the first Thom McAn shoe store; Melville Shoe Corporation, which will later be renamed Melville Corporation, is incorporated.

1936: Melville goes public, gaining a listing on the New York Stock Exchange.

1963: First Consumer Value Store (CVS) opens in Lowell, Massachusetts, as a discount health and beauty aid store in which customers bag their own merchandise; founders are brothers Sid and Stanley Goldstein and Ralph Hoagland.

1964: CVS name is used for the first time.

1968: Melville begins diversifying outside of shoes with the opening of the first Chess King clothing store; CVS outlets begin to add pharmacy departments, prompting CVS's development into a leading drugstore chain.

1969: Melville acquires the CVS chain.

1975: Melville acquires the Marshalls apparel store chain.

1981: Kay-Bee Toys chain is acquired by Melville.

1982: Linens 'n Things is added to the Melville roster.

1985: Stanley Goldstein is named president of Melville, becoming CEO and chairman the following year.

1990: Peoples Drug Stores, a 490-store chain, is acquired by Melville and is merged into the CVS chain during the early to mid-1990s.

1992: Restructuring of Melville, involving the closure of as many as 800 stores, is launched.

1993: Chess King and Accessory Lady chains are sold off.

1994: CVS enters the pharmacy benefit management field with the creation of PharmaCare Management Services.

1995: Melville announces a sweeping overhaul, aimed at concentrating on the CVS chain; Marshalls is sold to TJX Co.

1996: Kay-Bee Toys, the Wilsons leather goods chain, and the This End Up furniture chain are sold off; FootAction and Meldisco are spun off into a new public company called Footstar, Inc.; the Thom McAn chain is folded; Melville moves its headquarters to that of CVS, in Woonsocket, Rhode Island; Melville Corporation changes its name to CVS Corporation; CVS completes an IPO of 67.5 percent of Linens 'n Things.

1997: Company acquires Revco D.S., Inc., and its more than 2,500 drugstores; CVS divests its remaining interest in Linens 'n Things and sells Bob's Stores to a management-led group, thereby jettisoning its last non-drugstore operations.

1998: CVS pays $1.48 billion for Arbor Drugs, Inc., a chain with more than 200 stores mainly in southeastern Michigan.

1999: Goldstein retires as chairman of CVS; Thomas M. Ryan succeeds him as chairman and CEO; Soma.com, the first major online pharmacy, is acquired and is rebranded CVS.com; CVS ProCare, a chain of specialty pharmacies, is launched to serve patients with chronic diseases and conditions.

2000: Stadtlander Pharmacy, a mail-order specialty pharmacy serving patients with chronic diseases, is acquired.

2004: CVS reenters California market with acquisition of Eckerd Stores and Eckerd Health Services.

2006: CVS acquires 700 Sav-On and Osco drugstores.

2007: Merger with Caremark Rx creates the largest, fully integrated pharmacy in the United States.

2008: CVS Caremark acquires Longs Drugs store chain, involving 541 units in four states.

departments in self-service discount department stores. That year, however, earnings declined slightly from the 1959 totals, to $6 million in profit on sales of $151 million. The trend continued in 1962, as sales climbed to $176 million while net income dropped to about $5 million.

In 1964 Francis C. Rooney, a vice president, succeeded Robert Erb as president. Over the next two decades, Rooney oversaw tremendous growth at Melville that transformed the nature, breadth, and scope of Melville's operations. Between 1962 and 1967, sales jumped 50 percent and net profits tripled. By 1967 sales topped $260 million. At the end of the 1960s, Melville was the nation's largest shoe retailer, operating 1,400 Thom McAn, Miles, and Meldisco outlets. The growth also brought increasing differentiation and specialization, as Thom McAn turned into a suburban-based family chain, whereas Miles specialized in women's and girls' shoes.

DIVERSIFICATION OF MELVILLE: LATE SIXTIES TO SEVENTIES

In 1968 Melville made one of its most important moves of the decade, opening the first of its Chess King stores, a clothing chain geared toward fashion-conscious teens and youth. This was Melville's first venture into the fashion industry, but it was not to be its last. In 1968 Melville also acquired Foxwood, renamed Foxmoor, a 16-store apparel chain that catered to young women.

The following year brought even more expansion. Melville bought three companies: the Consumer Value Stores (CVS) chain of drug retail outlets; Mark Steven, Inc., a firm that distributed products to CVS; and Retail Store Management, Inc. The first Consumer Value Store opened in Lowell, Massachusetts, in 1963 as a discount health and beauty aid store in which customers bagged their own merchandise. It was founded by brothers Sid and Stanley Goldstein and Ralph Hoagland. The CVS name was first used in 1964, by which time the founders were running a 17-store chain. A key development came in 1968 when pharmacy departments began to be added to the CVS outlets, prompting the company's eventual emergence as a leading drugstore chain. At the time of its acquisition by Melville, the CVS chain consisted of 40 stores.

Buoyed by these acquisitions, Rooney boldly predicted in 1969 that Melville would attain total sales of $1 billion by 1975. By 1970 Melville, the fifth-largest and most profitable U.S. shoemaker, operated 1,644 total retail outlets. In 1972 Melville was ranked as the 43rd-largest retailing company in the United States, with sales of $512 million, and more than 15,000 employees.

Not satisfied with this accretion, Melville continued to expand. In 1972 Melville acquired Clinton Merchandising, Inc., which operated 80 Clinton Drug and Discount stores in the Midwest and Northeast, as well as Metro Pants Co. and Spotwood Apparel, Inc., both manufacturers of men's and boys' clothing. The Clinton stores were merged into the CVS chain. That year Melville left its longtime midtown Manhattan headquarters for a larger building in Westchester County, New York.

Melville's expansion took on an international character in the 1970s as well. In 1971 Melville entered into a joint venture with C.F. Bally of Switzerland, contracting to sell the upscale Bally shoe line in the United States. The same year, Melville formed a European buying company. In 1973 Melville initiated a venture to market Thom McAn shoes in Japan.

Despite the diversification, shoes still accounted for 71 percent of Melville's $765 million in sales in 1974. That year, the CVS chain generated sales in excess of $100 million and had grown to include 232 units, although only 45 of the locations had pharmacies. In 1975 Melville branched out further into nonshoe retailing when it bought Marshalls Inc., then a chain of 32 retail apparel stores. Expansion continued apace in 1977, when Melville bought the 36-unit Mack Drug Co. chain and merged it into the CVS unit.

In 1976 Melville, then the nation's 32nd largest retailing company, belatedly reached Rooney's vaunted goal of $1 billion in sales, due to the combination of acquiring new chains and expanding existing units. In 1976 receipts from the firm's 3,300 outlets totaled $1.2 billion. As part of a continuing trend, the footwear sales portion declined to 60 percent.

Upon Ward Melville's death in June 1977, Francis Rooney, who already held the posts of president and chief executive officer, was named chairman of the board. The transition marked the end of an era and the beginning of a new one in which shoes would play an increasingly smaller role in the Melville scheme. By 1978 Melville operated 3,812 stores and had sales of $1.75 billion. Shoes accounted for about 53 percent of the total.

ACCELERATING DIVERSIFICATION IN THE EIGHTIES AND EARLY NINETIES

As the 1970s came to a close, Melville continued to boom. In 1980, Melville, with 48,000 employees and more than 4,500 stores, saw its 26th straight year of increased sales. CVS had grown to 408 locations, with sales totaling $414 million, making the chain one of the top 10 drugstore chains in the United States. That year, Kenneth Berland was named to the post of president.

The following year, in which sales soared to $2.8 billion, Melville acquired Kay-Bee Toy and Hobby

Shops Inc. By 1982 Melville, the largest U.S. shoe retailer, operated nearly 5,200 total stores. These included 470 Chess King, 588 Foxmoor, 433 CVS, and 1,200 Thom McAn outlets. In 1982 Melville added leather retailer Wilsons to its roster, and the following year it acquired home furnishings specialist Linens 'n Things, which had been founded in 1975.

Despite the recession of the early 1980s, sales rose to $3.3 billion in 1983; nevertheless, Melville suffered some retrenchment during the 1980s. The firm began to phase out six of its seven shoe factories in late 1983, eventually terminating about 2,000 jobs. In 1985 Melville sold the 614-store Foxmoor chain, whose sales were declining. The same year, Melville shut down 72 Thom McAn outlets. Despite the closures or sales of various stores, 1985 receipts rose to $4.7 billion, and profits surged to $219 million. CVS sales surpassed the $1 billion mark for the first time. In 1985 Stanley Goldstein, the CVS cofounder who joined Melville when his corporation was acquired by the shoe giant, succeeded Berland as president and took his place as heir apparent. The following year, Goldstein was named chairman and chief executive officer, replacing the retiring Rooney. To Goldstein fell the task of building on Rooney's phenomenal record. Rooney had transformed the firm from a successful shoe company into a diversified retailing giant.

Melville's expansion continued under Goldstein. In 1987, while amassing $5.9 billion in sales, Melville acquired 25 Heartland and Pharmacity drugstores and 36 Leather Loft stores. In 1988 Melville bought athletic footwear retailer Finish Line as well as Bermans Specialty Stores. In 1989 Melville underwent some structural renovation. The firm created a profit-sharing plan and an employee stock ownership plan, under which about 6 percent of the company's common stock was distributed among its employees.

The year 1989 brought to a close a remarkably successful decade, one in which sales and earnings both increased more than threefold. The Melville that left the 1980s was vastly different from the one that entered that decade. In 1989 shoes, once the firm's mainstay, accounted for only 22.5 percent of total sales; the apparel sections accounted for 36 percent; and the drugstore business accounted for 28 percent. The toys and household furnishing division accounted for the remainder of sales.

This trend continued in 1990, as Melville acquired more non-footwear retail outlets. Melville bought both Circus World Toy Stores Inc., which it folded into the Kay-Bee division, and Peoples Drug Stores, a 490-store chain. By the end of 1990, Melville operated 7,754 stores and listed 119,000 employees on its payroll. Sales

for 1990 totaled $8.68 billion. Further expansion came in 1991, when Melville acquired Foot Action Inc., a Dallas-based chain of 128 athletic footwear stores, for $46 million.

RETRENCHMENT, RESTRUCTURING, EMERGENCE OF CVS CORPORATION

Retrenchment came to the fore in 1992 and 1993, however, as Melville struggled in a more difficult environment for retailers. In early 1992 CVS exited from the California market when it sold all 85 of its stores in that state to American Drug Stores Inc., a unit of American Stores Company, for $60 million. In December of that same year Melville announced a major restructuring involving the closure of up to 800 stores and a pretax charge of $347 million. About 390 of the 730 Thom McAn locations were subsequently shuttered, as were 240 of its 1,250 Kay-Bee stores and 75 smaller Linens 'n Things outlets. In addition, the 500-plus-unit Chess King chain was sold off in the spring of 1993 to Merry-Go-Round Enterprises Inc. and the 114-store Accessory Lady chain was sold to Woolworth Corporation in November 1993. Of the closed units, about 100 of them were converted to faster-growing formats, most notably, FootAction. With these series of moves, Melville was focusing more strongly on CVS and Marshalls, which together accounted for more than 60 percent of the company's sales and operating profits, as well as Kay-Bee Toys and the up-and-comers FootAction and Linens 'n Things.

Another development in the early to mid-1990s was the merger of Peoples Drug Stores into CVS, which thereby gained locations in Maryland, Pennsylvania, Virginia, West Virginia, and the District of Columbia. In 1994 Thomas M. Ryan, a pharmacist, was named CEO of CVS, which had more than 1,350 locations. CVS was by far the largest of Melville's chains, with 1994 revenues of $4.3 billion, or 38 percent of Melville's overall revenues of $11.3 billion. During 1994 CVS entered the burgeoning market for PBM services by forming PharmaCare Management Services to serve managed care and other organizations.

With its financial performance faltering and shareholders increasingly agitating for change, Melville in October 1995 announced a sweeping restructuring through which it planned to spin or sell off several of its businesses to focus primarily on its most profitable unit, the CVS drugstore chain. Melville had already agreed to sell Marshalls, its second largest chain, to archrival TJX Cos., in a $600 million deal that closed in November 1995. Next to go, during the first half of 1996, were Kay-Bee Toys, which was sold to Consolidated Stores

Corp. for about $315 million, and the Wilsons leather goods chain and the This End Up chain of furniture stores, both of which were sold off through management-led buyouts. Later in 1996, Melville spun off two of its footwear operations, the 444-unit FootAction chain and Meldisco, operator of leased shoe departments in nearly 2,200 Kmarts and almost 400 Payless Drug Stores, into a new public company called Footstar, Incorporated. The Thom McAn chain was closed down, after the conversion of about 100 of the stores to Foot-Action outlets.

In addition to CVS, Melville also had planned initially to retain the Linens 'n Things chain and Bob's Stores, a 34-unit chain selling off-price active apparel. In mid-1996, however, the company announced that it would shed those operations as well by the end of 1997. In September 1996 Melville moved its corporate headquarters from Rye, New York, to the headquarters of CVS in Woonsocket, Rhode Island. Two months later, Melville changed its name to CVS Corporation. Goldstein continued to serve as chairman and CEO, and Ryan was named vice-chairman and chief operating officer. Shortly after becoming CVS Corporation, the company completed an initial public offering in which it sold a 67.5 percent interest in Linens 'n Things to the public. CVS sold its remaining interest in Linens 'n Things during 1997.

LATE NINETIES AND BEYOND: REACHING FOR THE TOP THROUGH MAJOR ACQUISITIONS

The newly focused CVS moved quickly to become one of the top players in the rapidly consolidating U.S. drugstore industry. In May 1997 CVS acquired Twinsburg, Ohio-based Revco D.S., Inc., for $2.8 billion in stock plus the assumption of $900 million of Revco debt. Revco had about 2,600 drugstores located in 17 midwestern, southeastern, and eastern states. To gain regulatory approval, CVS had to sell 120 Revco drugstores, mainly located in Virginia. As a result, CVS emerged from the deal with nearly 4,000 drugstores in 24 states and the District of Columbia, giving it the largest store count in the industry. In terms of revenues, however, it ranked number two behind Walgreen Co. CVS, in the meantime, sold the last of its non-drugstore units in November 1997 when it sold Bob's Stores to a management-led group.

In early 1998 Ryan was named president and CEO of CVS, with Goldstein remaining chairman. The company completed another significant, albeit much smaller, acquisition in March 1998, a $1.48 billion deal for Troy, Michigan-based Arbor Drugs, Inc. Operating primarily in southeastern Michigan, Arbor had more than 200 stores and nearly $1 billion in revenue during fiscal 1997. The addition of Arbor increased CVS's store count to nearly 4,100 and also made CVS the country's largest dispenser of prescription drugs as it filled more than 11 percent of all prescriptions. CVS still trailed Walgreen in revenue, but its 1998 sales of $15.27 billion were nearly three times the level of 1996.

In addition to pursuing acquisitions, CVS also was growing organically by aggressively opening new locations. In 1998, for example, the company announced plans to open as many as 200 stores in New York City over a three-year period. At the same time, some of the older locations, particularly those in strip malls, were being closed down in favor of freestanding sites, some of which began featuring drive-through pharmacies.

An end of another era occurred in April 1999 when Goldstein retired as chairman of CVS, 36 years after cofounding the first Consumer Value Store. Ryan was named chairman and CEO. Later in 1999 CVS acquired Soma.com, the first major online pharmacy, for $30 million in stock. The Web site, soon rebranded CVS.com, enabled customers to order prescriptions and general merchandise for either in-store pickup or mail delivery. Another initiative in 1999 was the launching of CVS ProCare, a chain of specialty pharmacies, about 1,500 square feet in size, serving patients with chronic diseases and conditions that require complex and expensive drug regimens. The market for specialty pharmaceuticals, estimated at about $16 billion in 1999, was a particularly fast-growing segment of the drug industry, but it was highly fragmented, consisting mostly of mom-and-pop operations. CVS clearly saw the potential for being a consolidator in this segment of the market.

Its first such acquisition came in September 2000 with the purchase of Stadtlander Pharmacy, a Pittsburgh-based subsidiary of Bergen Brunswig Corporation, for $124 million. Stadtlander generated annual revenues of $500 million by selling drugs by mail-order to patients with chronic conditions. By the end of 2000, CVS's specialty pharmacy business consisted of mail-order operations and 46 CVS ProCare pharmacies located in 17 states and the District of Columbia. Overall, CVS saw its revenues surpass the $20 billion mark for the first time in 2000, while net income reached a record $746 million.

After entering four new markets in 2000 (Chicago; Tampa and Orlando, Florida; and Grand Rapids, Michigan), CVS continued to enter new territories in 2001, expanding into Fort Lauderdale, Florida, and Las Vegas, Nevada. The latter would represent the chain's first presence west of the Mississippi since selling its

California stores in 1992. CVS also announced in 2001 plans to expand into Phoenix, Arizona; Miami Beach, Florida; and three new markets in Texas: Dallas, Houston, and Fort Worth. In February 2001 CVS launched a chainwide loyalty card program called Extra-Care that would offer cardholders exclusive savings, mailings, and health information. The company's fortunes turned south later in the year, however, as profits began to decline. Management cited a lack of new prescription drug introductions, the growth of mail-order prescription services, and increasing competition. CVS had also had difficulty filling positions for pharmacists and been forced to shut down some pharmacy counters as a result. Furthermore, the general economic slowdown had taken a toll on sales of general merchandise. In October a major restructuring was launched, involving the elimination of 300 jobs, the closure of 200 underperforming stores (including 10 CVS ProCare units), and a $350 million charge. It was difficult to foresee whether these events were a momentary blip in a record of consistently positive performance for CVS since its emergence out of Melville in 1996 or the beginning of a deeper crisis.

FIVE-YEAR SURGE IN GROWTH AND PROFITABILITY: 2004–09

CVS emerged from its financial difficulties by implementing strategies to expand geographically and to improve its product and service offerings. Initiatives included brand development, acquisition of established drugstore chains, introduction of private-label brand goods, and the addition of pharmacy and health-care services. The creation of high-margin "front of the store" products, such as the upscale Essence of Beauty cosmetics, facilitated profitability and sales at the store level. Other new private-label products included Gold Emblem foods and CVS over-the-counter health products. A revamped logo and upscale store interior conveyed a contemporary atmosphere, and the online retail site and customer loyalty program raised customer awareness of private-label products. As the company entered new markets, CVS's private-label brands gained parity with known national brands.

In addition to pursuing organic growth by opening new stores, CVS acquired smaller drugstore chains in order to establish market presence without the costly process of scouting locations. In 2004 the company purchased the 1,268-unit Eckerd Store chain, with locations in Texas and Florida. The acquisition included Eckerd Health Services, a PBM business. The 2006 CVS acquisition of Sav-On and Osco drugstores further established a CVS presence in Southern California and in the Midwest.

CVS sought to attract and retain customers by providing services that reduced health-care costs and resulted in positive outcomes. Hence, in 2006 CVS acquired MinuteClinic, a chain of in-store health clinics. Nurse practitioners and physician assistants attended to minor health complaints, and they offered preventative health-care services, including vaccinations and health screenings.

Development of CVS pharmacy services occurred through a merger with Caremark Rx, which created the largest integrated pharmacy services company in the United States. Its 2003 merger with Advance PCS established Caremark as the leading PBM service, a $23 billion company. Likewise, CVS was the largest pharmacy in the country, with 6,200 drugstores drawing $44 billion in revenues. CVS and Caremark completed the merger in early 2007, when CVS acquired Caremark for $21.3 billion. CVS shareholders owned 54.5 percent of CVS Caremark, while Caremark shareholders owned the balance. As a merger of equals, the companies held an equal number of seats on the board of directors. CVS CEO Tom Ryan retained his position at the new enterprise, eventually becoming chairman.

CVS Caremark sought to grow by improving communication with customers by obtaining information about their experience and providing more information. Hence, the company developed the Consumer Engagement Engine, a technology that integrated and analyzed customer information from a variety of sources, such as the ExtraCare loyalty program, the pharmacy, Minute-Clinic, and the online business. By determining health issues and purchasing patterns, the company could offer customers and health-care payers cost-saving options, such as generic drug alternatives.

CVS Caremark continued to expand its pharmacy markets through acquisition. The August 2008 acquisition of Longs Drug Stores Corporation included 541 units in Arizona, Nevada, Hawaii, and California as well as the PBM service RxAmerica. CVS Caremark gained access to 10 important health-care markets, mainly in central and northern markets of California. The acquisition of 11 Kerr Drugs Stores in Charleston, South Carolina, followed in 2009.

Daniel Gross
Updated, David E. Salamie; Mary Tradii

PRINCIPAL OPERATING DIVISIONS

CVS Pharmacy; MinuteClinic; Pharmacy Benefit Management Services.

PRINCIPAL COMPETITORS

Walgreen Co.; Wal-Mart Stores, Inc.; Rite Aid Corporation; Eckerd Corporation; The Kroger Co.

FURTHER READING

Arditi, Lynn, "CVS Prescribes $30-Million Internet Dosage," *Providence Journal,* May 18, 1999, p. E1.

———, "CVS to Take Over Midwestern Chain," *Providence Journal-Bulletin,* February 10, 1998, p. A1.

"At CVS, It's All in a Day's Work," *Research,* December 2005, p. 72.

Auerbach, Jon G., "CVS Unit Chief Ryan Says Purchase of Revco Enhances Managed-Care Ties," *Wall Street Journal,* February 10, 1997, p. B8.

Barmash, Isadore, "Retailing: The Special Case of Melville Corp.," *New York Times,* April 4, 1982.

Berner, Robert, "CVS: Will Its Growth Elixir Work?" *Business Week,* July 9, 2001, pp. 50, 53.

———, "Merck, CVS Agree to Link Internet Sites," *Wall Street Journal,* October 6, 1999, p. A3.

Bird, Laura, "Melville Is Jarred by Shot Across the Bow from Calpers," *Wall Street Journal,* February 16, 1995, p. B4.

———, "Melville Plans Spinoffs, Sales of Businesses: Firm, Pressed by Holders, to Focus on Drugstores After Split into Three," *Wall Street Journal,* October 25, 1995, p. A3.

———, "Melville to Close Thom McAn Shoe Chain in Effort to Focus on CVS Drugstores," *Wall Street Journal,* June 4, 1996, p. B9.

Bulkeley, William M., "CVS to Buy Arbor Drugs for $1.48 Billion," *Wall Street Journal,* February 10, 1998, p. A3.

Chakravarty, Subrata N., "Reshaping the Last," *Forbes,* September 17, 1990.

"CVS Caremark Corporation to Acquire Longs Drug Stores Corporation," *Biotech Week,* August 27, 2008, p. 4507.

"CVS Caremark Is Proactive About Pharmacy," *Chain Drug Review,* August 3, 2009, p. 70.

"CVS Merger with Caremark Offers Significantly Greater Long-Term Value Creation for Caremark Shareholders Than Express Scripts Unsolicited Takeover Bid," *Business Wire,* January 4, 2007.

Fasig, Lisa Biank, "CVS: Falling Profits Lead Drugstore Chain to Close 200 Stores," *Providence Journal,* October 31, 2001, p. E1.

Fleming, Harris, Jr., "For Better," *Drug Topics,* March 2, 1998, pp. 104, 106.

"Grooving Shoe Sales to a Young Market," *Business Week,* April 27, 1968.

Hackney, Holt, "Melville Corp.: Portrait of a False Bargain," *Financial World,* November 23, 1993, p. 21.

Hechinger, John, "CVS to Shut 200 Stores, Trim 300 Jobs," *Wall Street Journal,* October 31, 2001, p. B9.

Henderson, Barry, "Drugstore Cowboys?: Riding the Accounting Bronco at CVS," *Barron's,* June 5, 2000, pp. 19, 21.

Johannes, Laura, "CVS Pushes Online Plans with Purchase of Soma.com for $30 Million in Stock," *Wall Street Journal,* May 18, 1999, p. B8.

Mammarella, James, "Melville De-Diversifies," *Discount Store News,* November 6, 1995, p. 1.

"Melville Steps into the Billion-Dollar Class," *Business Week,* April 11, 1977.

Muirhead, Greg, "CVS-Revco Merger Will Create $13 Billion Chain," *Drug Topics,* February 17, 1997, p. 19.

Nelson, Emily, "Consolidated Stores to Buy KayBee Toys from Melville Corp. for $315 Million," *Wall Street Journal,* March 26, 1996, p. A4.

Philippidis, Alex, "Melville Looks to Improve Performance," *Westchester County Business Journal,* April 17, 1995, p. 1.

———, "Splits-ville for Melville and City It Called Home," *Westchester County Business Journal,* April 29, 1996, p. 1.

Pressler, Margaret Webb, "Chain's Expansion Gives Headaches to Rivals, Critics," *Washington Post,* February 3, 1998, p. D1.

Rooney, Francis C., *Creative Merchandising in an Era of Change,* New York: Newcomen Society in North America, 1970.

Rudnitsky, Howard, "Fancy Footwork," *Forbes,* March 29, 1982.

Rundle, Rhonda L., "CVS to Buy Most of Bergen Unit for $124 Million," *Wall Street Journal,* July 6, 2000, p. 12.

Sloane, Leonard, "Ward Melville, 90s Shoe Magnate, Dies," *New York Times,* June 6, 1977.

Thayer, Warren, "CVS Store Brands Climb 13% and Aim Higher: The Drug Store Chain Expands into New Categories and New Markets," *Private Label Buyer,* October 2002, p. 16.

Tooher, Nora Lockwood, "CVS: On Its Own Again," *Providence Sunday Journal,* June 23, 1996, p. F1.

———, "New Boy on the Big Board," *Providence Journal-Bulletin,* October 16, 1996, p. F1.

———, "New Prescription for Leadership at CVS Corp.," *Providence Journal,* April 15, 1999, p. F1.

Trachtenberg, Jeffrey A., "Melville Corp. Plans to Close up to 800 Stores," *Wall Street Journal,* December 22, 1992, p. A2.

Deutsche Post AG

———————■———————

Charles-de-Gaulle-Strasse 20
Bonn, 53113
Germany
Telephone: (49 228) 182 0
Fax: (49 228) 14 88 72
Web site: http://www.dp-dhl.de

Public Company
Incorporated: 1490 as Kaiserliche Reichspost
Employees: 512,536
Sales: EUR 54.47 billion ($76.78 billion) (2008)
Stock Exchanges: Frankfurt
Ticker Symbol: DPWX
NAICS: 492110 Couriers; 491110 Postal Service

■ ■ ■

Operating under the Deutsche Post and DHL brand names, Deutsche Post AG is a leading provider of postal and logistics services. In addition to serving as the only universal provider of postal services in Germany, the company offers services such as air and ocean freight, road and rail transportation, international express, and contract logistics. Deutsche Post also offers corporate communications solutions, as well as dialogue marketing and press distribution services. Deutsche Post ranks as one of the world's largest employers, on the strength of more than 500,000 employees at 18,500 locations in approximately 220 countries and territories.

ORIGINS OF POSTAL SERVICES IN GERMANY: 1490–1800

The year 1490 is considered the founding year of the German post office, when German emperor Maximilian I ordered that a regular messenger service be established from Austria to the Netherlands, France, and Rome, so that he would be able to efficiently reign from his Innsbruck headquarters over his realm, including the new possessions he gained through marriage. The first post line between Innsbruck and Mechelen in Belgium was established in the same year. Maximilian I assigned the organization of this network to the noble family of the Tassis (later spelled Taxis) from Bergano, North Italy, who had experience in providing messenger services to various courts.

A relay system was established in which post riders traveled five miles between posts and communicated with each other by blowing a horn. They rode without interruption to the next post at an assigned location where they handed over the mail. Thereby a letter could be delivered the 920 kilometers from Brussels to Innsbruck in five days during the summer, and in six days during the winter. In the 15th and 16th centuries members of the von Taxis family settled in the main cities of Europe as their postal system was steadily enlarged.

In exchange for running the postal service system, the von Taxis family was paid an annual reimbursement by the different royal courts. However, due to weak state finances, wartime losses, and the failure of noble families to settle their debts, the von Taxis were not always paid properly, and they started looking for additional sources of income. Although not technically allowed to deliver anything but "royal mail," the Taxis posts also delivered for private customers beginning at the latest in 1506. Financial difficulties were accompanied by tough competition from existing messenger systems, primarily those between specific cities and the so-called butcher posts. Since butchers often had to travel to buy livestock, they traditionally served as mail deliverers and charged their clientele by the piece. When emperor Rudolf II made the messenger business an imperial monopoly in 1597 these conflicts were only partially resolved, since some of his local opponents ignored his edicts. Beginning in June 1600, the general post master, Leonard de Tassis, was officially permitted to collect fees for mail delivery from private persons. The head of the imperial post was always appointed by the emperor. In 1615, however, Lamoral von Taxis persuaded German emperor Matthias to grant him the right to provide imperial postal service and to make it inheritable. With this security, the von Taxis family had an incentive to invest into the system's extension.

As early as 1516 the postal system was used to transport people as well as to deliver information. The Taxis postal system initiated a postal ride system from Leipzig to Hamburg in 1660 and additional routes were added soon after. However, traveling with the postal coach was anything but comfortable and secure. Like the horse riding posts, the postal coaches were used regularly to transport money and other valuables in addition to the mail and were often a target for highwaymen.

The time it took to deliver mail did not change much between 1500 and 1765. However, innovations such as the introduction of home mail delivery, drop-off mail boxes, and postal stamps improved the service. The first regulation regarding mail delivery personnel was enacted in Prussia in 1770. Improvements in the postal infrastructure, such as improved roads, were often interrupted by wars and slowed down by disputes between the various regional governors until well into the 19th century.

PEAK AND END OF THE TAXIS POST: 1806–67

At the peak of its success in the 18th century just before the French Revolution, the Kaiserliche Reichspost, run by the Thurn und Taxis family as it was then known, was the leading postal system in the Holy Roman Empire, serving 11.3 million people in an area of over 222,000 square kilometers. Transit postal routes also connected the empire to France, England, Scandinavia, Poland, Russia, and to the court of the Turkish sultan. However, the Holy Roman Empire was dissolved as a result of Napoleon's campaigns at the beginning of the 18th century. When emperor Franz II renounced the crown of the Holy Roman Empire in 1806, the scene was set for a series of wars of liberation throughout Europe which made it increasingly difficult for the Thurn und Taxis postal system to survive.

The Southern German states, which had collaborated with Napoleon, dropped out of the Reichspost after the German Confederation of the Rhine was founded in 1806. In 1810, 43 different postal administrations were fighting for share of the territory of the former Reichspost. This competition at times even took the form of "postal wars," such as occurred in the state of Baden. Efforts to unify the German postal system at the Congress of Vienna, where the new European order was worked out after the defeat of Napoleon, failed. A newly established confederation consisted of 39 independent German states, many of which had their own weights and measures, currencies, and tariffs. By 1824, the Thurn und Taxis principality had reached almost 80 separate agreements and treaties with members of the new German states and other countries.

The two leading powers of the German confederation, Austria and Prussia, proposed the basic guidelines for a German postal association established in 1847. However, no agreement could be reached, and in 1850 the two states founded the German-Austrian Postverein, a postal association which other German states eventually joined. Thurn und Taxis negotiated new agreements with Prussia and Austria in 1850 and 1851, and between 1851 and 1865, five postal congresses were held to update existing agreements which developed into a sophisticated system of postal law. After Austria's defeat by Prussia in 1866, the German confederation was dissolved and a number of formerly independent postal administrations were integrated into the Prussian system. This marked the end of the almost 400-year-old Thurn und Taxis postal empire. On January 28, 1867, an agreement was concluded in Berlin between the Thurn und Taxis principality and Prussia according to which Prince Maximilian Karl von Thurn und Taxis sur-

KEY DATES

■

1490: The German post office, Kaiserliche Reichs-post, is formed when German emperor Maximilian I orders that a regular messenger service be established from Austria to the Netherlands, France, and Rome.

1770: First regulation regarding mail delivery personnel is enacted in Prussia.

1866: After Austria's defeat by Prussia, a number of formerly independent postal administrations are integrated into the Prussian system, marking the end of the almost 400-year-old Thurn und Taxis postal empire.

1867: Agreement is concluded in Berlin between the Thurn und Taxis principality and Prussia, according to which Prince Maximilian Karl von Thurn und Taxis surrenders all his postal rights and possessions to Prussia, making the Prussian post office the largest German postal system.

1870: German Reich is established, and the new postal administration, the Reichspostverwaltung, begins issuing postage stamps valid in all of Germany.

1903: German Reichspost uses cars for the first time to deliver packages in the city of Cologne.

1912: First German airmail is delivered in a demonstration show between Darmstadt and Frankfurt.

1945: At the end of World War II, the German postal system collapses completely.

1949: Establishment of two separate German states leads to two separate German postal systems: the Deutsche Post in the German Democratic Republic (East Germany—GDR) and the Deutsche Bundespost in the Federal Republic of Germany (West Germany—FRG).

1954: Bundespost initiates a modernization program for letter sorting.

1961: Night airmail transportation system is established, carried out by the airline Deutsche Lufthansa.

1989: New law, the Poststrukturgesetz, transforms the Bundespost into three government-owned, independently managed businesses: Deutsche Bundespost Telekom, Deutsche Bundespost

Postbank, and Deutsche Bundespost Postdienst.

1990: Deutsche Bundespost and Deutsche Post are reunited following the reunion of the two German states, and the GDR postal system is integrated into the Deutsche Bundespost and completely reorganized.

1995: Largest privatization project in FRG history occurs when the Deutsche Bundespost Postdienst is transformed into the Deutsche Post AG and officially registered in Bonn on January 2.

1999: German government allows Deutsche Post to take over Deutsche Postbank AG for DEM 4.3 billion.

2000: Darien, Connecticut-based Air Express International Corp. is acquired for $1.14 billion; Deutsche Post is partially privatized via an initial public offering (IPO) in November.

2001: Deutsche Post World Net secures controlling interest in the air freight operator DHL International, obtaining a 21.38 percent stake for an estimated $800 million.

2002: Full ownership of DHL International is acquired for $396 million.

2003: Deutsche Post sells its stake in DHL Airways to CEO John Dasburg and two other investors.

2004: IPO for the company's Postbank subsidiary generates $1.87 billion.

2005: German government sells its interest in Deutsche Post for $6.04 billion to the state-owned German development bank KfW Group.

2008: German authorities raid the home and office of CEO Klaus Zumwinkel following allegations of tax evasion, and Zumwinkel is succeeded by Frank Appel; Deutsche Post reveals that its DHL business will halt domestic deliveries in the United States in January 2009, limiting its operations to international pickups and deliveries only.

2009: Zumwinkel is convicted of tax evasion; Appel unveils an initiative named Strategy 2015 to prepare the company for the future.

rendered all his postal rights and possessions to Prussia, making the Prussian post office the largest German postal system.

GROUNDBREAKING TECHNOLOGIES AND WORLD WAR I: 1868–1932

Although the history of the German post office was greatly influenced by the sweeping political change and manmade catastrophes of this period, it was most affected by the development of revolutionary new technologies that led to fundamental change in how messages were exchanged. Worldwide mail delivery was greatly enhanced, for example, by the introduction of steam ships. In 1886 the first postal ship left for the German colonies in East Asia. In 1870 it took mail from 25 to 30 days to travel from Western Europe to Shanghai, and about seven days to North America. However, the important invention of the electric telegraph, first used in Germany around 1844 and introduced as a postal service in the following decade, made it possible to cut those times down to two days and two hours, respectively. Under the leadership of Heinrich Stephan, who became German postmaster general in 1876, the new technologies were quickly used by the German Reichspost. Beginning in 1876, telegraph cable connections were set up between Berlin and 221 German cities, and by 1896 there were about 17,000 public telegraph offices in Germany. At the same time, realizing the immense potential of the new medium of the telephone for the exchange of messages, Stephan pushed through ambitious plans to introduce telephone service on a large scale. With two Bell telephones which he had received as a personal gift, he began experiments in Berlin and contracted his acquaintance, entrepreneur Werner Siemens, to begin manufacturing German telephones as early as 1877 when as yet no public telephone network existed. Three years later, when only a single city in the United States over 15,000 inhabitants was without long-distance telephone service, the first long-distance telephone center with eight users was opened in Berlin. However, the Berlin business world was slow to embrace the novelty and in 1888 the network only had about 9,100 participants. In the same year Stephan managed to secure the monopoly for the establishment and maintenance of telephone networks for the German Reichspost.

In 1870 the new postal administration, the Reichspostverwaltung, began issuing postage stamps valid in all of Germany. Under Otto von Bismarck's chancellorship, Prussian-dominated Germany underwent a period of fundamental political, technological, and social change

which crucially affected the nation's postal system. Bismarck's struggle against the socialist movement by means of extremely restrictive legislation was accompanied by the establishment of a revolutionary system of social welfare which radically improved the lot of the common people. The Reichspost became the institution through which welfare payments were channeled and with the rising number of benefits such as disability insurance, pensions for the elderly, and later the benefits for surviving dependents, the postal system had to adapt to meet the new demand. This service was offered free of charge until 1921 and was performed by the post office until the 1950s and 1960s, when cash-free transactions replaced the cash payments. Despite protests by the banking lobby, in 1912 the Reichspost was also granted the right to offer money deposit accounts and accompanying services. By 1920, before postwar hyperinflation hit the German economy, the number of the so-called postal check accounts exceeded 620,000 with deposits of 4.7 billion German Marks.

Beginning in the middle of the 19th century, railway transportation had become increasingly popular and successively replaced horse carriers. Mail could be sorted en route, and dropped off without stopping, thereby cutting delivery times. The second wave of innovation was brought about by the automobile. In 1903 the German Reichspost used cars for the first time to deliver packages in the city of Cologne. Bavaria, which maintained its political independence and its own postal administration, established the first cross-country motorized line for the transportation of mail and people in June 1905. By 1914 the Bavarian postal administration was running a total of 127 lines with 155 vehicles and 136 trailers. In other German cities, battery-powered electric delivery vehicles were in service as early as 1911. The third invention which had a fundamental impact was the airplane. In 1912 the first German airmail was delivered in a demonstration show between Darmstadt and Frankfurt. Beginning in 1912, zeppelins, huge gas-filled balloons operated by the Deutsche Luftschiffahrts Aktiengesellschaft, were used regularly for both mail and passenger transportation.

World War I interrupted these developments: vehicles were needed for the war effort and gasoline supplies were limited. Regular domestic airmail lines in Germany were opened again in 1919. International airmail delivery was difficult for the Reichspost after the war because the Treaty of Versailles banned it from using former military airplanes outside Germany. However, since the Versailles Treaty also forbid Germany from building new airplanes, those planes were used to expand the domestic airmail system. After those restrictions were lifted in 1926, international airmail took off. In 1928, the German postal airmail system consisted of over 100 connections over a 33,000-kilometer network. The number of airmail letters, packages, and newspapers grew 16-fold between 1919 and 1925, and had doubled again by 1933. Because early airplanes were not able to cross the Atlantic Ocean, mail was sorted on ships at sea and when they were close enough to the American continent, airplanes took off from the ships to speed the arrival of the mail.

After World War I, various transportation enterprises competed for shares of the postal market. However, the position of the Reichspost was considered secure since its wide network insured that mail would be delivered even in difficult to reach areas. It further expanded its capacity by purchasing private transportation businesses. An agreement was reached with its main competitor, the Reichsbahn, the German railways, which in general gave the Reichsbahn the right to long-distance traffic on highways, lines parallel to railways, and the railway replacement lines (*schienenersatzverkehr*), while the Reichspost was given the right to all additional cross-country traffic.

Another 1920s innovation for the Deutsche Reichspost was radio and television transmission. The first public radio show was broadcast in Germany in 1923 and the first television transmission in 1928. While other institutions were soon given the right to produce content for the new media, the Reichspost established and maintained the technical infrastructure and provided the transmission services. In 1920 the Postreklame, a business that offered advertising on postal vehicles, and so forth, was integrated into the Reichspost to increase its income.

THE REICHSPOST UNDER THE NAZI REGIME: 1933–45

The German postal system was used intensively for propaganda of Adolf Hitler's nationalist ideology after he came to power in 1933, in particular through postage stamps and radio broadcasts. The Deutsche Reichspost achieved a measure of independence under the Weimar Republic after it was taken out of the national budget but still required as a government-owned business to contribute significantly to the Weimar Republic. The Nazi government, however, reintegrated it as a ministry in 1934. Wilhelm Ohnesorge became postal minister in February 1937 and was a supporter of the Nazi regime until 1945. The post office not only paid Hitler considerable amounts of money to use his picture on numerous postal stamps, it also carried out Nazi policies by introducing special hours when Jews were allowed to use postal services, cutting them off from services such as newspaper delivery and long-distance telephone service, and not hiring them as employees. Ohnesorge

illegally lent money from the Reichspost budget to high Nazi officials and constantly monitored mail and phone messages, such as the long-distance telephone traffic between the United States and England, beginning in 1942.

In the first half of World War II, while Germany was conquering new territory, the main challenge for the Reichspost was to get close to the battlefields and deal with the increasing amount of mail and freight being delivered to increasingly distant locations. The amount of work done by the Reichspost grew by 50 percent between 1938 and 1943. At the same time, the number of Reichspost personnel lost to the army and war production rose steadily from about 50,000 in 1940 to 450,000 in the first half of 1945. Nonetheless, the number of post office employees, including those working part-time, rose from 565,000 in 1940 to a high of 631,000 by July 1944. Over 6,000 postal drivers and vehicles had to actively support the SS in 1943. Toward the end of the war when the German army was in retreat, more and more civil servants from the post office were required to support the defense effort, and more and more services were cut back in the homeland. Beginning in the second half of 1944, when the "total war" was proclaimed, most of the postal services were no longer available, and a rising number of postal facilities and the necessary transportation infrastructure was destroyed as Allied troops entered Germany. At the end of the war, the German postal system collapsed completely.

TWO GERMAN STATES AND COLD POSTAL WARS: 1946–89

After the Third Reich was defeated, the victors formed the Allierten Kontrollrat, consisting of representatives from the United States, Great Britain, France, and the Soviet Union, to govern the country. This group ruled that the borders separating the four zones of occupation were equivalent to postal zones. The exchange of private messages was forbidden for several months, and all the mail delivered later by the new Deutsche Post and all other forms of communication was censored. The June 1948 currency reform in the three Western German zones and the establishment of two separate German states in 1949 led to two separate German postal systems: the Deutsche Post in the German Democratic Republic (East Germany—GDR) and the Deutsche Bundespost in the Federal Republic of German (West Germany—FRG).

The Deutsche Post in East Germany had a monopoly of the delivery of messages in any form—radio and television broadcasts and the distribution of newspapers and magazines. It was headed by a ministry and had a service agreement with the government-owned lottery founded in 1954. The mail distribution was neither mechanized nor very well maintained because investment funding was lacking. Thus postal employees worked under ever more difficult conditions while their pay dropped toward the lower end of the scale. The quality of service declined too as the scarcity of workers became chronic. Home delivery was abolished and mail was delivered to mailbox-complexes on sidewalks in front of buildings while packages had to be picked up at the post office. The reputation of the Deutsche Post declined even more when otherwise unemployable people had to be hired, and cases of theft subsequently increased. The Deutsche Post was used intensively by the GDR government as a source of "hard currency."

After the Berlin Wall was built in 1961, East German authorities issued more and more restrictive regulations for gift parcels from the FRG to the GDR. The number of refused and confiscated packages rose steadily. Later the Stasi, the GDR secret service, systematically scanned packages for money and other valuables, which were then removed and sold. The same department organized the sale of postage stamps to collectors in the FRG through the VEB Philatelic Wermsdorf. Among their best sellers were stamps from the Third Reich which the GDR "inherited" in great numbers. Income from the trade in collectible stamps was estimated at 8 million to 12 million deutsche marks annually. Another source of money for the GDR was the so-called Postpauschale, a sum collected from the West German government in exchange for opening and maintaining communication channels to West Germany and West Berlin. The last Postpauschale agreement from November 15, 1983, increased the amount collected from DEM 85 million to DEM 200 million annually.

Because the East German government distrusted its citizens, it maintained its own telephone connections and mail delivery system. The carrier firm Zentraler Kurierdienst, which shared space with certain post offices, delivered mail and packages between government-owned companies and authorities, and was largely used for secret messages and supplies. In the 1980s economic problems worsened; raw materials were so scarce that the print runs for magazines were rationed and the Deutsche Post, which delivered about three periodicals to every customer, refused to take new subscriptions. Specially trained civil servants at the post ministry were assigned to answer the flood of complaints. Ten percent of all Deutsche Post employees quit their jobs the year before the Berlin Wall came down.

After the founding of the FRG, the Deutsche Bundespost became the "special property" of the West German government and was required to carry out government orders. Under the Postverwaltungsgesetz, the postal law of 1953, the postal minister was simultaneously the chief executive of the Bundespost and the organization was required to transfer about 10 percent of its total annual revenues, not profits, to the federal budget. Ironically, the Bundespost was in the red itself, partly because postal rates were considered politically sensitive and thus were not adjusted to match costs. As a result, the Bundespost had to take out loans to cover its operating costs as well as to make the required contributions to the federal budget. Changes were recommended by a number of expert commissions, but these were abandoned or ignored by the changing governments in Bonn.

Change did not finally occur until the early 1980s. When the FRG fell behind other countries in terms of competitiveness, primarily due to the telecommunications monopoly of the Bundespost, Christian Schwarz-Schilling, a former entrepreneur who had been postal minister since 1982, initiated postal reform. A new law, the Poststrukturgesetz, went into effect on June 8, 1989. The Bundespost was transformed into three government-owned businesses which were managed independently according to market-oriented principles: the Deutsche Bundespost Telekom for the telecommunications sector, the Deutsche Bundespost Postbank for the banking, and the Deutsche Bundespost Postdienst for the postal service. The ministry still approved short- and long-term plans and salary levels for those three enterprises.

From 1950 onward, the Deutsche Bundespost in West Germany ran advertising campaigns encouraging people to help their "brothers and sisters" in the Eastern part of the country by sending them parcels of food and other items scarce in the GDR. Bundespost employees were granted the status of civil servants, who could not be laid off. Their number rose from 260,000 in 1952 to 360,000 a decade later. In 1954 the Bundespost initiated a modernization program for the sorting of letters. The number of letter centers was cut from 3,600 to just 350 in 1970. The centralization of mail logistics was accompanied by mechanization of letter sorting which was eventually applied to parcel post sorting as well. In the fall of 1961, a night airmail transportation system was established, carried out by the airline Deutsche Lufthansa. At the end of the 1960s and beginning of the 1970s, the Deutsche Bundespost was the largest user of automatic data processing in the FRG, according to former Executive Manager Franz Scholl. However, another traditional part of the German postal system, the transportation of people, was finally abandoned. After World War II, the allied forces ruled that transportation services had to be run by local businesses;

government-owned companies were no longer allowed to offer those services. The postal Kraftpost bus lines were reestablished in the 1950s and in service until the early 1980s when the business was finally taken over by the new railway company Deutsche Bundesbahn.

THE POSTAL REUNIFICATION IN GERMANY: 1990–94

Just as the Deutsche Bundespost was about to realize far-reaching reforms, it was overwhelmed by a real revolution. On the evening of November 9, 1989, the government of the GDR, under immense political pressure, announced that citizens would be granted unrestricted rights to travel, and visas would be issued immediately. A few hours later, the first East Germans arrived at post offices in West Berlin to call their relatives from the other side of the Berlin Wall. Approximately four weeks later, the two postal ministers discussed cooperation between the Deutsche Bundespost and the Deutsche Post. The treaty that brought about the currency, economic, and social reunion of the two German states also reunited the two postal systems, and the two postal ministers ratified the agreement on May 17, 1990. The territory of the Deutsche Bundespost was suddenly enlarged by 44 percent, 26 percent more people had to be provided with service, the number of employees went up by 30 percent, and the number of branches grew by 68 percent.

Thereafter, the East German postal system was integrated into the Deutsche Bundespost and completely reorganized. This, however, was easier said than done. Numerous obstacles had to be overcome. For example, the Deutsche Post, like the Bundespost, had developed a four-digit system of postal codes. Many of these codes were the same for two different cities; for example, 5300 was the code for both Bonn in West Germany and Weimar in East Germany. This problem was resolved temporarily by adding a capital letter to each postal code: O for East and W for West.

There were other challenges as well. East German post office facilities could not be taken over immediately, because of unresolved ownership issues. Then, the first appointed head of the Bundespost in East Germany was outed as a former Stasi informant. Moreover, postage fees were significantly lower in East Germany, reflecting the lower personal income in East Germany. This issue in particular created tension in Berlin post offices where employees from both parts of the city worked together but were paid different wages. West German businesses and even government-owned institutions took advantage of the lower rates in East Germany and mailed a great deal of their correspondence through East German subsidiaries, or just by dropping it off at post offices in East Germany.

After the communication borders had fallen and the West German deutsche mark had been introduced to the so-called new German Lander, the eastern part of Germany was flooded with mail, in particular advertising and catalogs from mail-order businesses wanting to expand into the new market. The number of letters sent from West to East Germany rose by 300 to 500 percent between 1989 and 1990 while the amount of packages, due to mail-order buying, grew five- to tenfold. The East German postal infrastructure was completely unprepared for the increases. At some locations, warehouses had to be rented to accommodate the overwhelming volume of packages. Moreover, two out of three pieces of postal machinery in use at the time were completely worn out. The Bundespost helped immediately, offering 5,000 used vehicles and other desperately needed equipment. Spontaneously formed partnerships between postal workers from the East and West were followed by an exchange program where some 4,500 West German managers helped reorganize and modernize facilities in the east while East German post office employees were trained on the job in West German locations. However, it took until roughly 1993 before the service quality in the Eastern post offices was equal to Western standards.

The integration of the east, along with the first Bundespost reforms, left the company with a deficit of DEM 1.5 billion in 1990. At the same time, chaos of reunification hurt the quality of Bundespost service in the West as well, and the backlog of undelivered mail increased. The Bundespost started a publicity campaign in December 1991 to improve its image and stop the loss of business to private carriers. That was followed by a well-received advertising campaign worth DEM 80 million publicizing the new five-digit postal codes, which were introduced on July 1, 1993. By the end of 1994, the Deutsche Bundespost Postdienst employed 342,413 people, 14 percent less than it had in 1990. Between 1990 and 1994, investments totaled DEM 10 billion. Although modernization had made considerable progress, personnel costs made up about 73 percent of all costs in 1994. That year, however, the company also realized a profit of DEM 256.7 million out of DEM 28.8 billion total revenues, its first profitable year since German reunification.

ON THE WAY TO PRIVATIZATION: 1995–99

The second phase of the postal reform was the largest privatization project in FRG history. The Deutsche Bundespost Postdienst was transformed into the Deutsche Post AG and officially registered in Bonn on January 2, 1995. Chairman of the Executive Board was Dr. Klaus Zumwinkel, a Wharton Business School graduate, former senior partner at McKinsey & Company Inc., and CEO of Quelle, Europe's largest mail-order retailer, who had successfully led the Deutsche Bundespost since 1990. Under the new organizational structure, the executive board, which consisted of experienced managers from the private sector, made most decisions. However, Deutsche Post, like the other two Bundespost offspring, was overseen by the government holding company Bundesanstalt fur Post und Telekommunikation, which was responsible for the overall payment agreements with the postal union. The holding company was supervised by the Ministry for Post and Telecommunication and supported by an advisory board comprising 16 representatives from the federal and state parliaments which regulated the market and established rules for competition. Politicians were placed on the advisory board of Deutsche Post. The 1994 loss of DEM 2.9 billion was made up by transfers from Deutsche Telekom AG, and from 1996 on the company was taxed like any other business. At the same time the markets for mail delivery and telecommunications were gradually opened to increased competition. For example, beginning in 1995 private companies were eligible to deliver mass mailings weighing over 250 grams.

In January 1998, the new postal law went into effect in Germany. It renewed the constitutional obligation to provide postal infrastructure by means of appropriate services and within an economic framework and granted Deutsche Post the exclusive right to deliver letters and catalogs weighing less than 200 grams, with certain exceptions, until the end of 2002. The same year, however, 155 businesses were granted licenses to deliver certain kinds of letters under 200 grams, a move that prompted Deutsche Post to sue the government agency that had issued the licenses. One case was settled against the Deutsche Post in July 1999, as the 170 messenger firms were offering same-day delivery, a service Deutsche Post did not offer. In 1995 a new organizational structure was introduced, reducing the number of local offices from 385 to 172. The former 23 directorates were organized under the umbrella of five branches: Frachtpost (freight post), Briefpost (letter post), Postfilialen (post offices), Internationale Post (international mail), and Postphilatelie (postage stamps).

Besides the efficient organizational structure, large-scale rationalization was at the core of the new business strategy. Deutsche Post had invested heavily in new technologies during the first half of the 1990s to become competitive. In July 1995, the last of 33 new logistic centers worth DEM 4 billion for freight turnover went into service, accompanied by a new normative package format and a tracking and tracing system. In the mail delivery branch, which generated about 70 percent of all revenues, the concept "letter 2000" was inaugurated which significantly cut delivery times for letters. In 1998, 95 percent of all letters reached their destiny one day after being dropped off at a post office, in comparison to 86 percent in 1994. About DEM 4 billion was invested for 83 new logistic centers for letter turnover, which replaced about 1,000 locations where letters at the beginning of the 1990s had been sorted mostly by hand.

A new concept for the country's 14,000 post offices was developed with the Deutsche Postbank AG, the former financial services arm of the Deutsche Bundespost. Bundespost had been privatized, but the German government later decided to let Deutsche Post take it over for DEM 4.3 billion in January 1999. About one-third of all transactions in German post offices were Postbank transactions, and the fusion of the two companies gave Deutsche Post the opportunity to better utilize its network of post offices, the biggest and most concentrated branch network in Germany. The strategic goal of making the Postbank attractive for a public offering was to gain influence in the retail banking market. In addition, it was planned that new financial services such as construction loans, investment banking, and life insurance would be added beginning in 1999.

At the same time, new ways of offering postal services were explored. Inefficient post offices were closed, and retail businesses such as grocery stores and gas stations were allowed to offer postal services for longer hours. Moreover, 17,000 mail carriers offered a growing number of mobile services that spared people in rural areas the inconvenience of driving to the nearest post office. A shop-in-shop cooperation with the stationery retailer McPaper & Co. was so successful that the Deutsche Post acquired the company from the parent company Herlitz AG in January 1998, and to improve service quality it was regularly monitored by anonymous testers from a market research institute.

To increase its competitiveness in the market, Deutsche Post began expanding into new markets. In the domestic market, new business opportunities were explored in the fields of direct marketing, in-house postal services for big corporations, electronic transfer of letters from financial institutions which were then printed out and delivered from a post office branch close to the addressee, and online shopping. However, the most pressing demand from existing clients, since the formation of the European Community and economic globalization, was to handle mail throughout Europe and beyond. Within three years, Deutsche Post acquired major shares of ground parcel delivery companies in Austria, France, Poland, Belgium, Italy, Spain, Portugal, and the United States. The largest deal was the takeover in early 1999 of the Swiss logistics concern DANZAS with 16,000 employees and CHF 7 billion annual revenues. Financial results for the second half of the 1990s at Deutsche Post were very promising. Although annual revenues increased only slightly from DEM 27.4 billion in 1995 to DEM 28.7 billion in 1998, profits rose by 450 percent from DEM 282 million to DEM 1.27 billion during the same period. Moreover, the percentage of personnel costs went down from 70.6 percent in 1995 to 66.2 percent in 1998, when Deutsche Post employed 233,863 people.

Deutsche Post rounded out the 1990s by acquiring Orgadis in October 1999, and announcing aggressive expansion plans in the United Kingdom the following month. At that time, the company announced that it would part with $1.14 billion to acquire Darien, Connecticut-based Air Express International Corp., which employed 7,700 people and operated 705 offices in 130 countries worldwide.

GOING PUBLIC

Deutsche Post ushered in the new millennium with more acquisitions. After snapping up DSL Bank in January, the company finalized its acquisition of Air Express International, which became part of the company's Danzas business, in February. A deal for Herald International Mailings followed in March. The company ended 2000 by becoming partially privatized, via an initial public offering (IPO) in November.

Deutsche Post kicked off 2001 with a flurry of activity. In January, the company established an enterprise named Nuova AEI S.P.A. in Italy. In addition, the company formed Deutsche Postbank Fund Services GmbH in April and snapped up Norway-based Danzas Quality Cargo AS midway through the year. It also was in early 2001 that the company secured controlling interest in the air freight operator DHL International, obtaining a 21.38 percent stake for an estimated $800 million. Deutsche Post rounded out 2001 by investing more than $10 million in start-up companies within the logistics and Internet sectors, through its venture capital business, Deutsche Ventures.

Deutsche Post began 2002 by combining its international dispatch functions with those of DHL Worldwide Express. Following this development, DHL Worldwide Express concentrated on express services, while Deutsche Post Global Mail began handling non-urgent deliveries. It also was in early 2002 that Deutsche Post Euro Express Deutschland GmbH & Co. OHG was established. In August, Deutsche Post revealed plans to begin offering discount international mail service in Japan. The company rounded out the year by acquiring full ownership of DHL International for $396 million.

Acquisition activity continued in 2003. During the first half of that year, Deutsche Post's acquisitions included Stock Express S.A., Commercial Safeway S.A., and Casa di Spedizioni Ascoli S.p.A. Midway through the year Deutsche Post sold its stake in DHL Airways to CEO John Dasburg and two other investors. Finally, the company's DHL Holding (USA) Inc. subsidiary acquired Airborne Inc. in August.

Growth continued at Deutsche Post during the middle years of the decade. The company began 2004 with the acquisition of Speedmail International. In April, full ownership of the unaddressed mail distributor Interlanden B.V., which delivered approximately 70 million leaflets and 9 million free local newspapers weekly, was acquired from Royal Wegener. Prior to the deal, Deutsche Post had acquired a 70 percent stake in Interlanden. Other acquisitions during the first half of the year included the companies QuikPak and Smartmail.

In mid-2004, an IPO was made for the company's Postbank subsidiary, generating $1.87 billion. Progress continued in the fall. In October, Deutsche Post revealed a five-year plan to invest $616 million in DHL's new information technology service center, located in Prague, Czech Republic.

GOVERNMENT RELINQUISHES CONTROL

A number of major milestones were reached at Deutsche Post in 2005. In March of that year, the company's DHL Solutions business acquired the logistics arm of Karstadt Quelle AG, one of the largest logistics operations in Germany, for $216 million. The deal added 2,650 employees to the company's workforce, along with 15 distribution centers.

In June 2005, the German government sold its interest in Deutsche Post for $6.04 billion to the state-owned German development bank KfW Group, which saw its ownership stake in Deutsche Post increase to 44.7 percent. At this time, Deutsche Post ranked as the largest postal service in Europe. As its monopoly over mail delivery in Germany came to an end, the company continued to branch out into new areas. Greece-based Multicontainer S.A. was acquired in November. The following month, Deutsche Post became the world's largest warehouse and inventory management company via its acquisition of U.K.-based Exel plc for $6.7 billion.

In early 2006, Deutsche Post parted with approximately $440 million to acquire a 75 percent ownership interest in the U.K.-based document management, mail services, and direct marketing company Williams Lea Group Ltd. Other developments in 2006 included plans to expand DHL's South Korean facilities via a $50 million investment. In addition, $14 million was earmarked to improve DHL's operations in Vietnam via a joint venture named Vietnam Post & Telecommunication. Specifically, new facilities were planned in Haiphong, Danang, Ho Chi Minh, and Hanoi.

After acquiring The Stationery Office Holdings Ltd. via its Williams Lea business in 2007, Deutsche Post made headlines early the following year when German authorities raided the home and office of CEO Zumwinkel in February following allegations of tax evasion. Zumwinkel soon stepped down as CEO, following what was revealed to be one of the largest tax scandals in Germany's history. Following this setback, logistics unit head Frank Appel was named CEO.

CHALLENGING TIMES

The years leading to the close of the decade were marked by difficult economic conditions. Midway through 2008, Deutsche Post was faced with the need to cut operational costs. Subsequently, the company's DHL business gave up its North American air parcel deliveries to competitor UPS. In addition, it scaled back ground deliveries in the United States by about 33 percent. In October, Deutsche Post agreed to sell a 29.75 percent ownership interest in Deutsche Postbank AG to Deutsche Bank AG in a deal worth $3.97 billion.

Facing an annual loss of $1.5 billion, in November 2008 Deutsche Post revealed that its DHL business would halt domestic deliveries in the United States altogether in January 2009, limiting its operations to international pickups and deliveries only. The move would result in the loss of approximately 9,500 job losses.

In January 2009 Zumwinkel was convicted of tax evasion. He admitted to not paying approximately $1.3 million in taxes between 2002 and 2006 by funneling money into his Liechtenstein-based Devotion Family Foundation. In addition to paying $5.1 million in back taxes, Zumwinkel was ordered to pay a $1.3 million fine. However, he avoided a two-year prison sentence.

In March 2009 Deutsche Post CEO Frank Appel unveiled Strategy 2015 to prepare the company for the future. Specifically, the initiative was focused on increasing DHL's profitability and bolstering the company's position in the German mail market. According to the company, the strategy "provides for a two-tier structure with MAIL and DHL as well as tighter links between the three DHL divisions, the latter being facilitated by the creation of an additional overarching executive committee. Other steps will be the simplification of planning processes, an even more intense focus on the shifting needs of customers and the reinforcement of Appel's open leadership culture through a new incentive system that stresses performance and respectful interaction among employees."

Developments continued in mid-2009, when Deutsche Post generated about $7 billion by selling its remaining stake in Deutsche Bank. Finally, a special milestone was reached on September 25, when DHL celebrated its 40th anniversary.

Evelyn Hauser
Updated, Paul R. Greenland

PRINCIPAL SUBSIDIARIES

Deutsche Post Address GmbH & Co. KG; Deutsche Post Fleet GmbH; Deutsche Post Com GmbH; Williams Lea Germany; Deutsche Post Customer Service Centre GmbH; Deutsche Post Direkt GmbH.

PRINCIPAL DIVISIONS

Mail Communication; Direct Marketing; Press Distribution; Philately; Global Mail; Pension Service.

PRINCIPAL COMPETITORS

FedEx Corp.; TNT N.V.; United Parcel Service Inc.

FURTHER READING

Dade, Corey, Alex Roth, and Mike Esterl, "DHL Beats a Retreat from the U.S.: Deutsche Post Unit's Campaign Foiled by Souring Economy, Management Missteps," *Wall Street Journal Europe*, November 10, 2008.

"Deal in the Post," *Banker,* December 1995, p. 15.

"Deutsche Post CEO Frank Appel Presents Strategy 2015," Bonn, Germany: Deutsche Post AG, September 24, 2009.

"Deutsche Post: Im Jahr 2000 auf's Parkett," *Spiegel Online Aktuell,* February 12, 1999.

"Deutsche Post on Buying Spree," *American Shipper,* June 1999, p. 20.

"Deutsche Post Scraps Trans-O-Flex Takeover Plans in Face of Commission Objections," *European Report,* May 13, 1999.

"Deutsche Post to Purchase Danzas," *Transportation & Distribution,* January 1999, p. 14.

Dohmen, Frank, and Ulrich Schäfer, "Post Modern," *Spiegel,* July 19, 1999.

Echikson, William, et al., "Privatization: Posts with the Most," *Business Week International,* August 17, 1998, p. 18.

"Festakt mit Intrigen," *Spiegel,* December 23, 1994.

Gallagher, Thomas L., "Zumwinkel Convicted of Tax Evasion," *Traffic World,* January 26, 2009.

"German Government Sells Its Last Deutsche Post Shares," *ePostal News,* June 25, 2005.

Glaser, Hermann, and Thomas Werner, *Die Post in ihrer Zeit,* Heidelberg: R. v. Decker's Verlag, G. Schenk, 1990.

"Kein Briefmonopol fur Post AG," *Focus Online,* July 6, 1999.

Lotz, Wolfgang, *Deutsche Postgeschichte,* Berlin: Nicolaische Verlagsbuchhandlung Beuermann, 1989.

McCawley, Ian, "Deutsche Post Completes Takeover of Interlanden," *Precision Marketing,* May 7, 2004.

"Mit mehr Technik und weniger Personal in schwarze Zahlen," *Handelsblatt,* December 19, 1994.

"Postbank IPO Raises $1.87b," *ePostal News,* July 16, 2004.

"Post kauft weiteren Expressdienst," *Die Welt* (online edition), January 8, 1999.

Schmitz, Heinz, "Der Einfluß der Politiker bleibt," *Handelsblatt,* December 20, 1994.

Scholl, Franz, ed., *Einheitsfarbe Ginstergelb,* Berlin: Edition Hentrich, 1995.

Taverna, Michael A., "Deutsche Post Buys Control of DHL," *Aviation Week & Space Technology,* September 25, 2000.

"Zumwinkel Resigns as DPWN Chief," *Traffic World,* February 15, 2008.

Deutsche Telekom AG

Friedrich Ebert Allee 140
Bonn, 53113
Germany
Telephone: (+49 228) 181-4949
Fax: (+49 228) 181-9400-4
Web site: http://www.telekom.de

Public Company
Founded: 1877
Incorporated: 1995
Employees: 260,798
Sales: EUR 61.7 billion (2008)
Stock Exchanges: Frankfurt New York
Ticker Symbol: DT
NAICS: 517212 Cellular and Other Wireless Telecommunications; 517110 Wired Telecommunications Carriers

■ ■ ■

Deutsche Telekom AG is one of the leading telecommunications companies in Europe and the United States, with more than 128 million mobile telephone subscribers, nearly 34 million fixed-line subscribers, and more than 15 million broadband Internet subscribers. The company operates primarily under the T-Mobile and T-Home brands. Deutsche Telekom operates through four primary divisions: Mobile Communications Europe; Mobile Communications USA; Broadband/Fixed Network; and Business Customers. Mobile Communications Europe includes the company's 39 million subscribers in Germany, as well as

its operations in the United Kingdom, Poland, the Netherlands, Austria, the Czech Republic, Hungary, Croatia, and Slovakia, for a total of 95.6 million subscribers.

The Mobile Communications USA division oversees the group's nearly 33 million subscribers, making the company the sixth-largest wireless player in the U.S. market. The Broadband/Fixed Network division operates primarily through T-Home, which claims a 46 percent share of the German digital subscriber line (DSL) broadband Internet market. The company has rolled out a number of broadband products, such as the voice over Internet protocol (VoIP) telephony service Call & Surf, and the television over Internet protocol (TVoIP) service Entertain. Deutsche Telekom's broadband operations extend to the Central and Eastern European market, and include majority stakes in Croatia's T-Hjrvatski Telekom, Hungary's Magyar Telekom, and Slovak Telekom. Deutsche Telekom's Business Customers division focuses on such large-scale clients as Royal Dutch Shell, Siemens, Airbus, and Old Mutual Group, through subsidiary T-Systems.

Once Europe's leading telecommunications company, and the number three in the world, Deutsche Telekom has struggled to find its place within the rapidly consolidating global telecom market. The company faces difficulties at home, seeing its number of fixed-line customers slip as people shift to mobile-only and VoIP telephone access. The company has also been rocked with a number of scandals, including being the focus of a class-action lawsuit brought by 16,000 plaintiffs in 2008. Although privatized in 1995, the

COMPANY PERSPECTIVES

Our Vision: Deutsche Telekom: a global leader in "Connected Life and Work." Our Mission: We mobilize personal, social and business networking.

company is still 30 percent owned by the German government. Deutsche Telekom is led by CEO and Chairman René Obermann.

1833–1933: THE TELEPHONE CONQUERS GERMANY

The optical telegraph was first introduced in the German state of Prussia in 1833. Thirteen years later, the first telegraph line connected the two largest cities of the state, Berlin and Potsdam. However, it took another 31 years until the human voice was first successfully transmitted over a wire in Germany. In 1877 the first postmaster of Germany's united postal system Deutsche Bundespost, Heinrich von Stephan, approved an experiment with two telephones built by U.S. inventor Alexander Graham Bell. For the first time in Germany, voices were transmitted over a distance of more than two kilometers. Von Stephan realized the potential of the new medium and put telephone services under the control of his postal authority, the Bundespost.

By 1880, 16,000 German households subscribed to telephone services. In the following decades, the telephone won more and more acceptance in Germany and the technology was greatly improved. Beginning in 1881, telephone networks were being established in the country's largest cities such as Berlin, Hamburg, Frankfurt am Main, and Cologne. By 1898 the number of Berlin's telephone subscribers had climbed to 46,000, more subscribers than in all of France. From 1912 on, Germany's telephone cables were laid underground in a constantly expanding cable network.

Automated systems started replacing operator-based telephony around this time. Advances in telecommunications technology also made it possible to interconnect local networks and increase their capacity. The 1920s brought self-dialing, long-distance, and mobile phone service to Germany. In 1926, for the first time, train passengers traveling between Berlin and Hamburg could call anywhere in the world. In 1933 public telex service was introduced between the two cities.

USE UNDER HITLER, FOLLOWED BY WARTIME DESTRUCTION: 1933–49

After Adolf Hitler came to power in January 1933, the Bundespost became an instrument of the Nazi totalitarian state and, as such, its propaganda machine. Letters and telephone calls were routinely intercepted and used to identify Jews and dissidents. During World War II telephone services of the Bundespost continued to function right up until Allied occupation in all areas of Germany. However, the service was in chaos by the time of Germany's surrender on May 7, 1945. Of the 3,420 buildings the Bundespost had owned before the war, 1,483 had been completely destroyed or damaged by bombing between 1940 and 1945, as well as during the fighting within Germany before its surrender. Many of its former personnel were dead or missing, and many telephone lines were cut.

As U.S., British, and Soviet forces assumed control of government, they also took over postal and telephone services. Between 1945 and 1947, political rifts and eventually the Cold War broke out between the Western allies and the Soviet Union. In 1947 the British and American occupation zones were merged for economic purposes, and administration began to be handed back to the Germans. The Soviets' refusal to participate in the currency reforms of June 1948 and the Berlin blockade meant that a unified postal structure for all occupation zones was doomed. Postal services in the eastern part of Germany were turned over to the new East German state established by the Soviets in 1949. An elected Parliamentary council from all three western zones met at Bonn on September 1, 1948, to draw up the West German constitution or Basic Law. In April 1949, the U.S., British, and French governments guaranteed full powers of self-government to the new West German state. The Bundespost was reborn as a state body under the control of a cabinet ministry and assumed control over posts, telephones, and telegraphs in the new Federal Republic of Germany. The new constitution specifically forbade the privatization of posts and telecommunications.

1950–70: REBUILDING THE NETWORK

During the 1950s the Bundespost had to rebuild its communications network and hundreds of post office buildings. Much of prewar Germany's communications had centered on east-west communication networks between Berlin and western industrial cities. The new West Germany was a long, narrow country in which many lines of communication ran north-south. West Berlin had become an isolated city in an alien country.

KEY DATES

1877: Heinrich von Stephan puts telephone services under the control of his postal authority.

1912: Germany's telephone network is laid underground.

1933: Nazis take control of the Post Office.

1949: Deutsche Bundespost assumes control over posts, telephones, and telegraphs in the new Federal Republic of Germany.

1989: New legislation passes the German parliament, and Deutsche Bundespost Telekom is established.

1990: Telecommunications companies of former East and West Germany are merged.

1994: Posts and Telecommunications Reorganization Act passes the governing bodies.

1995: Deutsche Bundespost Telekom becomes a public stock company and is renamed Deutsche Telekom AG.

1996: Deutsche Telekom shares are traded at the New York Stock Exchange for the first time.

1997: Telephone network in the eastern German states is fully digitized.

1998: German fixed-network telephone market is opened to competition.

2001: Deutsche Telekom takes over U.S. mobile phone service providers VoiceStream and Powertel.

2002: Company rebrands its mobile telephone operations under the T-Mobile name; company posts the largest corporate loss in German history.

2004: Deutsche Telekom acquires the California and Nevada networks of Cingular.

2009: Company agrees to merge its U.K.-based mobile telephone network with that of Orange UK in a 50-50 joint venture.

After the war, the division into different occupation zones had fragmented communications and delayed the formation of an integrated network.

The reconstruction of the telephone service was accomplished by the end of 1951, but installation of new private telephones was slow. By 1952, there were still only five telephones per 100 inhabitants in Germany, compared to 28 and 11 per 100 inhabitants in United States and Britain, respectively. By the 1960s,

however, Germany's communications network had been fully restored, and telephone subscribership was on a par with other industrial countries. As postwar Germany's prosperity rose, the demand for telecommunications services grew. The Bundespost invested in satellite communications; new transatlantic self-dialing facilities from Bonn, Frankfurt, and Munich became available in 1970.

1970–89: FIRST STEPS TOWARD REFORM

Attempts to free the Bundespost, including its telephone service, from political control date back to the 1920s. Around that time the government of the Weimar Republic was looking for a structure that would allow the Bundespost a measure of independence as a profit-making organization. In 1924, laws were passed allowing the Bundespost a considerable degree of financial autonomy from government control. The success of this reform, however, was restricted by interference from politicians and trade unions, and was finally reversed altogether by the Nazis.

The issue came up again when Germany experienced an unprecedented economic boom after World War II and many business and consumer groups began criticizing the post office monopoly for inefficiency. A 1970 law formally stated that the monopoly had been effectively superseded by a reservation that prevented the establishment of a rival undertaking, but little changed. In 1973 a further reform, the Postal Organization Act, limited government intervention in the Bundespost "only to what is politically necessary and to facilitate post office management." Under the new structure, the Bundespost was headed by an executive committee assisted by a supervisory council. The committee, however, remained responsible to the government.

German business continued to complain that the Bundespost's phone network was inefficient and expensive and that German manufacturers might be disadvantaged by a backward telecommunications market. However, several powerful interest groups opposed change for fear of job losses and disappearance of preferential treatment under a more competitive system that included: the Social Democratic Party; the postal union Deutsche Postgewerkschaft; the Bavarian State Government; large contract suppliers to the Bundespost, including the German electronic giant Siemens AG; and the Bundespost's employees, who enjoyed the status of civil servants with considerable job security and pension benefits.

Pressures from both the European Community (EC) and the United States finally forced Bonn to make recommendations about the future of the Bundespost. Under Chancellor Kohl's Christian Democrat–dominated government, the so-called Witte Commission began to explore the possibility of privatization in 1985 and presented a report in September 1987. The commission recommended the opening of the telecommunications equipment and services market to outside bidders, a change that was likely to be required by EC competition law. The Bundespost would continue to operate in all its present fields, but some competition would be allowed in radio paging, mobile telephones, modems, videotext, and some satellite systems. However, the basic telephone monopoly, which earned 90 percent of the Bundespost's telecommunications income, would be retained. The commission also recommended that the Bundespost be divided into three businesses: Postdienst (postal services), Postbank (bank services), and Telekom (telecommunications), with a minimal level of political interference above the level of their respective management boards.

The report drew criticism from both sides. While liberals condemned it for not going far enough, opponents claimed it went too far. As a result, the original proposals were heavily altered before the new law passed the Bundestag, Germany's parliament, in 1989. Deutsche Bundespost, was divided into three separate companies: Deutsche Bundespost Postdienst, Deutsche Bundespost Postbank, and Deutsche Bundespost Telekom. Each company had its own board of management and separate accounts. However, a common directorate was added between the three businesses and a proposal for incentive-based pay was limited. The Ministry of Posts and Communication still had ultimate supervisory and regulatory authority in the public interest.

1990–94: THE TELEPHONE REUNIFICATION OF GERMANY

What the postal reformers could not foresee was the collapse of East Germany in November 1989 and Germany's reunification in October 1990. German reunification brought with it the integration of East Germany's own telecommunications monopoly, Deutsche Post, into the Bundespost. It soon became apparent that the necessary infrastructure investment was much larger than previously anticipated. Only 10 percent of East Germany's households had a telephone, compared to 98 percent of West Germany's. East Germans who applied for a telephone line often waited 10 years and longer to get it. By 1989 the number of applications had risen to 1.3 million. More than 3,500 small East German towns were left without a public phone. Every call to West Germany was channeled through one of 15

connection centers to East Berlin's foreign connections office which was equipped with 111 lines to the West. Moreover, much of the existing East German telephone equipment predated World War II. This bottleneck brought the quickly increasing telephone communication from East to West close to breakdown.

Within six months Deutsche Bundespost Telekom launched its ambitious Telekom 2000 program, a seven-year investment plan of DEM 60 billion. The program not only aimed for bringing the telecommunications network of former East Germany up to Western standards, but also for installing a state-of-the-art infrastructure good enough to meet the demands of the year 2000 and beyond. Telekom emerged as one of the largest employers in eastern Germany. The company took over almost all employees from Deutsche Post's Telekom division. Up to 4,000 of Deutsche Bundespost Telekom's employees were sent to eastern Germany to support their new colleagues.

To make telephone connections available quickly, Telekom made it a priority to establish a mobile telecommunications infrastructure in the eastern part of Germany. Its C- and the new digital D1-cell phone networks reached 80 percent of the population in the eastern German states by the end of 1991. Three years later former East Germany was covered by Telekom's digital mobile phone network. In August 1992 uniform area codes were introduced for the whole country. In mid-1991 Telekom established a digital overlay-network over the existing analog long-distance network. The first digital connection centers were set up in eight eastern German economic centers. From there the digital network was gradually expanded and by 1993 the number of telephone connections between East and West had grown from under 1,000 to 30,000.

In the final phase of the program Telekom technicians worked around the clock to finish the task. It took some 40,000 kilometers of optic fiber cable to build the new digital long-distance network and over 10 million kilometers of copper cable to expand the 1,500 local networks. By 1997, Telekom 2000 had reached its goals. The telephone network in the eastern German states was fully digitized and the number of telephone connections had quadrupled since 1990. According to Deutsche Telekom, the former East Germany had the most modern and efficient telecommunications infrastructure in the world.

MOBILE SPINOFF IN 1993

The enormous costs of updating the former East German telephone system caused many opposition politicians to drop their objections against privatizing Deutsche Bundespost. Privatization was increasingly regarded as a way to make profits and increase efficiency, and the support of the Social Democrats for the two-thirds majority vote in the Bundestag necessary to make changes in the constitution became more likely. In September 1991, the Social Democrat party said it would support privatization under certain circumstances. The negotiations that followed went slowly. Whenever a compromise was in sight, the party added new demands to its list.

Helmut Ricke, Telekom's CEO since 1990, and his management team decided to move ahead and completely reorganize Telekom. In September 1992 the company abandoned the government agency structure, and six months later Ricke presented a more customer-focused organization. Throughout the company he established separate divisions for private and business customers and a third one for key accounts. In mid-1993 Telekom spun off its mobile telecommunications business as a private company, Deutsche Telekom Mobilfunk GmbH, allowing it to better compete in the already liberalized market for mobile phone services. Meanwhile, the Christian Democrat Minister of Postal Services and Telecommunications, Christian Schwarz-Schilling, who had worked relentlessly for postal reform, resigned suddenly and was succeeded by Wolfgang Botsch.

The final impulse for Telekom's privatization came from the EC. At a meeting in Brussels in May 1993 Botsch and his European colleagues decided to open their markets for network-based telephone communication to competition by 1998. Six months later a new proposal for postal reform was presented in Bonn. The postal workers' union fought Telekom's privatization until the end and organized a major strike in the late spring of 1994. In July 1994, however, the Posts and Telecommunications Reorganization Act passed the Bundestag and the Bundesrat, the German parliament's upper house. However, the law required the German government to be the majority shareholder in the former Bundespost companies for at least five more years and extended the monopolies for postal and phone services until the end of 1997. On January 1st, 1995, Deutsche Bundespost Telekom was transformed into a public stock company and renamed Deutsche Telekom AG.

PRIVATIZATION IN 1996

Just a few weeks before Telekom's transformation into a public stock company, Ricke, who had put the reunited Deutsche Telekom on the track to privatization, resigned as CEO. Ex-Sony manager Ron Sommer became the company's new chairman, and his first big task was to attract investors who would buy Telekom shares at the

company's initial public offering (IPO). As a monopolist, Deutsche Bundespost Telekom had been a profitable business with considerable yields for the German federal budget. However, its capital base had suffered badly in the early 1990s because of the necessary infrastructure investments. An additional burden was the cost for its civil servants for whom Telekom had to pay the difference between the retirement benefits they received from public funds and 75 percent of their final salary. In 1994, the company's budget for retirement benefits exceeded the budget for basic salaries by 50 percent.

Deutsche Telekom launched a huge image campaign to attract private German investors, including a new "T" logo and brand name. Telekom's top management courted the world's largest banks as well as other large institutional and private investors. In the United States alone, Telekom organized 17 "road shows." Both measures were extremely successful. Within two years of its introduction, the pink "T" was recognized by nine out of ten Germans as Telekom's logo. Some 400,000 Germans bought Telekom shares which were termed T-Aktien or T-Shares. Some banks placed orders worth between DEM 500 million and DEM 1 billion.

On November 18, 1996, the largest European IPO to date took place. After the first Telekom stock quote was announced at Germany's major stock exchange in Frankfurt am Main, the CEO and CFO Joachim Kroske jetted to New York to be present at an IPO party at the Guggenheim Museum. There Liza Minnelli sang "Money Makes the World Go Round" under a dome of pink light. The heavily oversubscribed shares debuted at 19 percent over issue price on the first trading day. The more than 700 million T-shares sold to private investors accounted for about one-quarter of Deutsche Telekom's share capital. The rest was still held by the German government. An agreement guaranteed that the German government could only sell shares to third parties if Deutsche Telekom agreed.

While investors were told that new T-shares would not be issued in 1997 and 1998, a second batch was issued in mid-1999, raising EUR 15 billion for the company. The government's stake decreased to about two-thirds of the total share capital after that transaction. As in the IPO, Telekom was the beneficiary of the new stock offering, and the money was used to boost the company's capital base. In early March 2000 the T-shares reached an all-time high of seven times the initial issue price. Three months later the third issue was launched to benefit Deutsche Telekom's major shareholder, the government, which had "parked" its shares at the Kreditanstalt für Wiederaufbau, a government-dominated development bank. The government's stake stood at 60 percent.

1998: MARKET LIBERALIZATION SPURS NEW STRATEGY

On January 1, 1998, the German fixed-network telephone market was opened to competition. Almost immediately, the average cost for long-distance calls dropped by up to 30 percent. German consumers jumped at the opportunity, although with a healthy portion of skepticism. While they took advantage of "call-to-call" offers from Telekom's competitors for long-distance calls, they were hesitant to completely switch to a new provider.

From the beginning, Deutsche Telekom fought fiercely against its competitors by any means available. For example, the company placed newspaper ads asking businesses with large phone systems, such as hotels, to make the use of alternative providers impossible. The company also warned customers that it would charge high "compensation fees" should they switch to other providers. Telekom's competitors, which mostly depended on the former monopolist's infrastructure, were not only charged for renting the phone lines but were also charged high "takeover fees" not always related to real costs when customers switched to a new phone company. When customers nonetheless decided to switch, Deutsche Telekom, competitors complained, took a great deal of extra time to connect them with their new provider of choice. Finally, Deutsche Telekom challenged every directive made by the newly established regulation agency Regulierungsbehorde für Telekommunikation und Post in appeals court. About 250 such lawsuits were pending by mid-2001, and it was estimated that resolutions could take another three to five years.

Two years after the market was opened, about 50 companies competed with Deutsche Telekom. About two-thirds of all long-distance calls in 1999 were placed with an alternative "call-by-call" provider, saving customers up to 85 percent. However, Telekom recaptured about half of the competition's revenues through network usage fees. Thus, the company's long-distance market share in terms of revenues was around 90 percent. Furthermore, roughly four-fifths of German customers preferred Deutsche Telekom as their basic phone company and did not plan to switch providers.

In the face of fundamental changes in the market for telecommunications, with mobile telephony and Internet-based applications on the rise, Deutsche Telekom decided to focus on four growth areas and do away with activities that were not in line with them. The new

growth plan was given the acronym TIMES, identifying new markets as telecommunications, information technology, multimedia, entertainment, and security services. Deutsche Telekom announced that it would concentrate on mobile phone and Internet-based communication and data transfer, broadband network access, and systems applications software development. The company set up a subsidiary to sell a significant part of Deutsche Telekom's real estate and sold part of the shares the company held in German cable TV networks.

ROCKY ROAD TO INTERNATIONAL GROWTH DURING THE NINETIES

In June 1995 Deutsche Telekom announced a strategic alliance with French carrier France Telecom and American phone company Sprint called Global One. However, five years later the alliance which ex-CEO Ricke had pushed through against strong resistance, fell apart. Another deal fell through in 1999 when Olivetti SpA, not Deutsche Telekom, took over Telecom Italia. Instead, Deutsche Telekom acquired French fixed-line carrier Siris SAS and British mobile phone company One-2-One.

In May 2001 Deutsche Telekom finalized the takeover of U.S. mobile phone service providers VoiceStream Wireless Corporation, and Powertel, Inc. The transaction was financed by issuing 1.12 billion "T-Shares," a move that ultimately diminished the German government's stake in the company to about 43 percent. The new partnership enabled Deutsche Telekom to offer frequent travelers between Europe and the United States one phone number and one rate for voice and data services.

By mid-2000, the situation at the world's stock markets had become unfavorable. Share prices dropped in connection with the so-called burst of the Internet bubble, and Deutsche Telekom postponed the IPO of its subsidiary T-Mobile International AG, which the company had founded in the same year. The T-shares themselves came under pressure as investors lost their confidence in the stock market. In September 2001, five years after Deutsche Telekom's IPO, its shares were valued below the initial share price for institutional investors. Consequently, the company's plan to use its shares as an "acquisition currency" for international acquisitions came to a halt.

The company's IPO enabled Deutsche Telekom to get rid of about half of its DEM 125 billion of debt. Although it did not seem as if Deutsche Telekom was seriously threatened by competitors in its home market, the company was struggling with self-made problems. Some 190,000 employees kept personnel costs high. In 1997 alone, the company had encountered DEM 2 billion in losses from bad investments in Malaysia and Indonesia, the Global One alliance, and from selling telephones and fax machines. In 1998 mobile phone services accounted for about one-fifth of Deutsche Telekom's revenues. Rival Vodafone-owned Mannesmann, however, had become Germany's mobile phone market leader and made handsome profits while Deutsche Telekom lost money, mainly through its foreign subsidiaries. In 1999 and 2000 Deutsche Telekom's profits dropped dramatically, due to decreasing revenues from fixed-line network business.

In late 1999 Deutsche Telekom's Internet service provider T-Online was reorganized as T-Online International AG. The company was profitable in 1999, but slipped into the red in 2000, due mainly to the flat rate the company introduced for unlimited Internet access. At a time when many dot-coms went bankrupt in the United States, T-Online was planning to push up online advertising revenues and to develop online content that users would be willing to pay for, a business model that in general had not been successful. To generate more e-commerce traffic, T-Online cooperated with automaker DaimlerChrysler AG and tourism companies TUI and C&N.

INDIGESTION IN THE 21ST CENTURY

In the first quarter of 2001 Deutsche Telekom once again restructured its business organization. Corresponding with the company's new strategy, all activities were organized in four business divisions: T-Mobile, T-Online, T-Systems, and T-Com. In the new systems applications field, Deutsche Telekom took over software systems developer debis Systemhaus GmbH from DaimlerChrysler. In the area of network access the company focused on winning new customers for its highspeed digital ISDN and broadband T-DSL services. Deutsche Telekom was also working on T-NetCall, a new service for Internet-based phone calls between PCs and from PC to phone.

In 2001 a group of shareholders filed a lawsuit against Deutsche Telekom for undervaluing its real estate. The company had allegedly written down the balance-sheet value of its real estate by EUR 2 billion, which reduced profits for the year 2000 by EUR 1.5 billion, based on German accounting law. In September 2001, the federal administrative court ruled that some of Deutsche Telekom's "interconnection-fees" to its competitors were illegal. A month later another court ruling required Deutsche Telekom to make its local

network accessible to competitors for much less than the company had charged.

Like many of Europe's telecom giants, Deutsche Telekom limped into the new century with a bad case of indigestion: by 2001, the company's debt load had skyrocketed to EUR 67 billion ($60 billion) after spending more than EUR 80 billion on acquisitions, including EUR 11 billion acquiring a 3G (third-generation) license to operate a high-speed mobile telephone network in Germany.

The company's largest and boldest move came in 2001, when it paid EUR 30 billion for VoiceStream, the sixth-largest mobile telephone operator in the United States. The company then became, if temporarily, the world's second-largest mobile telephone operator, with 50 million subscribers, trailing only Vodaphone. Voicestream and Deutsche Telekom's One2One network in Europe became T-Mobile in 2002. The company had acquired VoiceStream at the height of the telecom cycle. Meanwhile, the company's losses, driven by interests payments on its massive debt, mounted to EUR 3.5 billion at the end of 2001.

EAST EUROPEAN EXPANSION

Deutsche Telekom's expansion plans hit a major snag when the company failed in its buyout offer for Telecom Italia. The company was also hit with the German regulatory board's refusal to allow it to sell its failing cable television subsidiary to Liberty Media, which offered $4.8 billion in 2002. The sale would have helped the company pay down its debt. When the cable operation was finally sold the following year, the company generated just $1.72 billion. At the same time, Deutsche Telekom, like its rivals, suffered from the delays in deploying its 3G mobile telephone network.

By then, the company's difficulties resulted in a new drop in its share price, which slipped below its initial IPO value. By the end of 2002, Deutsche Telekom revealed the largest loss ever reported in Germany's corporate history, a staggering EUR 24.6 billion ($27.1 billion). Much of that loss came from write-downs taken against the group's 3G licenses. Under pressure from its legions of shareholders, including the German government, the company dismissed CEO Sommer, who had led the group since its privatization, replacing him with Kai-Uwe Ricke, who had been head of the company's mobile telephone division.

Ricke pushed through a new restructuring of Deutsche Telekom's assets, including the sale of the cable television operation, successfully pushing debt down to $49 million. The company also slimmed its workforce by 12,000, who were transferred to a new subsidiary, Vivento, which began selling services outside of Deutsche Telekom. By the end of 2003, the company had returned to profitability, helping to raise its share price in the process.

Deutsche Telekom's operations were boosted again by the rollout of broadband Internet services. By 2004, the company had signed up more than four million DSL customers, claiming a 90 percent share of the German market. As a number of new competitors entered the market, however, this figure shrank steadily, dropping to just 46 percent by 2009.

With the mobile telephone market increasingly competitive and growing close to saturation in Germany and beyond, Deutsche Telecom turned its attention toward expansion elsewhere. In 2004, the company agreed to pay $2.5 billion to acquire Cingular Wireless's networks in California and Nevada. The company also expanded its operations into Eastern Europe, acquiring Matav Telecommunications (later Magyar Telekom) in Hungary, and Polska Telefonia Cyfrowa, the number one mobile phone provider in Poland.

SEEKING NEW GROWTH IN THE 21ST CENTURY

By the end of the decade, Deutsche Telekom had expanded T-Mobile European network to include operations in Germany, the United Kingdom, the Netherlands, Austria, the Czech Republic, Croatia, Hungary, Poland, and Slovakia, as well as stakes in operators in Montenegro and elsewhere. By 2009, the company boasted more than 95.6 million subscribers in Europe, and nearly 33 million in the United States. Altogether, the company's total subscriber base reached 176 million. However, the company increasingly found itself outpaced by its rivals, particularly Vodafone and Telefonica, which rushed into the European lead toward the end of the decade.

Deutsche Telekom attempted to fight back, launching a joint bid with KPN of the Netherlands for the United Kingdom's O2 Plc. That company, however, was snapped up by Telefonica, pushing T-Mobile into the number three position in the United Kingdom in 2005. In the United States, meanwhile, the company faced mounting pressure to improve its market share. The only potential candidate for acquisition that would give T-Mobile the necessary scale was money-losing Sprint Nextel. In Germany, meanwhile, the company was confronted with the loss of a growing number of its fixed-line customers, more than 1.5 million, as people adopted mobile-only and VoIP-based telephony. With its share price still lagging, the company let Ricke go in 2006, replacing him with René Obermann, then head of T-Mobile.

The continued decline of the company's share price, to just EUR 11 in 2008, re-sparked the company's battle with its shareholders, who launched Germany's first large-scale class-action lawsuit, joined by more than 16,000 plaintiffs. Nonetheless, 2008 provided some bright moments for the company. In 2008, the company rolled out its well-received Internet-based television package called Entertain. The company also acquired a 20 percent stake in Hellenic Telecommunications, paying $3.92 billion that year. In 2009, the company unveiled its G-1 handset, based on Google's Android operating system and expected to become a major rival for the highly popular Apple iPhone.

Deutsche Telekom continued to gear up for its next big deal. In September 2009, the company reportedly was preparing a multibillion-dollar bid for Sprint Nextel, a move that would vault the company into the second-place spot in the U.S. market, behind Verizon with a total subscriber base of 82.3 million. In the meantime, the company had found a way to leapfrog the competition in the United Kingdom with the announcement of an agreement to create a 50-50 joint venture with France Telecom, operator of Orange UK, to merge their U.K. operations. Deutsche Telekom set out to prove that it remained a viable player in the fast-moving telecommunications market in the new century.

Clark Siewert
Updated, Evelyn Hauser; M. L. Cohen

PRINCIPAL SUBSIDIARIES

Albanian Mobile Communications Sh.a (Albania); Magyar Telekom NyRt. (Hungary; 59.21%); Software Daten Service Gesellschaft m.b.H. (Austria); T SYSTEMS TELEKOMÜNIKASYON LIMITED SIRKETI (Turkey); T-Mobile Austria GmbH; T-Mobile Czech Republic, a.s. (60.77%); T-Mobile UK Limited; T-Mobile USA, Inc.; T-Systems Argentina S.A.; T-Systems Belgium NV; T-Systems Canada, Inc.; T-Systems China Limited (Hong Kong); T-Systems CIS (Russia); T-Systems do Brasil Ltda.; T-Systems France SAS; T-Systems Italia S.p.A. (Italy); T-Systems ITC Iberia, S.A. (Spain); T-Systems Japan K.K.; T-Systems Luxembourg S.A.; T-Systems Mexico S.A. de C.V.; T-Systems Nordic TC Services A/S (Denmark); T-Systems North America, Inc. (USA); T-Systems P.R. China Ltd.; T-Systems Schweiz AG (Switzerland); T-Systems Singapore Pte. Ltd.; T-Systems South Africa (Pty) Limited (70%).

PRINCIPAL DIVISIONS

Mobile Communications Europe; Mobile Communications USA; Broadband/Fixed Network; Business Customers.

PRINCIPAL OPERATING UNITS

T-Mobile; T-Home.

PRINCIPAL COMPETITORS

E.ON AG; Telenor ASA; Siemens AG; France Telecom S.A.; Telecom Italia S.p.A.; ENDESA S.A.; Telecom Italia Mobile S.p.A.; Bouygues S.A.; BT Group PLC; Centrica PLC.

FURTHER READING

"Auf Wiedersehen, Ron," *Economist*, July 20, 2002.

"Bad Connection," *Economist*, April 12, 2008, p. 72US.

"'Befreiungsanläufe' der deutschen Telekom; Gründung von Tochter-gesellschaften," *Neue Zürcher Zeitung*, March 13, 1993, p. 32.

"Bund parkt Telekom-Aktien bei der KfW," *Frankfurter Allgemeine Zeitung*, June 26, 1997, p. 15.

Christ, Peter, "Darüber lache ich nur," *Die Woche*, February 6, 1998, p. 13.

Davis, Bernard, ed., *Federal Republic of Germany*, Philadelphia: National Philatelic Museum, 1952.

"Der Ärger in Brüssel über die Telekom wächst," *Frankfurter Allgemeine Zeitung*, January 21, 1998, p. 14.

Die Deutsche Telekom—Schrittmacher für den Aufbau Ost, Bonn, Germany: Deutsche Telekom AG, 1997, 19 p.

Ewing, Jack, "A Broadband Battle at Last," *Business Week*, June 14, 2004, p. 31.

———, "Deutsche Telekom Needs More Than an Ax," *Business Week*, July 22, 2002, p. 32.

———, "What's Ricke's Next Trick?" *Business Week*, December 15, 2003, p. 30.

"Firing the Boss Won't Fix Deutsche Telekom," *Business Week*, March 12, 2001, p. 22.

Franke, Michael, and Matthias Kietzmann, "Telefonieren; Günstig ins Ortsnetz," *Focus*, August 20, 2001, p. 172.

Goerth, Charles L., *The Postal System of Germany*, Valparaiso, IN: Germany Philatelic Society, 1968.

Holzwart, Gerhard, "Vom Local Hero zum Global Player—Times solles rechten," *Computers oche*, June 23, 2000, p. 9.

"Is the Price Right?" *Economist*, November 23, 1996, p. 87.

Kharif, Olga, and Jack Ewing, "The Case Against Buying Sprint Nextel," *Business Week Online*, September 15, 2009.

"Kurth: Gute Chance für Wettbewerb im Ortsnetz," *Frankfurter Allgemeine Zeitung*, July 20, 2001, p. 13.

Laurent, Lionel, "Deutsche Telekom Torn in the USA," *Forbes*, September 14, 2009.

———, "Doors Open for Deutsche Telekom," *Forbes*, January 29, 2009.

"One Cingular Sensation," *Business Week*, June 7, 2004, p. 50.

"Opening Up," *Total Telecom Magazine*, April 7, 2009.

Piller, Tobias, "Aus der Traum," *Frankfurter Allgemeine Zeitung*, May 25, 1999, p. 23.

Preissner, Anne, "Feine Gesellschaft," *manager magazin*, January 1, 2001, p. 18.

Reiermann, Christian, "Postreform; Vorwarts in die Vergangenheit," *Focus*, May 21, 1994, p. 50.

"Send in the Bulldozer," *Economist*, November 18, 2006, p. 67US.

Stüwe, Heinz, "Gefährdeter Wettbewerb," *Frankfurter Allgemeine Zeitung*, December 28, 1999, p. 15.

Wild, Bernhard, "Die größte Aktienemission der Geschichte," *Süddeutsche Zeitung*, November 20, 1996.

Dodger Theatricals, Ltd.

230 West 41st Street
New York, New York 10036
U.S.A.
Telephone: (212) 575-9710
Fax: (212) 575-0520
Web site: http://www.dodger.com

Private Company
Incorporated: 1980
Employees: 6
NAICS: 711320 Promoters of Performing Arts, Sports, and Similar Events Without Facilities

■ ■ ■

Dodger Theatricals, Ltd., is a New York City-based theatrical production company partnership that has garnered nearly 50 Tony Awards and about 135 Tony Award Nominations since its launch in 1978. Notable original shows over the years include *Jersey Boys, Urinetown, The Who's Tommy, Footloose, Jelly's Last Jam, Prelude to a Kiss, The Secret Garden,* and *Pump Boys and Dinettes.* Revivals include *Guys and Dolls, How to Succeed in Business Without Really Trying, The King and I, A Funny Thing Happened on the Way to the Forum, Peter Pan, 42nd Street,* and *Into the Woods.* The company works with regional theaters to develop potential Broadway properties, and also creates touring companies of successful productions.

MICHAEL DAVID: FROM STAGEHAND TO EXECUTIVE DIRECTOR

Dodger's longtime President Michael David was born and raised in affluent Grosse Pointe, a suburb of Detroit, Michigan. Like many theater people his journey to Broadway began in a church. As an eight-year-old he began singing in the choir of an Episcopal church, rehearsing four times a week, and in addition to developing a love of music, he became enamored with the theatricality of the Episcopal church service. He became familiar with the commercial theater world as a teen, taking advantage of a family connection to intern as a stagehand in Detroit and find summer employment through his undergraduate years at Michigan's Albion College, where he majored in Latin and Greek while participating in theater projects on the side. His summer job provided him with a wide range of backstage experience, from running followspot lights to serving as the dresser for actress Florence Henderson. An altruistic young man, David joined the Peace Corps after graduating from Albion in 1965, but because of his girlfriend's pregnancy, he had to scrap his plans of teaching English in Afghanistan. Instead, he got married and in hopes of placating his disappointed parents he applied to the prestigious Yale Drama School and was accepted to study set design.

David's love for theater became firmly rooted during his time at Yale. Not only did he study set design, he audited theater administration classes and with a colleague launched a theater in a warehouse in a poor section of New Haven, Connecticut, where in their spare time they mounted shows with Yale students as well as

KEY DATES

1980: Company is formed.
1982: *Pump Boys and Dinettes* becomes company's first Broadway show.
1985: *Big River* wins Tony Award for Best Musical.
1992: Company mounts revival of *Guys and Dolls*.
1997: Endemol Entertainment forms production partnership with Dodger.
2004: Dutch backer withdraws support.
2006: *Jersey Boys* wins Tony Award for Best Musical.

local talent. The experience also revealed to David that he enjoyed the challenge of producing shows. Yale also provided David with helpful New York contacts, including the assistant general manager of the Metropolitan Opera, Herman Krawitz, and Broadway press agent Harvey Sabinson. They helped David secure the job as executive director for the Chelsea Theater Center, which in 1968 was invited to move from a Manhattan church where they were housed to the Brooklyn Academy of Music (BAM).

David served as Chelsea's executive director for 10 years, working with Artistic Director Robert Kalfin, who had founded Chelsea in 1965, to produce a number of shows in Brooklyn that made their way to Broadway, including Harold Prince's revival of *Candide* in 1974, *Yentl* a year later, and in 1974 *Happy End*, a Bertolt Brecht and Kurt Weill show starring Meryl Streep. David also met future Dodgers at BAM, including Director Des McAnuff, Producers Rocco Landesman and Ed Strong, Production Specialist Sherman Warner, and Illustrator Doug Johnson.

FORMATION OF DODGER THEATRICALS: 1980

To find a Manhattan outlet for some of its works, Chelsea in 1973 acquired a club on West 43rd Street, the site of a former church, and renamed it the Westside Theatre. The 299-seat space served as a showcase for some of Chelsea's less commercial and more provocative works. In 1980 David and Kalfin decided to go their separate ways, and as part of the dissolution of their partnership, Kalfin assumed control of the Westside Theatre and David continued to work out of BAM. Opting to remain with him were McAnuff, Strong, and Landesman, and together in 1980 they formed the Dodger Theatricals partnership, with David acting as president.

Dodger remained at BAM for two years, struggling to stay in operation, the principals scraping by on summer seasonal unemployment benefits. It was then that Dodger took up residence in Manhattan's Public Theater, invited by the company's legendary founder, Joseph Papp, who had been impressed by Dodger's work. Papp had made his mark with the creation of the Shakespeare in the Park program and in the 1970s was flush with cash after the Public developed and took to Broadway the seminal musical *A Chorus Line*. While McAnuff and Sherman found work with Shakespeare in the Park, David and the others discovered a musical called *Pump Boys and Dinettes* that they mounted in a space across from the Public. It proved so popular that in February 1982 it became Dodger's first Broadway production, running about 18 months.

BIG RIVER WINS 1985 TONY AWARD

Dodger spent two seasons at the Public, but the foundation money that had kept Chelsea and the Dodgers alive for the past 15 years was no longer readily available. The company decided that it would no longer pursue nonprofit theater but act solely as commercial producers. Thus, they left the Public to fend for themselves in the Broadway and off-Broadway arena. Their prospects for success were buoyed by the Dodgers' next Broadway production, a musical comedy revival called *Big River*, which premiered in April 1985 and that year won the Tony Award for Best Musical. The musical comedy *Into the Woods* followed in 1987 and ran for 765 performances at the Martin Beck Theatre. Broadway was always a hit-or-miss business, however. Another Dodger production, an original musical titled *The Gospel at Colonus*, opened in March 1988 but played only 61 performances at the Lunt-Fontanne Theatre before closing.

The Dodgers enjoyed a run of success in the early 1990s. The romantic comedy *Prelude to a Kiss* opened in May 1990 and ran for 440 performances at the Helen Hayes Theatre. The production was nominated for the 1990 Tony Award for Best Play and the script was nominated for the 1991 Pulitzer Prize for Drama. Shortly before *Prelude* closed in May 1991, *The Secret Garden* opened at the St. James Theater. The musical set in colonial India won the 1991 Tony Award for Best Book of a Musical, taking the comparable honor for the 1991 Drama Desk Awards. It was also nominated for Best Musical at the 1991 Tony Awards and Drama Desk Awards. While *The Secret Garden* was engaged in its run of more than 700 performances, the Dodgers launched a revival of one of Broadway's greatest musicals, *Guys and Dolls*, which opened in March 1992 at the Martin Beck

Theatre, the show's home for nearly three years and more than 1,100 performances. It won a host of honors, including the 1992 Tony Award and Drama Desk Award for Best Revival, as well as individual awards for actors Nathan Lane and Faith Prince and Director Jerry Saks.

JELLY'S LAST JAM OPENS: 1992

Less than two weeks after the premiere of *Guys and Dolls,* the Dodgers opened *Jelly's Last Jam,* the Tony Award winner for Best Musical in 1992, a show that also garnered best actor awards for Gregory Hines and Tonya Pinkins, among numerous other honors. A year later brought *The Who's Tommy* to the St. James Theatre. The show was nominated for the 1993 Tony Award and Drama Desk Awards for Best Musical, and while it enjoyed a lengthy run, lasting more than two years and nearly 900 performances, it was expensive to run and essentially a break-even endeavor. After *Tommy,* the Dodgers served as general managers of Walt Disney Production's *Beauty and the Beast,* the 1994 show that not only became a Broadway staple but brought Disney to Times Square and helped revitalize the entire theater district. In that same year the Dodgers also served as general managers of the original musical *The Best Little Whorehouse Goes Public,* a disastrous production that closed two weeks after opening.

As producers the Dodgers turned their attention once again to musical revivals, opening *How to Succeed in Business Without Really Trying* in 1995 and three shows in 1996: *The King and I, A Funny Thing Happened on the Way to the Forum,* and *Once upon a Mattress.* Of the three *The King and I* was the most successful, winning the 1996 Tony Award and Drama Desk for Best Musical Revival and running until February 1998 for a total of 780 performances.

FORMATION OF PARTNERSHIP WITH ENDEMOL ENTERTAINMENT: 1997

The Dodgers' strong performance as a commercial producer caught the attention of the Dutch entertainment company Endemol Entertainment, which in 1997 formed a production partnership with the Dodgers called Dodger Endemol Theatricals. In 1997 the company premiered *Titanic,* an original musical that won the Tony Award for Best Musical that year, along with a revival of the historical musical *1776.* A year later an original musical comedy, *High Society,* made its debut but failed to connect with theatergoers, closing after 144 performances. Another original musical, *Footloose,* opened a few weeks later and enjoyed a better fate, last-

ing more than two years at the Richard Rodgers Theatre and more than 700 performances.

Endemol's deep pockets also allowed the Dodgers to expand into touring, marketing, and management. In 1998 Endemol's cofounder and vice chairman, Joop van den Ende, acquired Endemol's live entertainment assets, including its half-interest in Dodger Endemol Theatricals. With Ende's backing, the Dodgers were able to diversify further. In 1998, Dodger acquired the Eaves-Brooks Costume Company, Inc., its lineage dating to the Civil War. The business was renamed Dodger Costumes.

The Dodgers began the new century with spotty achievements. The original comedy *The Wrong Mountain* opened in January 2000 but closed less than a month later. The company fared only slightly better with a revival of *The Music Man,* which opened in April of that year, and a revival of *42nd Street,* which ran from May 2001 to January 2005 after winning the Tony for Best Musical Revival. The Dodgers fared better with the original musical comedy *Urinetown.* Although critically acclaimed and performed nearly 1,000 times, the show was not especially profitable.

The Dodgers sought to build something of a mini-conglomerate in the new century. In 2002, with Ende's financial backing, the company acquired the Loews Cineplex Worldwide Plaza, a former midtown half-price movie theater. The plan was to convert the subterranean complex beneath the Worldwide Plaza skyscraper into an off-Broadway entertainment center that would include five theaters ranging in size from 200 to 499 seats, plus a rehearsal hall and restaurant. The multiplex opened in September 2004 under the Dodger Stages name but was short-lived. By this time Ende had grown disenchanted with the commercial failure of several Dodger productions in the early 2000s. To make matters worse, a production of *Dracula* opened in August 2004 to poor reviews and was fated to a short run and sizable losses. Even the Tony Award–winning *42nd Street* was losing business and soon slated to close after more than 1,500 performances. Despite the three-and-a-half-year run the show, according to *Variety,* would not recoup its investment. Thus, in the fall of 2004, Ende terminated his association with the Dodgers.

CHANGE IN OFFICES: 2005

Without Ende's backing, the Dodgers found themselves on the brink of ruin and forced to make drastic cuts. Matters only grew worse in the ensuing months. A new musical production, *Good Vibrations,* opened in February 2005 but closed after just 90 performances. More belt tightening for the Dodgers resulted. Dodger Costumes was sold in April 2005 and the company vacated its posh two-story Times Square office complex complete with roof garden, replaced by four rooms that had once been a rehearsal studio. The company name was scrawled on an envelope taped to the door. By the end of 2005, the company also turned over control of Dodger Stages to Ende's Stage Entertainment company.

The elements for a comeback were in place for the Dodgers, however. While the company was enduring problems on multiple fronts, Des McAnuff was developing a new musical based on the music of Frankie Valli & the Four Seasons, *The Jersey Boys,* at the La Jolla Playhouse, where he was the artistic director. The show made its premiere on Broadway in November 2005 at the August Wilson Theatre and became an instant hit, winning the 2006 Tony Award for Best Musical and playing to standing-room audiences. Having produced shows on Broadway for a quarter-century, the Dodgers hoped to apply lessons learned from previous disappointments to take full advantage of *Jersey Boys.* With *Jersey Boys,* the Dodgers "got the math right." The show was still running strong in 2009. In the meantime, the Dodgers produced a drama called *The Farnsworth Invention* that ran for more than 100 performances in 2007 and 2008. Another La Jolla Playhouse–developed show, a revival of *The Wiz,* was also scheduled for a Broadway debut. Dodger Theatricals boasted a seasoned production team, one that had seen its share of triumphs and disappointments, but was now flying high with a major moneymaking show in *Jersey Boys.* Whether the Dodgers could duplicate that success with *The Wiz* or any other property it brought to Broadway in the years to come

was a mystery, given the capriciousness of show business.

Ed Dinger

PRINCIPAL SUBSIDIARIES

Dodger Touring Limited.

PRINCIPAL COMPETITORS

Jujamcyn Theaters LLC; Nederlander Producing Company of America, Inc.; The Shubert Organization, Inc.

FURTHER READING

"Artful Dodgers," *New York Post,* January 11, 2002, p. 41.

Dorbian, Iris, *Great Producers: Visionaries of the American Theater,* New York: Allworth Press, 2008.

Edmunds, Marlene, "Endemol to Spin Off Legit Arm," *Variety,* October 19, 1998, p. 81.

Funke, Phyllis, "For Brooklyn's Chelsea Theater, Manhattan Is a Profitable Sideshow," *New York Times,* April 20, 1975.

Hofler, Robert, "'Vibrations' Not Good for Dodgers," *Daily Variety,* April 20, 2005, p. 4.

Jacobs, Leonard, "Dodger Theatricals Trims Staff, Hints at Internal 'Restructuring,'" *Back Stage,* October 29–November 4, 2004, p. 2.

McKinley, Jesse, "Broadway Company to Convert Former Movie Complex into Theaters," *New York Times,* July 26, 2002, p. B1.

———, "Starved for Hits, Producer Finds Hard Times on Street of Dreams," *New York Times,* March 17, 2005, p. A1.

Rothstein, Mervyn, "A Life in the Theatre: Michael David," *Playbill.com,* May 19, 2009.

Donaldson Company, Inc.

1400 West 94th Street
Minneapolis, Minnesota 55431-2301
U.S.A.
Telephone: (952) 887-3131
Fax: (952) 887-3155
Web site: http://www.donaldson.com

Public Company
Incorporated: 1918
Employees: 10,600
Sales: $1.87 billion (2009)
Stock Exchanges: New York
Ticker Symbol: DCI
NAICS: 336399 All Other Motor Vehicle Parts
   Manufacturing; 333411 Air Purification Equipment
   Manufacturing; 333298 All Other Industrial
   Machinery Manufacturing

■ ■ ■

With operations in North and South America, Europe, South Africa, and Asia, Donaldson Company, Inc., is one of the world's largest manufacturers of specialty air and liquid filters and filtration systems. Donaldson's products are used in applications ranging from whole factory air filters to tractors and construction equipment, to computer disk drives and semiconductor processing. Nearly 60 percent of the company's revenues are generated outside the United States, including about 30 percent in Europe and 22 percent in the Asia-Pacific region.

PRE–WORLD WAR I FOUNDATION

Founder and company namesake Frank Donaldson was born and raised in southern Minnesota. After earning a degree in engineering from the University of Minnesota in 1912, he went to work as the western U.S. sales representative of Bull Tractor Company in Minneapolis. Donaldson found that one unhappy customer in Utah was having a great deal of difficulty keeping his new Bull tractor running. Donaldson had the dust-choked vehicle completely refurbished, but within a few days it was again out of commission. Taking matters into his own hands, Donaldson improvised a filter from a wire cage, eiderdown cloth, and an eight-foot-long pipe. When the enterprising young salesman proudly told his supervisors of his "modification," he was promptly fired for pointing up Bull's flaws.

Donaldson realized that although he was out of a job, he had something better: an invention that could be sold to tractor companies throughout the Farm Belt. With some help from his father, W. H. L. Donaldson, who owned a St. Paul hardware store, and his brother Bob, a sheet-metal fabricator, Frank designed a filter he called the "Twister." The conical device used centrifugal force to spin dirt out of the air before it passed into the engine. In 1915 Frank and his father each made an initial $200 investment in the new enterprise and named it Donaldson Engineering Company. Frank began demonstrating prototypes to former employer Bull Tractor, as well as other major midwestern equipment manufacturers.

External and internal pressures made Donaldson's early years a bumpy roller-coaster ride. Sales were rather

COMPANY PERSPECTIVES

■

The three characteristics that distinguish Donaldson from our competitors are our unique technology, strong customer relationships and extensive global presence. Strategically cultivating each of these has allowed us to grow at an average rate of 9 percent per year and provide career opportunities for our 12,000 employees worldwide.

slow that first year, but in 1917 the company won a contract to manufacture air cleaners for artillery tractors used in World War I. Before the year was through, Frank was drafted into the Army Corps of Engineers, leaving his father to run the fast-growing business. Overwhelmed, W. H. L. brought Bob into the firm at a salary of $150 per month and 25 percent of the company's profits (or half of W. H. L.'s stake). When a competing filter company, Wilcox-Bennet, brought a potentially expensive patent infringement suit against Donaldson later that same year, the patriarch went back on his employment agreement with Bob, applying the funds he saved to the company's legal defense. Bob withheld access to his machine shop in retribution, throwing the business further into chaos. Worse yet, W. H. L. began claiming sole ownership of the busy company that Frank had founded.

INTERWAR REORGANIZATION AND EARLY GROWTH

Months of infighting followed Frank's postwar homecoming. In the fall of 1918, the family settled its disagreement by incorporating the business as Donaldson Company, Inc., Frank owned 45 percent of the new corporate entity, Bob got 25 percent, their sisters Amanda and Mae each owned 12.5 percent, and mother Lottie held 5 percent. W. H. L. relinquished corporate ownership, settling instead for a royalty on any air filter he invented. Because he never came up with a product for Donaldson, the company's incorporation marked his final formal involvement in the firm. (Lottie gave Frank her shares upon W. H. L.'s death in 1926.) The lawsuit that precipitated this ownership crisis remained unsettled until 1919, when Donaldson agreed to purchase a U.S. license for Wilcox-Bennet air filters for $15,000 and a royalty on each unit.

The 1920s brought stability, new products, and increased prosperity. In 1920 Donaldson launched a second type and brand of filter, the Simplex. This air cleaner used oil-soaked moss to trap dust before it could enter a motor or engine and cause damage. The company combined characteristics of both its filters with the introduction of the patented Duplex that same year. Donaldson also forged its first contract with the John Deere Tractor Company during the 1920s. John Deere would become a major customer, accounting for one-third of annual sales by the end of the decade. After suffering a $4,000 loss in 1921, the company saw its sales multiply from $19,554 in 1924 to $204,667 by 1928. By 1929, Donaldson was selling 200,000 units per year. In addition to new product development, Donaldson sought close involvement with its customers' design processes so that their filters would work as well as possible in each manufacturer's tractors. In fact, the company began producing oil-bath type air cleaners in response to customer demand. In 1929 the corporation hired William Lowther to design a proprietary oil-washed air cleaner. His N.S. Filter was patented in 1932, but by that time the company would be scrambling to come up with the funds needed to begin manufacturing the new product.

Donaldson also diversified into tractor seats and spark-arresting mufflers in the late 1920s. The company had hoped to use a stock offering to fund the launch of an aftermarket car heater during this period as well, but the stock market's 1929 crash postponed that first public equity flotation. Nature conspired with the worsening economy, wreaking havoc on the nation's farmers and the industries that served them. A five-year drought and grasshopper plagues denuded the midwestern landscape, turning the heartland into a dust bowl. When farmers hurt, tractor companies hurt and so did Donaldson. During the 1930s, the Minnesota manufacturer slashed its payroll by 70 percent, from 40 to 12, and its chief executives halved their own salaries and borrowed against life insurance policies to keep their business afloat. In 1934 Donaldson defaulted on payments to several suppliers.

It was then that Frank Donaldson and corporate attorney Ken Owen devised a plan to get the company's new oil-washed air cleaner into production and revive its cash flow. They sold the device's patent for $4,000 to a group of investors composed primarily of Donaldson stockholders. In exchange for a small royalty on each unit sold, the new owners licensed rights to produce the filter back to the company. Ford Motor Company started testing the filter midyear and soon found that the device served its purpose well without sacrificing speed or efficiency. The contract that resulted took Donaldson from famine back to feast within months. Sales to Caterpillar, John Deere, Cummins Engine, and many other manufacturers of heavy vehicles boosted sales to $465,000 and profits to $88,000 by 1935.

┌───┐

KEY DATES

∎

1915: Frank Donaldson and his father, W. H. L. Donaldson, found Donaldson Engineering Company to market an air filter that the son has designed.

1918: Business is incorporated as Donaldson Company, Inc.

1951: Three senior executives quit to form Crenlo Corp.; Frank Donaldson Jr. becomes company president at age 31.

1955: Company goes public.

Early 1970s: Company diversifies through the acquisitions of Torit Corp., Majac, Inc., and Kittell Muffler and Engineering.

1973: Frank Donaldson Jr. becomes chairman and CEO; William Hodder is named president.

1983: Severe early 1980s recession leads to Donaldson's first annual loss as a public company, a major reorganization, and a more thorough program of diversification.

1996: Hodder retires and is replaced as CEO by company veteran William Van Dyke.

2000: Donaldson acquires the DCE dust control business of Invensys plc; revenues surpass the $1 billion mark for the first time during the year ending in July.

2002: Ultrafilter International AG of Germany is acquired.

2004: William M. Cook succeeds Van Dyke as Donaldson's president and CEO.

2009: Streak of 19 consecutive years of record earnings ends as the global economic downturn hits the company hard.

└───┘

By the end of this traumatic decade, annual sales hovered near $1 million, and the company's 200 employees manufactured 300,000 air cleaners each year. With a dominant 90 percent share of the market for farm and construction engine air cleaners, Donaldson sought growth through exports to Great Britain, Sweden, New Zealand, and Australia.

WORLD WAR II AND BEYOND

During World War II, Donaldson manufactured bomber gun sights, bayonet holders, crankcase valves for tanks, and, most important, air cleaners for tanks used in the difficult and dusty conditions of the North African desert.

The early 1940s brought a management shakeup as well. After Frank Donaldson suffered a stroke in 1942, brother Bob retired from day-to-day oversight of the company to become chairman. While Frank Donaldson continued as president, John Enblom was promoted from acting general manager to executive vice president with effective control. This administrative arrangement lasted only two years. When Frank died of heart failure in 1945, John Enblom advanced to the presidency. Upon his return from World War II service, Frank Donaldson Jr. assumed the title of vice president.

In spite of this unexpected leadership transition and a month-long strike, Donaldson did well during the early 1940s. Having established its first branch office in Milwaukee, Wisconsin, in 1938, the company added satellite offices in Cleveland, Chicago, and Detroit, and launched its first international production facility in Canada. Sales multiplied from less than $1 million in 1939 to $3.5 million by 1947, with profits topping $359,000.

In the late 1940s, the Internal Revenue Service (IRS) began to question the royalty plan that had saved Donaldson from bankruptcy during the Great Depression. The government agency charged that the royalties were "dividends in disguise," and that the company owed back and current taxes on these diverted profits. The IRS contended that royalties are paid before taxes and, therefore, are considered a tax-deductible business expense and that dividends are paid out of after-tax profits. By paying "royalties" to what was essentially a group of shareholders, the company had avoided $1.3 million in taxes in the process. Donaldson, which was worth only $1.27 million at the time, struggled to reach a lower settlement with the IRS over the next two years, but finally had to go to court.

The legal crisis brought on a mutiny of sorts at Donaldson. President John Enblom, along with pivotal employees Bill Lowther and Roger Cresswell, all members of the executive committee, issued an ultimatum: either Frank Jr. sold 51 percent of the company to them for $200,000, or they would all quit and start a competing company. Frank Jr. marshaled the Donaldson family, which still owned the vast majority of the company's equity, and they agreed not to sell.

True to their word, the three executives quit to form Crenlo Corp. in 1951. At the age of 31, Frank Jr. became president of a company with $5.5 million in annual sales. Although he had a degree in engineering from Harvard University, where he minored in economics and graduated cum laude, his lack of day-to-day experience made the early 1950s a difficult period of transition for the business.

Frank Jr.'s first order of business was to replenish the "brain trust." He sought management help from his cousin, Dick Donaldson, who became vice president of sales and engineering. The new president established the company's first formal research and development department in 1951 and brought in consultants from the Stanford Research Institute the following year. Seven years of research and testing resulted in the 1959 launch of the "Donaclone," the first heavy-duty air cleaner to use a paper filter. The brand name combined Donaldson and cyclone, and the device hearkened back to the company's original Twister brand filter. It used a series of "cyclone tubes" to spin dirt out of the air. The Duralife paper filter served as a final dirt trap. The new product was such a success that, during its first year, it accounted for 20 percent of Donaldson's annual sales.

In the meantime, Donaldson had gone public in 1955 with a modest $124,000 offering. Frank Jr.'s first decade in office was incredibly successful. Sales nearly doubled, from $5.5 million in 1950 to a record $10.1 million in 1959, and profits more than doubled, from $315,000 to $669,000 during the same period.

This was only the beginning, however, of what a company history dubbed "the age of the Donaclone." Sales tripled over the course of the 1960s, to $35.9 million in 1969, as clients ranging from Caterpillar to the U.S. Army adopted the new filter for their heavy-duty machinery. Geographic expansion also contributed to this growth, as Donaldson established joint ventures and licensing agreements with businesses in Britain, France, Germany, Brazil, and Australia. By the end of the decade, it had wholly owned subsidiaries in Germany, Belgium, and South Africa as well. Formalized in 1963, the International Division grew 30-fold from 1963 to 1970.

Frank Donaldson Jr. advanced to chairman and CEO in 1973. In a departure from the traditional promotion from within, Donaldson hired William Hodder, formerly president of Target Stores and a director of Donaldson for just four years, to succeed the founder's son. Hodder took the company on something of an acquisition spree, merging with St. Paul, Minnesota's Torit Corp. and acquiring Majac, Inc., and Kittell Muffler and Engineering in rapid succession. The new affiliates helped diversify Donaldson from its core. Torit added dust collectors that could clear the air in whole factories, while Majac specialized in making dust (it disintegrated materials to specifically sized bits) and Kittell produced heavy-duty sound controllers. Donaldson also diversified from within, establishing a hydraulic fluid filter division in 1975.

In spite of inflation and the energy crunch, Donaldson's strategy of "focused diversification" kept the company's sales and earnings on a countercyclical rise throughout the decade. Sales broke both the $100 million and $200 million thresholds over the course of the decade, and net income more than doubled from $6 million to $14.2 million. In 1979 the company was listed on the New York Stock Exchange.

REORGANIZATION AND RETRENCHMENT IN THE EIGHTIES

After this stellar decade, however, "stagflation" hit Donaldson's core constituencies hard in the early 1980s. Two prominent examples of the recession in the heavy machinery industry were International Harvester, which lost $3 billion, and John Deere, whose plants came to a standstill for two months during the early 1980s. Donaldson's sales skidded from $264 million in 1981 to $203 million by 1983, when the company suffered its first annual loss as a public firm, a $3.5 million shortfall. Blaming its difficulties in part on overexpansion in the late 1970s, the company closed two plants and scaled back the remaining U.S. production to 50 percent of capacity. Employment was reduced by more than 25 percent from 1980 to 1985. Administrative personnel accepted mandatory unpaid leave and a salary freeze. Sales and profits began to recover in 1984, the same year that Frank Donaldson Jr. announced his retirement.

Perhaps most important, the early 1980s crisis highlighted Donaldson's dependence on a mature market and precipitated a more thorough diversification. From 1984 to 1990, the company poured $40 million into acquisitions and joint ventures and plowed another $50 million into research and development. Hoping to eliminate duplication of effort and gain efficiencies, top executives reorganized the company into five groups: Industrial, International, Original Equipment, Aftermarket, and Worldwide Support. Having focused almost exclusively on the original equipment market throughout its history, the company began to target the filter aftermarket. Research and development efforts paid off in the form of new products for industries ranging from computers to passenger autos to pharmaceuticals. Sales in nontraditional markets grew to $129.5 million by 1990, almost one-third of annual sales.

It took most of the 1980s for these new strategies to come to full fruition, but the geographic, product, and market diversification helped even out Donaldson's cyclical performance. The budding conglomerate began to realize its goal of steady growth in profitability in the early 1990s, when rising net sales combined with an annual return on sales of more than 5 percent. Revenues increased from $422.9 million in 1990 to $704 million in 1995, and net income jumped from $21 million to $38.5 million.

BUILDING TOWARD $1 BILLION IN SALES IN THE NINETIES

With Chairman and CEO Hodder nearing mandatory retirement, Donaldson settled the question of succession. In 1994 William Van Dyke capped a more than 20-year career at the company with his appointment to the positions of president and COO. He was promoted to CEO in August 1996. Also during that year Donaldson continued its overseas expansion by acquiring Tecnov S.A., a maker of heavy-duty exhaust mufflers based in France. The company also sold off the operations of its subsidiary in Brazil.

Growth in emerging markets in Asia was a high priority during this period. In 1996 Donaldson formed a joint venture to manufacture Torit industrial-filtration products in Guilin, China. The following year the company established a subsidiary in South Korea called Donaldson Korea Co., Ltd. During 1999 Donaldson opened a new facility in Wuxi, China, for the manufacture of computer disk drive filtration products. This facility and a sister facility in Hong Kong generated more than $50 million in revenue during 1999, which represented nearly 5 percent of the company total.

There were a number of acquisitions in the late 1990s that helped to keep Donaldson's revenue figures soaring ever upward, with two being particularly noteworthy. In April 1997 the company acquired the Armada Tube Group, a manufacturer of exhaust products, for $11.3 million. Old Saybrook, Connecticut-based Aercology Incorporated, maker of industrial air filtration products, was acquired for $9.8 million in July of that same year. During fiscal 1999, the pace of acquisition slowed as deteriorating market conditions led Donaldson to focus on cost containment. A number of efficiency measures were put into place, including a $20 million inventory reduction, and the company also announced plans to close its Oelwein, Iowa, manufacturing plant, a move that involved the elimination of 125 jobs. As a result, Donaldson managed to increase its net earnings by 9.5 percent to $62.4 million on revenues of $944.1 million. Helping to propel sales forward was the introduction of the next-generation PowerCore air-intake filtration system for heavy-duty on-road and off-road vehicles. A year later, the figures for fiscal 2000 showed that revenues had surpassed the $1 billion mark for the first time.

PURSUING LARGER DEALS, DEFYING AN ECONOMIC DOWNTURN

As Donaldson grew in size, its appetite for acquisitions grew as well, resulting in more expensive deals. In November 1999 the company acquired AirMaze Corporation for $31.9 million. AirMaze, which had manufacturing facilities in Stow, Ohio, and Greenville, Tennessee, was a supplier of heavy-duty air and liquid filters, air/oil separators, and high-purity air filter products. In February 2000 Donaldson acquired the DCE dust control business of Invensys plc for $56.4 million. Based in Leicester, England, DCE fit in very well alongside Donaldson's Torit business and provided Donaldson with a major presence in the industrial dust collection sector outside North America with its strong presence in the European market, where it generated 70 percent of its sales, and with its assembly operations in South Africa, Australia, and Japan.

In mid-2002 Donaldson paid about $68 million for Ultrafilter International AG, a Haan, Germany-based firm specializing in compressed-air filtration systems and related parts and equipment. Like DCE, Ultrafilter fit the three criteria that Donaldson had been emphasizing in its diversification; namely, according to Van Dyke, "it expands our presence in industrial markets; it focuses on replacement parts; and the majority of its revenues are outside of the U.S."

The economic downturn at the dawn of the 21st century halted Donaldson's streak of 18 consecutive increases in annual sales. Revenues for fiscal 2002 fell about 1 percent, to $1.13 billion. Nevertheless, the company, in sharp contrast with many other U.S. industrial concerns, not only stayed solidly in the black but also posted its 13th consecutive year of double-digit growth in earnings per share, a streak dating back to 1990. Donaldson executives identified the firm's product line and geographic diversification as a key to its successful defiance of the poor economic climate.

In August 2004, 24-year veteran William M. Cook was promoted from senior vice president to president and CEO, succeeding the retiring Van Dyke. Cook maintained a strategy similar to that of his predecessor, developing innovative new products to retain Donaldson's competitive edge, pursuing modest acquisitions, and keeping a tight rein on costs. As part of its continued geographic diversification and search for operational efficiencies, the company increasingly sought to site its manufacturing close to customers. For example, because at this time most of the world's disk drives used in personal computers and other electronics equipment were being built in China and Thailand,

Donaldson moved its production of the small filters embedded in these drives to these same nations.

By fiscal 2008, Donaldson had recorded its 19th consecutive year of record earnings per share, and sales had soared more than 16 percent to surpass the $2 billion mark for the first time, totaling $2.23 billion. One trend providing a boost for the company was the enactment of stricter emissions regulations in a number of countries, which fueled demand for Donaldson's cutting-edge filtration products.

In the second quarter of fiscal 2009, however, the firm's fortunes reversed course in the face of the sharp global economic downturn. Despite its diversification strategy, Donaldson was unable to overcome simultaneous weakness in several key markets, including heavy- and medium-duty trucks and construction, mining, agricultural, and industrial equipment. Sales for the fiscal year ending in July 2009 dropped 16.3 percent to $1.87 billion, while profits sank 23.3 percent to $131.9 million. A portion of the profit decline was attributable to restructuring charges as Donaldson acted aggressively to slash annual operating expenses by as much as $100 million. As part of the restructuring actions, the company workforce was slashed by 2,800, or 21 percent, over the course of fiscal 2009. By the end of that year, executives were able to see signs of stabilization in some of the company's key markets, but a robust recovery did not appear imminent.

April Dougal Gasbarre
Updated, David E. Salamie

PRINCIPAL SUBSIDIARIES

Donaldson Capital, Inc.; ASHC, Inc.; Aerospace Filtration Systems, Inc.; Donaldson Australasia Pty. Ltd.; Donaldson Filtration Österreich, GmbH (Austria); Donaldson Europe, b.v.b.a. (Belgium); Donaldson Coordination Center, b.v.b.a. (Belgium); Donaldson Belgie, b.v.b.a. (Belgium); Donaldson do Brasil Equipamentos Industriais Ltda (Brazil); Donaldson Canada, Inc.; Donaldson Far East Ltd. (China); Donaldson (Wuxi) Filters Co., Ltd. (China); Donaldson Czech Republic s.r.o.; Donaldson Industrial CR - Konzern s.r.o. (Czech Republic); Donaldson Filtration CR - Konzern s.r.o. (Czech Republic); Donaldson Scandinavia a.p.s. (Denmark); Donaldson, S.A.S. (France); Donaldson France, S.A.S.; Financiere de Segur S.A.S. (France); Le Bozec Filtration et Systèmes, S.A.S. (France); Ultrafilter S.A.S. (France); Donaldson GmbH (Germany); Torit DCE GmbH (Germany); Donaldson Filtration Deutschland GmbH (Germany); Ultratroc GmbH (Germany); Donaldson Filtration Magyarorszag Kft.

(Hungary); Donaldson India Filter Systems Pvt. Ltd.; P.T. Donaldson Systems Indonesia; P.T. Donaldson Filtration Indonesia; Donaldson Italia s.r.l. (Italy); Nippon Donaldson Ltd. (Japan); Donaldson Luxembourg S.a.r.l; Donaldson Filtration (Malaysia) Sdn. Bnd.; Donaldson, S.A. de C.V. (Mexico); Prestadora de Servicios Aguascalientes, S. de R.L. de C.V. (Mexico); Donaldson Torit, B.V. (Netherlands); Donaldson Nederland B.V. (Netherlands); Donaldson Filtration Norway a.s.; Donaldson Filtration (Philippines) Inc.; Donaldson Polska Sp. z.o.o. (Poland); Donaldson Filtration (Asia Pacific) Pte. Ltd. (Singapore); Donaldson Filtration Slovensko s.r.o. (Slovakia); Donaldson Filtration Systems (Pty) Ltd. (South Africa); Donaldson Korea Co., Ltd.; Donaldson Ibèrica Soluciones en Filtración, S.L. (Spain); Ultrafilter S.L. (Spain); Donaldson Schweiz GmbH (Switzerland); Donaldson Taiwan Ltd.; Donaldson Filtration (Thailand) Ltd.; Donaldson (Thailand) Ltd.; Donaldson Filtre Sistemleri Ticaret Limited Sirketi (Turkey); Donaldson Filter Components Ltd. (UK); Donaldson UK Holding Ltd.; Donaldson Filtration (GB) Ltd. (UK).

PRINCIPAL OPERATING UNITS

Engine Products; Industrial Products.

PRINCIPAL COMPETITORS

Cummins, Inc.; Pall Corporation; MFRI, Inc.; ESCO Technologies Inc.

FURTHER READING

Abelson, Reed, "Exhausting the Possibilities," *Forbes*, May 25, 1992, p. 260.

Croghan, Lore, "Don't Look Back," *Financial World*, July 18, 1995, p. 50.

DePass, Dee, "Donaldson Names New CEO," *Minneapolis Star Tribune*, March 25, 2004, p. 1D.

Fedor, Liz, "Donaldson Focuses on Product Innovation," *Minneapolis Star Tribune*, April 20, 2009, p. 1D.

Goodman, Jordan E., "These Baby Blue Chips Promise to Become Grown-up Champs," *Money*, May 1991, p. 65.

Jaffe, Thomas, "Cleaner Air Company," *Forbes*, September 14, 1992, p. 562.

Keenan, Tim, "Let's Clear the Air: Donaldson, Hoechst Celanese Develop New Filter," *Ward's Auto World*, September 1995, p. 85.

Martin, Norman, Christopher A. Sawyer, and Marjorie Sorge, "The Ultimate in Air Fresheners," *Automotive Industries*, February 1996, p. 173.

Morais, Richard C, "Hong Kong Is Just Around the Corner," *Forbes*, October 12, 1992, p. 50.

Peterson, Susan E., "Donaldson Buys Filter Company," *Minneapolis Star Tribune*, June 14, 2002, p. 1D.

————, "Hodder's Legacy: Donaldson CEO Leaves Company on Solid Ground After Years of Growth," *Minneapolis Star Tribune*, July 29, 1996, p. 1D.

————, "Van Dyke Heir Apparent to Take Over Donaldson," *Minneapolis Star Tribune*, August 11, 1994, p. 3D.

————, "Visible Success: Filter Maker Donaldson Co. Was in a Highly Cyclical Business, but Since Broadening Its Customer Base It Has Consistently Had Double-Digit Growth," *Minneapolis Star Tribune*, December 10, 2001, p. 1D.

St. Anthony, Neal, "Donaldson Filters Out Costs to Let Profits Flow," *Minneapolis Star Tribune*, February 26, 2008, p. 1D.

"Salesman's Solution to Tractor-Choking Dust Leads to Founding of Filter Manufacturing Company," *Hydraulics and Pneumatics*, May 1983, p. 80.

Toward a Cleaner, Quieter World: History of the Donaldson Company, 1915–1985, Minneapolis, MN: Donaldson Co., Inc., 1985, 175 p.

Youngblood, Dick, "Diversified Firm Yields Dividends," *Minneapolis Star Tribune*, February 4, 1991, p. 1D.

Doosan Heavy Industries and Construction Company Ltd.

555 Gwigok-dong
Changwon, 641 792
South Korea
Telephone: (+82 55) 278 6114
Fax: (+82 55) 264 5551
Web site: http://www.doosanheavy.com

Public Company
Incorporated: 1946
Employees: 5,440
Sales: KRW 5.71 trillion ($4.01 billion) (2008)
Stock Exchanges: Seoul
Ticker Symbol: 034020
NAICS: 234930 Industrial Nonbuilding Structure Construction; 234990 All Other Heavy Con- struction

∎ ∎ ∎

Doosan Heavy Industries and Construction Company Ltd. is a world-leading producer of power plants and other heavy equipment and installations for the global energy generation and related industries. Doosan operates through five primary divisions: Power Plants, Nuclear Power Plants, Water Plants, Castings & Forgings, and Construction. The Power Plants division includes the engineering and construction of thermal and hydroelectric power plants, as well as wind generation and other renewable energy-based power plants.

Power Plants is the group's largest division, accounting for over 60 percent of the group's 2008 revenues of KRW 5.71 trillion ($4.01 billion). The division also includes the production of turbine gensets (fossil-fuel-powered generators), materials handling equipment, boilers, and heat-recovery steam generators.

The Nuclear Power Plants division includes the production of nuclear steam supply systems; fuel storage equipment; instrumentation and control systems; and replacement, repair, and refurbishment services. The Water Plants division focuses primarily on the design, engineering, and construction of desalination plants, and also develops waste- and wastewater-treatment systems. The Castings & Forgings division, carried out especially through U.K.-based subsidiary Doosan Babcock, includes the production of crankshafts, general forgings, work rolls, and castings. Doosan's Construction division includes civil engineering and plant construction services in support of the group's other operations, as well as commercial and residential construction.

Doosan is South Korea's oldest *chaebol* (a highly diversified industrial conglomerate). Among its nonconsolidated operations, the company is engaged in clothing distribution, food, pharmaceuticals and related manufacturing, fast-food restaurant operations, automobile distribution, and bottle-cap manufacturing. The company also owns a professional baseball team, the Doosan Bears. Founded as a food store in 1896, Doosan is listed on the Seoul Stock Exchange and is led by Chairman Park Yong Seong and President and COO Shim Gyu Sang.

COMPANY PERSPECTIVES

We see the big picture. At Doosan Heavy Industries & Construction, we have a reputation for helping utilities and industries around the world achieve impressive results. Those results, like the tip of an iceberg, are supported by a massive body of decades of knowledge and experience. And a vision of global leadership in power and water that continues to drive us as we help bring more prosperity and abundance to your world. This is our mission.

FOOD STORE BEGINNINGS IN 1896

Doosan Heavy Industries and Construction Company Ltd. claims to be South Korea's oldest *chaebol*. The company originated as a small food store opened in Seoul in 1896 by Park Seung-jik. In 1946 Park's son, Park Too Pyung, took over the store and launched its transformation into one of South Korea's early industrial giants.

The first step toward this transformation was modest enough, as Park Too Pyung expanded the family's grocery shop into a larger store, called Doosan. The increased revenues, however, from this business enabled the company to launch its true expansion starting in the early 1950s. In 1951 the company founded its own import and distribution business, Doosan Trading Company. Over time, that operation developed a wide-ranging distribution portfolio of foods, clothing, pharmaceuticals, chemicals, and other goods.

Doosan next entered the food and beverage industry, establishing the Oriental Brewery (OB) in 1952. OB quickly became the leading domestic beer brand, with a market share that reached 70 percent. OB also provided a springboard for a wider diversification of the group's operations, leading to the development of operations in the construction, machinery, media, trade, and other sectors.

The construction industry took on a larger presence in Doosan's portfolio at the beginning of the 1960s, as the company founded Dongsan Construction and Engineering. In this way, Doosan positioned itself as a major participant in the great South Korean industrialization effort as the country transformed itself from one of the world's most impoverished to a financial and industrial powerhouse.

DIVERSIFIED CONGLOMERATE IN THE SIXTIES

Through the 1960s, Doosan continued in its diversification drive. In 1960 the company bought Hapdong News Agency, which, under the Yonhap News name, grew into South Korea's leading news agency. The company's food and beverage division grew in 1966 with the creation of Hanyang Food, which began bottling Coca-Cola for the South Korean market. The following year, the company launched Yoonhan Machinery, which became a major producer of industrial machinery. The company's growing beverage business, including the strong success of the OB beer brand, led to an investment in glass and bottle production in 1969.

The 1970s marked a new period of growth for the *chaebol*, as it entered the electronics, agricultural, and livestock industries. Most of the company's growth had occurred within the framework of the OB Group. In 1978 that company was renamed, becoming Doosan Group. OB remained a prominent name, nonetheless, and became the original name of the group's own baseball team, founded in 1982 as the OB Bears.

Doosan's growth remained steady through the 1980s, as it added such operations as whiskey production in 1980 through a joint venture with Seagram and Chivas Brothers. Doosan entered the publishing industry, buying Donga Publishing in 1985. In that year, the company also acquired a second brewery operation, Baekhwa Brewery, based in Northern Cheolla. Sports and leisure became new business areas for the group, starting with the formation of Doosan Cuvex in 1987. These interests, which included property development and golf course and sports club operations, led to the opening of the Chuncheon Country Club in 1990.

INDUSTRIAL TRANSFORMATION IN THE NINETIES

By the beginning of the 1990s, Doosan had grown into one of the largest of Korea's second-tier *chaebols*, and ranked 12th largest overall. The decade, however, marked a period of decline for the company. In particular, the group's flagship business, the OB Brewery and brand, suffered a major catastrophe at the beginning of the decade with the accidental release of phenol into Nakdong River. As the toxic chemical made its way into South Korea's water supply, OB found itself at the center of a growing scandal. In the meantime, smaller competitor Chosun released a new beer brand, Hite, brewed with natural spring water. OB never recovered, and quickly saw its market share slip below 40 percent.

To make matters worse for Doosan, other parts of its sprawling conglomerate were struggling as well. By

KEY DATES
◼

1896: Park Seung-jik opens a grocery store in Seoul, Korea.

1946: Park's son, Park Too Pyung, expands the store, which is renamed Doosan.

1951: Park founds Doosan Trading Company, then builds Oriental Brewery, which becomes South Korea's leading beer brand.

1960: Doosan launches a major diversification drive, entering a wide number of industries over the next two decades.

1962: Hyundai Yanghaeng is founded to produce heavy-industry equipment and machinery.

1980: Hyundai Yanghaeng becomes Hanjung (Korea Heavy Industries & Construction) under the control of the South Korean government.

1995: Amid losses, Doosan restructures and decides to focus on the heavy-industry sector, acquiring Hanjung from the Korean government.

2000: Hanjung is renamed Doosan Heavy Industries & Construction Company.

2001: Doosan acquires Hankuk Heavy Industry in South Korea and the reverse osmosis water treatment division from American Engineering Services Inc. in the United States.

2005: Doosan acquires Daewoo Heavy Industry & Machinery, which is renamed Doosan Infracore.

2006: Doosan purchases Mitsui Babcock in the United Kingdom and Kvaerner IMGB in Romania.

2007: Company acquires Yantai Machinery in China and three heavy-equipment divisions from Ingersoll-Rand in the United States.

2008: Doosan buys Dong Myung Mottrol in South Korea.

2009: Company completes construction of a $300 million manufacturing site in Vietnam.

the middle of the 1990s, the company's losses mounted to KRW 900 billion. With little hope for recovery for its core food and beverage operations in sight, Doosan made the dramatic decision to adopt an entirely new industrial strategy.

The company's opportunity came as the South Korean government prepared to privatize Korea Heavy Industries & Construction Co. Ltd., more commonly known as Hanjung. That company had been founded as a private enterprise in 1962 as part of the Hyundai group of companies. Originally named Hyundai Yanghaeng, the company's name was changed to Korea Heavy Industries & Construction Co., or Hanjung, in 1980. At that time, Hanjung was taken over by the South Korean government, through the Korea Development Bank. Other major shareholders included Korea Electric Power Corp. and Korean Exchange Bank.

Hanjung had begun construction of a major production facility in 1976 at Changwon. The site was completed in 1982, and enabled the company to emerge as one of South Korea's leading producers of power plants and industrial plants and facilities. The Changwon site allowed the company to operate across the full spectrum of power-plant operations, from the initial design to the construction and installation of power plants, and their service and repair.

Hanjung continued to expand its facilities through the 1980s and 1990s. The company added a facility for the manufacture of marine diesel engines in 1983. In 1987 the company launched its own technical research center. This helped support the group's entry into gas-turbine production, with the installation of a new factory in 1993. By then Hanjung had not only become one of Korea's leading heavy-industry manufacturers, it became the country's only producer of power plants. Hanjung's research and technological push also made it the world's leading producer of desalination plants.

NEW DIRECTION AT THE DAWN OF THE 21ST CENTURY

Doosan's bid in 1995 for Hanjung met with some skepticism, with the suggestion that the move was made only in order to build the group's revenues and not for long-term objectives. The company's bid, however, was helped by the Korean government's decision to bar the country's top four conglomerates from bidding for Hanjung.

Doosan soon proved the seriousness of its bid to acquire Hanjung. The company put into place a three-stage restructuring process, designed to transform the group from its consumer-products focus into a global heavy-industry powerhouse. The first phase, completed by 1997, involved a cash-generation exercise through the sale of large portions of the company's existing operations. These sales raised more than KRW 1 trillion, and allowed the company to return to profitability.

In the second phase, Doosan continued selling off assets. These included the sale of OB, starting with a 50 percent stake sold to Interbrew for KRW 350 billion in 1997. By the time the second stage was completed,

Doosan had reduced the number of its businesses from 29 to just 12. The company had also successfully paid down much of its debt.

With its balance sheet in order, Doosan was ready to proceed with the acquisition of Hanjung. That purchase was completed in 2000, at which time these operations were renamed Doosan Heavy Industries & Construction. As both a near- and long-term strategy, Doosan pledged to commit itself to its new core operations.

HEAVY ACQUISITIONS IN THE 21ST CENTURY

Doosan launched the third phase of its restructuring strategy following the Hanjung acquisition. The company began seeking new acquisition candidates in order to build itself into a truly global player in the heavy-industry sector. In 2001, among the group's first acquisitions was Hankuk Heavy Industry, also in South Korea, which specialized in power generation. This business was then folded into Doosan Heavy Industries & Construction.

The company also moved into the U.S. market that year, buying the reverse-osmosis water-treatment division from American Engineering Services Inc. In this way, Doosan gained a national sales network, as well as one of the world's leading specialists in desalination plants and reverse-osmosis water-treatment plants. That company was renamed Doosan Hydro Technology. In 2003 the company further boosted its engineering and construction operations, buying Koryo Industrial Development. This purchase was followed by that of main Korean rival Daewoo Heavy Industry & Machinery in 2005. The new operation, which also boasted an extensive presence in the United States, was renamed Doosan Infracore.

The company completed another major foreign acquisition soon after, taking over Kvaerner IMGB, a heavy-machine manufacturer based in Romania in 2006. This purchase more than doubled the company's production capacity, while also giving it a significant foothold in the European market. The company also that year bought U.K.-based Mitsui Babcock, a world-leading boiler manufacturer.

GLOBAL HEAVY INDUSTRY PLAYER FOR 2010

Doosan had by then successfully completed its restructuring program. Whereas consumer products had once represented more than 75 percent of the group's revenues, this sector had shrunk to below 25 percent.

Doosan continued to build its heavy-industry operations through the end of the first decade of the 2000s as it positioned itself among the global leaders.

In 2007, for example, the company acquired three small construction-equipment business units from Ingersoll-Rand in the United States. With these new units, which operated in the Bobcat, Attachment, and Utility Equipment segments, Doosan became the world's seventh-largest producer of industrial machinery. Other acquisitions included Collier Technologies, Inc., also in the United States, and China's Yantai Machinery Ltd., which specialized in the production of wheel loaders. The following year, Doosan acquired South Korea's Dong Myung Mottrol, the country's leading producer of hydraulic machinery.

Doosan had also begun preparations for the large-scale expansion of its production capacity. In 2007 the group launched construction of a major new $300 million manufacturing base in Vietnam. The site, located in the Dung Quat Economic Zone in Quang Ngai, launched production in May 2009. By then Doosan had completed a remarkable transformation from a small grocery shop opened in 1896 to a global heavy-industries and power-plant leader in the 21st century.

M. L. Cohen

PRINCIPAL SUBSIDIARIES

Ceylon Heavy Industries & Construction Co., Ltd.; Doosan Babcock Energy Ltd. (UK); Doosan Babcock Engineering & Services India Pvt. Ltd.; Doosan Bears Inc.; Doosan Capital Co., Ltd.; Doosan Corporation; Doosan Corporation–Fashion; Doosan Corporation–Glonet; Doosan Corporation–Electro-Materials; Doosan Corporation–Information & Communication; Doosan Cuvex Co., Ltd.; Doosan Donga; Doosan Engine Co., Ltd.; Doosan Engineering & Construction Co., Ltd.; Doosan Engineering & Services LLC (USA); Doosan Feed & Livestock Corporation; Doosan Heavy Industries & Construction Co., Ltd.; Doosan Heavy Industries America Corp.; Doosan Heavy Industries Vietnam Co., Ltd.; Doosan HF Controls Corp. (USA); Doosan Hydro Technology, Inc. (USA); Doosan IMGB (Romania); Doosan Infracore Co., Ltd.; Doosan Mecatec Co., Ltd.; Doosan Tower Corporation; Doosan Heavy Industries Japan Corp.; Hanjung Power Ltd.; Han-Viet Heavy Industry & Construction Corp.; Neoplux Co., Ltd.; Oricom Inc.; Samhwa Crown & Closure Co., Ltd.; SRS Korea Co., Ltd.

PRINCIPAL DIVISIONS

Castings & Forgings; Construction; Nuclear Power Plants; Power Plants; Water Plants.

PRINCIPAL COMPETITORS

Samsung Heavy Industries Company Ltd.; GS Engineering and Construction Corp.; Hyundai Engineering & Construction Company Ltd.; Daelim Industrial Company Ltd.; POSCO Engineering and Construction Company Ltd.; SK Engineering and Construction Ltd.; Hanjin Heavy Industries and Construction Company Ltd.; Hyundai Development Company–Engineering and Construction.

FURTHER READING

"Daewoo Becomes Doosan but It's Business as Usual," *Plant Manager's Journal*, June 2005, p. 5.

"Doosan Acquires Three Daewoo Divisions," *Tooling & Production*, July 2005, p. 7.

"Doosan Buys Mitsui Babcock for $169m," *Power Engineering International*, December 2006, p. 15.

"Doosan Heavy Expects Sales to Gain 22 Pct This Year," Yonhap News Agency of Korea, February 14, 2009.

"Doosan Heavy Inks Strategic Deal with U.S. Firm," Yonhap News Agency of Korea, September 9, 2008.

"Doosan Heavy Wins 70 Bln Won Power Equipment Order," Thai Press Reports, July 9, 2009.

"Doosan Heavy Wins 200-Bln-Won Deal from U.S. Firm," *Times of Central Asia*, July 25, 2008.

"Doosan Vina Wins Multimillion Dollar Contract," Vietnamese News Agency, July 9, 2009.

"Doosan Wins Order for Eco-Friendly Facilities for Yeosu Thermal Plant," *Power Engineering International*, March 2009, p. 10.

"A Footprint in the US," *US Business Review*, December 2006, p. 90.

Kang Won, "Reinventing Doosan," *SeriQuarterly*, July 2008.

The Durst Organization Inc.

1155 Avenue of the Americas
New York, New York 10036
U.S.A.
Telephone: (212) 789-1155
Fax: (212) 789-1198
Web site: http://www.durst.org

Private Company
Incorporated: 1927
Employees: 750
NAICS: 233110 Land Subdivision and Land Development; 531390 Other Activities Related to Real Estate; 431311 Residential Property Managers; 531312 Nonresidential Property Managers; 531120 Lessor of Nonresidential Buildings

■ ■ ■

The Durst Organization Inc. is one of the leading developers, owners, and managers of midtown Manhattan, New York, commercial real estate projects. On the westside, Durst controls five office towers, including the company's flagship property, 4 Times Square, which in 1999 set the standard for environmentally responsible buildings. Durst also controls four eastside office towers. To a lesser degree, Durst is involved in residential real estate, its portfolio including the 38-floor Helena, overlooking the Hudson River at 57th Street near Lincoln Center, and the 58-story Epic, at 31st Street and Sixth Avenue (also known as Avenue of the Americas). All told, the company controls more than eight million square feet of commercial space. In addi-

tion, Durst offers apartments from a slate of midtown brownstones and small apartment buildings. Durst also leases retail space in its office towers, The Helena, and a few of its smaller properties. The company is run by the third generation of the Durst family.

FOUNDER COMES TO THE UNITED STATES: 1902

The history of The Durst Organization, like many companies, is at heart an immigrant's tale. The founder, Joseph Durst, was born in Austria and came to the United States around the age of 20 in 1902 with $3 sewn in the lapel of his jacket. He became a dry goods store clerk, worked his way up to salesman, and in 1913 became a partner in a dress manufacturing company, Durst & Rubin. Two years later he bought a 34th Street office building and his focus turned to the buying and selling, and eventually construction, of Manhattan properties. He became a vice president and treasurer of the Capital National Bank, which he helped to found in 1922, and became a prominent figure in midtown real estate. Durst was known for not building anywhere he could not walk to. He later sold Capital National to Manufacturers Hanover Trust.

One of Durst's most prominent projects in the 1920s was the 1926 $7 million acquisition of the Temple Emanu-El site at Fifth Avenue and 43rd Street. He leased adjoining land and in 1927 erected a 33-story bank and office building. In that same year, The Durst Organization was created. During the Great Depression of the 1930s Durst bought mortgages and leases on eastside commercial buildings, always taking a long view of the New York real estate market. In addition to office buildings, Durst was involved in apartment buildings, but in the 1940s when rent control was introduced he quickly exited the sector. While other real estate families abandoned midtown altogether, choosing to turn their attention to downtown or the suburbs, Joseph Durst remained committed to that part of Manhattan Island he could walk to. Three of Durst's four sons became involved in the business. Seymour B. Durst, who eventually replaced his father, joined the company in 1940. His brothers Royal and David also became part of the organization.

THIRD AVENUE BUILDING BOOM BEGINS: 1957

The Durst Organization was adept at keeping its thumb on the pulse of the midtown real estate market. Developers believed that the market for office towers in the Grand Central area extended no farther east than Fifth Avenue. When the Third Avenue El was demolished in the 1950s, the Dursts recognized that the removal of the train tracks opened up the area for office towers. Joseph Durst acquired a number of parcels of land, many of which were dilapidated, and was so fervent in his belief that the area was on the verge of a building boom that in 1957 he divested some of his other Manhattan properties to support his Third Avenue projects, selling a pair of large department store buildings at prime locations: 57th Street at Fifth Avenue and 34th Avenue between Fifth and Sixth avenues. In the late 1950s and early 1960s, The Durst Organization completed several eastside projects, including 205 East 42nd Street, 200 East 42nd Street, 201 East 42nd Street, 733 Third Avenue, and 805 Third Avenue. Another tower was constructed at 757 Third Avenue, but it was on leased land, and in order to avoid any potential problems in the future, the company sold the building.

While his father was busy on the eastside, Seymour Durst was laying the groundwork for future development on the westside of midtown Manhattan, the family again bucking the conventional wisdom of developers

who believed that corporations would never consider establishing their headquarters west of Fifth Avenue. In the mid-1960s Seymour Durst began acquiring property and over the next 10 years The Durst Organization either owned or held options on some 10 acres of land, mostly situated between Sixth and Seventh avenues between 42nd Street and 47th Street. Hardly an attractive stretch of real estate at the time, it was the home to peep shows, pornographers, and massage parlors. In the early 1970s during the administration of New York City Mayor Abraham Beame, the Dursts were accused of coddling pornographers that occupied some of the properties they acquired. Angered that the city was not providing much help in their efforts to evict seedy tenants, the Dursts sold one of the buildings to a notorious massage parlor mistress, thus making her the city's problem. In the end she defaulted on the mortgage and the Dursts were able to take back the property minus the nettlesome tenant. The building was eventually demolished to create part of the site of the United States Trust Company of New York building that was constructed at 114 West 47th Street.

WESTSIDE BUILDING OPENS: 1969

The vision of Seymour Durst for these westside properties in the late 1960s was a 10-tower mixed-use complex that would rival Rockefeller Center. In 1969 an office tower was completed at 1133 Avenue of the Americas between 43rd and 44th Streets. Because the office market began to deteriorate, it would be the last major building The Durst Organization constructed for 15 years. Seymour Durst was forced to give up on his dream. Some of the parcels were used to build small stores, "taxpayers" as he called them, essentially place markers until the office market improved. In 1973 he allowed mortgage holders to foreclose on about a dozen of the westside properties. While that five-block portion of midtown would never become available again in a complete assemblage for development, The Durst Organization retained many of the parcels and did not lose interest in the area.

Joseph Durst remained very much involved in the company he founded until just months before his death at the age of 92 in early 1974. The 61-year-old Seymour Durst succeeded him as president of the firm, while brothers David and Roy remained partners. Seymour Durst had already made his mark and would continue to do so in the years to come. He became responsible for one of the most recognizable features of midtown Manhattan, the "national debt clock" that was erected on one of his taxpayers near 43rd Street on Sixth Avenue. Escalating at a dizzying pace, the electronic

```
┌─────────────────────────────────────────────────────┐
│                                                       │
│               KEY DATES                               │
│               ─────────■─────────                     │
│                                                       │
│   1902: Joseph Durst immigrates to the United States. │
│   1915: Durst acquires first office building.         │
│   1927: Durst Organization is formed.                 │
│   1940: Seymour Durst joins company.                  │
│   1957: Third Avenue development begins.              │
│   1974: Joseph Durst dies.                            │
│   1995: Seymour Durst dies.                           │
│   1999: 4 Times Square opens.                         │
│   2008: Bank of America Tower opens.                  │
│                                                       │
└─────────────────────────────────────────────────────┘
```

digital counter estimated the share of the national debt for each household in the country. He wrote articles and letters to the editor decrying government interference in the real estate market, and also assembled a massive collection of New York City historical materials, including books, maps, and signs that took up much of a five-story brownstone he owned.

DELAY OF TIMES SQUARE DEVELOPMENT

Although the recovery of the local and national economy was far from certain in 1980, The Durst Organization and other developers decided the time had come to renew efforts to develop the stretch of Sixth Avenue south of Rockefeller Center. A year later the city and state announced a plan to revitalize the theater district, which had become squalid and a local if not national embarrassment. In the 1970s Seymour Durst had advocated the building of casino hotels to revitalize Times Square. The government instead created a 13-acre redevelopment district and offered generous tax incentives to developers. The four corners at 42nd and Broadway were the crown jewels of the district and were awarded to a partnership between Prudential Insurance Co. of America and a Manhattan developer, George Klein. The Dursts were among the losers in the sweepstakes and angered that the tax incentives received by their rivals put them and their site at 42nd Street and Sixth Avenue at an unfair disadvantage. The Dursts and other opponents of the redevelopment scheme rallied together to delay the projects, altogether filing nearly 50 lawsuits. Tough economic conditions in the early 1990s were the final stroke that killed the projects. In the meantime, The Durst Organization completed an office tower in the late 1980s at 114 West 47th Street for United States Trust Company.

The Durst Organization considered doing business outside of Manhattan in the early 1990s when a contact

steered them to Portland, Oregon, where 40 blocks of the downtown area, the "Lloyd District," were put up for sale by PacifiCorp. With Jonathan Durst taking the lead, The Durst Organization developed an interest in Portland, one of the few U.S. markets that was not declining. Moreover, the large amount of available property that could be developed over time was in keeping with the family's experience in Manhattan. A sales agreement was reached in 1992, but a year later The Durst Organization took PacifiCorp to court, alleging that the seller had misrepresented the condition of three major office buildings that were part of the deal. Hence, the Dursts asked that $7 million be subtracted from the purchase price to pay for necessary repairs. In May 1994 the Dursts' complaint was dismissed by the court, which maintained that the two parties had never reached an enforceable sales contract. Following a Durst appeal, the two sides reached a settlement out of court, and the Dursts no longer pursued projects in Portland.

Well into his 70s, Seymour Durst was in semi-retirement by the early 1990s. Although he retained the title of president, the company was run by members of the next generation, his two sons, Robert and Douglas, and David Durst's two sons, Jonathan and Joshua. In May 1995, Seymour Durst suffered a stroke, did not regain consciousness, and died at New York Hospital about two weeks later.

4 TIMES SQUARE OPENS: 1999

Around the time of his father's death, Douglas Durst decided to build a skyscraper in Times Square on state-owned property at 42nd Street and Broadway, a surprising development given his family's 15-year crusade to block others from building on the site. As a result, the Dursts had created untold enemies who were more than willing to block the efforts of the Dursts in Times Square. Despite the obstacles, Douglas Durst succeeded in gaining the property and securing Condé Nast and Skadden Arps as anchor tenants. The result was the 4 Times Square building that opened in 1999, a project that spurred a redevelopment boom that spread as far north as 59th Street, west to Eighth Avenue where the Port Authority Bus Terminal was located, and south to the garment district, long known for prostitution but now billed by real estate brokers as Times Square South. Moreover, 4 Times Square led the effort to develop "green" projects. The tower was a testament to the latest in environmentally responsible buildings. Not only did construction make use of recycled and recyclable materials, 4 Times Square included an energy-efficient gas-fired, digitally monitored heating and air conditioning system; high-performance windows that retained inside air temperature while letting in light; and fresh air circulation that was four times the code requirement. After the building opened, The Durst Organization continued to upgrade the operation and encouraged tenants to take the environment into account in their activities. The Durst Organization also applied the environmental lessons learned with 4 Times Square to future projects, such as the Bank of America Tower that opened in 2008.

In addition to office towers, Durst looked to develop residential projects in the new century. The Helena apartment building with 600 rental units was completed in 2005, followed two years later by The Epic and its 458 rental units. The company also controlled a portfolio of midtown apartments in an assortment of smaller buildings and brownstones. In addition, The Durst Organization looked to become involved in the construction of nearly 1,000 high-end homes in Pine Plains, in Dutchess County, New York. There were also changes taking place in the top ranks of the organization. In 2009 Jonathan Durst, co-president of the company with his cousin Douglas, announced his intention to resign his position after a transition period that was expected to last until the spring of 2010. Fourth-generation members of the Durst family were already in place at the company, making it likely that The Durst Organization would remain a major Manhattan developer for years to come.

Ed Dinger

PRINCIPAL DIVISIONS
Commercial; Residential.

PRINCIPAL COMPETITORS
Macklowe Properties, Inc.; Tishman Reality & Construction Co., Inc.; The Trump Organization.

FURTHER READING

"Builder Planning Third Ave. Deals," *New York Times,* February 11, 1957.

Colby, Richard, "New York Property Firm Hopes to Expand to Portland," *Oregonian,* March 14, 1993, p. E1.

Croghan, Lore, "Douglas Durst Productions Give Times Square a New Beginning," *Crain's New York Business,* May 15, 2000, p. 26.

Deutsch, Claudia H., "A Savvy Developer Who Marches to His Own Beat," *New York Times,* November 12, 1995, p. 9.

Dunlap, David W., "Holdouts; For Durst, It's Now a Tower Instead of Taxpayers," *New York Times,* February 18, 1990, p. A16.

Horsley, Carter B., "On Ave. of Americas the Lull Is Ending," *New York Times,* May 4, 1980, p. R1.

"Joseph Durst, 92, Real Estate Man," *New York Times,* January 2, 1974, p. 43.

Marino, Vivian, "Jonathan Durst," *New York Times,* September 13, 2009, p. 9.

Oser, Alan S., "The Champion of Midtown Laissez-Faire," *New York Times,* August 30, 1992, p. A3.

———, "Seymour B. Durst, Real-Estate Developer Who Led Growth on West Side, Dies at 81," *New York Times,* May 20, 1995.

"Third Ave. Boom Seen by Builder," *New York Times,* July 30, 1957.

Enel S.p.A.

—■—

Viale Regina Margherita 137
Rome, I-00198
Italy
Telephone: (+39 06) 8305 1
Fax: (+39 06) 8305 3771
Web site: http://www.enel.it

Public Private Company
Incorporated: 1962 as Ente Nazionale per L'energia
   Elettrica
Employees: 83,700
Sales: EUR 61.2 billion ($86.5 billion) (2008)
Stock Exchanges: Borsa Italiana New York
Ticker Symbols: ENEL EN
NAICS: 221122 Electric Power Distribution

■ ■ ■

Enel S.p.A. is one of Europe's leading energy companies, overseeing a combined generation capacity of more than 95,400 megawatts (MW) based on fossil fuels and renewable energy sources. In 2009, the company also launched construction of the first of 10 nuclear power facilities. Enel, the former Ente Nazionale per L'energia Elettrica, has successfully negotiated the loss of its status as Italy's state-owned energy monopoly by refocusing itself as a multinational power player. In 2009, the company's operations reached 23 countries, and a total customer base of 60.5 million. The company's major international holdings include more than 92 percent of Spanish power giant Endesa; a 55.8 percent stake in OGK-5 (the shortened form of JCS

Fifth Generation Company of the Wholesale Electricity Market) in Russia; and control of Enel Green Power, the world's leading operator of renewable energy-based power plants with a total capacity of 4,500 MW.

The company's holdings include power plants in the United States, Argentina, Brazil, Chile, Colombia, Peru, and elsewhere in Central and South America; and in France, Bulgaria, Slovakia, and Romania. Together, Enel's operations combined to generate revenues of EUR 61.2 billion ($86.5 billion) in 2008. The company is listed on the Borsa Italiana and the New York Stock Exchange. The Italian government continues to hold more than 31 percent of the group's stock. Fulvio Conti is the company's CEO.

BACKGROUND TO ITALY'S ENERGY MONOPOLY

ENEL (Enel) was established on December 6, 1962, by a special nationalization law after a long and complex debate. With a few exceptions, the law defined Enel's task as the implementation of "all activities of production, import and export, transmission, transformation, distribution and sale of electricity from whatever source, on national territory." The exceptions included production and distribution of electricity by local authorities ("municipalities"), by smaller companies with annual production of less than 15 megawatt hours, and by industrial self-producers (subject to authorization).

In addition to the production, transport, and distribution of electricity, Enel performed a number of complementary activities: it operated as an electricity "bank" for the whole country, buying electricity from all

COMPANY PERSPECTIVES

Our mission is to create and distribute value in the international energy market, to the benefit of our customers' needs, our shareholders' investment, the competitiveness of the countries in which we operate and the expectations of all those who work with us. We serve the community, respecting the environment and the safety of individuals, with a commitment to creating a better world for future generations.

producers in the country and reallocating it to its customers; it attended to all stages of plant engineering and construction; it carried out research and development on electricity and related fields; it undertook consulting activity and technical assistance for foreign electric power companies and Italian companies operating abroad; and it pursued exploration and development of geothermic sources.

POST–WORLD WAR II DEBATES

After World War II the debate on energy issues in Italy was essentially limited to the desirable nature, private or public, of firms that might operate in this area. At the time, electricity was generated by a large number of private companies, a few municipal plants, and a few generating companies controlled by IRI (Instituto per la Ricostruzione Industriale), a public holding company founded in 1933 to save the substantial portion of Italy's industry that was involved in a major banking collapse.

The combined output of the public sector (IRI's public utilities, municipal plants, and the railways) accounted for about 30 percent of Italy's total electricity supply. In the Constitutional debate, the parties of the political left were in favor of the complete nationalization of the electricity industry, but these demands were blunted by a compromise: while the Constitution retained the principle of nationalizing entire sectors ("when related to essential public services, or energy sources, or situations of monopoly"), any implementation in the electricity industry was deferred.

The government formally regulated electricity rates, but the influence of the private sector utilities was strong: they subsidized political parties and newspapers in order to influence political decisions and public opinion, and the rates they charged their largest industrial customers were not fully revealed so that the

administrative bodies charged with the determination of rates lacked much of the information necessary to perform the function.

THE PUSH FOR NATIONALIZATION IN THE FIFTIES

Many felt that full nationalization was the only possible solution, as the decentralization of decision making was an obstacle to the integration of thermoelectric and hydroelectric power production as well as to the construction of the national power grid. Lobbying was strong, however, in favor of maintaining the status quo, and the anti-nationalization lobby also advocated the privatization of Agip, the national hydrocarbons corporation that was perceived as a remnant of the Benito Mussolini years. While the privatization of Agip was averted by the initiative and determination of Enrico Mattei, who strongly believed in the importance of an autonomous Italian presence in the world oil and gas scene, the utilities succeeded in stalling any nationalization plans for a considerable time.

The vested interests against nationalization were so strong that until 1962 no reform plan was brought to Parliament for discussion. In the meantime, in the absence of any explicit commitment toward a national energy policy from the government, a leading role was assumed by Ente Nazionale Idrocarburi (ENI), the national hydrocarbon corporation created in 1953 under the forceful management of Enrico Mattei. Not surprisingly, most of Italy's industry and its political referents were hostile to ENI, whose dynamism and ambitions served to highlight the stagnation of the electricity industry.

In the 1950s three main factors contributed to the acceleration of the drive toward nationalization: the development of nuclear technology in the production of electricity, which called for a substantial public intervention because of the massive investments involved; the long lead times (time necessary for project design, planning, and implementation) needed before reaching commercial generation; and the economic boom of the 1950s, which emphasized the risks and limits of thriving economic growth when not adequately supported by the necessary infrastructure.

The issue of a national energy policy was put back onto the agenda, and three main bodies of opinion formed: a defensive position, championed by the private electricity companies, supporters of the status quo; the concentration in ENI of all activities related to the production of energy, including electricity from all sources; and the creation of a separate national electricity board.

KEY DATES

1962: Italian government nationalizes the country's electrical power industry, forming ENEL (Ente Nazionale per L'energia Elettrica).

1992: ENEL is reincorporated as a joint-stock company wholly owned by the government, and becomes Enel S.p.A.

1999: Enel is privatized, with a listing on the Borsa Italiana and the New York Stock Exchange.

2000: Enel enters the United States, buying CHI Energy Inc., a specialist in renewable energy power generation.

2007: Enel enters Russia, acquiring majority control of OGK-5.

2008: Enel acquires Spain's electricity sector leader, Endesa.

2009: Enel begins construction of the first of 10 nuclear power plants in Italy.

The third lobby prevailed, and this was probably the most important and long-lasting achievement of the first center-left government in Italy's republican history. The Parliamentary debate was intense, but the decision was reached comparatively quickly, as the powerful avant-garde of Italy's industry had come to the conclusion that defending the status quo in electricity was no longer a primary concern.

CREATING A STATE MONOPOLY IN 1962

As for the choice of the legal status of the new body, the possible options included an IRI-type formula (a holding company of which the majority of shares would be held by the State); an ENI-type formula (a state-owned holding company with its own equity, which would carry out its statutory tasks via the creation of companies fully or partially controlled by the state); a full integration of the electricity sector in the public sector; or an autonomous public body that would finance itself by issuing bonds but could not create affiliated companies or hold shares in any other company.

The latter option prevailed, and 1,189 electricity companies of different sizes and with different structures were merged into a unified and integrated body for the production, transmission, and distribution of electricity throughout Italy. It was an operation of unprecedented complexity compared with electricity nationalizations in France (1946) and Britain (1947). In 1963, 73 companies were consolidated, representing about 85 percent of the total assets being nationalized. The companies consolidated in Enel rose to 221 at the end of 1964, representing around 92 percent of the industry's asset value, and to 905 at the end of 1966. This year marked the de facto completion of the nationalization process, as the 284 companies transferred to Enel in the following years were of relatively minor importance.

The nationalization law decreed that Enel's original assets were to be obtained through the transfer of assets from the former generating companies. Unlike ENI, Enel was not endowed by the state with any initial capital, and the nationalization law established that funds for the compensation of shareholders and for future investments were to be raised by issues of special Enel bonds guaranteed by the state, within the limits set on a case-by-case basis by an interministerial committee.

These conditions had the effect of imposing a heavy financial burden on Enel, given that Enel had to finance itself by external borrowing and bond issues. For several years the debt incurred for compensations to ex-producers severely affected Enel's balance sheet. Another burden for the newly created body was that nationalization, while creating some efficiency gains in transport and distribution, also generated pressure for an increased workforce and higher levels of wages and salaries. The total number of Enel's employees grew from nearly 68,000 in 1963 to an all-time high of nearly 118,000 in 1981.

RESTRUCTURING IN THE SIXTIES

On the technical front, the crucial challenge for the electricity industry was to undertake the transition from a structure predominantly based on hydroelectric generation to a system that was better equipped to meet the needs of fast industrial growth. In 1960 hydroelectric power was still the predominant source (about 75 percent of the total) while electricity from petroleum products (fuel oil), natural gas, and solid fuels represented 15 percent, 3 percent, and 7 percent, respectively.

This structure was bound to change rapidly. In order to meet the demand for electricity, Enel started a massive investment program focused on the construction of new thermoelectric plants. At the end of the 1960s thermoelectric production had come to represent 60 percent of the total, thus becoming the axis of the whole system. Within this share, electricity from fuel oil represented 80 percent. The policy of diversification of sources also embraced nuclear power generation, and three nuclear plants were built.

However, Enel's overall efficiency and productivity of labor in its first decade of activity was very low, largely because of two factors: the difficulties inherent in the nationalization process itself and the constraints imposed on personnel management by politicians and unions. As for the former, Enel had incorporated a large number of heterogeneous plants not adequately interconnected, and the rationalization and restructuring of plants and grids required massive investments in the first few years.

As for the latter, it was soon clear that for political reasons the creation of Enel was not to be allowed to result in any redundancies, and this led to a rapid expansion of the workforce. In short, in the first decade of nationalization, the dramatic expansion in the workforce and the rise in labor costs counterbalanced the advantages of nationalization in terms of scale and grid economies. Furthermore, for many years Enel had to suffer the consequences of a political ceiling imposed by government on the rates it could set and other allowances in favor of household users, which created distortions in the patterns of consumption and investment.

RESPONDING TO CRISIS IN THE SEVENTIES

The first oil crisis of 1973 transformed the underlying premise of Italy's electricity industry, an abundant availability of low-cost imported oil. At the time Italy was in a position of strong dependency on hydrocarbons for electricity generation, which made the need for a change of direction in national energy policy even more pressing. The approach chosen, in the Italian tradition, was to widen the scope of central planning in defining broad aims and policy lines, thus imposing a further layer of bureaucracy on the existing powers of guidance of the national energy boards (ENI and Enel). Furthermore, since the time involved in the preparation and discussion of these programs tended to be very long, it often happened that by the time definitive approval was given many of the key elements of the picture had become obsolete.

The 1975 and 1977 National Energy Plans (PENs) recommended a major shift toward coal and nuclear power stations, together with fuller exploitation of domestic energy sources, increased imports of natural gas, and the encouragement of energy conservation. In the Italian institutional system the planning stage was only the initial phase of a complex procedure to be completed before reaching the implementation stage. Very soon obstacles were put in the way of the implementation of these programs and the construction of planned capacity.

The debate over the future of energy policy became more intense in the wake of the second oil shock of 1979, which had grave consequences for domestic inflation rates. However, the seriousness of the situation did not stimulate a more decisive approach, and the 1981 and 1986 PENs essentially reiterated most of the previous documents' recommendations. The commitment to the nuclear sector remained, together with major emphases on coal, increased imports of natural gas, and the development of domestic sources of gas.

RATE INCREASES IN THE EIGHTIES

During the period from 1980 to 1987, the consumption of thermoelectric power stations increased to 33.3 Mtoe, of which 19.3 Mtoe was oil products. The only concession to diversification was the start-up of the Caorso nuclear station and the conversion of some power stations from fuel oil to coal. On the demand side, the transition from a model of economic development based on heavy industry (highly energy-intensive) to a lower energy intensity manufacturing industry caused a decline in industrial energy demand from 41.5 Mtoe in 1974 to 31.5 Mtoe in 1985. This was more than offset by an increase of electricity consumption in the household and service sectors.

On the whole, there was no doubt that Enel's efficiency had been heavily constrained by bureaucratic delays and the failure of government and parliament to devise and implement a workable energy policy. The major problem for Enel lay in the bureaucratic procedures for the authorization of new plants. Attempts were made to simplify and speed up procedures, but in essence the government lacked the power to authorize the construction of a plant against the wishes of local authorities.

Enel was also heavily dependent on the political authorities for investment financing, both because electricity rates were imposed for all users and because any recourse to external borrowing by Enel was subject to government authorization. The control of electricity rates was a sensitive political issue, as they had been used as an instrument for attaining more general policy objectives, such as the battle against inflation and the subsidization of particular consumer groups or areas.

This contributed to Enel's serious financial difficulties in the first part of the 1980s, when soaring production costs added to the burden of interest repayments. These difficulties were eased in the second part of the decade after a substantial increase in rates and an injection of funds from the government. Between 1986 and 1990 the ratio of overall financial charges on Enel's total assets declined from 65.4 percent to 58.6 percent.

Another substantial rate increase was granted in December 1990 after some years of steady or declining electricity prices. In the 1980s Enel also began an overdue rationalization of its workforce. The total number of employees declined to 112,000 in 1988. At the same time, electricity sales increased substantially. In 1990, 4.7 times as many kilowatt-hours (kWh) were sold as in 1963, with an associated growth of productivity measured in terms of sales of electricity per employee.

NUCLEAR BAN IN 1987

Enel faced new difficulties in the 1990s, including a ban on nuclear power generation and the growing hostility, for environmental reasons, toward thermoelectric plants, with the exception of natural gas. The consolidated features of Italy's energy policy were put into serious question by the Chernobyl accident in the Soviet Union in April 1986. The ensuing debate culminated in a National Energy Conference in February 1987. However, the fundamental problem of Italy's energy policy (the wealth of programs contrasted with the lack of implementation and choice) was not solved as the conference could not provide a definitive answer to the question of how to reconcile economic viability, environmental concerns, and safety.

Along with other factors, the failure of the political parties in the government coalition to reach agreement on these issues led in April 1987 to the fall of the government that had convened the conference and to an early general election. A referendum was held in November 1987 that revealed strong public hostility toward nuclear power. This referendum effectively marked the end of nuclear electricity in Italy, and Enel was forced at a huge overall cost to interrupt the operation of all existing plants and to convert plants under construction to coal-fired or oil-fired power stations. The major effect of this development was a dramatic rise in Italy's net electricity imports, which reached almost 35 billion kWh in 1990, equivalent to nearly 15 percent of all electricity consumed.

While the domestic supply/demand ratio improved between 1980 and 1985, in the second part of the decade the situation deteriorated considerably. Despite sustained demand growth and the closure of the existing nuclear plants, with capacity totaling approximately 1,300 MW, only a modest increase in capacity had been possible in hydroelectric, geothermic, and thermoelectric plants.

TOWARD PRIVATIZATION AND DEREGULATION IN THE EARLY NINETIES

The growth of electricity imports was responsible for a fall in productivity through the end of the decade. Enel's strategy in the early 1990s was to sign more long-term supply contracts with different suppliers: in addition to traditional imports from France, Switzerland, and Germany, Enel import contracts were being negotiated with Tunisia and the former Soviet Union. In short, despite having achieved many of the objectives it had originally set, Enel had not quite succeeded in fully providing for Italy's electricity requirements.

The movement toward the reform of Enel began when the Italian government set up a commission in 1984 tasked with developing proposals both for restructuring Enel's organization and its ownership. That commission concluded, however, to maintain Enel's position as a state-owned monopoly.

A new commission appointed by the Ministry of Industry in 1990 came to a different conclusion, in the face of the impending unification of the European market in 1992. In 1991, the Italian government enacted a new law that began the process of liberalizing the energy generation sector in Italy. The new law also encouraged the development of renewable energy sources, by permitting these energy producers to sell power directly to end-customers. Under the new legislation, Enel itself began setting up a series of dedicated power generation subsidiaries, including Elettrogen, Eurogen, and Interpower, separate from its power transmission operations.

This legislation became a first step toward Enel's privatization. In the summer of 1992, the Italian government passed a new law transforming the company into Enel S.p.A., a joint-stock company wholly owned by the Italian government. By 1995, the Italian government had formulated a new series of rules for the liberalization of the Italian energy sector. At that time the government established a new regulatory authority separate from Enel. Enel also received compensation for the costs of decommissioning the country's nuclear power facilities.

In their place, Enel launched a major investment into renewable energy sources. In 1994 and 1995 the company built several new plants, including a solar power plant in Serre Persano, Salerno, which at the time became the largest solar power facility in the world, generating 3 MW. The company also added an air-generation facility in AltaNurra, Sassari, and a wind farm in Collarmele, in Aquila. These and other projects helped Enel become the world's leading producer of renewable energy into the beginning of the next century.

PRIVATIZATION AND DIVERSIFICATION FROM THE MID-NINETIES

By the end of 1995, Enel had signed an agreement with the Ministry of Industry granting Enel the operating concession for Italy's electrical sector for a 40-year period (starting in 1992). This agreement helped pave the way toward the final deregulation of the Italian electricity market and the privatization of Enel through the "Bersani Decree" enacted in 1999.

As part of this new legislation, Enel split off its power grid and transmission operations into a separate company, Terna, which was placed under the management control of a new entity called Gestore della Rete di Trasmissione. Enel remained Terna's sole shareholder, until its public offering in 2004, at which time an additional 30 percent of Terna was transferred to the Italian government's Cassa Depositi e Prestiti.

Another consequence of the privatization of Enel involved the requirement that the company shed at least 15,000 MW of power generation capacity. To accomplish this, Enel began preparing the sale of three of its power generation companies, Elettrogen, Eurogen, and Interpower. The company launched the sale of the first of these, Elettrogen, in 2000. By 2003, all three had been sold, raising EUR 5.5 billion for Enel's expansion elsewhere.

Enel's privatization became fact in November 1999 when the company placed 3.9 billion shares, worth 31.74 percent of the company, on the Borsa Italiana and New York Stock Exchange, raising a total of EUR 16.55 billion ($15 billion). The offering became Europe's largest ever at the time, and, by attracting millions of individual investors, the world's second-largest in terms of number of subscribers.

By the time of its privatization, Enel had launched its first expansion effort. Under a new management team headed by Franco Tato since 1996, the company had completed a series of restructuring efforts. Among these, the group trimmed more than 9,000 jobs, an act once unheard of for the former state monopoly. Many of these cuts came from the group's broad managerial base, as Tato flattened the company's organization. Further cuts through the end of the decade ultimately reduced the company's payroll to just 73,000, from 96,000 at mid-decade.

REFOCUSED ON ENERGY

Formerly operated as a single company, Enel restructured into three operational companies focused on production, transmission, and distribution, as well as six service companies. Tato also pushed through a modernization of the company's aging power generation facilities, as the company sought to reduce its power rates, among the highest in Europe, ahead of the coming deregulation of the European energy sector.

Enel's strengthening bottom line encouraged Tato to lead the company on a diversification drive into the late 1990s. By the end of the decade, Enel had become, as the *Economist* put it: "saddled with a hodgepodge of assets." Among the group's investments at the time were an entry into the real estate market, and a series of investments in water and waste treatment services. Among the group's most high-profile diversification moves was its attempt to enter the telecommunications sector, with the founding of Wind, a mobile telephone services provider in partnership with France Telecom, in 1997. Wind struggled to find its place in the Italian market, particularly after the expensive acquisition of Infostrada, a fixed-line operator owned by Vodafone. By the beginning of the 2000s, Wind remained in third place in Italy's mobile telephone market, and was losing money.

The difficulties at Wind, the slow progress made in the liberalization of the Italian energy market, and Enel's poor performance on the stock market resulted in Tato's ouster in 2002. In his place, the company named Paolo Scaroni, a former McKinsey consultant who had completed the turnaround of struggling British glass manufacturer Pilkington. Scaroni immediately announced a reversal of Enel's diversification strategy, including plans to sell off Wind as early as possible. Instead, the company announced its intention to refocus around its core energy business.

GOING GLOBAL IN THE 21ST CENTURY

However, following the sell-off of generation assets required by the Bersani Decree, Enel's market share in Italy had dwindled to just 50 percent. The company had also been forced to sell off parts of its distribution wing, notably for the Milan, Rome, and Turin markets. At the same time, the company's power generation infrastructure continued to lag behind its European counterparts, which had invested heavily in new technologies, such as combine cycle gas turbine plants. In 2003, the company launched a new investment drive in order to modernize its existing power plants.

At the same time, Enel began looking overseas for growth. The company had entered the United States, buying CHI Energy Inc. for $312 million in 2000. That company, a renewable energy specialist based in Stamford, Connecticut, had expanded its operations to

16 states by 2003. By then, Enel had also made its first investment in Spain, paying nearly $3 billion to acquire that country's fourth-largest electricity company, Viesgo.

The company entered Bulgaria in 2003, buying the 602 MW Maritz East III power plant. By 2005, the company had acquired a 66 percent share of Slovenske Elektrame, Slovakia's top electricity producer, adding more than 5,700 MW of capacity. In that year, Enel also bought 51 percent of Electrica Banat and Electrica Distriubtie Dobrogea, two power distribution companies. Enel later reinforced its Romanian operations with the acquisition of the Bucharest region's Electrica Muntenia Sud in 2006.

In 2007 Enel, led by Fulvio Conti, became the first foreign company to take a chance on the breakup of the former Russian state-owned electricity monopoly. In June of that year, Enel beat out rivals E.On and Endesa to acquire 25 percent of JCS Fifth Generation Company of the Wholesale Electricity Market, or OGK-5. Enel later raised its share in that company, which operated four power generation plants for a total capacity of 8,200 MW, to 55.8 percent. Also in Russia, the company acquired a 49 percent share in Rusenergysbyt, the leading independent electricity distributor in the country.

NUCLEAR POWERED FOR THE FUTURE

These deals provided the groundwork for the company's largest acquisition to date. In 2008, Enel beat out E.On for control of Spain's energy giant, Endesa. Enel initially acquired 67 percent of Endesa in a partnership with Spain's Acciona, in part to overcome the Spanish government's resistance to allowing a foreign company to acquire control over its electricity sector. As part of the deal, Endesa granted Acciona voting control over Endesa. Ultimately, however, the arrangement failed to work, and in February 2009, Enel bought out Acciona's 25 percent stake in Endesa for EUR 11 billion ($14 billion). The Endesa acquisition also gave the company operations in a number of Latin American markets.

In 2008, Enel regrouped its renewable energy operations into a new internationally operating company, Enel Green Power. That company then became the world's leading renewable energy company with more than 4,500 MW of generating capacity. Enel also continued to invest in developing its other generation operations. In Russia, for example, OGK-5 launched a number of new plant projects, including two 410 MW combined cycle plants at Nevinnomysskaya and Sredneuralskaya.

Back in Italy, however, in face of the growing cost of fossil fuel-based power plants, the Italian government, then under Silvio Berlusconi, pushed through an end to the ban on nuclear reactors. In 2009, Enel reached an agreement with France's electrical energy leader Electricité de France (EDF) to establish a joint-venture operation to build at least 10 nuclear power plants in Italy through 2020. In the meantime, Enel had completed its transformation from a government-run monopoly to one of the world's largest and most geographically diversified power generation companies.

Cristina Caffarra
Updated, M. L. Cohen

PRINCIPAL SUBSIDIARIES

Deval S.p.A.; Endesa SA (Spain; 92%); Enel Distribuzione S.p.A.; Enel Energia S.p.A.; Enel Green Power S.p.A.; Enel North America Inc. (USA); Enel Produzione S.p.A.; Enel Rete Gas S.p.A.; Enel Servizio Elettrico S.p.A.; Enel Sole S.p.A.; Enel Stoccaggi S.p.A.; Enel Trade Hungary; Enel Trade Romania; Enel Trade S.p.A.; Hydro Dolomiti Enel; Nuove Energie S.p.A.; Vallenergie S.p.A.

PRINCIPAL DIVISIONS

Engineering and Innovation; Generation and Energy Management; Iberia and Latin America; Infrastructure and Networks; International; Renewable Energy; Sales; Services and Other Activities.

PRINCIPAL COMPETITORS

Electricité de France S.A.; Total Gas and Power Ltd.; ENI S.p.A.; E.ON AG; SUEZ; National Grid PLC; RWE AG; Zorlu Holding A.S; Abengoa S.A.; TRACTEBEL S.A.; Iberdrola S.A.

FURTHER READING

"Along Better Lines," *Economist*, October 18, 1997, p. 62.

Belton, Catherine, and Guy Dinmore, "Italy's Power Force Sees New Frontier in Russian Market," *Financial Times*, October 30, 2007, p. 2.

Crooks, Ed, "Egyptian Boost for Enel Energy," *Financial Times*, April 10, 2008, p. 17.

———, "Triumph for a Fading National Champion," *Financial Times*, June 19, 2007, p. 2.

Crooks, Ed, and Carola Hoyos, "Enel Considers Sale of Gas Network," *Financial Times*, April 22, 2008, p. 18.

Crooks, Ed, and Guy Dinmore, "EDF and Enel Strike Italian Nuclear Deal," *Financial Times*, February 25, 2009, p. 18.

Dinmore, Guy, Peggy Hollinger, and Adrian Michaels, "EDF and Enel Close to EUR 2bn Power Agreement," *Financial*

Times, November 29, 2007, p. 20.

"Enel: A Gradual Move from Monopoly to Open Market," *Business Week*, July 16, 2001, p. 5.

"Enel Builds on Its Russian Assets," *Modern Power Systems*, April 2009, p. 30.

"Enel's Not-So-New Look," *Economist*, October 14, 2000, p. 75.

"An Ill Wind," *Economist*, September 14, 2002.

"Italy's Big Nuclear Ambitions," *Utility Week*, October 2, 2009.

"Jolted," *Economist*, March 14, 1998, p. 71.

Newton, Paul, "Fighting Fit," *Utility Week*, January 24, 2003, p. 20.

"Power Games," *Economist*, February 28, 2009, p. 63EU.

Ram, Vidya, "From Russia with Love to Enel," *Forbes*, June 7, 2007.

Sylvers, Eric, "Enel of Italy Looks to U.S. to Expand," *New York Times*, May 2, 2003, p. W1.

———, "Italy to Sell Another Stake in Enel, Its Biggest Utility," *New York Times*, March 26, 2005, p. C3.

Energy Recovery, Inc.

1908 Doolittle Drive
San Leandro, California 94577-3235
U.S.A.
Telephone: (510) 483-7330
Fax: (510) 483-7371
Web site: http://www.energyrecovery.com

Public Company
Incorporated: 1992
Employees: 89
Sales: $52.1 million (2008)
Stock Exchanges: NASDAQ
Ticker Symbol: ERII
NAICS: 333298 All Other Industrial Machinery
Manufacturing

■ ■ ■

Energy Recovery, Inc., (ERI) is a San Leandro, California-based developer and manufacturer of energy recovery devices used in water desalination, focusing on the seawater reverse osmosis (SWRO) segment of the market. The company's primary product is the PX Pressure Exchanger device, which recycles much of the energy used in seawater desalination by continually reclaiming the otherwise lost pressure energy from the reject or brine water to up to 98 percent efficiency. This improves the energy efficiency of SWRO plants by up to 60 percent compared with no energy recovery technology. What typically costs $10 to produce a cubic meter of freshwater from seawater is lowered to less than $5 with the use of the device. With just one moving

part made from a highly engineered ceramic aluminum oxide material, the device is highly reliable, durable, and requires little or no maintenance.

ERI is especially active in Algeria, Australia, China, India, and Spain, but the underlying economics of water delivery and the potential loss of water sources due to possible global warming, provides considerable promise to the publicly traded company. In addition to its San Francisco-area research and development and manufacturing facilities, ERI maintains sales and support centers in Madrid, Dubai, and Shanghai.

INVENTOR, NORWEGIAN BORN

Energy Recovery, Inc., was founded by Norwegian Leif Hauge. A college dropout, Hauge made his living working construction and from a talent for inventing. His interest in desalination was accidental. In 1986 he tried to help his brother, a farmer, to keep his vegetables cool by devising a way to circulate cold water from a nearby fjord through pipes surrounding a storage area. As a result, Hauge learned about the energy requirements of pumping water uphill and the loss of energy that occurred when the water returned to the fjord by way of gravity. In order to recover as much of the energy as possible, he developed a positive displacement pump that included a rudimentary pressure exchanger. While his idea to cool the vegetables did not pan out because of an inherent lack of water pressure, Hauge did not forget the insights he gleaned in energy recovery. A year later he learned that pressure exchangers were a key component of water desalination plants and he began developing a saltwater pressure exchanger.

Energy Recovery, Inc., designs and develops energy recovery devices that help make seawater desalination affordable by significantly reducing energy consumption.

Large desalination plants relied on a thermal process that consumed excessive amounts of energy. Hence, the process was mostly used in the Middle East, where energy costs were low. The other method, SWRO, was more recent in development, but it too used a great deal of energy as seawater was blasted through a filtering polymer membrane to extract freshwater, leaving behind a briny residue and much spent energy. Engineers for large seawater desalination plants relied on turbine devices including Pelton wheels or Francis turbines to recover the energy, the exiting water essentially turning a shaft to power a pump to force more water through the filter. The technology was more than 100 years old, however, and only under optimum conditions could it hope to be as much as 80 percent efficient. It also relied on metal components that when subjected to high-velocity seawater were prone to erosion and corrosion.

The pressure exchanger was another attempt to harness that energy, to use it to jet more water through the membrane, losing as little of the energy as possible as each new cycle was completed. Hauge came to believe that the device he had created as part of his fjord water pump to recover energy could be developed into a pressure exchanger suitable for SWRO desalination plants.

HAUGE TAKEN WAR PRISONER: 1990

Hauge was able to interest the Kuwait Institute for Scientific Research in his ideas, and in 1988 they formed a joint venture that provided him with three years of salary along with a staff and research facilities in Kuwait. It was not the best time to be a researcher in Kuwait, however. In 1990 Iraq invaded and occupied the country. Hauge was taken prisoner and sent to Baghdad. Fortunately, important documents related to his research were destroyed and did not fall into the hands of the Iraqis searching for valuable technology properties. Hauge and his pregnant wife were held in Baghdad until Iraq was defeated in the Persian Gulf War.

Following the war Hauge came to the United States and continued his work on pressure exchangers, setting

up shop in Virginia, where in 1992 he incorporated Energy Recovery, Inc. To develop his device Hauge had spent $500,000 received from friends, grants from a Norwegian industrial foundation, and credit cards. He found more backers for his research through Thyssen Nordseewerke, a German submarine maker, and Virginia shipbuilder Newport News. Hauge developed an ingenious design for his positive displacement pump. As described by *Forbes,* the device greatly reduced the mechanical complexity of the Pelton wheel: "High-pressure exiting water enters columns in a rotor arranged like the bullet chambers in a six-shooter. This speeding water smashes into low-pressure water that has entered the same tubes at the other end of the rotor. Because water cannot compress, the high-pressure water transfers nearly all of its momentum to the low-pressure water, pressuring it, before turning back on itself and draining." The water entered and left at an angle that quickly spun the chamber so that the process could be repeated 1,000 times per second.

NORWEGIAN INVESTORS BECOME INVOLVED: 1993

Hauge's concept was elegant but there was a major obstacle to overcome in making it a viable device: finding a material that could withstand the water pressure and the corrosive nature of saltwater. As he experimented with various metals and alloys, all of which corroded or fused, he exhausted his funds. In 1993 Hauge found further financial backing from a group of Norwegian-born investors headed by Hans Peter Michelet, a University of Oregon graduate in finance who was the head of a Scandinavian bank and invested in ERI on the side. He was joined by a group of other wealthy Norwegians. Unlike venture capitalists, they were patient with Hauge, but as his need for more funding continued he eventually owned less of the company than did his investors.

Hauge finally completed the design for his pressure exchange device, when in 1995 after three years of working with metals he took the advice of a Danish company that had considered an early prototype and suggested he employ ceramic materials. With a pair of Kmart coffee mugs, Hauge fashioned ceramic rotors. He then traveled to Oak Ridge National Laboratory to take advantage of precision ceramic-grounding equipment, but after two months of effort he was told by the researchers at Oak Ridge that it would be impossible to manufacture a ceramic rotor to the tolerances a pressure exchanger required. Undeterred, Hauge further explored ceramic materials until finally settling on the equivalent of corundum, a crystalline form of aluminum oxide that when polished was better known as sapphire. Nearly as

KEY DATES

1992: Leif Hauge establishes company in Virginia.
1997: First pressure exchanger devices are installed.
2000: Company moves to San Leandro, California.
2005: General Electric contract for PX-220 leads to profitability.
2008: Company goes public on the NASDAQ.

hard as diamond, it was resistant to corrosion and could be lubricated by water. As a result the first ceramic rotor was developed as the heart of the pressure exchanger (PX) device. In 1997 the first devices were installed in small desalination plants in the Canary Islands at resorts and hotels. However, Hauge was unable to scale or sell the device for larger applications.

ERI received five U.S. patents and installed more of the PXs at small and medium desalination plants around the country. Michelet and the other majority owners of ERI were growing increasingly frustrated with the inventor, however. More an artist than a businessman, Hauge insisted on handcrafting each PX, an approach that would never work if ERI were to reach an industrial scale and make back its investment. Moreover, his investors did not believe Hauge was an experienced enough manager to grow and sustain a business.

INSTALLATION OF PROFESSIONAL MANAGEMENT: 2000

At the start of 2000, ERI's owners decided that the inventor was best suited for the role of technical manager and that a professional management team should be brought in to take the company to profitability. Hauge refused and tried to reclaim patents that he had previously assigned to the company. The matter went to the courts. As the result of an adverse ruling, Hauge settled with his previous employer and left the company. ERI's corporate headquarters was moved in 2000 to San Leandro, California, where Hauge lived. Just as ERI began to evolve into an operational company, Hauge was left with no stake in the company he founded.

With new headquarters and a professional management team in place, ERI was able to hire a new engineering team. Because of flow dynamics, creating a larger device was easier said than done, but the company managed to accomplish the task relatively quickly. In 2002, ERI introduced the PX-220 (200 gallons per minute), a device that was five times larger than the original PX-40 (40 gallons per minute) it replaced. At that time, the company also hired a new CEO, G. G. Pique, to take the company to the next stage in its development. Originally employed as a consultant for the company since 2000, Pique was already familiar with the technology and the market. With a chemical engineering degree from the University of Connecticut and an M.B.A., Pique had been working in the desalination field since the early 1980s and boasted more than 30 years of experience in the water-treatment industry, including experience with well recognized, public companies such as US Filter Corporation.

Annual sales hovered at the $4 million range in both 2003 and 2004. A major breakthrough came in June 2005 when the company received a large order for the PX-220 from General Electric (GE) for a high-capacity desalination plant in Algeria, at the time one of the largest in the world. Not only did the order, divided into smaller orders, provide steady cash flow, it placed GE's imprimatur on the technology, a valuable asset in the marketplace. As a result, sales more than doubled to $10.7 million in 2005 and ERI turned a profit of nearly $900,000. Moreover, with 2,500 PXs in operation the company became the largest manufacturer of energy recovery devices for SWRO desalination plants. A year later sales topped $20 million and the company posted net income of $2.4 million. In 2007 sales increased to $35.4 million while earnings totaled $5.8 million.

PUBLIC OFFERING: 2008

In July 2008 ERI was taken public, creating excitement in what had been a discouraging stock market, as ERI shares increased 15.7 percent in value on the first day of trading, an impressive start given the conditions. The initial offering of stock netted the company $76.7 million, earmarked for working capital and other general corporate purposes. Investor enthusiasm was understandable, given the company's upward trend. When 2008 came to a close, ERI recorded sales of $52.1 million and net income of $8.7 million.

In the near-term the company expected most of its growth to come from international sales, in particular, Algeria, Australia, China, and India, but there were also attractive potential markets in the Caribbean, Europe, the Middle East, and North America. Due to rising temperatures attributed to global warming, sources of freshwater were also drying up, making the desalination of saltwater an increasingly important option. The energy efficiency of SWRO plants using ERI PX technology also promised to make desalination attractive to areas such as California that had to pump water from long distances but had ample supplies of seawater closer at hand. These possible markets by themselves offered ERI a bright future, but the company's technology also held out the promise of Osmotic Power. Instead of going from saltwater to fresh, ERI's technology could potentially be reversed, forcing freshwater through a forward osmosis membrane to create saltwater. The difference in pressure between freshwater and saltwater that would be created could then run turbines to create a renewable source of electricity, a market far larger than desalination.

As of mid-2009, there were over 7,000 ERI PX devices on the market, saving more than 750 megawatts of energy and reducing carbon dioxide emissions by more than 4.6 million tons annually. ERI was helping to make desalination an environmentally sound and cost-effective solution to the water shortages worldwide, and was expected to thrive as conditions continued to worsen in years to come.

Ed Dinger

PRINCIPAL SUBSIDIARIES

Osmotic Power, Inc.; Energy Recovery Iberia, S.L. (Spain); Energy Recovery, Inc. International.

PRINCIPAL COMPETITORS

Calder (Flowserve); Pump Engineering Incorporated.

FURTHER READING

Abate, Tom, "New Pump Desalinates Water as It Saves Money," *San Francisco Chronicle,* August 3, 2008, p. D1.

Avalos, George, "San Leandro Firm Ends IPO Drought," *Alameda Times-Star,* July 2, 2008.

Cowan, Lynn, "Energy Recovery IPO Ends String of Losses," *Wall Street Journal,* July 3, 2008, p. C3.

Hoyt, Jennifer, "Firm Bets Big on Desalination," *Wall Street Journal,* May 6, 2009.

"Making Sweet Water from (Almost) Perpetual Motion," *Forbes,* September 7, 2009, p. 94.

Ernst & Young Global Limited

————————■————————

Becket House
1 Lambeth Palace Road
London, SE1 7EU
United Kingdom
Telephone: (+44-20) 7951-2000
Fax: (+44 20) 7951-1345
Web site: http://www.eyi.com

Private Company
Incorporated: 1989
Employees: 135,730
Sales: $24.5 billion (2008)
NAICS: 541211 Offices of Certified Public Accountants

■ ■ ■

Ernst & Young Global Limited is an umbrella organization for one of the world's leading assurance, tax, transaction, and advisory services networks. The London-based operation provides services through its member firms, which are separate legal entities. Ernst & Young formed in 1989 when the third-largest accounting firm at the time, Ernst & Whinney (based in Cleveland, Ohio), merged with the sixth-largest firm, Arthur Young & Co. (headquartered in New York). Once the world's largest accounting firm, Ernst & Young ranks third among the "Big Four" in terms of revenue. The organization is divided into five geographic areas: Americas; Europe, Middle East, India, and Africa; Far East; Japan; and Oceania. Its 709 offices are spread through 140 countries. During the early 2000s, corporate wrongdoing triggered a move toward increased scrutiny of the profession and the demise of one of the world's top five firms. Legal troubles continued to hound the Big Four in the latter years of the decade.

COMPANY ORIGINS

The roots of Ernst & Young can be traced back well over 100 years to the formation of the auditing business and the development of generally accepted accounting practices, rules that became increasingly necessary with the rise of the multinational corporation and the intrusion of complicated taxes into private business. Prior to the 1989 merger, each of the two firms had enjoyed rich histories.

Arthur Young and Ernst & Whinney both rose from very small beginnings by capitalizing on the enterprise potential of accounting in its early years. Pioneer Arthur Young founded and headed the original Arthur Young firm back in 1895 in Kansas City, following an earlier union of Stuart and Young in Chicago. Glasgow-born Young had moved to the United States in 1890 "to pursue his career in accounting," an Ernst & Young Web-based history retold. Trained as a lawyer, the young Scot had developed an interest in banking and investment.

During the first decade of the 20th century, Young was operating as Arthur Young & Company, along with his brother Stanley. Arthur Young & Company flourished for many years, slowly developing its reputation as "old reliable" for auditing, adding increasing numbers of partners. The other half of the marriage, Ernst & Whinney, can also be traced back to the early years of the century, when Ernst & Ernst was founded in Cleveland, Ohio, in 1903, as a partnership between bookkeeper Alwin C. Ernst and his older brother, Theodore Ernst. The public accounting firm took on its first additional partners in 1910 and from there the family tree expanded by immense and unforeseen proportions. By 1913, when income taxes began to be levied in the United States, the need for accountants swelled dramatically.

Separately, Ernst and Young influenced the development of the industry. "Ernst pioneered the idea that accounting information could be used to make business decisions and make a difference to clients' organizations," the Ernst & Young history proclaimed. "Young supported the development of professionals. In the 1920s he originated a staff school and, in the 1930s, the firm was the first to recruit from university campuses."

Moreover, the firm made early entries into global partnerships. In 1924, Ernst & Ernst joined with Whinney, Smith & Whinney, and Young allied with Broad Paterson & Co. Both were based in England. Whinney, Smith & Whinney was established as Harding & Pullein in 1849. Frederick Whinney joined the firm and was made partner 10 years later. In 1894, the firm took the name Whinney, Smith & Whinney.

Ernst & Young also included a 19th-century Canadian operation, Thomas Clarkson's Toronto-based trustee and receivership firm, in its family tree. In 1939, Clarkson joined with Woods Gordon & Co., taking the firm into management consulting. Clarkson Gordon & Company then allied with Arthur Young & Company in 1944.

MEGAMERGERS: 1979–89

Ernst & Whinney formed in 1979, as the world's fourth-largest accountancy firm. Among its more publicized actions of the time was the audit paving the way for the government bailout of the Chrysler Corporation. Meanwhile, Arthur Young's European offices joined with several large local European firms. Stateside, though, was another story.

Long known for its reliable auditing practice and a clean, conservative interpretation of tax law, Arthur Young found its image tarnished by events of the 1980s, many in the area of the national savings and loan (S&L) scandal. For instance, Arthur Young was sued for $560 million for allegedly allowing Western Savings Association of Dallas to overstate its net worth by more than $400 million. In 1988 Bank of England sued Arthur Young and collected $44 million after a bank that Young audited collapsed.

In contrast to the struggles of Arthur Young prior to the merger, Ernst & Whinney's business had thrived, with its management consulting practice growing faster than its audit and tax practice. In fact, at the time of the merger, consulting fees accounted for 24 percent of Ernst & Whinney's revenues, whereas only 17 percent of Arthur Young's revenues came from consulting.

In general, both firms thought that a merger represented a comparative advantage for each. Although both had heavy hitters for clients, Arthur Young's clients were mostly investment banks and high-tech firms on the East and West Coasts, while Ernst & Whinney had more health-care and manufacturing industry clients concentrated in the Midwest and South. Internationally, Arthur Young had more clients in Europe, while Ernst & Whinney had established a presence in the Pacific Rim countries. Arthur Young's clients included American Express, Mobil, and Texas Instruments, while Ernst & Whinney had BankAmerica, Time, Inc., and Eli Lilly.

Although touted as a merger, the evidence suggests that the 1989 transaction that created the firm Ernst & Young was, in fact, an acquisition in disguise, with the stronger Ernst & Whinney swallowing up the floundering Arthur Young practice. Arthur Young had established a strong reputation over many years although it was generally seen as a cautious and stodgy practice. By the 1980s, though, after much of its traditional audit practice started to collapse and massive leveraged buyouts became an increasingly common practice in the business world, Arthur Young had difficulty competing in the cutthroat environment of the accounting arena.

Historically, the accounting business had seen increasing numbers of partners concentrated in a decreasing number of firms. In this respect, the birth of Ernst & Young in 1989 was the natural outcome of the cycle of competition that bred concentration and expansion, thus leading to further rounds of competition. For

KEY DATES

1849: Frederick Whinney joins English firm Harding & Pullein.
1859: Whinney becomes a partner.
1895: Arthur Young forms his first firm.
1903: Brothers establish Ernst & Ernst in Cleveland.
1924: Both Arthur Young and Ernst & Ernst establish overseas alliances.
1979: Ernst & Whinney forms.
1989: Arthur Young and Ernst & Whinney merge.
1992: Ernst & Young pays federal fine to settle savings and loan scandal accusations.
1998: Ernst & Young stops planned merger with KPMG.
2000: Firm sells consulting practice to Cap Gemini for $11.1 billion.
2003: Securities and Exchange Commission imposes six-month ban on new audit clients.
2007: Emerging markets continue to help drive growth.

over half a century previous to the creation of Ernst & Young, though, eight firms had dominated the accounting business. The elite group was dubbed the "Big Eight" by *Fortune* magazine.

Following two major mergers in the 1980s (the Ernst & Young deal and the merger the same year between Deloitte, Haskins & Sells and Touche Ross), the Big Eight became the Big Six. All of the Big Six were private partnerships, meaning that all were owned by the firm's senior executives, which also meant that none of the firms was required to report its profits.

The Ernst & Young merger created a firm with 6,100 partners and two chief executive officers, Ray Groves from Ernst & Whinney and William Gladstone from Arthur Young. The newly formed firm had worldwide revenues in 1989 of $4.27 billion, and its total sales eclipsed that established by a merger in 1987 of Peat Marwick and KMG Main Hurdman.

The actual merger in 1989 was essentially viewed as a smart competitive move. Some observers thought the merger might be difficult due to perceived differences in management styles, with Ernst & Whinney governed from the top and Arthur Young favoring a more decentralized management system. At the time of the merger Ernst & Whinney had 1,276 partners and 14,739 total personnel in 118 U.S. offices as well as

3,159 partners and 35,600 total personnel in 89 countries. The smaller Arthur Young had 829 U.S.-based partners and 10,652 total U.S. personnel in 93 offices; worldwide, the company had 2,900 partners and 33,000 total personnel in 74 countries.

There was a conflict at the time of the merger over each firm's "cola" clients. A conflict of interest existed in that PepsiCo had been an Arthur Young client since 1965, while Coca-Cola had been an Ernst & Whinney client since 1924. Coca-Cola forced the firm to dump PepsiCo, as Ernst & Young noted that Coca-Cola had been a client for a longer time and that Coke's annual audit fee was $14 million, a much higher figure than Pepsi's $8.8 million audit fee.

In one of its first business decisions following the merger, Ernst & Young began to move into computer-aided software engineering. This step reflected Ernst & Young's diversification into management systems and strategic planning services for businesses. Under the general heading of Development Effectiveness, these services capped a string of moves into the field. The general thrust of the project incorporated management consulting, Total Quality Management, and process innovation. The process innovation services were sold worldwide, primarily to the insurance and banking industries.

PAYING FOR THE S&L SCANDAL

However, as the newly formed firm faced the 1990s, it was steeped in the controversy surrounding the crisis of the S&L industry. Ernst & Young's audits of 23 failed S&LS were investigated by the Office of Thrift Supervision (OTS) under a subpoena issued in June 1991. OTS was formed by the federal government to recover losses from accounting firms that should have discovered improprieties during S&L audits and to impose fines on auditors for violations of accounting rules. Some of the thrifts that Ernst & Young audited included Charles Keating's failed Lincoln Savings & Loan (Irvine, California), Silverado Banking (Denver, Colorado), Vernon Savings & Loan (Vernon, Texas), and Western Federal Savings & Loan (Dallas, Texas), all of which experienced total losses of over $5.5 billion. The OTS subpoena required that Ernst & Young surrender one million documents from its work for the 23 failed S&Ls.

Several judgments were rendered against Ernst & Young in connection with the investigation. In July 1992, for instance, the firm paid a fine of $1.66 million to settle accusations that it helped Charles H. Keating Jr., deceive the federal government about the health of his failing S&L. Moreover, former Ernst & Young partner Jack D. Atchison's license was suspended for four years by the accounting board of Arizona. He was accused of helping persuade five U.S. senators to intervene with federal regulators on Keating's behalf. In connection with this settlement, Ernst & Young paid $63 million to settle charges of wrongdoing in the Keating affair. Ernst & Young did not admit guilt, however, and the claim was paid largely by insurance. In total, some $204 million in fines were paid in this civil suit.

In another settlement, Ernst & Young paid $400 million to the federal government in compliance with a federal ruling against the company. The settlement secured recovery of losses attributable to audit failures. In addition, the settlement avoided huge litigation costs and assured that future audits of insured institutions would be conducted according to the highest professional standards. With potential claims that could have mounted to an estimated $1 billion, the ruling relieved Ernst & Young of concerns regarding future penalties involving S&L auditing improprieties. Ernst & Young also agreed to change its accounting practices and ensure that its partners meet federal guidelines for working with federally insured financial institutions. Some of Ernst & Young's partners were barred from doing such work and changes in banking laws required accounting firms to be legally responsible for sharing with regulators reports prepared for bank management.

EXPANSION: 1991–96

Despite these troubles, Ernst & Young defied the rumors that it would fold. To eliminate overlap created by the merger and to reduce its payroll expenses, the firm cut its staff in 1991 and eliminated many partner positions. Although revenues had fallen slightly in the late 1980s, by the early 1990s revenues were modestly but steadily rising. Sales from Ernst & Young's risk management and actuarial services group rose 7.4 percent from 1990 to 1991, from $9.5 million to $10.2 million. Overall revenues rose from $5 billion in 1990 to $5.4 billion in 1991 and $5.7 billion in 1992.

The company garnered an increasing number of clients, and their involvement in such large projects as municipal insurance and environmental risk management consulting continued to grow. Revenues in risk management consulting went from $10.3 million in 1991 to $10.9 million in 1992. This increase reflected a growing market for these kinds of services. Moreover, major restructuring was taking place in hospitals and in the health-care industry in general, creating a need for consultants. The traditional Ernst & Young mainstay, auditing, still fared quite well in the new firm's early years. By 1992, in fact, Ernst & Young performed the most audits of large publicly held multinational

companies. It audited 3,231 companies with a total value audited of $10.22 trillion (based on asset figures for financial companies and sales for all other firms audited).

Ernst & Young's costly legal battles encouraged several changes in the mid-1990s. First, the firm hired a new general legal counsel, Kathryn Oberly, who reputedly made keeping costs down a higher priority than battling on principle. Second, the firm stepped up its expansion into consulting, an area much less fraught with legal responsibilities and their concomitant lawsuits than auditing. In addition to increasing its consulting in risk management, the company moved into information software products.

Ernst & Young also entered new business areas in the mid-1990s by developing alliances and by acquiring smaller companies. In 1996 the firm forged an alliance with Tata Consulting, headquartered in India. The same year, its alliance with ISD/Shaw gave the firm an entree into banking industry consulting. The firm moved into the petroleum and petrochemical consulting business in 1996 when it purchased Wright Killen & Co. Ernst & Young created a new subsidiary with the Houston-based company, which they named Ernst & Young Wright Killen.

FAILED MERGER WITH KPMG

In 1997 Ernst & Young forged an agreement to merge with KPMG International, another Big Six accounting firm. The agreement came only weeks after the announcement of a merger between Price Waterhouse and Coopers & Lybrand, which would have created the world's largest accounting firm, with $12 billion in revenues and a staff of 135,000. However, the proposed Ernst & Young-KPMG International merger overshadowed that, with combined revenues of $16 billion and 160,000 people. According to Ernst & Young, the deal was designed to satisfy multinational clients who wanted an auditor and consultant with offices in every city in which the client had offices. In addition, the merger would have limited the risk of a liability suit severely damaging earnings and would have made greater economies of scale for developing new products or services.

Combining the two huge companies presented a formidable task, particularly because they were intense competitors. Between 1991 and 1997 KPMG had lost approximately 60 of its auditing clients in the United States to Ernst & Young. A larger problem than overcoming historic rivalries, however, was gaining regulatory approval. The Ernst & Young-KPMG International merger and the Price Waterhouse-Coopers

& Lybrand merger would have furthered the consolidation of the major accounting firms into the Big Four, an outcome disturbing to many industry analysts. Along with fears that the relative lack of choice would encourage a rise in prices, there were fears among clients that the combined firms would make company secrets vulnerable to rivals using the same firm.

Citing the high cost of pursuing the merger and the uncertain regulatory outcome, Ernst & Young suggested in early 1998 that the two firms abandon their merger plans. Some analysts thought that the money and attention required to integrate the firms, at a time when all Big Six firms were expanding rapidly, also discouraged the merger.

Ernst & Young experienced substantial growth in 1997, despite being hit by a $4 billion lawsuit alleging the firm mishandled the restructuring of Merry-Go-Round Enterprises in 1993. Overall revenues rose from $7.8 billion in 1996 to $9.1 billion in 1997. A substantial amount of this growth was fueled by a 30 percent surge in tax advice revenues and an 18 percent increase in worldwide tax revenues, an area in which Ernst & Young led the Big Six. The firm also boosted its efficiency in 1997, raising its revenue per employee 10 percent that year, to $238,360. Revenues continued to rise spectacularly in 1998, reaching $10.9 billion, a jump of almost 20 percent.

The Big Five, as they were called with the completion of the Price Waterhouse-Coopers & Lybrand merger in 1998, continued to diversify their services in the late 1990s. Revenues from consulting on tax issues, personnel, management, property, and personal finance swamped revenues from auditing for Ernst & Young. In 1999 the firm had plans to add a worldwide law practice to its stable of services. Ernst & Young had associated law practices in several countries by the end of the century and planned to build a global staff of 4,000 by the year 2005.

INDUSTRY UPHEAVAL: 2000–06

At the cusp of the new century, Ernst & Young stood as one of the Big Five accounting firms that dominated the accounting business. A private partnership, Ernst & Young was owned by its senior partners and provided auditing services primarily to the world's largest corporations. In addition, it specialized in tax advice for multinational firms. Its increasing engagement in non-audit and non-tax businesses, though, would be a sticking point for the firm and its counterparts in the first decade of the 2000s.

In 2000, Europe's largest computer services company, France-based Cap Gemini, S.A., agreed to acquire Ernst & Young's consulting practice. The $11.1 billion cash and shares deal moved 1,000 consulting partners to Cap Gemini with 4,000 accounting and tax partners remaining with the auditing firm headed by Philip A. Laskawy, according to the *New York Times*. The largest accounting firms' consulting businesses had become their fastest growing and most profitable segments. The Securities and Exchange Commission (SEC) harbored concerns regarding the potential for conflicts of interest in terms of auditing, pushing the Big Five to address the problem.

The latter half of the year brought more changes. Ernst & Young created a global leadership team, part of a move toward greater global integration. More than 60 countries were divided into 10 geographic areas (Americas, Australia, Far East, France, Germany, Italy, Netherlands, Nordic, Switzerland, and the United Kingdom) under global CEO William L. Kimsey. The new structure, eventually to encompass all practices worldwide, was intended to improve the response to clients' global needs. New York Area Managing Partner James S. Turley had been appointed deputy chair and would succeed Laskawy upon his retirement in 2001.

Worldwide revenue climbed to $9.2 billion in 2000. Ernst & Young was the first of the Big Five to separate out its consulting services. Its key business lines included assurance and advisory, tax and law, and corporate finance. The latter led the segments in growth, climbing 32.2 percent.

The following year, Ernst & Young worldwide revenues topped $10 billion. The close of the fiscal year marked the end of Laskawy's 40-year tenure with the firm. Also in 2001, the U.K. partnership converted to a limited liability company, the first of the Big Five to do so under new legislation. PricewaterhouseCoopers had also lobbied for the status and was expected to make the shift as well, according to the *Daily Telegraph*.

In March 2002, Arthur Andersen was indicted on a single count of obstruction of justice. "Longtime clients, the federal government and even some of its own foreign affiliates abandoned Arthur Andersen yesterday, a day after the accounting firm was indicted for destroying Enron documents," the *New York Times* reported. Lake Forest, Illinois-based Brunswick, for one, took its business to Ernst & Young.

Kimsey, chief executive of Ernst & Young's international operation, meanwhile, had been pursuing the troubled firm's global partners. He continued to do so despite word of a deal between Andersen's non-U.S. network and a rival firm. KPMG International's merger attempt failed, however, as partnerships struck their own deals. Kimsey's tenacity and "wide leeway to make independent decisions" facilitated his efforts, according to the *Asian Wall Street Journal*. Andersen's Russian and New Zealand practices signed on with Ernst & Young. PricewaterhouseCoopers and Deloitte Touche Tohmatsu also picked up Andersen firms that KPMG had hoped to absorb.

Ernst & Young faced its own problems in the first half of 2002. The SEC slapped the firm with rule violation charges revolving around its former consulting business relationship with software-company Peoplesoft Inc. "The news comes at a time of intense scrutiny of company financial statements in the wake of the collapse of Enron, the bankrupt energy trader," Abigail Rayner reported for the *Times* (London) in May.

In July 2002, a new system to regulate accountants was created by the Sarbanes-Oxley Act. The legislation had an impact, going forward, on auditor training, business lines, and client relationships. The industry also contended with shockwaves of another kind. The Enron-related federal indictment of Arthur Andersen and subsequent client exodus had led to the firm's failure, making the Big Five, the Big Four.

In 2003, the SEC proposed a six-month ban on new audit clients against Ernst & Young for violating conflict of interest rules during its 1990s relationship with Peoplesoft. Ernst & Young also faced congressional hearings, dealing with its audits of HealthSouth Corporation. The rehabilitation and surgical center chain had been accused of widespread accounting fraud, according to the *New York Times*. In addition, Ernst & Young had been hit by a fine and lawsuits linked to improprieties related to tax shelter sales.

Despite the turmoil, worldwide revenues climbed 29.8 percent to $13.1 billion in 2003. Assurance and Advisory Business Services led the way followed by Transaction Advisory Services (formerly Corporate Finance), with 35 percent and 31 percent growth, respectively. The addition of former Andersen practices and clients and global organic growth also factored into the strong results. On the personnel side, James S. Turley took the role of global CEO.

In 2004, a judge upheld the SEC's Peoplesoft-related punishment, imposed a fine, and warned against future violations. Ernst & Young spokesman Charlie Perkins explained the former to the *Independent* in April: "While the order will prevent us from accepting new public company audits for the next six months, it will not impair our ability to continue to serve our existing public company audit clients, accept new audit work from privately held companies, or to accept non-audit work from public companies we do not audit."

At the end of the year, Giuliani Partners announced plans to acquire Ernst & Young Corporate Finance

L.L.C. The firm, headed by former New York City Mayor Rudolph W. Giuliani, was established in 2002 in affiliation with Ernst & Young. The accounting firm would also sell its interest in Giuliani Partners, according to the *New York Times*.

TACTICAL SUCCESS: 2005–09

Worldwide revenues continued to climb in fiscal 2005. In a press release Turley said: "We have worked hard to rebuild the reputation of the profession and to enhance confidence in the capital market system. We have been engaged in an active dialogue with many of its participants—client management and audit committees, regulators and investors—and other key stakeholders, as a means of improving standards of financial reporting and governance at every level." In 2006 Transaction Advisory Services led in growth among the service lines, as the number of corporate deals rose across the globe. In geographic terms, emerging markets produced the greatest growth for Ernst & Young, thanks to strategic investments in those regions.

For the fiscal year ending June 30, 2007, Transaction Advisory Services again led the pack, producing a 29 percent gain. As in previous years, significant geographic growth correlated with the company's investment strategy: China, India, and Russia all recorded increases of more than 30 percent.

During 2007, the Big Four climbed back among the top 10 consultancy fee generators in the United Kingdom, according to a November *Financial Times* article. All, save Deloitte, had sold their consultancy businesses, but with the expiration of non-compete agreements, posted double-digit growth. Globally, though, the reconstituted consulting business was less robust.

Addressing the resurrection, Richard Pile, managing director at Parson Consulting, told the *Financial Times*: "Now, safely protected behind newly-created limited liability partnership structures, and with more pricing power than ever in a smaller oligopoly (since the collapse of Arthur Andersen, the Big Fifth), audit firms are once again making consulting hay from their audit relationships."

New clients, new services, and advances in merging markets pushed combined revenues to $24.5 billion in 2008, despite the spreading economic downturn. Organizationally, Ernst & Young linked 87 national practices across Europe, the Middle East, India, and Africa and 15 national practices in Asia. Ernst & Young's three other linked areas included the previously integrated Americas, Japan, and Oceania (Australia, New Zealand, Fiji, and Indonesia).

Despite the increase in corporate monitoring, a new wave of wrongdoing arose in the second half of the decade. In early 2007, Ernst & Young audit client Broadcom Corporation "took charges of $2.2 billion to past earnings to fix misdated options," the *Orange County Business Journal* reported. The chipmaker was slated to go to trial over the issue in 2010. Ernst and Young LLP in Irvine remained in the clear as of July 2008. "In Broadcom's case, it could be argued executives went out of their way to keep Ernst & Young from knowing about options backdating," Jessica C. Lee wrote. "So far accounting firms haven't taken too much heat for the sins of stock options backdating. Some industry watchers think it's too early to tell what the fallout will be from the mortgage meltdown, which might bring specific auditors into the fire." Auditor KPMG LLC was under examination in regard to the failed subprime mortgage maker New Century Financial.

Fingers pointed once again in the direction of auditors, when details of Bernard Madoff's multibillion-dollar fraud against investors were revealed in late 2008. Ernst & Young, KPMG, PricewaterhouseCoopers, and an arm of the fifth-largest auditor, BDO International, "were all auditors of the feeder funds which channeled money into accounts at Mr. Madoff's New York brokerage," the *Financial Times* reported in December. The New York Law School, a victim of the Ponzi scheme, filed a lawsuit against BDO Seidman. The SEC also was taking heat in the matter, for failing "to investigate warnings alleging 'financial wrongdoing' by Madoff."

Ernst & Young settled with HealthSouth shareholders in March 2009, for $109 million. HealthSouth paid plaintiffs $445 million in January 2007, for its accounting misdeeds. Cries continued, nevertheless, for more accountability. "Auditors are also facing a legal threat to their structure. The unlimited liability auditors face in most countries has led them to form networks of national partnerships with a thin global umbrella with the aim of protecting the whole organisation from catastrophic litigation against a single member firm," the *Financial Times* stated. Nonetheless, for both its clients and itself, Ernst & Young recognized considerable opportunity for future growth, despite the difficult economic, political, and legal landscape.

John A. Sarich
Updated, Susan Windisch Brown; Kathleen Peippo

PRINCIPAL COMPETITORS

Deloitte & Touche Tohmatsu; KPMG International; PricewaterhouseCoopers International Limited.

FURTHER READING

"Bean-Counters Unite," *Economist,* October 25, 1997, pp. 67–68.

Berton, Lee, "Arthur Young, and Ernst Firm Plan to Merge," *Wall Street Journal,* May 19, 1989.

Burton, J. C., ed., *Arthur Young and the Business He Founded,* New York: Arthur Young & Company, 1948.

Cannon, Phillippa, "Ernst & Young Tax Breaks $2 Billion Barrier," *International Tax Review,* February 1998, p. 9.

Carswell, Simon, "Anglo Irish Bank Appoints Deloitte as Auditor," *Irish Times,* August 8, 2009, p. 16.

"E&W, AY, DH&S, and TR Financial Data Creates Public Stir," *Emerson's Professional Services Review,* March 1990.

"E&Y: The Masters of Total Quality Management," *Emerson's Professional Services Review,* March 1992.

"Entrepreneurial Services: Ernst & Young's Territory," *Emerson's Professional Services Review,* November 1991.

Ernst & Ernst: A History of the Firm, Cleveland: Ernst & Ernst, 1960.

"Ernst & Young Announces Global Revenues Increased to US$18.4 Billion," *NoticiasFinancieras* (Miami), September 29, 2006.

"Ernst & Young Changes Error Liability," *Daily Telegraph,* June 30, 2001, p. 27.

"Ernst & Young: Driving for Specialization and Service Integration Leadership," *Emerson's Professional Services Review,* March 1990.

"Ernst & Young Reaches 15% Increase in Global Revenues in Fiscal Year 2007," *NoticiasFinancieras* (Miami), November 5, 2007.

"Ernst & Young Settles Lincoln Savings Case," *New York Times,* July 15, 1992.

"Finance and Economics: Disciplinary Measures," *Economist,* March 6, 1999, pp. 68–69.

Frizell, Amy, "SEC Puts Six-Month Ban on Ernst & Young," *Independent* (London), April 17, 2004, p. 49.

Glater, Jonathan D., "Longtime Clients Abandon Auditor," *New York Times,* March 16, 2002, p. A1.

———, "S.E.C. Demands 6-Month Ban on New Ernst & Young Clients," *New York Times,* July 19, 2003, p. C3.

Hernandez, Raymond, "Giuliani's Firm to Acquire Investment Bank Business," *New York Times,* December 2, 2004, p. B4.

Hughes, Jennifer, "Audit Firms Once Again Making 'Consulting Hay,'" *Financial Times,* November 19, 2007, p. 4.

———, "Ernst & Young in $109m HealthSouth Settlement," *Financial Times,* March 26, 2009, p. 15.

Johnson, Carrie, "Surviving the Accounting Upheaval," *Washington Post,* July 30, 2003, p. E1.

Jones, Edgar, *Accountancy and the British Economy 1840–1980: The Evolution of Ernst & Whinney,* London: B.T. Batsford, Ltd., 1981.

Labaton, Stephen, "$400 Million Bargain for Ernst," *New York Times,* November 25, 1992.

Law, Donald M., "Business Tycoon Arthur Young Loved Life in Aiken at Crossways," *Aiken Standard,* April 19, 1987.

Lee, Jessica C., "Fallen Giants," *Orange County Business Journal,* July 21–July 27, 2008, pp. 28+.

Mackintosh, James, "Accounting Firms Drawn In to Madoff Scandal," *FT.com,* December 18, 2008.

McBride, Sarah, "How Ernst & Young Got Upper Hand—Point Man William Kimsey Never Stopped Wooing Andersen's Asia Partners," *Asian Wall Street Journal,* April 10, 2002, p. A1.

Moskowitz, Milton, et al., *Everybody's Business: A Field Guide to the 400 Leading Companies in America,* New York: Doubleday, 1990.

Murphy, Megan, "Law Lords; Ruling Limits Auditor Liability in Madoff-Style Frauds," *Financial Times,* July 31, 2009,

p. 1.

Rayner, Abigail, "Ernst & Young Accused of Breaking SEC Rules," *Times* (London), May 22, 2002, p. 25.

Stevens, Mark, *The Accounting Wars,* New York: Macmillan, 1985.

———, *The Big Eight,* New York: Macmillan, 1981.

———, *The Big Six: The Selling Out of America's Top Accounting Firms,* New York: Simon & Schuster, 1991.

Tagliabue, John, "Cap Gemini to Acquire Ernst & Young's Consulting Business," *New York Times,* March 1, 2000, p. C1.

Temkin, Sanchia, "Ernst & Young Has African Success," *Business Day* (Johannesburg), February 6, 2008, p. 12.

Willis, Clint, "How Winners Do It," *Forbes,* August 24, 1998, pp. 88–92.

HITACHI
Inspire the Next

Hitachi, Ltd.

■

6-6, Marunouchi 1-chome
Chiyoda-ku
Tokyo, 100-8280
Japan
Telephone: (+81 3) 3258-1111
Fax: (+81 3) 3258-2375
Web site: http://www.hitachi.co.jp

Public Company
Incorporated: 1920
Employees: 400,129
Sales: ¥10 trillion ($102.79 billion) (2009)
Stock Exchanges: Tokyo New York
Ticker Symbols: 6501 (Tokyo); HIT (NYSE)
NAICS: 334413 Semiconductor and Related Device
Manufacturing; 331513 Steel Foundries (Except
Investment); 334111 Electronic Computer
Manufacturing; 334220 Radio and Television
Broadcasting and Wireless Communications Equip-
ment Manufacturing; 334310 Audio and Video
Equipment Manufacturing; 334412 Printed Circuit
Board Manufacturing; 334419 Other Electronic
Component Manufacturing; 334515 Instrument
Manufacturing for Measuring and Testing Electric-
ity and Electrical Signals; 335228 Other Household
Appliance Manufacturing; 339113 Surgical Appli-
ance and Supplies Manufacturing

■ ■ ■

Hitachi, Ltd., is a leading electronics manufacturer and
one of the largest conglomerates in the world. The
company's full range of electronics products includes
semiconductors, personal computers, computer
peripherals, consumer audio and video equipment,
telecommunications equipment, and medical electronics
equipment. Beyond electronics, the company is involved
in financial services; property management; power and
industrial systems, including nuclear and hydroelectric
power plants; control equipment; elevators and escala-
tors; trains; automotive equipment and construction
machinery; home appliances such as air conditioners,
refrigerators, washing machines, microwave ovens, and
vacuum cleaners; and materials manufacturing, including pipes, wires, cables, and products made from iron,
steel, copper, and rubber.

ROOTS IN MOTORS

Hitachi's historical foundations can be traced back to
1910, when Namihei Odaira took his first engineering
job with Kuhara Mining. The graduate of the Tokyo
Institute of Science soon became frustrated with his
company's reliance on technology imported from
Europe and the United States. Odaira used his engineering skills to build small five-horsepower electric motors
that rivaled the imports in quality and durability. His
employer soon became his first, and, for a few years,
only customer.

While Odaira's motors worked efficiently for the
copper mine, he had trouble selling them to other
Japanese firms. It was not until the outbreak of World
War I that he was able to gain some large customers. A
major power company found that, because of the war, it
could not obtain the three large turbines it had ordered

from Germany and was forced to turn to Hitachi in the absence of a better alternative. Odaira made the most of his opportunity, delivering the 10,000-horsepower generators in five months. Impressed with his work, the power company ordered more equipment. Soon other corporations came to Odaira for help in improving their industrial capabilities.

Odaira incorporated his company in 1920 and named it for the town of Hitachi, where he had made his first sale. True to the company name, which means "rising sun," Odaira's success increased rapidly in the interwar era. In the 1920s Hitachi expanded its operations to meet the growing demand of Japan's burgeoning industrial economy. Through the acquisition of other companies, Hitachi evolved into the nation's largest manufacturer of pumps, blowers, and other mechanical equipment. The company also became involved in metal working and began manufacturing copper cable and rolling stock. These developments served to consolidate Hitachi's ability to build and supply a major manufacturer without outside help. In 1924 it also built Japan's first electric locomotive.

The ascendancy of the Japanese military government in the 1930s forced some changes at Hitachi. Although Odaira struggled to maintain corporate independence, his company was nonetheless pressured into manufacturing war material, including radar and sonar equipment for the Imperial Navy. Odaira, however, was successful in preventing Hitachi from manufacturing actual weapons.

World War II and its aftermath devastated the company. Many of its factories were destroyed by Allied bombing raids, and after the war, U.S. occupational forces tried to disband Hitachi altogether. Founder Odaira was removed from the company. Nevertheless, as a result of three years of negotiations, Hitachi was permitted to maintain all but 19 of its manufacturing plants. The cost of such a production shutdown, though, compounded by a three-month labor strike in 1950, severely hindered Hitachi's reconstruction efforts. Only the Korean War saved the company from complete collapse. Hitachi and many other struggling Japanese industrial firms benefited from defense contracts offered by the U.S. military. Meanwhile, Hitachi went public in 1949.

POSTWAR MOVES INTO ELECTRONICS AND HOUSEHOLD APPLIANCES

During the 1950s Chikara Kurata, who had succeeded Odaira as president of Hitachi, directed the company into an era of market expansion. Anticipating the future of electronic engineering, he established technology exchanges with General Electric and RCA. He also initiated a number of licensing agreements which allowed Hitachi to compete, through affiliates, in the worldwide market. In the 1960s the firm also began marketing consumer goods, introducing its own brand of household appliances and entertainment equipment.

Perhaps Hitachi's most important decision, however, was investing in computer research. In 1957 Hitachi built its first computer and entered into the high-tech age. During the 1960s Hitachi developed Japan's first online computer system, and emerged as the world's largest producer of analog computers, which were used in scientific research to compile complex statistical data. Despite its technical advances, Hitachi and most other Japanese electronics companies still lagged behind U.S.-based International Business Machines Corporation (IBM). The Japanese Ministry of International Trade and Industry took direct action to narrow the gap and make Japan competitive. It funded a cooperative research and development (R&D) effort which involved most of Japan's major technical firms. Hitachi benefited greatly from this program, and ended its overseas policy of non-confrontation. From that point forward, the high-tech competition between the United States and Japan, and between IBM and Hitachi in particular, was underway. In 1974 Hitachi developed and launched what were then known as "plug compatible mainframes." These "clones" cost less than, but were compatible with, IBM's machines, which set the industry standard.

Long recognized for its ability to adapt to changing economic conditions, Hitachi's flexibility was especially evident during the 1974 OPEC oil crisis that devastated Japan (which imported nearly 95 percent of its energy) and its industrial sector. Drastic cost-cutting measures were taken to keep the firm financially solvent, and company executives voluntarily took 15 percent pay cuts. Following 1975, when the company had its first disappointing fiscal year, sales and profits at Hitachi began to increase dramatically.

KEY DATES

■

1910: Namihei Odaira begins making small five-horsepower electric motors.

1915: Company manufactures a large 10,000-horsepower generator.

1920: Odaira incorporates his company as Hitachi, Ltd.

1924: Company builds Japan's first electric locomotive.

1939–45: Company is forced to make war material, and many of its factories are destroyed by Allied bombing raids.

1949: Hitachi goes public.

1957: Hitachi builds its first computer, marking the beginning of electronics production.

1960s: Production of household appliances begins.

1964: Hitachi builds the first cars for Japan's bullet train.

1974: Company produces its first IBM-compatible computer.

1982: Hitachi and 11 of its employees are indicted on charges of stealing confidential design secrets from IBM.

1988: Company forms joint venture with Texas Instruments to develop a 16-megabyte DRAM chip.

1989: Hitachi acquires controlling interest in National Advanced Systems, a U.S. distributor of mainframe computers; National is renamed Hitachi Data Systems.

1991: Through an alliance with IBM, Hitachi begins reselling IBM notebook computers in Japan under the Hitachi name.

1999: Company announces a ¥336.92 billion ($3 billion) net loss for the fiscal year ending in March; major restructuring efforts ensue.

2002: IBM Corp.'s disk drive manufacturing operations are acquired for $2.05 billion.

2003: Hitachi agrees to merge its semiconductor operations with those of Mitsubishi Electric Corp., resulting in a new company named Renesas Technology Corp. that is the world's third-largest semiconductor firm.

2006: President and CEO Etsuhiko Shoyama is named chairman, and Executive Vice President Kazuo Furukawa is named president.

2009: Takashi Kawamura, chairman of affiliate Hitachi Maxell Ltd., is named president; Hitachi announces plans to spin off its TV and auto parts businesses as separate companies.

SCANDALS AND OTHER PROBLEMS IN THE EIGHTIES

Hitachi worked hard, many said too hard, to transform itself into the IBM of Asia in the 1980s. In July 1982, Hitachi and 11 of its employees were indicted on charges of commercial bribery and theft. Apparently some employees at Hitachi had been stealing confidential design secrets from IBM so as not to lose ground in the intense race for technological superiority. The FBI and the U.S. Justice Department arranged an operation that caught Hitachi employees paying for IBM documents.

Penalties for the offense were, on the surface, quite light. Hitachi was fined $24,000 and only two employees were given jail sentences. The negative publicity caused by the scandal damaged Hitachi considerably, however. News of the trial appeared just as the company was beginning a full-scale marketing campaign for its products in the United States. Many U.S. companies canceled their orders or refused to receive shipments. A civil suit brought by IBM won the U.S. company at least $24 million in annual royalty payments over the ensuing eight years and the right to examine Hitachi's new software releases for five of those years.

Hitachi recovered from this unfortunate set of circumstances, but soon faced other problems. Marketing had always been the company's weakest department, seriously hampering its competitiveness abroad. For many years, Hitachi's products were sold under competitors' names, thereby undermining the company's brand recognition. In 1986, profits dropped for the first time in a decade, down 29 percent from 1985 to $884 million. Part of the decline could be attributed to external market factors: the strong yen made Hitachi's products comparatively more expensive; a global decline in semiconductor sales hamstrung that industry; and competition from low-cost manufacturers in Korea and Taiwan put a squeeze on profit margins.

Hitachi's sliding profits were also attributable to its concentration in mature and slow-growth markets. Its two largest sectors, industrial equipment and consumer products, were not all that promising: the conglomerate's large industrial customers had cut back on orders, and lackluster marketing efforts made Hitachi virtually indiscernible from the plethora of consumer electronics brands. The company was simply not positioned to enter into fast-growing markets.

To deal with these problems, Hitachi President Katsushige Mita sought to change the company's approach to its business. "We cannot live with tradition alone," he said. "I have to make Hitachi a more modern company." To this end, Mita reorganized Hitachi's operations and instituted new business strategies in the mid-1980s. Cost-cutting measures such as increased automation helped reduce labor expenses and helped the corporation compete more effectively with its rivals in Southeast Asia. The transfer of production to other countries helped diffuse fluctuations in the exchange rate. The 1989 purchase of a controlling interest in National Advanced Systems (NAS), a U.S. distributor of mainframe computers, helped shore up Hitachi's sales efforts in that important market. The subsidiary, renamed Hitachi Data Systems, hoped to challenge segment leaders IBM and Amdahl Corporation with machines that ran 20 percent faster than their competitors.

Increased investments in R&D helped the company stay in the technological vanguard, especially in semiconductors, consumer electronics, and computers. With the support of the Japanese government, Hitachi and its domestic competitors formed an R&D alliance known as the Very Large Scale Integration (VLSI) Project. The joint effort proved very fruitful, enabling Hitachi to stay one technological step ahead of its overseas competitors, continuously developing semiconductors with ever-higher memory capacity. By the early 1990s, Hitachi's R&D expenditures amounted to 6 percent of all corporate R&D spending in Japan. It also ranked as that country's top patent holder, and was even a contender for that standing in the United States.

Technical superiority, however, proved insufficient for the company; it also sought market share dominance. A 1985 memo leaked to the public revealed what U.S. competitors had suspected: Hitachi was "dumping" its semiconductors on overseas markets. Dumping, or selling goods in foreign markets at significantly lower prices than those set in domestic markets, is an anticompetitive practice. Once again, the company faced the wrath of the U.S. government.

DIFFICULT TIMES

An apparently contrite Hitachi charted a new, more cooperative course in the late 1980s and early 1990s. In 1988 it formed a trendsetting venture with Texas Instruments Incorporated to jointly develop a 16-megabyte dynamic random-access memory (DRAM) chip. In the early 1990s, Hitachi formed alliances with Hewlett-Packard Company, TRW Inc., and even longtime rival IBM. The latter partnership, which began in 1991, involved Hitachi reselling IBM notebooks in Japan under the Hitachi name.

Still, Hitachi was unable to parlay its technological leadership into earnings growth: while the conglomerate's sales were essentially flat at around ¥7 trillion from 1991 to 1994, its profits dropped more than 71 percent, from ¥230 billion to ¥65 billion. In 1990, President Mita announced a reorganization that focused, in part, on transforming the conservative corporate culture that some observers blamed for Hitachi's declining earnings. The leader shifted the company's primary emphasis from heavy industrial equipment to information systems. Organizational changes focused on the dismantling of a "plant profit center" scheme. Sometimes known as just "pc," this system integrated production, quality, and cost control as well as product design and planning within each factory. The new plan reorganized some divisions into autonomous operations in an effort to emphasize consumer demands over production requirements. Pay freezes and cuts of up to 15 percent for white-collar workers were also instituted.

Mita became chairman in 1991 as Tsutomu Kanai took the reins as president. As Hitachi struggled to improve its profitability, it continued to gain renown in Japan for the bullet trains that it built. Having built the first cars for the bullet train in 1964, Hitachi introduced a new model in 1993 that boasted maximum speeds of 270 kilometers (167 miles) per hour. This achievement was a prime example of why Hitachi suffered from such low profit margins throughout the 1990s. Although best known as an electronics manufacturer, the company was saddled with numerous slow-growth, low-margin product lines that were holdovers from earlier decades in the company's history. At mid-decade Hitachi's workforce totaled more than 330,000 workers, comprising the largest private labor force in Japan, and the company had more than 860 subsidiaries. Many U.S. observers believed that Hitachi and the other Japanese conglomerates needed massive restructurings involving huge workforce reductions and the selling off or closing down of large numbers of noncore operations. Although often compared to General Electric, Hitachi had nothing like the strategy of GE chief Jack Welch, who professed to abandon any business in which his company could not attain the number one or number two position. Such ruthless business practices, particularly any action involving mass layoffs or firings, remained taboo in Japan. Hitachi was seen by many as a lumbering giant, unable to move quickly enough to improve profitability or develop new products in a timely manner.

Compounding Hitachi's travails was the prolonged economic stagnation that afflicted Japan in the wake of the bursting of the bubble economy of the late 1980s. Then the Asian economic crisis erupted in mid-1997, sending demand for, and the prices of, semiconductors and other electronics products tumbling. Hitachi barely eked out a profit for the fiscal year ending in March 1998, before plunging into the red the following year, posting a net loss of ¥336.92 billion ($3.33 billion). This was the company's first loss since it began using consolidated accounting in 1963 and one of the largest on record in corporate Japan.

RESTRUCTURING BEGINS

Kanai in 1998 announced a restructuring involving a workforce reduction of 4,000. Then in April 1999 Kanai was named chairman, and Etsuhiko Shoyama was promoted from executive vice president to president. Shoyama began implementing other restructuring efforts, including the reorganization of the company into 10 divisions (which Hitachi called "companies"), each of which had its own president with broad autonomy whose pay was linked to performance. The size of the company's board of directors was cut to help speed up decision making. A semiconductor plant in Irving, Texas, was shut down and 650 people were laid off. Certain product lines, such as mainframe computers, were abandoned. To counter the company's engineering-driven culture, which tended to create products without regard to market needs, product developers were forced to get feedback from the marketing staff.

In another break with tradition, Hitachi abandoned its insistence on developing major products internally and turned to alliances and joint ventures with its competitors. In November 1999 Hitachi and NEC formed a joint venture, Elpida Memory Inc., to make DRAM memory chips. One month later, Hitachi joined with Taiwan-based United Microelectronics Corporation to form Trecenti Technologies, Inc., a venture focusing on the fabrication of semiconductor wafers. By early 2001 Hitachi had similarly entered into several other alliances, including ventures with: Fujitsu to develop, make, and sell large-screen plasma display panels for the widescreen television market; Computer Sciences Corporation of El Segundo, California, to offer informa-

tion technology systems and services in Japan; Clarity Group, to develop optical components for telecommunications through a U.S. venture called OpNext, Inc.; NEC to develop next-generation optical transport systems; Omron Corporation of Japan to design factory automation control systems; Fuji Electric Co., Ltd., and Meidensha Corporation to develop, design, and produce equipment and components for facilities devoted to the transmission and distribution of electric power; and Kawasaki Heavy Industries to pursue contracts for overseas railway systems.

Hitachi also began pursuing acquisitions as a means of gaining positions in burgeoning high-tech companies in the United States and Japan. One of the company's main strengths was its huge hoard of cash, which totaled $15 billion at the end of the 1990s. Leveraging this asset, Hitachi planned to spend about $3 billion on acquisitions from 2000 through 2003. One of the first purchases was a $175 million deal for U.S.-based e-Business Consulting Group, which was renamed Experio Solutions Corporation. In another streamlining move, Hitachi announced in February 2001 that its instruments group and its semiconductor manufacturing equipment group would be merged into Nissei Sangyo Co., Ltd., a publicly traded firm controlled by Hitachi through a majority ownership. Nissei Sangyo had already been handling sales for the two groups, and this move was aimed at improving efficiency. Other mergers of subsidiaries and affiliates were accomplished as well.

Although relatively tame by U.S. standards, the restructuring efforts undertaken were certainly significant for a Japanese giant such as Hitachi. Less certain was the program's chances for success. The emphasis on profitability, though, was never more prominent: Shoyama made delivering a return on equity of 8 percent by March 2003 the main goal of the restructuring.

Other developments during 2001 included the European Commission's approval of the company's plans to acquire Borg Warner Inc. and Hitachi Warner Turbo Systems midway through the year. That October, Hitachi revealed plans to spin off its Consumer Products Group and Industrial Components & Equipment Group.

GROWTH AND CHANGE DURING THE NEW MILLENNIUM

In mid-2002, a major deal unfolded when Hitachi acquired Comstock Systems Corp., strengthening its storage software business in a deal worth $20 million. Activity continued to heat up during the latter part of the year when Hitachi acquired IBM's disk drive manufacturing operations in December for $2.05 billion.

In April 2003, Hitachi agreed to merge its semiconductor operations with those of Mitsubishi Electric Corp., resulting in a new company named Renesas Technology Corp. The deal created the world's third-largest semiconductor firm by sales. That year, the company also made several key advancements within the medical industry. These included the development and commercialization of a high-speed finger vein authentication system, as well as the use of optical topography to measure the brain functions of infants.

Progress continued in 2004. In August of that year, Hitachi's Renesas Technology joint venture parted with $10.9 million to acquire two chip-making plants in the Tokyo area from Hitachi, Ltd. Importantly, the purchases enabled the joint venture's subsidiary, Renesas Eastern Japan Semiconductor Inc., to boost its production capacity by about 20 percent.

Hitachi made several advancements within its consumer electronics business during the middle of the decade. As part of a strategy to ramp up global market share for plasma television displays to 15 percent by 2006, the company agreed to acquire a portion of Fujitsu Hitachi Plasma Display Ltd. from partner Fujitsu Ltd. Around the same time, the company established a plasma television joint venture with Matsushita Electric Industrial Co.

Other developments in 2005 included the acquisition of the Santa Clara, California-based fiber-optic communications company Salira Optical Network Systems Inc. in conjunction with Hitachi Communications Technology Ltd. In addition, the company established an R&D hub in China, forming Hitachi (China) R&D Corp., and merged Hitachi Home & Life Solutions Inc., its electrical appliance business, with Hitachi Air Conditioning Systems Co.

LEADERSHIP CHANGES

Hitachi kicked off 2006 with a focus on its consulting business, revealing plans to expand the number of its consultants from 952 to roughly 3,000. During the early part of the year, the company's Hitachi Consulting Corp. subsidiary grew via the acquisition of the business intelligence and corporate performance management firm Navigator Systems Inc. In addition, Hitachi Consulting Europe Ltd. commenced operations.

Several leadership changes also occurred in 2006. In April, President and CEO Etsuhiko Shoyama was named chairman, and Executive Vice President Kazuo Furukawa was named president. During the latter part of the year, plans were made to construct a new flat-panel-display manufacturing facility in the Czech Republic, and the company announced that it would combine its nuclear power business with that of General Electric.

Hitachi began 2007 by announcing that its Hitachi Data Systems subsidiary had agreed to acquire the Waltham, Massachusetts-based digital archiving company Archivas Inc. The acquisition furthered the growth of a subsidiary that already employed 3,200 employees and served more than half of the *Fortune* 100. By this time, Hitachi itself employed a workforce of some 356,000 people throughout the world.

In November 2007, Hitachi revealed plans to significantly ramp up capacity at its Japan-based nuclear power equipment factory via a $265 million investment. In addition, Hitachi Appliances Inc. laid plans to commence production of Hitachi-branded commercial air conditioners for sale in India.

Progress continued at Hitachi as the company headed into the closing years of the decade. A new line of ultrathin high-definition television monitors was introduced in the United States during the early part of the year. Around the same time, the company established a liquid crystal display (LCD) business alliance with Canon Inc., and Hitachi Consulting acquired the San Francisco, California-based consulting firm JMN Associates.

Leadership changes were a major theme during this period. In September 2008, Kiyoshi Kinugawa was named president and CEO of Hitachi America Ltd. In early 2009, Nobuyuki Ohno became chief executive and chief innovation officer of the company's Hitachi China business. In February, Masao Hisada succeeded Tadahiko Ishigaki as chief executive for the Americas and chairman of Hitachi America Ltd. The following month, Hitachi Consulting named Philip R. Parr as its president and CEO. Changes continued in April, when Takashi Kawamura, chairman of affiliate Hitachi Maxell Ltd., was named president of Hitachi, Ltd.

In mid-2009, Hitachi announced that it would spin off its television and auto parts businesses as separate companies. In addition, the company revealed that five of its group firms, including Hitachi Software Engineering Co., Hitachi Systems & Services Ltd., Hitachi Maxell Ltd., Hitachi Plant Technologies Ltd., and Hitachi Information Systems Ltd., would become wholly owned subsidiaries.

Other significant developments occurred during the last half of 2009. In addition to finalizing its acquisition of Maxell, Hitachi's Data Systems Corp. business established the Yokohama Third Center in Yokohama,

Japan, which it dubbed one of the world's leading "green data centers."

April Dougal Gasbarre
Updated, David E. Salamie; Paul R. Greenland

PRINCIPAL SUBSIDIARIES

Hitachi Communication Technology Ltd.; Hitachi Electronics Service Co. Ltd.; Hitachi Information & Control Solutions Ltd.; Hitachi Koki Co. Ltd. (23.3%); Hitachi Information Systems Ltd. (52%); Shin Meiwa Kogyo Co. Ltd. (28.6%); Hitachi Kokusai Electric Inc. (52.5%); Tokiko Co. Ltd. (21.7%); Hitachi Kokusai Denki Co. Ltd. (36.5%); Hitachi-Omron Terminal Solutions Corp. (55%); Hitachi Software Engineering Co. Ltd. (53%); Hitachi System & Service Co. Ltd. (51.20%); Hitachi Computer Products (Europe) S.A.S. (France); Hitachi Global Storage Technologies Netherlands B.V.; Hitachi Information & Telecommunication Systems Global Holding Corp. (USA); Hitachi Displays Ltd. (50.2%); Hitachi High-Technologies Co. Ltd. (51.8%); Hitachi Medico Corp. (63.2%); Babcock-Hitachi K.K. Clarion Co. Ltd. (64%); Hitachi Building Systems Co. Ltd.; Hitachi Construction Machinery Co. Ltd. (53.1%); Hitachi Engineering & Services Co. Ltd.; Hitachi-GE Nuclear Energy Ltd. (80%); Hitachi Industrial Equipment Systems Co. Ltd.; Hitachi Koki Co. Ltd. (51.3%); Hitachi Mobile Co. Ltd.; Hitachi Plant Technologies Ltd. (69.8%); Hitachi Via Mechanics Ltd.; Hitachi Power Europe GmbH (Germany); Hitachi Appliances Inc.; Hitachi Maxell Ltd. (53.6%); Hitachi Media Electronics Co. Ltd.; Hitachi Plasma Display Ltd.; Hitachi Cable Ltd. (53.2%); Hitachi Chemical Co. Ltd. (51.4%); Hitachi Metals Ltd. (55.7%); Chuo Shoji Ltd.; Hitachi Life Corp.; Hitachi Logistics Co. Ltd. (59%); Nikkyo Create Co. Ltd.; Hitachi America Ltd. (USA); Hitachi Asia Ltd. (Singapore); Hitachi China Co. Ltd.; Hitachi Europe Ltd. (UK); Hitachi Capital Co. Ltd. (60.7%); Hitachi Computer Products (America) Inc. (USA); Hitachi Data Systems Corp. (USA); Hitachi Display Device (Suzhou) Co. Ltd. (China); Hitachi Automotive Products (USA) Inc. (USA); Hitachi Elevator (China) Co. Ltd. (70%); Hitachi Home Electronics (America) Inc. (USA); Shanghai Hitachi Home Electronics Co. Ltd. (China; 95%); Hitachi Insurance Services Ltd.

PRINCIPAL COMPETITORS

Fujitsu Limited; Panasonic Corp.; Toshiba Corporation.

FURTHER READING

Anchordoguy, Marie, *Computers, Inc.: Japan's Challenge to IBM*, Cambridge, MA: Harvard University Press, 1989.

Beauchamp, Marc, "'We Have to Change,'" *Forbes*, September 22, 1986, pp. 84–92.

Fulford, Benjamin, "Jack Welch Lite," *Forbes*, June 14, 1999, pp. 64–68.

Gross, Neil, "Inside Hitachi," *Business Week*, September 28, 1992, pp. 92–98, 100.

Hamilton, David P., "Harder Drive: Decade After Failing, Japan Firms Try Anew to Sell PCs in U.S.," *Wall Street Journal*, June 5, 1996, pp. A1+.

———, "Japan's PC Firms Boot Up to Invade U.S.: Hitachi and Fujitsu Are Leading Latest Foray," *Wall Street Journal*, November 3, 1995, p. A10.

Hara, Eijiro, "Hitachi: The Shackles of Past Glory, and Faith in Technology," *Tokyo Business Today*, March 1991, pp. 34–37.

"Hitachi, Canon Finalize LCD Business Alliance Deal," *Japan Consumer Electronics Scan*, March 2, 2008.

"Hitachi Completes Purchase of IBM Drive Business; Company to Form Hitachi Global Storage Technologies," *InfoWorld.com*, December 31, 2002.

"Hitachi Consulting Acquires Leading Financial Services Industry Consulting Firm JMN Associates," *Business Wire*, March 10, 2008.

"Hitachi Data Systems Unveils One of the Industry's Most Robust and Reliable Green Data Centers," *Information Technology Business*, September 8, 2009.

"Hitachi Forms China R&D Hub," *R&D*, May 2005.

"Hitachi Launches Ultra-Thin HDTVs for U.S. Market," *InformationWeek*, January 8, 2008.

"Hitachi Ltd.," *Notable Corporate Chronologies*, Online Ed., Farmington Hills, MI: Thomson Gale, 2007.

"Hitachi, Ltd. Appoints Masao Hisada Chief Executive for the Americas," *Business Wire*, February 3, 2009.

"Hitachi Names Nobuyuki Ohno as China Chief Executive," *SinoCast Daily Business Beat*, February 4, 2009.

"Hitachi Purchases Comstock," *eWeek*, June 24, 2002.

"Hitachi Set to Turn 5 Group Firms into Wholly Owned Subsidiaries," *Kyodo News International*, July 27, 2009.

"Hitachi's Snail-Like Progress," *Economist*, October 3, 1998, pp. 69–70.

"Hitachi to Have New President, Spin Off Car Parts, TV Operations," *Kyodo News International*, March 16, 2009.

"Hitachi Wraps Up Maxell Buy," *Europe Intelligence Wire*, August 8, 2009.

Hof, Robert D., "'The Japanese Threat in Mainframes Has Finally Arrived,'" *Business Week*, April 9, 1990, p. 24.

Imori, Takeo, "Hitachi: Too Little Too Late?" *Tokyo Business Today*, December 1992, pp. 12–13.

Keenan, Faith, and Peter Landers, "Staggering Giants," *Far Eastern Economic Review*, April 1, 1999, pp. 10–13.

Kunii, Irene M., "High-Tech Giants on the Ropes," *Business Week*, November 30, 1998, p. 74.

Landers, Peter, "Broken Up: Japan's Biggest Players Get Serious About Restructuring," *Far Eastern Economic Review*, February 11, 1999, p. 50.

Landers, Peter, and Robert A. Guth, "Japan's Hitachi Plans High-Tech Shopping Spree: Domestic and U.S. Stakes Are Sought as a Giant Changes," *Wall Street Journal*, January 5, 2000, p. Al9.

Mattera, Philip, *World Class Business: A Guide to the 100 Most Powerful Global Corporations*, New York: Holt, 1992.

Port, Otis, "What's Behind the Texas Instruments-Hitachi Deal," *Business Week*, January 16, 1989, pp. 93, 96.

Rowley, Ian, "Stimulus Spending Boosts Japan's Train Manufacturers," *Business Week Online*, March 10, 2009.

Smith, Lee, "Hitachi: Gliding Nowhere?" *Fortune*, August 5, 1996, pp. 81–84.

Sobel, Robert, *IBM vs. Japan: The Struggle for the Future*, Briarcliff Manor, NY: Stein & Day, 1985.

Tsurumi, Yoshi, *Multinational Management: Business Strategy and Government Policy*, Cambridge, MA: Ballinger, 1977.

Wald, Matthew L., "G.E. and Hitachi Will Merge Their Nuclear Power Units," *New York Times*, November 14, 2006.

Holland America Line Inc.

———— ■ ————

300 Elliott Avenue West
Seattle, Washington 98119
U.S.A.
Telephone: (206) 281-3535
Toll Free: (877) 724-5425
Fax: (206) 281-7110
Web site: http://www.hollandamerica.com

Wholly Owned Subsidiary of Carnival Corporation and Carnival plc
Incorporated: 1873 as Nederlandsch-Amerikaansche Stoomvaart Maatschappij
Employees: 14,000
Sales: $220.9 million (2008 est.)
NAICS: 483112 Deep Sea Passenger Transportation

■ ■ ■

Holland America Line Inc. (HAL) is a cruise ship operator offering vacation packages to 320 destinations in more than 100 countries on all seven continents. The company owns a fleet of 14 vessels ranging in age from the 1988 *Prinsendam* to the 2008 *Eurodam* with a total passenger capacity of 21,088. The majority of HAL's cruises last from seven to 21 days. Its longest cruise is the 118-day "Grand World Voyage," which circumnavigates the world. The majority of the company's Caribbean cruises visit Half Moon Cay, an island owned by HAL. In Alaska, where HAL ranks as the dominant cruise ship operator, the company owns a chain of 16 hotels, 24 domed railcars, 560 motor coaches, and two day boats. HAL is a subsidiary of the largest cruise ship operator in the world, Carnival Corporation and Carnival plc.

19TH-CENTURY ORIGINS

One of the oldest competitors in the cruise ship industry, HAL began operating 20 years before it offered its first cruise. The company was founded in Rotterdam in 1873 as Nederlandsch-Amerikaansche Stoomvaart Maatschappij (Netherlands-America Steamship Company, or NASM), its formation the result of another Rotterdam-based company, Plate, Reuchlin & Co., reorganizing itself. NASM shipped freight and transported passengers, its two principal lines of business for a century. Its first ship, *Rotterdam*, had sailed her 15-day, maiden voyage from the Netherlands to New York six months before the company was created, establishing the transfer points NASM would use to carry passengers and cargo, although the company, from 1882 forward, used facilities in Hoboken, New Jersey, as its western terminus. During its first 25 years of business, the company expanded its fleet to six ships, carrying 90,000 cabin passengers, 400,000 steerage passengers, and five million tons of cargo, primarily flower bulbs, herring, and gin.

NASM generated nearly all of its income from transportation and shipping during its early years, but it also ventured into a third business area. In 1895, one year before NASM changed its name to Holland Amerika Lijn (Holland America Line), the company offered its first vacation cruise aboard the 3,300-ton *Rotterdam II*. It was a significant moment in the company's history, but the trip itself was modest in scope. Tourists

For more than 136 years, Holland America Line has been a recognized leader in cruising, taking our guests to exotic destinations around the world. If you are looking for some of the most spacious and comfortable ships at sea, award-winning service, five star dining, extensive activities and enrichment programs and compelling worldwide itineraries, you've come to the right place. We are committed to our mission: through excellence, we create once-in-a-lifetime experiences, every time.

boarded the ship for a short voyage from Rotterdam to Copenhagen and back, inaugurating a service that years later would represent HAL's financial lifeblood. The company waited 15 years before offering its second vacation cruise, a voyage that was decidedly more ambitious than its first cruise. In 1910, HAL offered a cruise that departed from New York City and stopped in the Mediterranean before taking its passengers to the Holy Land. HAL continued to offer cruises in succeeding years; *Veendam II* completed the company's first Caribbean cruise in 1926, the same year *Rijndam I* completed the company's first around-the-world voyage, but shipping and transportation remained HAL's mainstay.

During its first half-century of business, HAL experimented with cruises and made a substantial percentage of its revenue hauling cargo, but the company devoted the bulk of its resources to transporting passengers. Millions of Europeans made the transatlantic trek to the United States between 1880 and 1920, a period of intense emigration from the Old World to the New World. HAL played a substantial role in the western exodus, carrying more than 10 percent of the passengers traveling steerage from Europe to the United States during the period.

TWO WORLD WARS AND THE GREAT DEPRESSION

For a 30-year period stretching from World War I, through the Great Depression, and to the end of World War II, HAL's business bowed to the influence of world events. The company lost six vessels during World War I, which reduced its fleet to 10 ships after the war. The worldwide economic collapse a decade later delivered a more painful blow to the company's operations. Between 1931 and 1933, HAL sold a dozen of its ships for scrap, closed or consolidated its offices in Europe

and North America, and cut its payroll by 34 percent. The company survived the crucible of the Great Depression, but just as HAL righted itself (the company offered 36 vacation cruises in 1938) another global conflict interrupted its normal course of business. HAL's fleet aided in the prosecution of the war effort, transporting military personnel and equipment and drawing fire from enemy forces. *Nieuw Amsterdam*, flagship of the HAL line, sailed 500,000 miles and carried 400,000 troops during World War II. Another HAL vessel, *Westernland*, served as the seat of the Netherlands government for a brief period during the war. A heavy toll was exacted upon HAL's fleet during World War II, reducing the size of its fleet from 25 ships to nine ships by the end of the war.

CRUISES TAKE PRECEDENCE

During the postwar era, the modern version of HAL took shape, as an extended period of peace and prosperity saw the company turn increasingly to cruises as its primary means of financial support. In 1951, *Ryndam II* and *Maasdam III*, dubbed the "Economy Twins," became the first HAL ships to allow tourist-class passengers to roam about; the upper deck on the vessels was the only area restricted to first-class passengers. In 1958, the 24,200-ton SS *Statendam IV* departed Hoboken on HAL's first Grand World voyage. As cruises became a more prominent facet of HAL's operations, the importance of shipping and transportation, the two pillars that had supported the company since its inception, began to fade. In 1971, the company stopped offering transatlantic passenger service and two years later, after hauling 76 million tons of freight during the previous century, sold its cargo shipping division. From the early 1970s forward, HAL focused its efforts on the cruise business.

ACQUISITION OF WESTOURS

The most significant event during HAL's transition from a cargo and passenger operator into a cruise operator occurred in 1971. The company paid $1.25 million to gain a controlling interest in Westours, Inc., a publicly traded tour company based in Seattle, Washington, that operated in Alaska. HAL bought out minority shareholders in 1977, and converted Westours into a private company, committing its resources to offering vacation itineraries in Alaska. It was a significant change in strategy and geography. HAL moved its headquarters from Rotterdam to Stamford, Connecticut, in 1978, and five years later, in an effort to save money, relocated its main offices again, occupying Westour's headquarters in Seattle. The move in 1983 led to a

---

KEY DATES

1873: Holland America is founded as Nederlandsch-Amerikaansche Stoomvaart Maatschappij.
1895: Company offers its first vacation cruise.
1896: Company changes its name to Holland Amerika Lijn (Holland America Line).
1920: During the previous 40 years, Holland America carries more than 10 percent of the passengers traveling steerage from Europe to the United States.
1931: Economic turmoil forces the company to sell a dozen of its ships for scrap.
1945: By the end of World War II, Holland America loses more than half its fleet.
1971: Holland America stops offering transatlantic passenger service and acquires a controlling interest in Westours, Inc.
1973: Company sells its cargo shipping division, leaving it focused on offering cruises.
1983: Holland America establishes its headquarters in Seattle, Washington.
1989: Carnival Cruise Lines pays $625 million to acquire Holland America.
1996: Holland America acquires an island in the Bahamas.
2002: *Zuiderdam*, the first of five Vista-class vessels, enters service.
2004: Stein Kruse is named chief executive officer.
2008: *Eurodam*, the largest ship in Holland America's fleet, enters service.

---

name change, the unfurling of the "Holland America Line-Westours Inc." corporate banner. Kirk Lanterman, the president of Westours, became the president of the newly christened company, marking the beginning of a leadership tenure that would stretch into the 21st century.

Committed to a future as cruise operator, HAL focused all its efforts on creating attractive itineraries for tourists. The company built its business around Westours, which owned day boats, railcars, and motor coaches that carried passengers to popular destinations and attractions in Alaska. In 1986, HAL acquired the 18-unit Westmark Hotel chain, which operated in Alaska and western Canada, enabling it to offer its customers comprehensive vacation packages. HAL invested in properties outside of Alaska as well, purchasing Windstar Sail Cruises in 1988. Windstar operated

three, four-masted, 148-passenger sailing ships that toured the Mediterranean, the Caribbean, and French Polynesia.

MERGER IN 1989

The year HAL acquired Windstar marked a significant moment in the company's history. Miami-based Carnival Cruise Lines, the largest cruise ship operator in the world, was looking to build on its leadership position in the industry. Led by Ted Arison, the company completed its initial public offering of stock in 1987 to finance an expansion campaign. Arison quickly moved to gain control of Royal Admiral Ltd., a cruise ship operator that owned Royal Caribbean Cruise Line and Admiral Cruises, offering $561 million to acquire a 70 percent stake in the company. His advances were rebuffed, prompting him to approach Nico van der Vorm, HAL's chairman, in November 1988. HAL, the dominant operator in Alaska, with holdings in various marine businesses such as steel cables, tarpaulins, navigational instruments, and ship chandlery, was a $328 million business at the time, generating nearly $50 million in annual profit. Arison offered approximately $625 million for HAL, and van der Norm agreed to the deal, ending more than a century of independence for the Seattle-based company.

The merger, the largest in the cruise liner industry at the time, was completed in January 1989, combining the largest mass-market line and the second-largest line in the mid-level premium market. With the acquisition, Carnival increased its passenger capacity by more than 50 percent. The company gained 5 day boats, 8 railcars, roughly 200 motor coaches, the Westmark Hotel Chain, Windstar, and HAL's cruise ship line: the 1,114-passenger *Rotterdam*, the 1,214-passenger *Nieuw Amsterdam*, the 1,214-passenger *Noordam*, and the 1,140-passenger *Westerdam*. For its part, HAL became part of an organization with deep financial pockets and was promised relative autonomy within the Carnival fold. Lanterman remained in charge of the company, adding the title of chief executive officer when the transaction was completed, and HAL remained based in Seattle, where it operated as an independent subsidiary of Carnival.

FLEET EXPANDS DURING THE NINETIES

The benefits of the merger with Carnival were evident shortly after the deal was completed. At the time of the transaction the HAL fleet ranged in age from the 1959 *Rotterdam* to the 1986 *Westerdam*. In 1990, with financial backing from Carnival, an order was placed with Italian shipyard Fincantieri Cantieri Navali S.p.A. for four, 1,266-passenger sister ships. In 1996, Carnival ordered two more ships from Fincantieri Cantieri Navali, spending $600 million to increase HAL's fleet to 10 vessels and consolidate its position as the industry's fourth-largest line. At the end of the decade, another building program was announced, as the Italian shipyard began building five, 1,848-passenger Vista-class vessels. The ships, costing $400 million each, became the signature vessels of the HAL fleet in the 21st century.

HAL expanded aggressively during the 1990s, increasing the size of its fleet substantially and even going as far as buying its own island. In December 1996, the company paid $6 million for Little San Salvador, an uninhabited island in the Bahamas. HAL renamed the 2,400-acre island Half Moon Cay and developed a 45-acre, $16 million property on the island, using it as a port of call for nearly every Caribbean cruise the company offered.

HOLLAND AMERICA IN THE 21ST CENTURY

As HAL entered its third century of business, its eagerly awaited Vista-class vessels entered service. *Zuiderdam*, completed in 2002, was the first of five, 85,800-ton Vista-class liners to carry passengers. Larger than any of the company's other ships, *Zuiderdam* was capable of accommodating 1,916 passengers and featured a brighter, more contemporary décor designed to attract younger customers. *Oosterdam* followed in 2003, a year that saw Lanterman pass the duties of president to Stein Kruse, HAL's senior vice president of fleet operations. Lanterman relinquished his responsibilities as chief executive officer the following year, ending a more than 20-year tenure at the helm of HAL. Kruse was appointed as his successor, taking charge of the company the same year the third Vista-class vessel, the 1,916-passenger *Westerdam*, entered service.

Under Kruse's stewardship, HAL's fleet expanded and the entire line underwent an ambitious renovation program. During his first years in command, two new Vista-class vessels joined the fleet, the 1,918-passenger *Noordam* in 2006 and the 2,104-passenger *Eurodam* in 2008. The period also saw HAL launch its "Signature of

Excellence" program, initially a $225 million renovation program that included sweeping interior and exterior improvements to the company's fleet. The first phase, completed in 2006, was followed by a $200 million program launched in 2008. The project was expected to be completed by 2010, by which time the 15th member of the fleet, *Nieuw Amsterdam*, was expected to be in service.

Jeffrey L. Covell

PRINCIPAL SUBSIDIARIES

HAL Antilles N.V.; Holland America Line N.V.; Holland America Tours; Holland America Westours Inc; Westours Motor Coaches Inc.

PRINCIPAL COMPETITORS

Royal Caribbean Cruises Ltd.; Star Cruises Limited; Nippon Yusen Kabushiki Kaisha.

FURTHER READING

Blum, Ernest, "Carnival Buys Holland America," *Travel Weekly*, December 5, 1988, p. 1.

———, "Carnival Orders 2 Larger-Class Cruise Ships for Holland America," *Travel Weekly*, July 25, 1996, p. 5.

"Cruise Line Buys Bahamas Island," *Travel Weekly*, January 16, 1997, p. 97.

"HAL's Lanterman to Step Down as CEO," *Travel Weekly*, November 1, 2004, p. 4.

"Holland America Will Start Seattle-Based Cruises in '02," *Puget Sound Business Journal*, May 18, 2001, p. 14.

"Kruse Steps Up to Run Holland America Line," *Europe Intelligence Wire*, November 10, 2003.

Mott, David, "$225M Facelift for the HAL Fleet," *International Cruise & Ferry Review*, Spring–Summer 2005, p. 31.

O'Dell, Larry, "Holland America Line Announces $200 Million in Enhancements to Five Ships as Part of Ongoing Signature of Excellence," *America's Intelligence Wire*, September 4, 2008.

Tobin, Rebecca, "*Zuiderdam*: The New Face of Holland America," *Travel Weekly*, February 3, 2003, p. C1.

Hoover's, Inc.

5800 Airport Boulevard
Austin, Texas 78752
U.S.A.
Telephone: (512) 374-4500
Toll Free: (800) 486-8666
Fax: (512) 374-4501
Web site: http://www.hoovers.com

Subsidiary of The Dun & Bradstreet Corporation
Incorporated: 1990 as The Reference Press
Employees: 383
Sales: $124.9 million (2008)
NAICS: 518111 On-Line Information Services; 511140 Database and Directory Publishers; 511130 Book Publishers; 541990 All Other Professional, Scientific, and Technical Services

■ ■ ■

Hoover's, Inc., markets business information on U.S. and international companies and industries, using a database of proprietary content covering public and private companies. The company publishes reference books, but concentrates primarily on electronic publishing, distributing its content through the Internet, data feeds, wireless devices, and e-commerce agreements with other vendors. Hoover's, Inc., maintains its own Web site, which offers free and for-pay content. The company generates the majority of its revenue by selling subscriptions on its Web site. Hoover's, Inc., is a subsidiary of The Dun & Bradstreet Corporation, a provider of credit information on corporations.

GARY HOOVER: SUCCESS AS AN ENTREPRENEUR

Gary Hoover laid the groundwork for his entrepreneurial career at an early age. He began subscribing to *Fortune* magazine when he was 12 years old, demonstrating an interest in the intricacies of the business world that led him to major in economics at the University of Chicago. Hoover founded three campus-based businesses during his college years, leaving with a degree in 1973 that he used to gain entry to Wall Street. Citibank hired him to work as a stock analyst for the retail industry, an industry Hoover joined when he left Citibank after a two-year stint and spent the next two years as a buyer for Sanger-Harris, the leading department store in Dallas, Texas. Next, Hoover served as vice president of May Department Stores, a job that took him to St. Louis, where he spent five years working on financial planning, competitive analysis, and strategic planning for the retail chain. After his experience in the securities and retail industries, Hoover was ready to start his own business, which he did in 1982 at the age of 30.

An Indiana native, Hoover returned to Texas and started a chain of discount bookstores in Austin that operated under the names BOOKSTOP and BOOKSTAR. Regarded as the first chain of superstores that sold books, the business expanded into Louisiana, Florida, and California by the end of the decade, drawing the attention of Barnes & Noble, a book retailer intent on becoming the dominant player in its industry. In 1987, Barnes & Noble acquired B. Dalton Bookseller from Dayton Hudson, giving it 797 retail locations that made it the second-largest bookseller in the United

COMPANY PERSPECTIVES

Hoover's, Inc., a D&B Company, puts you on the fastest path to business. We deliver comprehensive insight and analysis about the companies, industries, and people that drive the economy, along with the powerful tools to find and connect to the right people to get business done.

States. The company, which had been experimenting with different formats for its stores throughout the decade, found a blueprint for its sprawling chain when it acquired Hoover's business in 1989 for $41.5 million. Barnes & Noble credited the development of its superstore strategy to the acquisition of the Hoover's chain, gaining valuable insight into the particulars of real estate, operations, marketing, and merchandising. Hoover, after building his company into the fourth-largest bookseller in the nation, was free to start his next entrepreneurial venture.

HOOVER'S INC. BEGINS AS THE REFERENCE PRESS

While he presided over his chain of bookstores, Hoover noticed that the titles on his stores' shelves paid scant attention to his lifelong passion. He felt there were too few books devoted to companies and industries, a belief that prompted him to establish The Reference Press in 1990. In starting the company, which marked the beginning of Hoover's, Inc., Hoover enlisted the help of Alta Campbell, who served as the company's first editor-in-chief, and a friend from his years at the University of Chicago, Patrick Spain. Spain, who soon became The Reference Press's CEO, earned his degree from the University of Chicago a year after Hoover left and obtained a law degree from Boston University in 1979. After completing his education, Spain worked as an associate counsel for Extel, a company founded a century earlier to distribute financial and business information from commercial markets to subscribers.

The Reference Press published its first book before the end of 1990, *Hoover's Handbook 1991: Profiles of Over 500 Major Corporations*. The nearly 700-page book, which retailed for $19.95, gave a brief overview of each company, a short history, biographical sketches of senior executives, and financial and stock-related information. Hoover, Spain, and Campbell hoped to penetrate the mass-market with their first publication, but they were disappointed by the results. Greater disap-

pointment came with the 1991 release of the founders' first electronic product, a digital version of *Hoover's Handbook* made for Sony's Data Discman. The product flopped, exacerbating the founders' frustration.

Although The Reference Press failed to score a commercial success with its first efforts, the less-than-ideal start set the foundation for the company's future success. The collaboration with Sony introduced the founders to electronic publishing, which would become the primary focus of their business. The founders began moving toward electronic publishing when lackluster sales of the print edition of *Hoover's Handbook* prompted them to find other ways to market their content. The Reference Press signed its first online distribution deal in 1992, licensing its database of corporate information to America Online. America Online began publishing The Reference Press's company profiles, giving the founders their first taste of commercial success. Additional distribution deals followed, as The Reference Press negotiated deals with LexisNexis, Bloomberg, Dow Jones, the Microsoft Network, Yahoo!, and the *New York Times*.

DEBUT OF HOOVER'S ONLINE: 1994

Just as The Reference Press began to gravitate toward online publishing, Spain took over as CEO in 1993. Spain encouraged the move toward online publishing, signing Internet distribution deals with CompuServe, Apple, and AT&T. Soon, The Reference Press's success at finding a way to disseminate its content attracted the financial support of deep-pocketed companies. In 1994 Warner Books, a unit of Time Warner, invested in The Reference Press, which gave Spain the capital to launch Hoover's Online, a Web site offering access to the company's business information either for free or by subscription.

The Reference Press was an early entrant into the online realm, finding greater commercial success on the Internet than it did in traditional print publishing. The company continued to publish books in print, releasing annual titles such as *Hoover's Handbook of American Business* during the first half of the 1990s, but it increasingly emphasized online publishing as the way to distribute its content. By 1996, the year the company changed its name to Hoover's, Inc., it was distributing its content through more than 20 Web sites, in addition to its own. During the year, its revenues were evenly divided between print and electronic publishing, but by the following year electronic publishing accounted for 85 percent of the company's business. The Internet and online services, according to Spain in the September 22,

KEY DATES

1990: The Reference Press is formed and publishes its first book; later in the year, an electronic version of *Hoover's Handbook* is released for Sony's Data Discman, marking the company's entry into electronic publishing.

1994: Company launches its own Web site, Hoover's Online.

1996: The Reference Press changes its name to Hoover's, Inc.

1999: Company completes an initial public offering of stock.

2003: The Dun & Bradstreet Corporation acquires Hoover's, Inc., for $117 million.

2007: Coverage of private companies based in the United States is greatly increased.

1997, issue of *Publishers Weekly*, was "clearly the direction to go."

The turn of the millennium represented a period of fast-paced change and growth for Hoover's, Inc., as it did for the online world on which the company relied. In 1998 the company signed its first e-commerce agreement, forming a partnership with Amazon.com, and signed more than a dozen other agreements with vendors in the months that followed, enabling Hoover's Online to offer a variety of business-related products and services for a fee. In 1999 the need for capital to fund expansion led Spain to complete an initial public offering (IPO). The IPO raised $42 million in July and attracted AOL Time Warner as a major shareholder. With part of the proceeds, the company completed the fifth redesign of the Hoover's Online Web site, incorporating new features such as business news and information related to career development, business travel, and personal finance.

INTERNATIONAL EXPANSION IN 2000

Hoover's, Inc., expanded after its IPO, taking a 140 percent increase in revenues in 1999 as a signal that its strategy was sound. The company addressed the European market in 2000, forming Hoover's Online Europe, Ltd., as a London-based subsidiary. Hoover's Online Europe launched four Web sites, giving French, German, Italian, and Spanish business professionals access to business information tailored to their needs. "The new sites are part of Hoover's strategy of providing businesspeople around the world with information to help them do their jobs more efficiently," Spain said in the March 2001 issue of *Information Today*. "Now we can offer them information about companies in their own country and in their own language, as well as improve access to the wealth of information in the global Hoover's database."

Hoover's, Inc., reached out to new markets as it added to the features on its Web site. In mid-2001 the company released Hoover's Information Marketplace on Hoover's Online, giving visitors the ability to access a comprehensive collection of business research reports for a fee. Spain stepped down as CEO during the year and handed the reins of command to Jeff Tarr, the former CEO at a technology support Web service company named all.com. Hoover's Inc. finished the year on a celebratory note, turning its first profit during the fourth fiscal quarter.

As Hoover's, Inc., entered its second decade of business, it offered a full range of services and features to its subscribers. The company had transitioned from relying on advertisers as its primary source of revenue to selling subscriptions to build its business, a change in its business model that yielded its first profit. Although Hoover's, Inc., had steadily added to the range of its content offerings, the most distinctive elements of its branded business information were Company Capsules and Company Profiles. Company Capsules, the one-page narratives that debuted in *Hoover's Handbook 1991: Profiles of Over 500 Major Corporations*, gave the Hoover's Inc. database the breadth of its coverage, having developed into a collection covering 18,000 companies. Company Profiles, expanded versions of Company Capsules, provided coverage of 5,000 of the largest and most prominent companies, primarily publicly traded corporations.

HOOVER'S, INC., SEEKS A BUYER

Not willing to wait for its profits to finance expansion efforts, Hoover's, Inc., began looking to raise capital another way. In May 2002, the company contacted 18 other entities that might be interested in acquiring its operations. The search for a corporate suitor led to a $117 million offer by The Dun & Bradstreet Corporation (D&B) in early 2003. D&B, which owned a database of information on more than 12 million U.S. businesses and organizations, completed the acquisition before the end of the year.

Under D&B's ownership, Hoover's, Inc.'s database of content expanded rapidly. By the end of 2004, the number of companies included within its database increased from 18,000 to more than 40,000, while the number of industries it profiled doubled from 300 to 600. In 2007 the company launched a campaign to increase its coverage of private companies based in the United States, more than tripling its existing coverage to provide content for 250,000 private companies. While the number of Company Capsules and Company Profiles increased exponentially, Hoover's, Inc.'s subscribers, who gained access to D&B's content, were given a variety of ways to access information. Hoover's, Inc., placed a particular emphasis on providing wireless access. The use of Web-enabled cellular telephones and other devices was proliferating, creating a relatively new market that the company exploited by collaborating with technology firms.

As Hoover's, Inc., neared its 20th anniversary, it owed its growth to the decision made early in its development to use the Internet as the medium for distributing its content. The company had continued to publish in print during the late 1990s, releasing roughly a dozen of annual directories, but its online activities represented its lifeblood. In the years ahead, its most noteworthy progress was expected to involve increasing the depth and breadth of its content and finding new ways to deliver the information to the businesses and businesspeople that subscribed to its services.

Jeffrey L. Covell

PRINCIPAL SUBSIDIARIES

Hoover's Online, Inc.; Hoover's Online Europe, Ltd.; First Research, Inc.; AllBusiness.com, Inc.

PRINCIPAL COMPETITORS

OneSource Information Services, Inc.; Dow Jones & Company, Inc.; Zoom Information, Inc.

FURTHER READING

Cecil, Mark, "Street May Want More for Hoover's, but ...," *Mergers & Acquisitions Report,* January 20, 2003.

Hane, Paula J., "Hoover's: Solving Information Chaos," *Information Today,* June 2005, p. 30.

"Hoover's Launches Hoover's Information Marketplace, Joins with CCN Newswire," *Information Today,* July 2001, p. 24.

"Hoover's Online Europe Launches New Web Sites in France, Germany, Italy, and Spain," *Information Today,* March 2001, p. 35.

"Hoover's Signs E-Commerce, Advertising Agreement with USADATA.com," *Information Today,* October 1999, p. 18.

Milliot, Jim, "Hoover's Has New Investor, Will Boost Online," *Publishers Weekly,* September 22, 1997, p. 11.

"O'Leary, Mick, "The 'New' Hoover's: Complete Company Content," *Link-Up,* May 2002, p. 11.

"Online Content Drives Hoover's Sales," *Publishers Weekly,* August 30, 1999, p. 11.

"Steam for Hoover's," *Business Week,* February 28, 2000, p. 171.

ING Groep N.V.

Amstelveenseweg 500
Amsterdam, 1081 KL
Netherlands
Telephone: (+31 20) 541 5411
Fax: (+31 20) 541 5497
Web site: http://www.inggroup.com

Public Company
Incorporated: 1991 as Internationale Nederlanden Groep
Employees: 125,285
Total Assets: $1.33 trillion (2008)
Stock Exchanges: New York London
Ticker Symbol: ING
NAICS: 551111 Offices of Bank Holding Companies

■ ■ ■

ING Groep N.V. (ING Group) is one of the world's leading bancassurance (active in both banking and insurance) heavyweights. The Amsterdam, Netherlands-based company holds total assets of more than EUR 1.33 trillion ($800 billion), ranking it among the top 10 financial groups in the world. ING's operations span nearly 40 countries, with a total client base of more than 85 million private, corporate, and institutional customers. ING operates through two primary business units, ING Bank and ING Insurance, which are organized into six main divisions: Insurance Americas, Insurance Asia/Pacific, Insurance Europe, Retail Banking, Wholesale Banking, and ING Direct.

In 2008 ING received a EUR 10 billion bailout package amid the economic crisis caused by the banking

sector. The Dutch government also agreed to buy out $39 billion of the company's "toxic assets," largely U.S.-based housing securities, in 2009. The company's difficulties led to the departure of CEO Michel Tilmant that year. Tilmant was replaced by Jan Hommen, who also became the group's chairman. ING is listed on both the London and New York stock exchanges.

BANCASSURANCE TREND IN THE NINETIES

ING Group originated from the merger between two of the Netherlands' financial sector heavyweights in the early 1990s. This period was marked by the trend among banking and insurance companies toward developing integrated banking and insurance services and products. This new type of financial operation, which became known as "bancassurance," sought to achieve synergies and cost-reductions by cross-selling banking and insurance products through both sectors' extensive retail and corporate networks.

Many observers, both within the industry and without, were skeptical of the effectiveness, and even necessity, of such combined operations. This was in part because many financial institutions had achieved similar cross-marketing objectives through the creation of partnerships and cooperation agreements. Nonetheless, the bancassurance concept remained popular, especially among European corporations facing the creation of the European Union in 1992.

In the smaller European markets, such as the Netherlands, the bancassurance concept provided other advantages. Domestic financial players, while leaders in their home markets, would find it difficult to compete on a European-wide level. The merger between a bank and one of its counterparts in the insurance sector therefore provided both partners the opportunity to maintain their national identity, while providing the scale to compete on the international market.

Similar motivations were behind the creation of ING Group in 1991. In that year, two of the Netherlands' financial giants, Nationale-Nederlande, the leading insurance group in the Netherlands, and NMB Postbank, the country's third-largest bank, joined forces to create Internationale Nederlanden Groep, or ING as the company quickly became known.

INSURANCE ORIGINS IN 1845

Nationale-Nederlande traced its own beginnings back to the middle of the 19th century. Parts of the group, however, stemmed from as far back as 1743. In that year, a group of people in the village of Koog, in northern Holland, joined together to form one of the Netherlands' earliest mutual insurance funds, the Kooger Doodenbos. By the 19th century, such relatively small mutual insurance groups had become increasingly popular. In general, however, the insurance market remained dominated by Belgium, which controlled the regions that were later to become the Netherlands until 1830.

This break led to the creation of a truly Dutch insurance industry. Among the first companies to appear was Nederlandse Maatschappij van Brandverzekering, founded in Tiel in 1833. That company opened several agencies, establishing itself as an important regional force. A number of the Tiel company's agents also operated their own subagencies. Such was the case of the company's Zutphen agent, Gerrit Jan Dercksen, and his nephew Christiaan Marianus Henny. Dercksen and Henny owned several subagencies. However, when the Tiel company attempted to raise the subagents' status to full agencies, thus making them independent of the

Zutphen business, Dercksen and Henny responded by founding their own company.

The new company was called Assurantie Maatschappij tegen Brandschade de Nederlanden (for Netherlands Fire Insurance Company), and opened its doors in 1845. That company became one of the pillars of the future Nationale Nederlande. De Nederlanden, as the company later came to be known, grew quickly, establishing offices in the two primary Dutch markets, Amsterdam and Rotterdam. In addition, De Nederlanden began developing an international business, notably through following the Dutch interests to its colonies and foreign trading partners.

Among the company's important clients in this area was Nederlandsche Handel Maatschappij. In order to build its business with that company, De Nederlanden reinforced its operations with its own reinsurance wing, called De Nederlanden van 1859, founded that same year. The two businesses remained separate until 1888, when they were merged together into a single company, called "Assurantie Maatschappij tegen Brandschade De Nederlanden van 1845."

DUTCH INSURANCE LEADER IN THE SIXTIES

By 1900, De Nederlanden boasted an international network of nearly 140 agencies. The company moved its headquarters to The Hague, which was quickly becoming the political and financial capital of the Netherlands, in 1897. It also began expanding beyond its initial fire insurance market. In 1903, for example, the company launched its first life insurance policies. By the end of World War I, De Nederlanden's life insurance operations had grown enough for the company to create a new dedicated life insurance subsidiary.

Over the next two decades, the company added several new lines of insurance. This was accomplished through the acquisition of a number of existing businesses. De Nederlanden also acquired Fatum, a specialist in accident insurance, in 1917, and Labor, which provided insurance to businesses, in 1921. These were followed by an entry into the transport insurance market with the purchase of Binnenlands Vaaart Risico Societeit, in 1925. Other acquisitions included Haagse Assurantie Maatschappij in 1934 and Amsterdam-based Verzekeringsbank Victoria in 1938. In that year, also, the group completed its first foreign acquisition, of Belgium's De Vanderlandsche.

The company's international operations enabled it to switch its headquarters temporarily to its offices in the Dutch Indies following the German invasion of the Netherlands in 1940. The company then shifted its

KEY DATES

1845: De Nederlanden insurance group is founded in Zutphen, Netherlands, providing fire insurance.

1863: Nationale Levensverzekeringen Bank is founded in Rotterdam to provide life insurance.

1891: Netherlands government founds a savings bank, Rijkspostspaarbank.

1903: De Nederlanden begins offering life insurance products.

1918: Netherlands government founds a giro and checking service, Postcheque- en Girodienst.

1927: Nederlandsche Middenstandsbank (NMB) is founded.

1938: De Nederlanden completes its first international acquisition in Belgium.

1962: De Nederlanden and National Levensverzekeringen Bank merge to form Nationale-Nederlanden.

1977: Nationale-Nederlanden begins U.S. expansion with purchase of Security Life of Denver.

1986: Rijskpostspaarbank and Postcheque- en Girodiesnt merge to form Postbank.

1988: Postbank merges with NMB to form NMB Postbank.

1991: Nationale-Nederlanden and NMB Postbank merge to form Internationale Nederlanden Groep (ING).

1995: ING acquires Barings Bank for $1 billion.

1997: ING lists on the New York Stock Exchange.

1998: ING acquires Banque Bruxelles Lambert.

2005: ING acquires nearly 20 percent of Bank of Beijing.

2008: ING receives a EUR 10 billion bailout from the Dutch government.

2009: ING announces plans to exit 10 international markets.

headquarters again, to Curaçao, following the Japanese takeover of the Dutch Indies. In this way, De Nederlanden was able to continue doing business in a number of markets, including South Africa, the United States, and England.

Following the war, the company was forced to shift its focus to the West as the former Dutch colonies gained their independence. In Indonesia, for example,

De Nederlanden's operations were nationalized. Instead, De Nederlanden sought new markets such as Canada.

At the same time, the reconstruction of the Netherlands and the subsequent postwar economic boom led to a surge in demand for insurance products. By 1960, De Nederlanden had grown to become the leading home insurance provider, and the second-largest life insurance group in the Netherlands. Two years later, De Nederlanden completed a merger with its main life insurance rival, Nationale Levensverzekeringen Bank, itself established in 1863 in Rotterdam. The combined company then took on the name of Nationale-Nederlanden.

MERGING DUTCH INSURANCE AND BANKING GIANTS IN 1991

Nationale-Nederlanden became the dominant insurance group in the Netherlands. More than 75 percent of the Dutch population were said to have a relationship with the company, through at least one, and often several, of its branches. This also left more limited room for future growth, encouraging the company to continue to build its international business.

The United States became a major expansion target for Nationale-Nederlanden starting in the end of the 1970s. The company made its first acquisition there, in 1977, buying Security Life of Denver. Two years later, the company acquired Life of Georgia, a purchase that provided an important foothold for the group's growth across the United States. Into the mid-1980s, the company strengthened its presence in the Netherlands as well, buying AMFAS.

Despite its dominance of the Dutch market, Nationale-Nederlanden remained small compared to its major rivals in its neighboring European markets. The impending creation of the European Union, and the elimination of trade barriers among member nations, threatened to usher in a new and fiercely competitive era for the European financial sector. As a result, Nationale-Nederlanden began looking for a partner in order to achieve the scale needed to remain a competitor in the future market.

Nationale-Nederlanden found that partner in NMB Postbank, the Netherlands' third-largest bank, which itself had been created through the merger of Postbank and Nederlandsche Middenstandsbank in 1989. Postbank had been founded in 1891 as Rijkspostspaarbank, as the savings bank offshoot of the country's post office and telegraph service. The government later added the giro payment service, a type of check-based banking, in 1918, creating Postcheque- en Girodienst that year.

Both the saving bank and giro services operated from the national post-office network, and remained controlled by the Dutch government. Rising competition in the retail banking sector, and the run-up toward 1992, led the Dutch government to launch a privatization of its banking operations. In 1986, therefore, the two services were merged together, forming Postbank. Two years later, Postbank's merger with NMB, founded in 1927 as Nederlandsche Middenstandsbank and majority controlled by the Dutch government, was also completed. The government then reduced its stake in NMB Postbank, to 49 percent. NMB also brought the company a strong international operation, notably in South America and other emerging markets.

NMB Postbank and Nationale-Nederlanden agreed to merge together in 1991, forming the Dutch national financial champion Internationale Nederlanden Groep. The company quickly became known by its initials, and adopted the name ING Group soon after.

BUILDING INTERNATIONAL SCALE

ING quickly made good on its "International" name. The company began targeting the newly emerging Eastern European markets, starting with the Czech Republic in 1991. The group entered Romania in 1994, then Hungary in 1995. For the most part, the company's entry into these and other developing markets took place from the ground up, with start-up operations often based out of a single hotel room until the new subsidiary's business got fully underway.

Nonetheless, it was an acquisition that put ING on the map and made it a force to be reckoned with in the 1990s. In 1995, the company paid just $1 billion to acquire U.K.-based Barings Bank. That bank was then reeling from a major scandal and loss caused by one of its traders at its Singapore office. The bargain-price purchase of Barings not only brought ING's name to the international forefront, it also provided the company with the expertise of one of the industry's highest-rated financial staff.

Through the second half of the 1990s, ING completed a number of other acquisitions. These included Equitable of Iowa Companies in the United States in 1997; Belgium's Banque Bruxelles Lambert in 1998; BHF-Bank in Germany in 1999; and three U.S.-based insurance companies, ReliaStar, Aetna Financial Services, and Aetna International in 2000. ING also became one of the first major financial groups to launch a dedicated online bank, ING Direct, starting with operations in Canada in 1997. Over the next decade, the company rolled out ING Direct operations in France, the United States, the United Kingdom, Italy, Australia, and elsewhere. In the meantime, ING, which

had been listed on the London Stock Exchange, added a listing on the New York Stock Exchange as well in 1997.

ING completed several more acquisitions as it climbed into the top ranks of the world's financial markets. The company acquired Poland's Bank Slaski in 2001, added Indian operations through the creation of a Bangalore-based joint venture, and entered Mexico with the purchase of Seguros Comercial America that year. In 2002, ING reinforced its German operations with the acquisition of DiBa Bank. The company also boosted its presence in Canada, buying Allianz Canada in 2004. The company had entered China in 2000, acquiring a 50 percent stake in the joint venture Pacific Antai Life Insurance, originally formed by Aetna Financial Services. By 2005, the company had added a second presence in the Chinese market, acquiring nearly 20 percent of Bank of Beijing. This was followed by an entry into Taiwan in 2007, with the takeover of ABN AMRO's asset management business there.

STREAMLINING FOR THE CRISIS IN 2009

ING helped pay for its steady stream of acquisitions in part by shedding noncore holdings. The company raised nearly $500 million in 2004 through the sale of Baring Financial Services Group to Northern Trust Corporation. Other sell-offs included BHF-Bank in Germany, CenE, which had been part of NMB, Life of Georgia, and ING's 70 percent share of Banque Baring Brothers, in 2005.

Continued growth, however, remained the group's primary focus through the middle of the decade. ING entered Turkey in 2007, buying Oyak Bank. The group added ShareBuilder, an online stockbroker based in the United States that year, as well as a 30 percent share of Thailand's TMB Bank. In 2008, the company purchased U.S.-based Citistreet and also launched operations in Ukraine.

However, the international financial crisis soon caught up to the company, in part because of its exposure to the U.S. housing-based securities market. Despite the risky lending practices and heavy responsibility of the global financial industry in precipitating the worst economic crisis since the Great Depression, governments around the world rushed to bail out their financial institutions.

ING became one of the primary recipients of the Dutch government's financial aid package, grabbing EUR 10 billion in rescue funds in October 2008. By January 2009, the company had also offloaded more than $39 billion of its largely U.S.-based "toxic assets" to the Netherlands government as well, in a deal that would later bring ING under European Commission scrutiny. That same month, the company announced that it was laying off more than 7,000 employees. In addition, CEO Michel Tilmant was replaced by Jan Hommen. Part of the bailout money went to acquire the banking deposits of more than 160,000 U.K.-based clients of failed Icelandic bank Kaupthing Edge.

Through 2009, ING worked at adapting its strategy to the slowly recovering global market. The company streamlined its management structure, reducing the number of divisions to just six. ING also announced its decision to withdraw its operations from as many as 10 foreign markets, scaling back its international operations to just 38 countries. This led the group to announce the sale of its Asian private banking operations, as well as its Swiss private banking assets, in September 2009.

The company also sold off its ING Canada insurance operations that year. At the same time, ING completed the streamlining of its Dutch banking operations, a process launched in 2007 with the merger of Postbank into ING Bank. In China, the company announced its intention to sell off one of its Chinese businesses as well.

ING hoped that its restructuring effort would be enough to allow it to emerge strengthened from the economic crisis into the end of the decade. With total assets under management of more than EUR 551 billion ($800 million) and a balance sheet valuation of EUR 1.33 trillion, ING remained one of the world's leading and most international financial groups.

M. L. Cohen

PRINCIPAL SUBSIDIARIES

Insurance: AFP Capital S.A. (Chile); Belair Insurance Company Inc. (Canada); ING Afore S.A. de C.V. (Mexico); ING America Insurance Holdings, Inc. (USA); ING Asigurari de Viata S.A. (Romania); ING Australia Holdings Limited; ING Canada Inc.; ING Greek Life Insurance Company S.A.; ING Insurance Company of Canada; ING International Insurance Holdings, Inc. (USA); ING Life Insurance and Annuity Company (USA); ING Life Insurance Company (Japan) Limited; ING Life Insurance Company (Korea) Limited; ING Life Insurance Company of America (USA); ING Nationale-Nederlanden Magyarorszagi Biztosito Rt. (Hungary); ING Nationale-Nederlanden Polska S.A. (Poland); ING North America Insurance Corporation (USA); ING Novex Insurance Company of Canada; ING Re (Netherlands) N.V.; ING Seguros de Vida S.A. (Chile); ING USA Annuity and Life Insur-

ance Company (USA); ING Verzekeringen N.V.; ING Zivotna Poistovna a.s. (Slovakia); Lion Connecticut Holdings Inc. (USA); Movir N.V.; Nationale-Nederlanden Levensverzekering Maatschappij N.V.; Nationale-Nederlanden Vida, Compañia de Seguros y Reaseguros S.A. (Spain); Postbank Levensverzekering N.V.; Postbank Schadeverzekering N.V.; ReliaStar Life Insurance Company (USA); ReliaStar Life Insurance Company of New York (USA); RVS Levensverzekering N.V.; RVS Schadeverzekering N.V.; Security Life of Denver Insurance Company (USA).

Banking: Bank Mendes Gans N.V.; ING Bank A.S. (Turkey); ING Bank Deutschland A.G. (Germany); ING Bank N.V.; ING Bank Nederland N.V.; ING Bank Slaski S.A. (Poland); ING België N.V. (Belgium); ING Commercial Finance B.V.; ING Corporate Investments B.V.; ING Direct N.V.; ING Financial Holdings Corporation (USA); ING Lease Holding B.V.; ING Middenbank Curaçao N.V. (Netherlands Antilles); ING Vastgoed Management Holding B.V.; ING Vysya Bank Ltd. (India); InterAdvies N.V.; Nationale-Nederlanden Financiële Diensten B.V.; Postbank Groen N.V.; Postbank N.V.; Westland Utrecht Hypotheekbank N.V.

PRINCIPAL DIVISIONS

ING Direct; Insurance Americas; Insurance Asia/Pacific; Insurance Europe; Retail Banking; Wholesale Banking.

PRINCIPAL OPERATING UNITS

ING Bank; ING Insurance.

PRINCIPAL COMPETITORS

Bidvest Group Ltd.; Royal Bank of Scotland Group PLC; Barclays Bank PLC; JPMorgan Chase and Co.; Bank of America Corporation; ABN AMRO Holding N.V.; UniCredit S.p.A.; Société Générale Group; Wells Fargo and Company; Sumitomo Mitsui Financial Group Inc.; Wachovia Corporation.

FURTHER READING

Ackermann, Matt, "ING Group Acquires CitiStreet," *American Banker*, July 3, 2008, p. 8.

Bakker, Tino, "High Hopes in the Low Lands," *Banker*, April 1995, p. 65.

"Blazing a Trail," *LatinFinance*, November 1994, p. 41.

"Dutch Majors ING, Aegon Accept Bailout Package," *Financial Express*, October 29, 2008.

"EmergING Dutch Banking," *Economist*, July 16, 1994, p. 69.

"ING Bank, Postbank Merger to Save EUR400 in 2012," *Global Banking News*, April 10, 2009.

"ING Hits a Speed Bump," *Business Week*, July 3, 2000, p. 58.

"ING Receives Bids for Asian Private Banking Assets," *Global Banking News*, September 4, 2009.

"ING's Dutch Government Deal 'Too Good to Be True,'" *Euroweek*, January 30, 2009.

Jones, Marc, "ING Planning to Exit 10 Countries," *Best's Review*, July 2009, p. 11.

Marcial, Gene G., "Looking A-OK at ING," *Business Week*, July 25, 2005, p. 108.

McDougall, Paul, "ING Group Latest to Tap an Outsourcing Tag Team," *Bank Systems + Technology*, August 2006, p. 12.

Morais, Richard C., "Everyone Was Afraid," *Forbes*, September 9, 1996, p. 125.

"Old-Fashioned but Not Old Guard," *Banker*, February 1, 2008.

Rappleye, Willard C., Jr., "Nimble, Forceful, on a World Tear," *Financial World*, February 18, 1997, p. 87.

White, Aoife, "EU Deepens Probe into Dutch Aid for ING," *AP Worldstream*, September 15, 2009.

Yiu, Enoch, "ING Mulls Pulling out of Mainland Venture," *South China Morning Post*, March 9, 2009.

Israel Corporation Ltd.

Millennium Tower
23 Aranha Street
Tel Aviv, 61204
Israel
Telephone: (+972 3) 684-4531
Fax: (+972 3) 684-4565
Web site: http://www.israelcorp.com

Public Subsidiary of Ofer Brothers Group
Incorporated: 1968 as The Israel Corporation
Employees: 18,700
Sales: $19.8 billion (2008)
Stock Exchanges: Tel Aviv
Ticker Symbol: ILCO
NAICS: 551112 Offices of Other Holding Companies;
523999 Miscellaneous Financial Investment Activities; 211111 Crude Petroleum and Natural Gas Extraction; 325131 Inorganic Dye and Pigment Manufacturing; 531110 Lessors of Residential Buildings and Dwellings

■ ■ ■

Israel Corporation Ltd. is Israel's largest nongovernmental holding company with strategic investments in the chemicals, energy, shipping, and transportation industries. The company's Chemicals Division is focused around its 53 percent share of Israel Chemicals Ltd., a world-leading producer of fertilizers and other chemicals. The company's Energy Division includes a 45 percent interest in Oil Refineries Ltd., the largest Israeli-controlled oil refinery group. This division has also been investing in renewable energies, including a 33 percent stake in Better Place, a developer of refueling grids for electric vehicles. The Shipping Division controls ZIM Integrated Shipping Services Ltd., one of the world's top 20 container shipping services providers, which operates from hubs in Shekou, China; Hong Kong; Haifa, Israel; Kingston, Jamaica; Pusan, South Korea; Kelang, Malaysia; Singapore; and Barcelona, Spain. The Transportation Division includes Israel Corporation's 45 percent share of China-based Chery Quantum Auto Co., which is developing electric automobiles.

These holdings provided Israel Corporation with total annual revenues of $19.8 billion in 2008. The diversity of the group's holdings, especially the strong profits from Israel Chemicals, has enabled the company to continue to operate profitably despite the losses generated by much of its investment portfolio amid the economic downturn at the end of the first decade of the 21st century. Israel Corporation is listed on the Tel Aviv Stock Exchange. The Ofer family, through the Ofer Brothers Group, controls 55 percent of Israel Corporation. Nir Gilad is the company's president and CEO.

ENCOURAGING INVESTMENT IN ISRAEL IN 1968

The Six-Day War of 1967 marked a turning point in Israel's relationship with the global community. The country's victory (and its capture of Jerusalem and annexation of the West Bank and Gaza Strip and other territories) contributed to the loss of Israel's "underdog"

of the 1980s, the company boasted a shareholder base of 220 investors, most of whom lived outside of Israel.

EARLY INVESTMENTS AND SCANDAL IN THE SEVENTIES

Among The Israel Corporation's first and longest-lasting investments was a stake in ZIM Integrated Shipping Services Ltd. That company had been founded in 1945 as a partnership between the Jewish Agency, Israel Maritime League, and Histadrut labor federation in order to purchase ships to carry European immigrants and goods and supplies to Israel following World War II. The company acquired its first vessel, the *Kedmah*, in 1947, and by the mid-1950s had launched its global expansion.

The advent of widespread commercial airline services brought ZIM into difficulty by the end of the 1960s. This set the stage for Israel Corporation's first major investment, as it agreed to acquire 50 percent of the troubled shipper from the Israeli government in 1969. Israel Corporation mapped out a new strategy for the company, refocused around cargo shipping. By 1970 ZIM's fleet neared 150 vessels, including 70 wholly owned by the company. In that year, ZIM turned its attention to an entirely new sector in the global shipping industry, containerships. The company ordered its first six container vessels, as well as the corresponding onshore handling equipment. In this way, ZIM became one of the world's pioneering players in the containership market.

Israel Corporation's original investment interests focused on the shipping and oil-refining markets, as well as hotel developments and other tourism-related investments. The company also acquired stakes in cold-storage facilities and other similar industries. The company's early years, however, were marred by scandal. In 1975 the company's managing director, Michael Tzur, pleaded guilty to fraud charges in connection with the illegal funneling of some $17 million in investments from Israel Corporation and ZIM into the failed International Credit Bank in Geneva, Switzerland. The scandal endangered Israel Corporation's survival, as Rothschild threatened to pull out of the group and pull all of his other investments out of Israel.

EISENBERG'S BEGINNINGS

The aftermath of the scandal set the stage for Eisenberg to take control of Israel Corporation. Eisenberg by then was a major, if secretive, presence in the Israeli and global business worlds. Born in 1921 in Munich,

COMPANY PERSPECTIVES

Vision & Strategy: Israel Corporation's primary goal is the creation of shareholder value and its investments are made with that aim firmly in mind. The company's long-term, group-wide strategy balances economic value with an underlying responsibility to continue supplying major global basic materials in an environmentally and socially responsible manner.

status for many in the world, especially in the West. As a result, investment in the country dropped off sharply, particularly following Israel's refusal to restore its borders to their prewar limits.

In 1968, therefore, the Israeli government convened a "millionaires' conference" of wealthy Jews from around the world. Led by Finance Minister Pinchas Sapir, the conference was meant to stimulate foreign investment in Israel, especially in key areas of operations to help build the country's domestic economy and infrastructure, as well as its position in international markets. Among those attending the conference were such notables as Baron Edmond de Rothschild, of the French branch of the famous banking family; British financier Sigmund Warburg; Shoul Eisenberg; and members of the Ofer family.

Sapir proposed that the Israeli government establish a new investment company, called The Israel Corporation, which would make investments in support of Israel's growth. Each of the conference's attendees was then asked to invest $100,000 for a stake in the new company. Rothschild was named The Israel Corporation's first chairman, a position he held until 1984. Eisenberg, however, emerged as one of the largest investors in the new company.

In order to stimulate investment in Israel Corporation, the Israeli government passed special legislation in 1969 that provided income tax exemptions for the company's investors for a period lasting until 1999. This was not the only legislation developed by the Israeli government to favor investment in the country. A second piece of legislation was passed in 1970 specifically to encourage Eisenberg to relocate his own thriving business empire from Japan to Israel. As in the case of The Israel Corporation law, the Eisenberg law, as the measure came to be called, granted Eisenberg an exemption from income taxes for a 35-year period.

The country's legislative efforts succeeded in attracting strong backing for Israel Corporation. By the middle

KEY DATES

1968: Israeli government creates The Israel Corporation in order to stimulate foreign investment in Israel.

1980: Business tycoon Shoul Eisenberg acquires control of Israel Corporation.

1999: Ofer Brothers Group acquires 52 percent of Israel Corporation.

2008: Israel Corporation forms a joint venture with Chery Quantum Auto, in China, to produce electric automobiles.

Germany, Eisenberg had escaped to Shanghai, China, with his family in 1939. Shanghai, then under Japanese control, had become a center of Jewish immigration in the Far East, and provided Eisenberg with his first experiences in the business world.

Eisenberg quickly rose to become one of the most prominent members of the Shanghai Jewish community, where he developed relationships with members of the militant right-wing Betar and Irgun organizations. Eisenberg also began trading with people in the Japanese occupying force. As business opportunities in Shanghai dried up during World War II, these relationships enabled Eisenberg to gain rare permission to move to Tokyo.

While in Tokyo, Eisenberg met his future wife, whose father was a professor at Tokyo University and whose mother was a member of a prominent Japanese family. These connections allowed Eisenberg to develop a lucrative trade, importing iron ore from South America. Following the war, Eisenberg built the beginnings of his business empire by transforming scrap aluminum into household goods and appliances, which he sold to U.S. forces.

By the 1950s Eisenberg's business empire had expanded beyond Japan, to operations in Korea and elsewhere. Eisenberg, who gained Israeli citizenship in 1949, decided to move his family to Israel at the beginning of the 1960s. Nevertheless, in order to avoid paying the stiff taxes on his holdings, Eisenberg kept his business interests in Japan. It was only in 1970, following the passage of the so-called Eisenberg law, that the business tycoon agreed to relocate his company to Israel. At the same time, Eisenberg became one of the original investors in Israel Corporation.

EISENBERG AND ISRAEL CORPORATION: SEVENTIES THROUGH NINETIES

Israel Corporation's involvement in shipping and oil refining provided Eisenberg with an entry into these areas as well. By the late 1970s Eisenberg had boosted his stake in Israel Corporation to 49 percent. At the same time, Eisenberg had also become Israel's informal emissary to China, which had backed the Arab cause since the late 1940s. Over the next decade, Eisenberg brokered billions of dollars in deals (transferring Israeli weapons technology) between the Israeli government and China. These efforts were said to have laid the groundwork for China's official recognition of Israel in 1992.

They also enabled Eisenberg to take control of Israel Corporation during the 1980s. By 1980 Eisenberg had gained majority control of the company. Over the next several years many of the company's initial investors sold out their stakes as well. By 1984 Rothschild had stepped down as the group's chairman and Eisenberg himself filled the position.

As part of Eisenberg's business empire, Israel Corporation began to expand its range of investment interests. The company targeted a number of new areas, particularly the high-technology sector. Among the company's investments made during the 1980s were the purchases of Filtration Ltd., which focused on automated self-cleaning water-filter systems; Edunetics Ltd., which incorporated the use of computers into educational and training services; and Scinova Ltd., a developer of instruments for the health care and automotive industries.

Other holdings acquired during this time included Alumit Packaging, fire-extinguishing-equipment producer Spectronix Ltd., Israel Lighterage and Supply Company, Inter-Gamma Investment Company, and Rapac Electronics. Another major investment came with the purchase of control of Tower Semiconductor Ltd. Israel Corporation also gained a 26 percent stake in the government-owned Oil Refineries Ltd., Israel's largest oil refiner.

These investments allowed Israel Corporation to achieve strong growth despite a poor economic climate in Israel during the 1980s. From a market capitalization of just $110 million in the middle of the 1980s, the company emerged as one of the country's leaders, with revenues of $240 million at the end of 1991. Through the 1990s the group continued its somewhat scattershot investment policy, adding such disparate holdings as nursing homes and car rental operations.

NEW OWNERS AT THE START OF THE 21ST CENTURY

By the time of Eisenberg's death in 1997, Israel Corporation controlled a vast empire of more than 100 businesses. By then, the company had gained control of a major new prize, Israel Chemicals Ltd. (ICL), one of the leading industrial groups in Israel and one of the largest producers of fertilizers and other chemicals in the world. Formerly a state-owned company, ICL had begun its privatization process in 1995. At that time, Israel Corporation bought a 25 percent stake in the company, with an option to acquire a further 17 percent and gain effective control of ICL. Israel Corporation exercised that option in March 1997, just a few days after Eisenberg's death, and just a few hours before the option was due to expire.

Disagreements within Eisenberg's family, however, led son Erwin, who took over as head of his father's vast business empire, to decide to sell off the family's control of Israel Corporation. Eisenberg at first neared a deal to sell the family's 52 percent of Israel Corporation to Canada's Potash Corporation of Saskatchewan, which sought control of ICL. That deal appeared certain to face a great deal of opposition from Israel's regulatory authorities, reluctant to allow ICL to fall into foreign ownership. Instead, Eisenberg rushed into a new deal, agreeing to sell control of Israel Corporation to the Ofer Brothers Group, for $330 million.

Israel Corporation came under control of another of Israel's most prominent business families. Originally from Romania, the Ofer family, led by brothers Sammy and Yuli, had established their own fortune by building an internationally operating shipping empire. By the late 1990s, the family's holdings came under the leadership of Sammy's son Ilan. Following Ofer Brothers' purchase of control of Israel Corporation in 1999, Ilan Ofer became its chairman.

Seconded by Yossi Rosen, who became Israel Corporation's CEO in 1998, Ofer led a reorganization of Israel Corporation's investments. This reorganization targeted a dramatic streamlining of the company's holdings, which spanned dozens of smaller companies. As Rosen explained to Simon Clark of *Bloomberg* in 2009: "Management spent 80 percent of their time on these small businesses, and they had no time to deal with the core businesses. We decided that either we would gain control or we would come out."

STREAMLINED INVESTMENT PORTFOLIO FOR THE 21ST CENTURY

Israel Corporation narrowed its focus significantly over the next several years. By the midpoint of the first decade of the 2000s, the company had reduced its operations to the chemicals, energy, and shipping sectors, while maintaining its stake in Tower Semiconductor. The company also moved to gain controlling stakes in its major subsidiaries. In 1999, when the Israeli government completed the privatization of ICL, Israel Corporation boosted its stake in the company past 52 percent. The company also gained majority control of ZIM, buying out the Israeli government shares in 2004 and boosting its own stake in the company to 99 percent. Similarly Israel Corporation raised its stake in Oil Refineries Ltd. to 45 percent, while remaining the major shareholder of publicly listed Tower Semiconductor.

Ofer and Rosen pushed through a major restructuring program within its core holdings as well, helping to drive up their profitability. The company also backed their expansion. At ICL, for example, the company spent more than $700 million on acquisitions, boosting that company to the top ranks in the world's fertilizer and potash markets. ZIM also grew strongly, expanding its base of operations to eight major hubs, including in Spain, China, and Singapore. As a result of these investments, Israel Corporation's market value soared, topping $3.6 billion in the last half of the decade.

By then, Israel Corporation had begun to develop its interest in two new and related business areas. In 2008 the company formed a joint venture with China's Chery, that country's largest independent automotive producer, to develop electric automobile designs for the Chinese markets. Israel Corporation also invested in Better Place LLC, buying 33 percent of that company, which was pioneering development of refueling grids for electric vehicles.

Nevertheless, Israel Corporation hit a bump in the road as the group's operations suffered through the global economic crisis and the devaluation of the dollar as the first decade of the 2000s neared its close. By 2009 most of the group's operations were losing money, kept afloat largely by the continued strong profits of ICL. Nonetheless, Israel Corporation remained one of the motors of the Israeli economy in the new century.

M. L. Cohen

PRINCIPAL SUBSIDIARIES

Better Place LLC (33%); Chery Quantum Auto Co. (China; 45%); IC Green Energy Ltd.; Inkia Energy Ltd.; Israel Chemicals Limited (53%); Oil Refineries (45%); Tower Semiconductor Ltd. (39%); ZIM Integrated Shipping Services Ltd. (99%).

PRINCIPAL DIVISIONS

Chemicals; Energy; Other Investments; Shipping; Transportation.

PRINCIPAL COMPETITORS

IDB Holding Corporation Ltd.; Discount Investment Corporation Ltd.; Ampal-American Israel Corp.; Clal Industries and Investments Ltd.; Allied Investments Ltd.; Sadot Research and Development Fund Ltd.; Delta Ventures.

FURTHER READING

Ankori, Merav, "Israel Corp. Unit Invests $10m in Solar Power Co. HelioFocus," *Israel Business Arena*, August 27, 2008.

Ben-Israel, Adi, "Zim Losses to Weigh on Israel Corp., Leumi," *Globes*, August 26, 2009.

Clark, Simon, "Israel Corp., Palestinian Deal Blocked, Plans China Car Maker," *Bloomberg*, May 2, 2009.

Gaston-Breton, H., "Saul Eisenberg, l'Ami Israelien des Chinois," *Les Echos*, August 3, 2009.

"Israel Corp. CEO: We Won't Abandon Zim," *Globes*, August 27, 2009.

"Israel Corp. Makes 'Fortune' Global 500," *Globes*, July 13, 2009.

"Israel Corporation Buys 17% of ICL," *Israel Business Today*, September 15, 1997, p. 7.

"Israel Corporation Profits Soar," *Israel Business Today*, April 15, 1994, p. 10.

Nelan, Bruce W., "Israel's Secret Weapon," *Time*, July 21, 2008.

"Ofer Brothers Pull the Rug out from Under Potash Corporation of Saskatchewan and Take Control of the Israel Corporation," *Israel Business Today*, January 31, 1999, p. 16.

Rimon, Ran, and Sharon Baider, "Israel Corp. Stake in Chinese Car Venture to Grow," *Globes*, March 1, 2009.

Shalev, Shai, "Ofer Brothers Divide Control," *Globes*, September 29, 2002.

"Shaoul Eisenberg, 76, Developer of Israel's International Trade," *New York Times*, March 31, 1997.

Weiner, Joel, "Israel: Capital Opportunities," *Forbes*, April 22, 1985, p. 60.

Wollberg, Erez, "Ofer Family Increases Israel Chemicals Stake," *Globes*, September 11, 2006.

Japan Post Holdings Company Ltd.

———————■———————

1-3-2 Kasumigaseki, Chiyoda-ku
Tokyo, 100-8798
Japan
Telephone: (+81 03) 3504 4411
Fax: (+81 03) 3504 5399
Web site: http://www.japanpost.jp

Government-Owned Company
Incorporated: 2006
Employees: 229,134
Total Assets: ¥327.58 trillion ($1.7 trillion) (2008)
NAICS: 491110 Postal Service; 524113 Direct Life
  Insurance Carriers; 522120 Savings Institutions

■ ■ ■

Japan Post Holdings Company Ltd. oversees Japan's postal services and its network of more than 24,000 post offices, as well as one of the world's largest banks and one of the world's largest insurance companies, with total assets of nearly ¥328 trillion ($1.7 trillion). The company operates through four primary subsidiaries: Japan Post Service Co. Ltd., which provides mail delivery services throughout the country; Japan Post Network, which operates the post office network; Japan Post Bank; and Japan Post Insurance. Altogether, these operations employ over 200,000 people, including many through a hereditary system created at the time of the postal services founding in 1871.

Japan Post Holdings, also called Japan Post Group, was created in 2006 as the first step in the privatization of the Japanese post office. Under the privatization plan, both the banking and insurance arms are expected to be spun off as separate, publicly listed companies as early as 2010. The full-scale privatization of the company is scheduled to be completed by 2017. In mid-2009, the company remained 100 percent controlled by the Japanese government. However, the election of a new coalition government, ending the 50-year reign of the Liberal Democratic Party, in September 2009 threatened to disrupt the timing of the privatization. The new government announced its intention to reconsolidate the postal services and post office network into Japan Post Holdings.

MESSENGER SERVICES DATING FROM SEVENTH CENTURY

Japan marked the introduction of a modern postal service system only in 1871. However, the first organized postal services dated back to the Taika era in the seventh century. In 645, Japan's rulers instituted a messenger relay service based on the post-station model developed by the Tang dynasty in China.

The new messenger service, reserved exclusively for government use, employed riders on horseback along a network of relay stations. A formal system was laid out in 710, creating a system of main and secondary roads, and establishing relay stations every 16 kilometers apart along them. Operators of the relay stations paid for their expenses through fees levied on messages, as well as sales of crops and other goods to travelers. This system remained in place for the next three centuries, but fell into disuse as the cost of maintaining the relay stations became too heavy.

COMPANY PERSPECTIVES

"Atarashii-Futsu-wo-Tsukuru." We are dedicated to assisting people all over Japan lead more enjoyable lives. We sincerely provide services that people can trust and rely on. We will constantly redefine "Atarashii-Futsu" by evolving to meet the changing needs of our customers, serving people nationwide, one by one. We will unite for the purpose of changing in order to deepen relationships with our customers. We will be a corporate group that can grow together with our customers. The Japan Post Group will retain a tight focus on targeting customers' changing needs in step with social trends and other events. Through this process, we will use the group's resources to create more "universal services" that meet specific needs.

We have three business domains: postal, banking, and insurance services. Customers can access all three of these services through our vast network of post offices. We are determined to draw on our strengths to become an even more convenient source of products and services that our customers can use with complete confidence.

A next attempt to establish a postal system came during the Kamakura era at the end of the 12th century. An informal network of inns, teahouses, stables, and markets had taken the place of the former post-stations. The Kamakura government adapted this network into a relay system, which was placed under the control of military governors. While the new system continued to use horses for letter and parcel deliveries, a new type of messenger, the *hikyaku*, began carrying small packages and letters on foot. When the Kamakura government fell in the early 14th century, the relay network collapsed as well. The use of *hikyaku*, however, continued until well into the 19th century.

HIKYAKU INTO THE 19TH CENTURY

The Sengoku period and its network of warlords and feudal states broke up the national networks for much of the 15th and 16th centuries. Nonetheless, toward the end of the 16th century, the customs barriers set up among the feudal estates began to disappear, new provincial roads were built, and postal services based on relay stations were once again put into place. The new trade freedoms led the way to the Edo period and the creation of a newly centralized government at the beginning of the 17th century.

The rise of Edo as the Japanese capital brought about a major increase in the use of the relay stations, particularly along the five major arteries leading to the city. The increase in traffic led to a fortification of the relay station network, concentrating resources on these villages to the expense of more outlying regions. While horses continued to be used, the *hikyaku* became the backbone of the country's messenger system. Their importance was underscored by the creation of a partner system, in which every carrier was accompanied by a second carrier, who would take over the packet to be delivered in the event that the first carrier injured himself or otherwise fell ill.

The fast-moving *hikyaku*, traditionally clad only in loincloths, became ubiquitous on Japan's highways. They also enjoyed a certain esteem, including having the right of way over every other traveler. While the official postmen provided services only to the government, a secondary foot-based messenger system for private correspondence developed during the 18th century. This service was given official recognition by the military government in 1782.

ESTABLISHING A MODERN POSTAL SERVICE IN THE MEIJI PERIOD

The arrival of the Western powers, including the United Kingdom, France, and the United States, and the opening of Japan to the outside world in the middle of the 19th century, created the demand for modern postal services. The Western nations' establishment of outposts, trading centers, and consulates led to the need to develop postal services to communicate with their governments at home.

The British were among the first to establish postal services, with the creation of the British Postal Agency (BPA) starting as early as 1854, and the founding of the British Post Offices in Yokohama in 1859. The BPA opened several other post offices through the beginning of the Meiji period and the restoration of the imperial dynasty. France opened its own post office network, carrying mail from Shanghai as early as 1863. The French opened their own post office in Yokohama in 1865. Similarly, the United States had launched its own postal services into and out of Japan during the late 1850s. These activities were halted by the Civil War. Service resumed in 1867, with the creation of a series of Consular Postal Agencies operating, like the French and British systems, in parallel to the existing Japanese messenger system.

The restoration of the imperial government and the inauguration of the Meiji period in 1868 set the stage for the modern era both in Japan's postal system and its industrial development. Leading the creation of the modern postal system was Hisoka Maejima, who became the new government's Ministry for Popular Affairs. In 1870, Maejima was sent to the United Kingdom in order to examine the postal system there. Upon his return, the government took up his suggestions for the implementation of Japan's own national postal system.

The first link of that system, connecting Tokyo and Osaka with 65 post offices, was in place by April 1871. In order to develop the post office network, the cash-strapped service prevailed upon the nation's wealthy merchants, who donated land for the new post office buildings. The decline of the samurai, as Emperor Meiji imposed his political and military authority, provided the postal service with an early pool of employees. Many of the system's earliest postmasters came from the ranks of the country's former samurai. The company's postmasters benefited from a high degree of social and political prestige in their community, as well as a number of fiscal advantages. At the same time, the postmaster position was made hereditary, passing from father to son over generations. Even into the 21st century, many of the company's employees remained beneficiaries of this system.

The new service (referred to hereafter as Japan Post for convenience) issued its first stamps in 1871. By the end of the following year, the network had reached a national level. Japan Post at first operated in competition with the existing private postal services. In 1873, however, the Japanese government passed a law establishing a postal monopoly under government control. A number of private postal services, particularly those of the French and British, nonetheless continued to operate for several years. In 1873, the United States signed a convention with the Japanese government to dismantle the Consular Post Agencies, a move completed at the end of 1874. As part of that convention, Japan agreed to provide foreign mail services. These were instituted in 1875.

SAVINGS BANK FINANCING FROM 1874

Maejima, who became known as "The Father of the Post," established a system of uniform postal tariffs, meant to stimulate the use of postal services in Japan's rural and outlying regions. From the start, the development of the postal service was seen as an intrinsic component in the modernization, industrialization, and unification of Japan, as well as an instrument in carrying out the Japanese government's social policies. The creation of uniform postal rates made it possible for letters from Japan's remotest regions to be delivered for the same price as letters in its more populated areas.

The postal service's usefulness for the development of the country's commercial and industrial sectors led to the adoption of favorable rates for a variety of categories, such as books and newspapers. Later, special rates were also created for commercial samples, agricultural products, and other goods deemed important to the stimulation of the rural economy. The postal service had also begun to tackle the special requirements of transporting funds, starting with establishing maximum cash limits contained in letters in 1872.

Maejima also recognized the potential not only for allowing the postal service to become self-supporting, but also in supporting the country's vast industrial and infrastructure needs. In 1874, Japan Post inaugurated its own postal savings bank system. The system encouraged Japan's population to develop their savings, including allowing accounts to be created based on deposits of less than one-hundredth of a yen. Larger deposits paid modest interest rates. The development of the savings bank system also enabled Japan Post to launch postal money order services in 1875.

From the start, the postal service was required to place all of its deposits into a trust fund governed by the Ministry of Finance. This increasingly large pool of money was then made available for funding the vast program of public works and infrastructure projects launched by the Japanese government. As a result the postal savings bank played an integral role in Japan's rapid modernization.

GROWTH THROUGH THE 20TH CENTURY

The Japanese postal service itself developed quickly, joining the Universal Postal Union by 1877. By 1880, the service had extended its network to cover more than 30,000 miles, with nearly 700 post offices in operation, including more than 300 capable of providing and cashing money orders.

Japan Post developed strongly through into the next century. The company launched parcel post delivery services in 1892. In 1911, the company added an express delivery service, followed by the launch of airmail services in 1929. By then, Japan Post had come to resemble its Western counterparts, including establishing its own foreign post offices in China and elsewhere. These were closed in 1923 following the institution of the national Chinese postal system. At the same time, Japan Post had expanded its range of financial services, launching its first life insurance products in 1916. The new operations were part of the group's goal of providing affordable life insurance to a wide segment of the Japanese population. The insurance unit paralleled the growth of the savings bank, and would eventually become not only the largest life insurer in Japan, but the largest in the world as well.

The financial clout of Japan Post played a major role in the ability of the Liberal Democratic Party (LDP), which came to power in the aftermath of World War II, to dominate Japanese politics for 50 years. The use of the Post's massive savings deposits had permitted the country to develop its infrastructure, as well as a military machine, and emerge as a major new industrial and financial force in the Asian world in the first half of the century. In the second half of the decade, this same vast pool of money enabled the LDP to shore up its political control by funding a variety of politically motivated, and often unnecessary, infrastructure projects. At the same time, the LDP relied on the political clout of its huge employee base, which at one point neared 300,000 people, or approximately one-third of the nation's total civil servant workforce.

FIRST CALLS TO PRIVATIZE IN THE EIGHTIES

In the meantime, Japan Post's savings deposits and life insurance assets continued to swell, reaching total deposits of ¥162 trillion ($1.4 trillion) at the beginning of the 1990s, the largest single pool of money anywhere in the world. The presence of this pool, and the postal service's requirement to place its deposits in the finance ministry's trust fund, continued to fuel Japan's intensive industrial and financial growth during the postwar period.

However, as the country's economy cooled in the mid-1980s, an increasing number of observers had begun to criticize the policies surrounding the postal service. The first calls to privatize the service and split off its banking and insurance operations, in part to liberate the company's assets in order to stimulate the economy, began to appear in the late 1980s.

In the meantime, Japan Post kept apace with the modernization of its postal operations. In 1968, for example, the service joined in with much of the rest of the world, introducing the postal code address system. This in turn permitted the company to invest heavily in the mechanization and automation of its sorting systems. Japan Post also began expanding its range of banking services, including the introduction of a limited range of loan services in 1976.

FIRST STEP TO PRIVATIZATION IN 2006

By 2000, Japan Post's assets had continued to swell, nearing ¥328 trillion of largely underperforming funds at a time when the Japanese economy had limped through more than a decade and a half of economic stagnation. The political hurdles toward the privatization of the postal service especially its banking and insurance assets meant that progress toward the liberalization of the market came only slowly.

The election of Junichiro Koizumi to the prime minister's position in 2001 provided the signal that the long-awaited privatization of Japan Post might occur. Koizumi had long championed the breakup of what he considered an anticompetitive monster, freeing up the company's trillions in assets for more lucrative placement in the private sector. Over the next several years, Koizumi pushed through his vision of a privatized post office, adopting the privatization as part of his cabinet plan in 2004. Following the failure of a first privatization bill in 2005, Koizumi launched an early parliamentary election. His landslide victory during that election at last gave him enough votes to push through the privatization program.

The first step toward the postal service's privatization came in 2006, with the creation of a new holding company, Japan Post Holdings Co. Ltd. Preparations for the next step got underway, resulting in the breakup of Japan Post into four distinct companies: Japan Post

Service, which took over the postal delivery operations; Japan Post Network, which regrouped more than 24,000 post offices throughout the country; and the banking and insurance arms Japan Post Bank and Japan Post Insurance.

This restructuring was completed in October 2007, as the government announced its intention to spin off Japan Post Bank and Japan Post Insurance as publicly listed companies as early as 2010. The entire privatization process, including the sale of the government's 100 percent control of Japan Post Holdings, was slated for completion by 2017.

Nonetheless, the political and economic implications of the privatization of the world's largest financial operation provided plenty of potential hurdles before then. Amid the economic uncertainty of the period, a new election swept the LDP from power after more than 50 years. Within weeks of taking office, the new coalition government led by the Democratic Party of Japan had begun to indicate its willingness to rethink the privatization process.

In September 2009, the government announced its intention to reconsolidate Japan Post Service and Japan Post Network into Japan Post Holdings itself. The government also announced its plan to suspend the sale of stock in Japan Post Holdings, Japan Post Bank, and Japan Post Insurance, effectively placing the privatization process on hold. After more than 130 years as a key element of Japan's economic, social, and industrial success, Japan Post appeared likely to remain under the firm control of the Japanese government for some time to come.

M. L. Cohen

PRINCIPAL SUBSIDIARIES

Japan Post Bank Co. Ltd.; Japan Post Insurance Co. Ltd.; Japan Post Network Co. Ltd.; Japan Post Service Co. Ltd.; Japan Post Staff Co., Ltd.; Post Office Business Support Co., Ltd.; Yusei Challenge Co., Ltd.

PRINCIPAL DIVISIONS

Banking Business; Life Insurance Business; Parcel Delivery Business; Post Office Service; Postal Business.

PRINCIPAL OPERATING UNITS

Japan Post Bank; Japan Post Insurance; Japan Post Network; Japan Post Service.

PRINCIPAL COMPETITORS

Deutsche Post World Net; La Poste; Poste Italiane S.p. A.; Sofipost S.A.; TNT N.V.; Royal Mail Holdings PLC; Nexo Servicios Postales S.R.L.; Schweizerische Post; Organizacion Coordinadora Argentina S.A.

FURTHER READING

Ajima, Shinya, "Privatization Ends Postal Savings Safe Haven," *Japan Times*, October 2, 2007.

Callan, Eoin, and Michiyo Nakamoto, "Japan Reassures US over Post Office Break-up," *Financial Times*, February 16, 2007, p. 5.

Hitoshi, Chiba, "Special Delivery," *Look Again*, September 2003, p. 12.

"Japan Post President Nishikawa Offers to Discipline Himself," *Thai Press Reports*, June 21, 2009.

"Japan Post Puts Off Parcel Biz Consolidation Again," *Jiji*, September 11, 2009.

"Japan Post Service to Pull Out of Int'l Cargo JV with ANA," *Jiji*, August 8, 2009.

"Japan Post, TNT Join Forces," *Traffic World*, November 7, 2005, p. 31.

"Japan's Dangerous Post Office," *Economist*, October 29, 1994, p. 20.

"Japan's Post Offices Should Stop Being Banks," *Business Week*, February 19, 2001, p. 54.

Kite, Hanna, "Going Postal: Japan Post Is Under Fire. Here's Why," *Time International*, September 12, 2005, p. 50.

"Leviathan Unbound," *Economist*, March 29, 2003.

Pilling, David, "Storming the Castle," *Financial Times*, September 13, 2004, p. 19.

"Postal Privatization U-turn," *Yomiuri Shimbun*, September 18, 2009.

"Postal Shake-up," *Global Agenda*, October 4, 2007.

"Ready, Steady, Go: Japan Post," *Economist*, September 4, 2004, p. 68US.

"Reformable? Japan's Post Office," *Economist*, June 23, 2001, p. 6US.

"Return to Sender," *Economist*, October 18, 1997, p. 42.

"Snail Mail," *Economist*, June 11, 2005, p. 41US.

Summers, Adam B., "Japan Goes Postal: Freeing the Mail," *Reason*, June 2008, p. 9.

"Watch Out for Japan's Mighty Postal Bank," *Economist*, October 22, 1988, p. 81.

Wood, Carol, "Special Delivery: Japan Post to Be Privatized," *Business Week Online*, April 6, 2006.

Kayak.com

55 North Water Street, Suite 1
Norwalk, Connecticut 06854
U.S.A.
Telephone: (203) 899-3100
Fax: (203) 899-3125
Web site: http://www.kayak.com

Private Company
Incorporated: 2004 as Kayak Software Corporation
Employees: 50
Sales: $50 million (2007 est.)
NAICS: 561510 Travel Agencies; 561599 All Other
Travel Arrangement and Reservation Services

∎ ∎ ∎

Kayak.com is a global Internet travel company, operating Kayak.com, SideStep.com, and TravelPost.com. Originally founded as Kayak Software Corporation in 2004, the company launched Kayak.com to the public in 2005 as a travel search engine with a modest set of tools that enabled consumers to comparison shop for flight and hotel information. Since then, its search capabilities have increased to include travel tips, member discounts, user reviews, and destination information. Kayak.com has launched Web sites in France, the United Kingdom, Germany, Italy, and Spain. Investors include Sequoia Capital, America Online, General Catalyst, and Accel Partners.

FROM CONCEPT TO COMPANY: 2004

In 2003, the future cofounders of Kayak.com, Steve Hafner and Paul English, met to discuss issues facing the online travel industry. Chief among their concerns was the lack of customer loyalty. Studies had found that online travel shoppers visited several Web sites before making a purchase to take advantage of the significant price differences among companies. Studies also revealed that most shoppers ended up booking directly with a hotel, airline, or rental car company rather than through the agencies themselves.

Hafner, an executive vice president at Orbitz, and English, vice president of technology at Intuit, invited Terry Jones of Travelocity and Greg Slyngstad of Expedia to meet with them. The group agreed to tackle their problem in a new way. Instead of trying to sell products to consumers like a travel agency, they would create a search engine that mimicked consumer behavior. The search engine would collect data from hundreds of suppliers' and online travel agencies' Web sites and display prices and itineraries for flights, rental cars, and hotel rooms in one centralized location. The consumer could then purchase the travel product directly.

The search engine would be named Kayak.com, a name that represented a brand identity in the tradition of eBay, Google, and Yahoo!, and which Hafner said he hoped would conjure "self-powered and independent, a way to glide effortlessly through the information on the Web," according to a 2005 article in the *Fairfield County Business Journal*.

A few months later, in early January 2004, Hafner and English each kicked in $1.5 million of their own money and started Kayak Software Corporation in Norfolk, Connecticut. Their travel industry colleagues, who became shareholders in the company, joined them. Management quickly focused on building the technology to power Kayak.com.

Likewise, Hafner and English earnestly pursued fund-raising. The company's first round of financing, more than $8 million, came from General Catalyst and America Online. The second round came from Sequoia Capital in December 2004. In total, the company raised more than $15 million. "The concept was so strong, and the team was so strong, that getting capital wasn't all that difficult," Hafner said in a 2006 *Entrepreneur* article.

A FOCUS ON TECHNOLOGY BEFORE LAUNCH: 2004

Although the concept was strong, it was not new, however. Several other travel search engines already existed, including CheapFlights.com, SideStep.com, Mobissimo.com, and Yahoo!'s FareChase.com. All of these engines were in a race to become the Google of travel for good reason: The online travel industry was a $55 billion market and growing fast. According to Hafner in a 2004 *Boston Globe* article, research indicated that, in 1999, 6 percent of travelers booked online. By 2003 that number had jumped to 25 percent. Hafner predicted that in 2004 that percentage would rise to 30. In addition, Hafner foresaw that in coming years those numbers could skyrocket to as much as 60 to 70 percent.

To beat the competition in the race to the top, Kayak.com needed to focus its efforts on developing superior technology. It was crucial to be the best search engine with the most relevant results so that users did not have to search multiple Web sites to find the best deal.

Still, even if the company launched with impressive technological innovation, being the best search engine was not entirely in their control. Like many of its competitors, Kayak.com needed to convince suppliers that paying the company a referral fee was a worthwhile investment. When consumers clicked through from Kayak.com to a supplier's Web site, Kayak earned a small fee from the destination site regardless of whether or not the consumer made a purchase. "The way we make money is by providing consumer traffic to these online agencies as well as airlines and hotels directly, where consumers can actually complete a booking," Hafner said in a 2005 *Fairfield County Business Journal* article. Holdouts such as Southwest Airlines threatened to derail their strategy. If airlines refused to pay a fee, consumers would still need to leave Kayak.com to shop around.

The advantage of this model meant that prices did not vary from suppliers' Web sites (as they did on the most popular travel agency Web sites, such as Expedia, Travelocity, and Orbitz) because Kayak.com did not earn commissions. "We're a technology company that focuses on travel search, we're not a travel agency," Hafner said in a 2004 *New York Times* article.

When the alpha version of Kayak.com was launched to friends, family members, and colleagues in May 2004, Web site tools and functionality were quite modest. Users could search only for hotel rooms and round-trip flights. Broader searches that included multi-city stops and one-way tickets were not available. However, there was one unique feature that would eventually prove hugely popular: a slider that enabled users to narrow down their search criteria by restricting airlines or price ranges.

The beta version of Kayak.com launched in October 2004 with a significant number of vendors and suppliers signing agreements. The search engine scraped data from 60 online travel Web sites for information and provided prices and itineraries for more than 550 airlines and 85,000 hotels. However, Travelocity would not allow Kayak.com to scrape its Web site. In addition, there was a question of whether other online travel agencies would follow suit.

RAISING AWARENESS AND BUILDING RESOURCES: 2005–06

On February 7, 2005, Kayak.com was officially launched to the public. At the time, the company had 31 employees, with some based in the company's Norfolk headquarters and others in a research and development center in Concord, Massachusetts. The

KEY DATES

2004: Steve Hafner and Paul English cofound the Kayak Software Corporation.

2005: Kayak.com is officially launched; sales hit $3.6 million.

2006: Accel Partners invests $15 million; company opens a London office.

2007: Kayak.com launches Web sites in the United Kingdom, Germany, France, and Spain; company acquires SideStep, Inc.

2008: TravelPost.com is launched; Kayak.com enters Italian market.

2009: TravelPost.com is upgraded and relaunched.

company's short-term goals were simple: complete product buildup, raise awareness of Kayak.com, and draw consumers.

Building up Kayak.com was a matter of increasing partnerships with booking engine vendors and acquiring more supplier agreements so that search results could become ever more comprehensive. It also meant developing new technology so that search results were more compelling and customizable. By July 2005, Kayak.com had branched out from hotels and airlines with its launch of a rental car search feature. In addition, several new partners had joined as affiliates, including About.com, America Online, USA Today, Lonely Planet, and Smarter Travel.

As search results increased and improved, consumer awareness and traffic grew. By September, Kayak.com was culling data from more than 100 online travel Web sites and providing prices and itineraries for more than 550 airlines and 91,000 hotels and car rental agencies. The Web site was seeing an impressive 20 percent increase in traffic each month. At the end of 2005, sales had jumped to nearly $3.6 million from $3,000 in 2004. Kayak.com had more than five million users per month.

By April 2006, there were 115,000 searchable hotel properties on Kayak.com, which was more than any other travel Web site. With its steady growth, Kayak.com was able to attract more funding. Accel Partners led a Series C round of funding in May 2006, which raised another $15 million. Buoyed by the extra cash and its growing popularity, Kayak was feeling confident enough to launch a $10 million ad campaign in an effort to build brand awareness quickly a little more than a year after launch. Thirteen animated spots themed "Life's a

Trip" were broadcast on 20 cable stations in July.

As traffic grew rapidly, Kayak.com became increasingly eager to branch out globally and inch closer to winning the race to become the top travel search engine. At the end of 2006, Kayak.com opened an office in London.

GLOBAL EXPANSION, METEORIC RISE TO THE TOP: 2007

A few months later, in February 2007, Kayak.com launched its first international Web site in the United Kingdom. The Web site gathered data from more than 400 European-based travel Web sites and airline carriers. These partnerships and agreements eased the launches of two more Web sites in Europe two months later in France and Germany. Kayak.com kept expanding. Later in the year, Spain was added, and Italy came on board in April 2008.

At the same time, Kayak.com was garnering widespread attention domestically, winning more awards in 2007 than any other travel Web site, including "Best of the Web" by both *BusinessWeek* and *Forbes.com,* "Best Travel Search Engine" by the Associated Press, and "Best Search Aid" by *Travel + Leisure* magazine. It was included on *Time* magazine's "50 Coolest Websites" chart. The site had also been recognized by publications in the United Kingdom, including the *Telegraph*, the *Observer*, and the *Sunday Times*.

To ensure that it continued pleasing users and reviewers, in October 2007 Kayak.com launched a major redesign that included many enhancements and new functionalities based on user feedback. By the end of the year, in December, Kayak.com was looking to expand further in Europe and also had its eye on acquiring Santa Clara, California-based SideStep Inc. as a subsidiary.

Kayak.com obtained $196 million in financing for the SideStep deal. When the acquisition was complete in January, Kayak.com and its affiliate Web sites became the fifth-largest travel brand in the world. There was less than a 10 percent overlap between the two companies' users, which meant that each Web site gained millions of new users in the merger. According to a company press release, the acquisition meant that users would conduct more than 33 million searches on its Web sites in January 2008, up from 16 million in January 2007.

COMPETITION AND MARKET EXPANSION: 2008–09

A few months later, in March 2008, Kayak.com was ready to enter the travel user-review market. It launched its own user-review Web site, TravelPost.com, to compete with TripAdvisor.com, the number one online hotel and travel community Web site with more than eight million U.S. users per month.

A year later, TravelPost.com had yet to catch on. In order to make it more competitive, Kayak relaunched TravelPost.com in March 2009 as a powerful search engine that pulled 1.4 million hotel reviews from more than 200 Web sites. The upgrade was an escalation in an intensifying competition between Kayak.com and TripAdvisor.com, which had launched its own search engine, much like Kayak.com's. At the time, TravelPost.com attracted about 300,000 visitors per month.

By mid-2009, Kayak.com was searching more than 100 travel Web sites, hundreds of airlines, 158,000 hotels, all the major car rental agencies, and 17 cruise lines. During its four years in business, it had expanded from a modest and simple travel search engine to include destination information, travel tips, member discounts, user reviews, and hotel descriptions, as well as numerous tools such as fare alerts, a fuel cost calculator, and an iPhone application. Kayak.com had become a top travel search engine that was positioned to expand its reach exponentially in the years ahead, to India, China, and beyond.

Carrie Rothburd

PRINCIPAL COMPETITORS

Expedia Inc.; Orbitz Worldwide Inc.; Travelocity.com L.P.; Hotwire Inc.; Priceline.com Inc.; Travelzoo Inc.

FURTHER READING

Everson, Darren, "Kayak Merges with SideStep," *Wall Street Journal*, December 21, 2007, p. B4.

Kooser, Amanda C., "Hotter Than Hot," *Entrepreneur*, June 2006.

Mohl, Bruce, "Selling Travel … Sort Of," *Boston Globe*, December 19, 2004, p. M10.

Shattuck, Harry, "Kayak.com, Others Stick New Oars into River of Airfares," *Orlando Sentinel*, May 22, 2005, p. L8.

Stellin, Susan, "Kayak Is New Vehicle for Searching the Web," *New York Times*, November 28, 2004, p. 53.

Toth, David, "Kayak.com Navigates the Rapids of Online Travel," *Fairfield County Business Journal*, January 10, 2005, p. 2.

Wong, Nicole, "Kayak Aims to Land More Fans in Travel Web-site War; TravelPost Boosts Search Power to Take on TripAdvisor," *Boston Globe*, March 12, 2009, p. B5.

Zebora, Jim, "Kayak Expands Worldwide," *Connecticut Post*, December 21, 2007, p. G3.

Kiss My Face Corporation

———— ■ ————

144 Main Street
Gardiner, New York 12525
U.S.A.
Toll Free: (800) 262-5477
Fax: (845) 255-4312
Web site: http://www.kissmyface.com

Private Company
Incorporated: 1981
Employees: 55
Sales: $75 million (2008 est.)
NAICS: 325620 Toilet Preparation Manufacturing

■ ■ ■

Kiss My Face Corporation is a leading U.S. manufacturer of natural and organic health and beauty products. The company has a line of more than 200 products in all. These include body care products such as shaving creams, moisturizers, deodorants, and hand and foot care products; soaps and shower gels; beauty and face care items such as tinted moisturizers, lip care items, and shimmers and shines; hair care products; oral care products including toothpaste and mouthwash; sun care products; a line of children's products; and other products such as gift sets. The company sells through retailers across North America, in health food stores including well-known chains Whole Foods and Wild Oats. Kiss My Face products also have mainstream distribution through mass-market retailers such as Target and the drugstore chain CVS. Kiss My Face also sells its products through its Web site, and in some 20 countries

outside the United States. Almost all its products are manufactured in the United States, with the exception of its toothpaste, manufactured in Italy, and its olive oil soap, which is manufactured in Greece. Kiss My Face was founded by two partners who remain in control of the company.

BEGINNING IN THE COUNTRYSIDE

Kiss My Face Corporation began as a sideline in olive oil soap. Bob MacLeod, formerly a talent agent in New York City, and Steve Byckiewicz, a fellow New Yorker and flight attendant, moved together to a farm in upstate New York in 1980. The two men had found the city too hectic and expensive, and hoped to make a new life centered around organic produce. Both men were vegetarians with a penchant for gardening. They began growing their own vegetables, and sold what they could to stores in the nearby communities of New Paltz, Woodstock, and Kingston, New York. However, they discovered that in Manhattan they could command up to three times more for their vegetables than the small-town health food stores would pay them. Consequently, the two young entrepreneurs began trekking into the city several times a week.

They stumbled upon an interesting product one day while shopping in Woodstock. This was olive oil soap imported from Greece. The Greek importer was based in Manhattan, so they visited him and bought several cases. The men repackaged the soap and began selling it in the same health food stores that were buying their organic vegetables. The soap proved very popular, and the two men soon had orders for more.

At that point, MacLeod and Byckiewicz realized that natural health and beauty products was an inviting niche. There was little competition, and it seemed likely that consumers who liked the pure, natural olive oil soap might appreciate other similar products. They came up with the name Kiss My Face, hoping it was memorable. However, the young company had a rocky start. Revenues were only $30,000 to $45,000 in its first three years. The founders were unsure if they had a viable business, and they had no money for advertising or promotion. In an interview with *Natural Foods Merchandiser* in September 2004, the pair told the magazine, "We didn't think we'd make it at least once a week for the first three years."

Despite their uncertainty, MacLeod and Byckiewicz suddenly took the company to a bigger level when their importer moved. The importer told the men that he would be unable to supply them with soap for a few months while he relocated. Afraid to lose their most essential product, MacLeod and Byckiewicz bargained with the importer, ultimately buying up his entire inventory of 24,000 bars of soap, to be paid for in 90 days. This amounted to six tons of soap, most of which got stored in the men's garage and barn. The pair worked furiously to send samples to personal care product distributors. The earthy brown soap accompanied by hand-written notes sparked a lot of interest, and soon the men realized that even their six tons was not going to meet demand. In 1982, partner Byckiewicz next borrowed $20,000 from his parents and flew to Greece. He negotiated the purchase of a further 22 tons of the olive oil soap. This flew off store shelves, and Byckiewicz repaid his parents within 90 days.

BRANCHING OUT

Once the company was going well, the pair pressed their luck. In 1982, they arranged a marketing deal with BIC

Corporation. BIC was about to introduce a new disposable razor. Kiss My Face arranged to buy 200,000 razors, as well as 3,000 floor display units. The company set up displays of its natural soap and the new BIC razor in stores it had been doing business with in the East and Midwest. With both BIC and the display unit manufacturer, Kiss My Face arranged generous terms, so it would not have to pay for 45 days. The soap and razors sold so well that within three days they were all snapped up. The marketing stunt sparked orders from all sorts of new retailers, too. Orders rose precipitously that year. The company, which had been on rocky ground for three years, suddenly brought in $275,000. Earnings on that sum were a comfortable $150,000.

Kiss My Face then brought in a chemist to help it develop other natural health care products. The company created a lotion from olive oil and aloe vera, and another from local upstate New York honey and calendula flowers. MacLeod and Byckiewicz experimented with many formulas, testing them on friends and neighbors. Before long, the young company had a stable of products, all naturally formulated, designed to appeal to the same category of consumers who shopped in health food stores.

The company developed steadily over the next 10 years, adding more soaps and moisturizers and branching out into other health and beauty lines. By the mid-1990s, the Kiss My Face line had grown to more than 100 different products, including bath gels, lip balms, deodorant, mascara, sunscreen, and more. While bringing out new lines, the company had refrained from spending on advertising. Its progress was almost all made through word of mouth. The brand sold almost exclusively through natural food stores in its early years. Consumers who cared about what they put in their body might also care about what they put on their body, so the link to this type of store seemed to serve the brand well.

As some of these stores consolidated and grew, Kiss My Face followed along. In the 1980s, most natural food stores had been stand-alone operations. By the early 1990s, Kiss My Face was stocked in some of the new, fast-growing regional and national natural food store chains, including Fresh Fields and Wild Oats. These chains blossomed as the appeal of natural foods reached a wider swathe of consumers. Kiss My Face too was poised in the mid-1990s to enter broader distribution outside the natural foods niche.

MOVING INTO MASS MARKETS

Kiss My Face products were sold in some 10,000 retail outlets by the mid-1990s. The company's leaders

```
┌──────────────────────────────────────────┐
│                                            │
│              KEY DATES                     │
│              ─────■─────                    │
│  1981:  Company incorporates.              │
│  1982:  Company takes $20,000 loan to buy 22 tons │
│         of olive oil soap.                 │
│  1996:  Kiss My Face begins expanding into mass- │
│         market retailers.                  │
│  1997:  Fire destroys company warehouse and │
│         distribution center.               │
│  2004:  Product line grows to more than 200 items. │
│                                            │
└──────────────────────────────────────────┘
```

planned to double the brand's exposure very quickly, by seeking distribution in mass-market chains. The time was right for such a move. In the early 1990s, sales at natural food stores had grown at an average rate of 25 percent a year. Total sales for the industry were estimated at $10 billion by 1997. While traditional retailers often faced sluggish growth and struggled to differentiate products, the natural and organic categories were healthy and growing.

As consumer demand for natural products escalated in the 1990s, items previously found only in specialty natural food stores began to move into mainstream retail outlets. Perhaps the first natural health and beauty brand to break out of the natural food stores retailing niche was Tom's of Maine. In the late 1980s, Tom's all-natural toothpaste had been picked up by the drugstore chain CVS. Over the next 10 years, Tom's moved into 30,000 mass-market retailers. It could even be found at Wal-Mart, which was in some sense the antithesis of the small, privately or cooperatively owned natural food grocery.

Kiss My Face followed the boom in natural and organic products. Over 1996 and 1997, it doubled the number of retailers who stocked its products. It moved its lines into the drugstore chains Longs Drugs and Rite Aid, into the specialty shops Ulta3 and Grand Union, and into the discount department store chain Target. The company redesigned some of its packaging as it moved into more mainstream markets. Kiss My Face still did not do traditional media advertising, but it offered in-store displays with testers to tempt consumers to try the products.

The company also moved into product lines that might have more mainstream appeal. Its natural cosmetics seemed to be a big draw with drugstores. There were not many all-natural cosmetics available, and established brands such as Clairol who offered natural lines had done well. Kiss My Face brought out lipsticks and

mascaras packaged in birch cases. These looked upscale, and seemed to stand out among traditional makeup brands. The company also brought out a line of children's products as it moved into mass marketing. The hope was that adults who were buying Kiss My Face lotion or soap for themselves might also pick up one of the kids' products, such as Grape Jelli antibacterial soap, for their children. The move into mass marketing seemed to go smoothly for Kiss My Face. Sales were estimated at some $19 million by the mid-1990s.

CONTINUING EXPANSION

Not everything went well for Kiss My Face, though. In 1997, the company's warehouse and distribution center caught fire and had to be entirely rebuilt. In addition, not all of its new products attracted loyal consumers, and some formulations had to be remade. Still, the problems the company had seemed minor, and did not stop its advance into new markets and its increasing sales. The company did not release sales figures, but industry estimates showed sales growing from just under $20 million in the mid-1990s to around $75 million by 2004. The overall natural and organic foods market category also showed tremendous growth during this period. Within that category, the natural personal care market was also on a fast track. A report in *Drug Store News* from May 2, 2005 estimated that the total U.S. market for natural personal care products would reach $5.9 billion by 2008.

Although the natural personal care market had huge potential, it was still underdeveloped in the late 1990s and early 2000s. Kiss My Face had competitors in company's such as Nature's Gate, Jason Natural Products, and Burt's Bees. Nonetheless, room remained on drugstore shelves for natural health and beauty products. Consumers were coming to trust natural health care products more, as the science behind them had improved and they performed well against traditional formulations. Though natural health care products in most cases were more expensive than their traditional mass-market counterparts, consumers seemed willing to pay more for what they saw as pure and healthful goods.

These favorable market conditions meant Kiss My Face was able to unveil many new products and place itself in more and more retail outlets. By 2004, the company had over 200 different products. It sold these not only in unaffiliated natural food stores but in the chains Whole Foods, Wild Oats, Vitamin Cottage, Earthfare, and the Vitamin Shoppe. It was distributed in hundreds of CVS drugstores, with plans to move into as many as 1,000 CVS stores. It was carried by some 500

Target stores as well. Kiss My Face was also sold online, and in 20 countries outside the U.S. by the middle of the decade.

With sales growth estimated at more than 25 percent annually, the company could afford to innovate. It brought out a new line of skin care products called Obsessively Organic, designed to compete with mass-market skin care lines. These toners and facial cleansers used natural ingredients such as seaweed extract and ginger where more traditional products used chemicals such as alcohol. Kiss My Face dominated the shaving category for natural health care, with a market share of over 40 percent. As men's personal care items began to grow quickly, the company redesigned packaging to appeal to men, and also brought out more products designed for men.

Then in 2005, in partnership with the discount clothing company Old Navy, Kiss My Face launched a new line called OnBody. OnBody was to be sold inside Old Navy stores, and the line carried both companies' logos. Other new products included more cosmetics in 2006. Kiss My Face brought out its Color Line product assortment, which included tinted moisturizer and 3way Color for Lips, Cheeks & Eyes. This line stood out from traditional cosmetics in that they contained no animal ingredients, had not been tested on animals, and had no artificial colors, parabens, or other chemicals.

INCREASING COMPETITION

Kiss My Face had managed phenomenal growth while staying privately owned, eschewing most forms of advertising, and remaining true to its original orientation towards natural and organic ingredients. It had benefited from a growing tide of consumer interest in healthy living. By the end of the decade, this trend still seemed strong. In the early years of Kiss My Face, its competitors had been other small companies that were also doing so-called kitchen chemistry. A few of these, such as Burt's Bees and Tom's of Maine, gained wide distribution, as did Kiss My Face.

The success of these companies meant that many more raw materials became available to manufacturers. Formulations got better and more effective, and marketing became savvier. The strong sales of small companies also meant that the big health and beauty product manufacturers were eyeing the natural health care category. By 2006, sales of personal care products labeled organic grew almost 20 percent. Growth for personal care products overall was in the low single digits. Therefore, large manufacturers considered introducing natural and organic personal care products.

Companies such as Procter & Gamble, L'Oréal, and Unilever had extensive advertising budgets. They had the capacity to spend millions of dollars promoting new natural products, whereas companies such as Kiss My Face had never needed to do that. The shampoo maker L'Oréal, for example, had acquired a natural shampoo brand called PureOlogy in 2007. Industry estimates for the advertising budget for PureOlogy's mass-market rollout were $50 million or above. With Kiss My Face's overall revenues estimated at $75 million, a competitor with this much to spend may have seemed daunting.

However, Kiss My Face did not seem to suffer as bigger companies entered the natural personal care market. In fact, the company welcomed the broadening of interest that such competitors could bring. The natural health and beauty market evidently still had plenty of room to grow. In an interview with *WWD* (August 1, 2008), Kiss My Face's Byckiewicz noted that only 14 percent of customers who shopped at the natural grocery chain Whole Foods also shopped at the grocery's Whole Body health and beauty affiliate. If big companies put money into advertising their natural shampoos and lotions, that might draw more shoppers to the category as a whole. The entrance of big players, therefore, was not seen as a threat by Kiss My Face.

Even the sharp worldwide economic turndown that began in the fall of 2008 did not hit Kiss My Face hard. In spite of sinking consumer confidence and consumer spending in the United States, Kiss My Face claimed to have its best quarter ever at the beginning of 2009. The company had grown and prospered as the natural products market developed. After almost 30 years in business, Kiss My Face still seemed to have much growth in store.

A. Woodward

PRINCIPAL COMPETITORS

Burt's Bees, Inc.; Nature's Gate; Hain Celestial Group, Inc.

FURTHER READING

Alexander, Antoinette, "Organic Personal Care Category Ripe for Development in Drug," *Drug Store News*, May 2, 2005, p. 49.

Altmann, Allison, "Kiss My Face Expands Distribution, Products," *WWD*, July 23, 2004, p. 8.

Brookman, Faye, "Kiss My Face's Natural Moves," *WWD*, April 12, 1996, p. 9.

Coolidge, Carrie, "The Bootstrap Brigade," *Forbes*, December 28, 1998, pp. 90–91.

Hyde-Keller, O'rya, and Christian Spehar, "25 Who Made Naturals Beautiful," *Natural Foods Merchandiser*, September 2004, p. 40.

Nagel, Andrea, "Natural Players Ready for Competitors," *WWD*, August 1, 2008, p. 8.

"The Naturals," *FSB*, September 2009, p. 66.

Prior, Molly, "Old Navy to Enter Personal Care," *WWD*, July 29, 2005, p. 8.

Spehar, Christine, "The Guys Eye Personal Care," *Natural Grocery Buyer*, Winter 2005, pp. 22–23.

Tan, Cheryl Lu-Lien, "Shopping: Turning Your Skin Green," *Wall Street Journal*, July 14, 2007, p. 7.

Tode, Chantal, "Kiss My Face Takes a Look at Retail," *WWD*, October 20, 2000, p. 14S.

———, "Natural Brands Find New Home," *WWD*, August 15, 1997, p. 8.

"Trend Favors Kiss My Face," *Chain Drug Review*, June 29, 1998, p. 140.

Uhland, Vicki, "Q&A with Bob MacLeod and Steve Byckiewicz," *Natural Foods Merchandiser*, June 2009, p. 38.

Knitting Factory
Entertainment

—————■—————

361 Metropolitan Avenue
Brooklyn, New York 11211
U.S.A.
Telephone: (347) 529-6696
Web site: http://www.knittingfactory.com

Private Company
Incorporated: 1987
Employees: 130
Sales: $19 million (2008 est.)
NAICS: 711310 Promoters of Performing Arts, Sports,
and Similar Events with Facilities

■ ■ ■

Knitting Factory Entertainment is a New York City-based media company that focuses on live and recorded alternative music. The company maintains a performance space and bar in the Williamsburg section of Brooklyn as well as venues in Hollywood, California; Boise, Idaho; and Spokane, Washington. All the spaces are available for private bookings as well. The company also sponsors tours of its popular musical artists. In addition, Knitting Factory owns several recording labels, including Instinct Records, Shadow Records, Evolver, Knitting Factory Records, Knit Classics, JAM, and Shinny Disc.

FOUNDER, A LAW SCHOOL DROPOUT

The man behind the founding and rise to prominence of Knitting Factory was Michael Dorf. Born in

Milwaukee, he was studying law at the University of Wisconsin at Madison when a friend, Bob Appel, asked him to manage a band for which he played guitar called Swamp Thing. Dorf took a demo tape of the band to New York but failed to find any record label interested in signing Swamp Thing. Instead Dorf decided to start his own record label in Wisconsin in 1985, Flaming Pie Records, the first step in the creation of Knitting Factory Entertainment.

Although Flaming Pie Records, which also recorded other Madison bands, enjoyed meager success at best, Dorf decided to quit law school and move to New York City in the summer of 1986. In a rented Connecticut studio, Swamp Thing recorded a second album using the tentative title Mr. Blutdstein's Knitting Factory, a fictitious name coined by band member Jonathan Zarov and inspired by a Wisconsin sweater factory where he and Appel had once worked. Although the album was eventually called *A Cow Come True,* the Knitting Factory name was not forgotten and was soon applied to a performance space Dorf and a partner named Louis Spitzer created on Houston Street in Manhattan between Broadway and Bowery streets. It was financed by Dorf's $25,000 Bar Mitzvah savings.

A former Avon Products office, the property comprised 2,000 square feet on one floor of a four-story building. Initially Dorf was just looking for office space for Flaming Pie, but then decided to house an art gallery, Spitzer's area of interest, in front, and an office in back. Because it would be difficult to make enough money with a gallery alone, Dorf decided to sell coffee and muffins, and then realized he could use the gallery space at night for performances. The revised plan called for the space to serve as an art gallery and coffee shop during the day while evenings were devoted to "art in motion." The name was "___'s Knitting Factory," allowing for a limitless number of names to be substituted for Mr. Blutdstein. In time the space simply became known as Knitting Factory, although several years would pass before Dorf eliminated the "___'s" from the company's checkbook.

KNITTING FACTORY OPENS: 1987

When Knitting Factory opened in February 1987, Swamp Thing performed the first evening before a handful of Madison friends. Wednesday nights were then devoted to spoken-word performances, Thursday was designated jazz night, and the weekends offered an eclectic mix of whatever might draw a crowd, whether it be performance art or rock music. To book Thursday nights, Dorf turned to the classified ad section of the *Village Voice,* where he found jazz musician Wayne Horvitz. The resulting show was poorly promoted, drawing just eight people, but Horvitz liked the space and offered to program Thursday nights for Dorf, bringing in the artists that he knew would draw a crowd.

What Dorf did not realize when he and Spitzer opened Knitting Factory was that there was a lack of venues for non-mainstream musicians, both jazz and rock. With Horvitz's contacts, Knitting Factory started booking a wide variety of artists, who quickly developed an affection for the new club and made it the downtown space where musicians came to watch other musicians perform. As a result, Knitting Factory neglected other forms of art in motion, and the gallery required more energy than it was worth. As curator of the gallery, Spitzer was not especially interested in helping out with performances every night of the week and he was soon replaced by Appel, who was far better qualified to handle sound and cater to the other needs of the musicians playing the Knitting Factory stage.

Knitting Factory soon caught the attention of the *New York Times,* which reported in October 1987 that it

"had almost singlehandedly revived New York's downtown arts scene in its first six months of operation." The space was also noteworthy because it suffered a robbery a few weeks earlier, resulting in the loss of $10,000 in uninsured sound equipment and other materials. In order to replace the equipment, Dorf took out a loan, and when Spitzer declined to co-sign, the partnership formally came to an end and a new partnership between Dorf and Appel was established. The two men were already partners in Flaming Pie Records, which continued to pursue its own projects. They soon discovered that the radio stations and record stores they called about carrying Flaming Pie titles were more interested in the recordings of the artists playing at Knitting Factory, such as John Zorn and Cecil Taylor.

Knitting Factory began recording the shows, which led to the *Live at the Knitting Factory* radio series, which was initially carried by 30 radio stations agreeing to pay $5 a week to cover duplication and mailing. While the series did not make money, it built the Knitting Factory brand and generated interest in New York's budding downtown music scene. By 1990 the radio program found a sponsor in TDK Tapes and was carried by more than 200 stations.

A&M RELEASES LIVE SERIES: 1989

The show tapes also led to a deal with A&M Records to present a series of Live at the Knitting Factory recordings as well as compilation and full-artist records. Volumes 1 through 4 of the Live at the Knitting Factory series were released between May 1989 and June 1990. Sales were modest and when A&M was acquired by Polygram records the relationship was severed and Knitting Factory bought back its inventory of tapes and CDs. The loss of the record deal was a blessing in disguise, however. Dorf was forced to turn to independent distributors, which resulted in an important agreement with a Japanese label, Tokuma, which licensed all of the Knitting Factory recordings in Japan.

In the meantime, Knitting Factory began to take the artists it developed on the road. In 1988 the company sponsored a festival that garnered some press, including a lengthy article in a major Dutch newspaper, which led to a call from the programmer of a Dutch art center who invited Dorf to help her assemble a jazz marathon, which became a "Knitting Factory Festival" featuring 30 musicians from New York City. Knitting Factory also took some of its artists to Lincoln Center in New York for an event called "The Knitting Factory Goes Uptown."

The success of the Dutch jazz festival prompted Dorf to arrange a European tour in the summer of

KEY DATES

1987: Michael Dorf founds Knitting Factory in New York City.
1989: Radio series is introduced.
1990: Knitting Factory sponsors European tour.
1994: Knitting Factory moves to larger Leonard Street venue.
2000: Hollywood club opens.
2003: Dorf resigns as chief executive.
2006: Bravo Entertainment is acquired.
2009: Leonard Street Club closes, replaced by Brooklyn venue.

1990. It was a money-losing but educational experience. A year later Dorf proved he had learned his lessons, and a leaner lineup of jazz groups toured the continent and managed to break even, all while Knitting Factory continued to grow its brand. Earlier in 1991 Knitting Factory also sponsored its first West Coast tour, which was a modest success. Moreover, in preparation for the European tour, the company created a new record label, Knitting Factory Works. Its first project was a CD to promote and market the tour.

KNITTING FACTORY MOVES TO TRIBECA

In 1994 Knitting Factory moved to 74 Leonard Street in the Tribeca neighborhood of Manhattan. The new location was much larger than the Houston Street venue and included four performance spaces, the largest holding 400 standing customers, along with three bars and a recording studio. Dorf also installed Web cameras and began streaming concerts to its Web site, Knitmedia.com, becoming an early adopter of the new media. Dorf would later team up with MTV to develop an interactive live-music channel. Not only did Knitmedia stream concerts and sell Knitting Factory merchandise, it conducted distance learning seminars and took advantage of investor interest in anything related to the Internet in the late 1990s by raising nearly $5 million in venture capital. Knitmedia peaked in early 2000 and like many Internet companies was the victim of the bursting of the dot-com bubble.

Despite Dorf's infatuation with the Internet, music remained the heart of Knitting Factory, which finally turned a profit in 1996. The company acquired the Shimmy-Disc independent record label in 1997 from instrumentalist and producer Mark Kramer, who

founded the experimental rock imprint in the early 1990s but was forced to sell it as part of a settlement with a former partner. Knitting Factory then purchased about $200,000 in equipment from Kramer's New Jersey studio. Kramer also believed that Knitting Factory planned to hire him as house engineer and producer, but in the end only used him for a few production jobs, leading Kramer to sue Dorf for breach of contract and fraud.

Dorf also began arranging corporate sponsorships for Knitting Factory's annual summer What Is Jazz? festival. After Texaco supported the event in 1997, some of the musicians, who had paid $75 or less, rebelled the following year when Texaco provided a $440,000 sponsorship to the festival. A musician group called Noise Action Coalition then bargained with Dorf to double the rates.

HOLLYWOOD LEASE: 1999

Forever restless and ambitious, Dorf raised expansion capital from Leslie/Linton Entertainment Inc., an investment firm led by Robert Linton, the former chairman of Drexel Burnham. The funds were intended to take Knitting Factory beyond experimental music and make it into a broad-based entertainment company. The plan also called for Knitting Factory performance venues to open in Los Angeles, London, and Amsterdam by the end of the 1990s. The only one of the proposed clubs to come to fruition was the one slated for Los Angeles. In the spring of 1999 Knitting Factory signed a lease for a 10,000-square-foot space in the Hollywood Galaxy building.

Knitting Factory Hollywood finally opened in July 2000, but the project went $2 million over budget. Other setbacks for the company were to follow. The dot-com crash not only devastated the online aspirations of Knitmedia, it deprived Knitting Factory of potential investors. The September 11, 2001, terrorist attacks on the United States, which leveled the Twin Towers, also hampered business in Tribeca, resulting in the Leonard Street club being virtually unused for two weeks. Conditions grew so poor that Knitting Factory was close to ruin, and only a music-loving investor with an infusion of cash kept the operation afloat.

In 2002 Dorf used Knitting Factory stock to acquire another record label, Instinct Records, founded by Jared Hoffman, a Harvard University graduate who had worked in finance before deciding to pursue a career in music. Hoffman became Knitting Factory's chief operating officer. He was in a position to replace Dorf when Knitting Factory investors grew frustrated with Dorf's undisciplined way of running the company, and his eagerness to spread his energy in any number of directions. In 2003 Dorf was forced out and Hoffman took charge and began to return the company to profitability. Dorf remained on the board and looked to find new backers. In 2008 he launched City Winery, a wine and music venue in Manhattan's Soho district.

Hoffman took over a strong brand but also a company that was in need of redefinition, having long since lost its cachet as the center for avant-garde jazz. By 2006 he had at least stabilized Knitting Factory's finances enough to pursue a new expansion strategy, one that would take the company out of Manhattan. Since the time the Leonard Street complex opened, Tribeca had become too fashionable and expensive for clubs such as Knitting Factory and other entertainment venues, bars, and restaurants that had made the area trendy. It was hardly a shocking development. For decades artists in search of inexpensive space had revitalized rundown neighborhoods in New York City, only to see them gentrified and grow too expensive. Not only did Knitting Factory believe its future lay in the outer boroughs, it also saw promise in other parts of the country. In early 2006 the company acquired a majority stake in Bravo Entertainment, an independent regional concert and tour promotion company that operated across the country and owned The Big Easy Concert House venues in Boise, Idaho, and Spokane, Washington. Knitting Factory acquired the rest of Bravo in 2007 and the two venues were rebranded under the Knitting Factory Concert House name.

KNITTING FACTORY MOVES TO BROOKLYN: 2009

In 2008 Knitting Factory sold its Leonard Street space, which was supposed to close its doors on New Year's Eve at the end of the year, the same night Dorf's City Winery opened its doors. Instead the Tribeca space remained in use until July 2009. To replace the venue, the company acquired the site of the former Luna Lounge in Williamsburg, Brooklyn, an old industrial area along the East River that since the late 1990s had become a neighborhood to which artists had flocked for loft space and extremely low rents. The new Knitting Factory opened in September 2009. In many ways the company was returning to its roots. The space was much smaller, the main room able to hold only about 200 people, and the bar remained a community gathering place, open to everyone, not just ticket holders.

Noise ordinances also limited the type of performers the space could host. Consequently, the company planned to host louder shows in other New York venues, such as Webster Hall in Greenwich Village. While the Knitting Factory brand remained familiar to New Yorkers and music aficionados, it possessed little resonance in the heartland of the country. Whether the plan to take the Knitting Factory name to a wider audience would succeed remained to be seen.

Ed Dinger

PRINCIPAL SUBSIDIARIES

Knitting Factory Concert House; Knitting Factory Presents; Instinct Records; Shadow Records; Evolver.

PRINCIPAL COMPETITORS

HOB Entertainment, Inc.; Live Nation, Inc.; Sub Pop Ltd.; Wind-Up Entertainment, Inc.

FURTHER READING

Bambarger, Bradley, "At 10, the Knitting Factory Is a Powerhouse of New Music," *Billboard*, February 1, 1997, p. 1.

Block, Valerie, "King of the Nightclub," *Crain's New York Business*, January 16, 2006, p. 53.

———, "Weaving an Empire," *Crain's New York Business*, April 27, 1998, p. 3.

Kaplan, Fred, "New York's Knitting Factory Celebrates a Decade of Music Without Boundaries," *Boston Globe*, February 28, 1997, p. D15.

Pareles, Jon, "Eclectic Benefit for Downtown Club," *New York Times*, October 2, 1987.

Ratliff, Ben, "Michael Dorf of Knitmedia, the Entrepreneur of the Musically Avant," *New York Times*, May 16, 2001, p. E1.

Shapiro, Julie, "The Knit Cutting Out of Tribeca This Week," *Downtown Express*, January 2–8, 2009.

Sisario, Ben, "For Knitting Factory, Westward Ho (Brooklyn, Too)," *New York Times*, July 10, 2008.

Strauss, Neil, "Knitting Factory Goes Hollywood," *New York Times*, June 15, 2000, p. E3.

Verna, Paul, "Knitting Factory Puts Club's Music in Store," *Billboard*, December 4, 1993, p. 3.

Waddell, Ray, "Knitting Factory Buys Bravo, Plans Expansion," *Billboard*, February 11, 2006, p. 22.

KOHLER.

Kohler Co.

■

444 Highland Drive
Kohler, Wisconsin 53044-1515
U.S.A.
Telephone: (920) 457-4441
Toll Free: (800) 456-4537
Fax: (920) 457-1271
Web site: http://www.kohler.com

Private Company
Founded: 1873 as Kohler & Silberzahn
Incorporated: 1887 as Kohler, Hayssen & Stehn
   Manufacturing Company
Employees: 32,000
Sales: $5 billion (2008 est.)
NAICS: 326191 Plastics Plumbing Fixture Manufacturing; 327111 Vitreous China Plumbing Fixture and China and Earthenware Bathroom Accessories Manufacturing; 327122 Ceramic Wall and Floor Tile Manufacturing; 331511 Iron Foundries; 332913 Plumbing Fixture Fitting and Trim Manufacturing; 332998 Enameled Iron and Metal Sanitary Ware Manufacturing; 335312 Motor and Generator Manufacturing; 337110 Wood Kitchen Cabinet and Countertop Manufacturing; 337121 Upholstered Household Furniture Manufacturing; 337122 Nonupholstered Household Furniture Manufacturing; 337211 Wood Office Furniture Manufacturing; 713910 Golf Courses and Country Clubs; 721110 Hotels (Except Casino Hotels) and Motels

■ ■ ■

Kohler Co. is one of the largest privately operated firms in the United States. Unlike others that were once public companies but were taken private through debt-ridden leveraged buyouts, Kohler has always been owned and run by a circle of family members who descended from the founder. One of Wisconsin's largest employers, Kohler is best known for its line of baths, sinks, toilets, and other bathroom fixtures. The company is also a leading producer of electric generators and small engines, owns two distinguished furniture manufacturers and a leading tile maker, and operates successful hospitality and real estate businesses in Kohler, Wisconsin, where it has its corporate headquarters and largest manufacturing facilities.

LATE 19TH-CENTURY ROOTS

Kohler Co. was established in 1873, at the beginning of a debilitating five-year economic depression. That year the company's founders, John Michael Kohler and Charles Silberzahn, purchased an iron foundry from Kohler's employer and father-in-law, Jacob Vollrath, for $5,000. Kohler, a 29-year-old Austrian immigrant, was the senior partner in the business, which was located in Sheboygan, Wisconsin.

In their first year, Kohler & Silberzahn were hit hard by the depression. However, as manufacturers of agricultural implements, such as watering troughs and scalding vats (to remove hair from animal carcasses), they had a good market: People had to eat, and farmers had to feed them.

In November 1878, at the end of the depression, Silberzahn sold his interest in the business to Herman

COMPANY PERSPECTIVES

Kohler Co. and each of our more than 35,500 associates have the mission of contributing to a higher level of gracious living for those who are touched by our products and services.

Gracious living is marked by qualities of charm, good taste and generosity of spirit. It is further characterized by self-fulfillment and the enhancement of nature.

We reflect this mission in our work, in our team approach to meeting objectives, and in each of the products and services we provide.

Hayssen and John H. Stehn, who were employees of the enterprise. This prompted a company name change to Kohler, Hayssen & Stehn Manufacturing Company. In 1880, with improved business prospects, the company established a newer, larger machine shop; this plant, however, was destroyed by fire only months after opening, forcing the operation to move to a new location.

Rebounding from this costly setback, the small company introduced a line of unique enameled plumbing fixtures in 1883. While its significance was not yet fully realized, this line would propel Kohler into a period of strong growth. The company sold thousands of enameled sinks, cuspidors (spittoons), stove reservoirs, kettles, and pans, as well as the first Kohler bathtubs, fashioned from one of the company's watering troughs. By 1887, the year the company was formally incorporated (under the name assumed in 1878), these products accounted for 70 percent of Kohler's revenues.

The company encountered its first labor difficulties in March 1897, when 21 members of the AFL Iron Molder's Union struck over new pay rates. After some of the molders returned to work and others were replaced, the strike ended without any formal settlement.

EARLY 20TH CENTURY: ROCKY ROAD TO INDUSTRY LEADERSHIP

By 1900 Kohler employed more than 250 people, with 98 percent of its revenues coming from enameled iron products such as tubs, sinks, and water fountains. The factory in Sheboygan had become too small to meet growing production needs. Because it was not practical to expand the plant, which by that time was surrounded by homes, John Michael Kohler began building a new factory four miles west of Sheboygan in the small community of Riverside. The company entered a period of extraordinarily bad luck when John Michael Kohler died in November 1900 at the age of 56. Less than three months later, before a new chairman could be selected, the company's new iron foundry and machine and enamel shops burned down. Herman Hayssen and John Stehn's widow sold their interests in the company to the Kohler family, and in February 1901 the company was reorganized as J. M. Kohler Sons Co. under the leadership of Robert, Walter, and Carl Kohler, the oldest sons of John Michael Kohler. Three years later Carl died at the age of 24, and in 1905 Robert died at the age of 31, leaving the entire company to Walter Kohler.

Walter Kohler was a strong believer in corporate responsibility. As most of his employees were newly arrived immigrants, Kohler built the American Club, a stately boarding hotel where employees could live until they had enough money to purchase housing and send for their families. He established a benefit organization to provide employees with sickness and death benefits, and even provided lessons in civics, English, and American history so they could pass citizenship exams.

Kohler also laid plans to establish an entirely new community built around the company. He commissioned architects, city planners, and landscape architects, including the Olmsted Brothers (who designed New York's Central Park), to develop a city plan.

In 1911, after some years of stability, the workforce had grown to 950 and the company had ten sales offices, including one in London. That year the company introduced a revolutionary one-piece enamelware built-in bathtub with integral apron that was more sanitary than conventional two-piece tubs. The village of Kohler, meanwhile, had grown to 40 houses, and was incorporated in 1912 with a population of 254. In 1917 Kohler Improvement Company began building houses in the planned community, selling them to Kohler Co. employees at cost. A second development was started in 1923, and others followed. Another noteworthy development from 1912 was the shortening of the company name to Kohler Co.

By the mid-1920s Kohler had become the third-largest plumbing products company in the United States, adding such sales boosters as vitreous china toilets and wash basins and brass faucets, shower heads, and other fittings. The company also introduced a revolutionary new product called the "electric sink." Essentially a dishwasher, but 20 years ahead of its time,

KEY DATES

1873: John Michael Kohler and Charles Silberzahn establish Kohler & Silberzahn, initially a producer of agricultural implements.

1878: After Silberzahn sells his interest to two employees, the company name is changed to Kohler, Hayssen & Stehn Manufacturing Company.

1883: Line of enameled plumbing fixtures makes its debut.

1887: Company is formally incorporated.

1901: Following the death of the founding Kohler, the Kohler family buys full control of the company and renames it J. M. Kohler Sons Co.

1905: Cofounder's son, Walter Kohler, takes over company leadership.

1912: Village of Kohler is incorporated; company name is shortened to Kohler Co.

1940: Walter's younger brother, Herbert Kohler, takes control of company.

1954: Six-year-long strike against the company begins.

1968: Nonfamily members lead the company for the first time.

1972: Herbert Kohler Jr. is named chairman and CEO of Kohler Co.

1984: Sterling Faucet Company of Schaumburg, Illinois, is acquired.

1985: Kohler Design Center opens.

1998: Kohler Co. cements its status as a private company via a reorganization of the ownership shares; a resultant lawsuit filed by dissident shareholders is later settled out of court.

2001: In the largest acquisition in its history, Kohler purchases Mira, the leading producer of showers in the United Kingdom.

the device did not catch on. Shortly afterward, Kohler introduced a slightly more successful novelty, the electric clothes washer.

In 1929 the company's products were chosen on the basis of their excellent design for inclusion in an exhibition at New York's Museum of Modern Art celebrating "the artistic qualities of the bath." The following year Kohler began manufacturing cast-iron boil-ers and radiators for increasingly popular hot water and steam heat systems.

As one of the leaders in Wisconsin industry, Walter Kohler held substantial political power. In 1928 he ran successfully as a Republican for governor of Wisconsin. Distinguished for his administrative acumen rather than his political instincts, he was termed a "poor politician." He sought reelection in 1930 but was defeated by Philip La Follette in the Republican primary. When Kohler ran again in 1932, he triumphed over La Follette in the primary but lost the general election, a defeat largely attributed to Kohler's vigorous support for the unpopular President Herbert Hoover.

Inspired by the growth of electrical appliances but faced with poor electrical distribution, Kohler began developing small electrical generators. The first unit, introduced in 1920 as the Kohler Automatic Power & Light, provided 1,500 watts of 110-volt DC power from a generator driven by a four-cylinder gasoline engine. The small generator marked a significant improvement over existing generators, which merely charged batteries at 32 volts and were not as portable.

While the generators were intended for farm electrification, they were pressed into service by maritime and railroad companies, European castle owners, and others in need of portable power sources. Admiral Richard Byrd later took five Kohler generators with him on his first expedition to the South Pole in 1926, and he took seven Kohler generators with him on his return in 1933. Revisiting his original base station on the frozen continent, his team found the generators from the first expedition in perfect working order. Byrd named an Antarctic mountain range for Kohler and later became a close friend of the family.

GREAT DEPRESSION AND WORLD WAR II: ADJUSTING TO NEW CIRCUMSTANCES

By 1932, however, residential building rates had fallen to just 11 percent of their 1928 levels, and Kohler was facing the prospect of massive employee layoffs. Because the company was not in debt and retained favorable terms for raw materials, Kohler resolved to keep the company in operation and to stockpile whatever products could not be sold. This full-employment policy had the effect of saving the local economy from ruin.

The company was revisited by labor unrest in July 1934 when a portion of the workforce struck Kohler for the right to be represented by the Federal Union, a local union of the American Federation of Labor. The strike was canceled later that year when the union lost an employee vote to represent all of Kohler's production and maintenance employees. In arbitration, however, the National Labor Relations Board instructed the company to recognize a smaller, independent union, the Kohler Workers' Association.

In 1940 Walter Kohler died, and a battle for control of the firm broke out between Walter's children and their father's younger brother, Herbert Kohler, who was running the company. While the children argued for strict hereditary succession, the situation was further complicated by the fact that Herbert's mother and Walter's mother were sisters. In the end, Herbert prevailed.

When the United States became involved in World War II, much of Kohler's commercial operations ground to a halt. Iron, brass, and chrome supplies were diverted for war use by the government, which asked Kohler to resume production of military wares (during World War I Kohler had made mine anchors, projectiles, and shells). The company's first military products were precision valves and fittings for use in aircraft, such as the DC-3 and B-29. Kohler also built a variety of electric generators for the armed forces.

Based on Kohler's experience in precision crafted metallurgy, the government asked the company to produce 105mm and 3-inch artillery shells, as well as forgings for rockets and other shells, fuses, torpedo tubes, piston rings, shell rotating bands, and engine bearings. After the war, Kohler discontinued much of its military production, but resumed building 105mm shells during the Korean War. The company did, however, continue to manufacture precision products and generators, albeit for different markets.

POSTWAR DEVELOPMENTS

Given the occasional unreliability of utility-supplied power, many hospitals, banks, and other offices had to have their own emergency standby power but required larger capacities than the 10-megawatt models Kohler manufactured. Eager to supply this market, Kohler began development of 100-kilowatt diesel-powered systems. As the market continued to grow, Kohler introduced a 230-kilowatt model and, some years later, a massive 500-kilowatt system.

Kohler also manufactured small gasoline engines, which were first built to power the company's electric generators. During the 1950s, the small engines found an explosive market in Thailand and Vietnam, where they were used to power boats, pump water on rice paddies, and drive air compressors. Virtually all the air-cooled engines in Southeast Asia at this time were made by Kohler and sold through a distributor in Hong Kong.

In 1951 Walter Kohler Jr., a former officer and director of the company, followed in his father's footsteps to become the governor of Wisconsin. He was reelected twice, serving until 1957. At the company, labor trouble arose again in April 1954 when the UAW-CIO local called a walkout to protest changes in union shop rules, seniority, and pay increases without regard to merit. Seeing these demands as unfair and potentially crippling to the profitable operation of the corporation, the company resisted. The strike continued until September 1960, when bargaining resumed, and a new contract was concluded two years later. The strike ranked for decades as the longest major strike in U.S. history.

Entering the 1960s, the company's engine division, still strong in Asia, gained momentum in the United States, where Kohler motors were used to power lawnmowers, garden tractors, construction equipment, and even snowmobiles. International Harvester, John Deere, Wheel-Horse, Jacobsen, and Bombardier (inventor of the snowmobile) incorporated Kohler engines in their products. By 1963 Kohler was one of the leading small engine suppliers in the industry.

In order to keep pace with this growing demand, Kohler established two new production facilities, in Mexico City and Toronto. The company ran into strong competition, however, from Japanese and German manufacturers who had extensive experience with two- and four-stroke engines. Kohler suffered market share loss, but won back a significant share of the market by introducing higher technology two-cycle engines in 1968. It later won a suit against market leader Briggs & Stratton, which had tried to coerce its distributors to stop handling Kohler engines. Meanwhile, on the company's plumbing products side, Kohler introduced its long-running advertising theme, "The Bold Look of Kohler."

The company experienced another leadership crisis in 1968 when Kohler's president, James L. Kuplic, died unexpectedly. Only six days later, Herbert Kohler Sr., chairman and CEO of the company for 28 years, also died. Herbert Kohler Jr., heir to the company, was at the time a self-described "hippie," pursuing a career outside the company. He later told *Supply House Times,* "By preplanning my life, my father removed my right to fail. As a result, for a portion of my life I experienced nothing but failure. That led me to become a substantial rebel."

Company directors elected to pass over the younger Kohler, and named an interim chairman. In an unusual departure from company traditions, the directors named nonfamily members Lyman Conger and Walter Cleveland as chairman and president, respectively. When

Conger retired in 1972, Herb Kohler was appointed chairman and CEO, and two years later he succeeded Cleveland as company president. In 1978, concerned about the company slipping from family control, Kohler engineered a 1-for-20 reverse stock split, which reduced the number of shareholders in the private company from more than 400 to about 250 and the number of outstanding shares from 161,105 to about 8,000. The maneuver also forced a number of nonfamily shareholders to sell out at $412.50 per share, leaving the Kohler family with 96 percent of the voting shares.

LATE 20TH CENTURY: GROWTH THROUGH ACQUISITION

Under Herb Kohler's leadership, Kohler Co. more than tripled in size to an estimated $1.34 billion in annual sales by the late 1980s. After 110 years of strictly internal growth, much of the expansion came from the company's new venture into acquisitions. In 1984 the company acquired the Schaumburg, Illinois-based Sterling Faucet Company, a firm whose lower to middle-priced plumbing products were complementary to the higher-priced Kohler lines. Two years later, Kohler purchased Baker, Knapp & Tubbs, Inc., a high-end furniture manufacturer headquartered in Grand Rapids, Michigan, and Jacob Delafon, a plumbing products manufacturer headquartered in Paris. The company also established a Japanese subsidiary. In 1989 Kohler purchased Oakland, California-based Kallista, Inc.; Portland, Oregon-based Ann Sacks Tile & Stone; and Dupont Sanitaire-Chauffage, in Paris. McGuire Furniture Company, a San Francisco-based manufacturer, was acquired in 1990.

By this time, Kohler had also expanded into the leisure industry, turning the company's onetime workers' hotel, the American Club, into a successful full-scale convention and recreation resort. Having poured about $50 million into the resort from 1978 through the mid-1990s, Kohler created the only resort in the Midwest to receive AAA's top five-diamond rating. The resort's centerpiece was Blackwolf Run, which offered two world championship golf courses created by a top course designer, Pete Dye. Blackwolf Run hosted the 1998 U.S. Women's Open Championship. The bathrooms in the American Club's fancy guest rooms also served as showcases for Kohler Co. products. Serving a similar function was the Kohler Design Center, which opened in Sheboygan in 1985 as a 36,000-square-foot showcase of Kohler plumbing fixtures, faucets, engines, and generators; Baker and McGuire furniture; Ann Sacks tile and stone; and other company products.

Kohler continued to expand in the 1990s through acquisition, increasingly venturing overseas to do so. In

1993 the company acquired Sanijura, S.A., a French maker of bathroom cabinets. The following year, Kohler purchased Osio, a maker of enamel baths based in Italy. The company ventured further into the cabinet sector through the 1995 acquisition of Pennsylvania-based Robern, Inc., which specialized in mirrored cabinets, lighting fixtures, and accessories; and the 1996 addition of Canac Kitchens, Ltd., a maker of wood kitchen cabinets based in Ontario, Canada. Another France-based firm, Holdiam, S.A., was added in 1995, bringing to Kohler the leading French maker of acrylic baths, whirlpools, synthetic kitchen sinks, and artistic faucets. In the late 1990s the company established Kohler China Ltd., which had locations in Shanghai, Beijing, and Guangzhou Province, from which it manufactured and distributed throughout the People's Republic of China a full line of plumbing products.

In the meantime, back home, the company broke with its longstanding tradition of distributing the Kohler brand exclusively through a network of independent wholesalers. Faced with the trend of major home center chains grabbing a larger and larger portion of plumbing product sales, the company in 1995 began selling Kohler brand products directly to The Home Depot chain. Later, its retail distribution was widened to include The Home Depot's chief rival, Lowe's.

1998 STOCK RESTRUCTURING

In 1993 Kohler Co. sales reached a record $1.53 billion; earnings stood at $15.5 million, a figure substantially reduced by a $33 million charge resulting from a change in accounting for retiree health benefits. By 1997 earnings had increased to $88 million on sales of $2.2 billion. Concerned again about the loss of family control as well as anticipating the need to hold down estate taxes, Herb Kohler proposed another restructuring of the company's stock in early 1998. At the time, there were 7,445 shares outstanding, with 75 percent of them controlled by Herb and his sister, Ruth DeYoung Kohler. Over the years, about 4 percent of the stock had fallen into the hands of nonfamily members through the sale of the thinly traded stock by family members. In April 1998 Kohler shareholders approved a plan whereby all the nonfamily shareholders would be bought out at $55,400 per share. The plan also offered other family members the option of cashing in their stock or taking a mix of voting and nonvoting shares, with the added stipulation that if they chose the latter they could only sell their shares at a later date back to the company.

At the end of 1997 Kohler stock had a book value of about $100,000 per share and shares had been selling in early 1998 for as high as $137,500 per share. The plan therefore angered the outside shareholders, some of whom felt the stock was worth as much as $273,000 per share, as well as dissident members of the Kohler family, who bristled both at the buyback offer and at the plan's restrictions on selling to outsiders. Under Wisconsin law, shareholders had the ability to take a disputed stock valuation to court and ask a judge to increase the per share offer. A trial was therefore set for April 2000 in Sheboygan County Circuit Court to determine the value of Kohler Co. stock, with owners of 811 shares asking for redress. That month, however, the two sides reached an out-of-court settlement whereby these shareholders were bought out at $135,000 per share. Although the settlement meant that Kohler had to pay out nearly $80 million more than the original restructuring plan had called for, it also left Herb Kohler and his sister, Ruth, firmly in control of the company and preserved its status as a private firm.

CONTINUED EXPANSION, PARTICULARLY OVERSEAS

During the early 21st century, Kohler Co. remained on a growth trajectory as it completed a number of additional acquisitions, most of which occurred overseas. The high-growth Asia-Pacific region was a particular target, and in 2001 Kohler acquired Englefield Bathroomware of Auckland, New Zealand. This firm held the number one position in its home country and the number two position in Australia in acrylic bathroom fixtures, including shower enclosures, baths, and vanities. Englefield was especially attractive because of its plants and distribution capabilities throughout the Pacific Rim, but the firm also distributed its products in Europe, the Middle East, and South America. Most of Englefield's products were subsequently rebranded under the Kohler name. In 2002 Kohler acquired Karat Sanitaryware, a Thailand-based producer of vitreous china bath products, including toilets, sinks, bathtubs, and accessories.

In 2001 Kohler completed the largest acquisition in its history, the purchase of Mira, the leading producer of showers in the United Kingdom, from HSBC Private Equity for around $430 million. In addition to the Mira Showers brand, this deal also brought into the Kohler fold three other brands: Alstone shower enclosures, Meynell valves, and Rada shower controls. This latest string of deals helped propel Kohler's sales past $3 billion in 2002.

Kohler's hospitality unit continued to expand as well in the early 21st century. At "Destination Kohler," the company's name for its resort in its headquarters town, Kohler in 2000 opened the Kohler Waters Spa, a 16,000-square-foot facility offering a variety of water treatments, pools, steam rooms, and saunas. Earlier, in

1998, Kohler had expanded its golf operation through the opening of Whistling Straits, which included two top-rated 18-hole courses located on the shore of Lake Michigan, northeast of the town of Kohler. In 2004 Whistling Straits played host to the PGA Championship, one of the four "majors" of men's golf. That same year, Kohler ventured overseas to purchase the Old Course Hotel Golf Resort and Spa in St. Andrews, Scotland. Included in the purchase were the hotel and spa as well as restaurants on the property and the nearby Dukes Golf Course but not the Old Course itself, a course managed by a trust and considered the birthplace of golf.

In 2005 the company began experimenting with retailing, opening the first Kohler retail store in Chicago's Merchandise Mart, where Kohler bath and kitchen fixtures were sold directly to consumers. Its Baker furniture unit had earlier moved into the retail realm, and by 2007 more than a dozen Baker stores were open for business around the United States. In 2008 Kohler ventured further into the furniture field via the acquisition of High Point, North Carolina-based Mark David, an upscale provider of interior and outdoor furnishings for hotels, resorts, country clubs, and restaurants. Around this same time, Kohler was launching an aggressive push into India, which initially concentrated on marketing a line of bath products. The firm also earmarked $200 million to create a manufacturing hub in Gujarat for the production of kitchen and bath products, some of which were slated for export to Europe and the United States.

In 2008 and 2009 Kohler implemented a series of layoffs as its core kitchen and bath fixture business felt the effects of the global economic downturn. Slumping new home construction and consumer spending cutbacks forced the company to trim both production and costs. In April 2009, in this very challenging economic environment, David Kohler was named president and COO of Kohler Co. His father, Herb Kohler, remained chairman and CEO.

John Simley
Updated, David E. Salamie

PRINCIPAL SUBSIDIARIES

Baker Knapp & Tubbs, Inc.; McGuire Furniture Company; Kohler Co. Australia; Kohler (China) Investment Co., Ltd.; Kohler GmbH (Germany); Kohler New Zealand Ltd.; Kohler (Thailand) Public Co., Ltd.; Kohler Mira Limited (UK).

PRINCIPAL OPERATING UNITS

Kitchen and Bath Group; Interiors Group; Global Power Group; Hospitality and Real Estate Group.

PRINCIPAL COMPETITORS

Moen Incorporated; Trane Inc.; Masco Corporation; Price Pfister, Inc.; Elkay Manufacturing Company; Geberit AG; The Chicago Faucet Company.

FURTHER READING

The American Club: A Heritage and History Remembered, Kohler, WI: Kohler Co., 1993.

Blodgett, Richard E., *A Sense of Higher Design: The Kohlers of Kohler*, Lyme, CT: Greenwich Publishing Group, 2003, 328 p.

Bold Craftsmen, Kohler, WI: Kohler Co., 1973.

Christy, John H., and Shlomo Reifman, "The Importance of Being Private," *Forbes*, November 29, 2004, p. 201.

Daykin, Tom, "Kohler Co. Laying Off 455 Workers: Slump in Residential Construction to Blame," *Milwaukee Journal Sentinel*, April 3, 2009, p. D1.

Hill, J. Dee, "Reigniting Kohler's 'Bold' Look," *Adweek*, January 14, 2002, p. 4.

Kilman, Scott, "Family Squabble Brews at Kohler over Control," *Wall Street Journal*, March 23, 1998, p. A4.

———, "Head of Kohler Family Unveils Plan to Buy Out Holders of Fixtures Firm," *Wall Street Journal*, April 7, 1998, p. B16.

Koselka, Rita, Fleming Meeks, and Laura Saunders, "Family Affairs," *Forbes*, December 11, 1989, pp. 212+.

Lambert, Emily, "Splash: Is a Toilet a Work of Art? Herbert Kohler Has Some Novel Ways to Sell Plumbing Fixtures," *Forbes*, July 23, 2007, p. 66.

Lank, Avrum D., "Agreement on Kohler Stock Presents New Challenges," *Milwaukee Journal Sentinel*, April 16, 2000, p. 15D.

———, "Kohler Plans to Shut Down on Outsiders," *Milwaukee Journal Sentinel*, April 7, 1998, p. D1.

Lank, Avrum D., and Kathleen Gallagher, "Kohler Stock Challenge Considered: Proposed Restructuring Pushes Down Price Being Offered for Stock," *Milwaukee Journal Sentinel*, April 10, 1998, p. D1.

Malkani, Gautam, "Mira Showers Sold for £301m," *Financial Times*, July 20, 2001, p. 25.

McCune, Heather, "Kohler Co. Establishes Global Faucet Operations," *Supply House Times*, March 1998, p. 16.

McNamee, Tom, "Plumbing Kohler's Pleasures," *North Shore*, July 1999, pp. 52–62.

Melcher, Richard A., "Can Kohler Keep It All in the Family?" *Business Week*, May 4, 1998, p. 98.

Murphy, H. Lee, "Kohler Dips Toe into Retail," *Crain's Chicago Business*, November 19, 2007, p. 13.

"Rub-a-Dub-Dub," *Time*, July 26, 1982, p. 47.

Samuels, Gary, "Generational Investor," *Forbes*, October 16, 1995, p. 70.

Smith, Steve, "Kohler Opens Retail Stores, May Go National with Distributors," *Supply House Times*, December 2005, p. 16.

"This Is Herb Kohler, Like Him or Not," *Supply House Times*, November 1986.

Tracy, Eleanor Johnson, "How Herbert Kohler Won His Bid for Privacy," *Fortune*, February 12, 1979, pp. 84+.

Updegrave, Walter L., "Master of the Bath," *Builder*, June 1985, pp. 92+.

KPMG International

—————— ■ ——————

Burgemeester Rijnderslaan 10
Amstelveen, 1185 MC
Netherlands
Telephone: (+31 20) 656 7890
Fax: (+31 20) 656 7700
Web site: http://www.kpmg.com

Cooperative
Incorporated: 1897 as Marwick, Mitchell & Company
Employees: 135,000
Sales: $22.69 billion (2008)
NAICS: 541211 Offices of Certified Public Accountants;
541219 Other Accounting Services; 541618 Other
Management Consulting Services

■ ■ ■

KPMG International, the smallest of the Big Four accounting firms, operates across the globe. The cooperative's network of independent firms offers audit, advisory, and tax services in more than 140 countries. In the late 1990s, the company focused on unifying its historically loose federation of member firms to build a cohesive global image and offer a consistent array of products and services. Today, KPMG's three operating regions consist of Europe, the Middle East, South Asia, and Africa (EMA); the Americas; and Australia and Asia Pacific. Clients come from the corporate, government, and public sectors, and from nonprofit organizations.

A DEMANDING AND REWARDING
FIRST CENTURY: 1897–1979

KPMG got its start in 1897, just a few years after the first U.S. accounting firm had been established. The company was formed by James Marwick and Roger Mitchell, who had both immigrated to the new world from Scotland. They set up their new partnership, called Marwick, Mitchell & Company, in New York City. Eight years after its founding, Marwick, Mitchell & Company launched a banking practice, focusing its efforts on one industry for the first time. This effort proved so successful that the firm later went on to offer tailored services to companies in the insurance industry, the thrift field, and to mutual fund brokers.

In 1911 Marwick, Mitchell & Company merged with a British accounting firm headed by Sir William B. Peat. The new transatlantic company was called Peat, Marwick, Mitchell & Company. Through the merger, Marwick, Mitchell & Company strengthened its operations in Europe, while Peat gained greater access to the rapidly growing North American market. This configuration of the company remained in effect for the next three-quarters of a century.

During this time, Peat Marwick grew steadily, becoming one of the "Big Eight" major public accounting firms in the United States. In the late 1960s and early 1970s, Peat Marwick's business and revenues began to grow dramatically, as did those of their competitors. This boom in demand for accounting services came as a result of increasingly complex tax laws, securities laws, and industry regulations. Between 1973 and 1976, for example, the Securities and

Exchange Commission (SEC) added 16 new disclosure requirements for publicly held companies. With the ever increasing mandated need for accounting services, Peat Marwick's revenues grew steadily as demand outstripped supply.

In addition to the welter of new federal regulations, accounting industry standards became more exacting. The Accounting Principles Board and the Financial Accounting Standards Board issued a wide variety of directives to members of the industry in response to complaints that the accounting industry was not fulfilling its watchdog role in corporate America stringently enough. Like the rest of its peers in the industry, Peat Marwick was a defendant in several lawsuits, charged with failing to prevent or expose financial malfeasance.

In the early 1970s, the legal entanglements continued. In May 1972, for example, Raytheon Company sued the accounting firm over its audits of Visual Electronics Corporation from 1968 to 1970, charging that its work failed to show how dire the company's financial straits were.

LARGEST PUBLIC ACCOUNTING FIRM IN NATION

Nevertheless, by this time Peat Marwick had become the largest public accounting firm in the nation. The company had grown by providing services to corporations and also by winning government contracts. In 1972, for instance, it won a Department of Transportation contract to analyze the department's planning techniques.

In response to a general consensus that the financial industry was moving toward greater accountability, Peat Marwick took steps in 1975 to shore up the controls on its accounting practice. "We have a little bit of an image problem, and we'd better start doing something about

it," Peat Marwick's senior partner told the *Wall Street Journal*. The firm was concerned that its recent bad publicity was causing local government units, highly sensitive to public opinion, to seek other firms for their auditing business.

Hoping to clear its name, Peat Marwick engaged another Big Eight accounting firm, Arthur Young & Company, to audit its quality control procedures and make the results available to its clients and staff. In taking this step, Peat Marwick became the first public accounting firm to inaugurate a peer review process. The audit was scheduled to begin in June, in place of an earlier planned process that would have been conducted by the American Institute of Certified Public Accountants. Peat Marwick abandoned its plan for this review because it wished to make the results of the audit public.

In November 1975, Peat Marwick released the study of its operations by Arthur Young & Company in an effort to bolster its reputation for reliability. The report, which cost the company more than half a million dollars, was favorable in its account of the company's activities. In April 1976, the company revised its audit manual to include more use of internal auditors.

PREPARING FOR GLOBALIZATION

Just two months after this report, Peat Marwick won a major new governmental client when it was selected to audit New York City, a job that brought with it an annual fee of nearly $1 million. In addition to its other big clients, the firm was engaged by the General Electric Company for an audit so broad in scope that it required 429 employees in 38 different offices. In 1978 Peat Marwick formed Peat Marwick International to oversee the firm's activities outside the United States. With this change, the company set up a multinational umbrella partnership of different firms in locations around the world. By doing this, Peat Marwick hoped to prepare itself for further globalization of the world economy and financial markets by combining a single firm image with well respected and established local accounting organizations.

In 1979 Peat Marwick reported record revenues from its worldwide operations, which yielded $673.8 million in revenues over a 12-month period, an increase of 15 percent from the previous year. As Peat Marwick entered the 1980s with this strong financial performance behind it, the company began to face a maturing market for its services and growing competition from the other Big Eight firms. In addition, under pressure from the federal government, the accounting industry was forced

KEY DATES
■

1897: James Marwick and Roger Mitchell found Marwick, Mitchell & Company in New York City.

1925: Company creates alliance with British accounting firm W.B. Peat & Co. and forms Peat, Marwick, Mitchell & Company.

1978: Company changes name to Peat Marwick International.

1987: Peat Marwick International merges with Klynveld, Main, Goerdeler to form Klynveld Peat Marwick Goerdeler, based in the Netherlands; the U.S. arm is named Peat, Marwick, Main & Company.

1989: U.S. branch is renamed KPMG Peat Marwick.

1999: KPMG Peat Marwick shortens its name to KPMG LLP, a branch of KPMG International.

2003: KPMG International acquires Arthur Andersen's Japanese firm.

2007: Subprime mortgage client New Century folds, ushering in a broad financial meltdown.

2009: KPMG contends with a work slowdown in key Hong Kong and China markets.

to abandon its self-imposed prohibition on advertising. This resulted in a far more hotly contested market for accounting services.

INCREASING COMPETITION AND NEW OWNERSHIP: 1980–91

Entering a new decade, Peat Marwick and the accounting business both appeared to be in solid positions. Although Peat Marwick was somewhat narrow in its focus, primarily handling auditing and accounting services in the early 1980s, the company's revenues for the year ending June 1981 reached $979 million, a 20 percent increase compared to fiscal 1980 results. Business seemed to be increasing as well; workload figures rose by more than 8 percent over 1980. About 80 percent of the firm's revenues were generated from auditing and accounting, about 14 percent was attributed to tax advice, and the remainder came from management consultancy services. Peat Marwick earned more than half of its sales in North America. Among the firm's significant new clients were Vickers Ltd. of Britain, which included Rolls-Royce Motors, and the

State of California, for which Peat Marwick was hired to develop and install a major accounting system.

Despite significant growth, competition in the accounting industry was heating up, and in 1981 Peat Marwick moved to counter rising competition by automating the audit process. As a first step in this process, Peat Marwick developed a program called SeaCas, an abbreviation for Systems Evaluation Approach-Computerized Audit Support. Three years later, the company switched to the Apple Macintosh for all its future computer applications. Also in 1984, Peat Marwick purchased another accounting firm, W.O. Daley & Company, based in Orlando, Florida. With this move, the company added eight new partners to its worldwide tally of 1,284. Major diversification and expansion finally arrived at Peat Marwick in 1986, when the company agreed to merge with Klynveld Main Goerdeler (KMG), a Dutch accounting firm. KMG had been formed in the early 1980s through the merger of German company Deutsche Treuhand-Gesellschaft, Dutch firm Klynveld Kraayenhoff & Co., U.S. company Main Hurdman & Cranstoun, and several other European and Canadian accounting firms. The resultant international accounting federation, KMG, was based in the Netherlands, and the U.S. arm had become known as KMG Main Hurdman.

KMG was the ninth-largest accounting firm in the United States in 1986, while Peat Marwick was number two. The merger of KMG and Peat Marwick created the largest accounting firm in the world in terms of size and revenue. In its new configuration, Peat Marwick enhanced its ability to attract as audit clients large U.S. companies with multinational operations. After approval by Peat Marwick's 2,733 partners and KMG's 2,827 partners, the joined companies were to be known as Klynveld Peat Marwick Goerdeler, or KPMG, and were to be headquartered in Amsterdam. In September 1986, Peat Marwick announced that it had opened negotiations to buy a public relations company and a consulting business, both with ties to the high-tech industry. In the wake of its proposed merger with KMG, this move was seen as a bid by the company to enhance its profile in the consulting field.

COMPLETION OF MERGER: 1987

On January 1, 1987, the merger between Peat Marwick and KMG was officially completed, capping the largest merger in the history of the accounting business. The new firm instantly inherited worldwide revenues of $2.7 billion, with $1.7 billion contributed by Peat Marwick. In the United States, the operations of both KMG, with 79 U.S. offices, and Peat Marwick, with 91, were combined into one organization, which was to be known as Peat Marwick. Peat Marwick was the more dominant of the two companies in the United States, with annual revenues of about $1.1 billion, compared to KMG's $249 million. In Europe, however, KMG was stronger than Peat Marwick. KMG had more than 13,000 European employees and just under 200 locations, while Peat Marwick had only 34 offices and about 2,000 employees. With combined power, KPMG hoped to hold a leadership position across the world.

The combining of two large firms with varying operating cultures and management styles proved difficult, and integration of the merger occurred slowly. Member firms in Australia and New Zealand, for example, opted not to join the new company. KMG Hungerfords, the Australian branch of KMG, began investigating merger deals with competing accounting firms after voting against the merger. Establishing agreements with other partners, including firms in West Germany, Switzerland, Spain, and France, the situation lingered past the final merger date as questions regarding partnership details arose.

As the 1980s came to an end, the accounting business once again found itself in a period of transition. During the previous decade, booming business conditions had produced brisk growth for accounting firms, and KPMG had expanded rapidly along with the rest of the industry. By the end of the decade, the firm's client base had started to shrink as a result of changes in the financial world, such as the collapse of the savings and loan industry. Peat Marwick, which changed its name to KPMG Peat Marwick in 1989, found itself the object of a sweeping inquiry into its audits of savings institutions by the Office of Thrift Supervision due to the firm's involvement with the San Francisco Savings and Loan Association. In addition, the wave of bankruptcies that followed the frenzy for mergers and leveraged buyouts in the 1980s led to a reduction in need for accounting services and also generated a large number of lawsuits for public accounting firms as a result of their participation in these activities.

These factors combined to flatten KPMG's revenues in 1988 and 1989. In late 1990 the partnership elected a new chairman, Jon C. Madonna, and KPMG Peat Marwick began to implement changes to improve its profitability. In February 1991, the company announced that 265 partners, or one in seven, would be laid off from the firm in a streamlining effort. KPMG Peat Marwick predicted that severance costs would amount to $52 million. Despite this drain on U.S. earnings, the company's worldwide returns remained strong, as it posted annual revenues of $6 billion.

CONSOLIDATION AND INTERNATIONAL GROWTH: 1992–99

In March 1992, KPMG began to reorganize its operations under the aegis of a Future Directions Committee. Relying on input from the company's Client Service Measurement Process, a survey of customer satisfaction inaugurated in 1989, the firm chose six lines of business: financial services; government; health care and life sciences; information and communications; manufacturing, retailing, and distribution; and special markets and designated services. In addition, KPMG Peat Marwick divided the country into 10 separate geographical practice areas. The company then organized accountants, tax specialists, and consultants into industry-specific teams. Within this framework, KPMG Peat Marwick sought to develop specialists with certain areas of expertise who would entice new clients and bring high-paying tax and consulting jobs.

In September 1993, as growth in the company's targeted industries remained sluggish, KPMG Peat Marwick launched an advertising campaign for the first time. Focusing on the company's international stature, the ads urged companies to "go global—but not without a map." KPMG Peat Marwick enjoyed increased revenues following its launch, recording revenue for 1996 of $2.53 billion, a rise of 10 percent over 1995 revenues of $2.29 billion. Fiscal 1996 was the third year of revenue growth for KPMG Peat Marwick, a welcome relief after five years of little increase.

KPMG Peat Marwick also gained a new CEO and chairman in 1996 with the hiring of Stephen G. Butler, while Jon Madonna continued as chairman of KPMG International. Butler indicated the company would strengthen its consultancy services, a market with significant growth potential, and offer new services. Expanding existing services into new markets was another strategy for company growth. "Our plan is to increase revenue more than 10% a year," Butler stated confidently in the *Wall Street Journal*. "We have every expectation we'll be able to do that," he asserted.

KPMG's strategy proved successful, with the firm growing 11.1 percent in 1997 compared to 1996. In 1998, revenues grew 15.6 percent over 1997 to reach $10.4 billion. The firm attempted to unify its operations to form a more centralized operation and also sought to boost brand recognition, initiating a $60 million global branding campaign. The campaign, which included television, radio, and print ads, adopted the tagline, "It's time for clarity." KPMG Marketing Officer Tim Pearson explained the tagline in a company statement, noting, "The emphasis on clarity—not simply knowledge management or insight—in our brand advertising campaign strongly differentiates KPMG in the increasingly crowded business advisory arena and articulates KPMG's business strategy." To further enhance the brand, KPMG Peat Marwick shortened its name to KPMG LLP at the end of 1998.

STRENGTHENING CORE BUSINESSES, OVERCOMING SETBACKS

In the late 1990s the firm took additional action to strengthen and unify its core businesses of audit, tax, and consulting services. In August 1998 the U.S. arm announced plans to sell its compensation consulting practice to human resources consulting firm William M. Mercer, Inc. The decision marked KPMG's move away from noncore operations. In March 1999 KPMG restructured its operations to create global operating regions. The newly formed KPMG "Americas" group included 19 member firms in Mexico, Latin America, the Caribbean, Australia, and New Zealand. These partners combined operations with the U.S. firm of KPMG LLP. The "EMA" group covered Europe, the Middle East, and Africa and included member firms in such countries as France, the Netherlands, Germany, and the United Kingdom. The firm planned to form an Asia-Pacific group at a later date. In September 1999 Stephen G. Butler became the chairman of KPMG International, succeeding Colin Sharman, who had been the firm's chairman since 1997. Butler's new position was in addition to his continuing roles as chairman and CEO of KPMG LLP.

Despite KPMG's continued growth, the firm suffered a few setbacks in its expansion efforts. In late 1997 KPMG's Canadian arm announced plans to merge with accounting firm Ernst & Young. The deal, which fell through in early 1998, would have created the largest accounting and consulting firm in the world. The firms hoped their combined strength would help make inroads in the emerging markets of Latin America and China and enhance global opportunities. In 1999 KPMG Canada faced another failed merger attempt. On March 25 the firm declared its plans to separate from KPMG International and merge with Arthur Andersen, but the deal was called off just over a week later, on April 5. The soured deal left KPMG divided into opposing groups. Also that year KPMG's consulting practice in Belgium was acquired by rival PricewaterhouseCoopers.

The setbacks did little to slow the firm down, however, and KPMG made some acquisitions itself. In May 1999 the firm expanded its consulting business by acquiring Softline Consulting & Integrators, Inc., a firm based in San Jose, California. KPMG also added new

partners, many of whom had defected from PricewaterhouseCoopers, in Taiwan, Israel, Indonesia, and the Philippines. In the United States, KPMG separated its consulting business from its accounting operations and planned to sell stock in the entity, if approved by the SEC. In August 1999 Cisco Systems Inc. agreed to purchase a 20 percent stake in the consulting business for about $1 billion. KPMG intended to use the funds to further invest in its expanding Internet services. The partnership provided Cisco with access to KPMG's international corporate clients, while KPMG gained access to Cisco's equipment and expertise in computer networking. David Crawford, chairman of KPMG Australia, commented on the deal in the *Age,* noting, "This is a very significant development. … It puts us at the forefront of e-commerce development and the exploitation of the Internet." In January 2000 KPMG Consulting, LLC, was incorporated. The new business included KPMG's consulting operations in the United States and Mexico. KPMG expected to add additional firms, including those in Asia, Canada, and Latin America, during the course of the year.

As KPMG entered a new century, the company appeared headed for continued growth and success. The firm had expanded significantly in the late 1990s while also integrating operations into a more centrally run entity. KPMG reported record revenues of $12.2 billion for the year ended September 30, 1999, up 17 percent over 1998 revenues. All business areas enjoyed substantial growth during 1999: the consulting services division grew 32 percent to reach $3.5 billion, financial advisory services grew 39 percent, tax services increased 16.5 percent, and assurance services rose 9 percent. The firm's geographic regions experienced growth as well, with the Americas group surging 19 percent, Asia Pacific growing 20 percent, and the EMA region expanding 15 percent. Chairman Butler looked forward to the continued globalization of KPMG and indicated that the firm would take advantage of opportunities for growth, particularly regarding the Internet. "I'm enthused about KPMG's future prospects," Butler stated in a prepared statement. He remarked: "We'll continue moving KPMG toward a vision that emphasizes a cohesive and capable firm that effectively serves multinational clients anywhere they operate."

TRYING TIMES: 2000–04

The earlier effort to split off the U.S. consulting business was driven in part to attain a "degree of separation between the consulting practice and the traditional audit and tax practices," the *CPA Journal* reported. The SEC had voiced concerns about the Big Five's consulting services and their potential threat to the integrity of their auditing practices. The issue arose when a company hired one of the Big Five for both audit and consulting services.

The Big Five audited the largest publicly held companies in the world, all the while driving the accounting industry's self-regulatory process. In 1933, Congress limited "government's role to setting broad standards for company audits," *Business Week* recounted. Industry watchers pointed out inherent weakness in self-regulation, among them concerns linked to the Big Five's common liability insurance pool. Peers, some felt, might be disinclined to call attention to violations, fearing rising insurance costs for all.

In April 2002, the SEC filed a complaint against KPMG related to Xerox Corporation audits. Across the pond, bad news came to light in Europe's largest market. A former KPMG Germany client was charged with attributing sales to a nonexistent company. Coupled with earlier audit problems in Belgium in 2000 and Germany in 2001, and one looming in Switzerland, KPMG contended with erosion of trust in its key U.S. and European markets. Meanwhile, the industry as a whole suffered with the scandal ridden demise of Arthur Andersen. The firm was hit by federal obstruction of justice charges in regard to Enron Corp., which led to the loss of its right to conduct audits.

KPMG International returned to double-digit global growth in fiscal 2003, posting its largest gains since 1999. In 2000, KPMG saw negative growth, followed by an increase of 8.3 percent in fiscal 2001, before dropping back to 3.9 percent in 2002. The 13.4 percent growth rate placed the company third, behind Ernst & Young and Deloitte and ahead of PricewaterhouseCoopers.

During 2003, KPMG acquired Arthur Andersen's Japanese practice. Ashai & Co. propelled KPMG International into the top spot among "major audit, tax and advisory organizations in Japan, with more than 3,000 partners and staff," according to *Public Accounting Report.* KPMG also acquired Arthur Andersen's Thailand practice, with competitors Ernst & Young and Deloitte picking up other Andersen firms around the world.

LOSSES AMONG BIG FOUR, PROBLEMS WITH FANNIE MAE

The year also had a downside. The now "Big Four," after more than a decade of gains, experienced a net loss of public company audit clients, although KPMG saw the smallest decline. "After the rapid growth of the Big Four's audit client lists in the wake of the 2002 collapse of Andersen, we expected 2003 would be a year of rationalization of their client bases—that has clearly taken place. Also, we expected to see increased client selectivity on the part of the firms in light of the new Sarbanes-Oxley environment. However, these circumstances alone do not seem to fully explain the extent of client losses," Richard Ossoff, publisher of Auditor-Trak, said in *Insurance Advocate.* Smaller national, regional, and local firms gained defecting clients.

In December 2004, the SEC revealed longtime KPMG client Fannie Mae had been out of compliance with accounting rules and required the mortgage maker to restate earnings. The government-sponsored enterprise (GSE) dismissed KPMG as its auditor, a role it had held since 1969. The Office of Federal Housing Enterprise Oversight, Fannie Mae's regulator, said the GSE had improperly bypassed mark-to-market accounting of derivative transactions, according to the *Financial Times.* The restatement revealed earnings volatility and triggered elevated capital requirements.

Fears regarding the GSE's massive mortgage and derivative portfolios and the risk they posed to the U.S. financial system were fanned by the news. Foreign purchases of U.S. debt securities supported the country's deficit spending. Questions regarding the soundness of U.S. securities also threatened the health of the market. As for KPMG, the firm faced the scrutiny of the Public Company Accounting Oversight Board, established in 2003 in response to the Enron and WorldCom Inc. accounting scandals. "The inquiry is unwelcome news for Eugene O'Kelly, chief executive of KPMG's U.S. business since 2002, who has spent considerable time trying to draw a line under various audit and tax problems," Andrew Parker and Jenny Wiggins reported for the *Financial Times.*

MORE GOOD NEWS, BAD NEWS: 2005–07

KPMG had topped the Big Four in global growth in fiscal 2004, climbing 14.7 percent in U.S. dollars, to $13.4 billion in revenue. During the year the firm discontinued or divested businesses to focus on higher demand services. Double-digit growth continued in fiscal 2005, driven by economic resurgence, the new regulatory requirements placed on businesses, and prior internal investments.

A drawn out legal problem was resolved in August 2005. KPMG admitted wrongdoing and agreed to a $456 million settlement with the Department of Justice. The government maintained KPMG sold fraudulent tax shelters to wealthy clients, who filed for $11 billion in tax losses resulting in $2.5 billion in lost tax receipts.

KPMG generated $115 million in fees from 1996 to 2003 from the products. In addition to the fine, KPMG agreed to shut down its profitable tax practice for high net-worth individuals, according to the *Turkish Daily News*. The action ended the criminal probe against the firm, but civil lawsuits were pending and eight former partners had been indicted. Industry-wide, firms had pulled back from the tainted tax shelter business.

During fiscal 2006, the Advisory business and Asia Pacific region posted the greatest growth. Regulatory changes in the European Union allowed KPMG to merge its U.K. and German member firms, effective 2007, en route to building Europe's largest accountancy practice. Meanwhile, KPMG promoted a move toward global auditing and accounting standards.

At the end of January 2007, KPMG and New Century Financial accountants disclosed to the mortgage lender's board, reserves on troubled home loans had been miscalculated negating profits recorded for the later half of 2006. Investors bailed and New Century failed. As trouble in the subprime mortgage market spread like wildfire, rating agencies, regulators, and then accountants heard the cry: "Where were you?" KPMG had been examining New Century's books as it wrote and resold billions in mortgages.

GLOBAL ECONOMIC CRISIS: 2008–09

In March 2008 KPMG eliminated an earlier problem with the settlement of the Xerox securities lawsuit. For the fiscal year, KPMG repeated its performance in 2007, reporting double-digit growth across all its service lines: audit, tax and advisory. Regionally, Asia-Pacific continued to outperform the EMA (Europe, Middle East, and Africa) and the Americas. In the United States, KPMG maintained the top spot in terms of big bank audits, Citigroup, Wachovia, and Wells Fargo among them.

In April 2009 New Century's trustee filed a suit against KPMG. Roughly two years earlier, the firm engaged in countersuits with Fannie Mae. Timothy Flynn, named head of the U.S. operation following the death of O'Kelly in 2005 and chairman of KPMG International since October 2007, faced this latest legal challenge in a period marked by an ongoing global financial crisis. Hong Kong and China firms experienced cutbacks in staff hours in 2009, as initial public offerings, mergers and acquisition activity, and expansion slowed. Anticipating a turnaround, however, KPMG continued to recruit in the region, seeking accountants with "forensic knowledge and experience with complex

financial instruments," the *South China Morning Post* reported in July.

Elizabeth Rourke
Updated, Mariko Fujinaka; Kathleen Peippo

PRINCIPAL COMPETITORS

Deloitte Touche Tohmatsu; Ernst & Young Global Limited; PricewaterhouseCoopers International Limited.

FURTHER READING
"Accounting Business Is Thriving," *Globe and Mail,* January 4, 1982, p. B5.

Andrews, Frederick, "Fraud Trial of Peat Marwick Attracts Anxious Attention of Other Accountants," *Wall Street Journal,* October 29, 1974.

———, "Peat Marwick Is the First Big CPA Firm to Submit to 'Quality Review' by Peers," *Wall Street Journal,* June 17, 1974.

———, "Two Auditors Are Convicted of Stock Fraud," *Wall Street Journal,* November 15, 1974.

Bajaj, Vikas, and Julie Creswell, "Attention Turns to Another Subprime Player: The Accountant," *International Herald Tribune* (Paris), April 14, 2008, p. 16.

Barker, Garry, "Cisco Buys into KPMG US," *Age,* August 10, 1999, p. 1.

Berton, Lee, "Peat-KMG Merger Proposal Strained as Units in Some Countries Drop Off," *Wall Street Journal,* January 6, 1987.

———, "Peat-KMG Merger Will Form a Goliath," *Wall Street Journal,* September 12, 1986.

———, "Peat Marwick and KMG Main Agree to Merge," *Wall Street Journal,* September 4, 1986.

Bevan, Judi, "The 'Tough Nut' at Accountancy's Core," *Sunday Telegraph* (London), July 23, 1995, p. 12.

"Big Five Firms in 2000 and Beyond," *CPA Journal,* January 2000, p. 21.

"The Big Five's Credibility Gap Is Getting Wider," *Business Week,* October 30, 2000, p. 90.

Cowan, Alison Leigh, "Regulators Investigate Peat on Its Auditing of S.&L.'s," *New York Times,* May 23, 1991.

"Dismal Year for Accounting Profession," *Insurance Advocate,* February 2, 2004, p. 35.

Ewing, Jack, and Nanette Byrnes, "Continental Drift at KPMG," *Business Week,* May 27, 2002, pp. 70–71.

Gibb-Clark, Margot, "KPMG Suffers Internal Blows from Aborted Union," *Globe and Mail,* April 15, 1999, p. B13.

Heffes, Ellen M., "KPMG Chief Flynn Confronts 'the Age of Oversight,'" *Financial Executive,* May 2007, pp. 14+.

Heinzl, John, "Ernst & Young, KPMG to Create Global Giant," *Globe and Mail,* October 21, 1997, p. B6.

Hilzenrath, David S., "Fannie Mae Accused of Deceiving KPMG, Its Former Auditor," *Washington Post,* April 21, 2007, p. D1.

Hughes, Jennifer, "Accountant in Earnest; Power Player Timothy Flynn KPMG Chairman," *Financial Times,* May 31, 2007, p. 22.

———, "Timothy Flynn Follows Sir Michael at KPMG," *Financial Times,* May 31, 2007, p. 30.

Johnson, Jim, "Tax Giant Proposes a Different Kind of Cut," *Waste News,* April 28, 2008.

"July Ruling Expected on Andersen's Supreme Court Appeal," *Public Accounting Report,* January 31, 2005, pp. 1, 5.

Kardos, Donna, "KPMG Is Sued over New Century," *Wall Street Journal,* April 2, 2009, p. C3.

"KPMG Continues to Lead in Top Bank Audits," *Public Accounting Report,* July 31, 2008, pp. 6–8.

"KPMG Posts Double-Digit Global Growth Rate," *Public Accounting Report,* December 15, 2008, p. 5.

"KPMG Posts Highest Global Growth Rate Among Big Four," *Public Accounting Report,* January 31, 2005, pp. 1, 5.

"KPMG's Global Gross Revenue Tops $19.8 Billion," *Public Accounting Report,* November 30, 2007, pp. 1, 5.

"KPMG Sued for $1bn over New Century Collapse," *Europe Intelligence Wire,* April 2, 2009.

"KPMG to Pay $456 MLN in Tax Shelter Case," *Turkish Daily News,* August 31, 2005.

"KPMG Turns in Double-Digit Worldwide Revenue Growth Rate," *Public Accounting Report,* January 31, 2004, pp. 4, 8.

MacDonald, Elizabeth, "KPMG International Chooses Butler as Its Chairman, Succeeding Sharman," *Wall Street Journal,* July 1, 1999, p. B13.

Mann, Simon, "Peat and KMG Call Off Plans for Merger," *Sydney Morning Herald,* December 19, 1986, p. 13.

Minard, Lawrence, and Brian McGlynn, "The U.S.' Newest Glamour Job," *Forbes,* September 1, 1977.

Nuttall, Chris, "Xerox and Its Former Auditor to Settle Lawsuit," *Financial Times,* March 28, 2008, p. 20.

Parker, Andrew, and Jenny Wiggins, "A Broken Home: Fannie Mae Faces an Uncertain Future as Its Accounts Unravel," *Financial Times* (London), December 23, 2004, p. 19.

"The Power of Four," *Economist,* September 16, 2006, p. 18.

Richard, Patrick J., "Viewpoint: Where Were the Auditors as Companies Collapsed?" *American Banker,* October 10, 2008, p. 11.

Stodghill, Ron, "Who Says Accountants Can't Jump?" *Business Week,* October 26, 1992.

Tannenbaum, Jeffrey A., "Butler, Elected Peat Marwick CEO, Plans to Increase Revenue 10% a Year," *Wall Street Journal,* October 4, 1996, p. A3.

Weiss, Stuart, "Peat Marwick Merges Its Way to the Top," *Business Week,* September 15, 1986.

"WorldCom Won't Sue KPMG," *Public Accounting Report,* January 31, 2004, p. 4.

Yiu, Enoch, "Thousands of New Jobs; KPMG's Vote for Future," *South China Morning Post,* July 27, 2009.

Kratos Defense & Security Solutions, Inc.

4810 Eastgate Mall
San Diego, California 92121-1977
U.S.A.
Telephone: (858) 812-7300
Toll Free: (866) 606-5867
Fax: (858) 812-7301
Web site: http://www.kratosdefense.com

Public Company
Incorporated: 1994 as Wireless Facilities, Inc.
Employees: 2,000
Sales: $297.3 million (2008)
Stock Exchanges: NASDAQ
Ticker Symbol: KTOS
NAICS: 513390 Other Telecommunications; 541512
  Computer Systems Design Services

■ ■ ■

A NASDAQ-listed company based in San Diego, California, Kratos Defense & Security Solutions, Inc., is a provider of mission critical engineering and information technology (IT) solutions, primarily serving the U.S. military but also other federal, state, and local government agencies. Major services include weapon systems life-cycle support, military weapon range and technical services, command and control communication, surveillance and reconnaissance systems, security and surveillance systems, critical infrastructure design and integration services, and advanced IT services. In addition to the branches of the U.S. military, Kratos's customers include the U.S. Department of Homeland Security, Defense Contract Management Agency, Defense Logistics Agency, National Aeronautics and Space Agency (NASA), U.S. Postal Service, U.S. Department of Transportation, and Internal Revenue Service. Kratos maintains offices in about 25 locations in the United States.

INCORPORATION OF PREDECESSOR COMPANY: 1994

Kratos was originally known as Wireless Facilities, Inc. Incorporated in New York in 1994, it was an independent provider of outsourced services for the wireless communications industry. Its cofounders were Iranian-born brothers Masood and Massih Tayebi. Their family was part of a minority community in Iran, members of the Ghashghai nomad tribe who practiced the Baha'i faith and were far outnumbered by the dominant Shiite Muslim population. Moreover, the family moved from the countryside to the city to provide the children with better education, subjecting them to further discrimination. Matters only grew worse in the late 1970s when the Iranian government was toppled and an Islamic republic took its place. Because the Tayebi children were no longer permitted to attend school, they were sent to England. Here Masood Tayebi earned a master's degree in electronics engineering from the University of Southampton and a doctorate in mobile radio propagation from the University of Liverpool.

During his college days in England, Masood Tayebi had already begun to demonstrate entrepreneurial talents. As an undergraduate he earned extra money by

COMPANY PERSPECTIVES

■

Our vision is to be the trusted, innovative provider of Advanced Engineering, IT Services, War Fighter Solutions and Security and Surveillance Systems that will ensure the security and freedom of our nation and its allies.

repairing and selling television sets, and as a graduate student he outsourced software coding contracts to fellow students. After completing his education, he provided wireless technology consulting services to telecommunications companies in the United Kingdom.

By this time, one of his six siblings, his brother Sean, had found his way to the United States to study medicine, and urged Masood to pay a visit. Although his brother claimed the United States was an ideal place for his personality, Masood, knowing little more about the country than Hollywood movies, had some misgivings. "I thought of the U.S. as this violent place where everyone was killing each other," he told Rachel Laing of the *San Diego Union-Tribune* in a 2006 interview. When he made a two-week trip to Washington, D.C., in 1993, however, he became so enamored with the United States that he decided not to return to England.

COMPANY RELOCATES TO SAN DIEGO: 1995

Massih Tayebi joined his brother Masood in the United States in 1994. For the previous five years he had been a senior faculty member of the Engineering Department and director of Computer Integrated Product Life Cycle Research for the University of Paisley in Great Britain. Together the Tayebi brothers established an engineering-services firm under the name Wireless Facilities Inc. in New York City to provide consulting for telecommunications companies. A year later they moved the business to San Diego, which their research revealed was an emerging wireless research center.

In San Diego they enjoyed immediate success as a telecommunications infrastructure design and development company. Sales improved from about $1 million in 1995 to $15.4 million in 1996. A year later revenues increased to $22.7 million and surged to nearly $60 million in 1998. Part of that growth was the result of four acquisitions, including the 1998 purchase of

Virginia-based Entel Technologies, Inc., which provided microwave relocation, site acquisition, and construction services.

The additional capabilities allowed Wireless Facilities to serve wireless network operators as well as original equipment manufacturers. Wireless Facilities customers included such carriers as PacBell Wireless, Sprint PCS, PageNet, AT&T Wireless Services, and Next Link; and equipment makers Siemens AG, Motorola, Ericsson, and Lucent Technologies.

COMPANY GOES PUBLIC: 1999

In 1997 Tom Munro was hired as Wireless Facilities' first chief financial officer. He then helped shepherd the company through the process of going public to raise funds to maintain growth and take advantage of an explosive increase in mobile voice and data subscribers. Carriers faced competition and price pressure as they attempted to quickly build out their networks, and increasingly they looked to outsource both network construction and maintenance to companies such as Wireless Facilities. (Venture-capital firm Oak Investment Partners had provided previous backing and taken a stake in the company of about 18 percent.) The initial public offering (IPO) of stock was held in November 1999. Offered at $15 a share, the stock soared to $62 on the first day of trading on the NASDAQ. After some fluctuation it reached $150 in February 2000 to give Wireless Facilities a market capitalization of $7 billion.

Wireless Facilities was far from the only company in the telecommunications sector with an unsustainable market cap. The entire technology sector proved to be little more than a bubble that burst, leaving many customers of Wireless Facilities out of business. In 2001 alone a dozen customers filed for bankruptcy, and the ones that remained were forced to slash their budgets. As its business evaporated, Wireless Facilities saw its stock price collapse, dipping as low as $3.

The sector did not reach bottom until 2002. To avoid cutting staff, which it had assembled during the late 1990s at a time when its largest challenge had been recruiting, the Tayebi brothers no longer accepted their salaries, but given business conditions it was little more than a gesture and eventually they had no choice but to lay off nearly half their workers. "We kept delaying it, and the pain kept growing," Masood Tayebi told the *San Diego Union-Tribune* in the 2006 interview. "For years, we'd built this family culture, but then how can you cut your brothers and sisters? Every time you let someone go, you let go of a family—a spouse, their kids." Also in 2002 Masood Tayebi figuratively lost his brother when Massih Tayebi left the company to

```
┌─────────────────────────────────────────────┐
│                                               │
│              KEY DATES                        │
│                    ■                          │
│  ─────────────────────────────────────        │
│                                               │
│  1994:  Company is founded in New York as Wireless │
│         Facilities, Inc.                      │
│  1995:  Company moves to San Diego.           │
│  1999:  Wireless Facilities is taken public.  │
│  2004:  Eric DeMarco is named CEO.            │
│  2007:  Company is renamed Kratos Defense &   │
│         Security Solutions, Inc.              │
│                                               │
└─────────────────────────────────────────────┘
```

become chairman of MIR3, Inc., although Massih retained a 10 percent stake in Wireless Facilities.

RETURN TO PROFITABILITY: 2002

Wireless Facilities managed to return to profitability by the second quarter of 2002, due in part to the use of contract workers, and decided to be aggressive in rebuilding its business, actively courting the major wireless carriers. Eventually it landed Cingular, T-Mobile, Verizon, and other top companies in the industry, helping them to upgrade their networks. In order to pay down debt and replenish cash reserves, the company looked to the capital markets. Rather than attempt a secondary public offering of stock, it engineered a $45 million private placement in 2002. Further fund-raising allowed Wireless Facilities to retire nearly all of its debt and grow cash reserves to about $100 million by the summer of 2003.

Although pleased to have escaped catastrophe at the start of the 21st century, Wireless Facilities still found itself in a precarious position. Because carriers needed to upgrade their networks at a time of continued austerity, Wireless Facilities picked up a good deal of contract work but found itself in the unusual position of competing with its important customers' internal departments, which at the time were unable to add staff. How long the contracts might remain available once these departments were allowed to hire again was uncertain. Moreover, there was also the specter of new competition willing to underbid Wireless Facilities, resulting in slim margins.

The company began to seek diversity to become less dependent on AT&T and Cingular. In October 2002 Wireless Facilities added an enterprise solutions division to become involved in such areas as digital surveillance systems and wireless local area networks. It also broadened its business through acquisitions, including the purchase of Georgia-based Suntech Systems Inc., a provider of wireless, security, and voice/data services.

NEW CEO, ERIC M. DEMARCO: 2004

In November 2003 Eric M. DeMarco was hired as president and chief operating officer. Six months later he replaced Masood Tayebi as chief executive officer, although Tayebi remained chairman. It was DeMarco who directed Wireless Technologies toward the defense and federal government sectors, an area with which he was well familiar. In his previous post as president and chief operating officer of defense contractor Titan Corporation, DeMarco had helped to build Titan into one of the largest government IT companies in the country. He also had experience as a public accountant working for multinational corporations that served the U.S. Department of Defense.

DeMarco engineered a number of acquisitions to refocus Wireless Facilities on the public sector and to hedge against the unpredictable commercial cell-phone business. With the passing of the Cold War, the U.S. military was looking to maintain a smaller number of troops, but ones that relied on flexible, efficient technology and timely information. In late 2003 San Diego's High Technology Solutions was purchased for $48.8 million. The company had served as a defense contractor since 1990 when it began offering technical services to the U.S. Navy. In August 2004 Wireless Facilities spent $6.6 million for Manassas, Virginia-based Defense Systems Inc., a provider of IT services to the Department of Defense. Another significant acquisition, completed in early 2002, was Alexandria, Virginia-based TLA Associates, which sold voice and data network services to the Defense Department.

While looking to the future of Wireless Facilities, DeMarco also had to clean up problems from the past. In 2004 the company was forced to restate its earnings for 2001 through 2003. Further difficulties arose in 2006 when backdated stock options were uncovered, an illegal practice if not disclosed to shareholders and one that could result in high profits for anyone in a position to cash in the options. The stock-option accounts in question were created for employees years before they were even hired. The resulting investigation prevented Wireless Facilities from filing its 2006 annual report on time, leading to a notice from the NASDAQ in 2007 threatening to delist the company. In the end the company's former stock-options administrator, Vencent A. Donlan, pleaded guilty in 2007 to wire fraud and tax evasion charges related to bilking Wireless Technologies of more than $6.3 million in a backdated stock-option scheme.

In the meantime, DeMarco continued to transform Wireless Facilities. In the final months of 2006 the company paid $69 million for Huntsville, Alabama-based Madison Research Corp., provider of telecommunications and IT services to such clients as the U.S. Army, the U.S. Air Force, and NASA. At the start of 2007 Wireless Facilities began a restructuring plan. Not only did it divest some money-losing international businesses, it consolidated other operations to trim overhead and improve margins. More significantly in 2007, the company sold what for many years had been its core business, its wireless deployment operations. As a result, the company was no longer a commercial wireless network contractor but a government contractor of technical and IT services to the Department of Defense, the Department of Homeland Security, and other federal, state, and local government customers.

ADOPTION OF KRATOS NAME: 2007

Because of the company's new focus, a change in name was in order and in 2007 Wireless Facilities became Kratos Defense & Security Solutions, Inc. (Kratos was the Greek god of strength.) As such, the company, with the stock-option matter behind it, was finally able to state its 2006 earnings and retain its NASDAQ listing.

Kratos looked to build its business in 2008. Early in the year it used stock to acquire another San Diego-based company, SYS Technologies, a provider of information connectivity solutions to the Defense Department and others. Late in 2008 Kratos used $37.7 million in stock to acquire Huntsville, Alabama-based Digital Fusion, which mostly served the Department of Defense and specialized in simulation, engineering, space systems, and optics. For his efforts in turning Wireless Facilities into Kratos, DeMarco in 2009 won the Corporate Turnaround Executive Award from The Global M&A Network. The metamorphosis complete, the time had come to grow Kratos. Its future appeared promising but by no means guaranteed.

Ed Dinger

PRINCIPAL SUBSIDIARIES

Defense Systems, Incorporated; Kratos Commercial Solutions, Inc.; Kratos Government Solutions, Inc.; Kratos Mid-Atlantic, Inc.; Kratos Southeast, Inc.; Kratos Southwest L.P.; Madison Research Corporation.

PRINCIPAL COMPETITORS

Computer Sciences Corporation; Electronic Data Systems, LLC; Lockheed Martin Corporation.

FURTHER READING

Balint, Kathryn, "Company Sheds Wireless Focus for $24 Million," *San Diego Union-Tribune*, July 10, 2007.

———, "San Diego Wireless Company Plans Restructuring," *San Diego Union-Tribune*, January 4, 2007.

———, "Wireless Facilities Purchases Virginia Company," *San Diego Union-Tribune*, January 28, 2005.

Bigelow, Bruce V., "Kratos Expects to Be Relisted," *San Diego Union-Tribune*, October 6, 2007.

Davies, Jennifer, "San Diego-Based Builder of Cell-Phone Networks Proves to Be Resilient," *San Diego Union-Tribune*, July 8, 2003.

———, "San Diego's Wireless Facilities Buys Defense Contractor for $48.8 Million," *San Diego Union-Tribune*, December 24, 2003.

Douglas, Elizabeth, "Wireless Facilities, PacWest Hope to Plug into Interest in Telecom," *Los Angeles Times*, October 25, 1999, p. 1.

Freeman, Mike, "Defense Contractor Kratos Set to Acquire Info Tech Company," *San Diego Union-Tribune*, November 25, 2008.

Laing, Rachel, "Telecom Exec Eager for Biotech Venture," *San Diego Union-Tribune*, April 18, 2006.

Ryan, Vincent, "Woe Is This Wireless Stock," *Telephony*, January 31, 2000, p. 70.

Shinkle, Kirk, "Life After Tech Bust? Just Fine, Thank You," *Investor's Business Daily*, August 18, 2003, p. A07.

LACOSTE
Lacoste S.A.

8 Rue de Castiglione
Paris, 75001
France
Telephone: (33 1) 44 58 12 12
Fax: (33 1) 44 58 12 19
Web site: http://www.lacoste.fr

Private Company
Incorporated: 1933 as Société Chemise Lacoste
Employees: 25,000
Sales: EUR 1.56 billion (2007)
NAICS: 315211 Men's and Boys' Cut and Sew Apparel Contractors; 315212 Women's, Girls', and Infants' Cut and Sew Apparel Contractors; 533110 Lessors of Nonfinancial Intangible Assets (Except Copyrighted Works)

■ ■ ■

Lacoste S.A. produces a leading brand of high-end sportswear. It stays close to its sporting origins by also selling athletic apparel and accessories. Company founder René Lacoste is credited with bringing short sleeves to tennis and introducing a number of other innovations. The company's products are sold globally through upscale department stores and boutiques.

The Lacoste polo shirt, believed to be the first fashion item to feature a logo on the exterior, was successfully exported to the United States in the 1950s and became a cultural phenomenon spawning dozens of imitators. While the brand remained strong in France and other countries, U.S. sales collapsed in the 1980s,

leading to the brand's withdrawal from that market before a successful relaunch by Devanlay S.A.

Lacoste remains majority owned by its namesake family, with the rest in the hands of the company's worldwide licensee, Devanlay S.A., which is itself controlled by Swiss retail group Maus Frères S.A. Ninety percent of revenues come from outside of France, with the largest market being the United States, followed by France, Italy, the United Kingdom, and Spain, while China has been both a central front in its battle versus counterfeiters and efforts to expand the brand.

ORIGINS

The origins of Lacoste S.A. are firmly rooted in the glory days of tennis, and in French national pride. Company founder René Lacoste was one of the Four Musketeers, the first French team to wrest the Davis Cup away from the United States. Lacoste was ranked the number one player in the world in 1926 and 1927 and won several titles at the French Open, Wimbledon, and the U.S. Open. His wife, Simone Thion de la Chaume, was a golf champion (as was their daughter Catherine).

Lacoste picked up his famous nickname, "Le Crocodile," in the United States in 1927. The French Davis Cup captain promised to buy him an alligator suitcase if he won a certain match. The press and the public were taken with the name, which resonated with Lacoste's tenacity on the court as well as his long nose and toothy grin. He soon had a snapping crocodile embroidered on the breast of his tennis blazer.

The LACOSTE legend is born in 1933, when René Lacoste revolutionizes men's fashion replacing the classical woven fabric, long-sleeved and starched shirts on the courts, by what has now become the classic LACOSTE polo shirt. More than 75 years after its creation, LACOSTE has become a "lifestyle" brand which allies elegance and comfort. The LACOSTE art of living expresses itself today through a large collection of apparel for women, men and children, footwear, fragrances, leather goods, eyewear, watches, belts and home textiles. LACOSTE founds its success on the essential values of authenticity, performance, and elegance. The crocodile incarnates today the elegance of the champion, René Lacoste, as well as of his wife Simone Lacoste and their daughter Catherine Lacoste, both also champions, in everyday life as on the tennis courts and golf courses.

Lacoste reportedly used his reputation to reform the dress code of the era by insisting on defending his French Open title wearing a short-sleeved shirt similar to ones worn by polo players, rather than the starched long-sleeved shirts that were then standard. Later, perceiving a commercial opportunity, Lacoste went into business with knitwear manufacturer André Gillier in 1933 to manufacture the polo shirts. The crocodile logo which appeared on them is believed to be the first appearance of an external logo in the fashion industry.

The company's polo shirt would remain Lacoste's best-known product for decades. Code-named the "1212," it was made from an airy weave of knit cotton called Jersey petit piqué and available only in white at first. Advertisements touted its suitability for tennis, golf, and the beach.

Lacoste's impact on the game, and the industry, of tennis went far beyond clothing. The company introduced the first steel racquets to the game in 1963. Licensed to U.S. manufacturer Wilson, these brought Jimmy Connors several Grand Slam championships and served as a bridge in the evolution of tennis racquets between wood and composite construction. Lacoste also introduced string dampeners (1960), among other innovations.

A pioneering lifestyle brand, Lacoste ventured into a wide range of products. It began producing tennis shoes in 1963. In 1968 an eau de toilette produced with Jean Patou brought the label into the fragrance market. A series of brand extensions followed. Sunglasses debuted in 1981, manufactured under license by L'Amy. Over the years, the crocodile appeared on everything from bed linens to cars (on a 1984 edition of the Peugeot 205).

Production was suspended during World War II. When it resumed, the company began making shirts for women as well as men. A range of colors was added to the basic white in 1951.

EXPORTING STYLE

In 1952 Lacoste began exporting to the United States. Its shirts sold well, particularly after a photo of President Dwight Eisenhower wearing one appeared in *Life* magazine. By the 1960s, the crocodile-logo shirts were a favorite of the leisure set.

Minneapolis-based cereal giant General Mills Inc. acquired the North American license through its 1969 purchase of David Crystal Inc. It combined the Lacoste business with that of the venerable clothing manufacturer Izod.

Under General Mills ownership, the brand in the United States evolved from a niche status symbol to a mass-market phenomenon. Successive generations of youth adapted the country-club clothes of their parents to meet their own ends. In the preppy look of the 1970s and 1980s, the Izod Lacoste polos were worn untucked, with the collars flipped up, suggesting carefree affluence.

GENERAL MILLS UNLOADS THE BRAND

The highly visible success spawned legions of imitators. Munsingwear, with its Penguin-branded golf shirts, had been an imitator since the 1960s. Cheaper knockoffs followed from Le Tigre; J.C. Penney's Fox brand; Sears, Roebuck & Co.; and many others. At the same time, General Mills began making the shirts in the Far East and incorporating synthetic materials into the blend. In the mid-1970s, Ralph Lauren launched an all-cotton knockoff under the "Polo" brand that eclipsed Lacoste at upscale retailers such as Bloomingdale's.

As knit polo shirts became a commodity, both profits and volume fell. Izod Lacoste's revenues peaked around $400 million in 1982, but by the time the shirts were taken off the U.S. market in 1992, annual sales had slipped to less than $50 million and the brand was beginning to worry investors in publicly traded General Mills.

In 1985 General Mills spun off its fashion business into Crystal Brands, Inc. Devanlay S.A. acquired La-

KEY DATES

1933: French tennis champion René Lacoste forms joint venture to produce the first branded polo shirts.
1952: Lacoste begins exporting to the United States.
1963: Firm introduces the first steel tennis racquets.
1969: General Mills Inc. acquires Lacoste's North American licensee, David Crystal Inc., and combines it with Izod.
1985: After sales decline, General Mills spins off the U.S. business as part of Crystal Brands, Inc.
1994: Devanlay S.A. relaunches the Lacoste brand in the United States, focusing on exclusivity.
1999: Devanlay acquires the worldwide license to distribute the brand.
2004: United States resumes position as Lacoste's leading international market.
2005: Michel Lacoste is named chairman and CEO.

coste's North American and Caribbean distribution rights in 1992 while Izod became a part of Phillips-Van Heusen.

RENAISSANCE UNDER DEVANLAY

While the business suffered in the United States, it maintained its reputation in Europe, Japan, and Latin America. It was strong as ever in France. Lacoste outfitted the country's Davis Cup team, which in 1991 won the trophy in a repeat of the Musketeers' triumph 59 years earlier. (One of the victors, Guy Forget, wielded the company's novel Equijet racquet.) In the decade that followed, winning the Davis Cup, and the ladies' equivalent, the Fed Cup, soon became a routine event for Lacoste-wearing French teams.

In 1994 Devanlay S.A. relaunched the Lacoste brand in the United States, focusing on reclaiming its reputation for exclusivity. This time the shirts were again made of 100 percent cotton and boasted such refinements as mother-of-pearl buttons. They were also priced at the top end of the market, even higher than Ralph Lauren's Polo brand.

Robert Siegel took charge of Lacoste's U.S. operations via the Devanlay subsidiary Lacoste Inc. in January 2002. He had led the ultra-successful launch of Dockers 15 years earlier.

Timing played on Lacoste's side, noted *Brandweek*, as the grunge fad of the 1990s faded. Retro was a

popular theme, calling for at least the appearance of nostalgia and authenticity. Lacoste was embraced by youth perhaps unaware of the brand's heritage, including its more recent preppy past.

With a smaller market base, the company took the opportunity to experiment with its product mix. Around 2005 Lacoste wooed women by introducing a more fitted polo made with a stretchy Lycra-cotton blend fabric, in more than two dozen colors.

The brand's relaunch was so successful that the United States again became Lacoste's leading international market in 2004, when sales there doubled. In April 2005 the label signed a six-year endorsement deal with Andy Roddick, the leading U.S. tennis player.

LOOKING EAST

China became increasingly important as a market after joining the World Trade Organization in 2001 and agreeing to crack down on piracy. At least 100 manufacturers had been involved in counterfeiting Lacoste's designs. In 2003 Bernard Lacoste stated the aim of making it the company's top market within 10 years. It accounted for sales of about $70 million in 2004.

In 2006 *WWD* reported that the traditionally status-conscious Chinese were beginning to merge casual and business attire, as had been the trend in the West. By this time, the brand was available in 130 locations in China, including about three-dozen boutiques. Most of Lacoste's product for this market was made locally.

MILESTONES

Switzerland's Maus family acquired a 90 percent stake in Devanlay S.A., which held a 35 percent shareholding in Lacoste S.A., in 1998. Devanlay, France's leading underwear manufacturer, was reportedly valued at FRF 2 billion, twice as much as Lacoste. It acquired a worldwide license to distribute the brand in 1999.

Michel Lacoste became Lacoste S.A. chairman and CEO in 2005. He succeeded his older brother, Bernard Lacoste, the firm's leader for 42 years, who died in March 2006. By this time Lacoste was a much different company in terms of product mix. Clothing made up only 60 percent of Lacoste's sales by 2007.

There was much to celebrate at the time of Lacoste's 75th anniversary in 2008. The rejuvenated brand reported worldwide wholesale revenue of EUR 1.56 billion for the previous year. U.S. sales were $300 million and reportedly growing, even in a dismal economy. Lacoste had a presence in 112 countries and was particularly strong in the United States, France, Italy, the United Kingdom, and Spain.

Frederick C. Ingram

PRINCIPAL COMPETITORS

Fred Perry Limited; Polo/Ralph Lauren Corporation; Nautica Apparel, Inc.

FURTHER READING

Dell, Kristina, "Lacoste's Riposte: How the Once Flailing French Brand Regained Its Mojo in the U.S., Even If Andy Roddick Didn't," *Time,* Global Business/Brands Sec., September 26, 2005, p. A15.

"Devanlay May Take Total Control of Lacoste," *Les Echos,* March 18, 1997, p. 10.

Gogoi, Pallavi, "Lacoste's Alligator Sheds Its Skin," *Business Week Online,* February 27, 2006.

Haber, Holly, "Lacoste Looks to Propagate," *WWD,* January 22, 2003, p. 29.

Hollie, Pamela G., "Izod's Fall from Vogue a Drag on General Mills," *New York Times,* Bus. Sec., November 15, 1984.

Kapferer, Patricia, and Tristan Gaston-Breton, *La légende Lacoste,* Paris: Le Cherche Midi, 2002.

———, *Lacoste the Legend,* Paris: Cherche midi, 2002.

———, *Le style René Lacoste,* Paris: L'équipe, 2008.

Lee, Lena, "Lacoste Expects to Make China Its Top Market in 10 Years' Time," *Wall Street Journal Europe,* October 27, 2003, p. A4.

Levine, Joshua, "Anemic Crocodile," *Forbes,* August 15, 1994, p. 116.

Moin, David, "Lacoste Serves Up Active Style to Women," *WWD,* April 9, 2008, p. 9.

Monget, Karyn, "The Crocodile Makes a Comeback," *WWD,* April 27, 1994, p. 9.

Movius, Lisa, "Lacoste Gaining Popularity as China Embraces Casual," *WWD,* May 3, 2006, p. 9.

O'Loughlin, Sandra, "Robert Siegel: You'll See This Alligator Later," *Brandweek,* October 11, 2004, pp. M24–M28.

Schwartz, Judith D., "The Alligator Returns After Being Left for Dead," *Adweek's Marketing Week,* January 2, 1989, pp. 44+.

Loblaw Companies Limited

———————— ■ ————————

1 President's Choice Circle
Brampton, Ontario L6Y 5S5
Canada
Telephone: (905) 459-2500
Fax: (905) 861-2206
Web site: http://www.loblaw.com

Subsidiary of George Weston Limited
Incorporated: 1956
Employees: 139,000
Sales: CAD 30.8 billion (2008)
Stock Exchanges: Toronto
Ticker Symbol: L
NAICS: 445110 Supermarkets and Other Grocery
     (Except Convenience) Stores; 424410 General Line
     Grocery Merchant Wholesalers; 522110 Com-
     mercial Banking

■ ■ ■

Loblaw Companies Limited is the largest supermarket chain and the largest food distributor in Canada. Loblaw operates more than 1,000 company-owned and franchised stores that operate in all 10 provinces under more than a dozen different names, including Loblaws, The Real Canadian Superstore, Dominion, Extra Foods, and Provigo. The company categorizes its retail units into four types of formats: Superstore, Great Food, Hard Discount, and Wholesale. A portion of the inventory in Loblaw's stores consists of brands it has developed, including President's Choice, its signature label. More than 1,500 products are sold under the President's Choice brand name, including financial services and insurance. George Weston Limited, a baked goods company based in Toronto, Ontario, owns 63 percent of Loblaw.

EARLY 20TH-CENTURY ORIGINS

For Theodore Pringle Loblaw, the creation of Loblaw was his second attempt at building a chain of grocery stores. The Ontario native was hired by the United Farmers Cooperative Company in 1919 to develop a chain of cooperative grocery stores, but the venture quickly foundered. Loblaw launched his second, infinitely more successful attempt at creating a grocery chain before the end of the year, founding the company that bore his name with the help of an Ontario businessman, Justin Cork. Within 20 years, Loblaw developed into a chain of more than 80 grocery stores, spreading its physical presence outward from its base in Ontario.

As Loblaw developed into a major competitor in the grocery business, it attracted the attention of one of Canada's most powerful companies. George Weston Limited, based in Toronto, Ontario, was founded in 1882 by George Weston, who used the skills he learned as a baker's apprentice to build his company into Toronto's largest bakery. Upon his death in 1924, his son W. Garfield Weston took control of the company and made the family business a multibillion-dollar empire, creating Canada's largest food processing and distribution company. The Weston scion vertically integrated the company's operations, establishing a sugar refinery business, for instance. He also diversified, acquiring E. B.

Eddy Company, a pulp and paper business, in 1943. In 1947, W. Garfield Weston took another step toward vertical integration by giving his company control over the retail sale of the foods it distributed, acquiring a controlling interest in Loblaw. With George Weston Limited's backing, Loblaw developed into the largest grocery chain in Canada.

DAVE NICHOL AND THE CREATION OF PRESIDENT'S CHOICE

Loblaw was a nearly 50-year-old business when the defining period in its history occurred. The company, during its half-century of development, had expanded across Canada, operating clusters of chains under several different names. It was at this point when Dave Nichol joined the company. Nichol, who would go on to become an award-winning product-marketing expert, earned his undergraduate degree at the University of Western Ontario, where one of his roommates was Willard Gordon Galen Weston, the son of W. Garfield Weston. Nichol earned a law degree at Harvard Law School and began working in Toronto for McKinsey & Co., a management consulting company, when Galen Weston asked for his help in running the family's supermarket business. Nichol joined Loblaw in 1972, hired as the company's executive vice president.

Nichol spearheaded Loblaw's foray into developing its own brand of grocery items, the distinctive element of the company's success in the decades to follow. Nichol became Loblaw's president in 1975, putting him in a position of power to implement profound changes. In 1984 he collaborated with a team of senior executives that included Galen Weston, Richard Currie, Brian Davidson, and Don Watt to create the President's Choice brand, a "super premium" brand Loblaw would use to sell grocery items in its stores. Unlike other brands created by retailers, the President's Choice label and packaging was designed to confer superiority over national brands, bearing "no resemblance to the sad-looking cans of lima beans and cut-rate instant coffee that supermarkets normally slap their own labels on," the May 29, 1989, issue of *Forbes* noted.

Loblaw's development of its own brand became a massive business for the company, strengthening its already stalwart position as Canada's largest grocery store chain. Other lines supported President's Choice, labels such as "no name" for Loblaw's generic items and TGTBT, an acronym for "Too Good to Be True," which consisted of nutritious products, but President's Choice represented the most important component of the company's branded business. The strength of the brand was most evident when Loblaw introduced its own chocolate cookie, The Decadent, using President's Choice-branded Decadent chocolate chips, to compete against Nabisco's Chips Ahoy. "When we launched The Decadent Chocolate Chip Cookie," Nichol said in the November 1995 issue of *Progressive Grocer*, "Chips Ahoy was the leading chocolate chip cookie in Canada. Chips Ahoy was made with coconut oil, contained 26 percent chocolate chips, and was in distribution in 98 percent of all the stores in the country. The Decadent was made with 100 percent butter, contained 40 percent chocolate chips, and was only distributed in 17 percent of the stores. Within two years, the Decadent was the leading chocolate chip cookie in the country."

The combination of a retailer-controlled brand and the largest retailer of its kind in Canada proved to be a potent pairing, injecting vitality in a company that had grown listless before Nichol's arrival. Nichol oversaw the development and marketing of hundreds of President's Choice products covering the gamut of food, drinks, and consumer products stocked in Loblaw's stores. He became the company's spokesman, appearing in dozens of commercials and radio advertisements. He borrowed an idea from another retailer, California-based Trader Joe's, and began producing the *Insider's Report*, a flyer published four times a year that described the special qualities of President's Choice products. As evidence of the importance of Loblaw's branded business, the company reorganized in 1985, creating Loblaw International Merchants, the product development arm of Loblaw that counted Nichol as its president.

EXPANSION IN THE NINETIES

Drawing strength from its Loblaw International Merchants arm, Loblaw flourished during the 1990s, becoming a case study for success in the supermarket industry. The company tightened its stranglehold on the grocery market late in the decade, fleshing out its geographic presence and extending its reach into the one area it had yet to penetrate. In December 1998, the company completed a hostile takeover of Montreal-based Provigo, an acquisition that strengthened Loblaw's presence in Ontario and made it a major competitor in the Quebec market. Provigo became one of the numerous banners the company operated under, a roster that included Loblaws, Real Canadian Superstore, Zehr Mart, Dominion, Maxi & Maxi, Fortino's, and Extra Foods. The Provigo acquisition was completed the same month Loblaw purchased 198 stores from Sobeys, a Nova Scotia-based retailer. The purchase extended Loblaw's reach into the Maritime provinces for the first time. With the addition of Provigo and Sobeys, Loblaw towered over all competitors, casting a formidable presence. The company was larger than the next three largest food retailers combined.

LEDERER ERA BEGINS IN 2001

The start of the 21st century marked a new era in Loblaw's history, one that would see Canada's premier retail chain struggle after decades of enviable success. The new era began with the appointment of a new president, John Lederer, who replaced Richard Currie, one of the architects of the President's Choice brand, in 2001. When Lederer took charge of the company, it was generating $20 billion in sales from roughly 1,000 stores, 40 percent of which were franchised No Frills locations. Loblaw's private-label business had developed into a $2.3 billion business, having expanded the President's Choice brand considerably, going as far as to delve into banking through PC Financial. The company was performing well, but Lederer was troubled by what he saw when he assumed his responsibilities.

Lederer saw the imminent arrival of arguably the most feared retailer in the world. Arkansas-based Wal-Mart Stores, a retail juggernaut with more than $300 billion in sales, was about to increase its involvement in the Canadian market. The sprawling retailer announced plans to open its warehouse club format, Sam's Club, in the fall of 2003, and Lederer feared the arrival of the company's superstores next. Lederer took action, bracing Loblaw for Wal-Mart's incursion. He began emphasizing discount pricing and a focus on nonfood items, using the company's Real Canadian Superstore banner to implement his push into general merchandise. The chain, which had begun in 1979 in Saskatchewan, remained largely in western Canada until Lederer opened eight units, each measuring between 100,000 square feet and 150,000 square feet, in Ontario in 2003.

The additions brought the number of Real Canadian Superstores to 65, a total Lederer planned to double in the coming years. "What they're doing is Wal-Mart-proofing their stores across the country by lowering prices and adding general merchandise to discourage Wal-Mart from bringing in their superstores," an analyst noted in the May 12, 2003, issue of *Supermarket News*. Another analyst echoed the assessment two years later in the July 25, 2005, issue of *Supermarket News*, saying, "What Loblaw has done over the last five or six years is really shift the playing field in Canada, tipping it way more toward discount, so Wal-Mart has to think a lot harder about whether or not they can play here."

Wal-Mart, despite Lederer's efforts, brought its superstore format to Canada, opening three units in Ontario in November 2006. Within two years, there were 39 Wal-Mart Supercentres operating in Canada. Ironically, Loblaw's main concern was not the expansion of Wal-Mart, but the effect of the changes implemented to combat Wal-Mart. By 2006, the company's stock value and profits were shrinking, undercut by efforts to revamp distribution and procurement for the company's headlong foray into general merchandise. Lederer remained committed to Loblaw's overhaul. "We are changing the company from what it was to what it can be and what it must be," he said in the May 22, 2006, issue of *Supermarket News*. The company's poor financial performance, however, fueled criticism of his actions. Loblaw recorded its first annual loss in 19 years in 2006, posting a CAD 219 million deficit one year after recording a gain of CAD 746 million.

LEADERSHIP CHANGE IN 2006

Part of the loss recorded in 2006 stemmed from a one-time charge related to the acquisition of Provigo eight years earlier, but the company's deteriorating financial condition was enough to bring an end to Lederer's leadership tenure. In September 2006 he was replaced by Mark Foote, who joined Loblaw five months earlier after spending 27 years working for Canadian Tire, a retailer of automobile supplies and sporting goods.

Loblaw announced a five-year turnaround plan in 2007, as the company sought to restore the vitality it had enjoyed during the 1980s and 1990s. The program failed to meet expectations, which led to Foote's ouster in early 2008 and the appointment of Allan Leighton, a longtime adviser to the Weston family, as Loblaw's new leader. "We feel that we have been on defense, not on offense," Leighton said in the May 5, 2008, issue of *Supermarket News*. "We feel that we've been a bit more reactive than we should have been."

In leading Loblaw's offensive charge forward, Leighton favored an emphasis on service and marketing over cutting prices. "We are the No. 1 player in this market," he said in the May 5, 2008, issue of *Supermarket News*. "We have the big market share, we have the assets, we have the brands, and I think you will just see that we will now start to utilize those." Leighton perceived Loblaw's strengths to be the company's branded business and its service, both of which suffered as the company repositioned itself to compete against Wal-Mart. He implemented a major renovation program, remodeling 25 superstore locations in western Canada, and he began converting the 106-store Extra Foods chain to the company's No Frills discount format.

As he prepared for a 25th anniversary program for the President's Choice brand in 2009, Leighton also demonstrated the aggressive posture he said Loblaw had lacked in recent years. In September 2009, he completed the acquisition of the largest Asian food retailer in Canada, T&T Supermarket Inc. Loblaw paid $225 million for the chain's 17 stores and four distribution centers, adding T&T's more than $500 million in an-

nual sales to its business volume and another banner to the long roster of Loblaw-controlled retail chains.

Michelle Fedder
Updated, Jeffrey L. Covell

PRINCIPAL SUBSIDIARIES

Atlantic Wholesalers Ltd.; Fortinos Supermarket Ltd.; Glenhuron Bank Limited (Barbados); Kelly, Douglas & Company, Limited; Loblaw Alberta Inc.; Loblaw Brands Limited; Loblaw Financial Holdings Inc.; Loblaw Properties Limited; Loblaw Properties West Inc.; Loblaws Inc.; Loblaws Supermarkets Limited; National Grocers Co. Ltd.; PGV Acquisition Inc.; President's Choice Bank; Provigo Distribution Inc.; Provigo Properties Limited; Provigo Quebec Inc.; Westfair Foods Ltd.; Zehrmart Inc.

PRINCIPAL COMPETITORS

METRO Inc.; Canada Safeway Limited; Walmart Canada.

FURTHER READING

Dunn, Brian, "Loblaw Experiments with On-Line Shopping," *Supermarket News*, February 7, 2000, p. 22.

———, "Loblaw in Transition," *Supermarket News*, May 22, 2006, p. 34.

———, "Loblaw May Expand Brand Beyond Supermarket," *Supermarket News*, March 6, 2000, p. 25.

———, "Loblaw Prepares for Wal-Mart's Canadian Invasion," *Supermarket News*, May 12, 2003, p. 26.

Kosub, David, "Loblaw Leads Charge in Canada," *Supermarket News*, December 6, 2004, p. 31.

Levine, Joshua, "The Chill Wind from Canada," *Forbes*, May 29, 1989, p. 308.

"Loblaw Announces Completion of the Acquisition of T&T Supermarket, Canada's Largest Asian Food Retailer," *CNW Group*, September 28, 2009.

"Loblaw Cos. Posts First Full-Year Loss in Nearly 20 Years," *Progressive Grocer*, March 16, 2007.

Mathews, Ryan, "A Passion for Excellence," *Progressive Grocer*, November 1995, p. B21.

Springer, Jon, "Loblaw Debuts 'Great Food' Banner, Focuses on Fresh," *Supermarket News*, April 21, 2008.

———, "Loblaw Steps Up Non-Food Focus," *Supermarket News*, September 18, 2000, p. 16.

———, "Loblaw to Accelerate Turnaround," *Supermarket News*, May 5, 2008.

Vosburgh, Robert, "John Lederer; President, Loblaw Cos.," *Supermarket News*, July 25, 2005, p. 56.

Zweibach, Elliot, "Consolidation Heats Up in Canada," *Supermarket News,* September 20, 1999, p. 42.

———, "Lederer Out as Loblaw Shakes Up Top Manage-ment," *Supermarket News,* September 25, 2006, p. 8.

———, "Loblaw: Streamlining Infrastructure on Track," *Supermarket News,* March 13, 2006, p. 60.

Maple Leaf Foods Inc.

———————————■———————————

30 St. Clair Avenue West, Suite 1500
Toronto, Ontario M4V 3A2
Canada
Telephone: (416) 926-2000
Fax: (416) 926-2018
Web site: http://www.mapleleaf.com

Public Company
Incorporated: 1927 as Canada Packers Limited
Employees: 24,000
Sales: CAD 5.24 billion ($4.28 billion) (2008)
Stock Exchanges: Toronto
Ticker Symbol: MFI
NAICS: 112210 Hog and Pig Farming; 311119 Other
    Animal Food Manufacturing; 311412 Frozen
    Specialty Food Manufacturing; 311611 Animal
    (Except Poultry) Slaughtering; 311612 Meat
    Processed from Carcasses; 311613 Rendering and
    Meat By-Product Processing; 311615 Poultry
    Processing; 311812 Commercial Bakeries; 311991
    Perishable Prepared Food Manufacturing

■ ■ ■

Maple Leaf Foods Inc. is one of Canada's largest food
processors and that nation's largest pork processor. The
company produces fresh and frozen pork and poultry
products and sells them under such brands as Maple
Leaf and Schneider as well as through private-label,
foodservice, and industrial channels. Pork products
include bacon, hams, sausages, hot dogs, and delicates-
sen products, while poultry items include fully cooked

chicken breasts and turkey breast roasts. Maple Leaf
Foods also holds a nearly 90 percent interest in Canada
Bread Company, Limited, a leading manufacturer and
marketer of fresh and frozen bread and specialty bakery
products in Canada, frozen bread in the United States,
and bagels and specialty baked goods in the United
Kingdom. Although the company distributes its
products to customers in 50 countries around the world,
Canada accounts for 76 percent of overall sales with 12
percent generated in the United States. Maple Leaf
Foods' stock is publicly traded, but a branch of the
McCain family controls nearly 39 percent of the voting
shares while Ontario Teachers' Pension Plan Board holds
more than 19 percent.

THE EARLY YEARS: MERGERS AND ACQUISITIONS

Maple Leaf's origins stem back to 1836, and its history
covers more than a century of mergers and acquisitions.
The completion of the Welland Canal in 1833 initiated
the beginning of industrial-scale milling in Canada. In
1896 Grantham Mills, the forerunner of Maple Leaf
Mills Limited, was built in St. Catharines, Ontario. The
Maple Leaf brand first appeared in 1898.

In 1901 Grantham Mills and Thorold Mills merged
to form Hedley Shaw Milling Company. Maple Leaf
Flour Mills Company was incorporated under the
Dominion of Canada letters patent in 1904. In 1907
Maple Leaf Flour Mills Company acquired Hedley Shaw
Milling Company and Grantham Mills. Three years
later Maple Leaf Milling Company Limited was formed
to take over the assets of Maple Leaf Flour. The Canada

Bread Company Limited, later to play a major role in Maple Leaf's history, was founded in 1911 through the amalgamation of five companies.

The 1920s were a time of consolidation for Canadian meatpackers who, increasingly, were relying on the export market to survive. In the latter years of the 19th century, miners and settlers had provided an expanding market for packers, but this demand leveled off around 1900. Worldwide demand for meat increased, however, and Canadian production increased correspondingly. Meat production grew to meet the demand created during World War I. Unfortunately, at war's end, the demand for Canadian meat dropped when Canada was cut off from the European market. Demand dropped again in 1921 when the United States imposed a tariff on Canadian beef. Within a few years, Canada was facing severe competition for the U.S. market from such countries as Argentina and Australia. The decreased demand for Canadian meat led to a decrease in the number of meat-processing plants in the country.

Meanwhile, the Harris Abattoir Company of Toronto had succeeded during the 1920s by lowering production costs. In 1927 Canada Packers Limited was formed as a holding company when Harris purchased Gunns Limited and Canadian Packing Company Limited and then merged with William Davies Limited. J. Stanley McLean, secretary-treasurer of Harris Abattoir, became the first president of Canada Packers and held the post for 30 years. Canada Packers realized a profit of more than CAD 1 million during its first year of operation.

After the merger, the four companies that made up Canada Packers remained as separate operating units and continued to compete with each other until the Great Depression forced a change in their operations. Meat prices were high, and a drought in the prairies resulted in high unemployment and a decreased demand for meat. The William Davies Toronto plant closed in 1931, and the four companies formed a single company in 1932. By 1933, operating expenses had been cut by CAD 7 million annually.

The company revived during the mid-1930s, largely because of the Ottawa Agreements, which allowed Canadian packers to export 280 million pounds of bacon a year to England. At the same time that production was increasing for the meatpacking side of the business, the by-product division began to sell a mixture of scraps as a feed concentrate for animal food. This was a new venture and one that was to prove extremely profitable. Animal feed consistently remained a reliable division of the company.

Canada Packers began expanding in 1936 with the building of a meat-processing plant in Alberta and the acquisition of a tannery in Ontario. In 1938 the company opened an additional packinghouse and renovated other plants. The capital investment between 1935 and 1938 came to more than CAD 2.5 million.

During World War II, Canada continued to supply meat to England, doubling the export of bacon. Despite a labor shortage, the number of people employed by Canada Packers doubled to more than 11,000. The war years and those that followed heralded two significant events for Canada Packers. First, driven by a need for increased efficiency during wartime, the company established a research laboratory, which led them into the production of synthetic vitamins, gelatin, synthetic detergents, and dairy products. By 1946, the chemical application of animal by-products was playing such a significant role that it was awarded the status of a separate division.

Second, in 1943 and 1944, workers at Canada Packers were organized by the United Packinghouse Workers of America, later to become the Canadian Food and Allied Workers Union. This event was to have an impact on earnings for years to come. In 1947 a nationwide strike involved 16,000 meatpacking workers across the country. Canada Packers negotiated new contracts two months later.

Anticipating a recession, Canada Packers stepped up its diversification efforts. The expected recession, however, did not materialize. Population growth coupled with an era of prosperity led to an increased demand for meat and meat products. The research laboratory began to focus on improved production methods, and automated slaughtering operations replaced the manual process. Similarly, the company applied new technology to the mass production of poultry. Canada Packers' sales were greater than those of its two closest competitors combined.

In the 1950s, per capita consumption of poultry doubled and continued to increase in each decade. Through investments, acquisitions, and the development of a feather-cleaning company, Canada Packers began to expand its operations in the poultry industry. In 1954 William McLean became president of the company.

KEY DATES

1898: Maple Leaf Brand first appears.

1904: Maple Leaf Flour Mills Company Limited is incorporated.

1907: Maple Leaf Flour Mills Company acquires Hedley Shaw Milling Company and Grantham Mills.

1910: Maple Leaf Milling Company Limited is formed to take over the assets of Maple Leaf Flour.

1911: Canada Bread Company Limited is founded.

1927: Canada Packers Limited is formed through a merger of other companies.

1961: Maple Leaf Mills Limited is formed from the amalgamation of Maple Leaf Milling Company Limited, Toronto Elevators Limited, and Purity Flour Mills Limited.

1969: Canada Bread Company is renamed Corporate Foods Limited.

1987: Hillsdown Holdings plc acquires Maple Leaf Mills; the latter holds a majority stake in Corporate Foods.

1991: Hillsdown merges Maple Leaf Mills into Canada Packers, forming Maple Leaf Foods Inc.; Hillsdown holds majority stake.

1995: McCain Capital Corporation and the Ontario Teachers' Pension Plan Board acquire controlling interest in Maple Leaf Foods from Hillsdown.

1997: Maple Leaf Foods divests the last of its flour-milling operations; Corporate Foods changes its name back to Canada Bread Company, Limited.

2004: Maple Leaf acquires Schneider Corporation in a CAD 500 million deal.

2006: In an important strategic shift, Maple Leaf begins a major downsizing of its pork-processing operations as it places greater emphasis on value-added consumer products.

2007: Company divests its animal feed unit.

2008: Outbreak of listeria infection, traced back to contaminated machinery at Maple Leaf Foods' Toronto factory, is blamed for the deaths of 20 Canadians.

In 1955 the company purchased two packers, initiating a dispute with the Restrictive Trade Commission. Canada Packers successfully argued, however, that industry-wide competition had increased and that the purchase would have no restraining effect. Also in the 1950s, Canada Packers reorganized its many interests into separate divisions: feed and fertilizer, consumer products, and canned and frozen vegetables. By 1958, only 55 percent of sales were from meat.

DRAMATIC CHANGES IN THE SIXTIES AND SEVENTIES

In 1961 Maple Leaf Mills Limited was officially formed from the amalgamation of Maple Leaf Milling Company Limited, Toronto Elevators Limited, and Purity Flour Mills Limited. Maple Leaf Mills Limited grew to be a prominent force in the production and distribution of flour-based products in Canada.

Within Canada Packers, expansion and diversification continued. The company built two poultry plants in New Brunswick and Quebec, expanded operations in Ontario and Manitoba, and purchased a plant in Alberta. By 1963, livestock production accounted for only 36 percent of the company's assets.

The 1960s brought about the most dramatic changes that Canada Packers had seen to date. International distribution became more commonplace, and production became more specialized. North American beef was spending more time in transit than any other meat because of the specialized processes of raising and producing beef. During this decade, Canada Packers created the largest private food-research facility in Canada, including new data-processing centers in Edmonton, Winnipeg, Toronto, and Montreal. Also, Canada Packers sold its fertilizer assets, and the feed operation became known as the Shur-Gain division.

The 1960s were a time of international expansion. Canada Packers purchased meatpackers in England, West Germany, and Australia. It set up trading companies in London and Hamburg and increased trading operations with the United States and Southeast Asia. At the end of the decade, exports accounted for CAD 145 million, or 16.5 percent of sales.

Labor disputes arose again, with a national strike in 1966 that hit Canada Packers the hardest of all the packing companies. A second strike followed in 1969. The strikes had an impact on earnings, but Canada Packers continued to increase capital spending throughout the 1970s. In this decade, the meatpacker expanded its facilities at a cost of CAD 137 million and purchased two additional Australian meat processors. The subsidiaries did not perform well for several years but were expected to ultimately fill the growing demand in Asia.

Canada Packers continued to diversify during the 1970s. It separated the management of its meatpacking unit from its other food-production groups. The fruit and vegetable segment was given division status in 1970, poultry in 1971, and edible oils and dairy in 1975. In 1975 Harris Laboratories was established to develop pharmaceuticals for human use. This enhanced the operations of the chemical division. The division also created MTC Pharmaceuticals for the veterinary-product industry.

Although the economic climate was not the best during this decade, Canada Packers continued to maintain acceptable earnings. The nonfood sector was the only one to show significant increases in the early 1970s. Animal feeds grew steadily, but the meat division was experiencing an earnings drain.

In 1978 Valentine N. Stock became president of Canada Packers. By the time of his death in 1987, the company had experienced a continued decline in beef demand and completed a 10-year consolidation. Stock turned Canada Packers toward the more profitable areas of fish farming, processed foods, salad oils, and pharmaceuticals.

Food packers in Canada suffered through a tough year in 1979. Costs increased and a seven-week labor dispute affected the industry, closing some plants. At the same time, McCain Foods, Canada Packers' major competitor, increased its holdings in Canada Packers to 10.3 percent. Fearing a takeover, Canada Packers repurchased 3.5 percent of its shares. No takeover occurred.

Canada Packers strengthened its nonfood exports when it acquired Delmar Chemicals Limited for CAD 18.2 million. Delmar joined the existing pharmaceutical division. Also in 1979, the Ontario government gave Canada Packers a CAD 4 million grant to construct a canola processing plant.

As the decade came to a close, profit margins were less than 1 percent for the third year in a row. Sales values had increased, adding to higher-cost inventories. Because the company had CAD 34.7 million in long-term debt, it grew through acquisitions and through higher profit margins from packaged meats. As consumer demand rose for convenience foods, meat processing was the only growth area.

THE TROUBLED EIGHTIES

For a variety of economic reasons, the 1980s were the most difficult time for Canada Packers since 1927. Thanks to geographic and product diversification, the company was able to withstand the serious blow to its beef business that occurred during this decade.

The year 1981 looked promising. Profits had reached a record CAD 30 million. However, when the industry went into another cyclical downturn, pork operations were disappointing, carcass prices rose, consumer demand lowered, and industry competition eroded earnings.

In 1983 profits plunged, while sales continued to grow. Expenses associated with plant closings, poor performances in fresh meat operations, and foreign subsidiaries eroded the bottom line. Processed meat remained profitable, but the packinghouse division performed the worst in its history. Canada Packers responded by cutting hundreds of jobs in the fresh meat division and earmarking CAD 50 million for structural improvements in the profitable areas.

Surprisingly, nonfood products showed a profit decrease in 1983. The company realized that meats were its core products. Despite fiercely competitive profit margins, meat realized a proven cash flow.

Another labor strike occurred in 1984. Involving 3,700 employees in the company's 12 plants, the labor action cost the company CAD 7.5 million. The strike prevented the Maple Leaf brand from appearing in retail markets and effectively strengthened competitors' products. Earnings declined.

Between 1984 and 1985, the company undertook the largest and most costly reorganization in its history. Canada Packers sold a number of unprofitable businesses, while purchasing meat plants and oil refineries. Over the next four years, earnings climbed at record rates to more than CAD 38 million. A joint venture with SEA Farm of Norway brought the company into fish farming. By decade's end, Canada Packers had fish production facilities on both coasts and was optimistic about the future of its fish farming activities.

Another strike loomed in 1986 but was prevented by reducing the scope of nationwide bargaining. The company managed to keep negotiations on a provincial and single-plant level. Two years after Valentine Stock's death in 1987, A. Roger Perretti became CEO. Perretti planned further acquisitions beyond the meat industry, and as Canada Packers approached the new decade it had exited the beef businesses and was focusing on pork and poultry.

CREATION OF MAPLE LEAF FOODS INC. IN THE EARLY NINETIES

An economic recession was on its way. Market sluggishness contributed to a drop in net income to CAD 12.59 million from sales of over CAD 3 billion. At this time, the U.K. firm Hillsdown Holdings plc stepped into the picture for Canada Packers. Hillsdown had in 1987 acquired Maple Leaf Mills, which itself had earlier purchased majority control of Corporate Foods Limited, the name adopted by the Canada Bread Company in 1969. In 1991 Hillsdown merged Maple Leaf Mills into Canada Packers, forming Maple Leaf Foods Inc. Hillsdown emerged with a controlling majority stake in Maple Leaf Foods. In the wake of these transactions, Maple Leaf Foods shut down a number of underperforming divisions, and the company entered a period of top-to-bottom reorganizing.

When the North American Free Trade Agreement (NAFTA) was signed with the United States and Mexico, Maple Leaf increased its focus on international operations. The company followed a strategy termed "in-filling," buying strategically placed companies that fill holes in the core business of processed meats and baked goods. By 1994, Maple Leaf generated 8 percent of its sales from the United States, while subsidiaries in Britain, Germany, and Japan were showing promising results.

Margins were lean during the early 1990s, but the company continued to show a profit and maintained a market share of almost half of all Canadian meatpacking. Despite sluggish sales, the company realized profits through cost-cutting.

WALLACE MCCAIN–LED TAKEOVER IN 1995

Following a contentious fight for control of his family's business (Maple Leaf's rival, McCain Foods), Wallace McCain was expelled from joint command of the family empire but remained as vice chairman. Stating he saw no conflict of interest in the arrangement, McCain then launched a billion-dollar debt-propelled bid for Maple Leaf Foods. Backed by the Ontario Teachers' Pension Plan Board, the McCain bid (conducted through McCain Capital Corporation) offered a combined stock-and-cash offer for Maple Leaf. Hillsdown announced its interest in selling its 56 percent of shares, hoping to raise cash for European investments. Hillsdown stated it would sell to McCain if no better offers arose. After looking fruitlessly for better offers, Maple Leaf's shareholders voted to accept Wallace McCain's takeover bid. As a result of this leveraged buyout, Maple Leaf Foods went from holding over CAD 100 million in cash to owing about CAD 575 million in long-term bank debt.

Wallace McCain assumed the position of CEO of Maple Leaf. McCain believed he could wring more profits from Maple Leaf Foods than had previously been

realized. His strategy was to turn Maple Leaf into a lean, low-cost maker of high-value-added foods, making it more of a market-driven rather than production-driven company. The CEO's son, Michael McCain, served as company president.

Under the McCains' leadership, the company continued to expand in the United States. Initiating a strategic thrust into the specialty bread-and-roll market in the United States, Maple Leaf built a CAD 30 million bakery in Virginia, bought bakeries in New Jersey and California, and purchased a bagel plant in Brooklyn, New York. Michael McCain indicated that the bakery business in the United States was to be the most significant growth area. In 1997, following a strategy of focusing on core business categories, Maple Leaf divested the last of its flour-milling operations. That same year, Corporate Foods was renamed Canada Bread Company, Limited.

The McCains' strategy of keeping profits high by reducing operating expenses led to a period of bitter labor disputes. In 1997 the workers at Gainers, a 91-year-old slaughtering plant in Edmonton, went on strike. Michael McCain followed through on his promise to shut the doors of the old plant if a strike occurred, stating his intent to build a massive new production complex in Brandon, Manitoba. About the same time, two meat-cutting plants in Ontario struck, while 200 butchers in Saskatchewan were locked out over a wage and benefit dispute.

Also in 1997, McCain attempted a hostile takeover bid to gain control of a rival company, Schneider Corporation. In 1998 Maple Leaf Foods formally abandoned its bid and announced an intent to sell its controlling stake in the Ontario company to Smithfield Foods, Inc., a hog producer in the United States. Later, in early 2001, Maple Leaf acquired Schneider's fresh pork operations in Manitoba.

The year 1998 proved to be Maple Leaf's worst since the McCain takeover. Weak earnings in the bread division, combined with labor disputes at Maple Leaf Meats and expenses associated with firing staff, led to the worst annual performance since 1995. In May 1999, however, shareholders were told that the company was back on track, posting its best first-quarter profit and announcing the sale of a coffee shop chain that had been deemed noncore. That year, Michael McCain was named CEO of Maple Leaf Foods, with his father remaining chairman.

Profits in 2000 fell to CAD 36.8 million compared to CAD 77.2 million in 1999. The company attributed the reduction to the decline in the pork business itself.

The Brandon plant, opened in 1999, lost CAD 20 million in the first quarter of 2000, and it continued to operate in the red until the fourth quarter of 2001. This turnaround, coupled with improvements in international markets and in value-added poultry products, helped propel Maple Leaf Foods in 2001 to record sales of CAD 4.78 billion and record operating profits of CAD 157.5 million.

DEAL MAKING AND RESTRUCTURING IN EARLY 21ST CENTURY

Also performing well at this time was the majority-owned, publicly traded Canada Bread Company, which had developed into a leading supplier of so-called par-baked bread, loaves partially baked, frozen, and then shipped to customers for final baking. In 2002 Maple Leaf helped strengthen Canada Bread by selling its U.S. and U.K. bakery units to its affiliate in a CAD 266 million deal. Canada Bread thus gained market leading positions in the U.S. par-based market and the U.K. bagel market. As part of the deal, Maple Leaf acquired a further four million shares of Canada Bread stock, increasing its stake to 73 percent. Over the next several years, Maple Leaf increased its interest in Canada Bread to nearly 90 percent.

Another important deal was completed in April 2004 when Maple Leaf Foods gained the firm it had unsuccessfully pursued half a decade earlier: Schneider Corporation. The Kitchener, Ontario-based Schneider was acquired from Smithfield Foods for approximately CAD 500 million in cash and assumed debt. Schneider specialized in premium, value-added products, including packaged processed meat, deli, and poultry products. The combination of Maple Leaf and Schneider created a company with about 35 percent of the Canadian market for prepared meat products. Following the deal, the Maple Leaf stable included three flagship consumer brands: Maple Leaf, Schneiders, and Dempster's.

The purchase of Schneider helped push the company's sales up to CAD 6.46 billion by 2005. The most significant development that year was a streamlining that saw Maple Leaf's operating companies reduced in number from 14 to 10. Several consumer food businesses, including Schneider Foods, were merged as Maple Leaf Consumer Foods, while the firm's fresh pork and poultry operations were consolidated as Maple Leaf Fresh Foods. The company's animal nutrition operations were combined as Maple Leaf Animal Nutrition. In addition, the international trading business was reorganized as Maple Leaf Global Foods, and this unit was charged with expanding beyond trading and diversifying into value-added products.

A further restructuring in 2006 was sparked by a sharp rise in the value of the Canadian dollar versus the U.S. dollar and the Japanese yen. This development severely undermined Maple Leaf's fresh pork business, prompting the company to shift strategy away from being a primary pork processor and increase its emphasis on value-added consumer products, including packaged meats and ready-to-eat meals. Maple Leaf launched a multiyear rationalization of its pork-processing operations whereby it consolidated this business within its flagship plant in Brandon, Manitoba, and sold, converted, or closed its other six pork-processing plants. In a further shift, this slimmed-down pork-processing business was turned into a largely internal operation, one that focused on supplying Maple Leaf's own value-added meat business rather than shipping production to outside customers. The company also elected to narrow its focus even more by placing its animal feed unit up for sale. In July 2007 Maple Leaf Animal Nutrition was sold to Netherlands-based Nutreco Holding BV for CAD 524.8 million.

2008 LISTERIA OUTBREAK

This restructuring was still being carried out in the summer of 2008 when Maple Leaf Foods was forced into crisis mode after a deadly outbreak of listeria infection was traced back to contaminated machinery at the company's Toronto factory. The company temporarily shut the plant down and recalled nearly 200 products, but not before the outbreak was blamed for the deaths of 20 Canadians and for making more than 30 others seriously ill. Michael McCain received some kudos for his handling of the crisis, with his repeated apologies for the outbreak and for quickly implementing enhanced safety protocols at his company's plants. Maple Leaf also had to contend with a series of class-action lawsuits filed by victims and victims' relatives, and in December 2008 the company agreed to make payments totaling CAD 27 million to settle the suits.

With the costs of the product recall totaling CAD 37.5 million, and the firm recording an additional CAD 65.3 million in restructuring costs, Maple Leaf ended up posting a net loss of CAD 36.8 million for 2008. The company was hurt further by a surge in commodity prices that year. During 2009 Maple Leaf continued implementing the restructuring launched three years earlier, while also retaining its heightened attention to food safety with the appointment of the firm's first chief food safety officer. The latter was one of a number of initiatives aimed at repairing the damage to the Maple

Leaf brand that had been caused by the listeria outbreak.

June Campbell
Updated, David E. Salamie

PRINCIPAL SUBSIDIARIES

Canada Bread Company, Limited (89.8%); Canada Bread Frozen Bakery Ltd. (89.8%); Canada Bread Atlantic Limited (89.8%); Multi-Marques Inc. (89.8%); Maple Leaf Bakery Inc. (U.S.A.; 89.8%); Maple Leaf Bakery UK Limited (89.8%); Aliments Martel Inc. (89.8%); Schneider Corporation; Maple Leaf Consumer Foods Inc.; Cold Springs Farm Limited (99.99%); Larsen Packers Limited; Maple Leaf Foods USA Inc.

PRINCIPAL DIVISIONS

Maple Leaf Consumer Foods; Maple Leaf Agri-Farms; Rothsay Rendering; Fresh Bakery Group; Frozen Bakery Group.

PRINCIPAL OPERATING UNITS

Meat Products Group; Agribusiness Group; Bakery Products Group.

PRINCIPAL COMPETITORS

Tyson Foods, Inc.; Smithfield Foods, Inc.; Premium Brands Income Fund; Cargill, Incorporated; Pilgrim's Pride Corporation; Hormel Foods Corporation; ConAgra Foods, Inc.; George Weston Limited; Interstate Bakeries Corporation.

FURTHER READING

Bertin, Oliver, "Maple Leaf Foods Buys Two Hog Plants," *Globe and Mail*, January 16, 2001, p. B12.

———, "Maple Leaf Looks at Expansion," *Globe and Mail*, May 21, 1992, p. B6.

———, "Maple Leaf Seeks Major Food Role," *Globe and Mail*, April 7, 1992, p. B3.

Blackwell, Richard, "Less Fresh Pork, More Stock Volatility," *Globe and Mail*, October 12, 2007, p. B9.

———, "Tough Times for Maple Leaf," *Globe and Mail*, September 8, 2008, p. B6.

Bourette, Susan, "Maple Leaf Backs McCain Bid," *Globe and Mail*, April 8, 1995, pp. Bl, B2.

———, "McCain Takes Helm at Maple Leaf," *Globe and Mail*, April 20, 1995, p. B3.

Campbell, Matthew, "Nationwide Outbreak Spurs Massive Meat Recall," *Globe and Mail*, August 21, 2008, p. A1.

Galloway, Gloria, "Company, Government Faulted in Listeria Deaths," *Globe and Mail*, July 22, 2009, p. A4.

Heinrich, Kim, "Maple Leaf Takeover New Incentive for Bakery," *Vancouver Sun*, July 14, 1992, p. D2.

Laghi, Brian, "When the Maple Leaf Isn't Forever," *Globe and Mail*, December 5, 1997, p. A2.

"Maple Leaf Says It's Back on Profit Track," *Vancouver Sun*, May 4, 1999, p. D4.

Marotte, Bertrand, "Maple Leaf Buys Schneider," *Globe and Mail*, September 26, 2003, p. B1.

"Michael McCain to Add Title of Chief Executive at Maple Leaf Foods," *Vancouver Sun*, September 15, 1998.

Olijnyk, Zena, "Hot Dog!" *Canadian Business*, October 14, 2003, p. 47.

Owram, Kristine, "Maple Leaf Claims 'Progress' After Recall," *Globe and Mail*, February 25, 2009, p. B5.

Parkinson, David, and Andy Hoffman, "Maple Leaf Takes an Axe to Pork Operations," *Globe and Mail*, October 13, 2006, p. B1.

Pitts, Gordon, "McCain Brothers Unlikely to End Feud," *Globe and Mail*, December 24, 2001, p. B1.

———, "The Testing of Michael McCain," *Globe and Mail*, November 28, 2008, pp. 60+.

Saunders, John, "Wallace McCain Foresees Maple Leaf as Grade A Prize," *Globe and Mail*, March 5, 1995, p. Bl.

———, "Wallace McCain Seeks New Food Empire," *Globe and Mail*, March 7, 1995, p. A1.

Simon, Bernard, "Maple Leaf Strives to Contain Damage After Listeria Deaths," *Financial Times*, August 27, 2008, p. 15.

McKesson Corporation

One Post Street
San Francisco, California 94104
U.S.A.
Telephone: (415) 983-8300
Fax: (415) 983-7160
Web site: http://www.mckesson.com

Public Company
Incorporated: 1928 as McKesson & Robbins
Employees: 32,000
Sales: $106.63 billion (2009)
Stock Exchanges: New York
Ticker Symbol: MCK
NAICS: 424210 Drugs and Druggists' Sundries Merchant Wholesalers; 541611 Administrative Management and General Management Consulting Services; 541614 Process, Physical Distribution, and Logistics Consulting Services

■ ■ ■

McKesson Corporation is the largest pharmaceutical distributor in North America, responsible for supplying one-third of medicines used each day. The company divides its business into two segments, McKesson Distribution Solutions and McKesson Technology Solutions. By far the larger of the two segments, McKesson Distribution Solutions distributes ethical and proprietary drugs, surgical supplies and equipment, and health and beauty care products to more than 40,000 retail stores, hospitals, and physician practices. McKesson Distribution Solutions accounts for 97 percent of the company's annual revenues. The much smaller segment, McKesson Technology Solutions, provides a full range of management and consulting services to hospitals, retail pharmacies, health-care insurers, and physicians in North America, Europe, and the Asia-Pacific region. The company's hardware and software technology is installed in more than 70 percent of U.S.-based hospitals with more than 200 beds. McKesson ranks as the 15th-largest company in the United States.

ORIGINS AND CHANGES IN THE 19TH AND EARLY 20TH CENTURY

In 1833 John McKesson and partner Charles Olcott founded Olcott & McKesson, a wholesale and import drug company in Manhattan that provided herbal products. Twenty years later with the addition of Daniel Robbins and the death of Olcott, the firm changed its name to McKesson & Robbins. Yet this was just the beginning of the changes experienced by McKesson. When McKesson died in 1893, the McKesson heirs left the company in order to form the New York Quinine and Chemical Works. By 1900 McKesson & Robbins had partially consolidated its industry by persuading several large wholesale drug distributors to become McKesson subsidiaries.

In 1926, McKesson & Robbins was sold to Frank D. Coster. The ownership transition plunged McKesson & Robbins into 13 years of disrepute attributed directly to its new owner and his crime-prone family. Coster, whose real name was Philip Musica, was the son of a New York importer of Italian foods. The Musica family had prospered in the import trade primarily by bribing dock customs officials to falsify shipment weights. When the Musica team was arrested in 1909, Philip paid a $5,000 fine and served five months in prison for the crime.

The prison experience did not reform the criminal family, however, and they were again arrested in 1913 on similar charges. This time, a hair importing business started after Philip Musica left prison had racked up $500,000 in bank debt based on virtually nonexistent security. A bank investigation revealed that the supposedly valuable hair pieces being used for collateral were in fact only worthless ends and short pieces of hair. The Musica family was caught trying to escape on a departing New Orleans ship. Once again, Philip was the scapegoat for the family escapades; he served three years in prison. When he was released in 1916 he worked for the district attorney's office as an undercover agent named William Johnson.

During World War I, Musica began a poultry business, but his entanglement with the law was not over. After evading conviction for a 1920 murder, he changed his business interests from poultry to pharmaceuticals, posing as president of Adelphi Pharmaceutical Manufacturing Company in Brooklyn. In spite of many "second chances," Musica appeared unable to avoid a life of crime; his new venture, a partnership with Joseph Brandino, was actually a front for a bootlegging concern.

When Adelphi failed, Musica changed his name to Frank D. Coster. Hoping to put his criminal past behind him, Coster managed to establish himself as a respectable businessman by starting a hair tonic company that had a supposedly large customer list. With this apparently firm collateral, Coster seemed a viable acquirer when he offered to purchase McKesson & Robbins in 1926. In fact, for 13 years thereafter, Coster was able to keep his identity a secret; he was even listed in *Who's Who in America*, where he was described as a

businessman as well as a "practicing physician" from 1912 to 1914.

Coster went on an acquisition spree when the Great Depression weakened many competitors. In 1928 and 1929 alone, he added wholesale drug companies in 42 cities to McKesson & Robbins's U.S. and Canadian operations. Five more firms were acquired from 1930 to 1937. Meanwhile, 1929 sales had reached $140 million, and the company earned $4.1 million in profits.

Coster's true identity was revealed in 1938 when a treasurer at McKesson & Robbins became concerned over the way the profits were being handled. That curiosity soon led to an investigation that revealed a $3 million embezzlement scheme perpetrated by Coster. Some of the money was used to pay blackmail fees to his former partner, Brandino, who had discovered Coster's true identity and threatened to expose him. In 1939 Coster shot himself and Brandino was convicted of blackmail.

POST–WORLD WAR II HISTORY

The company reorganized in the early 1940s and returned to private ownership. Its operations were presumably closely held during this period. The company's calm and relatively quiet existence was intruded upon in 1967, however, when Foremost Dairies of California implemented a hostile takeover. Acrimony over the conduct of the buyout fostered an unhappy relationship between the managers of the new "partners" for several years after the merger. In fact, it was three years before McKesson offices were even moved to San Francisco, the headquarters of Foremost.

The new company formed by this merger, Foremost-McKesson, Inc., had no corporate strategy and appeared to be moving in several different directions at the same time. Rudolph Drews, head of the unified firm, was described by *Forbes* magazine as the "freewheeling" president who had acquired several diverse companies from "sporting goods to candy" after the merger with McKesson and who was better at making acquisitions than managing them. In 1974 Drews was forced from the corporation after a daylong board meeting; his management style was considered the cause for a "flattening" of earnings.

MID-SEVENTIES: COMPANY FENDS OFF A TAKEOVER

Drews's response, "I'll be back," after he was fired from Foremost-McKesson was no idle threat. Drews established his own corporate merger consulting business and found an opportunity in 1976 to orchestrate a

KEY DATES

■

1833: Partnership of Olcott & McKesson is founded.

1853: Business is renamed McKesson & Robbins.

1893: Founder John McKesson dies and his heirs leave the company.

1926: Frank D. Coster, a criminal whose real name was Philip Musica, buys the company.

1928: McKesson & Robbins is incorporated.

c. 1940: Company becomes privately owned after Coster kills himself in 1939.

1967: Foremost Dairies takes over the company, which becomes Foremost-McKesson, Inc.

1970: Company moves its headquarters to San Francisco.

1976: Company avoids a hostile takeover, is reorganized, and acquires C.F. Mueller Company and Gentry International.

1979: Armor All Products is acquired as McKesson enters the car protection products industry.

1983: Company acquires Zee Medical, Inc., and sells C.F. Mueller and Foremost Dairies.

1984: Company is renamed McKesson Corporation.

1986: McKesson Chemical Division is sold to Univar Corporation.

1989: McKesson gains Wal-Mart Stores as a major customer.

1990: Company gains control of Medis Health and Pharmaceutical, Canada's major drug wholesaler.

1994: McKesson acquires Integrated Medical Systems Inc. and decides to sell PCS Health Systems to Eli Lilly & Company.

1998: Company acquires Red Line HealthCare Corporation.

1999: January merger with HBO & Company creates McKesson HBOC Inc.; Kelly/Waldron & Company and Kelly Waldron/Technologies Solutions are acquired.

2000: McKesson acquires Prospective Health, Inc., and sells its Water Products business; company renews its contract with ShopKo Stores for five years.

2001: Firm introduces Supply Management Online to increase its Internet capabilities.

2002: John H. Hammergren adds the duties of chairman to his responsibilities as chief executive officer and president.

2005: McKesson pays $960 million to settle a lawsuit related to its purchase of HBO & Co.

2007: McKesson pays $1.8 billion for Per-Se Technologies Inc.

2008: Revenues exceed $100 billion for the first time.

takeover bid of his former company. Drews's middleman for the corporate raid was Victor Posner, a Miami multimillionaire who saw his own opportunity to buy out Foremost-McKesson. William Morison, who had succeeded Drews as president of Foremost-McKesson, worked hard to prevent Sharon Steel, Posner's Pennsylvania firm, from acquiring his company's stock. Although Posner was able to obtain 10 percent of Foremost-McKesson's equity, he soon found that the price of the stock could be measured in more than dollars and cents.

Morison's defense strategy focused on a negative public relations campaign that targeted Posner and Sharon Steel. Careful, well-publicized research revealed that Sharon Steel Corporation had overstated its earnings for 1975 by 45 percent in order to support its takeover offer. According to *Forbes*, Posner was

"scourged coast to coast" for his tactics as a "corporate marauder." Having repulsed Posner and Drews's takeover attempt, Foremost-McKesson stockholders approved a charter change that prohibited any "unsuitable" party from acquiring more than 10 percent of the company's common stock. An unsuitable party was defined as any business that might jeopardize Foremost's liquor or drug licenses.

Although the takeover crisis only lasted a few months, Foremost-McKesson suffered long-term consequences. The company had lost valuable time in executing the turnaround plans devised by the new president, Morison. Morison was determined to make the company a more dynamic, streamlined operation. Up to this point, Foremost-McKesson had been viewed as two companies wedded together with no real direction or focus. Morison complained that "people on the

East Coast think of us as McKesson the drug company, and people on the West Coast think of us as Foremost the dairy company, and we don't think either one really fits anymore." Morison hoped not only to turn Foremost-McKesson around operationally, but also to create a new corporate image. In 1977, Executive Vice-President Thomas E. Drohan compared the company to an elephant that, under the new direction of Morison, was "off its knees and ambling noisily."

Morison had, in fact, worked to implement a reorganization in the midst of the 1976 battle to maintain autonomy. That year, Foremost-McKesson made two major acquisitions and sold or combined 11 of its less vital operations. Morison wanted to move the company away from its role of middleman as a wholesale distributor of pharmaceutical products, beverages, and liquor, and emphasize production of proprietary products. His objective was to streamline the company by selling its low-profit operations and investing $200 million into new businesses by 1990. Although the battle with Posner sidelined many of these goals, Foremost's acquisitions of C.F. Mueller Company, the country's largest pasta marker, and Gentry International, a processor of onion and garlic, were two significant acquisitions made in 1976 that met the objectives set by Morison.

Over the course of the two years before Morison's retirement, he reorganized the company into four major operating groups: drugs and health care, wine and spirits, foods, and chemicals, as well as a small home-building division. This new strategic plan was the first of its kind for Foremost-McKesson, and it was one factor that placed the company in a more comfortable position for the future.

Thomas P. Drohan, who was elected president upon Morison's 1978 retirement, continued his predecessor's strategy. Drohan's defense against corporate raids was to maintain a prohibitively high stock price. His management style focused on productivity and efficiency. Specifically, he automated inventory and stock procedures, allowing Foremost to reduce personnel costs by a third.

Drohan also redefined the company's "middleman" role in the distribution chain by establishing data-processing procedures that would be valuable to both suppliers and customers, placing Foremost-McKesson in the position of acting as part of the marketing teams. This business strategy has been characterized by one *Harvard Business Review* analyst as a "value adding partnership." Over the course of the 1980s, independent druggists were faced with competition from powerful mass and discount drug chains. Foremost-McKesson's value adding partnership offered these small business owners, many of whom could not afford the computerized inventory controls that were a key to the national chains' success, the benefits of automated systems without the expense. These practices catapulted the company to the vanguard of wholesale practices and contributed to average annual profit increases of 20 percent, 10 times the rate recorded before 1976.

DIVESTITURES AND ACQUISITIONS IN THE EARLY EIGHTIES

Neil Harlan succeeded to the chairmanship of Foremost-McKesson in 1979. A former army captain, Harvard business professor, and McKinsey & Company director, Harlan soon initiated a second restructuring, selling the pieces of the company that did not fit its distribution image. In 1983 alone, Harlan divested more than one-third of the conglomerate's holdings to focus on health-care and retail products. Divisions sold included C.F. Mueller as well as Foremost Dairies and its food processing and residential construction subsidiaries.

In 1983 McKesson acquired Zee Medical, Inc. Formed in 1959, Zee Medical provided occupational safety and first-aid products. This McKesson subsidiary had grown rapidly after the federal government in 1971 increased workplace safety demands through the Occupational Safety and Health Administration. By around 2000 Zee Medical was a $100 million business that served more than 300,000 manufacturing plants, hotels, and other facilities.

Acquisitions made in the early part of the decade strengthened Foremost-McKesson's role as a major distributor of health-care products. In 1982 the drug distribution business contributed $2.1 billion to the company's $4 billion in sales. Fueled by $90 million in acquisitions of distribution and distribution-related businesses, revenues increased steadily in the early 1980s. Harlan's aggressive consolidation helped make McKesson one of the leaders in wholesale distribution. His strategy was twofold; he believed that "any company that doesn't stick to what it does best is inviting trouble" and that "anybody who doesn't prepare [for a raider] is living in a dreamworld." A 1984 name change, to McKesson Corporation, reflected the declining influence of food operations.

Harlan, a popular leader, retired in 1986 and was succeeded by Thomas W. Field Jr., formerly of American Stores Co., a national grocery chain. That same year, McKesson sold its poorly performing chemical distribution division, McKesson Chemical, to Univar Corp. for $76 million. Proceeds of the sale funded acquisitions of additional drug and health-care-product distributors, software firms, and medical equipment distributors. The company also raised funds for capital investments through the public offering of shares amounting to about 15 percent of subsidiary Armor All Products Corp. and a similar stake in prescription reimbursement division PCS Health Systems Inc. in 1986. Part of the proceeds went toward a $115 million expenditure on increased automation and efficient new distribution hubs.

McKesson had acquired Armor All, the company that launched the automotive protective market, in 1979. After suffering five years of limited profits, Armor All took off in the late 1980s. Within four years of entering the Japanese market in 1984, the product had captured one-fourth of the market. By the late 1980s, Armor All had achieved $126 million in annual sales and held 90 percent of the U.S. auto protectant market. Hoping to parlay its complete dominance of this category into continuously increasing sales, McKesson expanded Armor All's product line to include car waxes, detergents, and spray cleaners. By 1993, the products were offered in more than 50 countries. McKesson's bottled water subsidiary also paid off during this period: From 1980 to 1990, the U.S. market for bottled water grew by 250 percent, and McKesson's Sparklett's brand enjoyed a number-two ranking in that industry.

Although profits rose 33 percent and sales increased 46 percent over the course of CEO Field's term in office, he abruptly resigned in September 1989 amid difficulties related to McKesson's prescription reimbursement division, PCS Health Systems Inc. PCS managed pharmaceutical costs for the sponsors of corporate, government, and insurance health-care plans by performing cost-benefit analyses of drugs and recommending the top candidates to its customers. Under pressure from insurance companies to cut costs, PCS had tried to reduce reimbursements to pharmacists and drugstore chains. When major customers, including Rite Aid Corp. and Wal-Mart Stores, balked at the cuts, McKesson scrambled to keep both its constituencies satisfied. Harlan came out of retirement to serve as McKesson's interim CEO. Harlan was able to rejoin the ranks of the retired by the end of the year, when Alan Seelenfreund, a 14-year veteran of McKesson, advanced to chairman and CEO.

By 1990 McKesson was the industry leader in the drug wholesaling business. Its 27 percent market share was twice the percentage of its main competitor, Bergen Brunswig. McKesson in 1990 sold about 120,000 different products ranging from over-the-counter medicines to prescription drugs. Its customers included 2,500 hospitals, 14,000 independent drugstores, and 3,000 chain stores. Its annual sales of $7.6 billion and profits

of $106 million came from the hard work of 15,800 employees.

EXPANSION AND CHANGES IN THE NINETIES AND THE NEW MILLENNIUM

Ironically, after causing such an uproar in the late 1980s, PCS evolved into a vital segment of McKesson's business in the early 1990s. During that time, PCS recorded sales and earnings increases of 50 percent annually, and although the company only contributed 2 percent of McKesson's annual sales, it brought in 20 percent of its profits. The parent company moved to transform PCS into what *Business Week* called "a full-fledged medical-services-management company" through the early 1994 acquisition of Integrated Medical Systems Inc., an electronic network designed to connect doctors, hospitals, medical laboratories, and pharmacies. Although these two acquisitions improved McKesson's operations, they also attracted the attention of an increasingly acquisitive pharmaceutical industry. In 1993, Merck & Co., then the world's largest ethical drug company, or producer of doctor-prescribed drugs, bought Medco Containment, a rival drug distributor, for $6.6 billion.

Merck's move prompted speculation that PCS and parent McKesson were the next logical takeover targets. McKesson's stock increased by more than 40 percent from July 1993 (when the Medco deal was announced) to February 1994. To a limited extent that speculation became reality later that year, when McKesson agreed to sell PCS to Eli Lilly & Co. for $4 billion in cash.

McKesson used the sale as an opportunity to restructure its finances: The company gave shareholders $76 plus a new share in McKesson in exchange for each old McKesson share they held. The remaining $600 million in proceeds from the sale were reinvested in the company. CEO Seelenfreund looked to McKesson's future in the company's annual report for 1993. He noted, "In the competitive environment created by efforts to bring rising health care costs under control, the winners will be those organizations that have both the financial strength and the technological skills needed to improve the quality of care while cutting their own costs and those of their customers. McKesson is one of the few companies that possess both these strengths." McKesson's expansion in the 1990s was fueled by several acquisitions. On November 17, 1998, it announced the acquisition of Red Line HealthCare Corporation, a Novartis subsidiary whose headquarters remained in Golden Valley, Minnesota. A distributor of medical services and supplies for extended care facilities,

Red Line reported sales of about $375 million for the fiscal year that ended on August 31, 1998.

ACQUISITION OF HBO & CO. IN 1999

In January 1999 McKesson through a subsidiary completed its merger with HBO & Company (NAS-DAQ: HBOC) to form McKesson HBOC, Inc. The merged business that began operations on January 13, 1999 was "the world's largest healthcare services company," according to a press release.

In 1999 McKesson HBOC acquired two other companies. First it acquired Kelly/Waldron & Company and Kelly Waldron/Technologies Solutions, which provided market research, database services, and automated systems to help strengthen the corporation's sales and marketing efforts. The two acquired businesses had revenue of about $25 million in 1998. Later in 1999 McKesson acquired the Minneapolis company of Abaton.com, Inc., a private firm that offered Internet based prescribing, laboratory requests and results, and related services to doctors' offices. Prospective Health, Inc., (PHI)'s acquisition by McKesson HBOC was announced in a press release dated January 31, 2000. Headquartered in Palos Heights, Illinois, PHI and its 50 employees developed software for the health-care industry.

MCKESSON IN THE 21ST CENTURY

About a month later, on February 29, 2000, McKesson announced the sale of subsidiary McKesson Water Products Company to Groupe Danone for $1.1 billion in cash. That was the final step that began in the 1980s to end the company's diverse operations. "This sale completes the company's transition to a focused health care company, with market-leading positions in health-care information technology and supply management," said John H. Hammergren and David L. Mahoney, company co-CEOs and co-presidents, in a February 29, 2000 announcement.

At the end of fiscal 2000, which ended March 31, 2000, McKesson HBOC reported total revenues of $36.7 billion, a 22.3 percent increase over its $30 billion in total revenues for fiscal 1999. The corporation's fiscal year 2000 total revenues came from four sources: (1) pharmaceutical distribution and services, $24.1 billion; (2) medical-surgical distribution, $2.7 billion; (3) sales to customers' warehouses, $8.7 billion; and (4) information technology, $1.2 billion. Including special items, the company in fiscal 2000 earned a net income

of $723.7 million, up from $84.9 million the year before.

The company on July 24, 2000 announced it had signed a three-year contract with Wal-Mart Stores to continue providing pharmaceuticals for the chain of 1,773 Wal-Mart stores, 780 Supercenters, 466 Sam's Clubs, and five Wal-Mart warehouses. A Wal-Mart executive praised McKesson for its innovative service and technological prowess that led to the renewal of a business relationship that began in 1989.

In September 2000 McKesson HBOC Information Technology Business signed an agreement to acquire the MED-Solution system of Montgomery, Alabama's Health Care Systems, Inc. This was part of the company's efforts to improve the reliability and safety of drug dispensing in hospitals and other institutions. Through its automated systems, the company planned to ensure that the right patients received the right medications at the right times. Adverse drug events that led to deaths and suffering were a major problem according to the Institute of Medicine's 1999 study called *To Err Is Human: Building a Safer Health System.*

In early December 2000 McKesson HBOC's Clinical and Biological Services announced a strategic alliance with DHP Ltd., an Abergavenny, United Kingdom, clinical trial supplies company. This agreement resulted from increased globalization of the pharmaceutical and biotechnology industries that both companies served.

McKesson in late 2001 announced another expansion of its U.K. operations. In 1990 its Information Solutions business had started in the United Kingdom, but in 2001 it signed a $480 million 10-year contract to provide automated human resources and payroll systems to the government's National Health Service Information Authority.

During the first decade of the 21st century, McKesson enjoyed phenomenal financial growth. Between 2001 and 2009, the company's revenues leaped from $42 billion to a staggering $106 billion, an increase that made the San Francisco-based distributor the 15th-largest company in the United States. McKesson reigned supreme, eclipsing its closest rivals, Cardinal Health, Inc., and AmerisourceBergen Corp., to stand atop its industry, but the mood was not entirely carefree at company headquarters. McKesson suffered from a persisting and frustrating condition, one that had plagued the company for decades. Profits, no matter the size of the company, were hard to come by in the drug distribution business.

"McKesson Corp. holds the unenviable distinction of being one of the world's largest yet least profitable companies," *Business Week* noted in an August 7, 2006 article. The company subsisted on gross profit margins of just 3 percent, earning a fraction of what similarly sized companies earned in other industries. The challenge of increasing the company's profitability was taken on by Hammergren, who was appointed president and chief executive officer in 2001 and chairman in 2002.

TECHNOLOGY UNIT DRIVES
PROFIT GROWTH

One of the ways McKesson sought to increase its profit margin was to diversify into the lucrative business of marketing technology to hospitals, insurance companies, and doctors, a facet of the company's operations organized in its McKesson Technology Solutions segment. Execution of the strategy began in 1999 with the $12 billion acquisition of HBO & Co. and the results were disastrous. Soon after the acquisition was completed, McKesson discovered that HBO's previous management had inflated the company's revenues, which forced McKesson to restate its financial totals in 1999. The accounting improprieties touched off a securities class-action lawsuit that McKesson settled in 2005, paying a hefty $960 million to HBO and McKesson shareholders.

Despite the miserable start to the diversification campaign, Hammergren pressed forward with expanding McKesson Technology Solutions' capabilities. Rather than develop the business internally, he looked to build the segment through acquisitions, seeking innovative companies whose software provided clinical, patient care, financial, strategic, and supply chain solutions. By 2006, Hammergren could point to positive results, a year that saw McKesson purchase a billing software developer, HealthCom Partners, and RelayHealth, a developer of an Internet-based office management system for doctors. McKesson generated $88 billion in sales during the year, collecting only a fraction, $1.5 billion, from its technology unit, but McKesson Technology Solutions posted a gross profit margin of 46.7 percent, exponentially higher than the 3 percent registered by the drug distribution business.

As McKesson's 80th anniversary neared, Hammergren continued to add to the company's technology business, but he did not ignore its lifeblood: drug distribution. In late 2006, McKesson renewed its contract with the largest retailer in the world, Wal-Mart Stores Inc. The agreement signed in November maintained McKesson as the primary supplier of branded pharmaceutical products to the chain's 4,000 stores in the United States. In 2007, the company spent $519 million to acquire San Francisco-based OTN, a distributor of specialty pharmaceuticals in the United States. The year's largest purchase occurred within the McKesson Technology Solutions segment. At the beginning of the year, McKesson paid $1.8 billion for Per-Se Technologies Inc., an Alpharetta, Georgia-based provider of administrative services to hospitals, doctors, and pharmacies. Per-Se served 100,000 physicians in small practices, 17,000 hospital-affiliated physicians, 3,000 hospitals, and 50,000 retail pharmacies. The addition of Per-Se more than doubled the number of transactions McKesson processed for physicians and hospitals to 560 million annually. One month after the Per-Se acquisition, McKesson acquired Physician Micro Systems, Inc., for an undisclosed sum. Physician Micro, operating under the name Practice Partner, was a developer of software that provided clinical and administrative tools to physicians.

MCKESSON TURNS 80

In 2008, McKesson's 80th anniversary, the company reached a major financial milestone, posting $101 billion in revenues. Perhaps of greater significance was the company's profit total, which had increased substantially as its McKesson Technology Systems segment grew into a $3 billion business. Thanks largely to the acquisitions completed with the technology segment, McKesson's net income swelled from $751 million in 2006 to $990 million in 2008. In the years ahead, Hammergren intended to continue developing McKesson's technology arm while also paying close attention to the company's mainstay drug distribution business.

Updated, April Dougal Gasbarre;
David M. Walden; Jeffrey L. Covell

PRINCIPAL SUBSIDIARIES

Moore Medical LLC; McKesson Medical-Surgical, Inc.; McKesson Canada; McKesson Information Solutions UK Ltd.; McKesson United Kingdom; McKesson France; McKesson Netherlands; McKesson Asia-Pacific (Australia); Zee Medical Inc.; McKesson Pharmaceutical; McKesson Provider Technologies; Parata Systems; McKesson Pharmacy Systems; McKesson Health Solutions; McKesson Specialty Care Solutions; McKesson Patient Relationship Solutions; RelayHealth.

PRINCIPAL COMPETITORS

Cardinal Health, Inc.; AmerisourceBergen Corporation; Owens & Minor, Inc.

FURTHER READING

Byrne, Harlan S., "McKesson Corp.: Big Drug Distributor Bounces Back from a Bummer Year," *Barron's*, June 25,

1990, pp. 51–52.

Fox, Ben, "McKesson Acquires Practice Partner for Undisclosed Sum," *America's Intelligence Wire,* February 26, 2007.

"A Healthy Outlook for McKesson," *Business Week Online,* April 4, 2006.

Hof, Robert, "McKesson Dumps Another Asset: The Boss," *Business Week,* September 25, 1989, p. 47.

Johnston, Russell, "Beyond Vertical Integration: The Rise of the Value-Adding Partnership," *Harvard Business Review,* July/ August 1988, pp. 94–101.

"McKesson Agrees to Pay $960 Million to Settle Class Suit," *America's Intelligence Wire,* January 12, 2005.

"McKesson Corp. Completes Acquisition of Medical Records Provider," *America's Intelligence Wire,* February 27, 2007.

Mitchell, Russell, and Joseph Weber, "And the Next Juicy Plum May Be McKesson?" *Business Week,* February 28, 1994, p. 36.

Moskowitz, Milton, Robert Levering, and Michael Katz, editors, "McKesson," in *Everybody's Business: A Field Guide to the 400 Leading Companies in America,* New York: Doubleday/Currency, 1990, pp. 228–30.

Schlax, Julie, "Strategies: A Good Reason to Mess with Success," *Forbes,* September 19, 1988, pp. 95–96.

Stringer, David, "McKesson, Wal-Mart Continue Supply Agreement," *America's Intelligence Wire,* November 24, 2006.

"Update 4—McKesson to Acquire Per-Se Technologies in $1.8 Billion Deal," *America's Intelligence Wire,* November 6, 2006.

Mettler-Toledo
International Inc.

———— ■ ————

Im Langacher
P.O. Box MT-100
Greifensee, CH 8606
Switzerland
Telephone: (+41-44) 944-22-11
Fax: (+44-41) 944-24-70
Web site: http://www.mt.com

Public Company
Founded: 1945 as Einzelfirma E. Mettler
Employees: 10,000
Sales: $1.97 billion (2008)
Stock Exchanges: New York
Ticker Symbol: MTD
NAICS: 333997 Scale and Balance Manufacturing; 334513 Instruments and Related Products Manufacturing for Measuring, Displaying, and Controlling Industrial Process Variables; 334516 Analytical Laboratory Instrument Manufacturing; 334517 Irradiation Apparatus Manufacturing; 334519 Other Measuring and Controlling Device Manufacturing; 511210 Software Publishers; 811219 Other Electronic and Precision Equipment Repair and Maintenance; 811310 Commercial and Industrial Machinery and Equipment (Except Automotive and Electronic) Repair and Maintenance

■ ■ ■

Mettler-Toledo International Inc. is the world's leading manufacturer of precision weighing instruments and a leading producer of other precision analytical instruments for the laboratory and industrial/retail markets. The company holds leading positions in most of its product categories, including the global laboratory balance market. Other major lines include laboratory pipettes for measuring and dispensing liquids; analytical instruments such as titrators, thermal analysis systems, pH meters, and automated lab reactors; industrial weighing instruments; and food retailing weighing, packaging, pricing, wrapping, and labeling equipment. Mettler-Toledo is also a world leader in product inspection equipment, including metal detectors and X-ray visioning equipment, used in the cosmetics, food processing, pharmaceutical, and other industries. The company markets and services its products in 35 countries around the world, with Europe accounting for about 43 percent of sales; the Americas, 22 percent; and China, 11 percent. More than half of the firm's workforce consists of sales, marketing, customer service, and post-sales technical service personnel. Based in Greifensee, Switzerland, with its U.S. headquarters in Columbus, Ohio, Mettler-Toledo trades on the New York Stock Exchange.

MID-20TH-CENTURY BALANCING ACT

Mettler-Toledo built its global leadership position both through internal growth and a long history of acquisitions, enabling the company to strengthen its core market areas while expanding into diversified markets. Although parts of the company, including its Toledo line, established in 1901 as the Toledo Scale Company in the United States, predate the company, Mettler

342   INTERNATIONAL DIRECTORY OF COMPANY HISTORIES, VOLUME 108

COMPANY PERSPECTIVES

Innovation means traditional research and development, but it goes beyond technology and involves all of our employees. Mettler Toledo has long been a leader in innovation—not only in products and services, but in the way we think about everything. Innovation is the art of finding answers before the question is asked.

Our Company's culture centers on innovation. We spend considerably more than our peers on product development. Originally known for weighing technologies, today we are a recognized leader in communications, optics, robotics and other technologies as well as software to integrate these technologies into powerful lab, industrial and retail solutions. We are committed to ensuring our innovations translate into real value for customers like you.

traces its official origins to 1945 and the invention of the single-pan analytical balance by company founder Erhard Mettler. The company was established as Einzelfirma E. Mettler, in Küsnacht, Switzerland. With the introduction of its scale, the company broke the less accurate two-pan weighing mold, using Mettler's so-called substitution principle to achieve more accurate measurements. Large-scale production of the unit began in 1946. From the start, the company looked toward the international market for its sales.

Mettler continued to refine its technology. In 1952 it introduced the Mettler Mikrowaage ("Microscale"), capable of measurements to 0.000001 grams. Several years later, the company was able to increase the accuracy of its measurements still further, bringing measurements to the seventh place after the decimal point. At the same time, the company began marketing a range of precision scales for weight measurements from 0.1 grams to 0.01 grams.

The company's increasing sales brought it to its first expansion moves in 1952, with the opening of the Stäfa, Switzerland, production facility, which would undergo a series of extensions and remain in use into the 1990s. Two years later, the company's increasing international presence, in particular in the United States, led it to open its first international subsidiary, Mettler Instrument Corp., in Hightstown, New Jersey. This international expansion would be followed by the company's move into Giessen, Germany, in 1957. From

there, the company expanded throughout Europe, and later throughout much of the world, to place its subsidiaries and its products closer to its clients. This would form the basis of the company's sales strategy, centered around a locally based sales staff.

After more than a decade of strong internal growth, Mettler prepared for its first acquisition. In 1962 the company acquired Dr. Ernst Rüst AG, a maker of high-precision mechanical scales, which had been founded just three years before. The newly added division was subsequently renamed Mettler Optic AG. Mettler also made its first moves at expanding its product categories, introducing a thermal analyzer, the TA 1, in 1964. By the end of the decade, the company had delivered more than 100 units of this product.

In 1965 Mettler opened a new assembly facility, in Uznach, Switzerland, which initially employed just three people for the assembly of the company's precision balances. At the company's Stäfa production facility, Mettler was preparing the rollout of a new product group, the FP line, an apparatus for melting point determination. Initial production was 100 units; the product line would retain a key place in the company's catalog, while undergoing successive technological improvements in the coming decades. The FP line was joined by the TM line of temperature analysis instruments, introduced in 1968, as well as the PE line of precision balances, the company's first scales to incorporate emerging electronic technology. By then, Mettler also had moved into new facilities, with the construction of the first building of its Greifensee campus, which remained the company's headquarters into the 21st century.

DIVERSIFICATION IN THE SEVENTIES

The company took a new step toward a diversified product line with the 1970 introduction of its DV and DK lines of automated titration systems. At the same time, Mettler strengthened its core scales component with the acquisition of balance manufacturer Microwa AG. The following year, another acquisition, of August Sauter KG, of Albstadt-Ebingen, in Germany, added that company's specialized industrial and retail scales, as well as more than 500 employees to the Mettler payroll. By then, Mettler had taken its place among the world's leading manufacturers of specialized scales and other analytical apparatus.

Advances in microelectronics technology made possible the next step in Mettler's history: the conversion to electronic systems. In 1973 Mettler debuted its PT 1200 scale, the industry's first fully electronic precision

```
┌─────────────────────────────────────────────┐
│                                               │
│              KEY DATES                        │
│                   ■                           │
│                                               │
│  1945:  Erhard Mettler establishes Einzelfirma E. │
│         Mettler in Küsnacht, Switzerland, to begin │
│         production of the single-pan analytical bal- │
│         ance he has invented.                 │
│  1954:  Company's first international subsidiary is │
│         established in the United States.     │
│  1962:  Diversification begins with the introduction │
│         of a thermal analyzer.                │
│  1973:  Mettler introduces the industry's first fully │
│         electronic precision balance.         │
│  1980:  Company founder sells Mettler to the Swiss │
│         firm Ciba-Geigy AG.                   │
│  1989:  Mettler acquires the Ohio-based Toledo Scale │
│         Corporation and subsequently renames itself │
│         Mettler-Toledo AG.                    │
│  1996:  Mettler-Toledo gains its independence from │
│         Ciba-Geigy via a management buyout assisted │
│         by AEA Investors Inc.                 │
│  1997:  Company is taken public as Mettler-Toledo │
│         International Inc. with a listing on the New │
│         York Stock Exchange.                  │
│  2001:  Leading pipette producer Rainin Instrument, │
│         LLC, is acquired.                     │
│                                               │
└─────────────────────────────────────────────┘
```

balance. With a capacity of 0 to 1,200 grams, the PT 1200 had a sensitivity to 0.01 grams. The new balance proved immediately successful upon its official 1974 launch. The success of the PT 1200, and its successors, enabled the company to open an additional production facility, in Uznach, with an initial floorspace of 2,100 square meters. The company continued to refine its electronics technology, and in 1979 rolled out its DeltaRange, which was awarded the IR100 Award and voted one of the most significant technical achievements for the year.

In 1980 Mettler's shares were bought by Swiss giant Ciba-Geigy AG. Mettler was added to Ciba-Geigy's industrial division. The purchase enabled the company's founder to retire, while ensuring Mettler the resources for future growth. Mettler continued, however, to operate independently and manage its own development.

By then, Mettler had begun to expand beyond its original laboratory market to produce balances and other equipment for the industrial and retail, especially food retailing, markets. In 1982 the company presented its first electronic precision balance for industrial applications, the Sauter MultiRange. The company also

introduced its PE precision scale, which featured an extremely compact form. A new product line was launched in 1985, when Mettler, in a collaboration with Ciba-Geigy, introduced its first automated lab reactor, the Mettler RCI. The company also moved into the Asian market, opening a joint venture operation in China, where it began production of laboratory equipment in 1987.

ACQUIRING INDEPENDENCE IN THE NINETIES

The second half of the 1980s was marked by three significant acquisitions. The first took place in 1986, when Mettler acquired fellow Swiss company Ingold Firmengruppe and its line of laboratory and industrial-use electrodes and sensors. Next, in 1987, Mettler took over Garvens Automation GmbH, near Hanover, Germany, and that company's dynamic checkweighers, dosage control, and other processing systems. Whereas these acquisitions would bring Mettler into new product territories, Mettler's next major acquisition would bring the company something else: a new name.

In 1989 Mettler acquired the Toledo Scale Corporation, based in Worthington, Ohio. Toledo, which had been founded in 1901, was then the largest producer of industrial and food retailing scale systems in the United States. The acquisition enabled Mettler to capitalize on Toledo's strong brand recognition. Following the acquisition, Mettler changed its name to Mettler-Toledo AG. The company also restructured, placing its European subsidiaries under the Mettler-Toledo name.

Mettler-Toledo continued its product line expansion when it acquired the rheology and laboratory automation systems from Contraves AG in Zurich in 1990. Another acquisition made that year brought the laboratory balance production of Ohaus Corporation into the Mettler-Toledo group of products. After launching the microscale Mettler MT 5 in 1991, with sensitivity to 0.000001 grams, the company introduced the Mettler UMT 2, a fully automated balance capable of reading weights from 0.0000001 grams to 2 grams, in 1992. On a larger scale, Mettler-Toledo inaugurated new production facilities in Albstadt and Giessen, in Germany, as well as a new office in Schwerzenbach, in Switzerland.

In 1993 Mettler-Toledo reorganized its Swiss operations into a more vertically integrated structure under the Mettler-Toledo AG structure. At the same time, the company delineated its balance line into three categories: Basic, Standard, and Professional. In that same year, Mettler debuted two new products: the TA 8000 thermal analysis system and the AT 10005 mass comparator.

In 1996 Mettler-Toledo regained its independence from Ciba-Geigy after a management buyout, assisted by AEA Investors Inc., a New York-based investment group, worth $402 million. The following year, AEA Investors brought the firm to the public as Mettler-Toledo International Inc., listing the company on the New York Stock Exchange. This marked the first time that a Swiss company had gained a full U.S. stock listing. The listing gave the newly independent Mettler-Toledo the capital to increase its acquisition drive, as the company set out to expand its product offerings and consolidate its leadership positions in its various markets. An important acquisition was the 1997 purchase of the United Kingdom's Safeline Limited, the leading manufacturer of metal detection systems destined for the food, pharmaceutical, cosmetics, chemicals, and other industries requiring security testing procedures for their packaged products.

The year 1998 saw three more important acquisitions. The first took place in July 1998, with the purchase of Illinois-based Bohdan Automation Inc., a maker of laboratory automation and automated synthesis equipment. The move marked a further enhancement of Mettler-Toledo's position in the growing laboratory automation markets, especially in the synthesis reactor product category. At the end of 1998, Mettler-Toledo was able to boost this segment still further, as it announced the acquisitions of two drug and chemical compound automated discovery and development systems manufacturers, Applied Systems, of Annapolis, Maryland, and Myriad Synthesizer Technology, based in Cambridge, England. By then, Mettler-Toledo had elected a new company chairman, Robert Spoerry, who had been serving as company CEO since 1993.

Mettler-Toledo continued on its acquisition march in 1999. In May of that year, the company acquired French industrial and retail scale manufacturer Testut-Lustrana, a firm with annual sales of roughly $50 million. The move pointed the way to a further consolidation of the highly fragmented laboratory equipment market. In April 1999, Mettler-Toledo completed the acquisition of full control of its Chinese joint-venture partnership, which, combined with company-owned production facilities in Shanghai, enabled the company to expand its sales throughout the Asia-Pacific region.

With 46 percent of sales in Europe and 43 percent of sales in the United States, Mettler-Toledo had become one of the most global of laboratory equipment manufacturers. Its growing operations in the Asian region, which provided some 11 percent of company sales, gave it a strong foothold there, despite the region's economic difficulties in the late 1990s. By then, industrial products had risen to become the company's largest product area, with 49 percent of annual sales, as compared with just 38 percent for sales of laboratory products. Mettler-Toledo ended the decade reporting net income of $48.1 million on sales of $1.07 billion.

EARLY 21ST-CENTURY ACQUISITIONS

Mettler-Toledo continued on a growth trajectory in the early 21st century, purchasing no fewer than three companies in 2000 alone: AVS, Berger Instruments, and Thornton Inc. The acquisition of AVS, a U.K.-based producer of X-ray visioning equipment used to inspect packaged goods, augmented Mettler-Toledo's existing metal-detection-based packaging inspection lines. Headquartered in Newark, Delaware, Berger specialized in supercritical fluid chromatography products, which were used to analyze and purify chemical compounds during drug discovery. The Bedford, Massachusetts-based Thornton was a leading producer of pure and ultrapure industrial water-monitoring instruments used in microelectronics, semiconductor, biotechnology, and pharmaceutical applications. On the product development front, Mettler-Toledo in 2000 introduced the AX line of analytical balances, which featured an Internet connection for remote monitoring and downloadable applications and sensors that enabled one-handed operation.

Mettler-Toledo's push into the fast-growing life sciences market continued in 2001 with the purchase of Rainin Instrument, LLC, of Emeryville, California, for $294.2 million in cash and stock. Rainin ranked as the leading manufacturing of pipettes and related products used to measure and dispense liquids in the pharmaceutical, biotechnology, and medical research fields. At the time this acquisition was completed in November 2001, Rainin's annual revenues totaled approximately $66 million. Nearly 85 percent of these sales were generated in the United States, so Mettler-Toledo moved swiftly to expand the Rainin line globally via its strong international marketing and sales network.

Over the next few years, acquisitions took a back seat to organic growth initiatives, including the development and release of new products, the further expansion of operations in China and the pursuit of growth in other emerging markets such as India and Russia, and the extension of Mettler-Toledo's service offerings. Sales marched steadily upward during this period, reaching $1.59 billion by 2006, while profits soared by that same year to $157.5 million, a figure 45 percent higher than the preceding year.

Mettler-Toledo maintained its momentum through 2008 despite the downturn in the global economic environment that began in the latter months of the year. New highs in profits, $202.8 million, and sales, $1.97 billion, were both set. At the beginning of the year, Olivier Filliol became the company's president and CEO, replacing Spoerry, who assumed the role of executive chairman. Filliol had joined Mettler-Toledo in 1998 and had served as head of the firm's global sales, service, and marketing operations and its operations in China as well. By 2008, Mettler-Toledo's emerging markets push was clearly paying off as about 27 percent of total sales were generated in these fast-growing markets. In response to the economic downturn, the company by May 2009 was working to cut its annual operating costs by $100 million in part via a 1,000-person workforce reduction. Sales were down 18 percent and profits down 29 percent through the first six months of 2009 as the downturn finally ended the company's upward trajectory. Executives at Mettler-Toledo were nevertheless confident that the firm would emerge from the downturn a stronger company because of its restructuring efforts and concurrent initiatives to improve sales and marketing operations.

M. L. Cohen
Updated, David E. Salamie

PRINCIPAL SUBSIDIARIES

Mettler-Toledo (Schweiz) GmbH; Mettler-Toledo AG; Mettler-Toledo Holding AG; Mettler-Toledo Instrumente AG; Mettler-Toledo Logistik GmbH; Mettler-Toledo Logistik International GmbH; Mettler-Toledo Pac Rim AG; Mettler-Toledo OnLine GmbH; Microwa AG; Ohaus Europe GmbH; Mettler-Toledo Limited (Australia); Ohaus Australia Pty. Ltd.; Mettler-Toledo Ges.m.b.H. (Austria); Mettler-Toledo N.V. (Belgium); Mettler-Toledo Indústria e Comércio Ltda. (Brazil); Mettler-Toledo Inc. (Canada); Mettler-Toledo (Changzhou) Precision Instruments Ltd. (China); Mettler-Toledo (Changzhou) Scale & System Ltd. (China); Mettler-Toledo (Changzhou) Measurement Technology Ltd. (China); Mettler-Toledo Instruments (Shanghai) Co., Ltd. (China); Mettler-Toledo International Trading (Shanghai) Co., Ltd. (China); Ohaus International Trading (Shanghai) Co., Ltd. (China); Ohaus Instruments (Shanghai) Co. Ltd. (China); Panzhihua Toledo Electronic Scale Ltd. (Panzhihua) (China); Mettler-Toledo (Xinjiang) Electronic Scale Ltd. (China); Mettler-Toledo d.o.o. (Croatia); Mettler-Toledo spol. s.r.o. (Czech Republic); Mettler-Toledo A/S (Denmark); Mettler-Toledo EPEC SAS (France); Mettler-Toledo Analyse Industrielle S.a.r.l. (France); Mettler-Toledo Flexilab SAS (France); Mettler-Toledo Holding (France) SAS; Mettler-Toledo SA (France); Mettler-Toledo Garvens GmbH (Germany); Getmore Ges. für Marketing & Media Service mbH (Germany); Mesoma Verwaltungs GmbH (Germany); Mettler-Toledo (Albstadt) GmbH (Germany); Mettler-Toledo GmbH (Germany); Mettler-Toledo Management Holding Deutschland GmbH (Germany); Mettler-Toledo (HK) Ltd. (Hong Kong); Mettler-Toledo (HK) Holding Ltd. (Hong Kong); Mettler-Toledo (HK) MTCN Ltd. (Hong Kong); Mettler-Toledo (HK) MTCS Ltd. (Hong Kong); Mettler-Toledo (HK) MTCZ Ltd. (Hong Kong); Mettler-Toledo Kereskedelmi Kft. (Hungary); Mettler-Toledo India Private Limited; Turing Softwares Private Limited (India); Ohaus India Private Limited; Mettler-Toledo S.p.A. (Italy); Mettler-Toledo K.K. (Japan); Mettler-Toledo Kazakhstan; Mettler-Toledo (Korea) Ltd.; Mettler-Toledo (M) Sdn. Bhd. (Malaysia); Ohaus (SEA) Sdn. Bhd. (Malaysia); Mettler-Toledo S.A. de C.V. (Mexico); Ohaus de México S.A. de C.V.; Gelan Detectiesystemen B.V. (Netherlands); Gelan Holding B.V. (Netherlands); Mettler-Toledo B.V. (Netherlands); Mettler-Toledo Product Inspection B.V. (Netherlands); Mettler-Toledo Cargoscan AS (Norway); Mettler-Toledo A/S (Norway); Mettler-Toledo Sp.z.o.o. (Poland); ZAO Mettler-Toledo Vostok (Russia); Mettler-Toledo (S) Pte. Ltd. (Singapore); Mettler-Toledo spol. s.r.o. (Slovak Republic); Mettler-Toledo d.o.o. (Slovenia); Mettler-Toledo S.A.E. (Spain); Mettler-Toledo AB (Sweden); Mettler-Toledo (Thailand) Ltd.; Ohaus Indochina Limited (Thailand); Mettler-Toledo Ukraine Ltd.; Mettler-Toledo Ltd. (UK); Mettler-Toledo UK Holding Company; Mettler-Toledo UK Holdings Limited; Ohaus UK Ltd.; Mettler-Toledo Safeline X-Ray Limited (UK); Mettler-Toledo Safeline Limited (UK); Mettler-Toledo AutoChem, Inc. (USA); Mettler-Toledo, Inc. (USA); Mettler-Toledo Northwest LLC (USA); Mettler-Toledo Ingold, Inc. (USA); Ohaus Corporation (USA); Rainin Instrument, LLC (USA); SofTechnics, Inc. (USA); Mettler-Toledo Thornton, Inc. (USA); Mettler-Toledo International Finance, Inc. (USA).

PRINCIPAL COMPETITORS

Beckman Coulter, Inc.; Agilent Technologies, Inc.; Danaher Corporation; PerkinElmer, Inc.; Thermo Fisher Scientific Inc.

FURTHER READING

"Batch Plant," *Glass*, August 1996, p. 342.

"Mettler Targets $100 Million in Cost Savings," *Instrument Business Outlook*, May 15, 2009, p. 2.

"Mettler Toledo Acquires Two Companies," *Instrument Business Outlook*, December 1998.

"Mettler Toledo Gets the Balance Right," *Cosmetics International*, April 10, 1999, p. 13.

"Mettler Toledo Set to Jump Swiss New Equity Pipeline," *Euroweek*, January 8, 1999, p. 20.

"Mettler-Toledo to Acquire Rainin Instrument," *Instrument Business Outlook*, October 15, 2001, p. 2.

Terry, Bob, *Honest Weight: The Story of Toledo Scale*, New Jersey: Xlibris, 2000, 386 p.

Miami Subs Corporation

———— ■ ————

6300 NW 31st Avenue
Fort Lauderdale, Florida 33309
U.S.A.
Telephone: (954) 973-0000
Fax: (954) 973-0159
Web site: http://www.miamisubs.com

Private Company
Incorporated: 1989
Employees: 475
Sales: $150 million (2008 est.)
NAICS: 722110 Full-Service Restaurants

■ ■ ■

Miami Subs Corporation is a growing regional chain of quick-service restaurants headquartered in south Florida. The company operates mainly through its Miami Subs Pizza and Grill franchised shops, which offer a menu of submarine sandwiches, pizza, gyros, chicken, salads, and other casual meals. Its approximately 70 restaurants are found principally along the East Coast. Between 1999 and 2007, Miami Subs was owned by another quick-service restaurant chain, Nathan's Famous. During this era, many Miami Subs shops were co-branded with Nathan's, the fish-and-chips shop Arthur Treacher's, and with Kenny Rogers chicken, all brands owned by Nathan's Famous. Nathan's sold Miami Subs in 2007 to private investors, who launched a new plan for domestic and international growth. As of 2009, the company had franchise agreements with operators in Turkey and Romania, and hoped to add some 500 shops within the United States.

FROM TORONTO TO FLORIDA

Miami Subs Corporation began as one of several ventures run by Greek immigrant Konstantin "Gus" Boulis. Boulis died a multimillionaire, considered one of Florida's most powerful and influential businessmen. His story began quite humbly. As a teenage merchant marine, Boulis stepped ashore in Nova Scotia in 1968. He stayed in Canada, winding up in Toronto, where he washed dishes at a sandwich shop called Mr. Submarine. In classic rags-to-riches fashion, the hardworking Boulis eventually became part-owner of the Mr. Submarine chain. The chain had grown to 200 units by the 1970s. At that point, the enterprise was sold, and Boulis made enough money on the deal to retire to Florida.

Boulis, however, was still in his 20s, much too young to settle down in the sun. Consequently, in 1983 he opened a Mr. Submarine shop in Key West. Within a few years, Boulis's holdings had grown to three Mr. Submarine shops. Although still only a small enterprise, Boulis's business attracted the attention of some other investors in so-called quick-service restaurants. In the late 1980s, Boulis was approached by a group comprising the former owner of the Kentucky Fried Chicken chain and former Kentucky governor, John Y. Brown, and entrepreneur Don Perlyn. The group combined Boulis's three sub shops with a 20-year-old chain of taco shops called Taco Viva. Then all the shops were converted to a new concept, Miami Subs.

The Miami Subs shops stood out because they were designed in emblematic Florida colors of pastel pink and turquoise, amply festooned with neon signage. The restaurants offered a relatively large menu of around 70 items, from submarine sandwiches to gyros to chicken wings. The stores also sold wine, beer, and even $89 bottles of the famed champagne Dom Perignon. The industry journal *Nation's Restaurant News* (February 11, 1991) characterized the new chain as a "personality hangout." It occupied something of a middle ground between truly fast-food chains such as McDonald's and Burger King and traditional sit-down restaurants. Some units had drive-through service, but customers could also eat in. Prices were low, but not as low as those of its fast-food competitors.

EARLY GROWTH AND CHANGE

The chain quickly expanded, opening both company stores and franchised units. Boulis had many contacts in the Greek immigrant community, whom he brought into the business as franchisees. He was apparently a tireless worker, with knowledge both of the intimate details of restaurant operation and a grander vision. The company incorporated in 1989, and in 1990 was listed on the NASDAQ. Young as Miami Subs was, it made a strong impact on the industry. In 1991, the chief executive of Burger King, Barry Gibbons, told an audience that he feared Miami Subs as an up-and-coming rival. Business magazine *Fortune* (February 25, 1991) passed on the comment, quipping "Miami who?" Gibbons was right to take notice of the small chain, though. It had several formidable industry veterans in its management ranks, including Burger King's own past president, Ronald Petty. When Petty quit Burger King in 1990 after 12 years with the company, he joined Miami Subs. Petty had earlier taken Burger King's international unit from sales of $180 million to $800 million in four years. When Miami Subs announced it was poised to

grow rapidly from its approximately 50 units in 1991 to over 100, the restaurant industry paid attention.

However, expansion did not go smoothly. In 1992, the company reorganized, merging with the umbrella entity that had owned the firm's franchise rights in Florida. It announced a three-year plan to grow to 110 units, moving into markets in North and South Carolina, New Jersey, New York, and Texas. Part of the growth was to come from a joint venture with the Rax chain of sandwich restaurants, which was to convert some of its stores to Miami Subs. An owner of some 50 Burger King shops in the South also agreed to conversion. Some of the paperwork resulted in one-time charges. The growing chain was intermittently profitable, and at times in the red. A former Burger King president, Petty left after only a year with Miami Subs, evidently after quarreling with Boulis.

By 1994, the firm's stock price had sunk to less than $2 and franchise development had slowed. The company got a new head that year in Thomas J. Russo. Russo had previously been chief executive of the restaurant chain Howard Johnson and of Ponderosa Steakhouses. He was heading a housewares company when Miami Subs cofounder Perlyn convinced him to take significant stock in the sub chain and try to get its growth on track.

Russo seemed excited by the challenge, and made several changes right away. Miami Subs had a long and complex menu, offering more than 70 items. Russo brought that down to 50 items. While trimming some offerings, he also added a children's menu and a senior citizens' menu. Russo and his team made a point of working late, visiting stores between 6 P.M. and 3 A.M., trying to hone the concept. Russo told *Nation's Restaurant News* (December 5, 1994) that Miami Subs was not fast food, but "quality food served quick." This was its key identifier in a crowded market, and Russo hoped to bring the company's focus back to that. As part of this new sharpened image, Russo embarked on television marketing for the first time. Russo also brought in other restaurant industry talent, and tried to boost employee morale and improve training. His ambitious program was designed to bring the chain, which had grown to 160 units, back to profitability. The company anticipated further growth, to perhaps as many as 500 stores.

Russo's tenure was also short-lived. In 1997 he resigned, and the top management position reverted to founder Boulis. The chain had grown to 185 units over three years, remaining far smaller than it had hoped. Although the company reported year-end profits of $305,000 in 1996, the next year ended in a loss of $391,000. Revenue stood at approximately $34 million

KEY DATES

1968: Gus Boulis begins working in Toronto sub shop.
1989: Boulis and partners launch Miami Subs by combining two existing Florida chains.
1990: Company goes public, lists on the NASDAQ.
1999: Nathan's Famous buys Miami Subs.
2001: Founder Boulis is murdered.
2007: Nathan's Famous sells Miami Subs to a group of private investors.
2008: Company announces ambitious expansion plan.

in 1997, which was over 9 percent lower than that reported a year earlier. All in all, the company's promise seemed to have dulled, and by the late 1990s, Miami Subs was looking for a new plan.

CO-BRANDING AND SALE

The company's next move was to negotiate a merger with another restaurant chain. In May 1998, Miami Subs announced that it had found a partner in another Florida quick-service chain, Arthur Treacher's. Arthur Treacher's served fish and chips and other seafood. Its chairman and chief executive also served on the board of directors for Miami Subs. Thus the companies had some familiarity with each other. The deal was to be a stock swap, and the resulting company would operate co-branded shops that sold the menus of both Arthur Treacher's and Miami Subs.

The deal was complicated because Arthur Treacher's was already in the midst of acquiring a West Coast chain of seafood restaurants called Skipper's, owned by Seattle Crab Company. This was the fourth-largest quick-service seafood chain in the country, with 94 units. If the Arthur Treacher's deal had gone through, the new firm would have had some 400 units from the three combined chains. However, with the stock prices of both Arthur Treacher's and Miami Subs falling, and the Skipper's negotiations still unfirm, conditions were not right for the merger. Both companies called it off after a few months. The two companies still proceeded with the co-branding concept. Miami Subs opened several co-branded units even as the merger was falling apart. Because Treacher's was most popular at dinner time, and Miami Subs did most of its business at lunch and late at night, the combination was beneficial for both.

Nevertheless, changes were difficult for Miami Subs. It had changed course several times, under successive management plans. During the year before the Arthur Treacher's merger was proposed and then dismantled, Miami Subs cofounder Perlyn had tried to trim the average meal price at the restaurants. He had determined that the average meal check of $5.50 was too much for the chain's core customers. If the average meal price came down, then the loss in revenue would eventually be made up by more customers. Perlyn's plan brought the average check down to $4.70. He also made other menu changes and put funds toward renovating and painting franchised shops. A month after the breakup of the Treacher's deal, Perlyn replaced Boulis as chief executive. Boulis remained chairman although he also had other Florida business interests, principally hotels and casinos. In 1998 U.S. customs agents seized Boulis's financial records as part of an investigation into money laundering. Although Boulis's problems were apparently not directly related to Miami Subs, the change in leadership occurred at the same time as the records seizure. Miami Subs' share price fell to around 40 cents.

Just a few months later, Miami Subs had a new merger partner. A New York-based chain of hot dog restaurants, Nathan's Famous, first bought out Boulis's 30 percent share in the company for $4.2 million. Then it announced that it would eventually acquired the rest of the company in a stock swap. Nathan's traced its history back to 1916. By the late 1990s, it had grown to more than 190 restaurants, plus some 400 other retail outlets such as units in airports. Its units were spread across nearly 30 states. Like Arthur Treacher's, Nathan's saw the benefit of co-branding its shops with Miami Subs. Miami Subs opened co-branded units with both Nathan's and Treacher's over 1999. The acquisition of the rest of Miami Subs was completed in 2000, for a price of around $14 million.

SUBSIDIARY OF NATHAN'S FAMOUS

Miami Subs President Perlyn believed the company had turned around by the time of the Nathan's acquisition. It reported sales of $149 million for 1999, with profits of $547,000. A succession of false starts had hampered the company's growth. Under Nathan's, the chain ramped up its co-branding strategy, with four brands possible under one roof. A single Miami Subs outlet could offer the traditional Miami Subs menu, plus the Arthur Treacher's seafood menu, Nathan's hot dogs and French fries, and finally Kenny Rogers chicken. Kenny Rogers Roasters was a Florida-based chain that sold wood-fired rotisserie chicken. In the mid-1990s it had been very popular, and had over 300 locations. It was in bankruptcy and down to 40 U.S. shops (with another 50 abroad) when Nathan's acquired it in 1999.

Nathan's had overseen the conversion of about 90 Miami Subs shops by 2001 into what it called Miami Subs Plus restaurants. These offered all four branded menus. Nathan's also closed some 20 stores that were not performing well. Average sales per shop rose sharply, while costs were trimmed or remained steady. The diverse menu attracted new customers, and the four different branded offerings appealed to eaters at complementary times of day.

Nathan's began looking into international sales. It also moved its branded items into many different retail outlets. It sold its hot dogs in supermarkets and food club stores, and in casinos, gas stations, sports arenas, and convenience stores. Some aspects of its business seemed to be growing nicely. However, the co-branded restaurants were at times a sore spot. Nathan's had about 350 quick-service restaurants (various combinations of Miami Subs, Nathan's, and its other brands) by 2003. These had posted a profit of $1.24 million in fiscal 2003. In fiscal 2004, the chains lost about $14 million.

Meanwhile, Miami Subs founder Gus Boulis was murdered in 2001. Boulis had been investigated and fined by the federal government in connection with his SunCruz casino business. He had been forced to sell SunCruz, and then was involved in suits and countersuits with the buyers. Boulis was gunned down in his car one evening in Fort Lauderdale. He drove several blocks before passing out and crashing into a tree in front of a Miami Subs shop. He no longer had any financial connection to the business, yet it may have been the last thing he saw. His death was later alleged to have been a murder-for-hire. A trial was underway but still not resolved by 2009.

PRIVATE COMPANY AGAIN

From mid-decade on, the Miami Subs chain got smaller. By 2007, it had only 59 franchised units. All of these continued the co-branding strategy, and offered at least one of the other Nathan's brands. In 2007, Nathan's sold the chain for $3.3 million to private investors. It was bought up by a firm led by Bruce Galloway and Gary Herman. The pair put up $850,000 in cash, with another $2.4 million to be paid over the next four years.

On its own again, Miami Subs came up with a new plan for expansion into both domestic and international markets. The stores changed their name to Miami Subs Pizza & Grill. This meant that the restaurants added a full line of pizzas to the menu. The chain also promised a new delivery system in south Florida, with a central ordering system serving homes and offices in the area. New management aimed to refine the Miami Subs menu, keeping such classics as its popular Philly cheese steak. Other items on the menu, though, were open to evaluation. The new owners also hoped to begin remodeling and updating existing stores, while opening new ones. The firm opened three stores in New York, two in Florida and one in South Carolina in 2008. The company's long-range plan called for the addition of 100 stores in New York, then expansion to a total of 500 stores chainwide within five years.

The company also began expanding internationally. It opened a shop in the Cayman Islands and another in Turkey in 2008. Several more stores were under construction in Romania. In 2009, Miami Subs hired the former president of the Papa John's pizza chain, Dan Holland, to be its director of global franchising. Holland announced that Miami Subs had agreements to open 40 stores in Turkey, and that it had an agreement for a total of 20 outlets in Romania. Holland told industry journal *Chain Leader* (June 10, 2009) that he was pleased with Miami Subs' new management and direction. "This is not some start up but a proven concept that needed the infusion of capital and the creative and financial ability to take it to the next level." With a new name, new menu, and new management, the chain seemed to have another chance to reach its goals.

A. Woodward

PRINCIPAL COMPETITORS

Doctors' Associates Inc.; The Quiznos Master LLC; Blimpie International Inc.

FURTHER READING

Allen, Robin Lee, "Miami Subs Elevates Perlyn to Chain's Top Post," *Nation's Restaurant News*, August 17, 1998, p. 3.

Blum, Vanessa, "Businessman's Fraud Sentence Cut in Half for Helping Gus Boulis Murder Investigation," *Fort Lauderdale Sun-Sentinel*, June 26, 2008.

Colodny, Mark M., "Up from Whoppers," *Fortune*, February 25, 1991, p. 155.

Crownover, Catherine, "Arthur Treacher's, Miami Subs Call Off Merger Agreement," *Florida Times-Union* (Jacksonville), July 17, 1998.

Cukier, Eileen, "Newest Co-Branding Concept Tastes Great for Miami Subs Plus," *South Florida Business Journal*, June 29, 2001, p. 3.

"Former Papa John's President Joins Miami Subs," *Chain Leader*, June 10, 2009.

Frumkin, Paul, "Nathan's Is Red-Hot for Growth, Serves Up Diversity with New Brands," *Nation's Restaurant News*, March 27, 2000, pp. 4, 75.

———, "On a Roll," *Nation's Restaurant News*, April 2, 2001, pp. 8, 11.

———, "Slain Miami Subs Founder, Boulis, 51, Drew Ire and Admiration," *Nation's Restaurant News*, February 19, 2001, pp. 8, 91.

Hayes, Jack, "Miami Subs Dives into Uncharted Waters," *Nation's Restaurant News*, February 11, 1991, p. 7.

Kramer, Louise, "Nathan's Spicy Profit Fails to Boost Stock," *Crain's New York Business*, August 14, 2000, p. 4.

"Miami Subs Chief Russo Hands in Resignation," *Nation's Restaurant News*, March 24, 1997, p. 2.

"Miami Subs Posts Decline in 2nd-Q Profits, Revenues," *Nation's Restaurant News*, January 19, 1998, p. 14.

"Miami Subs Posts Profits of $547,000 for Fiscal 1999," *Nation's Restaurant News*, September 6, 1999, p. 12.

"Miami Subs Reorganizes," *South Florida Business Journal*, October 7, 1991, p. 4.

"Miami Subs to Open 110 Sites," *South Florida Business Journal*, January 20, 1992, p. 4.

"Nathan's Famous Sells Miami Subs for $3.3M," *Nation's Restaurant News*, June 18, 2007, p. 3.

Paperniek, Richard L., "Miami Subs Cites Charges in $391K Year-End Losses," *Nation's Restaurant News*, September 1, 1997, p. 12.

Prewitt, Milford, "Miami Subs Execs Get Turnaround in Sights," *Nation's Restaurant News*, December 5, 1994, p. 1.

Ramseyer, Rick, "Missing Links," *Restaurant Business*, October 15, 2003, p. 40.

"Six Locations Race to Be the First 'New' Miami Subs Pizza & Grill Locations," *Internet Wire*, November 19, 2008.

Walker, Elaine, "Founder of Miami Subs Sandwich Company Missed by Colleagues," *Miami Herald*, February 8, 2001.

———, "Miami Subs, Arthur Treacher's to Merge," *Miami Herald*, May 26, 1998.

———, "New York Hot Dog Chain Nathan's Famous to Buy Miami Subs," *Miami Herald*, December 1, 1998.

Mohawk Fine Papers, Inc.

465 Saratoga Street
Cohoes, New York 12047
U.S.A.
Telephone: (518) 237-1740
Toll Free: (800) 843-6455
Fax: (518) 233-7102
Web site: http://www.mohawkpaper.com

Private Company
Incorporated: 1931 as Mohawk Papermakers, Inc.
Employees: 650
Sales: $250 million (2007 est.)
NAICS: 322222 Coated and Laminated Paper
    Manufacturing; 322121 Paper (Except Newsprint)
    Mills; 322122 Newsprint Mills; 322212 Folding
    Paperboard Box Manufacturing

■ ■ ■

Mohawk Fine Papers, Inc., is one of the leading worldwide manufacturers of fine coated and uncoated papers, and the leading North American manufacturer of uncoated fine papers. The company supplies fine papers for formal and informal business communications, publishing text and cover stock, writing and artistic papers, packaging, on-demand photo books, and many everyday uses. Papers are available in a variety of weights, textures, colors, finishes, and hues. Premium brands include Mohawk Superfine, Mohawk Digital Papers, Mohawk Color Copy, Strathmore, Beckett, and the patented Inxwell papers Navajo and Options.

The company operates three paper mills, in Waterford and Cohoes, New York, and in Hamilton, Ohio, and four converting centers. Paper products are shipped from four warehouses, and more than 400 distributors market fine papers in Europe, the Middle East, Asia, and South America, as well as in Australia, New Zealand, and South Africa. Green Seal Certified, Mohawk Fine Papers is the industry leader in environmental stewardship, producing more than 2,000 papers with recycled content and more than 3,000 papers with wind energy; nearly 900 varieties of paper are carbon neutral through renewable energy offsets. Family-owned and -operated, Mohawk Fine Papers is headquartered in Cohoes.

LONG HISTORY DEFINES COMPANY

Mohawk Fine Papers traces its history to the post–Civil War era, when Mohawk and Hudson Paper Company began operations in a former ax handle factory in Waterford, New York. Frank Gilbert, one of the founders, obtained full ownership of the company in 1866 and gave it his name, Frank Gilbert Paper Company. Located on Kings Canal, the paper mill employed 40 people who turned rags, straw, and wood into three tons of printing paper each day. The primitive conditions earned the facility the nickname "mud mill." By 1878, though, the mill produced 900 tons of paper per year employing three machines. Gilbert purchased the factory building in 1881.

As Frank Gilbert Paper Company expanded with the prosperous economy of the early 1900s, Gilbert

COMPANY PERSPECTIVES

Mohawk Fine Papers' mission is to: Provide innovative, high quality products and superior customer service at a competitive price. Provide employees with a safe and respectful working environment that encourages personal development. Pursue the highest standards of environmental stewardship and sustainable practices. Contribute to the economic and social development of our communities. Strive for the highest quality results and honor our commitment to customers, stakeholders, partners and employees without compromising ethical standards.

constructed a new mill in Cohoes, south of the juncture of the Erie and Champlain canals. Commencing operations in 1917, the Cohoes mill produced base stock for bond, mimeo, and wallpaper. During the 1920s production shifted to base stock for box liner, and box covering, with less than 20 percent of output in printing papers. The company made boxes for Old Spice aftershave and paper for Monopoly money. As the Great Depression altered the economy, bankruptcy brought operations to a halt in 1930.

The mill survived bankruptcy and the Great Depression due to the skills of Waterford lawyer George E. O'Connor. As appointed receiver, he reorganized the company under the name Mohawk Papermakers, Inc., in 1931. That year, O'Connor purchased Mohawk Papermakers although he had no knowledge of papermaking. O'Connor obtained that expertise by inviting the International Brotherhood of Papermakers to form a local union. With their experience in papermaking, union officers and the 200 mill workers played a vital role in transforming the paper mill into a viable enterprise. Until World War II, Mohawk continued to make box stock, primarily. However, the need for printing paper combined with raw material shortages, led Mohawk to develop an alpha-cellulose paper. After a decade of struggle, the company became profitable manufacturing printing paper during World War II.

POSTWAR ERA REDEFINES PAPERMAKING ENTERPRISE

After World War II, Mohawk continued to make commercial printing paper. The company introduced the Halfmoon Vellum brand in 1946, followed by a line of text and cover stock, sold under the brand name Mo-

hawk Superfine. Success with the commercial printing papers gave the company a new identity. Mohawk concentrated its production and marketing on the growing advertising industry during the 1950s and 1960s. A reputation for high-quality papers and attentive, knowledgeable service attracted business from large advertising agencies in New York, Boston, Philadelphia, and Washington, D.C. The company developed a wide variety of paper stock, from opaque papers used by finance companies to construction paper for children. Brands included Poseidon, Cortlea, and Artemis.

By the late 1960s, changes were afoot as the company changed hands before returning to the O'Connor family. The Reigl Paper Company acquired Mohawk in 1969, and then Federal Paperboard acquired Reigl. Thomas D. O'Connor, son of George O'Connor, purchased the business in 1972, with investment support from other members of the O'Connor family. His two sisters, Frances Hardart and Annabel Strife, participated in managing the extensive modernization that followed.

MOHAWK INVESTS IN PRODUCTION AND ENVIRONMENTAL TECHNOLOGY

Under this second generation of O'Connor family leadership, Mohawk Paper Mills underwent a series of substantial capital projects. During the next two decades, the company invested $90 million in updating its facilities. A new folio sheeter automated the paper finishing department, and the company replaced one of the papermaking machines at the Waterford mill. Federal clean air and clean water legislation prompted Mohawk to replace existing paper dyes with safer, less polluting dyes. The surface action of the dyes led to the development of a high-quality acid-free paper, which held color better than acid-based paper. The quality of color print on Mohawk's innovative alkaline cover and text paper attracted business from book publishers worldwide.

Another phase of capital investment involved the 1989 refurbishment of a 1969 Fourdinier paper machine, which limited production to 1,200 sheets of paper per minute. To increase efficiency, the company replaced the mechanical gears and the line shaft drive of the dryer section and added 16 new driver felt rolls. Installation of 31 sectional drives, at one to 250 horsepower, replaced a single 500 horsepower drive. The setup reduced energy consumption, improved flexibility, and facilitated entry into the coated paper market.

During the early 1990s, Mohawk began to distinguish itself through the first of many

KEY DATES

1866: Frank Gilbert purchases the Mohawk and Hudson Paper Company.
1881: Frank Gilbert Paper Company purchases the building where it makes paper.
1917: Company builds a second paper mill in Cohoes, New York.
1931: George E. O'Connor purchases newly renamed Mohawk Papermakers out of bankruptcy.
1946: Mohawk introduces its first brand name papers, Halfmoon Vellum and Mohawk Superfine.
1972: Second generation of the O'Connor family modernizes company operations.
1989: Equipment refurbishment contributes to manufacturing flexibility and provides entry into coated paper market.
1990: Mohawk introduces first recycled coated paper in the industry; other environmental production changes follow.
1999: Mohawk receives a patent for its Inxwell uncoated paper for the digital printing market.
2003: Mohawk is the first paper manufacturer to implement wind-generated energy; a third generation guides company as Tom O'Connor Jr. becomes chief executive officer.
2005: Acquisition of fine papers business from International Paper makes the company the largest fine papers manufacturer worldwide.

were made available with recycled content in 4 whites and 12 colors. In 1993 Mohawk earned the Green Seal certification for recycled paper, the first fine papers manufacturer to do so.

Other manufacturing process initiatives addressed related environmental concerns. Mohawk replaced the steam-powered equipment with natural gas–fired boilers. Fuel consumption declined 14 percent, resulting in cost savings and a 43 percent reduction of combustion emissions. During the mid-1990s, Mohawk stopped using elemental chlorine for whitening and brightening paper stock, due to the toxic effects of dioxin to aquatic systems. The company stopped purchasing pulp treated with elemental chlorine as well. To reduce emissions of the harmful by-products of chlorine bleach, Mohawk used alternative chlorine compounds to whiten virgin pulp. The company applied a chlorine-free process to whiten its recycled papers.

MEETING TECHNOLOGY CHALLENGES, REVISING MARKETING STRATEGY

Mohawk entered the 1990s with a focus on developing customer service, in particular on anticipating needs and assisting in paper choices. Toward that end, Mohawk revamped its corporate identity and initiated a new marketing program. Taking its design from the company's long history, a new logo suggested experience and stability. Employee training about papers and their appropriate applications improved customer service, while the introduction of a specifications manual with paper samples provided customers with practical tactile and visual understanding of paper differences. The sleek design, ease of use, and customer service support attracted new business, and revenues increased 7 percent in 1991, to $80 million.

The idea to anticipate customer needs involved confronting a changing business environment with the advent of digital technology. Desktop publishing and digital printing technology decentralized production of printed materials, and much industry growth occurred outside of Mohawk's geographic range, in the West, Midwest, and South, and in Asia. Also, competition intensified as papermakers consolidated into large national companies.

Mohawk distinguished itself in the new business environment through innovation. The company formed alliances with manufacturers of digital printers, including Xerox, Heidelberg, Epson, Kodak, Hewlett-Packard, and Xeikon. In particular, research and development needed to address the differences between traditional printing ink and the new toners used in laser and ink-jet

environmental initiatives. In 1990 Mohawk introduced recycled coated paper, the first stock of its kind to use postconsumer waste. Shredded computer paper collected from local businesses supplied the waste content, at 10 percent, and waste from the manufacture of paper and envelopes supplied an additional 50 percent recycled content. Virgin pulp constituted the remaining 40 percent. Beginning in 1993, Mohawk purchased pulp only from vendors that followed sustainable forestry practices.

Mohawk offered a variety of recycled papers under the 50/10 brand name and expanded the product line. The Vellum product line became available in 100 percent postconsumer waste content in 5 whites and 20 colors, and Irish Linen and Tomohawk brand papers

printers. Concerns included ink adhesion, clarity, and color quality. Mohawk developed its proprietary Inxwell uncoated paper, featuring a surface texture that greatly increased ink opacity for better-quality print. Mohawk adapted the Options line of papers to Inxwell technology in 1995, and the Navajo line followed in 1996. The Satin and 5010 product lines were introduced as digital papers in 1998.

Mohawk's paper products quickly established a foothold in the digital printing market. Several *Fortune* 500 companies used them for their annual reports, and book designers using short-run digital presses favored the product as well. The papers found a niche market in fine press editions, illustrated books, and museum catalogs. New business included the supply of premium cover paper for the popular Harry Potter books. Due to the decentralized nature of much digital publishing, the new papers represented the company's entry into the consumer market, as the products became available in office supply stores. In 1999 the company obtained a patent for its Inxwell uncoated paper.

Mohawk continued to address its competitive challenges through capital investment and innovation. Automation improved speed and efficiency, and a new regional distribution center in Reno, Nevada, opened in 1998, improving product availability and service to distant customers.

DIGITAL PAPER SELECTION EXPANDS

Mohawk offered the most comprehensive selection of digital papers in the United States, and in 2001 Mohawk introduced improved versions of the Satin, Options, and Vellum lines. The company offered Satin 2.0 in multiple weights and hues of white for digital printing in color copiers, ink-jet, and offset printers. The Options line was reintroduced for digital and offset printing, and the Vellum line was expanded to include commercial papers for four-color press, letterpress, foil stamping, and embossing.

Mohawk continued to address environmental concerns, and in October 2003 the company became the first in the paper industry to implement the use of wind power to supply energy for manufacturing. The company purchased four million kilowatt hours of wind power from Community Energy, of Syracuse, enough energy to make 12,000 tons of paper per year or approximately 12 percent of the company's output.

2005 ACQUISITION OFFSETS DECLINE IN PAPER INDUSTRY

As computer technology reduced paper consumption, especially premium text and cover paper, Mohawk

sought to expand its market niche in fine papers. In the fall of 2004 Tom O'Connor Sr. wrote a letter to International Paper (IP), asking the multibillion-dollar corporation if it was interested in selling its fine papers operations. IP had obtained the businesses as part of larger acquisitions, but fine papers constituted a very small portion of the company's revenues. IP had no interest in promoting fine papers, so willingly answered "yes." The response came the same day the Tom O'Connor Sr. died, in late November 2004. His son, Tom O'Connor Jr., chief executive officer since 2003, became chairman of the company just as Mohawk doubled its revenues. Mohawk completed the $65 million acquisition the following May.

Mohawk gained several revered fine paper brands, including some lines that strengthened the company's offering for the consumer market. Beckett Paper Company, the oldest paper company west of the Allegheny Mountains, dated to 1848. Beckett Paper started as a newsprint manufacturer, using 100 percent rag content, but over the years the company created several new paper styles, including colored cover, lithographic, fluorescent, duplex, and linen papers. The Beckett acquisition included the Hamilton, Ohio, paper mill, with three fine paper machines, a converting center in Saybrook, Ohio, and artist papers operations in Westfield, Massachusetts. Recognized brands included Brite Hue, Via, and Beckett. The Strathmore brand, which dated to the late 1800s, was internationally recognized for its corporate identity writing paper and finely textured cover papers, as well as its artist papers and sketch books.

The acquisition nearly tripled annual revenues to $250 million, and Mohawk became the leader in fine papers and the largest supplier of premium uncoated papers. The Beckett brands complemented Mohawk's existing line of papers, with minor redundancies, and the acquisition gave Mohawk access to new distribution networks. Production capacity increased to 175,000 tons of fine paper annually. To reflect its enlarged identity, the company took the name Mohawk Fine Papers in September 2005.

Mohawk applied its environmental initiatives across the new business operations. At the Beckett Mill, Mohawk significantly reduced manufacturing by-products, hazardous waste, and energy consumption. Also, the company increased its access to wind power to 45 million kilowatt hours. This brought the two New York mills to 21 percent of total power from wind energy and the Ohio mill to 50 percent usage. While alternative energy sources increased the company's utility costs, it attracted new business from The Nature Conservancy, Sierra Club, and General Electric.

In 2007 Mohawk increased wind energy usage to 60 million kilowatt hours and implemented a carbon offset program. Verified emission reductions (VERs, or carbon offsets) involved contributions to alternative energy projects elsewhere that compensated for the company's greenhouse gas emissions. VERs reduced the company's greenhouse gas emissions by 14,000 tons annually. Mohawk applied the VERs to production of the Beckett Concept and Expression and Strathmore Writing and Script papers. Hence, these brands became the first papers to become carbon neutral.

In July 2008 Mohawk laid off employees at the Beckett mill, due to stagnating sales, along with higher prices of imported raw materials and a local increase in utility costs. The company reduced production from three machines in operation simultaneously, down to two machines. The company hoped to rehire employees by the end of the year, but the worldwide economic crisis delayed further action.

LEADER IN PREMIUM UNCOATED PAPER

Mohawk strengthened its position in fine papers when the company acquired SMART Papers' premium uncoated papers brands, including Pegasus, Passport, Carnival, Synergy, Genesis, SMART Brights, Feltweave, Magna Carta, Nekosa Linen, Nekosa 25 % Cotton, Nekosa Bond, Skytone, Solutions, and Proterra. The March 2009 acquisition gave Mohawk the lead position as supplier of premium uncoated paper in North American markets. Also, Mohawk became the exclusive worldwide sales representative of the SMART premium coated paper brands, Kromekote and Knightkote Matte for writing text and cover papers.

Mohawk continued to develop environmental stewardship. The company purchased additional VERs in June 2009, supporting alternative energy projects in Greenville, South Carolina, and Brazil. To analyze and reduce its own energy consumption, the company installed sensors throughout its facilities to monitor energy usage. Although the technology cost millions to install, the information feedback led to equipment changes that reduced energy consumption by 10 percent within a year. Mohawk became a featured supplier on the Environmental Paper Assessment Tool (EPAT) of Metafore, Inc., an Internet-based carbon footprint calculator that provided information for making environmentally responsible paper choices. Mohawk's environmental initiative earned the company the Green

Power Partner of the Year award from the U.S. Environmental Protection Agency in 2009.

Mary Tradii

PRINCIPAL OPERATING UNITS

Beckett Mill; Headquarters and Cohoes Mill: Saybrook Converting Center; Waterford Mill and Samples Department.

PRINCIPAL COMPETITORS

Domtar Corporation; Finch, Pruyn & Company; New-Page Group, Inc; Wausau Paper Corporation.

FURTHER READING

"Company Introduces Line of Recycled Paper," *Capital District Business Review,* October 29, 1990, p. 6.

D'Errico, Richard A. "Paper Maker Turns Page to Thrive in 21st Century Market," *Business Review,* December 30, 2005, p. 3.

Heffner, Jessica, "Hamilton, Ohio, Paper Mill to Lay off 27 Employees," *Middleton Journal,* July 29, 2008.

Higgins, Dan, "Building Future with Fine Paper," *Albany Times Union,* July 11, 2005.

Johnson, Jim, "N.Y. Paper Firm First to Use Wind to Power Production," *Waste News,* October 13, 2003, p. 9.

"The Many Faces of Mohawk: 70th Anniversary Celebration," Cohoes, NY: Mohawk Paper Mills, Inc., 2001.

Mitchell, Robert L., "Mohawk Fine Papers Inc.: Thousands of Sensors Monitor Everything from Office Light to Smokestack Emissions," *Computerworld,* April 20, 2009, p. 24.

"Mohawk Fine Papers Purchases Additional VER Contracts to Offset Carbon Footprint," *Energy Resource,* June 18, 2009.

"Mohawk Papers Mills, Inc. for All the Ways You Print," *Electronic Publishing,* June 2004, p. 44.

"Mohawk Purchases SMART Papers Premium Uncoated," *American Printer,* March 3, 2009.

Moorse, Alan, "Spirit of Cooperation Keeps Paper Mill Turning," *Capital District Business Review,* November 15, 1999, p. 7.

"Rebuild Gives Mohawk New Drive for Increased Production," *PIMA Magazine,* December 1989, p. 65.

Tresslar, Tim, "Paper Company Seeks to Cut Emissions at Ohio, New York," *Hamilton Journal-News,* May 18, 2007.

Wechsler, Alan, "Quality Time for Paper Company: Mohawk Fine Papers Records Best Quarter Ever After Buyout of International Paper Unit," *Albany Times Union,* April 20, 2007.

Yeich, Christopher R., "Just-in-Time Crunch," *Graphics Arts Monthly,* September 1998, p. 136.

Nationwide Mutual Insurance Company

———————————■———————————

1 Nationwide Plaza
Columbus, Ohio 43215-2220
U.S.A.
Telephone: (614) 249-7111
Toll Free: (877) 669-6877
Fax: (614) 854-3676
Web site: http://www.nationwide.com

Private Company
Incorporated: 1925 as Farm Bureau Mutual Automobile
    Insurance Co.
Employees: 36,032
Total Assets: $161.09 billion (2008)
NAICS: 524126 Direct Property and Casualty Insurance
    Carriers; 524113 Direct Life Insurance Carriers

■ ■ ■

Based in Columbus, Ohio, Nationwide Mutual Insurance Company is a major insurance and financial services firm. Primarily known for automobile insurance, Nationwide offers other property and casualty insurance as well as life insurance through scores of subsidiaries. The company also sells retirement and investment products and offers asset management services and strategic investment advice. In addition to serving individuals, Nationwide markets a variety of products, including commercial auto insurance, liability insurance, workers' compensation insurance, accidental medical insurance, travel insurance, employee benefits, retirement plans including 401(k) pensions, and farm and

ranch insurance. As a mutual company, Nationwide is technically owned by its policyholders.

COMPANY GROWS OUT OF THE FARM BUREAU MOVEMENT

Nationwide, like a number of insurance companies, emerged from the Farm Bureau movement of the early 1900s. The first county farm bureau was established in 1911 by the Binghamton, New York, Chamber of Commerce to sponsor an extension agent from the U.S. Department of Agriculture. The tag "bureau" was soon applied to all state farming organizations. In 1919 the Ohio Farm Bureau Federation was formed to assist Ohio farmers by lobbying for farmer-friendly legislation. In that same year, hundreds of delegates from state farm bureaus (or representing states that were in the process of organizing) gathered in Chicago to form a national organization that would become the American Farm Bureau Federation (AFBF), commonly called the Farm Bureau.

From the beginning, the Farm Bureau had to decide whether its focus was to be on education or commerce. One of the earliest commercial ventures, and most helpful to farmers, was auto insurance. Pioneering this "service to member" operation was George Mecherle of Bloomington, Illinois, the founder of State Farm Insurance. He created a mutual automobile insurance company in the early 1920s to serve rural and small-town drivers who were paying higher premiums despite having fewer accidents than urban drivers. By tying insurance rates to risk levels, Mecherle could offer premiums that were significantly lower than the competition. Mecherle signed agreements with state farm bureaus, which received a fee for each of its members who purchased policies. Rather than join forces with the insurer, some state farm bureaus emulated Mecherle and created their own mutual auto insurance companies.

In December 1925 the Ohio Farm Bureau took this approach and with a $10,000 loan incorporated Farm Bureau Mutual Automobile Insurance Co. Spearheading the effort was the executive secretary of the Ohio Farm Bureau, Murray D. Lincoln. Born in Massachusetts, Lincoln had served as a county agricultural agent, establishing the first cooperative milk distributing plant in New England. He joined the Ohio Farm Bureau in 1920.

GAINING A STATE LICENSE: 1926

Setting up a one-room office in Columbus, the three-person venture took applications over the next few months and by April 1926 had signed up 1,000 Ohio farmers, far more than the 100 the state required. At that point the company received a state license and became operational. Lincoln would eventually become president of the company in 1939. Like many Farm Bureau automobile insurance companies, Farm Bureau Mutual initially limited its sales to farmers but soon changed its approach. In a book about the Farm Bureau movement, Lincoln recalled, "When we first started our insurance company, it never dawned on me that we would ever insure anyone but farmers. But once we started insuring farmers other than Farm Bureau members, we found that we simply could not keep out the barber in the small town, the grocer, the gas-station attendant, the shopkeeper, or any other type of small businessman. Finally, as our company grew, we had to throw out the window the concept of restricting our insurance only to farmers."

The Farm Bureau brand carried a great deal of weight in rural communities and played a major role in the success of Farm Bureau Mutual. Moreover, because a large number of county agricultural agents sold Farm Bureau memberships, the Farm Bureau became a government agency in the eyes of many people, lending further credibility to Farm Bureau–affiliated insurance and helping to spur the growth of Farm Bureau Mutual. Just two years after its founding the company allied itself with local organizations and began selling policies in North Carolina, Delaware, Maryland, West Virginia, and Vermont. Rather than being limited to rural customers, the company began selling auto insurance to residents of small towns in 1931 and larger cities three years later.

ADDING LIFE INSURANCE: 1935

Success in auto insurance led Farm Bureau Mutual to become involved in other insurance products in the 1930s. The company began selling fire insurance in 1934, a business supplemented a year later by the acquisition of a struggling fire insurance company. Also in October 1935 Farm Bureau Mutual acquired American Insurance Union Inc. to begin selling life insurance. Farm Bureau Mutual then had its agents sell both property and casualty insurance and life insurance, a practice that was simply not done at the time.

Despite the Great Depression, Farm Bureau Mutual enjoyed strong enough growth that in 1936 the company moved into a new headquarters in Columbus. The advent of World War II hindered growth somewhat, yet by 1943 the company was doing business in 12 states and Washington, D.C. Following the war, the company resumed its pattern of strong growth and in 1946 diversified beyond insurance when it acquired a radio station in Columbus. Initially it was not intended as a revenue generator. Rather, the purpose was to provide farmers with a voice in the city. Over the years, Farm Bureau Mutual became comfortable with the media business and began adding other assets.

Increasing demand for its insurance products during the postwar years caused Farm Bureau Mutual to outgrow its Columbus offices, leading in 1951 to the opening of regional businesses. The company began offering mutual funds in the 1950s and became the first major insurance company to authorize agents to sell life insurance as well as mutual funds. The company was also a pioneer on other fronts during this period. In 1950 it began offering a premium discount to policyholders who took driver training courses. In 1955 it introduced the industry's first easy-to-understand illustrated contract, and later in the decade began mass merchandising auto insurance. Moreover, the company established a merit-based insurance subsidiary in 1956.

KEY DATES

1925: Farm Bureau Mutual Automobile Insurance Co. is incorporated.

1934: Company begins selling fire insurance.

1935: American Insurance Union is acquired and company begins selling life insurance.

1946: Company diversifies into radio stations.

1955: Company changes name to Nationwide Mutual Insurance Company.

1965: Nationwide expands beyond United States with the formation of a West German subsidiary.

1997: Nationwide Financial, the company's life insurance and savings unit, goes public in $524 million IPO.

1998: Nationwide Mutual divests its radio stations.

2007: Nationwide Bank is formed.

2008: Nationwide Financial is reacquired.

FARM BUREAU ADOPTS NATIONWIDE NAME: 1955

By the mid-1950s the company found that the Farm Bureau name was actually a hindrance to further growth because a large number of states already had their own Farm Bureau insurance companies. Thus, in 1955 Farm Bureau Mutual adopted a new name, one that also reflected its ambitions: Nationwide Mutual Insurance Company. A year later a stock company, Nationwide Corporation, was taken public. The mutual company along with Nationwide Mutual Fire Insurance Company, owned all of the B shares, while the A stock was sold to the public. Nationwide Corporation then used the proceeds of the sale to acquire a controlling interest in Nationwide Life Insurance Company and Detroit-based National Casualty Company, and substantial interests in Sun Life Assurance Company of Canada and Boston-based Columbia Life Insurance Company.

The switch to the Nationwide name led the company to expand into 20 additional states over the next decade, so that by 1965 Nationwide was doing business in 32 states and the District of Columbia. A year earlier the 72-year-old Murray Lincoln stepped aside as president and general manager after nearly 25 years in office. He was succeeded by Senior Vice President Bowman Doss.

Although there was a change in leadership, Nationwide remained in the forefront of advances in the automobile insurance field. In 1963 the company offered extra medical benefits to policyholders who wore seat belts, helping to stimulate the adoption of the safety feature that was still in its infancy. In a similar vein 12 years later the company offered discounts to policyholders whose cars were equipped with air bags. Nationwide opened the first customer service department in its home office in 1964. Ahead of the industry, Nationwide in 1969 began levying a surcharge to policyholders who owned high-performance, low-miles-per-gallon vehicles.

Nationwide's expansion efforts continued under new leadership. In 1965 Nationwide began doing business internationally for the first time, teaming up with the West German mail-order company Neckermann Versand to create Neckuna Neckermann Insurance Company, to sell automobile insurance in West Germany. The company expanded into the employee benefits management field through the 1969 acquisition of Columbus-based Gates McDonald Co.

FORMATION OF NATIONWIDE PROPERTY AND CASUALTY: 1979

Nationwide's growth in the 1970s led to the company constructing a 40-story skyscraper in Columbus, One National Plaza, to serve as the company's new international headquarters. The building's opening in 1978 ushered in a period of robust expansion for Nationwide. A new subsidiary, Nationwide Property and Casualty was formed in 1979 and all of the company's property/casualty assets were folded into it. A year later Colonial Insurance of California was acquired. Other purchases followed in the 1980s. Financial Horizons Life was added in 1981. A year later Farmland Insurance, a top farm insurer, was acquired to create Nationwide Agribusiness Insurance. In 1985 Nationwide took over some struggling operations: Wausau Insurance Cos., which required an infusion of $250 million, and Cal-Farm Insurance Co. and Cal-Farm Life Insurance Co., both owned by the California Farm Bureau Federation but placed under the authority of a state agency because they faced possible insolvency due to the sale of some bonds.

While Nationwide was building a portfolio of insurance subsidiaries, it continued to add radio stations and other media assets. By 1982 Nationwide Communications Inc. included seven radio states, three television stations, and a small cable TV company in Houston, Texas. In a deal completed in 1985 the company paid $40 million to Western Cities Broadcasting for eight radio stations located in Sacramento and San Jose, California; Las Vegas, Nevada; and Phoenix and Tucson, Arizona. The demand for radio properties soon increased, however, and Nationwide was content to wait for the market to settle. It also took the long view with its individual stations, willing to hire from within while gaining a reputation for taking deliberate actions. Unlike other radio operators, Nationwide did not hastily change course as new programming formats came and went. This measured approach served Nationwide Communications well. When station prices ebbed in the early 1990s, the company resumed expansion, adding five stations over the next few years.

NATIONWIDE FINANCIAL TAKEN PUBLIC: 1997

D. Richard McFerson became Nationwide's CEO in late 1992, taking over at a time when the entire industry was staggered by several disasters, natural and manmade, including Hurricane Andrew, a spate of midwest tornados, and civil disorder in Los Angeles. As a result, the Nationwide family of insurance companies saw its earnings drop from $261 million in 1992 to $22.2 million in 1993. Over the next few years Nationwide transformed itself from a personal-lines company that did most of its business in the East through agents to a multichannel distribution company that spread its business around the country. A major move McFerson made was to sell a 20 percent stake of Nationwide Financial, the company's life insurance and savings unit. The March 1997 offering not only raised $524 million, it allowed Nationwide to double the $1 billion book value of the remaining 80 percent of the unit. Moreover, Nationwide Mutual increased its capital base to support further growth through acquisition.

Under McFerson, Nationwide was especially aggressive in the acquisition of Allied Group in 1998. What started out as a friendly takeover of the publicly traded car and home insurer, became a successful $1.46 billion hostile takeover, a deal that would not have been possible without the benefits supplied by taking Nationwide Financial public. Also in 1998, Nationwide acquired the personal lines of TIG Countrywide along with its network of 3,000 independent agencies to bolster its distribution operations. To better focus its resources on its core insurance and financial services businesses, Nationwide elected in 1998 to divest its media holdings, selling 17 radio stations to Jacor Communications Inc. for $620 million. In 1999 Nationwide decided to sell its reinsurance unit as well.

Nationwide suffered a public relations problem in the 1990s when the company was accused of engaging in the illegal act of redlining, or refusing to sell insurance to people, mostly African American, who lived in certain poor urban areas. In 1998 Nationwide was found guilty in Virginia of discriminating against African Americans. In that same year, the company was sued in Cincinnati by a fair-housing organization, the local branch of the National Association for the Advancement of Colored People, and six individual homeowners. A year later Nationwide reached an out-of-court settlement for $1.3 million, the money earmarked for the creation of a program for low-interest loans to help homeowners pay for mortgages and make home repairs, and a contribution to a program that provided individual development accounts to help people save the money needed to buy a home.

McFerson retired at the end of 2000. During his time at the helm, Nationwide increased its assets from $37.6 billion to $115 billion, due in large part to its booming 401(k) business. Succeeding McFerson as CEO and chairman was W. G. "Jerry" Jurgensen, who would hold both posts until June 2003. Due to a number of corporate scandals, including those involving Enron and WorldCom, Nationwide decided like many companies to separate its board and operational roles as a way to avoid placing too much power in the hands of the CEO and increase public faith in the integrity of the company. Jurgensen relinquished the chairmanship and remained CEO.

Under Jurgensen, Nationwide continued to expand through acquisitions but eventually ran into problems. United Kingdom-based Gartmore Investment Management was purchased in 2001. Nationwide added Prudential Financial's special automobile insurance unit, THI Holdings Inc., in 2003. In 2007 Nationwide Financial added Nationwide Bank to offer a full-range of banking products. A year later Nationwide bought back the outstanding stock of Nationwide Financial, a deal that was not well received by the ratings agencies, which cut Nationwide's credit rating because the deal was financed by internal funds and, as a result, reduced the company's capital below rating guidelines. Moreover, the agencies expressed concern about Nationwide's 2008 investment losses and poor operating performance. In February 2009 the Nationwide board and Jurgensen reached a mutual agreement on his resignation. He was replaced as CEO by Chief Operating Officer Steve Rasmussen. Nationwide was not unique in being saddled with poor investments in 2008 and 2009. There was good reason to believe the company would bounce back as the economy rebounded.

Ed Dinger

PRINCIPAL SUBSIDIARIES

Nationwide Affinity Insurance Company of America; Nationwide Corporation; Nationwide Indemnity Company; Nationwide Mutual Fire Insurance

Company; Nationwide Property and Casualty Insurance Company; Nationwide Securities, LLC; Allied Group, Inc.; Nationwide Asset Management Holdings; Nationwide Advantage Mortgage Company; Nationwide Asset Management, LLC.

PRINCIPAL COMPETITORS

The Allstate Corporation; Prudential Financial, Inc.; State Farm Mutual Automobile Insurance Company.

FURTHER READING

Amatos, Christopher A., "Agent System Gives Nationwide a Jump," *Columbus Dispatch,* October 6, 1985, p. 2D.

Berger, Samuel R., *Dollar Harvest,* Lexington, MA: Heath Lexington Books, 1971, 221 p.

Bowers, Barbara, "Profiting from Experience," *Best's Review,* January 1, 2004.

Cosgrove, John, "Nationwide and Consumerism," *National Underwriter,* July 25, 1988, p. 21.

Koselka, Rita, "Give 'em What They Want," *Forbes,* September 30, 1991, p. 96.

Lohse, Deborah, "Nationwide Mutual Wakes Up," *Wall Street Journal,* July 7, 1998, p. 1.

"Murray Lincoln Plans to Retire Next Month," *New York Times,* March 5, 1964.

Niquette, Mark, "Nationwide Financial Services Splits Chairman, Chief Executive Jobs," *Columbus Dispatch,* June 5, 2003, p. 1E.

O'Boyle, Maureen, "Nationwide CEO to Stay the Course," *Business First-Columbus,* March 15, 1993, p. 1.

Shwiff, Kathy, "Crisis on Wall Street: Rasmussen Named CEO of Nationwide," *Wall Street Journal,* February 20, 2009, p. C3.

Natori Company, Inc.

180 Madison Avenue, 18th Floor
New York, New York 10016-5267
U.S.A.
Telephone: (212) 532-7796
Fax: (212) 481-7282
Web site: http://www.natori.com

Private Company
Founded: 1977
Employees: 450
Sales: $100 million (2009 est.)
NAICS: 315231 Women's and Girls' Cut and Sew Lingerie, Loungewear, and Nightwear Manu- facturing

∎ ∎ ∎

Natori Company, Inc., founded in 1977 by Josefina "Josie" Almeda Cruz Natori, is famous for its ultrafeminine, sophisticated, and elegant lingerie lines, sold under several labels. The company's enduring appeal is its mix of the exotic and luxurious, influenced by Josie Natori's Filipino background. "My greatest assets have always been my Asian heritage and my entrepreneurial spirit," Josie Natori told Melanie Linder of *Forbes Asia* in March 2009. Natori sleepwear, intimates, accessories, fragrances, home collections, and ready-to-wear ensembles are sold through upscale retailers and specialty shops in more than 25 countries worldwide.

EAST MEETS WEST: FORTIES TO EARLY SEVENTIES

Josie Cruz was born in Manila, Philippines, on May 9, 1947. She was the eldest of six children and the daughter of two successful entrepreneurs: Her father founded and ran F.E. Cruz & Company, a construction firm, and her mother ran a pharmacy and other businesses. From an early age, Josie showed extraordinary talent as a pianist, performing her first solo concert with the Manila Philharmonic Orchestra when she was nine. As she matured, her interest in music waned as she became more interested in business.

After graduation from high school, 17-year-old Josie Cruz journeyed to the United States in 1964 to attend Manhattanville College in New York City. She began taking classes in business and studied abroad her sophomore year in Paris. While in Paris Cruz soaked in the beauty of the city and its status as a fashion mecca, both of which would influence her in later life. After returning to the States, Cruz continued working toward a business degree, specializing in economics. In addition to classes at Manhattanville College, she also took economic courses at Fordham University in the Bronx.

Cruz went corporate after receiving her bachelor's degree, working at financier Bache & Company as a broker in 1968. She was soon tapped to help open a Bache office in Manila and became the new location's broker and assistant manager. After two years, as the Philippine economy soured and Bache decided to close the Manila office, Cruz returned to New York City.

Cruz left Bache and joined Merrill Lynch in 1971 as an investment banker specializing in utility clients.

COMPANY PERSPECTIVES

Not everything about the Japanese culture gets lost in translation. Consider, for instance, *natori*, the Japanese word for "highest form of art." In the 30 years since Josie Cruz Natori founded the lingerie company that bears her name, she's been reaching for natori. She approaches everything she does—whether it is designing the many lingerie, loungewear, sleepwear, and other collections of the Natori Company or perfecting her skills as a concert pianist—as if it were a work of art. "Natori is my husband's name, but it's very much my philosophy," says the CEO and founder of the company. "I'm always trying to find the perfect note."

She was not the average investment banker: Instead of wearing dark, severely cut business suits, she embraced her femininity and wore stylish, sexy skirts and dresses. Regardless of what she wore, Cruz delivered results and was appointed the firm's first woman vice president in 1975.

While rising through the ranks, Cruz's personal side had gotten a boost as well. She met, fell in love with, and married fellow Wall Streeter Ken Natori, managing director at Shearson Lehman (later Smith Barney). Despite her professional and personal successes, however, Josie Cruz Natori's entrepreneurial side needed something more. She wanted to follow in the footsteps of her parents and start her own company.

A FIRM OF HER OWN: THE LATE SEVENTIES

Seeking to blend her roots and business acumen into a new venture, Josie Natori began sampling various Philippine products, believing there could be a substantial market for them in the United States. She settled on some beautifully embroidered blouses and showed them to Lee Fabris, a lingerie buyer from Bloomingdale's, who thought they would probably sell as sleepwear.

Lengthening the soft, billowy blouses and creating a collection of 20 items from a friend's Philippine factory, Natori left Wall Street and invested $150,000 in her new business, called Natori, in 1977. The business name had two meanings: first, it was Josie Natori's married surname; second, the word also had intrinsic value to what Josie hoped to create (*natori* meant "highest form of art" in Japanese).

To launch her new business Josie Natori began selling loungewear from her apartment as her newborn son slept in a crib nearby. After luxury retailer Saks Fifth Avenue placed an order, Natori Company was officially born and scored a full-page ad in the *New York Times* courtesy of Saks. Josie Natori was soon overwhelmed with orders and struggled to keep up with demand.

She contracted with two factories in the Philippines until her father bankrolled a new factory in Pasig, outside Manila, in 1979. As manufacturing began at the new Pasig facility, Josie Natori moved operations from her home to an 11,000-square-foot loft in midtown Manhattan. As more New Yorkers discovered her ultrafeminine, luxuriously soft loungewear, few realized the clothing reflected Josie Natori's belief that lingerie did not have to be trampy to be sexy and that comfort was as important as style, a style proudly reflecting her heritage with beautiful Filipino appliqués and embroidery.

STEADY GROWTH, EXPANSION IN EIGHTIES AND NINETIES

By the mid-1980s Natori had become a well-known brand, sold in over 500 high-end department stores such as Saks, Bloomingdale's, Macy's, Neiman Marcus, and Bergdorf Goodman, as well as smaller specialty boutiques. With an eye on careful expansion, Josie Natori in 1984 released a fragrance, Natori, then segued into lingerie-related accessories such as slippers and robes, as well as a linen collection. She also wanted to design a Natori apparel collection and tested the waters with an exclusive line for Bergdorf Goodman. As revenues climbed, Josie Natori sought a partner with experience in licensing deals and strategic joint ventures.

The perfect candidate soon emerged: her husband, Ken Natori. In late 1985 Ken left his post at Smith Barney to join Natori full time as chairman to Josie's president, handling daily operations, finance, and licensing/partnerships. For 1985 sales reached about $10 million; by 1988 Natori's revenues, still dominated by its lingerie lines, climbed to $20 million.

The growing Natori product line spurred sales to $30 million in 1990 and $40 million by 1993. Lingerie, still the heart of the company, was available in three distinctive styles: Natori, the original, sophisticated signature line for women aged 30 to about 50; Natori II, featuring less-formal loungewear; and Josie, designed for younger women who wanted luxurious yet still sexy lingerie. Although Natori had gained a loyal following, a new competitor burst on the scene: Victoria's Secret. The new rival was bold and unapologetic about its overtly sexy lingerie and loungewear, the opposite of Natori's quiet elegance and Eastern reserve.

KEY DATES

1977: Josefina "Josie" Cruz Natori invests $150,000 to create Natori, a sleepwear and lingerie company.

1979: Natori opens its own factory in Pasig, outside Manila.

1984: Company releases its first fragrance, Natori.

1985: Ken Natori joins his wife's business full time.

1995: Natori leases showroom space on Madison Avenue, near its offices.

1998: Josie label is relaunched with a new logo and in-store boutiques.

1999: Natori adds to its accessories collection with scarves and wraps.

2004: Natori begins selling a bra collection created in partnership with Dana-Co Apparel.

2007: Kenneth Cruz Natori, Josie's son, joins the family business.

2008: Company unveils Natorious, a new ready-to-wear collection.

2009: Natori signs with Parlux to market a new fragrance.

In 1995 Natori began leasing a showroom on Madison Avenue, around the corner from its 34th Street offices, an area densely populated with upscale retailers. Two years later the company had grown to about $50 million in sales. Natori had also opened small boutiques in Paris and Milan, maintained a warehouse in New Jersey, and manufactured its goods in factories in the Philippines. In late 1998 Kathy Nedorostek was hired as president and chief operating officer of Natori, with Josie Natori retaining the title of chief executive. Nedorostek's appointment came at a time when the company had begun offering its apparel line, previously exclusive to Bergdorf Goodman, to Saks Fifth Avenue and Neiman Marcus stores.

The same year Natori was pushing its Josie line with major advertising and merchandising campaigns both domestically and abroad. The lingerie and daywear brand was repackaged with a bright, bold new logo and in-store Josie boutiques at many of its retail outlets. While the Josie launch was underway, a new Natori collection called Cruz was slated to debut the following year, comprising tastefully casual daywear and sophisticated, elegant eveningwear. Hopes were high that the two apparel lines would double Natori's apparel sales.

NEW HORIZONS IN THE 21ST CENTURY

In the early 2000s as the economy softened, the Natori game plan remained unchanged. By 2002, as designers and retailers struggled in a crowded marketplace, Natori's popular intimates managed to hold their own. The firm had introduced additional products (scarves, wraps, handbags, and belts) and cultivated new customers through its established lingerie and daywear brands. As Victoria's Secret took the innerwear segment by storm, Natori remained solid despite the no-holds-barred approach of its rival.

Josie Natori decided to be aggressive herself, looking for ways to expand her empire. In a November 25, 2002, interview with Karyn Monget and Melanie Kletter of *Women's Wear Daily*, she explained her new emphasis on accessories: "We are very focused on building this business and I think accessories could be as big as intimates. Eventually, I would like the businesses to be about half and half," she said. "I'm a gambler and I believe in taking risks. If you don't move, you don't get anywhere. And if it's a mistake, time will tell."

In 2003 Natori Company joined the World Wide Web with its first Web site, www.natori.com, featuring information about its branded collections and the retailers who carried them, new product launches, and press coverage. The year also marked the expansion of Natori's foundation collection through a partnership with the New York-based Dana-Co Apparel Group. The new bra collections were to be sold under the established Natori (Natori Black and Natori White) and Josie labels beginning in 2004.

After more than two decades Natori moved its design shop and showroom in 2004 from 34th Street to 180 Madison Avenue, the building where its offices were located. Although previously only about a block away from each other, Josie Natori and her staff were happy to have everything at one address. In 2005 Natori Company signed a joint-venture agreement with California-based JLA Home to create and market a line of home products including towels, linens, throw pillows, and window treatments. Natori had sold linens back in the 1980s, but the new Natori Home collection featured a wider range of products and was set to launch in late 2006.

ONWARD AND UPWARD: 2007 AND BEYOND

Natori's successful joint venture with Dana-Co was expanded in early 2007 to include coordinated intimates the following year. As the company celebrated 30 years in business, Josie Natori received two prestigious honors:

the Lakandula Award, presented by Filipino President Gloria Macapagal-Arroyo in Manila in March, followed by the Ellis Island Family Heritage Award in New York City in April. Another milestone occurred in April as the Natoris' son Kenneth Cruz Natori joined the family business. Formerly of Lehman Brothers, Kenneth Natori signed on as a vice president in finance. Chief among his responsibilities was turning the company's Web site into an e-commerce portal for increased sales.

Josie Natori also publicized the release of a coffee-table book, *The Art of Natori*, in 2007 as the company prepared for the 2008 launch of its first in-house designed, full ready-to-wear collection, Natorious. Sold exclusively at Saks, Natori's first customer back in 1977, the collection featured sleek, sophisticated, Asian-flavored separates in silk and satin for women on the go. With lots of black and bold accessories, the collection received rave reviews from fashionistas, who helped propel annual sales to more than $75 million annually.

In 2009 Natori launched a new fragrance through a partnership with Parlux Fragrances Inc., a new eyewear collection with Zyloware, and a bath and beach towel line with Loftex USA. Despite worldwide economic turmoil, the company went ahead with expansion plans believing the Natori brand was strong enough to weather the storm. As Josie Natori told Linder and *Forbes Asia* in 2009, "We've been grounded in lingerie for more than 30 years and have always been conservative about expanding. We're realistic about the times, but this is the time for us."

Nelson Rhodes

PRINCIPAL COMPETITORS

Calvin Klein, Inc.; Limited Brands, Inc.; Liz Claiborne, Inc.; Vera Wang Bridal House Ltd.; The Warnaco Group, Inc.

FURTHER READING

Eng, Dinah, "A Stylish Evolution (Interview with Josie Natori)," *FSB*, July/August 2009, p. 65.

Friedman, Arthur, "Natori's Brand Push," *WWD*, March 2, 1999, p. 12.

Hessen, Wendy, "Natori's Inspiration: Asia and Antiques," *WWD*, March 5, 2001.

Koenig, Gillian, "Natori Updates Original for Sister Scent," *WWD*, May 8, 2009, p. 8.

Linder, Melanie, "Intimate Objects," *Forbes Asia*, March 16, 2009.

Monget, Karyn, "All in the Family," *WWD*, January 29, 2008, p. 44B.

———, "Natori at 30," *WWD*, October 22, 2007, p. 10.

———, "Natori Receives Ellis Island Award," *WWD*, April 30, 2007, p. 23.

———, "Natori's Aggressive Strategy for Josie," *WWD*, March 8, 1999, p. 26.

———, "Natori's New Deal," *WWD*, April 21, 2003, p. 10.

———, "Turning Point for Spring," *WWD*, July 31, 2000, p. 2B.

Monget, Karyn, and Melanie Kletter, "Natori's 25-Year Mystique," *WWD*, November 25, 2002, p. 6.

Montandon, Maccabee, "Josie Natori: Natori Company Founder, CEO," *FSB*, November 1, 2001, p. 26.

Natori, Josie, *The Art of Natori*, New York: Glitterati, 2007, 160 p.

———, "Business as Symphony," *New York Times*, June 12, 2009, p. E14.

SanFilippo, Michele, "Natori and JLA Home Sign Licensing Agreement," *Home Textiles Today*, April 25, 2005, p. 4.

Van Dyk, Deirdre, "Josie Natori Turns Dressing Inside Out," *Time*, September 17, 2007, p. 92.

Webber, Kathleen Nicholson, "Natori's Lesson Plan: Sex Doesn't Always Sell," *WWD*, February 23, 2004, p. 4C.

Weisman, Katherine, "Cementing a Marriage," *Forbes*, July 22, 1991, p. 312.

Willen, Janet L., "Fashioning a Business," *Nation's Business*, February 1995, p. 14.

Nederlander Producing Company of America, Inc.

1450 Broadway, Floor 6
New York, New York 10018-2206
U.S.A.
Telephone: (212) 840-5577
Fax: (212) 840-3326
Web site: http://www.nederlander.com

Private Company
Incorporated: 1912
Employees: 50
Sales: $18 million (2008 est.)
NAICS: 711310 Promoters of Performing Arts, Sports, and Similar Events with Facilities

■ ■ ■

Nederlander Producing Company of America, Inc., also known as the Nederlander Organization, is a major New York City-based entertainment company that is involved in Broadway productions, Broadway touring attractions, London theater productions, concerts, and other events. Nederlander owns and/or operates nine Broadway theaters, three London theaters, as well as theaters in Chicago, Illinois; Detroit, Michigan; Durham, North Carolina; North Charleston, South Carolina; Tucson, Arizona; and Los Angeles, San Diego, Riverside, and San Jose, California. The company also operates several concert venues in California, including the Greek Theatre in Los Angeles, the Santa Barbara Bowl, the Grove of Anaheim, the San Jose Civic Auditorium, the Arlington Theatre in Santa Barbara, and the Balboa Theatre in San Diego. The Nederlander Organization

has been involved in some capacity with such major Broadway productions as *Fiddler on the Roof, Hairspray, Wicked, Rent, Chicago, Beauty and the Beast, The Lion King, Annie, Me and My Girl, La Cage aux Folles, Noises Off, The Dresser,* and *Nine.* The company is owned and managed by the third generation of the Nederlander family.

BIRTH OF NEDERLANDER ORGANIZATION: 1912

The Nederlander Organization was founded in Detroit in 1912 by David T. Nederlander, a businessman who owned a jewelry store and contract loan office and at the age of 26 bought a 99-year lease on the Detroit Opera House. Here he offered vaudeville featuring W. C. Fields, Al Jolson, and other notable performers. Unfamiliar with show business, he took in Lee and Jacob J. Shubert as partners. The Shubert brothers hailed from Syracuse, where they got their start in the theater business. In 1900 they moved to New York City and began their meteoric rise in the theater world, acquiring theaters and producing plays. By 1916 they were the most powerful theater owners and managers in the country, making Nederlander's alliance with them highly valuable. Later he would tell interviewers that the Shuberts taught him everything he knew about show business.

David Nederlander passed on his show business knowledge to his five sons who helped him grow his own theater organization. All the brothers played at least a small part in the family business, even Fred who manufactured auto parts but served as an investor.

COMPANY PERSPECTIVES

Now into their third generation of theatre development, ownership, management and production, the Nederlander Organization is one of the largest, most experienced operators of live theatre.

Another brother, Harry, acted as project developer for non-theater business, and Robert became the family attorney. It was James M. Nederlander and Joseph Nederlander, however, who took more active roles in their father's theater concern. Joseph supervised the general operations, while James was in charge of booking and was responsible for taking the family to New York City.

PURCHASE OF FIRST BROADWAY THEATER: 1965

Born in 1922, James Nederlander had designs on becoming a lawyer but in 1940 when he was a prelaw school student and strapped for cash he accepted a job from his father who had taken over the management of the Shubert Theatre in Detroit. Paid $25 a week, the younger Nederlander worked in the box office selling tickets. He would take on greater responsibilities as his father expanded the family's theater holdings in the post–World War II era. Because of his responsibility booking Broadway shows for the family's theaters, James Nederlander did business in New York City on regular visits. In 1964 he was in the city when a friend suggested the Nederlanders purchase a New York theater, in particular the Palace. The friend then walked Nederlander to see the president of RKO Theatres, Inc., which owned the former vaudeville house turned movie theater. A $1.6 million price was quickly agreed upon, and the Nederlanders became Broadway landlords in 1965. After $500,000 in renovations, the Palace soon became the home of a hit musical, *Sweet Charity.* In rooms above the theater the Nederlander Organization would also set up a modest office, making do with secondhand furniture.

Early in 1967 a second Broadway house, Henry Miller's Theatre on West 43rd Street, was acquired for $500,000. A year later it was sold and leased back to the Nederlanders for five years. (Like many Times Square theaters, however, the Henry Miller then suffered a serious decline, falling out of grace with Broadway and eventually becoming a notorious pornographic movie palace before returning to more respectable fare in the late 1970s.) The Nederlanders also purchased a half-

interest in the Brooks Atkinson Theatre for $1.6 million. In 1967 James Nederlander co-produced a pair of shows at the Biltmore Theatre: *On a Clear Day You Can See Forever* and *The Ninety Day Mistress,* and in preparation of becoming full-fledged Broadway producers, the family formed Nederlander Productions in 1967. Also in that year the Nederlanders for the first time independently produced a road show of a Broadway production, *The Impossible Years.* Their investment partner was Cleveland financier and shipbuilder George Steinbrenner, a name that would become better known to New Yorkers in a few years when he, along with backing from the Nederlanders, bought the New York Yankees Major League baseball team.

DAVID NEDERLANDER DIES: 1967

In October 1967, David Nederlander died at the age of 81. He left behind a portfolio of 10 theaters, and four movie theaters leased on a long-term basis to a local operator. In addition to two-and-half Broadway houses, the theater holdings included Detroit's Fisher Theater and Orchestra Hall; the Civic, McVickers, and Studebaker in Chicago; and the Morris A. Mechanic in Baltimore. Plans were also being laid for the addition of further theaters, both in New York and elsewhere around the country.

The late 1960s hardly seemed to be the ideal time to move aggressively into the Broadway scene when many observers were lamenting the death of the legitimate theater, the "fabulous invalid" as it was called by the playwriting team of Moss Hart and George S. Kaufman, or according to some wags, the "fabulous hypochondriac." The 1967 season, in fact, saw the fewest number of Broadway productions, 47, since the start of the century. James Nederlander would later say the theater had been in its death throes ever since he began his show business career, and he and his family proved the doubters wrong by finding a way to make a profit in the unpredictable world of Broadway. In addition, by 1970 the Nederlanders added theaters in Phoenix, Arizona, and Woodridge, New Jersey, as well as a 22-year lease on the Historic National Theater in Washington, D.C. In 1972 the Nederlanders began managing the 1,800-seat Uris Theater, which along with the smaller Circle in the Square Theater located in the same skyscraper, became the first new Broadway houses in 44 years.

ANNIE DEBUTS: 1977

Because most of the Nederlander theaters were large, they were ideal for musicals, and as a result the company specialized in musicals. Only three of the

KEY DATES

1912: David T. Nederlander acquires lease on Detroit Opera House.
1940: James L. Nederlander joins father.
1965: Nederlander Organization acquires first Broadway theater, the Palace.
1967: Company begins producing Broadway shows.
1972: Uris Theatre is added to Broadway holdings.
1977: *Annie* premiers in Nederlander house.
1985: Company begins managing new theater in New York's Marriott Marquis Hotel.
1994: *Beauty and the Beast* opens in the Palace.
2000: Renovated Pantages Theatre opens in Los Angeles.
2009: Broadway in Riverside and Broadway San Jose venues are added.

BALLET AND CONCERTS FILL DARK HOUSES

The Nederlander Organization did not limit itself to theatrical productions. Eager to keep its houses occupied, the company became involved in ballet. In 1976 a production called "Nureyev and Friends," featuring the famous Russian dancer Rudolf Nureyev, was booked in the Uris but the producers at the last minute had to withdraw. Rather than lose the date, the Nederlanders took over and earned a handsome profit as both the theater owner and producer. This success led to further ballet productions that toured Nederlander theaters across the country. The Nederlanders also booked concerts, leading to a subsidiary devoted to musical events based in Los Angeles, Nederlander Concerts. When Broadway underwent another fallow period, the Nederlanders could rely on concerts to generate some income and limit the number of nights their houses were dark. In the early 1980s the Nederlander Organization also teamed up with RKO to tape Broadway shows for cable TV presentation.

Just when Broadway came to believe it was immune from the recession that beset the rest of the country, the cyclical nature of Broadway once again became readily evident in the early 1980s. After enjoying record box-office business in 1981, just two years later the Street of Dreams was enduring a nightmare period of new shows opening to poor reviews and dampening attendance. Once again the death of legitimate theater was proclaimed, the prime culprit this time was the lack of talented playwrights, their ranks thinned by more profitable work to be found in film and television.

For James Nederlander the problems of the early 1980s were no different than slumps in the 1970s, 1960s, or earlier. His operating philosophy was simple, as he explained to the *New York Times*. "Being a theater owner means you're really in the moving business," he said in 1981. "You move 'em in, you move 'em out. I've been involved in a lot of flops. No question about it. When you have a show the people don't want, you just close it and go on to the next one." The theater business was also a numbers game. "If you have 10 theaters and five shows that are successful, they will make enough to carry those theaters. If you have one theater in New York and the show is a flop, you're out of business."

The Nederlander Organization was willing to hedge its bets in other ways as well. In 1984 the company sold an interest in six of its underperforming Broadway theaters to film producer Jerry Weintraub. The Nederlander Organization remained committed to theater ownership, however. In 1985 the company took over management of a new theater that was part of the Marriott Marquis Hotel that opened its doors in Times

theaters were considered dramatic houses. In 1977 one of the Nederlander Organization's most profitable shows, *Annie,* made its debut at the Alvin Theater. The production almost failed to make its tryout at the Kennedy Center in Washington, D.C., when the producers came up $300,000 short in their funding. The Nederlanders, along with the Kennedy Center, stepped up with a $150,000 investment to save the show. In a matter of five years, that $150,000 produced a profit of more than $1 million, in addition to the company's weekly one-third take of the gross ticket sales. The Nederlander Organization would also do a strong business importing shows from London's West End.

Believing in Broadway at the time was a testament to the optimism of the Nederlanders: The city was going bankrupt and Times Square was becoming a squalid eyesore. The bleak climate for the theater soon brightened, however. Broadway was on the cusp of a revival, so that by the end of the 1970s one of the greatest concerns of producers was finding an available theater from the Shuberts or the Nederlanders. As the decade came to a close, the Nederlanders and their partners were operating 23 theaters, rivaling the holdings of the Shubert Organization. With the addition of the Minskoff, Lunt-Fontanne, Mark Hellinger, and 46th Street theaters, they included seven legitimate houses in New York City as well as a part-time lease on the New York State Theater at Lincoln Center, and seven legitimate and six outdoor theaters elsewhere in the country.

Square in September of that year. At the time, about half of the district's 35 legitimate theaters were dark, unable to find shows that theatergoers were willing to pay to see.

BEAUTY AND THE BEAST, 1994, TRANSFORMS BROADWAY

The prospects for Broadway and Times Square in general brightened in the 1990s with the arrival of The Walt Disney Company, which rented a Nederlander theater, the Palace, for a staged version of its popular animated film *Beauty and the Beast,* which opened in April 1994. The show was a major success, leading Disney to make a commitment to bring more of its properties to Broadway, such as *The Lion King,* another hit that would become a Broadway mainstay. Instead of procuring an available Nederlander or Shubert theater, Disney renovated one of the empty and decaying theaters on 42nd Street, the New Amsterdam, leading to the restoration of other houses on the street that had been reduced to showing adult movies or left empty to become impromptu homeless shelters. As a result, a longtime effort to revitalize Times Square was given a much needed boost and the entire district was transformed into a family-friendly entertainment mecca. While some New Yorkers regretted the Disney-fication of Broadway, there was no denying that Disney's commitment to Broadway was a great help to everyone involved in the industry. Grittier theater continued to be developed in off-off Broadway venues farther downtown, such as the musical *Rent,* but that show's popularity led to it finding a Broadway audience as well, as the Nederlander Organization secured the rights to *Rent* and the show played at the Nederlander Theatre for a dozen years.

James M. Nederlander, approaching 80 years of age, remained very much in charge of the Nederlander Organization as the new century dawned, although a third generation of the family was also heavily involved in the running of the business. The company continued to produce and house Broadway shows, send touring productions of those show to its other theaters and elsewhere, and book concerts at its venues. In 2000 the Nederlander Organization opened the renovated Pantages Theatre, acquired a year earlier, to house a Los Angeles production of *The Lion King.* In that same year, Nederlander Concerts was named the exclusive live music promoter for Los Angeles's new 20,000-seat Staples Center. The company already had a similar arrangement with Arrowhead Pond in Anaheim and also booked its artists at the Los Angeles Forum. In addition, the Nederlander Organization became directly involved in London's West End theater through the theaters it owned or managed there.

The company did not neglect its holdings elsewhere in the United States, making an effort to enter cities it considered growth areas. In 2004 it began booking Broadway shows to a Tucson, Arizona, theater, billed as Broadway in Tucson, and to Knoxville, Tennessee, under the Broadway in Knoxville banner. The company also began booking Broadway tours to Dallas, and in 2008 added the Durham Performing Arts Center in North Carolina. The openings of Broadway in Riverside and Broadway San Jose followed in 2009, extending Nederlander's reach in California. As a result the Nederlander Organization, with a third generation already groomed and in place, was well positioned for further growth in the years to come.

Ed Dinger

PRINCIPAL SUBSIDIARIES

Nederlander Concerts, Inc.; Nederlander Alliances, Inc.

PRINCIPAL COMPETITORS

Dodger Theatricals, Ltd.; Jujamcyn Theaters LLC; The Shubert Organization, Inc.

FURTHER READING

Allen, Kathleen, "Nederlander: Broadway Royalty from Way Back," *Arizona Daily Star,* June 6, 2004, p. E1.

Calta, Louis, "Nederlander Family Adds Alvin to Its Holdings," *New York Times,* November 26, 1975.

Canby, Vincent, "Nederlander Family Building a Theater Empire," *New York Times,* July 18, 1967.

Croyden, Margaret, "The Box-Office Boom," *New York Times,* May 10, 1981.

"David R. Nederlander, 81 Dies," *New York Times,* October 17, 1967.

Freedman, Samuel G., "Weintraub Buys Interest in Nederlander Theaters," *New York Times,* September 26, 1984, p. C21.

Lawson, Carol, "Broadway Is in Its Worst Slump in a Decade," *New York Times,* January 3, 1983.

———, "He's the Avis of the Theater World," *New York Times,* November 29, 1981.

Nemy, Enid, "14 Years of Downs and Ups," *New York Times,* April 23, 1983.

"Pantages Restored to Former Glory," *Loveland (CO) Daily Reporter-Herald,* April 20, 2008, p. B4.

Rothstein, Mervyn, "Empty Theaters Bringing Concerts to Broadway," *New York Times,* May 24, 1989.

Zolotow, Sam, "A Detroit Family Buys the Palace," *New York Times,* July 9, 1965.

———, "Detroit Family Profits by Its Plays," *New York Times,* April 12, 1970.

Old Vic Productions plc

The Old Vic, The Cut
London, SE1 8NB
United Kingdom
Telephone: (44 20) 7928 2651
Fax: (44 20) 7261 9161
Web site: http://www.oldvicproductions.com

Private Company
Incorporated: 1993 as Criterion Productions
Sales: $3.2 million (2008)
NAICS: 711310 Promoters of Performing Arts, Sports, and Similar Events with Facilities

∎ ∎ ∎

Headquartered in London, Old Vic Productions plc is the production arm for England's venerable Old Vic Theatre, nearly 200 years old and the former home of Laurence Olivier's National Theatre Company. Old Vic Productions itself is of a more recent vintage. Since its launch in the early 1990s, it has been involved in the production of about 75 plays performed in London's West End theaters, some of which have been transferred to Broadway houses in New York or remounted for worldwide tours. Old Vic Productions' most successful production has been *Billy Elliot,* a musical that completed a successful transfer to Broadway in 2008, where it won the 2009 Tony Award for Best Musical and other honors. To hedge against the financial risk involved in theatrical productions, Old Vic shows are only partly financed by company funds. Outside inves-

tors are brought in to supply the balance of the necessary capital.

Although a private company, Old Vic is owned by numerous shareholders, and the company holds out the possibility that some day its shares might be listed on PLUS Markets, the London stock exchange for small and mid-cap companies. Lord Richard Attenborough serves as Old Vic's chairman while the driving force on a day-to-day basis is CEO Sally Greene. The artistic director of the Old Vic Company that mounts the projects of Old Vic Productions is U.S. actor Kevin Spacey.

SALLY GREENE ABANDONS ACTING FOR MANAGEMENT

Sally Ann Greene became involved with the Old Vic on the strength of her success with Criterion Productions, which she established in 1993. Born in London in 1961, she attended the Guildhall School of Music and Drama in London from 1984 to 1986 to study acting but found she was not suited for the stage. She did not begin her career in show business until prompted by her father, a lawyer, who held an interest in the Richmond Theatre and suggested she become involved with the operation. She did and fell in love with the theater and show business. The Victorian playhouse located in the London borough of Richmond was in need of repair and in 1986 Greene helped raise the necessary funds with her husband, property developer Robert Bourne. Her husband assumed the lease, and in 1991 she became managing director.

COMPANY PERSPECTIVES

■

Old Vic Productions has come a long way in 15 years. Contributing to over 75 leading West End and Broadway plays to date, co-producing the box office smash *Billy Elliot the Musical* with Working Title and helping to establish the Old Vic Theatre Company as a West End force to be reckoned with under the leadership of Kevin Spacey as Artistic Director.

Greene's success with the Richmond led to her taking on a new theater reclamation project in 1992 when she became chief executive officer of the Criterion Theatre Trust, which she founded to restore the Criterion, established in Piccadilly Circus in 1874. Using her considerable social skills Greene was able to persuade Richard Attenborough to chair the charitable trust, thus making the Criterion the first West End theater to be run as a charitable organization. Moreover, Greene hired a little-known designer, Laurence Llewelyn-Brown, to restore the Criterion. The £1 million project received excellent reviews and launched his career, as Llewelyn-Brown became a celebrity designer, famous for his work on the British do-it-yourself television show *Changing Rooms*.

The success of the Criterion's makeover helped to further solidify Greene's reputation. She established a separate enterprise, Criterion Productions, to bring shows to the Criterion stage. She enjoyed a number of successes including the award-winning *My Night with Reg* and the Reduced Shakespeare Company, which performed two of their popular comedic works in repertory. Given Greene's impressive record of restoring the Richmond and Criterion theaters, it was not surprising that she should be recruited in 1998 to save an even more renowned West End theater, the Old Vic.

OLD VIC OPENS DOORS: 1818

The Old Vic was established in 1818 as the Royal Coburg, a minor theater that according to the law at the time was not permitted to present serious drama but rather entertainment fare for the masses. Nevertheless, the tragedian Edmund Kean was brought in to perform some of his greatest Shakespearean roles in 1831 and according to lore admonished the unruly audience at his curtain call, exclaiming "I have never acted to such a set of ignorant, unmitigated brutes as I have before me." In 1833 the theater was renamed the Royal Victorian Theatre, named for Princess Victoria, the future queen.

Despite the change, the theater's reputation did not improve. It was sold off in 1871 and reopened as the New Victoria, but over the next decade was forced into auction and eventually shut down. In 1880 social reformer Emma Cons reopened the theater as the Royal Victoria Hall and Music Hall, and four years later it became the Royal Victoria Hall and Coffee Tavern, but the theater was commonly known as the "Old Vic."

It was Emma Cons's niece, Lilian Baylis, who began to transform the Old Vic into a respectable theatrical venue. She was appointed manager in 1889, and upon the death of her aunt in 1912 she assumed the lease and obtained a theater license. The Old Vic offered operas and in 1914 began staging Shakespeare productions. In the late 1920s and 1930s the Old Vic gave birth to some of the era's greatest Shakespearean actors, John Gielgud and Ralph Richardson, and such accomplished actors as Charles Laughton, Michael Redgrave, and Alec Guinness.

THEATER SEVERELY DAMAGED DURING WORLD WAR II

Following the death of Baylis in 1937, the old Vic received state funding to tour Shakespeare throughout England. Soon the country would be embroiled in World War II. The Old Vic did not remain unscathed, badly damaged in 1941 by German bombers. Nevertheless, the theater was repaired and reopened in 1950. In the meantime, Ralph Richardson and Laurence Olivier led the Old Vic company at temporary quarters at the New Theatre. In 1962 Olivier was named the first director of the National Theatre, which made its home at the Old Vic. The following year the Old Vic company disbanded, replaced by the National Theatre Company under Olivier's direction until 1973. Three years later the National Theatre's last performance was held at the Old Vic. The theater was leased out to visiting companies and also served as the home of the Prospect at the Old Vic production company.

The Old Vic was put on the block and sold in 1982 to Canadian department store mogul and Toronto theater owner Edwin "Honest Ed" Mirvish, who then restored the theater to a look reminiscent of its earlier days. Over the next 16 years the stage at the Old Vic saw numerous well-received productions and garnered more awards for them than any other theater in the country. The Old Vic did not, however, turn a profit. As a result, the Mirvish family put the Old Vic up for sale in 1998 with an asking price of £7.5 million. A public outcry ensued when word leaked out that the Old Vic might well become a bingo hall, pub, or gentlemen's club. Politicians felt the pressure and launched an effort to save the Old Vic.

KEY DATES

1818: Old Vic Theatre is established as Royal Coburg in London.
1950: After sustaining damage during World War II, Old Vic reopens.
1962: Old Vic becomes home to the National Theatre.
1982: Mirvish family acquires Old Vic.
1993: Sally Greene founds Criterion Productions.
1998: Greene heads trust to acquire Old Vic.
2000: Criterion Productions is restructured as Old Vic Productions.
2003: Kevin Spacey is named artistic director of Old Vic Theatre Company.
2004: *Billy Elliot the Musical* opens in London.
2009: *Billy Elliot* wins Tony Award for best musical.

RECRUITING SALLY GREENE TO SAVE OLD VIC: 1998

The United Kingdom's secretary of state for culture, Chris Smith, decided that Sally Greene, who had succeeded in similar efforts with the Richmond and Criterion, was the ideal person to rescue the Old Vic, and in 1998 he persuaded her to accept the challenge. She was able to cut the price of the theater in half and then formed the Old Vic Theatre Trust 2000 to raise the necessary cash, a task that proved difficult. Greene again used her social skills and tapped into her deep pool of friends on both sides of the Atlantic Ocean to develop a board of trustees to help in fund-raising. They included captains of industry as well as famous musicians including Elton John and actors including Willem Dafoe and John Malkovich.

After Greene assumed ownership of the Old Vic, the theater's first production under trust ownership, a revival of *Amadeus,* was nominated for five Olivier Awards. Nevertheless, she wanted to be more than just a landlord and sought to make the theater a producing house once again. In 2000 Criterion Productions was renamed Old Vic Productions to take on this task. To raise the company's profile she enlisted Lord Attenborough to serve as chairman and Dame Judi Dench, Jeremy Irons, and David Suchet to join the board of directors. Playing a major role in fund-raising was Oscar award-winning U.S. actor Kevin Spacey, who had a deep love for the Old Vic ever since the age of five, when he attended a performance there with his parents.

A troubled teen, Spacey turned to acting as a way to find purpose in his life. His first public stage role was as a messenger in a production of *Henry IV* in Shakespeare in the Park in New York City. While he learned his craft he also served as an assistant to the legendary founder of Shakespeare in the Park and the Public Theater, Joseph Papp. Spacey revered Papp, a ferocious champion of the theater who became something of a father figure to the young man. "I remember the day in 1982 when they knocked down two theatres in New York that Joe had campaigned to save, to build a hotel," Spacey recalled in an interview with the *Financial Times.* "I vowed then that if there was ever a time when I could pick up Joe's mantle. I would do the same."

Not only did Spacey help raise funds to save the Old Vic, but he also became a tireless promoter of Old Vic Productions and invested £500,000 out of his own pocket. The goal was to find another 300 investors willing to contribute at least £2,000. To entice well-heeled backers, the company offered people investing the minimum amount a free ticket to opening night of all productions as well as regular newsletters and priority bookings. Investors of £25,000 or more, primarily corporations, received 10 opening night tickets and the chance to enjoy backstage champagne receptions and cast dinners.

BILLY ELLIOT PRODUCTION: 2003

While the money was being harvested to fund production, Greene in 2000 was sowing the seeds for *Billy Elliot the Musical* after she and Elton John attended the premiere of the film *Billy Elliot* at the Cannes film festival. While the project was in development, Greene also moved behind the scenes to create Old Vic Theatre Company to mount shows for the production arm. The person she targeted as artistic director was Spacey. The two had lunch together in 2001. Greene, not fully realizing Spacey's deep affection for the Old Vic, did not have to expend much effort to persuade him to take up the challenge of heading Old Vic Theatre Company. Spacey would eventually sign a 10-year contract. Together they kept the theater company and his appointment as artistic director under wraps until 2003 when it was also announced that Old Vic Productions in association with Working Title Films was going to produce *Billy Elliot the Musical,* featuring songs by Elton John. Old Vic agreed to contribute 40 percent of the financing for the show. By this time, the company was grabbing headlines and filling seats with the co-produced play *The Vagina Monologues,* written by Eve Ensler and originally performed in New York City in 1996.

In 2004 Spacey's new company launched its first season and received a good deal of criticism as the initial plays, *Cloaca* and *National Anthems,* were poorly received by reviewers. The situation improved later in 2004 during the company's second season. As an actor, Spacey won the Critics' Circle Award for Best Actor in a Shakespeare Production for his role as Richard II. Also in June 2004 *Billy Elliot the Musical* opened at London's Victoria Palace Theatre to critical acclaim, the show winning numerous awards. Old Vic Productions also ventured beyond the theater in 2004, entering into a partnership to operate Ronnie Scott's Jazz Club in London, one of the world's most famous jazz clubs.

Spacey continued to experience problems with his programming for Old Vic. In 2006, for example, a production of Arthur Miller's *Resurrection Blues* directed by the well-respected filmmaker Robert Altman, was ravaged by the critics, causing the show to close a week earlier than scheduled. While Old Vic Productions had to write off £400,000 in 2006, the success of *Billy Elliot* kept the company profitable. *Billy Elliot* was set to be a moneymaker for years to come at the Victoria Palace. In December 2007 the show made a successful debut in Sydney, Australia, and in November 2008 the show was taken to Broadway where it was equally well received, winning the 2009 Tony Award for Best Musical. At the very least, the success of *Billy Elliot* provided a strong foundation for Old Vic Productions for years to come.

Ed Dinger

PRINCIPAL SUBSIDIARIES

Ronnie Scott's.

PRINCIPAL COMPETITORS

Dodger Theatricals, Ltd.; Nederlander Producing Company of America, Inc.; The Really Useful Theater Company Ltd.

FURTHER READING

Byrnes, Sholto, and Louise Jury, "The Power Couple—Why Two Heads Are Better Than One," *Independent* (London), November 19, 2000, p. 15.

Cassy, John, "Financiers Have Stars in Their Eyes: Spacey Sales Pitch Makes Dramatic Converts in City," *Guardian* (London), September 1, 2000, p. 23.

Edmands, Michael, "Now the Old Vic's Saviour Is Really Motoring," *Guardian* (London), October 7, 2000, p. 32.

Hattenstone, Simon, "The Queen of Flirts," *Guardian* (London), March 3, 2003.

Hemming, Sarah, "A Crowd-Pleaser Who Plays to Her Investors," *Financial Times,* May 3, 2005, p. 15.

Lloyd, Oliver, "Theatre Impresario Sally Greene Cashes In on 'Billy' Mania," *Daily Mail* (London), September 18, 2005.

Rosenthal, Daniel, "'It's Going to Be Buzzing,'" *Independent* (London), April 29, 2004, p. 8.

Strachan, Alan, "The Partnership of Kevin Spacey and Sally Greene Has Given the Old Vic Its Highest Profile for Years," *Independent* (London), November 18, 2004, p. 8.

Thomcroft, Tony, "'Theatre's More Important to Me Than Acting,'" *Financial Times,* September 2, 2000, p. 3.

OUTOKUMPU

Outokumpu Oyj

Riihitontuntie 7 B
Espoo, 02201
Finland
Telephone: (+358-9) 4211
Fax: (+358-9) 421-3888
Web site: http://www.outokumpu.com

Public Company
Incorporated: 1932
Employees: 8,471
Sales: EUR 5.47 billion ($7.62 billion) (2008)
Stock Exchanges: NASDAQ OMX Helsinki
Ticker Symbol: OUT1V
NAICS: 331111 Iron and Steel Mills

■ ■ ■

The Finnish firm Outokumpu Oyj is one of the world's largest producers of stainless steel. Its output, from its main plants in Finland, Sweden, the United Kingdom, the Netherlands, and the United States, includes cold and hot rolled stainless steel coil, sheet, and plate, along with quarto plate, thin strip, tubular, and long products. The company distributes these products through a network of sales subsidiaries and service centers located in around 30 countries, with about 78 percent of sales generated in Europe, 11 percent in the Americas, and 8 percent in Asia. In stainless steel coil, Outokumpu has captured an 18 percent share of the European market and 6 percent of the world market. Founded in the early 20th century as a copper mining operation, Outokumpu eventually developed into a diversified metals company

involved in the exploration and mining, smelting and refining, and fabrication of copper, zinc, nickel, and stainless steel. A series of divestments in the early 21st century enabled the company to concentrate on its strongest area, stainless steel. The Finnish State continues to hold a stake in Outokumpu of approximately 31 percent.

ORIGINS

The Finnish word *outokumpu* can be translated as "mysterious" or "strange hill," a reference to a specific hill in eastern Finland where both Outokumpu Oyj and Outokumpu, the community that developed around the company, were located. Local lore held that the "strange hill" in the wooded hills of eastern Finland contained valuable mineral deposits. Local prospectors needed no further encouragement to begin scrutinizing the *outokumpu*, their interest piqued by the promise of hidden wealth. From as early as 1725, samples from the hill were sent to the national College of Mines for analysis, but all hopes were dashed when scientific examination revealed that the prospectors had discovered iron pyrite, more commonly known as "fool's gold." In fact, the fabled hill did contain hidden wealth, but it took until the early 19th century for the value of the subterranean treasure to be identified.

In 1908 a discovery was made 40 miles outside of Outokumpu that triggered the formation of Outokumpu Oyj. A massive metallic boulder was found, prompting further analysis. Tests revealed that the giant orb contained valuable copper ore, carried, scientists theorized, by the movement of ice sheets during the most recent Ice Age. The glacial pattern of movement directed scientists northwest of the metallic boulder, toward the mysterious hill in Outokumpu. In 1910 test drilling at the hill confirmed the existence of a substantial copper ore deposit, leading to the establishment of a mining operation that formed the foundation for Outokumpu Oyj.

To add value to the ore at the hill, a small smelter was constructed alongside the mining operation, as preparations immediately commenced to turn the site into a commercial concern. Outokumpu Oyj experienced a somewhat fitful start to its business life, its birth giving rise to a divisive struggle over control. Finnish businessmen battled with government officials, with each side claiming ownership of the copper resources. The contentious debate was exacerbated by the hovering presence of foreign mining companies, who sniffed opportunity and tried to insinuate themselves into the picture. Operationally, the mining and smelting operations suffered at first from an insufficient number of employees with the technical acumen to solve problems that arose. When a certain aspect of the operations failed to work properly, the only recourse in many instances was to keep making adjustments until the problem was solved. It was a slow, sometimes painstaking, process, but eventually lessons were learned. By 1914, the company's first shipment was made: 60 metric tons of copper ingots sold in St. Petersburg, Russia.

Over time, the operational aspects of the smelting and mining operations improved, but the thorny question of ownership persisted. The individual responsible for solving this fundamental dilemma was Dr. Eero Mäkinen, the most influential figure during Outokumpu Oyj's development. Dr. Mäkinen joined the company as a 32-year-old mining engineer in 1918. Among his numerous contributions to the company, perhaps none was more important than his persistent effort to lend stability to the organization. During its first decade of existence, the company struggled in vain to secure private capital from Finnish sources, which left the company vulnerable to the covetous interests of foreign parties. In order to stave off a hostile takeover,

Dr. Mäkinen argued strongly for government intervention, believing ownership by the Finnish State would end the threat of foreign mining concerns. Dr. Mäkinen prevailed, persuading the Finnish State to assume ownership of Outokumpu Oyj in 1924. It was not until 1932, however, that the company was formally incorporated.

From its outset, Outokumpu Oyj was an export-driven company, relying heavily on supplying unprocessed ore and smelted ore to neighboring nations. During the 1920s, for instance, the company sold raw ore to Germany and refined copper to Sweden. The company's first appreciable surge of growth occurred during the late 1920s and early 1930s, when Finland's rapid industrialization propelled the company much closer to the forefront of technology. The paucity of technical expertise, which had hobbled Outokumpu's progress during its first years in business, no longer was a problem. Evidence of the greatly improved technological sophistication of the company's engineers was on display in 1935, when Outokumpu constructed what was then the largest electric copper smelter in the world. Located near Finland's eastern border in Imatra, the smelter was moved in 1944 to distance the valuable facility from the looming threat of Soviet troops. Dismantled and then rebuilt near Finland's west coast, the massive smelter found a permanent home in Harjavalta, the site of Outokumpu's greatest achievement.

FLASH SMELTING AND POSTWAR DIVERSIFICATION

At Harjavalta in the late 1940s, Outokumpu Oyj's scientists and engineers developed a new process of extracting metal from its ore. Called flash smelting, the closed extraction process captured nearly all of the sulfur-rich gases from the smelting furnace. Developed by Petri Bryk and John Ryselin, flash smelting was regarded as the most significant metallurgical breakthrough of the 20th century, an appraisal that had not changed by the century's end. The success of flash smelting, which later was licensed to other metallurgical companies, eventually led to the formation of an Outokumpu technology division. To aid in the development of further metallurgical innovations, the company relied on its metallurgical lab, first established in Pori in 1942. The formation of a full-scale metallurgical lab and the widespread acceptance of flash smelting testified to the evolutionary leap the company had achieved in the technical aspects of its business. The early days of solving problems by trial and error had given way to world-recognized sophistication in metallurgical science, securing a lasting market position for Outokumpu Oyj during the latter half of the 20th century.

KEY DATES

1914: First shipment of metal is made.
1924: Finnish government assumes ownership of Outokumpu Oyj.
Late 1940s: Flash smelting is developed.
1951: Exploration department is established.
1959: Company diversifies into steel production.
1976: Stainless steel plant in Tornio goes online.
1988: Outokumpu Oyj debuts on the Helsinki Stock Exchange.
2001: AvestaPolarit is created through the merger of Outokumpu Steel and Avesta Sheffield.
2003: Outokumpu acquires full ownership of AvestaPolarit; zinc business and copper mining and smelting operations are divested.
2005: Company sells its copper products division and focuses solely on stainless steel.

As the company's expertise blossomed, so too did the scope of its business. Initially, the company vertically integrated its copper operations by taking control over the various processing stages of the copper ore mined at Outokumpu. Such vertical integration brought the company closer to the end user, or "downstream," enabling it to reap profits and to better control costs along the downstream stages of copper processing. In 1940, for example, the company began producing copper semi-products in Pori. The facilities in Pori had begun producing a number of nonferrous alloys by the late 1940s, but, unlike with copper, the company did not possess the raw materials to produce the other alloys. Consequently, the company was forced to purchase the basic materials from other companies, an arrangement that did not suit Outokumpu Oyj officials. The company resolved to develop its own sources for the raw materials it needed, leading to the formation of an exploration department in 1951. Not long after the hunt for new ore deposits began, the mining and production of other metals commenced. Outokumpu would no longer exist as a copper-only company.

The company's quest for self-sufficiency recorded its first success several years after the creation of an exploration department. In 1954, a deposit of nickel-bearing pyrrhotite ore was found in Kotalahti, ushering the company into the nickel production business. A nickel plant, completed by 1960, was constructed in Harjavalta, where Outokumpu's engineers were able to incorporate flash smelting technology into nickel production. Also in 1954, the company opened its Vihanti mine, which added zinc to its growing portfolio of metals. Next, cobalt and sulfur production fell under Outokumpu's purview, with the company's decade of diversification ending in 1959, when a chromite deposit discovered in northern Finland led Outokumpu into steel production.

FOCUSING ON EXPORTS AND FOREIGN SUPPLIERS: FIFTIES TO SEVENTIES

As the company diversified its involvement in metal production, it also strengthened and expanded its network of sales offices. Outokumpu's initial focus on export markets endured throughout the 1930s, but the company redirected its efforts inward during subsequent years, as it focused on meeting domestic metal demands. In the 1950s, however, the company began focusing on export sales with renewed vigor. Sales representatives were established in Norway, Sweden, and Denmark during the decade, as the company's steadily increasing capacity necessitated a larger customer base. By 1964, as was true during the company's formative years, export sales exceeded domestic sales.

Outokumpu's physical expansion beyond Finland's borders was not limited to its marketing functions only. Although the company was beginning to greatly expand and diversify its exploration efforts, by the 1960s it could no longer supply its refining operations with enough ore by relying exclusively on Finnish sources. Outokumpu's production capacity had increased to the point where foreign sources of ore were required to keep the company's facilities operating at optimal efficiency. To answer the call for a greater supply of ore, the company brokered several extended purchase agreements with overseas mines. Not long after securing these agreements, the company demonstrated its penchant for self-reliance by forming an international department in 1974 to foster its own exploration and development efforts overseas. Because of these efforts, the company secured stakes in mining operations in Canada and Norway.

The 1950s and 1960s were years of aggressive expansion, time spent building the infrastructure and assembling the resources to support a multinational mining, refining, and production organization. The years of steady growth set the stage for what promised to be a profitable decade ahead, when the sprawling yet integrated mining operations would find full expression. The 1970s proved to be a difficult decade, however, witnessing the company's first annual losses in 40 years. The oil embargo during the early 1970s caused production costs to escalate, a pattern aped by labor costs. Instead of being a decade of progress, the 1970s forced Outokumpu into its shell, restricting capital improvements substantially. With the exception of a new stainless steel plant in Tornio that became operational in 1976, Outokumpu made no capacity expansions during the decade, choosing to wait until a more stable economic climate returned.

A MINING GIANT TAKES SHAPE IN THE EIGHTIES

The 1980s brought Outokumpu a return to prosperity and expansion. Much of the growth occurred on the international front, as the company significantly strengthened its presence overseas. The roster of company-controlled sales offices overseas grew to include facilities in the United States, the Netherlands, Singapore, Japan, Italy, Mexico, Switzerland, Chile, and elsewhere, accounting for one-third of Outokumpu's total sales by the early 1990s. The company grew via acquisition during the 1980s as well, purchasing an Ohio-based fabricator of zirconium copper in 1983 and a Wisconsin-based producer of specialty alloy wire in 1985. Other important additions included the purchase of a controlling interest in Tara Mines in Ireland and the acquisition of the Viscaria copper mine in Sweden.

Domestically, one of the most significant developments during the 1980s concerned Outokumpu's ownership. Since the 1960s, the company had offered employees the option of retiring with full pension benefits at the age of 52. In the 1980s, company officials feared the payment of pension benefits in the coming years could trigger a financial crisis. As a precaution, Outokumpu offered shares in the company to those Finnish employees who were eligible for pension benefits, hoping such employees would accept an ownership stake in exchange for their benefits. Nearly all of the employees agreed to the proposal. The crisis was averted and, in October 1988, Outokumpu Oyj shares debuted on the Helsinki Stock Exchange.

As Outokumpu prepared for the 1990s, an exhaustive reorganization occurred that altered the relationship among the company's scores of businesses. During the late 1980s, centralized management was shelved, replaced by a more autonomous organization that ceded authority to individual business units. Many of the company's subsidiaries and divisions were restructured as independent corporations, enabling the organization as a whole to react more nimbly to changing market conditions.

SHIFT TO STAINLESS STEEL BEGINS IN LATE NINETIES

During the 1990s, under the leadership of Jyrki Juusela, who was named chief executive in 1992, Outokumpu sharpened its focus on its core metal businesses. Between 1993 and 1996, the company invested in a major expansion and modernization program that increased the copper smelting capacity at Harjavalta by three-fifths and doubled the company's nickel smelting capacity. Although copper and nickel were important metals, particularly copper, Outokumpu was recording its greatest profit gains with its stainless steel businesses. By the late 1990s, the consistently strong performance of stainless steel convinced management to direct much of the company's capital resources toward strengthening its involvement in stainless steel. In December 1999 Outokumpu executives decided to launch a major expansion program at Tornio. The project, which ended up taking much more time than originally anticipated, doubled the plant's capacity when it was finally completed in 2005, at which point this plant ranked as the largest single-site stainless steel production facility in the world.

The most significant event concerning Outokumpu's involvement in stainless steel occurred in January 2001, when the company's steel businesses merged with the Avesta Sheffield Group, owned by Sweden-based Avesta Sheffield AB. The merger created AvestaPolarit, the second-largest independent stainless steel producer in the world. AvestaPolarit, 55 percent owned by Outokumpu, generated more than EUR 3 billion in annual sales, supported by facilities in Finland, Sweden, the United Kingdom, and the United States. During 2000, as this merger went through the process of gaining shareholder and regulatory approval, Outokumpu sold its nickel refinery in Harjavalta to OM Group, Inc., for about EUR 180 million. In April 2001 Outokumpu bolstered its zinc operations via the purchase of Norzink AS, a Norwegian zinc smelting and refining company, for around EUR 204 million.

Stainless steel came further to the fore in 2003. By March of that year, Outokumpu had acquired full ownership of AvestaPolarit by buying out the minority shareholders in that company for a total of EUR 1.1 billion. AvestaPolarit was subsequently renamed Outokumpu Stainless. Outokumpu that same year acquired the quarto plate business of ThyssenKrupp Nirosta GmbH for EUR 59 million. Quarto plate was a hot rolled stainless steel product that was extremely resistant to corrosion and wear resistant as well and thus used in challenging applications in the petroleum and pulp and paper industries and in chemical tankers. In late 2003 Outokumpu sold its zinc business and its copper mining and smelting operations to Boliden AB of Sweden. In return for these assets, Outokumpu received EUR 373 million in cash, a EUR 146 million subordinated note, and a 49 percent stake in Boliden. Outokumpu sold its entire stake in Boliden in stepwise fashion over the next few years, a process that essentially ended Outokumpu's participation in its founding mining business.

During the final months of 2004, a leadership transition occurred in which Juusela relinquished his chief executive position to Juha Rantanen, who was hired away from the Swedish machinery company Ahlstrom Corporation, where he had also served as chief executive. Rantanen soon completed the transformation of Outokumpu his predecessor had begun. In June 2005 the company sold its copper products division to private-equity firm Nordic Capital for EUR 612 million ($751 million). This divestment enabled Outokumpu to concentrate solely on stainless steel and devote more resources toward achieving its goal of becoming the number one stainless steelmaker in the world. Outokumpu ended 2005 ranked third in the world in stainless steel slab capacity, trailing only Germany's Thyssen-Krupp Stainless AG and Arcelor S.A. of Luxembourg (later the much larger ArcelorMittal).

FACING ECONOMIC CHALLENGES: 2008–09

Over the next few years, Outokumpu took a number of steps to build a more stable business model in a typically cyclical industry. Among these initiatives were increasing business with end users compared to distributors, shifting to a product mix with a greater proportion of value-added stainless steel products, and capturing more business outside of Western Europe. The EUR 224 million acquisition of SoGePar Group, an Italian distributor, in the summer of 2008 was one move that helped increase business with end users, while Outokumpu also launched major investments in a number of its plants to increase capacity and begin production of new value-added products. Additional investments were made to set up new service centers in Poland, India, and China and thus create a more geographically diverse company.

During the second half of 2008, however, the company was forced to pull back on some of its investment plans when the global financial meltdown led to greatly reduced demand for stainless steel. Outokumpu also implemented workforce reductions as part of an effort to trim annual operating costs by EUR 100 million. Its results for 2008 were bleak: a net loss of EUR 189 million ($263 million) on sales of EUR 5.47 billion ($7.62 billion), a 21 percent decline over the previous year. Demand for stainless steel remained depressed and the company continued to operate in the red during the

first half of 2009, although Outokumpu executives had begun to detect some signs of improvement in the marketplace.

Jeffrey L. Covell
Updated, David E. Salamie

PRINCIPAL SUBSIDIARIES

General Stainless: Contisteel N.V. (Belgium); Eurotec N.V. (Belgium); Finsogepar S.p.A. (Italy); Outokumpu AS (Norway); Outokumpu A/S (Denmark); Outokumpu Asia Pacific Ltd (China); Outokumpu Baltic Oü (Estonia); Outokumpu Benelux B.V. (Netherlands); Outokumpu Brasil Comercio de Metais Ltda. (Brazil); Outokumpu B.V. (Netherlands); Outokumpu Chrome Oy; Outokumpu Distribution Oy; Outokumpu Gebouwen B.V. (Netherlands); Outokumpu Ges.m.b.H (Austria); Outokumpu GmbH (Germany); Outokumpu India Private Limited; Outokumpu Istanbul Dis Ticaret Limited Sirketi (Turkey); Outokumpu Kft. (Hungary); Outokumpu K.K. (Japan); Outokumpu, Lda. (Portugal); Outokumpu Ltd (Ireland); Outokumpu Middle East FZCO (United Arab Emirates); Outokumpu Nordic AB (Sweden); Outokumpu N.V. (Belgium); Outokumpu Pty Ltd (Australia); Outokumpu (Pty) Ltd (South Africa); Outokumpu Rossija Oy; Outokumpu S.A.S. (France); Outokumpu S.A. (Spain); Outokumpu (S.E.A.) Pte. Ltd. (Singapore); Outokumpu Shipping Oy; Outokumpu S.p.A. (Italy); Outokumpu Sp. z o.o. (Poland); Outokumpu S.R.L. (Romania); Outokumpu s.r.o. (Czech Republic); Outokumpu Stainless B.V. (Netherlands); Outokumpu Stainless Coil, Inc. (USA); Outokumpu Stainless Holding GmbH (Germany); Outokumpu Stainless Ltd (UK); Outokumpu Stainless Oy; Outokumpu UAB (Lithuania); Sogepar Deutschland GmbH (Germany); Sogepar France s.a.r.l.; Sogepar Ireland Limited; So.Ge.Par S.p.A. (Italy); Sogepar UK Limited; ZAO Outokumpu (Russia). Specialty Stainless: Avesta Klippcenter AB (Sweden); Outokumpu Armetal Stainless Pipe Co. Ltd. (Saudi Arabia; 51%); Outokumpu Prefab AB (Sweden); Outokumpu Press Plate AB (Sweden); Outokumpu PSC Benelux B.V. (Netherlands); Outokumpu PSC Germany GmbH; Outokumpu Stainless AB (Sweden); Outokumpu Stainless Bar, Inc. (USA); Outokumpu Stainless Pipe, Inc. (USA); Outokumpu Stainless Plate, Inc. (USA); Outokumpu Stainless Steel (China) Co. Ltd.; Outokumpu Stainless Trading (Shanghai) Co. Ltd. (China); AS Outokumpu Stainless Tubular Products (Estonia); Outokumpu Stainless Tubular Products AB (Sweden); Outokumpu Stainless Tubular Products Ltd. (Canada); Outokumpu Stainless Tubular Products Oy Ab; Polarit Welding, Inc. (USA); SH-Trade Oy; AB Örnsköldsviks Mekaniska Verkstad (Sweden).

PRINCIPAL OPERATING UNITS

General Stainless; Specialty Stainless.

PRINCIPAL COMPETITORS

ArcelorMittal; Acerinox, S.A.; ThyssenKrupp Stainless AG; POSCO; Taiyuan Iron and Steel (Group) Co., Ltd.

FURTHER READING

Bergstrom, Rupini, "Outokumpu Plans to Cut Costs," *Financial Times*, September 27, 2005, p. 32.

"Boliden Acquires Outokumpu Assets," *Metal Bulletin*, September 11, 2003.

Brown-Humes, Christopher, "Deal Gives Outokumpu 49% of Boliden," *Financial Times*, September 9, 2003, p. 30.

Casteel, Kyran, "Building a Giant," *World Mining Equipment*, November 2001, pp. 37–38.

Francis-Grey, Paul, "Outokumpu to Sell Mines, Take 49% Stake in Boliden," *American Metal Market*, September 9, 2003, p. 1.

Kantrow, Buster, "Finnish Firm to Buy 23% Stake in Avesta-Polarit from Corus," *Wall Street Journal Europe*, July 2, 2002, p. A4.

Kuisma, Markku, *A History of Outokumpu*, Jyväskylä, Finland: Gummerus, 1989, 240 p.

Marsh, Peter, "Stainless Steel Makers Set to Merge," *Financial Times*, September 27, 2000.

Millbank, Paul, "Pushing for Profitability," *Metal Bulletin*, January 22, 2003.

"Outokumpu Buys Big to Balance Range," *Metal Bulletin Monthly*, October 31, 2008.

"Outokumpu on the Move," *Mining Journal*, October 13, 2000, pp. 291–292.

"Outokumpu Picks Ahlstrom Chief to Be New CEO," *Wall Street Journal Europe*, July 23, 2004, p. A9.

"Outokumpu Sells Its Harjavalta Refinery," *Metal Bulletin*, February 29, 2000.

"Outokumpu Takes Control in Merger with Avesta Sheffield," *Metal Bulletin*, October 2, 2000.

"Outokumpu to Buy Avesta, Creating Giant Steelmaker," *Wall Street Journal Europe*, September 29, 2000, p. 5.

"Repositioning Outokumpu," *Mining Magazine*, February 2001, p. 104.

Reynolds, Vicki, "Finnish Miner Outokumpu Shifting Focus to Metals, Technology," *American Metal Market*, October 23, 2000, p. 8.

Särkikoski, Tuomo, *A Flash of Knowledge: How an Outokumpu Innovation Became a Culture*, Espoo, Finland: Outokumpu Oyj, 1999, 304 p.

Smith, David A., "Outokumpu Sells Copper Divisions to Nordic Capital," *Waterbury (CT) Republican-American*, April 8, 2005.

Petroplus Holdings AG

Industriestrasse 24
Zug, CH-6300
Switzerland
Telephone: (+41 058) 580 11 00
Fax: (+41 058) 580 11 91
Web site: http://www.petroplusholdings.com

Public Company
Incorporated: 1993
Employees: 1,500
Sales: $28.05 billion (2008)
Stock Exchanges: Swiss
Ticker Symbol: PPHN
NAICS: 424690 Other Chemical and Allied Products Merchant Wholesalers; 424720 Petroleum and Petroleum Products Merchant Wholesalers (Except Bulk Stations and Terminals)

∎ ∎ ∎

Petroplus Holdings AG is Europe's leading independent petroleum refinery group. The Zug, Switzerland-based company operates seven petroleum refineries in strategic locations throughout Europe. At the end of 2009, the company's total refining capacity neared 865,000 barrels per day. Petroplus is a "pure-play" refining group. Petroplus groups its refinery operations into two primary divisions: North Sea Refining System and Inland Refining System. The North Sea System encompasses the group's refinery operations at Coryton and Teesside in the United Kingdom, and in Antwerp, Belgium. The Inland Sea System includes refineries in Couronne and Reichstett in France; Cressier in Switzerland, and Ingolstadt in Germany. These refineries primarily distribute finished petroleum products to their local markets; this proximity allows Petroplus to compete with its far larger integrated rivals. Petroplus focuses especially on the light products category, which includes gasoline, diesel and jet fuel, petrochemicals and naphtha, and liquefied petroleum gas. Light products account for 82 percent of the group's total volume. The company also produces bitumen-based home heating fuel oil, which accounts for 14 percent of the group's production volume. Petroplus is listed on the Swiss Stock Exchange and is led by CEO Robert Lavinia. In 2008, the company generated revenues of $28.05 billion.

"PETROPRENEURS" IN 1993

Petroplus originated in 1993 as the result of a management buyout of a Netherlands-based petroleum products trader called Vanol Rotterdam Olieproducten BV. Vanol, set up in 1989, had developed operations in the storage, marketing, and distribution of petroleum products. Vanol primarily focused on supplying household fuel oil in the Netherlands, Germany, and the United Kingdom. The company struggled, however, to find its footing in the early years of the 1990s. By the end of 1992, Petroplus was bankrupt, with losses reportedly mounting to $35 million. While Vanol's history remained obscure, the company was also said to have held assets worth approximately $100 million in the United Kingdom.

Vanol nonetheless provided the vehicle for the entrepreneurial ambitions of two business school

COMPANY PERSPECTIVES

Our Vision: Our goal is to be the leading independent refiner and supplier of unbranded petroleum products in Europe and to be an industry leader in returning value to our shareholders.

We are a "pure-play" refiner without the obligation to supply retail outlets or the cost of supporting a retail brand. As a result, we are free to supply our products into the distribution channel or market that we believe will maximize profit.

classmates, Marcel van Poecke and Willem Willemstein. Van Poecke's career background lay in the oil industry, starting with a position as the commercial director of Calpalm International Petroleum Company BV. Willemstein's own background originated in the financial sector, including a stint as the deputy general manager for international corporate banker NMB Bank (later part of the ING banking and insurance group). In 1990, Willemstein too joined Calpalm, becoming its financial director.

Van Poecke and Willemstein had initially met as students completing their M.B.A. studies at the University of Rochester in New York. While in the United States, Van Poecke and Willemstein decided to go into business together. Their target quickly fell on the petroleum sector, which was undergoing a number of significant changes in the United States in the late 1980s. Most notable of these was an increasing trend of the highly integrated major petroleum players to begin focusing more sharply on a smaller core of operations. This led these companies to shed parts of their ongoing operations, particularly those areas where achieving profitability remained difficult for the larger companies. As a result, a new generation of petroleum companies came into being, many of which were focused on the petroleum products storage, handling, trading, and marketing areas. Other companies took parts of the major players' refinery operations. The people behind this new breed of petroleum company were sometimes referred to as "petropreneurs."

Willemstein and Van Poecke recognized an opportunity to develop their own operations based on a similar model in Europe, which remained dominated by the major oil groups, with few smaller players competing for the fringes of the region's petroleum market. Their opportunity came amid the collapse of Vanol. By 1992, both Van Poecke and Willemstein had joined

Vanol, with Willemstein taking up the position of managing director. The partners then led a management buyout of Vanol, with backing from Nederlandse Participatie Maatschappij. Van Poecke and Willemstein then changed the company's name, to Petroplus International BV.

PUBLIC OFFERING IN 1998

Willemstein and Van Poecke immediately began putting into place their strategy of building a diversified petroleum products storage and trading company. For this, the company targeted the acquisition of a range of smaller European companies active in the market.

Over the next several years, Petroplus built up a portfolio of operations ranging from retail and wholesale trading companies, storage facilities, pipe laying and engineering operations, ship and tanker terminals, to other companies focused on the oil trading, logistics, and storage sectors. These purchases gave the company a presence across Europe, including operations in Russia. Petroplus also built a strong list of customers, including much of the Netherlands' inland shipping market, and the fuel-supply contract for Belgian aviation group Sabena. The company became market leader in a number of product categories, such as monoethyleneglycol, used in the production of polyester and antifreeze.

In 1997, Petroplus took its first steps into the petroleum refining market, buying up control of a petroleum storage and refinery complex in Antwerp from Daewoo of South Korea. The company then sold 40 percent of the Antwerp facility to Kuwait investment group IPG. The Antwerp facility also featured a neighboring bitumen plant, originally constructed as part of the refinery complex but sold off in the 1980s to the Swedish group Nynas.

Petroplus continued its search for new acquisition candidates, targeting especially the expansion of its refinery capacity. In 1998, the company gained the option to acquire Gulf Oil Refining, a refinery and oil terminal complex in Wales from Chevron. In order to provide a treasury for the purchase, Petroplus decided to go public, and in 1998 listed its shares on the Amsterdam Stock Exchange. By then, Petroplus had expanded its revenues to some NLG 1.2 billion (approximately $600 million), which enabled the company to list directly on the Amsterdam main board. The public offering helped Petroplus build a war chest of some $100 million to pay for the Milford Haven acquisition and others.

Petroplus completed the Gulf Oil Refining acquisition in 1998, boosting its sales past NLG 2 billion ($1

KEY DATES

1993: Willem Willemstein and Marcel van Poecke lead a management buyout of failed Dutch petroleum products trading group Vanol, changing its name to Petroplus.
1997: Petroplus acquires its first refinery, in Antwerp.
1998: Petroplus goes public, listing on the Amsterdam Stock Exchange.
2000: Petroplus acquires the Cressier Refinery in Switzerland and the Teesside Refinery in the United Kingdom.
2005: Petroplus delists from the Amsterdam Stock Exchange.
2006: A new management team, led by Thomas O'Malley, moves Petroplus to Switzerland where it re-lists on the Swiss Stock Exchange and launches its pure-play refinery strategy.
2007: Petroplus acquires the Ingolstadt refinery in Germany.
2008: Petroplus acquires the Petit Couronne and Reichstett refineries in France.

billion). The company quickly moved onto its next acquisition target, buying fellow Netherlands oil trading company North Sea Trading. That purchase added another NLG 1 billion ($500 million) to Petroplus's revenues. This expansion fit in with the company's strategy of becoming the leading independent petroleum products player in Europe, a position that was relatively easy to achieve, in that most, if not all of the group's rivals remained affiliated with the major petroleum groups.

BUILDING REFINERY OPERATIONS

The company's interest in Gulf Oil Refining lay principally in that operation's extensive petroleum storage facilities, and not in its small refinery complex. Into the beginning of the next decade, Petroplus's strategy increasingly began to focus on developing its refinery capacity. This increase in capacity led the group to redefine its strategy toward becoming a "pure-play" petroleum products refinery company. The company was aided in achieving this goal by the difficulties faced by the major petroleum groups during this period. Amid a turbulent petroleum market, coupled with increasing shareholder pressure to achieve short-term profit gains, a

number of oil groups had begun to adopt the U.S. model of streamlining their operations, including reducing their exposure to local refinery markets.

The company took an important step to what was to become its future direction in the year 2000, when it completed two major acquisitions. In that year, the company bought up all of Shell's petroleum operations in Switzerland, including its Cressier refinery. That complex, a 74-hectare site located near the French border, had been commissioned in 1966 and had expanded to achieve total production capacity of 68,000 barrels per day.

At the same time, Petroplus completed its second major refinery purchase, buying the Teesside refinery in the United Kingdom from PIP Ltd. This 40-hectare complex, also built in 1966, added another 117,000 barrels per day of capacity to Petroplus's rapidly growing refining operations.

In the early years of the new century, Petroplus continued to build up its non-refinery businesses. In 2000, for example, the company entered the retail market, launching a self-service, unmanned gas-station network under the Tango name. That network grew quickly, boasting 25 stations across the Netherlands by 2002, with plans to double that number by the end of the year. These plans included the opening of the first Tango stations outside of the Netherlands, with Belgium, Spain, and Hungary as the initial targets.

In another extension of its business, Petroplus acquired the bitumen facility at its Antwerp site from Nynas in 2003. The purchase agreement also included a contract to continue to supply Nynas with bitumen. Following that purchase, Petroplus restructured the Antwerp site, shutting down most of its refinery operations to focus the site on bitumen production. The costs of the shut-down, however, proved a heavy burden for the company, resulting in a net loss for the year.

BECOMING A PURE-PLAY REFINERY GROUP

The company's situation was buoyed somewhat at the beginning of 2004. At that time, Petroplus announced an agreement to sell off the Tango network of filling stations, to Kuwait Petroleum, for EUR 72 million ($89 million). The sale enabled the company to post a profit at the end of the first quarter of that year, while also pointing the way toward its future pure-play strategy.

Petroplus's difficulties, and an overall lack of investor confidence in the petroleum sector, prompted founders Willemstein and Van Poecke to lead a buyout of the company in May 2004. At that time, the company agreed to be acquired by RIVR Acquisition, an investment consortium including Willemstein, Van Poecek, and a number of funds associated with the Carlyle group. Following the offer, which was completed in 2005, Petroplus removed its listing from the Amsterdam exchange.

In 2006, Petroplus brought in a new management team, led by industry notable Thomas O'Malley as chief executive officer. Under O'Malley, Petroplus put into place its pure-play refinery strategy. Thus the company's other operations, including Petroplus Tankstorage, Oxyde Chemical, and Frisol, were sold in August 2006. At the same time, Petroplus, which no longer had any operations in the Netherlands, moved its headquarters to Zug, Switzerland. Soon after, Petroplus went public again with a listing on the Swiss Stock Exchange.

O'Malley quickly set into motion a new expansion drive for the company, more than quadrupling its refinery capacity by the end of the decade. The company acquired European Petroleum Holdings, which operated the BRC Refinery in Antwerp, in 2006, adding 110,000 barrels per day to its capacity. In March 2007, the group added another 110,000 barrels-per-day refinery, in Ingolstadt, Germany. This was followed soon after by the purchase of a refinery in Coryton, in the United Kingdom, in May 2007.

The next piece in Petroplus's puzzle came in March 2008, when the company completed the purchase of two refineries in France, in Petit Couronne, on the Seine River north of Paris, and in Reichstett. The former became the company's largest single refinery, with a capacity of 154,000 barrels per day, while the latter added 85,000 barrels per day. By 2009, Petroplus's total capacity had risen to nearly 865,000 barrels per day. In this way, Petroplus had grown to become the largest independent specialist refinery group in Europe.

M. L. Cohen

PRINCIPAL SUBSIDIARIES

Argus International Ltd. (Bermuda); Belgian Refining Corporation N.V.; European Petroleum Corporation (EPC) B.V. (Netherlands); Marimpex Mineralöl-Handelsgesellschaft mbH (Germany); Marimpex Prague (Czech Republic); Oléoduc du Jura Neuchâtelois S.A.; Petrobel N.V. (Belgium); Petroplus Czech Republic s.r.o.; Petroplus Deutschland GmbH (Germany); Petroplus Holdings B.V. (Netherlands); Petroplus Holdings France SAS; Petroplus International B.V. (Netherlands); Petroplus Marketing AG; Petroplus Marketing Ltd. (UK); Petroplus Refining Cressier SA; Petroplus Refining Teesside Ltd. (UK); Petroplus

Switzerland; Petroplus Tankstorage AG; Petrotrade B.V. (Netherlands).

PRINCIPAL DIVISIONS

Inland Refining System; North Sea Refining System.

PRINCIPAL OPERATING UNITS

APF Antwerp Processing Facility (Belgium); BRC Refinery (Belgium); Coryton Refinery (UK); Cressier Refinery; Ingolstadt Refinery (Germany); Petit Couronne Refinery (France); Reichstett Refinery (France); Teesside Refinery (UK).

PRINCIPAL COMPETITORS

Royal Dutch Shell PLC; Chevron Corp.; Glencore International AG; China National Petroleum Corp.; Elf Aquitaine S.A.; Vitol Holding B.V.; StatoilHydro ASA; Petrobras Distribuidora S.A.

FURTHER READING

Bickerton, Ian, "Petroplus Set to Go Private in Consortium Deal," *Financial Times*, May 19, 2004, p. 27.

"Dutch Refiner Moving Closer to Privatization," *Global Refining & Fuels Report*, September 15, 2004.

"EU Refiner Petroplus Sees Diesel More Profitable Than Gasoline in 2009," *Diesel Fuel News*, February 16, 2009.

"European Commission Approves Purchase of BP Refinery by Petroplus," *Global Refining & Fuels Report*, May 9, 2007.

"Good Time to Expand Capacity," *World Refining*, July–August 2002, p. 56.

Haldis, Peter, "Petroplus, LyondellBasell Complete Purchases of Shell's French Refineries," *Global Refining & Fuels Report*, April 9, 2008.

———, "Petroplus May Sell U.K. Refinery, Loses $775 Million in Q4," *Global Refining & Fuels Report*, February 11, 2009.

"Petroplus Acquires Teesside (UK) Refinery," *World Refining*, January–February 2001, p. 16.

"Petroplus Announces Formation of Growth Vehicle for US Refinery Acquisitions," *Space Daily*, February 29, 2008.

"Petroplus Forms Partnership to Pursue U.S. Acquisitions," *World Refining & Fuels Today*, February 28, 2008.

"Petroplus Has Purchased the Bitumen Plant on the Site of Its Antwerp Refinery from Sweden's Nynas," *Petroleum Economist*, April 2003, p. 41.

"Petroplus IPO Sold Four Times as Investors Buy O'Malley Effect," *Euroweek*, December 1, 2006.

"Petroplus Loses $11.3 Million in Q1," *Global Refining & Fuels Report*, May 20, 2009.

"Petroplus Names New CEO," *Professional Services Close-Up*, May 25, 2009.

Plains All American
Pipeline, L.P.

—■—

333 Clay Street, Suite 1600
Houston, Texas 77002
U.S.A.
Telephone: (713) 646-4100
Toll Free: (800) 564-3036
Fax: (713) 646-4572
Web site: http://www.plainsallamerican.com

Public Company
Incorporated: 1998
Employees: 3,302
Sales: $30.06 billion (2008)
Stock Exchanges: New York
Ticker Symbol: PAA
NAICS: 486110 Pipeline Transportation of Crude Oil

■ ■ ■

Plains All American Pipeline, L.P. (PAAP) transports, stores, and markets crude oil, refined oil, and liquefied petroleum gas. PAAP owns more than 17,000 miles of pipelines that move more than three million barrels of petroleum products per day. The company's network of pipelines and its storage facilities in Cushing, Oklahoma, carry oil and other petroleum products from the Gulf Coast to markets in the Midwest. PAAP also owns pipelines and storage facilities in Canada. The company operates as a master limited partnership, which spares it from paying taxes at the corporate level provided it distributes all its free cash flow to investors.

ORIGINS

PAAP developed within the corporate folds of another company, originating as a strategic decision to diversify by Houston, Texas-based Plains Resources, Inc. The architect of the plan, and the single most important person in PAAP's first decade of existence, was Greg L. Armstrong, who envisioned a business opportunity that blossomed into PAAP.

Armstrong, a graduate of Southeastern Oklahoma State University, rose through the executive ranks at Plains Resources, an independent energy company involved in the exploration and production of crude oil and natural gas. After spending more than a decade serving in various capacities such as chief financial officer and chief operating officer, Armstrong completed his climb to the top in 1992, when he was promoted to the posts of president and chief executive officer. From his leadership position, Armstrong oversaw the genesis of PAAP, inheriting control over a diversification program that began while he served as Plains Resources' chief financial officer.

During the late 1970s, at the height of the oil industry's boom period, Plains Resources nearly collapsed, saddled with marginal properties and debt. The company's fortunes changed in the 1980s when it discovered two significant oilfields that greatly increased its oil and gas reserves. The profits from the discoveries funded the exploration of a property in Louisiana in 1988 that catapulted the company in the ranks of the fastest-growing exploration and production firms in the country. Financially healthy, Plains Resources began to broaden its interests in the energy industry, delving into

COMPANY PERSPECTIVES

Our principal business strategy is to provide competitive and efficient midstream transportation, terminalling, storage and marketing services to our producer, refiner and other customers. Toward this end, we endeavor to address regional supply and demand imbalances for crude oil, refined products and LPG in the United States and Canada by combining the strategic location and capabilities of our transportation, terminalling and storage assets with our extensive marketing and distribution expertise.

the purchasing and marketing of crude oil in 1989. Within two years, the foray developed into a $50 million business, encouraging the company's senior executives, Armstrong included, to diversify again. The Plains Resources executives turned their attention to Cushing, Oklahoma, where they saw an opportunity for a potentially bustling business.

THE IMPORTANCE OF CUSHING

Cushing, known as the "Pipeline Crossroads of the World," served as a major hub in the storage and transportation of oil, home to as much as 10 percent of the United States' crude oil inventory and the site where oil was delivered to satisfy futures contracts bought and sold on the New York Mercantile Exchange. The price of oil set in Cushing determined the price of oil nationally, which led numerous industry experts to refer to Cushing as the most significant trading hub for oil in North America. A maze of pipelines spread out from Cushing, connecting oil producers from the Gulf of Mexico to consumers in the north, transporting millions of barrels of oil every day to markets such as St. Louis, Chicago, Salt Lake City, and Minneapolis.

In the early 1990s, Armstrong and the rest of Plains Resources' management team studied the facilities in Cushing and predicted a storage shortage in the near future, one that would be exacerbated by an increased need to transport oil to the Midwest. At the time, Cushing had a storage capacity of 21 million barrels of oil, nearly all of which was owned by major oil companies. "We started looking for capacity in Cushing for ourselves and just couldn't find any," Armstrong said in the October 28, 1991 issue of the *Houston Business Journal.* "We walked the ground to see what was there and found most of it to be dilapidated and barely getting by."

CUSHING TERMINAL BUILT IN 1993

One year after Plains Resources assayed storage capacity in Cushing, Armstrong was promoted from chief financial officer to chief executive officer. One of his first accomplishments was overseeing the construction of Plains Resources' Cushing Terminal, which was completed in 1993. The facility, capable of storing two million barrels of oil, became the foundation of PAAP, the heart of the company's operations located in the epicenter of the Gulf Coast oil industry.

Although the Cushing Terminal figured as PAAP's seminal asset, the company was not formed until five years after the storage facility began operating. The event that triggered its formation was the purchase of two pipelines, one large and one small, by Plains Resources. In July 1998, Plains Resources struck a deal with Wingfoot Ventures Seven, Inc., a subsidiary of The Goodyear Tire & Rubber Company, that gave it the capability of transporting oil. Plains Resources paid $400 million for the SJV Gathering System, a 45-mile, 16-inch, crude oil gathering system in California's San Joaquin Valley, and the jewel of the acquisition, the 1,233-mile, 30-inch All American Pipeline extending from California to Texas. The pipeline, which interconnected with other pipelines serving the Gulf Coast and Cushing, was built by Goodyear between 1985 and 1987 for $1.6 billion. Capable of transporting 300,000 barrels of oil per day, the All American Pipeline, coupled with the Cushing Terminal, gave Armstrong the basis for a separate company, an entity that became PAAP.

In November 1998, Plains Resources formed PAAP to acquire the two pipelines and the Cushing Terminal and spun the company off as a master limited partnership in an initial public offering (IPO) of stock. Although PAAP was a separate company, its shares trading on the New York Stock Exchange under their own ticker symbol, the relationship between PAAP and Plains Resources remained close, particularly during the first three years of PAAP's existence. Plains Resources held a 54 percent stake in PAAP after the spinoff, and Armstrong, chief executive officer of Plains Resources, served as PAAP's chairman and chief executive officer.

ACQUISITIONS FUEL EXPANSION

The story of PAAP's development during its first decade of business centered on acquisitions, as Armstrong struck an aggressive posture and completed a flurry of deals that extended PAAP's service territory and its storage capacity. Armstrong was intent on making PAAP a dominant, midsized provider of interstate and intrastate crude oil transportation and terminal and storage services.

KEY DATES

1998: Plains All American Pipeline (PAAP) is spun off from Plains Resources, Inc.
1999: Company acquires Scurlock Permian LLC.
2001: Company enters Canada through the acquisition of assets owned by Murphy Oil Company Ltd.
2002: PAAP pays $315 million for three pipeline systems owned by Shell Pipeline Co.
2006: PAAP completes a $2.4 billion merger with Pacific Energy Partners, L.P.
2008: PAAP acquires Rainbow Pipe Line Company for $534 million.

PAAP's acquisition campaign commenced in 1999. During the year, the company completed the first expansion of its Cushing Terminal, adding 1.1 million barrels of capacity in what became known as the Phase I expansion project. The year also included the company's first major acquisition, the purchase of Houston-based Scurlock Permian LLC, a subsidiary of Marathon Ashland Petroleum LLC. The transaction, completed for $138 million, made PAAP one of the largest independent crude oil gatherers and marketers in the United States. Scurlock Permian, which operated in 14 states, primarily in the Rocky Mountains and Gulf Coast markets, owned gathering operations that averaged 250,000 barrels of oil per day, exponentially increasing PAAP's existing gathering rate of 110,000 barrels of oil per day. The acquisition included 2,400 miles of pipelines, numerous storage terminals, and a fleet of 225 trucks.

PAAP ENTERS CANADA IN 2001

Armstrong's next significant move made the "All American" in PAAP's corporate title a misnomer. In 2001, he followed an industry trend and marched into Canada, acquiring the Canadian crude oil and trucking business of El Dorado, Arkansas-based Murphy Oil Company Ltd. PAAP paid $163 million for 450 miles of pipelines, 1.1 million barrels of storage and terminal capacity, and 121 crude transport trailers. Armstrong followed up the purchase of the Murphy Oil assets with another Canadian purchase in 2001, acquiring CAPNET Energy Group Inc., a Calgary-based crude oil gathering and marketing company. PAAP paid $42 million for CAPNET, which gathered 75,000 barrels of oil per day, marketed 26,000 barrels of natural gas liquids per day, and owned an oil storage facility with a capacity of 130,000 barrels.

As PAAP pushed into Canada, Plains Resources began to back away from its offspring. In mid-2001, Plains Resources reduced its ownership stake in PAAP from 54 percent to 39 percent by selling its interest to an investment group for $150 million. "This transaction will greatly simplify the corporate structure and capital structure of Plains Resources, while substantially improving its liquidity and financial strength," Armstrong said in the May 10, 2001, edition of the *Houston Chronicle*. Armstrong began devoting all his energies to PAAP after the sale, handing his executive responsibilities at Plains Resources to James Flores, a member of the investment group, and restricting his duties to serving as PAAP's chairman and chief executive officer.

SHELL PIPELINE ACQUISITION IN 2002

Armstrong spurred PAAP forward after leaving his corner office at Plains Resources, completing acquisitions that fleshed out the company's operations. In mid-2002, he brokered a deal with Shell Pipeline Co., the largest transaction in the company's history. PAAP paid $315 million for three pipeline systems, the Basin Pipeline System, the Rancho Pipeline System, and the Permian Basin Gathering System, that provided direct access to the Permian Basin in western Texas as well as to crude oil imports transported from the Gulf Coast into Cushing. At roughly the same time, PAAP completed Phase II of its expansion project at the Cushing Terminal, increasing the facility's storage capacity to 4.2 million barrels, and immediately began working on Phase III of its expansion efforts.

By the time Phase III of the Cushing Terminal expansion was completed in 2003, PAAP had spent five years adding to its assets through acquisitions. More than $1.2 billion was spent on acquisitions during the period, making PAAP one of the most aggressive pipeline operators in the country. After three expansion projects at the Cushing Terminal, with more to follow in the years ahead, PAAP owned 20 percent of the storage capacity in Cushing, able to store 5.3 million barrels in an array of tanks by 2003.

For the next five years, Armstrong intended to pursue the same acquisition-oriented strategy he employed during PAAP's first five years of business. He searched for assets throughout the North American oil industry, seeking properties that fit strategically with PAAP's existing network of pipelines and its storage and terminal facilities. In 2003, he completed 10 small acquisitions. In 2004, he purchased an ownership stake in the Capline Pipeline System, which served as a major transportation route between the Gulf of Mexico and the Midwest, and he acquired Link Energy LLC's North American crude oil and pipeline operations. Armstrong spent $165 million on seven acquisitions in 2005 and doubled the outlay in 2006, acquiring eight companies for an average price of nearly $40 million.

MERGER WITH PACIFIC ENERGY PARTNERS IN 2006

Among the deals concluded in 2006 was PAAP's largest transaction in its history. Midway through the year, the company reached an agreement to merge with Pacific Energy Partners, L.P., a Long Beach, California-based master limited partnership. Pacific Energy owned 4,000 miles of crude oil pipelines, 550 miles of refined products pipelines, and 21 million barrels of storage capacity in the Rocky Mountains region. The merger, valued at a staggering $2.4 billion, was completed in November 2006, significantly increasing PAAP's stature. "We view this as a transforming transaction and by that we mean one that positions [PAAP] for long-term stability and growth for many years to come," Armstrong said in the June 13, 2006 issue of the *Oil Daily.* "Pacific Energy has been on our radar screen for quite some time and at or near the top of our list of large attractive acquisition opportunities."

At the end of 2008, PAAP celebrated the conclusion of its first decade of business. During the year, the company acquired Rainbow Pipe Line Company, adding to its asset base in Canada. PAAP paid $534 million for a 480-mile pipeline stretching from Zama in northwest Alberta to Edmonton that was capable of carrying 200,000 barrels of oil per day. The acquisition marked the end of a decade-long spree, a period during which roughly $6 billion was spent on 52 acquisitions, but it did not signal the end of Armstrong's efforts to expand PAAP via purchases. In the years ahead, the company was expected to remain on the prowl for strong acquisition candidates, fueled by a $300 million annual budget.

Jeffrey L. Covell

PRINCIPAL SUBSIDIARIES

PAA Finance Corp.; Plains Marketing, L.P.; Plains Pipeline, L.P.; Plains Marketing GP Inc.; Plains Marketing Canada LLC; Plains Marketing Canada, L.P.; PMC (Nova Scotia) Company (Canada); Basin Holdings GP LLC; Basin Pipeline Holdings, L.P.; Rancho LPG Holdings LLC; Plains LPG Services GP LLC; Plains LPG Services, L.P.; PICSCO LLC; Lone Star Trucking, LLC; Plains Towing LLC; Pacific Energy GP, LP; Pacific Energy Management LLC; Pacific Energy Group LLC; Pacific Pipeline System LLC; Pacific Terminals LLC; Pacific LA Marine Terminal LLC; Rocky Mountain Pipeline System LLC; SLC Pipeline LLC; Pacific Atlantic Terminals LLC; PEG Canada GP LLC; Aurora Pipeline Company; Plains Midstream GP LLC; Plains Midstream, L.P.; Plains Midstream Canada ULC.

PRINCIPAL COMPETITORS

Sunoco Logistics Partners L.P.; TEPPCO Partners, L.P.; TransMontaigne Inc.

FURTHER READING

Brideau, Alexander, "Plains Shuts Part of All American Pipeline, Plans Sale of Crude Line Fill for $100 Million," *Oil Daily,* November 4, 1999.

Davis, Michael, "Plains, Shell in 3-Line Deal," *Houston Chronicle,* May 7, 2002, p. 1.

Douglas, Michael, "Texas Wildcatter Wows Wall Street: Gas Gusher Pumps Up Stock Price of Rags-to-Riches Plains Resources," *Houston Business Journal,* October 28, 1991, p. 1A.

Ivanovich, David, "Plains Resources to Sell Part of Stake in Pipeline Firm," *Houston Chronicle,* May 10, 2001, p. 1.

Kelly, Andrew, "Rising Imports Spur Plains-Pacific Deal," *Oil Daily,* June 13, 2006.

Kronenwetter, Eric, "Plains All American Finalizes Deal to Buy Scurlock Permian Assets," *Oil Daily,* March 22, 1999.

"PAA to Acquire Crude Oil Pipeline Systems," *CNW Group,* May 24, 2006.

Page, David, "Houston-Based Plains All American Expands Cushing Terminal," *Oklahoma City Journal Record,* June 26, 2001.

"Plains All American Joins Dive into Canada," *Oil Daily,* March 2, 2001.

"Plains All American Looks for Additional Acquisitions," *Daily Deal,* October 19, 2001.

"Plains All American Pipeline L.P. to Acquire CAPNET Energy Group Inc.," *Market News Publishing,* May 21, 2001.

"Plains' Road to Profits Runs Through Cushing," *Weekly Petroleum Argus,* July 21, 2003, p. 7.

"Plains Shuts Gulf Pipeline After Spill," *America's Intelligence Wire,* December 26, 2006.

"Plains to Buy Canada Pipeline," *Oil Daily,* April 9, 2008.

"Plains to Sell Pipeline Stake," *Oil Daily,* May 10, 2001.

Wilmoth, Adam, "Oil's Still Big Business in Cushing, Okla.," *Daily Oklahoman,* September 30, 2005.

Planet Hollywood
International, Inc.

— ■ —

7598 West Sand Lake Road
Orlando, Florida 32819
U.S.A.
Telephone: (407) 903-5500
Fax: (407) 370-0344
Web site: http://www.planethollywood.com

Private Company
Incorporated: 1991
Employees: 5,652
NAICS: 722110 Full-Service Restaurants; 721120
    Casino Hotels; 722410 Drinking Places (Alcoholic
    Beverages); 452990 All Other General Merchandise
    Stores

■ ■ ■

Planet Hollywood International, Inc., is a private
company jointly controlled by its founder Robert Earl
and the private-equity firm Bay Harbour Management.
Planet Hollywood International operates as the controlling body for about 25 entertainment-based theme
restaurants located throughout the world, primarily in
major metropolitan tourist areas including Las Vegas,
London, and Paris. The company's name reflects its
most well-known venture, a chain of company-owned
and franchised Planet Hollywood restaurants that offer
patrons a chance to dine in the midst of various film
and television props and memorabilia. Planet Hollywood International also owns the Buca di Beppo
casual-dining chain of restaurants, but since that chain's
acquisition in 2008, the traditional Italian fare has been

supplemented with other entrees. The Planet Hollywood
name is also found on a Las Vegas casino and resort,
jointly owned by Planet Hollywood founder Robert
Earl, Bay Harbour Management, and Starwood Hotels
& Resorts. A second Vegas hospitality enterprise, the
50-story condominium and timeshare Planet Hollywood
Towers, was expected to open in late 2009.

ORIGINS

The first Planet Hollywood restaurant opened in New
York City in 1991, but the events leading to its inception can be traced back almost 20 years before that date.
In 1972, a young man named Robert Earl opened a
dinner theater in London called The Beefeater, which
offered customers (mainly tourists) a medieval-theme
dining experience. Earl, who had graduated with a
degree in hotel and restaurant management from the
University of Surrey, possessed a talent for creating
entertainment-based restaurant concepts that drew large
numbers of customers. He soon developed The
Beefeater into a popular local success, which prompted
him to open other theme restaurants nearby. In the late
1970s, he created Talk of London, Shakespeare's Tavern,
and The Cockney Club.

Although successful in London, Earl saw greater
growth potential in the U.S. market, and therefore came
to the United States in the early 1980s to sell his
concepts to the developers of a then-new Disney World
attraction called EPCOT Center. The deal fell through,
but Earl decided to stay in Florida anyway and try his
luck in the Orlando restaurant business. He opened
several theme restaurants using medieval and Wild West

COMPANY PERSPECTIVES

Planet Hollywood International, Inc., is the creator and worldwide developer of consumer brands that capitalize on the universal appeal of movies, television, sports, music, and other leisure time activities. The company's worldwide operations offer products and services in the restaurant, retail, leisure, and entertainment sectors including, under license, the Planet Hollywood Resort & Casino, the hottest new property on the Las Vegas Strip featuring over 100,000 square feet of gaming, fine dining restaurants, an award-winning buffet, casual dining options, lounges and nightclubs.

ideas, nurturing his new restaurant group until he sold it to a larger holding company in the mid-1980s.

After changing hands again numerous times, his enterprise landed in the lap of Mecca Leisure, which had just purchased rights to Hard Rock International's eastern region. Hard Rock International was the controlling body for the Hard Rock Café chain of music industry-based theme restaurants. In 1989, Mecca appointed Earl as the new chief executive of their portion of the Hard Rock operation and put him in charge of expanding the chain in the eastern United States.

Within two years, Earl had helped the eastern-region Hard Rock Café chain grow from 7 units to 20. During that time, Earl met film producer Keith Barish, who soon became his business partner and the cofounder of Planet Hollywood International, Inc. Earl and Barish shared a belief that music, movies, and sports could transcend all barriers, language and otherwise, that separated the people of the world. The two men decided to capitalize on the worldwide appeal of the film and television entertainment industry by opening a restaurant based on that theme. Dubbing their creation Planet Hollywood, Earl and Barish opened the restaurant in New York City in late 1991.

QUICK SUCCESS IN THE EARLY NINETIES

Planet Hollywood was immediately successful, drawing crowds of people who often lined up outside the restaurant for hours to get tables. Part of the restaurant's appeal lay in its museum-like quality; its decor consisted of a multitude of real film and television costumes, props, and memorabilia. The genius marketing strategy used by the restaurant's founders accounted for the rest

of the attraction. They asked celebrities such as Arnold Schwarzenegger, Sylvester Stallone, Bruce Willis, Demi Moore, and Whoopi Goldberg to act as the restaurant's investor/owners. Every once in a while, these celebrities would stop by "their restaurant" to check in and mingle briefly with their fans. Although this did not occur all that often, customers still flocked to the restaurant in hopes that they would be one of the lucky few to dine with the stars.

A year after launching Planet Hollywood, Earl left behind his post at Hard Rock and also severed ties to his original theme restaurant group in Orlando. He and Barish began planning the worldwide introduction of additional Planet Hollywood restaurants and started by recruiting more celebrity investors for the new locations. Climbing on board were film actors Don Johnson and his then wife Melanie Griffith, director John Hughes, comedienne Roseanne Barr, and actors Tom Arnold, Wesley Snipes, and Danny Glover. By mid-1993, Planet Hollywood International had opened new restaurants in London and Southern California and was completing the construction of a fourth unit in Chicago.

Earl and Barish hired the New York City architect David Rockwell to design the new units, each of which typically seated over 200 people and contained film props and floor layouts that were unique to their locations. Different items on display throughout the chain included Dorothy's dress from *The Wizard of Oz,* the pottery wheel used by Demi Moore and Patrick Swayze in *Ghost,* a replica of the castle from *Dracula,* the Batmobile, the Flintstone buggy, and a plastic model of the meat slab that was pulverized by Stallone in the film *Rocky.* Customers were also treated to celebrity hand print walls and big-screen televisions, which played promotional clips for upcoming movies.

Meanwhile, a Hard Rock International executive, Peter Morton, filed suit against Earl and Planet Hollywood, alleging that Earl had engaged in the appropriation of trade secrets. Morton, a cofounder of Hard Rock International and the CEO of its western region, believed that Earl's Planet Hollywood chain was a ripoff of the Hard Rock concept. Earl nonchalantly dismissed the charges, however, and the case against Planet Hollywood never amounted to much in court. Furthermore, Morton's complaint did little to deter Planet Hollywood from expanding further, nor did it curb the public's desire to patronize the new and rapidly blossoming chain. Soon Planet Hollywood was known as a worldwide leader in the theme restaurant business.

By the end of 1993, Planet Hollywood had not only opened two new restaurants in Washington, D.C., and Cancún, Mexico, but it had also signed leases for five new units in Phoenix, Arizona; New Orleans,

KEY DATES

1991: Planet Hollywood is established.

1993: Famous actors begin promoting and investing in the firm.

1995: Development begins on Official All Star Café concept.

1996: Planet Hollywood goes public.

1997: Company begins to lose money and stock price falters.

1998: Robert Earl takes over as chairman and CEO.

1999: Firm files for Chapter 11 bankruptcy.

2000: Company emerges from Chapter 11 under a new reorganization plan.

2001: Planet Hollywood launches its entertainment Web site; company again files for Chapter 11.

2002: Planet Hollywood emerges from Chapter 11 as a private company.

2003: Company bids $637 million for the bankrupt Aladdin Resort and Casino in Las Vegas, Nevada.

2004: Planet Hollywood acquires the Aladdin through a partnership.

2007: Company announces plans to establish Planet Hollywood restaurants and hotels in India; renovation of the former Aladdin is finished, new Planet Hollywood Resort & Casino opens.

2009: Financially strapped, company sells $140 million in debt to Harrah's Entertainment.

Louisiana; Aspen, Colorado; Maui, Hawaii; and Minneapolis's Mall of America (the largest shopping mall in the United States). Each opening was a gala event, drawing enormous crowds of people to catch a glimpse of the many media personalities who made appearances and celebrated the new successes. However, the true test of a new location occurred the day after the "official" opening, when a restaurant actually opened its doors to the general public. Without fail, each new Planet Hollywood passed these tests with ease, and in the first year of operation, most were generating revenues of almost $15 million per unit.

A strong asset of the Planet Hollywood concept was that each unit sold licensed Planet Hollywood merchandise as well as serving food and drinks. Items of all kinds were sold, from key rings and T-shirts, to sweatshirts, watches, and leather coats. Sales of this merchandise helped boost Planet Hollywood's profit margins considerably above those achieved at other restaurants that relied solely on food to bring in profits. Merchandise became so popular that within a few years, the company began to open separate retail stores called Planet Hollywood Superstores, a move that further increased yearly profits.

EXPANSION IN THE MID-NINETIES

In 1994, Planet Hollywood continued its aggressive expansion program, and units continued to open worldwide. The company also began developing additional theme restaurant ideas, including the concept for the Official All Star Café. Acknowledging the success that Planet Hollywood had achieved from drawing upon the public's interest in celebrity life, Earl and Barish decided that the Official All Star Café would be the perfect sports-based equivalent. They began recruiting professional sports figures to invest in the concept, drawing in people such as hockey great Wayne Gretzky, football icon Joe Montana, and basketball superstar Shaquille O'Neal. Plans for the new restaurants included a menu of "stadium cuisine" supplemented by home cooking and sales of professional sports merchandise and souvenirs.

Also in 1994, the company opened what would soon become its highest-grossing Planet Hollywood unit, in Las Vegas. Unlike most previous units, which seated approximately 250 people, the Las Vegas restaurant was designed to seat 500 and was planned by Rockwell so that there would be no "bad" seats. The unit's opening rivaled a sporting event or the Academy Awards in magnitude, in that it drew a crowd of more than 10,000 people who packed themselves into stadium-like bleachers nearby to witness the stars' arrivals at the event. Even former President George H. W. Bush and First Lady Barbara Bush were on hand to celebrate. Later that year, the entrepreneurs opened another 500-seater in Orlando's Disney World, which made Earl and Barish owners of the two highest-grossing restaurants in the United States.

At that point, Planet Hollywood was composed of 18 units around the world, and the company was projecting the addition of 17 more during 1995. The Planet Hollywood chain was expanding almost on its own, so Earl decided to begin focusing his attention and energy on other avenues of growth while the chain took care of itself. In August 1995, ground was broken in New York City near the original Planet Hollywood, and construction of the first Official All Star Café began. Meanwhile, plans were in the works to develop a theme restaurant chain based on characters from the Marvel Comics series. Also, television game-show producer

King World began working with Roseanne Barr's production company on a Planet Hollywood Squares television game show, which was to be a revival of the original *Hollywood Squares* from decades past with a new Planet Hollywood twist.

With Planet Hollywood quickly becoming a household name, the company decided to go public in 1996. Not only was stock offered to the public, but the company also convinced MBNA to issue Planet Hollywood VISA credit cards, which gave cardholders priority seating at the restaurants. A joint venture with ITT Corporation was also formed to develop Planet Hollywood casinos in Las Vegas and Atlantic City in the future. Furthermore, Marvel Entertainment Group, Inc., and Planet Hollywood International decided to move ahead with the comic book character-based restaurant concept, calling it Marvel Mania. Ideas for a new concept called Chefs of the World, which was to feature a "star-studded" culinary staff, also began to arise.

Some began to wonder whether Planet Hollywood was spreading its resources too thin, and speculations surfaced as to whether the company would be able to continue the growth trend that it had been experiencing for the past five years. Earl maintained ambitious goals to keep the company expanding by 30 to 40 percent each year, in both the number of restaurant locations and in annual revenues. Criticisms of that plan, however, focused on the idea that the more units that were opened, the less novel a customer's experience in patronizing the restaurant chain, which could lead to a drop in sales. Furthermore, theme restaurants were popping up all over the country, providing Earl and Barish with intense competition. The Harley-Davidson Café was gaining popularity, as were other concepts such as Robert DeNiro's Tribeca Grill, the Country Star chain (backed by Wynonna Judd, Vince Gill, and Reba McEntire), and the Thunder Roadhouse (backed by Dennis Hopper, Dwight Yoakam, and Peter Fonda).

However, Planet Hollywood and the Official All Star Café did possess one major advantage over their competition, which was the celebrity endorsement received through stars' ownership and investment in the chains. Many customers thus viewed these restaurants as the "originals." As for continued growth potential, Earl dismissed skepticism with easy confidence, given that in only five years the company had grown from one $3.5 million restaurant in New York to an almost $300 million operation with approximately 50 units throughout the world.

FINANCIAL WOES

Nevertheless, stock price began to falter as skepticism about the future of the company increased. Despite a rise in profits and revenues in 1996, an aggressive growth strategy fueled speculation that Planet Hollywood would not be able to finance its rapid expansion. One year later, those doubts became certainties as the firm reported a $40 million loss in the fourth quarter. Management's narrow focus on diversification became apparent as the firm's core business, the Planet Hollywood restaurants, began to show signs of neglect: menu prices were high, food was mediocre, and service was below average.

In 1998, cofounder Barish resigned, leaving Earl chairman and CEO. William Baumhauer was then hired as president, and the management looked to his turnaround skills to have a positive impact on the company's finances. In August of that year, Planet Hollywood had to deal with another problem when a bomb exploded in one of its franchise restaurants in Cape Town, South Africa. It seemed that a black cloud had settled over the firm as a loss of $244 million was recorded that year.

BANKRUPTCY AND RESTRUCTURING IN THE NEW MILLENNIUM

In June 1999, Baumhauer resigned after having little effect on Planet Hollywood's bottom line. The company's once bright future was tarnished as it lay under $359 million in debt. Left with few options, the company declared Chapter 11 bankruptcy on October 12, 1999. The management placed blame on a loss in revenues, increasing costs, including those related to expansion, a decrease in customers, and an increase in competition.

Planet Hollywood set out to restructure itself. Its efforts included closing and selling poorly performing Planet Hollywood restaurants and Official All Star Cafés. The management also began to put into effect a strategy to focus on its core operation, its original restaurant theme. The company stopped operation of its Planet Movies by AMC, created in July 1999, and sold its Sound Republic units. It also cut costs by halting any ventures not closely related to its core focus. During its bankruptcy reorganization, the company eliminated 3,800 jobs.

On May 9, 2000, Planet Hollywood emerged from Chapter 11 after receiving approval for its reorganization plan involving its remaining 22 restaurants. The restructuring left the firm with a cash infusion of $30 million in new investments as well as $25 million more in credit, allowing it to rebuild without the burden of major debt. The reorganization plan called for updated restaurant décor, new menu items, and increased attention to food quality, something Earl and others admitted had been lacking. The firms' managers also set out to develop new celebrity relationships and endorsements. One of the first deals to be struck was with NBA star Shaquille O'Neal. The company also launched its entertainment Web site, which featured live celebrity chats, coverage of celebrity events, entertainment news, and merchandise.

Before the full effects of its reorganization plan could be felt, in October 2001, Planet Hollywood was again forced to declare bankruptcy and file for Chapter 11 protection claiming that the September 11, 2001, terrorist attacks on the United States, and a subsequent decline in tourist traffic, had severely impacted sales. The company was forced to slash overhead any way possible. As a result, management and other personnel numbers were pared to a bare minimum, and the company moved its flagship headquarters and remaining 85 staff into the Orlando warehouse used to store Planet Hollywood's memorabilia.

In late 2002, with financing from the private-equity firm Bay Harbour Management, Planet Hollywood emerged from bankruptcy as a private firm with only 10 company-owned restaurants. Under the second reorganization plan, Robert Earl took ownership of 10 percent of Planet Hollywood while the remainder was controlled by three investors and lenders.

EXPANSION INTO THE CASINO AND RESORT INDUSTRY

Planet Hollywood made its initial foray into the hospitality market in 2003 when it bid $637 million for the bankrupt Las Vegas Aladdin Resort and Casino located on the famous Strip in Las Vegas, Nevada. After receiving approval from the Nevada Gaming Commission, in September 2004, Planet Hollywood acquired the Aladdin through a partnership involving Earl, Bay Harbour Management, and Starwood Hotels & Resorts. The following year, a complete renovation of the Aladdin began.

In 2007, the company officially entered the hospitality industry when in April the Aladdin renovations were finished and the new Planet Hollywood Resort & Casino opened its doors to a two-day star-studded grand opening. Billed as "the hottest property on the Las Vegas Strip," the 100,000-square-foot resort and casino facility featured 2,500 remodeled rooms and suites along with numerous restaurants and lounges and was encircled by the Miracle Mile Shops, 170 specialty shops and restaurants. After opening its first mega-resort in 2007, Planet Hollywood began construction of Planet Hollywood Towers on the southeast corner of the Casino & Resort property. The $750 million, 50-story condominium and timeshare structure, developed with Westgate Resorts, a subsidiary of Central Florida Investments, was expected to include 1,200 vacation villas and 28 penthouse suites and be connected to the Planet Hollywood resort complex on the Strip.

Robert Earl also announced in 2007 that Planet Hollywood would invest $15 million by 2010 to expand the firm's restaurant/hotel operations into India with five hotels, the first being planned for Mumbai, home to Bollywood, with others to follow in Delhi, Bangalore, Goa, and Hyderabad. The Indian expansion involved a master franchise agreement with U.S.-based Arch Millennium Corp. with resulting new facilities expected to combine the excitement of Bollywood with Hollywood.

In 2008, Planet Hollywood created a new division to coordinate its international brand expansion, including the development of overseas hotel and vacation sites. Concurrently, the company named longtime Starwood Hotels & Resorts executive William (Bill) Feather as president of Planet Hollywood Resorts Management LLC. As part of his duties, Feather was put in charge of launching and coordinating the new management of Planet Hollywood Towers.

In a move to become a multi-branded restaurant firm, in 2008 Planet Hollywood expanded its dining operations by acquiring Buca, Inc., operator of the Italian restaurant chain Buca di Beppo, for nearly $10 million. Planet Hollywood assumed almost $20 million in Buca debt to take over the financially struggling casual dining company, known for its Italian dishes and casual atmosphere. Just months after Planet Hollywood took over Buca, the chain added new dishes to its traditional fare of home-style Italian food.

CONTINUING CHALLENGES

In 2009, Planet Hollywood Resort & Casino posted consecutive quarters of declining revenues for the first time since the Aladdin renovations were completed. That August, company officials conceded in a filing with the Securities and Exchange Commission that the firm would likely be unable to make interest payments on an $860 million loan. In September 2009, though, Harrah's Entertainment, one of the world's largest private gaming corporations with properties in Las Vegas, bought $140 million of the Resort & Casino's debt a day before Planet Hollywood would have defaulted on its mortgage. While the resort remained afloat, the move by Harrah's fueled speculation that the major casino corporation could be positioning itself to take over Planet Hollywood Resort & Casino.

During the first decade of the 21st century, Planet Hollywood transformed itself three times: twice through

Chapter 11 reorganizations and once when it entered the hospitality industry through its resort and casino. As the company neared the end of the decade, another bankruptcy did not appear imminent, but the company's status as an operator of resorts was being challenged by debt that Planet Hollywood had racked up by entering the resort industry. Over the two decades of the company's existence, though, founder Robert Earl had gained a reputation as an entrepreneur that never gave up and always found a way to remake his company. Such an approach by Earl, if Planet Hollywood Resort & Casino's financial picture did not improve, again could be necessary in the 2010s.

Laura E. Whiteley
Updated, Christina M. Stansell; Roger Rouland

PRINCIPAL SUBSIDIARIES

Buca, Inc.; Planet Hollywood Resorts Management, LLC; Planet Hollywood Memorabilia, Inc.

PRINCIPAL DIVISIONS

International Brand Expansion.

PRINCIPAL COMPETITORS

Ark Restaurants Corp.; Hard Rock Café International, Inc., HOB Entertainment, Inc.

FURTHER READING

Ball, Aimee Lee, "Mr. Universe," *New York*, July 15, 1991, p. 38.

Bjorhus, Jennifer, "Buca Finds a Buyer: Planet Hollywood Acquires the Struggling Italian Restaurant Chain Once Mired in Legal Difficulties," *America's Intelligence Wire*, August 6, 2008.

"Can Planet Hollywood Survive Its Own Disaster Flick as Rough Year Nears End?" *Nation's Restaurant News*, December 8, 1998, p. 29.

Greenberg, Herb, "Earth to Planet Hollywood," *Fortune*, December 23, 1996.

Guttman, Monika, "Why the Stars Orbit Planet Hollywood: With Meteoric Growth, the Eateries May Go Public," *U.S. News & World Report*, November 27, 1995, p. 60.

Hayes, Jack, "Robert Earl: The King of Planet Hollywood Promises the Stars—and He Delivers," *Nation's Restaurant News*, October 9, 1995, p. 164.

Jackson, Jerry W., "India Enters Planet Hollywood's Orbit," *Orlando Sentinel*, May 25, 2005.

———, "Planet Hollywood Eatery Chain Can Stay in Business Until Year's End," *Knight-Ridder/Tribune Business News*, February 15, 2001.

Kachru, Seema Hakhu, "Planet Hollywood Enters Indian Market with Hotel in Mumbai," *PTI—The Press Trust of India Ltd.*, November 20, 2007.

Kapner, Suzanne, "'Starry' Vegas Night Shines on New Planet," *Nation's Restaurant News*, August 8, 1994, p. 7.

Knightly, Arnold M., "Planet Hollywood Narrows Loss Even During Renovation," *Las Vegas Review-Journal*, April 2, 2008.

———, "Planet Hollywood Resort Concerned About Debt Payments," *Las Vegas Review-Journal*, August 15, 2009.

———, "Stars Align for Newest Planet Hollywood Resort," *Las Vegas Review-Journal*, November 16, 2007.

Levine, Joshua, "Hamburgers and Tennis Socks," *Forbes*, November 20, 1995, p. 184.

Lohmeyer, Lori, "Philippe Villain: Giving the Fans of Planet Hollywood Something to Clap About," *Nation's Restaurant News*, January 27, 2003, p. 196.

Martin, Richard, "Hard Rock Hits Planet Hollywood with Copycat Suit," *Nation's Restaurant News*, March 16, 1992, p. 3.

McClellan, Steve, "King World Developing 'Planet Hollywood Squares,'" *Broadcasting & Cable*, September 25, 1995, p. 11.

Mervine, Bob, "What Makes Robert Run? An All-New Planet: Down but Not Out: British Businessman Says Planet Hollywood Can Be Revived," *Orlando Business Journal*, December 7, 2001, p. 3.

Miracle, Barbara, "Beyond Planet Hollywood," *Florida Trend*, December 1993, p. 10.

Nakashima, Ryan, "Casino Rolls Big, Rebuilds Brands," *Marketing News*, December 15, 2007, p. 38.

"O'Neal Signs to Endorse Planet Hollywood Chain," *Nation's Restaurant News*, July 17, 2000, p. 30.

Palmer, Mark, "Planet Hollywood Founder Robert Earl's Move into the World of Casinos Could Hardly Be Better-Timed," *Financial Times*, November 20, 2004, p. 3.

Papiernik, Richard L., "All Quiet on the Hollywood Front After 'Picture Perfect' IPO," *Nation's Restaurant News*, May 13, 1996, p. 11.

"Planet Hollywood, All-Star Units End AMC Venture," *Nation's Restaurant News*, January 22, 2001, p. 50.

"Planet Hollywood Files for Ch. 11, Shutters Nine Units," *Nation's Restaurant News*, October 25, 1999, p. 3.

"Planet Hollywood Launches New Web Site," *Newsbytes*, July 30, 2000.

"Planet Hollywood, Marvel Comics Team for Themer," *Nation's Restaurant News*, June 6, 1994, p. 2.

"Planet Hollywood to Set Up Hotels and Resorts in India," *India Business Insight*, June 27, 2005.

Prewitt, Milford, "Planet Hollywood Eyes New Concepts, Profits Up 82% in '96," *Nation's Restaurant News*, February 24, 1997, p. 11.

———, "Robert Earl: CEO Planet Hollywood Inc., Orlando, Florida," *Nation's Restaurant News*, January 1995, p. 54.

Rawe, Julie, "Relaunching Planet Earl: After Two Bankruptcies, Robert Earl Is Heaving Planet Hollywood Back into Orbit," *Time*, October 13, 2003, p. A17.

St. Onge, Jeff, "You Heard It Here First: DJ Planet Hollywood CEO Sees Co. Returning to Past Glory," *Bankruptcy Newswire*, January 25, 2000.

Selinger, Iris Cohen, "Lights! Camera! But Can We Get a Table?" *Advertising Age*, April 17, 1995, p. 48.

Smith, Rod, "Groundbreaking Slated for Planet Hollywood Towers," *Las Vegas Review-Journal*, January 19, 2006.

———, "A New Plan, a New Planet," *Las Vegas Review-Journal*, September 8, 2005.

"That's Eatertainment: Baumhauer Out at Planet Hollywood," *Nation's Restaurant News,* July 5, 1999, p. 3.

Walkup, Carolyn, "Planet Hollywood Gears to Launch Unit in Chicago," *Nation's Restaurant News*, July 15, 1993, p. 94.

Wells, Melanie, "Flip Cards, Not Burgers," *Forbes Global*, October 27, 2003, p. 62.

Popular, Inc.

P.O. Box 362708
San Juan, 00936-2708
Puerto Rico
Telephone: (787) 765-9800
Toll Free: (888) 724-3659
Web site: http://www.popular.com

Public Company
Incorporated: 1893 as Sociedad Anónima de Economías
    y Préstamos: Banco Popular
Employees: 10,110
Total Assets: $38.9 billion (2008)
Stock Exchanges: NASDAQ
Ticker Symbol: BPOP
NAICS: 522110 Commercial Banking; 522310
    Mortgage and Nonmortgage Loan Brokers; 522291
    Consumer Lending; 523110 Investment Banking
    and Securities Dealing; 523120 Securities Broker-
    age; 524210 Insurance Agencies and Brokerages

■ ■ ■

Popular, Inc., is a full-service financial services provider, operating in its home base of Puerto Rico, as well as in the United States, the Caribbean, and Latin America. Principal subsidiary Banco Popular de Puerto Rico is the island's largest bank. Through other subsidiaries, Popular offers automobile and equipment leasing and financing, mortgage loans, consumer lending, investment banking, and broker-dealer and insurance services. Mainland-based Banco Popular North America holds community bank branches in New York, California, Illinois, New Jersey, and Florida, and wholly owned subsidiary E-LOAN. Transaction processing company EVERTEC provides processing and technology services to Popular and third parties. Deteriorating economic conditions during 2008 and 2009 forced a rollback in U.S. operations.

HOMELAND CHALLENGES: 1893–1957

Popular, Inc., was founded in 1893 in Puerto Rico's capital, San Juan, as Sociedad Anónima de Economías y Préstamos: Banco Popular (Savings and Loan Corporation: The People's Bank). Its goal, as set forth in the first article of incorporation, was to "foster the spirit of economy in all social classes, especially in that of the poor, by means of savings." Fifty-two stockholders provided the initial capital of 5,000 Mexican silver pesos. The number of shareholders tripled in the first four years, and the institution prospered by making loans, including mortgage loans. With regard to savings, however, fewer than 5 percent of the depositors belonged to the working class.

Five years later, the United States occupied and annexed Puerto Rico in the Spanish-American War in 1898. Banco Popular's deposits dropped by two-thirds in that year, and a hurricane devastated the island in 1899. The following year, Congress declared the Puerto Rican peso worth only 60 cents (rather than a dollar), reducing the bank's capital funds to only $18,000. In 1906 the bank introduced checking accounts, and in 1912 it circulated piggy banks for savings accounts; only the bank could open them with a key. Representatives of

COMPANY PERSPECTIVES

Our Creed: Banco Popular is a local institution dedicating its efforts exclusively to the enhancement of the social and economic conditions in the communities we serve and inspired by the most sound principles and fundamental practices of good banking.

Banco Popular pledges its efforts and resources to the development of banking services for its customers within strict commercial practices and so efficient that it could meet the requirements of the most progressive communities of the world.

Spanish import trading houses were the main stockholders and customers in this period (and still among the bank's largest customers 35 years later). Deposits of $921,090.98 in 1913 set a record not surpassed for more than a decade thereafter. Banco Popular was the first, and for many years the only, bank to make loans to the Puerto Rican government and to many island municipalities.

In order to conform to the island's first banking law, Banco Popular de Puerto Rico was founded again as a commercial bank (rather than a savings bank) in 1923. Rafael Carrión Pacheco became the majority stockholder in 1927. Personal loans were made available without collateral the following year. Banco Popular survived the banking crisis of the Great Depression while many other banks fell into receivership; in fact, it purchased Banco Comercial de Puerto Rico, the oldest and most respected banking institution on the island. In 1937 Banco Popular became the biggest bank in Puerto Rico, taking in $8.82 million in deposits that year. Work began on an Art Deco headquarters building that was completed in 1939.

Banco Popular established its first branch in 1934, and had eight on the island by 1942. In 1951 it established a mobile bank-on-wheels at Fort Buchanan. This format was adopted to serve much of Puerto Rico, including even remote mountain villages, between 1957 and 1974. The number of fixed branches reached 20 in 1954. Auto loans were introduced in 1957.

MAINLAND EXPANSION: 1961–2001

By this time, a vast post–World War II migration had created a large Puerto Rican community in New York City. In 1961 Banco Popular opened its first U.S. mainland branch, in the city's borough of the Bronx. A second one, in Manhattan's Rockefeller Center, was established in 1964. That year the bank also established its first foreign branch, in the Dominican Republic. Rafael Carrión Jr. succeeded his father as president of Banco Popular in 1965. Also that year, the bank moved its headquarters to a newly constructed building in Hato Rey, a suburb of San Juan.

Banco Popular established its first U.S. branch outside New York City in 1973, and its first outside the New York area, in Los Angeles, in 1975. It joined the Visa credit card system in 1975. The bank acquired the insolvent Banco Credito y Ahorro Ponceno (Ponce Credit and Savings Bank) in 1978, including 36 of that bank's 50 branches. With $1.7 billion in deposits, Banco Popular had grown to be included among the list of the 60 largest U.S. banks. There were 110 branches in 1980. The following year, the company opened a branch in Saint Croix, which was the capital of the U.S. Virgin Islands. It entered Chicago in 1984 by purchasing a locally owned, failed Hispanic bank from federal regulators. Richard L. Carrión, son of Rafael Carrión Jr., became the chief executive of Banco Popular in 1985.

Banco Popular had grown to 125 branches in 1989, including 10 on the U.S. mainland and three in the Virgin Islands. That year, it purchased BanPonce Corporation for cash and stock valued at between $278 million and $324 million. Founded in 1971 as Banco de Ponce, BanPonce was the fourth-largest Puerto Rican bank, with 40 branches on the island and 14 in New York, where it was the pioneering Puerto Rican bank. The acquired branches took the Banco Popular name, but a new holding company was established bearing the BanPonce Corporation name until 1997, when this parent firm was renamed Popular, Inc.

Banco Popular enhanced its position as the leading choice for New York City's growing Hispanic population in 1991, when it purchased the failed Bronx-based New York Capital Bank. New York Capital was an institution with five New York branches. The following year, Banco Popular acquired seven American Savings Bank branches in Manhattan and Brooklyn, bringing its number of New York branches to 28. At that point, Banco Popular had $1.5 billion in deposits in New York and had, in addition to making mortgage loans, become the city's top originator of federal Small Business Administration loans. These small business loans were made primarily to taxi owners, but also to importers, distributors, and wholesalers seeking to borrow less than $500,000.

In order to continue to thrive, the New York operation was looking beyond Hispanic customers after commissioning a study that showed more than one-fourth of

```
┌─────────────────────────────────────────────┐
│                                               │
│                KEY DATES                      │
│             ─────────■─────────               │
│                                               │
│  1893:  Banco Popular is founded as a savings bank.│
│  1923:  Banco Popular is reorganized as a commercial│
│         bank.                                 │
│  1937:  Banco Popular becomes the largest bank in│
│         Puerto Rico.                          │
│  1961:  Banco Popular opens its first mainland U.S.│
│         branch, in New York City.             │
│  1989:  Banco Popular acquires Banco de Ponce (Ban-│
│         Ponce Corporation), Puerto Rico's fourth-│
│         largest bank.                         │
│  1992:  Popular completes its initial public offering│
│         on the NASDAQ.                        │
│  2000:  Popular has 302 bank branches and 382 non-│
│         bank offices.                         │
│  2002:  North American unit sets goal of doubling│
│         assets in two years.                  │
│  2006:  Income slides after two decades of growth.│
│  2008:  Worsening economic conditions contribute to│
│         growing losses.                       │
│                                               │
└─────────────────────────────────────────────┘
```

its depositors were born in the United States. Furthermore, the study showed that fewer than one-third were from Puerto Rico. Also in 1992, BanPonce became a publicly traded stock on the NASDAQ.

Banco Popular began selling mutual funds and annuities in its New York branches in 1994. By the fall of 1997, it had six branches in neighboring New Jersey as well as 29 in New York. That fall, it also made its Texas debut by purchasing Citizens National Bank, which had been serving Houston's blue-collar Hispanic population. The bank also entered Florida that year by acquiring Seminole National Bank in Sanford, and by the spring of 1999 held eight branches in that state. It opened its first Miami branch in 2001 and announced plans to establish at least 20 more in south Florida.

Meanwhile, Popular had purchased Chicago's Pioneer Bank in 1993 and soon added two others, enhancing its presence in the city to 13 locations. It also chose Chicago as its official U.S. headquarters in 1997. In 1998, Banco Popular began offering a check cashing service in the United States which was named Popular Cash Express. A mainland-U.S. credit card operation based in Orlando, Florida, was already in existence, with nearly 200,000 customers.

In 1999 Banco Popular launched a nationwide mortgage loan program aimed at the Hispanic market. It was supported by a national advertising campaign featuring the bank's existing national spokesman, Don Francisco. Francisco was well known, having also served at the time as the master of ceremonies of the popular Saturday night variety show *Sábado Gigante,* telecast on Univision, the leading Spanish-language network in the United States.

Banco Popular's U.S. credit card operation was sold to Metris Companies Inc. in 2000. That year, the North American subsidiary (by then headquartered in Melrose Park, Illinois, a suburb of Chicago) launched a payday loan program, a common but controversial product offered at most traditional check cashing operations in the United States. This program with implied interest rates could run as high as the triple digits and catered to people who could not obtain funds through conventional loans. These payday loans were available in Texas through the bank's Cash Express outlets. A spokesman for the bank told Julie Johnsson of *Crain's Chicago Business* that its Texas payday lending was a pilot program that the bank was "not at liberty to discuss." The pilot program was never implemented into an ongoing service offering, and was discontinued approximately six months after rollout.

TAKING STOCK

Popular, Inc., was the 35th-largest bank holding company in the United States at the end of 2000, with consolidated assets of $28.1 billion and total deposits of $14.8 billion. Its income that year of $1.45 billion, and net income of $276.1 million, were both company records. Puerto Rico accounted for 72 percent of its assets, and the continental United States for 26 percent (compared to only 4 percent in 1980). Of the company's 302 banking branches, 199 were in Puerto Rico, 95 in the continental United States, and 8 in the Virgin Islands. Of the 382 non-banking offices, Equity One had 136; Popular Cash Express, 132; Popular Finance, 61; Popular Mortgage, 21; Popular Leasing & Rental, 12; and Popular Leasing, U.S.A., 11 (during 2000 a subsidiary sold its investment in Banco Fiduciario, S.A., a commercial bank in the Dominican Republic with 31 branches).

Banco Popular de Puerto Rico, Popular, Inc.'s principal subsidiary, was operating seven branches in the U.S. Virgin Islands, one branch in the British Virgin Islands, and one branch in New York, as well as its 199 branches in Puerto Rico. It included as its subsidiaries both Popular Leasing & Rental and Popular Finance, incorporated in 1989, and Popular Mortgage, incorporated in 1995. Popular Leasing & Rental was Puerto Rico's largest vehicle leasing and daily rental company. Popular Finance offered small loans and second mortgages. Popular Mortgage offered mortgage loans.

Popular Securities, a subsidiary of the parent company, was a securities broker-dealer in Puerto Rico with financial advisory, investment, and security brokerage operations for institutional and retail customers. GM Group, incorporated in 1989, was providing electronic data processing and consulting services, sale and rental of electronic data processing equipment, and sale and maintenance of computer software to clients in 10 countries. Popular, Inc., also held an 85 percent interest in Newco Mortgage Holding Corp., a mortgage banking organization with operations in Puerto Rico.

The other subsidiary of the parent, Popular International Bank, incorporated in 1992, held as its main subsidiary Popular North America. This was a holding company incorporated in 1991 for Banco Popular North America, a full-service commercial bank with branches in six states. Banco Popular North America, incorporated in 1998, held in turn as its subsidiary Popular Leasing U.S.A., which was incorporated in 1997 and was providing small-ticket equipment leasing in eight states.

The other direct subsidiaries of Popular North America were Equity One, incorporated in 1980, which was granting personal and mortgage loans and providing dealer financing through offices in 30 states; Popular Cash Express, incorporated in 1997 and offering services such as check cashing, money transfers to other countries, money order sales and processing of payments through offices and units in five states and the District of Columbia; Popular Insurance, incorporated in 2000 to offer insurance products in Puerto Rico; and Banco Popular National Association, a full-service commercial bank chartered in Orlando, Florida, that commenced operations in 2000. Popular International Bank also owned ATH Costa Rica and Crest, which were providing automated teller machine (ATM) switching and driving services in San Jose, Costa Rica.

Popular, Inc.'s largest shareholder in 2001 consisted of the employee retirement and profit sharing plans that owned 8.1 percent of the common stock. Next largest was State Farm Mutual Automobile Insurance Co., which owned 6.4 percent of the common stock. Of the company's offices, branch premises, and other facilities, the majority were leased rather than owned.

AMBITIOUS MOVES: 2002–05

In 2002, Popular, Inc., set plans in motion to double its mainland assets in two years, via acquisitions and internal growth. The $5.5 billion asset Banco Popular North America division would "reposition itself as a 'su-

percommunity' bank with a diverse customer base— while retaining its image as the premier Hispanic bank," Ben Jackson wrote in a July *American Banker* article. Citigroup Inc., as well as other competitors, had begun to court the Hispanic community, especially in California. The giant financial company acquired Mexico's second largest banking company in 2001. In the last decade of the 20th century, the U.S. Hispanic population had grown 58 percent.

Popular, meanwhile, sought to purchase non-Hispanic banks in the $3 billion to $5 billion asset range, in an area such as Chicago. More than 50 percent of its customers were non-Hispanic, primarily brought aboard through branch and bank acquisitions. Keeping the important Hispanic population in mind, Popular launched a bilingual ad campaign in New York, Chicago, Houston, Los Angeles, and central Florida and was developing targeted products and services.

Banco Popular North America moved closer to its two-year goal of achieving $11 billion in assets, upon its August 2004 agreement to buy a privately held $998 million asset Florida bank. The Federal Reserve had previously approved the acquisition of a $1.8 billion asset California bank, Quaker City Bancorp Inc. of Whittier. These were the first purchases in several years. Popular's decade-long buying spree had come to a halt in 2000, in the wake of Federal Reserve Board action centering on regulatory compliance.

Back in the market for other banks, Roberto R. Herencia, head of the mainland unit, envisioned reaching $15 billion to $20 billion in assets in three years, according to *American Banker*. Also needing double digit organic growth to advance such a cause, Banco Popular North America opened three branches in 2004, with three to six more planned for subsequent years.

The January 2005 Kislak National Bank of Miami purchase dovetailed with Popular's niche based commercial banking strategy. The newly acquired bank emphasized loans to condominium and housing associations. Additionally, Kislak National Bank held eight branches in the Miami area, where Popular had just one. Miami's large Hispanic population and business ties to Puerto Rico enticed Popular. "The brand recognition is instantaneous," Herencia told *American Banker*'s Matthias Rieker.

CEO Richard Carrión, backed by his own form of brand recognition, represented the third generation of his family (which controlled the second-largest block of common stock) to lead the company. He told *American Banker* in 2005 that Popular "is my purpose in life." He also spoke of the company's commitment to serving low income communities. "We are in tough neighborhoods, and we are there by choice." In the United States, 80 percent of its branches operated out of low- and moderate-income neighborhoods.

Carrión hoped to gather half of Popular's revenue from the mainland by the end of the decade. Banco Popular North America ranked as the 22nd-largest U.S. banking company and Popular, Inc., ranked 28th in *Fortune*'s list of the 100 best large companies to work for in 2005. Striving to raise its profile, Popular entered into a five-year agreement with the New York Mets, as the major league baseball club's official bank. Attracting new checking accounts and growing small business loans topped the growth to-do list in the states. The mainland operation was also wrapping up an efficiency improvement program, begun in 2002 and including systems integration, back office centralization, and staff reduction.

Profitability had proved to be an ongoing issue for one key unit. Cash Express posted earnings in only one year. Rieker wrote for *American Banker*: "Mr. Carrión said Cash Express has a role to play in Popular's mission to serve the underserved. The business 'is strategically very important to us,' and half of Cash Express customers have a bank account with Popular, he said." The mortgage and consumer finance businesses, meanwhile, were consolidated under New Jersey-based Popular Financial Holding Inc. The $9 billion asset operation generated 12 percent of the parent company's profits during 2004.

Also that year, Popular combined the technology solution, ATM, and transaction processing businesses under the EVERTEC Inc. subsidiary. Technology savvy Carrión believed the business could triple its profit contribution by the end of the decade, to between 15 and 20 percent from just 3 percent. Plans were on the drawing board to introduce transaction processing to small merchants on the mainland.

One-time gains from a sale of the check cashing unit and of property, elevated earnings in the fourth quarter of 2005, according to *American Banker*. Income also rose with sales from E-Loan Inc., acquired in November, and from Small Business Administration loans. For the year as a whole, Popular earned $540.7 million. On the down side, its market capitalization had fallen by one-fourth, dragged down in part by mortgage market accounting woes of Puerto Rican-based peers.

TREND DOWNWARD: 2006–09

After more than two decades of climbing earnings, the trend reversed in 2006. Popular saw its earnings drop by 34 percent, to $357.7 million. A revamping of the U.S. business, including a pullback from the subprime mortgage market and the investment in E-Loan, contributed to the decline. Puerto Rican operations

fared better, despite an economic downturn on the island.

Troubles mounted stateside during 2007. A move toward a full-scale online bank stalled, the entire consumer finance arm merged into U.S. bank operations, and bank acquisitions went nowhere. At year end Popular recorded a net loss of $64.5 million.

Popular agreed in early 2008 to sell subprime and prime assets of Equity One Inc. to an American International Group Inc. unit for $1.5 billion. Popular previously dropped its wholesale subprime mortgage lending and Texas retail banking businesses. The looming U.S. economic crisis pushed Popular back toward its core banking operations.

As mainland consumer and residential construction loan portfolios continued to deteriorate, Popular shored up its home base. The company acquired Citigroup Inc.'s 17-branch Puerto Rican retail banking network in 2007, for example, positioning for further growth upon improvement of the island's economy.

In September 2008, Popular agreed to sell $1.17 billion in subprime mortgage assets and servicing rights to Goldman Sachs Group Inc., closing out its U.S. consumer finance business. "There's no real market out there. There are very few buyers," Carrión told *American Banker*. "It's not easy. We felt, one, we had to address the liquidity situation, and secondly, we want to strengthen the balance sheet as much as possible. Probably sometime down the road, this will look like we sold them too cheap."

The cessation of Popular Financial Holdings' operation and a precipitous rise in the provision for loan losses were among the contributing factors in a net loss of $1.2 billion in 2008. The company had implemented tactics such as a dividend cut and stock and note offerings to try to stem the tide. Popular also entered into the U.S. Treasury Department's TARP Capital Purchase Program. The federal government had taken unprecedented action to upright the financial system, in a failure precipitated by the subprime mortgage market collapse.

In Puerto Rico, revenues grew by 9 percent, although credit quality deterioration necessitated a significant provision for loan losses. The company responded with actions to address problems in commercial and individual credit areas. EVERTEC sounded an upbeat note, with a 40 percent rise in net income year-over-year.

Popular continued to make difficult choices in 2009, suspending its dividend and preparing to exchange preferred stock and trust preferred securities for common shares. In regard to the latter, Joe Gladue,

B. Riley & Co. Inc. analyst, told *American Banker:* "It's unpleasant for the company and for common shareholders, but I think it's something they needed to do to get their capital ratios in line with what regulators are looking for."

Robert Halasz
Updated, Kathleen Peippo

PRINCIPAL SUBSIDIARIES

Popular International Bank, Inc.; Banco Popular de Puerto Rico; Banco Popular North America; EVERTEC Inc.

PRINCIPAL COMPETITORS

First BanCorp (Puerto Rico); Santander BanCorp; W Holding Company.

FURTHER READING

Baralt, Guillermo A., *Tradition into the Future: The First Century of the Banco Popular de Puerto Rico: 1893–1993*, San Juan: Banco Popular de Puerto Rico, 1993.

Davenport, Todd, "Popular Uses Gains to Top Expectations," *American Banker*, January 18, 2006, p. 18.

Dobbs, Kevin, "1Q Earnings: Popular's Results: Recession Effects," *American Banker*, April 21, 2008, p. 2.

Flynn, Barry, "Puerto Rico's Banco Popular Adds Florida Operations in Manageable Pieces," *Knight-Ridder/Tribune Business News*, April 5, 1999.

Hemlock, Doreen, "Puerto Rican Banking Firm Opens First Branch in Miami," *Knight-Ridder/Tribune Business News*, January 24, 2001.

Jackson, Ben, "Popular Aims to Double in U.S.," *American Banker*, July 15, 2002, p. 1.

Johnsson, Julie, "Bank's Bid for Payday Loan Riches," *Crain's Chicago Business*, February 14, 2000, pp. 1, 60.

Leuchter, Miriam, "A Bank's Popular Moves," *Crain's New York Business*, May 24, 1993, pp. 3, 37.

Mazzucca, Tim, "4Q Earnings: Popular Off 54% but Upbeat," *American Banker*, January 18, 2007, p. 2.

Monks, Matthew, "Popular CEO: Revamping Nearly Done at U.S. Unit," *American Banker*, June 10, 2009, p. 16.

Penn, Monica, "Hispanic Banks Go Head to Head," *Houston Business Journal*, March 12, 1999, pp. A1+.

"Popular, Inc. Reduces Dividend," *Investment Weekly News*, March 7, 2009, p. 166.

Quint, Michael, "Generosity Leads to a Bank Merger," *New York Times*, October 26, 1989, p. D2.

Rieker, Matthias, "High Note Ends a Tough Year for P.R. Banks," *American Banker*, December 29, 2005, p. 1.

———, "Popular's Aim in Mainland: Double Again," *American Banker*, April 6, 2006, p. 1.

———, "Popular's Low-Key CEO Expands on Urban Agenda," *American Banker*, March 30, 2005, p. 1.

———, "Popular's Work in Progress," *American Banker*, August 1, 2007, p. 1.

———, "A Reluctant Exit by Popular," *American Banker*, January 24, 2008, p. 1.

———, "Step by Step for Popular on Mainland," *American Banker*, August 19, 2004, p. 1.

Rose, Barbara, "Pioneer Buy a Foothold for Puerto Rico Bank," *Crain's Chicago Business*, September 20, 1993, p. 44.

Terris, Harry, "Last Piece of Popular Arm Finds Buyer," *American Banker*, September 2, 2008, p. 1.

Wahl, Melissa, "Banco Popular Becoming Just That," *Chicago Tribune*, June 24, 1999, Sec. 3, pp. 1, 4.

———, "San Juan Bank Picks Chicago as U.S. Base," *Chicago Tribune*, June 11, 1998, Sec. 3, pp. 1, 3.

Poste Italiane S.p.A.

Viale Europa 190
Rome, I-00144
Italy
Telephone: (+39 06) 59581
Fax: (+39 06) 59589100
Web site: http://www.poste.it

State-Owned Company
Founded: 1862
Incorporated: 1998 as Poste Italiane S.p.A.
Employees: 155,732
Sales: EUR 17.85 billion ($25.2 billion) (2008)
NAICS: 491110 Postal Service

■ ■ ■

Poste Italiane S.p.A. operates Italy's postal services system, with nearly 14,000 post offices and more than 155,000 employees throughout the country. Once one of Europe's most notoriously inefficient postal services, Poste Italiane has reinvented itself for the new millenium as one of the European Union's most dynamic, and most profitable. In addition to its postal services, Poste Italiane has expanded its services range to include Financial Services, through BancoPosta and its widely popular prepaid Postepay credit cards, and Insurance, including life insurance products.

Since 2008, Poste Italiane has become the first postal service in the world to launch its own mobile telephone operations, setting up the PosteMobile virtual operator service through Vodafone's mobile network. Poste Italiane's turnaround has earned the company a

place among *Fortune* magazine's World's Most Admired Companies list in 2008. Poste Italiane is a limited liability company 100 percent controlled by the Italian government. The company is expected to go public ahead of the full liberalization of the European postal market, slated for 2011. Massimo Sarmi is Poste Italiane's CEO.

ROOTS IN ROME

Italy can lay claim to one of the world's oldest known postal services, with the creation of the Roman Empire's *cursus publicus* under Augustus Caesar, who reigned from approximately 27 BCE to 14 CE The *cursus publicus* utilized light carriages drawn by fast horses; a second service provided slower deliveries with carriages drawn by two horses. The original services were reserved for government use; a third service was later added to provide postal deliveries for private use. The Roman service also provided the basis for the word *post,* which was derived from the resting points, or *posata,* used by the services' messengers during deliveries.

The *cursus publicus* remained in use, in various forms, through much of the Middle Ages. By the 13th century, however, unified postal delivery services had ceased to exist. Instead, these services were taken over by private courier operations. The most well-known of these was developed by the Tassis family (later known as the von Thurn und Taxis family), starting in 1290 in the Lombardy region of the future Italy.

Moving toward more modern times, Italy remained at the center of the development of European postal services. In the late 15th century, the region's rulers,

Poste Italiane is based on 6 fundamental assets: logistics infrastructure and ICT; payment management systems; image of trust/reliability; role of certifying body; multiple channels; widespread presence throughout the country. Each of these interacts with the others and serves to meet and satisfy customers' requests.

while recognizing the need for postal services, were reluctant to provide the financing for them. The Tassis family became one of the first to develop organized postal services, with scheduled delivery times and stopping points. By the end of the century, Francisco de Tassis and his brothers Ruggiero, Leonardo, and Janetto created a private postal delivery service linking Rome and Naples.

The brothers soon added Milan and Vienna, and by 1500 had begun to deliver mail as far away as Belgium. In 1505, the Tassis brothers were granted the monopoly on developing postal services throughout the Holy Roman Empire. In just 10 years, the family had extended their reach into Germany, France, Spain, Austria, and ultimately throughout the Austrian Habsburg Empire. The Tassis family later gained nobility in Germany, becoming the Von Thurn und Taxis family, and maintained their postal monopoly for more than 300 years.

STATE-OWNED POSTAL SERVICES IN THE 19TH CENTURY

The first moves toward developing nationally operating, government-controlled postal services took place during the 17th century. The Kingdom of Savoy, for example, established a state-controlled monopoly for private correspondence in 1604. France established its national monopoly in 1624, while England created a centralized post office in 1635. Nonetheless, the dominance of privately held mail delivery services remained in place through most of Europe through the end of the 18th century. The von Thurn und Taxis family remained the most prominent of these, with more than 20,000 messengers serving routes throughout Austria, Germany, Hungary, Italy, Belgium, and the Netherlands in the second half of the 19th century. The family's business was finally taken over by the Prussian government in 1867.

Italy had begun moving toward a national postal service, even before the country's unification in 1862. Lombardy and Veneto adopted centralized mail services at the end of the 18th century. Piedmont imposed its monopoly starting in 1818 and became one of the first postal services to provide extended services, such as money orders and post office boxes. The Piedmont system also established a network of post offices, including into the kingdom's most remote regions. In Sardinia, the government imposed the use of *cavallini*, stamped postal paper, for correspondence throughout the island in 1818. The *cavallini* provided the basis for the postage stamp system adopted throughout the world in the 19th century.

Other parts of the future Italy were also developing state-owned postal services, including the Papal States, starting in 1817, the Kingdom of Two Sicilies, from 1819, and the Grand Duchy of Tuscany, starting from 1827. Development of postal services took on fresh impetus with the development of the region's first railroads. The invention of the telegraph, which quickly fell under the competence of postal authorities, added new movement toward the creation of modern postal services. The Grand Duchy of Tuscany became one of the first in Italy to inaugurate telegraph services as part of its postal service.

MODERN BEGINNINGS FROM 1862

Through the middle of the 19th century, the development of a national post office network was well underway, with post offices established in 50 percent of Italy's towns. The various Italian postal services had also begun to issue stamps, starting with Piedmont, which imposed the use of stamps from 1851. By the end of the decade, stamps had been put into service throughout most of the Italian states. By then, too, the development of the rail network, largely confined to northern Italy, had replaced the coach system, providing faster and more reliable deliveries.

At the same time, Italy had steadily been approaching its unification into a single kingdom, which was largely completed in 1860. Two years later, the new state created its state-owned postal monopoly, which became the Poste Italiane, under the authority of the Directorate of Posts. Under the National Postal Law, enacted in 1862, the postal service was granted the monopoly over mail delivery, and took control of a national network of nearly 2,400 post offices. These were further regrouped into 18 regional branches. The new postal service started out with just 7,305 employees.

KEY DATES

1862: Unification of Italy leads to the creation of a state-controlled postal monopoly.
1888: Poste Italiane introduces home mail delivery.
1994: Poste Italiane converts from a government ministry to a state entity.
1998: Poste Italiane S.p.A. adopts limited liability status as a first step toward its future privatization.
1999: Poste Italiane begins selling life insurance products.
2000: Company launches new banking services, under the BancoPosta name.
2002: Poste Italiane achieves its first profit in 50 years.
2004: Poste Italiane launches the popular prepaid credit card Postepay.
2007: Poste Italiane launches its own virtual mobile telephone operator, PosteMobile.

The Poste Italiane joined in the creation of the Universal Postal Union, established in 1874. The new body, which initially represented 22 countries, established uniform international postal standards and rates. The conference also established guarantees for the confidentiality of private correspondence.

Two further milestones in Poste Italiane's development took place in the late 19th century. In 1876, the post office, like many of its counterparts in Europe, began offering banking services, establishing its own savings bank that year. Savings books were also extended to Italy's strong immigrant community, who remained an important source of foreign currency for the Italian state.

Other features of the modern post office also appeared during this time. The company introduced the use of postcards in 1874 and in 1881 took over parcel deliveries as well. The rapid growth of the use of postal services also led Poste Italiane to introduce home mail delivery, starting in 1888.

The next major milestone came with proliferation of telephone networks in Italy starting in the late 1870s. At first operated on a private basis, these networks were taken over by the Italian government in 1889, with the creation of the Ministry of Posts and Telegraphs (later Telecommunications). As in most European countries, the deployment of a national telephone system was joined to that of the postal service.

MODERNIZING IN THE POSTWAR ERA

During the 20th century, the Poste Italiane continued its development. The company introduced its first commemorative stamp in 1910. In 1913, the company introduced the use of pneumatic tube systems, which used compressed air to transport mail, in Milan, Naples, and Rome. Regular airmail service was launched in 1917. In the 1920s, the company began adopting the use of trucks and automobiles for use in domestic mail deliveries, while the company introduced the first sorting machinery during that decade. Also during this period, Poste Italiane introduced highly popular interest-bearing savings accounts.

The strategic importance of the post office meant that the Poste Italiane grew strongly throughout the years of Italy's fascist regime and World War II. The government invested heavily in the post office, expanding its network with a major construction program. This same strategic importance, however, meant that the country's post offices and other postal installations were vulnerable to attack by Allied bombing raids. By the end of the war, many of the country's post offices had suffered significant damage.

The reconstruction of the post office system began in earnest following the creation of the new Italian republic in 1946 and the creation of the new Posts and Telecommunications administration, which effectively separated the postal service and telephone system. As part of the reorganization, the Italian government also abolished Poste Italiane's monopoly on parcel delivery.

Poste Italiane launched a modernization effort in the 1950s, introducing its first computer-based systems in 1951. The postal service also benefited from the early successes of Italian computer maker Olivetti, which developed the first transistor-based computer in the late 1950s. Poste Italiane then added its first automated sorting equipment in 1967, and launched a national Postal (ZIP) Code system that year. Also during the 1960s, Poste Italiane outfitted its branch offices with telex machines, enabling customers to transmit data for the first time.

TOWARD PRIVATIZATION IN 1998

Poste Italiane's operations, however, remained notoriously inefficient and unprofitable throughout most of the second half of the 20th century. In fact, the postwar period saw the postal service enter more than 50 years of money-losing operations. By the early 1990s, the service's payroll had swelled to nearly 200,000 employees, a significant number of whom had been hired as a result of political cronyism. The company was also hampered by often unreliable equipment supplied through a monopoly contract from Olivetti, a contract at the center of a major corruption scandal at the beginning of the 1990s. Visits to an Italian post office at the time were described by the *Financial Times* in March 2002 as "Kafka-esque." By 1997, Poste Italiane's losses had mounted to EUR 1.4 billion per year.

Poste Italiane's renaissance began in 1994, when the postal service's status was converted to a state entity. No longer a ministry of the government, the postal service could also no longer serve as a channel for vote-gaining cronyism. By 1998, the postal service had been reincorporated as a limited liability company, Poste Italiane S.p.A. The move, a first step toward the privatization of the postal service, was made in compliance with European Union directives to liberalize Europe's postal services market by 2011.

Taking charge of the new company was Corrado Passero, a former McKinsey consultant who had previously served as managing director at Olivetti. Passero set into place a five-year plan, which included the hiring of new professionally trained managers, instituting performance-based measurements, and trimming the company's workforce by more than 33,000. The company also launched a major investment into a new technological infrastructure that transformed Poste Italiane into one of the most modern in Europe. The company also lowered its priority mail rates and promised overnight delivery for 80 percent of priority mail. As a result, businesses flocked to use Poste Italiane's services.

MULTISERVICE CHAMPION IN THE NEW CENTURY

Passero also recognized the need to expand Poste Italiane's range of services in order to ensure the group's growth and profitability. The company's vast network of 14,000 post offices provided the company with an unparalleled backbone for its development into a provider of a range of new services. This effort got off to a start with the launch of the group's first life insurance products in 1999. The move was a strong success: In less than three years, Poste Italiane had become the country's third-largest life insurance provider.

Poste Italiane next decided to expand its range of financial services beyond savings accounts. In 2000, despite intense resistance from Italy's commercial banks, Poste Italiane launched its own debit-card and credit-card accounts, quickly attracting more than two million clients. BancoPosta, as the new bank was called, became a major revenue generator for the company. By the early 2000s, the banking unit accounted for some 40 percent

of the group's total revenues, which topped EUR 3.8 billion in 2003. By then, Poste Italiane had achieved the primary objective of Passero's five-year plan, turning its first profit in 50 years by the end of 2002.

Passero left the company that year to take over as head of banking giant IntesaBCI. The CEO spot was then taken up by Massimo Sarmi, formerly general manager with TIM, an early Italian mobile phone operator. Sarmi set out not merely to maintain Poste Italiane's profitability, but also to transform it into one of the leaders in the European market. As part of that effort, Sarmi launched a major investment drive, spending $756 million to upgrade the company's technology, including equipping most of its network with broadband, and establishing online extensions of much of the group's postal, banking, and insurance services.

A major factor behind the company's success leading into the second half of the decade came with the 2004 launch of its prepaid, VISA-backed credit card, called Postepay. Based on the successful prepaid SIM card concept that Sarmi had helped pioneer for TIM, the Postepay card opened up credit card services to a vast new market in Italy. The cards, which were rechargeable at Poste Italiane's vast network of 14,000 post offices and 4,500 ATMs, quickly grew in popularity. By 2006, the company had issued more than 2.2 million Postepay cards.

RUN-UP TO LIBERALIZATION IN 2011

Poste Italiane continued to prepare itself for its coming privatization, and the impending deregulation of the European postal market. In 2006, the company reached an agreement with UPS to take over its international express shipments, while the Italian company would begin to handle parts of UPS's Italian pickup and delivery services. At the same time, Poste Italiane continued to expand the range of services offered through its network of post offices to include in-store and catalog-based retail sales of items ranging from books and calendars to televisions, bicycles, and cameras.

In another move, Poste Italiane became the first postal service in the world to enter the mobile telecommunications field. For this, the company reached a partnership agreement with Vodafone, which agreed to provide wholesale service for the launch of Poste Italiane's virtual operator, PosteMobile. Launched in 2007, the new service attracted more than 630,000 customers within its first year of operations.

By the end of 2008, Poste Italiane had become one of Europe's most profitable postal service operators, earning profits of EUR 883 million ($1.2 billion) on total revenues of nearly EUR 18 billion ($25 billion). By then, the company had been named by *Fortune* magazine in the top 10 of its World's Most Admired Companies for two years in a row. The company had also benefited from the economic downturn, as Italian savers abandoned traditional banks for Poste Italiane's own financial services. At the end of 2008, despite the group's lack of a banking license, Poste Italiane's deposits of more than EUR 340 billion made it the single largest bank in Italy.

Poste Italiane also responded to criticism that its diversification had come at a cost of its postal services, as waiting lines grew longer and longer with each new service. The company launched a redesign of its post office network, introducing a multi-window format, including a window dedicated solely to postal services. As the European postal system prepared to come full circle, to the privately owned postal services of its past, Poste Italiane had transformed itself into one of the top contenders for the future liberalized market.

M. L. Cohen

PRINCIPAL SUBSIDIARIES

BancoPosta Fondi S.p.A.; Consorzio Logistica Pacchi ScpA; Consorzio per I Servizi di Telefonia Mobile ScpA; Europa Gestioni Immobiliari S.p.A.; Mistral Air Srl; Poste Energia S.p.A.; Poste Italiane Trasporti S.p.A.; Poste Link Scrl; Poste Tutela S.p.A.; Poste Vita S.p.A.; Postecom S.p.A.; Postel S.p.A.; PostelPrint S.p.A.; Poste-Mobile S.p.A.; PosteShop S.p.A.; SDA Express Courier S.p.A.

PRINCIPAL DIVISIONS

Postal Services; Financial Services; Insurance Services; Other Services.

PRINCIPAL COMPETITORS

Deutsche Post AG; La Poste; Sofipost S.A.; TNT N.V.; Royal Mail Holdings PLC; Schweizerische Post; Oesterreichische Post AG.

FURTHER READING

Borlenghi, Laura, "14,000 Post Offices in Italy Will Access Internet with Italtel Core Network Services," *Total Telecom Online*, March 9, 2009.

De Mas, Italo, "Sorting Italian Postal System," *Precision Marketing*, March 12, 2004, p. 9.

Dinmore, Guy, "How Poste Italiane Is Truly Delivering," *Financial Times*, January 3, 2008, p. 14.

Faris, Stephan, "Special Delivery," *Fortune*, July 24, 2006, p. 35.

Klapner, Fred, "Pushing the Envelope," *Financial Times*, March 1, 2002, p. 14.

Michaels, Adrian, and Andrew Parker, "Mobile Tie-Up with Post Italiane to Likely Slow Growth," *Financial Times*, April 5, 2007, p. 25.

Minder, Raphael, "La Poste Set to Link up with Poste Italiane," *Financial Times*, May 31, 2001, p. 32.

"Pitney Bowes and Poste Italiane Introduce Internet Postage in Italy," *Direct Marketing*, August 2000, p. 11.

Rubach, Emma, "Italian Post Office Strikes Up Partnership with TNT," *Precision Marketing*, July 13, 2001, p. 9.

Segreti, Giulia, "Wary Savers Flee from Banks to Poste Italiane," *Financial Times*, December 8, 2008, p. 16.

Sylvers, Eric, "Pitfalls Abound for the New Poste Italiane," *International Herald Tribune*, November 1, 2006, p. 13.

———, "Poste Joins Italy's Love Affair with the Mobile," *International Herald Tribune*, March 27, 2007, p. 13.

"UPS Mails Italy," *Traffic World*, October 30, 2006, p. 35.

R&R Partners Inc.

900 South Pavilion Center Drive
Las Vegas, Nevada 89144
U.S.A.
Telephone: (702) 228-0222
Fax: (702) 228-7171
Web site: http://www.rrpartners.com

Private Company
Founded: 1974
Employees: 250
Gross Billings: $265 million (2009 est.)
NAICS: 541810 Advertising Agencies

■ ■ ■

R&R Partners Inc. is perhaps best known for the "What happens here, stays here" ad campaign for the Las Vegas Convention and Visitors Authority. Founded in Las Vegas in 1974, R&R Partners has grown from a local ad agency to a nationally recognized media dynamo with offices in Las Vegas, Reno, Phoenix, Salt Lake City, and Washington, D.C. R&R Partners caters to a diverse customer base including corporations, casino/resorts, sports venues, and mainstream brands, as well as governmental and public affairs clients.

FINDING A NICHE IN THE SEVENTIES AND EIGHTIES

R&R Partners was formed by Sid Rogich, a man with ties to the Las Vegas community and a bevy of political connections. Rogich's creativity made him a good friend to have, especially among folks with political aspirations. What Rogich could do in advertising for local businesses and casinos, he did on a larger scale for candidates looking to win over constituents. Rogich soon became the go-to man for effective public relations (PR) campaigns, both within and beyond Las Vegas.

In the 1970s Las Vegas was in transition. While beauty pageants, boxing matches, and risque dance revues still predominated, the city did not hold its previous allure. Headliners were not top talent and crime and drugs were taking their toll. The biggest threat to Vegas, however, was the legalization of gaming in Atlantic City, New Jersey. The struggling city had to find a way to attract new visitors and gamblers. The rise of huge hotel-casino resorts began in the late 1970s and throughout the next two decades. The megaresorts hit their stride in the 1990s and R&R Partners was there to represent them, to restore luster to the Vegas strip and its many businesses. One such client was the Las Vegas Convention and Visitors Authority (LVCVA), which relied on hotel room taxes as its major source of funding. The LVCVA needed some fresh ideas to keep tourism dollars flowing into the city and hired R&R Partners in 1980.

As R&R Partners gained a substantial foothold in the region, representing businesses both on and off the strip, Rogich's skills got him noticed by Ronald Reagan's political machine. Rogich not only helped shape Reagan's political message but also fashioned the governor of California's image with Republicans throughout the West Coast and beyond, preparing the former actor for national exposure.

With Rogich devoting the bulk of his time to Reagan and running mate George H. W. Bush's accelerating political careers, Billy Vassiliadis, Rogich's right-hand man, had been picking up the slack. Vassiliadis, an outspoken, brash Chicagoan who graduated from the University of Nevada, Las Vegas, took the reins of R&R Partners when Rogich left to run Reagan's and Bush's presidential campaigns.

GROWTH AND EXPANSION

In the early 1990s R&R Partners was the quiet agency with tons of Vegas and West Coast clout. The agency specialized in tourism, but also represented area and regional utility and health care providers. Satellite offices in Phoenix, Reno, and Salt Lake City had been added to handle non-Vegas clients. Although Sid Rogich was not getting prime-time exposure, insiders knew he was the man behind Presidents Reagan and George H. W. Bush, and a major political operator.

Like his boss before him, Vassiliadis had become a Vegas mover-and-shaker with a myriad of clients and connections. He had not only learned many tricks of the trade from Rogich, but had his own cadre of political hopefuls, party leaders, and celebrities who turned to him and R&R Partners for advice. The agency also represented several Vegas hotels and casinos, and still had the city's largest contract, LVCVA, which had been renewed twice.

With the addition of top-notch shopping and gourmet dining to the Vegas Strip, heralded by the arrival of the Forum Shops at Caesars Palace in 1992, Vegas had begun to attract more than hardcore gamblers. It became clear R&R Partners needed hands-on management and ownership, so Vassiliadis and Bob Henrie, another manager based in Salt Lake City, bought the agency from Rogich. By 1994 the city was averaging more than 28 million visitors to its hotels, casinos, and convention center.

Perhaps to offset Billy's tough guy image, Mary Ann Mele, daughter of a Vegas bandleader and a former PR guru for Caesars, bought into the agency and became a partner in 1996. Mele had been rising through the ranks at R&R for several years, and decided to buy in with another manager, Jim King. Rogich, meanwhile, had added George W. Bush as a client, as well as a major challenge: representing boxer Mike Tyson after his infamous ring snack of Evander Holyfield's ear in 1997.

While R&R Partners had plenty to keep it busy with customers in and around Las Vegas, the firm had been attracting a growing number of clients outside Nevada. In 1999 the Phoenix shop relocated and expanded its staff to handle additional clients, including the Arizona Water Pollution Control Association, CCBG Architects Inc., and Cox Communications, Inc.

HITTING THE BIG TIME

By the early 2000s R&R Partners had three popular hotel-casinos as clients: the Luxor, famous for its huge pyramid and Egyptian theme; Circus Circus, one of the earliest megaresorts with fun for both adults and kids; and Excalibur, the King Arthur/Camelot–themed resort, all owned by Mandalay Bay Resorts. While it perhaps appeared a conflict of interest to represent the hotels and the LVCVA, the agency had enough staff (more than 175 individuals) to work independently and not muddy the waters. Annual billings by the early 2000s reached around $115 million annually, with a substantial chunk coming from the LVCVA (approximately $25 million).

In 2001 R&R Partners landed new clients including Motor City Casino and the Utah Transit Authority, but lost part of its Mandalay Bay contract. In the Vegas office, staffers were working on a new LVCVA ad, one that would change the agency forever. R&R's other locations were also doing well, with Phoenix winning foodservice/hospitality giant Aramark's account, while Henrie's Salt Lake City office won the Public Relations Society of America's prestigious Silver Anvil award for outstanding promotional work in the public affairs/government category.

In 2002 R&R Partners promoted itself with a glittery bash, moving its headquarters to new 45,000-square-foot offices in Vegas. More good news came when the agency won Park Place Entertainment's $20 million advertising account, covering eight of its Nevada properties including the legendary Caesars Palace. Bigger and better was yet to come as the new LVCVA ad was launched. The "What happens here, stays here," tagline

KEY DATES

1974: R&R Partners is founded in Las Vegas by Sid Rogich.
1980: R&R Partners lands Las Vegas Convention and Visitors Authority (LVCVA) account.
1994: Billy Vassiliadis and Bob Henrie buy into R&R Partners.
1996: Mary Ann Mele and Jim King buy into R&R Partners; office in Phoenix opens.
2000: Phoenix office relocates and adds staff.
2002: R&R Partners moves to a new Las Vegas office complex.
2004: Brown & Partners and Peter Ernaut agency merge with R&R Partners.
2006: Firm opens a new office in Washington, D.C.
2009: R&R Partners wins the LVCVA contract for another three years, marking almost 30 years of representation.

hit national airwaves in 2003 and quickly struck a chord with viewers. The tagline proved so popular it was featured in prime-time television shows such as CBS's racy comedy *Two and a Half Men* and was wryly dropped by celebrities, athletes, and news personalities.

As tourism climbed and the slogan's punch continued to resonate with television and print audiences, additional spots were crafted and the LVCVA renewed its account for another five years. Flush with success and billings reaching over $175 million annually, R&R Partners broadened its client base by merging in 2004 with two other independent ad shops, Vegas-based Brown & Partners and Reno-based Peter Ernaut. All three agencies operated under the R&R Partners name while Mark Brown and Peter Ernaut became partners with Vassiliadis, Henrie, Mele, and King. Combined billings for the new R&R Partners was in excess of $225 million with staffing of 240 workers.

In 2005 Las Vegas celebrated its centennial in May, while R&R Partners debuted a new television ad for Caesars, the first for the venerable casino and hotel in more than a decade. Further, R&R Partners scored a literary coup when a twist of its ever popular LVCVA campaign was on the *New Yorker* magazine's cover (July 4, 2005), in a cartoon featuring a priest standing outside a church, stating to one of his parishioners, "*He* knows what you did in Vegas."

NEW DIRECTIONS: 2006 AND BEYOND

In 2006 R&R Partners opened a new office in Washington, D.C., not such a surprise considering the agency's political history and entrenchment. While the agency's other offices handled various political campaigns, the new D.C. office provided an important asset in expanding R&R's public affairs and governmental clientele. Back in the West, partner and owner Mark Brown left the agency to pursue outside interests, while R&R Partners geared up to bring more professional sporting events to Vegas as part of a joint Playboy Enterprises and LVCVA ad campaign.

As the decade progressed, R&R Partners signed Harrah's Entertainment, continued to create quirky spots for the LVCVA, and tried to lure additional sporting events to the city. One such project was getting *Sports Illustrated* to launch its annual swimsuit issue from Vegas. While the agency spent about $1 million, the event generated close to $20 million in national media attention for the agency, the city, and tourism. On the downside, R&R Partners lost the coveted Caesars Entertainment account to the Chicago-based Leo Burnett shop, and the economy took a nosedive.

In early 2009 R&R Partners absorbed a small Washington, D.C., agency, Gallatin Public Affairs, and incorporated it into its D.C. office to help generate additional business. As the country's finances and confidence collapsed, so did much of its travel and tourism. Luckily for R&R Partners, its mini-empire encompassed more than just Vegas gaming and tourism, so the downturn was not catastrophic. Still, Vegas visitor numbers had fallen by several percentage points according to the LVCVA. As a testament to its ongoing confidence in R&R Partners, the LVCVA renewed its contract with the agency for another three years to bring the gamers, tourists, and sports fans back.

As the first decade of the 2000s came to a close, R&R Partners remained a tour de force in creativity, reaching millions with its television and print ads for an ever evolving roster of customers. While few recognized the agency's name or clout, its pedigree was solid. The company had proven itself particularly valuable to a wide range of clients in the gaming, public affairs, health care, utility, and sports industries with nearly $270 million in annual billings.

Nelson Rhodes

PRINCIPAL SUBSIDIARIES

AirWave Productions.

R&R Partners Inc.

PRINCIPAL COMPETITORS

Dailey & Associates Advertising; E.B. Lane; Effler & Partners; Gavin & Gavin Advertising, Inc.; Grey Worldwide; Leo Burnett; Merica Agency; TBWA Worldwide; Young & Rubicam.

FURTHER READING

Audi, Tamara, "Vegas Plans a New Push to Attract More People," *Wall Street Journal,* January 7, 2008, p. B2.

Beirne, Mike, "Grand Marketers of the Year," *Brandweek,* October 11, 2004, pp. 1+.

———, "Las Vegas Makes a Play for Music, Sports Fans," *Brandweek,* November 6, 2006, p. 8.

———, "Vegas or Bust," *Brandweek,* January 15, 2001, p. 24.

Berke, Richard, "Younger Bush Looks to Father's Image Burnisher," *New York Times,* March 26, 2000, p. 28.

Comiteau, Jennifer, "R&R Partners," *Adweek,* June 15, 2009, p. AM8.

Fisher, Ann, "R&R Partners Promotes R&R in Vegas," *Post,* October 2001, p. 6.

Flass, Rebecca, "R&R Gains $320 Mil. Vegas Tourism Extension," *Adweek Western Edition,* November 12, 2003.

———, "Vegas Calls in New Campaign: R&R's Freedom Positioning Key to Selling the Land of Liberace," *Adweek Western Edition,* June 17, 2002, p. 5.

Goldrich, Robert, "Daniel Russ: Executive Creative Director of R&R Partners Reflects on the Past Year," *Shoot,* July 20, 2007, p. 13.

Hayes, Stephanie, "Ready to Strut," *Adweek Western Edition,* February 18, 2002, p. 3.

Jones, Chris, "Co-Owner at R&R Partners Plans to Leave Firm," *Las Vegas Review-Journal,* June 8, 2006.

O'Keefe, Rob, "WHHSH. Story," *Travel Marketing Decisions,* Fall 2007, pp. 1+.

Robertson, Anne, "Phoenix Is 'Sleeping Giant' to R&R Partners Executive," *Phoenix Business Journal,* October 27, 2000, p. 63.

Schmelzer, Randi, "Las Vegas' R&R Partners Looks Ahead with Merger," *Adweek Western Edition,* September 20, 2004, p. 12.

———, "R&R, Brown, Ernaut to Merge in Vegas," *Adweek Western Edition,* September 9, 2004.

———, "R&R Heads to the 'Burbs for New Vegas Spot," *Adweek Western Edition,* May 5, 2005.

———, "R&R Partners Taps D.C. Head," *Adweek,* December 5, 2005, p. 28.

Solman, Gregory, "For R&R, What Happens in 'Playboy' …," *Adweek Western Edition,* October 9, 2006.

———, "R&R Returns Caesars Palace to TV," *Adweek Western Edition,* June 13, 2005.

Spillman, Benjamin, "Las Vegas Showing Off," *Las Vegas Review-Journal,* January 14, 2009.

———, "LVCVA: What Works Here, Stays Here," *Las Vegas Review-Journal,* April 15, 2009.

Stewart, Al, "R&R Adds Park Place Business: Vegas Shop Gets Caesars, Bally's, Other Projects in Consolidation," *Adweek Western Edition,* February 11, 2002, p. 3.

"Vegas Bets on the Spontaneous: Effort Woos Last-Minute Travelers," *Brandweek,* July 14, 2008, p. 6.

Voight, Joan, "R&R Lets Freedom Ring in Vegas," *Adweek Western Edition,* September 25, 2000, p. 6.

———, "Striptease," *Adweek Eastern Edition,* June 12, 2000, p. 44.

Ricoh Company, Ltd.

Ricoh Building
8-13-1 Ginza
Chuo-ku
Tokyo, 104-8222
Japan
Telephone: (+81-3) 6278-2111
Fax: (+81-3) 6278-2997
Web site: http://www.ricoh.com

Public Company
Incorporated: 1936 as Riken Kankoshi Co., Ltd.
Employees: 108,500
Sales: ¥2.09 trillion ($21.13 billion) (2009)
Stock Exchanges: Tokyo Osaka Nagoya Fukuoka Sapporo
  Amsterdam Frankfurt Paris
Ticker Symbol: 7752
NAICS: 333315 Photographic and Photocopying Equip-
  ment Manufacturing; 334111 Electronic Computer
  Manufacturing; 334112 Computer Storage Device
  Manufacturing; 334119 Other Computer
  Peripheral Equipment Manufacturing; 334210
  Telephone Apparatus Manufacturing; 334413
  Semiconductor and Related Device Manufacturing;
  532420 Office Machinery and Equipment Rental
  and Leasing; 541511 Custom Computer Program-
  ming Services; 541512 Computer Systems Design
  Services; 561439 Other Business Service Centers
  (Including Copy Shops)

■ ■ ■

Ricoh Company, Ltd., is a leading maker of office
automation equipment, including copiers, printers,

facsimile machines, and related supplies. Other products
that the company manufactures and/or markets include
personal computers, servers, network devices,
semiconductors, and digital cameras. Ricoh, however, is
far more than a manufacturer, as it has transformed
itself in the early 21st century into a global leader in
imaging solutions with its revenue generated not only
through hardware but also through software, systems
design, and services. With factories, sales affiliates, and
service centers located throughout Asia, Europe, and
North and South America, Ricoh generates about 55
percent of its revenues outside of Japan, with about 25
percent stemming from Europe and 24 percent from the
Americas.

EARLY HISTORY: FROM PHOTO EQUIPMENT TO OFFICE EQUIPMENT

The company's initial efforts focused on photography,
and its ability to win market share was evident as far
back as 1936, when Riken Kankoshi Co., Ltd., was
formed to produce positive sensitive paper, used to
develop film. Under the leadership of Kiyoshi Ichimura
the firm instantly took the lead in the Japanese
sensitized paper market. In 1938, after deciding to
produce cameras as well, Ichimura changed the
company's name to Riken Optical Co., Ltd., and
introduced the Olympic 4.

The flashbulb and color film invented during the
1930s, and other innovations such as new chemicals for
film developing and computer-designed lenses originated
during World War II, were marketed to the public after

the war. In 1950 Riken introduced another camera, the Ricohflex III.

Five years later the company entered the copier market when it developed its first diazo copier, the Ricopy 101. This was followed by the Ricoh Synchrofax in 1959, two micro-enlargement copiers in 1960 and 1962, and two duplicators, also introduced in 1960 and 1962.

With a handful of employees and $100,000, the company established its first overseas subsidiary, Ricoh Industries, U.S.A., Inc., in 1962. The subsidiary initially imported cameras, but it soon began marketing copiers when it realized the sales potential in the United States.

In 1963, following the establishment of its successful subsidiary, the Japanese parent company changed its name to Ricoh Company, Ltd., and continued its success in both copier and photographic equipment.

In 1965 Ricoh entered the budding field of office computers with the debut of the Ricoh Typer Standard, a data-processing system. It also introduced the Ricopy BS-1, and electrostatic coated-paper copier.

PRODUCT EXPANSION AND U.S. GROWTH

The 1970s marked a decade of growth and change for Ricoh and its U.S. subsidiary. During the 1970s Ricoh began to sell cameras and other electronic goods on the U.S. market. Ricoh Industries U.S.A., whose annual sales had climbed to $1.3 million by 1970, was renamed Ricoh of America, Inc. In 1973 Ricoh established its second U.S. subsidiary, Ricoh Electronics Co., Ltd., in Irvine, California. Created to assemble copier supplies and parts, the subsidiary made Ricoh the first Japanese company to produce copiers in the United States.

During the mid-1970s Ricoh made advances in three important markets. The Rifax 600S, the world's first high-speed digital facsimile machine, made its debut in 1974 along with the Rinac 1000 System, an information-retrieval system. This was followed by the Ricopy DT1200, the company's first plain-paper copier, in 1975. Also in 1975, Ricoh was honored with Japan's highest award for quality control, the Deming Prize.

In 1976 Ricoh introduced the Ricoh Printer 40, an impact (daisy-wheel) printer, followed by the Ricoh WP-1, a word processor. By this time the company's products covered the field of office automation.

In 1978 Ricoh established Rapicom, formed to develop and market stand-alone, high-speed digital facsimile products, as well as satellite facsimile equipment. Ricoh of America opened a research and development facility in Santa Clara, California, in 1977. In 1979, however, the company assigned U.S. research and development functions to a new entity, Ricoh Systems, Inc.

EXPANDING THE RICOH BRAND

Although it had established four U.S.-based companies, Ricoh did not have much U.S. visibility, in part because of the company's agreement to sell copy machines in the United States under the labels of Savin and Pitney Bowes, two U.S. manufacturers. Early in the 1980s Ricoh announced its intention to market copiers under its own name and to become a major player in the worldwide office-automation market. Takeshi Ouye, president of Ricoh, planned to move carefully into the office-automation market, predicting in June 1980 in *Modern Office Procedures:* "We will be in a position to market a total automation system within ten years." Ricoh already held the leading position in the international plain-paper copier market, and its additional office products (offset duplicating equipment and systems, diazo copiers, and facsimile, microfilm, word-processing, document, and storage-retrieval equipment) gave the company a boost in its quest for a leading rank in office automation.

In 1981 Ricoh of America began to market Ricoh copiers in the United States. By 1984 the company had achieved a 7 percent share of the U.S. market. The firm

KEY DATES

■

1936: Riken Kankoshi Co., Ltd., is formed to produce sensitized paper.

1938: After camera production commences, company changes its name to Riken Optical Co., Ltd.

1955: Production of office equipment begins, with the debut of the company's first copier.

1962: First overseas subsidiary is established in the United States.

1963: Company changes its name to Ricoh Company, Ltd.

1973: Ricoh becomes the first Japanese company to make copiers in the United States.

1974: Company produces its first fax machine.

1975: Ricoh is awarded the Deming Prize for excellence in quality control.

1981: Ricoh-brand copiers are marketed for the first time in the United States.

1983: Company introduces its first personal computer and first laser printer.

1987: The Imagio line of digital office automation equipment makes its debut.

1992: Ricoh posts its first operating loss.

1995: Company acquires Savin Corporation and Gestetner Holdings PLC.

2001: Ricoh purchases Atlanta-based Lanier Worldwide, Inc.

2007: Ricoh and IBM Corporation form the joint venture InfoPrint Solutions Company.

2008: In the largest acquisition in its history, Ricoh acquires IKON Office Solutions, Inc.

then decided to venture into more advanced copying machines, moving from the $5,000-and-under price range to the $6,000-to-$13,000 range. This step put Ricoh in direct competition with Xerox Corporation.

Ricoh's four-year-old Rapicom subsidiary landed a major account for Telepress, Ricoh's satellite facsimile product, when it agreed in 1982 to supply the product to Gannett Company, publisher of *USA Today*. Telepress eliminated the practice of physically transporting the newspaper for printing and then again for distribution.

In 1983 Ricoh introduced an ultracompact hand-held business computer, the Ricoh SP25, in addition to its first personal computer, the Ricoh SP200, and its first laser printer, the Ricoh LP4120. The company also

added two more printers to its line the following year: the Ricoh JP5320, an ink-jet model, and the Ricoh TP3220, a thermal printer.

Longtime Ricoh President Takeshi Ouye was elected chairman in 1983, while Hiroshi Hamada became president. Under their leadership, the company continued to globalize. Previously, much of the company's new product research was done overseas, particularly in the United States, and then transferred to Japan, where the products were manufactured. Hamada felt that Ricoh should develop more products domestically and boost production capacity by manufacturing the products both at home and overseas. In the United States, for example, the company made its operation more independent and more responsive to the U.S. economy, merging its U.S. research and development operation, Ricoh Systems, with Ricoh Electronics, the production facility, both of which had reported separately to Ricoh in Japan. In addition, the company established Ricoh UK Products Ltd. in the United Kingdom in 1983, while Ricoh Nederlands opened offices in France and Italy in 1984, as well as a Belgian office in 1985.

In the mid-1980s the company continued aggressive marketing and product development efforts with the introduction of the RINNET System, a local area network; a color copier; an electronic filing system; an electronic whiteboard; and two minicomputers developed in cooperation with AT&T. As a result, sales grew 20 percent annually from 1982 to 1985. Ricoh's alliance with AT&T began with a three-year original-equipment-manufacturing (OEM) contract, in which Ricoh agreed to equip its facsimile machines with AT&T telephones. This was followed, in 1984, by an agreement allowing Ricoh to market AT&T's minicomputers in Japan. In 1985 the two firms created AT&T Ricoh Company, a joint venture to produce and market modified versions of AT&T's compact telephone systems. Ricoh lent its Japanese marketing-and-service network to AT&T, and AT&T helped Ricoh enter the telecommunications field.

In 1984 the company's Atsugi, Japan, plant established a production-technology research center and received the *Nihon Keizai Shimbun* Award for factory automation. Ricoh also established the Ricoh Research Institute of General Electronics Company, and Ricoh Finance. In addition, the company added a thermal paper and toner-production facility to its Fukui plant, while Sindo Ricoh Company began producing zoom plain-paper copiers and toner.

In the United States, Ricoh Electronics opened a fully automated thermal paper manufacturing plant in Irvine, California. In addition, Ricoh began construction of Ricoh Research and Development Center, which opened in Yokohama, Japan, in April 1986.

FURTHER GLOBALIZING AND INCREASING OVERSEAS PRODUCTION

In 1985 Ricoh Corporation (Canada), formerly Rapifax of Canada, opened a new facility in Nepean, Ontario. Ricoh also established two marketing companies in 1986: Ricoh España S.A., a joint venture with a Spanish distributor of Ricoh products, and Ricoh France S.A., a wholly owned subsidiary. When Ricoh UK Products began production in May, Ricoh became the first Japanese company to manufacture copiers in the United Kingdom. By 1988 the firm had also added facsimile equipment and supplies to its production capabilities.

Under the guidance of President Hiroshi Hamada, Ricoh in 1987 established its second European manufacturing subsidiary, Ricoh Industrie France S.A., which produced plain-paper copiers and other office-automation equipment and supplies at a new plant in Alsace. That same year, the firm also strengthened its position in the semiconductor arena with the purchase of Panatech Research & Development Corporation's semiconductor division. In May 1987 Ricoh opened a semiconductor-design center in San Jose, California. The center expanded research and development efforts for Ricoh's semiconductor products, which at this stage included CMOS, a large-scale integrated device that was incorporated in its copiers, facsimiles, and cameras.

In Japan in 1987 Ricoh introduced Imagio, a new line of office-automation equipment featuring a digital system that processed images, produced 20 copies a minute, and functioned as an input/output station for electronic filing systems. In addition, the introduction of several new copiers, including a high-speed, multifunctional desktop model, enabled Ricoh to maintain its position as Japan's leading plain-paper-copier company.

In April 1987 Ricoh reorganized and consolidated its U.S. subsidiaries. The move, calculated to create a "separate Ricoh in North America," was another move toward globalization for Ricoh. According to Hamada in the company's annual report for 1988, the new unit, called Ricoh Corporation, was to "gradually assume greater independence in virtually all aspects of its operations." Hamada also revealed plans to create another independent Ricoh in Europe, a plan that would begin by increasing production capacity.

In 1988 the company released a lightweight, compact eight-millimeter camcorder in the United States and Japan. The company also opened Ricoh Software Research in Santa Clara, California, to develop custom software for three-dimensional computer-aided design and database markets. The software products were designed for existing and future OEM clients. Also that year, Ricoh's overseas sales exceeded domestic sales for the first time although that proved to be a short-lived development. Ricoh's product line included facsimile machines, data-processing equipment, cameras, and copying machines and supplies. It was one of only a few companies making four different types of copying machines: the diazo, the electrofax, the plain-paper copier, and the duplicator.

While many Japanese companies suffered decreases in their export businesses during the mid- to late 1980s because of the high value of the yen, Ricoh's overseas sales grew. Its success was attributed to substantial gains in sales of facsimile machines and laser printers. In addition, Ricoh's two main office products, copiers and facsimile machines, had earned a major share of the U.S. market. In 1987 Ricoh's share of the laser printer and scanner market was about 24 percent. Ricoh's goal was to double that share by employing more aggressive marketing efforts through an expanded sales force and its U.S. network of dealers, distributors, and OEM arrangements.

Despite the aggressive sales strategy, Ricoh suffered profit declines in 1986 and 1987 that stemmed in part from the appreciation of the yen. To cope with the high yen, the company planned to continue increasing overseas production. In the late 1980s, it began making copiers at its third U.S. manufacturing plant. This, and a fourth plant, which opened in Lawrenceville, Georgia, in 1990, doubled Ricoh's U.S. production. About 20 percent of the products made at these facilities, which included copiers, facsimiles, sorters, automatic document feeders, and supplies, were exported to Japan and Europe.

WEATHERING RECESSION AND DIGITALIZING THE PRODUCT LINES

During the early 1990s Ricoh had to contend with the difficulties of the recessionary Japanese economy, which cut demand for office machinery, as well as the high yen, which made exports from Japan more expensive. Despite its efforts at increasing overseas sales and production, only about 27 percent of revenues were derived outside of Japan at the beginning of the decade, while most of its products were still built in Japan. The culmination of these trends came in the fiscal year ending in March 1992, when Ricoh posted its first operating loss. Net income for that year was just $15.4 million on sales of $7.65 billion, the latter figure a modest 7 percent increase over the previous year.

Ricoh embarked on a major cost-cutting initiative in the wake of the disappointing 1992 results. No workers were laid off, but the company no longer replaced every worker who resigned or retired. Ricoh also made major cuts in the products and parts it sold, reducing the number from 5,000 to 3,100. Work was halted on several new products. The company's management was also restructured. Attempting to bolster its overseas operations, Ricoh took a 24 percent stake in Gestetner Holdings PLC, a U.K.-based office equipment firm. Ricoh and Gestetner had worked together since the mid-1960s, and in the early 1990s Ricoh was selling office equipment to Gestetner, which marketed the products in Europe under its own name. Ricoh shifted production of low-end office automation products for the U.S. market from Japan to South Korea. In addition, the company established several subsidiaries and joint ventures in China and Hong Kong for the manufacture of copiers, fax machines, and parts.

On the product development side, Ricoh began revitalizing its product lineup through an increased emphasis on digital products. The company had introduced its first full-color plain-paper digital copier, the Artage 8000, in 1990, and moved into the burgeoning market for multifunctional digital copiers the following year with the Imagio MF530 (multifunctional copiers were also able to perform other functions, such as sending faxes and/or serving as a computer printer). Ricoh made an early entrance into the CD-recordable (CD-R) device sector, introducing both CD-R discs and CD-R drives in 1992. Making its debut in 1993 was the Preter 500/550, a full-color multifunctional digital copier. The company moved into the scanner market in 1994 with the Ricoh IS20 and into the digital camera field in 1995 with the Ricoh DC-1, which recorded both still and moving images as well as sound.

Ricoh's restructuring and new product development prowess paid off by the mid-1990s as the company posted healthy net income of $214.8 million on sales of $11.79 billion for fiscal 1995. Ricoh continued its drive to boost international sales by acquiring Savin Corporation for about $42 million and taking over Gestetner Holdings for about $286 million, with both purchases occurring in 1995. Based in Stamford, Connecticut, the financially troubled Savin had been marketing Savin-brand copiers and fax machines made by Ricoh and continued to do so as a Ricoh subsidiary.

Longtime President Hiroshi Hamada was named chairman and CEO in 1996, while Masamitsu Sakurai was promoted to president and COO, becoming the first head of the company with a technology background. That year, Ricoh helped develop the CD-ReWritable (CD-RW) platform, which enabled users to read, write, and rewrite computer data on compact discs. It introduced the first CD-RW drives and discs in late 1996 and early 1997. Also in 1996 the company began using the Aficio brand for all of its digital copiers sold outside of Japan. In 1997 Ricoh established a new research and development and venture-capital financing subsidiary in San Jose, California, called Ricoh Silicon Valley, Inc. (later renamed Ricoh Innovations, Inc.).

Ricoh was spared the worst effects of the Asian economic crisis of the late 1990s, thanks to its drive to increase overseas sales. By 2000, nearly 40 percent of revenues were derived outside Japan, with the company aiming for a 50-50 split. Sales and net income fell only slightly in fiscal 1998, while the next two years saw Ricoh post solid gains, culminating in net income of $407 million on sales of $14.05 billion for fiscal 2000.

Among the company's many product introductions of the late 1990s were the Imagio MF105 Pro, an ultrafast digital copier capable of printing 105 copies per minute (debuting in May 1999); the IPSiO Color 2000, the company's first color laser printer (July 1998); the Ricoh Image Scanner IS450, a flatbed scanner (March 1999); and several increasingly powerful and compact digital cameras. Ricoh was also placing increasing emphasis on semiconductor devices, including application-specific integrated circuits (ASICs), which were used in such areas as central processing units and facsimile engine controllers; and application-specific standard products (ASSPs), which included chip sets for digital cameras and PC card controllers for notebook computers. In mid-2000 Ricoh launched a proactive management restructuring to adopt a U.S.-style separation of executive and operating functions, with the heads of the company's divisions and subsidiaries gaining much more authority and responsibility than before.

FURTHER ACQUISITIONS AND AN INCREASED EMPHASIS ON SOFTWARE AND SERVICES

In January 2001, in a continuation of its strategy of buying copier companies selling products it manufactured, Ricoh acquired Lanier Worldwide, Inc., for around $250 million. Based in Atlanta, Lanier marketed office imaging equipment from about 1,600 sales and service locations in the Americas and Europe. This purchase strengthened Ricoh within its traditionally strong customer base of small and medium-sized companies while also providing inroads into the higher-end large-company sector where margins were higher. As with its previous takeovers of Savin and Gestetner, Ricoh continued to use the Lanier brand. Ricoh's multi-brand strategy enabled it to leverage the goodwill that the various brands had built up over the years and their strengths in particular areas, Savin in the government and education markets, for example, and Gestetner in hospitals. The Gestetner brand remained in use even after Gestetner Holdings was renamed NRG Group PLC, later in 2001.

As it continued to seek growth outside Japan, Ricoh placed particular emphasis on fast-growing China. To aid this effort, the company in October 2002 established Ricoh China Co., Ltd., as a regional headquarters for this important market. In 2003 and 2004, Ricoh pulled out of two markets, the film camera business and optical disk drive business, respectively. The withdrawal from the former was precipitated by the growing popularity of digital cameras, which Ricoh continued to produce, while the company exited from the latter because of fierce price competition. Also in 2004, Ricoh acquired Hitachi Printing Solutions, Ltd., from Hitachi, Ltd. The acquired company, subsequently renamed Ricoh Printing Systems, Ltd., specialized in the production of large printers for commercial use as well as laser printers.

Fueling Ricoh's growth in the early 21st century was the company's increasing emphasis not only on networked imaging equipment but also on the delivery and management of complete document processing systems. A number of Ricoh's initiatives during this period were designed to widen the company's product line as well as its software and services capabilities. As it evolved from an office machine maker into a provider of technology systems, Ricoh generated an increasing portion of revenues from software and services. By 2009, the revenue split between hardware on the one hand and software and services on the other was about 50-50.

A series of acquisitions and the establishment of a joint venture aided in this evolution. Most of these occurred under the leadership of Shiro Kondo, named president and CEO in April 2007. Just a few months earlier, Ricoh acquired the European office-equipment sales and services operations of Danka Business Systems PLC for $210 million. Under Ricoh, this business became known as Infotec Europe B.V. In June 2007 Ricoh paid IBM Corporation $725 million for a majority stake in IBM's printing systems division. The newly created joint venture, called InfoPrint Solutions Company, LLC, and based in Boulder, Colorado, specialized in high-speed, high-volume printing services for banks, insurance companies, and other financial institutions.

Ricoh next concluded the largest acquisition in its history, the $1.63 billion purchase of IKON Office Solutions, Inc., based in Malvern, Pennsylvania. IKON distributed and leased office equipment made by other companies, including Ricoh and main rival Canon,

although under Ricoh's ownership, IKON began to convert Canon customers into Ricoh users. The addition of IKON aided Ricoh in its move into services given that the former offered document- and business-processing services. The October 2008 deal also supported Ricoh's global growth ambitions as IKON's main markets were the United States and Western Europe.

Adding IKON helped push the portion of revenues that Ricoh generated outside Japan up to 55 percent for the fiscal year ending in March 2009. That year, however, after posting solid profits every year since the beginning of the 21st century, Ricoh managed to generate net income of just ¥6.53 billion ($66 million), a 94 percent plunge over the previous year. The company blamed this turn of events and the year's 5.8 percent drop in net sales to ¥2.09 trillion ($21.13 billion) on the global economic downturn and the effects of a stronger yen. In addition to contending with the sluggish global economy, Ricoh faced two other major challenges at this time: integrating the various acquisitions it had made over the previous decade and managing the bulging load of debt taken on to compete the deals.

Kim M. Magon
Updated, David E. Salamie

PRINCIPAL SUBSIDIARIES

Ricoh Optical Industries Co., Ltd.; Tohoku Ricoh Co., Ltd.; Ricoh Unitechno Co., Ltd.; Ricoh Elemex Corporation; Ricoh Microelectronics Co., Ltd.; Ricoh Keiki Co., Ltd.; Ricoh Printing Systems, Ltd.; Ricoh Tohoku Co., Ltd.; Ricoh Chubu Co., Ltd.; Ricoh Kansai Co., Ltd.; Ricoh Chugoku Co., Ltd.; Ricoh Kyushu Co., Ltd.; Hokkaido Ricoh Co., Ltd.; Ricoh Sales Co., Ltd.; Ricoh Technosystems Co., Ltd.; Ricoh Logistics System Co., Ltd.; Ricoh Leasing Co., Ltd. (51.1%); Ricoh Electronics, Inc. (USA); Ricoh UK Products Ltd.; Ricoh Industrie France S.A.S.; Ricoh Asia Industry (Shenzhen) Ltd. (China); Shanghai Ricoh Digital Equipment Co., Ltd. (China); Ricoh Americas Corporation (USA); InfoPrint Solutions Company, LLC (U.S.A.; 79.5%); IKON Office Solutions, Inc. (USA); Ricoh Europe Holdings PLC (UK); NRG Group PLC (UK); Ricoh Asia Industry Ltd. (China); Ricoh Asia Pacific Pte Ltd. (Singapore); Ricoh China Co., Ltd.; Ricoh Finance Nederland B.V. (Netherlands).

PRINCIPAL COMPETITORS

Canon Inc.; Xerox Corporation; Sharp Corporation; Eastman Kodak Company; Hewlett-Packard Company; Konica Minolta Holdings, Inc.; Lexmark International, Inc.; Seiko Epson Corporation.

FURTHER READING

Brubaker, Harold, "Ricoh to Buy Malvern's Ikon Office Solutions," *Philadelphia Inquirer*, August 28, 2008.

Caplan, Brian, "When Politics Beats Profits," *Asian Business*, March 1990, pp. 55+.

DeTar, Jim, "Low-Profile Ricoh Gets Aggressive," *Electronic News*, May 11, 1998, pp. 1, 70.

Deutsch, Claudia H., "Ricoh Tries to Put Multiple Brands Under One Roof," *New York Times*, February 5, 2001, pp. C1, C3.

The First Fifty Years of Ricoh: Insights and Innovations, Tokyo: Ricoh Company, Ltd., 1986.

Friedland, Jonathan, "Setting an Example: Japanese Manufacturer Ricoh Slashes Costs," *Far Eastern Economic Review*, October 8, 1992, pp. 81–82.

Helm, Leslie, and Rebecca Aikman, "Office Products: A Japanese Slugfest for U.S. Turf," *Business Week*, May 13, 1985, pp. 98 +.

Martin, Neil A., "An Original Copier: Ricoh Leads the Industry with Advanced Digital Office Machines," *Barron's*, January 6, 2003, pp. 20, 22.

———, "Ricoh: Getting Ready to Rumble," *Barron's*, August 3, 2009, p. 17.

Naruse, Miwa, "Technology Drives Ricoh's Growth," *Nikkei Weekly*, July 12, 2004.

Prystay, Cris, "Ricoh Campaigns for Global Exposure," *Wall Street Journal*, November 20, 2002, p. B5C.

"Ricoh Eyeing Growth in U.S. with New Global Marketing Strategy," *Nikkei Report*, July 1, 2009.

"Ricoh Racing to Reinvent Copier-Focused Strategy," *Nikkei Report*, June 30, 2009.

Taylor, Paul, "IBM Agrees Printing Deal with Ricoh," *Financial Times*, January 26, 2007, p. 26.

Tracy, Eleanor Johnson, "Ricoh's Foray into Xerox's Heartland," *Fortune*, May 28, 1984, p. 94.

Wada, Shigeru, and Miwa Naruse, "Ricoh Gears Up for Another Run at Glory," *Nikkei Report*, March 10, 2004.

Robert Bosch GmbH

Postfach 10 60 50
Stuttgart, D-70049
Germany
Telephone: (+49 711) 811-0
Fax: (+49 711) 811-6630
Web site: http://www.bosch.com

Private Company
Founded: 1886
Incorporated: 1917 as Robert Bosch AG
Employees: 281,717
Sales: EUR 45.13 billion ($66.34 billion) (2008)
NAICS: 332212 Hand and Edge Tool Manufacturing; 332213 Saw Blade and Handsaw Manufacturing; 333112 Lawn and Garden Tractor and Home Lawn and Garden Equipment Manufacturing; 333414 Heating Equipment (Except Warm Air Furnaces) Manufacturing; 333415 Air-Conditioning and Warm Air Heating Equipment and Commercial and Industrial Refrigeration Equipment Manufacturing; 333991 Power-Driven Handtool Manufacturing; 333993 Packaging Machinery Manufacturing; 334290 Other Communications Equipment Manufacturing; 334413 Semiconductor and Related Device Manufacturing; 334511 Search, Detection, Navigation, Guidance, Aeronautical, and Nautical System and Instrument Manufacturing; 335211 Electric Housewares and Household Fan Manufacturing; 335212 Household Vacuum Cleaner Manufacturing; 335221 Household Cooking Appliance Manufacturing; 335222 Household Refrigerator and Home Freezer Manufacturing; 335224 Household Laundry Equipment Manufac-

turing; 335228 Other Major Household Appliance Manufacturing; 335312 Motor and Generator Manufacturing; 335314 Relay and Industrial Control Manufacturing; 336312 Gasoline Engine and Engine Parts Manufacturing; 336322 Other Motor Vehicle Electrical and Electronic Equipment Manufacturing; 336340 Motor Vehicle Brake System Manufacturing; 336399 All Other Motor Vehicle Parts Manufacturing; 551112 Offices of Other Holding Companies

■ ■ ■

One of Germany's largest corporations, Robert Bosch GmbH is best known as the world's leading automotive supplier. The company derives nearly 60 percent of its revenues from automotive technology, where its specialties include fuel injection systems, vehicle safety equipment such as antilock brakes, electrical machinery such as starters and alternators, and communications gear such as automotive navigation systems. The company has also developed into a world leader in a variety of other fields, including automation technology, packaging machinery, solar energy equipment, power tools, heating and hot-water systems, security systems, and household appliances, the latter via a joint venture with Siemens AG. Bosch has operations in more than 60 countries around the world through its subsidiaries and associated companies, while its sales and service network encompasses no fewer than 150 nations.

Only about one-quarter of the company's revenues originate in Germany, with Europe as a whole account-

COMPANY PERSPECTIVES

As a leading technology and services company, we take advantage of our global opportunities for a strong and meaningful development. Our ambition is to enhance the quality of life with solutions that are both innovative and beneficial. We focus on our core competencies in automotive and industrial technologies as well as in products and services for professional and private use.

We strive for sustained economic success and a leading market position in all that we do. Entrepreneurial freedom and financial independence allow our actions to be guided by a long-term perspective. In the spirit of our founder, we particularly demonstrate social and environmental responsibility—wherever we do business.

Our customers choose us for our innovative strength and efficiency, for our reliability and quality of work. Our organizational structures, processes, and leadership tools are clear and effective, and support the requirements of our various businesses. We act according to common principles. We are strongly determined to jointly achieve the goals we have agreed upon.

As associates worldwide, we feel a special bond in our values that we live by day by day. The diversity of our cultures is a source of additional strength. We experience our task as challenging, we are dedicated to our work, and we are proud to be part of Bosch.

ing for about two-thirds. The remaining one-third is split about equally between the Americas and the Asia-Pacific region plus other regions. Since 1964, 92 percent of the company's share capital has been owned by a foundation called the Robert Bosch Stiftung GmbH (the Bosch family owns most of the remaining 8 percent), while most of the voting rights are held by an industrial trust, the Robert Bosch Industrietreuhand KG, which runs the company on behalf of the foundation. The foundation uses its share of company profits to fund various philanthropic programs.

EARLY HISTORY

Robert Bosch, a highly motivated, self-educated electrical engineer, founded what was originally known as the Werkstätte für Feinmechanik und Elektrotechnik (Workshop for Precision Mechanics and Electrical Engineering) in Stuttgart, Germany, in 1886. The initial focus was on building and installing various electrical devices such as telephone installations. A key early turning point came in 1887 when the firm, at the request of a customer, built a magneto ignition device for a stationary internal-combustion engine. This device was used to generate the electric spark needed to cause the air-fuel mixture in such engines to explode.

Magneto ignition systems proved to be the young company's first commercial success. They also led the company directly into the automotive industry. In 1897 Robert Bosch's company achieved the milestone of adapting its magneto ignition device for a vehicle engine. The company quickly entrenched itself as the world leader in automotive ignition systems and grew rapidly as automobile sales began booming. During the first decade of the 20th century, the workforce expanded from fewer than 40 to more than 2,000. Sales offices were set up throughout Europe and beyond as well, including the United States, which by 1914 accounted for 70 percent of the company's sales.

Robert Bosch, who was more talented as an administrator than as an engineer, gained a reputation for innovation in industrial relations. He instituted an eight-hour workday (which was uncommon at the time) and paid employees at a higher standard rate in the belief that superior working conditions would encourage better employee performance. Bosch readily acknowledged ability and creativity in his employees, assigning the most talented among them to positions in the most promising areas. He also recognized the need for a diverse, high-quality product line as the most direct means to growth.

An early diversification occurred in 1913 when the company introduced an automotive lighting system consisting of a generator, battery, and headlights. The outbreak of World War I the following year resulted in a U.S. trade embargo against Germany. Bosch was prevented from doing any more business in the United States and was forced to rely solely on European sales under a wartime economy. In 1917 Robert Bosch incorporated his firm as a public limited company (or stock corporation) under the name Robert Bosch AG.

DIVERSIFYING BEYOND THE AUTOMOTIVE SECTOR

When the war ended in 1918 the German economy was in a state of complete disarray. The nation fell into a serious economic depression during the 1920s, which caused many businesses to fail. Bosch, however, managed to remain in business, partly as a result of its

---

KEY DATES

1886: In Stuttgart, Germany, Robert Bosch founds a company initially called the Werkstätte für Feinmechanik und Elektrotechnik (Workshop for Precision Mechanics and Electrical Engineering).

1887: Company constructs a magneto ignition device for a stationary internal-combustion engine.

1897: Involvement in automotive industry begins with development of an ignition device for a vehicle engine.

1917: Founder incorporates his company as Robert Bosch AG.

1927: Production of diesel-engine fuel injection system begins.

1928: First Bosch power tools are introduced.

1932: Company expands in to thermotechnology via the purchase of a maker of natural-gas-fired water heaters.

1933: First Bosch refrigerator marks the firm's household appliance debut.

1937: Firm is changed into a private limited company called Robert Bosch GmbH.

1942: Robert Bosch dies and is succeeded by Hans Walz.

1951: Company introduces a mechanical fuel injection system for vehicles powered by gasoline engines.

1962: Walz retires as chief executive and is replaced by Hans Merkle.

1964: Ownership of the firm is largely transferred to a foundation called the Robert Bosch Stiftung GmbH.

1967: Bosch and Siemens AG combine their household appliance operations into a joint venture.

1978: Company launches the world's first series-produced antilock braking system.

1984: Marcus Bierich is named CEO.

1993: Bierich is succeeded by Hermann Scholl.

1996: Bosch acquires Allied Signal Inc.'s hydraulic- and antilock-braking business for light vehicles.

2001: Automation technology operations are enlarged via the purchase of Mannesmann Rexroth AG.

2003: Bosch becomes Europe's heating technology leader by acquiring Buderus AG; Franz Fehrenbach becomes the sixth chief executive in Bosch history.

2008: Company ventures into the alternative energy sector via the acquisition of Ersol Solar Energy AG.

---

diversification and good management. Bosch reduced its reliance on the automotive industry both through the development of new products and via acquisitions. The company produced its first power tools in 1928 and entered the household appliance sector in 1933 when the first Bosch refrigerator debuted. Bosch's entrance into thermotechnology occurred in 1932 with the acquisition of Junkers & Co. GmbH, a producer of natural-gas-fired water heaters based in Dessau, Germany. The following year, Bosch purchased the Berlin-based household and car radio manufacturer Ideal-Werke für drahtlose Telephonie AG, which was later known as Blaupunkt GmbH. An important development on the automotive side during this period was the production, in 1927, of a fuel injection system for truck diesel engines. This technology was later adapted for gasoline engines in passengers cars and became one of Bosch's key product lines.

As the economic situation stabilized, public discontent in Germany began to rise. In 1933 the Nazis under Adolf Hitler seized power and initiated a new economic order characterized by industrial growth and rearmament. The company enjoyed several periods of strong growth during the 1930s, primarily because of strong demand from German industry and the military for electronic and mechanical products. The company's growth necessitated a new form of organization, and in 1937 it was changed into a private limited company under the name Robert Bosch GmbH.

German military adventurism and territorial expansion precipitated World War II, which again eliminated foreign markets for companies such as Bosch. Robert Bosch died in 1942, during the height of Germany's success in the war, and was succeeded by Hans Walz. As outlined in Robert Bosch's will, ownership of the company eventually in 1964 was to be transferred in large part to the Robert Bosch Stiftung GmbH, with the balance remaining in the hands of the Bosch family.

POSTWAR REBUILDING

For Germany, the remainder of the war was characterized by severe shortages of all kinds and extensive war damage. At the end of the war Germany was partitioned into occupied Soviet and Western powers' zones (later East and West Germany). The more heavily industrialized western zone, where Bosch was located, was in ruins. Bosch reorganized and its factories were rebuilt. The U.S. market, however, remained closed to Bosch after the war, again forcing the company to strengthen its connections with smaller European manufacturers. New efforts were made to develop more advanced products, and in 1951 Bosch introduced a mechanical fuel injection system for vehicle engines running on gasoline.

West Germany was "readmitted" to the world market system in the early 1950s, during which time Bosch became a major supplier of automotive products to foreign manufacturers. During the 1950s the consumer automobile market experienced strong growth as a result of an expanding world economy and new levels of prosperity.

Also during the 1950s, Bosch commenced another diversification effort. For example, the range of Bosch household appliances gradually widened, extending to small kitchen appliances in 1952, washing machines in 1958, and dishwashers in 1964. Later, in 1967, Bosch and Siemens AG merged their household appliance operations into a joint venture originally called Bosch-Siemens Hausgeräte GmbH but later renamed BSH Bosch und Siemens Hausgeräte GmbH. In the meantime, in 1952, Bosch began manufacturing hydraulic equipment and do-it-yourself power tools. The move into hydraulics and also pneumatics formed the underpinnings of Bosch's later business in automation technology. In the early 1960s a series of acquisitions moved the company into the field of packaging machinery.

Walz retired in 1962 after 20 years as the company's chief executive. He was replaced by Hans Merkle, a self-taught and apprenticed engineer and businessman, known for his ability to predict changing market conditions. Merkle recognized pollution control and fuel economy as key factors in future automobile sales. Under Merkle's leadership, Bosch began to devote more of its resources to the development of electronic products and later produced a new fuel injection system that promoted a smoother running engine and reduced fuel consumption.

Competitors of Bosch, including Siemens and Bendix, largely ignored the potential of fuel injection systems while Bosch continually perfected new and better versions. When strict new antipollution regulations were enacted in the United States, automobiles equipped with Bosch fuel injectors, such as the Volkswagen Beetle, became extremely popular. Soon afterward, other European manufacturers, including Daimler-Benz and Volvo, decided to integrate the Bosch system into their product line. When the 1973 OPEC oil crisis caused dramatic increases in the price of petroleum, the highly efficient Bosch fuel injection systems became virtually indispensable.

EXPANDING AND DIVERSIFYING FURTHER IN THE SEVENTIES AND EIGHTIES

Throughout the 1970s Bosch expanded its operations overseas, moving into Japan and Malaysia in 1972, Turkey in 1973, and Spain in 1978. By the mid-1970s, Bosch had made strong progress in regaining its prewar market share in the United States. Bosch purchased a plant in Charleston, Virginia, in 1974 to produce fuel injection systems in the United States. The company also acquired a 25 percent share of American Microsystems, a manufacturer of integrated circuitry, and a 9.3 percent stake in Borg-Warner, which was well established in the area of microcircuitry. Bosch planned to apply technologies developed by these two companies to produce even more advanced automotive systems.

The Charleston plant was subsequently expanded three times. Through the late 1970s fuel injection systems, Bosch's primary product, became the most important electronic component to automobile manufacturers. By 1984, nearly half of the cars sold in the U.S. were equipped with fuel injection systems.

Around this same time, Bosch broadened its position in automotive technology by branching into an increasingly important area: safety systems. In 1978 Bosch introduced the world's first series-produced antilock braking system (ABS). This device prevented brakes from locking by means of an electronic gauge wired to the brake pedal. In addition to being an important safety feature, it made a number of other wires and cables redundant, allowing physical space for "cruise control" and other features. By 1985 the Bosch ABS system was standard on many European automobiles and had also been introduced on luxury cars in the United States. Despite competition in this area from Alfred Teves (a subsidiary of ITT) and Honda, Bosch developed additional facilities to build ABS systems in order to meet the anticipated increased demand.

Marcus Bierich, named CEO of Bosch in 1984, continued to push to expand the firm's product lines. Following the success of ABS, Bosch was involved in the development of electronic traction control, which involved sensors to measure wheel speed and adjust the speed as necessary to keep the car under control. Bosch began production of its first traction control system in 1986.

As car features grew more sophisticated, Bosch continued to develop systems to aid the driver. A new device called the digital trip meter calculated the course and direction of a car by measuring heat levels of the terrain and posting a computerized map on the driver's dashboard. In addition to making the driver aware of the most efficient available routes, the meter could also detect traffic jams. The product was introduced in 1989 as the Travelpilot navigation system. A more sophisticated version using CD-ROMs and providing data to the driver via voice and symbols was later introduced in 1995 on Japanese luxury-model vehicles.

Fierce competition and a 1984 metalworkers' strike seriously affected the company's production for several months and weakened its lead over competitors. For virtually the first time, clients were forced to evaluate alternative suppliers.

The 1980s also saw Bosch enter the telecommunications market through the acquisition of or the purchase of stakes in various companies involved in the manufacturing of equipment and the development of systems, including Telefonbau und Normalzeit, a German telecommunications company, and Telenorma, the exclusive supplier of communications systems to Bundespost, the national postal and telecommunications group. In 1989 these various activities were consolidated with the creation of the Bosch Communications Technology business sector. By 1990 Bosch's explosive growth over the previous three decades was evident as revenues reached nearly DEM 32 billion, compared with the DEM 2.2 billion total for 1963. During this same period, the portion of sales generated outside Germany increased from 35 percent to more than 50 percent.

EXPANDING INTERNATIONALLY IN AN INCREASINGLY COMPETITIVE GLOBAL MARKETPLACE

In addition to expansion into the newly merged areas of former East Germany, Bosch continued to expand internationally in the early 1990s. The opened markets of Eastern Europe were one targeted area, as marketing operations were established in Poland, Hungary, and the Czech Republic in 1992; in Bulgaria, Croatia, Latvia, Russia, Slovenia, Ukraine, and Belarus in 1993; and in Romania in 1994. On the manufacturing side, two Czech Republic-based joint ventures were formed in 1992 to produce automotive equipment. In the Asia-Pacific region, Bosch entered into a joint venture to form Korea Automotive Motor Corp. in South Korea in 1993; was involved in another South Korean joint venture the following year, Korea Mechanics and Electronics Corporation; established a sales company in the Philippines in 1995; and entered into no less than six joint ventures in China also in 1995. Finally, in the United States in 1992, Bosch joined Penske Transportation in setting up a joint venture called Diesel Technology Company to develop and produce injector technology for diesel engines used by heavy-duty commercial vehicles.

Bosch continued to refine its electronic automotive components in the 1990s, introducing the Vehicle Dynamics Control system in 1994, designed to improve the stability of vehicles in critical situations by detecting all rotational movements of the car around its vertical axis. The company also entered into the increasingly lucrative market for air bags through a joint venture with Morton International called United Airbag Systems. Bosch was contributing its expertise in electronic components by developing triggering devices for side-impact air bags.

Despite continuing its long tradition of innovation, Bosch entered a difficult period in the early 1990s under the combined pressure of depressed markets for automobiles and increased competition. Although known for the high quality of its products, Bosch had also over the years developed a reputation for high prices and inflexibility in its relations with its clients. Automakers were increasingly turning to other less expensive and more cooperative suppliers for parts they used to purchase from Bosch, or manufacturing the parts themselves. The latter occurred in 1991 when General Motors suddenly cut in half what was previously a standing order for fuel injection parts. Also contributing to Bosch's difficulties was its telecommunications business that, although profitable and contributing nearly a quarter of overall sales, was finding it increasingly difficult to compete against the giants of the industry: Siemens, Alcatel, and Northern Telecom.

In response to these challenges, Bosch in late 1991 instituted a cost-cutting program and process improvement initiative, and also cut its workforce by about 8,000. The company continued to struggle, however, as market conditions failed to improve, leading in 1993 to the company's first sales decline since 1967. At the same time, net income fell every year from 1989 to 1993, overall going from DEM 626 million in 1989 to DEM 426 million in 1993. Further moves were taken in 1993 to turn the company around, including the elimination of 13,000 additional jobs and the institution of team-oriented work groups. Leading this latest makeover was Hermann Scholl, who succeeded Bierich as CEO in 1993.

The next two years showed modest improvements for Bosch as sales increased 6.2 percent in 1994 and 4 percent in 1995, while net income increased to DEM 512 million in 1994 and DEM 550 million in 1995. Even if not completely recovered, the company was feeling healthy enough by early 1996 to make a $1.5 billion acquisition of Allied Signal Inc.'s hydraulic- and antilock-braking business for light vehicles. The purchase enabled Bosch for the first time to provide its customers with complete brake systems.

ALTERING GROUP STRUCTURE VIA SERIES OF DEALS

Over the next few years, a series of transactions significantly altered the array of operations within the Bosch group. In a further push into the rapidly growing Asia-Pacific region, Bosch in 1999 acquired majority control of Zexel Corporation, a Japanese automotive components company that ranked as that nation's largest manufacturer of fuel injection pumps for diesel engines. Zexel, which had a longstanding relationship with Bosch, was renamed Bosch Automotive Systems Corporation in 2000. At the beginning of 1999 Bosch transferred its entire passenger car and commercial vehicle steering systems operations into a joint venture with ZF Friedrichshafen AG called ZF Lenksysteme GmbH. Similarly, Bosch placed another of its smaller automotive operations, its lighting technology unit, into a joint venture with Magneti Marelli Holding S.p.A. ZF Lenksysteme, however, proved to be lasting, whereas Bosch in 2003 sold its holding in the joint venture with Magneti Marelli and thus exited from the automotive lighting sector.

Also reshaping the group was the divestment of the bulk of the company's communications operating unit in piecemeal fashion. Unable to compete with much larger competitors, Bosch's businesses in this area had suffered losses in the late 1990s. In 2000 Bosch sold its public-networks division to Marconi plc, its private-networks division to Kohlberg Kravis Roberts & Co., and its mobile-telephone business to Siemens. Bosch retained its security systems unit, which was placed within a newly enlarged Consumer Goods and Business Technology division, which also included the power tools, household appliances, and thermotechnology operations.

Seeking to lessen the predominance of automotive technology within its business portfolio, Bosch engineered two other key deals in the first years of the 21st century. In April 2001 the company acquired Mannesmann Rexroth AG from Mannesmann AG. Bosch then merged its existing automation technology division with the acquired unit to form Bosch Rexroth AG, which became the core of the Industrial Technology division alongside the packaging technology operations. Bosch Rexroth boasted a product range encompassing industrial hydraulics, pneumatics, assembly and linear technology, electric motors and controls, and mobile hydraulics. By 2002 the Industrial Technology division's sales had ballooned to EUR 4 billion ($4.2 billion), more than 11 percent of overall sales. In 2003 Bosch significantly enlarged its position in heating technology, and in fact gained the top spot in Europe in that sector, by acquiring Buderus AG for about EUR 1.7 billion ($2 billion). This deal brought together Bosch's strength in wall-mounted conventional boilers with Buderus's specialty, cast-iron floor-standing boilers.

ANOTHER ROUND OF ACQUISITIONS UNDER NEW LEADERSHIP

In mid-2003 Franz Fehrenbach became just the sixth chief executive in Bosch's long history, succeeding Scholl. While being much more open and accessible to the press than his predecessors, Fehrenbach continued the company's traditional emphasis on investing in research and development and pushed for additional diversification of the group's activities and strived to further reduce its dependence on the European market. Ironically, even as the company continued to bulk up its non-automotive activities, Bosch in 2005 overtook the struggling Delphi Corporation to become the largest supplier of car parts in the world.

Among the acquisitions that Fehrenbach engineered was the 2006 takeover of Telex Communications, Inc., for $420 million. Based in Minneapolis, Telex produced audio and electroacoustic systems for installation in such facilities as airports, railway stations, and stadiums. Telex became part of Bosch's security systems unit. In 2007 Bosch bolstered its packaging technology business through the purchase of Pharmatec GmbH, a specialist in pharmaceutical packaging lines, based in Dresden, Germany. Bosch that same year gained a foothold in the U.S. heat pump market by acquiring FHP Manufacturing Company of Fort Lauderdale, Florida. Fehrenbach made his boldest move yet in 2008 by venturing into the alternative energy sector via the acquisition of Ersol Solar Energy AG for EUR 1.12 billion ($1.67 billion). Based in Erfurt, Germany, with 2007 sales totaling EUR

160 million ($240 million), Ersol developed and manufactured solar cells used in electricity-generation modules. It operated four plants in Germany and California and was involved in a joint venture in China. Its name was subsequently changed to Bosch Solar Energy AG. Bosch delved deeper into the solar field in 2009 when it gained majority control of Aleo Solar AG, a German producer of solar modules with manufacturing facilities in Prenzlau, Germany, and near Barcelona, Spain.

Bosch's need to diversify was never more evident than in 2008, when the global economic downturn particularly battered the automotive industry, sending the company's revenues down 2.6 percent to EUR 45.13 billion ($66.34 billion) and its pretax profits down 75 percent to EUR 942 million ($1.38 billion). In response, Fehrenbach launched a concerted effort to cut costs while vowing not to slash research and development investments. The company permanently laid off a number of workers at its plants outside Germany while also temporarily idling 17,000 German employees. Fehrenbach also made the difficult decision of selling the loss-making car radio subsidiary Blaupunkt, which had been part of the group for more than 70 years. As Bosch continued its efforts to lessen its dependence on the troubled automotive industry, the company's strong balance sheet, a product in part of its traditionally conservative financial policies, boded well for its ability to survive the economic crisis intact. Bosch had entered 2009 with nearly EUR 8 billion ($11.1 billion) in cash and debt load that totaled only a little more than EUR 2 billion ($2.8 billion).

Updated, David E. Salamie

PRINCIPAL SUBSIDIARIES

Bosch Engineering GmbH; Bosch Rexroth AG; Bosch Sensortec GmbH; Bosch Sicherheitssysteme GmbH; Bosch Solar Energy AG; Bosch Thermotechnik GmbH; BSH Bosch und Siemens Hausgeräte GmbH (50%); Robert Bosch Car Multimedia GmbH; Robert Bosch Healthcare GmbH; ZF Lenksysteme GmbH (50%); Robert Bosch AG (Austria); Robert Bosch S.A. (Belgium); Robert Bosch odbytová s.r.o. (Czech Republic); Robert Bosch A/S (Denmark); Robert Bosch Oy (Finland); Robert Bosch (France) SAS; Robert Bosch S.A. (Greece); Robert Bosch Kft. (Hungary); Robert Bosch S.p.A. (Italy); Robert Bosch AS (Norway); Robert Bosch Sp. z o.o. (Poland); Vulcano Termodomésticos, SA (Portugal); Robert Bosch OOO (Russia); Robert Bosch spol. s.r.o. (Slovakia); Robert Bosch d.o.o. (Slovakia); Robert Bosch España S.A. (Spain); Robert Bosch AB (Sweden); Robert Bosch AG (Switzerland); Bosch

Sanayi ve Ticaret A.Ş. (Turkey); Robert Bosch OOO (Ukraine); Robert Bosch Ltd. (UK); Bosch Security Systems Ltd. (UK); Robert Bosch Argentina Industrial S.A. (Argentina); Robert Bosch (Australia) Pty. Ltd.; Robert Bosch Ltda. (Brazil); Robert Bosch Inc. (Canada); Bosch (China) Investment Ltd.; Bosch Limited (India); Bosch Corporation (Japan); Korea Automotive Motor Corporation; Robert Bosch Korea Mechanics and Electronics Ltd.; Robert Bosch Sdn. Bhd. (Malaysia); Robert Bosch S.A. de C.V. (Mexico); Robert Bosch (SEA) Pte. Ltd. (Singapore); Robert Bosch (Pty) Ltd. (South Africa); Robert Bosch Limited (Thailand); Robert Bosch Corporation (USA).

PRINCIPAL DIVISIONS

Automotive Technology; Industrial Technology; Consumer Goods and Building Technology.

PRINCIPAL COMPETITORS

Delphi Corporation; Eaton Corporation; DENSO Corporation; Johnson Controls, Inc.; Visteon Corporation; Magna International Inc.; Magneti Marelli Holding S.p.A.; Federal-Mogul Corporation.

FURTHER READING

Abrahams, Paul, Alexandra Harney, and Haig Simonian, "Bosch Assumes Control of Zexel," *Financial Times*, February 24, 1999, p. 35.

Banham, Russ, *Bosch in the United States: The First 100 Years*, Farmington Hills, MI: Robert Bosch Corporation, 2006, 93 p.

Becker, Rolf, "Robert Bosch: His Life and Work," *Journal of Bosch History*, suppl. 1, Stuttgart, Germany: Robert Bosch GmbH, 2004, 55 p.

Blau, John R., "As Bosch Gets Tougher, Will Customers Get Going?" *Electronic Business*, January 8, 1990, pp. 81–85.

"Braking," *Economist*, April 25, 1992, pp. 75–76.

Brooke, Lindsay, "No Strong Recovery," *Automotive Industries*, December 1991, pp. 36–38.

Burt, Tim, and Peter Marsh, "Bosch Enjoys the Benefits of a Varied Portfolio," *Financial Times*, July 6, 2000, p. 30.

Fuhrman, Peter, "Euro-Thrash," *Forbes*, July 22, 1991, pp. 66–67.

Herdt, Hans Konradin, and Dieter Blum, *Bosch, 1886–1986: Porträt eines Unternehmens*, Stuttgart, Germany: Deutsche Verlags-Anstalt, 1986, 174 p.

Heuss, Theodor, *Robert Bosch: His Life and Achievements*, translated by Susan Gillespie and Jennifer Kapczynski, New York: Henry Holt, 1994, 612 p.

Higgins, Amy, and Sherri Koucky, "Bosch and Rexroth Merge," *Machine Design*, June 7, 2001, p. 28.

"Knowing Who's Bosch," *Economist*, February 27, 1993, p. 61.

Kobe, Gerry, "Robert Bosch Corp. Automotive Group," *Automotive Industries*, February 1990, pp. 69–70.

Lessing, Hans-Erhard, *Robert Bosch*, Reinbek bei Hamburg, Germany: Rowohlt Taschenbuch Verlag, 2007, 158 p.

Marsh, Peter, "Bosch Chief Ends the Reign of the Quiet Men," *Financial Times*, January 9, 2004, p. 10.

Milne, Richard, "Bosch Takes the Long View," *Financial Times*, September 25, 2006, p. 11.

Naj, Amal Kumar, "Allied Signal Selling Piece of Auto Unit," *Wall Street Journal*, March 1, 1996, pp. A3, A4.

Plumb, Stephen E., "All Quiet on the Eastern Front? Not at Bosch," *Ward's Auto World*, July 1993, p. 104.

Reier, Sharon, "Components: Robert Bosch," *Financial World*, April 14, 1992, p. 56.

Schaefer, Daniel, "Space to Breathe amid the Crisis," *Financial Times*, March 2, 2009, p. 12.

Schroter, Harm G., "The German Question, the Unification of Europe, and the European Market Strategies of Germany's Chemical and Electrical Industries, 1900–1992," *Business History Review*, Autumn 1993, p. 369.

Siekman, Philip, "Bosch Wants to Build More of Your Car," *Fortune*, January 11, 1999, pp. 144B+.

"Success by Stealth," *Economist*, July 9, 1988, p. 69.

Way, Arthur, "A Mark of Respect for German Supplier," *Financial Times*, July 12, 1994, p. FTS3.

Whitbread, Colin, "Bosch Begins to Feel Pain of Slowdown," *Automotive News*, May 7, 2001, p. H24.

Royal Dutch Shell plc

Carel Van Bylandtlaan 30
The Hague, 2596 HR
Netherlands
Telephone: (31 70) 377 9111
Fax: (31 70) 377 4848
Web site: http://www.shell.com

Public Company
Incorporated: 1890 as Koninklijke Nederlandsche Maatschappig Tot Exploitatie van Petroleumbronnen in Nederlandschindie
Employees: 102,000
Sales: $458.36 billion (2008)
Stock Exchanges: London New York
Ticker Symbols: RDSA (London); RDS.A (New York)
NAICS: 324110 Petroleum Refineries; 324191 Petroleum Lubricating Oil and Grease Manufacturing; 324199 All Other Petroleum and Coal Products Manufacturing; 424720 Petroleum and Petroleum Products Merchant Wholesalers; 211111 Crude Petroleum and Natural Gas Extraction; 211112 Natural Gas Liquid Extraction; 213111 Drilling Oil and Gas Wells; 213112 Support Activities for Oil and Gas Field Exploration

■ ■ ■

Royal Dutch Shell plc is the world's second-largest oil and gas company, trailing industry leader Exxon Mobil Corporation. The company is involved in oil and gas exploration, production, refining, transportation, and marketing. The company boasts worldwide proved reserves of 10.9 billion barrels of oil equivalent, producing 3.2 million barrels of oil and gas per day. Royal Dutch Shell operates 45,000 Shell service stations, which constitutes the world's largest retail fuel network, serving 10 million customers each day. The company operates more than 25 refineries and chemical plants and maintains a presence in more than 100 countries. Royal Dutch Shell also develops renewable energy sources, transports natural gas, and produces chemicals and refined products.

LATE 19TH CENTURY: TWO OIL COMPANIES GET THEIR START

The Royal Dutch/Shell Group was formed in 1907 when a merging of the interests of Royal Dutch and Shell Transport took place, in which each company retained its separate identity. Royal Dutch was established in The Hague in 1890 after receiving a concession to drill for oil in Sumatra, in the Dutch East Indies. It had the support of King William III, hence the name Royal Dutch. The promoters of this venture had found oil in 1885, but needed funds to exploit their discovery. In the early years the firm was directed by J. B. August Kessler under whom, in 1892, it exported its first oil. In 1896 a 30-year-old bookkeeper, Henri Deterding, joined the company and in 1901 he became its chief executive. The predominant use for petroleum in the late 19th century was as paraffin or kerosene, which was used for heating and lighting. However, Sumatra's oil was particularly rich in gasoline, the product used by the internal combustion engine, and it was therefore well placed to take advantage of the growth in demand for oil which the automobile was to bring.

Deterding was one of the great entrepreneurial figures of the 20th century. He combined remarkable strategic vision with acute financial awareness born of his early training as a bookkeeper. His ambition was to build a company to rival the world's largest oil enterprise, John D. Rockefeller's Standard Oil Company of the United States. Deterding preferred to achieve this ambition through alliances and agreements rather than competition. In 1903, as part of this strategy, he formed a marketing company, the Asiatic Petroleum Company, owned jointly by Royal Dutch, Shell, and the Paris branch of the Rothschild family, the last of which had substantial Russian production interests. A crucial intermediary figure in making this alliance was Fred Lane, who had been one of the original directors of Shell Transport, but who had become closely identified with the Paris Rothschilds and, by the early 1900s, with Deterding.

The Shell Transport and Trading Company's origins lay in the activities of a London merchant, Marcus Samuel, who began his career in the 1830s selling boxes made from shells brought from the East. The business gradually expanded the number of commodities in which it traded. When Marcus Samuel Sr. died in 1870, his son Marcus continued to be involved in Far Eastern trade. In 1878 he established with his brother Samuel a partnership known as Marcus Samuel & Co. in London, and Samuel Samuel & Co. in Japan, which became a leading shipping and trading enterprise in the Far East. During the 1880s the Samuels, through intermediary Fred Lane, began selling the Russian oil of the Rothschilds to the Far East, breaking the monopoly previously held by Standard Oil. In 1892 the Suez Canal Company was persuaded to allow oil tankers to pass through the canal, which lowered the cost of Russian oil in the Far East, and allowed the Samuel partnership to rapidly increase its market share. Later in the 1890s fears that Russian supplies might be reduced led the Samuels to search for a secure source of oil nearer their Far Eastern markets, and in 1898 a major oilfield was discovered in Dutch Borneo, a year after the launch of Shell Transport and Trading.

MERGER OF ROYAL DUTCH AND SHELL: EARLY 20TH CENTURY

Shell Transport grew rapidly. By 1900 the company possessed oilfields and a refinery in Borneo and a fleet of oil tankers. However, Marcus Samuel was above all a merchant, lacking organizational skills and ignorant of the technicalities of the oil business. After 1900 he lost interest in the details of the business, and in 1902 became lord mayor of London. By the early 1900s Shell Transport had made a series of costly mistakes, including a disastrous involvement with Texas oil. When Texaco hit a large oil gusher in 1901, Samuel agreed to buy the oil. The flow of oil was not continuous and stopped altogether in the summer of 1902. The formation of the Asiatic Petroleum Company left Deterding in control of Shell's sales in the East. By 1906 Shell's financial situation was so bad that Deterding was able to impose his own terms for a merger of the two concerns, with the Dutch holding 60 percent of what came to be known as the group.

The combined group expanded rapidly under Deterding's leadership. The total assets of Royal Dutch and Shell Transport grew by more than two and a half times between 1907 and 1914. Major production interests were acquired in Russia in 1910 and Venezuela in 1913. The group also moved into Standard Oil's homeland. In 1912 the Roxana Petroleum Company was formed to operate in Oklahoma, and in 1913 California Oilfields, Ltd., was acquired. By 1915 the group was producing nearly six million barrels of crude oil a year in the United States.

World War I brought mixed fortunes for the group. Its properties in Romania were destroyed, and those in Russia were confiscated after the Russian Revolution in 1917. Shell's exploitation of the Venezuelan oilfields was delayed until late in the war due to difficulties in importing equipment. Shell's cosmopolitan structure was also held in suspicion by some civil servants and ministers within the U.K. government, who feared that it was pro-German and engaged in supplying oil to the enemy through subsidiaries in neutral countries. Various proposals were made by civil servants and several businessmen to merge the group with the Anglo-Persian Oil Company, Burmah Oil, or other U.K. interests in

```
┌─────────────────────────────────────┐
│                                      │
│            KEY DATES                 │
│               ■                      │
│  ─────────────────────────────────  │
```

1878: The Samuel brothers establish trading companies in London and Japan, which soon begin selling Russian oil to the Far East.

1890: Royal Dutch Petroleum Company is established in The Hague.

1892: Royal Dutch exports its first oil.

1897: The Samuel brothers establish The Shell Transport and Trading Company and begin searching for oil in the Far East.

1898: Shell discovers oil in Dutch Borneo.

1907: Royal Dutch and Shell merge, with Royal Dutch holding 60 percent of the group.

1910: Royal Dutch/Shell obtains production properties in Russia.

1912: Company begins operating in the United States.

1913: Company acquires production properties in Venezuela.

1922: Shell Union Oil is formed in the United States, consolidating Shell's U.S. interests with Union Oil Company of Delaware.

1929: Shell Chemical Company is formed.

1959: Joint Shell and Esso venture discovers one of the world's largest natural gas fields, in the Netherlands.

1971: Shell finds oil in the North Sea.

1974: Shell Coal International is formed.

1995: Shell initiates restructuring.

1998: Shell unveils five-year plan for reducing costs and improving bottom line.

2002: Company acquires Pennzoil-Quaker State.

2004: Company reveals it overestimated the size of its proved oil and gas reserves by 24 percent.

2005: British and Dutch entities merge, creating Royal Dutch Shell plc.

2009: Peter Voser is promoted to chief executive officer of Royal Dutch Shell.

order to make it truly British. However, these wartime proposals were unsuccessful, and regardless of its mixed ownership, the group played an important role in the Allied war effort. In 1919 an agreement was initialed by Deterding and a representative of the U.K. government that provided for an internal rearrangement of the group to allow U.K. interests majority control, but the agreement was never implemented, chiefly because of the delays caused by incoherence and confusion in the of-

ficial U.K. oil policy of the period. Royal Dutch retained the larger interest in the group.

UPS AND DOWNS: TWENTIES THROUGH FORTIES

The 1920s were a decade of growth. In 1919 Shell purchased the large Mexican oilfields controlled by the U.K. oil company Mexican Eagle, led by Lord Cowdray. In 1920 a marketing company was set up in the United Kingdom, Shell-Mex, which represented the Shell and Mexican Eagle interests. Venezuelan oil production expanded very rapidly, much of it controlled by Shell. In 1922 the Shell Union Oil Corporation was formed in the United States to consolidate Shell interests there with those of the Union Oil Company of Delaware, and the U.S. business increased rapidly. By 1929 its U.S. activities had spread to the Atlantic Coast. This decade also saw the first steps in product diversification. In 1929 a new company, N.V. Mekog, was established in the Netherlands to produce nitrogenous fertilizer from coke-oven gases. This was the group's first venture into chemicals. In the same year the Shell Chemical Company was formed in the United States to produce nitrogenous fertilizer from natural gas.

The Depression years brought problems. From the late 1920s there was a chronic problem of overcapacity in the oil industry. Deterding's response was to form a worldwide cartel, and in 1928 he organized a meeting in a Scottish castle at Achnacarry with the heads of Standard Oil of New Jersey and the Anglo-Persian Oil Company to achieve this goal. The Achnacarry agreement became an infamous example of cartel exploitation in the oil industry, but the large oil companies were actually unable to control all sources of supply in the world. Achnacarry and subsequent cartel agreements did not last long. The group's oil interests in Mexico were nationalized in 1938, an early warning of later problems in developing countries. Meanwhile Deterding's leadership of the group became suspect. Some managers felt that his leadership style had become very erratic. After his marriage to a German woman in 1936, he resigned as general managing director of Royal Dutch and went to live in Germany.

During World War II and the invasion of the Netherlands, the head offices of the Dutch companies moved to Curaçao in the Dutch West Indies. Once again, Shell played a major role in the Allied war effort. The refineries in the United States produced large quantities of high octane aviation fuel, while the Shell Chemical Company manufactured butadiene for synthetic rubber. All of the group's tankers were placed under U.K. government control, and 87 Shell ships were lost in enemy action.

EXPANSION AND DIVERSIFICATION: FIFTIES THROUGH EIGHTIES

The 1950s and 1960s were golden years of growth for oil companies, as demand for petroleum products expanded. The Shell group and the rest of the "seven sisters" of leading international oil companies—British Petroleum (BP), Exxon, Texaco, Chevron, Mobil, and Gulf—retained a strong hold over petroleum production and marketing. The group supplied nearly one-seventh of the world's oil products in these decades. After Deterding's departure, the group was run on a committee basis with no single dominant personality. A stable and respectable image was projected, symbolized by the advertising slogan "You can be sure of Shell." Few Americans, for example, realized that the Shell Oil Company of the United States was not a wholly U.S. oil company.

During the 1950s and 1960s Shell diversified into natural gas and offshore oil production and further expanded its chemicals operations. In 1959 a joint Shell/Esso venture found natural gas in the Netherlands in Groningen. This turned out to be one of the world's largest natural gas fields, and by the early 1970s it provided about half of the natural gas consumed in Europe. Shell was active in the exploration of North Sea oil, and it found oil in the northern North Sea in 1971. In the same year a major offshore gas discovery was made on the Australian northwest shelf. By the end of the 1960s the Shell group was also manufacturing several hundred chemicals in locations all over the world.

In the late 1960s the group, as well as BP, attracted widespread criticism because, despite the application of United Nations sanctions, the illegal regime in Rhodesia continued to obtain oil products which were supplied from South Africa. South Africa, of course, made no secret of its support for the illegal regime and did not apply United Nations sanctions. In the early 1970s it was revealed that the U.K. government had become a party to this discreditable behavior. The Shell group later became the subject of public criticism because of its substantial investment in South Africa.

1973: A CRITICAL YEAR

The structure of the world oil industry was radically altered during the 1973 oil crisis when the Organization of Petroleum Exporting Countries (OPEC) unilaterally raised crude oil prices. The oil companies found themselves forced to allocate scarce oil supplies during the crisis, causing severe problems with several governments. In the United Kingdom, Shell and BP had

a major clash with the Conservative government led by Edward Heath. Heath demanded that the United Kingdom receive preferential supplies of oil, which the oil companies were trying to ration between countries. Heath attempted to use the British government's 51 percent shareholding in BP to force that company to supply Britain first, but BP declined. The Shell group, like all the Western oil companies, had much of its crude oil production in developing countries nationalized. The search for oil in non-OPEC areas was stepped up successfully and in the late 1980s it remained responsible for producing 5 percent of the world's oil and 7 percent of its gas.

In response to the problems of the oil industry, the Shell group diversified its business in the 1970s, acquiring coal and metal interests. In 1974 Shell Coal International was established. In 1970 the company acquired the Billiton mining and metals business in the United Kingdom. Chemical manufacture was particularly expanded. This expansion proved unfortunate, since world economic growth after 1973 was much slower than anticipated, with the major recession of the late 1970s and early 1980s causing acute problems. As a result, severe overcapacity developed in the chemical industry. The U.K. company Shell Chemicals experienced problems and was obliged to restructure and reduce capacity. Similar overcapacity occurred in the oil refinery business throughout most of the 1980s. In the 1980s the group rationalized its exposure to chemicals and other noncore businesses. However, the group remained the world's largest producer of petrochemicals and a leading supplier of agrochemicals, in particular insecticides, herbicides, and animal health products and substantial profits were made in the chemicals business.

As the Shell group entered the 1990s, it was an enormous business enterprise and, alongside Unilever, one of the few examples of a successful venture owned and managed by more than one country. The group was the most highly decentralized enterprise in the world oil industry, with its nationally based, integrated operating companies given almost complete autonomy.

RESTRUCTURING IN THE NINETIES

The early 1990s saw higher costs associated with finding and developing oilfields and with refining operations, which had to operate under increasingly stringent environmental controls. At the same time, an abundance of oil on the world market kept prices depressed. While many oil companies scaled back their spending, Shell continued to pump money into both upstream and downstream growth. With Shell aggressively jumping ahead and its competitors drawing back, in 1991 the company overtook Exxon to become the world's largest public oil company.

In 1993, Cornelius Herkstroter became Shell's chairman. He was not in office long before he began to make some radical changes. Despite the fact that Shell was highly profitable, earning a record net profit of $6.3 billion in 1994, it was not performing as well as it should have been. The company's return on average capital employed, which is the key success indicator in the oil industry, had fallen well behind the returns of its competitors. Herkstroter became convinced that Shell's long-standing, extremely decentralized management structure was no longer giving it an advantage. Although the structure had once provided a strategic agility in independent units, it had come to be an unwieldy, inefficient, and expensive bureaucracy.

Herkstroter called in a team of consultants to evaluate the business. The result was a major restructuring that eliminated almost one-third of the jobs at Shell's headquarters. The reorganization also removed some of the power from Shell's dozens of country-specific operating companies, which were accustomed to functioning more as independent companies than as affiliates, and made them accountable to global committees appointed to oversee major areas of operation.

PUBLIC RELATIONS PROBLEMS

Meanwhile, Shell was coming under heavy fire from environmental groups. In 1995, the company tangled with Germany's Greenpeace group when it attempted to sink its Brent Spar, an offshore oil platform that was no longer used, in the Atlantic Ocean. Enraged environmentalists protested the sinking of the large storage buoy, with its attendant masses of waste that would pollute the waters. As Shell made preparations to tow the Brent Spar from its original location in the North Sea to its planned dumping ground, Greenpeace activists occupied the platform in protest. On land, the group organized a massive boycott of Shell products. Facing a public relations nightmare, Shell ultimately relented, agreeing to dismantle the platform on land, a project that cost exponentially more than sinking it would have. Just a few months after the Brent Spar incident, Shell was again the target of the environmentalists' ire. In November 1995, the Nigerian government executed Ken Saro-Wiwa, an author and activist who had protested the environment-exploiting activities of the oil multinationals in Nigeria, in particular, Shell. Saro-Wiwa's supporters subsequently accused Shell of colluding with the Nigerian government. The year 1998 was a difficult one for Shell. The company posted its largest ever annual loss: $2.47 billion. On top of that,

consolidation in the industry (the BP-Amoco merger, and the planned merger of Exxon and Mobil) bumped the company from its post as the largest oil company in the world.

Near the middle of 1998, Herkstroter retired from his position as Royal Dutch/Shell's chairman, and was replaced by Mark Moody-Stuart. Under the new leadership, Shell's move toward a more centralized, global structure was immediately accelerated. In December 1998, Moody-Stuart unveiled a five-year plan aimed at streamlining operations, lowering costs, and improving returns. As part of the restructuring, the company announced plans to sell off almost half of its chemicals business, focusing primarily on those chemicals that were most tightly linked to oil refining. It also began consolidating functions wherever possible, more closely integrating its globally far-flung businesses and eliminating some 6,000 jobs in 1999. Along with the divestitures and job cuts came a scaling back in investment; the company reduced overall capital spending by 41 percent in the first three quarters of 1999.

One of the by-products of the company's more tightly integrated, global structure was its ability to make more consistent and better environmental decisions. In 1997, Shell made a public commitment to contributing to sustainable development. In 1998, it released its first *Shell Report*, an annual publication that documented the actions the company had taken to meet its environmental and social responsibilities.

Shell's efforts to reduce costs proved very effective. While the company had originally expected a $2.5 billion annual savings from its 1998 restructuring, in late 1999 it raised that estimate to $4 billion. The company also continued to cut thousands of jobs and to sell off noncore businesses.

In 2001 and the first part of 2002, although oil and gas prices were volatile, Shell reported solid earnings. In March 2002, the company made a significant acquisition, obtaining Pennzoil-Quaker State Company for $1.8 billion. Pennzoil-Quaker State, the world's largest independent lubricants company, gave Shell a global leadership position in lubricants.

AN EMBARRASSING ADMISSION
IN 2004

The years immediately following the purchase of Pennzoil-Quaker State represented a period of fantastic growth for the oil industry. The price of oil leaped upward and the major oil companies reaped record profits, but at Royal Dutch/Shell the mood was far from celebratory. The organization was in crisis mode. In January 2004, Royal Dutch/Shell revealed it had overestimated the size of its proved oil and gas reserves by 20 percent (in subsequent months the figure rose to 24 percent), mistakenly booking assets that should have been recorded in two other, more speculative categories. "It's not uncommon for reserves to be cut," an industry analyst said in the January 26, 2004 issue of *Business Week*, "but from what we know, nothing of this magnitude has ever happened before." Aside from tainting one of the primary indicators of Royal Dutch/Shell's health—Royal Dutch Petroleum's stock plunged 10 percent in value when the error was reported—the revelation put the group's operations in the spotlight. Royal Dutch/Shell, upon close examination, was struggling.

The group's primary problem was that it was finding far less oil and gas than it was consuming. Royal Dutch/Shell was replacing 60 percent of the reserves it produced, far less than the industry average, and it possessed the shortest reserve life, 10.2 years, of any major oil company. Further, the cost of finding and developing reserves was substantially higher than the figures averaged by its two main rivals, BP p.l.c. and Exxon Mobil. Industry observers blamed the group's passive stance during the 1990s, when it cut back on exploration efforts and stood on the sidelines while its rivals acquired other oil and gas concerns. The criticism drew attention to the unusual attribute of the group, a peculiarity that had disturbed analysts and investors for years. The complex, Dutch/English ownership structure of Royal Dutch/Shell contributed to some of its problems, entrammeling decision making, blurring accountability, and impeding mergers because the dual share structure made it difficult to finance acquisitions with stock. An investigation by a law firm hired by Royal Dutch/Shell after the misstatement of reserves also found the ownership structure had created a schism within the group, revealing "a dysfunctional company where the top two executives, chairman Philip Watts and head of exploration and production Walter van de Vijyer, were on increasingly hostile terms," as reported in the May 3, 2004, issue of *Business Week*.

UNIFICATION IN 2005

Within months of the announcement that Royal Dutch/Shell had far less proved reserves than it had stated, Watts, van de Vijyer, and another senior executive were stripped from their duties. Watts was replaced by Jeroen van der Veer, president of Royal Dutch Petroleum, who took on the formidable challenge of righting a floundering organization. He immediately tended to the group's dwindling reserves, increasing exploration spending to $1.8 billion per year, reportedly the largest exploration budget in the industry. Van der Veer's most impressive

accomplishment occurred in 2005, when he eliminated the group's complex ownership structure and created a single entity, Royal Dutch Shell plc, a company based in The Hague but incorporated in Great Britain. The year also saw the company hire Jorma Ollila, the chief executive officer of Finnish cellular telephone giant Nokia Corp., as Royal Dutch Shell's non-executive chairman, effective June 2006.

Royal Dutch Shell's most pressing concern, boosting reserves, was not a problem that could be resolved immediately. "It can take years before exploration efforts turn into profits," *Business Week* noted in a July 18, 2005, article. "Shell estimates that its production will grow slightly until 2009, but as big projects kick in, output could grow from between 3.8 million and four million barrels per day in 2009 to between 4.5 million and five million by 2014." The task of ensuring that the company met its expectations was handed to van der Veer's successor, Peter Voser, who was promoted to chief executive officer in July 2009. Voser joined Royal Dutch Shell in 1982 and served in a variety of finance and business capacities until being named the group's chief financial officer in 2004. A Swiss citizen, Voser became the first leader not of Dutch or British ancestry in the history of Royal Dutch Shell, marking the beginning of a new era for the oil giant and one of the most critical periods it had faced in decades.

Geoffrey Jones
Updated, Shawna Brynildssen; Jeffrey L. Covell

PRINCIPAL SUBSIDIARIES

International Energy Bank Ltd. (Barbados); Shell Holdings (Bermuda) Ltd.; Solen Insurance Ltd. (Bermuda); Shell Treasury Hong Kong Ltd. (Bermuda); Shell Finance Luxembourg SARL; Shell Treasury Luxembourg SARL; Shell Treasury Centre East (PTE) Ltd. (Singapore); Shell Finance Switzerland AG; Solen Versicherungen AG (Switzerland); Shell Finance (Netherlands) B.V.; Shell International B.V.; Shell International Finance B.V.; Shell Overseas Investments B.V.; Shell Petroleum N.V.; Shell Treasury Netherlands B.V.; Shell Energy Investments Ltd. (UK); Shell International Investments Ltd. (UK); Shell Overseas Holdings Ltd. (UK); Shell Treasury Centre Ltd. (UK); Shell Treasury Dollar Company Ltd. (UK); Shell Treasury Euro Company Ltd. (UK); Shell Treasury UK Ltd.; The Shell Transport and Trading Company Ltd. (UK); Shell Petroleum Inc. (USA).

PRINCIPAL COMPETITORS

BP p.l.c.; Exxon Mobil Corporation; TOTAL S.A.

FURTHER READING

Beaton, K., *Enterprise in Oil: A History of "Shell" in the United States*, New York: Brill, 1957.

Carey, John, "Shell: The Case of the Missing Oil," *Business Week,* January 26, 2004, p. 45.

The First Hundred Years, The Hague: Royal Dutch Petroleum Company, 1990.

Gerretson, F. C., *History of the Royal Dutch*, 4 vols., Leiden: E.J. Brill, 1953–57.

Guyon, Janet, "Now If Only Shell Could Find Some Oil," *Fortune,* May 17, 2004, p. 38.

———, "Why Is the World's Most Profitable Company Turning Itself Inside Out?" *Fortune*, August 4, 1997, p. 120.

Henriques, Robert, *Marcus Samuel, First Viscount Bearsted and Founder of the "Shell" Transport and Trading Company, 1853–1927*, London: Barrie and Rockliff, 1960.

A History of the Royal Dutch/Shell Group of Companies, London: Shell, 1988.

Howarth, Stephen, *A Century in Oil: The "Shell" Transport and Trading Company 1897–1997*, London: Weidenfeld & Nicolson Ltd., 1998.

Jones, Geoffrey, "Frederick Lane" and "Marcus Samuel," in *Dictionary of Business Biography: A Biographical Dictionary of Business Leaders Active in Britain in the Period, 1860–1980*, 5 vols., edited by David Jeremy, London: Butterworth, 1984–86.

———, *The State and the Emergence of the British Oil Industry*, London: Macmillan, 1981.

Jordan, A. J., and Grant Jordan, *Shell, Greenpeace and the Brent Spar*, New York: Palmgrave, 2001.

Reed, Stanley, "Can Shell Put Out This Oil Fire?" *Business Week,* May 3, 2004, p. 32.

———, "He's Brave Enough to Shake Up Shell," *Business Week,* July 18, 2005, p. 53.

———, "Shell's Drama Isn't Over," *Business Week,* February 23, 2004, p. 28.

Sampson, A., *The Seven Sisters: The Great Oil Companies and the World They Made*, London: Hodder and Stoughton, 1975.

Schwartz, Nelson D., "A Shell of Itself," *Fortune,* March 6, 2006, p. 26.

"Shell on the Rocks," *Economist,* June 24, 1996, p. 57.

Samsung Electronics Co., Ltd.

---

250 2-ga, Taepyong-ro
Jung-gu
Seoul, 100-742
South Korea
Telephone: (+82 2) 727-7114
Fax: (+82 2) 727-7892
Web site: http://www.samsung.com

Public Subsidiary of Samsung Group
Founded: 1969
Employees: 84,462
Sales: $121.3 billion (2008)
Stock Exchanges: Korea
Ticker Symbol: 005930
NAICS: 335221 Household Cooking Appliance Manufacturing; 334310 Audio and Video Equipment Manufacturing; 334411 Electron Tube Manufacturing; 334413 Semiconductor and Related Device Manufacturing; 335222 Household Refrigerator and Home and Farm Freezer Manufacturing; 335224 Household Laundry Equipment Manufacturing

∎ ∎ ∎

The chief member of South Korea's giant Samsung Group, Samsung Electronics Co., Ltd., ranks as one of the world's largest electronics producers. Samsung Electronics operates two main divisions: Device Solutions (Semiconductor Business and LCD Business) and Digital Media and Communications (Telecommunica- tions Network Business and Digital Media Business). The company manufactures a wide variety of products, including televisions, video, and audio equipment; computers and related products; telephones, cellular phones, and fax machines; home appliances; semiconductors; and network-related equipment.

EARLY HISTORY OF SAMSUNG GROUP

Samsung Electronics was created in 1969 as a division of the mammoth Samsung Group, a Korean *chaebol* (a highly diversified industrial conglomerate). It was established as a means of getting Samsung into the burgeoning television and consumer electronics industry. The division's first product was a small and simple black-and-white television that it began selling in the early 1970s. From that product, Samsung Electronics gradually developed a diverse line of consumer electron- ics that it first sold domestically, and later began exporting. The company also began branching out into color televisions, and later into a variety of consumer electronics and appliances. By the 1980s Samsung was manufacturing, shipping, and selling a wide range of ap- pliances and electronic products throughout the world.

Although the rapid growth of Samsung Electronics during the 1970s and early 1980s was impressive, it did not surprise observers who were familiar with Samsung Group, which was founded in 1938 by Lee Byung-chull, a celebrated Korean entrepreneur. Lee started a small trading company with a $2,000 nest egg and 40 employees. He called it Samsung, which means "three stars" in Korean. The company enjoyed moderate

COMPANY PERSPECTIVES

For more than 70 years, Samsung has been at the forefront of innovation. Our discoveries, inventions and breakthrough products have helped shape the history of the digital revolution.

growth before the Communist invasion in 1950 forced Lee to abandon his operations in Seoul. Looting soldiers and politicians on both sides of the conflict diminished his inventories to almost nothing. With savings contributed by one of his managers, Lee started over in 1951 and within one year had grown his company's assets 20-fold.

Lee established a sugar refinery in 1953, a move that was criticized at the time because sugar could be obtained easily through U.S. aid. For Lee, however, the act was important because it was the first manufacturing facility built in South Korea after the Korean War. From sugar, wool, and other commodity businesses, Lee moved into heavier manufacturing. The company prospered under Lee's philosophy of making Samsung the leader in each industry he entered.

From manufacturing, Samsung moved into various service businesses during the 1960s, including insurance, broadcasting, securities, and even a department store. Lee experienced several major setbacks during the period. For example, in the late 1960s, shortly before Samsung Electronics was created, Lee was charged with an illegal sale of about $50,000 worth of goods. The charges turned out to be the fabrication of a disgruntled government official to whom Lee had refused to pay a bribe. Nevertheless, one of Lee's sons was arrested and Lee was forced to donate a fertilizer plant to the government to win his release. Despite that and other problems, Samsung continued to flourish. By the end of the 1960s the conglomerate was generating more than $100 million in annual revenues.

Shortly after his son was arrested, Lee decided to break into the mass communication industry by launching a radio and television station, as well as by manufacturing televisions and electronic components through the Samsung Electronics division. The industry was dominated at the time by several U.S. and European manufacturers, and some Japanese companies were beginning to enter the industry. Nevertheless, Lee was confident that Samsung could stake its claim on the local market and eventually become a global contender.

During the early 1970s, the company invested heavily, borrowed and coaxed technology from foreign competitors, and drew on its business and political connections to begin carving out a niche in the consumer electronics industry. In addition to televisions, Samsung branched out into other consumer electronics products and appliances.

GOVERNMENT INVOLVEMENT DURING THE SEVENTIES

Samsung Electronics' gains during the 1970s were achieved with the assistance of the national government. During the 1950s and 1960s, Samsung and other Korean conglomerates struggled as the Rhee Syngman administration increasingly resorted to favoritism and corruption to maintain power. Student revolts in the 1960s finally forced Rhee into exile. The ruling party that emerged from the ensuing political fray was headed by military leader Park Chung-hee. His regime during the 1960s and 1970s was characterized by increasing centralization of power, both political and industrial, as his government was obsessed with economic growth and development. Although Park was widely criticized for his authoritarian style, his government is credited with laying the foundation for South Korea's economic renaissance.

To develop the economy rapidly, Park identified key industries and large, profitable companies within them. The government worked with the companies, providing protection from competition and financial assistance as part of a series of five-year national economic growth plans. By concentrating power in the hands of a few giant companies (the *chaebols*), Park reasoned, roadblocks would be minimized and efficiencies would result. Between 1960 and 1980, South Korea's annual exports surged from $33 million to more than $17 billion.

Samsung Electronics and the entire Samsung *chaebol* were beneficiaries of Rhee's policies. Several countries, including Japan, were barred from selling consumer electronics in South Korea, eliminating significant competition for Samsung. Furthermore, although Samsung Electronics was free to invest in overseas companies, foreign investors were forbidden to buy into Samsung. As a result, Samsung was able to quickly develop a thriving television and electronics division that controlled niches of the domestic market and even had an edge in some export arenas.

During the 1970s and 1980s, Samsung Group created a number of electronics-related divisions, several of which were later grouped into a single entity known as Samsung Electronics Co., Ltd. Samsung Electron

KEY DATES

1969: Samsung Electronics is established.

1978: Samsung Group enters the semiconductor market by forming Samsung Semiconductor and Telecommunications Co.

1994: Sales increase after the 4-megabit dynamic random-access memory chip is developed.

1995: Exports reach $10 billion.

1997: Company battles the Asian economic crisis.

1999: Firm undergoes a major restructuring, and profits reach $2.4 billion.

2000: Sales reach $26 billion and net profits climb to $4.7 billion.

2001: Company secures the top spot on *Business Week*'s list of the world's top 100 information technology companies.

2003: Samsung reveals plans to invest approximately $7.3 billion in China.

2004: U.S. Justice Department accuses the company of participating in a price-fixing cartel.

2005: Samsung plans to invest $33 billion to more than triple its memory chip sales by 2012; company pleads guilty to criminal charges of price-fixing and agrees to pay $300 million in fines.

2006: Samsung Semiconductor President Park Young-hwan pleads guilty to price-fixing and agrees to pay a $250,000 fine and serve 10 months in prison.

2007: South Korean government begins a probe into alleged bribery and accounting fraud at Samsung.

2009: Samsung reorganizes into two main divisions: Device Solutions and Digital Media and Communications.

Devices Co. manufactured picture tubes, display monitors, and related parts. Samsung Electro-Mechanics Co. made VHF and UHF tuners, condensers, speakers, and other gear. Samsung Corning Co. produced television glass bulbs, computer displays, and other components. Finally, Samsung Semiconductor & Telecommunications Co. represented Samsung in the high-tech microchip industry. Rapid growth in those industries, combined with savvy management, allowed the combined Samsung Electronics Co., Ltd., to become Samsung Group's chief subsidiary by the end of the 1980s.

ENTERING THE SEMICONDUCTOR MARKET: LATE SEVENTIES TO EARLY EIGHTIES

Samsung's entry into the semiconductor business was pivotal for the company. Lee had determined in the mid-1970s that high-tech electronics was the growth industry of the future, and that Samsung was to be a major player. To that end, he formed Samsung Semiconductor and Telecommunications Co. in 1978. To make up for a lack of technological expertise in South Korea, the South Korean government effectively required foreign telecommunications equipment manufacturers who wanted access to the Korean market to hand over advanced semiconductor technology in return. This proved crucial for Samsung, which obtained proprietary technology from Micron of the United States and Sharp of Japan in 1983. Using its newly acquired knowledge, Samsung became the first Korean manufacturer of low-cost, relatively low-tech, 64-kilobit dynamic random-access memory (DRAM) chips.

Shortly after introducing its 64-kilobit chip, Samsung teamed up with some Korean competitors in a research project that was coordinated by the government Electronics and Telecommunications Research Institute. The result was a 1-megabit DRAM (and later a 4-megabit DRAM) chip. During the middle and late 1980s, Samsung parlayed knowledge from the venture to become a significant supplier of low-cost, commodity-like DRAM chips to computer and electronics manufacturers throughout the world. Meanwhile, its other electronics operations continued to grow, both domestically and abroad. Samsung opened a television assembly plant in Portugal in 1982 to supply the European market with 300,000 units annually. In 1984 it built a $25 million plant in New York that could manufacture 1 million televisions and 400,000 microwave ovens per year. Then, in 1987 it opened another $25 million facility in England with capacity for 400,000 color televisions, 300,000 videocassette recorders, and 300,000 microwave ovens.

Between 1977 and 1987, Samsung Group's annual revenues surged from $1.3 billion to $24 billion (or about 20 percent of South Korea's entire gross domestic product). Much of that growth was attributable to Samsung Electronics. Lee Byung-chull died in 1987 and was succeeded by his son, Lee Kun-hee. Lee Kun-hee recognized the importance of the electronics division and moved quickly to make it the centerpiece of Samsung Group. To that end, he consolidated many of the group's divisions and eliminated some operations. He also introduced various initiatives designed to improve employee motivation and product quality. Lee Kun-hee was credited with stepping up Samsung Electronics' partnering efforts with foreign companies as part of his goal to place Samsung at the forefront of semiconductor technology.

FOCUS ON ELECTRONICS AND
RESEARCH AND DEVELOPMENT

Sales at Samsung Group grew more than 2.5 times between 1987 and 1992. More important, Samsung drew from potential profit gains to more than double research and development investments as part of Lee Kun-hee's aggressive bid to make Samsung a technological leader in the electronics, semiconductor, and communications industries. Besides partnering with U.S. and Japanese electronics companies, Samsung Electronics acquired firms that possessed important technology, including Harris Microwave Semiconductors and Integrated Telecom Technologies. In 1993 Lee Kun-hee sold off 10 of Samsung Group's subsidiaries, downsized the company, and merged other operations to concentrate on three industries: electronics, engineering, and chemicals.

Under the leadership of Chief Executive Officer Kim Kwang-ho, Samsung Electronics took the microchip world by storm when it introduced its 4-megabit DRAM chip in 1994. Sales of that chip helped to push Samsung's sales from $10.77 billion in 1993 to $14.94 billion in 1994. Profits, moreover, spiraled from $173,000 to nearly $1.3 billion. In addition, Samsung had staged a bold grab for domestic market share in 1995 by slashing prices for consumer electronics and home appliances by as much as 16 percent and had wowed industry insiders when it unveiled an advanced liquid crystal display (LCD) screen, used for laptop computers, at a world trade show in Japan.

Samsung Electronics' rapid rise and technical achievements put the company in the spotlight in the semiconductor industry. Its 4-megabit DRAM chip had, in fact, made it the leading global producer of DRAM chips by early 1995. Furthermore, Samsung Electronics was increasing its investment in R&D still further, as evidenced by a $2.5 billion outlay to produce a 64-megabit DRAM chip by 1998. In December 1995, development on the world's first 1-gigabit synchronous DRAM chip was also in the works. Exports for the year increased to more than $10 billion.

RESTRUCTURING UNDER YUN
JONG-YONG: LATE NINETIES

In just one short year, however, the market for the company's largest revenue producer became unstable. In 1996 DRAM prices fell drastically because of oversupply in the industry. Although the company's telecommunications equipment and computer segment showed substantial growth, Samsung's semiconductor-related sales fell by 31.8 percent. In response, the firm implemented a new management structure that focused on increasing efficiency. The initiative included reforming price management to better recognize growth markets, improving communication between company managers, increasing overseas management support, implementing a new marketing strategy, and focusing on growth in telecommunications, microprocessors, and other non-memory products. Yun Jong-yong was named CEO in January 1997 to oversee the new strategy.

As part of the firm's new focus, Samsung continued to pare down its dependency on memory chips. It developed new technologies and quickly made a name for itself in the telecommunications and cellular phone market. In May 1997 the company was named the official Olympic partner for wireless communications equipment for the 1998 Winter Games and the 2000 Sydney games. The firm also established a telephone switching system in Ecuador, entered the Chinese wireless market by teaming up with Shanghai Great Wall Mobile Communications Co., and began selling its cellular phones to AT&T in the United States.

A crisis hit the Asian economy in the fall of 1997, and by early 1998 the Korean won, the nation's currency, was valued at 1,800 won to the dollar, less than half of its value just one year earlier. Samsung was forced to drastically change the way it had operated in the past and it began selling off segments that were not related to its core business. In addition, it cut 26 percent of its domestic workforce and 33 percent of its international workforce, and it slowed production.

While many Asian-based companies faltered, Samsung continued to forge ahead. The company established U.S.-based subsidiary Alpha Processor Inc. to oversee sales and marketing for its 64-bit Alpha processor product line. The firm also secured the top position in the LCD global market by capturing 18 percent of the market. In August 1998 the firm developed a flat-screen television. Despite the trying economic times, Samsung recorded a greater than 8 percent increase in gross sales. In January 1999 *Forbes Global* recognized the firm as the world's premier consumer goods and services company.

Under the leadership of Yun, Samsung had successfully diversified its product line from dependence on memory chips despite the trying economic times. By the end of 1999, the chips accounted for 20 percent of sales; in 1995 they had secured 90 percent of profits and half of total sales. The company divested more than 57 of its businesses and decreased long-term debt by $10.8 billion. In addition, all of its product groups were able to secure profits during the year. Samsung also held a strong share of the cellular phone market and was one of the six top manufacturers of wireless phones and the leading producer of computer monitors. Sales for the year increased 24 percent to $22 billion while profits reached $2.4 billion. The firm's stock also rose dramatically, increasing by 233 percent to $227 a share.

ALLIANCES FOR THE NEW MILLENNIUM

Yun's successful leadership of the company during its restructuring and the Asian crisis was noted throughout the industry. In January 2000 *Fortune* magazine named Yun Asia's Businessman of the Year. The firm, which had adopted the phrase "Leading the Digital Convergence Revolution" for the new millennium, continued to develop new technologies and seek growth in high-margin markets. The company partnered with Yahoo! to use its network to sell its products online. It also teamed up with Microsoft to design and develop a line of cellular phones. At the same time, Samsung's exports of cellular phones increased in Kazakhstan, Mexico, Central Asia, and Central and South America. By this time, it was operating as the fourth-largest producer of such phones.

Samsung's positive results continued in 2000 as the firm secured $26 billion in sales and $4.7 billion in net profits. Memory chips accounted for 38 percent of sales, information and telecommunications equipment secured 22 percent, digital media took 27 percent, and home appliances accounted for 8 percent. The company looked to strategic partnerships, research and development, and growth, to maintain its positive financial record. In March 2001 it teamed up with Dell Computer Corporation in a $16 billion technology and research and development agreement. In addition, the company was selected by China to provide code division multiple access (CDMA) cellular phone networks in four of its major cities. That year, the company also secured the top spot on *BusinessWeek*'s list of the world's top 100 information technology companies.

Progress continued in 2002 when the company agreed to invest $200 million for the expansion of its semiconductor plant in the Philippines. Midway through the year, Samsung agreed to sell the controller division of its Mechatronics business to Rockwell Automation Inc. In late 2002 Samsung announced plans to construct a $10 million factory in Indonesia, in order to capitalize on the emerging information technology market in that country.

Two other developments in 2002 included Dell Computer's decision to begin selling Samsung laptop computers under its brand name, and the introduction of a 54-inch digital LCD television monitor, which was the largest in the world at the time. In addition, Samsung devoted $400 million toward advertising efforts in the United States.

FOCUSING ON CHINA: 2003

In early 2003 Samsung revealed plans to invest approximately $7.3 billion in China, which was becoming a critical aspect of its global strategy. Accomplishments that year included the rollout of the first high-definition (HD) digital video disc (DVD) combo unit. Progress continued in 2004, when Samsung's cellular phone sales surpassed 20 million units in the United States alone. The company also secured leading mobile phone sales positions in other countries, including Russia. New product rollouts included the world's very first 46-inch LCD television. By mid-2004 Samsung held a leading position in the flash memory chip category, with 21 percent market share.

In September 2004 Samsung revealed plans to buy back $1.75 billion worth of its stock. A setback occurred three months later, when the U.S. Department of Justice included the company on a list of memory chip manufacturers accused of participating in a price-fixing cartel. The situation prompted Samsung to earmark $100 million for legal costs.

In early 2005 Samsung parted with $558.8 million to acquire 111.5 million additional shares of Samsung Card, its struggling credit-card operation. By this time, the company's leading market-share position in the memory chip sector had grown to 32 percent. In what was described as its largest single investment since 1974, when the company entered the semiconductor business, in September 2005 Samsung revealed plans to invest $33 billion to more than triple its memory chip sales by 2012. Specifically, the company planned to construct eight new chip fabrication lines, as well as a research and development line.

It also was in 2005 that Samsung and Sony revealed plans to invest approximately $2 billion for the construction of a new LCD television panel factory, capable of producing the largest television glass panels in the world. A major setback occurred that October, when Samsung pleaded guilty to criminal charges of price-fixing. In what was considered the second-largest antitrust penalty in corporate history, Samsung agreed to pay fines totaling $300 million.

Samsung continued to grow at a strong pace in 2006. In September the company announced plans to partner with Siltronic AG and establish a $1 billion,

300-millimeter-wafer fabrication operation in Singapore named Siltronic Samsung Wafer Pte. Ltd. Around the same time, plans were made to build a $100 million home-appliance plant in Kaluga, Russia, as well as a $100 million television and monitor production plant in Chennai (formerly Madras), India.

ETHICS CHALLENGES IN THE 21ST CENTURY

In December 2006 Samsung Semiconductor President Park Young-hwan agreed to pay a $250,000 fine and serve 10 months in prison after pleading guilty to price-fixing. An important leadership change unfolded early the following year, when Lee Jae-yong, the son of Samsung Group Chairman Lee Kun-hee, was selected to become the company's executive director. New product development continued, as Samsung made plans to introduce its Duo HD player, which supported either the HD DVD or Blu-ray format.

Despite its many accomplishments, Samsung continued to struggle in other areas. For example, the South Korean government began a probe into alleged bribery and accounting fraud at the company in 2007. Early the following year, special prosecutors raided the homes of several Samsung executives, as well as the office of Chairman Lee Kun-hee, who was charged with breach of duty and tax evasion. In April, he stepped down as co-CEO. In addition, Vice Chairman Lee Hak-soo also tendered his resignation. Yun Jong-yong was chosen to serve as co-CEO, along with two other executives. In May, however, he announced his retirement, at which time he was succeeded by Vice Chairman Lee Yoon-woo.

PREPARING FOR THE FUTURE

Following these setbacks, Samsung continued to make progress. In mid-2008 the company formed a joint venture named Samsung Mobile Display with Samsung SDI Co. to develop displays for handsets and small televisions. In September the company offered to acquire SanDisk in a $5.85 billion cash deal. Financial concerns, however, led Samsung to withdraw its offer the following month. In one highlight of 2008, the company secured the leading spot in the U.S. cellular phone market.

A major development unfolded in 2009, at which time Samsung reorganized into two main divisions: Device Solutions and Digital Media and Communications. Also that year, the company formed a light-emitting diodes joint venture with Samsung Electro-Mechanics Co., and established a new office in

Amman, Jordan, furthering expansion in the Middle East. Another leadership change took place when Hong Wan-hoon was named president and CEO of Samsung Semiconductor Inc. Approaching the 21st century's second decade, Samsung employed a workforce that spanned 62 countries. The company continued to rank as the largest computer memory chip maker worldwide.

Dave Mote
Updated, Christina M. Stansell; Paul R. Greenland

PRINCIPAL SUBSIDIARIES

Beijing Samsung Telecom R&D Center (China); DNS Korea Co. Ltd. (63.12%); Hangzhou Samsung Eastcom Network Technology Co. Ltd. (China; 70%); Kdns America Inc. (USA); LLC Samsung Electronics Russia; P.T. Samsung Electronics (Indonesia; 99.99%); P.T. Samsung Telecommunications (Indonesia; 99%); Samsung (China) Investment Co. Ltd.; Samsung Asia Pte. Ltd. (Singapore; 70%); Samsung Austin Semiconductor L.P. (USA); Samsung Card Co. Ltd. (46.85%); Samsung Corning Co. Ltd. (45.29%); Samsung Electronica da Amazonia Ltda. (Brazil); Samsung Electronica Latino America Colombia; Samsung Electronica Portuguesa S.A. (Portugal); Samsung Electronics (UK) Ltd.; Samsung Electronics America, Inc. (USA); Samsung Electronics Argentina S.A.; Samsung Electronics Australia Pty Ltd.; Samsung Electronics Austria Gmbh; Samsung Electronics Beijing Service Co. Ltd. (China); Samsung Electronics Benelux B.V. (Netherlands); Samsung Electronics Canada Inc.; Samsung Electronics Chile Ltda. (99.99%); Samsung Electronics China R&D Center; Samsung Electronics Display (M) Sdn. Bhd. (Malaysia); Samsung Electronics Europe Logistics B.V. (Netherlands); Samsung Electronics France S.A.; Samsung Electronics Gmbh (Germany); Samsung Electronics Hainan Fiberoptics Co. Ltd. (China); Samsung Electronics Holding GmbH (Germany); Samsung Electronics Hong Kong Co. Ltd.; Samsung Electronics Huizhou Co. Ltd. (China; 99.56%); Samsung Electronics Hungarian RT Co. Ltd. (Hungary); Samsung Electronics Iberia S.A. (Spain); Samsung Electronics Italia S.p.A. (Italy); Samsung Electronics Latino America Miami Inc. (USA); Samsung Electronics Latino America Panama (Zone Libre) S.A.; Samsung Electronics (Malaysia) Sdn. Bhd.; Samsung Electronics Manufacturing UK Ltd.; Samsung Electronics (Mexico) S.A. de C.V.; Samsung Electronics Nordic Aktiebolag (Sweden); Samsung Electronics Overseas B.V. (Netherlands); Samsung Electronics (Philippines) Corp.; Samsung Electronics (Philippines) Manufacturing Corp.; Samsung Electronics Poland Sp. z.o.o.; Samsung Electronics Service Co. Ltd. (83.33%); Samsung Electronics Slovakia S.R.O.; Samsung Electronics South Africa (Pty) Ltd.; Samsung Electronics Suzhou Semiconductor Co. Ltd. (China); Samsung Electronics Suzhou Computer Co. Ltd. (China); Samsung Electronics Suzhou LCD Co. Ltd. (China); Samsung Electronics Taiwan Co. Ltd. (China; 99.99%); Samsung Electronics Ukraine (99.99%); Samsung Gulf Electronics Co. Ltd. (United Arab Emirates); Samsung (India) Electronics Ltd.; Samsung (India) Software Operations Pvt. Ltd.; Samsung Information Systems America Inc. (USA); Samsung International Inc. (USA); Samsung Japan Co. Ltd. (50.96%); Samsung Kwangju Electronics Co. Ltd. (94.25%); Samsung (Malaysia) Electronics Sdn Bhd; Samsung Mexicana S.A. de C.V. (Mexico); Samsung Receivables Corp. (USA); Samsung Russia Service Center Ltd.; Samsung Semiconductor China R&D Ltd.; Samsung Semiconductor Europe Gmbh (Germany); Samsung Semiconductor Europe Limited (UK); Samsung Semiconductor Inc. (USA); Samsung Semiconductor International Inc. (Mexico); Samsung Semiconductor (Mexico) S.A. de C.V.; Samsung Telecommunications America L.P. (USA); Samsung Telecommunications Benelux (Netherlands); Samsung Telecommunications (India); Samsung Vina Electronics Co. Ltd. (Vietnam; 80%); Samsung Yokohama Research Institute; Samsung-Crosna Joint Stock Co. (Russia; 67%); Shandong-Samsung Telecommunications Co. Ltd. (China; 98%); Shanghai Samsung Semiconductor Co. Ltd. (China); Shenzhen Samsung Kejian Mobile Technology Co. Ltd. (China; 60%); Souzhou Samsung Electronics Co. Ltd. (China; 88.28%); STECO Ltd. (51%); Thai-Samsung Electronics Co. Ltd. (Thailand; 91.83%); Tianjin Samsung Electronics Co. Ltd. (China; 91.07%); Tianjin Samsung Electronics Display Co. Ltd. (China; 79.95%); Tianjin Samsung Telecom Technology Co. Ltd. (China; 79.94%); Tianjin Tongguang Samsung Electronics Co. Ltd. (China; 96.02%).

PRINCIPAL DIVISIONS

Device Solutions (Semiconductor Business, LCD Business); Digital Media and Communications (Telecommunications Network Business, Digital Media Business).

PRINCIPAL COMPETITORS

Hynix Semiconductor, Inc.; Panasonic Corp.; Sony Corporation.

FURTHER READING

"China: Samsung Electronics Plans US$7.3 Billion in China," *IPR Strategic Business Information Database*, January 1, 2003.

Choe Sang-hun, "Prosecutors Raid Office of Samsung Chairman," *New York Times*, January 15, 2008.

"Dell, Samsung Electronics Enter $16 Billion Alliance Agreement," *Business Wire*, March 21, 2001.

Engardio, Pete, and Moon Ihlwan, "How a Korean Electronics Giant Came Out of the Crisis Stronger Than Ever," *BusinessWeek Online*, December 20, 1999.

"*Forbes Global* Selects Samsung Electronics as World's Premier Consumer Goods & Service Company," *Business Wire*, January 11, 1999, p. 1427.

"A Giant with Wings?" *Business Korea*, December 1994, pp. 21–23.

Ihlwan, Moon, "Another Shakeup at Samsung," *BusinessWeek Online*, May 15, 2008.

———, "Samsung Inside? Look Out, Intel. The Korean Giant Wants to Become the No. 1 Chipmaker," *BusinessWeek Online*, October 25, 2004.

Jameson, Sam, "Samsung Isn't Content to Be a Mere Giant," *Los Angeles Times*, July 5, 1990, p. Dl.

"Korea's Samsung Electronics Opens Office in Jordan," *AsiaPulse News*, July 3, 2009.

Kraar, Louis, "The Man Who Shook Up Samsung," *Fortune*, January 24, 2000, p. 28.

"Lee Quits as Samsung Electronics CEO," *AsiaPulse News*, April 28, 2008.

Nakarmi, Laxmi, with Kevin Kelly and Larry Armstrong, "Look Out, World—Samsung Is Coming," *Business Week*, July 10, 1995, pp. 52–53.

Ota, Alan K., "Samsung Expands Overseas in Drive to Transform Itself," *Oregonian*, July 2, 1995, p. F9.

Ramstad, Evan, "Samsung's Image May Face New Bruise: South Korea to Begin Bribery Probe, Adding to Conglomerate's Woes," *Wall Street Journal Europe*, November 28, 2007.

"Samsung and Microsoft Announce Strategic Alliance," *AsiaPulse News*, June 14, 2000.

"Samsung Chairman Lee Kun-hee: A Modern Day Fortune-teller?" *Business Korea*, August 1993, pp. 18–19.

"Samsung Drops $5.85 Billion Bid for SanDisk; Growing Uncertainty in the Flash Memory Maker's Business and Its Deteriorating Finances Were Reasons Samsung Said It Was Pulling Out of the Deal," *InformationWeek*, October 22, 2008.

"Samsung Electronics Records $26 BLN in Sales in 2000," *AsiaPulse News*, January 19, 2001.

"Samsung Electronics Records US$6.54 BLN in Q1 Sales," *AsiaPulse News*, April 23, 2001.

"Samsung Electronics to Expand Overseas Market for Mobile Phones," *AsiaPulse News*, March 23, 2000.

"Samsung Group: Lee Kun-hee's First Five Years," *Business Korea*, December 1992, p. 37.

"Samsung Heir to Be Promoted in Management Reshuffle," *AsiaPulse News*, January 17, 2007.

"Samsung Names W. H. Hong CEO and President of Samsung Semiconductor, Inc," *Business Wire*, March 10, 2009.

"Samsung Plans Blu-Ray-HD DVD Disc Player," *InformationWeek*, April 13, 2007.

"Samsung Ranks World's 4th Largest Mobile Phone Maker," *Korea Herald*, February 10, 2000.

"Samsung: Steering a New Course," *Business Korea*, February 1992, p. 26.

"Samsung to Invest $33 Billion in Chips," *eWeek*, September 29, 2005.

"Samsung to Raise Profit to 10% of Sales or Higher by 2005," *Korea Herald*, December 21, 1999.

"Samsung Undergoes Major Revamp; The Electronics Company Will Consolidate into a Consumer Electronics Division and a Device Component Division," *InformationWeek*, January 16, 2009.

Selwyn, Michael, and Erwin Shrader, "Samsung Takes on the Giant," *Asian Business*, October 1990, pp. 28–34.

Sohn, Jie-Ae, "Samsung Group Embracing Breathtaking Changes," *Business Korea*, August 1993, pp. 15–18.

Steers, Richard M., with Yoo Keun Shin and Gerardo R. Ungson, *The Chaebol*, New York: Harper & Row, 1989.

Tänzer, Andrew, "Samsung of South Korea Marches to Its Own Drummer," *Forbes*, May 16, 1988, pp. 84–89.

Schneider Electric SA

35 rue Joseph Monier
Rueil Malmaison, 92500
France
Telephone: (+33 1) 41 29 70 00
Fax: (+33 1) 41 29 71 00
Web site: http://www.schneider-electric.com

Public Company
Founded: 1836
Incorporated: 1966 as Schneider S.A.
Employees: 114,000
Sales: EUR 18.31 billion ($25.49 billion) (2008)
Stock Exchanges: Euronext Paris
Ticker Symbol: SU
NAICS: 333415 Air-Conditioning and Warm Air Heating Equipment and Commercial and Industrial Refrigeration Equipment Manufacturing; 334220 Radio and Television Broadcasting and Wireless Communications Equipment Manufacturing; 334290 Other Communications Equipment Manufacturing; 334419 Other Electronic Component Manufacturing; 334512 Automatic Environmental Control Manufacturing for Residential, Commercial, and Appliance Use; 334515 Instrument Manufacturing for Measuring and Testing Electricity and Electrical Signals; 335122 Commercial, Industrial, and Institutional Electric Lighting Fixture Manufacturing; 335311 Power, Distribution, and Specialty Transformer Manufacturing; 335313 Switchgear and Switchboard Apparatus Manufacturing; 335312 Motor and Generator Manufacturing; 335314 Relay and Industrial Control Manufacturing;

335931 Current-Carrying Wiring Device Manufacturing; 335932 Noncurrent-Carrying Wiring Device Manufacturing; 335999 All Other Miscellaneous Electrical Equipment and Component Manufacturing

■ ■ ■

Schneider Electric SA holds global leadership positions in a number of electricity-related energy management product and service areas. The company's product lines include circuit breakers, transformers, and other products for low- and medium-voltage electricity applications in industrial, commercial, and residential buildings; switches, sockets, thermostats, door control systems, and security, fire alarm, and intruder-alert systems for the residential market; industrial control and automation devices; building automation and security products; and products for renewable energy applications, such as inverters for solar and wind power installations.

Schneider's operations include more than 200 production facilities and 140 distribution centers located in more than 100 countries around the world. More than half of the company's revenues are generated outside of Europe, with 27 percent originating in North America and 19 percent in the Asia-Pacific region. From its initial interests in industrial machinery and steel in the mid-19th century, Schneider eventually developed into a huge, highly diversified conglomerate. After a dizzying series of complicated restructurings, acquisitions,

COMPANY PERSPECTIVES

Today, we are living in an increasingly booming and fast changing world where energy is key. More than never, the current situation compels each and everyone to achieve more while using less resources. Global specialist in energy management, Schneider Electric brings you solutions for energy efficiency, while making energy safe, reliable and productive, from plant to plug.

and divestments that began in 1980, the company emerged in the early 21st century focused solely on the electrical industry.

EARLY HISTORY

Schneider's predecessor was founded in 1782 to manufacture industrial machinery at Le Creusot, France. The Creusot foundries, mines, and forges were taken over by two Schneider brothers, Adolphe and Eugène, in 1836, at the dawn of the industrial age in France. This event is considered the official beginning of the Schneider enterprise although the brothers did not technically create the company until two years later, when Schneider Frères & Cie was formed as a limited partnership. Also in 1838, Schneider built the first French steam locomotive, and it later expanded into building other large, complex mechanical devices.

By the late 1800s it had become involved in a wide variety of heavy industries, including steel manufacturing. Also around the end of the 19th century, Schneider entered the electricity sector, dedicating a plant at Champagne-sur-Seine to this effort. By 1914 the plant had 1,200 employees and was producing such equipment as transformers, generators, and traction motors.

Schneider gained recognition as a major French company during World War I. It survived nationalization efforts during France's three-year popular-front government (1936–39) and was called upon to help mobilize French forces in the months before World War II. Overrun during the war by German troops, Schneider's factories were either closed or redirected to support the German war effort.

By the time the war ended in 1945, many of Schneider's factories had been bombed or were obsolete. Charles Schneider undertook a recovery effort in which the company was reorganized into a holding company.

In 1949 Schneider's industrial interests were transferred to three operating subsidiaries in civil and electrical engineering, manufacturing, and construction. The following year Charles Schneider was killed in an accident; he was the last member of the founding family to head the company.

EMPAIN-SCHNEIDER ERA: 1963–80

With the benefit of government direction and regulation, Schneider entered the 1960s fully recovered from war damage and well established in its various operations. In 1963, however, another family industrial group called Empain acquired a large financial stake in Schneider. Empain, founded in 1881 by Édouard Empain, was a pioneer in rail transit. The company installed the Paris Metro system in 1900 and later formed a successful rail-construction firm called Electrorail.

While the Empain and Schneider operating companies remained largely separate, the holding company conducted a series of further acquisitions that greatly expanded the subsidiaries' involvement in basic industries. The two operating companies grew increasingly close between 1966 and 1969, when they were merged into a single group called Empain-Schneider.

The new company's assets remained divided between Schneider S.A. (incorporated in France) and Electrorail (incorporated in Belgium), but they shared the same management structure and president, Baron Édouard Empain. By 1971 Empain-Schneider had become one of the most important industrial groups in the world, with interests in virtually every sector of heavy industry and infrastructure.

In 1972 Empain-Schneider took over the civil- and electrical-engineering group Spie Batignolles. With interests in nuclear power, construction, and oil platforms, Spie Batignolles was formed in 1968 by the merger of the Société de Construction des Batignolles (SCB; founded in 1846 by Ernest Gouin) and the Société Parisienne pour l'Industrie Electrique (SPIE; founded in 1902).

Three years later Empain-Schneider acquired control of another vital French company, the industrial electrical products supplier Merlin Gerin. Founded in Grenoble in 1920 by Paul-Louis Merlin and Gaston Gerin, the company was a leader in industrial circuit breakers and switching gear.

A third major industrial group controlled by Empain-Schneider was Creusot-Loire, a heavy-equipment and special-steels manufacturer. It was also a leading builder of nuclear power stations through its subsidiaries Framatome and Novatome and was heavily

KEY DATES

1836: Adolphe and Eugène Schneider take over the foundries, mines, and forges at Le Creusot, France.

1838: The Schneider brothers form Schneider Frères & Cie.

c. 1900: Company first enters the electricity sector.

1963: The Empain group attains a large financial take in Schneider.

1969: Empain and Schneider merge into a single group called Empain-Schneider.

1972: Empain-Schneider takes over the civil- and electrical-engineering group Spie-Batignolles.

1975: Empain-Schneider acquires control of industrial electrical products supplier Merlin Gerin.

1980: After the Empain family divests most of its interest in Empain-Schneider, the company's name is changed to Schneider S.A.

1981: New leader Didier Pineau-Valencienne launches major restructuring of the group.

1988: Schneider acquires industrial-automation company Telemecanique.

1991: Further inroads into the electrical products sector and a North American beachhead are gained via the purchase of the U.S. firm Square D Company.

1997: With the divestment of Spie-Batignolles, Schneider is fully focused on electrical equipment and industrial control and automation products.

1999: Company changes its name to Schneider Electric SA.

2001: Schneider acquires French rival Legrand SA for EUR 6.6 billion, but European regulators veto the deal on antitrust grounds.

2002: Schneider sells Legrand at a substantial loss.

2007: American Power Conversion Corporation is acquired for $6.1 billion.

involved in turnkey projects abroad. By the late 1970s Empain-Schneider had developed a fourth major subsidiary, an energy and communications products group called Jeumont-Schneider. This company consisted of existing Schneider enterprises and several others controlled by the Jeumont-Industrie industrial group.

RESTRUCTURING: 1980–87

In 1980, however, the Empain family divested itself of its interest in Empain-Schneider, forcing the reorganization of the company and reducing Empain's involvement in the group from 45 percent to about 5 percent of turnover. As a result, the company also changed its name back to Schneider S.A. A more serious restructuring took place the following year when a Socialist government under President François Mitterand came to power.

The government sought to nationalize major companies in an effort to better coordinate industry with its national objectives. Under the new program the first sector to be nationalized was banking; the state took control of all banks with more than $220 million in assets. This included Schneider's banking subsidiary, Banque de l'Union Européenne.

Between 1981 and 1987 Schneider undertook a restructuring program whose objective was to transform the company from a complex family financial trust with many diverse interests into a leading international industrial group. As part of this effort, Schneider divested its machine-tool, heavy-equipment, shipbuilding, and steel operations, and later sold its lower-margin rail transport, nuclear-power, and private-telecommunications businesses.

The sectors that remained under the new simplified structure included construction of electric-power plants and power-distribution systems, building and civil-engineering projects, industrial infrastructure, and a wide variety of industrial electronics systems. Schneider's primary operating subsidiaries remained Spie Batignolles, with 55 percent of total revenue; Merlin Gerin, with 31 percent; and Jeumont-Schneider Industries, with 14 percent in 1987. Reflecting Schneider's position in international markets, 41 percent of the company's revenues were generated through foreign projects.

The person who spearheaded the restructuring effort was Didier Pineau-Valencienne, who was appointed vice chairman and CEO late in 1980, then became chairman and CEO the following year. Pineau-Valencienne built his reputation by turning around a small French chemical company, then found further success at the French chemical giant Rhone-Poulenc before being asked to take command of Schneider.

During the difficult restructuring process, Pineau-Valencienne gained a reputation for waging controversial corporate battles, even earning the nickname "Dr. Attila." In 1984 he failed to win government support for his plan to restructure Schneider's troubled capital-goods subsidiary, Creusot-Loire. After declaring the subsidiary bankrupt, Pineau-Valencienne was roundly accused of mismanagement and incompetence.

Undaunted, Pineau-Valencienne continued with his restructuring plan and sold off those parts of the company he considered unrelated to Schneider's core operations. In the process, Schneider accumulated a large cash reserve that Pineau-Valencienne earmarked for strategic acquisitions.

MAJOR ACQUISITIONS AND FURTHER RESTRUCTURING

The first of these was for the industrial-automation company Telemecanique, which Pineau-Valencienne had hoped to merge with Merlin-Gerin. The takeover battle, launched in February 1988, involved many bitter and complicated legal and labor disputes and finally government intervention. By July Schneider had won permission to acquire Telemecanique, but in the process had inspired a national debate on hostile takeovers. At the time of the takeover, Telemecanique had a workforce of 14,500, 32 subsidiaries outside France, and sales of EUR 1.2 billion.

Pineau-Valencienne next turned his attention to the United States. In 1990 Federal Power, a maker of low-voltage distribution equipment and medium-voltage switchgear, was acquired. That same year, Schneider acquired EPE Technologies, a world leader in uninterruptible power supplies (UPS). Schneider subsequently, in 1996, sold most of its interest in EPE in a leveraged buyout after deeming UPS outside its core businesses. Schneider's U.S. spending spree reached a peak in 1991 when it acquired Square D Company, based in Palatine, Illinois, for $2.23 billion in another hostile takeover. Square D (founded in 1902 and with sales of $1.65 billion and operations in 23 countries) was a market leader in electrical distribution, industrial control, and automation products, systems, and services. It became the flagship for Schneider's North American division, which was headed by Charles W. Denny, who had spent more than 30 years at Square D before being placed in charge of Schneider North America as well as gaining a spot on the Schneider executive committee.

The acquisition of Square D led to the further restructuring of Schneider's industrial operations. In 1991 Schneider increased its interest in Merlin Gerin, and also formed an industrial sector called Schneider Industrie that pulled Schneider's major industrial subsidiaries (Square D, Merlin Gerin, Telemecanique, and Jeumont-Schneider Industries) into an umbrella group. The following year, Schneider divested Jeumont-Schneider, leaving Schneider Industrie with purely electrical industry operations. From that point forward it was clear that Pineau-Valencienne intended for Schneider to eventually reduce itself to its electrical holdings alone.

Further moves over the succeeding years bore this out. In 1992 Schneider gained full control of Merlin Gerin through a merger. The next year the operations of Merlin Gerin, Square D, and Telemecanique were brought together under an overall global management structure where, for example, Schneider North America included the operations of all three companies within North America. Then in 1994, Schneider's corporate structure was further rationalized when a new Schneider Electric S.A. subsidiary, based in France, was created and both Merlin Gerin S.A. and Telemecanique S.A. were merged into the new subsidiary and ceased to exist as separate companies. Although Square D Company technically remained a subsidiary, Schneider essentially positioned Square D, Merlin Gerin, and Telemecanique as its major brands within Schneider Electric.

On the heels of this flurry of activity, Pineau-Valencienne made world headlines when he was arrested in Belgium in May 1994 and jailed for 11 days pending trial in a complex criminal-fraud investigation that involved Schneider's takeover of two Belgian subsidiaries that were remnants of the Empain-Schneider era. After Pineau-Valencienne returned to France following his release on bail, an international warrant was issued for his arrest in early 1995, effectively barring him from leaving France for several months until Belgian authorities finally rescinded the arrest warrant. Over the next number of months, the case seemed to make little progress, and Pineau-Valencienne, who remained in charge of the company, and other Schneider officials continued to insist that the case was entirely groundless.

Meanwhile, Pineau-Valencienne was struggling to deal with Schneider's last remaining non-electrical holding, Spie Batignolles. Spie was active in two main areas: electrical contracting and construction. While the former was related to the activities of Schneider Electric, the latter was not. Furthermore, because of difficult conditions in the French real estate market, Spie's construction sector was performing poorly, posting losses of FRF 2.25 billion from 1991 to 1994. Wishing eventually to divest itself of its Spie holding, a 59 percent stake, or at least Spie's construction sector, Pineau-Valencienne decided to first gain full control of the troublesome unit. He did so by engineering a merger between the companies in July 1995, which also had the side benefit of garnering Schneider a large tax credit.

Although the acquisition of Square D had significantly increased Schneider's overseas holdings (more than 62 percent of overall revenue was derived from outside of France by 1995), Schneider had in the process saddled itself with a heavy debt burden. Pineau-Valencienne thus identified debt reduction as a key to

Schneider's future, and by 1995 the company's debt-to-equity ratio had been reduced to 46 percent. Schneider's chairman also wished to reduce the percentage of shareholdings held by other French firms; such cross holdings were typical of public companies in France, but Pineau-Valencienne wanted to create a shareholding structure along Anglo-American lines. He also sought to increase the percentage of international investors in Schneider.

SOLE FOCUS ON ELECTRICAL EQUIPMENT AS SCHNEIDER ELECTRIC

Pineau-Valencienne successfully concluded the transformation of Schneider in February 1997 by engineering the sale of the firm's controlling interest in Spie Batignolles to the U.K. building group Amec in partnership with the employees of Spie. The sale price was FRF 350 million. With this divestment, Schneider was focused solely on electrical equipment and industrial control and automation products. Just a year later, Pineau-Valencienne stepped down from his management posts and was named honorary chairman. Taking over as chairman and CEO was Henri Lachmann, who had previously headed Strafor Facom, a producer of hand tools, furniture, and other products, and had served on Schneider's board of directors since 1996. Much later, in 2005, Pineau-Valencienne stood trial for forgery and fraud in connection with the charges that had led to his arrest and jailing in 1994. Although he and several other defendants were found guilty, the Belgian court refused to sentence them because the case had been so slow in coming to trial.

A further culmination of the company's transformation occurred in 1999 when the firm changed its name to Schneider Electric SA. Its operations were centered on four international brands specializing in electrical equipment: Merlin Gerin, Modicon, Square D, and Telemecanique. Later in 1999, Schneider added another key brand to its stable through the FRF 6 billion ($1.06 billion) acquisition of Lexel, which had previously operated as a joint venture of Finland's Ahlstrom Corporation and Denmark's NKT Group. Lexel specialized in low-voltage electrical installation products and services, including switches and trunking and ducting equipment. Amid more than a dozen deals completed in 2000, the two most significant, the takeovers of the French firm Crouzet Automatismes and the Switzerland-based Positec, bolstered Schneider's positions in control devices, small automation systems, and motion control equipment.

In its boldest move yet, Schneider Electric in July 2001 completed a friendly, EUR 6.6 billion ($6.43 billion) takeover of Legrand SA. By acquiring its chief French rival, Schneider saw an opportunity to become a global giant in low-voltage electrical equipment, including switches and circuit breakers. The deal soon foundered, however. Although company officials claimed that regulatory authorities had indicated that the takeover was likely to be approved with some concessions, the European Commission (EC) in October 2001 vetoed the deal on antitrust grounds. Schneider fought to resurrect the deal, and the EC's decision was later overturned by the European Union's Court of Justice, but the company in December 2002 decided to scrap the merger because regulators sought concessions that company officials viewed as undermining the viability of the combination.

At the end of 2002, Schneider sold Legrand to a financial consortium consisting of Wendel Investissement and Kohlberg Kravis Roberts & Co. for EUR 3.6 billion, booking a loss of at least EUR 1.4 billion in the process. Schneider later sued the EC for damages, seeking EUR 1.7 billion to compensate for the losses it incurred in unwinding the takeover. A European court later ruled in Schneider's favor and ordered the EC to pay damages, but in July 2009 Europe's highest court, the Court of Justice in Luxembourg, overturned the lower-court ruling, apparently bringing Schneider's Legrand saga to an end.

AGGRESSIVE STRATEGY OF ACQUISITION-LED GROWTH

In the wake of the Legrand debacle, Schneider pursued an aggressive growth strategy that ultimately resulted in a doubling of revenues between 2002 and 2008, when sales totaled EUR 18.31 billion ($25.49 billion). The company became even more of a global organization thanks to a string of acquisitions, alliances, and partnerships not only in the existing strongholds of Europe and the United States but also in such emerging markets as South Korea, China, Malaysia, and Russia. By 2008, emerging economies accounted for 32 percent of sales. Schneider also diversified its product range, moving deeply into areas with high-growth potential, such as products and services related to energy efficiency, critical power and cooling applications, and renewable energy. By 2008, energy-efficiency products and services alone accounted for 30 percent of overall revenues.

Among the dozens of acquisitions completed during this period, a handful stood out as particularly significant. In 2003 Schneider spent about EUR 422 million for the Swedish firm TAC, a leading producer of building automation and control systems. It then further bulked up in this same sector via the 2004, $484 million deal for U.S.-based Andover Controls. Also in

2004, the company reentered the uninterruptible power supplies (UPS) business by purchasing the French firm MGE UPS Systems, which ranked number one in Europe and number three in the world in the UPS sector. Among the 2005 deals was the $562 million acquisition of U.S.-based BEI Technologies, a producer of electronic sensors for the defense and automotive industries. In May 2006 the company's board of directors was split into supervisory and management boards, and Lachmann became nonexecutive chairman of the supervisory board, while 20-year company veteran Jean-Pascal Tricoire was named CEO of Schneider Electric and head of the management board.

Under Tricoire's leadership, the acquisition spree continued unabated. In 2007 Schneider snapped up American Power Conversion Corporation (APC) for $6.1 billion in a substantial follow-up to its earlier takeover of MGE UPS. Based in West Kingston, Rhode Island, APC was a major player in the critical power sector, with products ranging from surge protectors and UPS devices designed to protect residential and business equipment from power failures and power surges to air conditioning equipment designed to prevent major data centers from getting too hot. To gain regulatory approval for its acquisition of APC, Schneider was forced to divest the small systems unit of MGE UPS. Another significant acquisition of 2007 was Pelco Inc., a world leader in video security systems with headquarters in Clovis, California. The purchase price totaled $1.54 billion. Schneider's move into the renewable energy sector was highlighted by the 2008 buyout of the Canadian firm Xantrex Technology Inc. for a little over $400 million. Xantrex ranked as the world's largest producer of inverters used to convert raw energy into power in solar and wind power installations.

Acquisitions were placed on the back burner during the second half of 2008 as the global economic crisis led to lessened demand for Schneider Electric products in key markets. The construction industry in particular was quickly hard hit by the downturn, resulting in reduced demand for electrical installation equipment, such as circuit breakers and switches. Schneider launched a major cost-cutting drive centered on trimming its suppliers and staff, and streamlining its businesses. The numerous acquisitions of the previous several years had created myriad opportunities to reduce redundant operations, and in addition the company elected to streamline its array of brands, working to combine its 120 brands into just 10 by 2011. By that year, Schneider aimed to slash its annual operating costs by EUR 600 million ($750 million). Reflecting the poor economic environment, sales during the first half of 2009 were down

nearly 18 percent, while net income plunged almost 60 percent.

Updated, David E. Salamie

PRINCIPAL SUBSIDIARIES

Schneider Electric Industries SAS; Cofibel (Belgium; 99.62%); Cofimines (Belgium; 99.8%).

PRINCIPAL DIVISIONS

North America; Asia-Pacific; Europe; International.

PRINCIPAL COMPETITORS

Siemens AG; ABB Ltd.; Legrand SA; Panasonic Corporation; Rockwell Automation, Inc.; Mitsubishi Corporation; Honeywell International Inc.; Emerson Electric Co.; Eaton Corporation; Johnson Controls, Inc.; General Electric Company; Omron Corporation; Cooper Industries, Ltd.; Tyco International Ltd.

FURTHER READING

Arnold, Martin, "Schneider Plugs into New Markets Because of Euro," *Financial Times*, February 21, 2004, p. 9.

———, "Schneider's Chief Plans to Head Upstairs into New Role as Chairman," *Financial Times*, January 10, 2006, p. 21.

———, "Schneider to Cut 1,000 Jobs in France," *Financial Times*, July 3, 2003, p. 16.

Blitz, Roger, Tobias Buck, and Kwan Yuk Pan, "EU to Pay Damages over Veto of Merger Deal," *Financial Times*, July 12, 2007, p. 7.

Cameron, Doug, "Schneider to Gain Control of MGE UPS Power Systems," *Financial Times*, December 23, 2003, p. 16.

Day, Charles R., Jr., "The Ecstasy Is Worth the Agony," *Industry Week*, November 15, 1993, p. 20.

Donlon, J. P., "Groupe Dynamic," *Chief Executive*, March 1994, p. 26.

Du Bois, Martin, "Claims Against Schneider SA Total Over $53.9 Million in Probe of Fraud," *Wall Street Journal*, May 19, 1995, p. B5D.

———, "Judge Affirms Schneider Head to Stay in Jail: Alleged Misappropriation or Embezzlement Put at Up to $141.6 Million," *Wall Street Journal*, June 2, 1994, p. A11.

———, "Schneider's Chairman Steers Globally While He's a 'Prisoner' in His Country," *Wall Street Journal*, February 2, 1995, p. A14.

Forelle, Charles, "EU High Court Overturns Penalty: Antitrust Regulator Won't Have to Pay Schneider for Blocking Legrand Deal," *Wall Street Journal*, July 17, 2009, p. B2.

Guerrera, Francesco, and Victor Mallet, "Schneider Sues Commission over Merger," *Financial Times*, January 17, 2003, p. 28.

Kamm, Thomas, "Schneider Weighs Merger with Unit, Spie Batignolles," *Wall Street Journal*, March 7, 1995, p. A15.

Keller, Greg, "Schneider Scraps Legrand Merger," *Wall Street Journal Europe*, December 4, 2002, p. A5.

La Broise, Tristan de, and Félix Torres, *Schneider: L'histoire en force*, Paris: Jean-Pierre de Monza, 1996, 492 p.

Levitz, Jennifer, "APC Deal Reflects Demand for Data Protection," *Wall Street Journal*, October 31, 2006, p. C6.

Mallet, Victor, "Separation Turns Bitter for French Groups," *Financial Times*, February 4, 2002.

Miller, James P., "Square D Accepts Sweetened Bid of $2.23 Billion from Schneider," *Wall Street Journal*, May 31, 1991, p. A3.

Milne, Richard, and Friederike Tiesenhausen Cave, "Schneider Buys Balfour Unit in $403m Deal," *Financial Times*, May 20, 2004, p. 27.

Moskal, Brian S., "After the Battle, Square D Works the Peace," *Industry Week*, December 2, 1991, p. 45.

Murdoch, Adrian, "The Strange Case of Didier Pineau-Valencienne," *Chief Executive*, October 1995, p. 24.

Owen, David, "Schneider in Agreed FFr6bn Takeover of Lexel," *Financial Times*, January 12, 1999, p. 26.

Pineau-Valencienne, Didier, with Félix Torres, *Dans la boucle de l'hirondelle: Mémoires d'entreprise*, Paris: A. Michel, 2004, 392 p.

"Schneider Electric: 170 Years of History," Rueil Malmaison, France: Schneider Electric, 2005, 31 p., http://www.schneider-electric.com/documents/presentation/en/local/2006/12/se_history_brands_march2005.pdf.

Shishkin, Philip, "European Court Overturns Ruling Blocking Merger of French Firms," *Wall Street Journal*, October 23, 2002, p. C3.

Woodruff, David, "French Appeals Court Annuls Schneider's Bid for Legrand," *Wall Street Journal Europe*, May 4, 2001, p. 1.

———, "Schneider Chief Seeks New Acquisitions, Best Way to Undo Vetoed Legrand Deal," *Wall Street Journal*, December 31, 2001, p. B5.

Woodruff, David, and Greg Keller, "Schneider Buys Legrand in 7.2 Billion Euro Deal," *Wall Street Journal Europe*, January 16, 2001, p. 1.

Yates, Ronald E., "Profits Come Around After Square D Deal," *Chicago Tribune*, December 3, 1996, pp. 1, 4.

Yuk, Pan Kwan, "Schneider Chief Makes His Power Plays Abroad," *Financial Times*, November 21, 2007, p. 19.

Sierra Nevada Corporation

444 Salomon Circle
Sparks, Nevada 89434-9651
U.S.A.
Telephone: (775) 331-0222
Fax: (775) 331-0359
Web site: http://www.sncorp.com

Private Company
Incorporated: 1963
Employees: 2,000
Sales: $690 million (2008 est.)
NAICS: 332995 Other Ordnance and Accessories Manufacturing; 334111 Electronic Computer Manufacturing; 334511 Search, Detection, Navigation, Guidance, Aeronautical, and Nautical System and Instrument Manufacturing; 336413 Other Aircraft Parts and Auxiliary Equipment Manufacturing; 336414 Guided Missile and Space Vehicle Manufacturing; 336992 Military Armored Vehicle, Tank, and Tank Component Manufacturing; 811219 Other Electronic and Precision Equipment Repair and Maintenance

∎ ∎ ∎

Sierra Nevada Corporation is a U.S. producer and integrator of advanced electronic technology for military, homeland defense, law enforcement, and commercial customers. It boasts applications on land, air, and sea. Although it has grown rapidly in the military buildup following the September 11, 2001, terrorist attacks on the United States (9/11), it has sought to diversify beyond reliance on the Defense Department by entering the commercial spacecraft and renewable energy markets.

The company's operations are scattered across 20 states, and it has additional support sites outside the country. Led by Eren Ozmen and her husband, Fatih, the company ranks as the largest woman-owned federal contractor in the United States. SNC involves itself in a wide range of complex projects at the frontiers of technology, including microsatellites, renewable energy, telemedicine, nanotechnology, and automated landing systems for unmanned aerial vehicle (UAVs) and helicopters. Most of its employees have advanced scientific and technical education.

ORIGINS

Sierra Nevada Corporation (SNC) was incorporated in Nevada in December 1963. It remained a relatively small defense contractor for three decades. By the mid-1980s SNC was working on a NASA contract to develop portable, all-weather landing systems for remote airfields. The U.S. Air Force became its largest client, assigning it projects such as building mobile command centers. According to government records, SNC did $2.7 million worth of research, development, test, and evaluation work for the Department of Defense in 1990.

In 1994 Eren and Fatih Ozmen bought SNC. At the time, the business had 20 employees. Eren Ozmen had joined the company in 1988, the same year she wed her husband, who had then been with the company for seven years.

COMPANY PERSPECTIVES

SNC is a world-class prime systems integrator and electronic systems provider known for its rapid, innovative, and agile technology solutions. Fast-growing and widely diversified, SNC is a high-tech electronics, engineering, and manufacturing corporation that continues to expand its impressive portfolio of capabilities, products and services. SNC has a 45 year tradition of developing and providing high technology Electronics, Avionics, and Communications systems. Investing heavily over the years in people, processes, modern facilities, and state-of-the-art equipment, SNC continues to enhance our technical advantage to provide innovative and cost-effective solutions to our customer's requirements. With numerous successful and diverse acquisitions, SNC continues to acquire new capabilities as we expand our tradition of excellence into the areas of Space, Telemedicine, Nanotechnology, Energy, and Net-Centric Operations.

Fatih Ozmen became the company's chief executive officer. He held a master's degree in electrical engineering from the University of Nevada, Reno. Eren Ozmen had earned her M.B.A. at the same school. She assumed the roles of chairwoman, president, and chief financial officer. With her at the helm, the company qualified as a woman-owned business when competing for federal contracts.

In the decade and a half that followed, the Ozmens led the company through the acquisition of 10 electronics firms, increasing its workforce to 2,000 employees in 2009. Among the more notable early purchases was the 1998 acquisition of Advanced CounterMeasure Systems (ACM Systems) of Rancho Cordova, California. Founded in 1983, the acquired company made training simulation systems, aircraft-radar simulators, and communications jammers. In 2001 ACM Systems was part of a group awarded a $4 billion Defense Department electronic training contract. Its share was worth a potential $160 million over eight years.

In October 2001, SNC added Plano Microwave Inc. (PMI), which possessed unique sensor technology. By year-end, the company had 450 employees in nine states and annual revenues of $94 million. It was growing 20 percent or more a year. SNC had a reputation as a good place to work. It was named Nevada Distinguished Business of the Year for 2001. Seeking to attract highly educated professionals, the company offered such perks as free energy-bars and on-site daycare.

POST-9/11 GROWTH

Turtle Mountain Communications, Inc., (TMC) was acquired in June 2003. TMC produced secure communications and video devices used by the military and law enforcement. It employed about 30 people in East Tennessee (having moved from Pennsylvania in 1991) and was expanding quickly to meet demand from U.S. forces in Iraq and Afghanistan. TMC also operated a sophisticated custom electronics shop and repair facility. A few months later, SNC acquired Inter-4, a San Francisco manufacturer of handheld computers for the military.

GUIDED LANDING SYSTEMS

SNC was involved in the Common Automatic Recovery System (CARS), launched in 1990. Seven years later, SNC was able to use it to successfully land a Pioneer UAV. By the end of the decade it had demonstrated the ability to automatically land UAVs on ships.

After the 9/11 terrorist attacks the wars in Afghanistan and Iraq brought new urgency to SNC's military projects. One of these was a system to guide manned-helicopter landings in brownout (extremely poor visibility) conditions for the U.S. Army's Aviation Applied Technology Directorate (AATD). In collaboration with Herley Industries, Inc., SNC was also working on an automatic carrier landing system (ACLS) for the latest generation of F-18 navy fighter aircraft. Other defense projects under development included a mobile air traffic control tower and unmanned aerial refueling system.

SNC was posting revenues of approximately $200 million in 2004. It had become a top-50 supplier to the U.S. Air Force. During the year the company was awarded exclusive rights to adapt airships from Columbus, Georgia's Techsphere Systems International (TSI) for government applications. TSI made low-, medium-, and high-altitude spherical airships for operations between 7,000 and 70,000 feet. The high-altitude airships could remain aloft for up to a year. As a substitute or improvement on towers or satellites, the craft had potential applications in battlefield intelligence and homeland security.

Seeking to expand its systems-integration capabilities, SNC bought Aviation Resources De., Inc. (ARDI), an aircraft maintenance, repair, and modification shop in Maryland, in June 2004. This provided an East Coast base for integrating SNC's technology into aerial

KEY DATES

1963: Company is established in Nevada.
1994: Eren and Fatih Ozmen buy Sierra Nevada Corporation (SNC).
1998: SNC acquires Advanced CounterMeasure Systems of Rancho Cordova, California.
2001: SNC acquires Plano Microwave, Inc.
2004: SNC acquires Maryland aircraft repair and modification shop ARDI.
2005: Company acquires California radar specialist WaveBand Corporation.
2007: Company acquires Denver aircraft repair and modification stations Straight Flight, Inc., and Straight Flight Conversions, Inc.
2008: MicroSat Systems, Inc., and SpaceDev, Inc., acquisitions form basis of new Space Systems division.

platforms. The May 2005 acquisition of California's WaveBand Corporation furthered SNC's capabilities with millimeter wave (MMW) radar technology. Among WaveBand's projects was a bird-detection radar system for use at airports. In 2007 SNC added Denver aircraft repair and modification stations Straight Flight, Inc., and Straight Flight Conversions, Inc.

SPACE AND ENERGY

SNC entered the growing field of small satellites with the acquisition of Littleton, Colorado's MicroSat Systems, Inc., in January 2008. SNC had been collaborating with MicroSat on the TacSat-2 optical imaging satellite developed for Air Force Research Labs, which was launched in December 2006. Relying on a standard UAV datalink, the low-earth-orbit (LEO) satellite cost only $65 million to develop at a time when conventional satellites could cost billions.

In May 2008 SNC brought this technology to the commercial sphere when Orbcomm Inc. hired it to build 18 communications satellites within 36 months at a cost of just $117 million, with an option for 30 more microsatellites. These were designed to operate for seven years. *Northern Nevada Business Weekly* noted this contract marked a key step for SNC to diversify beyond defense work.

SNC bought SpaceDev, Inc., for $38 million in December 2008. The company had been established in 1997 in Poway, California, by James Benson. It was best

known for supplying spacecraft motors for Space-CraftOne, the pioneering private-sector, manned spacecraft. The SpaceDev purchase was considered complementary to the MicroSat Systems acquisition. SNC grouped the two into a new Space Systems business area.

Annual revenues were nearly $500 million in 2007, when SNC had 1,200 employees, one-third of them at its four sites in the Sparks area, which totaled 175,000 square feet. A year later, sales approached $700 million and the workforce was reportedly up to 2,000 people. The company by this time ranked as one of the top 100 U.S. defense contractors.

The fast-growing company was looking for more space, and more employees, reported *Northern Nevada Business Weekly*. It was working with the Ozmens' alma mater, the University of Nevada, Reno, to find prospective recruits. SNC joined the University of Colorado at Boulder in launching the Center for Space Entrepreneurship (eSpace), a business incubator, in 2009.

SNC entered the renewable energy field in August 2009 via a joint venture with Gestamp Asetym–Solar North America, Inc., a subsidiary of a Spanish auto-components supplier. The venture's goal was to build solar energy plants in Nevada and surrounding states. The move came as federal and state governments pushed a number of initiatives to promote renewable energy development. The partnership soon announced an award to supply three Nevada Army National Guard bases with 3.4 megawatts of power from three solar parking lot structures.

SNC was part of the Next Step in Space coalition dedicated to commercializing manned space flight. An official told the *Houston Chronicle* that the company believed it could offer the best value for bringing crews to low-earth orbit, while keeping more money within the United States (versus launching from Russian or other foreign space programs).

The fighting in Afghanistan and Iraq continued to be a driver of the business. In June 2009 the company announced a contract worth at least $36.5 million and up to $248.3 million to provide radio-jamming devices as a defense against IEDs (improvised explosive devices).

STILL BIG ON DEFENSE

In the first five years of the War on Terror, SNC won federal contracts worth $602.5 million, most of it ($474.1 million) from the Air Force. The company's close ties to Nevada Governor Jim Gibbons drew some media scrutiny. SNC had hired Gibbons's wife, Dawn, as a public relations consultant during his time in the U.S. House of Representatives. However, the company maintained her work was unrelated to the contracts it had won. SNC contributed to a wide range of political campaigns, both Republican and Democrat, as it lobbied for government business. Working at the edge of technology in covert programs, the company won most of its work from sole-source or no-bid contracts.

Frederick C. Ingram

PRINCIPAL SUBSIDIARIES

SpaceDev, Inc.; MSI (MicroSat Systems Inc.); Straight Flight, Inc.

PRINCIPAL DIVISIONS

SS (Space Systems); CNS/ATM (Communication, Navigation, Surveillance and Air Traffic Management); ISR (Intelligence, Surveillance and Reconnaissance); C4N (Command, Control, Computers, Communications and Networks); IMS (Integrated Mission Systems); SST (Sensor Systems & Technologies); EWR (Electronic Warfare/Range Instrumentation).

PRINCIPAL COMPETITORS

ITT Defense Electronics & Services; L-3 Communications Corporation; Raytheon Company; General Atomics Aeronautical Systems Inc.

FURTHER READING

Ball, Molly, and David Kihara, "Gibbons Faces New Questions; Report: Then-Congressman Aided Firm That Hired Wife," *Las Vegas Review-Journal,* March 31, 2007.

Berger, Eric, "What's Next in Space? Private Firms Believe They Have an Important Role to Play; Ares Program May Be in for Changes," *Houston Chronicle,* August 22, 2009, p. 1.

"Bird Radar Experiment," *Airports International,* November 1, 2004, p. 8.

Buchanan, Leigh, "Legacy: James Benson, 1945–2008; A One-Man Space Program," *Inc.,* January/February 2009, p. 120.

De Selding, Peter B., "MicroSat to Build Orbcomm Satellites," *Space News,* May 12, 2008, pp. 1, 7.

"East Tennessee Companies Make Equipment for War," *Associated Press Newswires,* March 28, 2003.

German, Jeff, "Fatih Ozmen: Mystery Man Behind Sierra Nevada," *Las Vegas Sun,* April 8, 2007.

Merrifield, John T., "Ames Develops Remote Site Landing Aids," *Aviation Week & Space Technology,* June 10, 1985, p. 119.

"Pioneer Drone Demonstrates Auto Recovery," *Military Robotics,* January 10, 1997.

Seelmeyer, John, "New Defense Contract to Boost Employment at SNC," *Northern Nevada Business Weekly,* June 29, 2009.

———, "Sierra Nevada Corp. Diversifies Beyond Defense," *Northern Nevada Business Weekly,* May 19, 2008.

———, "Sierra Nevada Corp. Solar Plans Take Shape," *Northern Nevada Business Weekly,* August 17, 2009.

"Smallsats Could Get Boost in Global Financial Crisis," *Aviation Week & Space Technology,* March 29, 2009.

Swett, Clint, "Rancho Cordova, Calif., Electronics Company Lands Defense Contract," *Knight-Ridder/Tribune Business News,* March 22, 2001.

Tiron, Roxana, "Precision Systems Let Helos Land in Sandstorms, Snow," *National Defense,* February 1, 2004, p. 34.

Wall, Robert, "Out of the Dust," *Aviation Week & Space Technology,* September 22, 2003, p. 58.

Wilke, John R., "Nevada Company's Capitol Ties: Defense Contractor Paid Gov. Gibbons' Wife for Consulting Work," *Wall Street Journal,* March 30, 2007, p. A4.

Skype Technologies S.A.

22/24 Boulevard Royal, 6e Etage
Luxembourg, L-2449
Luxembourg
Telephone: (+352) 26-20-15-82
Fax: (+352) 26-27-05-88
Web site: http://www.skype.com

Private Company
Incorporated: 2002
Employees: 500
Sales: $600 million (2008 est.)
NAICS: 517910 Other Telecommunications

■ ■ ■

Skype Technologies S.A. offers Web-based software that enables users to make phone calls using the Internet. The company's application, available at no charge, relies on peer-to-peer network architecture to provide audio and video communication capabilities. There is no charge for calls placed between registered Skype users. The company charges a fee in the form of prepaid subscriptions for SkypeOut and SkypeIn, giving its users the ability to call and to receive calls from non-Skype users. Skype boasts more than 400 million registered users across the globe. The company maintains offices in Europe, North America, South America, and Asia. Formerly a wholly owned subsidiary of eBay Inc., Skype is majority controlled by investment firm Silver Lake Partners, L.P.

NIKLAS ZENNSTROM AND KAZAA

By his mid-30s, Niklas Zennstrom had cemented his reputation as an iconoclast in the technology sector, taking what he described in the May 30, 2005 issue of *Business Week* as a "radically disruptive" approach in his entrepreneurial career. Born in Sweden, Zennstrom attended Uppsala University in Uppsala, 35 miles northwest of Stockholm, where he earned dual degrees in business administration and engineering physics. After college, Zennstrom worked for a Swedish telecommunications operator, Tele2, spending three years in the late 1990s helping to build one of Europe's leading alternative phone companies. Tele2 provided him with the telecommunications experience he would put to use in launching Skype. His "radically disruptive" inclinations first appeared after he left Tele2, emerging when he collaborated with Janus Friis, a Danish entrepreneur, at the turn of the millennium and changed the dynamics of a $1 trillion industry.

In 2001, 36-year-old Zennstrom and 26-year-old Friis developed Kazaa, capitalized KaZaA, Media Desktop. Kazaa enabled users to share files, primarily music files, through a peer-to-peer (P2P) network, freeing Zennstrom and Friis from having to purchase and maintain central servers. A P2P network harnessed the processing power, disk storage, and network bandwidth of its participants, using the computers of the network's constituents as its infrastructure. Available for free, Kazaa became immensely popular, attracting an estimated 315 million users within months. The vast community of Kazaa users downloaded the application and began sharing music files. This ignited the furor of the music industry, emboldened by its success in shutting down

COMPANY PERSPECTIVES

Hello. We're Skype. Skype is software that enables the world's conversations. Millions of individuals and businesses use Skype to make free video and voice calls, send instant messages and share files with other Skype users. Everyday, people everywhere also use Skype to make low-cost calls to landlines and mobiles.

Napster, another file-sharing operator, four months after Kazaa was launched. Kazaa soon faced its own legal troubles, charged with enabling piracy on a massive scale.

FROM KAZAA TO SKYPE

Zennstrom and Friis had launched Kazaa in March 2001 through a Dutch company named Consumer Empowerment. A Dutch copyright collecting agency, Buma/Stemra, quickly filed a lawsuit against Consumer Empowerment, which led to a court ruling in November 2001 ordering the company to institute measures to prevent copyright infringement. Although the High Council of the Netherlands, the country's supreme court, eventually ruled in favor of Kazaa, Zennstrom and Friis began distancing themselves from their venture by the end of 2001. Kazaa was sold to Australia-based Sharman Networks, leaving Zennstrom and Friis free to develop their next radically disruptive business idea, Skype.

The partners formed Skype Technologies in 2002, registering the company in Luxembourg for tax purposes and establishing its operations in London. For the software engineers he needed to help develop Skype, Zennstrom traveled to Tallinn, the capital of Estonia, where he had discovered a rich talent pool while working for Tele2. From their offices in London, Tallinn, and Luxembourg, Zennstrom and Friis began hatching their plan to enter the $1 trillion telecommunications industry with the same network architecture that Kazaa used.

HOW SKYPE WORKS

Instead of using the public switched telephone network (PSTN), Skype was developed to use the Internet, employing voice over Internet protocol (VoIP) to transmit its phone calls. Sound carried on the PSTN was converted into electronic signals that traversed an elaborate network of switches in a dedicated circuit, but VoIP worked differently, using the same technology that transmitted e-mail messages and Web pages. VoIP converted audio into packets of data for their transmission across the Internet or a private network. Once the packets reached their destination (in Skype's case, the person on the other end of the phone call), they were reassembled and converted into sound. Zennstrom planned to use VoIP to enable participants of a P2P network to communicate with speech, creating Skype to transmit audio in much the same way Kazaa enabled people to share music files. To make a phone call, a Skype user needed a computer and a broadband Internet connection. Once the Skype software was downloaded and registration was completed, the user put on a headset equipped with a microphone, selected the name of a friend with Skype (calls could be made only between two Skype users) on the computer screen, and clicked a green telephone icon.

Like Kazaa, Zennstrom intended to offer Skype software free of charge. "We don't need to have any income because Skype uses peer-to-peer software so we don't have an incremental cost for each user or each phone call between Skype users," he said in the May–June 2004 issue of *Global Telecom Business*. "Since incremental cost is zero, we believe we cannot charge for it. We believe that phone calls on the Internet should be free, and will be free in the future." Zennstrom's first objective was to build the business and attract a vast number of Skype users, whose own computers would be used to power the Skype network. Free calls on the Internet, using a P2P network, was a self-sustaining business model as far as operating the network was concerned, but Zennstrom's eventual aim was to make money: his acceptance of venture capital necessitated a profitable enterprise, as did Skype's corporate overhead. Money would be made once the Skype community grew and the company could begin offering additional services, such as voice mail, conferencing, and the ability to call non-Skype users, for a fee.

RAPID INITIAL GROWTH

Although Skype relied on only word-of-mouth advertising to promote itself, the offer of free phone calls, particularly free international calls, did not take long to attract legions of users. The company released a beta version of Skype in August 2003 and signed up 1.3 million registered users from 170 countries by the end of the year. By April 2004, the company had 4.5 million registered users, finding its most receptive audience in Europe. By June 2004, 14 million users had downloaded the company's P2P telephony software, giving Skype a sufficient base of followers to begin offering its fee-based premium services.

```
┌─────────────────────────────────────────┐
│              KEY DATES                    │
│              ───────◆───────              │
│                                           │
│  2002:  Niklas Zennstrom and Janus Friis  │
│         form Skype Technologies.          │
│  2003:  Skype releases a beta version of  │
│         the Skype application in August.  │
│  2004:  Skype introduces SkypeOut,        │
│         enabling Skype users to call      │
│         non-Skype users for a fee.        │
│  2005:  Skype is acquired by eBay Inc.    │
│         in a $2.6 billion deal.           │
│  2006:  Skype signs up its 100 millionth  │
│         user.                             │
│  2007:  Zennstrom resigns as Skype's      │
│         chief executive officer.          │
│  2008:  Josh Silverman takes the helm at  │
│         Skype.                            │
│  2009:  eBay announces it intends to spin │
│         off Skype in an initial public    │
│         offering of stock slated for      │
│         2010; in September eBay decides   │
│         to sell a 65 percent stake in the │
│         company to Silver Lake Partners   │
│         for $1.9 billion.                 │
└─────────────────────────────────────────┘
```

Skype's development occurred in a rush. Milestones were achieved monthly. By July 2004, Skype users had spoken over the network a total of one billion minutes. By June 2005, less than a year later, the traffic carried by the Skype network reached 10 billion minutes. People (Skype's base could not be referred to as "customers") were downloading the software at a frenetic pace, giving Zennstrom the audience to begin turning his company into a profit-making enterprise.

PREMIUM SERVICES DEBUT IN 2004

In July 2004, he launched SkypeOut, a prepaid service that allowed Skype users to make long-distance calls to landlines and cellular phones for less than two cents per minute. In its first year of availability, SkypeOut attracted more than 1.8 million customers, the first genuine customers Skype could claim. In November 2004, the company offered its European users the opportunity to cut their tether to their computer, announcing Skype software's compatibility with the Siemens Gigset DECT cordless phone, which connected to a computer via a Universal Serial Bus port.

In February 2005, when Skype counted 23.9 million registered users and was signing up 130,000 new users each day, it broadened its potential base by releasing Skype software that was compatible with Linux and Apple operating systems. In April 2005, the company offered the other end of SkypeOut, releasing SkypeIn, a

subscription-based service costing $13 for three months, or $39 for a year, that allowed Skype users to receive calls from preselected, conventional phone numbers carried on the PSTN. With the release of SkypeIn, Skype users could call non-Skype users for a fee, non-Skype users could call Skype users for a fee, and, as it had been from the company's inception, Skype users could talk to Skype users for free.

The rapid growth of the Skype community and the introduction of fee-based premium services had a clear effect on the company's financial stature. Skype generated $7 million in revenue in 2004. In 2005, the company was headed toward $60 million in revenue when corporate suitors came calling, their interest piqued by projections that Skype would generate $200 million in revenue in 2006. Rumors of a possible sale began to circulate throughout the telephony industry in mid-2005, when reports surfaced of Yahoo!, News Corp., and Google expressing interest in acquiring Skype. A Skype public relations representative, quoted in the August 30, 2005 issue of *Information Week*, quashed the speculation, saying, "Skype is not for sale." Less than two weeks later, Skype was sold.

NEW OWNERSHIP IN 2005

On September 12, 2005, eBay Inc., the online auctioneer, acquired Skype, completing a corporate marriage hailed by eBay's chief executive officer, Meg Whitman. Whitman envisioned numerous synergies in the union, seeing Skype as an ideal complement to eBay's $1.5 billion purchase of online payment facilitator PayPal in 2002. Skype, Whitman believed, would open up new product categories for eBay such as new cars, travel, personal and business services, and real estate. Further, Skype flourished in international markets where eBay had only a small presence. Lastly, VoIP capabilities were expected to aid sales by increasing the level of trust between the parties involved in a transaction, as well as facilitating bartering among eBay users. The benefits were enticing, prompting Whitman to pay more than eBay had ever paid to complete an acquisition. eBay acquired Skype for the staggering sum of $2.6 billion, $1.3 billion in cash and $1.3 billion in eBay stock, plus the potential of an additional $1.5 billion if Skype met predetermined growth and profit goals in 2008 and 2009.

Zennstrom and Friis joined eBay's executive team following the purchase. Skype, with 54 million users when it became an eBay subsidiary, continued to grow at a rapid pace, signing up 150,000 new users each day. New services and capabilities were introduced, including the ability to make video calls, which debuted at the end of 2005. Skype for Business, targeted for companies with fewer than 10 employees, was released in March 2006, one month before the company signed up its 100 millionth user. Skype made progress, but many industry observers failed to see a successful integration of Skype into eBay; the synergies envisioned by Whitman failed to materialize. "I don't know what their strategy is," an analyst said, referring to eBay in the April 28, 2006 issue of *Internet Week*, "why they want more unpaying customers that add more cost to their network."

A FUTURE WITHOUT EBAY

By late 2007, eBay's acquisition of Skype was generally regarded as a misstep, "Meg Whitman's folly," according to the October 27, 2008 issue of *Fortune*. In October 2007, Whitman paid Zennstrom, Friis, and other Skype shareholders $503 million to terminate their incentive package. Zennstrom stepped down as Skype's chief executive officer and, together with Friis, launched Joost, a P2P Internet television service. Whitman resigned as eBay's chief executive officer in March 2008, and her replacement, John Donahoe, expressed interest in shedding Skype, stating publicly that he would sell the company if he received an acceptable offer.

Against the backdrop of the leadership change at eBay, Skype experienced a period of unsteady management. In March 2008, Josh Silverman became the third executive to lead the company since Zennstrom departed six months earlier. Silverman, who had launched eBay's European online classifieds business, took the helm and began developing a more focused strategy for Skype to pursue. The company, in his mind, had developed new features and services without devoting sufficient resources to promoting and supporting the new offerings. He terminated the least promising of Skype's projects, such as SkypeCast, billed as a "public conversation platform," and concentrated the company's resources on improving its core services.

Donahoe, meanwhile, ended his search to find a buyer for Skype. In April 2009, eBay announced it intended to spin off Skype in an initial public offering of stock scheduled for the first half of 2010. The stock offering was expected to raise between $3 billion and $5 billion, but according to industry pundits a sale was still possible, notably a sale to Zennstrom and Friis, who reportedly were talking to private-equity firms, intent on regaining control of the company they had founded. In September 2009 eBay changed course and sold a 65

percent stake in Skype to Menlo Park, California-based Silver Lake Partners, L.P. The investment firm paid $1.9 billion for majority control of the company, with eBay retaining a 35 percent interest.

Jeffrey L. Covell

PRINCIPAL COMPETITORS

Vonage Holdings Corp.; Net2Phone, Inc.; AT&T Inc.

FURTHER READING

Burkitt-Gray, Alan, "The Mysteries of Skype," *Global Telecoms Business*, May–June 2004, p. 28.

———, "Ten Billion Minute Man," *Global Telecoms Business*, May–June 2005, p. 32.

"eBay Plans to Keep Skype 'Separate,' for Now," *InternetWeek*, September 12, 2005.

Hof, Rob, "eBay Opens a Whole New Channel," *Business Week Online*, September 13, 2005.

Lashinsky, Adam, "Is Skype on Sale at eBay?" *Fortune*, October 27, 2008, p. 48.

Laughlin, Kirk, "The Sneak Attack of P2P Voice: Skype's New VoIP Model Borrows from Instant Messaging," *America's Network*, December 1, 2003, p. 12.

Maurer, Harry, "Selling Off Skype," *Business Week*, April 27, 2009, p. 6.

Moore, Matt, "Skype's Callers Can Now Dial Phones," *America's Intelligence Wire*, July 27, 2004.

Myerson, Bruce, "Skype Goes Mobile," *Business Week Online*, October 19, 2007.

Reinhardt, Andy, "Disruptive Telecom," *Business Week*, May 30, 2005, p. 60.

"Skype Blames Two-Day Service Collapse on Software Glitch," *InformationWeek*, August 20, 2007.

"Skype Dials for Business Dollars," *Business Week Online*, March 9, 2006.

"Skype Founders Want to Buy VoIP Service Back from eBay," *InformationWeek*, April 13, 2009.

"Skype Insists It Is Not for Sale," *InformationWeek*, August 30, 2005.

"Skype Loses Its CEO, eBay Takes a $1.4 Billion Charge," *InformationWeek*, October 1, 2007.

"Vonage and Skype Turn Up the Heat—on Each Other," *InformationWeek*, April 18, 2005.

Wilson, Carol, "eBay Sees Billions in Skype Synergies," *Telephony*, September 12, 2005.

Soft Pretzel Franchise Systems, Inc.

———— ∎ ————

7368 Frankford Avenue
Philadelphia, Pennsylvania 19136-3829
U.S.A.
Telephone: (215) 338-4606
Toll Free: (800) 679-4221
Fax: (215) 437-6830
Web site: http://www.phillysoftpretzelfactory.com

Private Company
Incorporated: 2004
Employees: 58
Sales: $40 million (2009 est.)
NAICS: 311910 Snack Food Manufacturing

∎ ∎ ∎

Doing business as Philly Pretzel Factory, or in some cases Philly Soft Pretzel Factory, Soft Pretzel Franchise Systems, Inc., operates a chain of about 160 company-owned and franchised bakery shops specializing in hand-twisted, seven-inch, fresh soft pretzels. Unlike most pretzel shops, Philly Pretzel Factory focuses on volume sales, offering value on purchases of large quantities of pretzels, boxes of 50 or 100 for coworkers or other large groups. The stores also offer unsalted pretzels, cinnamon pretzels, half-sizes, pretzel bites ("rivets"), pretzel dogs (hot dogs baked in pretzel dough), bottled soft drinks, and a variety of dipping sauces including yellow mustard, spicy mustard, hot mustard, honey mustard, cheddar cheese, cream cheese, cinnamon, and chocolate. Philly Pretzel Factory offers meal combinations, such as three regular pretzels and a soft drink, two pretzel dogs

and a soft drink, or a box of rivets and a soft drink. The stores sell party trays that offer additional pretzel flavors: poppy, sesame, garlic, and "Everything."

Although most of the stores are located in southeastern Pennsylvania and southern New Jersey, they are also found in Delaware, Georgia, Maryland, New York, North Carolina, South Carolina, and Virginia. The company is headed by cofounder, President, and Chief Executive Officer Dan DiZio.

PRETZELS: MEDIEVAL ORIGINS

Pretzels are generally considered to be the invention of a monk in southern France, who around A.D. 600 twisted leftover bread dough to create a treat as a reward for children who learned their prayers. The three rings of the traditional pretzel shape represented the Trinity, the inner lacing supposedly imitating hands folded across the chest in prayer. (Philadelphia soft pretzels, in contrast, are shaped similar to a figure eight.) The treat then made its way to Germany where it took the name "bretzels," eventually becoming known as pretzels. According to some sources they were first brought to North America on the *Mayflower*, but there is no doubt that the German and Swiss German immigrants who became known as the Pennsylvania Dutch made soft pretzels popular in the New World.

The pretzel took root in the New World in the heart of Pennsylvania Dutch country, Lancaster County, located about 60 miles west of Philadelphia. It was here in the late 1600s that the hard pretzel was developed by accident when an apprentice baker, according to lore, fell asleep and failed to tend his hearth. The overbaked pretzels were devoid of moisture and hard but were also tasty and offered a longer shelf life than soft pretzels, resulting in a new variety. It was also in the Lancaster County community of Lititz that the first commercial pretzel bakery in the United States opened in 1861.

Given the proximity of Lancaster County to Philadelphia, it was natural that pretzels would become popular in that city as well. According to the *New York Times*, pretzel twisting was the second-highest paying craft in the area by the Civil War, trailing only cigar wrapping. Although pretzels were considered a German treat, it was an Italian American, Edmund Nacchio, who established one of the first commercial soft pretzel bakeries in Philadelphia in 1922, the Federal Pretzel Baking Company. It was also around this time that hot-dog vendors in the city began to carry soft pretzels, which served to increase the popularity of the item. In time, soft pretzels seemed to be available on every Philadelphia street corner. Not surprisingly, the consumption of pretzels was far higher here than anywhere else in the United States. In 1988 the *New York Times* reported that Philadelphians consumed 300,000 soft pretzels each day. According to some sources, Philadelphians on average consumed twice as many pretzels each year as the rest of the country.

DIZIO SELLS PRETZELS AS A CHILD

One of those Philadelphians obsessed with pretzels was DiZio. He was just 11 years of age when in 1983 he began selling pretzels on a street corner in northeast Philadelphia, peddling the leftovers of Kensington Soft Pretzel. Selling the pretzels out of a plastic crate, five for a dollar, he was able to sell 1,000 on a weekend day. After splitting the take with the baker, he took home $100, a large amount of money given that his allowance was $3 a week.

By the time he was in high school, DiZio decided he wanted to own his own pretzel business. Nevertheless, he soon changed his plans. He enrolled at East Stroudsburg University and after graduation became a stockbroker. It was not, however, a career that he found especially satisfying. In an interview with Adam Stone of the *Philadelphia Business Journal* in 2007, he recalled, "at

the end of the day I felt like a used-car salesman. People trusted you, and you tried to do the best you could. But the truth is, who knows what's going to happen tomorrow?"

Disenchanted with his career, DiZio decided to start his own business and found a partner in his former college roommate, Len Lehman, who was working as a psychiatric counselor. DiZio persuaded him to go into business by promising Lehman he would have more time to play golf. Each young man contributed $17,000 in cash and credit-card debt for seed money, originally planning to open a bar until friends convinced them that it was a bad idea. Instead, DiZio and Lehman turned to DiZio's old love: pretzels. Because it was primarily a morning business, Lehman still hoped to free up his afternoons for golf. With other people, however, the idea of opening a pretzel bakery was met with as much skepticism as opening a bar had been. "Everyone thought we were crazy," DiZio told Michael Callahan of *Fortune Small Business* in 2009. Even the landlord of the store they rented predicted they would be out of business in a matter of weeks.

FIRST STORE OPENS: 1998

Despite the doubters, in 1998 DiZio and Lehman opened their first store under the Soft Pretzel Factory banner on Frankford Avenue in Philadelphia. Their plan was to act as a wholesale baker, supplying kiosks at Philadelphia International Airport. That all changed on the first morning they began baking soft pretzels. Their bakery was located next to a popular breakfast place, providing early morning foot traffic. The smell of fresh-baked pretzels caught the attention of passersby who began to line up when DiZio and Lehman pulled down the brown paper that covered the bakery windows. A line of more than 40 people had formed by 9 a.m., eager to purchase fresh-from-the-oven soft pretzels. It was an opportunity too good to pass up and the bakery became a de facto retail operation.

The Pretzel Factory's pretzels proved so popular that DiZio and Lehman kept the oven as busy as possible and still could not keep up with demand. Any ideas of afternoon golf were quickly quashed. Instead, the young partners found themselves ensnared in a daily grind that included working the ovens and counter all day, and at the end sitting exhausted on the floor to split the take, putting aside what was needed for utilities and rent. This was followed by a trip to Sam's Club to purchase more ingredients, a shower, and bed before repeating the routine the next day. DiZio claimed that he was so tired he could fall asleep in his car waiting at a red light. They were so busy they did not find the time to learn if there was any supplier that could deliver ingredients to them, or even hire people to reduce the workload. After three months, the time when their landlord said they would be out of business, Lehman handed DiZio the keys to the store, ready to quit not for the lack of business but the excess of it.

Realizing the need to make the business a bearable burden, DiZio took the time to find a flour distributor and hired some college friends to lessen the workload. They would also be groomed to open up additional shops. The Pretzel Factory operated in a realistic manner. Not only did DiZio and Lehman prove their landlord wrong, they bought the building a year later as well as two adjacent buildings. The resulting complex would house the store in addition to the company's corporate offices.

DiZio sought to keep the operation as simple as possible and offer value to his customers. Single pretzels were sold hot in tissue paper: $5 provided customers with 22 pretzels in a brown paper bag, while orders of 50 for $11 or 100 for $20 were packaged in boxes. Because pretzels could be substituted in Philadelphia for a meal any time of day, the store offered a combination deal: four pretzels and a 20-ounce bottle of Coke for $2. DiZio eschewed fountain drinks, willing to carry only bottled drinks for simplicity's sake. He was also loathe to expand the menu. The addition of pretzel dogs was the extent of his adventurousness.

FIRST FRANCHISE UNIT OPENS: 2003

The second Pretzel Factory opened on Sansom Street in Philadelphia in 1999 under the guidance of Michael Gabbett. DiZio then teamed with Brad Beaverson to open a shop in Bryn Mawr, Pennsylvania, in 2002. A year later these were followed by the Suburban Station (East) location on JFK Boulevard and Suburban Station (West) in Philadelphia, both shops run by Ron Heil.

It was the Sansom Street store that led to franchising. Working down the street from the bakeshop was a man named Jim Powers, a North New Jersey native who was not familiar with Philadelphians' love of soft pretzels. Watching from his window he observed the steady line of customers, many of whom he came to recognize as regulars, and he became convinced that because the product appealed to every demographic in the city and the operation was kept simple, the Pretzel Factory was a perfect franchise opportunity. Powers and his wife, Julie, lobbied DiZio to grant them a Philly Pretzel Factory franchise. Eventually DiZio relented, a handshake deal was reached over lunch, and in 2003 Jim and Julie Powers opened the first Pretzel Factory franchise in 2003, in West Chester, Pennsylvania.

The original store continued to enjoy strong growth, reaching $1.1 million in annual sales in 2004, an amount that improved to $1.7 million just two years later. DiZio and Lehman also opened another shop together in 2004, located in Philadelphia's Frankford transportation terminal, but the franchising operation would soon occupy all of DiZio's time. Franchising also allowed the Pretzel Factory to move outside of Philadelphia and its immediate suburbs. The franchising operation was incorporated in 2004, the same year the first New Jersey franchise store opened. A year later there were a dozen shops in the state.

Jim and Julie Powers took the concept to Delaware in 2005, opening a store in Newark. Other stores followed in Dover, Rehoboth Beach, and Bear, Delaware. Also in 2005 a franchisee introduced Philly Pretzel Factory to Cincinnati, Ohio, while others brought it to Orlando, Florida; Elkton, Maryland; and Staten Island, New York. As franchising picked up, the Pretzel Factory opened 47 new stores in 2007, expanding beyond main streets and transportation hubs to include strip malls and college locations.

NEW MARKETS: 2008

The Pretzel Factory entered additional new markets in 2008. It spread to western Pennsylvania where a former Philadelphia Eagles football player opened a unit. Other units were also opened in 2008 in Tucker, Georgia; Clifton Park, New York; Mooresville, North Carolina; Bluffton, South Carolina; and Norfolk, Williamsburg, and Yorktown, Virginia. By the end of the year the chain was approaching 160 units.

Many of the new stores were opened to build the Philly Pretzel Factory brand, but it was far from certain that the product would catch on in all of these new markets. In Florida, in fact, despite the presence of ex-Philadelphians, several franchise stores had to be closed for lack of sales. The company also had to contend with the adverse impact of fluctuating flour prices and a declining interest in pretzels among the general population. The product, however, had survived for centuries, and the appetite for soft pretzels among Philadelphians remained unabated, providing the Philly Pretzel Factory with ample opportunity for continued growth.

Ed Dinger

PRINCIPAL COMPETITORS

Auntie Anne's, Inc.; Jim's Soft Pretzel Bakery; Pretzel Boy's.

FURTHER READING

Callahan, Michael, "Pretzel Wars," *Fortune Small Business*, September 2009, p. 78.

Campisi, Jon, "Dough Woes," *Philadelphia Northeast Times*, March 27, 2008.

Dash, Julekha, "Philly Pretzel Maker Has Dough to Grow in Md.'s Suburbs," *Baltimore Business Journal*, September 19, 2008.

Goldstein, Eliane Dann, "Fare of the Country; Philadelphia's Twist in the Pretzel," *New York Times*, November 13, 1988.

Rademaekers, Brian, "Philly Pretzel Maker," *Philadelphia Northeast Times*, February 15, 2007.

Sastrowardoyo, Hartriono B., "Philly Pretzel Factory Puts a New Twist on Franchises," *Asbury Park Press*, November 7, 2007.

Stone, Adam, "Philly Soft Pretzel's Twisted Logic," *Philadelphia Business Journal*, February 9, 2007.

White, April, "Rolling in Dough," *Philadelphia Magazine*, April 2008, p. 58.

Sony Corporation

———■———

7-1 Konan, 1-chome
Minato-ku
Tokyo, 108-0075
Japan
Telephone: (+81 3) 6748-2111
Fax: (+81 3) 6748-2244
Web site: http://www.sony.net

Public Company
Incorporated: 1946 as Tokyo Tsushin Kogyo Kabushiki
  Kaisha
Employees: 171,000
Sales: ¥7.73 trillion ($79.46 billion) (2009)
Stock Exchanges: New York Tokyo
Ticker Symbol: SNE
NAICS: 334310 Audio and Video Equipment
  Manufacturing; 334111 Electronic Computer
  Manufacturing; 334210 Telephone Apparatus
  Manufacturing; 334413 Semiconductor and Related
  Device Manufacturing; 511210 Software Publishers;
  512110 Motion Picture and Video Production;
  524113 Direct Life Insurance Carriers; 541810
  Advertising Agencies; 541910 Marketing Research
  and Public Opinion Polling; 551112 Offices of
  Other Holding Companies

■ ■ ■

Sony Corporation is one of the best-known names in consumer electronics. Since it was established shortly after World War II, Sony has introduced a stream of revolutionary products, including the transistor radio, the Trinitron television, the Betamax VCR, the CD player, the Walkman portable cassette player, and the PlayStation game console. In addition to audio and video products, televisions, personal computers (PCs), monitors, computer peripherals, telecommunications devices, and game consoles, Sony generates considerable revenues from its entertainment businesses. These include Sony Music Entertainment, Sony Pictures Entertainment, Sony Digital Production, Sony Pictures Home Entertainment, and Sony Pictures Television.

EARLY HISTORY: FROM TAPE RECORDERS TO TRANSISTOR RADIOS TO THE TRINITRON

Sony was founded by a former naval lieutenant named Akio Morita and a defense contractor named Masaru Ibuka. Morita, a weapons researcher, first met Ibuka during World War II while developing a heat-seeking missile-guidance system and a night-vision gun scope. After the war Ibuka worked as a radio repairman for a bomb-damaged Tokyo department store. Morita found him again when he read in a newspaper that Ibuka had invented a shortwave converter. In May 1946 the two men established a partnership with $500 in borrowed capital, and registered their company as Tokyo Tsushin Kogyo Kabushiki Kaisha (Tokyo Telecommunications Engineering Corporation, or TTK). Morita and Ibuka moved their company to a crude facility on a hill in southern Tokyo where they developed their first consumer product: a rice cooker, which failed commercially. In its first year TTK registered a profit of $300 on sales of less than $7,000.

COMPANY PERSPECTIVES

The Sony Group is primarily focused on the Electronics (such as AV/IT products & components), Game (such as PlayStation), Entertainment (such as motion pictures and music), and Financial Services (such as insurance and banking) sectors. Not only do we represent a wide range of businesses, but we remain globally unique. Our aim is to fully leverage this uniqueness in aggressively carrying out our convergence strategy so that we can continue to emotionally touch and excite our customers.

However, as the Japanese economy grew stronger, demand for consumer goods increased. Morita and Ibuka abandoned the home-appliance market and, with injections of capital from Morita's father, concentrated on developing new electronic goods. Ibuka developed a tape recorder fashioned after a U.S. model he had seen at the Japan Broadcasting Corporation. Demand for the machine, which was introduced in 1950 and was the first Japanese tape recorder, remained low until Ibuka accidentally discovered a U.S. military booklet titled *Nine Hundred and Ninety-Nine Uses of the Tape Recorder.* Translated into Japanese, the booklet became an effective marketing tool. Once acquainted with its many uses, customers such as the Academy of Art in Tokyo purchased so many tape recorders that TTK was soon forced to move to a larger building in Shinagawa.

Norio Ohga, an opera student at the academy, wrote several letters to TTK criticizing the sound quality of its recorder. Impressed by the detail and constructive tone of the criticisms, Morita invited Ohga to participate in the development of a new recorder as a consultant. Ohga accepted, and subsequent models were vastly improved.

Constantly searching for new technological advances, Masaru Ibuka heard of a tiny new capacitor called a transistor in 1952. The transistor, developed by Bell Laboratories, could be used in place of larger, less-durable vacuum tubes. Western Electric purchased the technology in order to manufacture transistorized hearing aids. Ibuka acquired a patent license from Western Electric for $25,000 with the intention of developing a small tubeless radio.

TTK began mass production of transistor radios in 1955, only a few months after they were introduced by a small U.S. firm called Regency Electronics. The TTK radio was named Sony, from *sonus,* Latin for "sound."

The Sony radio had tremendous sales potential, not only in the limited Japanese market but also in the United States, where the economy was much stronger.

Traditionally, international sales by Japanese companies were conducted through trading houses such as Mitsui, Mitsubishi, and Sumitomo. Although these trading companies were well represented in the United States, Morita chose not to do business with them because they were unfamiliar with his company's products and did not share his business philosophy. Morita traveled to New York, where he met with representatives from several large retail firms. Morita refused an order from Bulova for 100,000 radios when that company required that each carry the Bulova name. Morita pledged that his company would not manufacture products for other companies and eventually secured a number of more modest orders that assured his company's growth at a measured pace. Another highlight of 1955 was the first listing of the company's stock on the over-the-counter market of the Tokyo Stock Exchange.

The rising popularity of the Sony name led Morita and Ibuka to change the name of their company to Sony Kabushiki Kaisha (Corporation) in January 1958. The following year Sony announced that it had developed a transistorized television, which was introduced in 1960. That same year, after a business dispute with Delmonico International, the company Morita had appointed to handle international sales, Sony established a trade office in New York City and another in Switzerland called Sony Overseas.

A subsidiary called Sony Chemicals was created in 1962 to produce adhesives and plastics to reduce the company's dependence on outside suppliers. In 1965 a joint venture with Tektronix was established to produce oscilloscopes in Japan.

During the early 1960s Sony engineers continued to introduce new, miniaturized products based on the transistor, including an AM/FM radio and a videotape recorder. By 1968 Sony engineers had developed new color-television technology. Using one electron gun, for more accurate beam alignment, and one lens, for better focus, the Sony Trinitron produced a clearer image than conventional three-gun, three-lens sets. In what has been described as its biggest gamble, Sony, confident that technology alone would create new markets, invested a large amount of capital in the Trinitron.

Also in 1968, Sony Overseas established a trading office in England and entered into a joint venture with CBS Inc. to produce phonograph records. The venture was under the direction of Ohga, the art student who had complained about Sony's early tape recorder, whom Morita had persuaded in 1959 to give up opera and join

---

KEY DATES

1946: Akio Monta and Masaru Ibuka found Tokyo Tsushin Kogyo Kabushiki Kaisha (TTK).

1950: TTK introduces the first Japanese tape recorder.

1955: TTK begins selling Japan's first transistor radio; company goes public.

1958: Company's name is changed to Sony Corporation.

1960: Sony introduces the world's first transistor television.

1968: Revolutionary Sony Trinitron color television debuts; Sony enters record business through a joint venture with CBS Inc.

1975: Company launches the Betamax VCR.

1979: Sony Walkman is introduced.

1982: Sony introduces the first CD player.

1985: Company introduces its first 8-millimeter video camera.

1987: CBS Records, and its Epic and Columbia labels, is acquired for $2 billion.

1989: Columbia Pictures is acquired for $3.4 billion.

1994: Sony PlayStation debuts.

1997: VAIO line of PCs for the home market is launched.

2000: PlayStation 2, featuring enhanced graphics, processing power, and DVD and broadband capabilities, is released.

2003: Howard Stringer is named vice chairman; Sony and Bertelsmann agree to merge their recorded music operations into a new joint venture named Sony BMG.

2004: Sony acquires the world's largest content library when it agrees to buy Metro-Goldwyn-Mayer (MGM) Inc. in a $4.85 billion deal.

2005: Stringer succeeds Nobuyuki Idei at the company's helm, becoming Sony's first foreign-born chairman and CEO.

2006: European Court of First Instance annuls the Sony-Bertelsmann merger.

2007: European Commission opens a new investigation into the 2004 Sony-Bertelsmann merger, and grants its final approval of the deal in October.

2008: In a deal worth $900 million, Sony agrees to buy Bertelsmann AG out of Sony BMG Music Entertainment, which is renamed Sony Music Entertainment Inc.

Sony. The company, called CBS/Sony, later became the largest record manufacturer in Japan. In 1970 Sony Overseas established a subsidiary in West Germany to handle sales in that country.

BETAMAX AND THE WALKMAN IN THE SEVENTIES

After a decade of experience in videotape technology, Sony introduced the U-matic three-quarter-inch videocassette recorder (VCR) in 1971. Intended for institutions such as television stations, the U-matic received an Emmy Award for engineering excellence from the National Academy of Television Arts and Sciences. In 1973, the year Sony Overseas created a French subsidiary, the academy honored the Trinitron series with another Emmy.

Sony developed its first VCR for the consumer market, the Betamax, in 1975. The following year The Walt Disney Company and Universal Pictures filed a lawsuit against Sony, complaining that the new machine would enable widespread copyright infringement of television programs. A judgment in favor of Sony in 1979 was reversed two years later. Litigation continued, but by the time the matter reached the U.S. Supreme Court the plaintiffs' original case had been severely undermined by the proliferation of VCRs, making any legal restriction on copying television programs for private use nearly impossible to enforce.

During the mid-1970s, competitors such as U.S.-based RCA and Zenith and Japanese-based Toshiba and Victor Company of Japan (JVC) effectively adopted and improved upon technologies developed by Sony. For the first time, Sony began to lose significant market share, often in lines that it had pioneered. Strong competition, however, was only one factor that caused Sony's sales growth to fall (after growing 166 percent between 1970 and 1974, it grew only 35 percent between 1974 and 1978).

Like many Sony officials, Akio Morita lacked formal management training. Instead, he relied on his personal persuasive skills and his unusual ability to anticipate or create markets for new products. In typical fashion, Sony introduced the Betamax VCR well before its competitors, in effect creating a market in which it would enjoy a short-term monopoly. At this stage, however, Morita failed to establish the Betamax format as the industry standard by inviting the participation of other companies.

Matsushita Electric (which owned half of JVC) developed a separate VCR format called VHS (video home system), which permitted as many as three additional hours of playing time on a tape, but which was incompatible with Sony's Betamax. When the VHS was introduced in 1977, Morita was reported to have felt betrayed that Sony's competitors did not adopt the Betamax format. He appealed to 81-year-old Konosuke Matsushita, in many ways a patriarch of Japanese industry, to discontinue the VHS format in favor of Betamax. When Matsushita refused, many believed it was because he felt insulted by Morita's failure to offer earlier collaboration. Matsushita launched a vigorous marketing campaign to convince customers and other manufacturers not only that VHS was superior, but that Betamax would soon be obsolete. The marketing war between Matsushita and Sony was neither constructive nor profitable; both companies were forced to lower prices so much that profits were greatly depressed. Although Betamax was generally considered a technically superior product, the VHS format grew in popularity and gradually displaced Betamax as a standard format. Despite its falling market share (from 13 percent in 1982 to 5 percent in 1987), Sony refused to introduce a VHS line until the late 1980s.

In 1979 Morita personally oversaw the development of a compact cassette tape player called the Walkman. Inspired by Ohga's desire to listen to music while walking, Morita ordered the development of a small, high-fidelity tape player to be paired with the small, lightweight headphones that were already under development. The entire program took only five months from start to finish, and the product's success is legendary. Walkman even became the generic term for similar devices produced by Sony's competitors.

CD PLAYER, VIDEO CAMERAS, CBS RECORDS, COLUMBIA PICTURES: THE EIGHTIES

During the 1970s, Masaru Ibuka, 12 years Morita's senior, gradually relinquished many of his duties to younger managers such as Ohga, who was named president of Sony in 1982. Ohga became president shortly after a corporate reorganization that split Sony into five operating groups (marketing and sales, manufacturing, service, engineering, and diversified operations). While not formally trained in business,

Ohga nonetheless understood that Sony was too dependent on an unstable consumer electronics market. In one of his first acts, he inaugurated the 50-50 program to increase sales in institutional markets from 15 to 50 percent by 1990.

During this time, Sony's research and development budget consumed approximately 9 percent of sales (Matsushita budgeted only 4 percent). Another groundbreaking result of Sony's commitment to research and development was a machine that used a laser to reproduce music recorded digitally on a small plastic disk. The compact disk (or CD) player, introduced by Sony in 1982, eliminated much of the noise common to conventional, analog phonograph records. Sony developed the CD in association with the Dutch electronics firm Philips, partly in an effort to ensure broad format standardization. Philips, which had developed the most advanced laser technology, was an ideal partner for Sony, which led in the pulse-code technology that made digital sound reproduction possible. Soon the CD format was adopted by competing manufacturers; by the mid-1990s it had virtually replaced phonograph systems as the recording medium of choice.

Early in the 1980s, Morita began ceding some of his duties to Sony's president, Ohga, the young opera student hired 30 years earlier to improve Sony's tape recorders. Under Ohga, Sony entered into a new acquisitions phase with the intent of protecting itself from the costly mistake it had made with Betamax. One example of the changes Ohga brought about was Sony's video camera, introduced in 1985. Lighter, less expensive, and more portable than VHS cameras, the camera used 8-millimeter videotape, and was incompatible with both Betamax and VHS machines. The key difference between this and earlier Sony products was that Sony developed the new 8-millimeter video format in conjunction with over 100 competitors. While the camera may have been incompatible with the older Betamax and VHS technologies, Sony ensured that it would be compatible with the next generation of video cameras. Within three years of its introduction, the camera captured over 50 percent of the European, 30 percent of the Japanese, and 20 percent of the North American markets.

In May 1984 Sony purchased Apple Computer's hard-disk-technology operations. As a result of this acquisition, Sony was able to control about 20 percent of the Japanese market for workstations, PCs used in business offices, thus helping to increase the proportion of its sales derived from institutional customers. Ohga also broke a decades-old tradition in 1984 when he established a division to manufacture and market electronics components for other companies. By 1988, fueled by strong sales of semiconductors (once manufactured only for Sony products), the components division had grown to represent about 11 percent of Sony's total sales.

Sony also sought to gain control of the software end of the electronics/entertainment industry. On November 29, 1985 the Sony Corporation of America, which operated several assembly plants in the United States, purchased the Digital Audio Disk Corporation from its affiliate CBS/Sony. Two years later, Sony purchased CBS Records for $2 billion. CBS Records, whose labels included Epic and Columbia, was during this time the largest producer of records and tapes in the world.

Sony had learned through its Betamax experience that a superior product alone would not ensure market dominance; had Sony been able to flood the market with exclusively Beta-formatted movies, the VCR battle might have turned out differently. Looking toward the future development of audio equipment, including digital audio tape, Sony bought the record manufacturer with an eye toward guaranteeing that the products it manufactured to play music would remain compatible with the medium used to record music. The acquisition marked less of a diversification for Sony than an evolution toward dominance in a specific market.

Sony sought further diversification in U.S. entertainment companies. In 1988, the company considered an acquisition of MGM/UA Communications Company, but decided the price was too high. Then in 1989 Sony made headlines around the world when it bought Columbia Pictures Entertainment, Inc., from Coca-Cola for $3.4 billion. Columbia provided Sony with an extensive film library and a strong U.S. distribution system. It also carried $1 billion in debt, which almost tripled Sony's short-term debt to around ¥8 billion. Industry analysts applauded the move; when a recession hit the film industry shortly after Sony's purchase, however, some began to question Sony's ability to deliver its traditionally strong profits.

PLAYSTATION AND PREPARING FOR THE NETWORKED FUTURE: THE NINETIES

Sony did deliver, however, posting record earnings in 1990 of ¥58.2 billion ($384 million), a 38.5 percent increase over 1989. In 1992, Columbia Pictures and its subsidiary TriStar jointly captured 20 percent of the U.S. market share, far above the shares held by competing studios. By this time the entertainment operation had been renamed Sony Pictures Entertainment, Inc. The complexities of operating a truly multinational

corporation, however, began taking their toll on Sony. Most of the world's largest economies (Europe, Japan, and the United States) were experiencing a slowdown in the early 1990s. This factor created what Sony called "an unprecedentedly challenging operating environment." Although sales in most of Sony's businesses increased in 1992, operating income dropped 44 percent to ¥166 billion ($1.2 billion). Net income increased slightly to ¥120 billion.

The ongoing appreciation of the yen against most major currencies had an even more adverse effect on Sony's bottom line in 1993: net income fell a dramatic 70 percent to ¥36 billion ($313 million) on sales of ¥3.99 trillion ($34.4 billion). Had the yen's value held steady at 1992 figures, Sony's net income would have totaled about ¥190 billion ($1.3 billion).

During that year, Ohga assumed the duties of chief executive in addition to his role as president. He and Morita responded to Sony's tough economic situation by bolstering marketing, reducing inventory levels, streamlining operations, and keeping a watchful control of capital investments. The company also embarked on an extensive reorganization effort with the goal of decentralizing operations and reducing unnecessary management. Despite these measures, Sony was unable to stem the slide. Net income plummeted another 50 percent in 1994 to ¥15 billion, on sales of ¥3.73 trillion.

By this time Morita had relinquished virtually all his duties in the company, having suffered a stroke in late 1993. In Sony's 1994 annual report, his picture and signature were conspicuously absent from the letter to shareholders, implicitly announcing Ohga's new leadership position. Under Morita's leadership, Sony's rise to preeminence in the world consumer electronics market was almost entirely self-achieved; Sony outperformed not only its Japanese rivals, among them associates of the former *zaibatsu* (conglomerate) companies, but also larger U.S. firms, which by 1995 had all but abandoned the consumer electronics market.

In the late 1980s Morita told *Business Week* that he regarded Sony Corporation as a "venture business" for the Morita family, which had produced several generations of mayors and whose primary business remained the 300-year-old Morita & Company. Under the direction of Akio Morita's younger brother Kuzuaki, Morita & Company produced sake, soy sauce, and Ninohimatsu brand rice wine in Nagoya. The company, whose initial $500 investment in TTK was worth $430 million in 1995, owned a 9.4 percent share of Sony.

In April 1995, Ohga ascended to the chairmanship of Sony, and Morita was made an honorary chairman. The company's new president was Nobuyuki Idei, a 34-

year veteran of the company, who had founded Sony's French subsidiary in 1970 and had since played a role in many of the company's major accomplishments, including audio CD technology, computer workstations, and the 8-millimeter video camcorder.

Sony's success had been a direct result of the wisdom of its founders, who had the talent to anticipate the demands of consumers and to develop products to meet those demands. Idei's presidency, some suggested, signaled a new era for the company.

Immediate among Idei's concerns were helping Sony become an integral player in the information highway industry. He also hoped to help the company establish an industry standard for DVDs, or digital videodisks, CD-like disks capable of holding full-length films for play on television screens via players. Once again, Sony had teamed up with Philips to develop a DVD format, but the partners quickly discovered they were facing a rival format developed by Toshiba and Time Warner. This rival format quickly gained the support of a number of the world's consumer electronics powerhouses. Rather than face a replay of the bloody battle between the Betamax and VHS formats, Sony and Philips in late 1995 agreed to support the DVD format developed by Toshiba and Time Warner. Sony subsequently introduced its first DVD player in March 1997.

Meanwhile, Sony unexpectedly entered the video-game market in the mid-1990s, making an immediate splash. The development of the Sony PlayStation had actually begun in the late 1980s as a joint project with game giant Nintendo Co. Ltd. Nintendo had agreed to help develop a new game console that would combine the graphic capabilities of a computer workstation with Sony's CD-ROM drive, but then pulled out of the project in 1992. Sony decided to develop the new machine solo, introducing the 32-bit PlayStation to the Japanese market in 1994 and the U.S. market one year later. It was an immediate and huge success, in part because of the hundreds of software titles that were quickly available for the console thanks to Sony's ability to entice top Japanese and U.S. developers to create games for the PlayStation. By 1998, the PlayStation had grabbed about 40 percent of the worldwide game market, and Sony's game unit, Sony Computer Entertainment, accounted for 10 percent of the company's worldwide revenue and an impressive 22.5 percent of its operating income.

PROBLEMS AT SONY PICTURES, SUCCESS WITH VAIO

Unfortunately, the mid-1990s were also marked by continued problems at Sony Pictures Entertainment.

Top management at the motion-picture arm spent hundreds of millions of dollars on a string of flops, such as *Last Action Hero* and *Geronimo*, in addition to spending lavishly on hiring, studio renovations, and other expenses. Sony ended up taking a $3.2 billion write-off, one of the largest ever by a Japanese company, related to the entertainment unit during the fiscal year ending in March 1995; consequently, the company posted a net loss for the year of $2.8 billion (on sales of $44.76 billion). A major management shakeup occurred as well.

As Sony attempted to turn around its motion-picture unit, in electronics the company surprised many observers by entering the crowded and low-margin PC business in 1997. That year, through a partnership with Intel, Sony began selling its VAIO line of PCs. Including both desktop and notebook models, the line received plaudits for its quality but got off to a slow start in the United States thanks to its above-average price tags. Sony designed the VAIO computers specifically for the home market, and they sported unique features that made them particularly well-suited to consumers who owned other Sony products. For example, software and ports were included to allow owners of Sony camcorders to transfer their home videos to the VAIO PC and to edit and manipulate the videos in a variety of ways. Sony also continued to stay on the cutting edge in the venerable television field, introducing its first flat-screen TV in 1996 and its first digital, high-definition model two years later. Also in 1998 came the launch of AIBO, a robot dog, which was touted as having the capability of expressing emotions and learning.

During 1999, a year that saw the passing of company cofounder Morita (the other founder, Ibuka, had died in 1997), Idei launched a sweeping reorganization to position the company for the future: in Sony's vision, "the network era of the 21st century." In March 1999 Sony announced that it planned to cut its workforce by 10 percent and its manufacturing capacity by one-third before 2003. The cutbacks were slated for areas where growth had been slowing: analog televisions, VCRs, and Walkmans. The company planned to increase the amount of resources committed to such hot areas as digital products and the PlayStation, as well as placing increased emphasis on developing software, hardware, and services for the new networks (home networks, broadband networks, wireless networks) that were beginning to emerge at the end of the 20th century. For Idei, the key for Sony was a historic shift in focus: Hardware had traditionally driven product development, but Idei instead wanted software development and services to drive hardware design.

A NEW MILLENNIUM BEGINS

Perhaps the first example of such an approach came with the 2000 introduction of the Sony PlayStation 2. Although it was a technical marvel featuring high-end 3-D graphics and more processing power than most desktop PCs, the 128-bit PlayStation 2 was much more than a souped-up version of the original. It was of course designed for game software but it was not just a game console, having been conceived as a home entertainment center. Its DVD drive not only played game software but also audio CDs and DVD movies. It had the capability of connecting to the Internet and as such could be used as a broadband device controlling an Internet-connected home network. Despite manufacturing difficulties that limited production during the first year, the PlayStation 2 had a stellar debut, with about nine million units sold in the first 12 months. The high costs associated with developing and manufacturing the machines, however, depressed profits at Sony for the 2001 fiscal year. Also in the wake of its debut came rival Sega's exit from the game console business in favor of concentrating on developing game titles for other companies' machines, including the PlayStation 2. Sony continued to face competition in the game field from Nintendo, which planned to release a new machine in the fall of 2001, and faced the prospect of a new competitor, Microsoft Corporation, which was also planning a fall 2001 release of its Xbox machine.

In June 2000 Idei was named chairman and CEO of Sony, while Kunitake Ando, who had headed the VAIO unit, was named president and COO. Rounding out the new management team was Teruhisa Tokunaka, a former head of the PlayStation unit, who was named deputy president and CFO. The new team faced a myriad of challenges in the rapidly changing high-tech world of the early 21st century. One example was in Sony's music business, which was being rocked by the industry-wide threat of the rampant and unauthorized downloading of digital music files over the Internet. Sony joined other music giants in suing Napster, the most obvious threat to their hegemony. The company also entered into a joint venture with Vivendi Universal S.A. to develop an online subscription service that would allow music downloads through what was called a "virtual jukebox." Such a service was part of a new push by Sony into broadband delivery of the audio and video material owned by its content arms.

ENTERTAINMENT FOCUS

Several major developments within Sony's semiconductor business soon followed. After announcing plans for a $936 million semiconductor fabrication plant in Japan's Kumamoto Technology Park #2 in late 2000, Sony revealed plans to spin off its three semiconductor businesses into one separate subsidiary early the following year.

It also was in early 2001 that Sony Pictures Entertainment sold its 50 percent interest in the Game Show Network in a $275 million deal with Liberty Digital Inc. In addition, Sony also established both Sony Semiconductor Kyushu Co. Ltd. and Sony EMC Corporation and agreed to merge its mobile phone unit with that of Ericsson, creating a new entity named Sony Ericsson Mobile Communications.

Developments continued in 2002. In conjunction with Liberty Media Corporation and a group of other investors, Sony Pictures Entertainment struck a $2.7 billion deal with NBC for the sale of its 24-hour Spanish-language network, Telemundo Communications Group Inc. Sony rounded out the year by establishing Aiwa Co. Ltd. as a wholly owned subsidiary, which it then merged into the larger organization.

Several leadership changes took place in 2003. Early in the year, Howard Stringer was named vice chairman. In addition, games division head Ken Kutaragi was named the company's executive deputy president, in addition to his role as president of Sony Computer Entertainment.

As Sony headed into the middle years of the decade, the company remained heavily focused on its entertainment business. In late 2003 Sony and Bertelsmann agreed to merge their recorded music operations into a new joint venture named Sony BMG that stood to challenge Universal Music as the world's leading recorded music business by market share. Another major development in 2003 occurred when Sony announced plans to trim approximately 20,000 jobs from its workforce by 2006. The eliminations were part of a restructuring effort aimed at readying Sony's technology and content for a wireless, broadband world. In that vein, a new online music service named Sony Connect was established the following year, offering consumers approximately 500,000 music tracks.

After it initially raised objections to the deal, the European Union ultimately approved the Sony-Bertelsmann merger in mid-2004. In September of that year, Sony acquired the world's largest content library when it agreed to buy Metro-Goldwyn-Mayer (MGM) Inc. for $4.85 billion, adding more than 7,600 titles to its library. Sony ended 2004 on a sour note when several independent music businesses filed a lawsuit to block the Sony-Bertelsmann merger.

LEADERSHIP CHANGES

A number of major leadership changes occurred in early 2005. Stringer succeeded Idei at the company's helm, becoming Sony's first foreign-born chairman and CEO. In addition, the company reduced the size of its board from 16 members to 12, and announced the departure of half its members. Other leadership changes occurred when President Ando was replaced by Ryoji Chubachi, who also was named CEO of the company's electronics business. Andrew House, a marketing vice president at Sony Computer Entertainment America, also was named to the newly created position of global chief marketing officer.

Progress continued in 2006. In April, Sony and Samsung Electronics revealed joint plans to build a massive $2 billion liquid crystal display (LCD) television panel factory. In September, Sony announced that it was investing $90 million to construct a new LCD television plant in Nitra, Slovakia, providing employment for approximately 3,000 people. A worldwide launch of the company's PlayStation 3 video-game console was slated for November. At that time, Kazuo Hirai succeeded Kutaragi as president and chief operating officer of Sony Computer Entertainment Inc. Kutaragi then became chairman and group CEO of the company's Sony Computer unit.

In early 2007, an initial public offering (IPO) was planned for Sony Financial Holdings, the company's banking and insurance business. In March, the European Commission began investigating the 2004 merger of Sony Music and BMG, which had been annulled by the European Court of First Instance in 2006 following the objection of independent music labels. Despite continued objections, the European Commission granted its final approval of the deal in October 2007.

Sony bade farewell to Kutaragi, inventor of the PlayStation video-game console, who retired in April and was named honorary chairman of Sony Computer Entertainment Inc. The company's focus on digital entertainment continued, leading to the formation of an in-game advertising unit at Sony Computer Electronics America in October. The following month, the private-equity firm Dubai International Capital acquired a substantial, undisclosed stake in Sony.

Progress continued at Sony during the closing years of the decade, especially in the company's entertainment business. In early 2008, Sony BMG Norte snapped up the Mexican management firm Westwood Entertainment. In April of that year, Sony Corporation of America agreed to acquire the Emeryville, California-based digital media products firm Gracenote in a $260 million deal. Later in the summer, a deal worth $900 million unfolded when Sony agreed to buy Bertelsmann AG out of Sony BMG Music Entertainment. Completed in October, the deal resulted in the renaming of Sony BMG Music Entertainment as Sony Music Entertainment Inc.

More leadership changes took place in 2009. In April of that year, Sony President Chubachi tendered his resignation and Chairman Stringer assumed the additional role of president. In September, Sony announced plans to realign its LCD manufacturing operations in the Americas via the formation of a strategic alliance with Taiwan-based Hon Hai Precision Industry.

PRINCIPAL SUBSIDIARIES

AVIC Group Corporation; C3D Corporation (USA); Califon Productions Inc. (USA); Columbia TriStar Home Entertainment Inc. (USA); CPE Holdings Inc. (USA); CPT Holdings Inc. (USA); Frontage Inc. (60%); Gracenote Inc. (USA); Jeopardy Productions Inc. (USA); LEP Holdings Inc. (USA); Lot Inc. (USA); PEP Communications (USA); Quadra Productions Inc. (USA); Screen Gems Inc. (USA); Shanghai Suoguang Electronics Co. Ltd. (China; 70%); Shanghai Suoguang Visual Products Co. Ltd. (China; 70%); S-LCD Holdings AB (Sweden); So-net Entertainment Corporation (45.6%); Sony (China) Ltd.; Sony Americas Holding Inc. (USA); Sony Australia Ltd.; Sony Bank Inc.; Sony Benelux B.V. (Netherlands); Sony Brasil Ltda (Brazil); Sony Broadcasting Media Corporation; Sony Capital Corporation (USA); Sony Casualty Insurance Co. Ltd.; Sony Chemical & Information Device Corporation; Sony Computer Devices (Huizhou) Co. Ltd. (China); Sony Computer Entertainment America Inc. (USA; 99.7%); Sony Computer Entertainment Europe Ltd. (U.K.; 99.7%); Sony Computer Entertainment Hong Kong Limited; Sony Computer Entertainment Inc. (99.7%); Sony Corporation of America (USA); Sony Corporation of Hong Kong Ltd.; Sony DADC Austria A.G.; Sony de Mexico S.A. de C.V.; Sony Device Technology (Thailand) Co. Ltd.; Sony Electronics Asia Pacific Pte Ltd. (Singapore); Sony Electronics Inc. (USA); Sony Electronics of Korea Corporation (South Korea); Sony EMCS (Malaysia) Sdn Bhd.; Sony EMCS Corporation; Sony Energy Device Corporation; Sony Enterprise Co. Ltd.; Sony Entertainment Inc. (USA); Sony Ericsson Mobile Communications A.B. (Sweden; 50%); Sony Espana S.A. (Spain); Sony Europe (Belgium) N.V.; Sony Europe Holding B.V. (Netherlands); Sony Film Holdings Inc. (USA); Sony Finance International Inc.; Sony Financial Holdings Inc. (60%); Sony France S.A.; Sony Global Solutions Inc.; Sony Global Treasury Service Plc (UK); Sony Global Treasury Services (Thailand) Co. Ltd.; Sony Gulf FZE (United Arab Emirates); Sony Holding (Asia) B.V. (Netherlands); Sony Hungaria kft (Hungary); Sony India Pvt. Ltd.; Sony Inter-American S.A. (Panama);

Sony International (Hong Kong) Ltd.; Sony Italia S.p.A. (Italy); Sony Korea Corporation (South Korea); Sony Latin America Inc. (USA); Sony Life Insurance Co. Ltd.; Sony Manufacturing Systems Corporation; Sony Marketing Co. Ltd.; Sony Mobile Display Corporation; Sony Mobile Electronics (Singapore) Pte. Ltd.; Sony Music Communications Inc.; Sony Music Distribution (Japan) Inc.; Sony Music Entertainment (Japan) Inc.; Sony Music Entertainment (USA); Sony Music Entertainment B.V. (Netherlands); Sony Music Holdings Inc. (USA); Sony Music Manufacturing Inc.; Sony Music Manufacturing Inc.; Sony Nordic A/S (Denmark); Sony of Canada Ltd.; Sony Optiarc Inc. (99%); Sony Overseas S.A. (Switzerland); Sony Pictures Animation Inc. (USA); Sony Pictures Cable Ventures Inc. (USA); Sony Pictures Digital Production Inc. (USA); Sony Pictures Entertainment Inc. (USA); Sony Pictures Home Entertainment Inc. (USA); Sony Pictures Releasing Corporation (USA); Sony Pictures Releasing International Corporation (USA); Sony Pictures Television Inc. (USA); Sony Precision Devices (Huizhou) Co. Ltd. (China); Sony Semiconductor Kyushu Co. Ltd.; Sony Slovakia Spol. s.r.o.; Sony Supply Chain Solutions (Korea) Co. Ltd. (South Korea); Sony Supply Chain Solutions (Malaysia) Sdn Bhd.; Sony Supply Chain Solutions Inc.; Sony Taiwan Limited; Sony Technology (Thailand) Co. Ltd.; Sony Thai Company Ltd. (Thailand); Sony U.S. Funding Corporation (USA); Sony United Kingdom Ltd.; SPE Corporate Services Inc. (USA); ST. LCD Co. Ltd. (50%); Tandem Licensing Corporation (USA); TriStar Pictures Inc. (USA); TriStar Television Inc. (USA); Worldwide SPE Acquisitions Inc. (USA); ZAO Sony Electronics (Russia).

Maura Troester
Updated, David E. Salamie; Paul R. Greenland

PRINCIPAL COMPETITORS

Panasonic Corporation; Royal Philips Electronics N.V.; SANYO Electric Co. Ltd.

FURTHER READING

Armstrong, Larry, Christopher Power, and G. David Wallace, "Sony's Challenge," *Business Week*, June 1, 1987, pp. 64+.

Browning, E. S., "Japan's Sony, Famous for Consumer Electronics, Decides That the Future Lies in Sales to Business," *Wall Street Journal*, October 9, 1984.

Bruii, Steven V., Neil Gross, and Robert D. Hof, "Sony's New World," *Business Week*, May 27, 1996, pp. 100+.

Carvell, Tim, "How Sony Created a Monster," *Fortune*, June 8, 1998, pp. 162+.

Cieply, Michael, "Sony's Profitless Prosperity," *Forbes*, October 24, 1983, pp. 128+.

Fildes, Nic, "Outcry as EC Greenlights Sony BMG Merger," *Independent*, October 4, 2007.

Fulford, Benjamin, "Godzilla Needs Batteries: Sony, Japan's Most Famous Company, Is in a Slump," *Forbes*, September 18, 2000, p. 66.

Gross, Neil, and William J. Holstein, "Why Sony Is Plugging into Columbia," *Business Week*, October 16, 1989, pp. 56+.

Kunii, Irene M., and Ron Grover, "Sony Slides into a Slump," *Business Week*, June 5, 2000, p. 68.

Kunii, Irene M., Emily Thornton, and Janet Rae-Dupree, "Sony's Shakeup," *Business Week*, March 22, 1999, pp. 52–53.

Kunii, Irene M., et al., "The Games Sony Plays," *Business Week*, June 15, 1998, pp. 128–30.

Landro, Laura, Yumiko Ono, and Elisabeth Rubinfein, "A Changing Sony Aims to Own the 'Software' That Its Products Need," *Wall Street Journal*, December 30, 1988, p. 1.

Lubove, Seth, and Neil Weinberg, "Creating a Seamless Company," *Forbes*, December 20, 1993, p. 152.

Lyons, Nick, *The Sony Vision*, New York: Crown, 1976.

"Media Colossus: Sony Is Out to Be the World's One-Stop Shop for Entertainment," *Business Week*, March 25, 1991, p. 64.

Monta, Akio, *From a 500-Dollar Company to a Global Corporation: The Growth of Sony*, Pittsburgh: Carnegie-Mellon University Press, 1985, 41 p.

———, *Made in Japan: Akio Monta and Sony*, New York: Dutton, 1986, 309 p.

———, "When Sony Was an Up-and-Comer," *Forbes*, October 6, 1986, pp. 98+.

Morris, Kathleen, "Lonesome Samurai: Under Major Pressure on a Number of Fronts, Sony Goes It Alone as Usual," *Financial World*, May 23, 1995, pp. 26–29.

Nathan, John, *Sony: The Private Life*, Boston: Houghton Mifflin, 1999, 347 p.

Palmer, Jay, "Back in the Game," *Barron's*, April 15, 1996, pp. 31–35.

Schlender, Brent, "Sony on the Brink," *Fortune*, June 12, 1995, pp. 60+.

———, "Sony Plays to Win," *Fortune*, May 1, 2000, pp. 143–46+.

———, "Sony's New President: Here's the Plan," *Fortune*, April 17, 1995, pp. 18–19.

Siklos, Richard, Ronald Grover, and Irene M. Kunii, "Does Sony Really Need a Partner?" *Business Week*, October 11, 1999, pp. 118–19.

Smith, Ethan, "Sony to Take Over Music Partnership: Firm Raises Its Bet on Ailing Industry; Bertelsmann Exits," *Wall Street Journal Europe*, August 6, 2008.

Smith, Lee, "Sony Battles Back," *Fortune*, April 15, 1985, pp. 26+.

"Sony: A Diversification Plan Tuned to the People Factor," *Business Week*, February 9, 1981, p. 88.

"Sony Amasses World's Largest Media Library," *Online Reporter*, September 18, 2004.

"Sony-BMG Music Merger Clears Hurdle," *Online Reporter*, June 26, 2004.

"Sony Buys Gracenote," *Online Reporter*, April 26, 2008.

"Sony Completes Acquisition of Bertelsmann's 50% Stake in Sony BMG," *Japan Consumer Electronics Scan*, October 6, 2008.

"Sony Corporation," *Notable Corporate Chronologies*, Online Ed., Farmington Hills, MI: Thomson Gale, 2007.

"Sony Music and BMG Plan to Join Music Units in a 50-50 Venture," *Brandweek*, November 10, 2003.

"Sony Names Stringer First Foreign CEO," *PC Magazine Online*, March 7, 2005.

"Sony President Chubachi to Step Down in April," *Kyodo News International*, February 27, 2009.

"Sony's 'Father of PlayStation' to Retire," *InformationWeek*, April 26, 2007.

"Sony's Game Unit Names Hirai President, Kutaragi Chairman," *Europe Intelligence Wire*, November 30, 2006.

State Grid Corporation of China

86 Xichang'an Ave.
Beijing, 100031
China
Telephone: (+86 10) 6659 7221
Fax: (+86 10) 6659 7224
Web site: http://www.sgcc.com.cn

State-Owned Company
Incorporated: 2002
Employees: 728,000
Operating Revenues: $164.13 billion (2008)
NAICS: 221122 Electric Power Distribution

■ ■ ■

With 2008 revenues of more than $164 billion, State Grid Corporation of China (SGCC) ranks as the largest utility company in the world, the third largest company in China, and the 15th largest company on the *Fortune Global 500*. SGCC was formed in 2002 as part of the restructuring of China's electrical power generation industry. As such, SGCC was established in order to oversee approximately 80 percent of China's vast power grid network. The company operates through five regional power grid companies located in China's east, central, north, northeast, and northwest regions. SGCC also operates the power grid in Tibet. Altogether, SGCC oversees more than 250,000 kilometers of power transmission lines. SGCC is responsible for expanding China's power transmission network in order to meet the country's surging demand for electrical power.

To this end, the company has been investing on a massive scale, particularly focusing on developing its network of ultra-high-voltage transmission lines. The company has pledged to spend up to $170 billion in the years 2009 and 2010. This, however, will pale in comparison to funding needed for the construction of the company's proposed "smart grid," incorporating digital technology, two-way communication and other advanced features to automate power transmission requirements. The deployment of a smart grid may cost State Grid as much as CNY 4 trillion ($585 billion). SGCC remains a state-owned company wholly controlled by the Chinese government, and led by CEO and President Liu Zhenya.

BUILDING AN ELECTRIC POWER INFRASTRUCTURE FROM THE 19TH CENTURY

The earliest power plant to be built in China appeared in Shanghai in 1882. Constructed and operated by U.S. interests, the power plant generated just 654 kilowatts. The power plant nonetheless set the tone for the early period of China's electrical power infrastructure development. The next decades witnessed the construction of many more power plants. Like the Shanghai plant, these tended to be small, and located along the Chinese coast. They were also largely built and operated by foreign interests. Among the early players in the Chinese market were such U.S. electrical giants as Westinghouse and General Electric.

Increases in power generation technology into the early decades of the 20th century nonetheless permitted

power plants to develop higher capacity levels. In 1913,
for example, a British company built a new coal-fired
power plant in Shanghai. That plant was sold to U.S.
Electric Bond and Share Corporation in 1927, and
renamed Shanghai Power Company. With a total capacity of more than 16 megawatts, this plant became the
largest in the Asian region at the time.

By the late 1930s, China boasted more than 460
power plants and a total power generation capacity of
630 megawatts. Foreign ownership remained the
hallmark of the Chinese power grid, with more than 95
percent of power plants owned by foreign interests.
These included U.S., British, German, and French
interests, and, especially in the 1920s and 1930s,
Japanese interests. By the outbreak of World War II,
nearly 60 percent of China's power plants had been
built by or owned by Japanese interests.

NATIONAL POWER GRID FROM 1949

Under Japanese domination, China's power grid
continued to expand through the late 1930s and even
through World War II. By the end of the war, the
country's total power capacity had climbed as high as
1.85 gigawatts, for a total output of more than 4.3 billion kilowatt hours (kWh) per year. This, however,
compared to the more than 64 gigawatts of installed
capacity and more than 269 billion kWh output in the
United States at the time.

The arrival of the Communist government under
Mao Zedong and the establishment of the People's
Republic of China in 1949 brought the country's entire
power generation network under Chinese control for the
first time. Electrical power became a crucial and central
element of the Communist government's plans for the
country's industrial and economic development. The
Chinese government adopted policies inspired by
Vladimir Lenin's famed equation of "Communism
equals Soviet power plus electrification."

Self-sufficiency became the Chinese government's
watchword, as it nationalized the country's existing
power generation infrastructure and laid the framework

for its future development. During the first Five-Year
Plan of 1953, the Chinese government initially set out
to build a highly centralized power grid inspired by that
constructed in the Soviet Union. The country launched
construction of a number of large-scale power plant
projects during this period. While the Soviet Union
provided the Chinese with technological expertise and
assistance, the Chinese government insisted that the
country's power plants be designed and built by its own
engineers. In addition, China's own industrial and
manufacturing sectors provided the new plants with
their controls and equipment.

"TWO-LEGS" STRATEGY IN THE SIXTIES

China broke off relations with the Soviet Union toward
the end of the 1950s, however. This led to the first of
many about-face changes in the country's power grid
development programs. China adopted its so-called
walking on two legs strategy of expanding the country's
power generation capacity.

The first leg of the new strategy involved a continuation of the existing model of building large-scale,
modernized power plants to serve the country's cities
and large urban areas. These large-scale projects also
provided the Chinese government with no small amount
of propaganda, as the country sought to prove that its
engineering and technological expertise rivaled that of
both the Soviets and the Western nations. Most of these
large-scale plants were based, however, on the use of
coal, a readily abundant resource in China. In fact, the
construction of the country's network of large-scale
power plants paralleled the huge investments behind its
"Third Front" coal industry expansion program in the
1960s and 1970s.

While this first leg provided a viable means of
meeting the growing energy demand in the country's
major urban centers, the Chinese government was still
faced with supplying electrical power to its vast inland
and rural populations. Toward this end, the government
adopted its second development leg, which involved the
decentralized construction of a vast army of small-scale
power plants.

The decentralized leg, launched during the Great
Leap Forward from 1958 to 1960, at first emphasized
the construction of a series of small hydroelectric power
plants in order to harness rural China's vast hydropower
potential. This policy was reversed, however, during the
devastating years of the Cultural Revolution, when the
Chinese government instead chose to transmit surplus
electrical power from the urban centers to the rural
regions. This led to the construction of the country's

```
┌─────────────────────────────────────────┐
│                                           │
│              KEY DATES                    │
│                  ──■──                     │
│                                           │
│  1987:  Chinese government establishes the Ministry │
│         of Electric Power (MOEP) to oversee the │
│         country's power generation and transmission │
│         infrastructure.                   │
│  1997:  As part of restructuring of the electric power │
│         industry, the MOEP is converted to the State │
│         Power Corporation of China (SPCC). │
│  2002:  SPCC is broken up and State Grid Corpora- │
│         tion of China (SGCC) is created to oversee │
│         development of most of the country's power │
│         transmission grid.                │
│  2005:  SGCC begins construction of new ultra-high- │
│         voltage transmission lines.       │
│  2009:  SGCC announces plans to incorporate smart │
│         grid technology into its power transmission │
│         grid.                             │
│                                           │
└─────────────────────────────────────────┘
```

first long-range transmission lines and the first steps toward the development of a national power grid.

RESTRUCTURING IN THE EIGHTIES

Through the 1970s, however, the government reversed course again, promoting a higher degree of self-reliance in the rural provinces. Local and regional governments were expected to carry out their own power plant infrastructure development, albeit with some funding and technical assistance from the state. On the whole, however, the decentralized policy permitted the expansion of the country's power generating capacity while reducing the financial burden on the central government. By insisting on local self-reliance, the decentralized leg also helped reinforce local industrial development as well.

This policy led to a surge in new power plant construction, particularly during the period from 1970 to 1971 when the country more than doubled the number of hydroelectric plants in operation. Emphasis on hydroelectric power, at least in the rural provinces, played a key role in bringing electricity to outlying areas where building a power transmission infrastructure was impractical. By the late 1980s, China boasted more than 63,000 small hydropower plants. Together with a growing number of small coal-fired plants, as well as a limited number of plants using other fuels, such as diesel, these smaller power plants accounted for more than 20 percent of the rural regions' power supply.

The country's two-legged approach had permitted the country to extend electrical power to nearly all of China. However, the reliance on development at a local or at best regional level, meant that the country lacked a truly nationally operating power grid. Even where power grids had been put into place on a regional level, they often lacked connectivity among them. The lack of connectivity and inefficiency of the system became a major obstacle to China's development, as demand for electricity surged during the 1980s and 1990s.

The launch of China's economic reforms in the late 1970s also sparked the first steps toward a restructuring of its energy sector. Until this point, the country's power generation and transmission infrastructure had been governed by the Ministry of Water Resources and Electricity. However, the often contradictory interests between the electric power generation and water resources elements of the ministry had led to a great deal of inner conflict. Through the early 1980s, several efforts were taken to restructure the ministry, which remained one of the most powerful in the country. At last, in 1987, the Chinese government succeeded in hiving off the country's electric power infrastructure into a separate ministry, the Ministry of Electric Power (MOEP).

CREATING SGCC IN 2002

The MOEP established a new structure for China's electric power industry. The country's provinces established monopoly control over their own power generation and transmission operations. This policy fell into place with the Chinese government's overall aim of reducing the influence of the central state government while transferring control of business and industrial interests to the country's provincial governments.

The next step toward the restructuring of China's power industry came in 1995 and the passage of a new Electricity Law. The new legislation established a policy of removing the country's power generation industries from government control to the private sector. This led to the creation of the State Power Corporation of China (SPCC) in 1997, operated as a state-owned company under the control of former premier, and former MOEP head, Li Peng.

SPCC made a brief attempt to introduce a competitive energy market at the end of the 1990s. In 1999, the corporation ran a limited experiment, selecting six provinces that were to operate competitive power pools. That effort quickly failed amid a new surge in electric power demand, and the reluctance of SPCC to relinquish its own monopolistic control over the country's power market.

This failure, however, convinced the Chinese government of the need to carry out a full-scale reform of the Chinese electric power sector. In 2002, SPCC was broken up into three separate components. This led to the creation of five power generation companies, which operated largely on a regional basis. The operation of the country's power grid and transmission facilities were split into two power grid operators, State Power Grid Corporation (later State Grid Corporation of China, of SGCC) and Southern Power Grid Corporation. Oversight of the industry was given to an independent regulator, the State Electricity Regulatory Commission (SERC).

SGCC became the larger of the two power grid companies, taking over the operations of 80 percent of the country's total power grid network. SGCC put into place an organizational structure based on five regional power grid subsidiaries covering provinces in the east, central, north, northeast, and northwest regions of China, as well as the power grid in Tibet.

TRANSMISSION LINE EXPANSION FROM 2005

Among SGCC's imperatives was resolving the chronic power shortages that continued to affect much of China into the new century. While per-capita consumption in the country remained many times lower than in the West, the country's total energy consumption had outpaced even the United States, which had led the world in energy consumption for most of the 20th century. However, SGCC inherited a vast network, nearly 1.2 million kilometers, of largely outdated transmission lines. Only about 200,000 kilometers of the company's transmission network were capable of carrying loads greater than 220 kilovolts (kV).

SGCC immediately launched a massive investment program in upgrading and expanding its power grid. Starting in 2005, the company focused particularly on building a new network of ultra-high-voltage transmission lines. Ultra-high-voltage lines provided transmission capacity generally from 500 kV to 750 kV. In 2005, however, the company launched construction of a 618-kilometer 1,000 kV line to Shanghai.

Through the second half of the decade, SGCC's transmission line construction program included nearly 100,000 kilometers of new transmission lines. Even so, SGCC's operations barely kept ahead of the continuing surge in demand for electrical power. The company therefore moved to step up the expansion of its power grid. At the end of 2008, the company announced that it would double its proposed investment program, promising to spend as much as CNY 1.16 trillion ($170 billion) before the end of 2010.

SGCC was also eyeing expansion into other areas. In 2008, the company began working with automakers, including General Motors, to build a national network of charging stations for electric vehicles. In another direction, the company entered the power equipment manufacturing sector, buying Henan Pinggao Electric Co. and XI Group Corporation in 2009. Also that year, SGCC established subsidiary State Grid Xin Yuan Co., Ltd., which launched development of a vast wind and solar energy generation and storage complex in Hebei Province.

SMART GRID PLANS

SGCC, the third-largest corporation in China and the single-largest utility company in the world, made a first move into the international market in 2009, as well. In March of that year, the company joined a consortium with two Filipino companies that successfully bid for the 25-year concession to operate that country's power grid.

Back at home, in the meantime, SGCC increasingly turned its attention toward the future development of a so-called smart grid. The new-generation power infrastructure, in development by General Electric and others, proposed to incorporate digital technology and advanced communication features in order to maintain a more efficient power transmission network. SGCC announced its intention to invest heavily in the new technology, with some reports suggesting that the company prepare to spend as much as CNY 4 trillion ($585 billion) on the deployment of a smart grid. SGCC had become the backbone of China's effort to develop its electrical power generation infrastructure in the new century.

M. L. Cohen

PRINCIPAL SUBSIDIARIES

Central China Grid Co. Ltd.; China Anneng Construction Corp.; China Electric Power Technology Import & Export Corp.; China Electric Research Institute; China Power Finance Co.; East China Grid Co. Ltd.; North China Grid Company Ltd.; Northeast China Grid Co. Ltd.; Northwest China Grid Co. Ltd.; Yingda International Trust and Investment Co. Ltd.; Zhengxing Power Industrial and Commercial Development Company.

PRINCIPAL DIVISIONS

Regional Power Grid Companies; Scientific Research Institutes.

PRINCIPAL COMPETITORS

China Southern Power Grid Company Ltd.; Alstom (China) Investment Company Ltd.; China Shenhua Energy Company Ltd.; Huaneng Power International Inc.; Zhangjiakou Power Plant.

FURTHER READING

"China's New Installed Power Gen Capacity in HI Hits 27.51 Mln KW," *AsiaPulse News*, July 22, 2009.

"China State Grid to Add Investments in Nanjing," *SinoCast Daily Business Beat*, July 27, 2009.

"China State Power Company to Run Philippines' Network," *China Law & Practice*, March 2009.

"China to Invest $170bn in Grid over Next Two Years," *Power Engineering International*, December 2008, p. 10.

"China to Step Up Building of Smart Electricity Grid," *AsiaPulse News*, July 15, 2009.

"Coalbed Gas-Fired Power Capacity Triples in SGCC Area," *Reuters*, September 8, 2009.

"Electric Giants Eye Future Prosperity of Smart Grid in China," *AsiaPulse News*, July 20, 2009.

Fu Chenghao, "China Gets Smart on Power Supply," *China People's Daily*, June 1, 2009.

"Power to the People," *Economist*, February 11, 2006, p. 42US.

"State Grid Corporation Sets Targets for Development over Next Five Years," *China Business News*, January 6, 2006.

"State Grid Corporation Signs Agreements with Three Regions on Future Development," *China Business News*, May 10, 2006.

"State Grid Corporation to Focus on Extra High Voltage Power Grids in 2005," *China Business News*, January 24, 2005.

"State Grid Earns $109.49 Billion in 2006," *China Business News*, January 16, 2007.

"State Grid Enters Power Transmission & Transformation Sector," *SinoCast Daily Business Beat*, July 22, 2009.

"State Grid Transfers Huaxia Shares to Asset Management Arm," *Xinhua Economic News*, September 25, 2009.

"State Grid Xin Yuan to Spend CNY 10bn Building Energy Base," *SinoCast Daily Business Beat*, July 21, 2009.

"State Power Grid Corporation to Invest More Than $100 Bln in Grid Construction," *China Business News*, September 1, 2005.

Yang, Jing, "China's Wind Farms Bring Coal Plants," *Wall Street Journal*, September 29, 2009.

Yeh, Emily T., and Joanna I. Lewis, "State Power and the Logic of Reform in China's Electricity Sector," *Pacific Affairs*, Fall 2004, p. 437.

Telefónica S.A.

Gran Via 28-3a
Madrid, E-28013
Spain
Telephone: (+34 91) 584 09 20
Fax: (+34 91) 531 99 75
Web site: http://www.telefonica.com

Public Company
Incorporated: 1924 as Compania Telefónica Nacional de España S.A.
Employees: 257,035
Sales: EUR 57.95 billion ($75 billion) (2008)
Stock Exchanges: Madrid New York
Ticker Symbol: TEF
NAICS: 517212 Cellular and Other Wireless Telecommunications; 517110 Wired Telecommunications Carriers

■ ■ ■

Telefónica S.A. is one of the world's largest telecommunications companies, ranking number three behind China Mobile and Vodafone. The former Spanish telephone monopoly has expanded beyond its home market to become the dominant telecommunications provider in Spain and Latin America, and a major force in the United Kingdom, Germany, the Czech Republic, Ireland, and Slovakia. Altogether, Telefónica operates in 25 countries, serving more than 260 million customers. Telefónica is led by Chairman César Alierta.

EARLY HISTORY

Compania Telefónica Nacional de España S.A. (CTNE), as it was officially called until 1988, was founded in Madrid on April 19, 1924. Until then, the Spanish telephone service had been a muddle, supplied since its inception in 1877 by private individuals and small French and Spanish companies holding government concessions.

These companies operated incompatible and inefficient manual systems under severe government restrictions, paying heavy royalties to the state. In the first decade of the 20th century, Barcelona, with 3,000 telephones, possessed the largest of such systems. Successive royal decrees from 1882 onward had failed to bring order out of the chaos created by these concession holders, so the Spanish government decided that the responsibility for Spain's telephones should be entrusted to a single body.

On August 25, 1924, the government was empowered by another royal decree to sign a contract with the new Compañia Telefónica Nacional de España, conferring upon it the monopoly for operating the national telephone service. CTNE's task was to acquire the telephone operations and premises belonging to the existing private companies, or those that had reverted to the state, and to organize, integrate, develop, and modernize Spain's urban and trunk telephone networks. One condition of the contract was that at least 80 percent of CTNE's employees must be Spanish nationals.

CTNE came into being as a result of a takeover by the International Telephone & Telegraph Corporation

We want to improve people's lives, foster business growth and contribute to progress in the communities where we operate by providing innovative services based on information and communication technologies.

(ITT) of one of the existing Spanish telephone companies, created in 1899. The brothers Sosthenes and Hernand Behn, who had previously operated telephone companies in Puerto Rico and Cuba, set up ITT in 1920 as a U.S. holding company for their current and future enterprises. The companies were destined to become an international telephone system with corporate headquarters in New York.

When in 1924 Spain was chosen for ITT's entry into Europe, local investors came forward, influential Spaniards were invited to serve on the board of the new subsidiary, and the goodwill of Miguel Primo de Rivera's authoritarian government was secured. As a private-sector company providing a public service, CTNE would be subject to tensions between national- and shareholder-oriented strategies.

BUILDING A NETWORK INTO THE CIVIL WAR

In CTNE's early years, its efforts were concentrated on the arduous task of extending and improving the existing telephone service. It was operating in a largely agricultural, undercapitalized economy, and its geographical context was a vast mountainous central region, sparsely populated and difficult to access, bordered by coastal strips and plains containing most of the population. Prosperity varied sharply between regions and classes. The political background was unstable and would eventually erupt into the Spanish Civil War.

The new company set to work briskly in September 1924 and by the end of 1925 had 1,135 exchanges and "centers," nearly twice as many as it originally had. Some that were very small were operated by a family or individual, and some village centers consisted of a single pay phone in a private house. In 1925, CTNE's first underground cable was laid in the Escorial Palace near Madrid, and the site of the company's imposing headquarters in Madrid's Gran Via was purchased.

In 1926, new manual exchanges were built in 48 cities, and in 37 other cities existing exchanges were

refurbished. When King Alfonso XIII opened the new Spanish intercity telephone network in December, its 3,800-kilometer circuit constituted a European long-distance telephone record. By then, the number of manual exchanges in operation had risen to 1,397.

In 1926, the company's long-term drive toward the full automation of Spain's telephone system was underway. The automation process, which had actually begun just before CTNE's time, in 1923 (with an automatic exchange in Balaguer), would be finally completed in 1988. Between 1926 and 1929, automated rotary switching systems were installed first in San Sebastián and then in 19 other city exchanges.

NATIONALIZED BY FRANCO IN 1945

In 1928, Madrid had acquired its first prepaid call token-operated telephones. In the same year, telephone communication had been established between Spain and Cuba, and the telephone link was made with Argentina and Uruguay in 1929. In 1930, the two main islands of the Canaries, Tenerife and Gran Canaria, were telephonically linked by underwater cable, while the next year a radiotelephone service was established between the Canaries and the Iberian Peninsula. Mallorca's telephone link with the mainland was also established in 1931.

Between 1936 and the early 1950s, CTNE's development suffered severely, first from the upheaval and destruction of the civil war and then from Spain's political and economic isolation, both during World War II and after the defeat of the Axis powers, which had been favored by the government of General Francisco Franco. Until 1945, most of CTNE's capital was held by ITT.

At that point, Franco's government (1939–75) nationalized the company, taking over its stock from ITT and retaining 41 percent of the share capital, the rest going to more than 700,000 shareholders. In 1946, the state renewed CTNE's contract. The company kept its monopoly over all civil domestic telephone services in Spain and was obligated to develop and extend them according to certain state requirements.

EXPANSION AND MODERNIZATION: LATE FORTIES THROUGH SEVENTIES

Under the chairmanship, from 1945 to 1956, of José Navarro Reverter y Gomis, Compania Telefónica expanded its facilities and continued the modernization of its equipment. In 1952, Madrid and Barcelona saw their first in-city radio car phones. The next year the

KEY DATES
■

1924: Compania Telefónica Nacional de España S.A. (CTNE) is established.

1964: CTNE inaugurates Spain's first experimental earth station.

1985: CTNE becomes the first Spanish company to list on the London Stock Exchange.

1988: Spain passes telecommunications law; company's telephone service becomes fully automated.

1990: Firm acquires a stake in Telefónica de Argentina.

1994: Company begins to reorganize in preparation for deregulation.

1998: Telefónica S.A. is formed to act as a parent company; basic telephony in Spain is deregulated.

1999: Domestic telecommunications business is transferred to a subsidiary, which adopts the name Telefónica de España.

2000: Telefónica completes Operation Verónica, gaining control of its four major Latin American operations; Terra Networks S.A. merges with Lycos Inc.

2003: Telefónica acquires BellSouth's Latin American operations, adding 10 million customers.

2005: Telefónica pays $31 billion for O2 Plc; company extends the O2 brand to the Czech and Slovak markets.

2007: Telefónica becomes the largest shareholder in Telecom Italia.

2009: Telefónica and China Unicom strengthen their strategic alliance; Telefónica launches informal offer for T-Mobile UK.

company installed its first pulse code modulation radiolink, between Madrid and the Escurial. In 1955 it connected its millionth telephone, making Spain one of the most advanced telephone markets in the world at the time. In 1957, a coaxial cable carrying 432 telephone circuits went into service, linking Madrid, Saragossa, and Barcelona, and the following year it became possible for Spaniards to telephone to ships at sea and planes in flight.

From the early 1960s until the first oil crisis in 1973, Spain and CTNE enjoyed the *años de desarrollo*,

or years of development. During most of this period, in which the national standard of living rose, Telefónica was headed by Antonio Barrera.

TOTAL AUTOMATION IN THE SEVENTIES

In 1964, CTNE inaugurated Spain's first experimental earth station, designed to work in conjunction with international communication satellites Relay and Telstar. This was followed by other such ventures, notably in 1970 the company's earth station at Buitrago, to be used for telephone communication, data transmission, telegraphy, and black-and-white and color television, via the INTELSAT (International Organization for Telecommunications via Satellites) satellites, or a combination of satellite and submarine cable.

The goal of total automation was close to being accomplished. Automatic trunk dialing was introduced in 1960, and international trunk dialing appeared in 1972. In July 1971, a telephone service to the former Soviet Union was established, routed manually via Paris, and later the same year the company opened Europe's first dedicated public packet-switched data transmission network. Toward the end of 1978, the first computer-controlled electromagnetic network exchange was installed in Madrid.

In 1980, the first digital exchange systems were installed, and in the early 1990s, the digitalization of lines and exchanges continued to advance rapidly. By 1985, Telefónica was providing a network for the transmission of national and international television.

CHANGES IN THE TELECOMMUNICATIONS INDUSTRY DURING THE EIGHTIES

As the range of products and services grew and competition increased, there was a tendency for European countries to deregulate their telecommunications industries. Spain began planning to depart from its protectionist tradition at the end of the 1950s.

Events contributing to this liberalizing tendency and paving the way for a more outward looking policy for Compania Telefónica included the election of the first socialist government in 1982, the entry of Spain into the European Economic Community (EEC, later EC) in 1986, the 1987 EEC Green Paper proposing the deregulation of the newer parts of the European telecommunications market, and Spain's 1988 telecommunications law, the Ley de Ordenación de las Telecomunicaciones (LOT). The LOT implemented some of the EEC proposals, but the Spanish government contested some of the Green Paper's provisions, being particularly reluctant to see inroads made on its revenue from data transmission services.

At the end of 1982, the new Socialist government brought in the energetic Luis Solana as president of the Telefónica board. His objectives were to float the company on world markets, reduce the formidable backlog of telephone customers waiting to be connected, and make the company profitable after the recession of the late 1970s and early 1980s.

In 1983, net profits were up 11 percent over the previous year, and by 1985 Solana could claim that Telefónica was recovering. By adopting a four-year purchasing plan aimed at procuring over 90 percent of hardware from Spanish suppliers, he helped save jobs in Telefónica's subsidiaries. He announced various projects for research and development and promotion of exports, as well as for cooperative agreements and joint ventures, Spanish and international, involving both industrial production and technology transfers.

In June 1985 Compania Telefónica became the first Spanish company to be listed on the London Stock Exchange. In the previous 20 years it had increased the number of telephone lines in service more than sixfold and the telephone penetration per capita more than fivefold. Spain, with 13 million telephones (35 per hundred inhabitants) had the ninth-largest network in the world.

INTERNATIONAL INVESTMENTS START FROM 1986

In 1986, Solana reaffirmed the company's international orientation. He announced strategic agreements and joint ventures with AT&T of the United States and a number of European companies, including SysScan, British Aerospace, Olivetti, Brown Boveri, Philips, Saab-Scania, and Telfin. Among the technologies involved were application-specific integrated circuits and digital mapping.

Through the late 1980s, profits and development continued their upward trend. World financial markets were opening up to Telefónica, which had shares quoted in Europe, the United States, and Japan. In 1988, Telefónica increased the number of seasonal telephone booths (booths installed at resorts and in population centers during tourist seasons to meet increased telephone traffic) and prepared for the introduction of cardphones.

In that same year, steps were taken to reverse the decline in the quality and efficiency of the telephone service arising from failure to keep pace with the surge in demand. Telefónica invested in new ventures, including the pan-European company Locstar and Geostar (U.S.), set up to develop radiopaging via satellite in their respective continents.

The first Spanish-Soviet enterprise was formed to produce telephones of Spanish design. International cooperation agreements were signed with other public networks operators, including France Telecom, British Telecom, STET of Italy, and, in the United States, NYNEX, Bell Atlantic, Ameritech, and Southwestern Bell. In May 1988, the firm officially adopted the name Telefónica de España S.A.

The year 1989, during the chairmanship of Cándido Velazquez, formerly head of the Spanish state-owned tobacco industry and the successor of Solana in January, brought improved service quality, decentralization, and investment in the urgently needed expansion of the network infrastructure. The company set ESP 582 billion aside for investment, 62.7 percent more than in 1988.

ADDING DATA SERVICES

Telefónica Servicios (TS-1) was created to provide value-added network services (VANS), including radiopaging, e-mail, voice mail, electronic data interchange, videotex, and international corporate communications. Telefónica installed nearly 1.5 million telephone lines in 1989, more than 87 percent of them digital. Spain had over 15 million telephones. The waiting list had been reduced under Cándido Velazquez, but it still stood at 600,000 at the end of 1989. At 30 lines per 100 inhabitants, Spain had a lower level of telephone service penetration than any other EEC member. Telefónica's good financial performance culminated in 1989 in a 16 percent increase in annual revenue to ESP 703 billion ($5.1 billion) and an 8 percent increase in profits to ESP 68.5 billion.

During this period, Telefónica ensured a strong hold over its supplies of telecommunications equipment, with an interest in Spain's largest manufacturers of telecom hardware, a 21.14 percent share in Alcatel Standard Electrica S.A., and a 12 percent in Amper S.A., the main Spanish manufacturer of telecommunications terminals. Telefónica's Plan Industrial de Compras put a severe limit on imports, thus protecting its native suppliers, which were largely its own subsidiaries.

Because of the government's controlling interest, Telefónica's policies were closely linked with those of the state, and its strategies were influenced by national unemployment and inflation figures. Government restrictions were evident in staffing policy (the company was obliged to maintain a larger workforce than it otherwise would) and in the fixing of telephone tariffs that resulted, until the late 1980s, in a constant cross-subsidy from international calls to local ones. The latter were traditionally very cheap by European standards, with some private domestic subscribers never exceeding their allowance of free calls and paying only the rental charge. Local tariffs were raised, by 14 percent in 1990, but such increases required government approval.

Governmental trends also had an effect on the company's funding, investment, and marketing policies. Telefónica had traditionally been able to rely on the Spanish Bourses for a large part of its funding, but until LOT it was inhibited from raising capital abroad by government policy, which constrained exports. Telefónica's tax liabilities were met by a government levy, based on its net profits, and were usually a set minimum of 6 percent of total revenue.

LATIN AMERICAN EXPANSION IN THE NINETIES

Until the late 1960s, the company had left most of its research to its main supplier, SESA. Once properly started, however, Telefónica's research and development division took off and by 1971 was employing about 100 people. In 1989, Telefónica, with the participation of Pacific Telesis and AT&T's Bell Communications Research, opened its new $53 million research and development center.

This center, occupying 21,000 square meters and employing a staff of 500, had developed a second-generation packet-switching system and was engaged in projects on optical communication, speech technology, and various EEC and European Space Agency projects.

As well as maintenance and extension of the basic telephone services, Telefónica's activities in the early 1990s covered data transmission; VANS, including radiopaging, e-mail, electronic data interchange, videotex, and international corporate communications; and satellite communications. There was also development of the supporting infrastructures: digitalization of transmission services, installation of optical fiber cables, extension of ISDN (integrated services digital network), and maintenance of Telefónica's position among world leaders for submarine cable networks.

In the early 1990s, Telefónica aimed at expansion into European and Latin American markets by acquisition. The telephone network also benefited from a program completed in 1993 that commercialized the first Spanish satellite, Hispasat, and saw the launch of an additional satellite as well. In Spain, Telefónica also made large-scale preparations to meet the extra demands

on its telephone and telecommunications services during 1992, the year Barcelona hosted the Olympic Games. The company also adopted the Cellular Access Rural Telephony system that year, which was designed to allow for cellular telephone service in rural areas.

During the 1990s, Telefónica continued to invest in international expansion as well as in developing technologies. In 1990, the firm acquired an interest in telecommunications network providers in Chile and in Telefónica de Argentina. The following year, it gained majority control over Telefónica Larga Distancia of Puerto Rico. The company also began to develop its mobile telephony service, the operations of which were organized under Movistar and eventually fell under control of the Telefónica Móviles subsidiary.

PRIVATIZATION AND DEREGULATION: NINETIES AND BEYOND

During the 1990s, the landscape of the telecommunications industry began to change dramatically. As such, the business operations of Telefónica were deeply affected. Beginning in 1994, the company reorganized itself in preparation for privatization as well as deregulation of basic telephony. The following year, the Spanish government began the privatization movement, selling off 12 percent of its holdings in the company by offering 100 million shares on the market.

The company also began its foray into the Internet arena in 1995 by launching InfoVia. The firm's mobile service offerings also began to develop rapidly, and by 1996 had secured 3 million users, 8 out of every 100 Spaniards. The government fully privatized Telefónica in 1997, selling off its remaining 20.9 percent interest in the company. The $4.4 billion offering, the largest in Spanish history, was followed by the creation of the Telecommunications Market Commission, which was developed to promote competition in the rapidly deregulating telecommunications industry.

Led by Juan Villalonga (elected chairman and CEO in 1996 by Spain's Prime Minister José María Aznar), Telefónica quickly began to create ventures that would ensure its stature in the competitive market. One such venture was formed in 1998, when the company teamed up with what was then known as MCI Communications Corp. to provide products and services to U.S.-based consumers and small businesses.

During 1998, basic telephony in Spain was deregulated. As part of Telefónica's reorganization, its domestic telecommunications business was transferred to a subsidiary, which took the name Telefónica de España. Telefónica S.A. was then created to act as a parent company for the firm's business lines. As a result of facing new competition in its home market, the company continued to focus its efforts on its international expansion.

ACQUIRING TELEBRAS IN 1998

The company entered the Brazilian market when that country's telephone company, Telebras, was privatized. During 1998, the firm secured $18.2 billion in revenues with nearly 26 percent stemming from operations outside of Spain. By this time, over 50 percent of its 37 million fixed lines were outside of its home country, 54 percent of its 14.4 million cellular phone customers did not reside in Spain, and 86 percent of its 2.3 million pay-television subscribers were international. Telefónica had also invested nearly $10.9 billion in the Latin American region by the late 1990s and controlled nearly 40 percent of its telecommunications.

Along with its international phone operations, Telefónica was also focused on its Internet and media-related businesses. In 1999, the firm's Terra Networks S.A. Internet subsidiary went public. On the first day of trading on the NASDAQ, Terra's stock price increased by as much as 198 percent. The firm then strengthened its Internet holdings in 2000, when Terra acquired Lycos Inc. in a $12.5 billion purchase. After the all-stock deal was finalized, the company became known as Terra Lycos S.A. Telefónica's stake in the company was diluted to less than 38 percent. Also that year, Telefónica paid EUR 4.5 billion in stock to acquire Endomol, the Dutch production company that had created the *Big Brother* reality television format.

Telefónica made several other strategic moves upon entering the new millennium. As part of its quest to become a leading global telecommunications firm, the company launched Operation Verónica, involving four simultaneous deals meant to increase Telefónica's Latin American presence. Operation Verónica allowed Telefónica to gain majority control of Telefónica de Argentina, Telesp, Telefónica de Peru, and Tele Sudeste, at a total cost of $16.7 billion. Again, Telefónica paid for these transactions with its own shares.

Telefónica regrouped all of its mobile telecommunications operations into Telefónica Móviles S.A. in 2000. Soon after, Telefónica spun off Telefónica Móviles as a public company. Telefónica nonetheless retained a 93 percent stake in Telefónica Móviles. The company also filled a major gap in its Latin American portfolio in 2000 when it acquired Motorola's cellular telephone operations in northern Mexico in a share-swap transaction.

Not all of Villalonga's empire-building attempts succeeded. The company, which remained a small player in the fast-growing European market, had launched a bid for 60 percent control of KPN, then still held by the Dutch government. Villalonga faced resistance in the deal both from Telefónica's shareholders, and from the Spanish government, and was forced to abandon the deal. Soon after, Villalonga, already the center of a personal scandal involving his high-profile extramarital affair with a Mexican actress, came under attack for the extravagant stock option package he had put into place for himself and other members of Telefónica's management.

By 2000, Villalonga had been accused, by the popular Spanish newspaper *El Mundo*, of using privileged information about the MCI Worldcom merger to buy and sell Telefónica stock at an advantage in 1998. Villalonga was placed under investigation, and eventually reached a plea deal with the Spanish government, agreeing to step down as head of Telefónica. In his place, César Alierta, who had overseen the privatization of Tabacalera, the state-owned tobacco company, took over as Telefónica's chairman in 2000.

TELECOMMUNICATIONS HANGOVER

Telefónica had in the meantime joined in the race to acquire licenses for the deployment of new high-speed "3G" (third-generation) mobile telephone networks. By the time the dust had settled, the global telecom players had spent more than $100 billion on acquiring licenses, with the prospect of at least $100 billion more to build the actual high-speed infrastructure. Telefónica, through Telefónica Móviles, had been an active player in the 3G market, spending more than EUR 6 billion on its own. Together with partner Sonera, of Finland, Telefónica also won an EUR 8.4 billion bid to acquire Germany's third 3G license.

The frenzy around 3G quickly deflated in the new century. The technology to deploy high-speed mobile communications networks had not yet been perfected. At the same time, doubts arose as to whether telephone customers, given the relative simplicity of existing handsets, would be willing to pay for such features as video and internet access. With the collapse of the global high-technology market in general at the beginning of the 2000s, the telecommunications sector emerged from its buying spree with a major hangover, and many billions in debt.

Nevertheless, Telefónica was one of the most stable telecom players in the early 2000s. While rivals such as France Telecom and Deutsche Telekom wrestled with debt loads in the tens of billions of euros, Telefónica's policy of swapping shares, rather than cash, for most of its major deals left it with comparatively little debt, and a strong treasury.

BECOMING NUMBER FOUR IN 2003

New Chairman Alierta quickly instituted a sweeping transformation of Telefónica, designed both to consolidate its financial stability and to expand its global reach. The company refocused its operations around its Spanish fixed line, Latin American fixed line, and worldwide mobile telephone operations. Telefónica also instituted a new high-level customer service component, recognizing that the key to its continued growth resided in customer satisfaction.

Telefónica's mobile telephone unit then became the group's spearhead for growth. Latin America remained a primary target for the company in the early 2000s as the group sought to build scale. In 2002, the company expanded its Mexican presence, paying $87 million in cash for a controlling stake in Pegaso PCS, the country's second-largest mobile telephone player.

The company followed this deal with a new landmark purchase in 2003, when the company reached an agreement to acquire all of BellSouth's operations in Latin America. The purchase added 10 mobile telephone companies in 10 countries, including Colombia, Ecuador, Uruguay, and Venezuela, all of which were new markets for Telefónica. As a result, Telefónica Móviles added 10.5 million new customers, boosting its total to 86.5 million, and became the world's fourth-largest mobile telephone player. The company's market share in Latin America alone topped 35 percent.

GAINING SCALE IN EUROPE FROM 2005

Telefónica's European competitors were also moving quickly to build their international mobile telephone empires. In order to remain competitive, Telefónica needed to complete a new milestone transaction. The company at first targeted the Central European market, buying 51.1 percent of Cesky Telecom, in the Czech Republic in 2004. The country's strong economic growth had made it a highly promising mobile telephone market. This transaction, and the surging demand for mobile telephone services, boosted the group's total subscriber base past 145 million.

Telefónica continued to seek a larger deal, however. In September 2005, the company tried again for KPN, which by then had become a public company, launching an unsuccessful offer worth $24 billion. Instead, the company turned to China, where it reached a strategic partnership with that country's up-and-comer China Netcom (later China Unicom), which had already built a subscriber base of 90 billion in what was soon to become the world's largest and fastest-growing mobile telecom market.

At last, in October 2005, Telefónica achieved its European objective, paying £17.7 billion ($31 billion) to acquire U.K.-based mobile telephone operator O2 Plc. That purchase gave the company control of a major European mobile telephone brand, with operations in the United Kingdom, Ireland, and Germany. The company quickly rolled out the O2 brand to its Czech operations. In 2006, the O2 brand entered Slovakia as well, becoming that country's third mobile services provider. By the end of 2009, Telefónica's European mobile telephone operations, including its 47 million customers in Spain, neared 95 million.

INVESTING IN INFRASTRUCTURE, EXPANDING VIA PARTNERSHIPS

Telefónica continued to strengthen its infrastructure, expanding both its fixed-line and wireless broadband networks. In 2007 alone the company invested more than EUR 2.4 billion ($3.2 billion) expanding its networks. While the company continued to develop its private customer business, it also moved to gain a greater share of the corporate and industrial segments. In 2007, the company forged a strategic alliance with Telecom Italia to build one of Europe's strongest industrial sector operations. By 2009, this alliance extended through 8 countries, and claimed more than 17 percent of the European market.

Telefónica remained on the lookout for new expansion opportunities. The company announced its interest in buying out Portugal Telecom's 50 percent stake in the two companies' Vivo joint venture in Brazil. The company also led the investment consortium Telco, which included Intesa Sanpaolo, Mediobanca, Generali, and the Benetton family, to acquire 80 percent of Olimpia, Telecom Italia's largest shareholder. Telefónica paid EUR 2.3 billion ($3.4 billion) for its 42 percent stake in Telco, giving it a 10 percent share of Telecom Italia.

The company's mobile telephone operations continued to boom as Telefónica deployed its high-speed wireless network. The company also gained exclusive licenses to roll out the Apple iPhone, one of the driving forces of the new high-speed mobile market, throughout its mobile telephone operations in Latin America, and in many of its European markets, including in the United Kingdom. By the end of 2008, the company had agreements to market the iPhone in 20 of its 25 markets.

Telefónica continued strengthening its partnership with China Unicom through 2009, boosting its shareholding in the Chinese company to more than 5 percent. In September 2009, the two companies took the alliance a step further, announcing an agreement to purchase $1 billion in each other's shares. This agreement boosted Telefónica's stake in the Chinese company to nearly 9 percent, while China Unicom acquired its first shareholding in Telefónica, of nearly 1 percent. The growing alliance between the two companies represented a major force in the global market, with a total customer base of more than 550 million.

AGREEMENT WITH RIVAL VODAFONE

Telefónica faced political pressure to reduce its holding in Telecom Italia toward the end of 2009. The company also faced a new challenge in the United Kingdom, where arch rival Vodafone launched an informal offer for T-Mobile UK, amid rumors that parent Deutsche Telekom was preparing its sale. The acquisition would allow Vodafone to take the U.K. lead away from Telefónica, forcing the Spanish company to counter with its own informal offer for the struggling operation.

The rivalry with Vodafone nonetheless did not prevent Telefónica from forming a new infrastructure sharing agreement with its German rival in 2009. The agreement called for the two companies to share antennas and base stations in Ireland, Spain, and Germany, providing both with a hedge against other potential competitors in the European market. Telefónica had by then raised itself to the global top three with China Mobile and Vodafone. Telefónica had transformed itself from a slow-moving state-owned telephone company to a global telecommunications giant with a customer base of more than 260 million.

Olive Classe
Updated, Christina M. Stansell; M. L. Cohen

PRINCIPAL SUBSIDIARIES

Telefónica de España S.A.; Telefónica Latinoamericana; Telefónica Móviles S.A.; Terra Lycos S.A.; Telefónica DataCorp; Atento Holding Telecomunicaciones S.A.; Admira S.A.; Telefónica Publicidad e Información S.A. (59.87%); Emergia (Uruguay); Adquira S.A.

PRINCIPAL DIVISIONS

Spain; Latin America; Europe.

PRINCIPAL OPERATING UNITS

Corporate Centre; Telefónica España; Telefónica Latinoamérica; Telefónica O2 Europe.

PRINCIPAL COMPETITORS

Grupo Salinas; E.ON AG; Telenor ASA; Siemens AG; Verizon Communications Inc.; France Telecom S.A.; Telecom Italia S.p.A.; ENDESA S.A.; Telecom Italia Mobile S.p.A.; Bouygues S.A.; Grupo Ferrovial S.A.; Acciona S.A.

FURTHER READING

Alberts, Hana R., "China Unicom and Telefónica Reach Deal," *Forbes*, September 7, 2009.

Automización integral de España, Madrid: Servicio de Publicaciones de Telefónica, 1989.

De Pablos, Emiliano, and John Hopewell, "Eyeing the Big Picture," *Variety*, January 24, 2000, p. 49.

Edmondson, Gail, and Margaret Popper, "Spain's Success," *Business Week, International Edition*, August 3, 1998.

Hooper, John, *The Spaniards*, Harmondsworth, U.K.: Penguin Books, 1986.

Koerner, Brendan L., "A Telephone Spam Scam," *U.S. News & World Report*, June 19, 2000, p. 45.

Lalaguna, Juan, *Spain*, Gloucestershire, U.K.: Windrush Press, 1990.

"Largest Privatization in Spanish History," *Privatization International*, February 1997, p. 40.

McDonald, Joe, "China Unicom, Spain's Telefónica Expand Alliance," *Forbes*, September 7, 2009.

Ockenden, Karma, "Calm amid the Storm," *Utility Europe*, May 1, 2002, p. 26.

Olson, Parmy, "Double Trouble from Vodafone, Telefónica," *Forbes*, March 23, 2009.

Parry, John N., "Telefónica Finds the Game Has Changed," *European*, April 24, 1997, p. 19.

Ram, Vidya, "Vivo Telefónica?" *Forbes*, July 10, 2007.

"Results of MCI/Worldcom/Telefónica Agreements," *Telephony*, March 16, 1998, p. 1.

Schmidt, Philip, "The Wrong Call on Telefónica?" *Business Week*, June 25, 2001.

"Spain—Adios Don Juan?" *Economist*, July 1, 2000, p. 49.

"Telefónica Cranks Up Profits," *Fiber Optic News*, November 22, 1999.

"Telefónica Leads the Way in Latin America," *Euromoney*, September 2005, p. 42.

"Telefónica's Bid to Be a Cyberstar," *Business Week*, May 29, 2000.

"Telefónica Shells Out $1.78 Billion for Motorola Mexico Mobile Holdings," *InfoLatina S.A. de C.V.*, October 12, 2000.

"Telefónica to Undergo Name Change, Restructuring Moves," *Telecommunications Reports*, March 23, 1998, p. 13.

Tomlinson, Richard, "Dialing In on Latin America," *Fortune*, October 25, 1999, p. 259.

Ten Thousand Villages U.S.

────────■────────

704 Main Street
Akron, Pennsylvania 17501-0500
U.S.A.
Telephone: (717) 859-8100
Fax: (717) 859-2622
Web site: http://www.tenthousandvillages.com

Nonprofit Company
Incorporated: 2002
Employees: 70
Sales: $24 million (2008 est.)
NAICS: 453220 Gift, Novelty, and Souvenir Stores

■ ■ ■

Wholly owned by the Mennonite Central Committee (MCC), Ten Thousand Villages U.S. is an Akron, Pennsylvania-based nonprofit marketer of handcrafted items produced by more than 130 artisan groups in 38 developing countries. Ten Thousand Villages is a fair-trade organization that endeavors to support the unemployed or underemployed, offering artisans higher than prevailing rates, a "fair wage" that takes into account the cost of living in their community. Artisans are paid half of their wage up front and the balance on delivery, while Ten Thousand Villages assumes the risk of selling the goods. The organization also makes an effort to nurture new artisan cooperatives, rather than support already successful ones. Artisans are encouraged to use local sustainable raw materials as well as recycled materials in an environmentally responsible way.

The company's designers and buyers also help artisan groups develop products that cater to the North American market. Ten Thousand Villages makes these unique products available to consumers in the United States through more than 150 retail shops, a festival sales program, and the Internet. Inspiration for the company name is drawn from a Mohandas Gandhi quote: "India is not to be found in its few cities but in the 700,000 villages. We have hardly ever paused to inquire if these folks get sufficient to eat and clothe themselves with." Such a concern for the less fortunate is in keeping with Mennonite beliefs. A sister charity under the Ten Thousand Villages name also serves Canada.

FOUNDER: EDNA RUTH BYLER

Ten Thousand Villages was established by Edna Ruth Byler, who was born in Hesston, Kansas, in 1904, and raised a Mennonite. After being graduated in 1923 from Hesston College, a two-year Mennonite college, she married one of the school's young professors, Joseph N. Byler, two years later.

With the introduction of a military draft in the months leading up to the United States' entry into World War II, Joseph Byler in 1941 was named MCC education director for a Civilian Public Service camp in Indiana, where conscientious objectors to the draft were sent to fulfill their military obligations by performing public works. (The MCC had been formed in 1920 to aid Russian Mennonites suffering famine in the wake of the Communist revolution.)

COMPANY PERSPECTIVES

One day all artisans in the developing countries will earn a fair wage, be treated with dignity and respect and be able to live a life of quality.

The family moved to Bluffton, Indiana, but upon their arrival Byler was asked by the MCC to go to Nazi-occupied France to serve as an MCC worker. He complied, and Edna Byler moved their belongings and two children to Akron, Pennsylvania, where the MCC maintained its headquarters. Akron, located in Lancaster County, was the heart of Pennsylvania Dutch country and the center of the Mennonite community in North America. It became her permanent home as she served as the hostess at the MCC Main House, working with other Mennonite women to make doughnuts and sticky buns that they sold at factories to raise funds to support MCC work.

CRAFT SALES BEGIN: 1946

Byler's husband was absent for more than a year, and when he returned he continued to work for the MCC, involved in relief efforts. Following the war, in 1946 Edna Byler overcame her fear of flying to accompany him on a trip to Puerto Rico. It was a providential journey, one that led to the creation of Ten Thousand Villages. Family friends Mary and Melville Lauver were working in the impoverished La Plata community, the former helping the women to find a way to earn an income by establishing a sewing class in which they produced beautiful embroidered linens. Mary Lauver persuaded Edna Byler, herself an embroiderer, to take home samples of the needlework to see if she could take orders from friends and neighbors in Akron.

Byler spent $5 on placemats, napkins, and hand towels in Puerto Rico but had no idea how to generate orders from her samples. When she returned home, however, she was asked to give a talk about this trip; she showed the linens and a few people placed orders. Six months later the goods arrived and what would become Ten Thousand Villages began to take shape as Byler found more willing buyers in Pennsylvania. She began to place regular orders for La Plata goods, samples of which she kept in her car to generate further orders from homes, churches, and schools. In a matter of five years Byler sold more than $30,000 worth of the community's needlework.

In the 1950s Byler broadened the scope of her makeshift program, then casually known as Mrs. Byler's Project. Her husband's travels for the MCC played a key role in the development, as she accompanied him on trips around the world. In 1950 she added Asian linens to the items she represented, the result of teaching sewing classes in Hong Kong. A year later the Bylers visited Jordan, where Edna was introduced to the red cross-stitched tablecloths that Palestinian refugees produced. She also expanded beyond needlework during this period, adding hand-carved Haitian woodenware into the mix.

FORMALIZING THE PROJECT: 1952

At the Mennonite World Conference held in Basel, Switzerland, in 1952, Byler and a colleague, Ruth Lederach, displayed Byler's linens and crafts, selling $300 worth. This effort resulted in Mrs. Byler's Project taking the name Overseas Needlepoint and Crafts Project. The breadth of her linen and craft items exceeded the capacity of her trunk, and Byler set up a gift shop in the basement of her home.

The variety of goods also meant that many of the items, jewelry in particular, would not appeal to her fellow Mennonites, who were extremely conservative in nature. Thus, she began to attend festivals in Pennsylvania to find further customers for her stable of artisans. She took samples with her when making regular speaking engagements at sewing circle groups held across the United States and Canada, and commissioned other volunteers to whom she sent sample kits to take orders in their communities. In the 1960s church-based consignment sales were launched. She also became a wholesaler to gift shops.

Joseph Byler died in 1962, at which point Edna Byler turned over control of the Overseas Needlepoint and Crafts Project to the MCC as part of its relief, rehabilitation, and development program in order to expand the operation. North American sales at the time totaled little more than $1,800. Although it was renamed the MCC Self Help Program in 1968, she remained the director until her retirement at the end of 1970. Under her direction, the program developed Self Help programs in 10 countries. About $50,000, excluding distribution costs, was made in direct payment to artisans each year. Byler remained involved, however, in her life's work, managing a gift shop until a few months before her death in 1976.

FIRST SELF HELP SHOPS OPEN: 1972

The first Self Help gift and thrift shop featuring crafts from around the world was opened in Bluffton, Ohio,

KEY DATES

1946: Edna Ruth Byler begins selling embroidered linens made by impoverished Puerto Rican women artisans.

1952: Byler's effort is formalized as the Overseas Needlepoint and Crafts Project.

1962: Mennonite Central Committee assumes control of project.

1972: First retail shops open.

1980: SELFHELP Crafts name is adopted.

1996: Name is changed to Ten Thousand Villages.

2002: Organization is incorporated as independent nonprofit.

2005: Web sales begin.

in 1972. The first Canadian shop was also opened that year, in Altona, Manitoba. Craft sales had begun in Canada the previous decade and by the end of the 1960s all of the provincial MCC offices had appointed directors to place Self Help sales. The first chief executive officer of the MCC Self Help Program, Paul Leatherman, was named in 1976. A former shoe salesman who had long been involved with the MCC, he immediately went on a year-long trip around the world to meet with artisans and assess the program he inherited. He encountered a common theme in his travels, telling Henry Neufeld of *Canadian Mennonite* in a 2006 interview that he regularly heard artisans say, "I don't want you to give me anything, just buy things from me regularly so I can earn food for my family." By the end of the 1970s he had expanded the number of retail stores to 60, supplied by crafts produced in 20 countries.

Leatherman served as CEO until 1988. During his tenure, the organization grew on a number of fronts. In a branding move the program's name was officially changed to SELFHELP Crafts in 1980. Two years later the operation acquired a building in Ephrata, Pennsylvania, a short distance from Akron, which housed not only a gift store but also the SELFHELP Crafts administrative offices, a warehouse, and the first office of the International Fair Trade Association. The change in venue led to a surge in sales, as revenues at the Ephrata store tripled in the first year. Because of strong growth, the organization quickly outgrew its new space and in a matter of just four years, the offices and warehouse had to be relocated to a larger building in Akron. Sales exceeded $3.6 million in 1986. In the meantime, the program underwent a self-evaluation

process that determined the program should become financially self-sufficient.

Paul E. Myers became the new CEO in 1989 following Leatherman's retirement. By this time there were more than 120 stores in operation in the United States and Canada, with crafts sourced from 30 countries. According to the *Lancaster Intelligencer Journal*, the U.S. stores, 75 in number, generated $5 million in 1990, benefiting about 30,000 artisans in 37 developing countries. Sales approached $6 million by 1993, when the organization developed a five-year strategic plan. It called for a mail-order retail catalog, which was launched in 1994. Because sales were less than $40,000, however, the catalog business was discontinued just a year later. Clothing product lines were also discontinued.

ADOPTION OF TEN THOUSAND VILLAGES NAME: 1996

In 1996 SELFHELP looked to the past, celebrating its 50th anniversary, while also looking to the future. In that year the organization decided the time had come for a name change, resulting in the switch to Ten Thousand Villages. In 1997 the first company stores under the Ten Thousand Villages banner opened. By the end of the decade there were 127 U.S. outlets and another 45 stores in Canada, both company owned and franchised.

The MCC decided in 2000 to spin off Ten Thousand Villages as an independent charity. Based in Akron, the organization assumed the mandate of promoting economic development through craft sales. In 2002 Ten Thousand Villages was incorporated as a 501(c)(3) independent nonprofit, charitable organization. Not only did the organization continue to add retail stores in the new century, it began generating sales from its Web site in 2005, and in the fall of 2008 it began selling products through eBay's Worldofgood. com.

In 2006 Myers announced his retirement, effective later in the year, but he soon found a new post, becoming chairman of the International Fair Trade Association (since renamed World Fair Trade Organization). His replacement at Ten Thousand Villages was Craig R. Schloneger, the lead pastor at Lancaster's Neffsville Mennonite Church who previously had served as president of Dutch Corporation, a hospitality company located in Ohio's Pennsylvania Dutch country. Schloneger took over an operation that in fiscal 2006 (the year ending March 31) generated more than $20 million in the United States from 110 artisan groups in 32 countries.

Under Schloneger's leadership, U.S. sales increased to $24 million in fiscal 2009, while the Canadian sister operation posted an additional $14 million. Moreover, products from new artisan groups were also added; in 2009 this included products from 11 groups in Bolivia, Cameroon, Ghana, Indonesia, Kenya, Nicaragua, South Africa, and Zimbabwe. All told, 600 new products were added over the course of the year. There was no shortage of artisans around the world in need of help. The quality of the goods, and the reasonable prices Ten Thousand Villages charged for them, ensured that the organization would continue to successfully pursue its humanitarian mission.

Ed Dinger

FURTHER READING

Bahrampour, Tara, "Shop Holds a World of Promise," *Washington Post*, June 2, 2005, p. T16.

Duroni, Charlene, "SELFHELP Crafts Founder's Vision Lives On," *Lancaster Intelligencer Journal*, June 7, 1994, p. A06.

Gee, Laura, "Shopping for a Cause," *Newport News Daily Press*, December 11, 2007.

Neufeld, Henry, "Ten Thousand Villages: A $5 Investment 60 Years Later," *Canadian Mennonite*, July 10, 2006, p. 21.

Palmer, Nancy Simon, "Art Against Poverty," *Lancaster Intelligencer Journal*, October 11, 1990, p. C01.

Sommer, Mimi G., "Hand-Made Craft Items from Around the World," *New York Times*, January 3, 1999, Sec. 14CN, p. 2.

"Ten Thousand Villages Grows with Fair Trade," *Forbes*, September 7, 2009, p. 66.

"Tribute to Edna Ruth Byler," *Gospel Herald*, July 27, 1976, p. 582.

White, Elizabeth Ross, "Shopping off the Beaten Mall Path," *Christian Science Monitor*, December 16, 1997, p. 12.

Thor Equities, LLC

25 West 39th Street
New York, New York 10018
U.S.A.
Telephone: (212) 529-5055
Fax: (212) 460-9243
Web site: http://www.thorequities.com

Private Company
Incorporated: 1986
NAICS: 531300 Activities Related to Real Estate

■ ■ ■

Thor Equities, LLC, is a privately held New York City-based real estate investment firm that focuses on the acquisition of undervalued urban properties on which to develop mixed-use facilities. The company also offers property management services. Thor owns properties in Manhattan as well as Brooklyn, where the company's ambitious plans for revitalizing Coney Island has placed it at loggerheads with the city. Thor's portfolio also includes properties in the Atlanta, Chicago, Detroit, Miami, Ft. Lauderdale, Houston, Los Angeles, New Orleans, and San Francisco metropolitan areas. Serving as chairman and chief executive is Thor's founder, Joseph J. Sitt.

FOUNDER, BROOKLYN BORN: 1965

The son of a children's apparel maker, Joseph Sitt was born in 1965 in the Bensonhurst section of Brooklyn and grew up in the Sephardic Jewish community of Gravesend, hardly an affluent neighborhood. On the verge of his 12th birthday, Sitt became all too aware how his urban neighborhood was underserved by retailers. His grandmother promised to either buy him an Atari game system or a parrot, but they soon discovered that neither was available in Brooklyn in the mid-1970s, forcing them to spend an hour on the bus and subway to travel to Manhattan for a shopping trip. Sitt's frustration as an inner-city shopper would not be forgotten by him, the experience proving to be a seminal moment in the life of the entrepreneur. Another influence at the age of 11 was meeting Sam Walton of Wal-Mart fame. Sitt was accompanying his father on a sales trip to Wal-Mart's Arkansas headquarters, wandered off, and found himself called into Sam Walton's office where the company owner offered him candy and kindly conversation. Wal-Mart was still a relatively small company at the time, but Sitt would follow the retailer's growth and come to admire the skills and temperament of Walton.

Although he did not plan to become a businessman, hoping instead to become a history teacher, Sitt displayed a penchant for business and by college scrapped the idea of teaching. As an undergraduate student at New York University he began operating flea markets, taking advantage of the Aqueduct and Roosevelt racetrack parking lots to provide space for vendors to sell a wide variety of goods. Again he learned the reality of inner-city commerce. "One thing it showed me," he told *Inc.* in 2006, "was how underserved the market was, how many people were desperate to buy toys. It's hard to imagine, but back then there weren't many Toys 'R' Us around."

THOR EQUITIES FORMED: 1986

In 1986, when he was 21 and still in school, Sitt learned of properties that were being sold at tax auctions and began acquiring these distressed properties. The first was located on East Tremont Avenue in the Bronx. With money raised from family and friends, Sitt erected a one-story retail site to which he eventually attracted a Payless ShoeSource store and a Rite Aid Pharmacy. To house his fledgling real estate business, Sitt formed Thor Equities. An avid comic-book collector as a child, he drew on one of his favorite characters, Thor, to create the name for his company. Sitt built or acquired more of these small inner-city strip centers and endured the frustration of convincing retailers that despite the bad, crime-ridden neighborhoods in which the facilities were located, there was a great deal of business to be done. Sitt tried to make the strip centers he acquired as enticing as possible to both customers and retail chains. Not only did he repave and restripe the parking lots, he also installed attractive fencing, brighter lights, and new sound systems to play music for shoppers. To find tenants for his shopping centers, Sitt relentlessly called on the national chains only to endure countless rejections. While Sitt was pursuing his real estate interests he also held a job developing sourcing plants for Novelty Philippines, Inc., a unit of a U.S. manufacturer.

Distraught over the difficulty in attracting quality retailers to his properties, Sitt decided in the late 1980s to create his own retail operations. He paid for market research to discover the greatest retail needs in the urban marketplace and learned that there was an excellent general retail opportunity in ladies' apparel. While women in the inner city were able to find an abundance of low cost leggings and T-shirts, they found it difficult to shop for nice clothes that could be worn to work. Because many of the women in his markets were full-figured, he decided to develop a clothing store concept that catered to plus-sized women. For a name he drew on two of his wife's favorite businesswomen, Laura Ash-

ley and Martha Stewart, to coin the name Ashley Stewart. Moreover, both Laura Ashley and Martha Stewart were upscale brands, which fed into Sitt's plan to offer a more upscale shopping experience than the inner city generally provided.

FORMATION OF ASHLEY STEWART CHAIN: 1991

The first Ashley Stewart store opened in Brooklyn in 1991. To build the Ashley Stewart brand, Sitt applied the name to all the merchandise, not just signage. He also made sure the stores became part of the community to develop goodwill. Ashley Stewart stores held hundreds of fashion shows each year to raise money for the community. Discount coupons were handed out, and as a result the brand was promoted and new business was brought into the store. Having established Ashley Stewart in Brooklyn, Sitt took the concept to other inner-city locations, after soon realizing that landlords in those markets were offering rents far lower than he was willing to pay. Rather than just becoming a tenant, Sitt took advantage of the situation by having Thor Equities begin to snap up inexpensive properties across the country to open strip malls anchored by Ashley Stewart stores. In time, Thor controlled about 14 million square feet of retail space in a dozen cities.

Sitt built the Ashley Stewart chain to more than 300 units generating more than $400 million in annual sales. In 1998 he sold a controlling interest in Ashley Stewart and its parent company, Urban Brands. He remained as chairman of Urban Brands and added or invested in other retail concepts, including Body and Soul, The Children's Place, 100% Girls, Marianne Stores, Kidspot, and House of Bargains. Sitt had especially high hopes for Kidspot and in a matter of just two years opened 106 stores. The chain did not turn profitable quickly enough for Urban Brands' owners, however. In late 2000 Sitt was removed as chairman and a few weeks later Kidspot was closed.

SITT FOCUSES ON THOR EQUITIES: 2001

No longer involved in the running of Ashley Stewart and Urban Brands, Sitt turned his attention completely to Thor Equities, looking to pursue further inner-city real estate development opportunities. In 2001 the company invested $260 million to acquire six urban properties. Thor bought a ramshackle strip mall in New Orleans's Gentilly Woods neighborhood. As he had done in the past, Sitt replaced the parking lot, installed new lights, and listened to the community to determine its needs, leading to the opening of a linens store. Also in 2001 Sitt made a deal in his home borough of Brooklyn, paying $25 million for Albee Square Mall, located in the middle of the Fulton Street shopping district overlooking the Brooklyn Bridge. Sitt's plan was to convert the two-story building into a small upscale mall renamed The Gallery. Other Thor purchases included 26-34 South State Street in Chicago, whose major tenant would be a Forever 21 apparel store; 560 Broadway in Bayonne, New Jersey; 208-220 West 125th Street in Manhattan's Harlem section; and 20 Marietta Street in Atlanta, which was purchased from Urban Brands.

In 2002 Thor acquired the 945,000-square-foot Military Circle Mall and adjacent Doubletree Club Hotel in Norfolk, Virginia, located close to the world's largest naval base. In a matter of 18 months, as a result, Thor assembled a portfolio of about three million square feet of retail, office, and residential properties. To add to that total, in 2002 Thor began negotiations to acquire another Atlanta property, the South DeKalb Mall, which opened in a predominantly affluent African-American suburb near I-20 in 1970. Since the 2001 opening of the Mall at Stonecrest less than 10 miles east on I-20, it had experienced difficulty in attracting both shoppers and tenants. Thor took on Hip Hop producer and entrepreneur Russell Simmons as a partner to complete the $26.7 million acquisition in early 2003.

Also in 2003, Sitt increased his Brooklyn holdings. Near Fulton Street he bought the Brooklyn Municipal Parking Garage on Livingston Street. His plan was to build a 300,000-square-foot retail facility that could house a number of off-price retailers that had not been able to find reasonably priced space on Fulton Street, such as Dress Barn and Ross Stores. Thor also began buying properties in Coney Island, Brooklyn's famous beach and amusement park area that had become rundown over the years and was the subject of multiple plans for revitalization. A new minor league baseball park that opened in 2001 helped to boost the prospects of the area, as did a new subway station and playgrounds. Sitt's idea was to build a $1.5 billion entertainment district, complete with hotels, shops, and rides. In 2003 the Coney Island Development Corporation (CIDC), composed of well-connected area businessmen and politicians, was convened by the city to develop its own plan for the area. Sitt would find himself at odds with the CIDC.

COMPANY EXPANDS TO FLORIDA AND PUERTO RICO: 2004

Thor was involved in projects outside of Brooklyn as well. In 2004 it acquired retail properties in Florida: Cocowalk in Miami's Coconut Grove, a 455,000-square-foot facility housing a movie theater, shops, and restaurants; and Ft. Lauderdale's Beach Place, a 95,000-square-foot three-level facility that with its well-known restaurants mostly catered to wealthy South Americans and other international tourists. Also in 2004 Thor bought the Centro Gran Caribe mall near San Juan, Puerto Rico. Because the mall was already well booked, Sitt elected to expand the mall to bring in major U.S. retailers.

Thor was active on a number of fronts in 2005 and 2006. The company paid about $250 million to acquire the historic Palmer House Hilton hotel in Chicago in June 2005. Later in the year Thor bought the shuttered Revere Sugar factory in the Red Hook district of Brooklyn. The area had long been an eyesore, but the ascent of the nearby neighborhood of Carroll Gardens made the area increasingly viable and valuable, attracting both residents and retailers. Ownership of the old factory provided Thor with a potential space to develop if conditions warranted in the years to come. In Brooklyn, in the meantime, Thor spent $13 million to acquire the Washington Bath site located to the west of the Coney Island baseball park. When the CIDC made it clear that it would allow residential development on that site, he sold at a $72 million profit just 14 months later. Sitt also sold The Gallery for a $100 million profit in 2007 without making any of the promised renovations beyond a new awning. As a result, Sitt's plans for Coney Island were viewed with skepticism in some corners.

Painstakingly, Sitt had acquired about 10.5 acres of Coney Island's 13-acre entertainment district at a cost of $100 million, putting a wrench in the city's plans for the neighborhood. Sitt announced a plan in 2006 to build a $1.5 billion hotel condominium complex in Coney Island, provided the city rezoned the area as residential, but his plan was rejected by the city and failed to win community support. It appeared that he would have to sell out, but he rejected an offer from the city of $105 million. Some suspected that he was merely trying to increase the price of his holdings when he took steps to put pressure on the city by evicting some of his tenants in late 2008, including the famous Astroland amusement park, which only made the neighborhood more desolate in appearance.

In 2009 the city pursued a plan that would designate parts of Coney Island, and the property owned by Thor, as parkland. Potentially, the city could then seize the property through the use of eminent domain. Sitt won some political allies who objected to the ploy and the matter remained unresolved in the fall of 2009. Even while Sitt was fighting with the city over Coney Island he was requesting permission to bring a BJ's Wholesale Club store to a bus parking lot in Bensonhurst. Whatever the outcome of the project or the battle over Coney Island, there was little doubt that Joe Sitt and Thor Equities would remain an urban developer to be reckoned with for some time to come.

Ed Dinger

PRINCIPAL SUBSIDIARIES

Thor Retail Consulting Corp.; Thor Properties; Thor Urban Development.

PRINCIPAL COMPETITORS

Equity One, Inc.; ING Clarion Partners, LLC; Vornado Realty Trust.

FURTHER READING

Bagli, Charles V., "Beyond Sideshows, the City and a Developer Face Off over Coney Island's Future," *New York Times,* April 11, 2009, p. A14.

———, "City and Developer Spar over Coney Island Visions," *New York Times,* February 17, 2009, p. A27.

Barnett, Megan, "Urban Makeover Artist," *U.S. News & World Report,* August 16, 2004.

DeCambre, Mark, "Thor Equities Making $3b Push into Inner-City Retail Markets," *Real Estate Finance and Investment,* April 21, 2003, p. 1.

DeMause, Neil, "Coney Island's Last Ride? The Bulldozer," *Village Voice,* April 11–April 17, 2007, p. 19.

Fung, Amanda, "Coney Island Keeper," *Crain's New York Business,* June 29, 2009, p. 1.

Issenberg, Sasha, "How I Did It: Joe Sitt," *Inc.,* January 2006, p. 86.

LeClaire, Jennifer, "Joseph Sitt: Thor Equities Uses Marketing Savvy to Revitalize Inner Cities," *National Real Estate Investor,* April 1, 2004.

"Retail Grows in Brooklyn," *Chain Store Age,* March 2002, p. 124.

Sargent, Greg, "The Incredibly Bold, Audaciously Cheesy, Jaw-Dropping, Vegasified, Billion-Dollar Glam-Rock Makeover of Coney Island," *New York,* September 26, 2005, p. 22.

Tommy Bahama®

Tommy Bahama Group, Inc.

———— ■ ————

428 Westlake Avenue North, Suite 388
Seattle, Washington 98109
U.S.A.
Telephone: (206) 622-8688
Toll Free: (800) 647-8688
Fax: (206) 622-4483
Web site: http://www.tommybahama.com

Wholly Owned Subsidiary of Oxford Industries, Inc.
Incorporated: 1992 as Viewpoint International, Inc.
Employees: 2,500
Sales: $421.68 million (2008)
NAICS: 424320 Men's and Boys' Clothing and Furnishings Merchant Wholesalers; 424330 Women's, Children's, and Infants' Clothing and Accessories Merchant Wholesalers; 424340 Footwear Merchant Wholesalers; 423220 Home Furnishing Merchant Wholesalers; 448110 Men's Clothing Stores; 448120 Women's Clothing Stores; 722110 Full-Service Restaurants

■ ■ ■

Tommy Bahama Group, Inc., markets apparel and a wide range of merchandise under the Tommy Bahama, Tommy Bahama Relax, and Indigo Palms labels. In addition to operating a wholesale business, the company operates 70 retail locations in 22 states in the United States. Internationally, it operates seven stores in Canada, three stores in Australia, and three stores in the United Arab Emirates. Tommy Bahama sells a full range of tropical-themed, silk, and linen apparel for men and women. Through licensing agreements, the Tommy Bahama brand appears on a variety of merchandise, including home furnishings, perfumes, and rum. Roughly half the company's revenues are generated from its retail operations. Approximately 80 percent of its sales are derived from men's apparel. Tommy Bahama is a subsidiary of Oxford Industries Inc.

THE BIRTH OF A BRAND

Fittingly for a brand that exuded a tropical lifestyle, Tommy Bahama was conceived on a beach. Founders Tony Margolis and Bob Emfield had known each other for more than a decade when they purchased neighboring beach homes on Florida's Gulf Coast during the 1980s. They had met in the late 1960s, when they both worked for blue jeans manufacturer Britannia Ltd., and, along with their wives, began spending their vacations together. "We spent a lot of time at the beach," Margolis said in a November 21, 2001 interview with *Display & Design News*, "and one day [Emfield] turned to me and said, 'Tell me why we have to go back to work?' That is when we started to joke around and create a character that didn't have to go back. We gave him the name Tommy Bahama."

The two couples spent hours walking on the beach creating Tommy Bahama lore. They exchanged ideas about who their fictional character was, what he did, where he lived, what he owned, and what he wore, shaping his identity and honing the particulars of the Tommy Bahama brand. In 1991, Margolis and Emfield decided to turn their discussions into a business and enlisted the help of a third partner, a designer living in

COMPANY PERSPECTIVES

There is a warm westerly breeze rustling the palms, the lulling roar of crashing waves—it's a celebration of island living, courtesy of Tony Margolis, Bob Emfield and Lucio Dalla Gasperina. In 1992, our fictional Tommy Bahama character became the inspiration behind the experience of traveling to exotic locales where the food is good, the beaches are hot and the mood is relaxed. Tommy Bahama and his tropical adventures command the finer things in life: casual, comfortable sportswear, golfwear, swimwear, footwear and accessories for men and women. As the purveyor of island lifestyles, Tommy Bahama has created a world where life moves at a more relaxed pace, where the enjoyment of the good life is the norm, rather than the exception.

Seattle, Lucio Dalla Gasperina. Together, the trio had nearly a century of experience in the apparel industry, experience they would put to use to create a line of merchandise that reflected the image of Tommy Bahama.

The partners set their sights on their target customers, males between the ages of 35 to 65, and began setting up a business. They reached an agreement for financial and manufacturing support from a Hong Kong factory that, combined with their savings, gave them $2 million to start their company, Viewpoint International, Inc., founded in 1992. Despite their years of experience, the partners faltered from the gate, making several mistakes that threatened to destroy their entrepreneurial venture. "We spent our first two years going out of business," Dalla Gasperina noted in the December 1, 2001 issue of *Inc.*

DISAPPOINTING DEBUT

From the start, the partners decided they needed more than Tommy Bahama to support Viewpoint. They created two other labels, Gear for Urban Training and Linguini & Bob, and developed lines for each brand, unveiling the three creations in the spring of 1993. Problems surfaced immediately, the effects of which were exacerbated by the lavish salaries the partners paid to each other. "We were all coming out of six-figure-salary jobs," Margolis explained in the December 1, 2001 issue of *Inc.* Decisions related to distribution were the first to haunt the trio. They had decided to sell Gear

for Urban Training and Linguini & Bob through Merry-Go-Round Enterprises Inc., a midsized retail chain based in Maryland that was suffering from financial difficulties that ultimately led to its collapse. While the two lines sat on the shelves of an anemic retailer, Tommy Bahama struggled to secure any space on retailers' shelves. The partners had decided to sell the line of tropical print shirts and linen shorts to large department stores just as the retailers were centralizing purchasing and reducing their number of buyers. "If it wasn't red-white-and-blue Hilfiger, Polo, or Nautica, they didn't want it," Emfield said, describing department stores' reaction to the Tommy Bahama brand in the December 1, 2001 issue of *Inc.*

Viewpoint was struggling on three fronts, failing to make any headway and chewing through its supply of capital. Desperate, Emfield began showing the Tommy Bahama line to specialty stores and found some interested buyers, registering one of his first big sales with Gary's Island, a small chain of stores located on the West Coast and Hawaii. Specialty stores, rather than large department stores, seemed the ideal distribution channel for Tommy Bahama, but before Emfield could build a sizable customer base, he and his partners exhausted their financial resources.

A CHANGE IN STRATEGY IN 1994

By 1994, Margolis, Emfield, and Dalla Gasperina had to decide whether to abandon their company or to devise a new, more effective strategy. They resolved to press ahead and invest more of their savings in the venture. They decided to drop the Gear for Urban Training and Linguini & Bob labels and focus their efforts on distributing the Tommy Bahama label to specialty stores throughout the country. They also decided to launch a private-label business and began manufacturing clothing for other companies. "We did it to pay the light bill and the phone bill," Dalla Gasperina said in the December 1, 2001 issue of *Inc.*, referring to the sideline venture that Margolis deemed "the one key thing that happened in our history."

The changes made in 1994 injected financial vitality into Viewpoint. By the beginning of 1995, the company had $2 million to spend on promoting the Tommy Bahama brand, but instead of spending the money on print or television advertisements, the three partners took an unconventional approach to marketing. They decided to open a retail location, not solely as a way to make money but as a way to promote the company's wholesale business and to give retailers an example of how the Tommy Bahama brand should be presented in stores. When they found vacant commercial space in Naples, Florida, the property owner of-

throughout the line. Arguably the greatest benefit of the Naples compound was the excitement it caused within the retail industry. Viewpoint's wholesale business, its lifeblood, began to record animated growth as retailers clamored for the elegant yet casual line.

KEY DATES

■

1992: Tony Margolis, Bob Emfield, and Lucio Dalla Gasperina form Viewpoint International, Inc., to market the Tommy Bahama brand and two other brands.

1994: Out of money, the founders decide to focus all their efforts on the Tommy Bahama label.

1995: First Tommy Bahama retail store opens in November in Naples, Florida, adjoined by a Tommy Bahama Café that opens three months later.

1999: Company opens its first freestanding retail store in Ft. Lauderdale, Florida, and begins signing licensing agreements for the use of the Tommy Bahama name on a range of merchandise.

2002: Indigo Palms label is created.

2003: Oxford Industries Inc. acquires Viewpoint; Viewpoint becomes known as Tommy Bahama Group, Inc.

2005: Tommy Bahama Relax label is introduced.

2006: Tommy Bahama Golf 18 label is introduced.

2007: Company signs a licensing agreement to produce Tommy Bahama rum.

2008: Margolis retires as chief executive officer and is replaced by Terry R. Pillow.

SURGING SALES IN THE LATE NINETIES

After a tepid start, Viewpoint enjoyed robust growth, becoming a phenomenon within the retail community. With Emfield serving as vice president of sales, Dalla Gasperina as executive vice president of design and operations, and Margolis as president, the company began to expand aggressively. Before the end of the 1990s, another compound was opened in Sarasota, Florida, and two more were established in California, one in Palm Desert and the other in Newport Beach. The partners also began developing a traditional retail chain, opening their first freestanding location in February 1999 in Ft. Lauderdale, Florida.

BRAND EXTENSION BEGINS IN 1999

Sales by the end of the 1990s reached $100 million, a total that swelled in the coming years as Viewpoint expanded its retail presence. New stores opened in Florida, California, Texas, Nevada, and Arizona, giving the company 15 retail locations, six which were compounds, by 2001. Sales shot upward, reaching $300 million by the end of the year, a total derived from Viewpoint's retail and wholesale activities and from the most remarkable aspect of its business, its diversification to an array of product categories. Tommy Bahama, as a brand, began to represent much more than apparel. Through licensing agreements, the partners delved into footwear in 1999, signing a deal with Paradise Shoe Co. The same year, the Tommy Bahama brand extended into home furnishings through licensing agreements with Wildwood Lamps & Accents, Shaw Rugs, and Lexington Home Brands. In 2001, the company signed an agreement with Apparel Ventures to produce a line of Tommy Bahama swimwear. Viewpoint launched another brand as well, creating Indigo Palms, a line of men's denim wear, in 2002 that added a women's line two years later.

A CORPORATE SUITOR COMES CALLING IN 2003

A decade after its formation, Viewpoint exuded admirable strength. Revenues by the end of 2002 exceeded $350 million, reflecting a bustling wholesale

---

fered additional space at an attractive price, prompting the partners to make their unconventional move. As a way to promote the Tommy Bahama apparel brand, they decided to open a restaurant. "It's the greatest advertising vehicle ever, and we made money doing it," Margolis said in the December 1, 2001 issue of *Inc.*

The retail store opened in November 1995 and an attached restaurant with a tropical menu and white tablecloths opened three months later, constituting the first of what the company called its "compound" format. Built at a cost of $1.2 million, the Naples compound proved to be an immediate financial success, generating $2 million in revenue during its first year. Equally as important, the Naples location let Margolis, Emfield, and Dalla Gasperina gauge the reaction of consumers to its apparel line. Cashiers at the Naples store noticed women were buying extra-small men's shirts for themselves, prompting the partners to create a women's line of Tommy Bahama apparel. The partners also noticed customers preferred linen apparel over cotton apparel, leading them to emphasize the use of linen

and retail business. The company had 30 retail locations in operation and continued to add to the range of Tommy Bahama offerings through licensing agreements, a deal with Brown Jordan International to produce Tommy Bahama outdoor furniture being the most recent addition. Viewpoint represented an attractive package, and rumors in the business press began to circulate that the company was being sold to a corporate suitor. "That would be great news, wouldn't it?," Margolis said in the March 14, 2003 issue of *WWD*. "Actually, I'm not aware any transaction is imminent. We've talked to a dozen people over the last couple of years to no avail." One month later, a deal was announced, marking the end of Viewpoint's independence and the beginning of its existence as a subsidiary of Oxford Industries Inc.

Based in Atlanta, Georgia, Oxford Industries needed a company with Viewpoint's strengths. Led by Chairman and CEO J. Hick Lanier, Oxford was licensed to make apparel for brands, including Nautica, Geoffrey Beene, Tommy Hilfiger, and Oscar de la Renta, but it did not own its own high-profile, lifestyle brand. The addition of Tommy Bahama promised to give Oxford Industries an identity in the marketplace, and the response from Wall Street reflected elation at the prospect of the company owning its own brand. Oxford Industries stock jumped from $25.67 per share when the acquisition was announced in April 2003 to $70 per share within seven months. "We were not in control of our destiny ... and we had to pay royalties on licensed products," Lanier said in the October 13, 2003 issue of *Daily News Record*. "Tommy Bahama takes us into the luxury end of the business and they brought us their own stores. Our tagline on our annual report is 'Perfect Fit,' which refers to Tommy Bahama. We really do feel it's a perfect fit."

Oxford Industries struck gold when it acquired Viewpoint. The company paid $240 million cash, $10 million in stock, and agreed to pay as much as $75 million in contingent payments to acquire Viewpoint, but it gained a financial mainstay, acquiring assets that would account for nearly half its annual sales at the end of the decade. For Viewpoint, the only change was cosmetic. The company, operating as a subsidiary of Oxford Industries, changed its name to Tommy Bahama Group, Inc., but continued to operate out of Seattle and it continued to be led by Margolis.

TOMMY BAHAMA FLOURISHES AFTER OXFORD INDUSTRIES ACQUISITION

Expansion and brand extension, the themes of the company's development before the acquisition,

continued to describe Tommy Bahama's progress after the acquisition. The Margolis-led team launched a new brand in the fall of 2003, Island Soft, a line of trousers, shorts, shirts, and jackets in cashmere, silk, linen, and suede. At the same time, the company opened its first stand-alone Indigo Palms store in Newport Beach. In 2005, the company released a new sportswear collection under the Tommy Bahama Relax label, a more casual iteration of the Tommy Bahama brand. The following year, Tommy Bahama Golf 18 label was launched, introducing a line of women's and men's golf apparel that was sold at golf specialty stores. Meanwhile, Margolis journeyed further into the realm of brand extension, signing a licensing agreement with Gemini Cosmetics Inc. in 2004 to produce a men's and women's line of fragrances and negotiating a deal with Sidney Frank Importing in 2007 to produce Tommy Bahama rum. "Any chance we get to bring the brand into an area where the consumer is pleased to find it, it helps build Tommy Bahama into something much larger than just an apparel company," Margolis said in the February 12, 2007 issue of *Brandweek*.

FOUNDER RETIRES IN 2008

In 2008, Margolis, after working in the apparel industry for 46 years, announced his retirement from Tommy Bahama. He was replaced by Terry R. Pillow, a 30-year veteran of the apparel and retail industries who had spent his career at Polo Ralph Lauren, Neiman Marcus, and Giorgio Armani. Pillow took charge of a company that was expanding its retail presence across U.S. borders (Tommy Bahama stores were opening in Canada, Australia, and the Middle East) and continuing to explore new areas in brand extension. Pillow inherited control over a highly successful brand, and it was his challenge to perpetuate the Tommy Bahama aura created by Margolis, Emfield, and Dalla Gasperina.

Jeffrey L. Covell

PRINCIPAL SUBSIDIARIES

Tommy Bahama Texas Beverages, LLC; Maxsend Trading Limited; Tommy Bahama R&R Holdings, Inc.; Tommy Bahama Beverages, LLC; Tommy Bahama Global Sourcing Limited (Hong Kong).

PRINCIPAL COMPETITORS

Tommy Hilfiger Corporation; Polo Ralph Lauren Corporation; Nautica Apparel, Inc.

FURTHER READING

Clark, Julie, "Do You Like Pina Coladas?" *Display & Design Ideas*, November 2001, p. 25.

Hein, Kenneth, "When Sidney Met Tommy: Rum for the (Middle) Ages," *Brandweek,* February 12, 2007, p. 6.

Hofman, Mike, "A Brand Is Born," *Inc.,* December 1, 2001.

Larson, Kristin, "Tommy Bahama Goes Beyond the Beach," *WWD,* June 13, 2001, p. 29.

Lipke, David, "Tommy Bahama Taps Pillow as New CEO," *Daily News Record,* March 17, 2008, p. 6.

———, "Tommy Bahama to Debut Relax Store Concept," *Daily News Record,* March 26, 2007, p. 7.

Lloyd, Brenda, "Tommy Bahama Sends Oxford Soaring," *Daily News Record,* October 13, 2003, p. 1A.

———, "Tommy Bahama to Launch Fragrance," *Daily News Record,* July 12, 2004, p. 65.

Moin, David, "Tommy Bahama Accepting Suitors," *WWD,* March 14, 2003, p. 3.

Newkirk, Margaret, "Oxford Buys a Piece of the Beach," *Atlanta Journal-Constitution,* April 29, 2003, p. D1.

Schneider-Levy, Barbara, "Island Breeze: Though He Doesn't Exist in the Real World, Tommy Bahama Knows How to Build a Brand, Mon," *Footwear News,* February 1, 1999, p. 68.

Stewart, Al, "Tommy Bahama Stretches Its Scions," *Daily News Record,* January 19, 2004, p. 4.

Tschorn, Adam, "Tommy Bahama Group Realigns Brands," *Daily News Record,* January 15, 2007, p. 7.

———, "Tommy Bahama to 'Relax' with New Collection," *Daily News Record,* July 18, 2005.

TravelCenters of America LLC

24601 Center Ridge Road, Suite 200
Westlake, Ohio 44145
U.S.A.
Telephone: (440) 808-9100
Toll Free: (888) 982-5528
Fax: (440) 808-3306
Web site: http://www.tatravelcenters.com

Public Company
Incorporated: 1992 as National Auto/Truckstops Holdings Corporation
Employees: 11,900
Sales: $7.66 billion (2008)
Stock Exchanges: NYSE Alternext
Ticker Symbol: TA
NAICS: 447110 Gasoline Stations with Convenience Stores; 811111 General Automotive Repair; 722110 Full-Service Restaurants; 722211 Limited-Service Restaurants; 721110 Hotels (Except Casino Hotels) and Motels

■ ■ ■

TravelCenters of America LLC (TA) operates and franchises travel centers that are primarily located along U.S. interstate highways. TA's network of travel centers, the largest in the United States, spans more than 40 states and Ontario, Canada, and includes about 235 sites operating under the TA, TravelCenters of America, and Petro brand names. TA offers diesel and gasoline fueling services, 24-hour convenience stores, full-service restaurants operating under the Country Pride and Buckhorn names, quick-serve restaurants, and lodging. For TA's primary customer base of long-haul fleet and independent truck drivers, some travel centers also provide trucker-only services that include laundry and shower facilities, telephone and TV lounges, electronic (WiFi) communication, and heavy-truck maintenance and repair. In 2009, TravelCenters of America LLC was ranked number 332 on the *Fortune* 500 list of the largest U.S. corporations.

EARLY HISTORY

TravelCenters of America LLC traces its roots to its predecessor company National Auto/Truckstops Holdings Corporation, which itself stems from a distinguished lineage of other oil, transportation, and truck stop firms. National was established in December 1992 by an institutional investor group that included Clipper Group, L.P. and potential franchisees who were members of the new company board. In 1993, National acquired two well-established travel center operations to serve as its foundation. In April, the company purchased the truck stop business of Unocal (an oil firm with roots in the 19th century) that included 139 sites; this 35-year-old chain, the largest in the country at the time, included sites operating under National Auto, Unocal 76, and other brands. In December, National acquired a 44-site network from one of the world's largest and oldest oil companies, British Petroleum (BP) Company p.l.c. (established in the 1970s by the Ryder System, Inc., the network was later acquired by the BP subsidiary The Standard Oil Company of Ohio, or Sohio, in the 1980s). The acquisition of BP subsidiaries included rights to the brand names of Truckstops of America, TA, and Country Pride.

The resulting corporate structure of the 1993 acquisitions was that National Auto/Truckstops Holdings became the parent of two wholly owned subsidiaries, National Auto/Truckstops, Inc., comprising the former Unocal sites, and TA Holdings Corporation, which was the parent of and doing business as Travel-Centers of America, which in turn was the parent of TA Franchise Systems, Inc. (TAFSI). To enhance its brand image and create travel centers appealing to both truckers and non-trucker customers, in 1995 National Auto/Truckstops initiated a market research program aimed at designing a prototype travel center as well as a "protolite" center for smaller markets.

LATE NINETIES: NAME CHANGE, CONSOLIDATION, AND ACQUISITION GROWTH

In 1997 the company changed its name to Travel-Centers of America, Inc., and consolidated its former Unocal and BP travel centers into one centralized network of 171 facilities under one management team. The restructuring resulted in a holding company with three wholly owned direct subsidiaries: TA Operating Corporation, doing business as TravelCenters of America (TA), National Auto/Truckstops, Inc. (National), and TA Franchise Systems, Inc. (TAFSI). The company also refinanced its debt and began shedding travel centers in non-strategic areas and sites formerly in competition

with each other. In 1997 alone, TA sold 15 company-owned sites and terminated more than two dozen franchise agreements. Additionally, it converted more than two dozen facilities from leased to company owned. Following the consolidation, the company began rebranding itself and its facilities under the names TravelCenters of America and TA.

The company also launched a re-imaging and facility upgrading and building program to entice non-truckers (leisure and business travelers) into its travel centers in hopes of moving its customer base from an 80–20 mix of truckers to motorists closer to a 50–50 mix. Acting on company research, TA invested $200 million to change its designs and site features and began constructing new facilities based on completed designs for prototype and protolite sites. With the travel center industry growing at a rate of 5 to 7 percent a year during the 1990s, by 1997, TA wanted to keep pace with the growing number of truck stops expanding their sites and providing fast-food outlets.

The prototype design used to construct and refurbish travel centers featured the TA logo on a large pylon rising above a vaulted roof, a red archway, and spaces on the building's facade for quick-serve restaurant signs. The facility's outside featured a pet-walk area, and the inside had a business center with fax and copy machines, telephones, and laptop computer data ports. For its mainstay trucker customers, TA provided refurbished showers, laundry area, and television and phone lounge as well as an automated diesel gas-pay system to reduce truckers' refueling time. Additionally, truck parking spaces offered in-cab Internet, phone, fax, cable TV, and wake-up call services.

During the late 1990s, TA further expanded the geographical scope of its travel center chain with two acquisitions. In December 1998, TA acquired the truck stop network of Burns Bros., Inc., with 17 sites in northwestern and western states. To facilitate the acquisition, the company again refinanced its debt and increased its loan capabilities by $150 million. This refinancing also helped fund a $40.5 million, June 1999 merger-acquisition of Travel Ports of America, Inc., with 16 company-operated sites, largely in the northeastern United States. As a result of the acquisition, the subsidiary Travel Ports Systems Inc. became a TA subsidiary, renamed TA Licensing. After the Burns and Travel Ports purchases, TA's travel center network stretched from coast to coast and included 162 facilities in 40 states.

In July 1999, TA became an authorized provider of express service, repair work, and warranty repairs after signing a pact with Freightliner Corporation, a division of Daimler-Benz and the world's largest manufacturer of

KEY DATES

1992: National Auto/Truckstops Holdings Corporation is incorporated.

1993: Company acquires 139-site Unocal chain of truck stops; company purchases 44-site network from British Petroleum Company p.l.c.

1997: Company changes its name to TravelCenters of America, Inc., and consolidates its travel centers into one centralized network.

1998: TA acquires Burns Bros., Inc., a chain of 17 truck stops located primarily in western and northwestern states.

1999: TA acquires TravelPorts of America, Inc., a 16-site chain with facilities mostly in northeastern states.

2000: Oak Hill Capital Partners, L.P. acquires TA for $712 million.

2004: TA acquires 11 travel centers, mostly in southwestern states, from Rip Griffin Truck Service Center, Inc.

2006: TA becomes a wholly owned subsidiary of Hospitality Properties Trust.

2007: Hospitality Properties Trust spins off the company, renamed TravelCenters of America LLC; TA acquires competitor Petro Stopping Centers Holdings, L.P.

heavy duty and semitrailer trucks. TA, the only industry provider of truck repairs at each company site, became the first travel center firm to join with a truck manufacturer for such a service. Additionally, as part of the agreement, Freightliner Corporation subsequently acquired a minority stake of slightly less than 10 percent in TA, and TA's truck repair facilities became part of Freightliner's customer-assistance database for roadside repairs.

By the end of the 1990s, TA had revenues of $1.45 billion. After employing a program of active acquisition and subsequent consolidation, along with strategic closings and sales of sites, the company had 158 travel facilities. In sum, during the second half of the decade, TA had eliminated two-thirds of its franchisee-owner sites and two-thirds of its leased sites. It had also more than doubled the number of company-operated sites. TA's acquisition strategy had helped the company quadruple its revenues in seven years.

A NEW OWNER AND NEW CAPITAL

TA entered the 21st century with the largest travel center chain in the country, but it had only nominal earnings. The company was in need of capital for facility upgrades and further strategic expansion, and TA's majority-owner Clipper Group opted to find a new investor to finance future growth. In 2000, the private-equity investment group Oak Hill Capital Partners, L.P., founded by Texas billionaire Robert Bass, led an acquisition of TA for $712 million, a deal that included Oak Hill's assumption of $420 million in TA debt. The financial reorganization of the company gave Oak Hill 60.5 percent of the company's stock. Other investors (Clipper Group, United Bank of Switzerland, and Olympus Partners, all of which owned a part of the original National Auto/Truckstop) cumulatively gained control of 32.7 percent, while Freightliner's stake was trimmed to 4.3 percent, and members of management received 2.5 percent.

Concurrent with the Oak Hill sale was both a recapitalization and refinancing of TA that included $328 million in bank loans to the company and a $100 million revolving credit deal. For the year 2000, TA's revenues topped $2 billion although the company posted a $38.67 million loss. The following year, TA's revenues began a two-year slide, and the company posted another loss, of $10 million, in 2001. Meanwhile, revenues continued to fall, dropping to $1.87 billion in 2002 before climbing to $2.67 billion in 2004 when TA logged a $14.86 million profit.

In December 2004, TA expanded its service area farther into the southwestern United States through the acquisition of 11 travel centers from Rip Griffin Truck Service Center, Inc., including those in Arizona, Arkansas, California, Colorado, New Mexico, Texas, and Wyoming. In conjunction with the acquisition, TA also refinanced its debt, with J.P. Morgan and Lehman Brothers providing the company $575 million in credit, including a $100 million revolving loan to back the $120 million Griffin deal.

At this time, TA focused on a gradual means of expanding its network and enhancing its service for its primary customers, truck drivers. In 2004, TA opened its first Canadian truck maintenance facility in Ontario, and that same year it began offering maintenance services for refrigerated trailers. The following year, the company, which had been reducing the number of its franchised sites, once again sought new franchisees to address targeted strategic markets along state and interstate highways. In 2005, TA also initiated a one-year $30 million program to expand the number of its truck service bays from 400 to 600. The next year, TA started installing idle-reduction technology in about one-third of its travel centers. The technology, which both saved fuel and reduced neighborhood noise, was designed to allow truck drivers to heat or air condition their cabs as well as run electronic devices without running their truck engines. The use of idle-reduction technology at TA centers was not unimportant. A 2006 nationwide survey from the American Transportation Research found that "one-third of truckers' idle time occurs at truck stops," with truckers idling at rest stops 21 percent of the time, more than the 20 percent which they spend loading and unloading.

SECOND SALE OF TRAVELCENTERS IN SIX YEARS

In October 2006, TA was acquired for $1.9 billion by Hospitality Properties Trust (HPT), a real estate investment trust. Just as with the sale of the company in 2000, TA remained intact through the acquisition. In January 2007, HPT spun off the company, renamed TravelCenters of America LLC, as a separate entity. In the process, HPT shareholders became TA shareholders while HPT maintained ownership of a majority of TA's real estate and properties and leased those back to the company.

HPT acted quickly to both recoup its investment in and exert its influence on TravelCenters. In February 2007, HPT announced a public offering of five million common shares of TA priced at more than $47 a share. The same month, President and CEO Timothy Doane and CFO James George (both with the company since its days as National Auto/Truckstops Holding) were replaced by Thomas O'Brien and John Hoadley, respectively. O'Brien, who was a senior vice president for Reit Management & Research LLC, the managing company responsible for the day-to-day operations of HPT and the TA managing partner since the acquisition, was named the new TA president and chief executive. Hoadley, another Reit Management senior vice president, was named TA's chief financial officer.

In May 2007, TA acquired a principal competitor, Petro Stopping Centers Holdings, L.P., for $700 million, picking up 69 Petro sites in 33 states and giving TA a total network of 233 sites spanning 41 states. TravelCenters and Petro sites continued to be operated separately although TA management assumed control of both. In the deal, HPT acquired for $630 million approximately two-thirds of Petro's truck stops and leased them back to TA, which purchased for $70 million the remaining assets of Petro, including its franchisee operations.

FINANCIAL WOES AND THE FUTURE

In June 2007, TA announced a secondary offering of nearly five million shares at more than $41 a share. In late 2007, TA signed a $100 million revolving credit agreement. The following year, the company entered into a rent-deferral pact with HPT that gave TA the option of deferring its individual rent payments of up to $5,000 per month through the end of 2010. For 2007, TA lost more than $101 million, and its financial woes continued the following year. In March 2008, the company's stock hit an all-time low of $9.29, down more than 75 percent from its all-time high the previous June. With economic conditions worsening and the trucking industry suffering from weak freight volumes, in early 2008 TA cut its executive staff by about 8 percent and announced it would pare back or eliminate development and expansion efforts until economic conditions improved. For 2008, TA reported a $40.2 million loss. Unfortunately for the company, economic conditions for the first half of 2009 were worse. With fuel sales declining due to an ongoing downturn in the trucking industry, TA lost $33.1 million during the first two quarters of 2009. In response, the company deferred $30 million in rent to HPT during the period.

TA expected its financial future to be closely tied to the vitality of the U.S. economy, especially the trucking industry. Thus it remained uncertain whether a turn in the economy would drive an increased demand for eighteen-wheel-carried freight and spur more four-wheel motorist travel, and, in the process, provide the fuel for increased revenues and consistent profits.

Roger Rouland

PRINCIPAL SUBSIDIARIES

TravelCenters of America Holding Company LLC; TA Leasing LLC; TA Franchise Systems LLC; TA Operating LLC; Petro Franchise Systems LLC; TA Operating Texas LLC; 3073000 Nova Scotia Company; TravelCentres Canada, Inc.; TravelCentres Canada, LP.

PRINCIPAL COMPETITORS

Flying J Inc.; Love's Travel Stops & Country Stores, Inc.; Pilot Corporation.

FURTHER READING

Cable, Josh, "Acquisition Should Drive Growth Plans for Travel-Centers," *Crain's Cleveland Business*, November 20, 2000, p. 3.

Hardin, Angela Y., "Freightliner Deal to Raise TravelCenters Profile," *Crain's Cleveland Business*, March 22, 1999 p. 8.

———, "TravelCenters to Undertake $200M Makeover," *Crain's Cleveland Business*, September 1, 1997, p. 1.

"Hospitality Properties Trust Acquires 40 Hospitality and Fuel Centers," *National Petroleum News*, June 2007, p. 16.

"HPT Buying TravelCenters for $1.9 Billion," *Europe Intelligence Wire*, September 18, 2006.

Kalinoski, Gail, "Hospitality Properties Trust to Repay Acquisition Costs with Sale of 5M Shares," *Commercial Property News*, February 13, 2007.

Kilcarr, Sean, "TA Acquiring Petro," *Fleet Owner*, May 31, 2007.

Kovski, Alan, "TravelCenters Blends Two Truckstop Chains," *Oil Daily*, May 21, 1997.

Krummert, Bob, "Midscale Eats, Big Rig Style," *Restaurant Hospitality*, April 2001, p. 28.

Mezger, Roger, "TravelCenters of America Loses $15 Million in Second Quarter," *Cleveland Plain Dealer*, August 5, 2009.

Murray, Barbra, "Truck Stop Portfolio Trades for $1.9B," *Commercial Property News*, February 16, 2007, p. 6.

"Oak Hill Capital to Buy Leading Truck Stop Operator," *New York Times*, June 2, 2000, p. C4.

"TA to Acquire Rip Griffin Travel Centers," *National Petroleum News*, December 2004, p. 33.

"TravelCenters of America Cuts Jobs, to Slow Expansion," *Reuters*, March 10, 2008.

"TravelCenters of America: Rare Value Investing Opportunity," *Seeking Alpha*, September 14, 2009.

"TravelCenters of America to Be Sold," *Fleet Owner Online*, September 19, 2006.

U.S. Music Corporation

444 East Courtland Street
Mundelein, Illinois 60060
U.S.A.
Telephone: (847) 949-0444
Toll Free: (800) 877-6863
Fax: (847) 949-8444
Web site: http://www.usmusiccorp.com

Private Company
Incorporated: 1977 as Fretted Industries, Inc.
Employees: 164
Sales: $66.8 million (2008 est.)
NAICS: 339992 Musical Instrument Manufacturing; 334310 Audio and Video Equipment Manu- fac- turing

■ ■ ■

U.S. Music Corporation is a holding company whose divisions manufacture musical instruments, strings, amplifiers, and related accessories and equipment. The firm's portfolio includes Washburn and Parker guitars; Randall and Eden amplifiers; Oscar Schmidt Autoharps and stringed instruments; Lyon and Little Lyon instruments and accessories; Vinci strings; and SoundTech professional audio equipment. U.S. Music's largest unit is Washburn, which is the top acoustic guitar maker worldwide and one of the best-selling guitar brands in the United States. The privately held firm is owned by CEO Rudy Schlacher.

BEGINNINGS

The roots of U.S. Music date to 1883, when George Washburn Lyon and Patrick Healy began manufacturing instruments for their music store, which had been founded in Chicago in 1864 as an affiliate of East Coast music publisher and retailer Oliver Ditson. By 1885 Lyon & Healy had established a six-story factory on Michigan Avenue to produce a broad line of instruments under the George Washburn brand (later shortened to Washburn) that included guitars, mandolins, banjos, violins, woodwinds, horns, drums, and more.

In addition to selling instruments in its store, Lyon & Healy soon positioned itself as a supplier to catalog retailers Montgomery Ward and Sears, both of which were based in Chicago, and within a few years the firm claimed production of more than 100,000 instruments per year. Of this figure, guitars constituted only about 2,000, which nonetheless made Lyon & Healy one of their leading manufacturers. They were produced in a number of woods that included sycamore, oak, mahogany, and rosewood, as well as various sizes, designs, and finishes. The firm was one of the first to use an assembly-line approach to speed production, as opposed to building one guitar at a time, and this system was taken up by many other firms in ensuing years.

In 1926 Lyon & Healy built a new factory in Chicago to produce stringed instruments, as interest in guitars began to grow due to the success of such early country singers as Jimmie Rodgers. However, in 1928 the company's management abruptly decided to shift its

COMPANY PERSPECTIVES

US Music Corporation is a uniquely positioned, fully integrated musical instrument company that manufactures and markets instruments, accessories and audio equipment for professionals, aspiring professionals, collectors, hobbyists and beginner musicians.

focus away from manufacturing and distribution to expanding its retail stores, and sold the operation to J.R. Stewart Company. After orders plummeted in the wake of the stock market crash of 1929, the Stewart firm went bankrupt.

In 1930 the Washburn name was purchased by distributor Tonk Brothers, which contracted out production to Regal Musical Instrument Co., a onetime unit of Lyon & Healy. Production continued on a small scale until World War II, when the company turned to producing defense-related goods. After the war guitar manufacturing did not resume, and in 1947 the Tonk company was absorbed by another firm. Although a separate company that made Lyon & Healy brand harmonicas continued to operate, and its retail operations would last for a few more decades, the Washburn name appeared extinct.

In the 1960s Beckman Musical Instruments of Los Angeles bought the brand, and in 1974 it resumed production of Washburn guitars. The instruments were built in the Far East for import to the United States, and sales soon reached several hundred instruments per month. When owner Tom Beckman founded Roland Corp. USA several years later to distribute Roland keyboard instruments, he decided to sell the guitar business.

RUDY SCHLACHER ACQUIRES WASHBURN IN 1977

In January 1977 Rudy Schlacher and partner Rich Johnstone bought the Washburn brand. Austrian-born Schlacher had learned guitar- and violin-making in his native country, and moved to the United States in 1966 to repair instruments. He opened a music store in the Chicago suburb of Evanston the following year with $2,300 in savings, and subsequently developed a guitar string that was sold flat, rather than coiled. When its sales grew to top $2 million, Schlacher decided to begin making guitars. He rejected several brands, before settling on Washburn because of its long history and

Chicago-area roots. Schlacher and Johnstone's firm Fretted Industries, Inc., would market the Japanese-made instruments.

A year later the partners bought bankrupt Oscar Schmidt International, a maker of stringed instruments including the Autoharp, and other instruments used by music educators. The Schmidt firm dated to 1871, and at its peak had operated factories in New Jersey and Europe. Over time it had acquired the trademarked Autoharp, a version of the harp-like zither that had preset bars for easily playing chords, a feature popular with music educators as well as traditional musicians of the Appalachians.

Soon after buying Washburn, Schlacher redesigned its guitar line and sales of the inexpensive instruments began to take off. In 1987 he bought Johnstone's share in the company and acquired SoundTech, a company that produced speaker enclosures, mixing boards, amplifiers, and other professional audio equipment. The new unit specialized in supplying churches, and employed a Baptist minister who traveled the country touting its products. During the year Fretted Industries also changed its name to Washburn International, Inc.

EXPANSION IN 1991

After outgrowing its original quarters in Evanston, Washburn moved its offices to Northbrook and then Buffalo Grove before settling in a 52,000-square-foot warehouse/office facility in Vernon Hills in 1991. The firm also built a 60,000-square-foot manufacturing plant in Elkhart, Indiana, for SoundTech, which like Washburn sourced most of its products from the Far East. During the year the company launched a new production facility in Chicago to build solid-body electric guitars, as well.

With sales growth averaging 30 percent per year, the firm's annual revenues reached $40 million. It was selling some 15,000 guitars a month, and had 175 employees in the United States and 50 in Asia. Washburn's guitars started at $189 and ranged up to $3,000, with the average model selling for about $550.

The company was benefiting from a jump in interest in acoustic guitars, sparked by improved microphone technology and hit acoustic-based albums by Eric Clapton and others. Washburn took the unusual step of advertising on MTV's popular *Unplugged* television series as well as other music-related cable networks. Additional marketing efforts included co-promotions with Budweiser, the sponsor of music concerts around the United States, and Paramount Pictures, whose *Wayne's World* prominently featured a Washburn guitar. For the latter, 60 Washburn guitars signed by the film's stars

```
┌─────────────────────────────────────────────────┐
│                                                   │
│               KEY DATES                           │
│                     ■                             │
│                                                   │
│  1883:  Music retailers Lyon & Healy begin making │
│         Washburn brand instruments.               │
│  1930:  Washburn name is acquired by distributor  │
│         Tonk Brothers.                            │
│  1940s: Guitar-making ends with conversion to     │
│         defense production.                        │
│  1974:  Los Angeles-based Beckman Musical Instru- │
│         ments revives Washburn brand.             │
│  1977:  Evanston, Illinois-based Fretted Industries│
│         buys Washburn name.                       │
│  1978:  Bankrupt instrument maker Oscar Schmidt   │
│         International is purchased.                │
│  1987:  SoundTech is acquired; Fretted Industries │
│         takes name Washburn International.         │
│  1991:  Company moves headquarters to Vernon      │
│         Hills, Illinois; U.S. guitar production begins.│
│  1995:  Washburn acquires Randall Amplifiers from │
│         U.S. Music Corp.                          │
│  1999:  Firm consolidates Chicago-area operations in│
│         suburban Mundelein.                       │
│  2001:  Company acquires Vinci strings maker U.S. │
│         Music.                                     │
│  2003:  Washburn International is renamed U.S.     │
│         Music Corp.; company purchases Eden       │
│         amplifier line.                           │
│  2004:  U.S. Music acquires Parker guitars.       │
│  2007:  Firm licenses Hannah Montana name from    │
│         Disney for guitars, amps.                 │
│                                                   │
└─────────────────────────────────────────────────┘
```

Dana Carvey and Mike Myers were given away in regional markets. Like other guitar makers, the company had begun to sign celebrity endorsers including Nuno Bettencourt of the band Extreme, whose signature model was priced at $1,799.

In 1993 Washburn hired noted Tennessee guitar builder Grover Jackson to boost production at its Chicago shop, and also launched the Panoramic mixer line and reorganized its management to better handle customer service. The firm had annual sales estimated at $47 million, about half of which came from guitars.

PURCHASE OF RANDALL AMPLIFIERS: 1995

In 1995 Washburn International bought the Randall Amplifier company from U.S. Music Corp. It had been founded in 1970 by Don Randall, who in the 1950s and 1960s had played a key role in top guitar-maker Fender's success.

Washburn had a promotional budget of $3 million per year which was used in part for such programs as donating instruments to schools and hiring musicians to teach beginners. It also received a boost from such famous Washburn players as Bob Dylan, Jimmy Page, U2's The Edge, and George Harrison, whom Schlacher had met in 1966 when he provided technical support at Beatles concerts in Chicago and Cleveland. Attracting celebrity players was a valuable marketing tool, and the firm built custom instruments to their specifications and sent its staff on the road to make sure they were happy. Rudy Schlacher continued to head the company, with his wife Marianna serving as vice president and children Carl and Lisa also involved.

Washburn produced about 80 models of guitars that ranged in price from $200 to $30,000 for a custom model that was made with gold, silver, and mother of pearl. It offered endorsed models from Gregg Allman, Sammy Hagar, Vince Neil, and Paul Stanley of the band Kiss. The latter's guitar, known as the Black Diamond, retailed for $10,000 and had a body covered in hand-mounted shards of glass, with only about 100 made. Washburn was the third-largest producer of guitars in the United States, behind Fender and Gibson, and boasted the best-selling acoustic guitar in the world, the model D10, which retailed for about $250.

MOVE TO MUNDELEIN IN 1999

In the summer of 1999 Washburn International consolidated operations at a vacant 130,000-square-foot building in the Chicago suburb of Mundelein, closing its headquarters in Vernon Hills and moving other operations from Chicago and Elkhart. The company-purchased facility, which had been designed by a student of Frank Lloyd Wright, was located on 17 acres of land. Renovated at a cost of nearly $2 million, it included office, warehouse, production, and showroom space.

That fall Washburn International pleaded guilty to two charges of mail fraud for selling guitars, mandolins, banjos, and bass guitars that were made in Korea but had had labels attesting to their origin removed and warranty brochures that implied they were U.S.-made attached. The fraud took place between 1980 and 1994, and was uncovered during a 1994 raid on the company's facilities. Washburn was ordered to pay $880,000 in fines and $120,000 in restitution to the U.S. Customs Service for unpaid duties, and was placed on five years' probation. The $1 million total was the maximum that could be assessed.

In the fall the firm linked with the International House of Blues Foundation and donated 200 guitars worth $100,000 to a program to teach music to needy Chicago-area children, and in 2000 inaugurated the Mundelein Guitar Festival, a daylong concert held on its factory grounds. During that year Washburn also introduced a custom guitar built of wood from Nashville's fabled Ryman Auditorium, home of the Grand Ole Opry. Just 243 examples would be made, priced at $6,250 each.

In 2001 Washburn bought U.S. Music Corp., the owner of Vinci Strings. U.S. Music had evolved out of the Wisconsin-based Faas company, which had acquired the Guild guitar brand in the late 1980s and over time added several other companies including Randall Amplifiers and Vinci. Guild had been sold to Fender Musical Instruments Corp. in 1995, when Washburn had purchased Randall. Vinci's roots dated to 1953, when Amelio Vinci and his son Tom invented a machine for winding strings automatically that enabled much faster production.

WASHBURN BECOMES U.S. MUSIC IN 2003

On January 1, 2003, Washburn International, Inc., changed its name to U.S. Music Corporation to help divisions Oscar Schmidt, Randall, SoundTech, and Vinci better establish their own identities. Soon afterward the firm bought Eden Electronics, a maker of bass guitar amplifiers that had been founded in 1976. Sales for 2003 were estimated at $58.7 million.

In early 2004 U.S. Music purchased Parker Guitars, which was known for its composite-material Fly model. Designer Ken Parker had worked with Larry Fishman to create a guitar made of wood and composite fibers that was light but produced a broad range of tones.

In 2005 U.S. Music bought a 57,000-square-foot distribution facility in Mundelein, a half mile from its headquarters, and also launched a new brand called Mojo Strings. Vinci had been making strings as original equipment for other manufacturers, but now sought to market its own line. During the year the firm's Washburn division sponsored Riot Fest, the largest punk rock music festival in the Midwest, which featured 20 bands. A number of the company's guitars were given away at the event.

Washburn re-signed Kiss guitarist Paul Stanley as an endorser in 2006. A full line of solid-body and acoustic guitars bearing his imprint was planned.

In late 2007 U.S. Music reached an agreement with The Walt Disney Company to make guitars and amplifiers branded with that firm's popular Hannah Montana character. Unlike the company's other instruments,

which were sold through music dealers, they would be available from mass-market retailers. The company already offered a line of child-size electric guitars under the Little Lyon name, and other Disney-related products were expected to appear in the future. For 2008, sales hit an estimated $66.8 million.

More than three decades after Rudy Schlacher acquired the Washburn brand, U.S. Music Corporation had become a major force in the industry through divisions that made Washburn and Parker guitars, Randall and Eden Amplifiers, Oscar Schmidt stringed instruments, Vinci strings, and SoundTech professional audio equipment. The firm continued to seek new markets with efforts including a Disney licensing agreement, and appeared well-positioned for future success.

Frank Uhle

PRINCIPAL DIVISIONS

Washburn Guitars; Parker Guitars; Oscar Schmidt; Vinci Strings; SoundTech Professional Audio Systems; Randall Amplifiers; Eden Amplifiers.

PRINCIPAL COMPETITORS

Fender Musical Instruments Corp.; Gibson Guitar Corp.; C.F. Martin & Co., Inc.; Taylor-Listug, Inc.; Yamaha Corporation of America; Harman International Co.; Peavey Electronics Corp.

FURTHER READING

Applegate, Jane, "Music Firm Hits the Right Chord," *Chicago Sun-Times*, May 2, 1996.

Buursma, Bruce, "Guitar-Maker Strikes Comeback Chord," *Chicago Tribune*, February 17, 1991.

Donley, Michele, "Guitarists Unplug, Maker Hits High Note," *Crain's Chicago Business*, July 22, 1991, p. 4.

Gowen, Anne, "The Pick of the Pickers—That's the Goal of the Makers of Washburn Guitars," *Chicago Tribune*, August 28, 1994.

Keoun, Bradley, "Guitarmaker Pleads Guilty to Mail Fraud," *Chicago Tribune*, October 30, 1999.

"Leveraging Disney's Marketing Muscle to Move Music Products," *Music Trades*, February 2008, p. 92.

Lissau, Russell, "Washburn Guitars Ready to Rock Mundelein," *Daily Herald*, July 9, 1999.

Orthey, Mary Lou, and Ivan Stiles, *The Autoharp Owner's Manual,* Pacific, MO: Mel Bay Publications, Inc., 2001.

Roszowski, John, "Washburn Has That Extra Edge," *Libertyville Review*, September 6, 2001.

Stone, Emily, "Guitar Maker Plays to Youth Set with Low-Cost Acoustic Models," *Crain's Chicago Business*, April 8, 1996, p. 40.

"Suburban Guitar Firm Pickin' Up the Cash," *Bloomington Pantagraph*, February 20, 1991.

"The Top 125 U.S.-Based Music & Audio Suppliers, Ranked by Sales Volume," *Music Trades*, April 2009, p. 98.

"U.S. Music Acquires Parker Guitar," *Music Trades*, May 2004, p. 32.

Vigil, Jennifer, "Mundelein Plays Base Guitar for Firm," *Chicago Tribune*, August 18, 1999.

"Washburn Acquires Eden Electronics," *Music Trades*, February 2001, p. 62.

"Washburn Acquires U.S. Music Corp.," *Music Trades*, February 2003, p. 116.

"Washburn Guitars Built from Ryman Relics," *Music Trades*, September 2000, p. 98.

"Washburn Is Now U.S. Music," *Music Trades*, February 2003.

"Washburn Takes to Cable TV to Tout Guitar," *Music Trades*, October 1992, p. 93.

Wright, Michael, "Washburn Guitars," *Acoustic Guitar*, January 2009, pp. 74–81.

UniCredit S.p.A.

Piazza Cordusio
Milan, 20123
Italy
Telephone: (+39 02) 88621
Fax: (+39 02) 8862 8503
Web site: http://www.unicreditgroup.eu

Public Company
Incorporated: 1998
Employees: 168,000
Total Assets: EUR 1.04 trillion ($1.47 trillion) (2008)
Stock Exchanges: Borsa Italiana
Ticker Symbol: UNCFF
NAICS: 551111 Offices of Bank Holding Companies;
524210 Insurance Agencies and Brokerages

■ ■ ■

UniCredit S.p.A. is the second-largest bank in Europe, after the United Kingdom's HSBC, and the largest bank in the "euro-zone." The Milan, Italy-based bank boasts total assets of EUR 1.04 trillion, generating total revenue of nearly EUR 27 billion in 2008. UniCredit has been one of the leaders of the internationalization of the European banking industry, operating 10,200 branches in 22 countries. While Italy remains the bank's primary market, accounting for 49 percent of revenues, UniCredit has expanded heavily into Central and Eastern European (CEE) markets, which generated 30 percent of the group's commercial banking revenues in 2008.

UniCredit is present in 19 CEE markets, including Poland, Turkey, Ukraine, Bulgaria, Romania, Bosnia, Kazakhstan, Hungary, and Russia. The bank, which also operates in Austria and southern Germany, has grown through several major acquisitions, including Poland's Bank Pekao, Germany's HVB Bank, Bank Austria Creditanstalt, and Italy's Capitalia. The transformation of UniCredit, once known as state-owned Credito Italiano, into one of Europe's most geographically diverse and financially solid banks, has largely been the work of CEO Alessandro Profumo. UniCredit is listed on the Borsa Italiana.

GENOVA ORIGINS IN 1870

The 1998 merger of Italy's sixth-largest bank, Credito Italiano with Unicredito, the country's eighth-largest bank, and seven other prominent regional Italian banks set the stage for the emergence of one of Europe's most powerful banking groups. Credito Italiano's origins, however, lay in the late 1870s, while parts of the company's operations dated back to as far as the 15th century.

Credito Italiano was founded as the publicly listed Banca di Genova in 1870. Within two years, the bank had added an international component, establishing Banco de Italia y Rio de la Plata in Buenos Aires, Argentina. By 1880, the bank had also begun investing in industrial and commercial businesses in its region, and then throughout Italy.

The move toward more national operations was accelerated by a grave financial crisis of the 1890s, which saw the collapse of a number of Italy's largest banks.

The crisis led to a restructuring of the Italian banking industry as a whole. The Genova bank itself completed a capital increase, financed largely by German banks, and changed its name to Credito Italiano in 1895. At the time, the company employed fewer than 100 people, and, with total deposits of just ITL 32 million, had a market share of 2 percent.

Credito Italiano quickly began expanding, however. The company opened a new head office in 1897, then added its first branch, in Florence, in 1898. The company had acquired Banca Manzi in Rome in 1901, and Banca Meuricoffre in Naples, and Banca Vito di Cagno in Bari, in 1905. The company's shareholder base had by then shifted, with major shareholders including France's Banque de l'Union Parisienne and Banque Française pour le Commerce et l'Industrie. By 1906, the bank had expanded its branch network to 12.

INTERNATIONAL STEPS FROM 1907

Credito Italiano by then had become one of the driving forces of Italy's industrialization in the years leading up to World War I, providing loans and investments to many of the country's major industrial groups. The bank had also launched its first international investments. In 1907, for example, the company joined Belgium's Société Générale in the creation of Banca Brasiliana Italo-Belga, operating in Brazil, Argentina, and Uruguay. The bank was also the first Italian bank to open a London branch in 1911.

By then, Credito Italiano had moved to Italy's financial capital, Milan, opening its headquarters there in 1907. The company continued to build its branch network, which reached 32 by the outbreak of World War I. The bank's total deposits had reached ITL 360 million, for a 7 percent share of the Italian banking market.

As one of Italy's four largest banks, Credito Italiano played an important role in financing the Italian war effort, ensuring the flow of food and goods into the country, as well as financing the growth of its industrial sector. By the end of the war, Credito Italiano had car-

ried out a new expansion of its capital, to ITL 150 million, bringing in new major shareholders, including prominent industrialists Giovanni Agnelli and Riccardo Gualino. As a result, Credito Italiano came under control of Italian interests for the first time since 1895.

In 1918, Credito Italiano joined in the creation of a banking cartel closely tied to Italy's fast-growing industrial interests. The cartel attempted to coordinate the rationing of credit in the postwar period. However, the collapse in industrial demand, which had been artificially inflated during the war, led to a severe depression in Italy. By 1921, a large number of banks and businesses had failed. This enabled Credito Italiano to build its national presence, notably through the takeover of several banks, including Banca del Monferrato, Banca di Legnano, Banca Unione, and Credito Varesino.

GROWTH DURING THE GREAT DEPRESSION

The bank had already begun expanding its international operations. In 1917, Credito Italiano opened a New York office in order to service the large Italian population there. Into the 1920s, the bank began acquiring stakes in a number of banks outside of Italy, including in Austria, China, Egypt, France, Germany, Romania, and Switzerland.

In China, for example, the company created Banca Italo-Cinese, with backing from the Ministry of Foreign Affairs and a number of Chinese investors. Credito Italiano also opened two Austrian banks, Banca Italo-Viennese and Tiroler Hauptbank, in 1920. The following year, Credito Italiano added offices in Paris and Berlin. Backed by this international experience, Credito Italiano was given the task of founding Albania's national bank and developing the country's own monetary system.

On the eve of the Great Depression, Credito Italiano had grown into Italy's second-largest bank, with a branch network of more than 121 offices and a total market share of nearly 8 percent. As one of Italy's healthiest banks, Credito Italiano was called on by the Italian government to take over its struggling number three rival, Banca Nazionale di Credito, in 1930. By 1933, however, Credito Italiano, like the rest of the Italian banking system, was on the verge of collapse. The Italian government stepped in, creating the Istituto per la Ricostruzione Industriale (IRI, for the Institute for Industrial Reconstruction) and nationalizing much of the Italian banking system. Consequently, the Italian government took control of 78 percent of Credito Italiano.

Two years later, however, as part of a reshuffling of the Italian banking industry, Credito Italiano acquired

KEY DATES

1870: Banca di Genova is founded as a public company in Italy.

1895: Banca di Genova becomes Credito Italiano as part of a restructuring of the Italian banking sector.

1930: Credito Italiano acquires Banca Nazionale di Credito, becoming Italy's largest bank; the IRI (Istituto per la Ricostruzione Industriale) takes control of Credito Italiano three years later.

1969: Credito Italiano completes a partial listing on the Borsa Italiana.

1993: Credito Italiano becomes the first IRI bank to be privatized.

1998: Under CEO Alessandro Profumo, Credito Italiano takes over Unicredito; new entity is named Unicredito Italiano.

1999: Company launches its foreign expansion, acquiring 51 percent of Pekao Bank in Poland.

2005: The bank group, now known as UniCredit, becomes a leading European bank with the purchase of HVB Bank in Germany.

2007: UniCredit takes over Capitalia and becomes Europe's second-largest bank.

2009: UniCredit announces plans to complete a EUR 4 billion share offering.

Credito Marittimo and its 50-branch network. The IRI then took full control of Credito Italiano, which was delisted from the stock exchange. The passage of the Banking Law of 1936 established Credito Italiano as one of three "banks of national interest." The bank's operations were restricted to short-term commercial banking. Further branch office openings were subject to government approval, and its investment banking operations were suspended. In 1938, the IRI pushed through a restructuring of the country's branch office networks. Credito Italiano lost 22 of its existing branches. In their place, the company was forced to take over eight others, including four in the economic backwaters of Sardinia and Istria.

POSTWAR BOOM

Following the war, however, Credito Italiano became a major component of the reorganization of Italy's bank-ing sector, promoting the country's postwar reconstruction and subsequent economic boom in the 1950s. In 1946, for example, the company, which remained limited to the short-term lending market, became one of the founding shareholders of Mediobanca. Originally created as a medium-term lender, Mediobanca grew into one of Italy's most powerful merchant banks. Credito Italiano focused its operations on the Italian market. As a result, the bank, which regained control of its foreign operations, restructured its international branches into a network of representative offices instead.

At the start of the 1950s, Credito Italiano's network had grown to 253 branches, sub-branches, agencies, and offices, with a total payroll of 9,000. The company introduced an automatic nightly deposit service in 1956, and introduced its first computerized data-processing operations in 1960. Credito Italiano also carried out a new series of capital increases, reaching ITL 15 billion in 1959 and then ITL 30 billion in 1966.

By the end of the 1960s, the bank had added traveler's check services. In 1969, as the Italian government relaxed some of its banking rules, Credito Italiano launched a U.S. dollar-denominated, Luxembourg-based investment fund, Capital Italia. Also that year, the company re-listed on the Borsa Italiana. The Italian government nonetheless remained the bank's controlling shareholder.

RETURN TO INTERNATIONAL GROWTH IN THE SEVENTIES

Credito Italiano returned its attention to the international market in the 1970s in order to provide services for its clients' own increasingly international operations. The bank relaunched its London branch in 1972, followed by New York in 1973, Los Angeles in 1977, and Tokyo in 1982. The bank also opened a series of representative offices starting in 1973, including in Chicago, Moscow, Hong Kong, and Houston. At the same time, Credito Italiano made a number of stock purchases in foreign banks, including London's Libra Bank, Paris's Banque Transatlantique, and Canada's Orion Bank.

Credito Italiano expanded its operation to include credit card factoring, acquiring a 50 percent stake in the Italian business of U.K.-based Credit Factoring International. This was followed by the purchase of 50 percent of Eurocard SpA in 1978. Credito Italiano escaped relatively unscathed by the difficulties affecting the Italian economy in the 1970s. These included the Arab oil crisis, soaring inflation, a collapsing lira, and political instability that caused a new collapse of the country's industrial sector. The bank, like the other banks of national interest, faced mounting government pressure to rescue the country's struggling industrial groups.

These difficulties, however, set in motion a relaxation of the government's tight banking rules. Credito Italiano was allowed to complete a new capital increase, to ITL 160 billion, at the beginning of the 1980s, and to sell as much as 41 percent of its stock to the public. By 1983, the Bank of Italy had lifted the ceiling on bank lending, while lowering the restrictions on new branch openings, and enabling the credit banks to enter other commercial banking areas. In 1984, following a new capital increase to ITL 320 billion, Credito Italiano established its own asset management operations. The company also created a new investment funds trading arm, Gesticredit, and a London-based merchant banking arm that year.

PRIVATIZATION IN 1993

By the end of the 1980s, Credito Italiano boasted over 1.5 million customers and a 500-strong branch network. The company's international operations had expanded to include the Cayman Islands, Madrid, Amsterdam, Cairo, Beijing, and Madrid. The company's capital base by then had also been expanded, to ITL 800 billion.

With the start of the new decade, Credito Italiano, like the rest of the European banking sector, began preparing for the impending unification of the European market, slated for 1992. Credito Italiano recognized that it needed to acquire scale if it wished to compete on a Europe-wide level. In 1989, the bank launched a takeover attempt for Banca Nazionale dell'Agricoltura. The effort failed, however. Banco Italiano instead contented itself with a major branch opening program, following the elimination of remaining branch opening restrictions. Between 1990 and 1992, the bank added more than 200 new branches. The company also made two acquisitions, of Sicily's Banca Mediterranea di Credito and of majority control of Banca Popolare Di Spoleto.

Credito Italiano's healthy operations allowed it to become the first of the IRI banks to be privatized in 1993. As a public company, Credito Italiano then launched its drive to become a major Italian, and European, bank. This effort began with the acquisitions of two new banks, Banca Agricola Nord Calabria and Sicily's Cassa Rurale e Artigiana di Palma di Montechiaro, in 1993. The following year, the group acquired a majority stake in Banca Cattolica di Molfetta.

The arrival of Alessandro Profumo, first as general manager in 1995, then as CEO in 1997, set the stage for Credito Italiano's true transformation. The company completed new acquisitions through the middle of the decade, including of Credito Romagnolo Group, which was merged into Carimonte Banca, forming Rolo Banca 1473, in 1995. Credito Italiano also launched a dedicated Private Banking division, as well as a telephone banking subsidiary, ProntoCredit, in 1997. Still, Credito Italiano remained a small player in the overall European banking market, placing increasing pressure on its profits.

Profumo found his first transformational deal in 1998, when Credito Italiano, then Italy's sixth-largest bank, agreed to merge with Unicredito, the country's number eight banking group, in a deal worth $26 billion. Unicredito had been established in 1994 as the holding company for three of northern Italy's leading savings banks, Cassa di Risparmio di Verona, Cassa di Risparmio di Torino, and Cassamarca. The first two banks had been founded in the late 19th century, while Cassamarca dated its own origins back to 1496. The newly enlarged company became known as Unicredito Italiano.

EASTERN EUROPEAN AMBITIONS

A power struggle broke out for control of Unicredito Italiano between Profumo and the foundations behind Unicredito. In the end, Profumo won the day, and by early 1999 had begun to scout out new acquisition candidates. Profumo targeted a takeover of a major Italian rival. However, his first attempts, for Banca Commerciale Italiana, Banca Nazionale del Lavoro, and Banca di Roma, failed, in large part because of political interference.

Profumo turned his attention instead to European expansion and particularly to the emerging Central and Eastern markets, which Profumo called "New Europe." In 1999, Unicredito completed its first major foreign acquisition, a 51 percent stake in former state-owned Bank Pekao, paying the Polish government $1 billion. This purchase was quickly followed by a flurry of new acquisitions in 2000.

By the end of that year, the company had taken over Bulbank, the largest bank in Bulgaria; Slovakia's Pol-nobanka; Croatia's number three bank Splitska Banka, as well as stakes in market leader Zagrebacka Banka and the Czech Republic's Zivnostenska Bank. The following year, the company acquired Demirbank Romania as well, as it searched for new targets in Turkey, Lithuania, and elsewhere.

At the same time, Unicredito began building up its profile as a major European fund manager, establishing EuroPlus Research in Ireland. In 2001, Unicredito catapulted to the number five position in the European market through its $1.2 billion acquisition of Pioneer Group, based in Boston, Massachusetts, one of the leading fund managers in the United States.

Unicredito's efforts to gain control of a major rival in the fast-consolidating Italian market remained fruitless. Instead, the group carried out a reorganization on a smaller scale, absorbing Rolo Banca 1473 and four other smaller banks in 2001. The following year, the bank moved into Turkey, acquiring a 50 percent stake in Koç. The company then completed its acquisition of the Zivnostenska and Zagrebacka banks. In 2003, the company completed its restructuring, creating a holding company under the UniCredit name.

EURO-ZONE LEADER IN 2009

UniCredit signaled its arrival at the top of the European market in 2005, when it carried out a merger with Germany's HVB Group, the new name for Hypovereinsbank, formed through the 1998 merger of Bayerische Vereinsbank and Bayerische Hypotheken-und Wechsel-Bank. The merger, which cost UniCredit EUR 19 billion ($23 billion), gave UniCredit a significant presence in the southern German market, as well as control of Bank Austria and Poland's BPH. Profumo became the head of one of Europe's largest multinational banking empires with a market value of EUR 79 billion ($107 billion).

Profumo immediately began looking for his next deal, reportedly beginning merger discussions with France's Société Générale. Back at home, however, UniCredit saw its own position shrink, as the ongoing consolidation of the Italian banking sector created a number of new leaders, especially Intesa Sanpaolo, which claimed the top spot. This consolidation nonetheless provided Profumo with his next opportunity, as Italy's third-largest bank, Capitalia, suddenly became a takeover target.

Profumo quickly completed the purchase of Capitalia, which was merged into UniCredit in July 2007. UniCredit became the second-largest banking group in Europe, behind HSBC, and the largest in the so-called euro-zone. The company also took a spot among the global top ten banks, with a market capitalization of more than $100 billion, and total assets of more than EUR 1 trillion at the end of 2008.

While carrying out the integration of Capitalia, UniCredit continued to seek new expansion opportunities. At the end of 2007, the bank entered Kazakhstan, buying 90.8 percent of that country's fourth-largest bank, ATF Bank. The company's expansion was cut short by the collapse of the subprime loan market and the subsequent failure of the global financial system

in 2008. By April 2008, UniCredit announced that it would write down more than EUR 1 billion ($1.6 billion) from its investment banking operations. UniCredit's international exposure, with foreign operations accounting for more than 50 percent of the group's revenues, also hurt the company.

Nonetheless, UniCredit's limited exposure to the subprime loan market left the bank relatively healthy. At the end of 2008, UniCredit was able to post net profits of EUR 4 billion ($5.8 billion). By the middle of 2009, with its quarterly profits beating expectations, UniCredit was able to reject the Italian government's rescue funding package. Instead the company announced plans to raise an additional EUR 4 billion ($5.8 billion) through a stock sale in October 2009. Under Alessandro Profumo, UniCredit had become one of Europe's flagship banking empires.

M. L. Cohen

PRINCIPAL SUBSIDIARIES

A.S. UniCredit Bank; UniCredit Banca di Roma S.p.A.; UniCredit Bank; UniCredit Bank a.d. Banja Luka; UniCredit Bank Austria AG; UniCredit Bank Czech Republic, A.S.; UniCredit Bank Hungary Zrt; UniCredit Bank Ireland PLC; UniCredit Bank Slovakia A.S.; UniCredit Banka Slovenija dd; UniCredit Bulbank AD; UniCredit Corporate Banking S.p.A.; UniCredit Credit Management Bank S.p.A.; UniCredit Global Information Services S.p.A.; UniCredit International Bank (Luxembourg) S.A.; UniCredit Leasing S.p.A.; UniCredit MedioCredito Centrale S.p.A.; UniCredit Private Banking S.p.A.; UniCredit Tiriac Bank S.A.; UniCredit Zagrebacka banka dd Mostar.

PRINCIPAL DIVISIONS

Asset Management; CEE; Corporate; Global Banking Services; Markets and Investment Banking; Poland's Markets; Private Banking; Retail.

PRINCIPAL COMPETITORS

Royal Bank of Scotland Group PLC; Barclays Bank PLC; ABN AMRO Holding N.V.; ING Groep N.V.; Société Générale Group; Banco Santander Central Hispano S.A.; Landesbank Baden-Wurttemberg AG; Interros Holding Co.; Landesbank Berlin Holding AG.

FURTHER READING

Boland, Vincent, "UniCredit Boosts Sector Hopes," *Financial Times*, August 5, 2009, p. 15.

Carruthers, Quentin, "Taking Politics out of Italian M&A," *Acquisitions Monthly*, July 2007, p. 22.

Dinmore, Guy, and Peter Thal Larsen, "UniCredit Plans Eastern Push," *Financial Times*, June 27, 2008, p. 13.

Edmondson, Gail, and Maureen Kline, "An Italian Bank Pulls the Trigger," *Business Week*, June 27, 2005, p. 34.

Espinoza, Javier, "U-turn for UniCredit," *Forbes*, October 6, 2008, p. 40.

Hughes, Chris, and Peter Thal Larsen, "UniCredit Focuses on Boosting Profitability on Its Home Ground," *Financial Times*, July 28, 2008, p. 18.

"Investment Banking Drags Down UniCredit's Annual Results," *Euroweek*, March 20, 2009.

Michaels, Adrian, "Italy's Big Banks Get Back to Business After Mergers," *Financial Times*, February 27, 2008, p. 31.

Michaels, Adrian, and Peter Thal Larsen, "UniCredit Creates Banking Giant with Capitalia Deal," *Financial Times*, May 21, 2007, p. 19.

Milne, Richard, "View from the Top: Alessandro Profumo," *Financial Times*, March 27, 2009, p. 12.

"The Profumo Flair," *Economist*, May 26, 2007, p. 82US.

"Profumo's Sense," *Economist*, June 18, 2005, p. 71US.

Ram, Vidya, "Unique Italian Problem for UniCredit," *Forbes*, March 18, 2009.

Simpson, Ian, "Italy Bank Aid Spurned as UniCredit Eyes Cap Hike," *Forbes*, September 22, 2009.

"UniCredit to Hire Banks for EUR 4bn Rights Offering," *Global Banking News*, October 1, 2009.

UNIPAR – União de Indústrias Petroquímicas S.A.

Rua Araujo Porto Alegre 36
Rio de Janeiro, Rio de Janeiro 20030-013
Brazil
Telephone: (55 21) 2128-5700
Fax: (55 21) 2220-9237
Web site: http://www.unipar.ind.br

Public Company
Incorporated: 1969 as União Participações Industrias Ltda.
Employees: 3,000
Sales: BRL 6.64 billion ($3.63 billion) (2008)
Stock Exchanges: São Paulo
Ticker Symbol: UNIP
NAICS: 325110 Petrochemical Manufacturing; 325181 Alkalies and Chlorine Manufacturing; 325211 Plastics Material and Resin Manufacturing; 551112 Offices of Other Holding Companies

■ ■ ■

UNIPAR – União de Indústrias Petroquímicas S.A. (Unipar) is the name of Brazil's second-largest petrochemicals group, focusing, mainly through its majority stake in Quattor Participações S.A., on the production of basic and intermediate petrochemicals and thermoplastic resins. Quattor subsidiaries convert naphtha and natural gas into raw materials that are subsequently converted into resins such as propylene and polyethylene. A large number of other unrelated companies then use these resins as the raw material to manufacture a wide range of plastic consumer goods and industrial products. Carbocloro S.A., a joint venture with a U.S. company, produces chlorine and caustic soda.

THE MAKING OF A PETROCHEMICALS POWER: 1946–90

Unipar began with the establishment, in 1946, of Refineria de Exportação de Petróleo União by Alberto Soares Sampaio. This oil refinery, located in Mauá, São Paulo, came to be a major Brazilian processor of crude oil, so much so that in 1953 it was forbidden to expand since state-owned Petróleo Brasileiro S.A. (Petrobrás) was granted a monopoly over producing crude oil and refining it in Brazil. Ten years later, Petróleo União was nationalized, but when a military government seized power in 1964, it returned the refinery to Soares Sampaio with the condition that the revenues generated be reinvested in the oil sector.

The business was reorganized in 1969 as a joint project by Soares Sampaio's son-in-law, Pedro Geyer, two privately owned groups, and Petrobrás Química S.A. (Petroquísa), the petrochemicals subsidiary of Petrobrás. Named União Participações Industrias Ltda., it was incorporated later that year and made its initial public offering (IPO) of stock in 1973. Unipar was owner of an industrial complex producing and selling chemicals and petrochemicals. Only a small minority of the shares actually passed into public hands, and the president was an admiral with close ties to the military government.

Unipar's chief holding was Petroquímica União S.A. (PQU). PQU was established in 1966 by the three aforementioned groups, including that of Soares Sampaio, and Phillips Petroleum Company, but the state sector took majority control in 1973. In 1990 Petroquísa held two-thirds of Petroquímica União and Unipar only 28.6 percent. In the 1970s and 1980s Unipar basically financed its growth through its profits without taking on debt. For most of the 1980s these profits were, on average, around $20 million a year, but in 1988 the sum rose to $52 million. The following year, despite low world prices for Unipar's products, profits reached $43 million. Unipar was a group of 17 enterprises, although Unipar held less than controlling stakes in some, employing 8,000 people.

GEYER FAMILY TENSIONS: 1990–94

Geyer turned over his leadership of Unipar in 1990 to his eldest daughter, Vera. She was the only one of his five children, four of them girls, interested in the family business. One of her first actions was to tighten control of the sprawling group by reducing the corps of executives, ousting many of her father's old associates, including the admiral. Besides appointing a new president, she created a central planning group to coordinate policy.

The Geyer family held 52 percent of Unipar, but Odebrecht S.A., a group that included Brazil's leading construction company, owned nearly 40 percent of the common stock as a result of acquisitions in 1986 and 1988. In a bizarre turn of events, Odebrecht was able, in 1993, to seize control of the company in collaboration with Vera's own mother, Maria Cecília Soares Sampaio Geyer. As daughter of Unipar's founder, she, not her husband nor her children, owned the family shares. Maria Cecília was unhappy because Unipar had lost $30 million in the previous year, endangering her dividends.

Odebrecht executives rigorously monitored Unipar's spending. Administrative costs were reduced by 75 percent. The number of executives fell from 100 to less than 30. Two companies were shed: a manufacturer of sodium and potassium sulfate and a chemical firm. A manufacturer of plastics products took on partners. Unipar was able to earn a small profit in 1993.

However, Maria Cecília soon repented of her decision. She and her husband not only felt ignored but suspected that Odebrecht was exploiting the situation at Unipar's expense. After 10 months, direction returned to the Geyers, although Odebrecht executives wrested certain concessions before agreeing to yield power. The family, for example, had to give up its practice of billing Unipar for personal expenses. An executive told Rubeny Goulart of the business magazine *Exame,* "It was absurd, even the family's butcher bill was paid by the company."

NEW ACQUISITIONS AND PARTNERSHIPS: 1992–2007

Brazil was entering a period of privatization in which the government was planning to reduce its participation in the petrochemical sector, principally by selling Petroquísa's majority control of firms such as Petroquímica União. Unipar, in 1992, quickly took stakes in Petroflex Indústria e Comércio S.A., a subsidiary of Petroquísa, and Poliolefinas S.A., another Petroquísa subsidiary. With the divestiture of most of Petroquísa's stake in Petroquímica União, Unipar soon became the controlling shareholder of this essential cracker of naphtha, one of only three such in Brazil.

Another important addition was Unipar's purchase of a stake in newly privatized Companhia Petroquímica do Sul (Copesul), established in 1982 and a strategic supplier of raw materials for the petrochemical complex in Triunfo, Rio Grande do Sul. Such acquisitions raised Unipar's holdings to 25 with collective annual sales of about $1 billion.

Petroflex, one of these holdings, was the world's leader in the sale of basic rubber (for tires and shoes) and held a near-monopoly in Brazilian production of synthetic rubber. Wholly state-owned for 30 years and a Petroquísa subsidiary since 1976, Petroflex was privatized in 1992, when a consortium of Companhia Petroquímica do Nordeste S.A. (Copene); Suzano Petroquímica S.A., principally a polypropylene producer; and Unipar acquired majority control. Unipar sold its stake in the enterprise in 2007.

Unipar, in 1996, negotiated a partnership with Companhia Suzano de Papel e Celulose S.A. and Petroquímica da Bahia S.A. to establish Rio Polímeros Ltda. (later S.A.), with each taking a one-third share of the enterprise. Rio Polímeros was constituted to be Brazil's fourth petrochemical complex, in Duque de Caxias, Rio de Janeiro. This complex, the first in Brazil to use byproducts of natural gas as a feedstock in its cracker, did not become operational until 2006.

KEY DATES

1946: Alberto Soares Sampiao establishes an oil refinery in metropolitan São Paulo.

1969: This business is reorganized as Unipar, a chemicals and petrochemicals complex.

1988: Unipar is a group of 17 enterprises employing 8,000 people.

1996: Unipar takes part in what is destined to be Brazil's fourth petrochemical complex.

2008: Founding of Quattor makes Unipar Brazil's second-largest petrochemicals group.

After poor group results in 1997, Maria Cecília convened a special meeting of the Unipar board to replace its board chairman, Edson Vaz Musa. He was succeeded by Alberto Geyer, the only son of Paulo and Maria Cecília. An observer told Kara Sissell of *Chemical Week,* "The [Geyer] family has tried several times to have Unipar managed by professionals, but they have never succeeded because they're always fighting."

Unipar's relations with Odebrecht, at once a partner and at the same time a competitor, underwent change in the first years of the 21st century. In 2000 Unipar concluded a process of eliminating crossed shareholdings with Odebrecht Química S.A. with the creation of Polietilenos União S.A. (formerly Poliolefinas), a polyethylene manufacturer in the Mauá complex. The following year Odebrecht and a partner, the Mariani group, purchased majority control of Copene and then merged six chemical and petrochemical holdings, along with Copene, into a new company, Braskem S.A., which immediately became the largest petrochemical producer in Latin America.

Carbocloro S.A. – Industrias Químicas, a joint holding of Unipar and the U.S.-based firm Occidental Chemical Company, was Brazil's leading producer of caustic soda and chlorine and the third-largest industrial company in the state of São Paulo in 2007. The business magazine *Exame* judged Carbocloro to be the year's best chemical and petrochemical company.

THE CREATION OF QUATTOR PARTICIPAÇÕES IN 2008

Having helped create Braskem by selling off some of Petrobrás' petrochemical assets, the Brazilian government began seeking the creation of another integrated petrochemical producer that, in partnership with Petroquísa, would act as a competitor. Unipar and Petrobrás,

in late 2008, established a new company, Quattor Participações S.A., by means of a series of transactions involving their holdings in Petroquímica União, Polietilenos União, Rio Polímeros, and the polypropylene units of the former Suzano Petroquímica, which Petrobrás had bought in 2007 and renamed Nova Petroquímica. With annual gross revenue of about BRL 9 billion (about $5 billion), Quattor immediately became the second-largest petrochemical company in South America, with Unipar holding 60 percent of the capital. (Quattor's name was intended to evoke the four natural "elements": earth, wind, fire, and water.)

Quattor had nine production units in three states. It was expected to account for nearly 40 percent of polyethylene and polypropylene production in Brazil. Quattor's industrial facilities had the advantage of being closer to the nation's chief markets, São Paulo and Rio de Janeiro, than those of Braskem, which were located farther north and south.

Unipar's cracker in Mauá generally acquired naphtha either from Petrobrás or by means of imports. Rio Polímeros, three-quarters owned by Quattor, offered an alternative; it was the only Brazilian petrochemical company to use as the basic raw material not petroleum-based naphtha but ethane and propane, obtained from natural gas. One of its proposed projects called for converting glycerin produced during biodiesel production into propylene in order to make so-called green plastics.

Petroquímica União, by this time fully owned by Quattor, became Quattor Químicos Básicos S.A. Unipar's chemical division became Quattor Químicos Intermediários. Nova Petroquímica became Quattor Petroquímica S.A. Quattor Químicos Básicos was merged into Polietilenos Uni o in 2009.

Unipar's directly controlled companies, besides Quattor Participações, were Unipar Comercial e Distribuidora S.A. (fully owned), Carbocloro (half-owned), and Polibutenos S.A. – Industrias Químicas (one-third owned). The indirectly controlled companies were Quattor Químicos Básicos (the former PQU, fully owned), Quattor Petroquímica (fully owned), Polietilenos Uni o (fully owned), Quattor Químicos Intermediários (fully owned), and Rio Polímeros (three-quarters owned),

OTHER UNIPAR HOLDINGS IN 2008

Unipar had become a holding company with 10 plants and almost 3,000 employees. Especially in the production of polyethylene and polypropylene, it appeared to be a formidable competitor to Braskem. The company listed 92 projects to reduce costs as a result of its merged assets. It was expanding an ethylene cracker and two polypropylene plants and was at work on building a third plant.

Unipar's finances were a source of concern to investors and the Brazilian government. After earning BRL 145 million ($75 million) in 2007, Unipar lost BRL 152.3 million ($82 million) in 2008, mostly because of falling demand due to the world financial crisis and the consequent appreciation of the dollar against Brazil's currency, the real. Its debt had reached BRL 9 billion ($5 billion).

In August 2009 Braskem stated in a regulatory filing that it was engaged in talks with Quattor on a possible alliance. The news agency Reuters reported that a source said to have direct knowledge described the discussion as involving a Braskem purchase of Quattor but indicated that it was too early to speak of a deal, which would depend on resolving the differences among some shareholders. Investment analysts said that a merger could face antitrust questions.

THE GEYERS IN 2008

Paulo Geyer died in 2004. In the decade following his accession as board chairman of Unipar, Alberto Geyer lost control of the family holding company, and consequently of Unipar, to three of his sisters: Vera, Maria, and Cecília. Frank Geyer Abubakir, Cecília's son, was elevated to president (chairman) of the board of Unipar in 2008. Maria was vice president, and Vera was also on the seven-member board, but Alberto and his sister Joanita were left on the sidelines. The family holding company, Vila Velha S.A. Administrações e Participações, held 57 percent of Unipar's common stock and 19 percent of the total capital.

Robert Halasz

PRINCIPAL SUBSIDIARIES

Carbicloro S.A. – Industrias Químicas (50%); Quattor Participações S.A. (60%); Unipar Comercial e Distribuidora S.A.

PRINCIPAL COMPETITORS

BASF Aktiengesellschaft; Braskem S.A.; Dow Chemical Company; E.I. du Pont de Nemours and Company; Solvay & Cie. S.A.

FURTHER READING

"Como a Odebrecht vai tomando conta de tudo," *Exame,* June 23, 1993, pp. 48–49.

Gaspar, Malu, "Os enrolados sócios da Petrobras," *Exame,* October 10, 2007, pp. 108–10.

Goulart, Rubeny, "A força do batom chega á Unipar," *Exame,* August 1990, pp. 60–62.

———, "Não havia química entre os sócios," *Exame,* March 2, 1994, pp. 38–39.

———, "Um negócio de US$40 milhões," *Exame,* July 20, 1994, p. 48.

Jagger, Anna, "A Star Is Born," *ICIS Chemical Business,* November 10, 2008.

Parra-Bernl, Guillermo, "Braskem, Quattor Deal Hinges on Stake Holders," *Reuters,* August 24, 2009.

Ramiro, Denise, "Energia para crescer," *Exame Melhores e Maiores,* October 7, 2008, pp. 290, 292.

Sissell, Kara, "Unipar Board Attempts to Oust Vaz Musa," *Chemical Week,* April 8, 1998, p. 15.

Tullo, Alex, "Quattor Rises," *Chemical & Engineering News,* December 8, 2008, p. 23.

United States Postal Service

———— ■ ————

475 L'Enfant Plaza Southwest
Washington, D.C. 20260-0010
U.S.A.
Telephone: (202) 268-2500
Fax: (202) 268-4860
Web site: http://www.usps.com

Government-Owned Company
Founded: 1775
Employees: 656,000
Operating Revenues: $74.97 billion (2008)
NAICS: 491110 Postal Services Operated by U.S. Postal
Service

■ ■ ■

The United States Postal Service (USPS) is an
independent government agency that generates income
through postage and other fees. With a monopoly on
the delivery of noncritical mail, the USPS delivers about
46 percent of the world's mail, or more than 203 billion
pieces of mail annually. Beginning in the 1990s, the
USPS faced increased competition from rival package
delivery and courier services, as well as the Internet. In
anticipation of the widespread use of e-mail and other
e-commerce services, the USPS focused on developing
Internet strategies, such as computerized postage and
online delivery tracking of packages. By 2009, some 1.2
million people visited the Postal Service's Web site,
www.usps.com, every day, making it one of the most
highly trafficked government sites.

EARLY HISTORY: BIRTH OF THE UNITED STATES AND THE FEDERAL POST OFFICE

The Post Office Department had roots in America dating back to the 17th century, when there was a need for
correspondence between colonial settlements and
transatlantic exchange of information with England, the
native country of most eastern seaboard settlers. The
earliest mail services were disorganized at best, with no
uniform system in place until 1691, when Thomas
Neale established a North American postal service under
a British Crown grant and, in absentia, appointed
Governor Andrew Hamilton of New Jersey his deputy
postmaster general. Thereafter, under the control of the
British government, a centralized if erratic postal service
operated in the colonies. In 1737, Deputy Postmaster
General Alexander Spotswood, who had served as
lieutenant governor of Virginia, named Benjamin Franklin, then 31, postmaster of Philadelphia. Franklin
became joint postmaster general of the colonies and
undertook important reforms that led to a more efficient, regular, and quicker mail service.

Mistrust of the royal postal service led to changes
on the eve of the American Revolution. In 1774, the
Crown dismissed Franklin because of his activities on
behalf of the rebellious colonies. The colonists
responded by setting up the separate Constitutional Post
under the leadership of William Goddard. At the time
of the first Continental Congress in 1775, Goddard's
service provided intercolonial service through 30
post offices operating between New Hampshire and
Virginia.

Our vision of the future begins with a strong foundation. We will continue to strengthen our core operations and services, balancing an immediate and urgent need to reduce costs with a continued commitment to strategies such as Intelligent Mail, which are essential to our future. We will be guided by one principle: we exist to serve our customers. This vision is our commitment to ensuring a vital Postal Service for future generations.

The Continental Congress named Franklin chairman of a committee empowered to make recommendations for the establishment of a postal service. On July 26, 1775, the Congress approved the committee's plans, establishing the organization from which the U.S. Postal Service traces its direct descent and which, after the Bureau of Indian Affairs, is the second oldest federal department. The Congress wisely appointed Franklin the first postmaster general. Although Franklin served just a brief period, until November 7, 1776, he is generally credited with being the chief architect of the modern postal service.

It was not until September 22, 1789, after the adoption of the Constitution, that a law was passed to create the federal post office under the new government of the United States. It also established the Office of the Postmaster General. President George Washington named Samuel Osgood to that post four days later. At the time there were 75 post offices and approximately 2,000 miles of post roads.

Additional legislation in the 1790s strengthened the U.S. Post Office by expanding its responsibilities and codifying its regulations. It remained in Philadelphia, the seat of the federal government, until 1800, when in just two wagons it moved all of its furniture, records, and supplies to Washington, D.C., the nation's new capital.

The chief focus of the efforts of postal officials from the inception of the Post Office was on ways to achieve a more efficient and effective mail service. Finding the best methods of transporting and directing mail was always of primary concern. As a result, the Post Office played a significant part in the development and subsidization of new modes of transportation. Willing to experiment in the handling and delivery of mail, the Post Office was quick to try out new inventions and policies, even some disastrous ones that led to scornful criticism and ridicule.

RAPID EXPANSION IN THE 19TH CENTURY

During the 19th century, a citizenry hesitant to accept things new and different watched comparatively rapid changes transform the postal service into a remarkable public convenience. By the start of the 1800s, the Post Office Department had bought several stagecoaches for transporting both mail and passengers on the nation's post roads. Its patronage led to better stagecoach design, ensuring improved comfort and safety, and to better roads. In addition, a full 10 years before waterways became official post roads in 1823, the Post Office had begun using steamboats to transport mail between river-linked towns that shared no common road. By 1831, it had begun sending mail short distances via trains—the "iron horses" that many people denounced as demonic devices—and five years later awarded its first mail contract to a rail carrier.

Until replaced by automobiles and trucks at the beginning of the 20th century, horses remained major mail carriers, even over long distances, particularly during the period of westward expansion preceding the establishment of transcontinental telegraph and railway services. With the end of the Mexican War and the California gold rush of 1848, the need for effective communication between Atlantic and Pacific coastal cities quickly intensified. In that same year, the Post Office Department contracted a steamship company to carry mail to California. Ships from New York carried mail to Panama, where it was transported across the isthmus, then by ship again to San Francisco. The service was supposed to take between three and four weeks, a goal seldom realized in practice, and the Post Office sought alternative methods for getting the mail across North America in a more expeditious fashion.

In 1858, an overland service was contracted with a stage line, the Overland Mail Company, operating on a 2,800-mile route between Tipton, Missouri, and San Francisco. Semiweekly stagecoaches began carrying mail in September of that year. The service was prone to problems, however, and the advertised delivery time of 24 days in practice often ran into months. A solution was attempted by the Central Overland California and Pike's Peak Express Company, which, without a contract with the Post Office, in 1860 began operating a mail carrier service between St. Joseph, Missouri, and California. It was popularly known as the Pony Express. Changing mounts at established relay stations, riders could cover more than 100 miles per day. In March 1861, the Pony Express carried President Abraham

KEY DATES

1691: American postal service, under control of the British government, is established.

1737: Benjamin Franklin becomes the postmaster general of the colonies.

1775: U.S. postal service is established.

1789: U.S. Constitution is adopted and the federal post office is formed.

1847: First postage stamp is issued.

1855: Prepayment for postage becomes mandatory.

1872: Postal service is officially recognized by Congress as the Post Office Department.

1914: Post Office Department forms its own fleet of motorized carriers.

1918: Formal airmail service is introduced.

1963: ZIP code system is introduced.

1970: Post Office Department is reorganized as the United States Postal Service (USPS) and becomes an independent agency.

1999: USPS introduces Delivery Confirmation service and PC Postage.

2001: John E. "Jack" Potter is named the 72nd postmaster general; five mail-sorting machines at the Morgan Processing and Distribution Center in New York are found to be contaminated with traces of anthrax.

2002: President's Commission on the United States Postal Service is established.

2004: Former Postmaster General Marvin Runyon dies at age 79.

2006: First major legislative change to the Postal Service since 1971 occurs, with passage of the Postal Accountability and Enhancement Act.

2008: USPS names its first vice president of sustainability, Sam Pulcrano, to oversee all environmental and energy programs.

Lincoln's inaugural address over the route in less than eight days, encouraging the Post Office to put the service under federal contract. It began operations under that arrangement in July 1861, but with the transcontinental telegraph hookup on October 24, 1861, the celebrated service, rendered instantly obsolete, was halted.

Some important procedural and organizational changes also marked the pre–Civil War development of the Post Office. In 1829, President Andrew Jackson invited Postmaster General William T. Barry to sit as a cabinet member, although Jackson had no formal authority for the move. Although Barry's predecessor, John McLean, had in fact begun calling the service the Post Office *Department* even earlier, it was not until 1872, after the Civil War, that Congress officially recognized it as such. A year after Barry took his cabinet seat under Jackson, the Office of Instructions and Mail Depredations was created as an investigative arm of the Post Office. It was headed by P. S. Loughborough, generally regarded as the first chief postal inspector. In addition, by 1840 all railroads in the United States had been designated as postal routes, which quickly expanded rail service, the main means of moving large quantities of mail well into the next century.

Initially, mail was not sent in envelopes. Writers would simply fold their letters and address them, then drop them off at post offices where their correspondents would pick them up. In larger cities, there was a local delivery system that charged an extra fee for carrying mail to homes and businesses. An important innovation was the postage stamp, first issued in 1847 and followed by its mandatory prepayment use in 1855. Prepaid postage helped facilitate a new system of free city delivery, which by 1863 was available in 49 cities.

During the Civil War, the Confederacy created its own Post Office Department, with John H. Reagan serving as postmaster general. Although Reagan was appointed on March 6, 1861, it was a full two months before the Union postmaster general, Montgomery Blair, stopped the federal mail service to the secessionist states. The war, with Union blockades of Confederate ports and its eventual invasion, seriously impeded postal service in the South. Even at the end of the war, with the restitution of the federal post, mail delivery was irregular. As late as November 1866, fewer than half of the post offices in the South had been fully restored to service.

After the Civil War, "post offices on wheels," or mail cars, came into rapidly expanding use. They had first appeared during the war, in 1862, but it was not until August 1864 that an official Post Office route was put in operation between Chicago and Clinton, Iowa. Other routes quickly followed, providing mail sorting and handling services while trains were in transit. At first only letters were handled on the postal cars, but by 1869 all other types except parcels were being processed. The use of "post offices on wheels" would continue to grow well into the 20th century. In 1930, when trains were still the most viable means of long-distance hauling, more than 10,000 of them were used to carry mail to every city and rural town in the country. They would still be used into the 1970s, after the reorganization of the Post Office Department as the U.S. Postal Service, but very sparingly. The Transportation Act of 1958 had earlier ensured their quick decline, so that by 1965 only 190 trains still carried and processed mail. The last to do so, which ran between New York and Washington, made its final run on June 30, 1977.

CONTINUED GROWTH IN THE EARLY 20TH CENTURY

The invention of the horseless carriage and the airplane had much to do with declining use of mail cars and railroading in general. Both were extremely important in the changing face of the Post Office as it sought to provide service to the most isolated communities. Near the end of the 19th century, it inaugurated a system of rural free delivery (RFD) in a nation still in the process of shifting from an agrarian to an industrial society. Experiments with RFD were begun in West Virginia in 1896, despite vituperative complaints about its exorbitant cost and general impracticality. It was, however, a great boon to farm residents throughout the United States. It also stimulated the building and improvement of roads and highways, because service was provided only in places that had acceptable roads. In order for local residents to qualify for RFD, town and county governments undertook these changes at public cost.

Improved roads were, of course, inevitable, thanks to the automobile. In the same year that it inaugurated RFD, the Post Office began experimenting with the "horseless wagon" and in 1901 awarded its first contract for a horseless carrier covering a short route in Buffalo. For the next decade the Post Office contracted such services through private companies, but in 1914, fed up with excessive charges and fraudulent practices, it requested and obtained the authority to establish its own motorized fleet of carriers. Two years before that, the Post Office had won another fight with private companies when it obtained permission to put in place its parcel post service, a move that stimulated the rapid growth of mail-order merchandising.

After World War I, which provided a proving ground for the flying machine, the Post Office undertook a serious expansion into airmail service. As early as 1911 it had experimented with the airplane, sponsoring several flights at fairs and meets in more than two dozen states. In 1916, during the war, Congress even authorized a transfer of funds for the purpose, but it was not until 1918 that airmail service was begun in earnest. Using planes and pilots on loan from the Army Signal Corps, the Post Office began the first regular airmail service, between New York and Washington, D.C., on May 15 of that year. The date marked an important moment both in the history of the Post Office and commercial aviation.

The Post Office soon took complete control of the service, using its own planes and pilots, and despite reliance on primitive equipment and a lack of all navigational aids and weather data, compiled a remarkable safety record. The public was at first reluctant to pay the 24 cents charged for airmail letters, but interest picked up by 1920, when, on September 8, the last links were made to connect New York and San Francisco. By 1926, when the Post Office began contracting service with commercial airlines, it had won several awards for its pioneer work in night flying, the development of navigational aids, and the general advance of aviation in the United States. The transfer of equipment and stations to the Department of Commerce and municipalities was completed by 1927, when the Post Office put all airmail service under contract to independent carriers.

The Post Office's methods of sorting and distributing of mail were, unfortunately, considerably less innovative. Despite some earlier experimentation with canceling and sorting machines, the old "pigeonhole" method of sorting and distributing mail remained in practice until the mid-1950s, when the Post Office began a serious effort to automate mail handling. It started issuing contracts for the development of a number of mechanical devices, from letter and parcel sorters to facer-cancelers and address readers.

Leading the way toward automation was a parcel sorting machine first used in Baltimore in 1956, but it was quickly followed by the importation and use of the Transmora, a foreign-manufactured, multi-position letter sorter. This was in turn superseded by a U.S. machine, first tested in 1959, which remained in wide use into the 1970s. Other devices placed in service in the 1960s, when the mechanization program greatly accelerated, included Mark II facer-cancelers and a high-speed optical character reader (OCR) capable of sorting mail by the new ZIP (Zoning Improvement Plan) Codes.

The ever-increasing volume and change in the principal type of mail had made the changes mandatory. Most mail sent before World War II had been private correspondence, but by 1963, 80 percent had become business mail. The computer, an indispensable business tool, had already begun to play an important part in the rapid growth of business mail.

REORGANIZATION AND MODERN INNOVATION: SEVENTIES THROUGH EIGHTIES

On August 12, 1970, President Richard M. Nixon signed Public Law 91-375, which reorganized the federal Post Office Department as the United States Postal Service. Under the new law, which went into effect on July 1, 1971, the Service emerged as an independent agency of the executive branch, no longer under the control of Congress. Operational authority passed to a president-appointed and Senate-approved board of governors and a managerial infrastructure, headed by the postmaster general named by the governors. No longer a cabinet member, the postmaster general became the Service CEO. The law gave the new agency the authority to issue public bonds to finance operations and to engage in collective bargaining between management and union representatives. It also established a postal rate-setting policy and procedure regulated by the independent Postal Rate Commission.

The reorganization and partial privatization of the Post Office Department was undertaken to solve difficulties that by the 1960s had made its traditional operation an ineffective and financially disastrous albatross for the American taxpayer. Because the rates charged for services no longer bore any relationship to their actual cost, the Post Office had come to depend heavily on federal subsidies, rendering it increasingly susceptible to the vicissitudes of partisan politics. Furthermore, the managerial organization had turned into a bureaucratic maze, with a blurring of the lines of authority and fragmented control. Underfunding also had meant a continued reliance on antiquated facilities and equipment and mail-handling methods that, except for the introduction of the ZIP code in 1963, had not changed since 1900, despite a vastly expanded volume of mail. The resulting inefficiency led to long delays in service, with jams that from time to time brought it to a virtual standstill, such as that at the Chicago Post Office in 1966.

Along with the need to update both equipment and procedures, there was a clear need to reorganize management. In particular, labor-management relations had badly deteriorated in the 1960s. In March 1970, during congressional deliberations on postal reforms, poor relations led to a six-day work stoppage involving about 152,000 employees at 671 locations. For many postal workers, the proposed changes, including a salary increase, were simply not substantial enough. The workers returned to their jobs, however, when the postmaster general agreed to give the postal workers' unions a major part in planning reforms.

The most important problem faced by the newly created USPS was the upward spiraling volume of mail and the lack of adequate physical resources and equipment for handling it. Between 1970 and 1980, the volume of mail grew from just less than 85 billion to 106.3 billion pieces, an increase of almost 20 percent.

Alarmingly, it grew to 166.3 billion by 1990, and although the rate of growth abated thereafter, the problem of handling that quantity of mail remained formidable.

To deal with the increasing volumes of mail, the U.S. Postal Service updated equipment and sought new methods of improving its mail-handling efficiency. In 1978, it developed an expanded ZIP code, which helped reduce the number of times mail had to be handled. In 1982, to exploit fully the revised ZIP codes, the Postal Service installed its first computer-operated OCRs and bar-code sorters and the next year introduced the ZIP + 4 code to further define address sectors in any geographical area. By 1985, the new equipment and ZIP code refinements had made it possible for each key postal center to process 24,000 pieces of mail per hour, making it approximately four times as efficient as it had been using older sorting machines. By 1992, the Service also began replacing older facer-cancelers, the Mark II and M-36 models, with a more advanced facer-canceler system, which, processing 30,000 pieces of mail per hour, proved twice as fast as the older models. Put in use, too, were multiline OCRs, which, in conjunction with remote bar-coding systems, were capable of sorting even hand-addressed envelopes after they had been sprayed with an identifying bar code. These automated mail-handling machines and procedures vastly improved the ability of the Service to handle the growing volume of mail efficiently.

Increased cost was the downside of improved efficiency, however. Between 1975 and 1985, the first-class letter rate rose from 10 to 22 cents, and by 1995 it had increased to 32 cents, with proportional increases in other classes and types of mail. The greater expense to customers joined with a general slowdown in the economy quickly led to a slower rate of growth in the volume of mail in the early 1990s. In fact, in 1991, it declined for the first time in 15 years. The drop was also the result of growing competition, made possible, ironically enough, by the computer, the device that had played such an important role in the growth in the mail volume during the 1970s and 1980s. Fax machines, e-mail on the Internet, electronic money transfers, and increasingly competitive telecommunications rates offered viable and often preferred alternatives to the "snail" mail handled by the Postal Service. Many businesses that traditionally circulated advertisements via third-class mail, unhappy with the increasing rates, sought relief in telemarketing alternatives. Many mail-order shippers also turned to USPS competitors including United Parcel Service (UPS), which offered a quicker and more convenient package delivery service.

RESTRUCTURING AND MEETING THE CHALLENGES OF THE FUTURE

That competition caused the USPS, led by Postmaster General Marvin Runyon, who began his tenure in 1992, to undertake some restructuring. Of particular concern were customer needs and how these might best be met. In response, the Service instituted Customer Advisory Councils, made up of groups of interested citizens who worked closely with local postal managers to identify public concerns. There were 500 such councils in place by the summer of 1993. The USPS also issued contracts with private firms to measure customer satisfaction with the mail service. Efforts to reduce bureaucracy and costs, improve customer relations, and stabilize postal rates followed. A downsizing program reduced the upper echelon personnel by one-half, and, without layoffs or furloughs, cut other overhead positions by 30,000 through a policy of early retirements and other incentives. At the same time, it made strides toward its automation goals, which by 1994 were less than half realized. Estimates in that year were that 12,000 automation units would be in place and operating by 1997, a considerable increase over the 4,000 put in place between 1991 and 1994.

Downsizing and restructuring helped the Postal Service considerably, but in the mid-1990s it still faced recurring problems that related to its massive size. For example, it was straddled with retirement benefit costs that totaled more than 10 percent of its sales, one of many reasons why it operated with an annual deficit. Its size, however, simply reflected the daunting nature of its task. The Postal Service handled 40 percent of the world's mail, processing about 580 million items per day. It employed the largest civilian workforce in the nation, operated a transportation network using more than 200,000 vehicles, and used more than 250 million square feet of owned or leased office and storage space. Moreover, despite its ungainly size, it remained doggedly efficient in its primary mission: to get mail where it was supposed to go and, usually, on time.

As the USPS headed toward the 21st century, it continued to focus on implementing its restructuring strategy and to keep pace with its competitors, which included the ever threatening Internet. By 1998, the Postal Service acknowledged, operations were being affected by the growing popularity of computerized banking and online bill-paying services. Bills, payments, and statements accounted for 25 percent of the USPS's business, and increased usage of online services threatened to significantly hurt the Service's revenues. As the Postal Service strove to function effectively in the competitive atmosphere, it faced criticism from various business

groups, particularly UPS, which contended that the USPS was a monopoly that used its revenues to finance products and projects that unfairly competed against private business.

The Postal Service also faced some internal challenges during the mid-1990s when Loren Smith, the senior vice president of marketing for the USPS from 1994 to 1996, confirmed that he exceeded his 1995 advertising budget of $140 million by 62 percent, or $87 million. Smith was also responsible for launching a variety of new marketing programs, including offering postal paraphernalia, such as T-shirts and mugs, at post offices, redesigning post offices, and selling prepaid phone cards. Although the sale of USPS logo-emblazoned products did well, the Service chose to discontinue the business in 1998 as it strayed a bit too far from the core mission of the USPS. The USPS also faced criticism from the General Accounting Office, which reported in late 1998 that the Postal Service had spent about $234 million since 1995 to develop new business but had only recovered $149 million in new revenues.

Despite these challenges, the USPS enjoyed strong revenues and growth in operations in the late 1990s. A five-year investment program of $17 billion was implemented in 1995, and the USPS committed to investing in modernizing and automating numerous operations and acquiring new vehicles and facilities. In 1998 alone, the Service spent more than $3 billion to improve facilities, purchase vehicles, and acquire mail processing equipment. Also in 1998, the USPS reported positive net income for the fourth consecutive year, lowered debt from $9.9 billion in 1992 to $6.4 billion, and maintained steady postal rates for the fourth straight year. William J. Henderson was named postmaster general in May when Runyon returned to the private sector. The Service attempted to update its stodgy image in 1998 as well with a $15 million advertising campaign. The campaign, which included television, print, and radio ads, used the theme, "Fly Like an Eagle," and television commercials employed the Steve Miller Band song of the same name. The ads were designed to position the USPS as a progressive and modern organization.

The U.S. Postal Service continued to improve operations and prepare for the future in 1999. At the beginning of the year postal rates increased by 2.9 percent, or one cent for standard letters. The rate increase was the first in four years and was also the lowest increase to date. In March the USPS launched its Delivery Confirmation service, enabling customers to track packages sent via Priority Mail and Parcel Post. The new service made the USPS more competitive with companies such as UPS and FedEx, which had long offered tracking services. A month later, the USPS introduced Priority Mail Global Guaranteed, which provided two-day guaranteed service to a number of countries in Western Europe. The service was available in major metropolitan markets and expansion to additional countries was planned.

Foreseeing the impact of the Internet on its business, the Postal Service explored various Internet opportunities and offered a number of services on its Web site, including information about the USPS and the ability to order supplies, calculate rates, and track the location of packages. In August 1999 the USPS introduced online postage services, known as PC Postage. The Service had worked for more than three years with private businesses to develop a standard for digital postage. Companies independently developed PC Postage products, which allowed customers to buy and print postage on their computers, and sought approval by the Postal Service. Two companies, E-Stamp Corporation and Stamps.com Inc., gained approval for commercial distribution in 1999. The USPS also launched a Web site, www.usprioritymail.com, designed to generate Priority Mail sales to online retailers. Generally, the majority of e-commerce companies used one delivery company, and the Postal Service hoped to increase its share. The site offered free software for online retailers to download and incorporate into their own Web sites. The USPS also worked on developing PostalOne!, an information system geared toward large customers that would support the acceptance of bulk mail, postage payment, transportation, and data exchange.

The USPS enjoyed a fifth consecutive year of positive net income in 1999, reporting net income of $363 million on revenues of $62.7 billion. The Service handled a record 200 billion pieces of mail and achieved increased productivity as well. Despite the positive figures, the USPS noted that unexpected expenses arose, including an additional $100 million for health benefits and an outlay of $300 million for Y2K issues. The postponement of a postal rate increase until January 1999 reduced the Service's projected income by $800 million. The cutting of expenditures by $1 billion, however, helped offset the declines.

CHALLENGES OF THE NEW MILLENNIUM

Although the USPS was forced to shift gears to remain viable in a rapidly changing environment, its fundamental purpose remained the same: to deliver mail. Postal Service spokesperson Judy de Torok commented on the changing climate in the *Boston Globe*:

"Our goal is to have mail remain relevant to the American public. ... For us the challenge is, how do we continue to reach customers in the electronic world?"

As the USPS entered the new millennium, the question remained unanswered, but the Service was committed to the ongoing search for solutions. In January 2000, Peter A. Jacobson was named senior vice president and chief technology officer, returning to the USPS after a five-year stint in the private sector.

A number of advancements were made in 2001. That year, the USPS established a business alliance with FedEx and introduced both its Signature Confirmation and Internet change of address services. On the leadership front, Chief Operating Officer and Executive Vice President John E. "Jack" Potter, who had begun his career as a part-time postal clerk in 1978, was named as the 72nd postmaster general.

The early 2000s also were marked by a number of setbacks. Projected budget deficits led the USPS to cancel plans for an 800,000-square-foot distribution center near Cincinnati in mid-2001. In October of that year, five mail-sorting machines at the Service's massive 2.2-million-square-foot Morgan Processing and Distribution Center in New York were found to be contaminated with traces of anthrax. Officials proceeded to decontaminate specific areas of the facility. The Postal Union filed an unsuccessful lawsuit in an attempt to close the facility until the anthrax had been completely removed.

More developments occurred in December, when an employee at a processing facility in Bellmawr, New Jersey, was suspected of contracting anthrax, resulting in two million pieces of mail being stranded at the facility. Then, additional traces of anthrax were again detected at the Morgan facility in early 2002. Despite the setbacks, developments continued at this facility, including the installation of new bar-code scanners to improve the accuracy of mail processing. Other developments in 2002 included the formation of the President's Commission on the United States Postal Service.

In mid-2004, former Postmaster General Runyon died at the age of 79, as a result of a lung disease called pulmonary fibrosis. That year, the Service deployed biohazard detection equipment and implemented a pay-for-performance plan. In addition, a partnership was established with the online auction Web site eBay. Specifically, the USPS and eBay rolled out an online shipping service that gave shippers the ability to buy postage and print shipping labels from their computer. In addition, free co-branded shipping supplies were introduced, including boxes that included each organization's logo.

POSTAL EVOLUTION

Progress continued as the USPS headed into the middle of the decade. In 2005, the Service announced that standard mail volume exceeded that of first-class mail. The following year, the first major legislative change to the Postal Service since 1971 occurred, with passage of the Postal Accountability and Enhancement Act. Specifically, the act gave the USPS additional flexibility in setting its prices, allowing it to be more responsive to both customer needs and market conditions. Finally, the testing of fuel-cell technology was expanded that year when the Service extended a research partnership with General Motors that involved experimentation with hydrogen fuel-cell vehicles.

In 2007, the Postal Service introduced its "Forever" stamp. More partnerships were developed that year, including a tie-up with the U.S. Small Business Administration to develop an Internet-based small business advertising tool.

The USPS was also focused on environmental issues. Midway through 2008, the agency named its first vice president of sustainability, Sam Pulcrano, to oversee all of its environmental and energy programs. Specifically, Pulcrano pledged to determine the Service's greenhouse gas emissions, and develop a plan for reducing them.

More partnerships were developed in early 2009. Early that year, the USPS partnered with UPS in a new pilot program called UPS Returns Flexible Access. Specifically, the program allowed consumers to use special packaging labels to send returns via UPS by leaving the packages for pickup by a USPS carrier, or dropping the packages off at a post office.

Another interesting development in 2009 occurred in August, when the USPS prepared to auction off its vacant, 2.7-million-square-foot central post office in Chicago. The Postal Service had been exploring various redevelopment schemes for the building for about 10 years, with no success. With bidding slated to begin at $300,000, the facility provided would-be buyers with a chance to secure a large amount of space in downtown Chicago for a reasonable price. However, the facility's annual maintenance and utility costs alone totaled approximately $2.5 million. Due to the dire economic conditions that existed in late 2009, many of the city's leading real estate developers had not expressed any interest in the property.

The Postal Service found itself in a difficult climate heading into late 2009. The USPS recorded a $2.4 billion net loss during the third quarter alone, despite efforts to reduce costs, bringing its year-to-date net loss to $4.7 billion. As more consumers turned to electronic forms of communication, and the economy continued to struggle, it appeared that difficult conditions would persist for the foreseeable future.

John W. Fiero
Updated, Mariko Fujinaka; Paul R. Greenland

PRINCIPAL COMPETITORS

United Parcel Service Inc.; FedEx Corp.; DHL International GmbH.

FURTHER READING

"Anthrax Again Found on New York Mail Machine," *Medical Letter on the CDC & FDA*, January 20, 2002.

Atkinson, Helen, "Postal Service to Compete for Delivery of Goods Bought Online," *Journal of Commerce*, August 30, 1999, p. 5.

Bruns, James H., *Mail on the Move*, Polo, IL: Transportation Trails, 1992.

Cullinan, Gerald, *The Office Department*, New York: Frederick A. Praeger, 1968.

———, *The United States Postal Service*, New York: Frederick A. Praeger, 1973.

Ferrara, Peter J., ed., *Free the Mail: Ending the Postal Monopoly*, Washington, DC: Cato Institute, 1990.

Fleishman, Joel L., ed., *The Future of the Postal Service*, New York: Frederick A. Praeger, 1983.

Gay, Lance, "Postal Service Losing Money in Its New Lines," *Houston Chronicle*, November 28, 1998, p. 19.

Jackson, Donald Dale, *Flying the Mail*, Alexandria, VA: Time-Life Books, 1982.

Krause, Kristin S., "USPS Stirs the Pot," *Traffic World*, May 4, 1998, p. 42.

Lewis, Diane E., "Postal Service Leans Toward Overhaul in E-Mail Era," *Boston Globe*, December 5, 1999, p. El.

Long, Bryant A., and William J. Dennis, *Mail by Rail: The Story of the Postal Transportation Service*, New York: Simmons-Boardman Publishing Corp., 1951.

"Marvin Runyon Dies at 79; Former Postmaster General," *New York Times*, May 4, 2004.

"Postal Service Expands Fuel Cell Testing," *Fleet Owner*, September 28, 2006.

"Potter Named 72nd Postmaster General," *American Printer*, August 2001.

Riggs, Larry, "USPS Names Pulcrano First Sustainability VP," *Direct*, May 20, 2008.

Scheele, Carl H., *A Short History of the Mail Service*, Washington, DC: Smithsonian Institution Press, 1970.

Sharoff, Robert, "Bids Start at $300,000 for Chicago's Old Post Office," *New York Times*, August 5, 2009.

Sorkin, Alan L., *The Economics of the Postal System: Alternatives and Reform*, Lexington, MA: Lexington Books, 1980.

Summerfield, Arthur E., *U.S. Mail: The Story of the United States Postal Service*, New York: Holt, Rinehart and Winston, 1960.

Teinowitz, Ira, "Postal 'Idea Man' Goes $87 Mil Overboard on Ad Plans," *Advertising Age*, October 21, 1996.

U.S. Post Office Department, *A Brief History of the United States Postal Service*, Washington, DC: Government Printing Office, 1933.

The U.S. Postal Service: Status and Prospects of a Public Enterprise, Dover, MA: Auburn House Publishing Co., 1992.

United States Soccer Federation

1801 South Prairie Avenue
Chicago, Illinois 60616
U.S.A.
Telephone: (312) 808-1300
Fax: (312) 808-1301
Web site: http://www.ussoccer.com

Private Company
Incorporated: 1914 as United States Football Association
Employees: 92
Operating Revenues: $50.6 million (2008)
NAICS: 711320 Promoters of Performing Arts, Sports, and Similar Events Without Facilities

■ ■ ■

United States Soccer Federation (USSF) is the governing body of soccer in the United States, presiding over the professional, amateur, and recreational aspects of the sport. The USSF supports men, women, and youth squads representing the United States in World Cup and Olympic Games tournaments. At the professional level, the organization oversees Major League Soccer, United Soccer Leagues, National Indoor Soccer League, and Women's Professional Soccer. The USSF also governs affiliates such as United States Youth Soccer Association, American Youth Soccer Organization, United States Adult Soccer Association, U.S. Club Soccer, and National Soccer Coaches Association of America, promoting and supporting soccer at the recreational level. The USSF operates the U.S. Soccer National Training Center in Carson, California, a complex of facilities used as a training site for U.S. national teams. The USSF is a member of the Confederation of North, Central America and Caribbean Association Football, the continental governing body of soccer, and the Fédération Internationale de Football Association, the worldwide governing body for the sport.

ORIGINS

For at least a century before the USSF was formed, organized soccer had existed in the United States. It would take the formation of a national governing body, though, to lend genuine cohesion to the sport. The formation of the first organized soccer club, the Oneidas of Boston, in 1862 represented one significant milestone, and the organization of soccer as a college sport following the Civil War (Princeton University and Rutgers University played the first intercollegiate soccer match in 1876) represented another meaningful milestone. The creation of the American Football Association in 1884 marked the first time a governing body for soccer was formed, but the Newark, New Jersey-based entity only presided over soccer clubs in metropolitan areas in the eastern United States. A national body charged with governing soccer activities throughout the nation did not emerge until the USSF was formed in 1913 as the United States Football Association. (The organization changed its name to United States Soccer Football Association in 1945 and to United States Soccer Federation in 1974.)

Countries across the globe formed their own national associations in the years preceding and following the creation of the USSF. A worldwide governing

COMPANY PERSPECTIVES

As the governing body of soccer in all its forms in the United States, U.S. Soccer has helped chart the course for the sport in the USA for more than 90 years. In this time, the Federation's mission statement has been very simple and very clear: to make soccer, in all its forms, a preeminent sport in the United States and to continue the development of soccer at all recreational and competitive levels.

body was created when the Fédération Internationale de Football Association (FIFA) was formed in Paris in 1904. The USSF joined FIFA on a provisional basis in 1913 and was granted full membership the following year, when the organization was incorporated under the laws of the state of New York.

As the USSF set out, its success would be measured by the popularity of soccer in the United States. The sport's popularity, in turn, was determined largely by the performance of U.S. national teams (both men and women) on the world stage, the success of professional leagues, and the level of participation on a recreational basis, all of which were intertwined and under the USSF's jurisdiction. Largely, the USSF's growth was pinned to the performance on the field of the teams and leagues it governed, making the history of the USSF tantamount to the history of soccer in the United States.

EARLY YEARS OF THE U.S. NATIONAL TEAM

Although the USSF was one of the first national associations outside of Europe to join FIFA, the popularity of soccer in the United States lagged behind the support the sport enjoyed in other nations. It took decades before the popularity of U.S. soccer reached anywhere near the levels existent in other countries. The U.S. national team made their first journey abroad in 1916, playing six matches in Norway and Sweden, ending the tour with three victories. The first professional league, the American Soccer League, was formed in 1921, but the seven-team league, comprising teams from a five-state region on the East Coast, disbanded in 1933. The first significant moment for U.S. soccer and the USSF occurred in 1930, when the U.S. national team played in FIFA's inaugural World Cup in 1930. The United States was one of 13 teams to play in the tournament and it distinguished itself; a U.S. player, Bert Patenaude scored the first hat trick (three goals) in World Cup his-

tory, advancing to the semifinals before being knocked out of the tournament by Argentina.

The U.S. national team's performance in the quadrennial World Cup became one of the most important indicators of the USSF's success. As the U.S. national team went, so did the USSF. After the 1930 World Cup, a tournament open to any member of FIFA, national teams had to qualify to participate, presenting the U.S. national team and the USSF with a test that had to be passed every four years to give the United States legitimacy as a soccer nation. The United States qualified for the 1934 World Cup, exiting in the first round of play, but it did not qualify for the 1938 World Cup. World War II suspended World Cup play until 1950, when the United States qualified and gave the USSF its first crowning achievement. The United States was eliminated in the group stage in the tournament, but it beat England, the overwhelming favorite, 1–0 on a goal by Joe Gaetjens that shocked the world and ignited interest in soccer in the United States. On the international stage, however, U.S. soccer disappeared from view following the 1950 World Cup, spending the next 40 years longing for a return to the glory engendered by Gaetjens' goal.

USSF EXPANDS AND A NATIONAL PROFESSIONAL LEAGUE DEBUTS: 1940–67

The USSF suffered from the inability of the United States to qualify for the World Cup, but the development of the sport did advance during the decades away from the world's largest sporting event. The National Soccer Coaches Association of America (NSCAA), an affiliate of the USSF, was organized in 1941 by 10 coaches attending the annual meeting of the Intercollegiate Soccer Football Association of America, providing a national education program for training coaches. In 1953, the USSF, after reaching an agreement with the Philadelphia Oldtimers Association, began administrating the National Soccer Hall of Fame (a facility dedicated to housing the national soccer archives opened in 1979 in Oneonta, New York). Structurally, the USSF's relationship with FIFA changed with the formation of the Confederation of North, Central America and Caribbean Association Football (CONCACAF) in 1961. One of what would be six continental confederations affiliated with FIFA, CONCACAF governed soccer in North America, Central America, and the Caribbean, positioned between FIFA and the USSF in the hierarchy of governance over the sport.

The decades away from the World Cup also witnessed the rise of the first, national professional league in the United States. (After the American Soccer

KEY DATES

1913: Organization is founded as the United States Football Association and gains full membership in the Fédération Internationale de Football Association the following year.
1930: U.S. national team plays in the first World Cup.
1950: In a major upset, the U.S. national team beats England in World Cup play.
1961: Confederation of North, Central America and Caribbean Association Football is formed, creating a continental governing body for soccer.
1967: North American Soccer League is formed, the first national professional soccer league in the United States.
1985: North American Soccer League ceases to operate.
1989: After a 40-year absence, the United States qualifies for the World Cup when Paul Caligiuri scores a goal against Trinidad and Tobago.
1994: United States hosts the World Cup.
2003: U.S. Soccer National Training Center is opened.
2006: Major League Soccer commences play.

country's professional league, whose existence was crucial to promoting soccer and to developing players to play on the U.S. national team, represented just one of the low points during the 1980s. The USSF had failed in its bid to host the 1986 World Cup, failed to enter a team in the World Cup for nearly 40 years, and it was severely strapped for cash. The organization's president, Werner Fricker, relied on banking relationships he had cultivated through his own construction company to secure loans to keep the USSF afloat. No greater sign of the organization's financial weakness occurred during the late 1980s than when the USSF proposed rescinding the $5 per diem paid to U.S. national team players during a 20-day training camp so it could afford an additional day of training. The USSF, representing a sport in the richest nation in the world, was trying to find a way to save $100.

THE SHOT HEARD 'ROUND THE WORLD

U.S. soccer, at its nadir in the late 1980s, staged a remarkable resurgence at its bleakest hour. The country's most important goal, Joe Gaetjens' winning shot against England in 1950, became the second greatest moment in U.S. soccer history when the national team faced Trinidad and Tobago in November 1989 in a World Cup qualifier. The United States needed a win to qualify for the 1990 World Cup, and the team sealed its victory when Paul Caligiuri scored the only goal in the game. Caligiuri's goal had a tremendous effect on the development of U.S. soccer, touching off a period of unprecedented success both on and off the field. Although the U.S. national team was eliminated from the 1990 World Cup quickly, losing all three games it played, its return to the world stage triggered a sequence of events that propelled the advancement of U.S. soccer.

Without qualifying for the 1990 World Cup, the United States likely would not have been selected to host the 1994 World Cup. Demonstrating the nation's passion for the sport, total attendance during the tournament was 3.6 million, the highest in World Cup history. Further, FIFA, as a condition of giving the United States the opportunity to host the 1994 World Cup, required the United States to establish a professional league, which gave birth to Major League Soccer (MLS) in 1996. World Cup qualification, a dream before Caligiuri's goal, became a common occurrence in succeeding years, with the U.S. national team qualifying for every World Cup through 2010.

The revival enjoyed during the 1990s drew meaningful momentum from the success of the U.S. women's national team, with its achievements on the field adding to the popularity of the sport across the

League folded in 1933, a second iteration, which also called itself the American Soccer League, was formed and existed for 50 years, but like its predecessor, it consisted only of teams from the northeastern United States.) In 1967, the USSF-sanctioned United Soccer Association started its first season, as did a competing league, the National Professional Soccer League. After the end of the first season, FIFA intervened, requesting that the two leagues merge. The USSF and the owners of the independent National Professional Soccer League agreed, which created the North American Soccer League (NASL), a professional league that comprised teams from the United States and Canada.

The NASL attracted attention to soccer, marking the sport's most ambitious attempt to compete alongside the country's three major sports, football, baseball, and basketball. The NASL secured a national television contract and it expanded to 24 teams, but it ultimately collapsed in 1985, ruined by over-expansion and an over-reliance on aging soccer players from Europe and South America. For the USSF, the failure of the

country. The United States won the inaugural Women's World Championship (the original name of the Women's World Cup) in 1991 and in 1999, when the tournament was hosted by the United States. Nearly 700,000 spectators attended the event, including more than 90,000 fans who watched the final between the United States and China.

THE USSF IN THE 21ST CENTURY

On all fronts, U.S. soccer surged forward during the 1990s, providing firm financial footing for the USSF that enabled it to pursue its mission of promoting soccer at all competitive and recreational levels. There was no greater symbol of the organization's vitality than the facility unveiled during its 90th anniversary. In 2003, the $130 million U.S. Soccer National Training Center in Carson, California, was completed. The complex included a 27,000-seat stadium for Major League Soccer's Los Angeles Galaxy, five training fields, office space, weight-training and physical-therapy rooms, and a residential area. "This is a landmark moment for [the USSF], the organization's president, S. Robert Contiguglia," said in the February 27, 2002 edition of the *Houston Chronicle*. "The importance of having a facility that can provide a world-class environment for the continued development of our players is immeasurable. Creating this icon for the sport will benefit every part of the [USSF] family, from the national team to our coaching and referee programs, enabling us to cast our nets wider in developing the sport in this country."

As the USSF neared its centennial, it watched over a healthy and growing sport. Perhaps the most remark-able aspect of its development was not how much it had achieved since 1913, but how much it had achieved during the previous quarter-century. U.S. soccer, at the international level, had faded into obscurity by the 1980s, but thanks to the USSF's persistence and Paul Caligiuri's goal, the sport and the organization it governed staged a remarkable rise to prominence, making the days when the USSF fretted over $5 per diem payments a distant memory.

Jeffrey L. Covell

PRINCIPAL COMPETITORS

National Football League; National Basketball Association, Inc.; Major League Baseball.

FURTHER READING

Burke, Monte, "Kicks Are for Kids," *Forbes,* June 10, 2002, p. 56.

Deady, Tim, "World Cup Will Bring Organizers $20 Million Net," *Los Angeles Business Journal,* June 13, 1994, p. 1.

McKenna, Jon, "U.S. Soccer Federation Has Itchy Feet," *Atlanta Business Chronicle,* March 18, 1991, p. 6A.

McTaggart, Brian, "U.S. Soccer Builds a Home in California," *Houston Chronicle,* February 27, 2002, p. 7.

"Mutiny in Search of Gold," *Tampa Tribune,* May 3, 1999, p. 10.

Rutherford, Erik, "How North America Got Offside: Why Has Professional Soccer Never Taken Hold on This Continent?" *Globe & Mail,* June 17, 2006, p. F9.

Whiteside, Kelly, "U.S. Soccer Then and Now," *USA Today,* May 2, 2006, p. 3C.

Vicarious Visions, Inc.

150 Broadway, Suite 205
Menands, New York 12204
U.S.A.
Telephone: (518) 701-2500
Fax: (518) 701-2501
Web site: http://www.vvisions.com

Subsidiary of Activision Blizzard, Inc.
Incorporated: 1994
Employees: 200
Sales: $200 million (2008 est.)
NAICS: 511210 Software Publishers

■ ■ ■

Vicarious Visions, Inc. (VV), is a developer of video-game software for a variety of gaming platforms, including personal computers, traditional consoles such as Sony Corporation's PlayStation 3, Microsoft Corporation's Xbox 360, and Nintendo Co.'s Wii, and handheld consoles such as Sony's PlayStation Portable and Nintendo's Nintendo DS. VV made a name for itself with the release of *Terminus* in 2000 and in succeeding years developed a number of successful titles for Nintendo's Game Boy Advance, notably a series of games based on professional skateboarder Tony Hawk. The company, owned by Activision Blizzard, Inc., helped develop *Guitar Hero III: Legends of Rock,* which became the first video game to generate more than $1 billion in overall retail sales. VV is based in Menands, New York, a small community near Albany.

ORIGINS

Brothers Karthik and Guha Bala founded VV while they were attending high school in Rochester, New York, launching a homespun business that one day would contribute to more than $1 billion in retail sales. The brothers started the business in 1991, using their parents' basement to fulfill the teenage fantasy of two self-described computer geeks. Karthik and Guha began making their own video games. They enlisted the help of several friends and set to work, using their earnings from checking coats at a local art gallery to fund their efforts.

After high school, the brothers went their separate ways, each choosing a different college to attend, but they did not abandon their video-game development venture. Guha enrolled at Harvard University, where he earned an honors degree in chemistry. Karthik opted for Rensselaer Polytechnic Institute in Troy, New York, choosing the private research university with VV in mind. In 1980, Rensselaer Polytechnic established the first university-based business incubator program in the United States, committing itself to helping fledgling startups by providing space, business counsel, and other resources. At Rensselaer Polytechnic, Karthik pursued a double major in computer science and psychology, but his primary objective was to give VV a nurturing environment in which to develop. The business moved from the Bala household in Rochester to Karthik's dormitory room at Rensselaer Polytechnic before moving into more substantial quarters at Rensselaer Technology Park, where it would remain for a decade.

COMPANY PERSPECTIVES

We are a team of talented, energetic, and highly motivated individuals. Our people come from all areas of the globe, so we bring a very diverse mix of styles to our games. It makes for a very cool place to work ... and we have the pictures to prove it! We make great games based on innovation and creativity. We work with leading game publishers to reach broad audiences with our content and technology. We succeed because of teamwork throughout the company. We ship product. If you've ever put your heart and soul into a game just to see it cancelled, you'll appreciate VV's reputation for delivering high quality games on-time. We believe in building a great entertainment company. We invest in our people, capabilities, and relationships for the long run.

VV RELEASES ITS FIRST GAME IN 1996

The first milestone in VV's development occurred in 1994. The company was incorporated during the year and it secured its first contract, a project to help develop a futuristic detective game for a British publisher, 21st Century. The game, *Synergist,* was released in Europe in 1996 and earned a modicum of praise from critics, but it failed to fulfill the commercial expectations of the handful of VV designers who worked on the project.

Greater success would be achieved with VV's second project, its first original game. Despite the somewhat lackluster commercial performance of *Synergist,* Karthik had distinguished himself in the eyes of observers, enough to attract the financial support of local investors. Michael Marvin, a leader of upstate New York's software industry and a partner in Exponential Business Development Corp., heaped praise on Karthik in the January 23, 1998 edition of *Albany Times Union,* saying, "What you have is one of the best entrepreneurs to come out of Rensselaer Polytechnic Institute in the last 10 years." Marvin, through Exponential Business Development Corp., invested an undisclosed amount of seed money in VV, which the company used to develop *Dark Angael.*

FROM *DARK ANGAEL* TO *TERMINUS*

Developed for $250,000, *Dark Angael* received three out of five stars from *Computer Gaming World*; it was not a critical masterpiece, but the game attracted a larger audience than *Synergist* had. *Dark Angael* was sold on VV's Web site, debuting in October 1997, and distributed electronically by gaming magazines. The lack of a publisher kept the game off retail shelves in the United States, but publishers in Europe distributed a French-language version of *Dark Angael* to stores in certain parts of Africa, Belgium, Canada, and Switzerland.

By the beginning of 1998, the Bala brothers were devoting all their efforts to VV, having earned their degrees and settled into offices at Rensselaer Technology Park. Karthik served as chief executive officer and chief creative officer, while Guha served as president. During the year, they were in the midst of discussions with U.S. game publishers to distribute *Dark Angael* to domestic retailers and they also were seeking a publisher for their next project, *Terminus.* A space-combat game set in 2197, *Terminus* became the game that made VV a recognized name in the game development industry, a project that stretched the financial capabilities of the startup and marked a turning point for the seven-member development team.

The first indication that VV developers had created their masterstroke occurred at the Electronic Entertainment Expo, or E3, in May 1998. Three weeks before the event, the development team, in a mad rush, rewrote the graphics engine for the game, finishing just in time to make the trek from Troy to Atlanta, the host city of E3 in 1998. The team packed a car with computers and the *Terminus* demo and drove 17 straight hours to Atlanta, where the game, which implemented Newtonian physics and advanced artificial intelligence, received an enthusiastic response from E3 attendees. *Terminus* won Best Programming and Best Audio at the 1st Independent Games Festival in 1999 and was released in 2000, drawing a sizable and loyal following that cemented the reputation of the Bala brothers.

FORAY INTO CROSS-PLATFORM BUSINESS LINES

Aside from its critical and commercial success, *Terminus* had another profound effect on VV. Development of the game had caused considerable strain on the company's finances, which prompted the Bala brothers to begin developing games for Nintendo's handheld Game Boy Color console as a way to pay for the cost of developing *Terminus.* VV introduced two games for Game Boy Color in 1999, *Vigilante 8* and *Zebco Fishing!,* and five more titles in 2000, including *Spider-Man.* Although VV did not disclose its financial results, the company revealed that its revenue volume increased 10-fold between 1998 and 1999. The games provided a significant stream of revenue, but more importantly the

KEY DATES

1991: In their parents' basement, Karthik and Guha Bala begin developing video games.

1994: The brothers incorporate Vicarious Visions, Inc. (VV).

1996: VV releases its first game, *Synnergist*.

1997: VV releases its first original game, *Dark Angael*.

2000: Release of *Terminus* brings critical and commercial success to VV.

2005: Activision acquires VV.

2007: VV develops the Wii version of *Guitar Hero III: Legends of Rock*.

2008: Activision merges with Vivendi Games, creating Activision Blizzard, Inc.

development of Game Boy Color games gave VV developers experience in working with non-desktop platforms. The ability to make games for different gaming platforms, such as personal computers and handheld consoles, became VV's signature strength, enabling the company to address distinct markets with a single game title.

The first example of VV applying its cross-platform skills on the development of a game was *Polaris SnoCross*. Polaris Industries, a major snowmobile manufacturer, conceived the idea of a snowmobile game as a marketing tool and awarded VV the development contract for the project. *Polaris SnoCross* was released in 2000, becoming VV's first cross-platform game, compatible with personal computers, conventional consoles PlayStation and Nintendo 64, and Game Boy Color handheld consoles. "We are the first company to create a game that three players with three different systems can all play online against each other," Guha noted in the February 23, 2000 edition of *Albany Times Union*.

VV picked up the pace of its development efforts following the release of its two defining games, *Terminus* and *Polaris SnoCross*. The company introduced nearly a dozen titles in 2001, primarily games developed for handheld consoles. The year's most notable achievement introduced gamers to a more sophisticated handheld console, Game Boy Advance. VV was selected to develop the launch title for Game Boy Advance, releasing *Tony Hawk's Pro Skater 2*, which won numerous awards, including "Best Handheld Game" at the 2001 E3 and "Best Mobile Game of the Year" from the Brit-

ish Academy of Film and Television Arts. In 2002, VV began developing games for the next generation of conventional consoles, releasing *Whiteout* and *Star Wars Jedi Knight II: Jedi Outcast* for Sony's PlayStation2, Microsoft's Xbox, and Nintendo's GameCube. In 2003, VV recorded the most productive year in its history, nearly doubling the number of games it had developed the previous year. The company released 15 titles in 2003, winning numerous awards with *Tony Hawk's Underground*, a game developed for Game Boy Advance, and displaying its cross-platform capabilities with the release of *Crash Nitro Kart*, a game compatible for PlayStation2, Xbox, GameCube, and Game Boy Advance.

VV ACQUIRED BY ACTIVISION IN 2005

For VV and all other game developers, the cost of doing business was escalating at a rapid rate. VV spent $250,000 to develop *Dark Angael*, a fraction of the sum required to develop a game less than a decade later. By 2004, development costs had soared to $20 million for some games, dramatically altering the dynamics of the industry. Although VV primarily focused on developing games for Game Boy Advance, sparing the company from the massive budgets required for more sophisticated consoles, it endured increasing financial pressure as development costs skyrocketed.

For VV, relief from much of the company's financial stress came after a major deal was announced in early 2005. By 2005, VV had developed five games that sold one million or more copies, including two titles for the industry's second-largest developer and publisher, Santa Monica-based Activision, Inc. In January 2005, Activision acquired VV for an undisclosed sum, gaining control of a 95-employee firm in the midst of developing Doom 3 for the Xbox console. The transaction marked the beginning of new chapter for VV, ushering in an era in which the company stood to benefit from the deep financial pockets of its new owner and its long-established ties with retailers. Several months after the deal was completed, VV moved from one nurturing environment to another, potentially more beneficent setting. In July 2005, the company left Rensselaer Technology Park and moved to its new offices in Menands, New York, where it occupied 37,000 square feet of space in Riverview Center.

In the wake of the Activision deal, the Bala brothers remained in charge of the company, continuing to pursue their mission of developing popular software. Under Activision's auspices, VV began to rely less heavily on developing games exclusively for Game Boy Advance and, instead, began developing cross-platform games. The company developed *Marvel: Ultimate Alli-*

ance in 2006, a game that served as the launch title for Nintendo's hugely popular Wii console.

VV WORKS ON THE *GUITAR HERO* SERIES

The company's experience in developing the game for Wii gave it the expertise for its greatest success during its first years under Activision's control. VV helped develop *Guitar Hero III: Legends of Rock,* the third major installment of the immensely popular *Guitar Hero* series, a franchise developed by Neversoft Entertainment and published by Activision. VV took responsibility for developing the game for Wii, which proved to be the best-selling version of the title. *Guitar Hero* became the first game to generate more than $1 billion in retail sales. VV's Wii version sold two million copies, making it the best-selling third-party game developed for Wii.

As VV plotted its future course, consolidation in its industry altered the profile of its parent company. In late 2007, Paris, France-based Vivendi S.A., a massive media conglomerate, announced it intended to merge its software unit, Vivendi Games, with Activision. The deal, completed in July 2008 for a staggering $9.85 billion, created Activision Blizzard, Inc., a company 52 percent owned by Vivendi. The merger gave VV a parent company whose stature rivaled that of the industry's largest competitor, Electronic Arts Inc., ensuring that

the Bala brothers could look forward to being part of one of the most powerful organizations in their industry. By the beginning of 2009, the brothers calculated that they had generated $500 million in revenue for their parent company since the acquisition in 2005, a figure that was expected to rise substantially in the years ahead.

Jeffrey L. Covell

PRINCIPAL COMPETITORS

Electronic Arts Inc.; Take-Two Interactive Software, Inc.; Sony Online Entertainment LLC.

FURTHER READING

Furfaro, Danielle T., "Vicarious Visions Seeing Success," *Albany Times Union,* February 23, 2000, p. E1.

Higgins, Dan, "Company Has Spidey in Hand," *Albany Times Union,* April 14, 2005, p. E1.

Orenstein, David, "His Visions Are a Dream Come True," *Albany Times Union,* January 23, 1998, p. E1.

"Splurging for the Real Thing," *Albany Times Union,* September 12, 2004, p. E1.

"Technology Briefing Deals: Activision Buys Game Developer," *New York Times,* January 21, 2005, p. C2.

"Video Game Developer Relocating to Menands," *Albany Times Union,* July 29, 2005, p. E1.

VSE Corporation

2550 Huntington Avenue
Alexandria, Virginia 22303-1499
U.S.A.
Telephone: (703) 960-4600
Fax: (703) 960-2688
Web site: http://www.vsecorp.com

Public Company
Incorporated: 1959 as Value Engineering Company
Employees: 1,920
Sales: $1.04 billion (2008)
Stock Exchanges: NASDAQ
Ticker Symbol: VSEC
NAICS: 541330 Engineering Services

■ ■ ■

VSE Corporation is a publicly traded, Alexandria, Virginia-based engineering and technical support company that helps to improve the operations of the U.S. military and government agencies. The company offers engineering services, including prototyping and fabrication, industrial engineering, and systems integration; logistics, including supply chain management, facilities management, and training; service life extension and other sustainment services; foreign military sales services; project management and consulting; information technology services; demilitarization and other energy/environmental services; and such program support services as acquisition and financial management. VSE also maintains an International Group that in addition to providing engineering, industrial,

logistics, and foreign military sales services to the U.S. military, also serves foreign governments by helping them with the transfer of U.S. ships, including overhaul and maintenance, and technical support.

FOUNDER'S BACKGROUND, EARLY YEARS WITH COMPANY: WORLD WAR II TO 1968

VSE was founded in Virginia in 1959 as Value Engineering Company by John B. Toomey, a man well familiar with the military. During World War II he served as a U.S. Navy pilot in the Pacific. After his discharge in 1946, Toomey enrolled at the Missouri School of Mines and Metallurgy (now known as Missouri S&T), earning a bachelor's degree in mechanical engineering in 1949, followed two years later by a master's degree in the same discipline. He then returned to the Navy from 1952 to 1954 and remained in the U.S. Naval Reserve for another 20 years. Following his second discharge from the Navy, Toomey began his engineering career and started Value Engineering with three employees in 1959 as a federal government services company. The goal was to help clients improve the reliability of equipment while lowering costs. This would be done through the application of the value engineering principles that grew out of the work of General Electric Company purchase engineer Lawrence Miles during World War II.

Despite a shortage of key materials and components, Miles had been charged with increasing the production of bomber superchargers from 50 to 1,000 per week. Not only did Miles discover that he

COMPANY PERSPECTIVES

Today, VSE is a broadly diversified company focused on creating, sustaining, and improving the systems, equipment, and processes of government through core competencies in legacy systems sustainment, obsolescence management, prototyping, reverse engineering, technology insertion, supply chain management, foreign military sales, management consulting, and process improvement. Our expanded mission now includes providing innovative services and technologies to help our customers succeed in the engineering, energy, environment, information technology, and defense services markets.

could find suitable substitute materials, in many cases they performed their tasks the same or better at less cost. Hence, value engineering in a nutshell became providing the same necessary function at a lower cost.

Given Toomey's ties to the U.S. Navy, it was not surprising that the first contract he performed in 1960 was to help the Navy choose between bids on missile rocket motors. The firm then opened a commercial laboratory, the first of its kind in the area to perform material and metallurgical analysis. The U.S. Army became a customer in 1963, when Value Engineering won a production engineering support contract for operations at Fort Belvoir, Virginia, home to the U.S. Army Engineer School and a host of Defense agencies, including the Defense Logistics Agency, the Defense Contract Audit Agency, the Defense Technical Information Center, and the Defense Threat Reduction Agency. Value Engineering began working for NASA (National Aeronautics and Space Administration) in 1965, establishing a field office in Hampton, Virginia, to design force measurement devices. As the company grew it required fabrication capabilities and in 1967 bought its first fabrication shop as well as adding a testing and inspection facility. A year later Value Engineering, employing more than 350 people, was doing in excess of $5 million a year in sales. To maintain growth and consolidate its offices in Alexandria, the company held an initial public offering of stock.

ENTERING THE MARINE
ENGINEERING SECTOR: 1973

Further expansion took place in the 1970s. The firm entered the marine engineering sector in 1973 when it

began helping the U.S. Navy in its overhaul and modernization program. Five years later the Navy supplied Value Engineering with its first $1 million contract to help with a shipboard equipment configuration audit services. By the end of the 1970s the firm was generating annual revenues of $38 million, not all of which came from engineering services.

Toomey also began making other investments to provide some diversity. Metropolitan Capital Corporation was formed as a small-business investment subsidiary. Among its activities were investments in the Long John Silver's Seafood Shoppe fast-food restaurant chain, and the Pohick Square town-house development in Lorton, Virginia. Other businesses that would be brought into the fold included D&P, a graphic communications firm; Starr Management Corp., a property management company; and Design & Production, an operator of museum exhibits. Because of its growing range of interests, the company changed its name in 1979 from Value Engineering to VSE Corporation.

ANNUAL SALES REACH $100
MILLION: 1986

In 1983 VSE completed a secondary stock offering of $8.8 million, some of which was paid to Toomey, who still controlled more than 40 percent of the company's stock. By this stage, the company's annual sales topped $50 million, 93 percent of which came from government contracts. VSE employed more than 1,500 people working out of 22 locations across the country. The main thrust of VSE through the rest of the 1980s remained its government contracts. In 1984 it gained certification as a Navy Master Ordnance Repair contractor. A year later it won its first major U.S. Air Force contract, providing test range support. Also in 1985 VSE opened a Reverse Engineering Center. In 1987 the U.S. Marine Corps contracted VSE to provide vehicle design support, and a year later VSE began offering similar services to the U.S. Army. Aside from branches of the U.S. military, VSE received contracts from the National Cancer Institute and the U.S. Postal Service during this period. Revenues increased at a steady pace, topping the $100 million mark by 1986.

Although familiar in military circles, VSE was little known to the general public until it became a side player in a 1980s espionage scandal, the John Walker spy ring that fed classified information to the Soviet Union from 1968 to 1985. One of the men recruited by ex-Navy officer Walker was his older brother Arthur, a retired Navy officer with financial troubles who in the late 1970s went to work for VSE. John Walker lured him into the ring by asking him to smuggle unclassified information out of the VSE office and paid him hand-

KEY DATES

1959: Company is founded by John Toomey as Value Engineering Company.

1968: Company goes public to finance further growth.

1978: Company receives its first $1 million contract.

1979: Name is changed to VSE Corporation.

1992: Toomey retires after more than 30 years at the helm.

2001: Company organizes into four groups, later changed to three.

2008: G&B Solutions is acquired in an effort to increase the company's nonmilitary business.

somely for the material, $6,000. Once Arthur Walker realized how easily he could smuggle documents out of the office and the kind of money he could receive, he eagerly joined his brother's spy network. John Walker later recruited his own son but the ring was exposed although not before the Soviets had received help in decoding more than 200,000 encrypted naval messages.

What no one realized at the time the Walker spy ring was exposed was how weak the Soviet Union had become. Within a few years its satellite states in Eastern Europe broke away and abandoned communism, and Russia itself eventually adopted a capitalist economic system. As a result, the Cold War between the United States and the Soviet Union that had dominated world politics during four decades since World War II came to a surprising end, reducing the need for military spending. While a positive development for the world, the passing of the Cold War adversely impacted VSE's business, dominated as it was by military contracts. Although Toomey had made an effort to diversify the company, VSE's outside investments did not fare well, a situation that grew worse with an economic recession.

PURCHASE OF SCHMOLDT ENGINEERING SERVICES: 1990

VSE's annual revenues peaked at $115.1 million in 1988 when the company also posted a $2.8 million net profit. A year later revenues dipped to $109.8 million and net income fell to $218,000. The downward trend continued in the early 1990s. Revenues decreased to $84.8 million in 1990 and $68.3 million in 1991, when VSE reported a $4.7 million loss. The company in the meantime looked to diversify further by acquiring

Oklahoma-based Schmoldt Engineering Services Company in 1990. The 38-year-old Schmoldt specialized in the cathodic protection of metallic structures buried in the ground or submerged in water, in particular to prevent corrosion in liquid and gas pipelines. Also in 1990 VSE formed Human Resources Systems, Inc., to provide health-care staffing personnel, such as nurses and pharmacists, mostly to the Navy.

Toomey had reached retirement age and in 1992 was interested in realizing the value of his stock while also providing a way for VSE to restructure its business. As a result Toomey exchanged his 48 percent stake in VSE for control of three subsidiaries: Starr Management, Metro Capital, and Design & Production. Together they generated about $10 million in annual revenue. The arrangement also allowed VSE to focus on its core engineering business, something that investors had advocated for some time.

After Toomey's departure, VSE launched a new division in 1993 to provide engineering and technical logistics support to the Naval aviation and weapons communities. For the year, revenues improved to $79.6 million. In 1994 revenues dipped to $65.6 million while net income improved to $1.55 million. In the meantime, VSE identified a new source of business that resulted from the end of the Cold War: the transfer of ships to foreign governments as the Navy sought to reduce the size of its fleet. In 1995 the firm received its first $1 billion contract, a 10-year effort to assist in the overhaul of ships to be transferred and to provide logistical support. Also in 1995 VSE expanded its nonmilitary business through the acquisition of Energetics Incorporated. Established in 1979, Energetics was a major support contractor for the Department of Energy, providing a full range of energy and environmental consulting services, including assessment, technical and economic feasibility analysis, technology transfer, research and development planning, engineering studies, market assessment, regulatory analysis, environmental compliance, and risk management.

Revenues increased to $128.8 million in 1998 before slipping to $110 million to end the decade. At that time, the U.S. Navy accounted for nearly 69 percent of VSE's annual revenues, while the Army contributed 12.7 percent and all other government clients about 17 percent. The firm's commercial business provided just $380,000, or 1.5 percent.

FORMATION OF MANAGEMENT SCIENCES DIVISION: 2001

VSE broadened its service offerings as it entered the new century. In 2000 the company began offering multimedia and audiovisual technology, network management, and information technology facilities installation and maintenance services. A year later VSE established its Management Sciences Divisions to provide consulting and systems training services to help clients implement Lean Six Sigma quality systems. Because of the growing range of services, VSE also reorganized itself in 2001, dividing its business among four operating groups: Federal, Energy and Environment, International, and Telecommunications Technologies. Two years later Telecommunications Technologies was folded into the Federal Group.

In 2004 revenues improved to a record $216 million, aided in part by wars in Afghanistan and Iraq. Helping to drive that growth was the Army CECOM Rapid Response Program contract signed in 2003, the firm's first multibillion-dollar IDIQ (indefinite delivery/indefinite quantity) contract. The following year VSE received two more IDIQ contracts that held a potential of exceeding $1 billion: a U.S. Navy Ship Support Contract and the U.S. Navy SeaPort Enhanced contract. This new business resulted in a surge in revenues, which topped $280 million in 2005 and $363 million in 2006.

To expand further in its existing markets, VSE acquired Integrated Concepts and Research Corp. (ICRC) in 2007 for $11.6 million in cash plus another $5.8 million in potential earn-out provisions. Serving federal customers, ICRC offered management services for civil engineering, utility, construction, and other major infrastructure projects. Another company was acquired in 2008, G&B Solutions, Inc., an information technology provider that served a variety of federal customers, including the Department of Homeland Security, the National Institutes of Health, the Department of Housing and Urban Development, Pension Benefits Guarantee Corporation, and the Departments of Agriculture, Interior, and Labor. G&B helped VSE to

increase its nonmilitary business to 20 percent. It also helped the firm to grow revenues beyond the $1 billion level in 2008. While it was unlikely that VSE could maintain such a strong rate of growth, there was every reason to believe that with a number of long-term contracts in hand the firm would enjoy a robust business for years to come.

Ed Dinger

PRINCIPAL SUBSIDIARIES

Energetics Incorporation; Integrated Concepts and Research Corp.; G&B Solutions, Inc.

PRINCIPAL COMPETITORS

General Dynamics Corporation; Northrop Grumman Corporation; Todd Shipyards Corporation.

FURTHER READING

"Bartlesville Company Schmoldt Engineering Merges with VSE," *Tulsa World,* July 15, 1990, p. G2.

Hinden, Stan, "Plan to Transfer Half of VSE to Chairman Draws Fire," *Washington Post,* October 12, 1992, p. F31.

Mount, Ian, "Procurement Trickles Down," *FSB,* July 2009.

Paton, Huntley, "VSE Writes Off Its Investment in Cruise Liner," *Washington Business Journal,* January 8, 1990, p. 1.

"S&T to Dedicate New Complex," *Rolla Daily News,* April 14, 2009.

"VSE Acquires Services Company ICRC," *Defense Daily,* June 6, 2007.

"VSE Corp. of Alexandria Reports $4.7 Million Loss," *Washington Post,* March 30, 1992, p. F18.

"VSE Offers 502,000 Shares to the Public at $17.50 Each," *Washington Post,* May 23, 1983, p. 3.

Wilmar International Ltd.

56 Neil Road
Singapore, 088830
Singapore
Telephone: (+65) 6216 0244
Fax: (+65) 6836 1709
Web site: http://www.wilmar-international.com

Public Company
Incorporated: 1991
Employees: 70,000
Sales: $29.15 billion (2008)
Stock Exchanges: Singapore
Ticker Symbol: WLMIF
NAICS: 111336 Fruit and Tree Nut Combination Farming; 311225 Fats and Oils Refining and Blending; 424590 Other Farm Product Raw Material Merchant Wholesalers

■ ■ ■

Wilmar International Ltd. is the world's leading integrated palm oils group, and the largest agro-industrial group in Asia. The Singapore- and Malaysia-based group operates through four primary divisions: Merchandising & Processing - Palm & Laurics; Merchandising & Processing - Oilseeds & Grains; Plantations & Palm Oil Mills; and Consumer Products. As a vertically integrated company, Wilmar controls more than 223,000 hectares of oil palm plantations, primarily in Indonesia and Malaysia, with increasing holdings in West Africa. The company owns palm oil processing facilities in Indonesia, Malaysia, China, Vietnam, the Netherlands, and Germany, and participates in joint-venture plants in India, Ivory Coast, Russia, Uganda, and Ukraine. The company's Oilseeds & Grains division is one of the largest in China, and processes a large variety of seeds and grains for edible oil and feed production. Wilmar has also been investing heavily in palm oil-based biodiesel production. The company's Consumer Division markets edible oils under the Sania brand in Malaysia and Indonesia, and the Arawana, Koufu, Orchid, and other brands in China, Vietnam, and Bangladesh. Other Wilmar operations include fertilizer production and distribution and bulk oil shipping.

Founded in 1991, Wilmar is led by Kuok Khoon Hong, founder, chairman, and CEO and a nephew of famed Singapore business magnate Robert Kuok. Cofounder Martua Sitorus is Wilmar's chief operating officer. Wilmar is listed on the Singapore Stock Exchange. Major shareholders include PPB Group Bhd. and Archer Daniels Midland. In 2008, Wilmar's revenues were $29.15 billion.

PALM OIL FAMILY TREE FROM 1986

Kuok Khoon Hong, also known as William Kuok, had a leg up in business when he cofounded Wilmar in 1991. Kuok was one of the nephews of Robert Kuok, one of the most dynamic business magnates in Asia. The Kuok family had immigrated to Malaysia at the beginning of the 20th century. Robert Kuok, born in 1927, took over as head of the family's rice trading business in the 1940s, then switched focus to the sugar industry in the

COMPANY PERSPECTIVES

Over the years, we have established a resilient integrated agribusiness model that captures the entire value chain of the agricultural commodity processing business, from origination and processing to the branding, merchandising and distribution of a wide range of agricultural products. Through scale, integration and the logistical advantages of our business model, we are able to extract margins at every step of the value chain, resulting in significant operational synergies and cost efficiencies.

We are today: the largest global processor and merchandiser of palm and lauric oils; one of the largest plantation companies in Indonesia/Malaysia; the largest palm biodiesel manufacturer in the world; a leading consumer pack edible oils producer, oilseeds crusher, edible oils refiner, specialty fats and oleochemicals manufacturer in China; one of the largest edible oils refiners and a leading producer of consumer pack edible oils in India; the largest edible oils refiner in Ukraine; and the leading importer of edible oils into East Africa and one of the largest importers of edible oils into Southeast Africa.

We will continue to leverage on the scale and strengths of our business model to benefit from the long term growth potential of the agricultural commodity business, especially in Asia.

late 1950s and flour milling in the 1960s. By the early 1970s, Robert Kuok had become known as "The Sugar King," and directly controlled more than 10 percent of the global sugar market. By then, Kuok had reorganized most of his Malaysian holdings into a new company, Perlis Plantations Bhd (PPB), formed in 1968.

Kuok Khoon Hong, born in 1949, began working for his uncle in the early 1970s. By 1973, the younger Kuok had joined the family's flour milling and grains operations. During the next decade, the Kuok's business interests expanded into oilseeds and edible oils. The rising promise of palm oil soon attracted the Kuok family's interest. In fact, palm oil boasted the highest oil-per-hectare content of any of the other major vegetable oil crops, significantly out-producing rapeseed (canola), soybean, and sunflower. As a result, palm oil developed into a major global commodity, and quickly became a primary processed foods ingredient.

Through PPB, the Kuok family launched its first investments into oil palm plantations started in 1986, when the company planted its first 9,000-hectare plantation. PPB added another 14,000 hectares as well as its first oil refinery the following year, and by the middle of the 1990s, PPB controlled nine plantations throughout Malaysia. Into the second half of the decade, PPB extended its reach into other markets, acquiring its first 10,000 hectare plantation in Indonesia.

In 1997, PPB reorganized all of its oil palm operations under a single company, PPB Oil Palms, which was then spun off as a publicly listed company under PPB's control. By the end of the decade, PPB Oil Palms had added its parent's oil palm plantations in Indonesia as well. By the middle of the next decade, PPB Oil Palms' total land bank neared 365,000 hectares, nearly 80 percent of which was located in Indonesia. By then, PPB's vertically integrated palm oil operations accounted for more than 70 percent of the Kuok group's total revenues.

FOUNDING A PALM OIL GIANT IN 1991

Kuok Khoon Hong spent his early career largely within his uncle's flour operations, conducted through Federal Flour Mills. By 1986, Kuok had been named general manager of that company. In 1989, Kuok took on a second position, as managing director of Kuok Oils & Grains Pte. By the early 1990s, however, the younger Kuok had become eager to strike out on his own and build his fortune in the palm oil market.

In 1991, Kuok Khoon Hong joined with a partner, Martua Sitorus, to buy a parcel of 7,100 hectares in Sumatra. The partners combined their names, using Kuok's anglicized name William, to form the name of their new company, Wilmar Trading. The partners were backed by an investment from stockbroker and family friend Peter Lim, who invested $10 million in the new company. As Lim told *Forbes*: "From the moment I first spoke to [Kuok], I thought: 'This man is really very clever. I'd better follow him because he can make a lot of money for me.'"

Wilmar started out with an eye toward vertical integration. The company quickly established itself as a palm oil trader, launching an oil distribution business in Indonesia. Wilmar also began planting its first oil palm plantation. At the same time, the company invested in the acquisition of palm seed processing facilities. By the end of its first year, the company had bought two 50 metric-ton-per-day seed crushing plants in northern Sumatra and Riau, as well as a 100 metric-ton-per-day palm oil refinery in southern Sumatra. The company

KEY DATES

■

1991: Kuok Khoon Hong, a nephew of Robert Kuok, and Martua Sitorus found an oil palm plantation and palm oil trading company, Wilmar Trading.

1995: Wilmar launches its vertical integration strategy with opening of its first oil milling plant.

2000: Company launches its own edible oil brand, Sania.

2003: Wilmar Holdings and major shareholder Archer Daniels Midland form a soybean oil refinery joint venture in China.

2006: Wilmar completes a reverse takeover of Ezy-health and lists part of its operations on the Singapore Stock Exchange as Wilmar International.

2007: Wilmar merges its assets with those of PPB Oil to form the Asian region's largest agro-industrial group.

2009: Wilmar announces its plan to spin off its Chinese assets as a new company listed on the Hong Kong Stock Exchange.

also launched construction of a new 700 metric ton refinery, in Riau, that year.

VERTICAL INTEGRATION IN THE MID-NINETIES

Wilmar opened its first milling plant in 1995, adding a capacity of 40 metric tons per hour. The company's vertical integration model led to the purchase of its first oil tanker vessel that year. The following year, the company added a new refinery and fractionation facility in Butterworth, in Malaysia. The group then invested in upgrading the new plants, doubling their capacity to 1,000 metric tons per day.

Vertical integration remained the group's keywords into the 2000s. The company launched a specialty fats production arm starting in 1998, generating increased profits through the addition of high value-added products.

Wilmar later boosted its specialty oils business in 2005, buying PT Cahaya Kalbar Tbk, which produced specialty oils for the chocolate and cocoa industries, as well as ingredients for the bakery products, processed foods, and beverages industries.

The company turned directly to the consumer market, developing its own line of edible oils under the Sania brand name, launched in 2000. At the opposite end of the integration spectrum, the company entered fertilizer production, adding a compound fertilizer factory in 2002.

Wilmar, which had reorganized its operations as a privately held holding company, Wilmar Holdings Pte., had also been expanding beyond the Malaysian and Indonesian markets. The company's palm oil distribution business had quickly extended to a global scale. The company had also entered the mainland Chinese market, the world's largest single palm oil market, by the beginning of the new century. Much of this growth took place through a number of joint-venture partnerships established with Archer Daniels Midland. That company also became a major shareholder in Wilmar Holdings, alongside COFCO (China National Cereals, Oils & Foodstuffs Corp.), the Chinese procurement agency.

These partnerships also came as part of Wilmar's extension of its operations beyond palm oil to include a wider variety of oilseeds. In 2003, for example, the company teamed up with Archer Daniels Midland to build a soy processing factory in Shanhaiguan, in China.

REVERSE TAKEOVER IN 2006

Wilmar set its sights on becoming one of the Asian region's leading agro-industrial companies. Toward this end the company launched a major investment program. Over the course of the year, the company acquired five oil palm plantation companies and a total of 85,000 hectares in Indonesia; another plantation company in Malaysia, with 30,000 hectares; as well as 25,000 hectares previously held by two Wilmar subsidiaries. The company's industrial investments that year included three new refineries, three fractionation facilities, four palm kernel crushing plants, four palm oil mills, and a 1,000 metric-ton-per-day fertilizer plant.

While part of this investment drive was carried out in partnership with Archer Daniels Midland, Wilmar also went in search of fresh capital for its expansion. This led the company to go public in 2006, listing its shares on the Singapore Stock Exchange. Rather than go through the lengthy and costly public offering process, Wilmar carried out a reverse-takeover of ailing Ezyhealth Asia Pacific Ltd. That company had previously operated in the managed health care field.

As part of the transaction, Wilmar agreed to inject part of its palm oil trading, plantation, refining, and distribution assets, worth approximately $1 billion, into Ezyhealth. The company also agreed to sell off Ezyhealth's prior assets to its founder. Ezyhealth was then renamed Wilmar International. Wilmar Holdings remained its majority shareholder, with Archer Daniel Midland becoming a major shareholder as well. Following the company's re-listing on the Singapore Stock Exchange, the company carried out a new share placement, raising another $153 million.

ASIAN AGRIBUSINESS LEADER

Toward the end of 2006, Wilmar announced its intention to enter the biodiesel market, as the world scrambled to find alternative fuel sources in the new century. The company launched construction of its first 350,000 ton per year biodiesel refinery that year, then announced plans to add two more similar facilities, with plants to raise its total output to more than one billion tons per year by the end of 2007.

Wilmar also went in search of new horizons. This led the company to form a joint-venture partnership with Olam International and SIFCA Group to develop palm oil, cotton seed oil, and other interests in Africa. In 2008, the company also entered the Russian and CIS markets, establishing a joint venture with Delta Exports Pte Ltd. and Nizhny Novgorod Fats & Oils Group. The deal helped establish Wilmar as the leading edible oils refiner in Ukraine.

By then, however, Wilmar had completed the deal that transformed it into a global powerhouse. At the end of 2006, Wilmar launched a takeover offer for PPB Oil Palms and other Kuok Group edible oils, grains, and related operations. Concurrent with that deal, Wilmar Holdings carried out its own restructuring exercise, transferring most of its own operations into Wilmar International. Archer Daniels Midland also agreed to transfer the two companies' China-based joint-venture operations into the newly expanded company. As a result, Archer Daniels Midland emerged as a major shareholder in Wilmar International.

The merger process was completed in 2007, and Wilmar International asserted itself as a leading player in the global palm oils market, while laying claim to the position of the leading agro-industrial group in the Asian region. Founders Kuok and Sitorus now joined the ranks of the world's billionaires, as did original investor Peter Lim. Those fortunes appeared certain to grow even more in the near future. In July 2009, Wilmar announced its plans to spin off its Chinese assets into a new company, which would then list on the Hong Kong Stock Exchange. That offering was expected to raise another $4 billion for Wilmar as it consolidated

its position as a global agribusiness player in the new century.

M. L. Cohen

PRINCIPAL SUBSIDIARIES

Cai Lan Oils & Fats Industries Company Ltd. (Vietnam); Delta Wilmar CIS (Ukraine; 50%); Intertrade (Bangladesh) Private Limited; Kerry (New Zealand) Limited; Kerry Oils & Grains (China) Limited; KNZ Australia Pty Limited; Myanmar Kuok Oils & Grains Limited; PPB Oil Palms Berhad; PT Kerry Sawit (Indonesia); Southseas Oils & Fats Industrial (Chiwan) Ltd. (China); Wilmar China Investments Pte Ltd.; Wilmar Edible Oils B.V. (Netherlands); Wilmar Edible Oils GmbH (Germany); Wilmar Edible Oils Sdn. Bhd.; Wilmar Europe Holdings B.V. (Netherlands); Wilmar Fertilizer Indonesia Pte Ltd. (1); Wilmar Holdings Sdn. Bhd.; Wilmar Iberia S.L. (Spain); Wilmar Plantations Limited (British Virgin Islands); Wilmar Renewable Energy Pte. Ltd.; Wilmar Seed Investments Pte. Ltd. (China); Wilmar Trading Pte Ltd.; Wilmar-ADM China Investments Pte. Ltd.; Yihai (Yantai) Oils & Grains Industries Co., Ltd. (China).

PRINCIPAL DIVISIONS

Associates; Consumer Products; Merchandising & Processing - Oilseeds & Grains; Merchandising & Processing - Palm & Laurics; Others; Plantations & Palm Oil Mills.

PRINCIPAL COMPETITORS

IOI Corporation; Sime Darby Bhd.; Genting Bhd.; FFM Bhd.; Kuala Lumpur Kepong Bhd.; FELDA Holdings Bhd.; PGEO Group Sdn Bhd; Felda Palm Industries Sdn Bhd; PPB Group Bhd; PGEO Edible Oils Sdn Bhd; Mewah-Oils Sdn Bhd.

FURTHER READING

Burton, John, "Unilever Sells Oil Unit, Buys Soaps," *Chemical Week*, December 15, 2008, p. 31.

Cameron, Doug, and Assif Shameen, "Wilmar in $4.3bn Palm-Oil Merger," *Financial Times*, December 15, 2006, p. 26.

De Guzman, Doris, "Palm Oil's Big Future," *ICIS Chemical Business Americas*, December 18, 2006, p. 37.

Hui, Cheok Soh, "Wilmar to Raise $153m, Eyes Indonesia Biodiesel," *Chemical Market Reporter*, July 24, 2006, p. 13.

Kovac, Matt, "Wilmar Quadruples Bio-Plan," *ICIS Chemical Business*, September 4, 2006, p. 34.

Lim, Jeanne, "Wilmar Denies Forest Burning Allegations," *ICIS Chemical Business Americas*, July 9, 2007.

Ooi Tee Ching, "PPB-Wilmar Deal a 'Logical Move,'" *Business Times Malaysia*, April 16, 2007.

Rovnick, Naomi, and Wong Ka-Chun, "Wilmar Picks Hong Kong over Shanghai for US$4b Float," *South China Morning Post*, July 20, 2009.

Tan, Jessica, "Palm Oil Pal," *Forbes*, September 1, 2008.

Van Gelder, Jan Willem, "Buyer and Financiers of the Wilmar Group," *Profundo*, July 2007.

"Wilmar Eyes Opportunities in Emerging Marts," *Business Times Malaysia*, August 15, 2008.

Wong, Chia-Peck, "Wilmar Bids for Palm Oil Refiner," *International Herald Tribune*, December 15, 2006, p. 18.

Zaidi Isham Ismail, and Ooi Tee Ching, "Kuok Family Merge Businesses," *Business Times Malaysia*, December 15, 2006.

Yak Pak

———■———

900 Broadway
New York, New York 10003
U.S.A.
Telephone: (718) 797-3671
Toll Free: (800) 292-5725
Fax: (718) 624-7460
Web site: http://www.yakpak.com

Private Company
Incorporated: 1989
Employees: 475
Sales: $50 million (2008 est.)
NAICS: 316991 Luggage Manufacturing; 316992
   Women's Handbag and Purse Manufacturing

■ ■ ■

Yak Pak is a New York City-based privately owned manufacturer of stylish yet functional carrying bags, catering primarily to college students and other young adult consumers. In addition to colorful double-strap backpacks, the company offers its signature single-strap messenger bags, inspired by the bags traditionally used by bicycle messengers but targeted to students as well as urban professionals. Yak Pak carries a line of handbags and small accessories bags, as well as larger totes. While some Yak Pak backpacks and courier bags are designed to accommodate laptops, the company produces dedicated laptop cases as well as strapless laptop sleeves. Yak Pak specialty products include diaper bags and duffles, yoga mat-carrying bags, guitar straps, iPod cases, wallets, luggage tag/keychains, and beanbag chairs. In

addition, Yak Pak produces a wide variety of colorful youth-oriented products under a licensing agreement with Dickies (Williamson-Dickie Manufacturing Company), including backpacks, messenger bags, totes, laptop sleeves, handbags, clutches, accessory cases, kitchen knife bags, and guitar straps.

Yak Pak products are sold through Urban Outfitters, Pacific Sunwear, and other specialty boutiques as well as the company's Web site. In addition to developing products for the Yak Pak and Dickies brands, the company is a private-label contractor that has designed and launched fashion bag programs for such prominent brands as Coleman, Levi's, and Wrangler. Manufacturing is primarily done at a company-owned factory in San Salvador, El Salvador, the hometown of the company's chief financial officer, Rolando Cohen. Some products are also sourced in China. Yak Pak maintains a warehouse in Santa Fe Springs, California. The company is headed by its founder, Chief Executive Officer Stephen Holt.

TIBET TRIP, 1988, PROVIDES INFLUENCE FOR COMPANY'S ORIGINS

While both Cohen and Holt are considered cofounders of Yak Pak, the inspiration for the company was provided by Holt, the son of a lawyer and a social worker. In the 1980s he was an undergraduate student at Georgetown University, majoring in Chinese with a minor in business, his career ambition to one day become the U.S. ambassador to China. Holt's interest shifted to business while studying abroad in China during his junior year in 1988. Paying a visit to Tibet with a friend on a backpacking trip he came across a holy lake, Lake Nam Co. "It was there that I came up with the idea of starting my own company," Holt told the *Daily News Record* years later. As a tribute to Tibet he also decided to include the Yak, the country's national animal, in the company name. All that was lacking was an idea for an actual product or service.

Several months passed before further inspiration struck. Like many college students Holt relied on bags to carry his textbooks and other materials from class to class. Around that time in the late 1980s backpack maker JanSport was having success in persuading retailers to carry their daypacks in back-to-school sections rather than just camping departments, leading to a sharp increase in market share for JanSport and a growing popularity for the products among college students like Holt. While the backpacks were functionally sound, Holt was not impressed by JanSport's mundane sense of style, and he believed there was an opening in the market for bookbags that were stylish and more appealing to his contemporaries.

TAKING A SMALL LOAN TO START COMPANY: 1988

In 1988 Holt took out a $5,000 loan and had 400 samples of suede bookbags in two different styles and colors made at a factory in China and shipped to his dorm room at Georgetown. Only then did he settle on the name of his company, using "Yak" to create Yak Pak. His housemate was Rolando Cohen, a native of El Salvador who quickly realized that Holt's bookbag concept was promising and began lobbying his friend to take him on as a partner in the business.

After they both graduated from Georgetown in 1989, Holt moved to Brooklyn, New York, to start his business, which he initially ran out of his apartment. To make ends meet while he operated his nascent business during the day, he waited tables at night. Going store-to-store in Manhattan to show his bags, Holt was able to place the bags in the trendy Canal Jean Co. By the end of the year his account base totaled about two dozen stores, including Urban Outfitters in Philadelphia

and Up Against the Wall in Washington, D.C. He was also able to move Yak Pak's headquarters out of his apartment to a space in the DUMBO (Down Under the Manhattan Bridge Overpass) section of Brooklyn along the East River. All told, Yak Pak shipped 5,000 bags in 1989.

It was at this point that Holt needed help with his taxes and turned to Cohen for help. After graduating from Georgetown, Holt's former housemate had taken an accounting job with Deloitte & Touche. Cohen provided his services and eventually quit his job to become Holt's partner and serve as chief financial officer. Together they gradually built up Yak Pak's business by paying sales calls to stores and attending trade shows, so that by 1995 annual sales reached $1.6 million. Yak Pak also made its mark on the daypack sector by employing bright nylon colors and pursuing a hip-hop DJ motif with a bag that included space to hold headphones and microphones as well as seven-inch vinyl albums that DJs usually lugged in milk crates. Also in an effort to appeal to its core urban customers, Yak Pak bags were designed to accommodate inline skates and water bottles.

EL SALVADOR FACTORY OPENS: 1996

At the start of 1996 Yak Pak opened a factory in Cohen's hometown of San Salvador, El Salvador, hiring about 40 people to produce Yak Pak bags using sewing machines bought in Brooklyn. The company also beefed up its marketing efforts in March 1996 by hiring Stephen Schactel, the former JanSport vice president of sales, who led Yak Pak's marketing department. Under Schactel, Yak Pak looked to move beyond specialty boutiques and begin selling its products in sporting goods and outdoor specialty stores. In July of that year, Yak Pak unveiled a new line of multipurpose packs at a National Sporting Goods Association show.

In 1997 Yak Pak became involved in the mass market by signing a licensing agreement with Williamson-Dickie Manufacturing Company to develop a bag line under the Dickies brand. Aside from tapping into new sales channels, the alliance allowed Yak Pak to expand beyond its core urban youth customer base to older work-oriented customers. From its perspective, the Fort Worth, Texas-based workwear manufacturer was interested in reaching out beyond its traditional customer base to a younger demographic, one that might perceive the old-guard Dickies brand as something of an anti-fashion fashion statement. The logic behind a marriage between Yak Pak and Dickies was not readily accepted by retail accounts, however. "When we first made calls trying to sell Dickies bags

[into] retail," Schactel told *Sporting Goods Business,* "we got a lot of people hanging up on us." The company did not give up and in time Yak Pak succeeded in making Dickies one of the most popular bag brands for teenage girls in the United States, as well as standard gear for the skate-punk crowd. As a result, Dickies became Yak Pak's most fashion-forward brand, drawing on influences from multiple sources to remain current with the ever changing moods and tastes of its customers. Because of the line's popularity Yak Pak also achieved its goal of breaking into mass-market channels, as Dickies bags were picked up by the major sporting goods chains.

A major part of the appeal of Yak Pak products was its emphasis on function. More than just appearance, the bags were utilitarian in nature. A prime example of merging style with function was the messenger bag line Yak Pak introduced in the late 1990s. With the company based in New York City, Yak Pak designers could not help but notice the bicycle messengers that traversed Manhattan's clogged streets to deliver packages tucked inside large pouches slung over a rider's back by way of a single, thick banana-shaped strap. Not only did it offer an iconic look, the messenger bag was nothing if not practical, designed to distribute weight over a broader surface to lighten the load, and so plain in appearance that it essentially offered designers a blank canvas on which to work. The re-imagined messenger bag with its easy-to-use yet secure Velcro strap also proved popular with consumers and became a major seller for Yak Pak. Also in the 1990s Yak Pak pioneered the mini backpack.

RETAIL STORE OPENS: 2000

Yak Pak's success with Dickies led to other licensing opportunities. In the late 1990s the company developed a bag program for Coleman, the venerable camping gear and outdoor equipment company. In 2000 Yak Pak

reached an agreement with Levi Strauss & Co. to license its highly recognizable Red Tab label. The company also licensed its Yak Pak brand in Japan to six separate companies to offer footwear, watches, bags, young men's apparel, children's apparel, and high-end women's apparel. A women's footwear collection was introduced in the United States in 2002. Another source of revenue was a concept retail store Yak Pak opened in San Francisco in September 2000 in the vicinity of the Haight-Ashbury intersection, the heart of the 1960s' counterculture. While the store was less than 400 square feet in size, it benefited from a good deal of street traffic, resulting in $700 per square foot in revenue from the sale of Yak Pak, Dickies, and Levi's bags. With both Dickies and Levi bags providing significant contributions, Yak Pak grew sales to about $20 million in 2002.

Restricting the company's growth at this point was an inadequate information technology (IT) infrastructure that forced Yak Pak to rely on a rudimentary supply chain system. The company was so hampered by its IT system, that it was unable to drill down into sales data to determine what products were selling where. Unable to answer these basic questions the management team was forced to make ill-informed decisions. Operating a remote warehouse was also out of the question. Since the mid-1990s the company flew in its bag production from the El Salvador plant once a week to a Brooklyn warehouse, where the products were then distributed throughout North America. With all of the operation, aside from manufacturing, confined to a single location, Yak Pak had to absorb higher overhead costs if it wanted to hire more personnel. This was directly due to the high cost of living in New York City, which inflated wages.

The inability to take advantage of remote locations was clearly an untenable situation, but Yak Pak found itself a small company with larger company needs, and the only solutions were outside of its price range. Finally the company became aware of a new small business solution, the enterprise resource planning software package from American Express Tax and Business Services. Yak Pak became an early adopter, installing the system in September 2003. No longer forced to maintain a nearby warehouse, Yak Pak was able to open a warehouse in Houston, allowing the company to ship its products from El Salvador by ocean, resulting in major savings in freight charges. Moreover, the rent for the warehouse was 30 percent less than the Brooklyn facility, and was larger, more modern, and more cost effective. The Houston operation was later replaced by a warehouse in Santa Fe Springs, California.

MORE LICENSING DEALS: 2004

Not only did Yak Pak move its warehouse out of Brooklyn, in the new century the company also moved its headquarters and design operations to Manhattan, procuring space in Manhattan's Flatiron district. Here Yak Pak continued to design innovative bags, many of which were geared toward the urban music culture. Yak Pak, for example, offered a "graf" bag for graffiti artists, designed to hold spray-paint cans and other items, though the company made it clear that it supported tag art, not the defacing of property. The company also continued to sign licensing deals. After the Levi license was terminated in 2004, Yak Pak signed development deals with MTV, Wrangler, and The Original Penguin.

In addition to introducing a wealth of new designs for its core bag collections, Yak Pak opened up a variety of new product categories. The Yak Baby Collection, featuring diaper bags and duffels, was introduced in March 2008, followed a month later by the Bladerunner line of kitchen knife cases and bags. Later in the year Yak Pak catered to technophiles by launching a line of laptop cases and sleeves. Early in 2009 Yak Pak introduced a small accessories line for women that included a wallet, wristlet, and ID sleeve that could also serve as a luggage tag. Yak Pak went even further afield in 2009 with the addition of beanbag chairs the company produced in partnership with Canada's NEON stores. In the meantime, Yak Pak opted not to renew the lease on its San Francisco store. Whether the company would open other stores in other major cities remained to be seen, but with about $50 million in annual sales, Yak Pak appeared well positioned to enjoy further growth in the years to come.

Ed Dinger

PRINCIPAL SUBSIDIARIES

Yak Pak El Salvador, SA de CV.

PRINCIPAL COMPETITORS

kay spade LLC; Kenneth Cole Productions, Inc.; Lands' End, Inc.

FURTHER READING

Askin, Ellen, "Yak Pak Bags Three Licenses," *Daily News Record,* August 30, 2004, p. 18.

Cuen, Leigh, "Yak Pak Closes, Shoe Repair Shop Feels Economic Hit," *Haight-Ashbury Beat,* January 7, 2009.

Gallagher, Leigh, "The Next Pack," *Sporting Goods Business,* August 1996, p. 68.

Griffin, Cara, "Yak Pak Is on the Mark with Trendsetting Bags," *Sporting Goods Business,* February 2003, p. 16.

Kareem, Nadra, "Pack It Away," *El Paso Times,* August 27, 2003, p. 3D.

Romero, Elena, "Yak of All Trades," *Daily News Record,* April 22, 2002, p. 16S.

YTB International, Inc.

1901 East Edwardsville Road
Wood River, Illinois 62095
U.S.A.
Telephone: (618) 655-9477
Toll Free: (800) 243-4450
Fax: (618) 659-9607
Web site: http://www.ytb.com

Public Company
Founded: 1982 as Travel Network, Ltd.
Employees: 275
Sales: $162.5 million (2008)
Stock Exchanges: Over the Counter (OTC)
Ticker Symbol: YTBLA
NAICS: 561510 Travel Agencies

■ ■ ■

YTB International, Inc., provides a variety of travel arrangements and services for small businesses, travel agencies, and independent travel agents. The company's roots began in New York with the formation of Travel Network, Ltd., in 1982 and after several name changes and mergers became YTB International, Inc., in 2004. Under the management of Lloyd "Coach" Tomer, Scott Tomer, and Kim Sorenson, who collectively own almost half of the company's stock, YTB is one of the country's largest travel services firms, consistently ranking in the top quarter of *Travel Weekly's* annual Power List.

BEGINNINGS: 1970–2003

YTB International, Inc., began as Travel Network, Ltd., in 1982, performing business transactions as Global Travel Network. The company was formed in New York by a group including Michael Y. Brent, who owned and operated his own travel agency. Upon the creation of Travel Network, Ltd., Brent served as the company's vice president until 1989 when he became chief operating officer and bought a substantial portion of the business. In 1994, when the firm reincorporated in New Jersey, Brent became president and CEO.

The company retooled and changed its name to Global Travel Network, LLC, in 1998. Late the following year, in September 1999, the company merged most of its assets with Playorena, Inc.; the remaining travel business, renamed Etravnet.com, Inc., and based in Englewood Cliffs, New Jersey, went public on the Over the Counter (OTC) market under the ticker symbol ETVT.

By 2000 Etravnet.com served 300 travel franchises and operated 50 store-within-a-store travel shops in Wal-Mart Super Centers nationwide and another 50 franchises worldwide. The company served its growing list of clients through three Web brands: Etravnet.com, a travel and hospitality site for private Web site owners; Hagglewithus.com, an auction booking service for travel and retail customers; and Rezconnect.com, a real-time online reservations system for hotels and restaurants.

In August 2002 Etravnet.com changed its name to REZconnect.com Technologies, Inc., to reflect its patented reservations system and again offered shares on the OTC market as REZT. The year also brought an

COMPANY PERSPECTIVES

YTB International, Inc., was recognized as the 25th largest seller of travel in the U.S. in *Travel Weekly*'s 2009 Power List, based on 2008 annual retail value of travel services booked. YTB provides Internet-based travel booking services for home-based independent representatives in the United States, Puerto Rico, the Bahamas, Canada, Bermuda, and the U.S. Virgin Islands. The Company operates through three subsidiaries: YTB Marketing, Inc. (formerly YourTravelBiz.com, Inc.), YTB Travel Network, Inc., and YTB Franchise Services, Inc.

extensive partnership with client YourTravelBiz.com, Inc., for REZconnect.com to provide Web site hosting services for its customers. YourTravelBiz.com, Inc., founded in 2001, was run by J. Lloyd Tomer (known as "Coach"), his son Scott Tomer, and J. Kim Sorenson. All three executives had worked in sales and marketing for A.L. Williams (the precursor of Primerica Financial Services) in the 1980s and 1990s before cofounding YourTravelBiz.com.

EXPLOSIVE GROWTH: 2004–06

In late 2004 the combined companies reincorporated in Delaware as YTB International, Inc., with a public offering on the OTC Bulletin Board. REZconnect.com became a wholly owned subsidiary, along with YTB Travel Network, Inc., and YourTravelBiz.com, Inc. (later renamed YTB Marketing, Inc.). Michael Brent and his two sons ran the New Jersey operations as a director and CEO team while Chairman Coach Tomer and his team (Scott Tomer as president and Kim Sorenson as vice president) operated from Alton, Illinois, near the Illinois-Missouri border and metro St. Louis area. The company also leased space in Puerto Rico for an international branch.

By offering clients travel booking programs and Web site training and hosting services, YTB hoped to dominate the rapidly growing Internet travel market. The firm generated fees through three major venues: Internet Business Centers, which charged for travel service setups; Referring Travel Agents (RTAs) who paid for training and YTB-hosted travel Web sites at brick-and-mortar agencies; and commissions received from travel bookings and transactions.

After bringing in net revenues of $3.2 million for its maiden year of business as YTB International, the company continued to capitalize on the Internet travel boom. Growth prompted a move to new office space in nearby Edwardsville, Illinois, in 2005. (Two years later, with a growing corporate staff, the company again relocated to Wood River, Illinois.)

In August 2005 the company held its third annual convention in St. Louis, with the theme "YTB: Your Time to Build." The premise proved immensely popular and helped propel annual revenues to $21.6 million for the year, with the company's corporate workforce increasing to more than 50 full-time employees. Plans for the following year included an enormous increase in advertising spending, from just over $23,000 in 2005 to $385,000 in 2006, to provide the YTB name with both national and international recognition.

The promotional gambit worked as YTB's next annual convention, deemed the "Business of Champions," was attended by over 3,000 current and new affiliated travel professionals. Throughout the year, YTB continued to grow at a rapid pace, especially the YourTravelBiz.com segment, which had franchises in all 50 states. To reflect its contributions, Scott Tomer was named YTB's chief executive (and continued his duties as CEO of YourTravelBiz.com), with Michael Brent taking over Scott's previous duties as president. YTB finished 2006 with revenues of $50.6 million and achieved another milestone by being named the 35th-largest U.S. travel firm by *Travel Weekly* magazine.

CHANGE IN THE AIR: 2007–08

YTB International continued its explosive growth in 2007 as further accolades and soaring revenues (over $141 million) brought the company additional exposure. Coach Tomer was named to *Travel Weekly*'s "Most Influential People in the Industry" list, while attendance at the company's annual national convention in August, "Cleared for Takeoff," exceeded 10,000 participants. YTB followed up in November with the "Funshine Travel" trade show in Orlando, with 5,000 travel agent attendees. The company also expanded its worldwide presence to include several new international travel offices in Canada, the Bahamas, and Bermuda.

As the decade began to wind down, change was in the air. YTB continued its unprecedented growth, again scoring high with its 2008 annual convention, featuring the slogan "Liberty and Travel for All." Attendance was off the charts at nearly 16,000. In the executive suite, changes signaled a new direction as the Brents left the business and Kim Sorenson was elevated from treasurer to president. The company also redesigned and relaunched its corporate Web site, www.ytb.com. While

KEY DATES

1982: Travel Network, Ltd., is formed in New York.

1994: Company is reincorporated in New Jersey.

1998: Firm undergoes a name change to Global Travel Network, LLC.

1999: Much of the company merges with Playorena, Inc., except Etravnet.com.

2002: Etravnet.com changes its name to REZconnect.com Technologies, Inc.

2004: YourTravelBiz.com and REZconnect.com merge to become YTB International, Inc.

2005: YTB moves to Edwardsville, Illinois; two years later the company relocates to Wood River, Illinois.

2006: Company is ranked as *Travel Weekly*'s 35th-largest travel company.

2007: Company Chairman J. Lloyd ("Coach") Tomer is named one of *Travel Weekly*'s Most Influential People in the travel industry.

2008: California Attorney General Jerry Brown files suit against YTB.

2009: YTB settles the California lawsuit and retools its business practices.

year-end revenues reached $162.5 million, the economy had soured and the travel industry took a nosedive.

WEATHERING THE RECESSION AND OTHER PROBLEMS

With the leisure industry particularly hard-hit in the recession, YTB lost more than 35,000 travel agents and their bookings. The company had also come under scrutiny after several lawsuits were filed in California. Amidst the deepening recession, YTB reduced its workforce, sold real estate in southern Illinois, and sold its private Lear jet. As the travel industry limped through the year, YTB managed to hold on, even scoring its fourth Pinnacle Award from Carnival Cruise Lines as a top marketer of "Fun Ship" cruise vacations.

In the boardroom, YTB brought in Robert Van Patten, a 25-year business veteran, to work as a consulting co-CEO alongside Scott Tomer and quiet growing criticism of the company. As YTB came under increasing fire, four board members departed. California Attorney General Jerry Brown had launched a full-scale investigation into the company for alleged deceptive marketing and unfair business practices.

The news got worse for YTB as Illinois Attorney General Lisa Madigan launched her own investigation into what many characterized as a pyramid scheme, and two more lawsuits were filed in East St. Louis, Illinois. YTB had a loss of $4.1 million for 2008 since the bulk of its income, over 75 percent, was derived from the start-up, Web site maintenance, and training fees for its dwindling independent travel agents. By mid-2009 the company had settled its California lawsuit, retooled its business structure, tightened oversight, and launched a new subsidiary, YTB Franchise Services, Inc., to oversee franchise opportunities in place of its RTA business model.

Despite a dire economy and continuing legal woes with Illinois's attorney general, YTB International, Inc., was focused on the future. CEO Scott Tomer commented in a company press release (August 10, 2009), "Looking to the second half of the year, we plan to continue to effectively manage our cost structure, ensuring that we are as agile as possible in order to take advantage of the inevitable market turnaround." YTB still ranked among *Travel Weekly*'s largest travel companies. The Tomers and Sorenson, who owned nearly half of the company's stock, were determined to grow their online business services and continue the climb toward the number-one slot on *Travel Weekly*'s annual power list.

Nelson Rhodes

PRINCIPAL SUBSIDIARIES

YTB Marketing, Inc.; YTB Travel Network, Inc.; YTB Franchise Services, Inc.

PRINCIPAL COMPETITORS

Expedia, Inc.; Kayak.com; Orbitz Worldwide, Inc.; Priceline.com Inc.; Travelocity.com LP.

FURTHER READING

Buss, Will, "Travel Website Moves to Wood River," *Belleville (IL) News-Democrat*, January 4, 2007.

"Change in Management for YTB International, Inc.," *Internet Wire*, January 12, 2006.

"Cruising News," *Cruise Guide*, June 8, 2009.

Ellis, Cynthia M., "Businessman Pays Off Church's Mortgage," *Alton (IL) Telegraph*, February 5, 2007.

———, "Old Kmart to Be HQ of Internet Travel Business," *Alton (IL) Telegraph*, December 10, 2006.

———, "Wood River May Get Hotel; Convention Center Also Part of YTB's Plans," *Alton (IL) Telegraph*, April 8, 2008.

Godwin, Nadine, "Card Mill? Pyramid Scheme? YTB Prefers the Term 'Travel Agency,'" *Travel Weekly*, January 8, 2007, p. 8.

———, "Lloyd Tomer, Chairman, YTB International," *Travel Weekly*, January 8, 2007, p. 4.

———, "2nd Class Action Filed Against YTB as Number of Suits Keeps Growing," *Travel Weekly*, August 25, 2008, p. 1.

Logan, Tim, "Embattled YTB Near Deal in California Suit," *St. Louis Post-Dispatch*, April 8, 2009.

———, "Illinois Wants to Shut Down YTB," *St. Louis Post-Dispatch*, May 16, 2009.

———, "Two More Quit YTB's Board," *St. Louis Post-Dispatch*, May 5, 2009.

———, "YTB Sells Dream of Prosperity," *St. Louis Post-Dispatch*, August 31, 2008.

———, "YTB Settles with California, Promises Big Changes," *St. Louis Post-Dispatch*, May 15, 2009.

Luzadder, Dan, "YTB Defends Its Business Practices," *Travel Weekly*, October 22, 2007, p. 71.

Schmidt, Sanford J., "Judge Wants Suits Against YTB Consolidated," *Telegraph*, December 16, 2008.

Zachary Confections, Inc.

2130 West State Road 28
Frankfort, Indiana 46041
U.S.A.
Telephone: (765) 659-4751
Fax: (765) 659-1491
Web site: http://www.zacharyconfections.com

Private Company
Incorporated: 1987
Employees: 250
Sales: $35.1 million (2008)
NAICS: 311330 Confectionery Manufacturing from Purchased Chocolate; 311340 Nonchocolate Confectionery Manufacturing

■ ■ ■

Family owned and operated since 1950, Zachary Confections, Inc., produces chocolates and candy in a large manufacturing facility located in Frankfort, Indiana. In addition to specializing in seasonal and holiday treats, the company also offers everyday, private-label, and corporate-gift candies. The product line features more than 150 items and includes candy corn, chocolate raisins, mints, caramels, chocolate bunnies, and big heart-shaped boxed bonbons.

A GROWING FAMILY-OWNED COMPANY: 1950–84

Zachary Confections, Inc., was founded in 1950 in Chicago, Illinois, by J. J. Zachary and his wife, Helen.

The pair focused on manufacturing and selling high-quality specialized chocolates. In the beginning, they ran the small business almost singlehandedly. When the couple's son, Jack, was old enough to join the company, they hired him as a salesman, eventually promoting him to a territory sales manager position in 1959. Thirteen years later, in 1972, J. J. retired as company president and appointed Jack in his place. Over the span of 22 years, Zachary Confections had grown from a simple family-owned operation into a large-scale candy factory.

By the early 1980s, the company's sales volume exceeded production capacity; a new facility was needed. In addition to searching for increased manufacturing space, better equipment, and room to grow, the Zacharys also wanted to find a family-oriented community where they could establish their operations permanently. They found the perfect plant in Frankfort, Indiana, a spacious 210,000-square-foot facility situated on 26 acres that had once been owned and operated by Peter Paul Cadbury. Designed to produce candy bars, not chocolate specialties (Zachary Confections' primary product), the facility needed some upgrades and remodeling. However, there were some well-designed aspects, including floor-to-ceiling glazed tiled walls and segregated enrobing and cooling halls, that made the building a good choice. The company relocated in 1984.

NEW PRODUCT LINES, REBRANDING, AND MACHINERY UPGRADES: 1994–2000

Ten years later, in 1994, the company was at a turning point again. "We thought collectively that there were opportunities in the [confectionery] industry and that Zachary Confections was probably in a better situation than some others to take advantage of them," Jack Zachary stated in a 1997 *Candy Industry* article. This realization was the driving force over the next several years behind a series of changes in the company's product line and marketing practices, as well as its significant investment in new factory machinery.

Until then, the company had strictly limited its product line to seasonal and holiday chocolates. By 1997, though, it was ready to expand into the "everyday" category. That year, chocolate panned goods joined Zachary's product offerings, and its cordial cherry program expanded beyond the Valentine's Day selling period. In 2000, the company added Gobblers, roasted peanuts and soft caramels covered in milk chocolate.

In addition to launching new products, the company also redesigned its branding with the goal of creating packaging that communicated the quality of Zachary's chocolates and was easily identifiable to consumers: "We want to be a brand that people recognize. Ultimately, we hope that we can create a look so that customers don't have to read the word 'Zachary' to know whose product it is," Jack Zachary said in a 1997 *Candy Industry* article.

To support the product line expansion and marketing efforts, the company made some significant investments in its machinery, installing a second NID Pty Ltd starch molding plant, a Hohberger automatic cream plant, and a Dumoulin chocolate panning system. "Our determination is, if we're going to go, we're going to go all the way!" Jack Zachary said in *Candy Industry* in 1997. These new machines also included screens and printouts that tracked exactly what was happening with temperature and speeds. The end result was a significant improvement in output. The company had taken a fairly labor intensive process and streamlined it, transforming

itself from a batch-based operation into an automatic, state-of-the-art computerized plant.

The confectionery industry took notice of Zachary Confections' considerable transformation. Two years later, in 1996, Jack Zachary was awarded the 51st Kettle Award by *Candy Industry* for his efforts in sales, marketing, and public relations, at the National Confectioners Association.

MARGINS SHRINK AS PRODUCTION CAPACITY INCREASES: 2000–02

However, although the company's significant improvements made it more competitive, it did not make it immune to industry trends. In early 2000, the candy industry was witnessing two major shifts: Value-oriented consumers began buying large boxes of chocolate to save money, and increasing numbers of consumers had developed a taste for premium designer chocolates.

As a low-cost producer of a value brand, Zachary Confections lost some customers to the premium brands. More problematic still was increasing holiday competition from national brands and retailers' demand for larger product presentations. As a result, the company saw its profit margin shrink.

Nevertheless, despite these market developments, the company was still "bursting at the seams," according to George Anichini, vice president of operations, during a 1997 *Candy Industry* interview. The company's loading area was jammed with 37 trailers full of packaging material because its storage area was at capacity.

As a result, in the fall of 2001 the company began construction on 80,000 square feet of cold storage space. The new facility would be ultra high-tech, equipped with radio frequency scanners that monitored the efficiency of storage space use. It would also double the facility's shipping and receiving capacity by increasing the total number of docks from four to eight.

MORE PRODUCT LINE EXPANSION AND NON-CHOCOLATE PRODUCTS: 2002–08

Another important goal for the expansion related to the company's long-term business strategy. Beginning in 2000, market shifts focused the company's attention on product-line expansion into non-chocolate items. After investing $3 million in machinery to produce candy corn, mello-cremes, and jellies, Zachary Confections launched its candy corn and mello-creme lines in 2002. "It's our first entry into becoming more of a general line

```
+---------------------------------------------+
|                 KEY DATES                   |
|                     ■                       |
|                                             |
| 1950: Zachary Confections, Inc., is founded |
|       by J. J. Zachary and his wife, Helen, |
|       in Chicago, Illinois.                 |
| 1972: Jack Zachary is appointed president   |
|       of Zachary Confections, Inc.          |
| 1984: Company moves to a new 210,000-square-|
|       foot facility in Frankfort, Indiana.  |
| 1996: Jack Zachary wins the 51st Kettle     |
|       Award.                                |
| 2002: Construction of 80,000 additional     |
|       square feet of cold storage space is  |
|       completed; company expands product    |
|       line outside the chocolate category,  |
|       adding candy corn and mello-cremes.   |
| 2003: Jellies are added to the product      |
|       lineup.                               |
| 2004: Patrick W. Zachary becomes Zachary    |
|       Confections' president and chief      |
|       executive officer.                    |
| 2005: Company's candy corn wins the         |
|       American Culinary ChefsBest Award.    |
| 2006: Company adds 10,000 more square feet  |
|       to its facility.                      |
| 2008: Company creates a West Coast territory|
|       sales manager position.               |
+---------------------------------------------+
```

candy company," Patrick Zachary said in a 2002 *Professional Candy Buyer* article. "We're trying to get more presence in the market, and these non-chocolate items will help," he further explained in *Candy Business* in 2003. This development also marked the company's foray into the Halloween candy market.

One year later, in 2003, Zachary Confections' candy corn received industry recognition by being nominated for the "Product of the Year Award" by the National Confectionery Sales Association. Then, in 2005, American Culinary ChefsBest awarded the company's candy corn its prestigious "2005 ChefsBest Award." Company leadership considered this a huge coup. "Quality is where we want to differentiate ourselves," Patrick told *Candy Industry* in a 2006 article. "We approached the project from the perspective that we wanted to make ... the best mass-produced candy corn in the world." By 2006, the company controlled about 15 percent of the candy corn market in the United States.

In all, by 2003, Zachary Confections manufactured more than 150 products, including double-dipped peanuts, bridge mix, peanut clusters, and chocolate-covered raisins, as well as jellies and other non-chocolate

items. However, Zachary Confections still remained focused on chocolate products manufactured with proprietary blends developed for the company by a handful of industrial chocolate manufacturers, including ADM Cocoa, Blommer Chocolate Company, and Wilbur Chocolate Company. At the time, the company had plans to continue to increase its competitive edge by extending its everyday chocolate line, relying upon chocolate-covered items.

CHANGES IN LEADERSHIP: 2004–06

Before it could tackle its business goals, the company faced a change in leadership. By 2004, Jack Zachary was ready to retire. Over the years, three of his six children had joined the business. In 1982, Jack's oldest son, Jack III, began working at the company; he became senior vice president by 1996. Jack's daughter, Susan Zachary, became a regional sales manager. His youngest son, Patrick, began working at the company as a manufacturing supervisor in 1995.

Having performed virtually every task in the plant at increasing levels of responsibility, 34-year-old Patrick Zachary was appointed president and chief executive when his father stepped down. In his new role, he continued to perform a wide range of duties, from sales and profits, to new product development and new product lines, to licensing and acquisition. At that same time, Jack III became executive vice president, overseeing Zachary Confections' sales force. Longtime employee George Anichini took Jack's position as senior vice president.

As head of the company, Patrick Zachary started looking at new ways of upgrading its sales capacity, and, in 2006, he hired a new director of marketing. That year, in a *Candy Industry* article, Zachary said that the company's goal was "to grow revenues at a minimum of 10 percent annually."

Zachary saw three areas for revenue growth with the highest potential for growth in the company's candy corn and mello-creme segments. Another opportunity existed in new product development with plans for new licensing deals (the company was the exclusive licensee for Garfield, the smart-alecky cartoon cat character), instant consumables (portion-sized treats), tray packs/party trays, unique packages, and tub items. The third revenue growth opportunity was in chocolate.

REMODELING, FACTORY UPGRADES, AND WEST COAST MARKET GROWTH: 2006–09

In 2006, the company completed a 10,000-square-foot plant addition that enabled it to turn out more than

75,000 pounds of product per shift. Three hundred and fifty employees kept the plan running three shifts a day. On this rigorous schedule, output increased by as much as 7 percent. With plans to implement a new company-wide computer system, the company expected output to increase even further.

That same year, the company's retail outlet store, dubbed The Candy Shoppe and located within the plant, underwent a remodel to allow for extra browsing space and a larger selection of products. The new store's hours increased, and with some local marketing, Zachary expected to quadruple the store's sales by 2007.

At the time, the company's most popular products were chocolate, which made up 70 percent of the company's sales. Seasonal sales accounted for 75 percent of total revenues, while everyday items made up the remaining 25 percent.

By 2008, the company was again looking to expand its market and refine its branding and marketing. Citing the company's strength in the Midwest and Northeast, it added a West Coast territory sales manager position. It also increased its focus on its growing jellies segment, adding sour-sanded jellies and experimenting with exotic and tropical flavors to attract younger consumers. As the company rounded out the decade, hopes were high for

increasing market penetration by launching new products, widening the consumer base, and extending the Zachary brand into new territories.

Carrie Rothburd

PRINCIPAL COMPETITORS

The Hershey Company; Mars, Incorporated; Nestlé S.A.; Asher's Chocolates, Inc.; Cadbury plc; Ghirardelli Chocolate Company; See's Candies, Inc.; Russell Stover Candies Inc.; Sherwood Brands, Inc.

FURTHER READING

Pacyniak, Bernard, "Staying Fit," *Candy Industry*, May 2006, p. 20.

Stall, Judah, "Inside Zachary: Zachary Confections' Hometown Appeal Translates into Steady Growth for This All-American Candy Maker," *Candy Business*, January–February 2003, p. 14.

Tiffany, Susan, "From Me-Too to Branded Player," *Candy Industry*, April 1997, p. 48.

"Zachary Enters Non-Chocolate Category," *Professional Candy Buyer*, May-June 2002, p. 10.

Cumulative Index to Companies

Bavaria S.A., 90 44–47

Baxi Group Ltd., 96 27–30

Baxter International Inc., I 627–29; 10
141–43 (upd.)

Baxters Food Group Ltd., 99 47–50

The Bay *see* The Hudson's Bay Co.

Bay State Gas Company, 38 79–82

Bayard SA, 49 46–49

BayBanks, Inc., 12 30–32

Bayer A.G., I 309–11; 13 75–77 (upd.);
41 44–48 (upd.)

Bayerische Hypotheken- und
Wechsel-Bank AG, II 238–40 *see also*
HVB Group.

Bayerische Motoren Werke AG, I
138–40; 11 31–33 (upd.); 38 83–87
(upd.); 108 95–101 (upd.)

Bayerische Vereinsbank A.G., II 241–43
see also HVB Group.

Bayernwerk AG, V 555–58; 23 43–47
(upd.) *see also* E.On AG.

Bayou Steel Corporation, 31 47–49

BB&T Corporation, 79 57–61

BB Holdings Limited, 77 50–53

BBA *see* Bush Boake Allen Inc.

BBA Aviation plc, 90 48–52

BBAG Osterreichische
Brau-Beteiligungs-AG, 38 88–90

BBC *see* British Broadcasting Corp.

BBDO Worldwide *see* Omnicom Group
Inc.

BBGI *see* Beasley Broadcast Group, Inc.

BBN Corp., 19 39–42

BBVA *see* Banco Bilbao Vizcaya Argentaria
S.A.

BCE, Inc., V 269–71; 44 46–50 (upd.)

Bci, 99 51–54

BDO Seidman LLP, 96 31–34

BE&K, Inc., 73 57–59

BEA *see* Bank of East Asia Ltd.

BEA Systems, Inc., 36 80–83

Beacon Roofing Supply, Inc., 75 59–61

Bear Creek Corporation, 38 91–94

Bear Stearns Companies, Inc., II
400–01; 10 144–45 (upd.); 52 41–44
(upd.)

Bearings, Inc., 13 78–80

Beasley Broadcast Group, Inc., 51
44–46

Beate Uhse AG, 96 35–39

Beatrice Company, II 467–69 *see also*
TLC Beatrice International Holdings,
Inc.

BeautiControl Cosmetics, Inc., 21
49–52

Beazer Homes USA, Inc., 17 38–41

bebe stores, inc., 31 50–52; 103 47–51
(upd.)

Bechtel Corporation, I 558–59; 24
64–67 (upd.); 99 55–60 (upd.)

Beckett Papers, 23 48–50

Beckman Coulter, Inc., 22 74–77

Beckman Instruments, Inc., 14 52–54

Becton, Dickinson and Company, I
630–31; 11 34–36 (upd.); 36 84–89
(upd.); 101 69–77 (upd.)

Bed Bath & Beyond Inc., 13 81–83; 41
49–52 (upd.)

Beech Aircraft Corporation, 8 49–52 *see
also* Raytheon Aircraft Holdings Inc.

Beech-Nut Nutrition Corporation, 21
53–56; 51 47–51 (upd.)

Beef O'Brady's *see* Family Sports
Concepts, Inc.

Beer Nuts, Inc., 86 30–33

Beggars Group Ltd., 99 61–65

Behr GmbH & Co. KG, 72 22–25

Behring Diagnostics *see* Dade Behring
Holdings Inc.

BEI Technologies, Inc., 65 74–76

Beiersdorf AG, 29 49–53

Bekaert S.A./N.V., 90 53–57

Bekins Company, 15 48–50

Bel *see* Fromageries Bel.

Bel Fuse, Inc., 53 59–62

Bel/Kaukauna USA, 76 46–48

Belco Oil & Gas Corp., 40 63–65

Belden CDT Inc., 19 43–45; 76 49–52
(upd.)

Belgacom, 6 302–04

Belk, Inc., V 12–13; 19 46–48 (upd.);
72 26–29 (upd.)

Bell and Howell Company, 9 61–64; 29
54–58 (upd.)

Bell Atlantic Corporation, V 272–74; 25
58–62 (upd.) *see also* Verizon
Communications.

Bell Canada Enterprises Inc. *see* BCE, Inc.

Bell Canada International, Inc., 6
305–08

Bell Helicopter Textron Inc., 46 64–67

Bell Industries, Inc., 47 40–43

Bell Resources *see* TPG NV.

Bell Sports Corporation, 16 51–53; 44
51–54 (upd.)

Bellcore *see* Telcordia Technologies, Inc.

Belleek Pottery Ltd., 71 50–53

Belleville Shoe Manufacturing
Company, 92 17–20

Bellisio Foods, Inc., 95 51–54

BellSouth Corporation, V 276–78; 29
59–62 (upd.) *see also* AT&T Corp.

Bellway Plc, 45 37–39

Belo Corporation, 98 19–25 (upd.)

Beloit Corporation, 14 55–57 *see also*
Metso Corp.

Belron International Ltd., 76 53–56

Belvedere S.A., 93 77–81

Bemis Company, Inc., 8 53–55; 91
53–60 (upd.)

Ben & Jerry's Homemade, Inc., 10
146–48; 35 58–62 (upd.); 80 22–28
(upd.)

Ben Bridge Jeweler, Inc., 60 52–54

Ben E. Keith Company, 76 57–59

Benchmark Capital, 49 50–52

Benchmark Electronics, Inc., 40 66–69

Benckiser N.V. *see* Reckitt Benckiser plc.

Bendix Corporation, I 141–43

Beneficial Corporation, 8 56–58

Benesse Corporation, 76 60–62

Bénéteau SA, 55 54–56

Benetton Group S.p.A., 10 149–52; 67
47–51 (upd.)

Benfield Greig Group plc, 53 63–65

Benguet Corporation, 58 21–24

Benihana, Inc., 18 56–59; 76 63–66
(upd.)

Benjamin Moore and Co., 13 84–87; 38
95–99 (upd.)

Benninger AG, 107 40–44

BenQ Corporation, 67 52–54

Benton Oil and Gas Company, 47
44–46

Berean Christian Stores, 96 40–43

Beretta *see* Fabbrica D' Armi Pietro
Beretta S.p.A.

Bergdorf Goodman Inc., 52 45–48

Bergen Brunswig Corporation, V
14–16; 13 88–90 (upd.) *see also*
AmerisourceBergen Corp.

Berger Bros Company, 62 31–33

Beringer Blass Wine Estates Ltd., 22
78–81; 66 34–37 (upd.)

Berjaya Group Bhd., 67 55–57

Berkeley Farms, Inc., 46 68–70

Berkshire Hathaway Inc., III 213–15;
18 60–63 (upd.); 42 31–36 (upd.);
89 92–99 (upd.)

Berkshire Realty Holdings, L.P., 49
53–55

Berlex Laboratories, Inc., 66 38–40

Berliner Stadtreinigungsbetriebe, 58
25–28

Berliner Verkehrsbetriebe (BVG), 58
29–31

Berlinwasser Holding AG, 90 58–62

Berlitz International, Inc., 13 91–93; 39
47–50 (upd.)

Bernard C. Harris Publishing Company,
Inc., 39 51–53

Bernard Chaus, Inc., 27 59–61

Bernard Hodes Group Inc., 86 34–37

Bernard L. Madoff Investment Securities
LLC, 106 58–62

Bernard Matthews Ltd., 89 100–04

The Bernick Companies, 75 62–65

Bernina Holding AG, 47 47–50

Bernstein-Rein,92 21–24

The Berry Company *see* L. M. Berry and
Company

Berry Petroleum Company, 47 51–53

Berry Plastics Group Inc., 21 57–59; 98
26–30 (upd.)

Bertelsmann A.G., IV 592–94; 43 63–67
(upd.); 91 61–68 (upd.)

Bertucci's Corporation, 16 54–56; 64
51–54 (upd.)

Berwick Offray, LLC, 70 17–19

Berwind Corporation, 100 61–64

Besix Group S.A./NV, 94 66–69

Besnier SA, 19 49–51 *see also* Groupe
Lactalis

Best Buy Co., Inc., 9 65–66; 23 51–53
(upd.); 63 61–66 (upd.)

Best Kosher Foods Corporation, 82
41–44

Best Maid Products, Inc., 107 45–48

Bestfoods, 22 82–86 (upd.)

Bestseller A/S, 90 63–66

Bestway Transportation *see* TNT
Freightways Corp.

BET Holdings, Inc., 18 64–66

Daily Journal Corporation, 101 152–55
Daily Mail and General Trust plc, 19 118–20
The Daimaru, Inc., V 41–42; 42 98–100 (upd.)
Daimler-Benz Aerospace AG, 16 150–52
Daimler-Benz AG, I 149–51; 15 140–44 (upd.)
DaimlerChrysler AG, 34 128–37 (upd.); 64 100–07 (upd.)
Dain Rauscher Corporation, 35 138–41 (upd.)
Daio Paper Corporation, IV 266–67; 84 86–89 (upd.)
Dairy Crest Group plc, 32 131–33
Dairy Farm International Holdings Ltd., 97 125–28
Dairy Farmers of America, Inc., 94 143–46
Dairy Mart Convenience Stores, Inc., 7 113–15; 25 124–27 (upd.) see also Alimentation Couche-Tard Inc.
Dairy Queen see International Dairy Queen, Inc.
Dairyland Healthcare Solutions, 73 99–101
Daishowa Paper Manufacturing Co., Ltd., IV 268–70; 57 100–03 (upd.)
Daisy Outdoor Products Inc., 58 85–88
Daisytek International Corporation, 18 128–30
Daiwa Bank, Ltd., II 276–77; 39 109–11 (upd.)
Daiwa Securities Company, Limited, II 405–06
Daiwa Securities Group Inc., 55 115–18 (upd.)
Daktronics, Inc., 32 134–37; 107 91–95 (upd.)
Dal-Tile International Inc., 22 169–71
Dale and Thomas Popcorn LLC, 100 131–34
Dale Carnegie & Associates Inc., 28 85–87; 78 78–82 (upd.)
Dalgety PLC, II 499–500 see also PIC International Group PLC
Dalhoff Larsen & Horneman A/S, 96 95–99
Dalian Shide Group, 91 136–39
Dalkia Holding, 66 68–70
Dallah Albaraka Group, 72 83–86
Dallas Cowboys Football Club, Ltd., 33 122–25
Dallas Semiconductor Corporation, 13 191–93; 31 143–46 (upd.)
Dalli-Werke GmbH & Co. KG, 86 105–10
Dallis Coffee, Inc., 86 111–14
Damark International, Inc., 18 131–34 see also Provell Inc.
Damartex S.A., 98 84–87
Dames & Moore, Inc., 25 128–31 see also URS Corp.
Dan River Inc., 35 142–46; 86 115–20 (upd.)
Dana Holding Corporation, I 152–53; 10 264–66 (upd.); 99 127–134 (upd.)

Danaher Corporation, 7 116–17; 77 129–33 (upd.)
Danaos Corporation, 91 140–43
Daniel Measurement and Control, Inc., 16 153–55; 74 96–99 (upd.)
Daniel Thwaites Plc, 95 122–25
Danisco A/S, 44 134–37
Dannon Company, Inc., 14 149–51; 106 138–42 (upd.)
Danone Group see Groupe Danone.
Danske Bank Aktieselskab, 50 148–51
Danskin, Inc., 12 93–95; 62 88–92 (upd.)
Danzas Group, V 441–43; 40 136–39 (upd.)
D'Arcy Masius Benton & Bowles, Inc., 6 20–22; 32 138–43 (upd.)
Darden Restaurants, Inc., 16 156–58; 44 138–42 (upd.)
Dare Foods Limited, 103 135–38
Darigold, Inc., 9 159–61
Darling International Inc., 85 81–84
Dart Group PLC, 16 159–62; 77 134–37 (upd.)
Darty S.A., 27 118–20
DASA see Daimler-Benz Aerospace AG.
Dassault-Breguet see Avions Marcel Dassault-Breguet Aviation.
Dassault Systèmes S.A., 25 132–34 see also Groupe Dassault Aviation SA.
Data Broadcasting Corporation, 31 147–50
Data General Corporation, 8 137–40 see also EMC Corp.
Datapoint Corporation, 11 67–70
Datascope Corporation, 39 112–14
Datek Online Holdings Corp., 32 144–46
Dauphin Deposit Corporation, 14 152–54
Dave & Buster's, Inc., 33 126–29; 104 98–103 (upd.)
The Davey Tree Expert Company, 11 71–73
The David and Lucile Packard Foundation, 41 117–19
The David J. Joseph Company, 14 155–56; 76 128–30 (upd.)
David Jones Ltd., 60 100–02
Davide Campari-Milano S.p.A., 57 104–06
David's Bridal, Inc., 33 130–32
Davis Polk & Wardwell, 36 151–54
Davis Service Group PLC, 45 139–41
DaVita Inc., 73 102–05
DAW Technologies, Inc., 25 135–37
Dawn Food Products, Inc., 17 126–28
Dawson Holdings PLC, 43 132–34
Day & Zimmermann Inc., 9 162–64; 31 151–55 (upd.)
Day International, Inc., 84 90–93
Day Runner, Inc., 14 157–58; 41 120–23 (upd.)
Dayton Hudson Corporation, V 43–44; 18 135–37 (upd.) see also Target Corp.
DB see Deutsche Bundesbahn.
dba Luftfahrtgesellschaft mbH, 76 131–33

DC Comics Inc., 25 138–41; 98 88–94 (upd.)
DC Shoes, Inc., 60 103–05
DCN S.A., 75 125–27
DDB Worldwide Communications, 14 159–61 see also Omnicom Group Inc.
DDi Corp., 7 118–20; 97 129–32 (upd.)
De Agostini Editore S.p.A., 103 139–43
De Beers Consolidated Mines Limited / De Beers Centenary AG, IV 64–68; 7 121–26 (upd.); 28 88–94 (upd.)
De Dietrich & Cie., 31 156–59
De La Rue plc, 10 267–69; 34 138–43 (upd.); 46 251
De Rigo S.p.A., 104 104–07
Dean & DeLuca, Inc., 36 155–57
Dean Foods Company, 7 127–29; 21 165–68 (upd.); 73 106–15 (upd.)
Dean Witter, Discover & Co., 12 96–98 see also Morgan Stanley Dean Witter & Co.
Dearborn Mid-West Conveyor Company, 56 78–80
Death Row Records, 27 121–23 see also Tha Row Records.
Deb Shops, Inc., 16 163–65; 76 134–37 (upd.)
Debeka Krankenversicherungsverein auf Gegenseitigkeit, 72 87–90
Debenhams plc, 28 95–97; 101 156–60 (upd.)
Debevoise & Plimpton, 39 115–17
DEC see Digital Equipment Corp.
Deceuninck N.V., 84 94–97
Dechert, 43 135–38
Deckers Outdoor Corporation, 22 172–74; 98 95–98 (upd.)
Decora Industries, Inc., 31 160–62
Decorator Industries Inc., 68 101–04
DeCrane Aircraft Holdings Inc., 36 158–60
DeepTech International Inc., 21 169–71
Deere & Company, III 462–64; 21 172–76 (upd.); 42 101–06 (upd.)
Defiance, Inc., 22 175–78
Degussa-Hüls AG, IV 69–72; 32 147–53 (upd.)
DeKalb Genetics Corporation, 17 129–31 see also Monsanto Co.
Del Laboratories, Inc., 28 98–100
Del Monte Foods Company, 7 130–32; 23 163–66 (upd.); 103 144–51 (upd.)
Del Taco, Inc., 58 89–92
Del Webb Corporation, 14 162–64 see also Pulte Homes, Inc.
Delachaux S.A., 76 138–40
Delaware North Companies Inc., 7 133–36; 96 100–05 (upd.)
Delco Electronics Corporation see GM Hughes Electronics Corp.
Delhaize Group, 44 143–46; 103 152–57 (upd.)
Deli Universal NV, 66 71–74
dELiA*s Inc., 29 141–44
Delicato Vineyards, Inc., 50 152–55
Dell Computer Corporation, 9 165–66; 31 163–66 (upd.); 63 122–26 (upd.)

Givaudan SA, 43 190–93
Given Imaging Ltd., 83 167–170
Givenchy *see* Parfums Givenchy S.A.
GKN plc, III 493–96; 38 208–13
   (upd.); 89 232–41 (upd.)
GL Events S.A., 107 150–53
Glaces Thiriet S.A., 76 164–66
Glacier Bancorp, Inc., 35 197–200
Glacier Water Services, Inc., 47 155–58
Glamis Gold, Ltd., 54 132–35
Glanbia plc, 59 204–07, 364
Glatfelter Wood Pulp Company *see* P.H.
   Glatfelter Company
Glaverbel Group, 80 130–33
Glaxo Holdings plc, I 639–41; 9
   263–65 (upd.)
GlaxoSmithKline plc, 46 201–08 (upd.)
Glazer's Wholesale Drug Company,
   Inc., 82 142–45
Gleason Corporation, 24 184–87
Glen Dimplex, 78 123–27
Glico *see* Ezaki Glico Company Ltd.
The Glidden Company, 8 222–24
Global Berry Farms LLC, 62 154–56
Global Crossing Ltd., 32 216–19
Global Hyatt Corporation, 75 159–63
   (upd.)
Global Imaging Systems, Inc., 73
   163–65
Global Industries, Ltd., 37 168–72
Global Marine Inc., 9 266–67
Global Outdoors, Inc., 49 173–76
Global Payments Inc., 91 206–10
Global Power Equipment Group Inc.,
   52 137–39
GlobalSantaFe Corporation, 48 187–92
   (upd.)
Globe Newspaper Company Inc., 106
   208–12
Globex Utilidades S.A., 103 188–91
Globo Comunicação e Participações
   S.A., 80 134–38
Glock Ges.m.b.H., 42 154–56
Glon *see* Groupe Glon.
Glotel plc, 53 149–51
Glu Mobile Inc., 95 163–66
Gluek Brewing Company, 75 164–66
GM *see* General Motors Corp.
GM Hughes Electronics Corporation, II
   32–36 *see also* Hughes Electronics
   Corp.
GMH Communities Trust, 87 176–178
GN ReSound A/S, 103 192–96
GNC Corporation, 98 149–55 (upd.)
GNMA *see* Government National
   Mortgage Association.
The Go-Ahead Group Plc, 28 155–57
The Go Daddy Group Inc., 102 142–45
Go Sport *see* Groupe Go Sport S.A.
Go-Video, Inc. *see* Sensory Science Corp.
Godfather's Pizza Incorporated, 25
   179–81
Godiva Chocolatier, Inc., 64 154–57
Goetze's Candy Company, Inc., 87
   179–182
Gol Linhas Aéreas Inteligentes S.A., 73
   166–68

Gold Fields Ltd., IV 94–97; 62 157–64
   (upd.)
Gold Kist Inc., 17 207–09; 26 166–68
   (upd.) *see also* Pilgrim's Pride Corp.
Goldcorp Inc., 87 183–186
Golden Belt Manufacturing Co., 16
   241–43
Golden Books Family Entertainment,
   Inc., 28 158–61 *see also* Random
   House, Inc.
Golden Corral Corporation, 10 331–33;
   66 143–46 (upd.)
Golden Enterprises, Inc., 26 163–65
Golden Krust Caribbean Bakery, Inc.,
   68 177–79
Golden Neo-Life Diamite International,
   Inc., 100 192–95
Golden State Foods Corporation, 32
   220–22
Golden State Vintners, Inc., 33 172–74
Golden Telecom, Inc., 59 208–11
Golden West Financial Corporation, 47
   159–61
The Goldman Sachs Group Inc., II
   414–16; 20 254–57 (upd.); 51
   144–48 (upd.)
Gold'n Plump Poultry, 54 136–38
Gold's Gym International, Inc., 71
   165–68
Goldstar Co., Ltd., 12 211–13 *see also*
   LG Corp.
GoldToeMoretz, LLC, 102 146–49
Golin/Harris International, Inc., 88
   126–30
Golub Corporation, 26 169–71; 96
   136–39 (upd.)
GOME Electrical Appliances Holding
   Ltd., 87 187–191
Gomez Inc., 104 166–69
Gonnella Baking Company, 102 150–53
Gonnella Baking Company, 40 211–13
The Good Guys!, Inc., 10 334–35; 30
   224–27 (upd.)
The Good Humor-Breyers Ice Cream
   Company, 14 203–05 *see also* Unilever
   PLC.
Goodby Silverstein & Partners, Inc., 75
   167–69
Goodman Fielder Ltd., 52 140–43
Goodman Holding Company, 42
   157–60
GoodMark Foods, Inc., 26 172–74
Goodrich Corporation, 46 209–13
   (upd.)
GoodTimes Entertainment Ltd., 48
   193–95
Goodwill Industries International, Inc.,
   16 244–46; 66 147–50 (upd.)
Goody Products, Inc., 12 214–16
The Goodyear Tire & Rubber
   Company, V 244–48; 20 259–64
   (upd.); 75 170–78 (upd.)
Goody's Family Clothing, Inc., 20
   265–67; 64 158–61 (upd.)
Google, Inc., 50 204–07; 101 214–19
   (upd.)
Gordmans, Inc., 74 125–27

Gordon Biersch Brewery Restaurant
   Group,Inc., 92229–32
Gordon Food Service Inc., 8 225–27; 39
   179–82 (upd.)
The Gorman-Rupp Company, 18
   201–03; 57 158–61 (upd.)
Gorton's, 13 243–44
Gosling Brothers Ltd., 82 146–49
Goss Holdings, Inc., 43 194–97
Gottschalks, Inc., 18 204–06; 91
   211–15 (upd.)
Gould Electronics, Inc., 14 206–08
Gould Paper Corporation, 82 150–53
Goulds Pumps Inc., 24 188–91
The Governor and Company of the
   Bank of Scotland, 10 336–38
Goya Foods Inc., 22 245–47; 91 216–21
   (upd.)
GP Strategies Corporation, 64 162–66
   (upd.)
GPS Industries, Inc., 81 169–72
GPU *see* General Public Utilities Corp.
GPU, Inc., 27 182–85 (upd.)
Grace *see* W.R. Grace & Co.
GraceKennedy Ltd., 92 143–47
Graco Inc., 19 178–80; 67 191–95
   (upd.)
Gradall Industries, Inc., 96 140–43
Graeter's Manufacturing Company, 86
   165–68
Grafton Group plc, 104 170–74
Graham Corporation, 62 165–67
Graham Packaging Holdings Company,
   87 192–196
Grameen Bank, 31 219–22
Grampian Country Food Group, Ltd.,
   85 155–59
Granada Group PLC, II 138–40; 24
   192–95 (upd.) *see also* ITV plc.
Granaria Holdings B.V., 66 151–53
GranCare, Inc., 14 209–11
Grand Casinos, Inc., 20 268–70
Grand Hotel Krasnapolsky N.V., 23
   227–29
Grand Metropolitan plc, I 247–49; 14
   212–15 (upd.) *see also* Diageo plc.
Grand Piano & Furniture Company, 72
   151–53
Grand Traverse Pie Company, 98
   156–59
Grand Union Company, 7 202–04; 28
   162–65 (upd.)
Grandoe Corporation, 98 160–63
Grands Vins Jean-Claude Boisset S.A.,
   98 164–67
GrandVision S.A., 43 198–200
Granite Broadcasting Corporation, 42
   161–64
Granite City Food & Brewery Ltd., 94
   214–17
Granite Construction Incorporated, 61
   119–21
Granite Industries of Vermont, Inc., 73
   169–72
Granite Rock Company, 26 175–78
Granite State Bankshares, Inc., 37
   173–75
Grant Prideco, Inc., 57 162–64

HSN, 64 181–85 (upd.)
Huawei Technologies Company Ltd., 87 228–231
Hub Group, Inc., 38 233–35
Hub International Limited, 89 260–64
Hubbard Broadcasting Inc., 24 226–28; 79 207–12 (upd.)
Hubbell Inc., 9 286–87; 31 257–59 (upd.); 76 183–86 (upd.)
Huddle House, Inc., 105 226–29
The Hudson Bay Mining and Smelting Company, Limited, 12 259–61
Hudson Foods Inc., 13 270–72 *see also* Tyson Foods, Inc.
Hudson River Bancorp, Inc., 41 210–13
Hudson's Bay Company, V 79–81; 25 219–22 (upd.); 83 187–194 (upd.)
Huffy Corporation, 7 225–27; 30 239–42 (upd.)
Hughes Electronics Corporation, 25 223–25
Hughes Hubbard & Reed LLP, 44 230–32
Hughes Markets, Inc., 22 271–73 *see also* Kroger Co.
Hughes Supply, Inc., 14 246–47
Hugo Boss AG, 48 206–09
Huhtamäki Oyj, 64 186–88
HUK-Coburg, 58 169–73
Hulman & Company, 44 233–36
Hüls A.G., I 349–50 *see also* Degussa-Hüls AG.
Human Factors International Inc., 100 229–32
Humana Inc., III 81–83; 24 229–32 (upd.); 101 250–56 (upd.)
The Humane Society of the United States, 54 170–73
Hummel International A/S, 68 199–201
Hummer Winblad Venture Partners, 97 218–21
Hungarian Telephone and Cable Corp., 75 193–95
Hungry Howie's Pizza and Subs, Inc., 25 226–28
Hunt Consolidated, Inc., 7 228–30; 27 215–18 (upd.)
Hunt Manufacturing Company, 12 262–64
Hunt-Wesson, Inc., 17 240–42 *see also* ConAgra Foods, Inc.
Hunter Fan Company, 13 273–75; 98 208–12 (upd.)
Hunting plc, 78 163–16
Huntingdon Life Sciences Group plc, 42 182–85
Huntington Bancshares Incorporated, 11 180–82; 87 232–238 (upd.)
Huntington Learning Centers, Inc., 55 212–14
Huntleigh Technology PLC, 77 199–202
Hunton & Williams, 35 223–26
Huntsman Corporation, 8 261–63; 98 213–17 (upd.)
Huron Consulting Group Inc., 87 239–243

Hurricane Hydrocarbons Ltd., 54 174–77
Husky Energy Inc., 47 179–82
Hutchinson Technology Incorporated, 18 248–51; 63 190–94 (upd.)
Hutchison Whampoa Limited, 18 252–55; 49 199–204 (upd.)
Huttig Building Products, Inc., 73 180–83
Huy Fong Foods, Inc., 107 206–09
HVB Group, 59 237–44 (upd.)
Hvide Marine Incorporated, 22 274–76
Hy-Vee, Inc., 36 275–78
Hyatt Corporation, III 96–97; 16 273–75 (upd.) *see* Global Hyatt Corp.
Hyde Athletic Industries, Inc., 17 243–45 *see also* Saucony Inc.
Hyder plc, 34 219–21
Hydril Company, 46 237–39
Hydro-Quebéc, 6 501–03; 32 266–69 (upd.)
Hylsamex, S.A. de C.V., 39 225–27
Hypercom Corporation, 27 219–21
Hyperion Software Corporation, 22 277–79
Hyperion Solutions Corporation, 76 187–91
Hyster Company, 17 246–48
Hyundai Group, III 515–17; 7 231–34 (upd.); 56 169–73 (upd.)

I

I Grandi Viaggi S.p.A., 105 230–33
I.C. Isaacs & Company, 31 260–62
I.M. Pei & Associates *see* Pei Cobb Freed & Partners Architects LLP.
i2 Technologies, Inc., 87 252–257
IAC Group, 96 194–98
Iams Company, 26 205–07
IAWS Group plc, 49 205–08
Iberdrola, S.A., 49 209–12
Iberia Líneas Aéreas De España S.A., 6 95–97; 36 279–83 (upd.); 91 247–54 (upd.)
IBERIABANK Corporation, 37 200–02
IBJ *see* The Industrial Bank of Japan Ltd.
IBM *see* International Business Machines Corp.
IBP, Inc., II 515–17; 21 287–90 (upd.)
Ibstock Brick Ltd., 37 203–06 (upd.)
Ibstock plc, 14 248–50
IC Industries Inc., I 456–58 *see also* Whitman Corp.
ICA AB, II 639–40
ICEE-USA *see* J & J Snack Foods Corp.
Iceland Group plc, 33 205–07 *see also* The Big Food Group plc.
Icelandair, 52 166–69
Icelandic Group hf, 81 182–85
ICF International, Inc., 28 200–04; 94 240–47 (upd.)
ICI *see* Imperial Chemical Industries plc.
ICL plc, 6 240–42
ICN Pharmaceuticals, Inc., 52 170–73
ICON Health & Fitness, Inc., 38 236–39; 102 175–79 (upd.)
ICU Medical, Inc., 106 237–42
Idaho Power Company, 12 265–67

IDB Communications Group, Inc., 11 183–85
IDB Holding Corporation Ltd., 97 222–25
Ideal Mortgage Bankers, Ltd., 105 234–37
Idealab, 105 238–42
Idearc Inc., 90 241–44
Idemitsu Kosan Co., Ltd., IV 434–36; 49 213–16 (upd.)
Identix Inc., 44 237–40
IDEO Inc., 65 171–73
IDEX Corp., 103 222–26
IDEXX Laboratories, Inc., 23 282–84; 107 210–14 (upd.)
IDG Books Worldwide, Inc., 27 222–24 *see also* International Data Group, Inc.
IDG Communications, Inc *see* International Data Group, Inc.
IdraPrince, Inc., 76 192–94
IDT Corporation, 34 222–24; 99 214–219 (upd.)
IDX Systems Corporation, 64 189–92
IEC Electronics Corp., 42 186–88
IFF *see* International Flavors & Fragrances Inc.
IG Group Holdings plc, 97 226–29
IGA, Inc., 99 220–224
Igloo Products Corp., 21 291–93; 105 243–47 (upd.)
IGT *see* International Game Technology.
IHC Caland N.V., 71 178–80
IHI *see* Ishikawajima-Harima Heavy Industries Co., Ltd.
IHOP Corporation, 17 249–51; 58 174–77 (upd.)
Ihr Platz GmbH + Company KG, 77 203–06
IHS Inc., 78 167–70
II-VI Incorporated, 69 353–55
IKEA Group, V 82–84; 26 208–11 (upd.); 94 248–53 (upd.)
IKON Office Solutions, Inc., 50 236–39
Ikonics Corporation, 99 225–228
Il Fornaio (America) Corporation, 27 225–28
ILFC *see* International Lease Finance Corp.
Ilitch Holdings Inc., 37 207–210; 86 195–200 (upd.)
Illinois Bell Telephone Company, 14 251–53
Illinois Central Corporation, 11 186–89
Illinois Power Company, 6 504–07 *see also* Ameren Corp.
Illinois Tool Works Inc., III 518–20; 22 280–83 (upd.); 81 186–91 (upd.)
Illumina, Inc., 93 246–49
illycaffè SpA, 50 240–44
ILX Resorts Incorporated, 65 174–76
Image Entertainment, Inc., 94 254–57
Imagine Entertainment, 91 255–58
Imagine Foods, Inc., 50 245–47
Imasco Limited, V 401–02
Imation Corporation, 20 301–04 *see also* 3M Co.
Imatra Steel Oy Ab, 55 215–17

International Management Group, 18 262–65 *see also* IMG.

International Multifoods Corporation, 7 241–43; 25 241–44 (upd.) *see also* The J. M. Smucker Co.

International Olympic Committee, 44 244–47

International Paper Company, IV 286–88; 15 227–30 (upd.); 47 187–92 (upd.); 97 234–43 (upd.)

International Power PLC, 50 280–85 (upd.)

International Profit Associates, Inc., 87 248–251

International Rectifier Corporation, 31 263–66; 71 181–84 (upd.)

International Shipbreaking Ltd. L.L.C., 67 213–15

International Shipholding Corporation, Inc., 27 241–44

International Speedway Corporation, 19 221–23; 74 157–60 (upd.)

International Telephone & Telegraph Corporation, I 462–64; 11 196–99 (upd.)

International Total Services, Inc., 37 215–18

Internationale Nederlanden Groep *see* ING Groep N.V.

Interpool, Inc., 92 176–79

The Interpublic Group of Companies, Inc., I 16–18; 22 294–97 (upd.); 75 202–05 (upd.)

Interscope Music Group, 31 267–69

Intersil Corporation, 93 250–54

Interstate Bakeries Corporation, 12 274–76; 38 249–52 (upd.)

Interstate Hotels & Resorts Inc., 58 192–94

Intertek Group plc, 95 208–11

InterVideo, Inc., 85 179–82

Intevac, Inc., 92 180–83

Intimate Brands, Inc., 24 237–39

Intrado Inc., 63 202–04

Intrawest Corporation, 15 234–36; 84 192–196 (upd.)

Intres B.V., 82 178–81

Intuit Inc., 14 262–64; 33 208–11 (upd.); 73 188–92 (upd.)

Intuitive Surgical, Inc., 79 217–20

Invacare Corporation, 11 200–02; 47 193–98 (upd.)

Invensys PLC, 50 286–90 (upd.)

inVentiv Health, Inc., 81 205–08

The Inventure Group, Inc., 96 199–202 (upd.)

Inverness Medical Innovations, Inc., 63 205–07

Inversiones Nacional de Chocolates S.A., 88 199–202

Investcorp SA, 57 179–82

Investor AB, 63 208–11

Invitrogen Corporation, 52 182–84

Invivo Corporation, 52 185–87

Iogen Corporation, 81 209–13

IOI Corporation Bhd, 107 220–24

Iomega Corporation, 21 294–97

IONA Technologies plc, 43 238–41

Ionatron, Inc., 85 183–86

Ionics, Incorporated, 52 188–90

Iowa Beef Processors *see* IBP, Inc.

Iowa Telecommunications Services, Inc., 85 187–90

Ipalco Enterprises, Inc., 6 508–09

IPC Magazines Limited, 7 244–47

Ipiranga S.A., 67 216–18

Ipsen International Inc., 72 192–95

Ipsos SA, 48 221–24

IranAir, 81 214–17

Irex Contracting Group, 90 245–48

IRIS International, Inc., 101 261–64

Irish Distillers Group, 96 203–07

Irish Life & Permanent Plc, 59 245–47

Irkut Corporation, 68 202–04

iRobot Corporation, 83 212–215

Iron Mountain, Inc., 33 212–14; 104 209–12 (upd.)

IRSA Inversiones y Representaciones S.A., 63 212–15

Irvin Feld & Kenneth Feld Productions, Inc., 15 237–39 *see also* Feld Entertainment, Inc.

Irwin Financial Corporation, 77 213–16

Irwin Toy Limited, 14 265–67

Isbank *see* Turkiye Is Bankasi A.S.

Iscor Limited, 57 183–86

Isetan Company Limited, V 85–87; 36 289–93 (upd.)

Ishikawajima-Harima Heavy Industries Company, Ltd., III 532–33; 86 211–15 (upd.)

The Island ECN, Inc., 48 225–29

Isle of Capri Casinos, Inc., 41 217–19

Ispat Inland Inc., 30 252–54; 40 267–72 (upd.)

Israel Aircraft Industries Ltd., 69 215–17

Israel Chemicals Ltd., 55 226–29

Israel Corporation Ltd., 108 276–80

ISS A/S, 49 221–23

Istituto per la Ricostruzione Industriale S.p.A., I 465–67; 11 203–06 (upd.)

Isuzu Motors, Ltd., 9 293–95; 23 288–91 (upd.); 57 187–91 (upd.)

Itaú *see* Banco Itaú S.A.

ITC Holdings Corp., 75 206–08

Itel Corporation, 9 296–99

Items International Airwalk Inc., 17 259–61

ITM Entreprises SA, 36 294–97

Ito En Ltd., 101 265–68

Ito-Yokado Co., Ltd., V 88–89; 42 189–92 (upd.)

ITOCHU Corporation, 32 283–87 (upd.)

Itoh *see* C. Itoh & Co.

Itoham Foods Inc., II 518–19; 61 138–40 (upd.)

Itron, Inc., 64 202–05

ITT Educational Services, Inc., 33 215–17; 76 200–03 (upd.)

ITT Sheraton Corporation, III 98–101 *see also* Starwood Hotels & Resorts Worldwide, Inc.

ITV plc, 104 213–20 (upd.)

ITW *see* Illinois Tool Works Inc.

Ivar's, Inc., 86 216–19

IVAX Corporation, 11 207–09; 55 230–33 (upd.)

IVC Industries, Inc., 45 208–11

iVillage Inc., 46 253–56

Iwerks Entertainment, Inc., 34 228–30

IXC Communications, Inc., 29 250–52

J

J & J Snack Foods Corporation, 24 240–42

J&R Electronics Inc., 26 224–26

The J. Paul Getty Trust, 105 255–59

J. & W. Seligman & Co. Inc., 61 141–43

J.A. Jones, Inc., 16 284–86

J. Alexander's Corporation, 65 177–79

J.B. Hunt Transport Services Inc., 12 277–79

J. Baker, Inc., 31 270–73

J C Bamford Excavators Ltd., 83 216–222

J. C. Penney Company, Inc., V 90–92; 18 269–73 (upd.); 43 245–50 (upd.); 91 263–72 (upd.)

J. Crew Group, Inc., 12 280–82; 34 231–34 (upd.); 88 203–08

J.D. Edwards & Company, 14 268–70 *see also* Oracle Corp.

J.D. Power and Associates, 32 297–301

J. D'Addario & Company, Inc., 48 230–33

J.F. Shea Co., Inc., 55 234–36

J.H. Findorff and Son, Inc., 60 175–78

J.I. Case Company, 10 377–81 *see also* CNH Global N.V.

J.J. Darboven GmbH & Co. KG, 96 208–12

J.J. Keller & Associates, Inc., 81 2180–21

The J. Jill Group, Inc., 35 239–41; 90 249–53 (upd.)

J.L. Hammett Company, 72 196–99

J Lauritzen A/S, 90 254–57

J. Lohr Winery Corporation, 99 229–232

The J. M. Smucker Company, 11 210–12; 87 258–265 (upd.)

J.M. Voith AG, 33 222–25

J.P. Morgan Chase & Co., II 329–32; 30 261–65 (upd.); 38 253–59 (upd.)

J.R. Simplot Company, 16 287–89; 60 179–82 (upd.)

J Sainsbury plc, II 657–59; 13 282–84 (upd.); 38 260–65 (upd.); 95 212–20 (upd.)

J. W. Pepper and Son Inc., 86 220–23

J. Walter Thompson Co. *see* JWT Group Inc.

j2 Global Communications, Inc., 75 219–21

Jabil Circuit, Inc., 36 298–301; 88 209–14

Jack B. Kelley, Inc., 102 184–87

Jack Henry and Associates, Inc., 17 262–65; 94 258–63 (upd.)

Jack in the Box Inc., 89 265–71 (upd.)

Jack Morton Worldwide, 88 215–18

National Medical Enterprises, Inc., III 87–88 *see also* Tenet Healthcare Corp.

National Medical Health Card Systems, Inc., 79 270–73

National Oil Corporation, 66 233–37 (upd.)

National Oilwell, Inc., 54 247–50

National Organization for Women, Inc., 55 274–76

National Patent Development Corporation, 13 365–68 *see also* GP Strategies Corp.

National Penn Bancshares, Inc., 103 271–75

National Picture & Frame Company, 24 345–47

National Power PLC, 12 349–51 *see also* International Power PLC.

National Presto Industries, Inc., 16 382–85; 43 286–90 (upd.)

National Public Radio, 19 280–82; 47 259–62 (upd.)

National R.V. Holdings, Inc., 32 348–51

National Railroad Passenger Corporation (Amtrak), 22 375–78; 66 238–42 (upd.)

National Record Mart, Inc., 29 348–50

National Research Corporation, 87 332–335

National Rifle Association of America, 37 265–68

National Sanitary Supply Co., 16 386–87

National Sea Products Ltd., 14 339–41

National Semiconductor Corporation, II 63–65; 6 261–63; 26 327–30 (upd.); 69 267–71 (upd.)

National Service Industries, Inc., 11 336–38; 54 251–55 (upd.)

National Standard Co., 13 369–71

National Starch and Chemical Company, 49 268–70

National Steel Corporation, 12 352–54 *see also* FoxMeyer Health Corp.

National TechTeam, Inc., 41 280–83

National Thoroughbred Racing Association, 58 244–47

National Transcommunications Ltd. *see* NTL Inc.

National Weather Service, 91 345–49

National Westminster Bank PLC, II 333–35

National Wildlife Federation, 103 276–80

National Wine & Spirits, Inc., 49 271–74

Nationale-Nederlanden N.V., III 308–11

Nationale Portefeuille Maatschappij (NPM) *see* Compagnie Nationale à Portefeuille.

NationsBank Corporation, 10 425–27 *see also* Bank of America Corporation

Nationwide Mutual Insurance Company, 108 358–62

Natori Company, Inc., 108 363–66

Natrol, Inc., 49 275–78

Natura Cosméticos S.A., 75 268–71

Natural Alternatives International, Inc., 49 279–82

Natural Gas Clearinghouse *see* NGC Corp.

Natural Ovens Bakery, Inc., 72 234–36

Natural Selection Foods, 54 256–58

Natural Wonders Inc., 14 342–44

Naturally Fresh, Inc., 88 272–75

The Nature Conservancy, 28 305–07

Nature's Path Foods, Inc., 87 336–340

Nature's Sunshine Products, Inc., 15 317–19; 102 291–96 (upd.)

Natuzzi Group *see* Industrie Natuzzi S.p.A.

NatWest Bank *see* National Westminster Bank PLC.

Naumes, Inc., 81 257–60

Nautica Enterprises, Inc., 18 357–60; 44 302–06 (upd.)

Navarre Corporation, 24 348–51

Navigant International, Inc., 47 263–66; 93 324–27 (upd.)

The Navigators Group, Inc., 92 261–64

Navistar International Corporation, I 180–82; 10 428–30 (upd.) *see also* International Harvester Co.

NAVTEQ Corporation, 69 272–75

Navy Exchange Service Command, 31 342–45

Navy Federal Credit Union, 33 315–17

NBC *see* National Broadcasting Company, Inc.

NBD Bancorp, Inc., 11 339–41 *see also* Bank One Corp.

NBGS International, Inc., 73 231–33

NBSC Corporation *see* National Bank of South Carolina.

NBTY, Inc., 31 346–48

NCAA *see* National Collegiate Athletic Assn.

NCH Corporation, 8 385–87

NCI Building Systems, Inc., 88 276–79

NCL Corporation, 79 274–77

NCNB Corporation, II 336–37 *see also* Bank of America Corp.

NCO Group, Inc., 42 258–60

NCR Corporation, III 150–53; 6 264–68 (upd.); 30 336–41 (upd.); 90 303–12 (upd.)

NDB *see* National Discount Brokers Group, Inc.

Nebraska Book Company, Inc., 65 257–59

Nebraska Furniture Mart, Inc., 94 323–26

Nebraska Public Power District, 29 351–54

NEBS *see* New England Business Services, Inc.

NEC Corporation, II 66–68; 21 388–91 (upd.); 57 261–67 (upd.)

Neckermann.de GmbH, 102 297–301

Nederlander Producing Company of America,Inc., 108 367–70

N.V. Nederlandse Gasunie, V 658–61

Nedlloyd Group *see* Koninklijke Nedlloyd N.V.

Neenah Foundry Company, 68 263–66

Neff Corp., 32 352–53

NeighborCare, Inc., 67 259–63 (upd.)

The Neiman Marcus Group, Inc., 12 355–57; 49 283–87 (upd.); 105 317–22 (upd.)

Nektar Therapeutics, 91 350–53

Nelsons *see* A. Nelson & Co. Ltd.

Neogen Corporation, 94 327–30

Neopost S.A., 53 237–40

Neptune Orient Lines Limited, 47 267–70

NERCO, Inc., 7 376–79 *see also* Rio Tinto PLC.

NES *see* National Equipment Services, Inc.

Neste Oil Corporation, IV 469–71; 85 295–302 (upd.)

Nestlé S.A., II 545–49; 7 380–84 (upd.); 28 308–13 (upd.); 71 240–46 (upd.)

Nestlé Waters, 73 234–37

NetCom Systems AB, 26 331–33

NetCracker Technology Corporation, 98 253–56

Netezza Corporation, 69 276–78

Netflix, Inc., 58 248–51

NETGEAR, Inc., 81 261–64

NetIQ Corporation, 79 278–81

NetJets Inc., 96 303–07 (upd.)

Netscape Communications Corporation, 15 320–22; 35 304–07 (upd.)

Netto International, 103 281–84

Network Appliance, Inc., 58 252–54

Network Associates, Inc., 25 347–49

Network Equipment Technologies Inc., 92 265–68

Neuberger Berman Inc., 57 268–71

NeuStar, Inc., 81 265–68

Neutrogena Corporation, 17 340–44

Nevada Bell Telephone Company, 14 345–47 *see also* AT&T Corp.

Nevada Power Company, 11 342–44

Nevamar Company, 82 255–58

New Balance Athletic Shoe, Inc., 25 350–52; 68 267–70 (upd.)

New Belgium Brewing Company, Inc., 68 271–74

New Brunswick Scientific Co., Inc., 45 285–87

New Chapter Inc., 96 308–11

New Clicks Holdings Ltd., 86 295–98

New Dana Perfumes Company, 37 269–71

New England Business Service, Inc., 18 361–64; 78 237–42 (upd.)

New England Confectionery Co., 15 323–25

New England Electric System, V 662–64 *see also* National Grid USA.

New England Mutual Life Insurance Co., III 312–14 *see also* Metropolitan Life Insurance Co.

New Flyer Industries Inc., 78 243–46

New Holland N.V., 22 379–81 *see also* CNH Global N.V.

New Jersey Devils, 84 281–285

New Jersey Manufacturers Insurance Company, 96 312–16

Pennon Group Plc, 45 338–41
Pennsylvania Blue Shield, III 325–27 *see also* Highmark Inc.
Pennsylvania Power & Light Company, V 693–94
Pennwalt Corporation, I 382–84
PennWell Corporation, 55 300–03
Pennzoil-Quaker State Company, IV 488–90; 20 418–22 (upd.); 50 350–55 (upd.)
Penske Corporation, V 494–95; 19 292–94 (upd.); 84 305–309 (upd.)
Pentair, Inc., 7 419–21; 26 361–64 (upd.); 81 281–87 (upd.)
Pentax Corporation, 78 301–05
Pentech International, Inc., 29 372–74
The Pentland Group plc, 20 423–25; 100 343–47 (upd.)
Penton Media, Inc., 27 360–62
Penzeys Spices, Inc., 79 314–16
People Express Airlines Inc., I 117–18
People's United Financial Inc. , 106 349–52
Peoples Energy Corporation, 6 543–44
PeopleSoft Inc., 14 381–83; 33 330–33 (upd.) *see also* Oracle Corp.
The Pep Boys—Manny, Moe & Jack, 11 391–93; 36 361–64 (upd.); 81 288–94 (upd.)
PEPCO *see* Potomac Electric Power Co.
Pepper *see* J. W. Pepper and Son Inc.
Pepper Hamilton LLP, 43 300–03
Pepperidge Farm, Incorporated, 81 295–300
The Pepsi Bottling Group, Inc., 40 350–53
PepsiAmericas, Inc., 67 297–300 (upd.)
PepsiCo, Inc., I 276–79; 10 450–54 (upd.); 38 347–54 (upd.); 93 333–44 (upd.)
Pequiven *see* Petroquímica de Venezuela S.A.
Perdigao SA, 52 276–79
Perdue Farms Inc., 7 422–24; 23 375–78 (upd.)
Perfetti Van Melle S.p.A., 72 270–73
Performance Food Group, 31 359–62; 96 329–34 (upd.)
Perini Corporation, 8 418–21; 82 274–79 (upd.)
PerkinElmer, Inc., 7 425–27; 78 306–10 (upd.)
Perkins & Marie Callender's Inc., 107 345–51 (upd.)
Perkins Coie LLP, 56 268–70
Perkins Family Restaurants, L.P., 22 417–19
Perkins Foods Holdings Ltd., 87 371–374
Perma-Fix Environmental Services, Inc., 99 338–341
Pernod Ricard S.A., I 280–81; 21 399–401 (upd.); 72 274–77 (upd.)
Perot Systems Corporation, 29 375–78
Perrigo Company, 12 387–89; 59 330–34 (upd.)
Perry Ellis International Inc., 41 291–94; 106 353–58 (upd.)

Perry's Ice Cream Company Inc., 90 326–29
The Perseus Books Group, 91 375–78
Perstorp AB, I 385–87; 51 289–92 (upd.)
Pertamina, IV 491–93; 56 271–74 (upd.)
Perusahaan Otomobil Nasional Bhd., 62 266–68
Pescanova S.A., 81 301–04
Pet Incorporated, 7 428–31
Petco Animal Supplies, Inc., 29 379–81; 74 231–34 (upd.)
Peter Kiewit Sons' Inc., 8 422–24
Peter Pan Bus Lines Inc., 106 359–63
Peter Piper, Inc., 70 217–19
Peterbilt Motors Company, 89 354–57
Petersen Publishing Company, 21 402–04
Peterson American Corporation, 55 304–06
Pete's Brewing Company, 22 420–22
Petit Bateau, 95 327–31
PetMed Express, Inc., 81 305–08
Petrie Stores Corporation, 8 425–27
Petro-Canada, IV 494–96; 99 342–349 (upd.)
Petrobrás *see* Petróleo Brasileiro S.A.
Petrobras Energia Participaciones S.A., 72 278–81
Petroecuador *see* Petróleos del Ecuador.
Petrof spol. S.R.O., 107 352–56
Petrofac Ltd., 95 332–35
PetroFina S.A., IV 497–500; 26 365–69 (upd.)
Petrogal *see* Petróleos de Portugal.
Petrohawk Energy Corporation, 79 317–20
Petróleo Brasileiro S.A., IV 501–03
Petróleos de Portugal S.A., IV 504–06
Petróleos de Venezuela S.A., IV 507–09; 74 235–39 (upd.)
Petróleos del Ecuador, IV 510–11
Petróleos Mexicanos (PEMEX), IV 512–14; 19 295–98 (upd.); 104 373–78 (upd.)
Petroleum Development Oman LLC, IV 515–16; 98 305–09 (upd.)
Petroleum Helicopters, Inc., 35 334–36
Petroliam Nasional Bhd (Petronas), 56 275–79 (upd.)
Petrolite Corporation, 15 350–52 *see also* Baker Hughes Inc.
Petromex *see* Petróleos de Mexico S.A.
Petron Corporation, 58 270–72
Petronas, IV 517–20 *see also* Petroliam Nasional Bhd.
Petroplus Holdings AG, 108 381–84
Petrossian Inc., 54 287–89
Petry Media Corporation, 102 326–29
PETsMART, Inc., 14 384–86; 41 295–98 (upd.)
Peugeot S.A., I 187–88 *see also* PSA Peugeot Citroen S.A.
The Pew Charitable Trusts, 35 337–40
Pez Candy, Inc., 38 355–57
The Pfaltzgraff Co. *see* Susquehanna Pfaltzgraff Co.

Pfizer Inc., I 661–63; 9 402–05 (upd.); 38 358–67 (upd.); 79 321–33 (upd.)
PFSweb, Inc., 73 254–56
PG&E Corporation, 26 370–73 (upd.)
PGA *see* The Professional Golfers' Association.
Phaidon Press Ltd., 98 310–14
Phantom Fireworks *see* B.J. Alan Co., Inc.
Phar-Mor Inc., 12 390–92
Pharmacia & Upjohn Inc., I 664–65; 25 374–78 (upd.) *see also* Pfizer Inc.
Pharmion Corporation, 91 379–82
Phat Fashions LLC, 49 322–24
Phelps Dodge Corporation, IV 176–79; 28 352–57 (upd.); 75 319–25 (upd.)
PHH Arval, V 496–97; 53 274–76 (upd.)
PHI, Inc., 80 282–86 (upd.)
Philadelphia Eagles, 37 305–08
Philadelphia Electric Company, V 695–97 *see also* Exelon Corp.
Philadelphia Gas Works Company, 92 301–05
Philadelphia Media Holdings LLC, 92 306–10
Philadelphia Suburban Corporation, 39 326–29
Philharmonic-Symphony Society of New York, Inc. (New York Philharmonic), 69 293–97
Philip Environmental Inc., 16 414–16
Philip Morris Companies Inc., V 405–07; 18 416–19 (upd.); 44 338–43 (upd.) *see also* Kraft Foods Inc.
Philip Services Corp., 73 257–60
Philipp Holzmann AG, 17 374–77
Philippine Airlines, Inc., 6 106–08; 23 379–82 (upd.)
Philips Electronics N.V., 13 400–03 (upd.) *see also* Koninklijke Philips Electronics N.V.
Philips Electronics North America Corp., 13 396–99
N.V. Philips Gloeilampenfabriken, II 78–80 *see also* Philips Electronics N.V.
The Phillies, 106 364–68
Phillips Foods, Inc., 63 320–22; 90 330–33 (upd.)
Phillips International, Inc., 78 311–14
Phillips Lytle LLP, 102 330–34
Phillips Petroleum Company, IV 521–23; 40 354–59 (upd.) *see also* ConocoPhillips.
Phillips-Van Heusen Corporation, 24 382–85
Phillips, de Pury & Luxembourg, 49 325–27
Philly Pretzel Factory *see* Soft Pretzel Franchise Systems, Inc.
Phoenix AG, 68 286–89
Phoenix Footwear Group, Inc., 70 220–22
Phoenix Mecano AG, 61 286–88
The Phoenix Media/Communications Group, 91 383–87
Phones 4u Ltd., 85 328–31
Photo-Me International Plc, 83 302–306

Puget Sound Energy Inc., 6 565–67; 50 365–68 (upd.)

Puig Beauty and Fashion Group S.L., 60 243–46

Pulaski Furniture Corporation, 33 349–52; 80 296–99 (upd.)

Pulitzer Inc., 15 375–77; 58 280–83 (upd.)

Pulsar Internacional S.A., 21 413–15

Pulte Homes, Inc., 8 436–38; 42 291–94 (upd.)

Puma AG Rudolf Dassler Sport, 35 360–63

Pumpkin Masters, Inc., 48 330–32

Punch International N.V., 66 258–60

Punch Taverns plc, 70 240–42

Puratos S.A./NV, 92 315–18

Pure World, Inc., 72 285–87

Purina Mills, Inc., 32 376–79

Puritan-Bennett Corporation, 13 419–21

Purolator Products Company, 21 416–18; 74 253–56 (upd.)

Putt-Putt Golf Courses of America, Inc., 23 396–98

PVC Container Corporation, 67 312–14

PW Eagle, Inc., 48 333–36

PWA Group, IV 323–25 *see also* Svenska Cellulosa.

Pyramid Breweries Inc., 33 353–55; 102 343–47 (upd.)

Pyramid Companies, 54 303–05

PZ Cussons plc, 72 288–90

Q

Q.E.P. Co., Inc., 65 292–94

Qantas Airways Ltd., 6 109–13; 24 396–401 (upd.); 68 301–07 (upd.)

Qatar Airways Company Q.C.S.C., 87 404–407

Qatar National Bank SAQ, 87 408–411

Qatar Petroleum, IV 524–26; 98 324–28 (upd.)

Qatar Telecom QSA, 87 412–415

Qdoba Restaurant Corporation, 93 358–62

Qiagen N.V., 39 333–35

QLT Inc., 71 291–94

QRS Music Technologies, Inc., 95 349–53

QSC Audio Products, Inc., 56 291–93

QSS Group, Inc., 100 358–61

Quad/Graphics, Inc., 19 333–36

Quaker Chemical Corp., 91 388–91

Quaker Fabric Corp., 19 337–39

Quaker Foods North America, II 558–60; 12 409–12 (upd.); 34 363–67 (upd.); 73 268–73 (upd.)

Quaker State Corporation, 7 443–45; 21 419–22 (upd.) *see also* Pennzoil-Quaker State Co.

QUALCOMM Incorporated, 20 438–41; 47 317–21 (upd.)

Quality Chekd Dairies, Inc., 48 337–39

Quality Dining, Inc., 18 437–40

Quality Food Centers, Inc., 17 386–88 *see also* Kroger Co.

Quality Systems, Inc., 81 328–31

Quanex Corporation, 13 422–24; 62 286–89 (upd.)

Quanta Computer Inc., 47 322–24

Quanta Services, Inc., 79 338–41

Quantum Chemical Corporation, 8 439–41

Quantum Corporation, 10 458–59; 62 290–93 (upd.)

Quark, Inc., 36 375–79

Québec Hydro-Electric Commission *see* Hydro-Québec.

Quebecor Inc., 12 412–14; 47 325–28 (upd.)

Quelle Group, V 165–67 *see also* Karstadt Quelle AG.

Quest Diagnostics Inc., 26 390–92; 106 383–87 (upd.)

Questar Corporation, 6 568–70; 26 386–89 (upd.)

The Quick & Reilly Group, Inc., 20 442–44

Quick Restaurants S.A., 94 357–60

Quicken Loans, Inc., 93 363–67

Quidel Corporation, 80 300–03

The Quigley Corporation, 62 294–97

Quiksilver, Inc., 18 441–43; 79 342–47 (upd.)

QuikTrip Corporation, 36 380–83

Quill Corporation, 28 375–77

Quilmes Industrial (QUINSA) S.A., 67 315–17

Quinn Emanuel Urquhart Oliver & Hedges, LLP, 99 350–353

Quintiles Transnational Corporation, 21 423–25; 68 308–12 (upd.)

Quixote Corporation, 15 378–80

The Quizno's Corporation, 42 295–98

Quovadx Inc., 70 243–46

QVC Inc., 9 428–29; 58 284–87 (upd.)

Qwest Communications International, Inc., 37 312–17

R

R&B, Inc., 51 305–07

R&R Partners Inc., 108 407–10

R.B. Pamplin Corp., 45 350–52

R.C. Bigelow, Inc., 49 334–36

R.C. Willey Home Furnishings, 72 291–93

R.G. Barry Corp., 17 389–91; 44 364–67 (upd.)

R. Griggs Group Limited, 23 399–402; 31 413–14

R.H. Macy & Co., Inc., V 168–70; 8 442–45 (upd.); 30 379–83 (upd.) *see also* Macy's, Inc.

R.J. Reynolds Tobacco Holdings, Inc., 30 384–87 (upd.)

R. M. Palmer Co., 89 362–64

R.P. Scherer Corporation, I 678–80 *see also* Cardinal Health, Inc.

R.R. Bowker LLC, 100 362–66

R.R. Donnelley & Sons Company, IV 660–62; 38 368–71 (upd.)

Rabobank Group, 26 419; 33 356–58

RAC *see* Roy Anderson Corp.

Racal-Datacom Inc., 11 408–10

Racal Electronics PLC, II 83–84 *see also* Thales S.A.

Racing Champions Corporation, 37 318–20

Rack Room Shoes, Inc., 84 314–317

Radeberger Gruppe AG, 75 332–35

Radian Group Inc., 42 299–301 *see also* Onex Corp.

Radiant Systems Inc., 104 383–87

Radiation Therapy Services, Inc., 85 344–47

@radical.media, 103 347–50

Radio Flyer Inc., 34 368–70

Radio One, Inc., 67 318–21

RadioShack Corporation, 36 384–88 (upd.); 101 416–23 (upd.)

Radius Inc., 16 417–19

RAE Systems Inc., 83 311–314

RAG AG, 35 364–67; 60 247–51 (upd.)

Rag Shops, Inc., 30 365–67

Ragdoll Productions Ltd., 51 308–11

Raiffeisen Zentralbank Österreich AG, 85 348–52

RailTex, Inc., 20 445–47

Railtrack Group PLC, 50 369–72

Rain Bird Corporation, 84 318–321

Rainforest Café, Inc., 25 386–88; 88 312–16 (upd.)

Rainier Brewing Company, 23 403–05

Raisio PLC, 99 354–357

Raleigh UK Ltd., 65 295–97

Raley's Inc., 14 396–98; 58 288–91 (upd.)

Rallye SA, 54 306–09

Rally's, 25 389–91; 68 313–16 (upd.)

Ralph Lauren *see* Polo/Ralph Lauren Corportion.

Ralphs Grocery Company, 35 368–70

Ralston Purina Company, II 561–63; 13 425–27 (upd.) *see also* Ralcorp Holdings, Inc.; Nestlé S.A.

Ramsay Youth Services, Inc., 41 322–24

Ramtron International Corporation, 89 365–68

Ranbaxy Laboratories Ltd., 70 247–49

Rand McNally & Company, 28 378–81; 53 122

Randall's Food Markets, Inc., 40 364–67 *see also* Safeway Inc.

Random House Inc., 13 428–30; 31 375–80 (upd.); 106 388–98 (upd.)

Randon S.A. Implementos e Participações, 79 348–52

Randstad Holding n.v., 16 420–22; 43 307–10 (upd.)

Range Resources Corporation, 45 353–55

The Rank Group plc, II 157–59; 14 399–402 (upd.); 64 317–21 (upd.)

Ranks Hovis McDougall Limited, II 564–65; 28 382–85 (upd.)

RAO Unified Energy System of Russia, 45 356–60

Rapala-Normark Group, Ltd., 30 368–71

Rare Hospitality International Inc., 19 340–42

SABIC *see* Saudi Basic Industries Corp.
SABMiller plc, 59 352–58 (upd.)
Sabratek Corporation, 29 410–12
Sabre Holdings Corporation, 26 427–30; 74 286–90 (upd.)
Sadia S.A., 59 359–62
Safe Flight Instrument Corporation, 71 321–23
SAFECO Corporation, III 352–54
Safeguard Scientifics, Inc., 10 473–75
Safelite Glass Corp., 19 371–73
SafeNet Inc., 101 438–42
Safeskin Corporation, 18 467–70 *see also* Kimberly-Clark Corp.
Safety 1st, Inc., 24 412–15
Safety Components International, Inc., 63 342–44
Safety-Kleen Systems Inc., 8 462–65; 82 314–20 (upd.)
Safeway Inc., II 654–56; 24 416–19 (upd.); 85 362–69 (upd.)
Safeway PLC, 50 401–06 (upd.)
Saffery Champness, 80 324–27
Safilo SpA, 40 155–56; 54 319–21
SAFRAN, 102 363–71 (upd.)
Saga Communications, Inc., 27 392–94
The Sage Group, 43 343–46
Sage Products, Inc., 105 369–72
SAGEM S.A., 37 346–48 *see also* SAFRAN.
Sagicor Life Inc., 98 337–40
Saia, Inc., 98 341–44
SAIC *see* Science Applications International Corp.
Sainsbury's *see* J Sainsbury PLC.
Saint-Gobain *see* Compagnie de Saint Gobain S.A.
Saks Inc., 24 420–23; 41 342–45 (upd.)
Salant Corporation, 12 430–32; 51 318–21 (upd.)
Salem Communications Corporation, 97 359–63
salesforce.com, Inc., 79 370–73
Salick Health Care, Inc., 53 290–92
Salix Pharmaceuticals, Ltd., 93 384–87
Sallie Mae *see* SLM Holding Corp.
Sally Beauty Company, Inc., 60 258–60
Sally Industries, Inc., 103 377–81
Salomon Inc., II 447–49; 13 447–50 (upd.) *see also* Citigroup Inc.
Salomon Worldwide, 20 458–60 *see also* adidas-Salomon AG.
Salt River Project, 19 374–76
Salton, Inc., 30 402–04; 88 343–48 (upd.)
The Salvation Army USA, 32 390–93
Salvatore Ferragamo Italia S.p.A., 62 311–13
Salzgitter AG, IV 200–01; 101 443–49 (upd.)
Sam Ash Music Corporation, 30 405–07
Sam Levin Inc., 80 328–31
Samick Musical Instruments Co., Ltd., 56 297–300
Sam's Club, 40 385–87
Sam's Wine & Spirits, 96 366–69
Samsonite Corporation, 13 451–53; 43 353–57 (upd.)

Samsung Electronics Co., Ltd., 14 416–18; 41 346–49 (upd.); 108 433–40 (upd.)
Samsung Group, I 515–17
Samuel Cabot Inc., 53 293–95
Samuels Jewelers Incorporated, 30 408–10
San Diego Gas & Electric Company, V 711–14; 107 389–95 (upd.)
San Diego Padres Baseball Club L.P., 78 324–27
San Francisco Baseball Associates, L.P., 55 340–43
San Miguel Corporation, 15 428–30; 57 303–08 (upd.)
Sanborn Hermanos, S.A., 20 461–63 *see also* Grupo Sanborns, S.A. de C.V.
Sanborn Map Company Inc., 82 321–24
SanCor Cooperativas Unidas Ltda., 101 450–53
The Sanctuary Group PLC, 69 314–17
Sandals Resorts International, 65 302–05
Sanders Morris Harris Group Inc., 70 285–87
Sanders\Wingo, 99 386–389
Sanderson Farms, Inc., 15 425–27
Sandia National Laboratories, 49 345–48
Sandoz Ltd., I 671–73 *see also* Novartis AG.
Sandvik AB, IV 202–04; 32 394–98 (upd.); 77 367–73 (upd.)
Sanford L.P., 82 325–29
Sanitec Corporation, 51 322–24
Sankyo Company, Ltd., I 674–75; 56 301–04 (upd.)
Sanlam Ltd., 68 331–34
SANLUIS Corporación, S.A.B. de C.V., 95 362–65
The Sanofi-Synthélabo Group, I 676–77; 49 349–51 (upd.)
SanomaWSOY Corporation, 51 325–28
Sanpaolo IMI S.p.A., 50 407–11
Sanrio Company, Ltd., 38 413–15; 104 404–07 (upd.)
Santa Barbara Restaurant Group, Inc., 37 349–52
The Santa Cruz Operation, Inc., 38 416–21
Santa Fe Gaming Corporation, 19 377–79 *see also* Archon Corp.
Santa Fe International Corporation, 38 422–24
Santa Fe Pacific Corporation, V 507–09 *see also* Burlington Northern Santa Fe Corp.
Santa Margherita S.p.A. *see* Industrie Zignago Santa Margherita S.p.A.
Santarus, Inc., 105 373–77
Santos Ltd., 81 360–63
Sanwa Bank, Ltd., II 347–48; 15 431–33 (upd.)
SANYO Electric Co., Ltd., II 91–92; 36 399–403 (upd.); 95 366–73 (upd.)
Sanyo-Kokusaku Pulp Co., Ltd., IV 327–28

Sao Paulo Alpargatas S.A., 75 347–49
SAP AG, 16 441–44; 43 358–63 (upd.)
Sapa AB, 84 342–345
Sapp Bros Travel Centers, Inc., 105 378–81
Sappi Ltd., 49 352–55; 107 396–400 (upd.)
Sapporo Holdings Limited, I 282–83; 13 454–56 (upd.); 36 404–07 (upd.); 97 364–69 (upd.)
Saputo Inc., 59 363–65
Sara Lee Corporation, II 571–73; 15 434–37 (upd.); 54 322–27 (upd.); 99 390–398 (upd.)
Sarnoff Corporation, 57 309–12
Sarris Candies Inc., 86 347–50
The SAS Group, 34 396–99 (upd.)
SAS Institute Inc., 10 476–78; 78 328–32 (upd.)
Sasol Limited, IV 533–35; 47 340–44 (upd.)
Saturn Corporation, 7 461–64; 21 449–53 (upd.); 80 332–38 (upd.)
Satyam Computer Services Ltd., 85 370–73
Saucony Inc., 35 386–89; 86 351–56 (upd.)
Sauder Woodworking Co., 12 433–34; 35 390–93 (upd.)
Saudi Arabian Airlines, 6 114–16; 27 395–98 (upd.)
Saudi Arabian Oil Company, IV 536–39; 17 411–15 (upd.); 50 412–17 (upd.)
Saudi Basic Industries Corporation (SABIC), 58 325–28
Sauer-Danfoss Inc., 61 320–22
Saul Ewing LLP, 74 291–94
Saur S.A.S., 92 327–30
Savannah Foods & Industries, Inc., 7 465–67 *see also* Imperial Sugar Co.
Savers, Inc., 99 399–403 (upd.)
Sawtek Inc., 43 364–66 (upd.)
Saxton Pierce Restaurant Corporation, 100 373–76
Sbarro, Inc., 16 445–47; 64 339–42 (upd.)
SBC Communications Inc., 32 399–403 (upd.)
SBC Warburg, 14 419–21 *see also* UBS AG.
Sberbank, 62 314–17
SBI *see* State Bank of India.
SBS Technologies, Inc., 25 405–07
SCA *see* Svenska Cellulosa AB.
SCANA Corporation, 6 574–76; 56 305–08 (upd.)
Scandinavian Airlines System, I 119–20 *see also* The SAS Group.
ScanSource, Inc., 29 413–15; 74 295–98 (upd.)
Scarborough Public Utilities Commission, 9 461–62
SCB Computer Technology, Inc., 29 416–18
SCEcorp, V 715–17 *see also* Edison International.
Schawk, Inc., 24 424–26

Svenska Handelsbanken AB, II 365–67; 50 460–63 (upd.)

Svenska Spel AB, 107 425–28

Sverdrup Corporation, 14 475–78 *see also* Jacobs Engineering Group Inc.

Sveriges Riksbank, 96 418–22

SWA *see* Southwest Airlines.

SWALEC *see* Scottish and Southern Energy plc.

Swales & Associates, Inc., 69 336–38

Swank, Inc., 17 464–66; 84 380–384 (upd.)

Swarovski International Holding AG, 40 422–25

The Swatch Group Ltd., 26 479–81; 107 429–33 (upd.)

Swedish Match AB, 12 462–64; 39 387–90 (upd.); 92 349–55 (upd.)

Swedish Telecom, V 331–33

SwedishAmerican Health System, 51 363–66

Sweet Candy Company, 60 295–97

Sweetbay Supermarket, 103 419–24 (upd.)

Sweetheart Cup Company, Inc., 36 460–64

The Swett & Crawford Group Inc., 84 385–389

SWH Corporation, 70 307–09

Swift & Company, 55 364–67

Swift Energy Company, 63 364–66

Swift Transportation Co., Inc., 42 363–66

Swinerton Inc., 43 397–400

Swire Pacific Ltd., I 521–22; 16 479–81 (upd.); 57 348–53 (upd.)

Swisher International Group Inc., 23 463–65

Swiss Air Transport Company Ltd., I 121–22

Swiss Army Brands, Inc. *see* Victorinox AG.

Swiss Bank Corporation, II 368–70 *see also* UBS AG.

The Swiss Colony, Inc., 97 395–98

Swiss Federal Railways (Schweizerische Bundesbahnen), V 519–22

Swiss International Air Lines Ltd., 48 379–81

Swiss Reinsurance Company (Schweizerische Rückversicherungs-Gesellschaft), III 375–78; 46 380–84 (upd.)

Swiss Valley Farms Company, 90 400–03

Swisscom AG, 58 336–39

Swissport International Ltd., 70 310–12

Sybase, Inc., 10 504–06; 27 447–50 (upd.)

Sybron International Corp., 14 479–81

Sycamore Networks, Inc., 45 388–91

Sykes Enterprises, Inc., 45 392–95

Sylvan, Inc., 22 496–99

Sylvan Learning Systems, Inc., 35 408–11 *see also* Educate Inc.

Symantec Corporation, 10 507–09; 82 372–77 (upd.)

Symbol Technologies, Inc., 15 482–84 *see also* Motorola, Inc.

Symrise GmbH and Company KG, 89 436–40

Syms Corporation, 29 456–58; 74 327–30 (upd.)

Symyx Technologies, Inc., 77 420–23

Synaptics Incorporated, 95 394–98

Synchronoss Technologies, Inc., 95 399–402

Syneron Medical Ltd., 91 471–74

Syngenta International AG, 83 391–394

Syniverse Holdings Inc., 97 399–402

SYNNEX Corporation, 73 328–30

Synopsys, Inc., 11 489–92; 69 339–43 (upd.)

SynOptics Communications, Inc., 10 510–12

Synovus Financial Corp., 12 465–67; 52 336–40 (upd.)

Syntax-Brillian Corporation, 102 405–09

Syntel, Inc., 92 356–60

Syntex Corporation, I 701–03

Synthes, Inc., 93 434–37

Sypris Solutions, Inc., 85 421–25

SyQuest Technology, Inc., 18 509–12

Syratech Corp., 14 482–84

SYSCO Corporation, II 675–76; 24 470–72 (upd.); 75 357–60 (upd.)

System Software Associates, Inc., 10 513–14

Systemax, Inc., 52 341–44

Systems & Computer Technology Corp., 19 437–39

Sytner Group plc, 45 396–98

T

T-Netix, Inc., 46 385–88

T-Online International AG, 61 349–51

T.J. Maxx *see* The TJX Companies, Inc.

T. Marzetti Company, 57 354–56

T. Rowe Price Associates, Inc., 11 493–96; 34 423–27 (upd.)

TA Triumph-Adler AG, 48 382–85

TAB Products Co., 17 467–69

Tabacalera, S.A., V 414–16; 17 470–73 (upd.) *see also* Altadis S.A.

TABCORP Holdings Limited, 44 407–10

TACA *see* Grupo TACA.

Taco Bell Corporation, 7 505–07; 21 485–88 (upd.); 74 331–34 (upd.)

Taco Cabana, Inc., 23 466–68; 72 344–47 (upd.)

Taco John's International Inc., 15 485–87; 63 367–70 (upd.)

Tacony Corporation, 70 313–15

TAG Heuer S.A., 25 459–61; 77 424–28 (upd.)

Tag-It Pacific, Inc., 85 426–29

Taiheiyo Cement Corporation, 60 298–301 (upd.)

Taittinger S.A., 43 401–05

Taiwan Semiconductor Manufacturing Company Ltd., 47 383–87

Taiwan Tobacco & Liquor Corporation, 75 361–63

Taiyo Fishery Company, Limited, II 578–79 *see also* Maruha Group Inc.

Taiyo Kobe Bank, Ltd., II 371–72

Takara Holdings Inc., 62 345–47

Takashimaya Company, Limited, V 193–96; 47 388–92 (upd.)

Take-Two Interactive Software, Inc., 46 389–91

Takeda Chemical Industries, Ltd., I 704–06; 46 392–95 (upd.)

The Talbots, Inc., 11 497–99; 31 429–32 (upd.); 88 393–98 (upd.)

Talisman Energy Inc., 9 490–93; 47 393–98 (upd.); 103 425–34 (upd.)

Talk America Holdings, Inc., 70 316–19

Talley Industries, Inc., 16 482–85

TALX Corporation, 92 361–64

TAM Linhas Aéreas S.A., 68 363–65

Tambrands Inc., 8 511–13 *see also* Procter & Gamble Co.

TAME (Transportes Aéreos Militares Ecuatorianos), 100 407–10

Tamedia AG, 53 323–26

Tamfelt Oyj Abp, 62 348–50

Tamron Company Ltd., 82 378–81

TAMSA *see* Tubos de Acero de Mexico, S.A.

Tandem Computers, Inc., 6 278–80 *see also* Hewlett-Packard Co.

Tandy Corporation, II 106–08; 12 468–70 (upd.) *see also* RadioShack Corp.

Tandycrafts, Inc., 31 433–37

Tanger Factory Outlet Centers, Inc., 49 386–89

Tanimura & Antle Fresh Foods, Inc., 98 379–83

Tanox, Inc., 77 429–32

TAP—Air Portugal Transportes Aéreos Portugueses S.A., 46 396–99 (upd.)

Tapemark Company Inc., 64 373–75

TAQA North Ltd., 95 403–06

Target Corporation, 10 515–17; 27 451–54 (upd.); 61 352–56 (upd.)

Targetti Sankey SpA, 86 385–88

Tarkett Sommer AG, 25 462–64

Tarmac Limited, III 751–54; 28 447–51 (upd.); 95 407–14 (upd.)

Taro Pharmaceutical Industries Ltd., 65 335–37

TAROM S.A., 64 376–78

Tarragon Realty Investors, Inc., 45 399–402

Tarrant Apparel Group, 62 351–53

Taschen GmbH, 101 465–68

Taser International, Inc., 62 354–57

Tastefully Simple Inc., 100 411–14

Tasty Baking Company, 14 485–87; 35 412–16 (upd.)

Tata Iron & Steel Co. Ltd., IV 217–19; 44 411–15 (upd.)

Tata Tea Ltd., 76 339–41

Tate & Lyle PLC, II 580–83; 42 367–72 (upd.); 101 469–77 (upd.)

Tati SA, 25 465–67

Tatneft *see* OAO Tatneft.

Tattered Cover Book Store, 43 406–09

Tatung Co., 23 469–71

Wenner Media, Inc., 32 506–09
Werhahn *see* Wilh. Werhahn KG.
Werner Enterprises, Inc., 26 531–33
Weru Aktiengesellschaft, 18 558–61
Wessanen *see* Koninklijke Wessanen nv.
West Bend Co., 14 546–48
West Coast Entertainment Corporation, 29 502–04
West Corporation, 42 435–37
West Fraser Timber Co. Ltd., 17 538–40; 91 512–18 (upd.)
West Group, 34 502–06 (upd.)
West Linn Paper Company, 91 519–22
West Marine, Inc., 17 541–43; 90 438–42 (upd.)
West One Bancorp, 11 552–55 *see also* U.S. Bancorp.
West Pharmaceutical Services, Inc., 42 438–41
West Point-Pepperell, Inc., 8 566–69 *see also* WestPoint Stevens Inc.; JPS Textile Group, Inc.
West Publishing Co., 7 579–81
Westaff Inc., 33 454–57
Westamerica Bancorporation, 17 544–47
Westar Energy, Inc., 57 404–07 (upd.)
WestCoast Hospitality Corporation, 59 410–13
Westcon Group, Inc., 67 392–94
Westdeutsche Landesbank Girozentrale, II 385–87; 46 458–61 (upd.)
Westell Technologies, Inc., 57 408–10
Western Atlas Inc., 12 538–40
Western Beef, Inc., 22 548–50
Western Company of North America, 15 534–36
Western Digital Corporation, 25 530–32; 92 411–15 (upd.)
Western Gas Resources, Inc., 45 435–37
Western Oil Sands Inc., 85 454–57
Western Publishing Group, Inc., 13 559–61 *see also* Thomson Corp.
Western Resources, Inc., 12 541–43
The WesterN SizzliN Corporation, 60 335–37
Western Union Financial Services, Inc., 54 413–16
Western Wireless Corporation, 36 514–16
Westfield Group, 69 366–69
Westin Hotels and Resorts Worldwide, 9 547–49; 29 505–08 (upd.)
Westinghouse Electric Corporation, II 120–22; 12 544–47 (upd.) *see also* CBS Radio Group.
WestJet Airlines Ltd., 38 493–95
Westmoreland Coal Company, 7 582–85
Weston Foods Inc. *see* George Weston Ltd.
Westpac Banking Corporation, II 388–90; 48 424–27 (upd.)
WestPoint Stevens Inc., 16 533–36 *see also* JPS Textile Group, Inc.
Westport Resources Corporation, 63 439–41

Westvaco Corporation, IV 351–54; 19 495–99 (upd.) *see also* MeadWestvaco Corp.
Westwood One Inc., 23 508–11; 106 490–96 (upd.)
The Wet Seal, Inc., 18 562–64; 70 353–57 (upd.)
Wetterau Incorporated, II 681–82 *see also* Supervalu Inc.
Weyco Group, Incorporated, 32 510–13
Weyerhaeuser Company, IV 355–56; 9 550–52 (upd.); 28 514–17 (upd.); 83 454–461 (upd.)
WFS Financial Inc., 70 358–60
WFSC *see* World Fuel Services Corp.
WGBH Educational Foundation, 66 366–68
WH Smith PLC, 42 442–47 (upd.)
Wham-O, Inc., 61 390–93
Whataburger Restaurants LP, 105 493–97
Whatman plc, 46 462–65
Wheaton Industries, 8 570–73
Wheaton Science Products, 60 338–42 (upd.)
Wheelabrator Technologies, Inc., 6 599–600; 60 343–45 (upd.)
Wheeling-Pittsburgh Corporation, 7 586–88; 58 360–64 (upd.)
Wheels Inc., 96 458–61
Wherehouse Entertainment Incorporated, 11 556–58
Whirlpool Corporation, III 653–55; 12 548–50 (upd.); 59 414–19 (upd.)
Whitbread PLC, I 293–94; 20 519–22 (upd.); 52 412–17 (upd.); 97 468–76 (upd.)
White & Case LLP, 35 466–69
White Castle Management Company, 12 551–53; 36 517–20 (upd.); 85 458–64 (upd.)
White Consolidated Industries Inc., 13 562–64 *see also* Electrolux.
The White House, Inc., 60 346–48
White Lily Foods Company, 88 435–38
White Mountains Insurance Group, Ltd., 48 428–31
White Rose, Inc., 24 527–29
White Wave, 43 462–64
Whitehall Jewellers, Inc., 82 429–34 (upd.)
Whiting Petroleum Corporation, 81 424–27
Whiting-Turner Contracting Company, 95 446–49
Whitman Corporation, 10 553–55 (upd.) *see also* PepsiAmericas, Inc.
Whitman Education Group, Inc., 41 419–21
Whitney Holding Corporation, 21 522–24
Whittaker Corporation, I 544–46; 48 432–35 (upd.)
Whittard of Chelsea Plc, 61 394–97
Whole Foods Market, Inc., 20 523–27; 50 530–34 (upd.)
WHX Corporation, 98 464–67

Wickes Inc., V 221–23; 25 533–36 (upd.)
Widmer Brothers Brewing Company, 76 379–82
Wieden + Kennedy, 75 403–05
Wienerberger AG, 70 361–63
Wikimedia Foundation, Inc., 91 523–26
Wilbert, Inc., 56 377–80
Wilbur Chocolate Company, 66 369–71
Wilco Farm Stores, 93 490–93
Wild Oats Markets, Inc., 19 500–02; 41 422–25 (upd.)
Wildlife Conservation Society, 31 462–64
Wilh. Werhahn KG, 101 491–94
Wilh. Wilhelmsen ASA, 94 459–62
Wilhelm Karmann GmbH, 94 463–68
Wilkinson Hardware Stores Ltd., 80 416–18
Wilkinson Sword Ltd., 60 349–52
Willamette Industries, Inc., IV 357–59; 31 465–68 (upd.) *see also* Weyerhaeuser Co.
Willamette Valley Vineyards, Inc., 85 465–69
Willbros Group, Inc., 56 381–83
William Grant & Sons Ltd., 60 353–55
William Hill Organization Limited, 49 449–52
William Jackson & Son Ltd., 101 495–99
William L. Bonnell Company, Inc., 66 372–74
William Lyon Homes, 59 420–22
William Morris Agency, Inc., 23 512–14; 102 448–52 (upd.)
William Reed Publishing Ltd., 78 467–70
William Zinsser & Company, Inc., 58 365–67
Williams & Connolly LLP, 47 445–48
Williams Communications Group, Inc., 34 507–10
The Williams Companies, Inc., IV 575–76; 31 469–72 (upd.)
Williams Scotsman, Inc., 65 361–64
Williams-Sonoma, Inc., 17 548–50; 44 447–50 (upd.); 103 515–20 (upd.)
Williamson-Dickie Manufacturing Company, 14 549–50; 45 438–41 (upd.)
Willis Group Holdings Ltd., 25 537–39; 100 456–60 (upd.)
Willkie Farr & Gallagher LLPLP, 95 450–53
Willow Run Foods, Inc., 100 461–64
Wilmar International Ltd., 108 537–41
Wilmington Trust Corporation, 25 540–43
Wilson Bowden Plc, 45 442–44
Wilson Sonsini Goodrich & Rosati, 34 511–13
Wilson Sporting Goods Company, 24 530–32; 84 431–436 (upd.)
Wilsons The Leather Experts Inc., 21 525–27; 58 368–71 (upd.)
Wilton Products, Inc., 97 477–80

Index to Industries

Accounting

American Institute of Certified Public
  Accountants (AICPA), 44
Andersen, 29 (upd.); 68 (upd.)
Automatic Data Processing, Inc., III; 9
  (upd.); 47 (upd.)
BDO Seidman LLP, 96
BKD LLP, 96
CPP International, LLC, 103
CROSSMARK, 79
Deloitte Touche Tohmatsu International,
  9; 29 (upd.)
Ernst & Young Global Limited, 9; 29
  (upd.); 108 (upd.)
FTI Consulting, Inc., 77
Grant Thornton International, 57
Huron Consulting Group Inc., 87
JKH Holding Co. LLC, 105
KPMG International, 33 (upd.); 108
  (upd.)
L.S. Starrett Co., 13
McLane Company, Inc., 13
NCO Group, Inc., 42
Paychex, Inc., 15; 46 (upd.)
PKF International 78
Plante & Moran, LLP, 71
PRG-Schultz International, Inc., 73
PricewaterhouseCoopers, 9; 29 (upd.)
Resources Connection, Inc., 81
Robert Wood Johnson Foundation, 35
RSM McGladrey Business Services Inc.,
  98
Saffery Champness, 80
Sanders\Wingo, 99
Schenck Business Solutions, 88
StarTek, Inc., 79
Travelzoo Inc., 79
Univision Communications Inc., 24; 83
  (upd.)

Advertising & Business Services

ABM Industries Incorporated, 25 (upd.)
Abt Associates Inc., 95
Accenture Ltd., 108 (upd.)
AchieveGlobal Inc., 90
Ackerley Communications, Inc., 9
ACNielsen Corporation, 13; 38 (upd.)
Acosta Sales and Marketing Company,
  Inc., 77
Acsys, Inc., 44
Adecco S.A., 36 (upd.)
Adelman Travel Group, 105
Adia S.A., 6
Administaff, Inc., 52
The Advertising Council, Inc., 76
The Advisory Board Company, 80
Advo, Inc., 6; 53 (upd.)
Aegis Group plc, 6
Affiliated Computer Services, Inc., 61
AHL Services, Inc., 27
Allegis Group, Inc., 95
Alloy, Inc., 55
Amdocs Ltd., 47
American Building Maintenance
  Industries, Inc., 6
Amey Plc, 47
Analysts International Corporation, 36
aQuantive, Inc., 81
The Arbitron Company, 38
Ariba, Inc., 57
Armor Holdings, Inc., 27
Asatsu-DK Inc., 82
Ashtead Group plc, 34
The Associated Press, 13
Avalon Correctional Services, Inc., 75
Bain & Company, 55
Barrett Business Services, Inc., 16

Barton Protective Services Inc., 53
Bates Worldwide, Inc., 14; 33 (upd.)
Bearings, Inc., 13
Berlitz International, Inc., 13; 39 (upd.)
Bernard Hodes Group Inc., 86
Bernstein-Rein, 92
Big Flower Press Holdings, Inc., 21
Billing Concepts, Inc., 26; 72 (upd.)
Billing Services Group Ltd., 102
The BISYS Group, Inc., 73
Booz Allen Hamilton Inc., 10; 101 (upd.)
Boron, LePore & Associates, Inc., 45
The Boston Consulting Group, 58
Bozell Worldwide Inc., 25
BrandPartners Group, Inc., 58
Bright Horizons Family Solutions, Inc., 31
The Brink's Company, 58 (upd.)
Broadcast Music Inc., 23; 90 (upd.)
Bronner Display & Sign Advertising, Inc.,
  82
Buck Consultants, Inc., 55
Bureau Veritas SA, 55
Burke, Inc., 88
Burns International Services Corporation,
  13; 41 (upd.)
Cambridge Technology Partners, Inc., 36
Campbell-Ewald Advertising, 86
Campbell-Mithun-Esty, Inc., 16
Cannon Design, 63
Capario, 104
Capita Group PLC, 69
Cardtronics, Inc., 93
Carmichael Lynch Inc., 28
Cash Systems, Inc., 93
Cazenove Group plc, 72
CCC Information Services Group Inc., 74
CDI Corporation, 6; 54 (upd.)
Cegedim S.A., 104
Central Parking System, 18; 104 (upd.)

Agribusiness & Farming

Airlines

Automotive

Beverages

Bio-Technology

Chemicals

ARCO Chemical Company, 10
Arkema S.A., 100
Asahi Denka Kogyo KK, 64
Atanor S.A., 62
Atochem S.A., I
Avantium Technologies BV, 79
Avecia Group PLC, 63
Azelis Group, 100
Baker Hughes Incorporated, III; 22 (upd.); 57 (upd.)
Balchem Corporation, 42
BASF SE, I; 18 (upd.); 50 (upd.); 108 (upd.)
Bayer A.G., I; 13 (upd.); 41 (upd.)
Betz Laboratories, Inc., I; 10 (upd.)
The BFGoodrich Company, 19 (upd.)
BOC Group plc, I; 25 (upd.); 78 (upd.)
Braskem S.A., 108
Brenntag Holding GmbH & Co. KG, 8; 23 (upd.); 101 (upd.)
Burmah Castrol PLC, 30 (upd.)
Cabot Corporation, 8; 29 (upd.); 91 (upd.)
Calgon Carbon Corporation, 73
Caliper Life Sciences, Inc., 70
Calumet Specialty Products Partners, L.P., 106
Cambrex Corporation, 16
Catalytica Energy Systems, Inc., 44
Celanese Corporation, I
Celanese Mexicana, S.A. de C.V., 54
CF Industries Holdings, Inc., 99
Chemcentral Corporation, 8
Chemi-Trol Chemical Co., 16
Chemtura Corporation, 91 (upd.)
Church & Dwight Co., Inc., 29
Ciba-Geigy Ltd., I; 8 (upd.)
The Clorox Company, III; 22 (upd.); 81 (upd.)
Croda International Plc, 45
Crompton Corporation, 9; 36 (upd.)
Cytec Industries Inc., 27
Degussa-Hüls AG, 32 (upd.)
DeKalb Genetics Corporation, 17
The Dexter Corporation, I; 12 (upd.)
Dionex Corporation, 46
The Dow Chemical Company, I; 8 (upd.); 50 (upd.)
DSM N.V., I; 56 (upd.)
Dynaction S.A., 67
E.I. du Pont de Nemours & Company, I; 8 (upd.); 26 (upd.)
Eastman Chemical Company, 14; 38 (upd.)
Ecolab Inc., I; 13 (upd.); 34 (upd.); 85 (upd.)
Eka Chemicals AB, 92
Elementis plc, 40 (upd.)
Engelhard Corporation, 72 (upd.)
English China Clays Ltd., 15 (upd.); 40 (upd.)
Enterprise Rent-A-Car Company, 69 (upd.)
Equistar Chemicals, LP, 71
Ercros S.A., 80
ERLY Industries Inc., 17
Ethyl Corporation, I; 10 (upd.)
Ferro Corporation, 8; 56 (upd.)

Firmenich International S.A., 60
First Mississippi Corporation, 8
FMC Corporation, 89 (upd.)
Formosa Plastics Corporation, 14; 58 (upd.)
Fort James Corporation, 22 (upd.)
Fuchs Petrolub AG, 102
G.A.F., I
The General Chemical Group Inc., 37
Georgia Gulf Corporation, 9; 61 (upd.)
Givaudan SA, 43
Great Lakes Chemical Corporation, I; 14 (upd.)
GROWMARK, Inc., 88
Guerbet Group, 46
H.B. Fuller Company, 8; 32 (upd.); 75 (upd.)
Hauser, Inc., 46
Hawkins Chemical, Inc., 16
Henkel KGaA, III; 34 (upd.); 95 (upd.)
Hercules Inc., I; 22 (upd.); 66 (upd.)
Hoechst A.G., I; 18 (upd.)
Hoechst Celanese Corporation, 13
Huls A.G., I
Huntsman Corporation, 8; 98 (upd.)
Ikonics Corporation, 99
IMC Fertilizer Group, Inc., 8
Imperial Chemical Industries PLC, I; 50 (upd.)
International Flavors & Fragrances Inc., 9; 38 (upd.)
Israel Chemicals Ltd., 55
KBR Inc., 106 (upd.)
Kemira Oyj, 70
KMG Chemicals, Inc., 101
Koppers Industries, Inc., I; 26 (upd.)
Kwizda Holding GmbH, 102 (upd.)
L'Air Liquide SA, I; 47 (upd.)
Lawter International Inc., 14
LeaRonal, Inc., 23
Loctite Corporation, 30 (upd.)
Loos & Dilworth, Inc., 100
Lonza Group Ltd., 73
The Lubrizol Corporation, I; 30 (upd.); 83 (upd.)
Lyondell Chemical Company, 45 (upd.)
M.A. Hanna Company, 8
MacDermid Incorporated, 32
Makhteshim-Agan Industries Ltd., 85
Mallinckrodt Group Inc., 19
MBC Holding Company, 40
Melamine Chemicals, Inc., 27
Methanex Corporation, 40
Mexichem, S.A.B. de C.V., 99
Minerals Technologies Inc., 52 (upd.)
Mississippi Chemical Corporation, 39
Mitsubishi Chemical Corporation, I; 56 (upd.)
Mitsui Petrochemical Industries, Ltd., 9
Monsanto Company, I; 9 (upd.); 29 (upd.)
Montedison SpA, I
Morton International Inc., I; 9 (upd.); 80 (upd.)
The Mosaic Company, 91
Nagase & Company, Ltd., 8
Nalco Holding Company, I; 12 (upd.); 89 (upd.)

National Distillers and Chemical Corporation, I
National Sanitary Supply Co., 16
National Starch and Chemical Company, 49
NCH Corporation, 8
Nippon Soda Co., Ltd., 85
Nisshin Seifun Group Inc., 66 (upd.)
NL Industries, Inc., 10
Nobel Industries AB, 9
NOF Corporation, 72
Norsk Hydro ASA, 35 (upd.)
North American Galvanizing & Coatings, Inc., 99
Novacor Chemicals Ltd., 12
Nufarm Ltd., 87
OAO Gazprom, 42; 107 (upd.)
Occidental Petroleum Corporation, 71 (upd.)
Olin Corporation, I; 13 (upd.); 78 (upd.)
OM Group, Inc., 17; 78 (upd.)
OMNOVA Solutions Inc., 59
Penford Corporation, 55
Pennwalt Corporation, I
Perstorp AB, I; 51 (upd.)
Petrolite Corporation, 15
Pfizer Inc., 79 (upd.)
Pioneer Hi-Bred International, Inc., 41 (upd.)
PolyOne Corporation, 87 (upd.)
Praxair, Inc., 11; 48 (upd.)
Quaker Chemical Corp., 91
Quantum Chemical Corporation, 8
Reichhold Chemicals, Inc., 10
Renner Herrmann S.A., 79
Rhodia SA, 38
Rhône-Poulenc S.A., I; 10 (upd.)
Robertet SA, 39
Rohm and Haas Company, I; 26 (upd.); 77 (upd.)
Roussel Uclaf, I; 8 (upd.)
RPM International Inc., 8; 36 (upd.); 91 (upd.)
RWE AG, 50 (upd.)
S.C. Johnson & Son, Inc., III; 28 (upd.); 89 (upd.)
The Scotts Company, 22
SCP Pool Corporation, 39
Sequa Corporation, 13; 54 (upd.)
Shanghai Petrochemical Co., Ltd., 18
Sigma-Aldrich Corporation, I; 36 (upd.); 93 (upd.)
Sociedad Química y Minera de Chile S.A., 103
Solutia, 52
Solvay S.A., I; 21 (upd.); 61 (upd.)
Stepan Company, 30; 105 (upd.)
Sterling Chemicals, Inc., 16; 78 (upd.)
Sumitomo Chemical Company Ltd., I; 98 (upd.)
Takeda Chemical Industries, Ltd., 46 (upd.)
Teknor Apex Company, 97
Terra Industries, Inc., 13
Tessenderlo Group, 76
Teva Pharmaceutical Industries Ltd., 22
Tosoh Corporation, 70
Total Fina Elf S.A., 24 (upd.); 50 (upd.)

Conglomerates

Construction

Containers

Drugs & Pharmaceuticals

Omnicare, Inc., 49
Omrix Biopharmaceuticals, Inc., 95
Par Pharmaceutical Companies, Inc., 65
PDL BioPharma, Inc., 90
Perrigo Company, 59 (upd.)
Pfizer Inc., I; 9 (upd.); 38 (upd.); 79
   (upd.)
Pharmacia & Upjohn Inc., I; 25 (upd.)
Pharmion Corporation, 91
PLIVA d.d., 70
PolyMedica Corporation, 77
POZEN Inc., 81
QLT Inc., 71
The Quigley Corporation, 62
Quintiles Transnational Corporation, 21
R.P. Scherer, I
Ranbaxy Laboratories Ltd., 70
ratiopharm Group, 84
Reckitt Benckiser plc, II; 42 (upd.); 91
   (upd.)
Recordati Industria Chimica e
   Farmaceutica S.p.A., 105
Roberts Pharmaceutical Corporation, 16
Roche Bioscience, 14 (upd.)
Rorer Group, I
Roussel Uclaf, I; 8 (upd.)
Salix Pharmaceuticals, Ltd., 93
Sandoz Ltd., I
Sankyo Company, Ltd., I; 56 (upd.)
The Sanofi-Synthélabo Group, I; 49
   (upd.)
Santarus, Inc., 105
Schering AG, I; 50 (upd.)
Schering-Plough Corporation, I; 14
   (upd.); 49 (upd.); 99 (upd.)
Sepracor Inc., 45
Serono S.A., 47
Shionogi & Co., Ltd., III; 17 (upd.); 98
   (upd.)
Sigma-Aldrich Corporation, I; 36 (upd.);
   93 (upd.)
SmithKline Beecham plc, I; 32 (upd.)
Solvay S.A., 61 (upd.)
Squibb Corporation, I
Sterling Drug, Inc., I
Stiefel Laboratories, Inc., 90
Sun Pharmaceutical Industries Ltd., 57
The Sunrider Corporation, 26
Syntex Corporation, I
Takeda Chemical Industries, Ltd., I
Taro Pharmaceutical Industries Ltd., 65
Teva Pharmaceutical Industries Ltd., 22;
   54 (upd.)
UCB Pharma SA, 98
The Upjohn Company, I; 8 (upd.)
Vertex Pharmaceuticals Incorporated, 83
Virbac Corporation, 74
Vitalink Pharmacy Services, Inc., 15
Warner Chilcott Limited, 85
Warner-Lambert Co., I; 10 (upd.)
Watson Pharmaceuticals Inc., 16; 56
   (upd.)
The Wellcome Foundation Ltd., I
WonderWorks, Inc., 103
Zentiva N.V./Zentiva, a.s., 99
Zila, Inc., 46

Education & Training
ABC Learning Centres Ltd., 93
American Management Association, 76
American Public Education, Inc., 108
Benesse Corporation, 76
Berlitz International, Inc., 13; 39 (upd.)
Bridgepoint Education, Inc., 108
Career Education Corporation, 45
ChartHouse International Learning
   Corporation, 49
Childtime Learning Centers, Inc., 34
Computer Learning Centers, Inc., 26
Corinthian Colleges, Inc., 39; 92 (upd.)
Council on International Educational
   Exchange Inc., 81
DeVry Inc., 29; 82 (upd.)
ECC International Corp., 42
Edison Schools Inc., 37
Educate Inc., 86 (upd.)
Education Management Corporation, 35
Educational Testing Service, 12; 62 (upd.)
GP Strategies Corporation, 64 (upd.)
Green Dot Public Schools, 99
Grupo Positivo, 105
Huntington Learning Centers, Inc., 55
ITT Educational Services, Inc., 39; 76
   (upd.)
Jones Knowledge Group, Inc., 97
Kaplan, Inc., 42; 90 (upd.)
KinderCare Learning Centers, Inc., 13
Knowledge Learning Corporation, 51
Kumon Institute of Education Co., Ltd.,
   72
LeapFrog Enterprises, Inc., 54
Learning Care Group, Inc., 76 (upd.)
The Learning Company Inc., 24
Learning Tree International Inc., 24
LPA Holding Corporation, 81
Management and Training Corporation,
   28
National Heritage Academies, Inc., 60
The New School, 103
Noah Education Holdings Ltd., 97
Nobel Learning Communities, Inc., 37;
   76 (upd.)
Plato Learning, Inc., 44
Renaissance Learning, Inc., 39; 100 (upd.)
Rosetta Stone Inc., 93
Scientific Learning Corporation, 95
Strayer Education, Inc., 53
Sylvan Learning Systems, Inc., 35
Whitman Education Group, Inc., 41
Youth Services International, Inc., 21

Electrical & Electronics
ABB ASEA Brown Boveri Ltd., II; 22
   (upd.)
ABB Ltd., 65 (upd.)
Acer Incorporated, 16; 73 (upd.)
Acuson Corporation, 10; 36 (upd.)
ADC Telecommunications, Inc., 30 (upd.)
Adtran Inc., 22
Advanced Circuits Inc., 67
Advanced Micro Devices, Inc., 6; 30
   (upd.); 99 (upd.)
Advanced Technology Laboratories, Inc., 9
Agere Systems Inc., 61
Agilent Technologies Inc., 38; 93 (upd.)

Agilysys Inc., 76 (upd.)
Aiwa Co., Ltd., 30
AKG Acoustics GmbH, 62
Akzo Nobel N.V., 13; 41 (upd.)
Alienware Corporation, 81
Alliant Techsystems Inc., 30 (upd.); 77
   (upd.)
AlliedSignal Inc., 9; 22 (upd.)
Alpine Electronics, Inc., 13
Alps Electric Co., Ltd., II; 44 (upd.)
Altera Corporation, 18; 43 (upd.)
Altron Incorporated, 20
Amdahl Corporation, 40 (upd.)
American Power Conversion Corporation,
   24; 67 (upd.)
American Superconductor Corporation,
   97
American Technical Ceramics Corp., 67
American Technology Corporation, 103
Amerigon Incorporated, 97
Amkor Technology, Inc., 69
AMP Incorporated, II; 14 (upd.)
Amphenol Corporation, 40
Amstrad plc, 48 (upd.)
Analog Devices, Inc., 10
Analogic Corporation, 23
Anam Group, 23
Anaren Microwave, Inc., 33
Andrew Corporation, 10; 32 (upd.)
Anixter International Inc., 88
Anritsu Corporation, 68
Anthem Electronics, Inc., 13
Apex Digital, Inc., 63
Apple Computer, Inc., 36 (upd.); 77
   (upd.)
Applied Micro Circuits Corporation, 38
Applied Power Inc., 9; 32 (upd.)
Applied Signal Technology, Inc., 87
Argon ST, Inc., 81
Arotech Corporation, 93
ARRIS Group, Inc., 89
Arrow Electronics, Inc., 10; 50 (upd.)
Artesyn Technologies Inc., 46 (upd.)
Ascend Communications, Inc., 24
Astronics Corporation, 35
ASUSTeK Computer Inc., 107
Atari Corporation, 9; 23 (upd.); 66 (upd.)
ATI Technologies Inc., 79
Atmel Corporation, 17
ATMI, Inc., 93
AU Optronics Corporation, 67
Audiovox Corporation, 34; 90 (upd.)
Ault Incorporated, 34
Autodesk, Inc., 10; 89 (upd.)
Avnet Inc., 9
AVX Corporation, 67
Axcelis Technologies, Inc., 95
Axsys Technologies, Inc., 93
Ballard Power Systems Inc., 73
Bang & Olufsen Holding A/S, 37; 86
   (upd.)
Barco NV, 44
Bel Fuse, Inc., 53
Belden CDT Inc., 19; 76 (upd.)
Bell Microproducts Inc., 69
Benchmark Electronics, Inc., 40
Bicoastal Corporation, II
Black Box Corporation, 20; 96 (upd.)

Telxon Corporation, 10
Teradyne, Inc., 11; 98 (upd.)
Texas Instruments Inc., II; 11 (upd.); 46 (upd.)
Thales S.A., 42
Thomas & Betts Corporation, 11; 54 (upd.)
THOMSON multimedia S.A., II; 42 (upd.)
THQ, Inc., 92 (upd.)
The Titan Corporation, 36
TiVo Inc., 75
TomTom N.V., 81
Tops Appliance City, Inc., 17
Toromont Industries, Ltd., 21
Trans-Lux Corporation, 51
Trimble Navigation Limited, 40
TriQuint Semiconductor, Inc., 63
Tweeter Home Entertainment Group, Inc., 30
Ultimate Electronics, Inc., 69 (upd.)
Ultrak Inc., 24
Uniden Corporation, 98
United Microelectronics Corporation, 98
Universal Electronics Inc., 39
Universal Security Instruments, Inc., 96
Varian, Inc., 12; 48 (upd.)
Veeco Instruments Inc., 32
VIASYS Healthcare, Inc., 52
Viasystems Group, Inc., 67
Vicon Industries, Inc., 44
Victor Company of Japan, Limited, II; 26 (upd.); 83 (upd.)
Vishay Intertechnology, Inc., 21; 80 (upd.)
Vitesse Semiconductor Corporation, 32
Vitro Corp., 10
Vizio, Inc., 100
VLSI Technology, Inc., 16
VTech Holdings Ltd., 77
Wells-Gardner Electronics Corporation, 43
Westinghouse Electric Corporation, II; 12 (upd.)
Winbond Electronics Corporation, 74
Wincor Nixdorf Holding GmbH, 69 (upd.)
WuXi AppTec Company Ltd., 103
Wyle Electronics, 14
Xantrex Technology Inc., 97
Xerox Corporation, III; 6 (upd.); 26 (upd.); 69 (upd.)
Yageo Corporation, 16; 98 (upd.)
York Research Corporation, 35
Zenith Data Systems, Inc., 10
Zenith Electronics Corporation, II; 13 (upd.); 34 (upd.); 89 (upd.)
Zoom Telephonics, Inc., 18
Zoran Corporation, 77
Zumtobel AG, 50
Zytec Corporation, 19

Engineering & Management Services

AAON, Inc., 22
Aavid Thermal Technologies, Inc., 29
Acergy SA, 97
AECOM Technology Corporation, 79

Alliant Techsystems Inc., 30 (upd.)
Altran Technologies, 51
Amey Plc, 47
American Science & Engineering, Inc., 81
Analytic Sciences Corporation, 10
Arcadis NV, 26
Arthur D. Little, Inc., 35
The Austin Company, 8; 72 (upd.)
Autostrada Torino-Milano S.p.A., 101
Babcock International Group PLC, 69
Balfour Beatty plc, 36 (upd.)
BE&K, Inc., 73
Bechtel Corporation, I; 24 (upd.); 99 (upd.)
Birse Group PLC, 77
Bowen Engineering Corporation, 105
Brown & Root, Inc., 13
Bufete Industrial, S.A. de C.V., 34
C.H. Heist Corporation, 24
Camp Dresser & McKee Inc., 104
CDI Corporation, 6; 54 (upd.)
CH2M HILL Companies Ltd., 22; 96 (upd.)
The Charles Stark Draper Laboratory, Inc., 35
Coflexip S.A., 25
CompuDyne Corporation, 51
Corrections Corporation of America, 23
CRSS Inc., 6
Dames & Moore, Inc., 25
DAW Technologies, Inc., 25
Day & Zimmermann Inc., 9; 31 (upd.)
Donaldson Company, Inc., 16; 49 (upd.); 108 (upd.)
Doosan Heavy Industries and Construction Company Ltd., 108
Dycom Industries, Inc., 57
Edwards and Kelcey, 70
EG&G Incorporated, 8; 29 (upd.)
Eiffage, 27
Elliott-Lewis Corporation, 100
Essef Corporation, 18
Exponent, Inc., 95
FKI Plc, 57
Fluor Corporation, 34 (upd.)
Forest City Enterprises, Inc., 52 (upd.)
Foster Wheeler Ltd., 6; 23 (upd.); 76 (upd.)
Framatome SA, 19
Fraport AG Frankfurt Airport Services Worldwide, 90
Freese and Nichols, Inc., 107
Fugro N.V., 98
Gale International Llc, 93
Georg Fischer AG Schaffhausen, 61
Gilbane, Inc., 34
Great Lakes Dredge & Dock Company, 69
Grupo Dragados SA, 55
Halliburton Company, III; 25 (upd.); 55 (upd.)
Halma plc, 104
Harding Lawson Associates Group, Inc., 16
Harley Ellis Devereaux Corporation, 101
Harza Engineering Company, 14
HDR Inc., 48
Hittite Microwave Corporation, 106

HOK Group, Inc., 59
ICF Kaiser International, Inc., 28
IHC Caland N.V., 71
Invensys PLC, 50 (upd.)
Jacobs Engineering Group Inc., 6; 26 (upd.); 106 (upd.)
Jacques Whitford, 92
Jaiprakash Associates Limited, 101
The Judge Group, Inc., 51
JWP Inc., 9
KBR Inc., 106 (upd.)
The Keith Companies Inc., 54
Keller Group PLC, 95
Klöckner-Werke AG, 58 (upd.)
Kvaerner ASA, 36
Layne Christensen Company, 19
The Louis Berger Group, Inc., 104
The MacNeal-Schwendler Corporation, 25
Malcolm Pirnie, Inc., 42
McDermott International, Inc., III; 37 (upd.)
McKinsey & Company, Inc., 9
Michael Baker Corporation, 51 (upd.)
Mota-Engil, SGPS, S.A., 97
Nooter Corporation, 61
NTD Architecture, 101
Oceaneering International, Inc., 63
Odebrecht S.A., 73
Ogden Corporation, 6
Opus Corporation, 34; 101 (upd.)
PAREXEL International Corporation, 84
Parsons Brinckerhoff Inc., 34; 104 (upd.)
The Parsons Corporation, 8; 56 (upd.)
The PBSJ Corporation, 82
Petrofac Ltd., 95
Quanta Services, Inc., 79
RCM Technologies, Inc., 34
Renishaw plc, 46
Ricardo plc, 90
Rosemount Inc., 15
Roy F. Weston, Inc., 33
Royal Vopak NV, 41
Rust International Inc., 11
Sandia National Laboratories, 49
Sandvik AB, IV; 32 (upd.); 77 (upd.)
Sarnoff Corporation, 57
Science Applications International Corporation, 15
SENTEL Corporation, 106
Serco Group plc, 47
Siegel & Gale, 64
Siemens AG, 57 (upd.)
SRI International, Inc., 57
SSOE Inc., 76
Stone & Webster, Inc., 13; 64 (upd.)
Sulzer Ltd., III; 68 (upd.)
Susquehanna Pfaltzgraff Company, 8
Sverdrup Corporation, 14
Tech-Sym Corporation, 44 (upd.)
Technip 78
Tetra Tech, Inc., 29
ThyssenKrupp AG, IV; 28 (upd.); 87 (upd.)
Towers Perrin, 32
Tracor Inc., 17
TRC Companies, Inc., 32
Underwriters Laboratories, Inc., 30

Financial Services: Banks

Financial Services: Excluding Banks

Food Services, Retailers, & Restaurants

Health, Personal & Medical Care Products

ICON Health & Fitness, Inc., 38; 102 (upd.)
Immucor, Inc., 81
Inamed Corporation, 79
Integra LifeSciences Holdings Corporation, 87
Integrated BioPharma, Inc., 83
Inter Parfums Inc., 35; 86 (upd.)
Intuitive Surgical, Inc., 79
Invacare Corporation, 11; 47 (upd.)
Invivo Corporation, 52
IRIS International, Inc., 101
IVAX Corporation, 11
IVC Industries, Inc., 45
The Jean Coutu Group (PJC) Inc., 46
John Frieda Professional Hair Care Inc., 70
John Paul Mitchell Systems, 24
Johnson & Johnson, III; 8 (upd.); 36 (upd.); 75 (upd.)
Kanebo, Ltd., 53
Kao Corporation, III; 79 (upd.)
Kendall International, Inc., 11
Kensey Nash Corporation, 71
Keys Fitness Products, LP, 83
Kimberly-Clark Corporation, III; 16 (upd.); 43 (upd.); 105 (upd.)
Kiss My Face Corporation, 108
Kolmar Laboratories Group, 96
Kyowa Hakko Kogyo Co., Ltd., III
Kyphon Inc., 87
L'Oréal SA, III; 8 (upd.); 46 (upd.)
Laboratoires de Biologie Végétale Yves Rocher, 35
The Lamaur Corporation, 41
Laserscope, 67
Lever Brothers Company, 9
Lion Corporation, III; 51 (upd.)
Lush Ltd., 93
Luxottica SpA, 17; 52 (upd.)
Mandom Corporation, 82
Mannatech Inc., 33
Mary Kay Inc., 9; 30 (upd.); 84 (upd.)
Matrix Essentials Inc., 90
Maxxim Medical Inc., 12
Medco Containment Services Inc., 9
MEDecision, Inc., 95
Medical Action Industries Inc., 101
Medicine Shoppe International, Inc., 102
Medifast, Inc., 97
Medline Industries, Inc., 61
Medtronic, Inc., 8; 30 (upd.); 67 (upd.)
Melaleuca Inc., 31
The Mentholatum Company Inc., 32
Mentor Corporation, 26
Merck & Co., Inc., I; 11 (upd.); 34 (upd.); 95 (upd.)
Merit Medical Systems, Inc., 29
Merz Group, 81
Mueller Sports Medicine, Inc., 102
Natura Cosméticos S.A., 75
Nature's Sunshine Products, Inc., 15; 102 (upd.)
NBTY, Inc., 31
NeighborCare, Inc., 67 (upd.)
Neutrogena Corporation, 17
New Dana Perfumes Company, 37
Neways Inc. 78

Nikken Global Inc., 32
NutriSystem, Inc., 71
Nutrition for Life International Inc., 22
Nutrition 21 Inc., 97
Ocular Sciences, Inc., 65
OEC Medical Systems, Inc., 27
Obagi Medical Products, Inc., 95
OraSure Technologies, Inc., 75
Orion Oyj, 72
Orthofix International NV, 72
Parfums Givenchy S.A., 100
Patterson Dental Co., 19
Perrigo Company, 12
Pfizer Inc., 79 (upd.)
Physician Sales & Service, Inc., 14
Physio-Control International Corp., 18
Playtex Products, Inc., 15
PolyMedica Corporation, 77
The Procter & Gamble Company, III; 8 (upd.); 26 (upd.); 67 (upd.)
Puritan-Bennett Corporation, 13
PZ Cussons plc, 72
Quest Diagnostics Inc., 26; 106 (upd.)
Quidel Corporation, 80
Reckitt Benckiser plc, II; 42 (upd.); 91 (upd.)
Redken Laboratories Inc., 84
Reliv International, Inc., 58
Remington Products Company, L.L.C., 42
Retractable Technologies, Inc., 99
Revlon Inc., III; 17 (upd.); 64 (upd.)
Roche Biomedical Laboratories, Inc., 11
Rockwell Medical Technologies, Inc., 88
S.C. Johnson & Son, Inc., III; 28 (upd.); 89 (upd.)
Safety 1st, Inc., 24
Sage Products Inc., 105
St. Jude Medical, Inc., 11; 43 (upd.); 97 (upd.)
Schering-Plough Corporation, I; 14 (upd.); 49 (upd.); 99 (upd.)
Sephora Holdings S.A., 82
Shaklee Corporation, 39 (upd.)
Shionogi & Co., Ltd., III; 17 (upd.); 98 (upd.)
Shiseido Company, Limited, III; 22 (upd.); 81 (upd.)
Slim-Fast Foods Company, 18; 66 (upd.)
Smith & Nephew plc, 17
SmithKline Beecham PLC, III
Soft Sheen Products, Inc., 31
Sola International Inc., 71
Sonic Innovations Inc., 56
SonoSite, Inc., 56
Spacelabs Medical, Inc., 71
STAAR Surgical Company, 57
The Stephan Company, 60
Straumann Holding AG, 79
Stryker Corporation, 11; 29 (upd.); 79 (upd.)
Sunrise Medical Inc., 11
Sybron International Corp., 14
Syneron Medical Ltd., 91
Synthes, Inc., 93
Tambrands Inc., 8
Thermo Fisher Scientific Inc., 105 (upd.)
Terumo Corporation, 48
Thane International, Inc., 84

Tom's of Maine, Inc., 45
Transitions Optical, Inc., 83
The Tranzonic Companies, 37
Turtle Wax, Inc., 15; 93 (upd.)
Tutogen Medical, Inc., 68
Unicharm Corporation, 84
United States Surgical Corporation, 10; 34 (upd.)
USANA, Inc., 29
Utah Medical Products, Inc., 36
Ventana Medical Systems, Inc., 75
VHA Inc., 53
VIASYS Healthcare, Inc., 52
Vion Food Group NV, 85
VISX, Incorporated, 30
Vitamin Shoppe Industries, Inc., 60
VNUS Medical Technologies, Inc., 103
Wahl Clipper Corporation, 86
Water Pik Technologies, Inc., 34; 83 (upd.)
Weider Nutrition International, Inc., 29
Weleda AG 78
Wella AG, III; 48 (upd.)
West Pharmaceutical Services, Inc., 42
Wright Medical Group, Inc., 61
Wyeth, 50 (upd.)
Zila, Inc., 46
Zimmer Holdings, Inc., 45

Health Care Services

Acadian Ambulance & Air Med Services, Inc., 39
Adventist Health, 53
Advocat Inc., 46
Allied Healthcare Products, Inc., 24
Almost Family, Inc., 93
Alterra Healthcare Corporation, 42
Alticor Inc., 71 (upd.)
Amedisys, Inc., 53; 106 (upd.)
The American Cancer Society, 24
American Healthways, Inc., 65
American Lung Association, 48
American Medical Alert Corporation, 103
American Medical Association, 39
American Medical International, Inc., III
American Medical Response, Inc., 39
American Nurses Association Inc., 102
American Red Cross, 40
AMERIGROUP Corporation, 69
AmeriSource Health Corporation, 37 (upd.)
Amil Participações S.A., 105
AmSurg Corporation, 48
The Andrews Institute, 99
Applied Bioscience International, Inc., 10
Assisted Living Concepts, Inc., 43
ATC Healthcare Inc., 64
Baptist Health Care Corporation, 82
Beverly Enterprises, Inc., III; 16 (upd.)
Bon Secours Health System, Inc., 24
Bravo Health Insurance Company, Inc., 107
Brookdale Senior Living, 91
C.R. Bard Inc., 9; 65 (upd.)
Cancer Treatment Centers of America, Inc., 85
Capital Senior Living Corporation, 75
Caremark Rx, Inc., 10; 54 (upd.)

Hotels

Information Technology

Insurance

Lloyd's, 74 (upd.)
Lloyd's of London, III; 22 (upd.)
The Loewen Group Inc., 40 (upd.)
Lutheran Brotherhood, 31
Manulife Financial Corporation, 85
Marsh & McLennan Companies, Inc., III; 45 (upd.)
Massachusetts Mutual Life Insurance Company, III; 53 (upd.)
MBIA Inc., 73
The Meiji Mutual Life Insurance Company, III
Mercury General Corporation, 25
Metropolitan Life Insurance Company, III; 52 (upd.)
MGIC Investment Corp., 52
The Midland Company, 65
Millea Holdings Inc., 64 (upd.)
Mitsui Marine and Fire Insurance Company, Limited, III
Mitsui Mutual Life Insurance Company, III; 39 (upd.)
Modern Woodmen of America, 66
Munich Re (Münchener Rückversicherungs-Gesellschaft Aktiengesellschaft in München), III; 46 (upd.)
The Mutual Benefit Life Insurance Company, III
The Mutual Life Insurance Company of New York, III
The Mutual of Omaha Companies, 98
Mutuelle Assurance des Commerçants et Industriels de France, 107
National Medical Health Card Systems, Inc., 79
Nationale-Nederlanden N.V., III
Nationwide Mutual Insurance Company, 108
The Navigators Group, Inc., 92
New England Mutual Life Insurance Company, III
New Jersey Manufacturers Insurance Company, 96
New York Life Insurance Company, III; 45 (upd.)
Nippon Life Insurance Company, III; 60 (upd.)
Northwestern Mutual Life Insurance Company, III; 45 (upd.)
NYMAGIC, Inc., 41
Ohio Casualty Corp., 11
Old Republic International Corporation, 11; 58 (upd.)
Oregon Dental Service Health Plan, Inc., 51
Pacific Mutual Holding Company, 98
Palmer & Cay, Inc., 69
Pan-American Life Insurance Company, 48
PartnerRe Ltd., 83
The Paul Revere Corporation, 12
Pennsylvania Blue Shield, III
The PMI Group, Inc., 49
Preserver Group, Inc., 44
Principal Mutual Life Insurance Company, III

The Progressive Corporation, 11; 29 (upd.)
Provident Life and Accident Insurance Company of America, III
Prudential Financial Inc., III; 30 (upd.); 82 (upd.)
Prudential plc, III; 48 (upd.)
Radian Group Inc., 42
The Regence Group, 74
Reliance Group Holdings, Inc., III
Riunione Adriatica di Sicurtà SpA, III
Royal & Sun Alliance Insurance Group plc, 55 (upd.)
Royal Insurance Holdings PLC, III
SAFECO Corporaton, III
Sagicor Life Inc., 98
The St. Paul Travelers Companies, Inc. III; 22 (upd.); 79 (upd.)
SCOR S.A., 20
Skandia Insurance Company, Ltd., 50
Sompo Japan Insurance, Inc., 98 (upd.)
StanCorp Financial Group, Inc., 56
The Standard Life Assurance Company, III
State Auto Financial Corporation, 77
State Farm Mutual Automobile Insurance Company, III; 51 (upd.)
State Financial Services Corporation, 51
Stewart Information Services Corporation 78
Sumitomo Life Insurance Company, III; 60 (upd.)
The Sumitomo Marine and Fire Insurance Company, Limited, III
Sun Alliance Group PLC, III
Sun Life Financial Inc., 85
SunAmerica Inc., 11
Suncorp-Metway Ltd., 91
Suramericana de Inversiones S.A., 88
Svenska Handelsbanken AB, 50 (upd.)
The Swett & Crawford Group Inc., 84
Swiss Reinsurance Company (Schweizerische Rückversicherungs-Gesellschaft), III; 46 (upd.)
Teachers Insurance and Annuity Association-College Retirement Equities Fund, III; 45 (upd.)
Texas Industries, Inc., 8
TIG Holdings, Inc., 26
The Tokio Marine and Fire Insurance Co., Ltd., III
Torchmark Corporation, 9; 33 (upd.)
Transatlantic Holdings, Inc., 11
The Travelers Corporation, III
UICI, 33
Union des Assurances de Pans, III
United National Group, Ltd., 63
Unitrin Inc., 16; 78 (upd.)
UNUM Corp., 13
UnumProvident Corporation, 52 (upd.)
USAA, 10
USF&G Corporation, III
UTG Inc., 100
Victoria Group, 44 (upd.)
VICTORIA Holding AG, III
Vision Service Plan Inc., 77
W.R. Berkley Corporation, 15; 74 (upd.)

Washington National Corporation, 12
The Wawanesa Mutual Insurance Company, 68
WellCare Health Plans, Inc., 101
WellChoice, Inc., 67 (upd.)
WellPoint, Inc., 25; 103 (upd.)
Westfield Group, 69
White Mountains Insurance Group, Ltd., 48
Willis Group Holdings Ltd., 25; 100 (upd.)
Winterthur Group, III; 68 (upd.)
The Yasuda Fire and Marine Insurance Company, Limited, III
The Yasuda Mutual Life Insurance Company, III; 39 (upd.)
Zurich Financial Services, 42 (upd.); 93 (upd.)
Zürich Versicherungs-Gesellschaft, III

Legal Services

Akin, Gump, Strauss, Hauer & Feld, L.L.P., 33
American Bar Association, 35
American Lawyer Media Holdings, Inc., 32
Amnesty International, 50
Andrews Kurth, LLP, 71
Arnold & Porter, 35
Baker & Daniels LLP, 88
Baker & Hostetler LLP, 40
Baker & McKenzie, 10; 42 (upd.)
Baker and Botts, L.L.P., 28
Bingham Dana LLP, 43
Brobeck, Phleger & Harrison, LLP, 31
Cadwalader, Wickersham & Taft, 32
Chadbourne & Parke, 36
Cleary, Gottlieb, Steen & Hamilton, 35
Clifford Chance LLP, 38
Coudert Brothers, 30
Covington & Burling, 40
CRA International, Inc., 93
Cravath, Swaine & Moore, 43
Davis Polk & Wardwell, 36
Debevoise & Plimpton, 39
Dechert, 43
Dewey Ballantine LLP, 48
DLA Piper, 106
Dorsey & Whitney LLP, 47
Drinker, Biddle and Reath L.L.P., 92
Faegre & Benson LLP, 97
Fenwick & West LLP, 34
Fish & Neave, 54
Foley & Lardner, 28
Fried, Frank, Harris, Shriver & Jacobson, 35
Fulbright & Jaworski L.L.P., 47
Gibson, Dunn & Crutcher LLP, 36
Greenberg Traurig, LLP, 65
Heller, Ehrman, White & McAuliffe, 41
Hildebrandt International, 29
Hogan & Hartson L.L.P., 44
Holland & Knight LLP, 60
Holme Roberts & Owen LLP, 28
Hughes Hubbard & Reed LLP, 44
Hunton & Williams, 35
Jenkens & Gilchrist, P.C., 65
Jones, Day, Reavis & Pogue, 33

Manufacturing

Materials

Mining & Metals

Nonprofit & Philanthropic Organizations

Paper & Forestry

Personal Services

Petroleum

Publishing & Printing

Retail & Wholesale

Rubber & Tires

Telecommunications

Textiles & Apparel

Tobacco

Transport Services

Utilities

Scottish and Southern Energy plc, 66 (upd.)
Scottish Hydro-Electric PLC, 13
Scottish Power plc, 19; 49 (upd.)
Seattle City Light, 50
SEMCO Energy, Inc., 44
Sempra Energy, 25 (upd.)
Severn Trent PLC, 12; 38 (upd.)
Shikoku Electric Power Company, Inc., V; 60 (upd.)
SJW Corporation, 70
Sonat, Inc., 6
South Jersey Industries, Inc., 42
The Southern Company, V; 38 (upd.)
Southern Connecticut Gas Company, 84
Southern Electric PLC, 13
Southern Indiana Gas and Electric Company, 13
Southern Union Company, 27
Southwest Gas Corporation, 19
Southwest Water Company, 47
Southwestern Electric Power Co., 21
Southwestern Public Service Company, 6
State Grid Corporation of China, 108
Suez Lyonnaise des Eaux, 36 (upd.)
SUEZ-TRACTEBEL S.A., 97 (upd.)
TECO Energy, Inc., 6
Tennessee Valley Authority, 50
Tennet BV 78
Texas Utilities Company, V; 25 (upd.)
Thames Water plc, 11; 90 (upd.)
Tohoku Electric Power Company, Inc., V
The Tokyo Electric Power Company, 74 (upd.)
The Tokyo Electric Power Company, Incorporated, V
Tokyo Gas Co., Ltd., V; 55 (upd.)
TransAlta Utilities Corporation, 6
TransCanada PipeLines Limited, V
Transco Energy Company, V
Tri-State Generation and Transmission Association, Inc., 103
Trigen Energy Corporation, 42
Tucson Electric Power Company, 6
UGI Corporation, 12
Unicom Corporation, 29 (upd.)

Union Electric Company, V
The United Illuminating Company, 21
United Utilities PLC, 52 (upd.)
United Water Resources, Inc., 40
Unitil Corporation, 37
Utah Power and Light Company, 27
UtiliCorp United Inc., 6
Vattenfall AB, 57
Vectren Corporation, 98 (upd.)
Vereinigte Elektrizitätswerke Westfalen AG, V
VEW AG, 39
Viridian Group plc, 64
Warwick Valley Telephone Company, 55
Washington Gas Light Company, 19
Washington Natural Gas Company, 9
Washington Water Power Company, 6
Westar Energy, Inc., 57 (upd.)
Western Resources, Inc., 12
Wheelabrator Technologies, Inc., 6
Wisconsin Energy Corporation, 6; 54 (upd.)
Wisconsin Public Service Corporation, 9
WPL Holdings, Inc., 6
WPS Resources Corporation, 53 (upd.)
Xcel Energy Inc., 73 (upd.)

Waste Services

Allied Waste Industries, Inc., 50
Allwaste, Inc., 18
American Ecology Corporation, 77
Appliance Recycling Centers of America, Inc., 42
Azcon Corporation, 23
Berliner Stadtreinigungsbetriebe, 58
Biffa plc, 92
Brambles Industries Limited, 42
Browning-Ferris Industries, Inc., V; 20 (upd.)
Casella Waste Systems Inc., 102
Chemical Waste Management, Inc., 9
CHHJ Franchising LLC, 105
Clean Harbors, Inc., 73
Clean Venture, Inc., 104
Copart Inc., 23
Darling International Inc., 85

E.On AG, 50 (upd.)
Ecolab Inc., I; 13 (upd.); 34 (upd.); 85 (upd.)
Ecology and Environment, Inc., 39
Empresas Públicas de Medellín S.A.E.S.P., 91
Fuel Tech, Inc., 85
Industrial Services of America, Inc., 46
Ionics, Incorporated, 52
ISS A/S, 49
Jani-King International, Inc., 85
Kelda Group plc, 45
McClain Industries, Inc., 51
MPW Industrial Services Group, Inc., 53
Newpark Resources, Inc., 63
Norcal Waste Systems, Inc., 60
Oakleaf Waste Management, LLC, 97
1-800-GOT-JUNK? LLC, 74
Onet S.A., 92
Pennon Group Plc, 45
Perma-Fix Environmental Services, Inc., 99
Philip Environmental Inc., 16
Philip Services Corp., 73
Republic Services, Inc., 92
Roto-Rooter, Inc., 15; 61 (upd.)
Safety-Kleen Systems Inc., 8; 82 (upd.)
Saur S.A.S., 92
Sevenson Environmental Services, Inc., 42
Severn Trent PLC, 38 (upd.)
Servpro Industries, Inc., 85
Shanks Group plc, 45
Shred-It Canada Corporation, 56
Stericycle, Inc., 33; 74 (upd.)
TRC Companies, Inc., 32
Valley Proteins, Inc., 91
Veit Companies, 43; 92 (upd.)
Waste Connections, Inc., 46
Waste Holdings, Inc., 41
Waste Management, Inc., V
Wheelabrator Technologies, Inc., 60 (upd.)
Windswept Environmental Group, Inc., 62
WMX Technologies Inc., 17

Geographic Index

South Korea (Republic of Korea)

Spain

Sweden

Switzerland

Herley Industries, Inc., 33
Herman Goelitz, Inc., 28
Herman Goldner Company, Inc., 100
Herman Miller, Inc., 8; 77 (upd.)
Herr Foods Inc., 84
Herschend Family Entertainment
   Corporation, 73
Hersha Hospitality Trust, 107
Hershey Foods Corporation, II; 15 (upd.);
   51 (upd.)
The Hertz Corporation, 9; 33 (upd.); 101
   (upd.)
Heska Corporation, 39
Heublein, Inc., I
Hewitt Associates, Inc., 77
Hewlett-Packard Company, III; 6 (upd.);
   28 (upd.); 50 (upd.)
Hexcel Corporation, 28
HFF, Inc., 103
hhgregg Inc., 98
Hibbett Sporting Goods, Inc., 26; 70
   (upd.)
Hibernia Corporation, 37
Hickory Farms, Inc., 17
HickoryTech Corporation, 92
High Falls Brewing Company LLC, 74
Highlights for Children, Inc., 95
Highmark Inc., 27
Highsmith Inc., 60
Hilb, Rogal & Hobbs Company, 77
Hildebrandt International, 29
Hill's Pet Nutrition, Inc., 27
Hillenbrand Industries, Inc., 10; 75 (upd.)
Hillerich & Bradsby Company, Inc., 51
The Hillhaven Corporation, 14
Hills Stores Company, 13
Hilmar Cheese Company, Inc., 98
Hilton Hotels Corporation, III; 19 (upd.);
   62 (upd.)
Hines Horticulture, Inc., 49
Hispanic Broadcasting Corporation, 35
Hitchiner Manufacturing Co., Inc., 23
Hittite Microwave Corporation, 106
HMI Industries, Inc., 17
HNI Corporation, 74 (upd.)
Ho-Chunk Inc., 61
HOB Entertainment, Inc., 37
Hobby Lobby Stores Inc., 80
Hobie Cat Company, 94
Hodgson Mill, Inc., 88
Hoechst Celanese Corporation, 13
Hoenig Group Inc., 41
Hoffman Corporation 78
Hogan & Hartson L.L.P., 44
HOK Group, Inc., 59
Holberg Industries, Inc., 36
Holiday Inns, Inc., III
Holiday Retirement Corp., 87
Holiday RV Superstores, Incorporated, 26
Holland & Knight LLP, 60
Holland America Line Inc., 108
Holland Burgerville USA, 44
The Holland Group, Inc., 82
Hollander Home Fashions Corp., 67
Holley Performance Products Inc., 52
Hollinger International Inc., 24
Holly Corporation, 12
Hollywood Casino Corporation, 21

Hollywood Entertainment Corporation,
   25
Hollywood Media Corporation, 58
Hollywood Park, Inc., 20
Holme Roberts & Owen LLP, 28
Holnam Inc., 8; 39 (upd.)
Hologic, Inc., 106
Holophane Corporation, 19
Horizon Food Group, Inc., 100
Holson Burnes Group, Inc., 14
Holt and Bugbee Company, 66
Holt's Cigar Holdings, Inc., 42
Homasote Company, 72
Home Box Office Inc., 7; 23 (upd.); 76
   (upd.)
The Home Depot, Inc., V; 18 (upd.); 97
   (upd.)
The Home Insurance Company, III
Home Interiors & Gifts, Inc., 55
Home Products International, Inc., 55
Home Properties of New York, Inc., 42
Home Shopping Network, Inc., V; 25
   (upd.)
HomeBase, Inc., 33 (upd.)
Homestake Mining Company, 12; 38
   (upd.)
Hometown Auto Retailers, Inc., 44
HomeVestors of America, Inc., 77
HON INDUSTRIES Inc., 13
Honda Motor Company Limited, I; 10
   (upd.); 29 (upd.)
Honeywell Inc., II; 12 (upd.); 50 (upd.)
Hooker Furniture Corporation, 80
Hooper Holmes, Inc., 22
Hooters of America, Inc., 18; 69 (upd.)
The Hoover Company, 12; 40 (upd.)
Hoover's, Inc., 108
HOP, LLC, 80
Hops Restaurant Bar and Brewery, 46
Horace Mann Educators Corporation, 22;
   90 (upd.)
Horizon Lines, Inc., 98
Horizon Organic Holding Corporation,
   37
Hormel Foods Corporation, 18 (upd.); 54
   (upd.)
Hornbeck Offshore Services, Inc., 101
Horsehead Industries, Inc., 51
Horseshoe Gaming Holding Corporation,
   62
Horton Homes, Inc., 25
Horween Leather Company, 83
Hospira, Inc., 71
Hospital Central Services, Inc., 56
Hospital Corporation of America, III
Hospitality Franchise Systems, Inc., 11
Hospitality Worldwide Services, Inc., 26
Hoss's Steak and Sea House Inc., 68
Host America Corporation 79
Hot Stuff Foods, 85
Hot Topic, Inc., 33; 86 (upd.)
Houchens Industries Inc., 51
Houghton Mifflin Company, 10; 36
   (upd.)
House of Fabrics, Inc., 21
Household International, Inc., II; 21
   (upd.)
Houston Industries Incorporated, V

Houston Wire & Cable Company, 97
Hovnanian Enterprises, Inc., 29; 89 (upd.)
Howard Hughes Medical Institute, 39
Howard Johnson International, Inc., 17;
   72 (upd.)
Howmet Corp., 12
HSN, 64 (upd.)
Hub Group, Inc., 38
Hub International Limited, 89
Hubbard Broadcasting Inc., 24; 79 (upd.)
Hubbell Inc., 9; 31 (upd.); 76 (upd.)
Huddle House, Inc., 105
Hudson Foods Inc., 13
Hudson River Bancorp, Inc., 41
Huffy Corporation, 7; 30 (upd.)
Hughes Electronics Corporation, 25
Hughes Hubbard & Reed LLP, 44
Hughes Markets, Inc., 22
Hughes Supply, Inc., 14
Hulman & Company, 44
Human Factors International Inc., 100
Humana Inc., III; 24 (upd.); 101 (upd.)
The Humane Society of the United States,
   54
Hummer Winblad Venture Partners, 97
Hungarian Telephone and Cable Corp.,
   75
Hungry Howie's Pizza and Subs, Inc., 25
Hunt Consolidated, Inc., 27 (upd.)
Hunt Manufacturing Company, 12
Hunt Oil Company, 7
Hunt-Wesson, Inc., 17
Hunter Fan Company, 13; 98 (upd.)
Huntington Bancshares Incorporated, 11;
   87 (upd.)
Huntington Learning Centers, Inc., 55
Hunton & Williams, 35
Huntsman Corporation, 8; 98 (upd.)
Huron Consulting Group Inc., 87
Hutchinson Technology Incorporated, 18;
   63 (upd.)
Huttig Building Products, Inc., 73
Huy Fong Foods, Inc., 107
Hvide Marine Incorporated, 22
Hy-Vee, Inc., 36
Hyatt Corporation, III; 16 (upd.)
Hyde Athletic Industries, Inc., 17
Hydril Company, 46
Hypercom Corporation, 27
Hyperion Software Corporation, 22
Hyperion Solutions Corporation, 76
Hyster Company, 17
I.C. Isaacs & Company, 31
Iams Company, 26
IBERIABANK Corporation, 37
IBP, Inc., II; 21 (upd.)
IC Industries, Inc., I
ICF International, Inc., 28; 94 (upd.)
ICN Pharmaceuticals, Inc., 52
ICON Health & Fitness, Inc., 38; 102
   (upd.)
ICU Medical, Inc., 106
Idaho Power Company, 12
IDB Communications Group, Inc., 11
Ideal Mortgage Bankers, Ltd., 105
Idealab, 105
Idearc Inc., 90
Identix Inc., 44

Skidmore, Owings & Merrill LLP, 13; 69 (upd.)
skinnyCorp, LLC, 97
Skyline Chili, Inc., 62
Skyline Corporation, 30
SkyMall, Inc., 26
SkyWest, Inc., 25
Skyy Spirits LLC 78
SL Green Realty Corporation, 44
SL Industries, Inc., 77
Sleepy's Inc., 32
SLI, Inc., 48
Slim-Fast Foods Company, 18; 66 (upd.)
SLM Holding Corp., 25 (upd.)
Small Planet Foods, Inc., 89
Smart & Final LLC, 16; 94 (upd.)
Smart Balance, Inc., 100
SMART Modular Technologies, Inc., 86
SmartForce PLC, 43
Smead Manufacturing Co., 17
Smith & Hawken, Ltd., 68
Smith & Wesson Corp., 30; 73 (upd.)
Smith Barney Inc., 15
Smith Corona Corp., 13
Smith International, Inc., 15; 59 (upd.)
The Smith & Wollensky Restaurant Group, Inc., 105
Smith's Food & Drug Centers, Inc., 8; 57 (upd.)
Smith-Midland Corporation, 56
Smithfield Foods, Inc., 7; 43 (upd.)
SmithKline Beckman Corporation, I
Smithsonian Institution, 27
Smithway Motor Xpress Corporation, 39
Smurfit-Stone Container Corporation, 26 (upd.); 83 (upd.)
Snap-on Incorporated, 7; 27 (upd.); 105 (upd.)
Snapfish, 83
Snapple Beverage Corporation, 11
Snell & Wilmer L.L.P., 28
Society Corporation, 9
Soft Pretzel Franchise Systems, Inc., 108
Soft Sheen Products, Inc., 31
Softbank Corporation, 77 (upd.)
Sola International Inc., 71
Solar Turbines Inc., 100
Sole Technology Inc., 93
Solectron Corporation, 12; 48 (upd.)
Solo Cup Company, 104
Solo Serve Corporation, 28
Solutia Inc., 52
Sonat, Inc., 6
Sonesta International Hotels Corporation, 44
Sonic Automotive, Inc., 77
Sonic Corp., 14; 37 (upd.); 103 (upd.)
Sonic Innovations Inc., 56
Sonic Solutions, Inc., 81
SonicWALL, Inc., 87
Sonnenschein Nath and Rosenthal LLP, 102
Sonoco Products Company, 8; 89 (upd.)
SonoSite, Inc., 56
Sorbee International Ltd., 74
Soros Fund Management LLC, 28
Sorrento, Inc., 24
SOS Staffing Services, 25

Sotheby's Holdings, Inc., 11; 29 (upd.); 84 (upd.)
Sound Advice, Inc., 41
Souper Salad, Inc., 98
The Source Enterprises, Inc., 65
Source Interlink Companies, Inc., 75
South Beach Beverage Company, Inc., 73
South Dakota Wheat Growers Association, 94
South Jersey Industries, Inc., 42
Southdown, Inc., 14
Southeast Frozen Foods Company, L.P., 99
The Southern Company, V; 38 (upd.)
Southern Connecticut Gas Company, 84
Southern Financial Bancorp, Inc., 56
Southern Indiana Gas and Electric Company, 13
Southern New England Telecommunications Corporation, 6
Southern Pacific Transportation Company, V
Southern Poverty Law Center, Inc., 74
Southern Progress Corporation, 102
Southern States Cooperative Incorporated, 36
Southern Union Company, 27
Southern Wine and Spirits of America, Inc., 84
The Southland Corporation, II; 7 (upd.)
Southtrust Corporation, 11
Southwest Airlines Co., 6; 24 (upd.); 71 (upd.)
Southwest Gas Corporation, 19
Southwest Water Company, 47
Southwestern Bell Corporation, V
Southwestern Electric Power Co., 21
Southwestern Public Service Company, 6
Southwire Company, Inc., 8; 23 (upd.)
Sovran Self Storage, Inc., 66
Sovereign Bancorp, Inc., 103
Spacehab, Inc., 37
Spacelabs Medical, Inc., 71
Spaghetti Warehouse, Inc., 25
Spangler Candy Company, 44
Spanish Broadcasting System, Inc., 41
Spansion Inc., 80
Spanx, Inc., 89
Spark Networks, Inc., 91
Spartan Motors Inc., 14
Spartan Stores Inc., 8; 66 (upd.)
Spartech Corporation, 19; 76 (upd.)
Sparton Corporation, 18
Spear & Jackson, Inc., 73
Spear, Leeds & Kellogg, 66
Spec's Music, Inc., 19
Special Olympics, Inc., 93
Specialized Bicycle Components Inc., 50
Specialty Coatings Inc., 8
Specialty Equipment Companies, Inc., 25
Specialty Products & Insulation Co., 59
Spectrum Control, Inc., 67
Spectrum Organic Products, Inc., 68
Spee-Dee Delivery Service, Inc., 93
SpeeDee Oil Change and Tune-Up, 25
Speedway Motorsports, Inc., 32
Speidel Inc., 96
Speizman Industries, Inc., 44

Spelling Entertainment, 14; 35 (upd.)
Spencer Stuart and Associates, Inc., 14
Spherion Corporation, 52
Spicy Pickle Franchising, Inc., 105
Spiegel, Inc., 10; 27 (upd.)
Spinnaker Exploration Company, 72
Spirit Airlines, Inc., 31
Sport Chalet, Inc., 16; 94 (upd.)
Sport Supply Group, Inc., 23; 106 (upd.)
Sportmart, Inc., 15
Sports & Recreation, Inc., 17
The Sports Authority, Inc., 16; 43 (upd.)
The Sports Club Company, 25
The Sportsman's Guide, Inc., 36
Springs Global US, Inc., V; 19 (upd.); 90 (upd.)
Sprint Corporation, 9; 46 (upd.)
SPS Technologies, Inc., 30
SPSS Inc., 64
SPX Corporation, 10; 47 (upd.); 103 (upd.)
Spyglass Entertainment Group, LLC, 91
Square D, 90
Squibb Corporation, I
SRA International, Inc., 77
SRAM Corporation, 65
SRC Holdings Corporation, 67
SRI International, Inc., 57
SSI (U.S.), Inc., 103 (upd.)
SSOE Inc., 76
STAAR Surgical Company, 57
Stabler Companies Inc. 78
Stage Stores, Inc., 24; 82 (upd.)
Stanadyne Automotive Corporation, 37
StanCorp Financial Group, Inc., 56
Standard Candy Company Inc., 86
Standard Commercial Corporation, 13; 62 (upd.)
Standard Federal Bank, 9
Standard Microsystems Corporation, 11
Standard Motor Products, Inc., 40
Standard Pacific Corporation, 52
The Standard Register Company, 15, 93 (upd.)
Standex International Corporation, 17; 44 (upd.)
Stanhome Inc., 15
Stanley Furniture Company, Inc., 34
The Stanley Works, III; 20 (upd.); 79 (upd.)
Staple Cotton Cooperative Association (Staplcotn), 86
Staples, Inc., 10; 55 (upd.)
Star Banc Corporation, 11
Star of the West Milling Co., 95
Starbucks Corporation, 13; 34 (upd.); 77 (upd.)
Starcraft Corporation, 30; 66 (upd.)
Starent Networks Corp., 106
Starkey Laboratories, Inc., 52
Starrett Corporation, 21
StarTek, Inc. 79
Starter Corp., 12
Starwood Hotels & Resorts Worldwide, Inc., 54
Starz LLC, 91
The Stash Tea Company, 50
State Auto Financial Corporation, 77